Lecture Notes in Electrical Engineering

Volume 1211

The book series *Lecture Notes in Electrical Engineering* (LNEE) publishes the latest developments in Electrical Engineering—quickly, informally and in high quality. While original research reported in proceedings and monographs has traditionally formed the core of LNEE, we also encourage authors to submit books devoted to supporting student education and professional training in the various fields and applications areas of electrical engineering. The series cover classical and emerging topics concerning:

- Communication Engineering, Information Theory and Networks
- Electronics Engineering and Microelectronics
- Signal, Image and Speech Processing
- Wireless and Mobile Communication
- Circuits and Systems
- Energy Systems, Power Electronics and Electrical Machines
- Electro-optical Engineering
- Instrumentation Engineering
- Avionics Engineering
- Control Systems
- Internet-of-Things and Cybersecurity
- Biomedical Devices, MEMS and NEMS

For general information about this book series, comments or suggestions, please contact leontina.dicecco@springer.com.

To submit a proposal or request further information, please contact the Publishing Editor in your country:

China

Jasmine Dou, Editor (jasmine.dou@springer.com)

India, Japan, Rest of Asia

Swati Meherishi, Editorial Director (Swati.Meherishi@springer.com)

Southeast Asia, Australia, New Zealand

Ramesh Nath Premnath, Editor (ramesh.premnath@springernature.com)

USA, Canada

Michael Luby, Senior Editor (michael.luby@springer.com)

All other Countries

Leontina Di Cecco, Senior Editor (leontina.dicecco@springer.com)

**** This series is indexed by EI Compendex and Scopus databases. ****

Koushlendra Kumar Singh · Sangeeta Singh ·
Subodh Srivastava · Manish Kumar Bajpai
Editors

Machine Vision and Augmented Intelligence

Select Proceedings of MAI 2023

Springer

Editors
Koushlendra Kumar Singh
Department of Computer Science
and Engineering
National Institute of Technology
Jamshedpur
Jamshedpur, Jharkhand, India

Subodh Srivastava
Department of Electronics
and Communication Engineering
National Institute of Technology Patna
Patna, Bihar, India

Sangeeta Singh
Department of Electronics
and Communication Engineering
National Institute of Technology Patna
Patna, Bihar, India

Manish Kumar Bajpai
Department of Computer Science
and Engineering
National Institute of Technology Warangal
Warangal, Telangana, India

ISSN 1876-1100 ISSN 1876-1119 (electronic)
Lecture Notes in Electrical Engineering
ISBN 978-981-97-4361-2 ISBN 978-981-97-4359-9 (eBook)
https://doi.org/10.1007/978-981-97-4359-9

This Springer imprint is published by the registered company Springer Nature Singapore Pte Ltd.
The registered company address is: 152 Beach Road, #21-01/04 Gateway East, Singapore 189721, Singapore

Preface

The third edition of Machine Vision and Augmented Intelligence: Selected Proceedings of MAI 2023 brings together academicians, researchers, industry people, and students to come together and discuss the current state-of-the-art research in the field of Machine Vision and Augmented Intelligence and its real-life applications. The book had provided a benchmark and platform to the "AATM NIRBHAR BHARAT" by using modern augmented intelligence. The theme of the book encompasses all industrial and non-industrial applications in which a combination of hardware and software provides operational guidance to devices in the execution of their functions based on the capture and processing of images. Today, manufacturers are using machine vision and augmented intelligence-based metrology to improve their productivity and reduce costs. Machine vision and augmented intelligence integrates optical components with computerized control systems to achieve greater productivity from existing automated manufacturing equipment. This will become very useful to improve the efficiency in different fields like security, crime detection, forensic, inventory control, different applications of artificial intelligence, etc.

Jamshedpur, India — Koushlendra Kumar Singh
Patna, India — Sangeeta Singh
Patna, India — Subodh Srivastava
Warangal, India — Manish Kumar Bajpai

Contents

About the Editors

Koushlendra Kumar Singh is currently working as an assistant professor in the Department of Computer Science and Engineering at the National Institute of Technology, Jamshedpur, India. He completed his doctoral degree and master's program from the Indian Institute of Information Technology, Design, and Manufacturing, Jabalpur, India, in 2016 and 2011, respectively. Dr. Singh graduated in computer science and engineering from Bhagalpur College of Engineering, Bhagalpur, in 2008. He has published several papers in international refereed journals and conferences. His current research interest areas are image processing, biometrics, and different applications of fractional derivatives, computational modeling, epidemic forecasting, etc.

Sangeeta Singh is an Assistant Professor in the Department of Electronics and Communication Engineering, NIT Patna, India. Her researches interests include beyond CMOS Devices Green Electronics steep switching transistors and soft computing techniques and applications. She has been recognized as an eminent scholar in the field of Electronics and Computer Engineering. She is editing two books. She is a member of IEEE, IEEE EDS Society, IET, etc. She received her Ph.D. degree in Electronics and communication engineering from IIITDM Jabalpur, India. She has handled many research projects and more than 100 research articles are in her credit.

Dr. Subodh Srivastava is working as an Assistant Professor in the Department of Electronics and Communications Engineering, and Professor-In charge of IEEE SB NIT Patna, Bihar, India. He has around 60 publications in reputed Journals and conferences. One Indian Patent (Granted) and 12 Book chapters to his credit. He is a member of the IEEE, and is also connected with the Indian Society of Technical Education through life. He received projects from BIRAC, TEQIP and WellM in the field of AI and medical Image Processing. He is also the reviewer of many International Journals and Conferences. He received his Ph.D. from IIT (BHU) in 2014. His research interests include Image processing, biomedical image analysis, pattern recognition, machine learning, computer vision, and their medical applications.

Manish Kumar Bajpai is an Associate professor in the Department of Computer Science and Engineering at the National Institute of Technology Warangal. Dr. Bajpai has published over 50 publications in international journals and conferences. He has several sponsored research and consultancy projects funded by agencies such as SPARC, MHRD, DST, USIEF, ATAL, BRNS, and NVIDIA. Eleven students have completed/pursuing their Ph.D. under his supervision. His areas of research are augmented intelligence, machine vision, brain-computer interface, medical imaging, and parallel algorithms design. Dr. Bajpai is a senior member of IEEE and a life member of the Indian Science Congress and Indian Nuclear Society.

Ultra Energy Efficient Reliable and Robust DLJLFET-Based-PUF for IoT Devices

Chithraja Rajan, Rakesh Kumar, Meena Panchore, and Jawar Singh

1 Introduction

Over the past two decades, the Internet of Things (IoTs) has emerged as a promising future electronics hardware in the world of computing and wireless communications [1–6]. Electronics hardware measures five main core elements of data security confidentiality, integrity, availability, authenticity, and non-repudiation [7]. To secure these devices, identifiers are used for authentication during the encryption and decryption process. The traditional technique to authenticate any device is usually a key stored in non-volatile memory (NVM) and subsequently used in a digital signature or keys generated from the software. However, these techniques are very easy to predict and vulnerable to key hacking. So these techniques promote invasive attacks. Hence, we need a better solution for key hacking and invasive attacks. Physically Unclonable Function (PUF) has the potential to create a better hardware security technology for Internet of Things (IoTs) devices [8]. A PUF is a circuit that produces unique hardware characteristics which come during manufacturing variations. So it can provide better security for IoT. PUF is used to authenticate devices and it does

C. Rajan (✉)
School of Computer Science and Engineering, Ramdeobaba University, Nagpur, Maharashtra 440013, India
e-mail: rajan.chithraja@gmail.com

R. Kumar · M. Panchore
Department of Electronics and Communication Engineering, National Institute of Technology Patna, Bihar 800005, India
e-mail: rakeshk.phd19@nitp.ac.in

M. Panchore
e-mail: meenap.ec@nitp.ac.in

J. Singh
Department of Electronics and Communication Engineering, Indian Institute of Technology Patna, Patna, India
e-mail: jawar@iitp.ac.in

K. Kumar Singh et al. (eds.), *Machine Vision and Augmented Intelligence*, Lecture Notes in Electrical Engineering 1211, https://doi.org/10.1007/978-981-97-4359-9_1

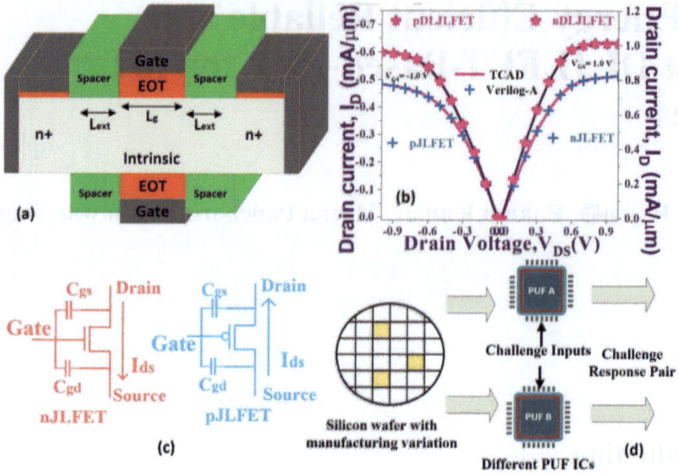

Fig. 1 3D Schematic view of **a** n-JLFET, **b** p-JLFET, **c** n-DLJLFET, and **d** p-DLJLFET

not require storing keys; however, it also mitigates the drawbacks of authentication of stored keys, so it is impossible to clone a PUF device [9]. PUF is like a digital fingerprint that can uniquely identify a device. It also has the ability to transfer data without human interaction [10]. Thus, the PUF circuit provides better hardware security for IoT devices. When some natural variations happened during the manufacturing of IC, these variations are inevitable and uncertain in nature. Each identical IC obtained by cutting wafers will give a different and unique random number as an output key for the same input even if this variation in output is too small. This whole process is shown in Fig. 1. The output key is a string of random binary numbers. This random binary bit is very unique for specific input. These random numbers can be used in high security applications specifically in IoT and cryptography.

IoT devices face many difficult challenges, such as low energy consumption, transmission speed, and reliability as well as security against cyber attacks [2, 3, 6]. In order to achieve this, various devices have been proposed which can overcome this shortcoming. Sahoo [11] analyzed a low power PUF using CMOS technology which consumes 42.75 μW average power but uniqueness of chip is 46.22%. Yanambaka [10] proposed a dopingless transistor-based PUF which increases the uniqueness to 48% but also average power is increased to 121.3 μW. In this article, we propose DLJLFET-based PUF which is more power efficient as well as gives high unique PUF. Its frequency of operation is high so it will encrypt and decrypt incoming and outgoing data more faster. The detailed performance comparison of different PUFs is shown in table-III. Nowadays, JLFET devices are promising over inversion mode transistors. It shows less sensitivity to short channel effects (SCE), smaller sub-threshold swing (SS), reduced drain-induced barrier lowering (DIBL), and higher Ion/Ioff but due to higher doping in the channel it shows high random dopant fluctuating (RDF) [12]. Therefore, dopingless JLFET (DLJLFET) could be the best alternative to mitigate this problem. In DLJLFET a thin layer of intrinsic silicon is used to form the source and drain region with proper S/D work function; therefore, during the manufacturing of ICs fabrication steps in DLJLFET little bit simpler than JLFET because DLJLFET does not utilize any external ion implantation [10, 13].

PUF takes input as a challenge and gives output as a response. These two put together are commonly known as Challenge-Response Pair (CRP). The response depends not only on the given input challenge but also on the device where the function is executing. When a different challenge is given to identical PUF, then we get different responses. This happens only because a good PUF is independent of input. These PUFs are completely mounted within a chip. So when we have two identical PUFs mounted on different chips and we provide the same challenge to both devices, it will give a different response. Essentially each device provides a unique response to the same challenge and the difference between these responses is significant. This paper proposes a DLJLFET-based RO-PUF for which 100 Monte Carlo simulations have been performed. The performance metrics of the proposed RO and PUF have been evaluated and compared with other works in the literature.

2 Device Structure and Simulation Parameters

The performances of JLFET and DLJLFET have been investigated using a SILVACO ATLAS 5.2.8.R [14]. Lookup tables have been generated using this TCAD simulator that helps to run circuit simulation using the Verilog-A model. Later, 100 Monte Carlo simulations have been carried out with 10 % deviation in different geometric parameters and I-V characteristics have been obtained. Figure 1 represents a schematic view of (a) n-JLFET, (b) p-JLFET, (c) n-DLJLFET, and (d) p-DLJLFET. Identical parameters are taken for the simulation of these devices except doping in channel and work function for gate [15]. In JLFET, Si layer is doped heavily with 10^{19}cm^{-3} doping concentration and 5.5 eV work function (ϕ_g) is applied on gate electrode. Alternatively, Si layer in DLJLFET is doped lightly with 10^{15}cm^{-3} concentration and the formation of the source/drain (S/D) regions in DLJLFET relies on the utilization of the charge-plasma (CP) concept. The CP concept offers enhanced resilience to random dopant fluctuations (RDFs) caused by process variations. In this paper, to induce charges in the S/D region in a DLJLFET, the gate metal work function has been taken 3.9 (hafnium). The essential requirements of the CP concept are explained in detail in [15]. Design parameters of the device are provided in Table 1.

Silvaco ATLAS faces TCAD mixed-mode simulation challenges and comparatively long simulation times and convergence issues. To overcome these limitations a two-dimension (2-D) lookup table-based Verilog-A small signal model is used. A 2-D lookup-table model is created to plot C-V and I-V characteristics of DLJLFET based on the device parameters. SPICE circuit simulations are employed in Verilog-A models and we further calibrate with TCAD simulation results. In this model, a three-terminal device with source, gate, and drain terminals is under consideration, with current measurements specifically focused on the flow between the source and drain

Table 1 Delay and frequency of oscillation with different V_{DD} of five-stage JLFET-RO and DLJLFET-RO

	Delay (ps)	Frequency (GHz)	Delay (ps)	Frequency (GHz)
0.4	74.57	1.34	43.95	2.28
0.5	21.13	4.73	8.16	12.3
0.6	12.44	8.04	5.63	17.8
0.7	9.02	11.1	4.29	23.3
0.8	7.16	14.0	3.58	27.9
0.9	6.15	16.3	3.06	32.6
1.0	5.30	18.9	2.73	36.6

terminals. This approach is justified by the use of high-k gate dielectrics, which effectively eliminate gate leakage. We included two parasitic capacitors, one in between gate and source terminal is C_{gs} and the other in between gate and drain terminal is C_{gd}. The channel of DLJLFET is fully depleted and the junction is not formed across the source and drain so the channel and junction capacitance are negligible, respectively. In order to obtain output characteristics of n-type and p-type JLFET and DLJLFET, we build three 2-D tables taking the two input voltages V_{gs} and V_{ds} for modeling of both devices: the transfer characteristics $[I_{ds}(V_{gs}, V_{ds})]$, the gate-drain capacitance $[C_{gd}(V_{gs}, V_{ds})]$, and the gate-source capacitance $[C_{gs}(V_{gs}, V_{ds})]$. The input voltages V_{gs} and V_{ds} are sweeping with 50 mV. Furthermore, based on three tables, stored on comma-separated values as CSV files. Figure 1c shows the Verilog-A small signal model of n-type and p-type DLJLFET, respectively. With the help of TCAD simulation data which is taken from device parameters, a lookup table is made for analysis of output characteristics. We do enough simulations to check the accuracy of the Verilog-A device model. Finally, we found the calibration difference between the Verilog-A and TCAD simulation is acceptable for output characteristics of n-type and p-type JLFET and DLJLFET in Fig. 1b, respectively.

3 Ring Oscillator

Ring oscillator is a primary element of PUF. It comprises an AND gate, an enable input, and an odd number of inverters and has feedback from the last inverter fed to the NAND gate. NAND gate is used to control the oscillation [11]. This circuit oscillates with a fixed frequency which depends on the delay of each phase. This delay is dependent upon the gate capacitance of the devices. During the manufacture of RO, some variations are introduced, so not every RO will give the same frequency of oscillation. There will be a slight difference in the frequency of two similar types of ROs. The frequency of oscillation of the RO is given as Eq. 1.

$$f = \frac{1}{2nt_d} \tag{1}$$

where f is frequency of ring oscillator, n is number of stages, and t_d is delay of each stage.

In this paper, one RO is made up of five inverters. It is shown in Fig. 2. Junctionless and dopingless FET devices are used to implement inverter and compare its performance. We considered performance parameters such as delay and power delay product (PDP) for both devices. The relationship between average power and V_{DD} in an inverter is described in Eq. 2.

$$P_{avg} = \frac{1}{2}\alpha f C_L V_{DD}^2 \tag{2}$$

where α is activity factor, f is the frequency of operation, C_L is load capacitance of all gates, and V_{DD} is the power supply.

Figure 3a, b shows delay and power delay product (PDP) against V_{DD} of JLFET and DLJLFET-based five-stage RO. It is observed that the delay in DLJLFET-based RO is 61 % less than JLFET-RO at supply voltage (V_{DD}) of 0.5 V. This is because of JLFET shows more parasitic capacitance than DLJLFET device. The Power delay product (PDP) gives an idea of how energy efficient a device is. DLJLFET-RO saves 47 % more energy than JLFET-RO during each transition at the same V_{DD} because JLFET shows a higher leakage current due to high doping in the channel. Further, we analyze the transient response of both RO. It is shown in Fig. 4a, b. It is observed that the frequency of oscillation of DLJLFET-RO is 2.59 times higher than JLFET-RO at same V_{DD}. This is because DLJLFET devices show less delay as compared to JLFET devices. This significant reduction in delay and PDP makes DJLET a higher frequency of oscillation and energy efficient. A comparative analysis of delay and frequency with different V_{DD} of the two ROs using JLFET and DLJLFET is presented in Table 2. From Table 2, it is clear that when V_{DD} is changing from 0.4 V to 1 V then the frequency of oscillation increases from 70 % to 94 % in DLJLFET-RO as compared to JLFET-RO because relative parasitic capacitance against V_{DD} increases in JLFET-RO.

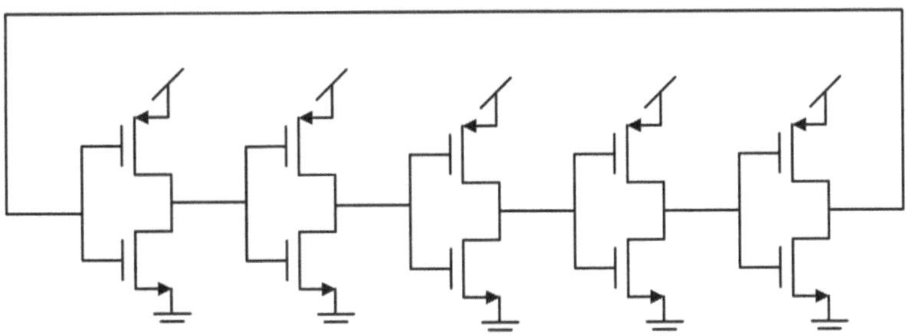

Fig. 2 Five-stage ring oscillator

Table 2 Performance comparison table of ROs

Metric	This work	Mondal [16]	Lee [17]	Coombs [18]	Ho [19]	Zhang [20]
Technology (nm)	DL JLFET (15)	CMOS (90)	CMOS (65)	CMOS (65)	CMOS (90)	CMOS (65)
RO Inverter stage (n)	5	5	5	5	5	–
Average power (mW)	0.0284	0.788	2.7	5.3	87.6	0.059
Frequency (GHz)	12.25	1	2	5	0.771	0.1
Power supply (V)	0.5	1.1	1.2	1	0.6	0.5

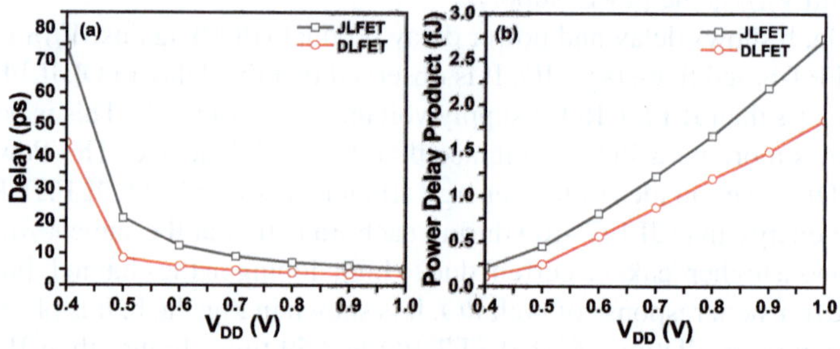

Fig. 3 **a** Delay and **b** power delay product (PDP) of JLFET and DLJLFET-based five-stage RO

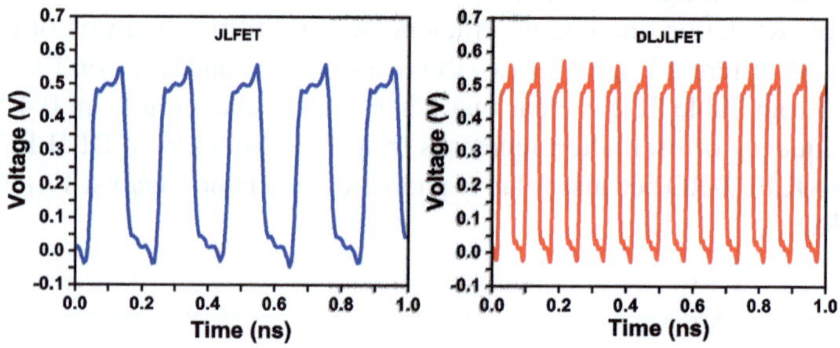

Fig. 4 Transient response of **a** JLFET and **b** DLJLFET-based five-stage RO

4 Ring Oscillator PUF Design

The implementation of a ring oscillator physical unclonable function (RO-PUF) is straightforward, and it consumes a smaller chip area that also consumes less power compared to other architecture; this delay-based PUFs were first proposed by Suh and Devadas [8]. The conventional RO-PUF design is shown in Fig. 5. In this architecture,

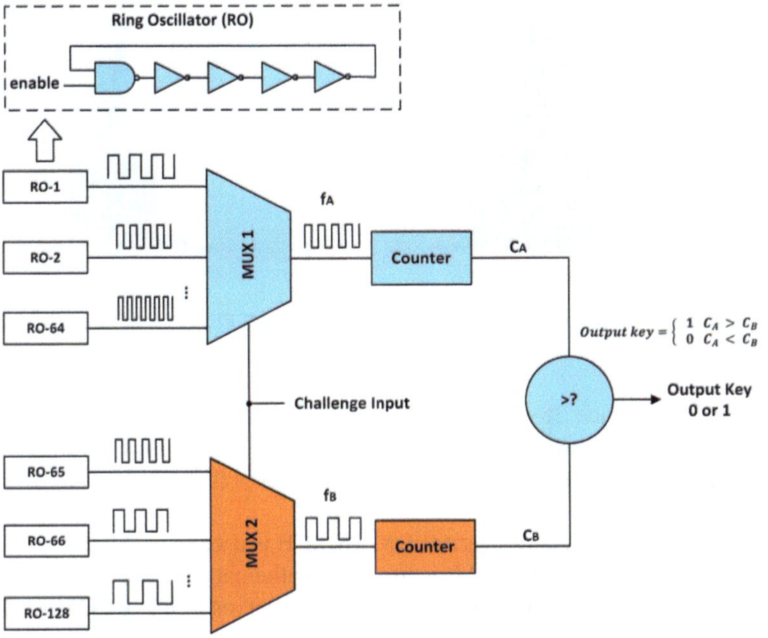

Fig. 5 Conventional design of RO-PUF

128 identical ring oscillators (ROs), two multiplexers, two frequency counters, and one comparator are used. The ROs are connected to counters through multiplexer (MUX). The MUX is used to select random ROs. The counter keeps track of the oscillation count generated by the randomly selected ring oscillators (ROs). One-half of the oscillators are linked to one counter, while the other half are connected to the second counter [21–23]. In this paper, 5 inverters are taken in one RO and 128 ROs are used to generate 64-bit key. Whenever an enable is set to 1, a signal will pass through the AND gate. If the enable bit is set to 1 and the other input value is 0, then the output of the AND gate will be 0 followed by the output of the first inverter as 1, and finally, the output of the RO is 1. The AND gate and output of RO are feedback so in the next time cycle the output of the AND gate will be 1 followed by the output of RO will be 0. So finally output essentially creates a periodic signal of 1's and 0's. The frequency of the output depends on the number of NOT gates present in RO and the delay present in each phase.

In this Fig. 5 MUX-1 and MUX-2 will select RO-2 and RO-66. Both oscillators RO-2 and RO-66 have different frequencies because of fabrication variations. A square waves pulse with frequency f_A and f_B is received by counter. Now both the counters start from 0 and they will start counting each and every positive pulse received from the multiplexer. The counter counts for a certain period of time. If the count value C_A is greater than C_B the output key will be 1 otherwise 0. The uniqueness of RO-PUF throughout the process is that its output response depends

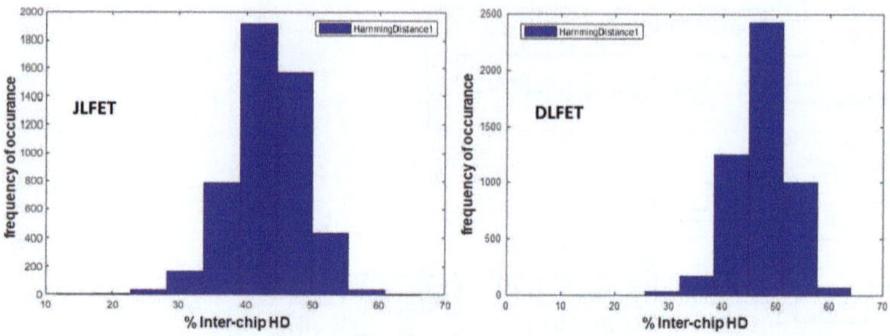

Fig. 6 Frequency of occurrence with Hamming distance for **a** JLFET-PUF and **b** DLJLFET-PUF

on the particular device. If we choose two identical RO-PUFs then each will give a different response to a particular challenge. So, if we run this RO with several different challenges, we can produce a string of output responses that will be independent of the other.

To find the PUF Figures of Merit (FOM), SPICE is used to do Monte Carlo simulations for 100 runs and MATLAB is used for mathematical calculations to obtain the final output. The Inter-chip Hamming Distance serves as a key FOM for PUFs. It is employed to assess the distinctions in the outputs of two PUFs when subjected to the same challenge [21]. Hamming distance (HD) is used to measure bit error rate (BER) which decides the uniqueness of a PUF by observing various PUF responses by changing challenge bits [7]. In the case of an ideal PUF, the Hamming Distance (HD) is expected to precisely equal 50% [10]. If the mean HD is exactly 50 %, it means no correlation between the chips exists. The underlying distribution is known as binomial distribution. Monte Carlo simulations were performed for 100 runs and the output keys were checked for uniqueness. Figure 6a, b shows the frequency of occurrence with Hamming distance between the different keys produced in different runs for JLFET and DLJLFET-PUF, respectively. We observed that for JLFET-PUF the mean HD is 48 % and for DLJLFET-PUF is 51%. It is clearly observed that DLJLFET devices have mean HD closer to 50 % which means DLJLFET devices give more unique PUF. We do Monte Carlo simulations for 100 runs of JLFET-PUF and DLJLFET-PUF at $V_{DD} = 0.9V$ and the frequencies of oscillation are shown in Fig. 7a, b, respectively. We observed that the frequency of oscillation of the DLJLFET is approx 2 times higher than JLFET due to the delay being minimum in DLJLFET as stated above in Eq. 1. Hence, DLJLFET-PUF will take less time during encryption and decryption for incoming and outgoing data, thus the output key generation will be faster.

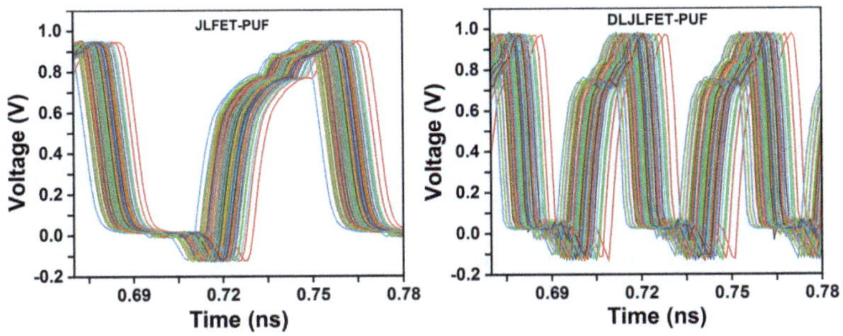

Fig. 7 Monte Carlo simulation is performed for 100 runs of **a** JLFET-PUF and **b** DLJLFET-PUF at $V_{DD} = 0.9V$

5 Conclusion

In this paper, we designed DLJLFET-based RO and a detailed comparative study with JLFET-RO further, a PUFs circuit made from these ROs. We observed that DLJLFET-RO has less delay and consumes less energy than JLFET-RO. The frequency of oscillation of DLJLFET-RO is higher. We did Monte Carlo simulation for 100 runs, and we observed that DLJLFET-PUF has less delay and gives more unique PUF than JLFET-PUF. Finally, DLJLFET-PUF is more reliable, energy efficient, and fast.

Acknowledgements The authors would like to thank the SERB, Government of India, for providing financial support (File No. EEQ/2021/001072).

References

1. Sicari S, Rizzardi A, Grieco LA, Coen-Porisini A (2015) Security, privacy and trust in internet of things: the road ahead. Comput Netw 76:146–164
2. Babaei A, Schiele G (2017) Spatial reconfigurable physical unclonable functions for the internet of things. In: Proceedings of the international conference on security privacy and anonymity in computation, communication and storage, Guangzhou, China, pp 312–321
3. Martinez B, Montón M, Vilajosana I, Prades JD (2015) The power of models: modeling power consumption for IoT devices. IEEE Sensors J 15(10):5777–5789. https://doi.org/10.1109/JSEN.2015.2445094
4. Babaei A, Schiele G (2019) Physical unclonable functions in the internet of things: state of the art and open challenges. Sensors 19:3208. https://doi.org/10.3390/s19143208
5. Chatterjee B, Das D, Maity S, Sen S (2019) RF-PUF: enhancing IoT security through authentication of wireless nodes using in-situ machine learning. IEEE Internet Things J 6(1):388–398. https://doi.org/10.1109/JIOT.2018.2849324
6. Khan S, Prasad A, Gupta C, Chouhan SS, Pandey JP, Vishvakarma SK (2019) An ultra-low power, reconfigurable, aging resilient RO PUF for IoT applications. Microelectron J 92:104605. https://doi.org/10.1016/j.mejo.2019.104605

7. Tumuganti N, Kong J, Choi JR (2017) Novel TCAM-based PUF with improved reliability for hardware-entangled security. IEICE Electron Express 14(17):1–11. https://doi.org/10.1587/elex.14.20170716
8. Rajan C, Sharma D, Samajdar DP (2019) Implementation of physical unclonable functions using hetero junction based GAA TFET. Superlattices Microstructures 126:72–82
9. Rajan C, Samajdar DP (2020) Design principles for a novel lightweight configurable PUF using a reconfigurable FET. IEEE Trans Electron Dev 67(12):5797–5803. https://doi.org/10.1109/TED.2020.3030868
10. Panchore M, Singh J, Mohanty SP, Kougianos E (2016) "Compact behavioral modeling and time dependent performance degradation analysis of junction and doping free transistors. IEEE International symposium on nanoelectronic and information systems (iNIS). Gwalior, India, pp 194–199. https://doi.org/10.1109/iNIS.2016.052
11. Sahoo SR, Kumar S, Mahapatra K, Swain A (2016) A novel aging tolerant RO-PUF for Low power application. In: 2016 IEEE international symposium on nanoelectronic and information systems (iNIS), pp 187–192, https://doi.org/10.1109/iNIS.2016.050
12. Priyanka, Singh S, Panchore M (2022) Dopingless-TFET leaky-integrated-fire (LIF) neuron for high-speed energy efficient applications. IEEE Trans Nanotechnol 21:110–117. https://doi.org/10.1109/TNANO.2022.3151241
13. Bramhane L, Salankar S, Gaikwad M et al. (2022) Impact of work function engineering in charge plasma based bipolar devices. Silicon 14:3993–3997. https://doi.org/10.1007/s12633-021-01146-9
14. ATLAS Users manual, Version 5.2.8.R (2019)
15. Panchore M, Singh J, Mohanty SP (2016) Impact of channel hot carrier effect in junction and doping-free devices and circuits. IEEE Trans. Electron Dev 63(12):5068–5071. https://doi.org/10.1109/TED.2016.2619621
16. Mondal AJ, Talukdar J, Bhattacharyya BK (2020) Estimation of frequency and amplitude of ring oscillator built using current sources. Ain Shams Eng J 11(3):677–686, https://doi.org/10.1016/j.asej.2020.01.006
17. Lee Y, Seong T, Yoo S, Choi J (2018) A low-jitter and low-reference-spur ring-VCO-based switched-loop filter PLL using a fast phase-error correction technique. IEEE J Solid-State Circuits 53(4):1192–1202. https://doi.org/10.1109/JSSC.2017.2768411
18. Coombs D, Elkholy A, Nandwana RK, Elmallah A, Hanumolu PK (2017) 8.6 A 2.5-to-5.75 GHz 5 mW 0.3 psrms-jitter cascaded ring-based digital injection-locked clock multiplier in 65nm CMOS. 2017 IEEE international solid-state circuits conference (ISSCC), pp 152–153, https://doi.org/10.1109/ISSCC.2017.7870306
19. Ho Y, Yang Y-S, Chang C, Su C (2013) A near-threshold 480 MHz 78μW all-digital PLL With a bootstrapped DCO. IEEE J Solid-State Circuits 48(11):2805–2814. https://doi.org/10.1109/JSSC.2013.2280409
20. Zhang Y, Rhee W, Kim T, Park H, Wang Z (2015) A 0.35-0.5-V 18-152 MHz digitally controlled relaxation oscillator with adaptive threshold calibration in 65-nm CMOS. IEEE Trans Circuits Syst II Express Briefs 62(8):736–740, https://doi.org/10.1109/TCSII.2015.2433531
21. Chaudhuri CR, Amsaad F, Niamat M (2016) Impact of temporal variations on the performance and reliability of configurable ring oscillator PUF. In: 2016 IEEE national aerospace and electronics conference (NAECON) and ohio innovation summit (OIS), pp 458–463, https://doi.org/10.1109/NAECON.2016.7856849
22. Xu W-X et al (2020) High-speed ring oscillator using skewed delay scheme integrated by metal-oxide TFTS. IEEE Trans Electron Dev 67(12):5526–5531. https://doi.org/10.1109/TED.2020.3029539
23. Garcia-Bosque M, Díez-SEñorans G, Sánchez-Azqueta C, Celma S (2020) Proposal and analysis of a novel class of PUFS based on Galois ring oscillators. IEEE Access 8:157830–157839. https://doi.org/10.1109/ACCESS.2020.3020020

Dopingless JLFET-Based 8T SRAM Cell Design for Enhanced Performance and Stability

Kanchan Cecil, Ashish Jha, Meena Panchore, and Pushpa Raikwal

1 Introduction

As scaling in MOS field–effect transistor (MOSFET) reaches to sub-nanometer regime, the fabrication of a p–n junction with extremely sharp doping concentration gradient is a significant issue. To address this issue, a new device structure known as junctionless field effect transistor (JLFET) has been proposed, which does not require any p–n junction [1]. This unique property makes JLFET as a promising candidate of modern CMOS technology and offers innate benefits than conventional MOSFET such as simple fabrication step and reduced short-channel effect (SCE) [2]. However, higher body doping in JLFETs to achieve the driving current criterion for high carrier concentration in the channel exaggerates variability issues. As a result, a lowly doped (or dopingless) JLFET, called dopingless (DL) JLFET, has recently been introduced as a potential candidate to counter process variation issues raised by random dopant fluctuations (RDFs) [3, 4]. The DLJLFET incorporates the charge-plasma (CP) theory to develop heavily doped source and drain regions without using ion implantation or chemical doping techniques. Due to the use of lightly doped channel, the DLJLFET is more immune from the process variability issue caused by RDF. At circuit level, the standard 6T static random-access memory (SRAM) cell configuration has been reported in the literature for DL and JLFETs

K. Cecil (✉)
Department of Electronics and Telecommunication Engineering, Jabalpur Engineering College, Jabalpur, M.P, India
e-mail: cecil.kanchan@gmail.com

A. Jha · M. Panchore
Department of Electronics and Communication Engineering, NIT Patna, Bihar 800005, India

P. Raikwal
Department of Electronics and Communication Engineering, PDPM IIITDM, Jabalpur, M.P 482005, India

K. Kumar Singh et al. (eds.), *Machine Vision and Augmented Intelligence*, Lecture Notes in Electrical Engineering 1211, https://doi.org/10.1007/978-981-97-4359-9_2

due to CHC effect. It was found that the DLJLFET 6T SRAM cell are less sensitive to CHC effect as compared to its conventional counterpart JLFET.

However, 6T SRAM has the lowest read stability (RSNM) of all of these topologies, indicating that the cell is most susceptible to noise during read operations. When the cell changes state, this could result in incorrect data being retrieved. In the past studies, the DLJLFET-based 8T SRAM cell has not been analyzed yet to improve the performance and stability of SRAM cell. Hence, in this article, for the first time, we analyzed 8T SRAM cell configuration by employing DL and JL structures in place of access transistors (ATs). With the help of device–circuit co-simulation approach, the performance metrics of 8T SRAM cells such as read static noise margin (RSNM) and read delay are analyzed and compared with their conventional counterpart 6T SRAM cells. We found that DLJLFET-based 8T SRAM cell shows significant improvement in RSNM and read delay than conventional JLFET.

2 Device Parameters and Characteristics

The cross-sectional views of both the conventional JLFET and DLJLFET are shown in Fig. 1a, b, respectively. Except for the gate work functions and the doping concentrations, the dimensions of both the devices are kept identical. The specifications of various parameters are as follows: Silicon film thickness (T_{si}) = 10 nm, gate length (L_G) = 15 nm, effective oxide thickness = 1 nm, and S/D extension (L_{ext}) = 15 nm. In a conventional n-type JLFET, the gate metalwork function is 5.5 eV, and the doping is kept uniform throughout the source/channel/drain region, i.e., (10^{19}cm^3). Similarly, the gate work function for n-type DLJLFETs is 4.73 eV with intrinsic silicon body (10^{15} cm^3) [5].

Figure 2a, b show the transfer characteristics of n- and p-type DL- and JLFET. The I–V characteristics produced by the Verilog-A model are calibrated with TCAD simulation result for both DL and JLFET and reproduced the earlier reported I–V characteristics of both devices [5], as shown in Fig. 2a, b. It is observed that the Verilog-A model characteristics of DL and JLFET show good agreement with TCAD results. One can also observe from Fig. 2 that the ON-state current of DLJLFET is increased by approximately 21% improvement in comparison with JLFET [6, 7].

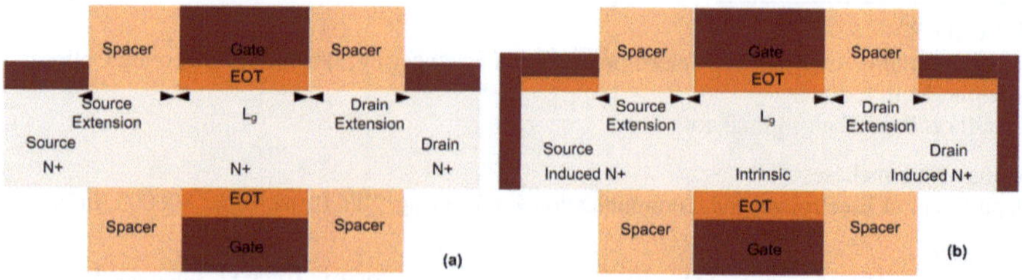

Fig. 1 Cross-sectional view of **a** Conventional JLFET **b** DLJLFET

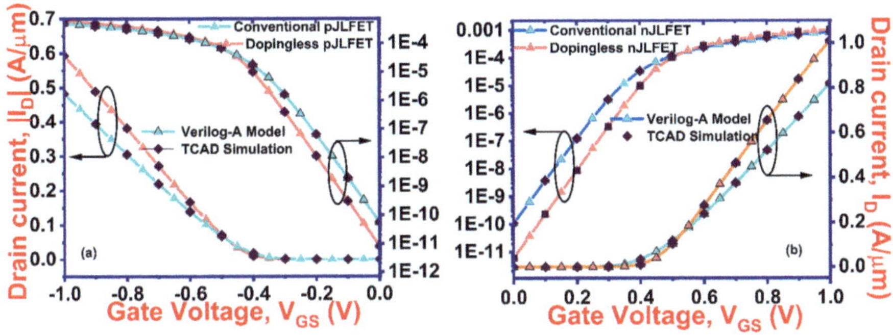

Fig. 2 Transfer characteristics of **a** p-type JLFET and DLJLFET **b** n-type JLFET and DLJLFET

It is because of considering low metal work function material at S/D contact, the DLJLFET shows a significant improvement in I_{ON} than conventional JLFET.

3 Circuit Simulation Methodology

Figure 3 represents the basic schematic circuit diagram of an 8T JLFET-based SRAM cell. It comprises of two sets of access transistors on each side of the storage node. This structure symmetrically resembles the 6T SRAM but the basic difference of this 8T SRAM cell from general 6T SRAM is that it consists of an extra storage line (SL) alongside WL and one extra pair of pass gate type of access transistors (ATs). The data present at the output nodes should be stored in the access transistors (MN_3 and MN_4) before the circuitry is disconnected from the supply. Initially, nodes Q and QB areas summed to be in high (logic 1) and low (logic 0) states, respectively. The storage line (SL) is generally calibrated to the supply voltage. As the left storage node (Q) is at logic high, hence the gate bias of MN_3 is 0. Similarly, the right storage node (QB) is at logic level low, hence the gate bias of MN_3 is VDD. In order to avoid discharging of node Q, the SL is pulled down to the ground before the power is off. During this stage, there is no any effect on the state of node QB [8, 9]. The supply may be disconnected once the data storage operation is completed. Word line is pulled up to V_{DD} before the 8T SRAM cell wakes up during the recall phase, providing a low-impedance path from node QB to ground and a high-impedance path from node Q to ground. Power supply is then pulled up to V_{DD} and charged at both the Q and QB cell storage nodes. Since the bitline capacitances have different strengths in pulling down Q and QB, hence, before the supply is off, the node voltages are restored to their earlier states. The SL is pulled up to V_{DD} after Q and QB have settled down, and the cell is all set to continue its working like a normal SRAM. During the recall operation, the polarization states of MN_3 and MN_4 are not modified. The bitlines are pre-charged to V_{DD} during the read operation. The storage line is increased to V_{DD} in order to provide low-impedance paths between output nodes and transistors

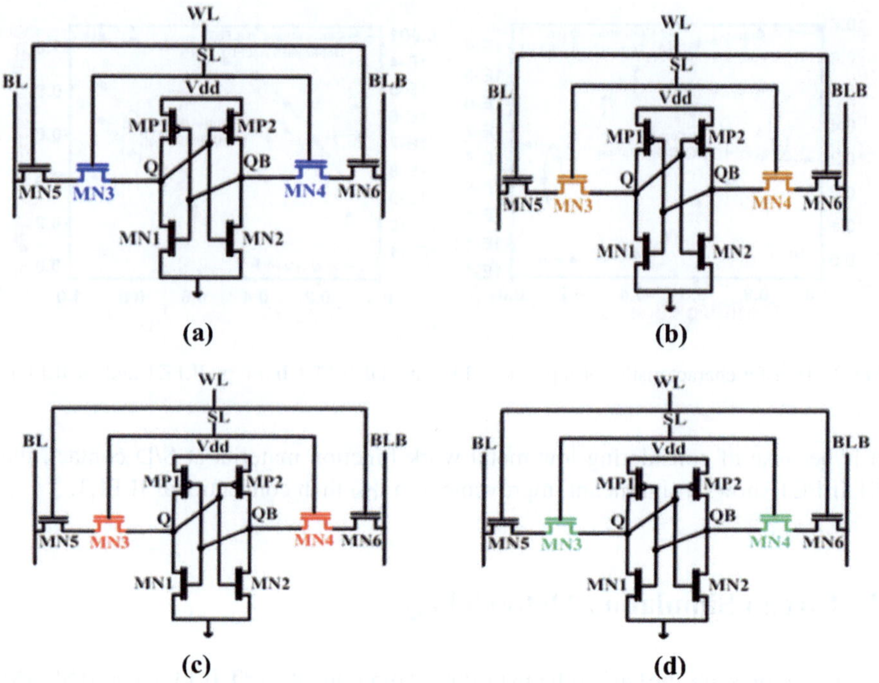

Fig. 3 Schematic of different 8T SRAM cells **a** JLFET **b** DLJLFET **c** AT-DLJLFET **d** AT-JLFET

MN_5 and MN_6. The process of read operation is still initiated by triggering the WL. During the read time, other voltage conditions are analogous to those of a standard 6T SRAM. The SL is raised to V_{DD} during the write operation. As soon as WL is enabled, the output nodes will change their states via bitlines. The writing process is then finished. Delay parameters such as read and write delays are used for the performance evaluation of the SRAM cells. Read and write delays are calculated for the 6T and 8T SRAM cells and compared to conventional and dopingless JLFETs for different configurations of access transistors (ATs). Leakage current is also a major factor for low-power applications.

4 Results and Discussion

Here, we have considered four different configurations by employing different DL- and JLFET-based architectures in place of access transistors of 8T SRAM cell. The simulation of different configurations has been performed on SPICE circuit simulator. In this section, the performance metrics of four different 8T SRAM cell configurations in terms of RSNM and read delay are analyzed and discussed.

A. *Rsnm*

Read Static Noise Margin (RSNM) serves as a scaling element to calculate the stability of SRAM cell during read operation. The width of ATs is kept same as that of pull-down transistors. The RSNM value is extracted using the traditional butterfly method. The RSNM is measured as the side of the maximum square that can be fitted inside the lobes of the butterfly curve. It is observed from Fig. 4 that the highest value of RSNM is calculated for the DLJLFET configuration. Almost 7.5% and 5% of increment have been observed in the RSNM value of DLJLFET configuration for 6T SRAM cell and 8T SRAM cell, respectively. This is due to better drive capability and higher threshold voltage of DLJLFET. Also, there is less fluctuation in threshold voltage (V_{TH}) as compared to that of other device configurations. There is improvement of 12 mV and 8 mV in RSNM, respectively, for conventional and dopingless devices for 6T and 8T SRAM cells, as shown in Fig. 5a.

B. *Read Delay*

Fig. 4 Butterfly curve of different JLFET 8T SRAM cell configurations

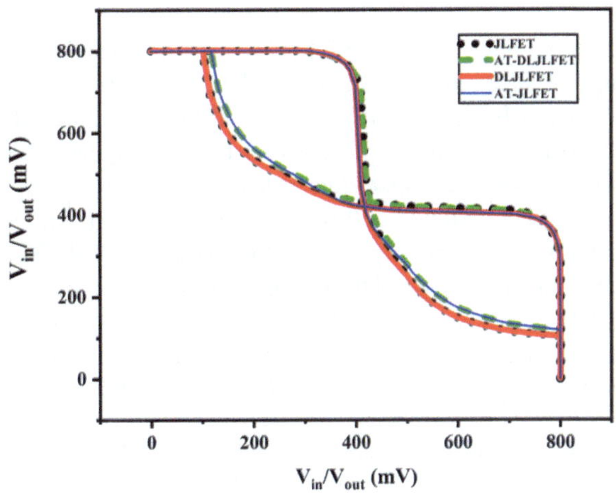

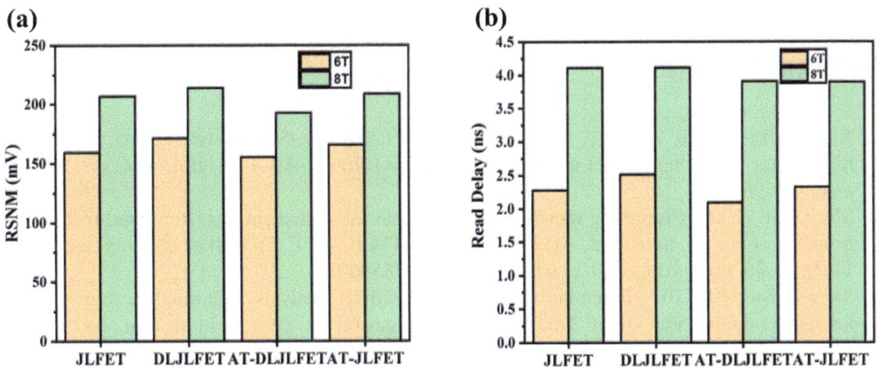

Fig. 5 **a** RSNM and **b** read delay of different 8T SRAM JLFET SRAM cells

Here, we have calculated read delay as the time difference between 90% of BL voltage (falling) and 50% of WL voltage (rising). The access transistors (ATs) have an aspect ratio of 2.5 for read delay measurement setup. For read delay calculation, bitline's capacitance has been set as 10pF. As the bitline(s) capacitance value is much greater than that of the storage node, hence it takes more effort to switch bit line than to switch storing nodes. Hence, read delays are more as compared to delays for write operation. In Fig. 5b, the last configuration in which ATs are made from dopingless JLFET has the minimum read delay for both types of SRAM cells. There is almost 10% and 5% reduction in delays for 6T and 8T cells, respectively. The shrinkage in read delay is because of the higher amount of drain current in DLJLFET after VTH as compared to that of conventional JLFET.

5 Conclusion

In this paper, the new 8T SRAM cell has been proposed by considering different device structures such as DL and JLFET in place of access transistor. From the set of butterfly curves for different 8T SRAM cell configurations, it is observed that DLJLFET-based 8T SRAM cell has the highest value of RSNM and hence it is more immuneto noise due to less fluctuation in V_{TH}. We have also examined the delay of 8T SRAM cell during read operation. The read delay of AT-DLJLFET is observed less as compared to other 6T and 8T SRAM cell configurations due to high driving capability of DL device. From the simulation result, it can be concluded that DLJLFET-based 8T SRAM cell configuration has worked well than other JLFET configuration. Hence, in future, the performance of higher-order SRAM cells such as 9T, 10T, 11T, etc., can also be analyzed using DL devices.

Acknowledgments The authors would like to thank the SERB, Government of India for providing financial support (File No. EEQ/2021/001072).

References

1. Xiang J, Lu W, Hu Y, Wu Y, Yan H, Lieber CM (2006) Ge/Si nanowire heterostructures as high-performance field-effect transistors. Nature 441(7092):489–493. https://doi.org/10.1038/nature04796
2. Moore GE (2009) Cramming more components onto integrated circuits, Reprinted from Electronics, volume 38, number 8, April 19, 1965, pp.114 ff. IEEE Solid-State Circuits Soc Newsl 11(3):33–35, https://doi.org/10.1109/n-ssc.2006.4785860
3. Sahu C, Singh J (2015) Potential benefits and sensitivity analysis of dopingless transistor for low power applications. IEEE Trans Electron Devices 62(3):729–735. https://doi.org/10.1109/TED.2015.2389900
4. Kumar MJ, Nadda K (2012) Bipolar charge-plasma transistor: a novel three terminal device. IEEE Trans Electron Devices 59(4):962–967. https://doi.org/10.1109/TED.2012.2184763

5. Panchore M, Cecil K, Singh J (2020) Impact of temporal variability on dopingless and junctionless FET based SRAM cells. Silicon, pp 1–7, https://doi.org/10.1007/s12633-020-00747-0.
6. Panchore M, Singh J, Mohanty SP (2016) Impact of channel hot carrier effect in junction-and doping-free devices and circuits. IEEE Trans Electron Dev 63(12):5068–5071. https://doi.org/10.1109/TED.2016.2619621
7. Panchore M, Singh J, Mohanty SP, Kougianos E (2017) Compact behavioral modeling and time dependent performance degradation analysis of junction and doping free transistors. In: Proceedings—2016 IEEE international symposium on nanoelectronic and information systems, iNIS 2016, pp 194–199, https://doi.org/10.1109/iNIS.2016.052
8. You WX, Su P, Hu C (2020) A new 8T hybrid nonvolatile SRAM with ferroelectric FET. IEEE J. Electron Devices Soc. 8:171–175. https://doi.org/10.1109/JEDS.2020.2972319
9. Sikarwar V, Khandelwal S, Akashe S (2013) Optimization of leakage current in SRAM cell using shorted Gate DG FinFET. International conference on advanced computing and communication technologies, ACCT, pp 166–170, https://doi.org/10.1109/ACCT.2013.41

Survey on Robustness of Deep Learning Techniques on Adversarial Attacks in WBAN

R. N. L. S. Kalpana, Ajit Kumar Patro, and D. Nageshwar Rao

1 Introduction

Remote healthcare system (WBAN) has got much popularity in recent years because of versatility. WBAN transmit various health-related parameters like BP, pulse, respiration rate, Heart Rate (HR), Electrocardiogram (ECG), and Oxygen Saturation (SpO_2) using local posting unit to authorized medical professional [1]. Probability of detecting diseases is increased with the help of WBAN sensors. With the help of integrated biological signals positioned in body for monitoring vital health signals given improved service delivery through early detection of degrading health condition and prevention of death.

WBAN senor uses transducers for signal detecting. It can be deployed in health care sector within or outside hospital. The WBAN receives and transmit signals over human body surface is more exposed to body fluids. Absorption capability of fluid, transducer, and data injection from outside world causes data anomalies and network faults. These sensor failures or adversarial attacks must be handled by the LPU unit of WBAN to avoid false alarm [2]. Besides WBAN requires higher confidentiality and proper maintains user privacy as number of users increases security vulnerabilities leading to information breach and performance degradation.

The LPU must be robust against adversaries should medially alarm in critical situations, medical emergency. Deep learning is the best technique used for this

R. N. L. S. Kalpana (✉)
Department of ECE, GIET University, Gunupur 765022, Odisha, India
e-mail: rns.kalapana@giet.edu

A. K. Patro
Department of ECE, SoET, GIET University, Gunupur 765022, Odisha, India
e-mail: ajitpatro@giet.edu

D. N. Rao
Department of ECE, TKRCET, Hyderabad 500097, Telangana, India
e-mail: nageshwarrao@tkrcet.com

K. Kumar Singh et al. (eds.), *Machine Vision and Augmented Intelligence*, Lecture Notes in Electrical Engineering 1211, https://doi.org/10.1007/978-981-97-4359-9_3

purpose. Deep learning is an important type of AI with more layers stacked for better reasoning and good level of abstraction for data over different ML techniques. The most popular CNN model of DL architecture with bootstrap performance has been used in many areas like computer vision [3], object detection [4], action recognition [5], pose estimation [6], image segmentation [7], and motion tracking [8].

Inaccurate diagnosis caused by anomalous observation which results from malicious attack targeting WBAN sensors to insert wrong data. So, anomaly detection has been the best solution for WBAN to distinguish between abnormal and normal data. Machine learning and statistical methods are applied to this problem over the past few years. But some solutions still have some limitations in terms of accuracy and features. Based on the challenges faced by the WBAN it is mandatory to focus on further health care, proper quality of service for efficient operations.

Methods and defenses for identifying adverse attacks against the deep learning model have become the greatest deal of interest in research. The step-by-step process of making a model robust against the adversarial attack is such that the model is not fooled by the out-of-distribution examples which are known or unknown attacks.

2 Challenges

Adversary is additional samples or data which is added to original data causes to mislead medical diagnosis, jam the communication network using of medical information misuse. Fast-growing WBAN commercialization raises security and privacy issues in addition to performance issues. As users increase, security vulnerability also increases in WBAN. Adversarial samples are created intentionally and maliciously by introducing an imperceptible perturbation, denoted as η, to clean samples x. When subjected to model F, this manipulation leads to misclassification, and the resulting output, x', exhibits a high confidence level according to the model.

$$F(x) \neq F(X\prime)x\prime - x \leq \eta$$

Important approaches for generating defense against attacks providing taxonomy description of methods results and approaches are concern in this section [1]. Target attack and non-target attack are two types of attacks based on the outcome of model.

1. **Non-target attacks**: in which attacker doesn't have predetermined outcome of target model misprediction means adversarial sample is misclassified by target model.
2. **Target attacks**: The misclassifying of adversarial samples into specified classification category for constructing adversarial samples by considering multiple features.

The adverse example-generating model attacks can be classified based on timing, information, goals, and attack frequency [9].

Timing: Timing is a very important feature when does attack occur. Based on possibility of occurring, it is divided into two types: Evasion and Poisoning attacks. Evasion attack occurs during the time of interference by assuming the model is already trained. Poison attack generally targets the data during the training phase of model.

Information attack: The attack can also occur on information based on the access to it. Attackers accessing level on information leads to dividing adversarial attack types into four categories.

White box attack: In this type of attacking, the attacker will have the deep learning model with full knowledge of target model such as its architecture, parameter values range, and training method information about data used for training. Adversary can unrestrictedly query the model such as gradient and hyperparameters prediction score.

Black box attack: The structure of model, training parameters are hidden to attacker in this type of attack. For developing attacking strategy observation and judging outout by indirect interaction with the model.

Grey box attack: Attacker working with only knowledge of future representation of model and type of model without access to dataset.

Restricted back box: no box attack: The attack aims to assess the feasibility of transferring an assault executed on one DNN to an inaccessible target model, with no information accessible to the attacker. Top of Form [10].

Goals: The goal of attacker in target attack is to give output a specific pattern with the help of algorithm, whereas, in non-targeted attack, it is to reduce the reliability of model or algorithm by forcing a mistake.

The objective of the attacker function is to generate perturbation in one step or in multiple steps based on the attack frequency.

The perturbed input which is close to the input data can be input specific, which will be effective to all inputs in training dataset is called input perturbation. perturbation measurement is the metric used for to measure magnitude. Commonly used metric is l_{norm}, l_2, l_2, l_∞. Robust accuracy is the measurement to compare the different methods of attack.

Attack success rate (ASR): It is the ratio of perturbed samples in dataset to that of all samples in dataset. It is the same as robust accuracy. It is the baseline for an attacker's ability to fool unprotected network.

Adversarial success rate under defense (ASRD): It is the ratio of undetected perturbation to that of all samples in dataset. The attacks have property of transferability which means that samples are global to all models [11]

Adversarial Attack Generation Methods:

For analysis of model performance, the attacker generates data using different methods of attack models. Different types of models are there for generation of adversaries.

L-BFGS: Attacking deep neural network model is first initiated by this algorithm. The goal of this attack is to find the minimum input perturbation in the constrained space of the input to make the model classify wrong. Because of unsolved problem of optimization, this has become unpopular [12].

$$r = x' - x \text{ which means} F(x) \neq F(x') = y'$$

It attacked the best image classification model of time causing the model to misclassify the large no of images. From this author, it is found that the adversaries can be generalized across models.

1. **Fast Gradient Signal Method (FGSM)**: This uses the gradient of deep neural network (DNN) to create adversarial examples [13]. Adversarial perturb is generated by adding noise to input samples, aiming to lower the gradient loss function. Perturb is added to input samples which will become adversarial samples. This process is $x\prime = x + \varepsilon.sign(\nabla j(x, y)$. It generates adversarial samples faster than L-FSGM. It is a simpler and faster method which only calculates gradient of loss function of high probability of adversarial examples that are having small perturbations will not be obtained. This model experimented with SoftMax and Maxout networks on MNIST dataset with high error rate.

R FGSM: $x\prime = x - \varepsilon.sign(\nabla j(x, y)$ adds perturbation in the opposite direction of gradient.

2. **Momentum iterative FGSM**: [14] It is extension of FGSM. increased gradient is calculated iteratively for each small step. It is more perfect than FGSM at a cost of more computational work.

MI-FGSM: [15] It is based on momentum iteration. applying signed gradient for updating of perturbation for generating final perturbation.it is designed with smoother update and faster convergence to avoid risk of local maxima in the process of increasing the success rate at a cost of less transferability.

BIM: It is an extension of FGSM it perturbs multiple small steps along the direction of increasing gradient by iterating along with recalculation of gradient [16]. It generates more accurate perturbation than FGSM with more cost of computational efforts and time.

3. **JSMA method**: It is a white box-based targeted attack algorithm by changing number of pixels in the picture for image [17]. The most influential samples will be used as Perturbance.
4. **Deep fool method**: This method is proposed by L2-based targeted attack called deep fool method [18]. The perturbation is generated by changing hyperplane. The gradient of loss function corresponding input samples and calculate adversarial samples resulting in misclassification. For multiple classification plane, hyperplane must be calculated for each plane individually. This is a reliable method of adversarial robustness to build a robust classifier.

5. **Optimization-based method**: C&W method [19] proposed three adversarial attack methods based on three metrics used for finding perturbations that minimizes similarity metrics. L0—the number of pixels in image that have been modified, L2—Euclidean distance for adversaries and clean samples, and $L\infty$—the max changing value of pixel in sample. The perturbation can be made approximately undetectable by changing these levels. It got 100% success rate of attack on normally trained DNN models of MNIST, CIFAR10, and ImageNet.
6. **Universal Adversarial Perturbation**: UAP (20) is used for different network models. It works by driving close to boundaries of classifier perturbs that are searched and added to each data samples and has the best transferability. Fast feature fool method is proposed by [21] allows training of target model without knowledge of dataset and internal structure of model itself.
7. **GAN-based attack**: [22] This is based on GAN method-based adversarial generative network. It consists of three main components: generator, discriminator, and target neural network. This network generates adversarial by mapping original samples by perturbations in GAN generator section. The discriminator checks the presence of adversarial or not. The target neural network is a spoof with generated adversarial samples. The attack success rate is higher than all network attacks.

Summary of attacks: Table with ref. no.

S no	Type of attack	Name of attack	
1.	White box attack	Non-targeted	FGSM[13]
			MI-FGSM[15]
			BIM-FGSM[16]
			DEEP FOOL[18]
		targeted	R + FGSM[14]
			C&W[19]
			JSAM[17]
2.	Black box attack	Non-targeted	FFF-UAP[20]
			GD-UAP[21]
			GAN-BASED[22]
		targeted	Not discussed in this paper

Defensive methods against adversarial samples:

1. Sample-based detection method: [23] adversarial samples of all DNN effectively detect adversaries using two new features like kernel density estimation, Bayesians neural network.
2. Adding detecting sub network: Adversary Detector Network [24] is pre trained network added with binary detector network which is trained for detection of maleficent samples. The detector is generally CNN. It if effective in finding FGSM 97%, deep fool, 82% BIM attacks 82%.

3. Adding Binary Classifier: [25] This method shows good performance on MNIST, CIFAR, SVM datasets. It is robust to second round adversarial attack with preprocessing step for model protections. It has got limited generalizing capability sensitive to different adversarial sample generation algorithm
4. Feature squeezing: [26] The author suggested the feature size is directly proportional to the attack probability. Following this principle, he suggested a detection method based on feature compression, wherein prediction results are compared between inputs that are compressed and those that are uncompressed.
5. Defensive Distillation: [27] It is an extension of distillation algorithm. The model is trained using original samples and spoofing rate against the adversarial sample is tested before and after applying defensive algorithm (MNIST, CIFAR) datasets are used.
6. Regularization: [28] The author used gradient regularization to improve the robustness against attack by penalizing the degree of output variations with respect to input on a trained object will give small adversarial perturbation which can't affect the prediction results. The author employed gradient regularization to enhance resilience against attacks, penalizing the extent of output fluctuations concerning input in a trained object. This approach results in minimal adversarial perturbation, ensuring negligible impact on prediction outcomes.
7. Deep contractive network: It is an idea based on CAE (Compressed Autoencoder) [29]. This method uses smoothing penalty term of compressed autoencoder which makes output much smoother by making small changes in input not in hidden layers activation values. A slight modification is introduced to the initial sample created by the model itself, and the deep neural network is adjusted to withstand unfamiliar adversarial samples. This process is laborious and requires significant computational resources during the training phase.
8. Defensive approach based on real-world observation: The author suggested two defensive techniques bounded ReLU and Gaussian data augmentation [30]. Bounded ReLU layer as activation layer allowing for enhancing generalization on noise added to original data means gaining robustness to the network this combination has got good results in resisting various adversarial attacks.
9. Magnet: [31] It is a defensive network that doesn't rely on adversarial samples but only by using features of itself like autoencoder.

It is not ideal for white box attacks, but it is good for black box attacks.

10. Defensive-based GAN: [31] It learns data distribution from generators. Generation of clean predictions with adversary inputs is supplied by generators. It is trained using unsupervised learning with original data the success rate is highly correlated with the performance of GAN.
11. Defense based on adversarial training: It is the most effective way for improving robustness of deep NN. A slight modification is introduced to the initial sample created by the model itself, and the deep neural network is adjusted to withstand unfamiliar adversarial samples. This process is laborious and requires significant computational resources during the training phase.

Robustness against the adverse attack is the combination of designing attacks with maximizing the loss of information and defenses with min loss of information. It is divided into two parts:

1. Characterization of attack, min–max optimization problem lower and upper bound approximations to generate models.
2. Investigation, analysis, and categorization of most recent approaches to generate adversarial examples and adversarial retraining.

Gaps:

- Lack of strong universal defense system for new threats and defensive countermeasures are not effective.
- Robustness of DNN is still not explored.
- The surveys on adversarial attacks predominantly focus on image data and neglect other domains such as NLP, voice recognition, and developments in cyberspace security.

For challenges 1 and 3, security system can be developed which can be used in a variety of domains. The model should train with many types of adversarial samples. And robustness of target can be calculated for target model promptly and give defense strategy with high degree of confidence, and for 2, further improvement of robustness evaluation methods with a variety of networks.

To overcome these challenges deep learning holds immense promise in addressing security concerns, showcasing strong capabilities in identifying anomalous behavior across diverse data sources, where other security model fails. Nonetheless, the substantial susceptibility of deep learning models to adversarial attacks poses a significant challenge in elucidating and ensuring their secure and reliable operation.

3 DL Application in Adversaries

An adversarial attack occurs where adverse attack data are fed an input into deep learning model, for example, some features in dataset have been purposefully perturbed to confuse deep learning model for production of incorrect prediction.

The author [32] WBAN depends on the idea of anomalies by using signals from sensors connected to accessing human health conditions using mean time failure which improved the performance of detection of anomalies the performance measure re MTFF is 43.0 s. Detection of failure is 95%.

Methods for detection of anomalies [33] from sensor data with fuzzy cluster and data compression using HADOOP map reduce MTF. This method can access 98–97% of data with few false alarms. The Kalman filter approach identified has great performance in finding physiological reaction in WBAN [34]. The disadvantage of this method is great computation cost for optimum reaction. Ref. [35] proposes An original approach utilizing Gaussian regression and majority voting. It is successful in terms of detection of false positive rate. At a cost of computing complexity and high false alarm rate and sample error. [36] Correlation-based method with threshold (dynamic) to detect anomalies results in degrading temporal correlation for each sensor. [37, 38] Unreliability of certain sensors is generating false alarm using dynamic sliding window with great attention of observer. [39] proposed anomaly detection algorithm for WBAN for claiming false alarm using the correlation between spatial and temporal elements, along with an approximation based on game theory, spatial–temporal correlation, and game theory approximation. The author crafted a novel adversarial attack to evaluate the performance of a network intrusion detection system based on deep learning. Disadvantage is not capable of detecting random charging in various physiological signals. [40] The author evaluated the performance of three intrusion detection models based on CNN, LSTM, and gated recurrent unit with adversarial example such as (FGSM) for checking robustness of three models. The outcome CNN is best and able to withstand such adversarial examples (GRU&LSTM). [41] Anomaly detection for WBAN-based data sampling techniques is for boosting detection speed. [42]. The author devised an innovative adversarial attack to assess the effectiveness of a deep learning-based network intrusion detection system. Two techniques: 1. Model extraction and 2. Saliency map. With these models, attack was successfully compromised attack success rate of 94.3%. [43] Deep autoencoder (DAE), shallow autoencoder (SAG) [44], Ensemble Autoencoder (SAE), 3 models used for anomaly detection with data poisoning attack challenged by and proved that DLL is more robust to attack. [45] With deep neural network and support vector machine, a frame work was proposed to detect data poison attack and evaluate with different state of art of data for several HAR, EEG, and ECG classes. It could detect data poisoning attack effect and remove specific poisoned. [46] Different kind of adversarial approach with adversarial ML classifier in WBAN which fail ML based WBAN [47]. Cognitive machine learning-assisted attack detection framework (CML-ADF) is used in anomaly detection with 95% detection attack prediction with 95% accuracy. [48] CNN + LSTM (conv LSTM) combines capability of hybrid conv LSTM with correlation in various physiological data to detect contextual data point's anomalies in measure data stream accuracy—99%, F1-score is 98%. Individual CNN and LSTM—64% and 64%, respectively.

Summary of Defense Methods

S. no	Study	Providing anomaly detection	Dealing with adversarial attack	Proposing defense method
1	32	√	X	X
2	33	√	X	X
3	34	√	X	X
4	35	√	X	X
5	36	√	X	X
6	37,38	√	X	X
7	39	√	X	X
8	40	√	√	X

(continued)

(continued)

S. no	Study	Providing anomaly detection	Dealing with adversarial attack	Proposing defense method
9	41	√	X	X
10	42	√	√	√
11	43	√	√	X
12	44	√	√	X
13	45	√	√	X
14	46	√	√	√
15	47	√	√	X
16	48	√	√	X

3.1 Conclusion and Future Scope

From the above survey, we can come to the conclusion that the CNN technique of deep learning is good at addressing adversaries and immune to it. If it is used in architecture with other techniques like BiLSTM, it will give good results in future. For further exploration of deep learning models on CNN + BiLSTM, other models need to be explored. A special focus on autoencoders is to be done to further explore of deep learning models.

References

1. Najafirad P (2020) Opportunities and challenges in deep learning adversarial robustness: a survey SH Silva. arXiv preprint arXiv:2007.00753, arxiv.org
2. A survey on deep learning techniques for anomaly detction in HAR, ICSST 2021, CONFERENCE (2021)
3. Voulodimos A, Doulamis N, Doulamis A, Protopapadakis E (2018) Deep learning for computer vision: a brief review. Comput Intell Neuroscience
4. Redmon J, Divvala S, Girshick R, Farhadi A (2016) You only look once: Unified, real-time object detection. In: Proceedings of the IEEE conference on computer vision and pattern recognition, pp 779–788
5. Varol G, Laptev I, Schmid C (2017) Long-term temporal convolutions for action recognition. IEEE Trans Pattern Anal Mach Intell 40(6):1510–1517
6. Cao Z, Simon T, Wei S-E, Sheikh Y (2017) Realtime multi-person 2d pose estimation using part affinity fields. In: Proceedings of the IEEE conference on computer vision and pattern recognition, pp 7291–7299
7. Badrinarayanan V, Kendall A, Cipolla R (2017) Segnet: a deep convolutional encoder-decoder architecture for image segmentation. IEEE Trans Pattern Anal Mach Intell 39(12):2481–2495
8. De La Torre G, Rad P, Choo K-KR (2018) Driverless vehicle security: Challenges and future research opportunities. Future Gen Comput Syst

9. Vorobeychik Y, Kantarcioglu M (2018), Adversarial machine learning. Morgan & Claypool Publishers
10. Chen P-Y, Zhang H, Sharma Y, Yi J, Hsieh C-J (2017) Zoo: Zeroth order optimization based black-box attacks to deep neural networks without training substitute models. In: Proceedings of the 10th ACM workshop on artificial intelligence and security, pp 15–26
11. Lei W, Zhanxing Z (2020) Towards understanding and improving the transferability of adversarial examples in deep neural networks. Proceedings of The 12th Asian conference on machine learning, Eds by Pan SJ, Sugiyama M. 129 of proceedings of machine learning research. PMLR, 2020. 18–20 Nov. P 837–850. https: //proceedings.mlr.press/v129/wu20a.html
12. Intriguing properties of neural networks / Christian Szegedy, Wojciech Zaremba, Ilya Sutskever et al. (2013). arXiv preprint arXiv:1312.6199
13. Goodfellow Ian J, Jonathon S, Christian S (2014) Explaining and harnessing adversarial examples. arXiv preprint arXiv:1412.6572
14. Ensemble adversarial training: aAttacks and defenses / Florian Tramèr, Alexey Kurakin, Nicolas Papernot et al. (2017). arXiv preprint arXiv:1705.07204
15. Dong Y, Liao F, Pang T et al. (2018) Boosting adversarial attacks with momentum. Proceedings of the IEEE conference on computer vision and pattern recognition, pp 9185–9193
16. Alexey K, Ian G, Samy Bet al. (2016) Adversarial examples in the physical world
17. Papernot N, McDaniel P, Jha S et al. (2016) The limitations of deep learning in adversarial settings. 2016 IEEE European symposium on security and privacy (EuroS&P). IEEE, pp 372–387
18. Seyed-Mohsen M-D, Alhussein F, Pascal F (2016) Deepfool: a simple and accurate method to fool deep neural networks. Proceedings of the IEEE conference on computer vision and pattern recognition, pp 2574–2582
19. Nicholas C, David W (2017) Towards evaluating the robustness of neural networks. 2017 IEEE symposium on security and privacy (sp). IEEE. pp 39–57
20. Moosavi-Dezfooli SM, Fawzi A, Fawzi O, Frossard P (2017) Universal adversarial perturbations. Proceedings of the IEEE conference on computer vision and pattern recognition, pp 1765–1773
21. Reddy MK, Utsav G, Venkatesh BR (2017) Fast feature fool: A data independent approach to universal adversarial perturbations. arXiv preprint arXiv:1707.05572
22. Xiao C, Li B, Zhu J-Yet al. (2018) Generating adversarial examples with adversarial networks. arXiv preprint arXiv:1801.02610
23. Feinman R, Curtin RR, Shintre S, Gardner AB (2017) Detecting adversarial samples from artifacts. arXiv preprint arXiv:1703.00410
24. Metzen JH, Genewein T, Fischer V, Bischoff B (2017) On detecting adversarial perturbations. arXiv preprint arXiv:1702.04267
25. Zhitao G, Wenlu W, Wei-Shinn K (2017) Adversarial and clean data are not twins. arXiv preprint arXiv:1704.04960
26. Weilin X, David E, Yanjun Q (2017). Feature squeezing: detecting adversarial examples in deep neural networks. arXiv preprint arXiv:1704.01155
27. Geoffrey H, Oriol V, Jeff D (2015) Distilling the knowledge in a neural network. arXiv preprint arXiv:1503.02531
28. Slavin RA, Finale D-V (2018) Improving the adversarial robustness and interpretability of deep neural networks by regularizing their input gradients. Thirty-second AAAI conference on artificial intelligence
29. Shixiang G, Luca R (2014) Towards deep neural network architectures robust to adversarial examples. arXiv preprint arXiv:1412.5068
30. Valentina Z, Maria-Irina N, Ambrish R (2017). Efficient defenses against adversarial attacks. Proceedings of the 10th ACM workshop on artificial intelligence and security, pp 39–49
31. Dongyu M, Hao C (2017) Magnet: a two-pronged defense against adversarial examples. Proceedings of the 2017 ACM SIGSAC conference on computer and communications security, pp 135–147

32. Dehabadi MSZ, Jahed M (2017) Reliability modeling of anomaly detection algorithms for Wireless Body Area networks. In: Proceedings of the 2017 Iranian conference on electrical engineering (ICEE), Tehran, Iran, 2–4 May 2017; pp. 70–75. [CrossRef].
33. Saneja B, Rani R (2018) An integrated framework for anomaly detection in big data of medical wireless sensors. Mod Phys Lett B 32:1850283. [CrossRef]
34. . Salem, Serhrouchni A, Mehaoua A, Boutaba R (2018) Event detection in wireless body area networks using Kalman filter and power divergence. IEEE Trans. Netw Serv Manag 15:1018–1034. [CrossRef]
35. . Al Rasyid MUH, Setiawan F, Nadhori IU, Sudarsonc A, Tamami N (2018) Anomalous data detection in WBAN measurements. In: Proceedings of the 2018 international electronics symposium on knowledge creation and intelligent computing (IES-KCIC), Bali, Indonesia, 29–30 October 2018; pp 303–309. [CrossRef]
36. Mohamed MB, Makhlouf AM, Fakhfakh A (2018) Correlation for efficient anomaly detection in medical environment. In: Proceedings of the 2018 14th international wireless communications & mobile computing conference (IWCMC), Limassol, Cyprus, 25–29 June 2018; pp 548–553. [CrossRef]
37. Nair SGS, Balakrishnan R (2018) Mitigating false alarms using accumulator rule and dynamic sliding window in wireless body area. CSI Trans ICT 2018, 6, 203–208. [CrossRef]
38. Smrithy GS, Balakrishnan R, Sivakumar N (2018) Anomaly detection using dynamic sliding window in wireless body area networks. In: Data science and big data analytics: ACM-WIR 2018; Springer: Berlin/Heidelberg, Germany, pp 99–108. [CrossRef] .
39. . Arfaoui A, Kribeche A, Senouci SM, Hamdi M (2019) Game-based adaptive anomaly detection in wireless body area networks. Comput Netw 163:106870
40. Nagdeo SK, Mahapatro J (2019) Wireless body area network sensor faults and anomalous data detection and classification using machine learning. In: Proceedings of the 2019 IEEE Bombay section signature conference (IBSSC), Mumbai, India, 26–28 July 2019; pp 1–6
41. Boudargham N, El Sibai R, Abdo JB, Demerjian J, Guyeux C, Makhoul A (2020) Toward fast and accurate emergency cases detection in BSNs. IET Wirel Sens Syst 10:47–60
42. Qiu H, Dong T, Zhang T, Lu J, Memmi G, Qiu M (2023) Adversarial attacks against network intrusion detection in IoT systems. IEEE Internet Things J 8:10327–10335. [CrossRef] Appl. Sci. 2023, 13, 6807 17 of 17
43. . Bovenzi G, Foggia A, Santella S, Testa A, Persico V, Pescape A (2022) Data poisoning attacks against Autoencoder-based anomaly detection models: a robustness analysis. In: Proceedings of the ICC 2022—IEEE international conference on communications, Seoul, Republic of Korea, 16–20 May 2022; pp 5427–5432. [CrossRef]
44. Watson M, Al Moubayed N (2021) Attack-agnostic adversarial detection on medical data using explainable machine learning. In: Proceedings of the 2020 25th international conference on pattern recognition (ICPR), Milan, Italy, 10–15 January 2021; pp 5427–5432
45. Raza A, Li S, Tran KP, Koehl L (2022) Detection of poisoning attacks with anomaly detection in federated learning for healthcare applications: a machine learning approach. arXiv 2022, arXiv:2207.08486. [CrossRef] .
46. Newaz AI, Haque NI, Sikder AK, Rahman MA, Uluagac AS (2020) Adversarial attacks to machine learning-based smart healthcare systems. In: Proceedings of the GLOBECOM 2020–2020 IEEE global communications conference, Taipei, Taiwan, 7–11 December 2020; pp 1–6. [CrossRef]
47. AlZubi AA, Al-Maitah M, Alarifi A (2021) Cyber-attack detection in healthcare using cyber-physical system and machine learning techniques. Soft Comput 25:12319–12332. [CrossRef]
48. Albattah A, Rassam MA (2022) A correlation-based anomaly detection model for wireless body area networks using convolutional long short-term memory neural network. Sensors 22:1951. [CrossRef]

Synergizing Collaborative and Content-Based Filtering for Enhanced Movie Recommendations

Madhav Walia, Shivanshu Raj, M. Aishwary, and T. Jaya Lakshmi

1 Introduction

Over the last few years, movie recommender systems have become important in decision-making. They are changing our experiences online. Internet, smartphones, and cute apps have changed the way people consume material. This new method for finding a movie is very different from the former ones. If recommender systems have more influence over our movie-watching choices, then they must be important to us.

Many years ago, shops such as Blockbuster and DVDs ruled the media entertainment industry. However, as communications technology advanced and the internet became an indispensable part of our lives, media consumption was transformed. With the development of streaming services, how we watch and consume media has been completely changed. With faster Internet speeds and the rise of smart gadgets, streaming services gained popularity. Today people can watch streaming versions of their favorite films and television shows, on computers, smart TVs, tablets, or cellular phones equipped with broadband-compatible systems or portals to clip online clips in real time on the Internet. Streaming services, however, are currently the most significant distribution channel. People can have a great deal of creative power in their free time with original content that is readily shared and paired with personalized recommendations. The choice of entertainment experience that suits your needs while streaming is totally in your hands. You have the freedom to view anything ranging from complete seasons of TV shows to individual episodes.

M. Walia · S. Raj · M. Aishwary (✉) · T. J. Lakshmi
Department of Computer Science and Engineering, School of Engineering and Applied Sciences, SRM University, Guntur, Andhra Pradesh, India
e-mail: aishwary_m@srmap.edu.in

M. Walia
e-mail: madhav_walia@srmap.edu.in

S. Raj
e-mail: raj_shivanshu@srmap.edu.in

K. Kumar Singh et al. (eds.), *Machine Vision and Augmented Intelligence*, Lecture Notes in Electrical Engineering 1211, https://doi.org/10.1007/978-981-97-4359-9_4

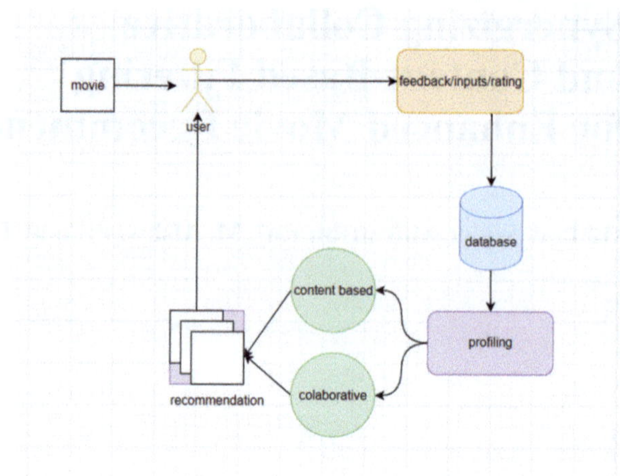

Fig. 1 Design of a recommender system

Due to the dynamic nature of the environment, the importance of recommendation systems has increased. Streaming services offer an abundance of high-quality content; nevertheless, clients are sometimes unsure about what to watch next. Recommendation systems, enabled by sophisticated algorithms and user data analysis, play a crucial role in providing personalized recommendations based on user preferences. Additionally, these algorithms forecast your interests (Fig. 1).

2 Literature

In our approach we begin with TF-IDF, a popular approach in information retrieval, and text mining. It is the statistical measure that shows how important or how frequent a term appears in a given document out of the whole document set (corpus or collection). TF-IDF combines two key components: TF and IDF. Term frequency (TF) determines how many times a term appears in a particular document. Such is done by dividing the frequency of occurrence of a particular term within the document in question by the number of terms in it. TF stands for the frequency of a term in a document and is equal to the number of times that term occurs in the document divided by the total number of terms in the document and demonstrates the importance of the term. Another measure used in vector space model [1] is the inverse document frequency (IDF) which describes how rare or unique a term is in the entire corpus. It is calculated by using the natural logarithm of the proportion of the corpus documents which contain a certain term from the whole set of documents in the corpus. According to IDF, rare words are more informative and possess more discriminative power. If we want to calculate the TF-IDF score for a certain word in a particular document, we would have to multiply together the term frequency (TF) and the inverse document frequency (IDF). The final score indicates the term's importance in a document. The TF-IDF technique is commissioned to evaluate the pertinence of

Fig. 2 Cosine similarity

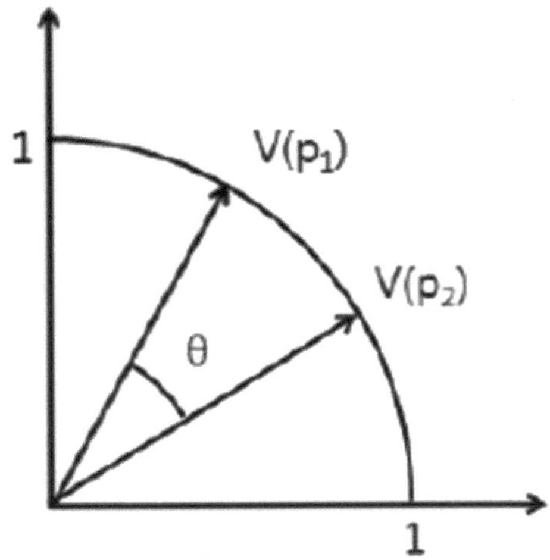

movies By calculating TF and IDF scores for every term in movie, it is possible to identify components that facilitate the recommendations (Fig. 2).

Cosine similarity is a metric used in this work for computer similarity. We use cosine similarity to determine how comparable movies are based on their descriptions. The dimensions of each movie's vector representation in a multidimensional space matched specific words and phrases [1].

The calculation of the cosine similarity between the two movies involves taking their dot product and dividing it by their respective magnitudes. At this stage, the resultant similarity score does not depend on the length of the vectors but on their directed nature instead. In general, for a system of recommendations based on its content, cosine similarity is especially helpful for the identification of films that possess identical text features. We can also use the textual cosine similarity between a target movie and every other movie in our dataset, allowing us to easily find which movies are most like it. More movie together with these similar movies would help users get a bit of an idea about more key in forming this type of compacted space.

The conclusion is that our content-based recommender system can find movies with similar content by utilizing cosine similarity. This enables us to offer users tailored suggestions based on their interests and preferences (Fig. 3).

Finally, we used singular value decomposition. SVD is a matrix factorization [2] technique that factorize given similarity matrix into basis matrices.

We applied SVD to collaborative filtering. The user–item rating matrix can be divided into three matrices using SVD: the user matrix, the item matrix, and the singular value matrix.

The similarity matrix stores the relationships between users and items. The values of each latent factor are represented by the elements of the singular value matrix. Singular Value Decomposition (SVD) accurately finds the latent factors that impact user preferences by decomposing the user–item rating matrix into three separate matrices. This method identifies underlying links between users and items [3].

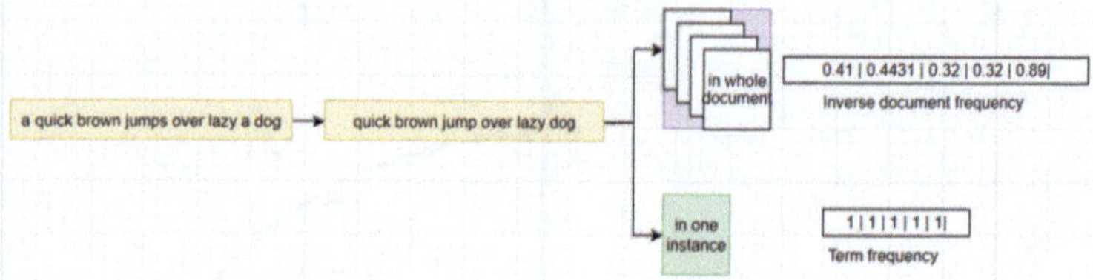

Fig. 3 The basic idea of TF-IDF

In order to attain the most accurate estimate, SVD chooses the dormant components that are associated with the largest singular values. This reduces calculation by selectively gathering crucial information and eliminating inappropriate data.

3 Recommender System Selection

3.1 Content-Based Recommender System

We at first created a recommender system that specifically points up content-based filtering. We use cosine similarity and TF-IDF (Term Frequency–Inverse Document Frequency) algorithm to produce suggestions from movie text. This procedure recommends movies based on their qualities by extracting pertinent information and computing similarity scores. There are limitations amalgamated with this approach in terms of accurately determining user preferences and providing recommendations across different genres [4].

3.2 Metadata-Based Recommender System

We next designed a recommender based on the content-based model, including actors, directors, and other related attributes. We improved the accuracy of the recommendation using more information, based on the CountVectorizer. A sophisticated content-driven mechanism takes advantage of the shared factors of movies and employs machine learning to deliver better recommendations suited to the individual preferences of users (Fig. 4).

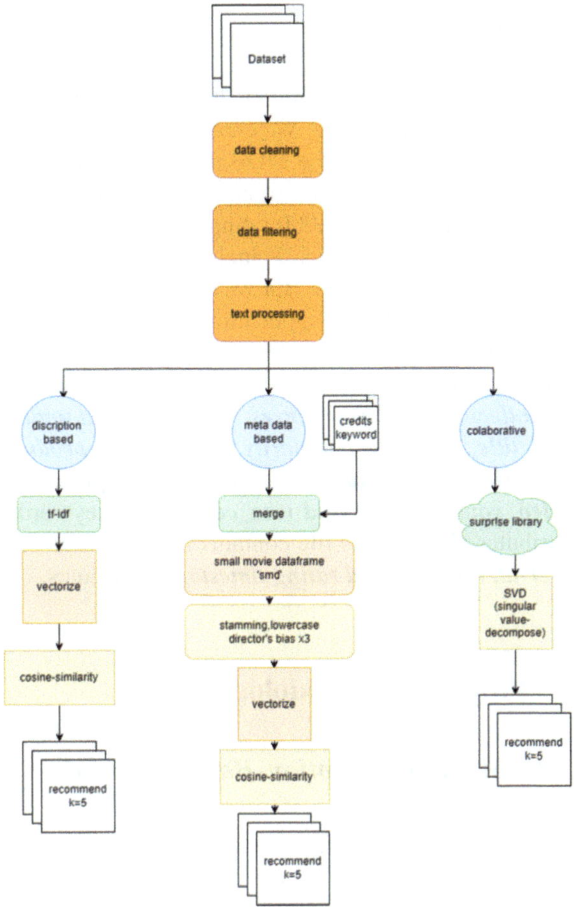

Fig. 4 An overview of our recommendation engine

3.3 Collaborative Filtering Recommender System

Recognizing the need for personalized recommendations, we implemented a collaborative filtering-based recommender system. Collaborative filtering relies on the concept that users similar to an individual can be used to predict their preferences for movies they have not yet experienced. By analyzing the preferences and ratings of similar users, this system captures the taste and preferences of an individual to offer personalized recommendations. Collaborative filtering provides a user-centric approach to recommendation, addressing the limitations of content-based systems and delivering recommendations based on user similarities.

4 Dataset

We picked up data from Kaggle by the name of TMDB datasets. TMDB will stand for The Movie Database. We chose the TMDB dataset because it provided a rating attribute in contrast to the MDB database, which lacked it. For the development of our recommender system, we need movie ratings from users.

It consists of 26,000,000 ratings and 750,000 tag applications applied to 45,000 movies by 270,000 users. It includes tag genome data with 12 million relevance scores across 1,100 tags. But we took a smaller version, which comprises 100,000 ratings and 1,300 tag applications applied to 9,000 movies by 700 users. The dataset consists of a file containing ratings, credits, keywords, movie metadata, and links. Metadata file contains 22 attributes for each movie ***namely, adult,belongs_to_collection, budget, genres, homepage, id,imdb_id, original_language, original_title, overview, popularity, poster_path, production_companies, production_countries, release_date, revenue, runtime, spoken_languages, status, tagline, title, video, vote_average, and vote_count.*** The keyword file contains ***id and keywords*** attributes. The credits file contains the ***cast, crew, and id.*** The rating file contains ***user-id, movieid, and rating timestamp*** attributes.

5 Proposed Methodology

5.1 Movie Description-Based Method

To implement the content-based recommendation algorithm, we first used a text vectorization technique to convert the text in the combined column of movie taglines and descriptions into a matrix of features. Specifically, we used the TfidfVectorizer function from the scikit-learn library to transform the text into a matrix of term frequency–inverse document frequency (TF-IDF) features. This feature matrix included both individual words and pairs of words, and common English stop words were removed to improve the quality of the features.

The cosine similarity between pair of movies is calculated. In our implementation, we computed the cosine similarity between movie TF-IDF vectors using the linear_kernel function from the scikit-learn library. The movies with the highest cosine similarity scores are used to generate recommendations for a particular film.

Overall, our implementation of the content-based recommendation algorithm successfully leverages the textual content of each movie's tagline and description columns to generate recommendations based on similarities between movies.

5.2 Movie Metadata-Based Method

The natural language processing approach, combined with machine learning algorithms, is used by movie metadata-based recommender systems to analyze movie descriptions and suggest personalized recommendations to users. These systems know what is in a movie and the context of the movie so that they can spot similarities and patterns of like-minded movies to recommend to a user. With this method, people find movies they like since those movies relate to what is written in their profiles.

In order to utilize the metadata-driven content recommender effectively, we need to merge our existing dataset and the crew's dataset with the keyword lists. Initially, we extract information from two distinct CSV files that contain data about keywords and credits. Subsequently, we transform all the attributes into integer values in order to facilitate the process of vectorization. This is done for the movie data, as well as for the keywords and credits. Ultimately, we perform the merging operation on the movie data frame by matching it with the shared column "id" from the "credits" and "keywords" data frames. Ultimately, we downsize the initial filmic data frame to obtain a compact data frame that exclusively includes movies that have matching ids. We have now reduced our cast, crew, genres, and credit information to single data points. To further refine our data, we will apply the following considerations:

- **Crew**: From the crew, we will exclusively select the "director" as our key feature, recognizing that their role has the most significant influence on the overall "feel" of the movie, in contrast to other crew members whose contributions may be comparatively less impactful.
- **Cast**: Choosing a cast is a little more tricky. We understand that lesser-known actors and minor roles have a relatively minor impact on viewers' opinions of a movie. Consequently, our selection criteria will focus solely on the major characters and their corresponding actors. As an arbitrary but practical choice, we will opt to include the top three actors who appear in the credits list for each movie. We now filter the original movie data frame based on the "id" values present in the list. This results in a smaller data frame called "smd", which focuses on a specific subset of movies for further analysis. The subsequent transformations applied to "smd" involve converting the "cast", "crew", and "keywords" columns from string representations to Python objects using the literal_eval function. This allows for easier manipulation and access to the respective data.

However, this is because this code enhances the usefulness of these transformed fields on the merged data frame, such as cast, crew, and keywords. Cast size and crew size, which are other important aspects, can contribute to future investigations or elements of a recommender system. Moreover, the "cast" column in the "smd" data frame provides crucial information about the cast, which is very helpful and easily understandable. It also helps in analysis because it presents summarized lists of how the cast of the movie is involved in their different aspects.

Table 1 Contains the most relevant keywords and their word count

Keywords	Count
Independent Film	610
Woman Director	550
Murder	399
Credits Stinger	327
Based on Novels	318

During our process, after lowercase conversion and white space removal, we generated credit and genre information useful in repeating the director's name three times to ensure the greater weight of the director rather than the cast. We pre-parse keywords for better utilization in future processing.

Firstly, in the initial stage of our survey, we calculate the frequency counts of all keywords. The analysis shows that the frequency of keywords ranges between one and six hundred and ten, as documented in Table 1 presented below. The keywords, which appear only once, are of no practical value to us, and therefore they can be deleted. Afterwards, we use stemming to normalize every word to treat words like "dogs" and "dog" equally in our research.

We now vectorize the data with the "CountVectorizer" function. The "soup" column in the "smd" data frame is converted into the form of a matrix representation where the word is considered to be an individual token, unigrams and bigrams are taken into account, all words that appear at least once across documents are included, and common English words are excluded.

Eventually, the cosine similarity is computed between every two films using the weight matrix. The cosine similarity measures how much a single vector is related to another one. It is commonly used as a measure of item similarity in the area of recommendation systems based on specific properties.

5.3 Collaborative Method

To address the limitations of our content-based recommendation engine and provide more personalized recommendations, we adopted collaborative filtering. Collaborative filtering leverages the preferences and ratings of similar users to predict a user's preferences or ratings for specific items. Therefore, in our case, we applied the Surprise library, which is a very efficient component for designing recommender systems. We used Surprise's SVD (Singular Value Decomposition) in a specific way. Matrix factorization [2] employing singular value decomposition (SVD) and minimizing RMSE can yield good prediction accuracy for recommendations [3].

First, we created a reader object from the Surprise library, which helped in the processing of rating information. Finally, we incorporated rating information from a file to prepare it for analysis. Using the Surprise library, we checked the first entries in the dataset. Through the use of the Surprise library, we created a dataset object ready for collaborative filtering. Hence, we were able to place the data in an appropriate order, taking into consideration only specific columns that facilitated collaborative filtering. Finally, we initialized the SVD model, which is one of the key elements of collaborative filtering in Surprise.

To analyze the performance of our SVD model, we utilized the Surprise library to perform cross-validation. The technique divided the data into multiple train–test folds and calculated evaluation metrics including RMSE and MAE [5]. We subsample the rating data to analyze the rates supplied by a specific user for a more complete study.

Lastly, we estimated ratings by using the SVD model to predict certain user and item characteristics. Noteworthy is the fact that we did not take into account the content or attributes of the items in our collaborative filtering process, which was carried out using the Surprise library and the SVD model [6]. Instead, we only took into account the user-assigned identifiers and ratings.

We successfully addressed our content-based engine's limitations by utilizing the SVD model and integrating collaborative filtering with the Surprise library. Our recommendations were tailored to each individual based on their ratings and preferences.

6 Results and Analysis

In this section, we present a comprehensive comparison of two content-based recommendation methods. We evaluate these methods using precision, recall, F1-score, and NDCG (Normalized Discounted Cumulative Gain) values. The results for the two different models, namely "Description Based" and "Metadata Based," are summarized in Table 2.

Precision Analysis

Precision refers to the degree to which the model correctly detects positives. The precision of the "description-based" and "metadata-based" models is amazing. "Description-based" gets a precision of up to 0.998417, and the precision for "metadata-based" is even greater, scoring at 0.999088. These findings show that the two approaches are effective in recognizing true cases; therefore, they can be used in tasks with low levels of tolerating misleading positives.

Recall Analysis

Table 2 Contains the performance scores of both methods

Performance	Description-Based	Metadata-Based
Precision	0.998417	0.999088
Recall	0.002343	0.003343
F1-Score	0.004675	0.006663
NDGC	0.988573	0.994544

Recall measures the ability of a model to capture a significant number of positive instances from the total pool. "Description Based" exhibits a relatively low recall of 0.002343, implying that it may struggle to identify a substantial portion of positive instances. On the other hand, "Metadata Based" performs slightly better with a recall of 0.003343. While the improvement is marginal, it suggests that "Metadata Based" has a better capacity to capture positive instances, providing a more balanced evaluation of the model's performance.

F1-Score Analysis

The F1-score encompasses precision and recall for evaluating model performance. Both models have low F1-scores. The F1-score of content-based method is 0.004675, whereas that of metadata-based is 0.006663. These results demonstrate the need for more optimization to attain a better balance.

NDCG Analysis

The ranking quality of the recommendations is measured by NDCG. The NDCG for "Description Based" is 0.988573, which signifies a high level of quality. With an NDCG of 0.994544, "Metadata Based" exhibits a marginally superior performance, thereby reasserting its preeminence in delivering pertinent and highly ranked suggestions. Metadata-based approaches appear to be more effective than description-based approaches with regard to precision, recall, F1-score, and NDGC. In spite of this, the recall values of both models remain comparatively low, indicating that they could be enhanced to capture a greater number of positive instances. Additional examination and inquiry are required in order to comprehend the particular attributes and constraints of the models and arrive at well-informed conclusions regarding improvements or optimizations. In response to the constraints of our content-based recommendation system and in an effort to deliver more tailored suggestions, we implemented collaborative filtering. We calculated the efficacy of this filter using the root mean square error (RMSE) and the mean square error (MSE).

7 Conclusion

This research paper presents a movie recommendation system that combines two techniques: collaborative filtering and content-based filtering. It generates individualized and reliable suggestions based on users' interactions with specific items as well as film attributes. This system uses various steps to acquire metadata and text-based attributes from the data. Various measures of assessing the system's performance are used by the system, which displays impressive accuracy and relevancy. The effectiveness of the recommended solution was evaluated through well-established measures, including various metrics. The system's predictive ability is measured using MAE and RMSE [5], which are classified as accuracy metrics. Also, relevance indices such as accuracy, recall, and F1-score help determine how a recommendation system is tailored toward user interests. The accuracy of descriptive and metadata-based recommendation systems is almost the same.

Though the recall score of a metadata-based system is higher than the other, it indicates that it is effective at identifying and suggesting relevant items to users, particularly in the context of information retrieval or recommendation tasks. In learning user profiles and providing a more luring recommendation, a metadata-based recommender outperforms the other. A similar outperformance can be observed with a higher F1-score for the metadata-based recommender. This means it will also recommend luring recommendations with more accuracy. To understand this better, the reader shall think of what accuracy means and how it is different from precession; they are not the same. Precision, on the other hand, measures the accuracy of positive predictions made by a model. It calculates the number or proportion of true positives out of all positives. In other words, in addition to enticing information, the recommended information from the metadata-based recommender has such accuracy that the chances of users spending more time on the website will greatly rise. Utilizing a recommendation engine for a movie, therefore, increases the time spent on the platform and consequently improves revenue for a media platform or e-commerce platform that operates using advertisement. However, an explanation-oriented model may yield relevant user recommendations but might not be effective enough. Hereby, we are unable to recommend users with high accuracy. Hence, these types of engines can be adopted on platforms whose recommendations are insufficient to sustain engagement among users on the platform. In a sense, this acts as a general recommendation service for an unregistered user on the platform. On the other hand, he will be told what people from his neighborhood like, though not exactly what suits him. Such a recommendation would be optimal for new users who are not logged in; the company does not have a user profile for that person, yet they need suggestions about what to consume based on their needs. Lastly, there is nothing notable regarding the mean differences in NDGC scores. While trying to make use of the idea as the reader, its essence does not require choosing between them since it's straightforward enough so it may be implemented. There is one less thing to worry about. How good that could be!

Future research can focus on incorporating additional data sources for improved personalization and the user experience. Exploring deep learning techniques and leveraging NLP can enhance system performance. User studies and feedback collection would provide valuable insights into refinement and addressing limitations.

References

1. Salton G, Wong A, Yang CS (1975) A vector space model for automatic indexing. Commun ACM 18(11):613–620
2. Koren Y, Bell R, Volinsky C (2009) Matrix factorization techniques for recommender systems. Computer 42(8):30–37. https://doi.org/10.1109/MC.2009.263
3. Golub GH, Reinsch C (1970) Singular value decomposition and least squares solutions Numerische Mathematik 14(5):403–420

4. Kumaar H, Srikumaran S, Veni S (2022) Content-based movie recommender system using keywords and plot overview 2022 international conference on wireless communications signal processing and networking (WiSPNET), 49–53
5. Sarwar B, Karypis G, Konstan J, Riedl J (2001) Item-based collaborative filtering recommendation algorithms. In: Proceedings of the 10th international conference on world wide web (WWW '01). association for computing machinery, New York, NY, USA, 285–295
6. Mu Y, Wu Y (2023) Multimodal movie recommendation system using deep learning. Mathematics 11(4):895

Exploring Transformer-Based Approaches for Hyperspectral Image Classification: A Comparative Analysis

Rajat Kumar Arya and Rajeev Srivastava

1 Introduction

High-dimensional data rich in spectral and spatial information is hyperspectral imagery (HSI). Numerous fields, such as object detection, mineral exploration, urban planning, precision agriculture, and ecological science, are valuable due to their fine-grained material discrimination [1]. Traditional feature selection focuses on retaining the most pertinent spectral channels while discarding those with minimal contribution to classification [2]. Recently, convolutional neural networks (CNNs) have been used in remote sensing more frequently due to their ability to extract local information automatically, which is crucial for hyperspectral classification. Significant instances are Siamese CNNs [3], multi-scale dense networks [5], and deep fusion residual networks [4]. Unfortunately, many CNN-based methods often achieve a limited receptive field by extracting data from the deepest convolutional or pooling layers.

Consequently, these models prioritize local features while overlooking the global context of the entire image [6]. The introduction of transformers has offered a solution to this issue. Transformers incorporate a self-attention mechanism that allows them to capture global data correlations more effectively, independent of external information. In computer vision, transformers have been adapted into vision transformers (ViTs) for processing images, proving effective in target detection, image recognition, video comprehension, and image enhancement.

R. K. Arya (✉) · R. Srivastava
Department of Computer Science and Engineering, Indian Institute of Technology-BHU, Varanasi, India
e-mail: rajatkumararya.rs.cse22@itbhu.ac.in

R. Srivastava
e-mail: rajeev.cse@itbhu.ac.in

K. Kumar Singh et al. (eds.), *Machine Vision and Augmented Intelligence*, Lecture Notes in Electrical Engineering 1211, https://doi.org/10.1007/978-981-97-4359-9_5

2 Literature Review

Established backbone networks have recently proven highly effective in task categorization of hyperspectral (HS) images [7]. These networks include types such as autoencoders (generative adversarial networks (GANs), recurrent neural networks (RNNs), capsule networks (CapsNet), graph convolutional networks (GCNs), and convolutional neural networks (CNNs) [8]. Principal component analysis (PCA) derived dimension-reduced images have been used to extract deep feature representations using Stacked AE networks [9]. CNNs with stacked AEs were employed by Chen et al. [10] to improve image classification accuracy by collecting features from HS images. An RNN model that efficiently captures the relationship between bands was presented by Hang et al. [11] for HSI classification. To solve HSI classification issue, three PCA components of noise were added to GANs [12]. Paoletti et al. [13] enhance a CNN-based model by incorporating a capsule unit, improving HSI classification and optimizing network architecture performance. Hong et al. [14] have compared CNNs and GCNs for HSI classification and suggested miniGCNs, a batch graph convolutional network, to tackle challenges caused by enormous graphs in GCNs, leading to state-of-the-art performance. Yadav et al. [15] introduced Pixel Certainity Active Learning (PCAL), which utilizes extended differential patterns (EDP) to improve image quality. They applied Histogram Equalization (HE) to improve the images and Distributed Intensity Filtering (DIF) for noise reduction. Jawaharlalnehru et al. [16] proposed an enhanced YOLO algorithm for better target object detection in UAV images. Their improvements addressed low accuracy, slow detection, missed targets, and mispredictions. Khan et al. [17] presented a crowd anomaly detection model based on AlexNet for video frames. The model comprises four convolution layers (CLs) and three Fully Connected layers (FC) with ReLU activation, employing backpropagation for weight adjustments.

However, specific limitations persist:

- CNNs excel in extracting spatial and local contextual information from HS images but struggle with capturing sequence attributes, especially mid and long-term dependencies. This limitation impacts classification tasks with diverse and highly similar spectral signatures.
- RNNs are designed for sequences and accumulate spectral features band-by-band from HS images. This approach is sensitive to spectral order and can struggle with learning long-term dependencies, leading to difficulty capturing significant spectral changes [18].
- Other backbone networks, such as GANs, CapsNet, and GCNs, have strengths in learning spectral representations but generally fall short in effectively modeling sequential information, which is crucial in HS image classification.

To address these limitations, we propose a new perspective for HS image classification using current state-of-the-art transformers [19]. Unlike CNNs and RNNs, transformers incorporate self-attention techniques, optimizing the processing and analysis of sequential (or time series) data. This aligns well with HS data processing, making transformers suitable for HS image classification. The self-attention block in transformers excels at capturing global sequential information with positional encoding [20]. However, transformers also exhibit drawbacks that hinder their performance improvement:

(1) While transformers handle long-term dependencies of spectral signatures effectively, they struggle with capturing local contextual or semantic features.
(2) Skip connections are pivotal in transformers, aiding gradient propagation and memory enhancement. Nevertheless, the connectivity across layers or blocks is weakened because the additive skip connection function is only available for each transformer block [21].

For these reasons, we conducted a comparative analysis to evaluate the performance of transformers in HS image classification.

3 Implemented Models

In our research, we developed and tested several models like ViT, SSRN-ViT, SpectralFormer, and double-ViT for hyperspectral image classification. We trained and assessed these models using various metrics to gauge their accuracy and suitability for handling hyperspectral data. Our findings compare these models. Emphasize the advantages of using approaches in classifying hyperspectral images.

3.1 ViT Model

The ViT (Vision Transformer) model [22] is an architecture based on transformers used for visual recognition tasks. It divides input images into patches. Processes them through self-attention and feed-forward networks to capture the relationships within the image. When classifying images, this model has been adapted to handle data leveraging self-attention to learn distinctive features. Its ability to handle data and long-range dependencies makes it well-suited for working with data. We have trained this model on the Indian Pines dataset. However, there is still a need for improvement to enhance the performance of this dataset (Fig. 1).

3.2 Double-ViT

The double-ViT model [23] combines two ViT models to capture both spectral details in hyperspectral image classification. It consists of two branches, one dedicated to information and the other focused on information. This combination provides

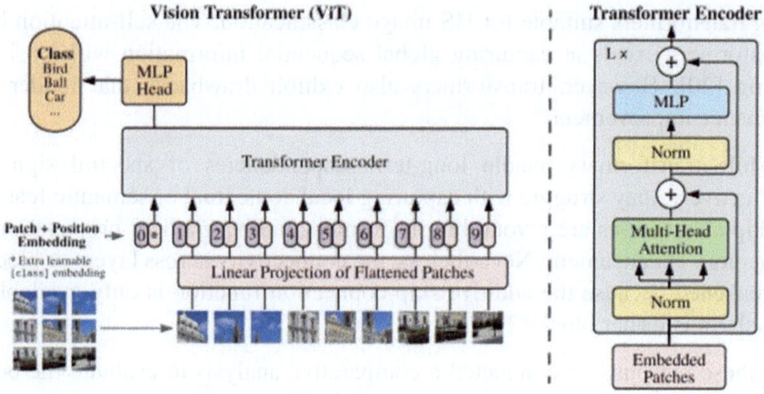

Fig. 1 Vision transformer architecture [22]

a representation for classification. However, it requires resources for training and inference due to the computational intensity of two ViT models.

3.2.1 SpectralFormer (Pixel Wise)

The SpectralFormer model [24] adopts a pixel-level approach for hyperspectral image classification. It treats each pixel as an input, enabling it to capture spectral information at the pixel level. SpectrualFormer excels in learning patterns across neighboring bands of images in a localized manner. It incorporates layer skip connections to preserve important information during propagation. Its objective is to extract spectral and spatial features to enhance classification accuracy (Fig. 2).

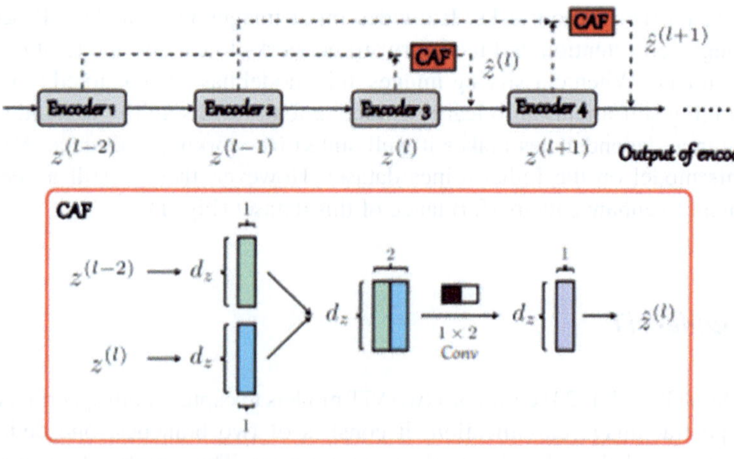

Fig. 2 SpectralFormer architecture [24]

3.2.2 SpectralFormer (Patch Wise)

This variation of SpectralFormer takes a patch approach by dividing the image into fixed-sized patches and treating each patch as an input for classification. More context and spatial relationships between pixels could be gathered using this procedure, enhancing the pixel-by-pixel method's accuracy. However, Improvements must be made using hybrid models that integrate structures.

3.3 SSRN-ViT

The spatial-spectral residual network (SSRN) and vision transformer (ViT) models are combined in this SSRN ViT model [25]. While the ViT enhances spectrum information using transformer-based architecture, the SSRN emphasizes details through layers. SSRN ViT can gather precise spatial and spectral information for HSI classification despite integrating both components. It achieves accuracy; however, significant fluctuations suggest that further research and improvements are needed. There is potential to enhance its architecture and training techniques for improvements.

4 Experiments

4.1 Dataset Description

Using an Airborne Visible/Infrared Imaging Spectrometer (AVIRIS) sensor, the Indian Pines Data [26] were first gathered in 1992 in Northwestern Indiana, USA. This is a 145 $\times$ 145 pixel hyperspectral (HS) image with a 20-m ground sampling distance (GSD). With a resolution of 10 m, the image is made up of 220 bands that span wavelengths from 400 to 2500 nm. The dataset contains 200 bands after 20 water absorption bands are removed, specifically bands 1–103, 109–149, and 164–219. This dataset is primarily focused on 16 specific categories within the scene.

4.2 Implementation Details

We used the PyTorch platform, with an i7 6850 K CPU, 128 GB RAM, and an NVIDIA GTX 1080Ti 11 GB GPU, to develop the implementation details of our models. Our optimizer of choice was Adam. We worked with a minibatch size of 64. Initially, we set the learning rate at 5e-4. It decreased it by 0.9 every tenth of the epochs. It is worth mentioning that the SpectralFormer model, which includes

Table 1 Results comparison analysis

Models	Dataset	Overall accuracy (%)	Average accuracy (%)	K (Cohen's Kappa)
ViT	Indian pines	71.86	78.97	0.6804
Double ViT		100	89.19	0.9821
Spectral former (Pixel-wise)		78.55	84.68	0.7554
Spectral former (Patch-wise)		81.76	87.81	0.7919
SSRN-ViT		91.90	77.94	0.8926

the CAF (Channel Attention Fusion) module, showed efficiency improvements as it achieved convergence in 300 epochs when applied to the Indian Pines dataset.

5 Results and Evaluation

During our evaluation of models, we tested ViT, ViT, SpectralFormer (pixel- and patch-wise), and SSRN ViT (Table 1).

In summary, the double ViT showed superior accuracy and a consistently high average accuracy, which makes it an attractive model. The evaluations of the SpectralFormer models showed good performance both pixel-wise and patch-wise. Overall, the SSRN ViT model showed good accuracy. The outcome demonstrates both weaknesses and benefits of different models for categorization in the Indian pines dataset.

6 Conclusions

This comparative study demonstrated that transformer-based models have proven valuable and feasible for classifying hyperspectral images. Conventional CNNs perform well at collecting features; the double-ViT model can handle spectral signatures. Using the Indian Pines dataset, the double ViT exhibited good accuracy and its potential as a hyperspectral image classification tool. Moreover, significant accuracy is observed using patch-wise and pixel-wise spectralformer models, emphasizing the crucial role of localized sequence features in classification applications. This comparative study shows that every model has advantages and disadvantages that must be investigated to improve effectiveness. The future of transformer-based imaging techniques and remote sensing is highlighted in this paper.

References

1. Wu C, Zhu S, Yang J, Hu M, Du B, Zhang L, Zhang L, Han C, Lan M (2021) Traffic density reduction caused by city lockdowns across the world during the COVID-19 epidemic: from the view of high-resolution remote sensing imagery. IEEE J Sel Topics Appl Earth Observ Remote Sens 14:5180–5193
2. Yang J, Wu C, Du B, Zhang L (2021) Enhanced multiscale feature fusion network for HSI classification. IEEE Trans Geosci Remote Sens 59(12):10328–10347
3. Rao M, Tang P, Zhang Z (2020) A developed siamese CNN with 3D adaptive spatial-spectral pyramid pooling for hyperspectral image classification. Remote Sensing 12(12):1964
4. Li G, Li L, Zhu H, Liu X, Jiao L (2019) Adaptive multiscale deep fusion residual network for remote sensing image classification. IEEE Trans Geosci Remote Sens 57(11):8506–8521
5. Zhang C, Li G, Du S (2019) Multi-scale dense networks for hyperspectral remote sensing image classification. IEEE Trans Geosci Remote Sens 57(11):9201–9222
6. Yang J, Du B, Wu C, Zhang L (2021) Automatically adjustable multi-scale feature extraction framework for hyperspectral image classification. In: 2021 IEEE international geoscience and remote sensing symposium IGARSS, pp 3649–3652. IEEE
7. Li S, Song W, Fang L, Chen Y, Ghamisi P, Benediktsson JA (2019) Deep learning for hyperspectral image classification: an overview. IEEE Trans Geosci Remote Sens 57(9):6690–6709
8. Chen Y, Lin Z, Zhao X, Wang G, Gu Y (2014) Deep learning-based classification of hyperspectral data. IEEE J Sel Topics Appl Earth Observ Remote Sens 7(6):2094–2107
9. Abdi H, Williams LJ (2010) Principal component analysis. Wiley Interdisciplinary Rev Comput Stat 2(4):433–459
10. Chen Y, Jiang H, Li C, Jia X, Ghamisi P (2016) Deep feature extraction and classification of hyperspectral images based on convolutional neural networks. IEEE Trans Geosci Remote Sens 54(10):6232–6251
11. Hang R, Liu Q, Hong D, Ghamisi P (2019) Cascaded recurrent neural networks for hyperspectral image classification. IEEE Trans Geosci Remote Sens 57(8):5384–5394
12. Zhu L, Chen Y, Ghamisi P, Benediktsson JA (2018) Generative adversarial networks for hyperspectral image classification. IEEE Trans Geosci Remote Sens 56(9):5046–5063
13. Paoletti ME, Haut JM, Fernandez-Beltran R, Plaza J, Plaza A, Li J, Pla F (2018) Capsule networks for hyperspectral image classification. IEEE Trans Geosci Remote Sens 57(4):2145–2160
14. Hong D, Gao L, Yao J, Zhang B, Plaza A, Chanussot J (2020) Graph convolutional networks for hyperspectral image classification. IEEE Trans Geosci Remote Sens 59(7):5966–5978
15. Yadav CS, Pradhan MK, Gangadharan SMP, Chaudhary JK, Singh J, Khan AA, Haq MA, Alhussen A, Wechtaisong C, Imran H, Alzamil ZS (2022) Multi-class pixel certainty active learning model for classification of land cover classes using hyperspectral imagery. Electronics 11(17):2799
16. Jawaharlalnehru A, Sambandham T, Sekar V, Ravikumar D, Loganathan V, Kannadasan R, Khan AA, Wechtaisong C, Haq MA, Alhussen A, Alzamil ZS (2022) Target object detection from Unmanned Aerial Vehicle (UAV) images based on improved YOLO algorithm. Electronics 11(15):2343
17. Khan AA, Nauman MA, Shoaib M, Jahangir R, Alroobaea R, Alsafyani M, Binmahfoudh A, Wechtaisong C (2022) Crowd anomaly detection in video frames using fine-tuned AlexNet model. Electronics 11(19):3105
18. Bengio Y, Simard P, Frasconi P (1994) Learning long-term dependencies with gradient descent is difficult. IEEE Trans Neural Networks 5(2):157–166
19. Vaswani A, Shazeer N, Parmar N, Uszkoreit J, Jones L, Gomez AN, Kaiser Ł, Polosukhin I (2017) Attention is all you need. Advances in neural information processing systems, 30
20. Ke G, He D, Liu TY (2020) Rethinking positional encoding in language pre-training. arXiv preprint arXiv:2006.15595

21. Dong Y, Cordonnier JB, Loukas A (2021) Attention is not all you need: Pure attention loses rank doubly exponentially with depth. In: International conference on machine learning, pp 2793–2803. PMLR
22. Dosovitskiy A, Beyer L, Kolesnikov A, Weissenborn D, Zhai X, Unterthiner T, Dehghani M, Minderer M, Heigold G, Gelly S, Uszkoreit J (2020) An image is worth 16x16 words: transformers for image recognition at scale. arXiv preprint arXiv:2010.11929
23. Shouhengx (2022) DB-ViT. GitHub. https://github.com/shouhengx/DB-ViT
24. Hong D, Han Z, Yao J, Gao L, Zhang B, Plaza A, Chanussot J (2021) SpectralFormer: rethinking hyperspectral image classification with transformers. IEEE Trans Geosci Remote Sens 60:1–15
25. Zhong Z, Li J, Luo Z, Chapman M (2017) Spectral–spatial residual network for hyperspectral image classification: a 3-D deep learning framework. IEEE Trans Geosci Remote Sens 56(2):847–858
26. "Hyperspectral Remote sensing Scenes Datasets." [Online]. Available at: https://www.ehu.eus/ccwintco/index.php?title=Hyperspectral_Remote_Sensing_Scenes. Accessed 20 Sept 2023

Deep Learning for Cognitive Task and Seizure Classification with Hilbert–Huang Transform and Variational Mode Decomposition

Shraddha Jain and Rajeev Srivastava

1 Introduction

The EEG signal is detected cognitive functions based on scalp EEG data. Electrical data of brain activity, called electroencephalogram signals, can be obtained without intervention from sensors mounted on the scalp. In the cognitive processes, the mental processes that can be examined through EEG signal analysis, including perception, attention, memory, and decision-making. Using this framework, EEG signals can be immediately classified and divided into various cognitive functions [1]. Understanding the differences between various cognitive states, such as motor planning, memory, and attention, can provide a better understanding of how the brain processes information. We use deep learning combined with signal processing techniques such as HHT and VMD to extract complex patterns from EEG data related to different tasks.

HHT and VMD apply an adaptive scheme for their removal while the essential non-stationary trace produces simple de-convolutions. The incorporation of self-developed features in an EEG-based classification algorithm can lead to a high specificity but low sensitivity and probably this is due either to regulatory restrictions or inadequate generalization capabilities [2].

EEG is a technique that records electricity generated in brain and is thus non-invasive. Deep learning algorithms utilize identified features or patterns extracted from EEG data for classification of such data. Several studies have demonstrated their usefulness when using EEG and deep learning in classification of brain's cognitive functions. Such an approach can enhance our knowledge on how the brain works,

S. Jain (✉) · R. Srivastava
Department of Computer Science and Engineering, Indian Institute of Technology, BHU, Varanasi, India
e-mail: shraddhajain.rs.cse22@itbhu.ac.in

R. Srivastava
e-mail: rajeev.cse@iitbhu.ac.in

K. Kumar Singh et al. (eds.), *Machine Vision and Augmented Intelligence*, Lecture Notes in Electrical Engineering 1211, https://doi.org/10.1007/978-981-97-4359-9_6

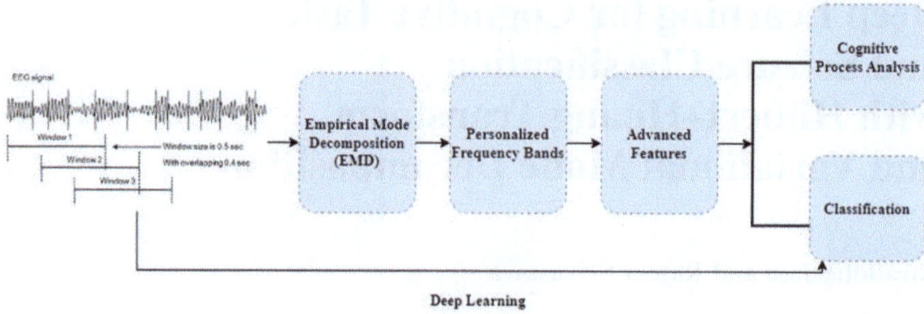

Fig. 1 Block diagram for the suggested approach

and it might also aid diagnosis as well as management of neurodegenerative diseases [3].

Ensemble deep learning uses recording the electrical activity of brain with classifying any visual stimulus through the combination of several deep neural networks. This is done by directly using EEG readings. Electrical recordings of brain activity give information about an individual's mental status. Automatic visual classification of EEG can detect brain diseases or cognitive states for a variety of uses including healthcare and gaming [4].

This research develops a seizure detection scheme via HHT and VMD collaboration. We propose these techniques would be used in the current algorithm pipeline in order to look for latent temporal and spectral artifacts pointing towards seizure onset. This approach will improve the quality of our results, which in turn will benefit patients' care and help us better understand epileptic discharges This represents a major progress in cognitive neuroscience since it provides a reliable and efficient method of categorizing cognitive tasks from the EEG signals captured in Fig. 1.

We aim to identify the hidden status of the signals in these signals in order to better capture the time-resolved frequency shifts and amplitude spectra of the high-dimensional non-linear and non-stationary EEG signals in distinctive feature sets.

The following is a list of our major contributions

(1) **Personalized frequency bands for brain waves can be obtained using a data-driven strategy**: We suggest a HHT (Hilbert–Huang Transform)-based technique to determine the frequency bands for every individual rather than using the predetermined as well as universally applicable fixed frequency bands. The findings demonstrate that although the personalized frequency bands closely resemble the traditional bands, they do differ depending on the subject.
(2) **Advanced metrics to measure brain wave activity**: We provide two unique approaches to evaluate the strength and frequency of the HHT-derived sub-signals that could be interpreted as brain waves. These metrics make advantage of the selected frequency bands. The freshly developed information-bearing metrics have higher discriminating abilities than the regularly utilized VMD

and wavelet transform-derived feature sets in the literature. Additionally, the suggested metrics have interpretation significance in the field of neurology.

(3) **Automated feature engineering for WT using deep learning**: Deep learning frameworks can be used to automate feature engineering using the time–frequency format of EEG data provided by HHT and VMD.

The remaining sections of this work are structured as follows: Several recent methods are reviewed in Section II. We provide our suggested strategy for identifying EEG signal seizures in Section III. We incorporate the Hilbert–Huang Transform (HHT) and Variational Mode Decomposition (VMD) integration into the analysis pipeline. In Section IV, we provide a full analysis of the results, complete with numerical performance indicators and visual representations. We offer actual applications for our novel features in Part V, which serves as the paper's conclusion.

2 Review of Some Existing Methods

In recent years, there has been significant activity in the field of automated cognitive task classification utilizing scalp EEG readings. One notable work in this field is 'NeuroClassify'. A Deep Learning Framework for Automated Cognitive Task Classification from Scalp EEG Signals. Several recent studies have explored the use of composite networks and deep learning methods for analyzing electroencephalogram (EEG) signals. Gao et al. [5] applied composite network analysis and EEG signal analysis using deep learning methods and classify cognitive tasks. Suchetha et al. [6] categorized cognitive tasks from EEG readings using successive convolutional neural networks.

Ieracitano et al. [7] and Ieracitano et al. [8] both utilized EEG data and convolutional neural networks, dementia phases are classified. Bao et al. [9] created a hybrid deep learning approach that can be easily interpreted for automatic elimination of scalp EEG artifact. Yin et al. [10] utilized physiological signal-based deep learning framework with transfer dynamic auto encoders to estimate mental illness. These works show the potential of merging deep learning method with complex network analysis for the study of EEG data and related applications.

Deep learning techniques have shown promise in analyzing electroencephalogram (EEG) signals for brain imaging and pathology detection [11, 12]. These approaches have also been utilized for cognitive healthcare and motor impairment neural disorder classification [13, 14]. A dual-stage deep learning architecture has been used to classify high-level motor imagery tasks in real time on the EEG [15]. All things considered, deep learning architecture has shown promise in improving EEG-based brain imaging and analysis.

3 Proposed Method

Our research aims to find hidden wave modes in high-dimensional non-linear and non-stationary EEG data and encourage to capture their time-resolved frequency shifts and amplitude spectra in novel feature set. The method can be described in line with the flowchart in Fig. 2.

We can use deep learning architecture to detect EEG signals and automate feature engineering by combining the prior processes.

3.1 Hilbert-Variational Mode Decomposition H-VMD

H-VMD, or Hilbert-Variational Mode Decomposition, is a signal processing approach that applies the Hilbert–Huang Transform (HHT) to a non-stationary signal in order to separate it into its constituent oscillatory components.

The steps of the H-VMD approach are as follows:

(1) ***Apply the empirical mode decomposition (EMD) algorithm to the creative signals to obtain its constituent intrinsic mode functions (IMFs)***: EMD is a completely data-driven method that breaks down a signal xi(t) into a number of sub-signals with distinct oscillation modes. The Intrinsic Mode Function (IMF) is a category for sub-signals si(t) that meet the first two criteria [16]:

The collection of IMFs si(t), where i = 1, … , n, provides a comprehensive, flexible, and almost orthogonal origin for the initial signals. A procedure of repeated sifting can be used to obtain the IMFs [17].

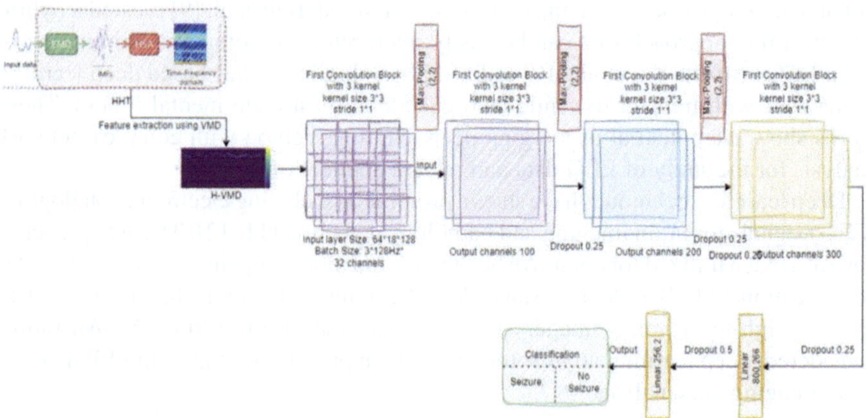

Fig. 2 Flowchart for the proposed HHT CNN-based algorithm

$$xi(t) = \sum_{i=1}^{n} (si(t) + r_n(t)) \tag{1}$$

where si(t) is the ith IMF and rn(t) is the residual signals after N iterations of EMD. The deconstructed IMFs by using the EEG signal, x ⁿ(t), which is a need for the instantaneous frequency estimated using the Hilbert transform to be physically meaningful [18].

(2) ***Apply the VMD (Variational Mode Decomposition) method to each IMF to decompose it into a finite number of modes with well-defined frequency bands***: To break each IMF down into a finite number of modes with clearly defined frequency bands, use the VMD approach. That is expressed in Eq. (2) as follows, is the key challenge for the VMD algorithm [19].

$$\min_{\{m_k\},\{n_k\}} \left\{ \sum_k \left\| \partial_t \left[\left(\partial(t) + \frac{j}{\pi t} \right) m_k(t) \right] e^{-jn_k t} \right\|_2^2 \right\} \tag{2}$$

where {mk} = {m1, m2, m3 … , mk} and {nk} represent the center frequency and each mode component individually. The original minimization problem is resolved utilizing the increased Lagrangian as well as the optimization scheme for the alternate direction method of multipliers (ADMM) [20]. Equation (3) provides the enforced convergence condition for ADMM optimization. The aforementioned iteration is completed when Eq. (3) is satisfied

$$\sum_k \left\| m_k^{u+1} - m_k^u \right\|_2^2 / \left\| m_k^u \right\|_2^2 / \in \tag{3}$$

where u is the number of updates needed for each VMF before receiving the final result, and **ε** is the value of the convergence tolerance.

(3) ***To determine the instant frequency and amplitude information for each mode, apply the Hilbert transform to It.***: Apply the Hilbert transform to every mode to determine the instant frequency and amplitude information for each mode. All 1D cosine functions are mapped into their corresponding sine functions by the linear, shift-invariant operator H, which is known as the 1D Hilbert transform [21]. The transfer function identifies it as an all-pass filter.

$$\hat{h}(\omega) = -jsgn(\omega) \tag{4}$$

$$\hat{h}(\omega) = -j\omega / |\omega| \tag{5}$$

As a result, the spectral domain multiplier operator is the Hilbert transform. The matching impulse reaction is h (t) = 1/ (πt). The Hilbert transform Hf(t) of a signal f(t) is derived as the Cauchy principal value (abbreviated p.v.) of the convolution integral because convolution with h(t) is not integrals [22]:

$$Hf(t) = \frac{1}{\pi} p.v. \int_{-\infty}^{\infty} \frac{f()}{} \tag{6}$$

(4) ***Combine the Hilbert spectra of the modes from all IMFs to achieve the Hilbert spectrum of the creative signal***: Combine the Hilbert spectra of the modes obtained from all IMFs to achieve the Hilbert spectrum of the original signal. This technique is called the Hilbert spectrum so the Hilbert transform to calculate the direct frequency of signals in accordance with Eq. (8) the initial signal x (t), since si(t) has mentioned values of zero [23]. For each si(t), we can use HT to determine the instantaneous frequency ω(t) and amplitude αi(t). Consequently, the initial signal x(t) can be written as

$$\omega = \frac{d\theta(t)}{dt} \tag{7}$$

$$x(t) = \sum_{i=1}^{j} \alpha_i(t) \exp\left(i \int \omega_i(t) dt \right) \tag{8}$$

Figure 3 shows the progressive steps for thoroughly analyzing EEG signals using this integrated signal analysis framework. In step (a), first, the empirical mode decomposition (EMD) method decomposes the EEG signal into intrinsic mode functions (IMFs) and a residual component. Variational Mode Decomposition (VMD), which further decomposes each IMF into different modes with clearly defined frequency regions, is introduced in step (b). The application of the Hilbert Transform to each mode in the following step, shown in (c), enables the extraction of instantaneous frequency and amplitude data. In step (d), the Hilbert–Huang Transform (HHT) spectrum in the time–frequency domain is produced by combining the Hilbert spectra of modes from all IMFs.

3.2 Personalized Frequency Bands

After applying the H-VMD process to decompose the EEG signal into oscillatory components, the personalized frequency bands aligning the dominant frequencies of the extracted IMFs with personalized frequency bands, that bridge the gap between signal decomposition and cognitive interpretation. The frequency bands for brain waves vary depending on the individual [24]. First, we break down x(t) into a collection of IMFs that are sorted by decreasing frequency. Most of the recent IMFs' instantaneous frequencies are <0.5 Hz. The priori research assumptions for both scalp EEG datasets concentrate on brain oscillations between 1 and 30 Hz [17, 19].

In Table 1, the signal indicating the conventional frequency bands that is delta is 1 Hz–4 Hz, theta is 4 Hz–8 Hz, alpha is 8 Hz–14 Hz, and beta is 14 Hz–30 Hz [25].

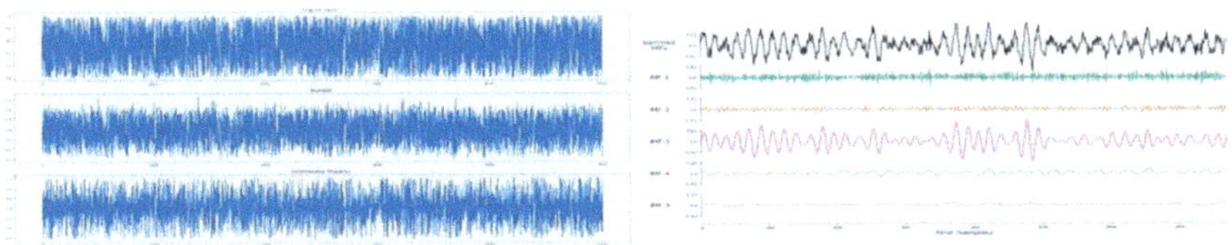

(a) **EMD of the EEG signal outputs** (b) **VMD of the EEG signal outputs**

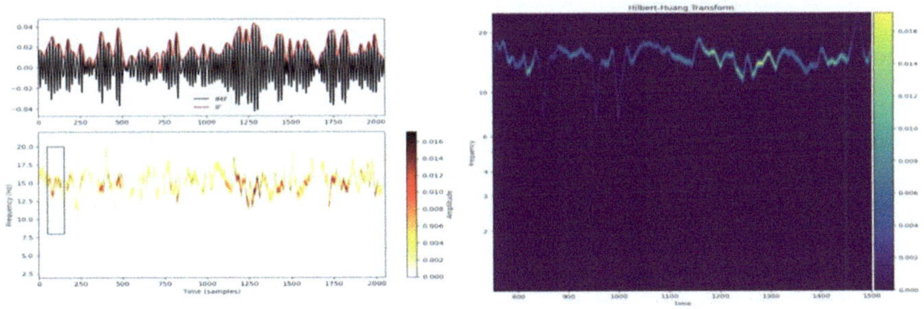

(c) **Hilbert transform of EEG signals** (d) **HHT spectrum with time-frequency domain**

Fig. 3 Framework for multi-step signal analysis

Table 1 Frequency band power of EEG signal

Frequency band	Speed (Hz)	EEG recording
Delta frequency band	1 Hz–4 Hz	
Theta frequency band	4 Hz–8 Hz	
Alpha frequency band	8 Hz–14 Hz	
Beta frequency band	14 Hz–30 Hz	

Individual differences in brain responses are evident in the subject-specific frequency bands, although they very closely resemble the canonical frequency bands.

3.3 *Advanced Features*

By generating customized frequency bands for each subject. This is done to adjust the analysis to each person's unique brain activity patterns, which might vary greatly from person to person. By concentrating on subject-specific oscillations, personalized frequency bands improve the precision and applicability of EEG data analysis. The

Hilbert spectrum shows that the overall relative frequency dropped down to a lower frequency range and the total amplitudes increased when the individual switched from closed to open eyes. It is common practice to sample a wide range of frequencies within a given frequency band in order to assess the strength of a specific brain wave. One is frequency ratio (FR) and another is average amplitude (AA) [26].

In frequency ratio

$$FR_{i,s} = \frac{1}{t}\left(\left|t/\,\omega_i(t) \in R\right|\right) \tag{9}$$

In the personalized frequency bands Rs, s = 1, ... , S, and i = 1, ... N. We keep track of the total quantity of time that its IFs ω (t) are in each of the bands of frequencies Rs. The four brainwaves that we are interested in are delta, theta, alpha, and beta waves. In our situation, S = 4 and N = 4 as the remaining IMFs occur below 0.5 Hz. FR1 = (76.1% 12.3, 3.0, 0.1%), for example, suggests that the first IMF may be indicative of beta oscillation [27].

In the averaged amplitude,

$$AA_{i,s} = \left\{m\left(H(\omega_i, t)/\,\omega_i(t) \in R_s\right)\right\} \tag{10}$$

It is based on the relationship between frequency, time, and amplitude, where the arithmetic mean is shown by m (.). The amplitude averaged throughout the intervals when the IFs are present in each of the 4 frequency bands Rs, s = 1... 4 are shown by the vector AAi = (aai1.... aai4).

In Eqs. (9) and (10) proposed metrics (FRi and AAi) escape the issue of sample frequencies and use a variety of measurements to determine the strength of brainwaves. This is in contrast to the conventional approach, which calls for frequency sampling and, separately, computing the power of each sampled frequency. Additionally, the measurements can significantly lower the size of the IMFs' Hilbert spectrum.

3.4 CNN Model

In the Advanced Features section, it is explained how certain metrics, such as the Frequency Ratio (FR) and Average Amplitude (AA), are calculated to measure the intensity of various brain waves within custom frequency bands. This highlights the value of precisely measuring brain wave properties in EEG recordings. Then, in "CNN Model," a deep learning framework based on 2D-CNN (Convolutional Neural Network) and Hilbert–Huang Transform (HHT) for seizure detection. In order to detect seizure activity, we have suggested a deep learning framework based on 2D-CNN and on an HHT. We created a CNN model that can be effectively taught to recognize ecliptic seizures. In our study, feature extraction and classification using the 2D-CNN are used to better understand the specifics of EEG signals linked to disease [28].

The suggested trained CNN model's primary parameters and associated details, such as their values or types, are shown in Table 2.

Table 2's input size is width x height, where width equals (18) the number of electrode channels and height equals 64. A 128-piece batch is used in the model. Thus, (64, 18, 128) is the form of the incoming data. The 2D convolutional layer, the 2D max pooling, the 2D batch normalization, and the fully connected layer, respectively, are all referred to as Conv2 and Pooling2D in the proposed architecture. In this model, the activation function is the ReLU with an alpha value of 0.3, and it follows each convolution layer. In the suggested model, there are three convolution layers, three batch normalization layers, three drop-out layers with a probability of 0.25, three max-pooling levels, and three fully linked layers.

Together, the aforementioned layers make up the two convolution blocks. To extract the pertinent characteristics, one convolution block comprises two convolution layers with two distinct convolution kernels. The two convolution kernels, specifically 5–1 and 1–3, have different kernel diameters. The first three convolution blocks are in fact connected to the max-pooling layers. Following the last convolution block, a fully connected layer with a dropout probability of 0.5 is connected to the final output fully connected layer. The final output of this model is the classification outcomes of seizure detection.

Table 2 An overview of our CNN architecture's most significant variables

CNN Hyper-parameter Modeling	Types
Batch Size	16
Learning Rate	0.01
Momentum	0.5
Dropout	0.25
Number of epochs	300
Pooling Layer	Max Pooling
Activation Function	Sigmoid
Optimizer	SGD (Stochastic Gradient Descent)
Loss Function	Binary_crossentropy

4 Results and Discussion

4.1 Dataset Description

The dataset from CHB-MIT [29] was used ([30] found at physionet.org). It includes 22 children's 686 scalp EEG records from Boston Children's Hospital. The dataset contains 23 sets of EEG recordings from 22 patients (5 males and 17 females), ranging in age from 1.5 to 22 years (mean, SD). One hundred and ninety-eight records out of these 686 contain seizures, and 1000 random samples, each including a recording of 20 s, were taken for seizure and non-seizure classes in the proposed work.

The CHB-MIT dataset that you brought up is unquestionably an EEG dataset that was recorded from the scalp, and it's well known to include a wide range of noise and artifacts, such as pulse interference, myoelectricity interference, electrocardio interference, power frequency interference, amplifier saturation, blink artifacts, and eye movement artifacts. Prior to processing the EEG data for analysis, it is essential to minimize or eliminate these interference signals [31].

4.2 Result Analysis

Publicly accessible EEG dataset is utilized in the proposed research CHB-MIT [30] has been used to employ the Hilbert–Huang Transform (HHT) after analyzing several EEG processing techniques. In order to obtain IMFs, signals are first applied with HHT to the datasets. The plot of amplitude (mV) for various IMF levels shown in Fig. 4 shows how much information is dispersed throughout a range. EEG characteristics are calculated for various IMF levels following decomposition. This work makes use of 16 time–frequency domain-based (amplitudes, phase, and frequency) characteristics, as well as 5 IMF levels.

The Hilbert spectrum (HS) and convolutional neural networks (CNN) have demonstrated remarkable efficacy in seizure diagnosis. The HS approach provides a useful level of detail regarding the instantaneous frequency, amplitude, and energy

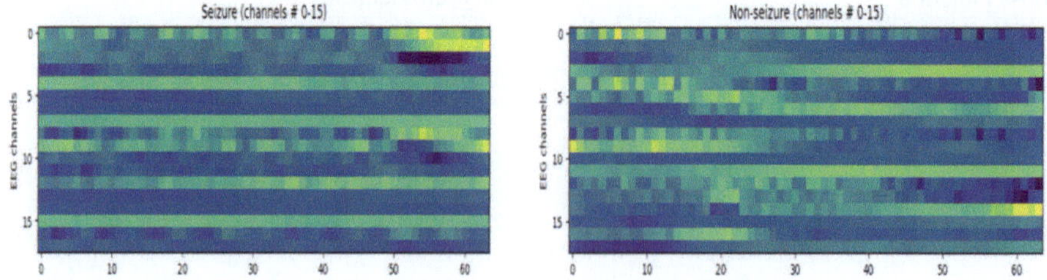

Fig. 4 Seizure identification by transformation into two-dimensional images

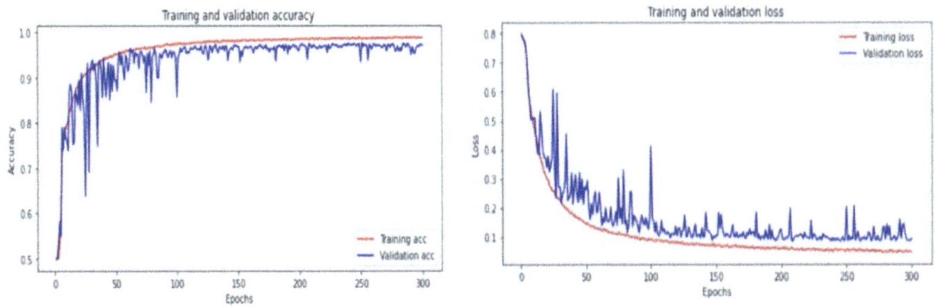

Fig. 5 CNN training and validation accuracy and loss

distribution properties within the time–frequency domain. A comprehensive understanding of signal characteristics is provided by the Hilbert Spectrum (HMS), which simultaneously estimates the energy contribution from individual frequency values. Our work leveraged the potential of HS time–frequency dynamics by converting recorded EEG time series signals into HS visuals, which enhanced our understanding of the underlying brain events. We were able to investigate the temporal variations in spectral content and gain understanding of potential seizure-related patterns. Convolutional neural networks (CNNs) and HS were combined to enable automated feature extraction and classification. The hierarchical architecture of CNNs makes it possible to precisely identify seizure-related patterns by collecting complex spatial patterns by HHT.

Figure 4 shows two 2-s segments, one with a seizure (top) and the other without one (bottom), with a sampling frequency of 64 Hz. This results in 128 distinct data points. Color maps are used to represent the EEG signals. The process of analyzing EEG data as time series, which results in the study of 2D images. Our model obtains a binary classification accuracy of 98.40%, respectively. Figure 5 displays the accuracy and classification of loss.

Figures 4 shows that the suggested model swiftly converged from epoch 0 to epoch 180. Figure 5 displays the accuracy and loss curves for the model across the first 300 epochs. After 300 iterations, the model accuracy has already attained 97.56%. The model's accuracy then gradually increased from epoch 180 to epoch 300. The model's accuracy is 98.18% up to the first 300 epochs. After stabilizing for 180–300 epochs, the model ultimately reaches high accuracy of 98.40%, respectively, sensitivity is 97.77%, specificity is 97.70%, and F1-score is 97.29%.

Table 3 compares the accuracy of binary classification to results from other studies that also used this dataset. According to Table 3, our method has the best performance out of all the ones mentioned above for epileptic seizure identification.

Table 3 Comparison with other studies that made use of the CHB-MIT dataset

Authors	Model	Accuracy (%)	Sensitivity (%)	Specificity (%)
Kukker et al. [32]	FQL, GAFQL	94.0	91.9	93.2
Zhou et al. [33]	CNN	96.7	95.4	94.3
Yuan et al. [34]	Spectrogram with STFT	94.3	92.6	93.8
Tsiouris et al. [35]	(DWT) + LSTM	95	88	89.6
Tsiouris et al. [36]	STFT + SSM	93	88.34	84.75
Fergus et al. [37]	Power spectral density + KNN	96.87	93	94
Xiang et al. [38]	FuzzyEn + SVM	98.31	98.27	96.36
Our Paper	**HHT + CNN**	**98.40**	**97.77**	**97.70**

5 Conclusion

In conclusion, In the Hilbert spectrum of sub-signals obtained from scalp EEG signals, this research suggests customized frequency bands and special metrics for compressing frequency and power information. Using the Hilbert–Huang Transform (HHT) and Variational Mode Decomposition (VMD), a unique method for the seizure detection in EEG signals. We have established the method's outstanding sensitivity in detecting seizures through thorough experimentation utilizing real-world scalp EEG recordings. Our method not only solves the problems posed by non-stationary and non-linearity but also presents intriguing directions for further investigation in neuroscience studies. We provide an important technique for improving early seizure detection and expanding our knowledge of brain dynamics in epilepsy by integrating computational intelligence and signal processing. Improved diagnostic and therapeutic approaches are made possible by this work, which advances the field of EEG signal processing more broadly.

References

1. Khezri MR, Setayeshi S, Abolghasemi V (2021) NeuroClassify: a deep learning framework for automated cognitive task classification from scalp EEG signals. J Neurosci Methods 357:109159. https://doi.org/10.1016/j.jneumeth.2021.109159
2. Sorna Meena M (2022) A deep learning approach for automatic classification of cognitive task using the scalp Electroencephalogram signals. In: Futuristic communication and network technologies: select proceedings of VICFCNT 2020, pp. 385–394. Springer Singapore
3. Sridhar S, Manian V (2020) Eeg and deep learning based brain cognitive function classification. Computers 9(4):104
4. Zheng X, Chen W, You Y, Jiang Y, Li M, Zhang T (2020) Ensemble deep learning for automated visual classification using EEG signals. Pattern Recogn 102:107147
5. Gao Z, Dang W, Wang X, Hong X, Hou L, Ma K, Perc M (2021) Complex networks and deep learning for EEG signal analysis. Cogn Neurodyn 15:369–388

6. Suchetha M, Madhumitha R, Sruthi R (2021) Sequential Convolutional Neural Networks for classification of cognitive tasks from EEG signals. Appl Soft Comput 111:107664
7. Ieracitano C, Mammone N, Bramanti A, Hussain A, Morabito FC (2019) A convolutional neural network approach for classification of dementia stages based on 2D-spectral representation of EEG recordings. Neurocomputing 323:96–107
8. Ieracitano C, Mammone N, Hussain A, Morabito FC (2020) A novel multi-modal machine learning based approach for automatic classification of EEG recordings in dementia. Neural Netw 123:176–190
9. Bao C, Hao Z, Dou W (2022) Automatic removal of scalp EEG artifacts using an interpretable hybrid deep learning method. In 2022 IEEE international conference on bioinformatics and biomedicine (BIBM), pp 1451–1456. IEEE
10. Yin Z, Zhao M, Zhang W, Wang Y, Wang Y, Zhang J (2019) Physiological-signal-based mental workload estimation via transfer dynamical autoencoders in a deep learning framework. Neurocomputing 347:212–229
11. Bozhkov L, Georgieva P (2018) Overview of deep learning architectures for EEG-based brain imaging. In: 2018 International joint conference on neural networks (IJCNN), pp 1–7. IEEE
12. Bajpai R, Yuvaraj R, Amalin Prince A (2021) Automated EEG pathology detection based on different convolutional neural network models: deep learning approach. Comput Biol Med 133:104434
13. Amin SU, Alsulaiman M, Muhammad G, Shamim Hossain M, Guizani M (2020) Deep learning for EEG motor imagery-based cognitive healthcare. Connected health in smart cities, pp 233–254
14. Vrbancic G, Podgorelec V (2018) Automatic classification of motor impairment neural disorders from EEG signals using deep convolutional neural networks. Elektronika ir Elektrotechnika 24(4):3–7
15. Cho J-H, Jeong J-H, Lee S-W (2021) Neurograsp: Real-time eeg classification of high-level motor imagery tasks using a dual-stage deep learning framework. IEEE Trans Cybern 52(12):13279–13292
16. Liang M, Zheng J, Isham E, Ekstrom A (2021) Common and distinct roles of frontal midline theta and occipital alpha oscillations in coding temporal intervals and spatial distances. J Cogn Neurosc,https://doi.org/10.1162/jocn_a_01765
17. Huang NE et al. (1998) The empirical mode decomposition and the Hilbert spectrum for nonlinear and non-stationary time series analysis. Proc Royal Soc London Series A Math Phys Eng Sci 454(1971):903–995
18. Liu Y (2015) The EMD decomposition of EEG signal (IMF1 to IMF9). ResearchGate
19. Dragomiretskiy K, Zosso D (2014) Variational mode decomposition. IEEE Trans Signal Process 62(3):531–544, https://doi.org/10.1109/TSP.2013.2288675
20. Bertsekas DP (1982) Constrained optimization and Lagrange multiplier methods. Academic Press, Cambridge
21. Singh SA, Singh SA, Devi ND, Majumder S (2021) A study on sleep stage classification based on a single-channel EEG signal. In: Electronic devices, circuits, and systems for biomedical applications, pp 135–152. Academic Press
22. Mert A, Akan A (2013) "Hilbert-Huang transform based hierarchical clustering for EEG denoising. In: 21st European signal processing conference (EUSIPCO 2013), pp 1–5. IEEE
23. Doppelmayr M, Klimesch W, Pachinger T, Ripper B (1998) Individual differences in brain dynamics: important implications for the calculation of event-related band power. Biol Cybern 79(1):49–57
24. Dimitriadis SI, Salis C, Tarnanas I, Linden DE (2018) Data-driven extraction of dynamic functional networks from brain activity. Hum Brain Mapp 39(5):2198–2217. https://doi.org/10.1002/hbm.23998
25. Mukhopadhyay A, Mitra M, Banerjee A (2020) Automated classification of EEG signals for cognitive task using deep learning and Hilbert-Huang Transform. Biomed Signal Process Control 59:101890. https://doi.org/10.1016/j.bspc.2020.101890

26. Smith JR, Johnson AB (2022) Deep learning framework for seizure detection using 2D- CNN and HHT. J Med Signal Process 7(3):123–136
27. Zhang G, Cheng Y, Shen W, Liu B, Huang L, Xie S (2018) Brain regional homogeneity changes in cirrhotic patients with or without hepatic encephalopathy revealed by multi-frequency bands analysis based on resting-state functional MRI. Korean J Radiol 19(3):452–462
28. Acharya UR, Oh SL, Hagiwara Y, Tan JH, Adeli H (2018) Deep convolutional neural network for the automated detection and diagnosis of seizure using EEG signals. Comput Biol Med 100:38–48
29. Shoeb AH (2009) Application of machine learning to epileptic seizure onset detection and treatment. PhD Thesis. Massachusetts Institute of Technology, pp 157–162.
30. http://ntsa.upf.edu/downloads/andrzejak-rg-schindler-k-rummel-c-2012-nonrandomness-non linear-dependence
31. https://physionet.org/content/chbmit/1.0.0
32. Kukker A, Sharma R (2021) A genetic algorithm assisted fuzzy Q-learning epileptic seizure classifier. Comput Electr Eng 92:107154
33. Zhou M, Tian C, Cao R, Wang B, Niu Y, Hu, Ting, Guo H, Xiang J (2018) Epileptic seizure detection based on EEG signals and CNN. Front Neuroinform 12:95
34. Yuan Y, Xun G, Jia K, Zhang AD (2019) A multi-view deep learning framework for EEG seizure detection. IEEE J Biomed Health Inform 23:83–94. https://doi.org/10.1109/JBHI.2018.2871678
35. Tsiouris KM, Markoula S, Konitsiotis S, Koutsouris DD, Fotiadis DI (2018) A robust unsupervised epileptic seizure detection methodology to accelerate large EEG database evaluation. Biomedical Signal Process Control 40:275–285
36. Tsiouris KM, Pezoulas VC, Zervakis M, Konitsiotis S, Koutsouris DD, Fotiadis DI (2018) A long short-term memory deep learning network for the prediction of epileptic seizures using EEG signals. Comput Biol Med 99:24–37.
37. Fergus P, Hignett D, Hussain A, Al-Jumeily D, Abdel-Aziz K (2015) Automatic epileptic seizure detection using scalps EEG and advanced artificial intelligence techniques. BioMed Res Int
38. Xiang J, Li C, Li H, Cao R, Wang B, Han X, Chen J (2015) The detection of epileptic seizure signals based on fuzzy entropy. J Neurosci Methods 243:18–25

Tracking of Ship and Plane in Satellite Videos Using a Convolutional Regression Network with Deep Features

Devendra Sharma and Rajeev Srivastava

1 Introduction

Visual object tracking (VOT) is a fundamental computer vision task with numerous applications. Object tracking is a process in which tracker follow a particular object by taking the first frame from sequence of frames and assign bounding box to the object. Object tracking can be divided into two parts: first is single object tracking (SOT) and second is multi-object tracking (MOT). In comparison to generic videos, in satellite videos the object tracking is a latest domain for research. The spatial pixels of satellite frames are up to 3840*2160 pixels which have more than eight million pixels and the size of moving objects like are car, plane, ship, and train are very small such as 17*18 pixels, so ratio of the object size to frame size becomes 1/100000. Small size object creates object detection problem and tracker suffers different kinds of problems like model drift, background clutter, rotation problem, and so on. Different types of tracking methods have been proposed and that performed well for generic videos such as OTB [1] and LaSOT [2]. In recent years, some methods have also been proposed for tracking the moving objects in the satellite videos [3–6]. The single object tracking in satellite videos is categorized into two parts generative method and detection-based method. In detection-based method, the motion information of inter-frames is used to detect and then track the moving objects. Detection-based method is also divided into two methods correlation filter (CF)-based tracker which is the mostly used method because of its processing speed and second is deep learning-based which is more expensive because a large amount of dataset is required for training the model.

D. Sharma (✉) · R. Srivastava
Computer Science and Engineering Department, Indian Institute of Technology, BHU, Varanasi, India
e-mail: devendrasharma.rs.cse21@itbhu.ac.in

R. Srivastava
e-mail: rajeev.cse@iitbhu.ac.in

K. Kumar Singh et al. (eds.), *Machine Vision and Augmented Intelligence*, Lecture Notes in Electrical Engineering 1211, https://doi.org/10.1007/978-981-97-4359-9_7

In this article, the overall motivation is inherited from the convolutional regression network with the appearance and motion features (CRAM) [7] model in which VGG16 is associated as a feature extractor and gives good performance. To further improve the results, this article proposes a method in which different kinds of feature extractors are used to extract the valuable features from the objects of satellite videos.

Our main contribution is use different kinds of pre-trained feature extractor such as VGG16, VGG19, and ResNet50 to extract the motion feature and appearance features of tinny objects in satellite videos where ResNet50 gives better result compare to others. PSR is used to fuse the response map of extracted features. In fused response map, the maximum value is used for calculate the location of target.

In this article, related research work on single object tracking is described in Sect. 2 and, in Sect. 3, tracking framework of the CRAM with ResNet50 which is used for feature extraction. Section 4 describes the experimental work on SVs and Sect. 5 concludes this article.

2 Related Work

In this section, explained the existing method for single objects tracking in generic videos and satellite videos. In object tracking, the first task is detection of moving object and second task is follow the object over the sequence of frames. AlexNet-based detection of objects are presented by [8] in which model is developed using four convolution layers and three fully connected layers followed by Rectified Linear Unit (ReLU). Some model faces the problem of glitches during detection such as missed targets and slow detection, to solve this issue the improved You Only Look Once (YOLO) algorithm is used which is effectively used for real-time target detection for dynamic size objects [9].

2.1 Single Object Tracking (SOT)

SOT is divided into discriminative and generative methods. In generative method, the model is developed to represent the objects and area is found which mostly looks as search area in upcoming frames. Some existing methods are particle filters [7] and mean shift [10]. The features of the object affect the accuracy and speed of the tracker. Generative method considers the feature of the objects itself which makes it easy for the sample for tracking [4]. The discriminative method is divided into two different methods: correlation filter (CF)-based and deep learning-based. Using kernel trick and circulant matrix with existing CF, trackers become kernelized correlation filter (KCF) in which the fast Fourier transform is used for various algebraic operation.

Correlation Filter-Based Tracking: First time MOSSE [11] proposed tracker using the CF. CSK [12] introduces the circulant matrix and kenrel trick based on MOSSE.

In recent years, tracking algorithm the discriminative correlation filter (DCF) has taken the leading position. The problem of regression is solved by the learning a mapping function from dense samples of the targets object to soft Gaussian labels for the target positions prediction [13]. The main goal of regression is to learn a function of linear mapping as $y = \theta\prime.x$, y is the corresponding label of the pixel and x is n-dimensional features of a sample pixel [13]. θ is regression coefficients which can be learned by the minimization problem:

$$\underset{\theta}{\arg min}\|X\theta - Y\|^2 + \lambda\|\theta\|^2 \tag{1}$$

where $X \in \mathbb{R}^{m\times n}$ is the matrix which contains n number of extracted feature samples from the search region and $Y \in \mathbb{R}^n$ shows the output of this n pixels in search area [13]. Notation λ which is a regularization parameter used to penalize to over-fitting [13]. The closed-form solution of the minimization problem is shown as

$$w = (\lambda I + X^T X)^{-1} X^T Y \tag{2}$$

where I is an identity matrix. CSK [12] tracker introduced a circularly shifting of samples and the kernel tricks to create a correlation filter for rapid computation.

Deep CNN-Based Tracking CNN-SVM [14] is a deep learning-based model which a convolutional neural network (CNN) associated with a support vector machine for single object tracking. The larger amount of data is used to train CNN model offline and fine-tune the parameter online for reconcile the changes in object. Feature extractors such as AlexNet [15] and VGG [13] are trained on a ImageNet dataset [16] which is studied in object tracking [13]. Deep regression-based trackers used CNN to solve regression problem in tracking.

2.2 *SOT in Satellite Videos*

There are two methods for single object tracking in satellite videos detection-based and discriminative. In detection-based method [2], a optical flow-based tracker is used multi-frame proposed in which the velocity feature, multi-frame difference, and integral image are fused. Detection-based trackers do not give better performance. Deep learning-based tracker Siamese [5] in which when the tracking is performed then there is a need of adjustment of parameters to achieve best tracking result. Deep learning methods face that deep sub-network in which low-resolution representation may not be suitable for tracking the small objects [7]. Inspired by Convolutional Regression and Appearance Motion (CRAM) model which have two regression network with two different types of features as motion features and appearance features. Results of two network are integrated together which improve the robustness of tracker in SVs. Recognition of objects using spatio-temporal motion feature over a sequence of frames is presented in [17].

3 Proposed Method

The proposed model is inspired by the CRAM [7]. The model has been designed for a robust object tracking using appearance and motion features of moving objects. This model is divided into two parts first one is the feature extraction part and second part is regression network that predict the target in upcoming frames based on Peak to Sidelobe Ratio (PSR) value. In feature extraction part, there are two branches appearance features (Net-A) which takes from the RGB image of the search window, and motion features (Net-M) takes from the optical flow of some consecutive frames. In feature extraction part features of image patch and optical flow image is extracted using VGG16.

The proposed method in Fig. 1 uses modified CRAM model in which for feature extraction it uses the pre-trained ResNet50 instead of VGG16 for feature extractor from an image patch in appearance features (Net-A) branch also in motion features (Net-M) branch. This method uses the ResNet architecture's (feature extractor in Fig. 1) first sequential block (layer1) and the first convolution block. The modified backbone has one max-pooling layer and one down sampling layer of Layer1. Thus, the resultant features are reduced to ¼ th the size of original search patch. Size reduction of feature channel is carried out to decrease the channel size of output features in both branches of the feature extraction. Then the feature channel is convolved with a Gaussian filter of the same size as the object's bounding box to generate corresponding response maps. These response maps are fused based on their Peak-to-Sidelobe Ratio (PSR), which helps to eliminate noise and false detection which separates object from background. The maximum value in the fused response map is used to calculate the location of the target.

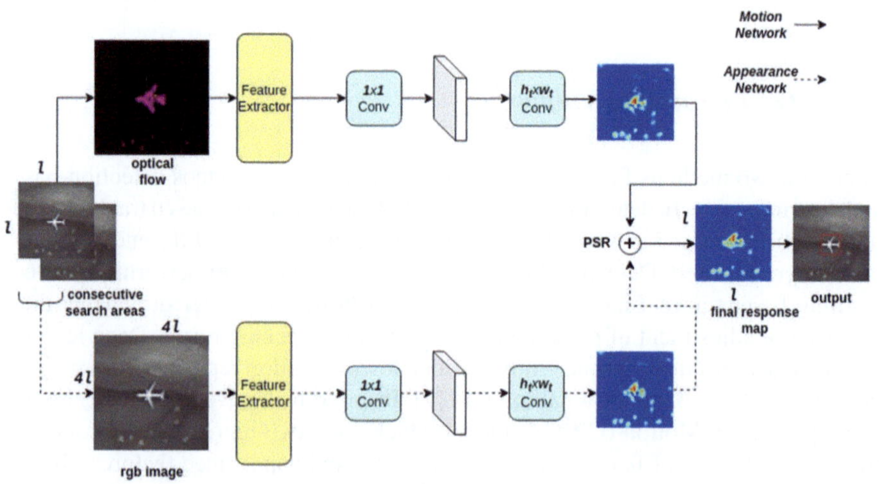

Fig. 1 Architecture of the tracking method CRAM with ResNet50

Search Window: This window is created in which a search patch contains the target as our Region of Interest (ROI). Initially, it is generated using the bounding box of the object in the first frame. The consequent search patches are generated from the object location which is predicted from the previous frames. The search window size (in square shape) is set to 4 times of the maximum value of the height and width of target. The search patch is again upsampled four times to balance the downsampling of the input image from the backbone [13].

Feature Extraction: The RGB image search patch is used to calculate appearance features and motion feature which is obtained using optical flow between the search patch and a reference frame. Optical flow is calculated using the inbuilt OpenCV function named cv.calcOpticalFlowPyrLK(). Before passing it to the feature extraction part, the 2D optical flow vector is transformed into pseudo-3D RGB spaces using (Hue-Saturation-Value) HSV transformation. The optical flow is used only after every five frames, and the reference frame, i.e., last frame is set to the initial frame.

Feature Fusion: The unwanted layers of the deep features are removed using one 1×1 convolutional layer [13]. The Gaussian filter is generated using the Gaussian distribution. In Fig. 1, w is width and h is the height of target, σ^2 variance which is set to 0.2 times of the average of the width and height of the target. To reduce mathematical complexity, convolution is performed after combining the 32 channels of the features into one channel rather than separately convolving each channel and then combining them into one. Motion features can't be directly fused with appearance features. Hence here each pixel values in motion feature is replaced with its local average computed using a square window of the same size as the target. The averaged features and the motion features are fused using following equation:

$$\underset{x_t, y_t}{\arg max} \alpha A(x_t, y_t) + (1 - \alpha)F(x_t, y_t) \tag{3}$$

The value of α is calculated by PSR (Peak-to-Sidelobe Ratio) of the appearance and motion features. A is the response map of *network-A* and $F(x_t, y_t)$ is the local average of motion feature around target position (x_t, y_t) [13]. The PSR value is calculated using the following equations

$$\text{PSR} = \frac{g_{max} - \mu_{\text{sl}}}{\sigma_{\text{sl}}} \tag{4}$$

where g_{max} is maximum response value, μ_{sl} is mean and σ_{sl} is standard deviation of the sidelobe. The peak area is 1/4th of the response map, while remaining part is denoted by sidelobe. Once PSR values are calculated, then α is calculated by following equation:

$$\alpha = \frac{\text{PSR}_A}{\text{PSR}_A + \text{PSR}_M} \tag{5}$$

where PSR_A is for appearance features and PSR_M is for motion features. The maximum value of fused response map gives the predicted location of the target. The size of the predicted bounding box is the same as the initial bounding box.

4 Experiment and Result Analysis

4.1 Dataset Description

For object tracking in satellite videos the dataset Satellite Video Single Object Tracking (SatSOT) [3] is used. This dataset is a large-scale dataset for moving object detection and tracking, which consists of 105 sequences with 27,664 frames, 11 attributes, and four categories of typical moving targets in satellite videos: car, plane, ship, and train are manually labeled. Each images have a resolution of 12,000 × 5000 and contains a large number of objects with different sizes. For our experiment take the Plane and Ship dataset for tracking and evaluate performance of our proposed tracking model. Five videos sequences of ship and five sequences of plane are used. Each sequence has bounding box values and sequence of images. Bounding box is described as x-coordinate, y-coordinate, width, height, i.e., [x, y, w, h].

4.2 Evaluation Metrics

Overlap Score (S): Overlap score is the ratio of the absolute intersection to the absolute union of the ground truth and the predicted bounding box. It is similar to the IOU in common machine learning terms. a_g is the area occupied by ground truth bounding box and a_p is the area occupied by predicted bounding box.

$$S = \frac{|a_g \bigcap a_p|}{|a_g \bigcup a_p|} \tag{6}$$

Accuracy(A): Accuracy is evaluated by averaging per-frame overlap score over valid number frames. Valid frames (N_{valid}) include all those frames for which re-initialization of the search window does not occur.

$$A = \frac{1}{N_{\text{valid}}} \sum_{t=1}^{N_{\text{valid}}} S_t \tag{7}$$

Average Overlap (AO): The average overlap is calculated as the mean of IOUs. In this case, we use the overlap score instead of IOU and calculate its mean over all the frames (N_{all}).

$$AO = \frac{1}{N_{\text{all}}} \sum_{t=1}^{N_{\text{all}}} S_t \tag{8}$$

Robustness (R): The robustness evaluates how many times the tracker fails (lose the object) during tracking. Per-sequence failure times is R_i, N_i is the range of failed sequence lengths, and m is the sequences in total as

$$R = \frac{1}{N_{\text{total}}} \sum_{i=1}^{m} N_i R_i \tag{9}$$

4.3 Result Analysis

The CRAM model has used VGG16 as its backbone. Using VGG16 as backbone in the proposed model did not give satisfactory results. So, to improve the performance of tracker, another pre-trained feature extractor as backbone is used like VGG19 and ResNet50 which are more efficient. VGG16 smoothly detects the object in the starting of videos but leaves the target after some frames of video, for example, when another plane comes inside the search patch.

VGG19: VGG19 has 19 layers and VGG16 has 16 layers. The additional layers allow for more complex feature extraction and better performance on specific tasks. Even though we take only the starting seven convolution layers of VGG19, the pre-trained weights of this model still performs better than the pre-trained weights of VGG16. VGG19 correctly detects the object in the plane dataset but loses the target in the ship dataset due to the background noise of water waves.

ResNet50: VGG16 is a relatively shallow network with 16 layers. ResNet50 has 50 layers which allows it to capture more complex and abstract features. ResNet50 has a more efficient architecture than VGG16, with fewer parameters and faster training times. ResNet50 correctly tracks both plane and ship objects till the last frame and outperforms VGG16 and VGG19.

Figures 2, 3, and 4 show the tracking results by VGG16, VGG19, and ResNet50 feature extractors, respectively. We have shown the frame120 and frame190 along with the initial frame out of the first 250 frames because they have the highest amount of noise and similar target structures within the search patch. Figure 1 shows detection by VGG16 architecture. VGG16 smoothly detects the object initially but leaves the target after some video frames, for example, when another plane or a similar structure enters the search patch (frame 120). Figure 2 shows detection by VGG19 architecture. VGG19 correctly detects the object in the plane dataset but loses the target in the ship dataset due to the background noise of water waves (frame 190). Figure 3 shows detection by ResNet50 architecture. ResNet50 correctly tracks plane and ship objects until the last frame and outperforms VGG16 and VGG19 (Table 1).

VGG19 has a deeper architecture than VGG16 architecture and this increased depth could potentially allow it to capture more complex and abstract features in the early stages of feature extraction. Though we use the same number of convolution layers in both architectures, VGG19 has better generalization ability which helps the

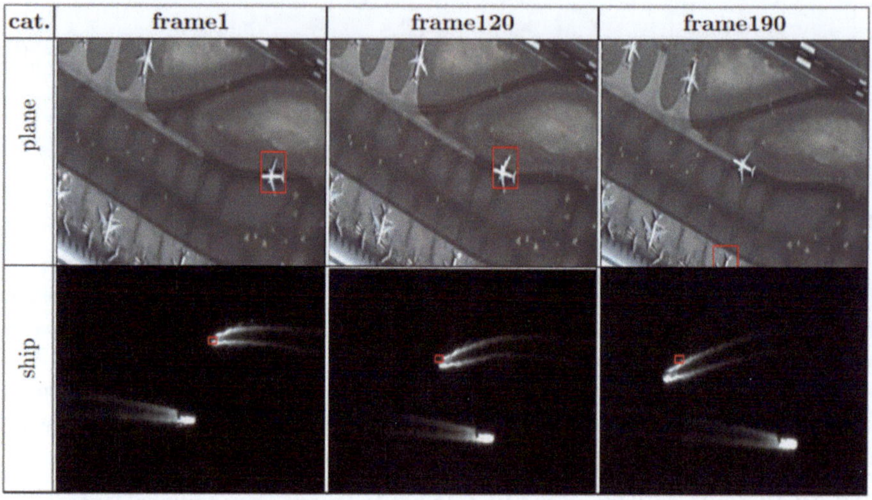

Fig. 2 Result of VGG16

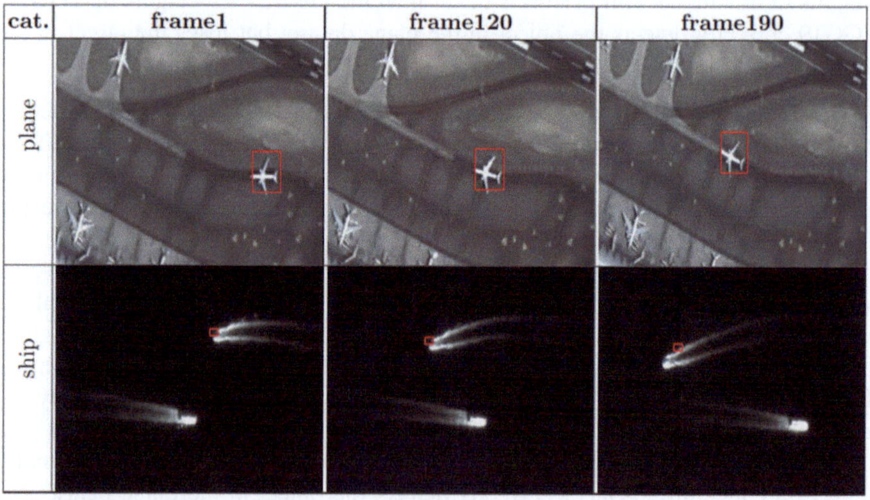

Fig. 3 Result of VGG19

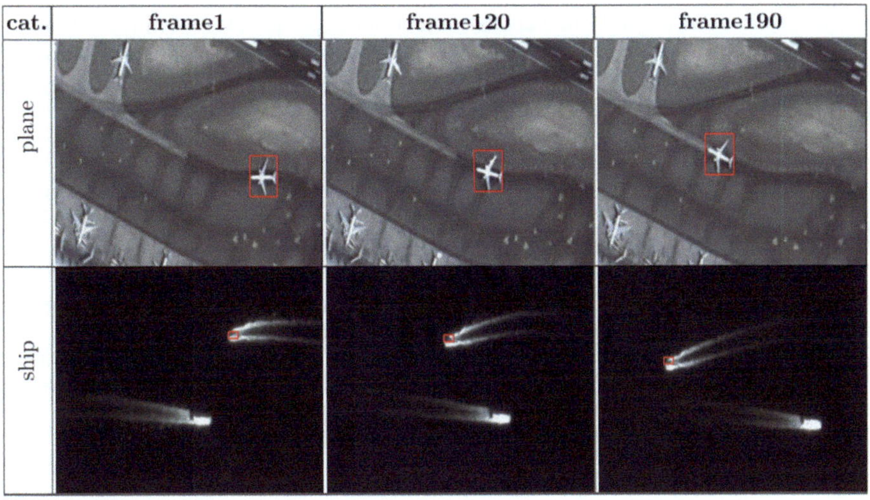

Fig. 4 Result of ResNet50

Table 1 Comparative analysis of the VGG16, VGG19, and ResNet50 feature extractor in CRAM for ship and plane objects in satellite video dataset

Method	Accuracy	Average overlap	Robustness
VGG16	0.45	0.43	0.54
VGG19	0.52	0.49	0.34
ResNet50	0.73	0.70	0.19

model learn more invariant and discriminating features, which leads to better performance. ResNet50 outperforms both the above architectures because it also employs skip connections (residual connections) apart from general convolutional layers. This facilitates smoother gradient flow during training, which often leads to faster convergence and better training stability. The residual connections in ResNet50 contribute to improved feature learning, leading to better generalization and robustness against variations and noise in the data, hence, it is able to detect the target object all the way to the last frame. However, as the architectures improve in accuracy, they take more time to train.

5 Conclusion

The model makes use of both appearance as well as motion features to track the object. VGG16 smoothly detects the object in the starting but loses track after some point (for example, when another plane comes inside the search patch in the plane dataset). VGG19 accurately detects the object in the plane dataset but loses track in the ship dataset due to the background noise of water waves. ResNet50 accurately tracks both plane and ship datasets till the last frame and outperforms VGG16 and VGG19 giving better results.

References

1. Wu Y, Lim J, Yang M-H (2013) Online object tracking: a benchmark. In: Proceedings of the IEEE conference on computer vision and pattern recognition, pp 2411–2418
2. Fan H, Lin L, Yang F, Chu P, Deng G, Yu S, BaiH, Xu Y, Liao C, Ling H (2019) Lasot: a high-quality benchmark for large-scale single object tracking. In: Proceedings of the IEEE/CVF conference on computer vision and pattern recognition, pp 5374–5383
3. Chen Y, Tang Y, Yin Z, Han T, Zou B, Feng H (2022) Single object tracking in satellite videos: a correlation filter-based dual-flow tracker. IEEE J Sel Topics Appl Earth Observ Remote Sens 15:6687–6698. https://doi.org/10.1109/JSTARS.2022.3185328
4. Zhao M, Li S, Xuan , S Kou L, Gong S, Zhou Z (2022) SatSOT: a benchmark dataset for satellite video single object tracking. IEEE Trans Geoscience Remote Sens 60:1–11, Art no. 5617611, https://doi.org/10.1109/TGRS.2022.3140809
5. Li S et al (2023) Recent advances in intelligent processing of satellite video: challenges, methods, and applications. IEEE J Sel Topics Appl Earth Observ Remote Sens 16:6776–6798. https://doi.org/10.1109/JSTARS.2023.3296451
6. Guo Y et al. (2022) The first challenge on moving object detection and tracking in satellite videos: methods and results. 2022 26th international conference on pattern recognition (ICPR), Montreal, QC, Canada, pp 4981–4988, https://doi.org/10.1109/ICPR56361.2022.9956153
7. Yin Q et al. (2022) Detecting and tracking small and dense moving objects in satellite videos: a benchmark. IEEE Trans Geoscience Remote Sens 60:1–18, Art no. 5612518, https://doi.org/10.1109/TGRS.2021.3130436
8. Hu Z, Yang D, Zhang K, Chen Z (2020) Object tracking in satellite videos based on convolutional regression network with appearance and motion features. IEEE J Sel Topics Appl Earth Observ Remote Sens 13:783–793
9. Arunnehru J, Thalapathiraj S, Dhanasekar R, Vijayaraja L, Kannadasan R, Khan AA, Haq MA, Alshehri M, Alwanain MI, Keshta I (2022) Machine vision-based human action recognition using spatio-temporal motion features (STMF) with difference intensity distance group pattern (DIDGP). Electronics 11(15):2363
10. Nummiaro K, Koller-Meier E, Van Gool L (2002) Object tracking with an adaptive color-based particle filter. In: Pattern recognition: 24th DAGM symposium Zurich, Switzerland, September 16–18, 2002 Proceedings 24, pp 353–360. Springer, Berlin, Heidelberg
11. Vojir T, Noskova J, Matas J (2014) Robust scale-adaptive mean-shift for tracking. Pattern Recogn Lett 49:250–258
12. Bolme DS, Ross Beveridge J, Draper BA, Lui YM (2010) Visual object tracking using adaptive correlation filters. In: 2010 IEEE computer society conference on computer vision and pattern recognition, pp 2544–2550. IEEE
13. Wang L, Ouyang W, Wang X, Lu H (2015) Visual tracking with fully convolutional networks. In: Proceedings of the IEEE international conference on computer vision, pp 3119–3127
14. Henriques JF, Caseiro R, Martins P, Batista J (2012) Exploiting the circulant structure of tracking-by-detection with kernels. In: Computer Vision–ECCV 2012: 12th European conference on computer vision, Florence, Italy, October 7–13, 2012, Proceedings, Part IV 12, pp 702–715. Springer, Berlin, Heidelberg, 2012
15. Zhang Z, Xie Y, Xing F, McGough M, Yang L (2017) Mdnet: a semantically and visually interpretable medical image diagnosis network. In: Proceedings of the IEEE conference on computer vision and pattern recognition, pp 6428–6436

16. Alippi C, Disabato S, Roveri M (2018) Moving convolutional neural networks to embedded systems: the alexnet and VGG-16 case. In: 2018 17th ACM/IEEE international conference on information processing in sensor networks (IPSN), pp 212–223. IEEE
17. Khan AA, Nauman MA, Shoaib M, Jahangir R, Alroobaea R, Alsafyani M, Binmahfoudh A, Wechtaisong C (2022) Crowd anomaly detection in video frames using fine-tuned AlexNet model. Electronics 11(19):3105

Tumor Detection and Analysis from Brain MRI Images Using Deep Learning

Shweta Singh and Rajeev Srivastava

1 Introduction

Brain, having several roles, coordinates and controls all systems of the body functions. One such organ is the brain that comprises millions of nerves which communicate with each other for information processing and regulate human behavior. Such an occurrence makes tumors in the brain. In India, as per the Indian Council of Medical Research (ICMR), brain tumor is the 10th most common type of cancer. India's health Ministry ICMR's National Cancer Registry Programme (NCRP) estimated incidence prevalence with a 0.5 incidence. In India, it is estimated that 100,000 people will be diagnosed with cancer of the brain and nervous system and 10,200 of these cases will be new ones by 2020 [1]. The NBTF says that brain tumor deaths have increased by nearly 300% over the last few years in wealthy countries [2].

The success in classification of brain tumors depends on early discovery and division of types of brain tumors. Brain tumors are some of the worst and deadliest types of adult cancers for which there is no known cure for adults and children. Brain tumors are caused by aberrant brain cell development. They are grouped based on their pace of growth and propensity to return following treatment. They can be roughly divided into malignant and benign forms. Benign tumors are benign, do not spread quickly, and are much less likely to return after treatment. Contrarily, malignant tumors contain cancer cells that can metastasize or move to other body areas from the original location, invading nearby tissues [3]. Three types of brain cancers with different traits and clinical symptoms include gliomas, meningiomas, and pituitary tumors.

S. Singh (✉) · R. Srivastava
Department of Computer Science and Engineering, Indian Institute of Technology, BHU Varanasi, Uttar Pradesh, Varanasi, India
e-mail: shwetasingh.rs.cse20@iitbhu.ac.in

R. Srivastava
e-mail: rajeev.cse@iitbhu.ac.in

K. Kumar Singh et al. (eds.), *Machine Vision and Augmented Intelligence*, Lecture Notes in Electrical Engineering 1211, https://doi.org/10.1007/978-981-97-4359-9_8

The location, histological subtype, and tumor margins are three characteristics that affect the prognosis of brain cancer over the long term. Cancer frequently returns and worsens to grade IV even after treatment. The early identification of cancer has the potential to improve treatment. Early intervention can be the difference between life and death since lesions are more likely to be treated in their early stages. Early detection of cancer may enhance the cure. Early intervention lesion is more liable to get cured when detected during its early stages because it may mean a life or death difference. Early identification is crucial. Different methods can be used in diagnosing brain tumors like computed tomography (CT), magnetic resonance imaging (MRI), positron emission tomography (PET), and magnetic resonance spectroscopy (MRS). These imaging methods provide the relevant information that is very important about the type, the site, and the size of a brain tumor. The main applications of MRI are during diagnosis and location determination of a tumor for future growth tracking and surgical planning [4]. In addition, MR imaging involves aspects of anatomy, physiology, metabolism, and so on, hemodynamics of the lesion. This in turn means that the best way of detecting brain tumors is by taking imaging scans still from magnetic resonance imaging [2].

2 Literature Review

Various other classification techniques that are based on different types of tumors have been developed in literature. The paper [5] proposed a method that uses ResNet-50 to build a transfer learning-based prediction model for brain tumor diagnosis. The accuracy of their experimental results was 95%. In a related study, [6] attained a five-fold cross-validation precision of 94.82% using block-wise transfer learning. They tested their theory using a benchmark dataset from T1-weighted contrast-enhanced magnetic resonance imaging (CEMRI). To distinguish between high and low grades of glioma, [7] used convolutional neural networks. They had precisions of 71% and 96%, respectively. Krol et al. [8] developed two main approaches for detection using CNN and trained on transverse brain tumor pictures, with an accuracy of 91.43%. Kumar et al. [9] offer a framework based on Grey Wolf Optimization (GWO) and SVM for classifying brain cancers in MR images. They demonstrated how the GWO outperforms other computations. They achieved a 95.23% classification accuracy as a result of their efforts.

A study [10] used a modified version of AlexNet CNN to establish a non-invasive approach for classifying glioma brain tumors. The categorization was performed using whole-brain MRI scans, with labels placed at the image level instead of the pixel level. The accuracy of the technique was found to be 91.15%. Utilizing segmented brain tumor MRI scans to categorize brain tumors, the research reported in the paper [11] proposed using CNN as a data improvement approach. For classification, they used a pre-trained VGG-19 CNN architecture, and for the data before and after augmentation, they obtained an accuracy of 87.39% and 90.66%, respectively.

Enhanced images from a previous pre-processing stage were used as input and sent through the convolution layer for feature extraction and downsampling (convolution, ReLU, maxpooling) in the study by [12], which initially demonstrated a 16-layer VGG-16 deep NN. The accuracy of multiple classifications of brain cancer MR images was improved by their proposed method. Linked layers and SoftMax were used to avoid overfitting. Following twenty training cycles, their suggested model attained 98% accuracy. Swati et al. [6] created a technique that combines fine-tuning and transfer learning to classify photos of brain tumors. The authors obtained an accuracy of 94.82% by applying a five-fold cross-validation strategy.

To differentiate BT from MR pictures, the research [13] proposed to use a network of two consolidated regulations composed of genetic algorithms and convolutional neural networks. They identified gliomas and their grades with an accuracy of 90.9% and 94.2%, respectively. First presented in [14], a Wavelet-based autoencoder with ANN splits the input image into a low-resolution image for classification. The created images are fed into CNN to minimize computer complexity while maintaining accuracy.

Verma et al. [15] employed HSADML with MobileNet as the backbone network to enhance MRI classification—their accuracy of 98.69% improved class separability. The study did not, however, concentrate enough on the backbone network, indicating that further attention-based domain-specific network research may be possible. To achieve 96.51% accuracy, Cherukuri et al. [16] created a multi-level attention network (MANet) for T1W-CE MRI data, using Xception as the backbone model. Compared to CNNs and RNNs, they pointed out that LSTM networks are more computationally expensive and difficult to debug.

A customized CNN model with five convolutional layers and two fully linked layers was created by Deepak et al. [17]. Using a 70–30% training–testing split, batch normalization, ReLU activation, and max pooling, they used CNN and an SVM to achieve a 95.8% classification accuracy on the T1W-CE MRI dataset. Nawaz et al. [18] categorized brain tumors in three stages: one-stage detector tumor detection/classification, deep feature extraction using a bespoke CornerNet with DenseNet-41, and exact region identification. With 98.8% accuracy on the T1W-CE MRI dataset, they provide an affordable option for classifying brain tumors.

Two methods were put out by Deepak et al. [19] to enhance brain tumor classification. The first method, "Deep Feature Fusion," blended CNN models' deep features with various loss functions to get an accuracy ranging from 94.8% to 95.6%. In the second, "Majority Voting," accuracies ranging from 94.1% to 94.8% were obtained by applying the same classifier to three feature sets derived from CNN models with different loss functions. These methods improved predictions but raised processing demands because they required several loss functions to be trained. Three CNN models (AlexNet, ResNet-50, and Inception V3) were employed by Kumar et al. [20] to identify MRI brain tumor images. Preprocessing consisted of augmentation, normalization, and scaling. They obtained accuracy percentages of 92.07%, 98.24%, and 93.51%. However, because they need training data, longer training times with more layers, and procedures like maxpooling, CNNs can be slow.

3 Methodology

3.1 Data Pre-processing

This research is conducted using a dataset comprising of MRI (Magnetic Resonance Imaging) images. Before analysis, the MRI images underwent a pre-processing pipeline, which involved the following steps:

Bilateral Filtering: Bilateral filter, an edge preserving smoothing non-linear filter was applied to the MRI images. In this respect, it was intended to minimize noise without losing important image edges and structures.

Normalization: Bilateral filter was adopted in normalizing the images before making comparison among various samples with matched scales. Normalization was carried out to adapt the intensity levels of the images to normal range, reducing the impact of pixel intensity fluctuations.

Mathematically, the normalization process involves the following steps:

Min–Max Scaling

Subtract the minimum intensity value of the image from the pixel's intensity value for every pixel. Find the ratio of result to the range of intensity values or difference between highest and lowest intensities in the image.

The formula for min–max scaling is as follows:

$$\text{normalized\_pixel\_value} = (\text{pixel\_value}-\text{min\_intensity})/(\text{max\_intensity} - \text{min\_intensity})$$

Input image size: Initially, it consists of a single channel at 64×64 pixels, then three channels obtained through a 3×3 filter.

3.2 Feature Extraction

The MRI images obtained after the pre-processing stage are then fed into a ResNet (Residual Neural Network) architecture. The ResNet leverage its deep convolutional layers to learn useful features from image and act as a feature extractor. The main purpose of feature extractor is to transform the complex raw image data into a more abstract and informative representation.

ResNet-50:

The deterioration issue that plagues typical CNN architectures are dealt using residual networks or ResNets. The network's efficiency reaches a saturation point as the depth of the network increases and soon begins to decline at a fast rate. ResNet addresses this issue by introducing shortcut connections between layers, allowing

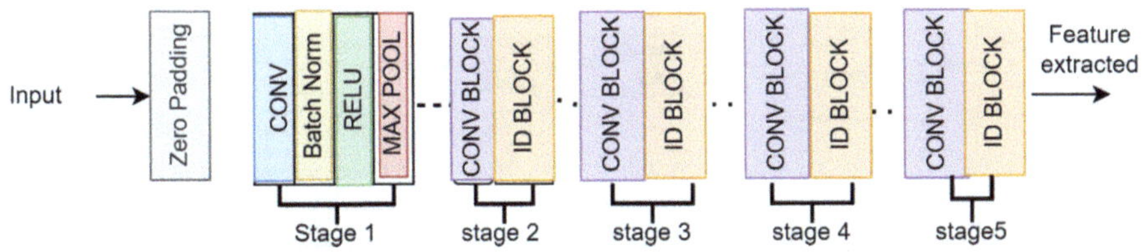

Fig. 1 ResNet-50 model architetcure

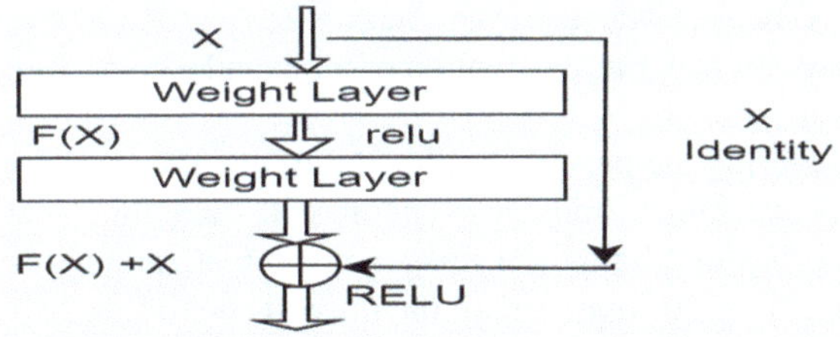

Fig. 2 A residual learning building block displaying a skip connection [21]

critical knowledge from the previous layer to be passed straight to succeeding levels. The shortcut connections directly link the nth layer's input to some (n + x)th layer. Furthermore, ResNet adds the original input to the output of the convolution block, which is then connected sequentially. As seen in Fig. 1, a residual block is generated, allowing information to be transferred across layers (Fig. 2).

3.3 Classification Algorithms

Once the features were extracted, classification algorithms were employed to classify the MRI images into predefined classes. The following classifiers were utilized:

k-Nearest Neighbors (kNN): This instance-based classifier assigns a class label to an image based on the class labels of its k-nearest neighbors in the feature space.

Random Forest Classifier: A collection of decision trees, where each tree votes to determine the final class label. This ensemble technique can handle complex relationships in the data.

Decision Tree Classifier: A single decision tree that recursively splits the feature space based on the most discriminative attributes to reach class assignments.

XGBoost Classifier: An optimized gradient boosting framework that constructs a series of weak learners to improve overall predictive accuracy.

Gradient Boosting Classifier: A boosting algorithm that builds an ensemble of weak learners, with each subsequent learner focusing on the mistakes made by the previous ones.

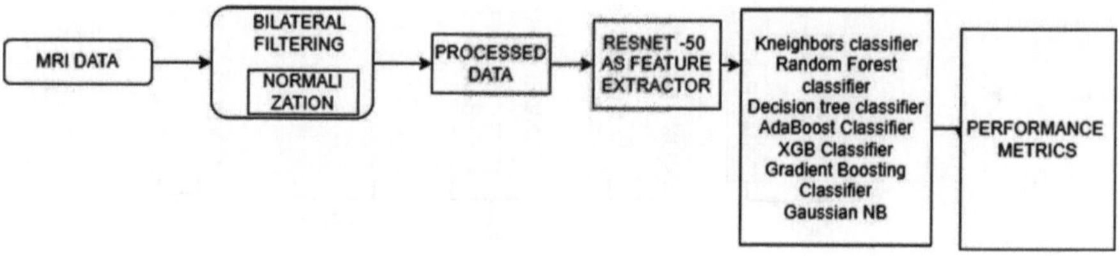

Fig. 3 Overview of the proposed architecture

Gaussian Naive Bayes Classifier: A probabilistic classifier that applies Bayes' theorem with the assumption of independence between features given the class label (Fig. 3).

During the pre-processing phase, the dataset is normalized and bilateral filtered. Normalization transforms numerical data into a standard range; then, bilateral filtering highlights the image. In normalization, a similar group of pixels comes together. The input size of the image is 64*64. Initially, the number of channels is 1, and it is enhanced to 3 by applying the filter of size 3*3. In our work, we have used ResNet-50 for feature extraction. It is pre-trained by default to classify 1000 classes. These are pre-trained models, so in our model, while using our dataset, every layer is trained. The trainable parameter accounts for 23,534,622, meaning some weights are again trained, and non-trainable params are 53,120, i.e., we have not applied the concept of transfer learning. Transfer learning uses weights from the network that have been previously trained with millions of data. The activation function used in neurons of each layer of the ResNet-50 model is RELU. The feature extracted by ResNet-50 is passed through various classifiers. The activation function used is RELU in the input and hidden layer. The output layer has a Sigmoid activation function. The categorical_crossentropy is used as the loss function and the Adam optimizer is used for training neural networks.

$$L(\hat{y}, y) = -\frac{1}{N}\sum_{i}^{N}\left[y_i \log \hat{y}_i + (1 - y_i)\log(1 - \hat{y}_i)\right] \tag{1}$$

Model Trainable Parameters:

The total number of trainable parameters in our model is 23,534,622, indicating that some weights are being trained from scratch during training.

The non-trainable parameters are 53,120, meaning that we have not used transfer learning to keep some layers' weights frozen.

4 Result and Analysis

4.1 Performance Evaluation

The following performance indicators were calculated in order to evaluate the effectiveness of the categorization algorithms:

Confusion Matrix: A matrix that summarizes the number of true negative, true positive, false negative, and false positive predictions, offering insight into the type and frequency of classification errors.

Accuracy: A measure of the overall performance of the classifier that compares the percentage of correctly categorized cases to the total number of occurrences.

$$\text{Accuracy} = \frac{\text{Number of correct predictions}}{\text{Total number of predictions}} \tag{2}$$

Precision: The ratio of true positive occurrence to the total predicted positive instances, indicating the classifier's ability to avoid false positives.

$$\text{Precision} = \frac{\text{True Positives}}{\text{True Positives} + \text{False Positives}} \tag{3}$$

Recall (Sensitivity): A measure of a classifier's accuracy in identifying positive cases, calculated as the ratio of true positive predictions to all real positive instances.

$$\text{Recall} = \frac{\text{True Positives}}{\text{True Positives} + \text{False Negatives}} \tag{4}$$

F1-Score: The harmonic mean of recall and precision offers a thorough assessment of classifier performance by striking a balance between the two variables.

$$F - \text{Measure} = \frac{(2 * \text{Precision}*\text{Recall})}{(\text{Precision} + \text{Recall})} \tag{5}$$

4.2 Dataset

We used a publicly accessible dataset from Figshare that Cheng et al. [22, 23] first published in 2015 and later revised by Cheng in 2017. The dataset includes 233 patients' 3064 T1-CE MR scans of three typical brain tumor types (meningioma, glioma, and pituitary) obtained between 2005 and 2010 from two Chinese medical facilities. Sagittal, axial, and coronal planes were used to obtain the images, which were initially 512 × 512 pixels but were later downsized to 224 × 224 pixels to accommodate the transfer deep learning network. Examples of various tumor types

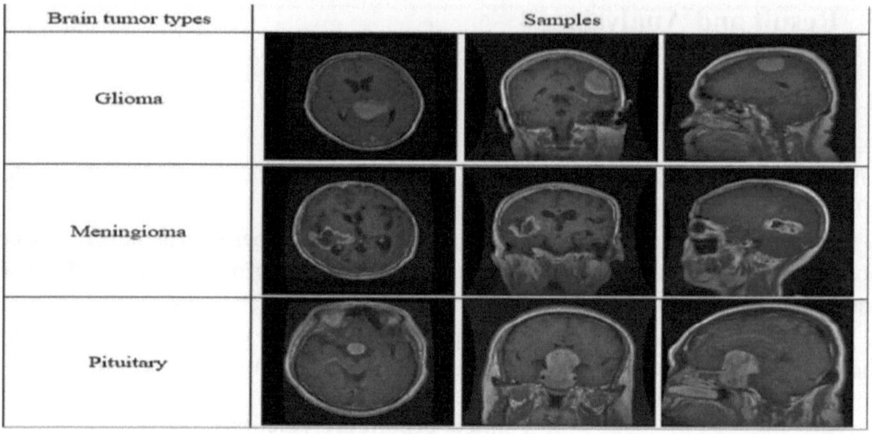

Fig. 4 Axial, sagittal, and coronal MR slices for brain tumor types [19]

and planes were displayed in Fig. 4 by the authors, who used 30% of the dataset for testing and 70% of the dataset for training.

4.3 Result

Among various classifier used Support Vector Classifier (SVC) outperform and was able to give an accuracy of 91.40%, when trained on the Figshare dataset.

MODEL	TN	FP	FN	TP	Accuracy	Precision	Recall	F1Score	Specificity
KNN	844	23	34	325	0.891789	0.824468	0.829665	0.826336	0.916175
Random Forest	821	46	28	331	0.873844	0.796838	0.790046	0.792179	0.897879
Decision Tree	799	60	91	276	0.811310	0.697890	0.690846	0.693697	0.851389
XGB	808	29	21	368	0.899946	0.840416	0.823433	0.829445	0.919549
Gradient Boosting	833	34	25	334	0.883089	0.819731	0.796757	0.803281	0.903542
Gaussian NB	736	129	103	258	0.733007	0.604386	0.612933	0.596070	0.805141
SVC	829	25	22	350	0.914084	0.866237	0.844512	0.852751	0.929130

The "SVC" (Support Vector Classifier) model achieves the highest accuracy (91.40%), indicating that it has the overall best ability to correctly classify instances. Precision: The "SVC" model has the maximum precision (86.62%), which indicates that it is comparatively dependable and has a reduced false positive rate when predicting a positive class. Recall: Its recall at 84.45% under the "SVC" model this implies that it can distinguish true positives. F1-Score: Combining recall and precision this is evident because "SVC" model scores a good F1-score of 85.28%. This means that it has a well balance and ensure that there is a balance in reducing the number of false positives versus accurately detecting true positives. Specificity: The "SVC" model has the highest maximum specificity, calculated as 92.91% accurately classifying negative cases. XGB (extreme gradient boosting) is a better than other. Some aspects such as the accuracy, precision, recall, F1 score, and specificity performed higher than others. The "Random Forest" and "Gradient Boosting" show good results. They showcase competitive performance in a number of different ways such as across multiple criteria. The fact that "GaussianNB" according to most criteria, (Gaussian Naive Bayes) seems to be the worst. This means that it might be among the last in some criteria. trouble classifying the dataset.. In comparison to the other models, the "Decision Tree" model performs worse in terms of accuracy, precision, recall, and F1-score. In summary, the "SVC" model appears to be the top performer based on the provided metrics, followed closely by the "XGB," "Random Forest," and "Gradient Boosting" models.

5 Conclusion

This study analyzed previous research and suggested an enhancement to the current models in order to increase the overall testing accuracy of the brain tumor MRI classification problem. Also, we performed a comparative analysis of different classifiers that can be used for the classification problem and used the most efficient classifier for our work. This helped in improving the accuracy from the existing state-of-the-art solutions.

References

1. Gibson W, Green LA (2016) Users of personal health records: an analysis of the needs, characteristics, and preferences of a cross-sectional sample of users. J Med Internet Res 18(8):e202. https://doi.org/10.2196/jmir.5486
2. Abd-Ellah MK, Awad AI, Khalaf AA, Hamed HF (2019) A review on brain tumor diagnosis from MRI images: practical implications, key achievements, and lessons learned. Mag Res Imaging 61:300–318
3. Fritz A, Percy C, Jack A, Shanmugaratnam K, Sobin L, Parkin DM, Whelan S (eds) (2001) International classification of diseases for oncology, vol 3. World Health Organization, Geneva
4. Claus EB, Walsh KM, Wiencke JK, Molinaro AM, Wiemels JL, Schildkraut JM, Bondy ML, Berger M, Jenkins R, Wrensch M (2015) Survival and low-grade glioma: the emergence of genetic information. Neurosurg Focus 38(1):E6
5. Saxena P, Maheshwari A, Tayal S, Maheshwari S (2019) Predictive modeling of brain tumor: A DEEP learning approach. arXiv preprint arXiv:1911.02265

6. Swati ZN, Khan QZ, Kabir M, Ali F, Ali Z, Ahmed S, Lu, Jianfeng (2019) Brain tumor classification for MR images using transfer learning and fine- tuning. Comput Med Imaging Graph 75:34–46
7. Ertosun MG, Rubin DL (2015) Automated grading of gliomas using deep learning in digital pathology images: a modular approach with ensemble of convolutional neural networks. In: AMIA annual symposium proceedings, vol 2015, p 1899. American Medical Informatics Association
8. Krol A, Gimi B (2017) Medical imaging 2017: biomedical applications in molecular, structural, and functional imaging. In: Society of photo-optical instrumentation engineers (SPIE) conference series, vol 10137
9. Kumar A, Ansari MA, Ashok A (2019) A hybrid framework for brain tumor classification using grey wolf optimization and multi-class support vector machine. Int J Recent Technol Eng
10. Khawaldeh S, Pervaiz U, Rafiq A, Alkhawaldeh RS (2017) Noninvasive grading of glioma tumor using magnetic resonance imaging with convolutional neural networks. Appl Sci 8(1):27
11. Sajjad M, Khan S, Muhammad K, Wu W, Ullah A, Wook Baik S (2019) Multi-grade brain tumor classification using deep CNN with extensive data augmentation. J Comput Sci 30:174–182
12. Srikanth B, Venkata Suryanarayana S (2021) WITHDRAWN: Multi-Class classification of brain tumor images using data augmentation with deep neural network
13. Anaraki AK, Ayati M, Kazemi F (2019) Magnetic resonance imaging-based brain tumor grades classification and grading via convolutional neural networks and genetic algorithms. Biocybernetics Biomedical Eng 39(1):63–74
14. Chen T, Lin L, Zuo W, Luo X, Zhang L (2018) Learning a wavelet- like auto-encoder to accelerate deep neural networks. In: Proceedings of the AAAI conference on artificial intelligence, vol 32, no 1
15. Verma A, Singh VP (2022) Hsadml: hyper-sphere angular deep metric based learning for brain tumor classification. In: Proceedings of the satellite workshops of ICVGIP 2021, pp 105–120, Springer
16. Shaik NS, Cherukuri TK (2022) Multi-level attention network: application to brain tumor classifcation. Signal Imag Video Process 16(3):817–824
17. Deepak S, Ameer P (2021) Automated categorization of brain tumor from mri using cnn features and svm. J Amb Intell Human Comput 12:8357–8369
18. Nawaz M, Nazir T, Masood M, Mehmood A, Mahum R, Khan MA, Kadry S, Thinnukool O (2021) Analysis of brain mri images using improved cornernet approach. Diagnostics 11(10):1856
19. Deepak S, Ameer P (2023) Brain tumor categorization from imbalanced mri dataset using weighted loss and deep feature fusion. Neurocomputing 520:94–102
20. Kumar KK, Dinesh P, Rayavel P, Vijayaraja L, Dhanasekar R, Kesavan R, Raju K, Khan AA,Wechtaisong C, Haq MA et al (2023) Brain tumor identifcation using data augmentation and transfer learning approach. Comput Syst Sci Eng 46(2)
21. He K, Zhang X, Ren S, Sun J (2016) Deep residual learning for image recognition. In: Proceedings of the IEEE conference on computer vision and pattern recognition, pp 770–778
22. Cheng J et al. (2015) %2522 enhanced performance of brain Tumor classification via Tumor region augmentation and partition. %2522 PloS One 10.10
23. Cheng J, Huang Z, Yang X, Li Y, Wang Y (2016) Retrieval of brain tumors by adaptive spatial pooling and Fisher vector representation. PloS One 11(6). The Matlab source codes for this paper are available on GitHub at https://github.com/chengjun583/brainTumorRetrieval

Software Maintenance Prediction Using Stack Ensemble Deep Learning Algorithms

Shristi Chirania, Hera Tahreem, Ayushi, Bikash Agrawalla, and B. Ramachandra Reddy

1 Introduction

A crucial step in development cycle of software is maintenance. It becomes extremely crucial for the software to be updated from time to time after the delivery of the product. Because it continues throughout the lifespan of the product, maintenance [1] is the phase of the project cycle that lasts the longest. It is also the most costly phase and takes a lot of effort.

After the program has been created and delivered, maintenance is crucial to its success. The basic work of this phase of the product life cycle is to keep the software updated and free from bugs. Due to the advancement in technology, new features are being added to this field regularly. So, it becomes necessary to keep our software updated with the new technologies so that it becomes compatible with the other software present in the market.

The main aim of software maintenance [1] is to fix bugs in the code, add new features launched in the market, and improve performance so that it works efficiently and correctly and continues to meet the needs of the customers. Maintenance also plays an important role in keeping up with emerging technologies and products over time. Software maintenance prediction saves a lot of effort and money, so it becomes quite important to have a very good model to solve this issue. Here, we will try to solve the problem using ensemble learning using deep neural networks.

There are several stages involved in the process of software maintenance [2]. In the first step, we need to identify the bugs or errors that occur and we need to form a document about these bugs and errors. After that, we need to analyze the bugs and find out what is the root cause for these errors. Then a plan is created to address these issues to the developer team and then they are responsible to correct the errors. After

S. Chirania · H. Tahreem · Ayushi · B. Agrawalla · B. R. Reddy (✉)
Department of Computer Science and Engineering, NIT Jamshedpur, Jamshedpur, India
e-mail: brcreddy.cse@nitjsr.ac.in

K. Kumar Singh et al. (eds.), *Machine Vision and Augmented Intelligence*, Lecture Notes in Electrical Engineering 1211, https://doi.org/10.1007/978-981-97-4359-9_9

that, again testing is performed and then the new software version is again deployed and this process continues until the users do not find any more bugs or errors.

Compared to conventional machine learning techniques, stacking deep learning algorithms has a number of significant benefits. By merging the results of several neural networks, it frequently produces better predicting performance and is adept at identifying intricate data patterns. Due to the ensemble variety resulting from various neural network designs and methodologies, stacking improves resilience by lowering overfitting. Particularly for jobs like image identification and natural language processing, it excels in feature extraction. Pre-trained models for transfer learning may be included into stacking, accelerating training and data efficiency. Although deep learning models are sometimes criticized for being difficult to comprehend, stacking can shed light on model contributions. There are additional computing requirements, lengthier training durations, and a requirement for careful model selection and optimization, too.

DNN [3] is similar to ANN [4]. The DNN having multiple inner layers called "hidden layers in between the input and output layers is basically said to be a DNN. Here, we have utilized the basic functionality of DNN, in which we will give it a number of inputs, and then neural networks will process the given inputs using complicated calculations. According to these calculations, it will try to find patterns in the given inputs and will give an output that will help us solve the maintenance classification problem [5, 6].

The remainder of the writing is organized as follows: The relevant research on software maintenance prediction using various machine learning models is summarized in Sect. 2. The suggested deep neural network model for forecasting software maintenance is briefly described in Sect. 3. Experimental results are shown in Sects. 4, and 5 concludes.

2 Related Work

Assessing the quality of a software product involves evaluating its maintainability, which refers to how simple it is to modify the system or component to correct errors, improve performance, or respond to environmental changes. Tracking maintenance habits, though, is challenging, making it difficult to predict the cost and risk of maintenance after delivery. The study makes numerous recommendations for machine learning algorithms that may be used to evaluate and forecast software maintainability, including the Genetic Algorithms (GA), Probabilistic Neural Network (PNN), and Group Method of Data Handling (GMDH) [7] using Gaussian activation function. The study used two commercial datasets, UIMS and QUES, which, respectively, have 39 and 71 courses and were written in traditional Ada. The performance of the proposed machine learning algorithms was compared with various models taken from the literature, such as the General Regression Neural Network (GRNN),

Bayesian Regression Tree (RT), Artificial Neural Network (ANN), Stepwise Selection, Multiple Adaptive Regression Splines (MARS), Backward Elimination, Generalized Regression (GN), TreeNets, Support Vector Machine (SVM), Adaptive Neuro Fuzzy Inference System (ANFIS), and Multiple Linear Regressions (MLR) models [1, 7].

In recent years, more and more organizations have adopted the object-oriented (OO) paradigm in their software development practices, as evidenced by Chidamber and Kemerer [4]. The introduction of OO methods and languages Proponents of OOP claim that it leads to easier maintenance due to better data encapsulation, and some evidence supports this assertion. Despite this, there is quite a low possibility that we will be able to eliminate the maintenance completely, and hence, maintenance of software after its deployment will likely be present enough to affect a major part of system costs. And hence, software maintenance remains a crucial area even in the object-oriented era.

In modern times, software maintainability is an essential quality attribute that must be considered for any system or software. This study introduces an improved version of the Random Forest Algorithm (RFA) for predicting software maintainability by Aggarwal and Singh [2]. To increase the precision of the fundamental RF algorithm, the suggested method combines the RFA with three popular feature selection methods—RF, Chi-Squared, and Linear Correlation Filter—as well as a resampling method. The evaluation of the enhanced-RFA approach's effectiveness is done using the R2 value after it has been applied to two commercially accessible datasets, QUES and UIMS.

The management of software maintenance is often an imprecise task due to uncertainties related to resource and service descriptions. Even when following a well-established maintenance process, task delays can occur if resources change while the procedure is being executed or if the new services are not adequately specified. In addition, depending on the complexity or dependability needs of the services, a task delay in an early process stage may cause a different delay towards the conclusion of the process. This study suggests using Bayesian networks [8], a knowledge-based representation, to simulate the delays of maintenance projects using the expertise of professionals. The paper also presents a tool designed to assist in managing software maintenance projects.

To categorize modules as fault-prone or not, Khoshgoftaar et al. [9] employed a one hidden layer neural network with a backpropagation training strategy. A fuzzy model has been created by Aggarwal et al. [10] to assess the maintainability of software. Comment ratio, average life span, average live variable, and cyclomatic complexity are the model's inputs. The model's output is the typical duration of corrective maintenance.

3 Proposed Method

In this section, we propose a method using ensemble DL models for software maintenance and prediction and then compare the accuracy of this model with other ML algorithms such as linear regression, SVR, decision trees, random forests, XGBoost, and CatBoost.

For the ensemble deep learning mode [11], we used stack ensemble learning, and in level 0 of the model, we took five different deep learning models. In each of these models, we used the Adam optimizer and ReLU activation function to increase the accuracy of each model and then trained each of these models with different datasets. For the meta-model, we made it a deep neural network model and used the same activation function and optimizer.

The below block diagram shows the basic structure of our ensemble deep neural network model (Fig. 1).

3.1 *Ensemble Learning*

- An arbitrator assists an ensemble of computational intelligence models in producing the final output by combining the results of all of its separate constituent prediction models, and a certain priority level is assigned to each of them.

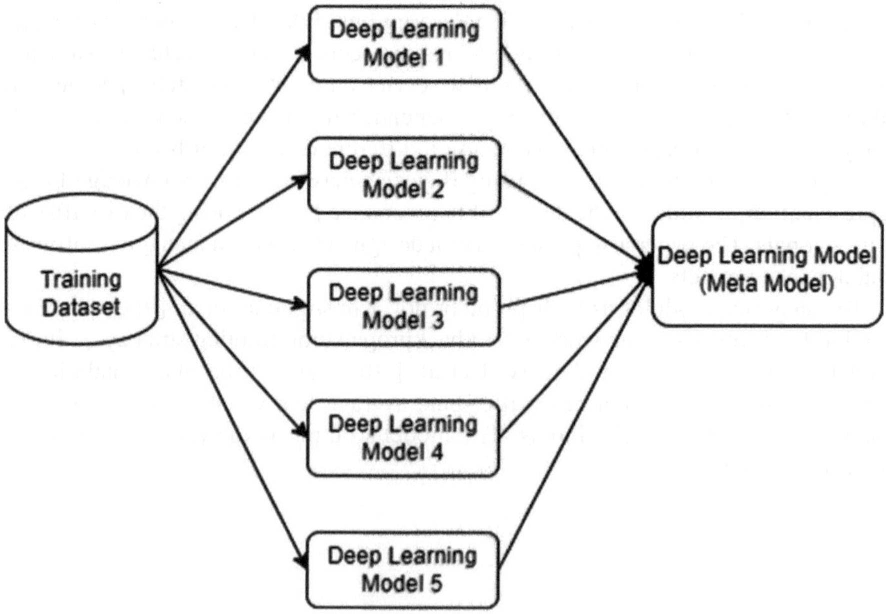

Fig. 1 Block diagram of the proposed method

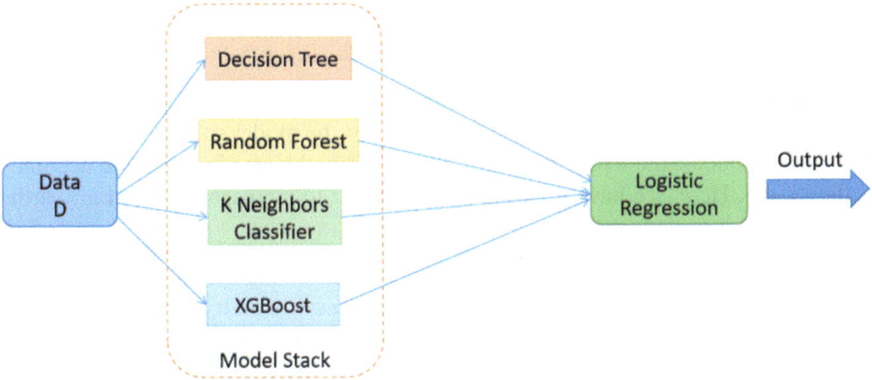

Fig. 2 Block of stacking with machine learning models

- Both single-model and multi-model ensembles exist. The individual constituent prediction models in single-model ensembles are all of the same kind, but they each have a training set that was produced randomly.
- Boosting and bagging are two instances of single-model ensembles. Different separate constituent prediction models make up multi-model ensembles.

3.2 *Stacking*

Stacking is one of the ensemble learning techniques, along with bagging and boosting. Stacking takes multiple heterogeneous weak learners, unlike bagging and boosting, which use homogeneous weak learners for ensemble learning. Stacking learns these heterogeneous learners in parallel, and then to form the meta-model, which will give the final result, it combines these weak learners and trains them to form the meta-model.

The phrase "stacked generalization" is another word for stacking. By applying the performance weights of all sub-models equally, this method generates a new model with predictions that are more accurate. This new model is referred to as a stacking model since it is placed on top of the previous iterations. The following diagram shows stacking for machine learning (Fig. 2).

3.3 *Deep Neural Network*

The fundamental task of deep neural network is to do mathematical calculations on the input fed to them in order to try to find a pattern between them and according to these calculations, give the final output. In a deep network, there is a flow of sequential data, an input, and an output. Inputs like × 1, × 2, and so forth are turned into outputs like z1, z2, and so forth in two (shallow networks) or several intermediary operations, also known as layers, in neural networks (deep networks).

Optimizer: Optimizer is defined as the methods that we use in our model (deep neural network models) to change the attributes of the model so that we can reduce the overall value of the loss function of our model and hence increase the accuracy of the model. Here, we have used Adam Optimizer to increase the accuracy of the model.

Adam Optimizer: Adam is an alternative optimization algorithm that is basically designed to be applied in the training of deep neural networks. It can be viewed as the fusion of momentum-based stochastic gradient descent, which can be used to train deep learning models instead of stochastic gradient descent, and RMSProp, which combines the best features of these algorithms. This method seems to be the most efficient for a problem with a lot of data and parameters. We have used the Adam optimizer in TensorFlow.

Activation Function: ReLU (Rectified Linear Unit): In a neural network, the activation function is responsible for activating the node or output for each input by transforming the node's summed weighted input. The rectified linear activation function (ReLU), if the input is positive, will output the input directly; if the input is negative, it will output zero.

3.4 Dataset Description

- For predicting the software maintainability, we made use of various datasets of same software in different versions and then prepared our own dataset of the software maintenance value of the older dataset by finding the difference in lines of code in the new version and the older version of same classes.
- We did this for four different software versions and then calculated their MSE and RMSE values for comparative study.
- In this study, we have taken four datasets for the evaluation of the proposed method.
- The datasets consist of 20 independent and 1 dependent feature.
- Our information was split into two sections. Data is utilized for testing in 10% of the cases, and training in 90% of the cases.
- To evaluate datasets, we have taken into account ensemble approaches and machine learning algorithms.

3.5 *Performance Measures*

RMSE and MSE are the two factors that are considered in determining the accuracy of each of the models.

Root Mean Square Error (RMSE): The prediction error for each data point is taken into consideration when calculating expected performance using the RMSE.

$$RMSE = \sqrt{\frac{1}{n}\sum_{i-1}^{n}(y_i - \hat{y}_i)^2} \tag{1}$$

Here, y_i is the actual value and $\hat{y}_i$ is the predicted value of house price.

Mean Square Error: Mean Square Error (MSE), which is frequently covered in machine learning classes, is a concept that most people are acquainted with and frequently utilize. MSE is unable to have a negative value since it applies the sum to a squared number. The following is a mathematical definition of the MSE:

$$MSE = \frac{1}{n}\sum_{i-1}^{n}(y_i - \hat{y}_i)^2 \tag{2}$$

4 Experimental Setup and Result Analysis

We took 4 datasets for the comparative study of the errors, and applied Linear Regression, Support Vector Regression, Decision Tree, Random Forest, XGBoost, CatBoost, and Ensemble Deep Neural Networks. In all the four datasets, ensemble deep neural networks algorithm outperformed all the other machine learning algorithms by giving the minimum RMSE and MSE values. The four datasets used are ant_1.5, camel_1.4, Xerces_1.2, and camel_1.2 (Fig. 3).

In the ant_1.5 dataset, it can be observed that using ensemble approach performed better than all other algorithms that are used with RMSE of around 162 and support vector regression method performed worst with RMSE of around 600. In the camel_1.4 dataset, it can be observed that using ensemble approach performed better than all other algorithms that are used with RMSE of around 95 and support vector regression method performed worst with RMSE of around 200 (Fig. 4).

In the Xerces_1.2 dataset, it can be observed that using ensemble approach performed better than all other algorithms that are used with RMSE around 41 with random forest having RMSE value around 45 and XGBoost method performed worst with RMSE around 135. In the camel_1.2 dataset, it can be observed that using ensemble approach performed better than all other algorithms that are used with RMSE around 175 with XGBoost almost performing similar to the ensemble

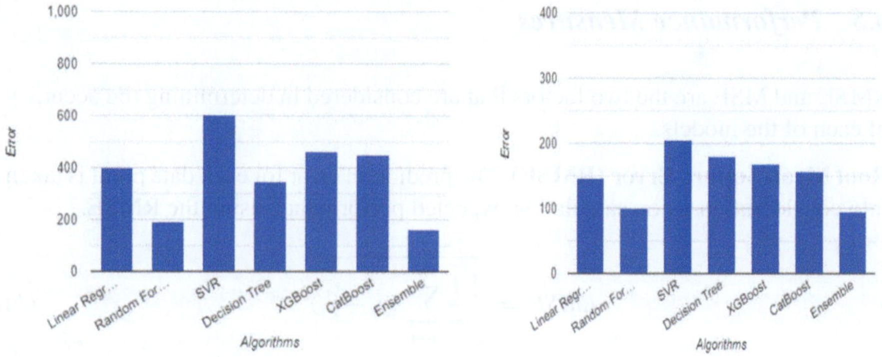

Fig. 3 Root mean squared error of ant V1.5 and camel V1.4

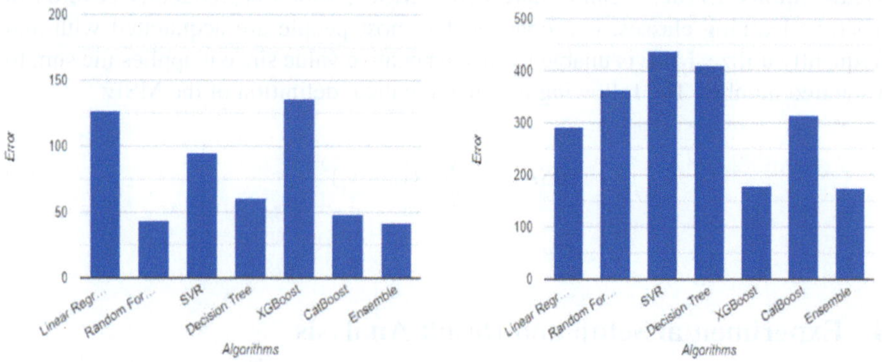

Fig. 4 Root mean squared error of Xerces V1.2 and camel V1.2

approach, having RMSE around 177 and support vector regression method performed worst with RMSE around 440.

From, the above graphs, we can easily compare the RMSE values of all the algorithms and see the difference. The ensemble method gave the best accuracy in all the datasets, followed by random forest, which also gave very good results in some of the datasets after hyper-parameter tuning by choosing the optimal values of the parameters.

From the above two tables, Tables 1 and 2, we can clearly see that the ensemble approach has outperformed all other algorithms for various datasets and we can clearly say that using ensemble techniques for software maintenance prediction will help in increasing the performance of the software or the system and enhancing the accuracy of the overall system.

Table 1 MSE comparison of ensemble method with machine learning algorithms

Methods	ant_1.5	camel_1.4	Xerces_1.2	camel_1.2
Linear regression	161,581	21,758.38	15,998.07	85,706.05
Random forest	36,346.39	8867.11	1018.01	131,342.9
Decision tree	11,861.7	32,367.37	3726.67	168,012.3
SVR	365,299.7	41,775.46	9007.77	192,168
XGBoost	215,685.4	28,093.34	18,311.36	31,425.63
CatBoost	203,682.1	24,539.58	2377.69	98,460.2
Ensemble method	26,256.3	9130.62	1758.27	30,810.57

Table 2 RMSE comparison of ensemble method with machine learning algorithms

Methods	ant_1.5	camel_1.4	Xerces_1.2	camel_1.2
Linear regression	401.97	147.5	126.48	292.75
Random forest	190.64	100.16	45.9	362.41
Decision tree	344.4	179.9	61.04	409.89
SVR	604.4	204.39	94.9	438.36
XGBoost	464.41	167.61	135.31	177.27
CatBoost	451.31	156.65	48.76	313.78
Ensemble method	162.03	95.55	41.93	175.52

5 Conclusion

In this research study, we used a wide range of datasets, including ant_1.5, camel_1.4, Xerces_1.2, and camel_1.2, to perform an exhaustive comparative analysis of software maintenance prediction. Linear Regression, Support Vector Regression, Decision Tree, Random Forest, XGBoost, CatBoost, and Ensemble Deep Neural Networks were just a few of the machine learning techniques that we evaluated.

With the lowest Mean Squared Error (MSE) and Root Mean Squared Error (RMSE) values across all four datasets, ensemble deep neural networks consistently outperformed all other machine learning techniques. When looking at certain datasets, this advantage becomes quite clear. As an illustration, in the ant_1.5 dataset, the ensemble technique greatly outperformed support vector regression, which had an RMSE of almost 600.

The ensemble technique consistently produced the greatest results, whereas support vector regression regularly rated as the least effective algorithm in terms of RMSE, according to similar tendencies that were seen in the camel_1.4, Xerces_1.2, and camel_1.2 datasets.

Our results show that the ensemble technique offers reliable forecasts for activities requiring software maintenance forecasting. Additionally, Tables 1 and 2 demonstrate a distinct performance benefit of the ensemble technique throughout the datasets under examination, reiterating its efficacy in boosting software maintenance forecast accuracy.

References

1. Li W, Henry S (1993) Object-oriented metrics that predict maintainability. J Syst Softw 23(2):111–122
2. Kaur A, Kaur K (2013) Statistical comparison of modelling methods for software maintainability prediction. Int J Software Eng Knowl Eng 23(06):43–774
3. Geirhos R, Jacobsen JH, Michaelis C, Zemel R, Brendel W, Bethge M, Wichmann FA (2000) Shortcut learning in deep neural networks. Nat Mach Intell 2(11):665–673
4. Thwin MMT, Quah TS (2005) Application of neural networks for software quality prediction using object-oriented metrics. J Syst Softw 76(2):147–156
5. Jha S, Kumar R, Abdel-Basset M, Priyadarshini I, Sharma R, Long HV (2019) Deep learning approach for software maintainability metrics prediction. IEEE Access 7:61840–61855
6. Mohana Ramya Y, Deepthi K, Vamsai A, Juhi Sai A, Sharma N, Ramachandra Reddy B (2023) Software fault prediction using deep neural networks. In: Machine vision and augmented intelligence: select proceedings of MAI 2022, pp 267–274 (2023)
7. Malhotra R, Chug A (2012) Software maintainability prediction using machine learning algorithms. Software Eng Int J (SeiJ) 2(2)
8. Zhou Y, Leung H (2007) Predicting object-oriented software maintainability using multivariate adaptive regression splines. J Syst Softw 80(8):1349–1361
9. Khoshgoftaar TM, Allen EB, Hudepohl JP, Aud SJ (1997) Application of neural networks to software quality modeling of a very large telecommunications system. IEEE Trans Neural Networks 8(4):902–909
10. Aggarwal KK, Singh Y, Chandra P, Puri M (2005) Measurement of software maintainability using a fuzzy model. J Comput Sci 1(4):538–542
11. Alsolai H, Roper M (2022) The impact of ensemble techniques on software maintenance change prediction: an empirical study. Appl Sci 12(10):5234
12. Elish MO, Aljamaan H, Ahmad I (2015) Three empirical studies on predicting software maintainability using ensemble methods. Soft Comput 19:2511–2524

Resource Allocation in 6G Network for High-Speed Train Using D2D Outband Communication

Aakansha Garg, Rajeev Arya, and Maheshwari Prasad Singh

1 Introduction

With the growth of 5G/6G, the enhanced communication meeting high quality of service in the moving vehicle is the demand of users [3]. There are various challenges for providing services in the moving train. Each train has different mobility model, i.e., due to its speed, halts at different station, targeted destinations and it's time to reach out that destination, etc. [9]. Fast fading varies according to the scenario for train travelers, i.e., fading depends on whether train is moving through the tunnel, open area and residential area, etc. To apply the correct model for operations is a challenge [7]. A particular coach in the train may be connected to one base station (BS), while the other may be connected to different base stations and the switching of base station varies according to the speed of train. For the low-speed train, pre-transmission processing may be predictive but, for the high-speed train, pre-transmission processing of data is difficult to obtain [10].

The above challenges are solved by using a variety of techniques like utilizing mobile relay is deployed at train's cabin rooftop using mm-Wave [14]. With multiple mobile relays, dynamic power allocation scheme is proposed for energy-efficient train to ground communications [12].The mobile relays and base station can serve as mobile edge computing server. The resource optimization along with mobile relay

A. Garg (✉) · R. Arya
Wireless Sensor Network Lab, Department of Electronics and Communication Engineering, Patna, India
e-mail: aakanshag.phd20.ec@nitp.ac.in

R. Arya
e-mail: rajeev.arya@nitp.ac.in

M. P. Singh
Department of Computer Science and Engineering, National Institute of Technology, Patna, India
e-mail: mps@nitp.ac.in

K. Kumar Singh et al. (eds.), *Machine Vision and Augmented Intelligence*, Lecture Notes in Electrical Engineering 1211, https://doi.org/10.1007/978-981-97-4359-9_10

allocation reduces the latency and energy consumption [5]. A non-uniform beam design reduces the effect of train track geometry and distance from base station [6].

The above analysis signifies that, to assign efficient resources for providing computational resources in a fast-moving train, there are various concerns: (a) *Change of base station for fast-speed train travelers*: The travelers traveling in fast-speed train faces the issues of weak signal strength, i.e., due to Doppler shift in frequency and base station. (b) *Reuse of frequency*: In fast-moving train, the channel allocated to one user may be reallocated to some other user in adjacent cell which may cause interference after sometime. (c) *Ineffectual to meet latency requirements* for various applications, i.e., availability of limited computation resources.

The above issues motivate us to impart efficient computation and communication. Presented work increases the network's computation and communication scope by offloading the tasks to idle traveler, mobile relay. The issue is contrived by taking into account many restrictions like utmost power transmission of mobile devices, latency, helpers, computing power of mobile devices, mobile relay capacity to save channel state information (CSI), etc. The constraints in discrete and continuous form are appraised, and this problem is contrived as an optimized non-linear mixed integer programming problem with constraints (MICONP).

The subsequent explanation mentioned below describes the offerings to provide constructive resources to provide computation in real time:

1. The base changes continuously with the train movement which leads to poor connectivity and can be avoided by utilizing mobile relay for storing channel state information of the base station to enhance communication.
2. In fast-moving train cells change continuously. Sometimes, a channel allocated to one user may be reallocated to another user in another cell so reuse of channel may cause severe interference. To avoid it, D2D communication in out band mode is used.
3. Many applications requires high computation resources. To get computation resources from edge servers causes high latency. Placement of small server enhance computation performance.

In the presented work, part 2 describes relevant work. In part 3, the system model has been explained. Improved grey wolf optimization algorithm is described in part 4. Part 5 converses about results obtained after simulation. In part 6, work come to conclusion.

2 Relevant Works

Communication in fast-speed train is really a challenging area. Various works has been proposed to improve performance for communication in train. Train to ground communication by using mobile relay is used. The bandwidth allocation optimization is performed by the sequential quadratic programming method. The communication is limited to line-of-sight communication as losses other than path loss are not considered [14]. Mobility support and communication challenges for mm-Wave are explained in [4]. There are various challenges for fast-moving train communication as channel are continuously changing. Sometime resources are not allocated according to the current state of channel due to fast state switching [2]. An analysis of channel state measurement and fast-speed train communication models is performed. Various fast-fading and small-fading channels are also presented. It is analyzed that fading varies according to the scenario [11]. An energy-efficient train to ground (TG) communication for fast-moving train using dynamic power allocation can be attained. The power is allocated on the basis of mobile relay connectivity to a cell or different cell [12]. The scope is limited for low latency applications. To reduce average latency during TG communication, the resource allocation and computation offloading is performed. The scope of work is limited to consider the fixed distance between mobile relay and base station [5]. An antenna system is connected to the central controller for ensuring communication and non-uniform beamforming to reduce the rate gap. But the scope is limited for hardware control [6].

From the above discussion it is evident that various systems are implemented for optimizing train communication. But many of them has not considered fading due to infrastructure. Some have used fast switching but Doppler shift is not considered and vice versa. Hence, there is a lack of work for resource allocation considering all dynamics. A framework has been implemented for resource allocation to ensure computation and communication in fast-speed train.

3 System Model

The mobile relay along with small server (SS) is placed at the rooftop of the coach. It works as a clone of base station and edge server. This relay gets the channel state information (CSI) from base station. The CSI for the base stations is stored in a stack memory. Based on CSI resource, allocation is performed. In railway coaches, there are many idle devices. The small server stores requested data in cache. The study of change in cell network with the movement of trains is done. Figure 1 indicates the scenario of the network in which the base station sends the CSI to the mobile relay. This information is stored in stack memory. The users send requests to the mobile relay (MR) which allocates resources as per the CSI. It is considered that users with available state help to communicate and compute. This work aims to improve the communication and computation capacity of the devices in moving trains for different scenarios.

A. *Path Loss Model:*

In the moving train the network switching is very fast with respect to ground. But the relative movement of the users with respect to train is almost negligible. The resources available in proximity to the user can be used to perform computation and communication with minimum latency. The available resources are allocated to the user based on signal to interference and noise ratio. The scenario of train coach is

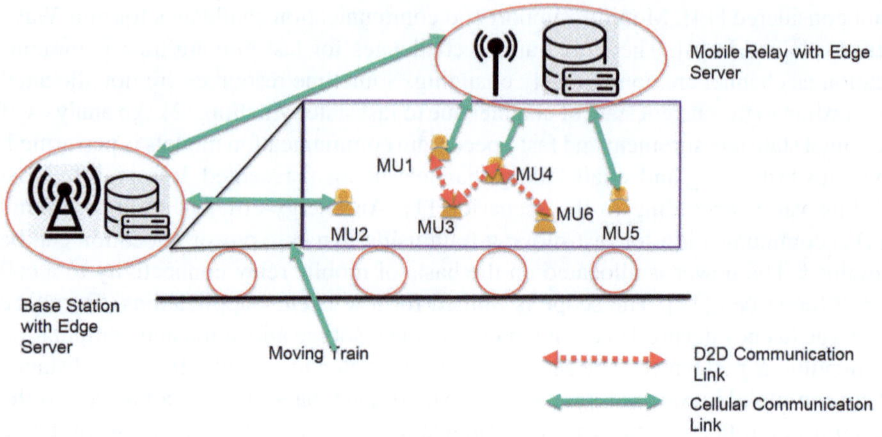

Fig. 1 System model

almost like urban micro scenario mentioned in [1]. The other losses due to wooden structures is also considered. Equation (1) represents it mathematically as follows:

$$PL = L_{path-travelled} + SF + L_{penetration} \tag{1}$$

$$L_{path-travelled} = 32.4 + 21(\log_{10} d) + 20\log_{10} f_c \tag{2}$$

$$SF = 4dB \tag{3}$$

$$L_{penetration} = 4.85 + 0.12f \tag{4}$$

Equation (1) represents that total loss in communication is due to the path traveled, shadow fading and penetration through wood. Equations (2), (3), and (4) represent the mathematical model for loss due to path, shadow fading, and penetration, respectively. In this, f_c is the central frequency in Hz. In this, frequency $f \in \left[f_c - \frac{B}{2}, f_c + \frac{B}{2}\right]$.

B. *Communication Model:*

The device-to-device communication is performed in underlay mode of communication. The rate of communication is defined as follows:

$$C_R = B\log_2(1 + \frac{P_{trans}|ga|^2}{\varsigma_0}) \tag{5}$$

In this, C_R is the communication rate, B is the bandwidth, P_{trans} is the transmitted power, ga is the channel gain, and ς_0 is the channel noise.

C. *Doppler Shift:*

The Doppler shift due to movement of train is as follows:

$$\Delta f = \pm\frac{|\Delta v|}{c} f_c \tag{6}$$

The above equation indicates that Δf is the change in frequency, Δv is the change in speed, and c is the speed of light. This equation explains that for fast-speed train the change in frequency is higher and shift in latency is very low.

D. *Computation Model:*

The users are limited in resources and requires more resources for computation to achieve low latency. It can be achieved by offloading task to proximity resources for computation. The best resources are identified, and task is divided among n number of resources for computation. The energy consumption and latency are calculated as follows:

$$E_{consumption} = E_{computation} + E_{transmission} \tag{7}$$

$$E_{computation} = t_s C_s C_p f_u^2 \tag{8}$$

$$E_{transmission} = P_t * latency \tag{9}$$

$$T_L = \frac{t_s}{C_R} + \frac{t_s C_p}{f_u} \tag{10}$$

In this, Eq. (7) represents that overall energy consumption is the energy consumption due to computation and communication, respectively. Equation (8) represents the energy consumption due to is computation, where t_s is the task size, C_s is the system capacitance, C_p is the number of computation cycles to execute 1-bit task, and f_u is the mobile user computation resources. Equation (9) represents energy consumption during transmission, where P_t is the transmitted power and Eq. (10) represents the latency to complete the task.

4 Modified Grey Wolf Optimization for Resource Allocation

This algorithm is used to allocate resources based on best quality of the signal. The mobile relay sends the idle use information to the user requesting resources. Then user selects the user with best signal quality user whose resource can be used for communication.

The referred grey wolf optimization algorithm is used for outage probability prediction [8, 13]. The presented work allocates the accessible users which are in idle state as alpha, beta, and omega, respectively. The fittest solution is termed as alpha and subsequent solutions are termed as beta and omega, respectively. At first, the user get resources from nearby idle user. In the next step, the remaining resources are analyzed, and next best resource is obtained. This process continues till availability of idle user or maximum three idle users allocated to one user. In this way, improved grey wolf optimization algorithm helps to lessen cost by making use of the idle nearby resources. The algorithm's flow chart is indicated in Fig. 2.

Fig. 2 Flow chart indicating improved grey wolf optimization algorithm

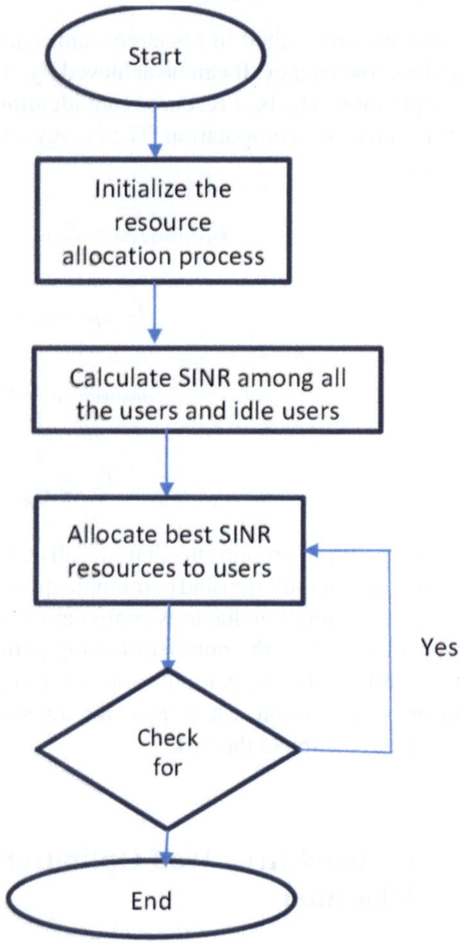

5 Simulated Results Discussion

The executed results show the competency of the presented algorithm. Figure 3 stipulates that consumption of energy in mobile edge computing system using IGWO algorithm is lower than Hungarian algorithm. The outcomes of presented algorithm are 1% better for low task size and with increase in task size, results are improved almost up to 400%. The reason behind it is that low task requires low resources and for higher task size energy consumption is optimized due to optimization of resource allocation.

Figure 4a, b represent latency versus energy consumption and throughput, respectively. It indicates that latency decreases with increase in maximum power as with more power the data can be transmitted in less time. The performance is improved by almost three times. The latency increases with the increase in carrier frequency and the performance is improved by more than three times.

Figure 4c, d represent throughput versus carrier frequency and maximum power, respectively. The result indicates that throughput reduces with increase in carries frequency due to high penetration losses. The performance is improved up to 2.5 times as compared to other. The throughput increases with change in transmit power. High data rate is achieved for more transmission power.

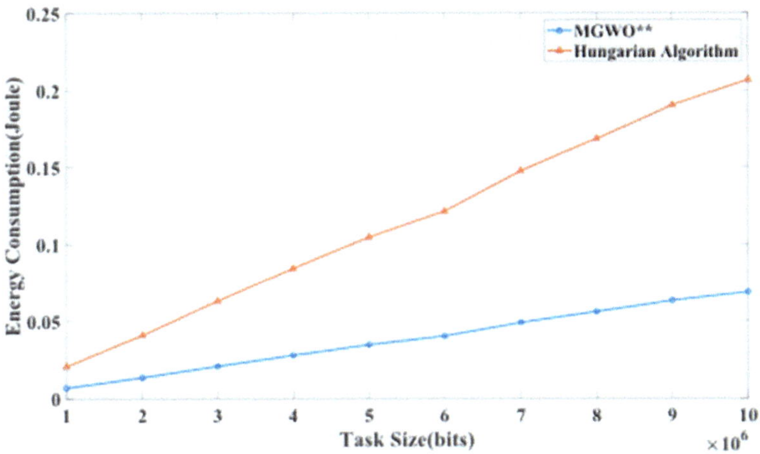

Fig. 3 Energy consumption versus Task size

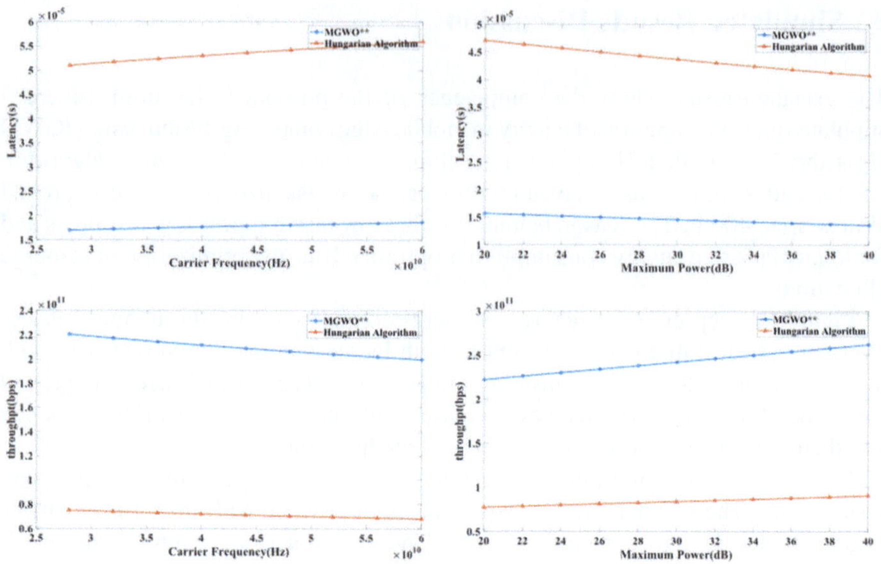

Fig. 4 **a** Latency versus carrier frequency **b** Latency versus Maximum power **c** throughput versus carrier frequency **d** Throughput versus maximum power

6 Conclusion and Future Works

The IGWO algorithm is used in present work to assign resources for computation. The assignment of resources is performed to improve connectivity and computation in high-speed train carrying out optimization of cost. The results simulated signifies that the consumption of energy and latency is reduced. It reduces overall cost in computation and communication. The throughput is also improved resulting in high data transmission rate. Thus, overall system performance is improved using the present algorithm.

In upcoming time, the presented algorithm can be examined for the real-time data in the network for high-speed train.

References

1. 3GPP (2017) TR 138 900—V14.2.0—LTE; 5G; Study on channel model for frequency spectrum above 6 GHz (3GPP TR 38.900 version 14.2.0 Release 14). https://portal.etsi.org/TB/ETSIDeliverableStatus.aspx
2. Ai B, Cheng X, Kurner T, Zhong ZD, Guan K, He RS, Xiong L, Matolak DW, Michelson DG, Briso-Rodriguez C (2014) Challenges toward wireless communications for high-speed railway. IEEE Trans Intell Transp Syst 15(5):2143–2158. https://doi.org/10.1109/TITS.2014.2310771

3. Ali W, Wang J, Zhu H, Wang J (2020) Seamless mobility under a dedicated distributed antenna system for high-speed rail networks. IEEE Trans Veh Technol 69(12):15427–15441. https://doi.org/10.1109/TVT.2020.3041156
4. Li J, Niu Y, Wu H, Ai B, Chen S, Feng Z, Zhong Z, Wang N (2022) Mobility support for millimeter wave communications: opportunities and challenges. IEEE Commun Surv Tutorials 24(3):1816–1842. https://doi.org/10.1109/COMST.2022.3176802
5. Li L, Niu Y, Mao S, Ai B, Zhong Z, Wang N, Chen Y (2022) Resource allocation and computation offloading in a millimeter-wave train-ground network. IEEE Trans Veh Technol 71(10):10615–10630. https://doi.org/10.1109/TVT.2022.3185331
6. Liu Y, Ai B, Niu Y, Han Z, Zhong Z, Qiao Y, Wang N, Stuber GL (2023) Adaptive non-uniform hybrid beamforming for mmwave train-to-ground communications in high-speed railway scenarios. IEEE Trans Veh Technol 72(7):9085–9098. https://doi.org/10.1109/TVT.2023.3249213
7. Micheli D, Barazzetta M, Diamanti R, Obino P, Lattanzi R, Bastianelli L, Primiani VM, Moglie F (2018) Over-the-air tests of high-speed moving LTE users in a reverberation chamber. IEEE Trans Veh Technol 67(5):4340–4349. https://doi.org/10.1109/TVT.2018.2795650
8. Nie X, Zhao F (2021) Pilot allocation and power optimization of massive MIMO cellular networks with underlaid D2D communications. IEEE Internet Things J 8(20):15317–15333. https://doi.org/10.1109/JIOT.2021.3061510
9. Saki M, Abolhasan M, Lipman J, Jamalipour A (2022) Mobility model for contact-aware data offloading through train-to-train communications in rail networks. IEEE Trans Intell Transp Syst 23(1):597–609. https://doi.org/10.1109/TITS.2020.3014588
10. Singh SK, Singh R, Kumbhani B (2023) TRASH: traffic aware hybrid-CRAN scheme for V2I connectivity enhancement. IEEE Trans Veh Technol PP 1–7. https://doi.org/10.1109/TVT.2023.3295244
11. Wang CX, Ghazal A, Ai B, Liu Y, Fan P (2016) Channel measurements and models for high-speed train communication systems: a survey. IEEE Commun Surv Tutorials 18(2):974–987. https://doi.org/10.1109/COMST.2015.2508442
12. Wang L, Ai B, Niu Y, Zhong Z, Mao S, Wang N, Han Z (2023) Energy efficient train-ground MMWAVE mobile relay system for high speed railways. IEEE Trans Green Commun Netw 7(1):16–28. https://doi.org/10.1109/TGCN.2022.3194036
13. Xu L, Wang H, Lin W, Gulliver TA, Le KN (2019) GWO-BP neural network based OP performance prediction for mobile multiuser communication networks. IEEE Access 7:152690–152700. https://doi.org/10.1109/ACCESS.2019.2948475
14. Zhang X, Niu Y, Mao S, Cai Y, He R, Ai B, Zhong Z, Liu Y (2021) Resource allocation for millimeter-wave train-ground communications in high-speed railway scenarios. IEEE Trans Veh Technol 70(5):4823–4838. https://doi.org/10.1109/TVT.2021.3075214

Controlling the Band-to-Band Tunneling Effect in Charge Plasma Based Dopingless Transistor

Nisha Dewagan, Meena Panchore, Ganesh Khekare, Chitraja Rajan, and Lokesh Kumar Bramhane

1 Introduction

Continuous growth in semiconductor industry is a result of constant increase in transistor performance year by year according to Moore's law. As devices are scaled down beyond 32 nm node, the problem of power consumption, short channel effects (SCEs) become more severe. Also complex process formation of the device requires costly millisecond annealing technique. To address these issues junction-less transistor (JLT) was proposed by Colinge et al. [1]. This device provides less thermal budget, less fabrication complexity, lesser SCEs and also facilitates full CMOS functionality [1]. Many junction-less structures like double gate, triple gate, gate all around (GAA) nanowire have been suggested to further enhance the performance of JLT [2–4]. However, many researchers have reported that JLT exhibits more V_{th} variability [5, 6] caused by Random dopant fluctuations (RDFs), increased parasitic capacitance [7], higher work-function to turn the device off [1]. To mitigate the drawbacks of JLT, charge plasma based doping-less transistor (DLT) has been recently proposed [8], which shows less process variability [9] along with all the benefits of JLT. Junctionless transistor is highly doped device (doping ranges from 10^{18} to 10^{20}) and it needs to be volume depleted in off state which results in significant band over-

N. Dewagan · M. Panchore · L. K. Bramhane (✉)
Department of ECE IIITDM, Jabalpur, Madhya Pradesh, India
e-mail: lokesh.bramhane@nitgoa.ac.in

M. Panchore
e-mail: Meenap.ec@nitp.ac.in

ECE NIT Goa, ECE NIT Patna, Patna, Bihar, India

G. Khekare
CSE Department of VIT Vellore, Vellore, India

C. Rajan
RCOEM, Nagpur, India

K. Kumar Singh et al. (eds.), *Machine Vision and Augmented Intelligence*, Lecture Notes in Electrical Engineering 1211, https://doi.org/10.1007/978-981-97-4359-9_11

lap between channel and drain region. When $V_{gs} \leq 0$ V and V_{ds} is sufficiently high resulting in unacceptable lateral BTBT leakage current formally known as GIDL current [10]. The tunneling of electrons from the channel region leaves behind the holes which introduces a parasitic BJT consisting of p-type channel as base and n-type source/drain as emitter/collector respectively. It has also been demonstrated that the lateral BTBT is more prominent compared with transverse BTBT due to the absence of sufficient vertical band bending in JLFET [10]. Also Lateral BTBT is reported as major leakage current component for today's CMOS technology [11]. Although DLT offers better performance in terms of less V_{th} variability, better SCEs controllability, less thermal budget [8, 9] compared with JLT.

Comparison of the performance of JLT and DLT for different silicon thicknesses shows that DLT is better. Further we propose a novel dual material gate along with vacuum gate dielectric [12, 13] DLT (DMG-VDLT) to further decrease the I_{off} current of DLT. The structure consists of asymmetric gate oxide having HfO_2 dielectric at source side and vacuum at drain side. We show that the BTBT effect is more in single material gate ($I_{on}/I_{off} \sim 10^6$) DLT using calibrated 2D-simulation. We investigate that using DMG-VDLT, we get I_{on}/I_{off} ratio as $\sim 10^{10}$. In addition we also demonstrate the temperature dependency of I_{off} current for various SMG and DMG DLT structures.

2 Device Structure and Simulation Parameters

The device structures of the JLT, DLT and DMG-VDLT used for the simulations are shown in Fig. 1a–c respectively. Device parameters used are given in Table 1. Parameters are same for JLT and DLT except for intrinsic silicon film concentration of $N_d = 10^{15}$ for DLT and gate workfunction to maintain V_{th} constant for fair comparison of both the devices [8]. To induce n^+ source/drain regions in classical DLT and DMG-VDLT appropriate source/drain workfunction of 3.9 eV is used [8]. Next, the Debye length criteria for charge plasma concept is fulfilled by varying the silicon film thickness from 7 nm to 9 nm which is less than the Debye length of the device [14].

The proposed DMG-VDLT consists of two gates: (1) control gate at source side having work-function as ϕ_1 and length L_1, (2) Tunnel gate at drain side having work-function as ϕ_2 and length L_2 [15]. The gate dielectric is composed of HfO_2 at source side and Vacuum at drain side. Many technologies for dual material gate fabrication have been proposed such as full silicidation of Co–Ni bi-layer with doped poly Si metal gate [16], metal inter-diffusion technique [17], and Dual metal gate using rapid-thermal chemical vapor deposition (RT-CVD) with Ti as gate metal [18]. Realization of vacuum as gate dielectric can be achieved by first deposition of sacrificial layer of SiO_2 using Chemical vapor deposition (CVD) and the removal of that layer using Hydrofluoric (HF) acid later on [12, 19]. We have chosen L_1/L_2 as 0.5 for best results as reported in [20]. Gate workfunctions ϕ_1 and ϕ_2 are varied from 3.9 eV to 4.94 eV for DMG-VDLT.

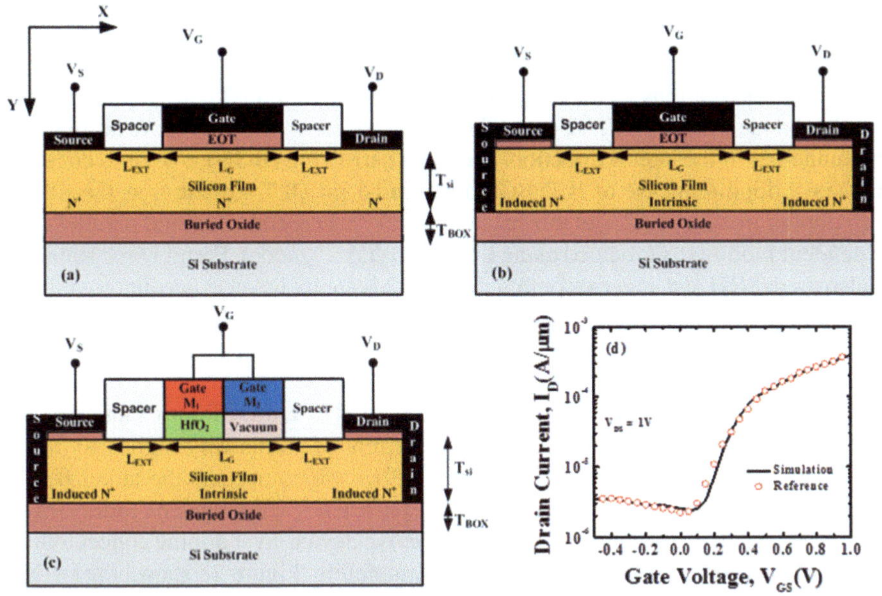

Fig. 1 Structure of **a** JLT, **b** DLT, and **c** Proposed DMG-VDLT **d** Calibration of simulation setup by reproducing the results of [10]

Table 1 Parameters used for device simulation

Parameters	JLT	DLT	Proposed DMG-HVDLT
Silicon Thickness (T_{Si})	7–9 nm	7–9 nm	7 nm
Gate Length (L_G)	20 nm	20 nm	20 nm
Channel Doping (N_D)	1×10^{19} cm^{-3}	1×10^{15} cm^{-3}	1×10^{15} cm^{-3}
Gate work-function (ϕ_m)	5.1 eV	4.74 eV	3.9–4.94 eV
Sourec/Drain work-function ($\phi_{S/D}$)	–	3.9 eV	3.9 eV
Effective Gate Oxide Thickness (EOT)	1 nm	1 nm	1 nm
Spacer Length (L_{EXT})	15 nm	15 nm	15 nm
Substrate Doping (N_D)	5×10^{18} cm^{-3}	5×10^{18} cm^{-3}	5×10^{18} cm^{-3}
Buried Oxide (T_{BOX})	30 nm	30 nm	30 nm

3 Results and Discussion

2-D device simulations have been performed using Silvaco ATLAS [21]. Nonlocal Band to band tunneling (BTBT) model has been incorporated in order to account for the tunneling in the lateral direction. Bandgap narrowing (BGN) is used to consider the heavy doping in case of JLT. BGN is not used for DLT structures as the silicon film doping in case of DLT is intrinsic ($N_d = 10^{15}$). Perpendicular and parallel field dependent mobility is modeled using Lombardi (CVT) model. Fermi Dirac statistics is also used. SRH and auger recombination models are included to account for minority recombination. The quantization effects due to thin device layers are considered using increased band gap obtained as done in [10]. All the models considered for the device depicted are in Fig. 1d.

Figure 2a shows the transfer characteristics of JLT and DLT for channel length (L_G = 20 nm) and T_{Si} = 6 nm. So off state current of JLT is very high $\sim 10^{-5}$ due to heavy doping concentration ($N_d = 10^{19}$) in JLT which triggers the larger BTBT induced BJT action [10]. However in case of DLT, the I_{off} current is 5 orders lesser compared with JLT owing to the fact that the active device layer doping concentration is intrinsic type ($N_d = 10^{15}$) resulting in less tunneling. Figure 2b shows the I_D–V_G characteristics of JLT and DLT for different silicon thicknesses (T_{Si}). Thicker silicon film results in higher I_{off} current in case of JLT due to increased tunneling width [10]. But in case of DLT the variation of I_{off} with respect to T_{Si} is not much significant because the device is less sensitive towards T_{Si} variation as proved in [8]. Figure 3a, b DLT larger depletion region in off state increases the tunneling width sufficiently of the device at channel-drain region, hence, it will reduce the possibility of the tunneling of electrons from the valence band of the channel to the conduction band of the drain. The less tunneling of electrons results in lesser hole accumulation in DLT compared with JLT as shown in Fig. 4a, b. This proves that the BTBT induced parasitic BJT has smaller gain for the DLT. It can also be shown from Fig. 3 that the barrier height between source and channel is more for DLT due to the fact that we have used BGN model for JLT to account for the heavy doping concentration.

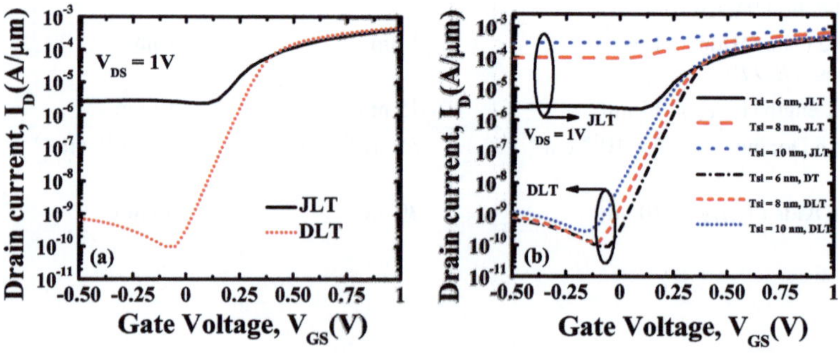

Fig. 2 Transfer characteristics of JLT and DLT **a** T_{si} = 7 nm **b** For different T_{si} for L_G = 20 nm at V_{DS} = 1V

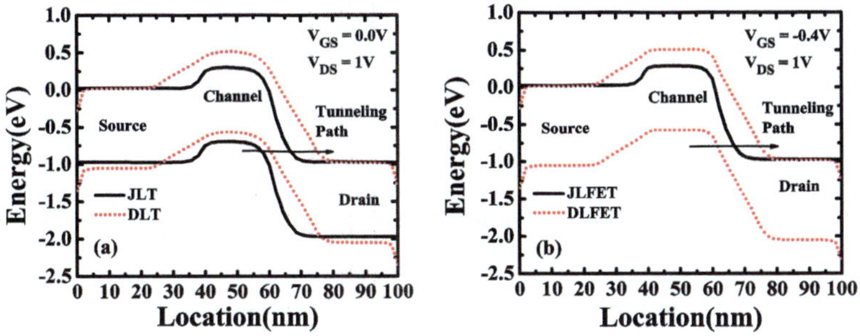

Fig. 3 Energy band profiles in the lateral channel direction for JLT and DLT in off state 1 nm below Si/SiO_2 interface **a** $V_{GS} = 0$ V and **b** $V_{GS} = -0.4$ V at $V_{DS} = 1$V, $T_{Si} = 7$ nm

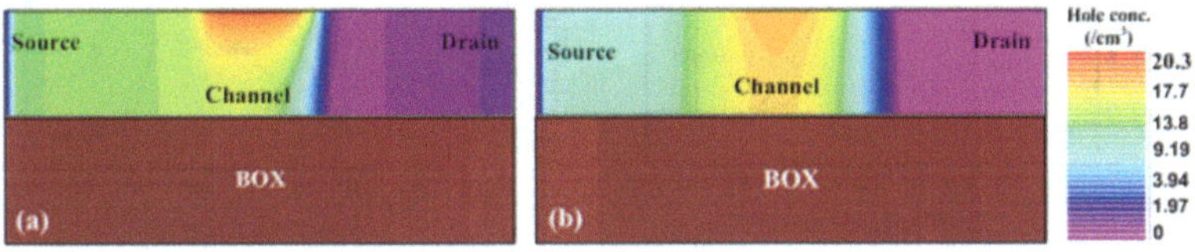

Fig. 4 Hole concentration contour plot of **a** JLT and **b** DLT during off state ($V_{GS} = 0$ V and V_{DS} = 1V) 1 nm below Si/SiO_2 interface

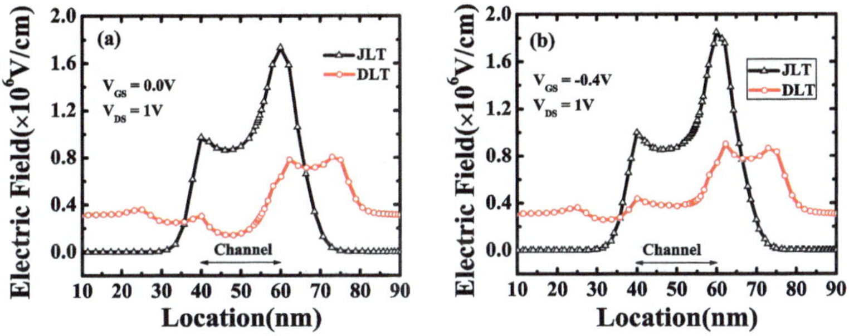

Fig. 5 Electric field distribution along channel direction for JLT and DLT in off state 1 nm below Si/SiO_2 interface **a** $V_{GS} = 0$ V and **b** $V_{GS} = -0.4$ V at $V_{DS} = 1$ V, $T_{Si} = 7$ nm

But in case of DLT, BGN has not been used as channel is intrinsically doped. This automatically reduces the off state current of DLT even if BTBT between channel and drain is not present. The electric field distributions of JLT and DLT along channel direction are compared in Fig. 5. The maximum electric field (E_{max}) at drain side in DLT is almost three times lesser than JLT resulting in lesser band bending and hence DLT suffers less BTBT and shows superior I_{on}/I_{off} ratio ($\sim 10^6$) compared with JLT ($\sim 10^3$).

Further, to diminish the effect of BTBT in DLT and to make this device even better we propose vacuum gate dielectric architecture for DLT (VDLT). In Fig. 6a, b, we observe that the hole concentration for SMG-VDLT is less than that of DLT,

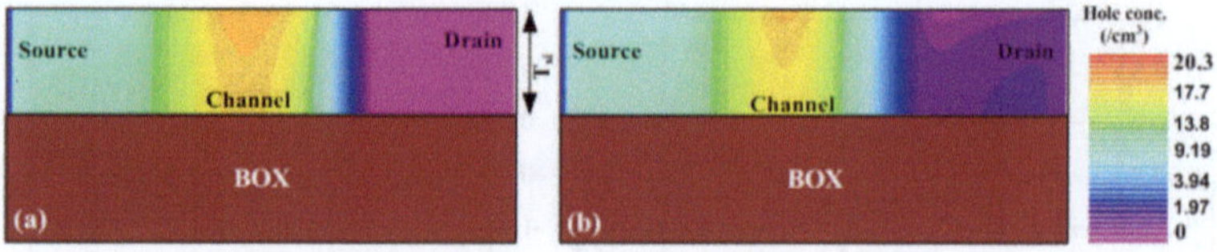

Fig. 6 Hole concentration contour plot of **a** JLT and **b** SMG-VDLT during off state(V_{GS} = 0 V and V_{DS} = 1 V) 1 nm below Si/SiO_2 interface

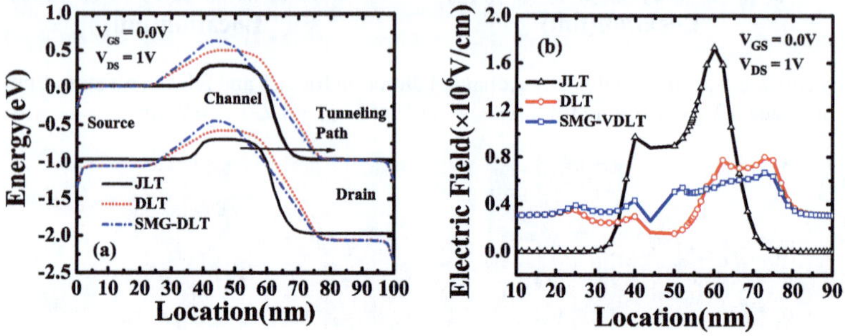

Fig. 7 **a** Energy band profiles and **b** Electric field distributions along channel direction for JLT, DLT and SMG-VDLT during off state (V_{GS} = 0 V and V_{DS} = 1 V), ϕ_1 = 4.74 eV and ϕ_2 = 4.74 eV

resulting in smaller BTBT. Figure 7a shows the energy band profiles along channel direction for JLT, DLT, and SMG-VDLT at V_{GS} = 0 V. It is clear from the fig that use of vacuum as dielectric widens the tunneling width. The maximum electric field at drain junction also gets reduced in case of SMG-VDLT compared with DLT as shown in Fig. 7b resulting in reduced tunneling width. Therefore asymmetric vacuum dielectric gate structure provides better immunity against band-to-band tunneling but at the cost of reduced on state current. Therefore to maintain the drive current for analog application without affecting the BTBT effect [13] we propose asymmetric vacuum gate dielectric with dual material gate (DMG-VDLT) architecture. This structure is realized by providing two metal gates of different workfunctions such that $\phi_1 > \phi_2$ on source and drain side. Figure 8a demonstrate the I-O characteristics of DLT, SMG-VDLT and DMG-VDLT in ϕ_1 = 4.74 eV and different ϕ_2 taking L_1/L_2 as 0.5. We see that the off state current of DMG-VDLT decreases as we decrease ϕ_2. From electric field profile comparison it can be analyzed that the peak electric field at channel-drain region decreases for decreasing ϕ_2, resulting in lesser band bending and hence reduced off state current. Further, the effect of variation of ϕ_1 on transfer characteristics of DMG-VDLT is shown in Fig. 9a for ϕ_2 = 3.9 eV. From the fig we conclude that the increase in ϕ_1 increases the V_{th} of the device. The increase in V_{th} results from the increase in Source-channel electric field as shown in Fig. 9b. We observe a reduction in I_{off} by two order in DMG-VDLT as compared to DLT and hence I_{on}/I_{off} ratio is found to be $\sim10^{10}$ for ϕ_1 = 4.94 eV and ϕ_2 = 3.9eV.

In addition, the temperature dependence of tunneling current is analyzed as shown in Fig. 10. The off-state leakage current is plotted for temperatures 300 K, 350 K,

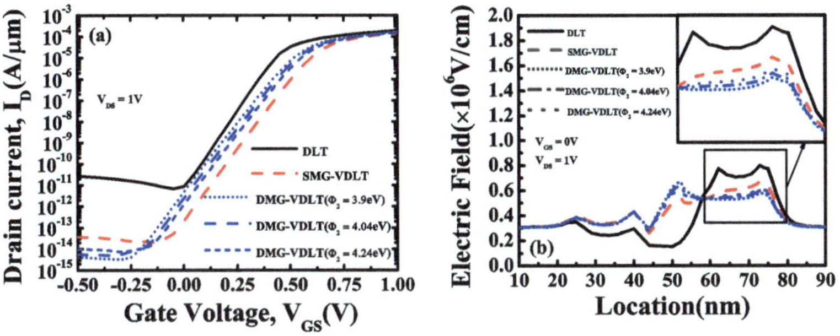

Fig. 8 **a** Transfer characteristics and **b** Energy band profiles taken at 1 nm below the Si/SiO2 interface of the DLT, SMG-VDLT, and DMG-VDLT with $\phi_1 = 4.74$ eV and varying ϕ_2

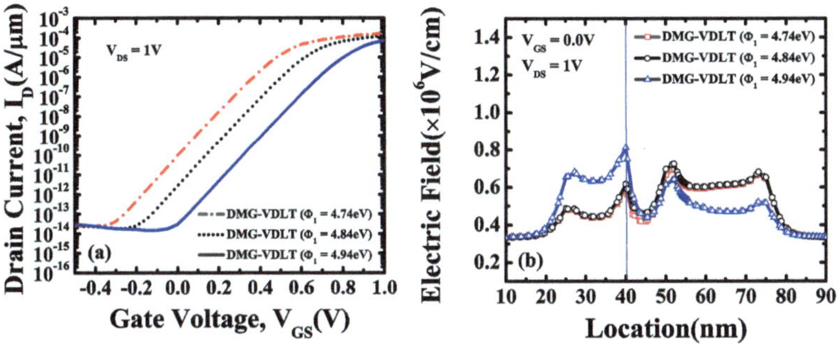

Fig. 9 **a** Transfer characteristics and **b** Energy band profiles taken at 1 nm below the Si/SiO2 interface of DMG-VDLT with $\phi_2 = 3.9$ eV and varying ϕ_1

Fig. 10 Tunneling currents at different temperatures (300 K, 350 K, 400 K) for DLT, SMG-VDLT, DMG-VDLT ($\phi_1 = 4.74$ eV $\phi_2 = 3.9$ eV)

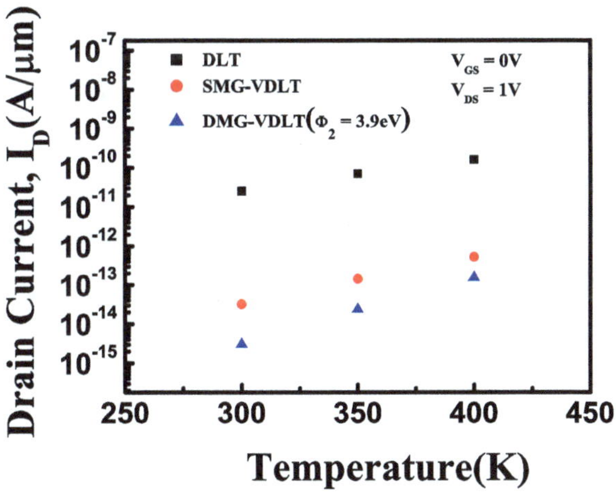

and 400 K at $V_{GS} = 0$ V and $V_{DS} = 1$ V for DLT, SMG-VDLT, and DMG-VDLT. We observe an increase in tunneling current for all the devices as we increase the temperature [11].

4 Conclusion

Comparing the effect of B2B tunneling for JLT and charge plasma based DLT. We demonstrate that the DLT suffers less BTBT leakage current compared with JLT. The off state leakage current in DLT is five orders less than that of JLT. We have proposed the application of vacuum as gate dielectric in DLT (SMG-VDLT) for the first time to further suppress the leakage current which results in I_{on}/I_{off} ratio as $\sim 10^9$. Furthermore we have proposed the DMG-VDLT to further improve the I_{on} current of SMG-VDLT. We have varied the control gate and tunnel gate workfunctions and found that for $\phi_1 = 4.94$ eV and $\phi_2 = 3.9$ eV we get I_{on}/I_{off} ratio as $\sim 10^{10}$. Therefore our proposed device shows excellent immunity against BTBT leakage current and can be considered as a lucrative alternative of conventional DLT. However dependency of tunneling current for DLT, SMG-VDLT, and DMG-VDLT and found the increase in tunneling current as we increase the temperature for all the devices.

References

1. Colinge J-P, Lee C-W, Afzalian A, Akhavan ND, Yan R, Ferain I, Razavi P, ONeill B, Blake A, White M, Kelleher A-M, McCarthy B, Murphy R (2010) Nanowire transistors without junctions. Nature Nanotechnol 5(3):225–229
2. Choi S-J, Moon D-I, Kim S, Duarte JP, Choi Y-K (2011) Sensitivity of threshold voltage to nanowire width variation in junctionless transistors. IEEE Electron Dev Lett 32(2):125–127 Feb
3. Sallese J-M, Chevillon N, Lallement C, Iniguez B, Pregaldiny F (2011) Charge-based modeling of junctionless double-gate field-effect transistors. IEEE Trans Electron Dev 58(8):2628–2637 Aug
4. Barraud S et al (2012) Scaling of trigate junctionless nanowire MOSFET with gate length down to 13 nm. IEEE Electron Dev Lett 33(9):1125–1127 Sep
5. Gnudi A, Reggiani S, Gnani E, Baccarani G (2012) Analysis of threshold voltage variability due to random dopant fluctuations in junctionless FETs. IEEE Electron Dev Lett 33(3):336–338 Mar
6. Aldegunde M, Martinez A, Barker JR (2012) Study of discrete doping-induced variability in junctionless nanowire MOSFETs using dissipative quantum transport simulations. IEEE Electron Dev Lett 33(2):194–196 Feb
7. Parihar MS, Ghosh D, Kranti A (2013) Ultra low power junctionless MOSFETs for subthreshold logic applications. IEEE Trans Electron Dev 60(5):1540–1546 May
8. Sahu C, Singh J (2014) Charge-Plasma based process variation immune junctionless transistor. IEEE Electron Dev Lett 35(3):411–413 March
9. Sahu C, Singh J (2015) Potential benefits and sensitivity analysis of dopingless transistor for low power applications. IEEE Trans Electron Dev 62(3):729–735 March

10. Gundapaneni S, Bajaj M, Pandey RK, Murali KVR, Ganguly S, Kottantharayil A (2012) Effect of band-to-band tunneling on junctionless transistors. IEEE Trans Electron Dev 59(4):1023–1029 Apr
11. Yuan X et al (2008) Gate-induced-drain-leakage current in 45-nm CMOS technology. IEEE Trans Dev Mater Reliab 8(3):501–508 Sept
12. Han W, Ahn JH, Choi Y (2011) Damage immune field effect transistors with vacuum gate dielectric. J Vac Sci Technol B 29:14 Feb
13. Pratap Y, Haldar S, Gupta RS, Gupta M (2016) Gate-material-engineered junctionless nanowire transistor (JNT) with vacuum gate dielectric for enhanced hot-carrier reliability. IEEE Trans Dev Mater Reliab 16(3):360–369 Sept
14. Hueting RJE, Rajasekharan B, Salm C, Schmitz J (2008) The charge Plasma P-N Diode. IEEE Electron Dev Lett 29(12):1367–1369 Dec
15. Sahay S, Kumar MJ (2016) Insight into lateral band-to-band-tunneling in nanowire junctionless FETs. IEEE Trans Electron Dev 63(10):4138–4142 Oct
16. Liu J, Wen HC, Lu JP, Kwong DL (2005) Dual-work-function metal gates by full silicidation of poly-Si with co-Ni bi-layers. IEEE Electron Dev Lett 26(4):228–230 Apr
17. Yeo Y-C (2004) Metal gate technology for nanoscale transistors-Material selection and process integration issues. Thin Solid Films 462(463):34–41
18. Lu Q et al. (2000) Dual metal gate technology for deep submicron CMOS transistors. In: Proceedings symposium VLSI technolology, pp 72–73
19. Griesbach T, Wurz M, Rissing-Leibniz L (2011) Application of sacrificial layers for the modular micro sensor fabrication on a flexible polymer substrate. In: Proceedings sensitive test conference sensitive, pp 355–360
20. Lou H et al (2012) A junctionless nanowire transistor with a dual-material gate. IEEE Trans Electron Dev 59(7):1829–1836 Jul.
21. ATLAS Device Simulator Software (2012) Silvaco. Santa Clara, CA, USA

Comparison of Different CIC Filter Architectures on the Basis of a Novel Parameter Called Noise Factor for Sigma-Delta Based ADCs

Pushpendra Dwivedi, Meena Panchore, Pushpa Raikwal, and Akash Agarwal

1 Introduction

Today's voice band and audio applications are dominated by Sigma-Delta Analog to Digital Converter [1]. A major benefit of the High Oversampling Rate, which is used in Sigma-Delta modulator, is that it simplifies the Analog Anti-Aliasing filter for the ADC and the Anti-Imaging filter for the DAC [2–4]. Additionally, with a small increase in overall Die Area, Power, and Cost, features like Digital Filter Programmability are made practical by the simplicity of adding Digital functions to a CMOS-based converter [5].

Decimation Filter is an important part of Sigma-Delta based ADC. The main functions of the decimation filter are: (1) Low pass filtering of the output of Sigma-Delta Modulator, (2) Decimating the output of Sigma-Delta Modulator to its Nyquist rate, so as to make it suitable for further processing by the Digital Signal Processors

P. Dwivedi (✉) · A. Agarwal
Department of Electronics and Communication Engineering, Bhagalpur College of Engineering, Bhagalpur 813210, Bihar, India
e-mail: pushpendra.ece.dstte@bihar.gov.in

A. Agarwal
e-mail: akash.ec@nitp.ac.in

M. Panchore
Department of Electronics and Communication Engineering, National Institute of Technology, Patna 800005, Bihar, India
e-mail: meenap.ec@nitp.ac.in

P. Raikwal
Department of Electronics and Communication Engineering, PDPM Indian Institute of Information Technology Design and Manufacturing, Jabalpur 482005, Madhya Pradesh, India
e-mail: praikwal@iiitdmj.ac.in

K. Kumar Singh et al. (eds.), *Machine Vision and Augmented Intelligence*, Lecture Notes in Electrical Engineering 1211, https://doi.org/10.1007/978-981-97-4359-9_12

and (3) Increase the resolution of the Sigma-Delta Modulator output from Single-Bit to Multi-Bit output [6–15].

Based on the Moving-Average (Boxcar) filter structure, a new class of CIC filters has been developed [16, 17]. For the implementation of comb filter, no multipliers are required because all its coefficients are equal to unity [17]. This filter class works well even at high frequencies and can be implemented using a single chip VLSI. Communication Systems use this type of filter in a variety of applications. The Comb filter is used for filtering very high-rate signals. Comb filters are used where a large conversion factor is desired [14, 18, 19]. A technique that improves the filter performance is Filter sharpening [20, 21]. CIC Decimator has been cascaded with a Sine Compensator and a Cosine filter. This Sine–cosine based compensator is used as a second stage for the improvement of passband characteristics of the CIC filter [22–24].

Section 1 covers the Introduction of the paper. Section 2 describes about the different CIC filter architectures. Section 3 explains the concept of Quantization Noise and derivation of Noise factor. Section 4 covers the plot of noise factor for various CIC filter architectures and its comparison. Section 5 concludes the paper.

2 Different CIC Filter Architectures

2.1 Basic Comb Decimation Filter

A Moving-Average (MA) digital filter is a simple low pass FIR filter. Its impulse response is of rectangular shape and is given by [16, 17, 22]:

$$g_c[n] = \frac{1}{N}\{^{1, for 0 \leq n \leq N-1}_{0, otherwise} \tag{1}$$

The z-transform representation of this comb filter is

$$G_c(z) = \frac{1}{N} * \sum_{k=0}^{N-1} z^{-k} \tag{2}$$

This transfer function could be modified as that of a Recursive filter of the form given below

$$G_c(z) = \frac{1}{N} * \frac{1 - z^{-N}}{1 - z^{-1}} \tag{3}$$

Putting $z = e^{j\omega}$, the Frequency Response of the above equation is found to be

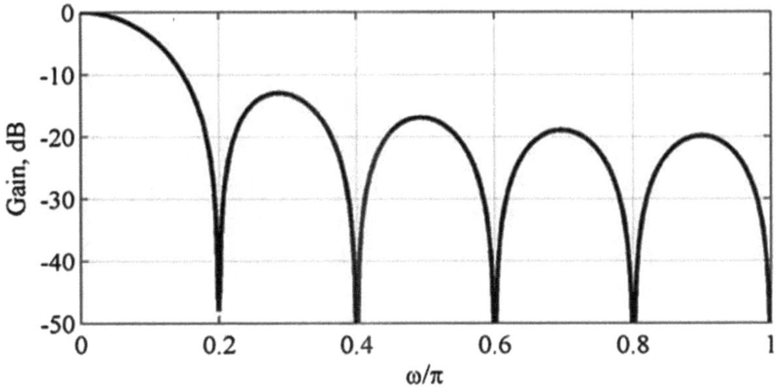

Fig. 1 Magnitude Response of the Comb filter

$$G_c\left(e^{j\omega}\right) = \frac{1}{N} * \frac{\sin\left(\frac{\omega N}{2}\right)}{\sin\left(\frac{\omega}{2}\right)} * e^{j\omega[(N-1)/2]} \tag{4}$$

Figure 1 shows the magnitude response of Eq. (4) for N = 10.

2.2 *K-Stage CIC Filter*

The transition width of CIC filter is very wide and its Stopband Attenuation is very poor. To improve the frequency response of this filter, cascading of several identical stages is done [18]. The Z-domain representation of CIC filter is written as

$$G_C^K(z) = \left[\frac{1}{N} * \frac{1 - z^{-N}}{1 - z^{-1}}\right]^K \tag{5}$$

And its Magnitude Frequency Response is given by

$$G_C^K\left(e^{j\omega}\right) = \left|\frac{1}{N} * \frac{\sin\left(\frac{\omega N}{2}\right)}{\sin\left(\frac{\omega}{2}\right)}\right|^K \tag{6}$$

Figure 2 shows the improvement in selectivity and stopband attenuation of the overall filter by use of Cascaded identical stages. An increase in the number of comb filter sections improves its Selectivity and Stopband Attenuation. From Fig. 2, it is observed that there is a continuous decrease of passband gain, which is referred to as Passband Droop.

The use of Comb Filter in multirate applications was first proposed by Hogenauer. Therefore, they are also referred to as Hogenauer filter [16].

Fig. 2 Magnitude Response of a Multirate Comb Realization

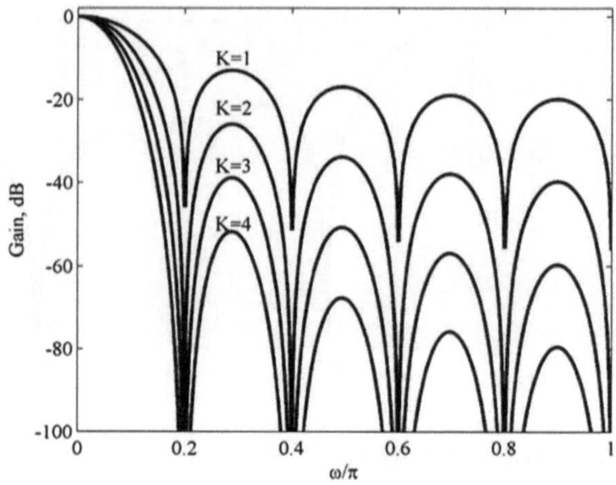

2.3 *Sharpened CIC Filter*

A technique, called as Filter sharpening, is used to improve the performance of filter, i.e., it provides less Passband gain and high Stopband Attenuation. The Digital Filter's Magnitude Response can be sharpened by the use of multiple versions of a basic lower order filter [20]. $H_{nm}(f)$ is a type of sharpened filter and it is expressed as

$$H_{nm}(f) = H_p^{n+1}(f) * \sum_{k=0}^{m} \frac{(n+k)!}{n! * k!}[1 - H_p(f)]^k, \quad (7)$$

$H_p(f)$ is a basic lower order filter. Here, n and m are non-negative integers and denote how many non-zero derivatives of $H_{nm}(f)$ occur at $H_{nm}(f) = 0$ and $H_{nm}(f) = 1$, respectively.

If $n = m = 1$, transfer function becomes

$$H_{11}(f) = H_p^2(f)\left[3 - 2 * H_p(f)\right] \quad (8)$$

The Kaiser-Hamming sharpening technique is valid for an FIR filter. If $H_p(z)$ is a causal FIR filter, then $H_{11}(z)$ becomes

$$H_{11}(z) = H_p^2(z) * \left[3z^{-D} - 2H_p(z)\right] \quad (9)$$

Here D is the group delay (in samples). Equation (8) leads to a transfer function $H_{11}(z)$, that improves both passband and stopband characteristics of lower order filter. The square bracket term of Eq. (9) leads to reduction of Passband Droop and $H_p^2(z)$ leads to improvement of Stopband Rejection.

Kwentus et al. [21] proposed Comb Filter $G_C^K(z)$ as the basic filter $H_p(z)$ in Eq. (9) to implement filter sharpening technique on CIC filter.

2.4 *CIC Filter Based on Architecture Developed by Dolecek [23, 24]*

In this method, CIC Decimator was cascaded with a Sine Compensator and a Cosine filter. CIC decimator, $G_C^K(z)$, is the first stage of the filter. Then Sine-based compensator is used as a second stage to enhance the characteristic of the filter in passband. It compensates for the passband droop observed in CIC filter. The system function of the Sine based compensator is

$$H_{SIN}(z) = \frac{1}{4}\left[-1 + 6z^{-M/2} - z^{-M}\right] \tag{10}$$

$$H_{SIN}\left(e^{j\omega}\right) = e^{-j\omega M/2}\left(1 + \sin^2(M\omega/4)\right) \tag{11}$$

$$\left|H_{SIN}\left(e^{j\omega}\right)\right| = \left|1 + \sin^2(M\omega/4)\right| \tag{12}$$

This compensation filter decreases the passband droop but increases side lobes in stopband. To reduce side lobes, a Cosine filter was used with system function as shown below:

$$H_{COS}(z) = (1 + z^{-L})/2 \tag{13}$$

$$\left|H_{COS}\left(e^{j\omega}\right)\right| = \cos(L\omega/2) \tag{14}$$

The complete transfer function of the compensated filter becomes

$$H_{2CCIC}(z) = G_C^K(z) * H_{SIN}(z) * H_{COS}(z) \tag{15}$$

3 Quantization Noise Analysis and Derivation of Noise Factor

Most of the Decimation Filter, designed for a very high Decimation Ratio, use CIC Decimator as the first stage, which decimates the input signal by a large factor of the total decimation ratio [18, 25]. In this section, the mathematical analysis of the Quantization Noise is done for the CIC Decimator as shown in Fig. 3.

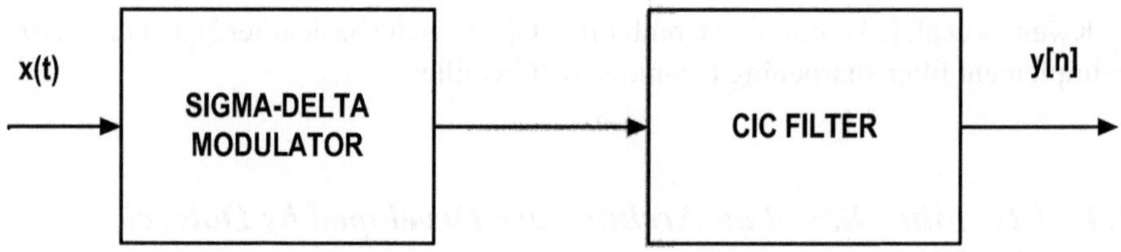

Fig. 3 Block diagram of sigma-delta modulator cascaded with CIC Filter

The Power Spectral Density of the Quantization Noise at the output of Lth-order Sigma-Delta Modulator [26, 27] is given by

$$|N_{TF}(F)|^2 * |V_{Qe}(F)|^2 \tag{16}$$

where

$$|N_{TF}(F)| = \left|2 * \sin\left(\frac{\pi * F}{F_s}\right)\right|^L \tag{17}$$

$$|V_{Qe}(F)| = \frac{\delta}{\sqrt{12F_s}} \tag{18}$$

Now, the RMS Quantization Noise in any frequency range $[F_1, F_2]$ is given by

$$V^2_{Qe,RMS}(F_1, F_2) = 2 * \int_{F_1}^{F_2} |N_{TF}(F)|^2 * |V_{Qe}(F)|^2 * dF \tag{19}$$

The output of Sigma-Delta Modulator (L^{th}-order) is passed through a CIC Decimation Filter to filter the out-of band signals and Quantization Noise. Let us define the transfer function of the CIC Decimator by

$$|H(F)| = \left|\frac{1}{N} * \frac{\sin\left(\frac{\pi * N * F}{F_s}\right)}{\sin\left(\frac{\pi * F}{F_s}\right)}\right|^K \tag{20}$$

where K is the filter order, N is the Decimation ratio of CIC Filter and F_s is the input sampling frequency.

The RMS Quantization Noise, at the output of the CIC Decimation Filter, for any frequency range $[F_1, F_2]$ is given by

$$V^2_{Qe,RMS}(F_1, F_2) = 2 * \int_{F_1}^{F_2} |N_{TF}(F)|^2 * |V_{Qe}(F)|^2 * |H(F)|^2 * dF \tag{21}$$

The terms that are used for our analysis of the Quantization Noise are defined as:

(i) Total RMS Quantization Noise,
(ii) In-band RMS Quantization Noise and
(iii) RMS Quantization Noise, aliased in the signal Bandwidth.

These terms are defined as:

Total RMS Quantization Noise,

$$V^2_{Qe,RMS} = 2 * \int_0^{F_S/2} |N_{TF}(F)|^2 * |V_{Qe}(F)|^2 * |H(F)|^2 * dF \quad (22)$$

In – band RMS Quantization Noise,

$$V^2_{QeIB,RMS} = 2 * \int_0^{F_m} |N_{TF}(F)|^2 * |V_{Qe}(F)|^2 * |H(F)|^2 * dF \quad (23)$$

RMS Quantization Noise that is aliased in the signal Bandwidth,

$$V^2_{QeFB,RMS} = \sum_{m=0}^{N-1}\left[\int_{\frac{mF_s}{N}-F_m}^{\frac{mF_s}{N}+F_m} |N_{TF}(F)|^2 * |V_{Qe}(F)|^2 * |H(F)|^2 * dF\right], \quad (24)$$

here FB in $V^2_{QeFB,RMS}$ denotes the Folding Bands.

By putting the values of $|N_{TF}(F)|$, $|V_{Qe}(F)|$and $|H(F)|$ from Eqs. 17, 18, and 20 in the above three Eqs. 22, 23 and 24, we get

$$V^2_{Qe,RMS} = \frac{\delta^2}{6 * F_s} * \frac{2^{2L}}{N^{2K}} * \int_0^{\frac{F_S}{2}} \frac{\left|\sin\left(\frac{\pi * N * F}{F_s}\right)\right|^{2K}}{\left|\sin\left(\frac{\pi * F}{F_s}\right)\right|^{2*(K-L)}} dF = C_0 * V_0 \quad (25)$$

$$V^2_{QeIB,RMS} = \frac{\delta^2}{6 * F_s} * \frac{2^{2L}}{N^{2K}} * \int_0^{F_m} \frac{\left|\sin\left(\frac{\pi * N * F}{F_s}\right)\right|^{2K}}{\left|\sin\left(\frac{\pi * F}{F_s}\right)\right|^{2*(K-L)}} dF = C_0 * V_1 \quad (26)$$

$$V^2_{QeFB,RMS} = \sum_{m=0}^{N-1}\left[\frac{\delta^2}{6 * F_s} * \frac{2^{2L}}{2 * N^{2K}} * \int_{\frac{mF_s}{N}-F_m}^{\frac{mF_s}{N}+F_m} \frac{\left|\sin\left(\frac{\pi * N * F}{F_s}\right)\right|^{2K}}{\left|\sin\left(\frac{\pi * F}{F_s}\right)\right|^{2*(K-L)}} dF\right] = C_0 * V_2 \quad (27)$$

where C0 is a constant and is equal to $\delta^2/6 * F_s$, and V_0, V_1 & V_2 are functions of N, L, and K.

For an Lth-order Sigma-Delta Modulator, the value of K is taken as (L + 1). Figure 4 shows the plot of V_0 versus $\log_2 N$ for L = 1, 2, 3 using MATLAB [28].

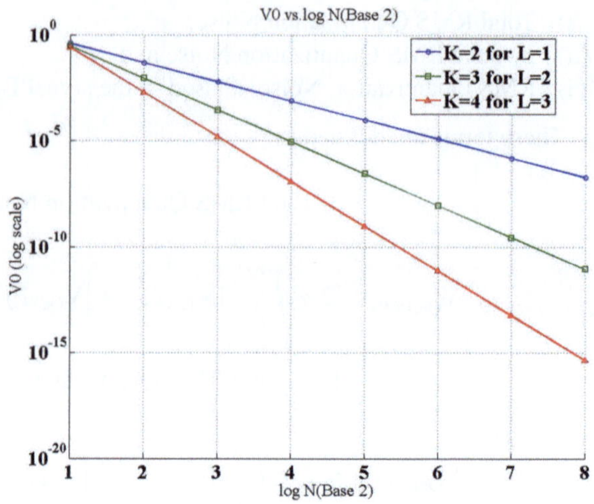

Fig. 4 Total quantization noise versus $\log_2 N$

This plot shows that the total Quantization Noise decreases with increase in value of N. For a particular value of N, the value of V_0 decreases as the order of the Sigma-Delta modulator increases.

Figure 5 shows the plot of V_1 vs $\log_2 N$ for $L = 1, 2, 3$. In-band quantization noise is almost constant and does not vary much w.r.t. N. Figure 6 shows the Plot of V_2 versus $\log_2 N$ for $L = 1, 2, 3$. This figure shows the plot of RMS Quantization Noise that alias in the signal bandwidth after the filtering operation by CIC Decimation Filter. The value of V_2 increases with increasing value of N for all any positive value of L. The order of magnitude of Fig. 5 is much greater than that of Fig. 6.

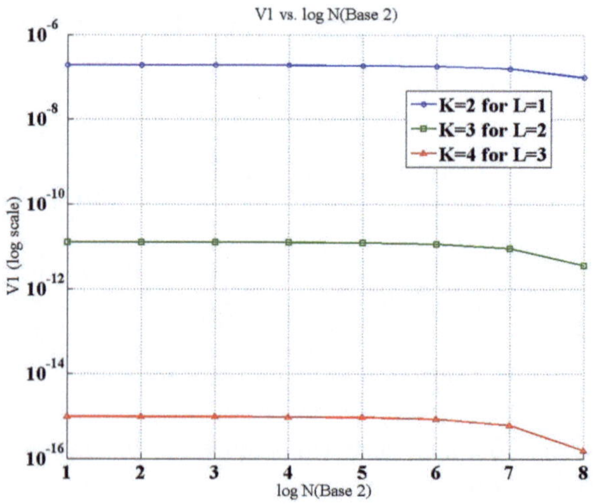

Fig. 5 In-band quantization noise versus $\log_2 N$

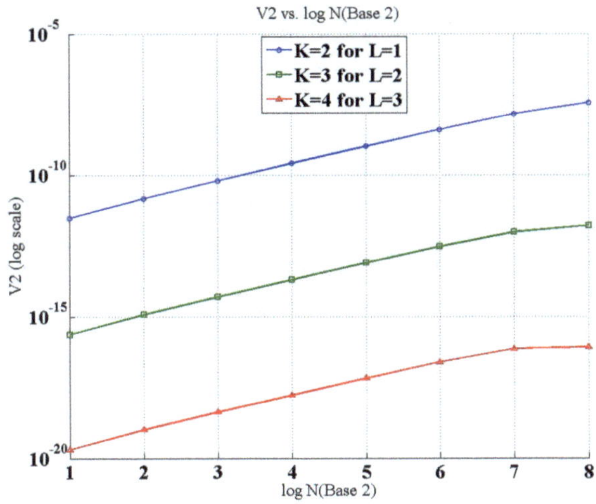

Fig. 6 RMS Quantization Noise that alias in the signal bandwidth after filtering operation

Figure 7 shows the plot of $(V_1 + V_2)$ versus $\log_2 N$ for $L = 1, 2, 3$. This figure shows the plot of variation of Total Quantization Noise present in the signal bandwidth. This plot shows that the value of $(V_1 + V_2)$ is approximately equal to V_1. Also, there is a variation of 4 orders of magnitude for each increment in L.

Here, we define Noise factor (NF) as the ratio of Quantization Noise in the Signal Bandwidth to the Total Quantization Noise at the output of the CIC Filter. Mathematically, it is given by

$$NF = \frac{C_0 * (V_1 + V_2)}{C_0 * V_0} = \frac{V_1 + V_2}{V_0} \tag{28}$$

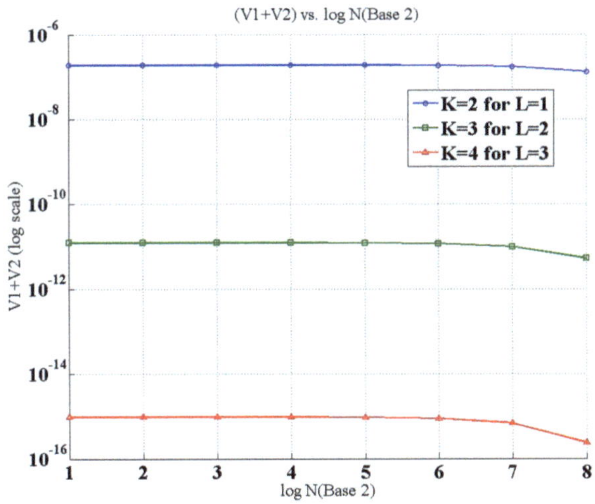

Fig. 7 Total Quantization Noise present in the signal bandwidth versus N

4 Noise Factor for Different CIC Filters

Figure 8 shows the plot of Noise Factor versus $\log_2 N$ of the basic CIC filter for different values of L = 1, 2, 3. With increase in value of N, Noise Factor also increases. This implies that larger values of Decimation Factor lead to more Noise Factor and thus to use CIC Decimation Filter with large values of N. Figure 9 shows the plot of Noise Factor versus $\log_2 N$, where the Noise Factor axis is made Linear.

Figure 10 shows the variation of Noise factor (Log scale) for different CIC filter architectures that were discussed in Sect. 2. This figure tells that Noise factor of Cascade of CIC, sine, and cosine filter is least and thus, it performs best in terms of noise factor. Figure 11 shows the same graph of Fig. 10 on linear scale.

Fig. 8 Noise Factor versus $\log_2 N$ (LOG PLOT)

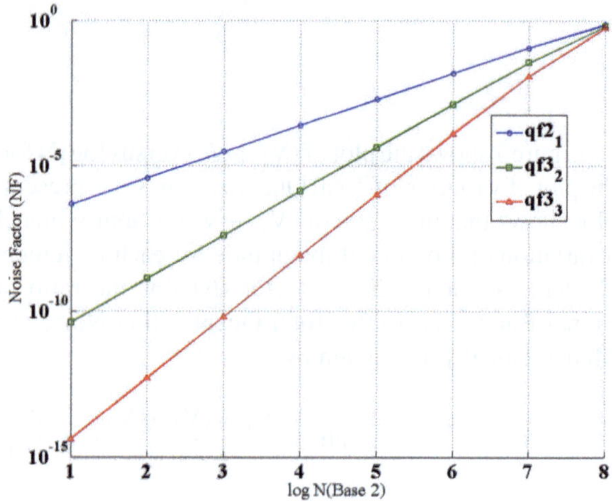

Fig. 9 Noise Factor versus $\log_2 N$ (LINEAR PLOT)

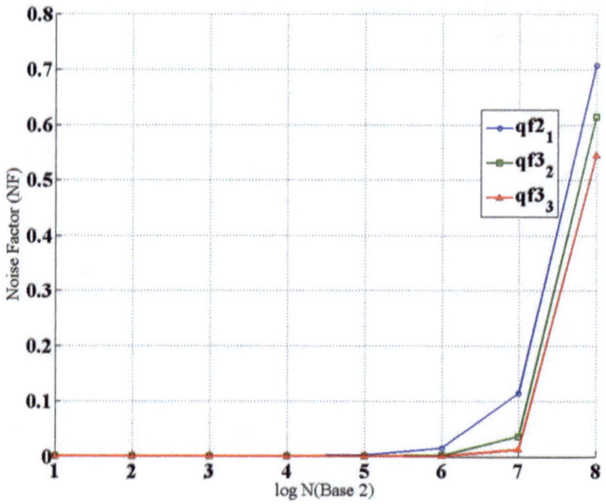

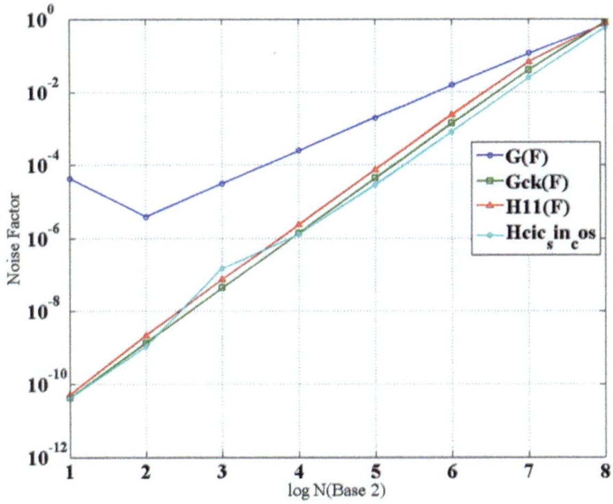

Fig. 10 Noise Factor versus log2N for Different CIC Filter Architectures (Log Plot)

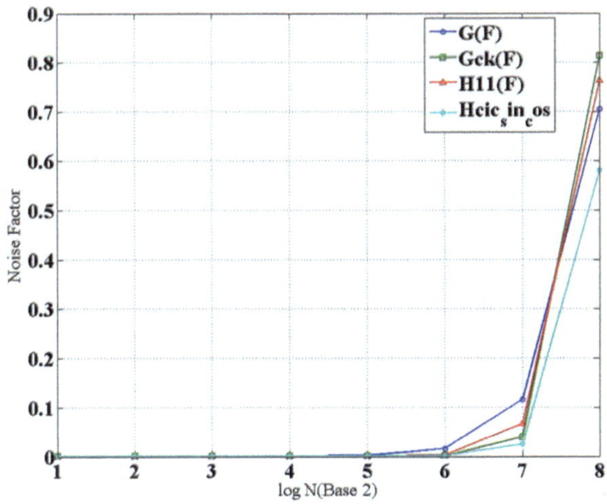

Fig. 11 Noise Factor versus $\log_2 N$ for Different CIC Filter Architectures (Linear Plot)

5 Conclusion

This paper covers different CIC filter architectures and their importance in Sigma-Delta based ADC. A new parameter called Noise factor is defined that indicates the fraction of noise present in the signal bandwidth as compared to the total quantization noise after decimation. Noise factor of CIC filter, for varying values of order sigma-delta modulator(L) and stages of CIC filter(K) is compared. It is found that Noise factor increases with increase in value of N and increase in value of L. The noise factor decreases, i.e., there is improvement in Noise factor. Also, it is observed that cascade of CIC, sine, and cosine filters performs best in terms of Noise factor for all values of Decimation ratio as compared to the other CIC filter architectures discussed in this paper.

References

1. Brandt BP, Wingard DE, Wooley BA (1991) Second-order sigma-delta modulation for digital-audio signal acquisition. IEEE J Solid-State Circuits 26(4):618–627. https://doi.org/10.1109/4.75064
2. Boser BE, Wooley BA (1988) The design of sigma-delta modulation analog-to-digital converters. IEEE J Solid-State Circuits 23(6):1298–1308. https://doi.org/10.1109/4.90025
3. Candy JC, Temes GC (1991) Oversampling methods for data conversion. In: IEEE Pacific Rim conference on communications, computers and signal processing conference proceedings, IEEE, pp 498–502. https://doi.org/10.1109/PACRIM.1991.160785
4. Gray R (1987) Oversampled sigma-delta modulation. IEEE Trans Commun 35(5):481–489. https://doi.org/10.1109/TCOM.1987.1096814
5. Kester W, others (2004) Analog-digital conversion. Analog Devices Norwood, MA
6. Hristov MH, Kuncheva S, Mougel T, Fujcik L, Donchev B, others (2005) Design of a decimation filter for novel sigma-delta modulator. ELECTRONICS'2005, 21–23 September, vol 5, pp 56–61
7. John B, Wagner F, Krautschneider WH (2005) Comparison of decimation filter architectures for a sigma-delta analog to digital converter. Institute of Nanoelectronics Hamburg University of Technology (TUHH)
8. Lei C et al. (2005) A decimation filter design and implementation for oversampled sigma delta a/d converters. In: Proceedings of 2005 IEEE international workshop on VLSI design and video technology, IEEE, pp 55–58. https://doi.org/10.1109/IWVDVT.2005.1504463
9. Candy J (1986) Decimation for sigma delta modulation. IEEE Trans Commun 34(1):72–76. https://doi.org/10.1109/TCOM.1986.1096432
10. Li H (2007) Digital decimation filter design and simulation for delta-sigma ADC with high performance. In: 2007 7th international conference on ASIC, IEEE, Oct. 2007, pp 922–925. https://doi.org/10.1109/ICASIC.2007.4415782
11. Zhaochun L, Xiaohong P, Wuchen W, Ligang H, Yong H (2010) Design of 16 bit digital filter used in delta-sigma A/D converter. In: 2010 2nd international conference on computer engineering and technology, IEEE, pp V4–484-V4–487. https://doi.org/10.1109/ICCET.2010.5485455
12. Sokolovic M, Jovanovic B, Damnjanovic M (2004) Decimation filter design. In: 2004 24th international conference on microelectronics (IEEE Cat. No.04TH8716), IEEE, pp 601–604. https://doi.org/10.1109/ICMEL.2004.1314899
13. Crochiere R, Rabiner L (1975) Optimum FIR digital filter implementations for decimation, interpolation, and narrow-band filtering. IEEE Trans Acoust 23(5):444–456. https://doi.org/10.1109/TASSP.1975.1162719
14. Park S (1992) Multi-stage decimation filter design technique for high-resolution sigma-delta A/D converters. IEEE Trans Instrum Meas 41(6):868–873. https://doi.org/10.1109/19.199424
15. Lian Y, Wei Y, Chandrasekaran R (2007) A 1 GHz decimation filter for Sigma-Delta ADC. In: 2007 50th midwest symposium on circuits and systems, IEEE, pp 401–404.https://doi.org/10.1109/MWSCAS.2007.4488614
16. Hogenauer E (1981) An economical class of digital filters for decimation and interpolation. IEEE Trans Acoust 29(2):155–162. https://doi.org/10.1109/TASSP.1981.1163535
17. Story MA (1997) Mutiplierless decimation and commercial postfiltering of a discrete-time signal. Massachusetts Inst Technol
18. Milic L (2009) Multirate filtering for digital signal processing: MATLAB applications: MATLAB applications. IGI Global

19. Yang H (2004) "Desing and implementation of a cascaded integrator comb (CIC) decimation filter. Carleton University
20. Kaiser J, Hamming R (1977) Sharpening the response of a symmetric nonrecursive filter by multiple use of the same filter. IEEE Trans Acoust 25(5):415–422. https://doi.org/10.1109/TASSP.1977.1162980
21. Kwentus AY, Jiang Z, Willson AN (1997) Application of filter sharpening to cascaded integrator-comb decimation filters. IEEE Trans Signal Process 45(2):457–467, https://doi.org/10.1109/78.554309
22. Dolecek GJ, Salgado GM (2012) Low power non-recursive comb-based decimation filter design. In: 2012 5th international symposium on communications, control and signal processing, IEEE, pp 1–4. https://doi.org/10.1109/ISCCSP.2012.6217826
23. Dolecek GJ, Mitra SK (2007) A new two-stage CIC-based decimation filter. In: 2007 5th International symposium on image and signal processing and analysis, IEEE, pp 218–223. https://doi.org/10.1109/ISPA.2007.4383693
24. Jovanovic-Dolecek G, Mitra SK (2005) A new two-stage sharpened comb decimator. IEEE Trans Circuits Syst I Regul Pap 52(7):1414–1420. https://doi.org/10.1109/TCSI.2005.851390
25. Crochiere RE, Rabiner LR (1983) Multirate digital signal processing, vol 18. Prentice-hall Englewood Cliffs, NJ
26. Baker RJ (2008) CMOS: mixed-signal circuit design. Wiley
27. Johns DA, Martin K (2008) Analog integrated circuit design. Wiley
28. Losada RA (2008) Digital filters with MATLAB. The Mathworks Inc, vol 4

The Scientific Analysis on Effective Yoga Posture Recognition Techniques

E. G. Rajgure and Raghavendra Patidar

1 Introduction

From ancient times, yoga has been practiced in the Hindu religion. Its curative effects have been well-documented in the West, and attaining it involves having total mastery over one's own body, emotions, and thoughts. Breathing exercises, physical postures called asanas, and mental practices like meditation and relaxation are the foundation of yoga [1, 2]. Literature indicates that these treatments are useful for improving respiratory muscle strength, enhancing lung capacity, alleviating shortness of breath, and facilitating breathing. The basic concepts of yoga originated in ancient Indian philosophy. Yoga effectively combines and proves its importance by combining different possibilities of physical exercises and asanas, sushupti, pranayama, and meditation practices which develop awareness and realize the higher levels of consciousness (samadhi) in an extensive variety of modern yoga methods [3].

People began utilizing yoga as a therapeutic intervention at the beginning of the twentieth century, taking advantage of the numerous psychological and physical benefits linked to its diverse components. The one hundred billion cells that make-up our bodies, and notably the Brain, rely on the oxygen supplied by our respiratory system. Asthma, bronchitis, the common cold, and respiratory allergies are just few of the diseases that can manifest themselves in the respiratory system. Symptoms of an asthma attack include abrupt shortness of breath, wheezing, and coughing [4–8]. The psychological condition known as bronchial asthma is characterized by recurrent episodes of airway blockage interspersed with periods of apparent health [9].

This research offers a way to recognize the yoga poses by utilizing various samples collected from different data acquisition techniques with the effect of yoga postures on body health parameters. Also, the novel model is presented which senses the pressure joints using force sensor while performing yoga and classifies the types of

E. G. Rajgure (✉) · R. Patidar
School of Engineering, ECE, University of Technology, Jaipur, India
e-mail: eshantraj1989@gmail.com

K. Kumar Singh et al. (eds.), *Machine Vision and Augmented Intelligence*, Lecture Notes in Electrical Engineering 1211, https://doi.org/10.1007/978-981-97-4359-9_13

yoga using machine learning classifier. The present paper is organized as, Section II covers the topic of yoga posture recognition utilizing different data inputs. Part III discusses how yoga practices affect various aspects of the human body. Section V discusses the results of Section IV's explanation of the suggested methodology. The general conclusion of the subject is finally provided in Section VI.

2 Related Work on Posture Recognition

Different researchers have implemented several techniques to recognize the posture which is mainly based on computer vision, kinetic sensor, and biomedical signal orientation which are discussed in this section.

2.1 Computer Vision Based Posture Recognition

The sun salutation yoga poses were categorized [10] using four machine learning models. The yoga page was broken because it incorrectly used the angle calculated by the KNN model used to estimate poses. In Yoga-82, which provided sequential labels for yoga positions with respect to individuals' human body related poses, state-of-the-art convolutional neural network (CNN) architectures were presented [11] for their classification accuracy. The hip and joint angles are two of the factors for classification that were proposed [5] in their posture recognition system. It was proposed by Maddala et al. [12] that we put our JADMs through their paces using a single-stream deep CNN model trained on yoga video sequences. The yoga poses were categorized using BP-ANN classifier, and then classified further within each category using fuzzy C-means (FCM), both of which were proposed by Wu et al. [13].

2.2 Kinetic Sensor Based Posture Recognition

A Yoga posture recognition system was proposed by Hua-Tsung Chen et al. which uses a Kinect sensor to capture the user's body map and extract the body features to identify the yoga posture being performed by the practitioner and then obtain online yoga instruction materials to draw the practitioner's attention to the position. Embedded based Assistive System for Yoga was designed and implemented by Shinde et al. [14] to analyze yoga postures. An algorithm based on a skeleton method to analyze images was created for studying yoga poses like Parsva Tadasana. Using a Kinect sensor and LabVIEW, we've implemented an Embedded based Assistive System for Yoga. In order to better assist the user in their yoga practice, Shaw and Routray [15] devised a system that can track the user's motion of various body parts and the precision with which they do various yoga positions. In order to gauge the precision with which a user performs various yoga postures, the Microsoft Kinect sensor is employed to identify several joint points simultaneously. Human subjects were asked to assume a variety of positions for the experiments. Dongjin Lee et al. demonstrated a Kinect-based system for analyzing children's posture as they do yoga postures with the Nao robot.

2.3 *Biomedical Signal-Based Posture Recognition*

Electromyography data were analyzed by Anantamek and Hnoohom [6] to determine how four thigh and calf muscles performed while walking. Three machine learning algorithms were employed to recognize the appropriateness of yoga poses by analyzing electromyographic (EMG) data, which tracked the activity of four muscles in the lower body. A total of 87.43% accuracy was achieved by the yoga posture identification model, with the findings showing that the Random Forest Decision Tree algorithm is the most effective at recognizing yoga poses.

The aim of the study by Hernando et al. [7] is to study the impact of yoga on the nervous system by analyzing the PRV obtained from the NIVA signal. Twenty healthy participants had their temporal, spectral, and nonlinear characteristics examined both before and after they participated in a yoga session.

3 Effect of Yoga Practices on Body Health Parameters

The many studies of yoga's health benefits that were considered here all pointed in the same direction. Therefore, more research is needed to determine what kinds of patients would respond positively to the therapies, as well as what parts of the yoga interventions (e.g., physical exercise and subsequent lifestyle modification) or yoga traditions proved most beneficial. Consistent yoga practice has been suggested to boost health-related fitness and well-being by Ghorpade-Aher et al. [16]. The purpose of the study by Dev et al. [4] was to use functional near infrared spectroscopy to compare the haemoglobin levels of yogis and non-yogis doing an attention task. Each group had 10 individuals, all of whom took a six-minute test measuring visual continuous performance before taking a break. Study participants in the yoga group had significantly higher concentrations of oxyhaemoglobin ($p = 0.04$) and lower concentrations of deoxyhaemoglobin ($p = 0.002$) compared to those in the non-yoga group. In this study, yoga was found to increase oxygen flow to the brain's prefrontal regions as participants performed an attention test. A methodology was provided by Islam et al. [17] to forecast the Pulse following Surya Namaskar for persons of varying Prakruti and Prahar. Lee et al. [18] put out the Time, disposition, make-up, chaos, and environments are the five factors that inform the system's operation, all of which were determined by a panel of ayurveda specialists. Inputting these values into the decision tree causes it to produce rules for making recommendations. For the purpose of predicting yoga and raga names, the created rules are passed to an artificial neural network. SVM and Kernel- SVM (k-SVM) have been compared in order to categorize the meditative state of the brain related with Kriya Yoga, as stated by Chen et al. [19]. Ten non-meditators (the "control group") and 23 meditators (the "test group") had their EEG signals recorded. The acquired findings demonstrate that the kernel-based SVM is superior to the traditional SVM in categorizing the EEGs of meditators and non-meditators alike. The Electroencephalography (EEG) recorded during brief sessions of Kriya Yoga meditation is characterized in the current work by Thanuja and Suganthi [20] by using a topographical method for the analysis of brain wave sub-bands.

The examination of physiological signals, such as an ECG and a photoplethysmogram, during yoga practice by pregnant women is described in detail by An [21]. The EEG signals that cause or contribute to stress or depression were studied and discussed by Ren [22]. Mood swings can be managed by identifying the underlying causes, which vary from person to person, and then modifying the corresponding behaviors. In order to combat this issue, Büssing et al. [23] created a section that introduces an integrated solution based on a smartphone app that employs Yoga and Music Therapy.

4 Proposed Methodology

The proposed yoga position identification and quantification methodology is as shown in Fig. 1, which utilized real-time yoga activity by collecting data values of wearable sensor from physical pressure nodes of FSR sensor and classifying the data pattern using a supervised machine learning approach. This is an innovative approach to improving the health benefits of conventional yoga postures.

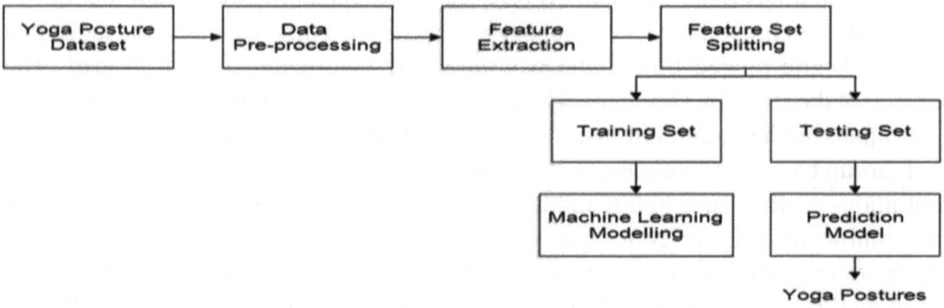

Fig. 1 Proposed structure for identification and quantification of yoga positions

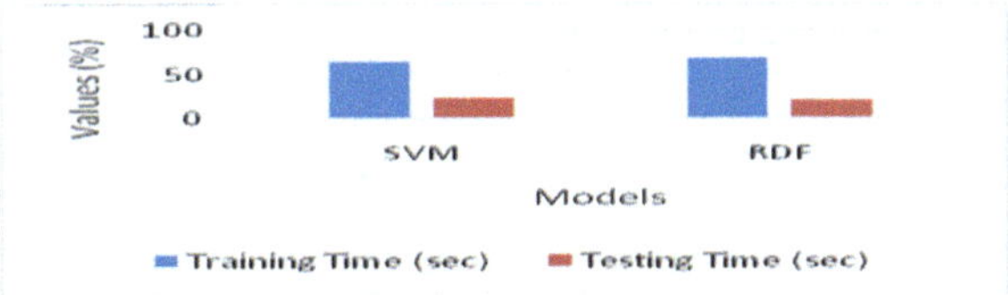

Fig. 2 Computation time performance

4.1 Time Series Dataset Based on Yoga Positions

Wearable sensor device is designed with Node MCU controller and force sensor interface to sense the pressure of joints during yoga practice and add it to the yoga posture dataset. We enlisted as many participants as possible to collect information on the most common yoga positions. Given the difficulty in locating volunteers who can successfully execute all or the vast majority of yoga postures, we recruited 20 volunteers which is gender wise divided equally for the dataset collecting. The median age of the participants was 31.5. All of the participants wore our custom-made wearable device on their shirts and slacks. The volunteers had all been doing yoga regularly for some time before the trial, with only a handful having never done so before. Shavasana, Balasana, Bhuijagasana, Tadasana, Uttanasana, Chakravakasana, and Setu Bandha Sarvangasana are among the yoga postures that have been considered for official acknowledgment. There were 7 participants, thus we took 20 samples for each stance, for a total of 980 samples. When a session is recorded, a.csv file is automatically exported.

4.2 Data Preprocessing

Information is processed when raw data is gathered and transformed into meaningful information. Collecting, sorting, processing, analyzing, storing, and finally presenting the raw data is the process. It's often done in a series of steps. Data preparation is the process of organizing and purging general data to get rid of copying, outdated information, and other mistakes. Raw data must first be checked for mistakes, duplication, incorrect computations, or missing data before being converted into an appropriate format and subjected to additional analysis and processing. This guarantees that the processor only receives the best information possible.

4.3 Feature Extraction

In feature extraction, time domain and frequency domain features are extracted. In time domain features, MAV, ZCR, WL, SSC, standard deviation (σ), and RMS are evaluated. In frequency domain features, Skewness (γ), kurtosis (K), and mean frequency are evaluated.

$$MAV = \frac{1}{n}\sum_{i=1}^{n}|x_i|$$

$$WL = \sum_{k=1}^{n-1}|x_{K+1} - x_k|$$

$$WL = \sum_{k=1}^{n-1}|x_{K+1} - x_k|$$

$$zcr = \frac{1}{T-1}\sum_{t=1}^{T-1} 1_{R<0}(s_t s_t - 1)$$

$$RMS = \sqrt{\frac{1}{n}\sum_{i=0}^{n} x_i^2}$$

$$\sigma = \sqrt{\frac{1}{n-1}\sum_{i=0}^{n}(x_i - \mu)^2}$$

$$\gamma = \frac{E\{x - \mu\}^3}{\sigma^3}$$

$$K = \frac{E\{x - \mu\}^4}{\sigma^4}$$

4.4 Feature Splitting

The train-test split can be used to estimate the performance of machine learning algorithms that are used for predictions. We can quickly and simply apply this method to assess the effectiveness of our own machine learning model. The training set receives 70% of the default data distribution, whereas the test set receives 30%. To assess the efficacy of our machine learning model, we must divide a dataset into train and test sets. Since the train set's statistics are accessible, they can be used to fit the model. The test data set, which is the second collection, is only used to make predictions.

4.5 Machine Learning Classification Modeling

In the last step, two supervised machine learning classifiers—Support Vector Machine (SVM) and Random Decision Forest (RDF)—are provided the feature data and labeled data for training and validation. For pattern classification, two machine learning models with various hyper-parameters are utilized. The remaining test feature data are evaluated on the trained model following the machine learning model's successful validation, ensuring that the system performance evaluation is accurate. Support Vector Machines (SVMs) are supervised learning models that analyze data for categorization and come with corresponding learning methods. SVM's ability to function well in high-dimensional domains and its relative memory efficiency are two of its key benefits. Random Decision Forest (RDF) aims to improve a dataset's prediction accuracy by averaging the outcomes of many decision trees trained on different subsets of the information. The primary benefit of RDF is that it uses several trees to minimize overfitting, resulting in more reliable and exact outputs.

5 Experimental Results and Discussion

This research presents a technique that utilizes many machine learning models to identify proper yoga poses. In this experiment, an NVIDIA GeForce GTX-1080 graphics processing unit and an Intel i5 processor were utilized. The accuracy of the training and testing datasets varies greatly until the different hyper-parameters are adjusted. To confirm the model's effectiveness, the suggested approach—which divides the dataset 70:30 between training and test data—was also put into practice.

Accuracy, sensitivity, specificity, and f-score are estimated using standard formulas consisting of TP—true positive, FP—false positive, TN—true negative, FN—false negative which are employed to evaluate the suggested model's performance in the context of the confusion matrix.

The computation time is evaluated for training and testing phase of two classifier models which is shown in Table 2. The training time is higher in case of RDF due to higher hyper-parameters to tune the algorithms as compared to SVM algorithm as depicted in Fig. 2 (Table 1).

Various assessment parameters, as stated in Table 2, are used to evaluate and analyze the proposed model using the SVM and RDF classifier models. As illustrated in Fig. 3, the accuracy performance of the suggested model utilizing RDF outperforms the SVM.

Table 1 Computation Time as per classifier models

Classifiers	Training Interval (sec)	Testing Interval (sec)
SVM	64.2	22.8
RDF	68.4	19.7

Table 2 Classification performance evaluation using classifier models

Classifiers	Accuracy (%)	Sensitivity (%)	Specificity (%)	F-score (%)
SVM	86.44	90.05	86.44	87.14
RDF	94.91	95.61	94.91	94.90

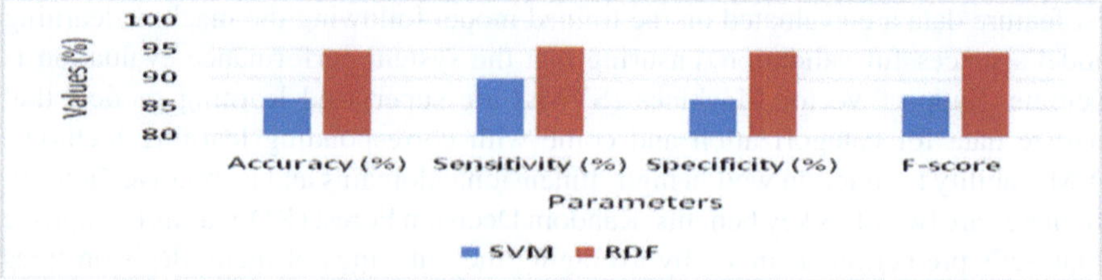

Fig. 3 Classification performance evaluation

The RDF classifier also improved the performance of all other performance metrics.

6 Conclusion

Many individuals all around the world now do yoga regularly. This fact underscores the necessity for yoga posture research. It has been concluded that the utilization of such self-learning-based position detection system can help practitioners to do yoga with more precision by identifying the correct postures. As it's a real-time based signal analysis, difficult to get standard data which is readily available. Although we get quantified results based on available systems but additional research is needed to reach up to firm conclusions. This research will create well awareness among practitioners to know the several benefits of doing yoga correctly. General trials give some predicted results but as doing yoga is an individual concern as per practitioner's personality, age, weight, place of practice, time of event, and many others, it is not easy to define standards for implementations. For many diseases and disorders, there is also a wide range of study demographics, yoga therapies, practice length and frequency, control groups, and outcome measurements. In many cases, meta-analyzes were inappropriate because of the condition's heterogeneity and the low quality of the primary trials. This study offers the first model construction and evaluation of the classification of yoga postures. It is recommended that more research be done in this area because the underlying psychophysiological explanation makes sense.

References

1. Upadhyay A, Basha NK, Ananthakrishnan B (2023) Deep learning- based yoga posture recognition using the Y_PN-MSSD model for yoga practitioners. Healthcare 11(4):609. MDPI
2. Ashraf FB, Islam MU, Kabir MR, Uddin J (2023) Yonet: a neural network for yoga pose classification. SN Comput Sci 4(2):198
3. Jain S, Rustagi A, Saurav S, Saini R, Singh S (2021) Three-dimensional CNN-inspired deep learning architecture for Yoga pose recognition in the real-world environment. Neural Comput Appl 33:6427–6441
4. Dev P, Lancet RS, Saurav S, Seshadri NG, Singh BK, Jha M (2019) Effect of yoga on hemodynamic changes at prefrontal cortex during sustained attention task. In: 2019 5th international conference on advanced computing & communication systems (ICACCS), pp 728–731. IEEE
5. Chezhiyan P, P D (2019) Joint-angle-based yoga posture recognition for prevention of falls among older people. Data Technol Appl 53(4):528–545
6. Anantamek P, Hnoohom N (2019) Recognition of yoga poses using EMG signals from lower limb muscles, 132–136. https://doi.org/10.1109/ECTI-NCON.2019.8692300
7. Hernando D, Nardelli M, Hocking K, Lázaro J, Alvis B, Gil E, Scilingo EP, Brophy DR, Valenza G, Laguna P, Brophy C (2019) Effect of yoga on pulse rate variability measured from a venous pressure waveform. In: 2019 41st annual international conference (EMBC), pp 372–375. IEEE
8. Budak FK, Yilmaz E (2019) The effect of yoga on clinical insight and medication adherence in patients with schizophrenia-A randomized controlled trial. Europ J Integr Med 30:100949
9. Chinnaiah MC, Nandan TK, Haritha P, Dubey S, Pasha IA (2018) A new deliberation of embedded based assistive system for Yoga. In: 2018 8th international symposium on embedded computing and system design (ISED) IEEE
10. Palanimeera J, Ponmozhi K (2021) Classification of yoga pose using machine learning techniques. Mater Today Proc 37:2930–2933
11. Verma M, Kumawat S, Nakashima Y, Raman S (2020) Yoga-82: a new dataset for fine-grained classification of human poses. In: Proceedings of the IEEE/CVF conference on computer vision and pattern recognition workshops, pp 1038–1039
12. Maddala TKK, Kishore PVV, Eepuri KK, Dande AK (2019) Yoganet: 3-d yoga asana recognition using joint angular displacement maps with convnets. IEEE Trans Multimedia 21(10):2492–2503
13. Wu Z, Zhang J, Chen K, Fu C (2019) Yoga posture recognition and quantitative evaluation with wearable sensors based on two-stage classifier and prior Bayesian network. Sensors 19(23):5129
14. Shinde DD, Srivastava M, Prasad R (2018) An initiative to enhance productivity in higher education (Technical) using yoga which interconnect human mind and body. In: 2018 global wireless summit (GWS), pp 190–193. IEEE
15. Shaw,L, Routray A (2017) Topographical sub-bands analysis of eeg during short kriya yoga meditation. In: 2017 14th IEEE INDICON, pp 1–5. IEEE
16. Ghorpade-Aher J, Patil A, Deshpande Y, Gaopande S, Phatak E (2017) A proposed framework for prediction of pulse, based on the effect of surya namaskar on different prakruti at different prahars of the day. In: 2017 international conference on big data analytics and computational intelligence (ICBDAC), pp 11–16. IEEE
17. Islam MU, Mahmud H, Ashraf FB, Hossain I, Hasan MK (2017) Yoga posture recognition by detecting human joint points in real time using microsoft kinect. In: 2017 IEEE Region 10 humanitarian technology conference, pp 668–673. IEEE
18. Lee D, Yun WH, Park C, Yoon H, Kim J (2015) Analysis of children's posture for the bodily kinesthetic test. In: 2015 12th international conference on ubiquitous robots and ambient intelligence (URAI), pp 408–410. IEEE
19. Chen HT, He YZ, Hsu CC, Chou CL, Lee SY, Lin BSP (2014) Yoga posture recognition for self-training. In: MultiMedia modeling: 20th anniversary international conference, MMM 2014, Dublin, Ireland, January 6–10, 2014, Proceedings, Part I 20, pp 496–505. Springer International Publishing

20. Thanuja ES, Suganthi L (2017) Effect of integrated yoga on cardiovascular parameters during pregnancy. In: 2017 international conference ICICCS .IEEE
21. An X (2016) Retracted: teaching level evaluation approach based on AHP for yoga training in colleges. In: 2016 international conference on smart city and systems engineering (ICSCSE), pp 406–410. IEEE
22. Ren N (2016) Plan of the arrangement of yoga movement in colleges and universities based on AHP. In: 2016 Eighth international conference on measuring technology and mechatronics automation (ICMTMA), pp 475–478. IEEE
23. Büssing A, Michalsen A, Khalsa SBS, Telles S, Sherman KJ (2012) Effects of yoga on mental and physical health: a short summary of reviews. evidence-based complementary and alternative medicine

Impact of Gamma Rays on Emerging Devices for Photonic Applications

Swati Verma, S. Harikiran, Pushpa Raikwal, and Meena Panchore

1 Introduction

Over the past few years, Junctionless field effect transistor (JLFET) has gathered attention as an alternative to conventional MOSFETs. This can be largely attributed to their simplified manufacturing process resulting from the lack of junctions at channel-drain and channel-source interface, thus eliminating the need for involuted thermal requirements [1]. However, JLFET in volume depletion at highly doped channel results in increased leakage current of inactive state. Hence, JLFET needs less than 5 nm of ultra-thin silicon over insulator (SOI) film, and work function surpassing 5.5 eV to attain volume depletion for highly doped n-channel device in OFF-state [2].

The immediate expansion of state of art technologies in electronic devices poses a challenge to keep pace with emerging electronic devices. These challenges extend to the systems when deployed in the harsh environments including rouged conditions like exposure to photon radiation. Radiation is defined as the state when radioactive element is structurally unstable and reverts to a more stable state when emits particle or energy. Photon radiation comprises of no mass but still it affects the device in system [3]. Consequently, these electronic devices may experience the effects of these phenomena and can lead to malfunction and failure of the entire system.

In this paper, the effect of gamma ray photon irradiation on regular SOI JLFET and high-K oxide layer JLFET (HL JLFET) has been carried out. Firstly, in order to suppress the constraint of SOI JLFET, high-K oxide layer with highly doped

S. Verma (✉) · S. Harikiran · P. Raikwal
Department of Electronics and Communication Engineering, Design and Manufacturing, PDPM, Indian Institute of Information Technology, Jabalpur, M.P 482005, India
e-mail: 21pece07@iiitdmj.ac.in

M. Panchore
Department of Electronics and Communication Engineering, National Institute of Technology, Patna, Bihar 800005, India

K. Kumar Singh et al. (eds.), *Machine Vision and Augmented Intelligence*, Lecture Notes in Electrical Engineering 1211, https://doi.org/10.1007/978-981-97-4359-9_14

ground plane has been incorporated instead of silicon dioxide SiO_2 layer. The use of high-K oxide layer enhances the depletion of device from bottom resulting in reduction of effective thickness of the device's active layer [4]. However, in this manuscript, the main work is to focus on how both the devices behave when exposed to gamma ray's photon irradiation. In earlier publication [5] as mentioned, JLFET focuses on attaining volume depletion even at $V_{GS} = 0$ V without using large gate bias voltage and unrealizable work function. Two-dimensional simulation is done for both the devices to obtain a reduction in leakage current at different channel lengths and thicknesses of the device. Further, the behaviour of devices under gamma ray photon irradiation has been investigated using different dose rates. The paper has been divided into two sections. Section I consists of regular JLFET and HL JLFET performance comparisons on the basis of transfer characteristics and leakage current [6]. Section II consists of photonic irradiation of JLFET for different dose rates showing the radiation and electric field contour plot along with this threshold plot is also being observed for the same.

2 Device Structures and Simulation Parameters

The schematic representation of regular SOI JLFET and HL JLFET are shown in Fig. 1a, b respectively. The device parameters of both the structures are same whereas the difference lies in the latter structure having high-K dielectric oxide layer as compared to the regular SOI JLFET. Earlier majority of publications and [7] in particular, have presented detailed fabrication techniques and steps of SiO_2 based SOI JLFET. Further, there are some reported works that have shown the potential trade-off for using high-K dielectric oxide layer.

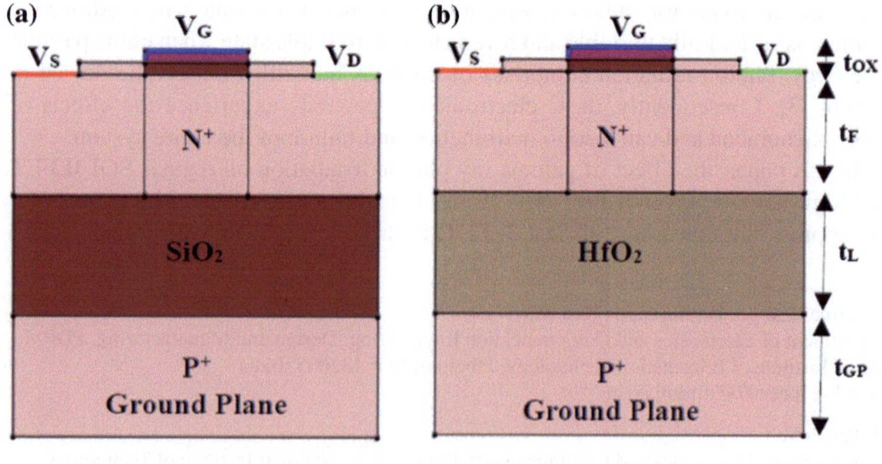

Fig. 1 Schematic representation [1] of a Regular SOI JLFET b HL JLFET

Table 1 Simulation parameter used for the device modeling

Parameter	JLFET	HL JLFET
Silicon film doping (N_D)	1×10^{19} cm^{-3}	1×10^{19} cm^{-3}
SOI film thickness (t_F)	10 nm	10 nm
Layer thickness (t_L)	10 nm	10 nm
Gate oxide thickness (t_{OX})	1 nm	1 nm
Gate length (L_G)	20 nm	20 nm
Gate work function	5.1 eV	5.1 eV
Ground plane doping (N_A)	1×10^{20} cm^{-3}	1×10^{20} cm^{-3}
Ground plane thickness (t_{GP})	20–50 nm	20–50 nm

The simulation parameters used for the device modeling are mentioned in Table 1. It may be highlighted that electrostatic effect and study of device for variation in different parameters are being examined.

3 I–V Characteristics of JLFET and HL JLFET Structures

Two-dimensional (2D) simulation is performed here using the Sentaurus Synopsys TCAD Software. The simulation setup utilized several models which included the Lombardi mobility model and the Philips unified mobility model leveraged for the doping-dependent mobility and transverse-field dependent mobility [8]. Along with this, the simulation setup also used the Shockley–Read–Hall (SRH) model, the Auger recombination model, and the Fermi–Dirac statistics. Tunneling models are not included in the simulation.

Transfer characteristics of regular SOI based JLFET and HL JLFET with layer thickness of 10 nm, 15 nm, and 20 nm above ground plane have been shown in Fig. 2. It can be observed that ON-state current and subthreshold swing is degraded with an increase in the thickness of high-K oxide layer [9]. However, this work mainly focuses on studying the electrostatic effect of high-K oxide layer on the overall characteristic of the device.

The comparison of off-state leakage current of the regular SOI JLFET and HL JLFET is also considered in this section. The off-state leakage current of the regular SOI JLFET is very high as compared to HL JLFET as there is no volume depletion attained [10]. Further, in HL JLFET, there is a huge variation of leakage current due to a change in high-K oxide layer thickness at $V_{GS} = 0$ V. However, there is a difference of four orders of magnitude in 10 nm device structure for regular SOI based JLFET and HL JLFET. Apart from this, it can also be observed that the current ratio (I_{ON}/I_{OFF}) is also improved for device structure with increasing layer thickness of HL JLFET.

The off-state current reduces with an increase in ground plane doping [11] that results in an increase in the effective work function of ground plane along with the

Fig. 2 Transfer characteristic of the regular SOI JLFET and HL JLFET with different layer thickness (t_L)

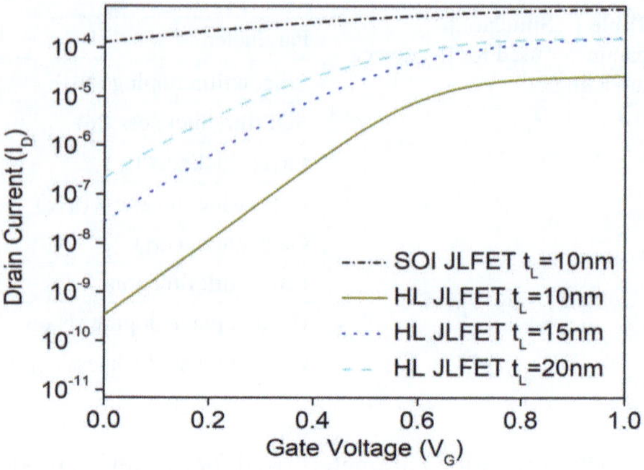

depletion layer of HL JLFET that leads to a decrease in OFF-state leakage current. Therefore, the transfer characteristic of HL JLFET for heavily doped ground plane results in better performance in terms of OFF-state leakage current of the device as shown in Fig. 3a. The HL JLFET outperforms regular SOI JLFET with gate electrodes featuring a substantial work function. This offers a straightforward and efficient approach to achieve effective volume depletion. The HL JLFET exhibits a lower OFF-state leakage current compared to regular SOI JLFET as can be seen in Fig. 3b.

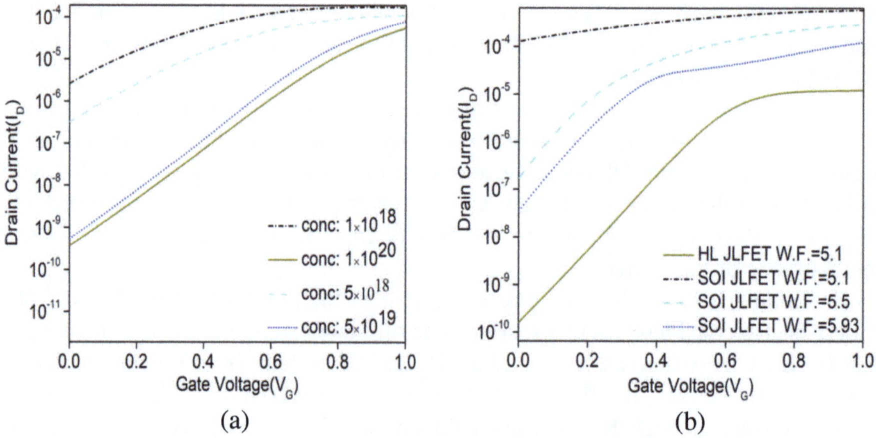

Fig. 3 Transfer characteristic of **a** HL JLFET with different ground plane doping concentrations and **b** the regular SOI JLFET and HL JLFET with different gate work functions (W.F.)

4 Photonic Irradiation on HL-JLFET and Its Impact

Nowadays, there are a number of steps involved to test the feasibility of the device in harsh environmental conditions including radiation pollution. Radiation is transmitted in three different energy forms in the harsh environment: (a) electromagnetic waves (b) rays and (c) particles. In the presence of radiation, empty space has electrically charged particle that consists of electromagnetic waves and this leads to energy in the form of waves or photons. Further, Radiation can be categorized in two types: (a) Photon radiation and (b) Particle radiation. In radiation, there are two factors that play a major role in mass and energy [12]. Photon radiation does not have mass but comprises of gamma rays and x-rays and also can lead to failure of device if ionization range is large enough. On the contrary, particle radiation does have mass and energy and comprises of alpha rays, protons, neutrons, and ions.

Electronic devices are affected by radiation pollution in two distinct ways: (a) cumulative effects and (b) Single Event Effects (SEE). The foremost one, i.e., cumulative effect involves gradual degradation of electronic device eventually after some time when exposed to radiation whereas the latter one occurs instantaneously as the radiation particle comes in contact with the device. If the radiation is very intense, it results in the immediate degradation of device. Understanding these effects is essential for ensuring the performance of JLFET in radiation-prone environments [13]. This study will explore the impact of photon radiation on the JLFET through the utilization of gamma ray irradiation mechanism.

Gamma ray are photon radiation within the range of electromagnetic energy spectrum. These photons bear the highest energy level and are capable of emission in less than a second. Within device simulation, gamma rays serve as the radiation source. All radiation parameters like dose rate, dose time, etc., are configured in the physics section [14, 15].

Transfer characteristics of regular SOI based JLFET and HL JLFET for different dose rates have been shown in Fig. 4. In regular SOI based JLFET, dose rate has a direct effect on both on-state and off-state currents due to dose time radiation penetration on the device. While, in HL JLFET as the dose rate of radiation is increased in the device off-state leakage current is increased while on-state current is not affected much.

When the device is being exposed to radiation, there is a formation of electric field density due to the generation of electron–hole pair in the device as the same can be observed in the electric field contour plot of devices at different dose rates in Figs. 5 and 6.

The effect of gamma ray's photon radiation on simulation of device at different dose rates can be observed in Fig. 5. The changes observed in radiation-prone area of the device affect the characteristics and mainly depend on two factors, i.e., dose rate and dose time. The estimated dose time used in simulation is $1 \times e^{-3}$ to $100 \times e^{-3}$ on the other hand it can be observed in HL JLFET that as dose rate increases drain current also increases along with there are changes observed in threshold values also.

Fig. 4 Transfer characteristic of HL JLFET with respect to different dose rate

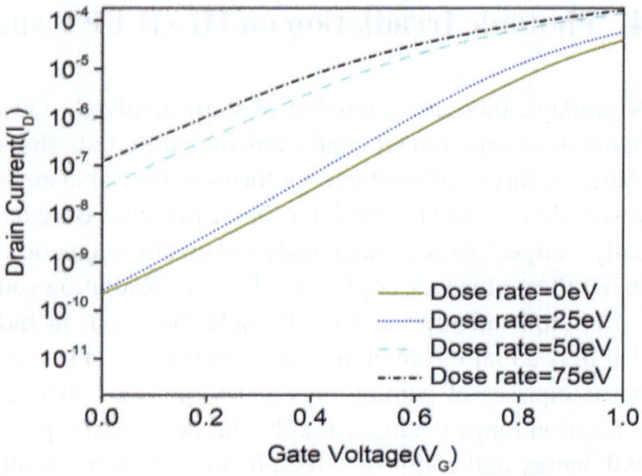

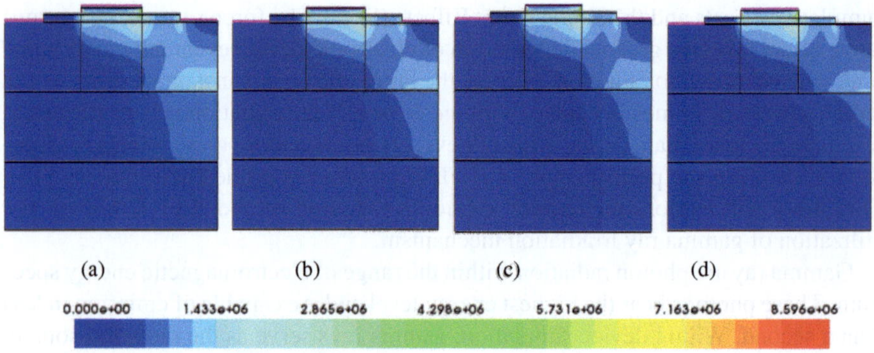

Fig. 5 Electric field contour plot on radiated device of the HL JLFET with dose rate of **a** 0 MeV **b** 25 MeV **c** 50 MeV **d** 75 MeV

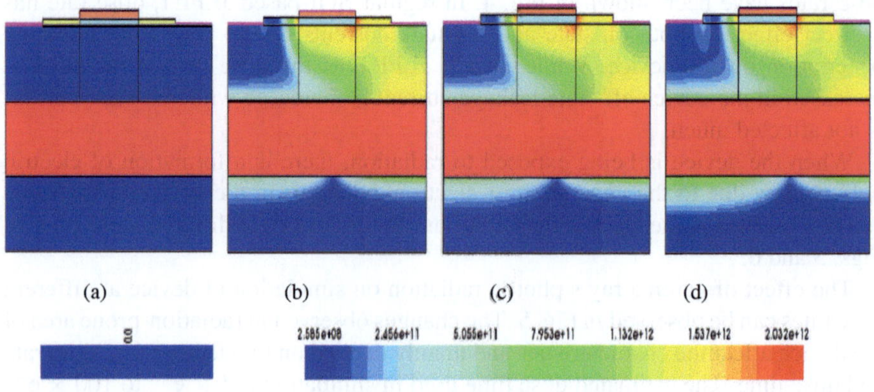

Fig. 6 Radiation contour plot of the HL JLFET with dose rate of **a** 0 MeV **b** 25 MeV **c** 50 MeV **d** 75 MeV

Fig. 7 Variation of threshold voltage for different dose rate for HL JLFET

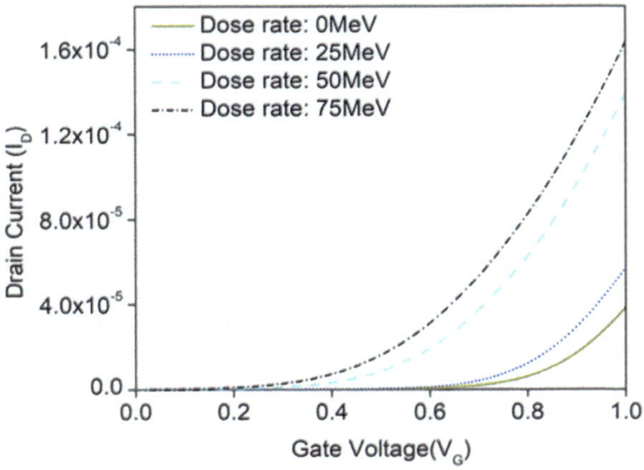

Figure 7 shows the transfer characteristic of HL JLFET after gamma rays photon radiation at different dose rates focusing on change in threshold values [16, 17].

5 Conclusion

In this paper, we have focused on two prospects. Initially, provided a simple and effective approach to decrease off-state leakage current by using high-K oxide layer in JLFET and compared it with SOI based JLFET for two-dimension device using a Sentaurus Synopsys TCAD tool. Secondly, the emphasis has been given on achieving the improved version of JLFET to withstand harsh environment conditions, i.e., during gamma rays photonic irradiation. The electric field behavior and radiation effect on the device are also analyzed at different dose rates of gamma radiation.

Acknowledgements This research work has received substantial funding from Madhya Pradesh Council of Science and Technology, Bhopal (File no. A/RD/RP-2/337). Pushpa Raikwal acknowledges the support from the Faculty Initiation Grant (FIG) PDPM IIITDM Jabalpur (Project No. IIITDMJ/ODRSPC/2021/80).

References

1. Sahay S, Kumar MJ (2016) Realizing efficient volume depletion in SOI junctionless FETs. IEEE J Electron Dev Soc 4(3):110–115.
2. Bramhane L et al. (2022) Impact of work function engineering in charge plasma based bipolar devices. Silicon, 1–5
3. Panchore M et al. (2016) Compact behavioral modeling and time dependent performance degradation analysis of junction and doping free transistors. 2016 IEEE international symposium on Nanoelectronic and information systems (iNIS). IEEE

4. Panchore M, Bramhane L, Singh J (2021) Channel-hot-carrier degradation in the channel of junctionless transistors: a device-and circuit-level perspective. J Comput Electron 20(3):1196–1201
5. Theja A, Panchore M (2022) Performance investigation of GaSb/Si heterojunction based gate underlap and overlap vertical TFET biosensor. IEEE Trans NanoBioscience 22(2):284–291
6. Kamal N, Panchore M, Singh J (2018) 3-D simulation of junction-and doping-free field-effect transistor under heavy ion irradiation. IEEE Trans Device Mater Reliab 18(2):173–179
7. Azwan E et al. (2018) Study the effects of photon radiation on power MOSFET for harsh environment application. MATEC web of conferences. Vol 225. EDP Sciences
8. Kumari V, Gupta M, Saxena M (2021) TCAD-based investigation of double gate junctionless transistor for UV photodetector. IEEE Trans Electron Devices 68(6):2841–2847
9. Jain AK, Kumar MJ (2020) Sub-10 nm scalability of junctionless FETs using a ground plane in high-k box: a simulation study. IEEE Access 8:137540–137548
10. Kamal N, Lahgere A, Singh J (2019) Evaluation of radiation resiliency on emerging junctionless/dopingless devices and circuits. IEEE Trans Device Mater Reliab 19(4):728–732
11. Gupta M, Hu, Vita Pi-Ho (2021) Sensitivity analysis and design of negative-capacitance junctionless transistor for high-performance applications. IEEE Trans Electron Devices 68(8):4136–4143
12. Gundapaneni S et al. (2012) Effect of band-to-band tunneling on junctionless transistors. IEEE Trans Electron Dev 59(4):1023–1029
13. Aishwarya K, Lakshmi B (2023) Radiation study of TFET and JLFET-based devices and circuits: a comprehensive review on the device structure and sensitivity. Radiat Eff Defects Solids 178(3–4):229–257
14. Raut P, Nanda U, Panda DK (2023) Recent trends on junction-less field effect transistors in terms of device topology, modeling, and application. ECS J Solid State Sci Technol
15. Singh S, Panchore M (2022) Dopingless-TFET leaky-integrated-fire (LIF) neuron for high-speed energy efficient applications. IEEE Trans Nanotechnol 21:110–117
16. Kumar P, Panchore M, Raikwal P, Cecil K (2022) Performance investigation of Ge DLTFET based digital integrated circuit. Int J Electron Lett Taylor Francis 11:1–7
17. Raikwal P, Kumar P, Panchore M, Dwivedi P, Cecil K (2023) Soft-error-aware radiation-hardened Ge-DLTFET-based SRAM cell design. Electronics 12(14):3198:1–10

Shaft Rotation Monitoring Using Radar Signal Processing and Wavelet Transform

Denis Valuyskiy, Sergey Vityazev, and Vladimir Vityazev

1 Introduction

Rotating shafts are currently key elements of many industrial machines and apparatuses. Stability and uniformity of rotation are an extremely important requirement for industrial shaft mechanisms, since it is the quality of rotation that determines the quality of products, the percentage of rejects, etc. In addition, the uneven rotation of the shafts due to the wear of the rotating mechanisms can lead to damage and destruction of industrial machines, which, in turn, leads to additional costs for the repair and replacement of equipment and may pose a threat to the life and health of the industrial machine's maintenance personnel. Thus, continuous and accurate monitoring of the state of rotating shafts of industrial machines is a topical and practical problem.

Monitoring the state of rotation of an industrial shaft can be implemented in various ways: using vibration sensors directly connected to an industrial apparatus, using optical analysis tools (cameras, lidars) or using radar sensors. The use of radar sensors and systems is of interest, as it allows diagnostics without direct contact with the industrial apparatus. In addition, radar sensors, unlike optical ones, retain their performance in conditions of insufficient illumination, dust or pollution, which is an important advantage in industrial production [1, 2].

Usually, to analyze the quality of shaft rotation, an analysis of the spectrum of the signal recorded using a vibrometer is used using the fast Fourier transform method. On the resulting spectrum, the side lobes will stand out more brightly—at frequencies that are 2x, 3x away from the main one, and so on [3–5, 18]. Further analysis of the obtained spectrum can be carried out in various ways, for example, using autocorrelation algorithms [3].

D. Valuyskiy (✉) · S. Vityazev · V. Vityazev
Ryazan State Radio Engineering University, Gagarina. 59/1, 390005 Ryazan, Russian Federation
e-mail: valuyskiy.d.v@mail.ru

K. Kumar Singh et al. (eds.), *Machine Vision and Augmented Intelligence*, Lecture Notes in Electrical Engineering 1211, https://doi.org/10.1007/978-981-97-4359-9_15

Recently, more and more attention has been paid to the possibility of assessing the quality of the shaft by means of radar systems. For example, in [6] the installation of a radar at a frequency of 24 GHz is implemented to investigate the possibility of monitoring the helicopter transmission. The signal spectrum was obtained and analyzed. However, an effective indicator of the transmission condition is not offered.

In [7], the AWR1642boost automotive radar evaluation board with a frequency of 77 Hz [8] is used to detect target vibrations in laboratory conditions and compare them with a laser vibrometer. The achievable performance of the radar system is evaluated in terms of the accuracy of the frequency and offset estimates. Rotation is not taken into account. The target state is also not evaluated.

The use of wavelet transform for processing radar signals reflected from a rotating shaft is one of the promising directions in the development of radar detectors of damage to rotating shafts [9, 16]. Moreover, by combining wavelet signal processing with deep learning techniques it can be possible to design industrial shaft rotation quality classifier based on a radar sensor [10, 11, 17].

In our research, we will consider the possibility of using radar signals with subsequent wavelet processing to assess the quality of shaft rotation. Experimental signals reflected from the intact and damaged industrial shafts are registered and analyzed. An approach to radar signal processing using wavelet transform and deep learning neural networks for automatic rotation evenness estimation is offered.

Section 2 provides the common of radiolocation and wavelet theory is used in our work. Section 3 describes the testbed represents the signals recorded during our experiments. In Sect. 4, experimental data is analyzed and a shaft fault detection algorithm is described. The results of the conducted research and further work are described in the conclusion.

2 Radar Detection Theory

2.1 Radiolocation Principles

General view of the radar operation process includes three main tasks: determining the range to the target, estimating the speed and determining the azimuthal direction [12–14]. The distance to the object is calculated based on the propagation time of the signal in both directions. The calculation of the object's speed involves an assessment of the Doppler frequency shift, and the azimuth angle is determined based on signals received through several receiving channels by separate antennas.

Using FMCW (frequency modulated continuous wave) signals allows you to simultaneously achieve high resolution in range and Doppler frequency, which is especially important for shaft rotation quality analysis tasks, since the estimation of motion parameters is the estimation of Doppler frequency shift. The radar produces a pack of pulses with linear frequency modulation. The reflected signal will be described with p indices that representing the number of pulse in a frame and n indices representing the samples of a signal in one pulse.

To estimate the direction to the detected object, the radar must process signals from several receiving antennas. The signal at the output of the demodulator and ADC is processed by multiplying by the reference chirp signal. The resulting IF signal is a three-dimensional signal (1):

$$s(l,n,p) = \alpha \cdot \exp\left(j2\pi \cdot \left(\left(\frac{2KR}{c} + f_d\right) \cdot \frac{n}{f_s} + \frac{f_c l d \sin\theta}{c} + f_d p T_0 + \frac{2f_c R}{c}\right)\right) + \omega(n,p), \quad (1)$$

where α represents attenuation, f_c is a carrier frequency, θ is the azimuth angle, f_d is a Doppler frequency, f_s is sampling frequency, c is the speed of light, d is the distance between the receiving antennas, T_0 is pulse duration, K is a modulation constant.

From expression (1), it can be deduced that information about the range, speed and azimuthal direction to the detected object can be obtained from the signal using three FFTs. The first FFT gives range resolution, the second—speed resolution, the third FFT allows you to get azimuth angle resolution. Radar signal processing basics described above are used in our research as a basis for experimental data collecting.

Instead of using second FFT, it is possible to use wavelet transform and reach the time–frequency map for the Doppler signal reflected from rotating shaft. The Morlet wavelet can be described as follows (2):

$$\psi_\sigma(t) = c_\sigma \pi^{-\frac{1}{4}} e^{-\frac{1}{2}t^2}\left(e^{i\sigma t} - k_\sigma\right), \quad (2)$$

where k_σ is a constant defined by an admissibility criterion, and c_σ is a normalization constant [15].

2.2 AWR1642boost Evaluation Board

The radar market offers a wide range of evaluation radar boards that can be used for experiments. Texas Instruments AWR1642boost is one of the most suitable radar modules for our purposes. This is a continuous wave frequency modulation (FMCW) radar module on a chip with an operating frequency of 77 GHz. The radar system we use includes three key components. An analog processing component with a transceiver module and a preprocessing device for the received radio signal. The digital processing component includes a high-performance DSP. It is designed for basic signal processing and target detection. In addition, a general-purpose processor with ARM architecture is used to control the rest of the units and control the target detection process.

Radar board used to build the experimental stand is depicted in Fig. 1.

Fig. 1 Appearance of TI AWR1642 radar module

AWR1642boost has parameters that allow analyzing the rotation parameters of industrial shafts with sufficient accuracy. With a range and speed resolution of 3.8 cm and 0.08 m/s, respectively, and an azimuthal resolution of up to 15 degrees, the information extracted from the signal will be complete enough to determine the quality of shaft rotation [8].

As part of the ongoing research, the radar system will be used to receive and record Doppler signals reflected from rotating shafts.

3 Description of the Experiments

3.1 Experimental Setup

The experiments carried out as part of the current research work are the recording, processing and subsequent analysis of the results of processing signals reflected from rotating metal shafts. The experimental stand is based on a lathe.

In our work, a test bench has been constructed consisting of the following components (Fig. 2). The AWR1642boost radar board is used as a detector. The Texas Instruments DCA 1000 evaluation board is used to record radar signals reflected from a lathe and pre-processed by the radar detector. The recorded signals are recorded on a personal computer and then processed using software developed during the research.

In the experiments, the signals recorded for various shaft rotation speeds. The metal rod modeling the shaft rotates without beats, but the beats are modeled by shifting the axis of the shaft attachment points in the machine. Thus, it is possible not only to simulate the beats of the shaft, but also to control the frequency and amplitude of these beats.

Fig. 2 Testbed

3.2 *Experimental Signals*

The form of reflected signals in the time domain, corresponding to the mathematical description given in expression (1), is shown in Fig. 3. It can be seen from Fig. 3, that the signal recorded for a damaged shaft has a pronounced low-frequency bursts. These bursts can be used for shaft damage classification using wavelets and deep learning neural networks.

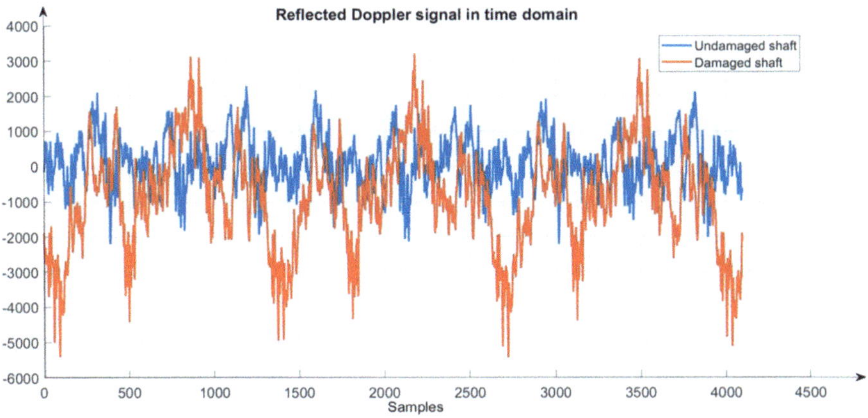

Fig. 3 Experimental signals in time domain

Time–frequency map can be reached by applying the wavelet transform to the reflected signal. In this work, continuous wavelet transform is applied to reflected signal. The base function is Morlet wavelet described in (2). The study of the wavelet transform of the signal on one revolution of the shaft makes it possible to avoid the influence of 2x, 3x, etc., frequencies on the resulting image. The comparison of time–frequency maps for the different signals reflected from damaged and undamaged shafts on one revolution of the shaft are shown on Fig. 4. It can be seen that the time–frequency map for signal reflected from damaged shaft has highly pronounced low-frequency components.

In the resulting image, three regions can be distinguished—high, medium and low scales. The high-frequency regions are approximately the same for signals reflected from damaged and undamaged shafts. Presumably they correspond to reflections from the shaft mounting elements. Important information for determining the quality of shaft rotation is contained in the area of medium and low frequencies. These regions are characterized by single bright bursts corresponding to the moments of the shaft beats.

4 The Proposed Method of Signal Processing

4.1 Analysis of the Results of the Experiment

According to the experimental results, it could be concluded that the signal reflected from the damaged shaft has a pronounced constant low-frequency component. Of interest is also the analysis of the results of the wavelet transform at one revolution of the shaft (about 1500 time samples of the signal). It can be seen that the signal reflected from the damaged shaft has repetitive low-frequency bursts, while the signal reflected from the intact shaft has only high-frequency oscillations repeated more than once within one revolution of the shaft.

4.2 A Novel Method for Shaft Rotation Evaluation

The approach consists in assessing the dynamics of changes in the time–frequency map of the signal reflected from the shaft within a single shaft revolution, as well as the dynamics of changes in the time–frequency map from one shaft revolution to another.

In Fig. 5, a comparison of signal processing using the wavelet transform and using the FFT is shown. As can be seen from the comparison of the resulting images, the use of the wavelet transform allows us to estimate changes in the signal spectrum over time with fairly high accuracy. At the same time, the spectrogram constructed

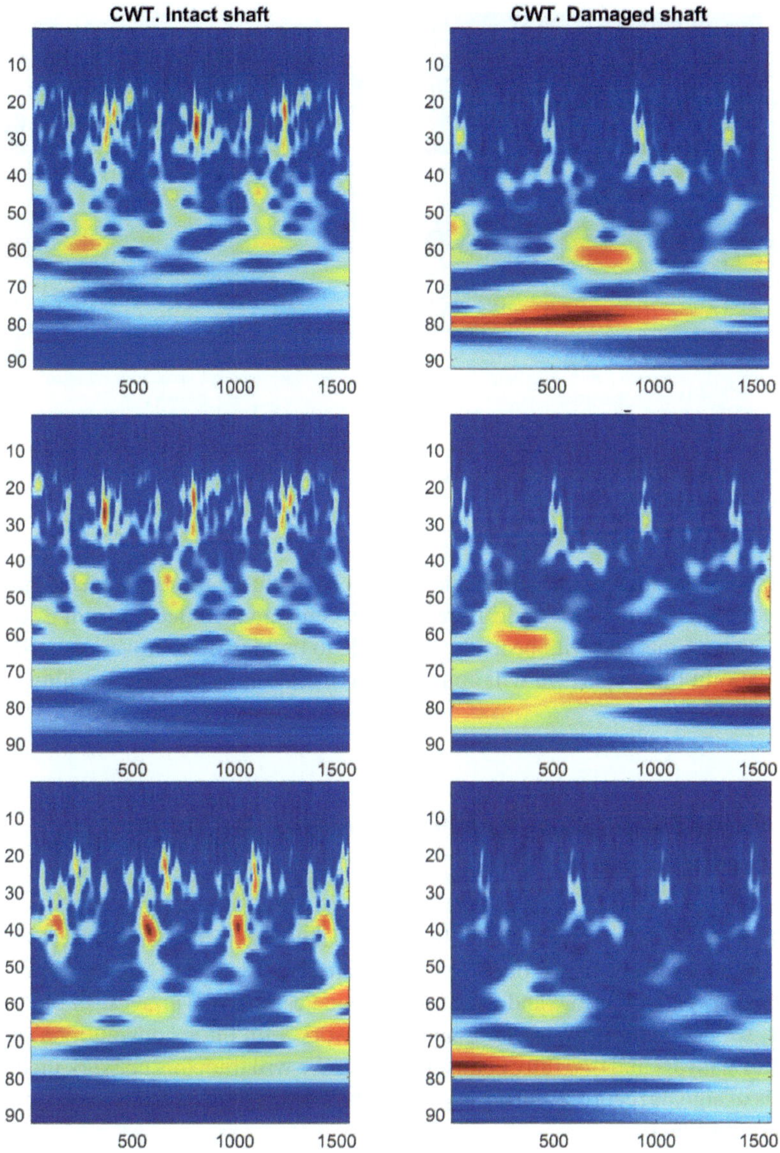

Fig. 4 Wavelet signal processing on one signal revolution for undamaged (**a**) and damaged (**b**) shaft

using the FFT does not allow a detailed analysis of the dynamics of the spectrum over time due to the averaging of the results over the entire observation interval.

Based on the analysis carried out, numerical models can be developed to estimate the dynamics of the spectrum of the signal reflected from the shaft over time.

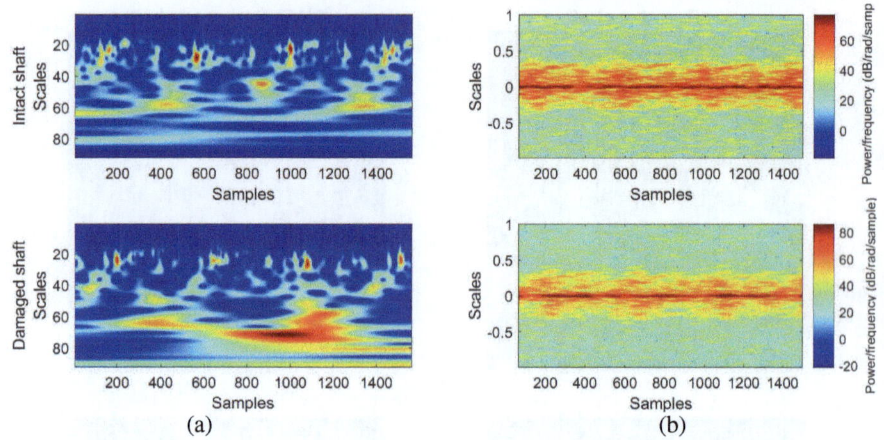

Fig. 5 Comparison of wavelet (**a**) and spectrogram (**b**) processing of the signal reflected from intact and damaged shafts

The obtained images show that the use of CWT with a Morlet wavelet makes it possible to clearly identify the difference between signals reflected from a rotating shaft without beats and with beats. It is possible to build various solvers according to CWT data. In this paper, we will consider classification using deep learning neural networks.

4.3 Using Deep Learning Neural Network for Shaft Classification

Consider the classification of shafts by the wavelet transform of the reflected radio signal is an analysis using deep learning neural networks to identify the beats described above in the low and medium frequencies in CWT images. In our experiments, we are using deep learning neural network with three convolutional layers, three ReLu layers and one fully connected layer. We will train this network on dataset consists of signals recorded during experiments. The result of neural network training is shown on Fig. 6.

Since the currently recorded dataset of experimental signals is small, it is impossible to achieve high accuracy of neural network training. However, even on such a data set, the accuracy of shaft classification (damaged/undamaged) is about 90%.

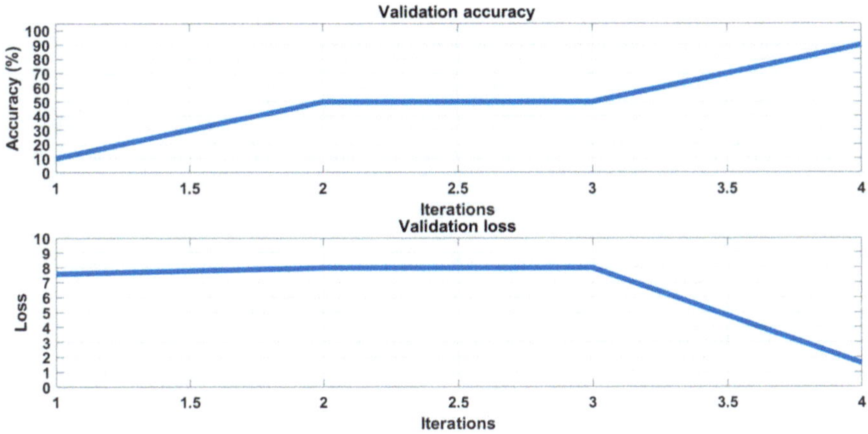

Fig. 6 Neural network training

5 Conclusion

Approaches for shaft rotation monitoring were discussed. An advantages of using radar signals to shaft damage detections are given. Based on the described theoretical foundations, a test stand was built to monitor the mine using a radar sensor. Signals for intact and damaged shafts were recorded and analyzed. It was concluded that the damaged shaft has a bright spikes in the time domain. It was proposed to base on this information an algorithm for processing wavelet signals in a device for shaft rotation monitoring. The brightness of low-frequency components during one shaft revolution and repeating bright low-frequency components during all observation intervals in time–frequency representation of the reflected signal can be used as a metric of unevenness of shaft rotation.

An approach to use deep learning neural network to classify the industrial shafts by time–frequency maps was offered. The effectiveness of this classification was demonstrated by a test neural network trained by experimental radar signals.

In future work, the accuracy of neural network training will be improved. Moreover, it should be investigated to use some numeric methods for shaft rotation classification by wavelet processing of the reflected radar signals.

References

1. Greco MS, Li J, Long T, Zoubir A (2019) Radar systems for modern civilian applications: Part 1. IEEE Signal Process Mag 36(4)
2. Greco MS, Li J, Long T, Zoubir A (2019) Radar systems for modern civilian applications: Part 2. IEEE Signal Process Mag 36(5)

3. Gradzki R, Kulesza Z, Bartoszewiczoster B (2019) Method of shaft crack detection based on squared gain of vibration amplitude. Nonlinear Dyn 98:671–690
4. Ma H, Zhao Q, Han Q, Wen B (2015) Dynamic characteristics analysis of a rotor–stator system under different rubbing forms. Appl Math Model 39:2392–2408
5. Patel TH, Darpe AK (2009) Vibration response of misaligned rotors. J Sound Vib 325:609–628
6. Bharadwaj R et al (2013) Condition monitoring using standoff vibration sensing radar. In: AHS airworthiness, CBM, and HUMS specialists' meeting, Huntsville, AL
7. Ciattaglia G et al (2021) Performance evaluation of vibrational measurements through mmWave automotive radars. Remote Sens 13(1)
8. (2020) AWR1642 evaluation module (AWR1642boost) single-chip mmWave sensing solution user's guide, Texas instruments
9. Vityazev S, Valuyskiy D (2023) Experimental study of the industrial shaft uneven rotation influence on the characteristics of probing radar signals. In: 2023 25th international conference on digital signal processing and its applications (DSPA)
10. Sahu PK, Rai RN (2023) Effect of time-frequency representations for fault classification of rolling bearing in noisy conditions using deep learning. In: 2023 25th international conference on digital signal processing and its applications (DSPA)
11. Russell B, Han J (2016) Jean Morlet and the continuous wavelet transform. CREWES Res Rep 28
12. Zeintl C, Eibensteiner F, Langer J (2019) Evaluation of FMCW radar for vibration sensing in industrial environments. In: 29th international conference radioelektronika (RADIOELEKTRONIKA). IEEE
13. Khablov D (2021) Signal processing of Doppler microwave vibration sensors with quadrature transformation. In: 23rd international conference on digital signal processing and its applications (DSPA). IEEE
14. Patole SM, Torlak M, Wang D, Ali M (2017) Automotive radars: a review of signal processing techniques. Signal Process Mag 34(2):22–35
15. Skolnik M (2008) Radar handbook, 3rd ed. McGraw Hill Companies
16. Orkisz M, Szewczuk A (2023) Spectrum shape based roller bearing fault detection and identification. IEEE Trans Ind Appl 59(2):1547–1556
17. Landi E et al (2023) A MobileNet neural network model for fault diagnosis in roller bearings. In: 2023 IEEE international instrumentation and measurement technology conference (I2MTC), Kuala Lumpur, Malaysia
18. Tang L, Wu X, Wang D, Liu X (2023) A comparative experimental study of vibration and acoustic emission on fault diagnosis of low-speed bearing. IEEE Trans Instrum Meas 72:1–11

Gysel Power Divider Miniaturization Using an Inter-Digital Capacitor-Based Slow-Wave Structure

Mukesh Kumar, Abhinav Kumar, Parimal Sah, Prashant Kumar, A. Vikas, and A. Theja

1 Introduction

Power dividers (PDs) are crucial parts of numerous microwave communication systems, including power amplifiers, antenna arrays, and feeding networks. A typical power divider (PD) is the Wilkinson power divider (WPD), which has a straightforward structure, good impedance matching, and good isolation features. However, a single isolation resistor linked between the output ports, which are unable to provide a suitable heat sink, prevents it from handling high microwave power. As a result, only low power applications can use it [1, 2]. GPD [3], which comprises of four λ/4 and λ/2 transmission lines and two resistors, overcomes this problem. Because there are numerous transmission line portions, the GPD's overall size is considerable, especially at lower frequencies. The key advantage of GPD over WPD is its ability to act as a heat sink and suitability for high power applications. Therefore, a low cast GPD must be designed for high power applications. Researchers have suggested a number of strategies to optimize the size and performance of power dividers [4–16]. The power divider's circuit size can also be reduced by defective ground structures (DGS) and electromagnetic band-gap (EBG) structures [4–6]. The physical area of

M. Kumar
GEC, Abhirajpur Bairiya, Seohar (Bihar), India

A. Kumar · P. Kumar
BCE, Bhagalpur, Bihar, India

P. Sah
PCE, Purnia, Bihar, India

A. Vikas · A. Theja (✉)
TKR College of Engineering & Technology, Hyderabad, Telangana, India
e-mail: thejaarkala@tkrcet.com

A. Vikas
e-mail: vikasambekar@tkrcet.com

K. Kumar Singh et al. (eds.), *Machine Vision and Augmented Intelligence*, Lecture Notes in Electrical Engineering 1211, https://doi.org/10.1007/978-981-97-4359-9_16

microwave circuits (PDs) is reduced in [7, 8] by studying slow-wave topologies. The size of the GPD is reduced in [9] using a composite right/left hand (CRLH) transmission line (TL), but the harmonics cannot be suppressed. [10] reduces the size of the structure by substituting a filter (low pass filter, LPF) circuit for the transmission line portion of the GPD. In [11], the typical line is swapped out for stub loaded lines whereas in [12], the design and performance of GPD are enhanced using a single isolation resistor. In [13], WPD and GPD are used in tandem to enhance GPD's performance. The size of the GPD circuit has recently been greatly reduced by the inclusion of lumped parts (inductor and capacitor) [14]. The author used composite dual transmission lines and linked line sections, respectively, to design compact GPDs in [15, 16]. Even though the size of the aforementioned approaches is substantially less, they have a smaller bandwidth and other limitations at higher frequencies. In order to achieve a good trade-off between size reduction and performance, a compact line with strong slow-wave properties must be designed.

In this paper, an IDC loaded transmission line is investigated. The proposed structure provides high value (minimum enhancement of 177% in the passband) of SWF compared to the traditional line (reference line). Based on the proposed structure a compact GPD is designed at 0.9 GHz. The physical area of the proposed GPD occupies 23% of the reference GPD at the design frequency. In addition to this, harmonic is suppressed below 30 dB.

2 Slow-Wave Transmission Line Based on Meander Line and IDC

Figure 1 shows the proposed slow-wave transmission line which consists of one-stepped impedance meander line and two inter-digital capacitors (IDCs). The meander line is made in such a way that it makes non-uniform impedance (step impedance) to provide a high value of slow-wave factor (SWF) compared to a conventional line of uniform impedance. The SWF of this line is further increased by adding two IDCs on both sides of the meander line. Due to this high value of slow-wave characteristics, the phase velocity of the proposed line is reduced greatly and thereby size reduction can be achieved to a large extent by replacing the conventional line maintaining the same characteristic impedance and electrical length at the design frequency. The physical parameters of the proposed line are depicted in Fig. 1. The lumped equivalent circuit is given in Fig. 2. From this figure, the lumped inductors L_1 and L_2, represent the meander line and capacitor, and C_2 arises due to its gap. The lumped elements L_3 and C_1 correspond to the IDC.

The capacitors, C_3 and C_4 are equivalent junction capacitances with respect to the ground due to the junction of the meander line and IDCs. The characteristic impedance (Z_c) is given by Eq. (1) and the guided wave number (β_g) of the line (assumed lossless) is given by

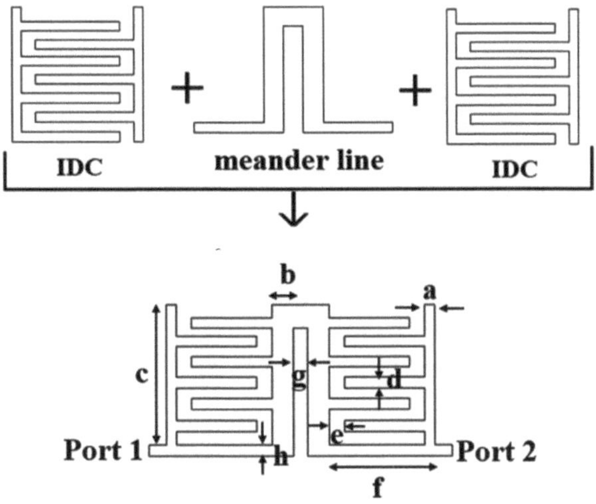

Fig. 1 Proposed slow-wave transmission line

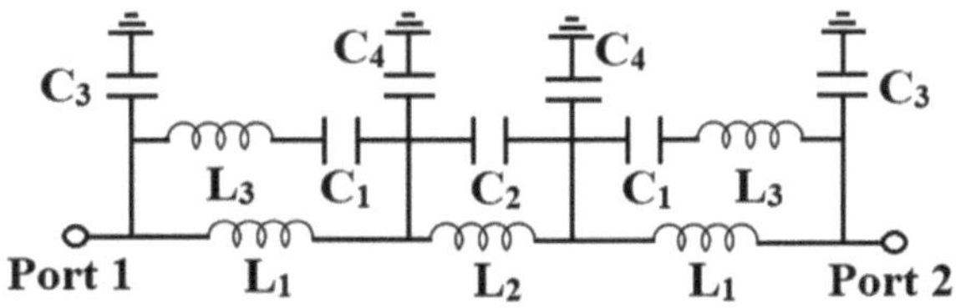

Fig. 2 Lumped equivalent circuit of proposed line

$$Z_c = \sqrt{\frac{Z_{\text{total}}}{Y_{\text{total}}}} \tag{1}$$

$$j\beta_g = \sqrt{Z_{\text{total}} Y_{\text{total}}} \tag{2}$$

where: ω is the angular frequency, total series impedance $Z_{\text{total}} = 2(j\omega L_1 \parallel (j\omega L_3 + 1/j\omega C_1)) + (j\omega L_2 \parallel 1/j\omega C_2)$, and total shunt admittance $Y_{\text{total}} = 2j\omega\ (C_3 + C_4)$. By the use of meander line and IDC, high values of L_1 and L_2 and effective shunt capacitance $(C_3 + C_4)$ are obtained. As a result of this, a high value of β_g is achieved. Consequently, the guided wavelength of the proposed line is effectively reduced. Hence the miniaturization of the microwave circuit can be achieved by using the proposed line. Furthermore, two different parallel LC resonators comprising L_1, L_3, C_1, and L_2, C_2 are connected in cascade. These resonators produce two transmission zeros (TZs) which help to improve the out-off band performance of microwave circuits. The Location of the TZs is obtained by using Eqs. (3–4) from the equivalent circuit model. The lumped element values of this equivalent LC model are obtained by using the formula documented in [1].

$$f_{TZ1} = \frac{1}{2\pi\sqrt{(L_1 + L_3)C_1}} \tag{3}$$

$$f_{TZ2} = \frac{1}{2\pi\sqrt{L_2 C_2}} \tag{4}$$

On an Arlon substrate of dielectric constant (ε_r) of 2.2 with thickness (h) of 0.787 mm, and a loss tangent of 0.0009, an IDC loaded line is constructed utilizing micro-strip technology. To obtain a high SWF in the line, the number of IDC fingers (N) = 20 is used. The Ansys HFSS full-wave EM simulator and CST microwave studio simulate the line's electromagnetic (EM) and electrical circuits. The frequency responses of the IDC loaded line, which is fed by a 50 micro-strip line, are displayed in Fig. 3. The figure shows that at 1.4 GHz and 1.55 GHz, respectively, two transmission zeros (TZs) are achieved with attenuation levels ($|S_{21}|$) better than 15 dB. These TZs may be helpful in improving the out-off band characteristics of microwave circuits. The physical dimensions of the IDC loaded line and the component values of its LC equivalent circuit are tabulated in Tables 1 and 2, respectively.

The phase responses of the line at different stages in comparison with reference line are compared in Fig. 4. Figure 4 shows the phase variation of the proposed line, meander line, and reference line. The SWF of the line is calculated by Eq. (5) [7].

$$\text{SWF} = \frac{\lambda_g \Delta\theta}{L} + \sqrt{\varepsilon_{\text{eff}}} \tag{5}$$

Following the above equations, the SWF of the line is compared with the reference line and shown in Fig. 5. From figure, the variation of SWF for different evolutionary

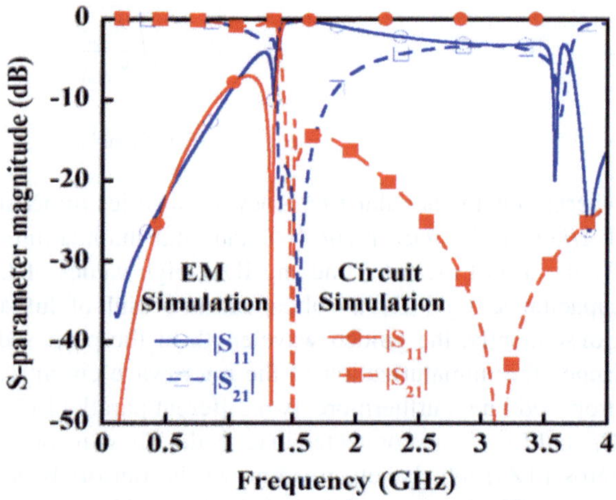

Fig. 3 Frequency response of proposed line

Table 1 Dimensions of the line (in 'mm')

a	b	C	d = e	f	g	h
0.5	1	9.8	0.3	4.8	0.4	0.5

Table 2 LC parameters of the line (L (nH) and C (pF))

L_1	L_2	L_3	C_1	C_2	C_3	C_4
2.7	8	2.5	1.9	0.3	1	1.7

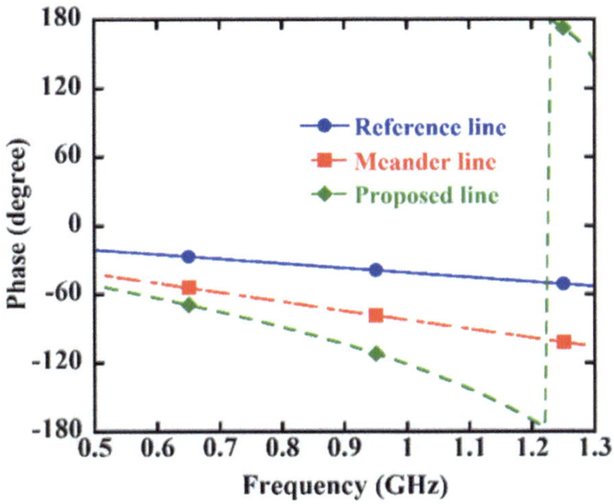

Fig. 4 Phase response of proposed line, meander line, and reference line

stages of the proposed line and compared with the reference line up to 1.3 GHz. The increase in SWF validates the size reduction capability of the proposed line for microwave circuits. Because the line loaded with IDC significantly affects the per-unit inductance and capacitance values. As a result, the phase constant, β_g of the loaded line is more than the phase constant of the reference line. Thus, the phase velocity of the proposed line is smaller (due to short wavelength) than the reference line. Hence, this results in a higher value of this SWF than the reference line. We used this proposed line to reduce the circuit area of a GPD.

3 Miniaturization of a GPD with IDC Loaded Line

Figure 6a depicts the transmission line model for a reference GPD. Six transmission lines and two resistors (R) make up this GPD. The lines' distinctive impedances are Z_1, Z_2, and Z_3. Similarly, the electrical lengths are θ_1, θ_2, and θ_3. This GPD provides equal power division by considering all the lines are of equal length ($\theta_1 = \theta_2 = \theta_3 = 90°$) with respect to design frequency and the same characteristic impedance ($Z_1 = Z_2 = Z_3 = 70.7\ \Omega$) by selecting $R = 100\ \Omega$ based on the work in [10]. The way this reference is organized Fig. 6b depicts a GPD operating at 0.85 GHz with $L_1 = 55.8$ mm, $W_1 = 2.4$ mm, and $W_2 = 1.4$ mm. This PD is composed of six quarter wavelength lines (QWLs) resulting in large circuit area. Each of the QWLs in this reference GPD is replaced by the suggested IDC loaded line, as illustrated in Fig. 7a,

Fig. 5 Variation of SWF of different stages of the proposed line in comparison with reference line

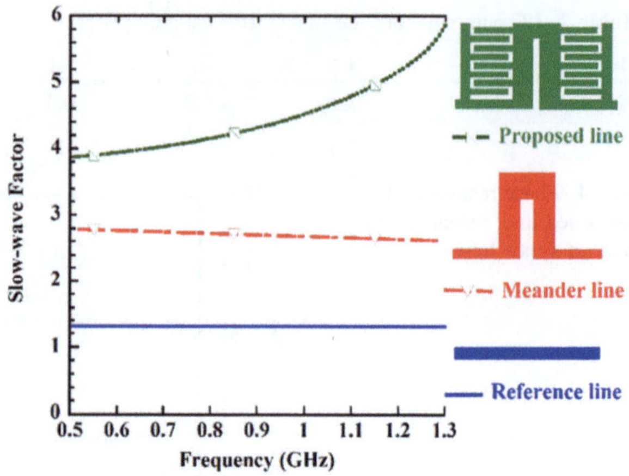

to decrease the circuit area. To obtain the desired characteristic impedance of 70.7 Ω and electrical length of 90° at the design frequency, the layout of this line is modified and optimized using full wave EM simulation by selecting port impedances (port 1 and port 2) of 70.7 Ω. Figure 7 shows the impedance and phase variation of the IDC line. From this figure, it is observed that the impedance and phase are 71 Ω and 92°, respectively which is nearly the same as the desired value at the design frequency of 0.85 GHz. The characteristic impedance of this proposed line is evaluated by following the well-known Eq. (6) where, $Z_0 = 50\ \Omega$, S_{11} is the reflection coefficient, and S_{21} is the transmission coefficient. Based on the above IDC based line, a compact GPD (proposed GPD) is designed and shown in Fig. 8. The size of this power divider has been decreased because, as mentioned in [7], the IDC line has a higher SWF than the normal line. Figure 8 provides the recommended physical dimensions of the reference and suggested GPDs. As a result, only around 23% of the reference GPD's circuit size is occupied by the total physical area of the proposed GPD.

$$Z_c = Z_o\sqrt{\frac{(1+S_{11})^2 - S_{21}^2}{(1-S_{11})^2 - S_{21}^2}} \tag{6}$$

3.1 Simulated Results

In Fig. 9a, b, the suggested GPD's simulated frequency responses are compared with those of the reference GPD. According to Fig. 9a, the proposed design offers, at the design frequency of 0.85 GHz, reflection coefficient ($|S_{11}|$) of −19.7 dB, insertion-loss ($|S_{21}|$ and $|S_{31}|$) of 3.27 dB, and isolation ($|S_{23}|$) of −32.1 dB, compared to the reference design's −33 dB, 3.1 dB, and −34 dB, respectively. Furthermore, the second order harmonic is effectively suppressed by more than 25 dB. The fractional

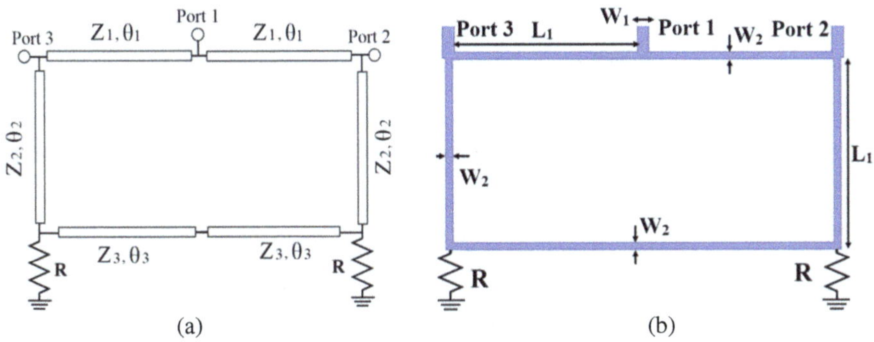

Fig. 6 GPD: **a** Transmission line mode, **b** Layout

Fig. 7 Slow-wave line: **a** Layout of proposed line with dimensions are in mm: a = 0.5, b = 1, c = 8.6, d = e = 0.3, f = 0.8, g = 0.4, l = 4.8, **b** Impedance and phase of proposed line

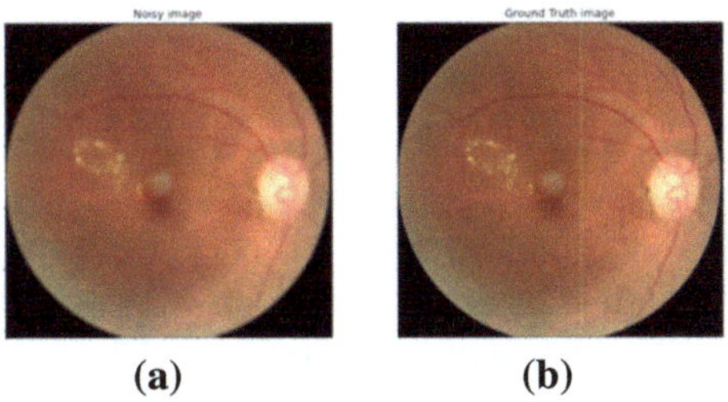

Fig. 8 Layout of proposed GPD (with optimum dimensions are in mm: W = 1.4, L = 51, a = 0.5, b = 1, c = 8.6, d = e = 0.3, f = 0.8, g = 0.4, k = 3 h = m = 1.7, j = i = 6, l = 4.8), N = 20

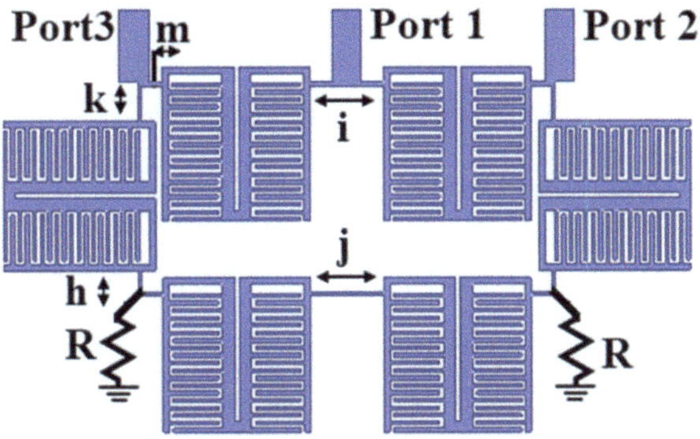

bandwidth (FBW) is found to be 35.5% for reflection coefficient and isolation better than 15 dB. While it is ±0.20 for the reference GPD in Fig. 9b, the phase difference between the output ports (Port 2 and Port 3) is ±0.250 within the operating band.

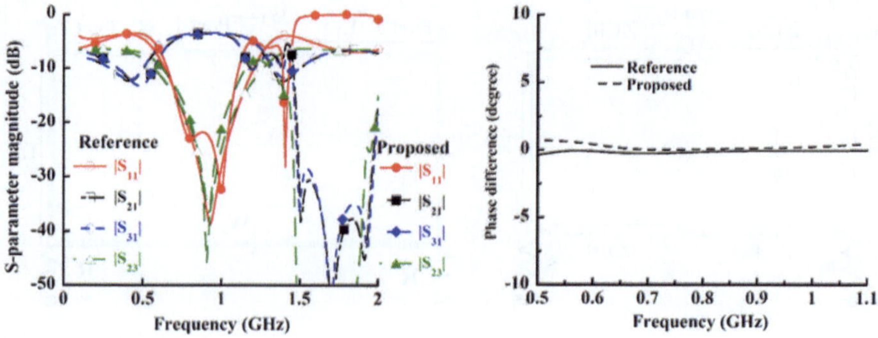

Fig. 9 Proposed GPD: **a** S-parameters of the proposed GPD, **b** Phase difference (∠S_{21}–∠S_{31}) of the proposed GPD

4 Conclusions

A compact Gysel power divider is designed at 0.85 GHz based on the slow-wave transmission line based on meander lines and inter-digital capacitors. Firstly, the slow-wave line is designed which provides a very high value of slow-wave factor (SWF) compared to the traditional line. Therefore, this line has the capability to reduce the circuit size due to high SWF. Because of this, as compared to the reference design, the suggested design's overall physical dimension only takes up 23% of the circuit space. Furthermore, the suppression of the second order harmonic is better than 25 dB.

References

1. Hong JS, Lancaster MJ (2001) Microstrip filters for RF/microwave applications. Wiley, New York, NY, USA
2. Wilkinson EJ (1960) An N-way hybrid power divider. IRE Trans Microw Theory Tech 8(1):116–118
3. Gysel UH (1975) A new N-way power divider/combiner suitable for high power applications. IEEE MTT-S Int Dig, 116–118
4. Zhang F, Li CF (2008) Power divider with microstrip electromagnetic bandgap element for miniaturization and harmonic rejection. Electron Lett 44(6):422–423
5. Woo DJ, Lee TK (2005) Suppression of harmonics in Wilkinson power divider using dual-band rejection by asymmetric DGS. IEEE Trans Microw Theory Tech 53(6):2139–2144
6. Yang J, Gu C, Wu W (2008) Design of novel compact coupled microstrip power divider with harmonic suppression. IEEE Microwave Wirel Compon Lett 18(9):572–574
7. Liu H, Li Z, Sun X (2005) Compact defected ground structure in microstrip technology. Electron Lett 41(3):132–134
8. Kanaparthi VPK, Karthikeyan SS (2015) A compact 1:4 lossless T-junction power divider using open complementary split ring resonator. Radio Eng 24(3):717–721

9. Zhang HL, Hu BJ, Zhang XY (2012) Compact equal and unequal dual-frequency power dividers based on composite right-/left handed transmission lines. IEEE Trans Ind Electron 59(9):3464–3472
10. Karimia G, Siahkamaria H, Khamin-Hamedani F (2015) A novel miniaturized Gysel power divider using low-pass filter with harmonic suppression. Int J Electron Commun (AEÜ) 69:856–860
11. Shahi H, Shamsi H (2017) Compact wideband Gysel power dividers with harmonic suppression and arbitrary power division ratios. AEU-Int J Electron Commun 79:16–25
12. Zaker R, Abdipour A, Mirzavand R (2014) Closed-form design of Gysel power divider with only one isolation resistor. IEEE Microw Wirel Compon Lett 24(8):527–529
13. Guan J, Zhang LJ, Sun ZY, Leng YQ, Peng YT (2012) Designing power divider by combining Wilkinson and Gysel structure. Electron Lett 48(13):769–770
14. Ryo U, Hitoshi H (2017) Miniaturized Gysel power dividers using lumped-element components. Prog Electromagn Res Lett 71:37–43
15. Kumar M, Sen G, Islam SN, Parui SK, Das S (2020) Composite dual transmission lines and ITS application to miniaturization of Gysel power divider. Prog Electromagn Res Lett 90:91–97
16. Kumar M, Sen G, Islam SK, Parui SK, Das S (2020) Miniaturization and harmonic suppression of power divider using coupled line section for high power application. Radioengineering 29(2):336–342

9. Zhang H, Xu F, Zhang K (2013) Compact equal and unequal dual-frequency power divider based on composite right-/left-handed transmission lines. IEEE Trans Ind Electron 60(9):3464–3472
10. Khandelwal S, Sinha N, Kumar S (2019) A novel miniaturized Gysel power divider using low-pass filter with harmonics suppression. In: [illegible] Commun [illegible] Syst [illegible] 560
11. Shahi H, Shamsi H (2017) Compact wideband Gysel power dividers with harmonic suppression and arbitrary power division ratios. AEU Int J Electron Commun 79:16–25
12. Zaidi R, Soliman A, Ahmed R (2017) Closed-form design of Gysel power divider with [illegible] ... IEEE Microw Wirel Compon Lett 27(3):[illegible]
13. [illegible] Zhang J, Sun [illegible], Leung [illegible] (2013) Bagging power divider ... Microwave [illegible] structure. Electron Lett [illegible]
14. [illegible] (2017) Miniaturized Gysel power dividers using ... [illegible] Prog Electromagn Res Lett [illegible]
15. [illegible] (2016) Compact unequal [illegible] dividers in LTCC application to [illegible] of Gysel power dividers. [illegible]
16. [illegible] (2018) [illegible] ... divider [illegible] ... Engineering [illegible]

Noise Estimation and Removal in Fundus Images Using Pyramid Real Image Denoising Network

Anuj Kumar Parashar and Bambam Kumar

1 Introduction

Denoising of Fundus Images is an active issue for many researchers these days due to real-time applications. In the image denoising task, clean and clear biomedical images are obtained from noisy biomedical images. The most significant noise component in the biomedical images can be modeled as additive white Gaussian noise (AWGN), Poisson noise, salt and pepper noise, and speckle noise [1]. Deep convolutional neural networks (CNN) have been widely used by researchers these days. It shows significant improvement in the denoising task for a specific noise level. Conventional filter-based approaches were used for removing the noise from the image. Then a deep convolutional encoder-decoder with skip connections, REDNet [2], was introduced by Mao. An approach that merges residual learning and batch normalization was introduced by Zhang et al. [3], again, a deep learning approach for denoising (DnCNN), which works better than non-CNN-based approaches. Other than DnCNN, some deep learning approaches [4, 5] show good results. However, these approaches show good results with specific noise levels. But the performance of conventional approaches such as BM3D [6] and some deep learning approaches becomes worse with real-world noise. DnCNN can work with blind noise (real-world noise), but some other approaches, such as FFDNet [7], have been developed in interactive settings with relatively higher noise levels, which can deal with more complex levels of noise (blind noise). CBDNet [8] has been introduced; it utilizes a sub-network that estimates the noise and achieves end-to-end blind denoising. A multi-path CNN named Path-Restore is proposed by Yu et al. [9], it can dynamically

A. K. Parashar (✉) · B. Kumar
Department of ECE, National Institute of Technology Patna, Patna, India
e-mail: anujp.ph21.ec@nitp.ac.in

B. Kumar
e-mail: bambam.ec@nitp.ac.in

K. Kumar Singh et al. (eds.), *Machine Vision and Augmented Intelligence*, Lecture Notes in Electrical Engineering 1211, https://doi.org/10.1007/978-981-97-4359-9_17

choose the route for each region of the image, especially where the noise levels are varied in nature (image with blind noise).

These approaches show promising results in image denoising, but there are still some issues that need to be addressed in the denoising of images with blind noise which are as follows:

1. In most deep learning-based approaches, there is no adjustment of channel-wise features according to their importance. They are all treated equally. Feature channels capture different kinds of noise from all regions of a noisy image. Some noise needs more attention, thus should be assigned more weights.
2. Some of the approaches previously mentioned with fixed receptive fields fail to carry information because of the diversity of the information. In method BM3D [6], it searches for similar blocks in the image by taking global information into consideration. As the features are not limited to a small area, hierarchical spatial features have been fully exploited by receptive fields with different scales. If the images have been suffering from heavy noise, context information becomes helpful.
3. Some of the approaches simply concatenate the features for the aggregation of multi-scale features [2]. Although they contain the information of all scales, they treat features with different scales indiscriminately and ignore the spatial and channel specificity of scale-wise features. Therefore, multi-scale features cannot be adaptively expressed. Section 2 describes the architecture of the PRIDNet model for denoising Findus images. Section 3 describes a description of the data. In Sect. 4, experiments using PRIDNet and comparisons with recent papers are presented.

2 Network Architecture

2.1 Pyramid Real Image Denoising Network (PRIDNet)

There are modules used in this network for denoising images with blind noise. First, it estimates the noise; second, it utilizes pyramid pooling to extract multi-scale features. Lastly, it fuses multi-scale features adaptively. Figure 1 represents the Pyramid real image denoising network (PRIDNet). There are three modules in this network noise estimation: multi-scale denoising and fusion of features.

2.2 Noise Estimation

It focuses on the extraction of discriminative features from the input image, which estimates the noise level [8]. In this module, a five-layer fully convolutional subnetwork without pooling and batch normalization is used. ReLU is used after each

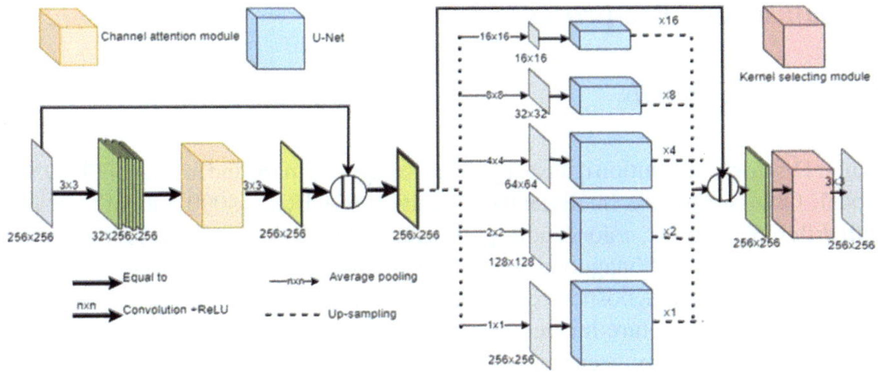

Fig.1 Architecture of PRIDNet

convolution layer. In each convolution layer, 32 feature maps with 3 × 3 filters have been used, except for the last layer (1 or 3). A channel attention block [10] has been used to calibrate the interconnections between feature channels explicitly.

2.3 *Multi-scale Denoising*

In a five-level pyramid structure, input feature maps have been sampled down to different sizes, which helps branches gain relatively scaled different receptive fields to capture original, local, and global information concurrently. Pooling kernels have been settled at 1 × 1, 2 × 2, 4 × 4, 8 × 8, and 16 × 16, respectively. Each feature is pooled, followed by U-Net [11], which consists of an encoder, decoder, and skip connections. It is noted that five U-Nets do not share weights; multi-level denoised features are up-sampled by bilinear interpolation to the same size and then concatenated together at the end of this stage.

2.4 *Feature Fusion*

In the feature fusion stage, different size kernels are chosen by each channel within concatenated multi-scale results, inspired by [12].

3 Dataset and Pre-processing

3.1 Dataset Details

Ocular Disease Recognition dataset has been used for training and testing of PRIDNet Modal. Oscular Disease Intelligent Recognition (ODIR), a 5000 patient's dataset with different ages, i.e., color fundus photograph of both eyes. It is a real-life dataset which is collected by Shanggong Medical Technology Co. Ltd. Dataset is collected from hospitals and diagnostics centers in China. In these centers, various cameras have been used to capture images, resulting in varied image resolution. Total 400 numbers of images have been randomly selected from ODIR dataset.

3.2 Steps of Preprocessing

Randomly 400 Images are selected from ODIR dataset for creating training and testing datasets. Dataset is set as per the requirement of the model. Model used color fundus images of 256 × 256 size as Input. The dimension of the images is converted into 256 × 256 as per the requirement of the model. Figure 2a represents the noisy image used for training and Fig. 2b represents the ground truth image used for training. Scaling and Augmentation are performed for increasing the size of the dataset. After the scaling and Augmentation Random noise is added for creating the noisy image. The whole dataset is divided into 70% and 30% for training and testing datasets, respectively.

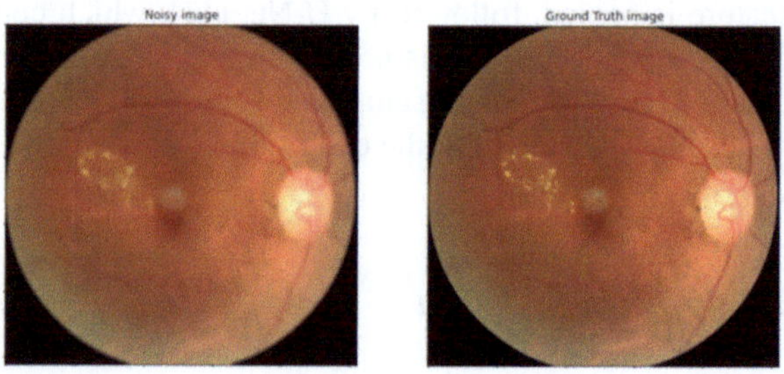

Fig. 2 **a** Noisy fundus imaget, **b** Ground truth fundus image

4 Experiments

4.1 Implementation Details

In the training process, 150 epochs and 32 batch sizes have been used. It means 32 samples have been passed at a time to train the model until all training data has passed to complete one single epoch. Before the training process, fundus images were resized. The fundus image dataset has been resized from 512 × 512 × 3 to 256 × 256 × 3. The proposed model has been trained on a 256 × 256 × 3 fundus image. The model has been implemented in a Python notebook using Adam Optimizer, and it has been trained on Google Collaborative, which consists of 24 GB of RAM for a large dataset with an NVIDIA Tesla K80 GPU.

4.2 Results

Results of fundus image denoising are obtained using PRIDnet, which shows that the results of the image denoising task are better than those of conventional filter-based approaches and state-of-the-art deep learning approaches. The results of PRIDNet are compared with conventional filter methods in Table 1 and deep learning methods in Table 2. PSNR and SSIM using PRIDNet are 41.20695608345564, 0.96168379076031, respectively, which is good in comparison with various filter-based methods and deep learning-based methods (CNN-DWT, GAN-CT, RED-CNN, SDCDAE, and DnCNN). PRIDNet outperforms in both kinds of methods. This shows the acceptance of this method among blind denoising tasks of fundus images. Figure 3a, d, g, j represents the noisy fundus images obtained after the preprocessing step applied to the ODIR dataset. Figure 3b, e, h, k shows the ground truth fundus images obtained from the ODIR dataset, and Fig. 3c, f, i, l represents the predicted fundus image using the PRIDNet model.

Table 1 Comparison of PRIDNet with basic filter methods

Method	PSNR	SSIM
Average filter	22.1463	0.196891
Gaussian filter	22.1669	0.199592
Median filter	22.5899	0.207295
Bilateral filter	26.0316	0.649345
Adaptive median Filter	25.1877	0.675843
Local noise reduction filter	25.6085	0.783475
PRIDNet (ours)	**41.2069**	**0.961683**

Table 2 Comparision of PRIDNet with deep learning techniques

Deep learning methods	PSNR	SSIM
CNN-DWT[13]	31.1307	0.9486
GAN-CT [14]	31.3581	0.9537
RED-CNN [15]	32.2434	0.9632
SDCDAE [16]	32.3844	0.9674
DnCNN [17]	33.5354	0.9233
PRIDNet (ours)	**41.2069**	**0.9616**

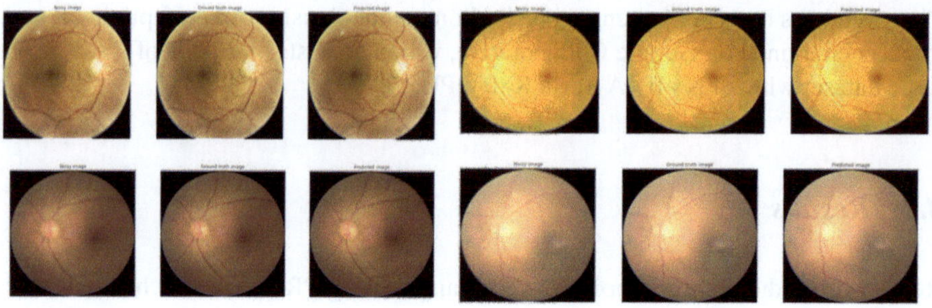

Fig. 3 **a, d, g, j** Noisy image, **b, e, h, k** Ground truth image, and **c, f, i, l** Predicted image

5 Conclusion

In this work, PRIDNet is used for blind denoising of fundus images. There are three steps in this model for the denoising task. The PRIDNet network performs denoising in three steps. First, it estimates the noise; second, it utilizes pyramid pooling to extract multi-scale features. Lastly, it fuses multi-scale features adaptively. PSNR and SSIM using PRIDNet are 41.2069 and 0.961683, respectively, which is good in comparison with various filter-based methods and deep learning-based methods (CNN-DWT, GAN-CT, RED-CNN, SDCDAE, and DnCNN). PRIDNet outperforms in both kinds of methods. This shows the acceptance of this method among blind denoising tasks of fundus images. Results show that PRIDNet performs better than filter denoising approaches as well as some deep learning approaches to denoising. Qualitative and quantitative experiments show the supremacy of PRIDNet over state-of-the-art methods.

References

1. Dhruv B, Mittal N, Modi M (2017) Analysis of different filters for noise reduction in images. In: 2017 recent developments in control, automation & power engineering (RDCAPE), 26–27 October 2017, Noida, India

2. Mao X-J, Shen C-H, Yang Y-B (2016) Image restoration using very deep convolutional encoder-decoder networks with symmetric skip connections. In: NIPS, pp 2802–2810
3. Zhang K, Zuo W, Chen Y, Meng D, Zhang L (2017) Beyond a Gaussian denoiser: residual learning of deep CNN for image denoising. IEEE Trans Image Process 26(7):3142–3155. https://doi.org/10.1109/TIP.2017.2662206
4. Plötz T, Roth S (2018) Neural nearest neighbor's networks. In: NIPS, pp 1087–1098
5. Tai Y, Yang J, Liu X-M, Xu C-Y (2017) Memnet: a persistent memory network for image restoration. In: ICCV, pp 4539–4547
6. Dabov K, Foi A, Katkovnik V, Egiazarian KO (2007) Color imagedenoising via sparse 3d collaborative filtering with grouping constraint in luminance-chrominance space. In: ICIP, pp 313–316
7. Zhang K, Zuo W-M, Zhang L (2018) Ffdnet: toward a fast and flexible solution for cnn-based image denoising. IEEE Trans Image Process 27(9):4608–4622
8. Guo S, Yan Z-F, Zhang K, Zuo W-M, Zhang L (2018) Towardconvolutional blind denoising of real photographs. arXiv:1807.04686
9. Yu K, Wang X-T, Dong C, Tang X-O, Loy CC (2019) Path-restore: learning network path selection for image restoration. arXiv:1904.10343
10. Lu Y, Jiang Z-Q, Ju G-D, Shen L-C, Men A-D (2019) Recursive multistage upscaling network with discriminative fusion for super-resolution. In: ICME, pp 574–579
11. Ronneberger O, Fischer P, Brox T (2015) U-net: convolutional networks for biomedical image segmentation. In: MICCAI, pp 234–241
12. Li X, Wang W-H, Hu X-L, Yang X-L (2019) Selective kernel networks. arXiv:1903.06586
13. Kang E, Min J, Ye JC et al (2016) A deep convolutional neural network using directional wavelets for low-dose CT X-ray reconstruction. Med Phys 44(10):e360–e375
14. Wolterink JM, Leiner T, Viergever MA et al (2017) Generative adversarial networks for noise reduction in low-dose CT. IEEE Trans Med Imaging 36(12):2536–2545
15. Chen H, Zhang Y, Kalra MK et al (2017) Low-dose CT with a residual encoder–decoder convolutional neural network. IEEE Trans Med Imaging 36(12):2524–2535
16. Ghosh SK, Biswas B, Ghosh A (2019) SDCA: a novel stack deep convolutional autoencoder—an application on retinal image denoising. IET Image Process Spec Sect: Advers Learn Image Process 13(14):2778–2789
17. Parashar AK, Phartiyal GS, Kumar B (2023) Denoising of fundus images using feed-forward convolutional neural networks. In: International conference on electrical, electronics, communication and computers. IEEE

Evaluation of Hybrid Encryption Method to Secure Healthcare Data

Sangjukta Das, Maheshwari Prasad Singh, and Suyel Namasudra

1 Introduction

The healthcare systems are continuously evolving with the advancement of various technologies. The modern healthcare systems, also called smart healthcare systems consist of different sensors and smart devices that make the data collection easier than it was in traditional healthcare systems. The collected or gathered data are sent to the next higher layer of the healthcare system for analysis and research purposes. Therefore, any kind of breach or modification of data may not provide the desired analytical outcome. This may even cause consequences to patients' lives if the diagnostics and the treatments are based on the tampered data. Here, data security comes into the picture in order to protect healthcare data from unauthorized modifications. Different security services provided by cryptography like confidentiality, integrity, and authentication, can build a secure healthcare system.

The security goal, confidentiality, can be achieved through encryption and decryption processes. The two categories of encryption and decryption are symmetric key and asymmetric key encryption and decryption [1]. Symmetric key encryption uses a single key while asymmetric key encryption uses two keys, one private and one public key, for the encryption and decryption process. Both processes have their advantage and disadvantages. For example, symmetric encryption is faster, yet, secret key management is challenging [2]. As a result, the hybrid encryption technique,

S. Das (✉) · M. P. Singh
Department of Computer Science and Engineering, National Institute of Technology Patna, Bihar, India
e-mail: sangjukta24@gmail.com

M. P. Singh
e-mail: mps@nitp.ac.in

S. Namasudra
Department of Computer Science and Engineering, National Institute of Technology Agartala, Agartala, India

K. Kumar Singh et al. (eds.), *Machine Vision and Augmented Intelligence*, Lecture Notes in Electrical Engineering 1211, https://doi.org/10.1007/978-981-97-4359-9_18

combining both symmetric and asymmetric encryption, has been used by researchers in the literature [3]. A hybrid encryption method is proposed by Tayel et al. [4] that uses Serpent and ECC-based encryption to provide security in the system. ECC-based encryption provides strong security but it slows down the system if the data size is large [2]. Still, it performs better than other asymmetric encryptions, such as RSA. Another issue faced by many of the encryption systems is the key generation process. If a key generation authority generates the user's key pair, then, that entity may illegally access encrypted data by using the private key. This raises the issue called key escrow [5]. This problem arises because of a centralized key generation authority that generates private keys for all users. This indicates that the centralized authority can control the user's private keys, which raises security and privacy-related concerns [6, 7]. Besides the above-discussed issues, a variety of other issues regarding security and privacy of data are discussed by many researchers in the literature [8–10].

The proposed scheme, called the Hybrid Encryption Method to Secure Healthcare Data (HEM-SHD), addresses the above-mentioned problems by reducing data encryption, and decryption times. HEM-SHD combines symmetric and asymmetric encryption for healthcare data encryption. It uses AES symmetric encryption to encrypt healthcare data. Then, the secret key is encrypted by using ECC-based asymmetric encryption. Here, to solve the key escrow problem, a different key generation process is proposed. Each user generates its public–private keys from construction components generated by the Key generation authority. Additionally, data integrity in the HEM-SHD is maintained by using digital signature.

2 Background Studies

2.1 *ECC-Based Encryption and Decryption*

In ECC-based encryption, a plaintext is mapped to a point PT on the elliptic curve E [11]. Two private keys p_a and p_b are chosen for two users A and B, respectively. The public keys for users A and B are computed as $q_a = p_a * P$ and $q_b = p_b * P$, where P is the generator point. User A encrypts a plaintext PT for B by using B's public key q_b. User A chooses $k \in z_r$ and computes ciphertext CT as shown in Eq. (1). The intended user B decrypts CT by using p_b, as shown in Eq. (2).

$$CT = [k.P, (PT + k.q_b)] \tag{1}$$

$$PT = (PT + k.q_b) - k.P.p_b \tag{2}$$

3 Proposed HEM-SHD

The proposed scheme (HEM-SHD) has three phases, namely user registration and key generation, encryption, and decryption. It also has three entities: Centralized Management (CM), user, and Data Owner (DO). A CM registers all users in the system. It also assists each user in generating key pairs. When a user requests healthcare data, the DO encrypts and sends the requested data to the user. A few assumptions were considered below:

- CM setups the model initially, registers all the users, and generates all necessary components for the users.
- Each user generates its key pair from the key construction components.

3.1 User Registration and Key Generation

The user selects a number K_u from z_r randomly and calculates $R_u = K_u.P$. The user sends R_u and the real identity ID. The CM starts the registration process by selecting K_{IM} from z_r to compute $P_{IM} = R_u + K_{IM}.P$. Again, the CM randomly selects $\propto$ and β from z_r and computes GID $= \{(ID+ \propto .\beta.P), \propto .P\}$ for the user. Again, the CM generates $C_U = \{P_{IM}, GID\}$ and generates hash value, $h_1 = \text{hash}(C_U)$ and $r_u = h_1.K_{IM} + IM_{PVT}$. Here, C_U and r_u are the key construction components of the user. The user generates the public–private key pair by using $\{C_U, r_u\}$ as follows:

$$K_{\text{pvt}} = h_1.K_u + r_u \text{ and } K_{\text{pub}} = K_{\text{pvt}}.P.$$

3.2 Encryption Process

At first, the DO generates the symmetric key SK_1 and encrypts the message PT using AES encryption technique. This produces CT_1 as output. The DO selects a random integer k to encrypt SK_1 using ECC encryption. This produces CT_2 as output. The DO concatenates CT_1 and CT_2 to generate CT. Then, the DO creates its signature (m, s). To generate a digital sign for CT, the DO calculates $z = H(CT, K_{\text{DO}_{\text{pub}}}, K_{\text{pub}})$, where $H(.)$ is the hash function. The DO chooses an integer c randomly from the range $(1, r - 1)$ and calculates m and s to generate digital sign (m, s). Then, the encrypted messages (CT_1, CT_2) and (m, s) are sent to the receiver. The entire encryption process is shown in Algorithm 1.

Algorithm 1: Encryption
Input: $K_{pub}, SK_1,$ PT, and PP
Output: (CT, m, s)

1. START
2. Take plaintext PT
3. Generate SK_1 for AES
4. Calculate $CT_1 = ENCRYPT_{AES}(SK_1, PT_1)$
5. Calculate $CT_2 = ENCRYPT_{ECC}(K_{pub}, SK_1) = [(k.P), (SK_1 + k.K_{pub})]$
6. Concatenate CT_1 and CT_2 to generate CT
7. Calculates the hash value of CT as $z = H(CT, K_{DO_{pub}}, K_{pub})$
8. Select random integer c from $(1, r-1)$
9. Calculate $c.P = (x_1, y_1)$
10. Calculate $m = x_1 \bmod r$, if $m = 0$ reselect c
11. Calculate $s = c^{-1}\left(z + K_{DO_{pvt}}.m\right) \bmod r$, if $s = 0$ reselect c
12. Create signature (m, s)
13. Send (CT, m, s) to U
14. STOP

3.3 Decryption Process

The user performs the decryption process shown in Algorithm 2. The user verifies, if m and s are within the valid range of $[1, r-1]$ or not. Then, the user calculates a point $T = (u_1.P + u_2.K_{DO\_pub})$. If $T \neq 0$, the user computes $v = x_T \bmod r$, where X_T is the X coordinate of T. If $v = m$ holds, the verification is successful. The user decrypts CT_2, which is equal to $[(k.P), (SK_1 + k.K_{pub})]$ by his/her K_{pvt}. The SK_1 can be obtained as:

$$SK_1 = \left(SK_1 + k.K_{pub}\right) - k.P.K_{pvt}$$

$$= \left(SK_1 + k.K_{pub}\right) - k.K_{pub}, \text{ where } K_{pub} = K_{pvt}.P$$

This SK_1 is used for decrypting CT_1 to the original message generate PT.

Algorithm 2: Decryption
Input: (CT, m, s), K_{pvt}, and PP
Output: PT

1. START
2. Verify m and s are in $(1,\ r-1)$
3. Calculate $z = H(CT, K_{DO_{pub}}, K_{pub})$
4. Calculate $u_1 = s^{-1}z \bmod r$ and $u_2 = s^{-1}m \bmod r$
5. Calculate $T = (u_1.P + u_2.K_{DO\_pub})$
6. Calculate $v = x_T \bmod r$
7. If $v = m$, Signature is Accepted
8. Calculate $SK_1 = DECRYPT_{ECC}(K_{pvt}, CT_2)$
9. Calculate $PT = DECRYPT_{AES}(SK_1, CT_1)$
10. STOP

4 Security Analysis

Theorem 1

If the OWHF assumption holds, the authenticity can be maintained.

OWHF, i.e., One Way Hash Function, is a hash function that generates a fixed-length hash value $H(CT, K_{DO_{pub}}, K_{pub})$ for $\{CT, K_{DO_{pub}}, K_{pub}\}$ of arbitrary length in such a way that it is easy to compute $H(CT, K_{DO_{pub}}, K_{pub})$. It is difficult to compute $\{CT, K_{DO_{pub}}, K_{pub}\}$ for given $H(\{CT, K_{DO_{pub}}, K_{pub}\})$. It is difficult to compute another message m_1 such that $H(\{CT, K_{DO_{pub}}, K_{pub}\}) = H(m_1)$.

Theorem 2

If $H(.)$ in ECC-based digital signature is preimage and collision resistance, the sign cannot be forged.

For a hash value of length t bit, an attacker needs to perform 2^t attempts to generate a preimage and $2^{t/2}$ operation for collision attack. Attacks on ECC-based digital signatures are computationally hard for a large value of t.

Theorem 3

The signature (m, s) can be verified by only the intended user.

If the signature (m, s) for $\{CT, K_{DO_{pub}}, K_{pub}\}$ is generated by the sender, then $s = c^{-1}(z + K_{DO\_pvt}.m) \bmod r$. Rearrangement of s generates:

$$c = s^{-1}(z + K_{DO\_pvt}.m) \bmod r = (s^{-1}.z + s^{-1}.K_{DO\_pvt}.m) \bmod r = (u_1 + u_2.K_{DO\_pvt}) \bmod r$$

$(u_1.P + u_2.K_{DO\_pub}) \bmod r = (u_1.P + u_2.K_{DO_{pvt}}.P) \bmod r = (u_1 + u_2.K_{DO_{pvt}})P \bmod r = c.P$ So $v = m$ can be proved as required.

Attack 1 An attacker tries to modify, delete, or replicate the encrypted data CT.

To generate digital sign, the DO computes $s = c^{-1}(z + K_{DO\_pvt}.m) \bmod r$, where $z = H(CT, K_{DO_{pub}}, K_{pub})$. If the attacker alters CT, then, z will also be altered. The sign verification will fail; thus, an attacker cannot be successful.

Attack 2 An attacker, attempts to retrieve SK_1 without valid K_{pvt}.

To retrieve SK_1 fromCT_2, i.e., $[(k.P), (SK_1 + k.K_{pub})]$, an attacker needs to solve the equation for SK_1. $\mathcal{A}$ cannot solve the equation as it does not have k and K_{pvt}. Therefore, it is almost impossible for the attacker cannot find SK_1.

5 Results and Discussion

To implement all the algorithms, the Java programming language is used. The encryption, decryption, and total execution time are considered as performance matrices. Two existing schemes, HLPRE [12] and ENPK [13], are used for comparisons. The experimental results show that the encryption and decryption time increases linearly as the message size increases. Figure 1a, b depict encryption and decryption times, respectively. It could be seen that HEM-SHD requires less time than ENPK and HLPRE.

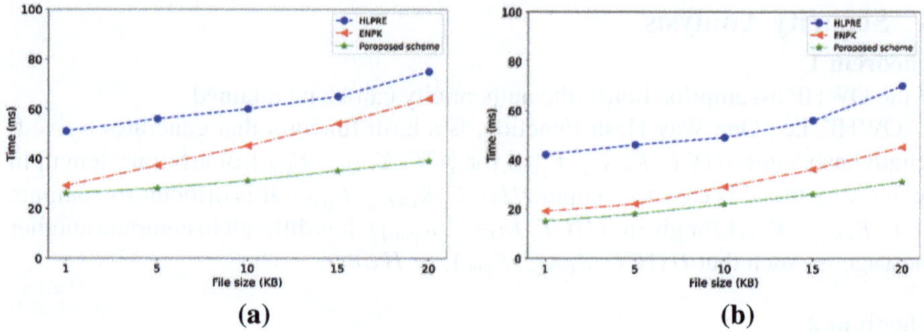

Fig. 1 **a** Encryption time and **b** Decryption time

Table 1 Total execution time

Scheme	Total execution time (ms)
HLPRE	165
ENPK	203
Proposed scheme (HEM-SHD)	134.96

As shown in Table 1, the total execution time of HEM-SHD is 134.96 ms. It incurs 62.56 ms, 23 ms, 18 ms, and 31.4 ms in total for key generation, encryption, decryption, and sign generation and verification, respectively.

6 Conclusions

In this paper, HEM-SHD employs a central management authority, responsible for user registration and key generation. In this model, symmetric encryption is employed to safeguard healthcare data, while asymmetric encryption ensures the secure transmission of symmetric encryption key. In HEM-SHD, ECC-based digital signature protects data against forgery and preserves data integrity. This approach prevents security threats like MITM, collision, and forgery attempts. Additionally, it exhibits better efficiency compared to existing solutions.

References

1. Hamouda BEHH (2020) Comparative study of different cryptographic algorithms. J Inf Secur 11:138–148
2. Kuppuswamy P, Khalidi SQYA (2014) Hybrid encryption/decryption technique using new public key and symmetric key algorithm. Int J Inf Comput Secur 6(4):372
3. Hafsa A et al (2020) An improved co-designed AES-ECC cryptosystem for secure data transmission. Int J Inf Comput Secur 13(1):118–140

4. Tayel M, Dawood G, Shawky H (2018) A proposed serpent-elliptic hybrid cryptosystem for multimedia protection. In: International conference on advances in computing, communications and informatics (ICACCI). IEEE, pp 387–39
5. Bhole D, Mote A, Patil PR (2016) A new security protocol using hybrid cryptography algorithms. Int J Comput Sci Eng 4(2):18–22
6. Coutinho RWL, Boukerche A (2020) Modeling and analysis of a shared edge caching system for connected cars and industrial IoT-based applications. IEEE Trans Industr Inf 16(3):2003–2012
7. Suganya S (2014) Enhancing security for storage services in cloud computing. IEEE Curr Trends Eng Technol 3(6):283–287
8. Das S, Namasudra S (2022) A novel hybrid encryption method to secure healthcare data in IoT-enabled healthcare infrastructure. Comput Electr Eng 101
9. Alemami Y, Mohamed MA, Atiewi S (2023) Advanced approach for encryption using advanced encryption standard with chaotic map. Int J Electr Comput Eng 13(2):1708
10. Qian Q, Jia Y, Zhang R (2016) A lightweight RFID security protocol based on elliptic curve cryptography. Int J Netw Secur 18(2):354–361
11. Sowjanya K, Dasgupta M (2020) A ciphertext-policy attribute based encryption scheme for wireless body area networks based on ECC. J Inf Secur Appl 54:1–10
12. Khashan OA (2020) Hybrid lightweight proxy re-encryption scheme for secure fog-to-things environment. IEEE Access 8:66878–66887
13. Thirumalai C, Mohan S, Srivastava G (2020) An efficient public key secure scheme for cloud and IoT security. Comput Commun 150:634–643

Multimodal Face Recognition System Using Hybrid Deep Learning Feature

Pradeep Kumar Jena, Bonomali Khuntia, Sarbajit Mohanty, and Charulata Palai

1 Introduction

All organizations need an attendance management system to track the attendance of their employees either manually or automatically. Daily attendance of a class is essential for performance assessment and quality monitoring [1, 2]. Naming or signing are traditional methods in most organizations that are time consuming and insecure. On the other hand, most automated human identification systems rely on traditional methods such as fingerprints, passwords and id scans [3]. However, all these methods have several limitations, such as forgetting a password or losing an id. Therefore, the most suitable method for complete security and historical data storage is an intelligent facial recognition and emotion classification [4, 5]. It is a rapidly growing field, and plays an important role in security and authentication. Transfer learning is a form of machine learning where the pre-trained models are again trained for a specific task to save time and enhance performance [6]. In this work, we present an attendance system using face detection through deep learning [7]. Here the transfer learning applied on three pre-trained convolutional neural networks and trained them with our data containing 31 different classes with 2562 face images in each class. The three networks showed very high performance in terms of high prediction accuracy and reasonable training time. Face detection and recognition applications help to find out if the face found on the camera matches the compiled database [8, 9]. CCTV

P. K. Jena (✉) · S. Mohanty · C. Palai
Department of Computer Science and Engineering, NIST Institute of Science and Technology, Berhampur, Odisha 761008, India
e-mail: pradeep@nist.edu

C. Palai
e-mail: charulata@nist.edu

B. Khuntia
Department of Computer Science, Berhampur University, Bhanjabihar, Berhampur, Odisha 760007, India

K. Kumar Singh et al. (eds.), *Machine Vision and Augmented Intelligence*, Lecture Notes in Electrical Engineering 1211, https://doi.org/10.1007/978-981-97-4359-9_19

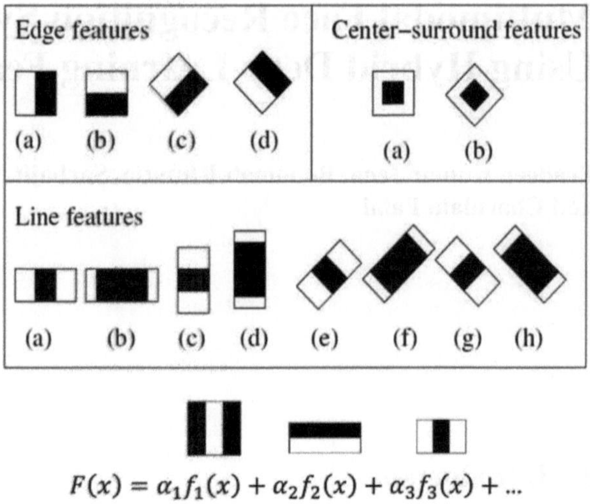

Fig. 1 Viola Jones's approach for Haar feature extraction [15]

is also used as a facial recognition camera in many places. Nowadays most of the school, college, hospital, and banks are having CCTV camera based surveillance systems. The real time face recognition can be helpful for attendance purpose and track the persons within the campus [10–12]. As all the face images are captured simultaneously in a group photo in an unconstrained environment [13], the orientation of the faces of the persons will be different that generate multimodal face images [14], moreover the size of the faces will differ as the persons stand away from the camera. So we have used the Haar feature and deep learning feature in this work.

1.1 Haar Features Extraction

Haar features are similar to this convolution kernel which is used to detect the presence of that feature in the given image. Each feature results in a single value which is calculated by subtracting the sum of pixels under white rectangle from the sum of pixels under black rectangle. The Fig. 1 shows the templates used for Haar features using Viola Jones Algorithm [15].

1.2 Deep Learning Architecture

Deep learning possesses the capability to automatically extract crucial features from extensive image datasets. It is important to recognize that deep learning fundamentally remains a variant of neural networks. Common deep learning models encompass the autoencoder [16], its extensions, and the convolutional neural network, which comprises multiple restricted Boltzmann machines.

These models are characterized by their hierarchical structure, numerous parameters, and substantial capacity, enabling them to better capture the inherent characteristics of the image dataset. Furthermore, deep learning exhibits the advantage of seamlessly integrating both the classifier and feature extraction within a unified framework, which is useful for image classification and image retrieval [17, 18]. The convolution and pooling operations are shown in Figs. 2 and 3 respectively.

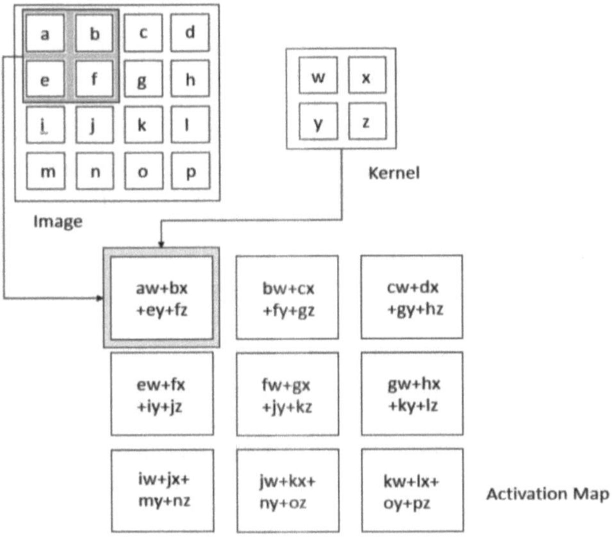

Fig. 2 Convolution operation

Fig. 3 Pooling operation

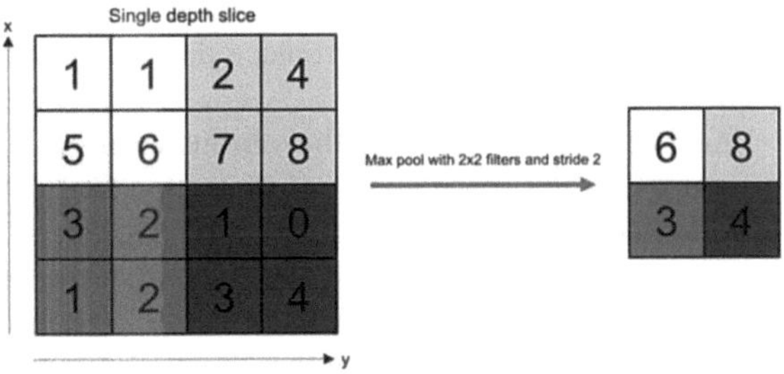

2 Liturature Survey

Alhanaee et al. [1] Proposed deep learning-based face detection, the authors used transfer learning using three pre-trained convolutional neural networks i.e. Squeeze-net, Google-net, and Alex-net. It is observed that the validation accuracy of Squeeze-net and Alex-net are more efficient than the Google-net. Jena et al. [4] proposed a NIR face detection model, which is tested with CASIA NIR face database. Here a feature fusion technique is proposed by combining the LBP and S-Sub-band of SVD features. It is observed that the performance of the proposed fused feature is better than that of the LBP and SVD feature; moreover the image retrieval performance using Chi-square distance is better than other distance measures. Verma et al. [5] presented a novel approach for multimodal fusion of information from a large number of channels i.e. Electroencephalogram (EEG), Galvanic skin response (GSR), blood volume pressure, respiration pattern, skin temperature, electromyogram (EMG) and electrooculogram (EOG) as given in the DEAP database to classify and predict emotions using four different classifiers such as SVM, MLP, KNN and MMC. Discrete Wavelet Transform, a classical transform for multi-resolution analysis of signals has been used for this study. Rouhsedaghat et al. [6] proposed a high-performance data-efficient low-resolution face recognition model called LRFRHop for resource-constrained environments. Here an emerging machine learning method i.e. Successive Subspace Learning (SSL) is used for an explainable non-parametric feature extraction submodel that flexibly deals the model size for the performance verification. Moreover the author claims that active learning can be conveniently incorporated to reduce the labeling cost. The effectiveness of the LRFRHop is verified using the LFW and the CMU Multi-PIE datasets. Sutabri et al. [9] introduced a Convolutional Neural Network to detect a face, i.e. Dlib's CNN or deep metric learning for facial embedding, and K-NN to classify faces, the system successfully recognises the face of a student who is making an attendance. Student data that has been identified in the form of the student's ID number, date and time, is used by the system to record student attendance. This system makes the student attendance process done automatically and is expected to be able to replace the old manual attendance process, which is currently used.

Patel et al. [10] discussed the various issues to design an automated attendance system using the traditional face detection and CNN based face detection. This includes the selection of suitable training dataset, selection of proper CNN architecture for feature extraction, and computational time to provide a real time solution. Ben Fredj et al. [13] used transfer learning to train the Res-Net 100 model for face recognition. The authors claim that the model is trained of face images in different conditions and different locations of the LFW face dataset, and it's performance is compared with the accuracy of FaceNet. Ding et al. [14] presented a comprehensive deep learning framework used to jointly learn face representation from the multimodal information. They proposed a deep learning structure consisting of a set of convolutional neural networks (CNNs), followed by three-layer stacked auto-encoder

(SAE). The set of CNNs extracts the complementary facial features from the multimodal data. Then, these features are concatenated to produce a high-dimensional feature vector and these dimensions are compressed by SAE. The proposed model performance is tested using CASIA-WebFace database.

The main objective of this paper is to develop multimodal face recognition based automated attendance system from group photos. In order to assure the quality of the face recognition the proposed model is restricted only to the frontal face images for the training and testing i.e. for the face detection both the eyes must be visible of a face image in the group photo.

3 Methodology

A face recognition problem (in computer vision) can be formulated in the following general statement: identify or authenticate one or more people in a scene based on certain images or video images using a database of stored faces. The solution mainly includes face segmentation (face detection), feature extraction, detection or verification of the face region. The structure of the face recognition system is shown in fig below and consists of steps such as image preprocessing, face recognition, face normalization, feature extraction (and feature reduction in complex face recognition systems), and classification. Our dataset is a collection of 2562 images. The data was classified into 31 classes, each individual class includes 30–120 images. Those 31 classes represent people from both genders. The collected data is used in a JPG file formatting. The image sizes are ranging between 9.0 and 15.0 KB. Each network has a different input size.

Therefore, we had to resize the images to the corresponding input dimensions of the network. AlexNet uses 227 × 227, while VGG16 uses 224 × 224. The collected data is used in a JPG file formatting. The image sizes are ranging between 90.0 and 400.0 KB. Each network has a different input size. Figure 4 shows the steps of face detection, feature extraction and face recognition using deep learning. Therefore, we had to resize the images to the corresponding input dimensions of the network. SqueezeNet and AlexNet use 227 × 227, while VGG16 uses 224 × 224. Figure 5 shows the model it using 224 × 224 as dimensions and 3 channels.

The standard procedure for training a neural network through transfer learning commences with adjustments to the parameters associated with the base architecture. This involves the selection of appropriate values for key parameters such as the learning rate, training duration, number of epochs, and validation frequency. If the initial learning rate is set too low, it may lead to training stagnation, whereas excessive high rate learning can reduce the training process unstable, hence a suboptimal weight convergence to be learned by the system during training. As a solution, we opted to employ the VGG16 architecture for our model training. An epoch signifies a single training cycle in which the model encounters the entire training dataset. This dataset was randomly divided into two segments: 70% of the data served as the training

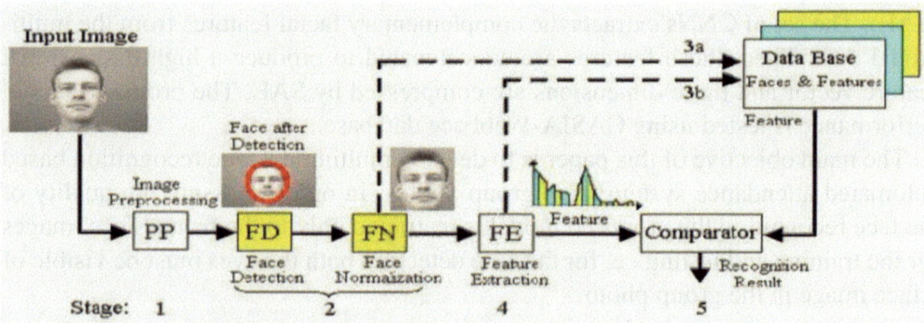

Fig. 4 Deep learning model for face recognition [14]

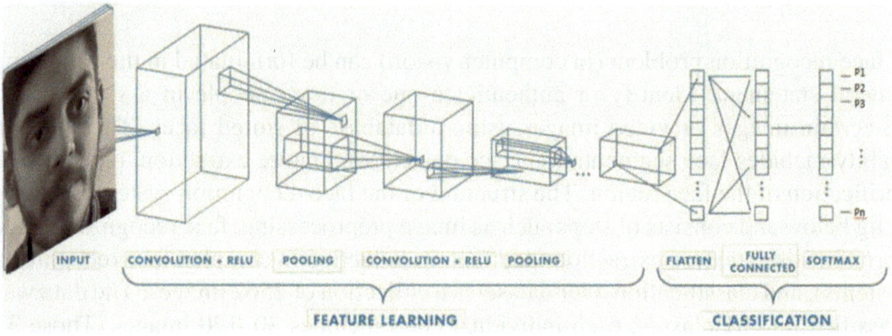

Fig. 5 Architecture of the proposed face recognition system

subset, while the remaining 30% was allocated for validation purposes. Figure 6 shows the architecture of the proposed face recognition model.

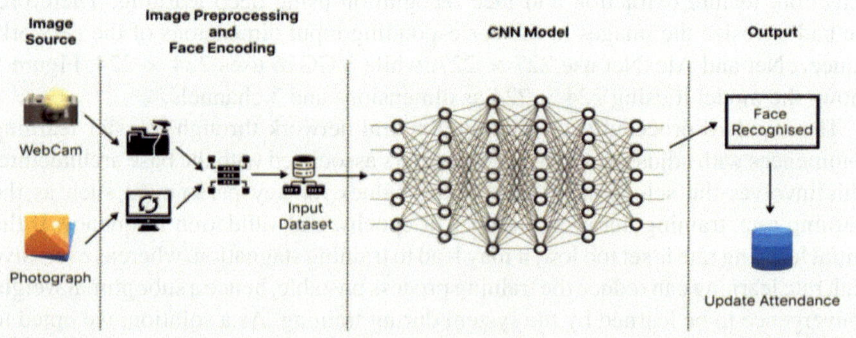

Fig. 6 Architecture of the proposed face recognition system

4 Results and Discussion

The proposed face recognition model is developed and trained using 2562 face images of 31 persons. For each epoch, 81 steps and 20 validation steps were performed and a total of 20 epochs were performed. We achieved an accuracy of 95% with a loss of 16% using the proposed CNN architecture to train the model which is fast and gives better accuracy. Figure 7 shows the training and validation accuracy, which shows the model is mostly stable after 30 epochs. Figure 8 shows the loss value with each epoch.

Figure 9 shows the Receiver Operating Characteristics (ROC) curve analysis and Figure show the recall versus precision curve for individual subjects (see Fig. 10).

Figure 11 shows the face detection in a group photo. Figure 12 presents the individual person identified by the face recognition system. The class-wise performance analysis is shown using a confusion matrix in Fig. 13. The validation performance

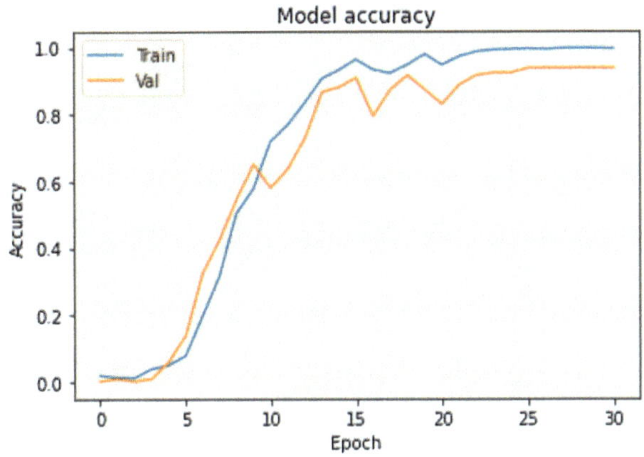

Fig. 7 Training accuracy of the proposed model

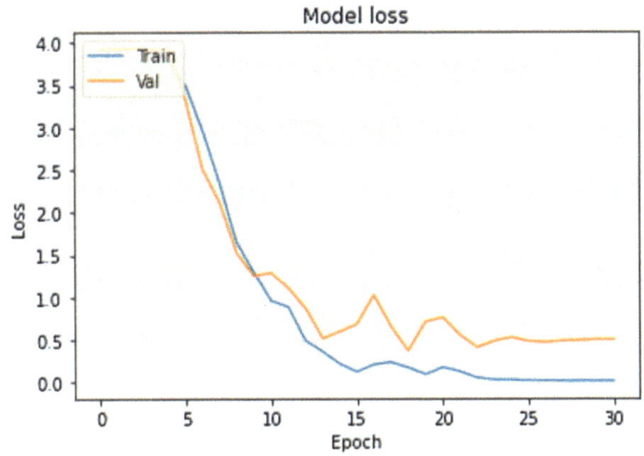

Fig. 8 Loss versus epoch graph

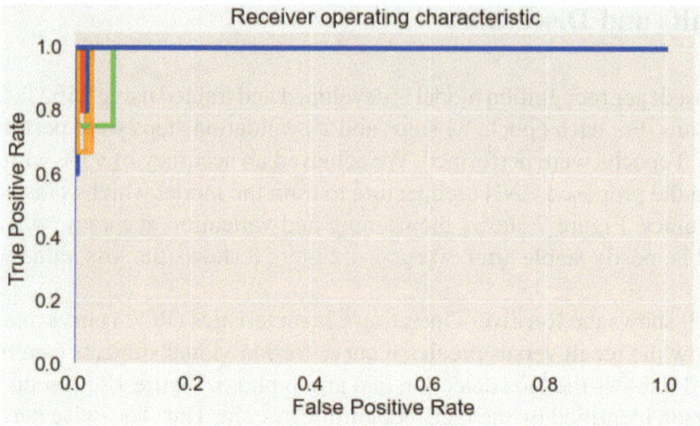

Fig. 9 Receiver operating characteristics of the proposed model

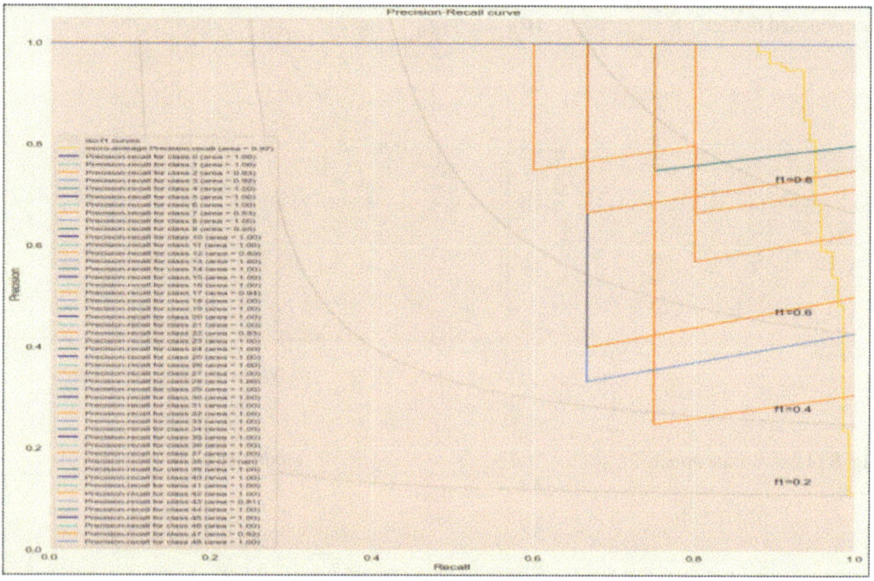

Fig. 10 Precision-recall curve of the proposed face recognition system

such as precision, recall and f1-score values and support i.e. the number of images given for each class are shown in Fig. 14.

Fig. 11 Detection of faces from a group photo

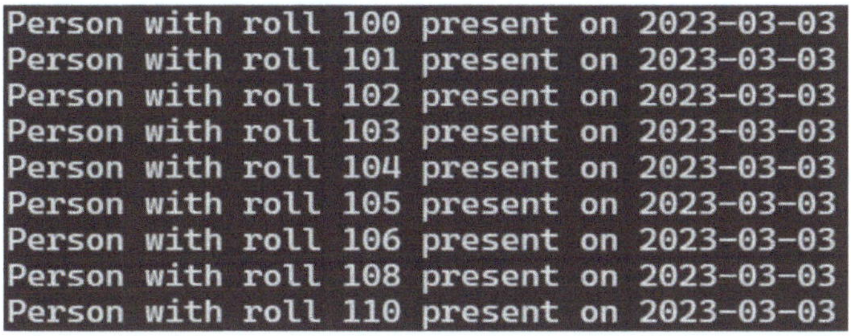

Fig. 12 Attendance update

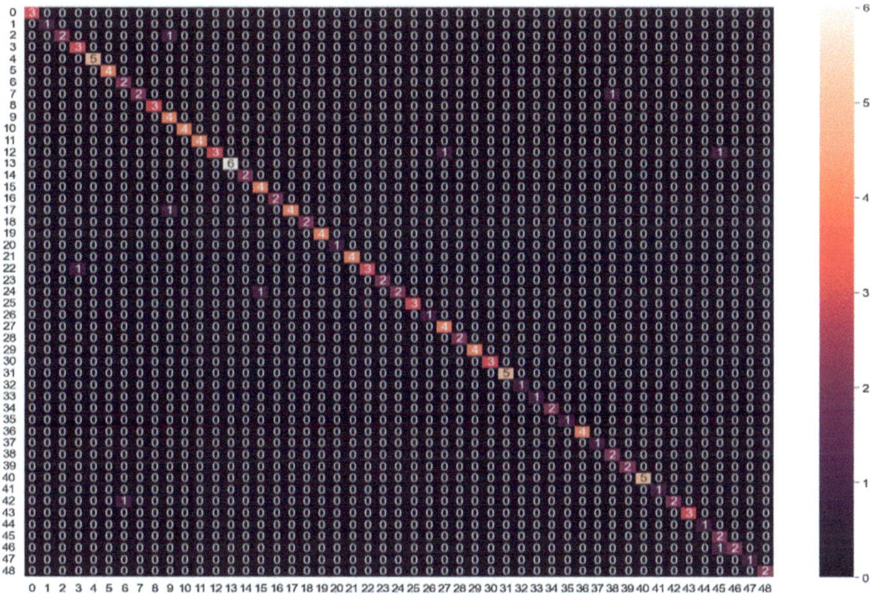

Fig. 13 Confusion matrix of the proposed model

Fig. 14 Performance matrix of the proposed face recognition system

classification_report

	precision	recall	f1-score	support
0	1.00	1.00	1.00	3
1	1.00	1.00	1.00	1
2	1.00	0.67	0.80	3
3	0.75	1.00	0.86	3
4	1.00	1.00	1.00	5
5	1.00	1.00	1.00	4
6	0.67	1.00	0.80	2
7	1.00	0.67	0.80	3
8	1.00	1.00	1.00	3
9	0.67	1.00	0.80	4
10	1.00	1.00	1.00	4
11	1.00	1.00	1.00	4
12	1.00	0.60	0.75	5
13	1.00	1.00	1.00	6
14	1.00	1.00	1.00	2
15	0.80	1.00	0.89	4
16	1.00	1.00	1.00	2
17	1.00	0.80	0.89	5
18	1.00	1.00	1.00	2
19	1.00	1.00	1.00	4
20	1.00	1.00	1.00	1
21	1.00	1.00	1.00	4
22	1.00	0.75	0.86	4
23	1.00	1.00	1.00	2
24	1.00	0.67	0.80	3
25	1.00	1.00	1.00	3
26	1.00	1.00	1.00	1
27	0.80	1.00	0.89	4
28	1.00	1.00	1.00	2
29	1.00	1.00	1.00	4
30	1.00	1.00	1.00	3
31	1.00	1.00	1.00	5
32	1.00	1.00	1.00	1
33	1.00	1.00	1.00	1
34	1.00	1.00	1.00	2
35	1.00	1.00	1.00	1
36	1.00	1.00	1.00	4
37	1.00	1.00	1.00	1
39	0.67	1.00	0.80	2
40	1.00	1.00	1.00	2
41	1.00	1.00	1.00	5
42	1.00	1.00	1.00	1
43	1.00	0.67	0.80	3
44	1.00	1.00	1.00	3
45	1.00	1.00	1.00	1
46	0.50	1.00	0.67	2
47	1.00	0.67	0.80	3
48	1.00	1.00	1.00	1
49	1.00	1.00	1.00	2
accuracy			0.94	140
macro avg	0.96	0.95	0.94	140
weighted avg	0.96	0.94	0.94	140

5 Conclusion

Developing a reliable face recognition system remains a major challenge for computer vision and pattern recognition researchers. The reasons for the recent increase interest in facial recognition, including the growing public concern about security, the need for identity verification in the digital world, facial analysis, and modeling techniques for managing multimedia data. This paper proposed a face detection and recognition system using a deep learning approach from group photographs. Here the face detection is restricted to only the frontal face images. Major challenges in face recognition using group photo is the size of the face becomes smaller as the person goes away from the camera, which results a low resolution face image. Finding the face features from a low resolution image for the face recognition is difficult for the classifier. To deal with the multimodal and multi-resolution face images in this work we have proposed a face recognition system using deep learning and the Haar feature of the face image. The average accuracy of the proposed model is 96% here we have used 30 epochs to train the model. Further analysis can be done for the person identification using side face images.

Acknowledgements We would like to acknowledge that the research work presented in this paper was conducted at Computer Vision Lab, NIST Institute of Science and Technology (Autonomous), Berhampur.

References

1. Alhanaee K, Alhammadi M, Almenhali N, Shatnawi M (2021) Face recognition smart attendance system using deep transfer learning. Procedia Comput Sci 192:4093–4102
2. Wang M, Deng W (2021) Deep face recognition: a survey. Neurocomputing 429:215–244
3. Sahu SK, Sahani S, Jena PK, Chattopadhyay S (2012) Fingerprint identification system using tree based matching. Int J Comput Appl 53(10)
4. Jena PK, Khuntia B, Anand R, Patnaik S, Palai C (Jan 2020) Significance of texture feature in NIR face recognition. In: 2020 first international conference on power, control and computing technologies (ICPC2T). IEEE, pp 21–26
5. Verma GK, Tiwary US (2014) Multimodal fusion framework: a multiresolution approach for emotion classification and recognition from physiological signals. Neuroimage 102:162–172
6. Rouhsedaghat M, Wang Y, Hu S, You S, Kuo CCJ (2021) Low-resolution face recognition in resource-constrained environments. Pattern Recogn Lett 149:193–199
7. Yu C, Pei H (2021) Face recognition framework based on effective computing and adversarial neural network and its implementation in machine vision for social robots. Comput Electr Eng 92:107128
8. Patil V, Kapadia K, Khokrale A, Jain P (Apr 2020) Intelligent college attendance system using image tagging. In: Proceedings of the 3rd international conference on advances in science & technology (ICAST)
9. Sutabri T, Pamungkur AK, Saragih RE (2019) Automatic attendance system for university student using face recognition based on deep learning. Int J Mach Learn Comput 9(5):668–674
10. Patel B, Patil V, Pawar O, Pawaskar O, Mahajan JR (2022) Attendance system using face recognition library. In: Applied information processing systems: proceedings of ICCET 2021. Springer Singapore, pp 247–254

11. Pooja GR, Poornima M, Palakshi S, Varma MBP, Krishna AN (2010) Automated attendance system using image processing. Int J Adv Netw Appl
12. Ahmedi A, Nandyal S (2015) An automatic attendance system using image processing. Int J Eng Sci (IJES) 4(11):1–8
13. Ben Fredj H, Bouguezzi S, Souani C (2021) Face recognition in unconstrained environment with CNN. Vis Comput 37:217–226
14. Ding C, Tao D (2015) Robust face recognition via multimodal deep face representation. IEEE Trans Multimedia 17(11):2049–2058
15. Kukharev G, Kuźmiński A (2003) Techniki biometryczne. Część 1. Metody Rozpoznawania Twarzy. Pracownia Poligraficzna WI PS, 310 s., Szczecin
16. Palai C, Jena PK, Pattanaik SR, Panigrahi T, Mishra TK (2023) Content-Based image retrieval using encoder based RGB and texture feature fusion. Int J Adv Comput Sci Appl 14(3)
17. Palai C, Jena PK, Khuntia B, Mishra TK, Pattanaik SR (2023) Content-based image retrieval using adaptive CIE color feature fusion. Revue d'Intelligence Artificielle 37(1):63
18. Jena PK, Khuntia B, Palai C, Pattanaik SR (Mar 2019) Content based image retrieval using adaptive semantic signature. In: 2019 IEEE 5th international conference for convergence in technology (I2CT). IEEE, pp 1–4

Classification of Copy and Move Image by Using HELM-FSK Method: An Efficient Approach

Mahesh K. Singh, Sanjeev Kumar, V. Satyanarayana, and Durgesh Nandan

1 Introduction

Due to the probability of additional modifications in forged locals or areas, detection of area duplicates is difficult. These additional modifications include blurring of the regions generated, adding noise to the field, geometric changes, scaling, etc. [1, 2]. These advances are intended to interfere with the complicated detection process. This highlights an important need for the professional identification of copy movements that are strongly inflamed, obscure, and other geometrical shifts. This thesis examines the use of location recognition for copy transfer forgery. The idea of image forgery is hidden from the object. This definition was only processed by pasting similar characteristics into the same picture [3]. In some cases, the picture of the classification is replaced by forgery traces. Figure 1 shows the difference between the normal picture and the fake picture.

The above-mentioned Copy-Move fake describes the connection between the copied and the authenticated piece. An effective detection is determined by the principle of defining this classification relationship [4]. The estimated image structure allows the image of the classification to be found when it is saved in JPEG standards. In this chapter, the most basic and obvious techniques establish a strategy for the detection and concentration of duplicated regions in an image. The movement of copies and splitting definitions was categorized according to the kind of passive detection of classification. The classical copy moves fake algorithms, followed simply by a sequence called block tiling, extraction, matching features, and verification. By insulation of the same image into different substrates, the usual frayed area or regions

M. K. Singh · S. Kumar · V. Satyanarayana
Department of ECE, Aditya University, Surampalem, India
e-mail: vasece_vella@aec.edu.in

D. Nandan (✉)
School of CS & AI, SR University, Warangal, India
e-mail: durgeshnandano51@gmail.com

K. Kumar Singh et al. (eds.), *Machine Vision and Augmented Intelligence*, Lecture Notes in Electrical Engineering 1211, https://doi.org/10.1007/978-981-97-4359-9_20

Fig. 1 **a** Original image. **b** Copy-move forgery

can be identified in an original image [5]. After the identification is completed, the characteristics extracted are matched to identify the corresponding function vectors in the same regions of the image. An efficient algorithm is needed to define such a method [6].

Image forensics is a well-established discipline in which photographs of special conditions are analyzed to create confidence and honesty. Due to many real-time application executions in various fields, the domain is quick and better-known, including intelligence, Sports, legitimate government, news reporting, and medical imagery [7]. By changing image attributes such as luminosity, darkness, or image parameters or by concealing data an image may be distorted. Picture classification means changing the digital image into useful or relevant data. It can simply be described as the insertion or disposal process of the specific features of an image without evidence of change and avoidance for malicious purposes [8, 9]. The altered image part of the authenticated image is often difficult to identify. For the originality and preservation of truthfulness, identification of a forged image is important. A forgery detection that tries to obscure the color hue of the changes in the image's lighting. To achieve separate textures and edge-based characteristics by consolidating data from material science and statistical illumination in image regions [10].

2 Related Work

New copy-move forgery detection architecture is built through the use of versatile division and feature point coordination. The proposed system plot makes forgery detection methods both block-based and keyboard-based. However, by separating the host input image into non-overlapped and irregular blocks, the proposed flexibility over the division is proposed [11, 12]. Thus, the component centers, organized to recognize the highlighted features that display effective classification detection from each block, are expelled from each block. The main point-based characteristics are Mirror Reflection Invariant Fake detection function and Kd-tree to fit similarity to reduce high dimensionality [1, 13]. It is used to estimate the relative variations of characteristics by gradually defining additional key points, hysteresis, threshold, and morphological operations. To assess the relative transition, the algorithm selects non-collinear key points from all likely pairs [3, 14]. The execution of an evaluation of the f-measure and retrieval, compared to other algorithms, is performed on the CASIA datasets.

An interesting point detector is proposed along with SIFT and KD-Tree descriptors to balance the similarity of copy-move classification. The Harris detector is used primarily to determine places where the signal variations occur in one or two directions [15]. The KD-tree is used to classify the close neighbors, and it pre-processes the data for a comprehensive range query structure. With low false-negative rates, less detection time, and a matching similarity according to the threshold values, the experimental results achieve reliable results [16]. The identification of images of classification with multiple cloning is seen. Analyzed swarm intelligence copy-move forgery segmentation. Swarm Intelligence is initially chosen to determine the perfect parameter for each sheet. The input image is divided primarily into a smooth and rough layer. The SI algorithm is used for the identification of forgery area parameters by keyboard location according to the SIFT scheme. SIFT and SI are divided into portions to differentiate between the smooth, raw regions and each layer of the test picture. The results show that the picture forgery in smaller or smoother areas is distinguished by a high positive false rate [4, 17]. The results show the prophesized results.

An algorithm to detect and locate images is proposed. The image is obtained through the composition of the image, which can discern traces of multiple devices. CNN is performed to remove features from image patches for the characteristic camera models. Iterative clustering techniques are used to identify the characteristics based on image classification as fiction or authentication of the image [5, 18]. The outcomes of the success are assessed and the results indicate an effective accuracy and true negative rates. However, they create the first network layer with an essential high-performance channel collection and distinguish the copy-move forgery similar to the splicing detection process. The forgery was proposed by using local Convolutionary features [19, 20]. The so-called local features recognize signature abnormalities in various regions to identify forged areas, while the data taken are based on Convolutional local features to detect key points. The evidence shows that the Convolution Kernel Network performs competitively at high rating accuracy compared to traditional local features [8].

3 Methodology for Image Detection HELM-FSK

Here, classifying the authentic and the annoyance picture using a novel HELM-FSK has been proposed. The proposed techniques are the filter term with the median filter principle and the overlapping units are discussed before processing. The function vector is extracted from the area indicated by the object boundary detection. The wavelet transformation is also defined. With the use of this tool, the work expands the forgery detection. The similarities are calculated by DBA between vectors. The flow graph of this proposed method is characterized as demonstrated in Fig. 2.

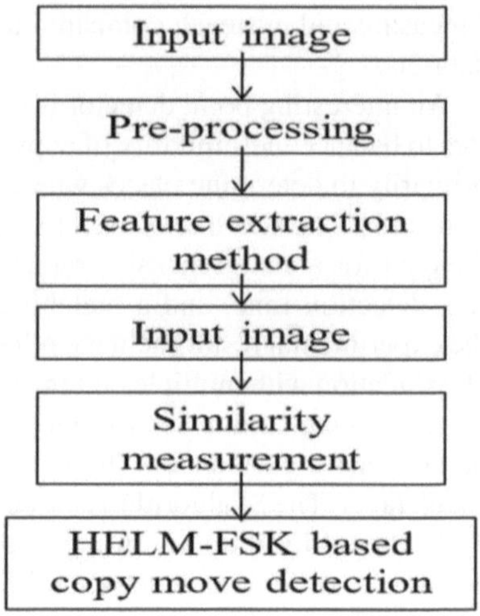

Fig. 2 The proposed method for copy-move detection using HELM-FSK

The median filter was initially used for the input image. Since the edge of the filter can also be predicted when noise is removed. Compared to other filters, it is effective. The pre-processing phase is here to eliminate the noise from the image to improve the quality of the image. Compared to the standard medium filter, the media filter has many merits, such as robustness, and a single deceptive pixel in one area would not significantly alter the median. Because of its characteristics, the critical selection of median filters does not produce new idealistic pixel values. The input pixel is processed into a median of pixel values of the neighborhoods, and then edges, to increase the accuracy of detection. The median selected is used to process the inner window and center pixel values that have been replaced by a local pixel intensity media.

The extraction method is the process used to decrease dimensionality. It is used to alter several highlighted features via the information in the picture. Function extraction requires the exact separation of features from the image and no loss of data in the image. A few image changes used as part of extraction are achieved. This is achieved. The pre-processed image can here be used for the extraction of features to improve the accuracy of detection. A Contourlet Transform (CT) was used to extract the features of the forgery image. The anisotropy and directions properties of this product are used here. Different images are extracted by some traditional device modules that produce various limitations such as inefficient computing.

The "BAT" algorithm detects the fabric image by analyzing reference and sample image similarities. Euclidean distance metrics predict that the image function vectors are similar and are defined as:

$$E_{OP_1,DP_1} = \sqrt{(V_{P1} - V_{P2})^2} \tag{1}$$

Table 1 The important formulation used for copy-move forgery detection

S. no.	Calculated parameter	Formulation
1	Accuracy	Accuracy (Acc) $= \frac{(T_p+T_n)}{(T_p+F_n+T_n+F_p)}$
2	Specificity	Specificity (Spc) $= \frac{(T_n)}{(T_n+F_p)}$
3	Precision	Precision$(p) = \frac{(T_p)}{(T_p+F_p)}$
4	Recall	Recall$(r) = \frac{(T_n)}{(T_n+F_p)}$
5	F-measure	$F -$ Measure $= 2\frac{(p.r)}{(p+r)}$
6	Sensitivity	Sensitivity (Sen.) $= \frac{(T_p)}{(T_p+F_n)}$

where 'VP1' and 'VP2' are denoted as feature vectors of 'OP1'. OP1 is denoted as the original image and 'DP1' is denoted as database image.

The distance function was optimized for this proposed scheme by using the Bat algorithm to calculate efficiencies of similarity to increase the classification detection precision. The parameter, for example, G-mean, F-measure, Recall (r), Precision (p), Accuracy (Acc), Specificity (Spc), and Sensitivity (Sen) are utilized. The 'r' and 'p' are evaluated as well tested with different obstruct sizes calculated as following in tabular form (see Table 1).

In the classification process of image processing, the extreme learning machine concepts with significant invention are one component. The general merits of the design of a learning machine are highly classified. Since classification restrictions have a minimum fitness value. The latest evolutionary algorithms have been deployed. Some cases are better achieved by combining and HLEM algorithms.

4 Result and Discussion for Copy and Move Detection

In the course portion, the images of the database are pre-processed to remove impulse noise and the image is split into blocks. Finishing the pre-processing phase leads to the extraction process for the feature. Following this, a forged boundary is identified by ACS procedure, as stated in previous sections. Finally, the HELM is used to obtain the input characteristics. The data was trained here by the ELM. DE function has been used to change the input function vector weights and hidden distortions in HELM. To improve your HELM training and testing performance, the kernel feature was stated as FSK. In the storage space, the training values are stored. The values and the image checked are listed as original or falsified. 100 photos and 100 pictures are being checked here. Figure 3 shows some genuine pictures and falsified ones.

Certain efficiency metrics and numerical values of the proposed HELM-FSK system have been forecast and evaluated. For example, in HELM-FSK, of 150 images,

(a) (b)

Fig. 3 **a** Samples of the original image. **b** Samples of the original image

100 authentic and forgery images have been properly classified by the efficient extraction of their characteristics. In such instances, due to its output loss, the limits of the forgery picture were not identified. It is obvious that the HELM-FSK proposed is highly predictive than other algorithms (see Table 2).

Compared to other systems, the HELM-FSK methodology has been quite effective. The performance of the proposed methods is then less degraded with increasing images; however, the overall performance is improved in Fig. 4. The values obtained are tabled and depicted in graphical formats. The following rate of each constraint is expressed. The current methods are assessed in each parameter. The database includes 500 pictures, which are divided into each collection of 100 pictures. To estimate the output of the proposed process, each set is evaluated by parameters. The series of images have been checked and educated and the average value of their parameters is forecast (see Tables 3 and 4).

Displays the efficiency of the proposed HELM-FSK and SVM-related forgery detection systems concerning precision, sensitivity, and specificity. Thanks to the

Table 2 Performance result based on all measures for the proposed method

Input set images	No. of images	Accuracy	Precision	Recall	Specificity	Sensitivity
Set_1	100	0.91	0.85	0.92	0.99	0.82
Set_2	100	0.84	0.83	0.98	0.89	0.87
Set_3	100	0.92	0.89	0.81	0.91	0.89
Set_4	100	0.97	0.91	0.88	0.85	0.90
Set_5	100	0.90	0.95	0.92	0.95	0.97
Set_6	100	0.98	0.87	0.95	0.92	0.89
Average	100	0.92	0.88	0.91	0.91	0.89

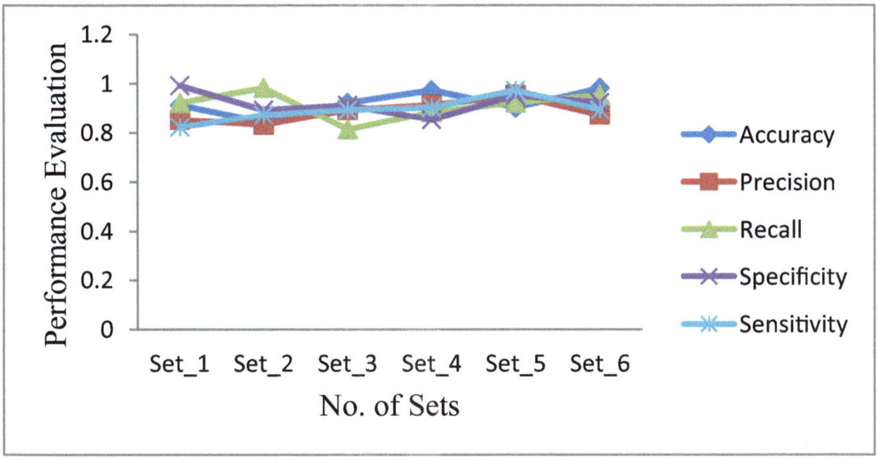

Fig. 4 Performance evolution result of different sets

Table 3 Performance result for image detection for HELM-FSK technique (proposed)

Input sets	No. of real images	No. of false images	True positive (Tp)	True negative (Tn)	False positive (Fp)	False negative (Fn)	Accuracy (Acc)	Specificity	Sensitivity
Set_ 1	100	100	92	98	2	8	95.00	98.00	92.00
Set_ 2	100	100	94	97	3	6	95.50	97.00	94.00
Set_ 3	100	100	84	96	4	16	90.00	96.00	84.00
Set_ 4	100	100	91	91	9	9	91.00	91.00	91.00
Set_ 5	100	100	96	94	6	4	95.00	94.00	96.00
Set_ 6	100	100	89	92	8	11	90.50	92.00	89.00
Total	600	600	546	568	32	54	92.83	94.67	91.00

excellent weight forecast and the SVD dependent stop running, which decreases process time and noise and improves efficiency the accuracy of the proposal is increased in Fig. 5. The proposed FSK is proven 92.8% percent accurate in all data sets, and the proposed method outside SVM systems was 84.83% percent accurate.

As an input for the classification procedure, the extracted functions are supplied to the images. At different points, the characteristics of the segmented image as a shape and texture image are calculated. To increase the classification rate, these features should be trained in classification systems. Classification is generally used

Table 4 Performance result for image detection SVM technique (Existing)

Input sets	No. of real images	No. of false images	True positive (Tp)	True negative (Tn)	False positive (Fp)	False negative (Fn)	Accuracy	Specificity	Sensitivity
Set_1	100	100	85	84	16	15	84.50	84.00	85.00
Set_2	100	100	92	83	17	8	87.50	83.00	92.00
Set_3	100	100	84	82	18	16	83.00	82.00	84.00
Set_4	100	100	86	84	16	14	85.00	84.00	86.00
Set_5	100	100	91	82	18	9	86.50	82.00	91.00
Set_6	100	100	85	80	20	15	82.50	80.00	85.00
Total	600	600	523	495	105	77	84.83	82.50	87.17

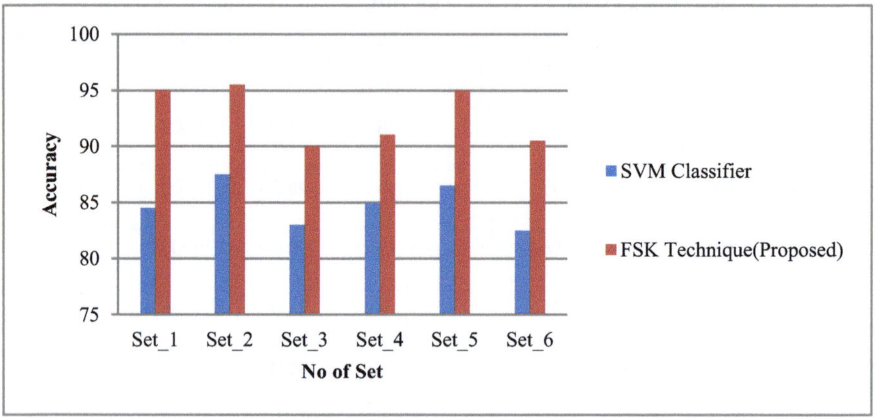

Fig. 5 Results for the proposed and existing method for accuracy comparison

to make decisions. Optimizing the Glow-worm swarm optimization to enhance accuracy optimizes the FSK weight parameter. This integrated technology has therefore been defined as improved. Due to its easy implementation and consistently high classification accuracy, the SVM approach is usual in many actual classification situations. The FSK classification results are based on the model's linear formulation, resulting in a satisfactory sparse preliminary presentation. It can therefore be generalized and deducted at low measurement costs.

5 Conclusion and Future Scope

The experimental findings conclude that the proposed HELM-FSK is ideally suited for the detection of forgery by copying and splicing images. Previous research issues such as filtering, feature extraction, rim detection, and classification are listed in every segment. Lower accuracy and sensitivity, maximum time, and low accuracy are its drawbacks. To prevent such effects, the median filter principles adjust the pre-processing stages. The median filter was used to reprocess noise reduction and to improve the image's visual appearance. Then the pre-processed image is passed to the extraction function transforming the Contourlet. Due to their directions and anisotropic properties, Contourlet efficiently processes the functions. The optimum detection of boundary values is then performed using the performance values dependent on the Active Contour. HELM-FSK approach proposed. Finally, the resemblance between the image pixels was balanced to detect the classification. The HELM-FSK classifies the tempered pictures and natural pictures effectively. In comparison with the current SVM system, the simulation results show that the Helm FSK has achieved a high efficiency. Copy moving as well as splicing classification was detected in this case, but picture color space and picture quality were not centered.

References

1. Qureshi MA, Deriche M (Feb 2014) A review on copy move image forgery detection techniques. In: 2014 IEEE 11th ınternational multi-conference on systems, signals & devices (SSD14). IEEE, pp 1–5
2. Lee JC, Chang CP, Chen WK (2015) Detection of copy–move image forgery using histogram of orientated gradients. Inf Sci 321:250–262
3. Meena KB, Tyagi V (2020) A copy-move image forgery detection technique based on tetrolet transform. J Inf Secur Appl 52:102481
4. Thirunavukkarasu V, Kumar JS, Chae GS, Kishorkumar J (2018) Non-intrusive forensic detection method using DSWT with reduced feature set for copy-move image tampering. Wireless Pers Commun 98(4):3039–3057
5. Singh MK, Kumar S, Nandan D (2023) Faulty voice diagnosis of automotive gearbox based on acoustic feature extraction and classification technique. J Eng Res 11(2):100051
6. Nandan D, Singh MK, Kumar S, Yadav HK (2022) Speaker identification based on physical variation of speech signal. Traitement du Signal 39(2):711
7. Abd Warif NB, Wahab AWA, Idris MYI, Ramli R, Salleh R, Shamshirband S, Choo KKR (2016) Copy-move forgery detection: survey, challenges and future directions. J Netw Comput Appl 75:259–278
8. Sushma K, Satyanarayana V, Singh MK (Dec 2021) A copy and move ımage forged classification by using hybrid neural networks. In: International conference on artificial ıntelligence and data science. Springer Nature Switzerland, Cham, pp 101–111
9. Kalyan MP, Kishore D, Singh MK (Dec 2021) Local binary pattern symmetric centre feature extraction method for detection of ımage forgery. In: International conference on artificial ıntelligence and data science. Springer Nature Switzerland, Cham, pp 89–100
10. Vaishnavi D, Subashini TS (2019) Application of local invariant symmetry features to detect and localize image copy move forgeries. J Inf Secur Appl 44:23–31

11. Chandana Sri K, Deepika Y, Radha N, Singh MK (Dec 2021) Using convolution networks to remove stripes noise from ınfrared cloud ımages. In: International conference on artificial ıntelligence and data science. Springer Nature Switzerland, Cham, pp 530–539
12. Silva E, Carvalho T, Ferreira A, Rocha A (2015) Going deeper into copy-move forgery detection: exploring image telltales via multi-scale analysis and voting processes. J Vis Commun Image Represent 29:16–32
13. Nandan D, Kumar K, Kanungo J, Mishra RK (Nov 2019) Compact and errorless 16-region error correction scheme for antilogarithm converter. In: 2019 ınternational conference on electrical, electronics and computer engineering (UPCON). IEEE, pp 1–5
14. Urmila S, Kumar RA, Singh MK (Dec 2021) Cardiac surveillance system using by the modified kalman filter. In: International conference on artificial ıntelligence and data science. Springer Nature Switzerland, Cham, pp 112–122
15. Zhang Z, Wang C, Zhou X (2018) A survey on passive image copy-move forgery detection. J Inf Process Syst 14(1):6–31
16. Nandan D, Mahajan A, Kanungo J (Sep 2017) An efficient antilogarithmic converter by using 11-regions error correction scheme. In: 2017 4th international conference on signal processing, computing and control (ISPCC). IEEE, pp 118–121
17. Ouyang J, Liu Y, Liao M (Oct 2017) Copy-move forgery detection based on deep learning. In: 2017 10th international congress on image and signal processing, biomedical engineering and informatics (CISP-BMEI). IEEE, pp 1–5
18. Li Y, Zhou J (2018) Fast and effective image copy-move forgery detection via hierarchical feature point matching. IEEE Trans Inf Forensics Secur 14(5):1307–1322
19. Cozzolino D, Poggi G, Verdoliva L (2015) Efficient dense-field copy–move forgery detection. IEEE Trans Inf Forensics Secur 10(11):2284–2297. Liu B, Zhang Y, He D, Li Y (2018) Identification of apple leaf diseases based on deep convolutional neural networks. Symmetry 10(1):11
20. Fang T, Chen P, Zhang J, Wang B (Aug 2019) Identification of apple leaf diseases based on convolutional neural network. In: International conference on ıntelligent computing. Springer, Cham, pp 553–564

Analysis of Energy Efficient Smart Home Based on IoT System

Mahesh K. Singh, Sanjeev Kumar, and Durgesh Nandan

1 Introduction

IoT is one of the most trending technologies in the present modern era. By using IoT one can connect and control any electronic device with the help of the internet. Wireless technology has become more popular and people are showing more interest in it. Designing smart home devices is not enough for eco-friendly users but conservation of energy is at most important key factor [1]. Automation using IOT reduces power consumption. It has wider applications. They are categorized into building, office, home, and industrial automation sectors. The home appliance manufacturers and service providers started the initiation of bringing smart homes in earlier days. The smart home devices are interconnected via wireless connections like Wi-Fi, Bluetooth, and internet [2]. There are several benefits to an Internet of Things (IoT)-based Energy Efficient Smart Home, including energy conversion, cost savings, environmental impact, remote monitoring and control, automation and optimization, data analytics, and more.

The smart home works on mainly six sensors. They are the Motion sensor, Weather sensor, Water sensor, Doorbell sensor, Light sensor, and Temperature sensor [2, 3]. Home automation techniques are based on the categories mentioned below:

1. Arduino based
2. Cloud-based

M. K. Singh · S. Kumar
Aditya University, Surampalem, India
e-mail: Mahesh.singh@aec.edu.in

S. Kumar
e-mail: sanjeev.kumar@aec.edu.in

D. Nandan (✉)
School of CS & AI, S R University, Warangal, India
e-mail: durgeshnandano51@gmail.com

K. Kumar Singh et al. (eds.), *Machine Vision and Augmented Intelligence*, Lecture Notes in Electrical Engineering 1211, https://doi.org/10.1007/978-981-97-4359-9_21

Fig. 1 Arduino hardware structure

3. Voice-based
4. Bluetooth/Pattern-based.

1.1 Arduino Based IoT System

Globally System for Mobile (GSM) is the simplest technology. This GSM protocol does not depend on mobiles. For the controlling of devices, GSM-SIM-900 and Arduino are used [3]. The relay module controls the on/off states of electronic devices [4]. Arduino is shown in Fig. 1.

1.2 Cloud Based IoT System

This type of home automation is cloud-based. This will assist the customer to feel an incursion of confidentiality, different from when a third revelry monitors their home for them. It can study input signals from numerous sensors in several places to stay in the house using RF and a support joint that is attached to multiple relays to power the home appliances [3, 5]. Cloud based IoT system is shown in Fig. 2.

1.3 Pattern-Based IoT Monitoring System

Initially, GSM module is used via SMS gateway later apple Siri is introduced. It works only on Apple mobiles but there is no application based on android mobiles. This pattern recognition helps the users to use this application in android mobiles. This system works on Bluetooth technology. To solve this challenge, Wi-Fi technology

Fig. 2 Cloud based IoT system

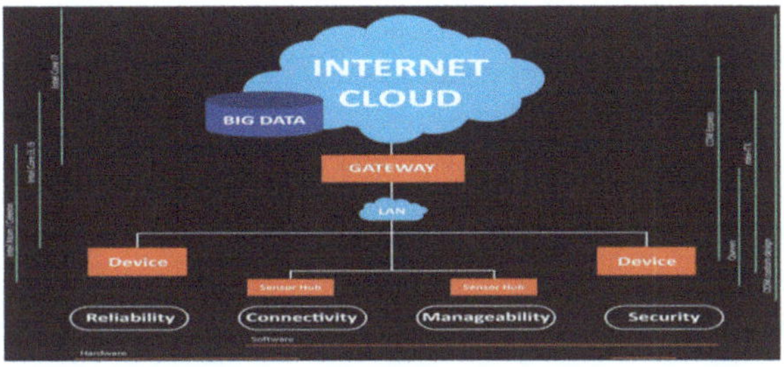

can be used for a wider scope of messages [6, 7]. Pattern-based IoT monitoring system is shown in Fig. 4.

2 Related Work for IOT Based Smart Home

Nowadays, the smart home is not adequate for the ecological cognizant consumer, but the important feature is the energy efficiency for the particular application. Designing of a prototype for controlling devices through GSM Module and Arduino is designed [8]. By using Arduino based microcontroller GSM module 900 works as an SMS gateway. The working principle of this prototype is Arduino takes the input signal from mobile through SMS and this input command passes to the relay module. This module makes the devices in on/off state [9]. It is connected to the cloud, where we can monitor our home or can be operated from any place in the world, where now a day's availability of the internet is not a big problem. It contains a base node that is cloud connected service superficially. This project is inspired by installing smart home devices and costly and its operation is also difficult. It is implemented by the Digilent Chip kit uno32 and Arduino [10, 11].

This type of automation is based on speech recognition using RF based Zig-Bee wireless communication module for low power that is comparatively not expensive [12]. This system is constructed in a manner based on these factors: easy to install, easy to operate and maintenance. This protocol works on the Zig-bee protocol, central controller module, and appliances control module. Prototype investigation can also be carried out on information composed by the sensors [13]. This will create the classification a great deal more energy efficient as it will have the capability to control Off/On equipment dynamically depending on a normal using prototype [14]. This type of operation can reduce man's effort and conserve more energy. IoT is a revolutionary technology creates a smart environment by sensors and actuators. The rapid increase of these many sensors can be seen in homeland security, military, and in industries. IoT enabled devices have been equipped with smart functionality through the use of different tools and technologies. IOT of a variety of areas like virtualized world, RFID, and artificial intelligence [15]. There are a number of problems with IoT implementation in smart homes:

Privacy and security issues.
Compatibility of protocols and devices.
Scalability problems.
Obstacles to energy efficiency.
Usability and user acceptance problems.

3 Method and Methodology for Energy Efficient IOT System

Arduin-Uno prototypes are designed for energy efficient IOT system. It is the most popular Arduino prototypes that use AT–Mega-328. This has 16 electronic in/output pins eight for analog inputs, eight of which could be used as PWM outputs, 8 MHZ crystal oscillators, USB interface, power socket IC's description, and reorganize switch. Block diagram of ARDUINO based automation system shown in Fig. 3.

SIM-900 is a complete GPRS/GSM module designed for SMT-type quad band with a very advanced and commanding chip notebook that integrates the AMR-926-EJ Score. The 32-bit ARM notebook base LPC-2148 microcontroller was linked up with a GSM module SIM-900. It is linked via USB to RS232 driver to LPC-2148.

3.1 *Voice Based IoT System*

The main objective of the wireless home automation system is to provide a method that responds to accent commands and can organize the on/off position of electrical devices, such as television, fans, light-lamps, air conditioners, etc., available in

Fig. 3 Pattern-based IoT monitoring system

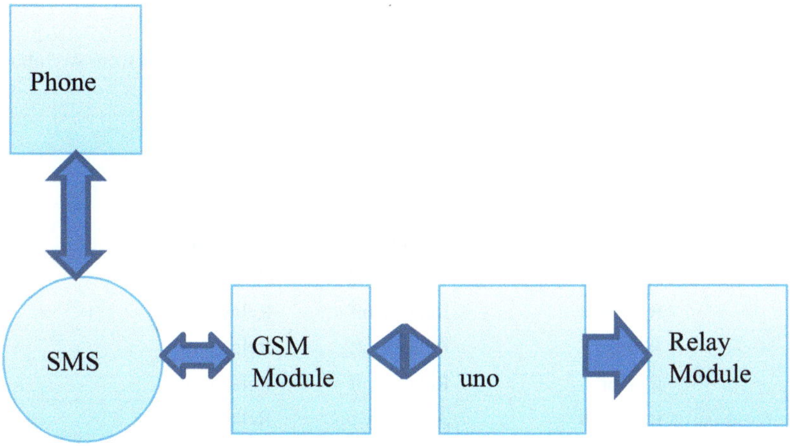

Fig. 4 Block diagram of ARDUINO based automation

the home. This type of automation based on voice-based recognition improves the security of your home [5]. Voice based IoT system is shown in Fig. 5.

The above figures show an incorporated display place for automation, monitoring, and home security. These electrical appliances are wirelessly connected to security alarms and your android mobile or any web application [5].

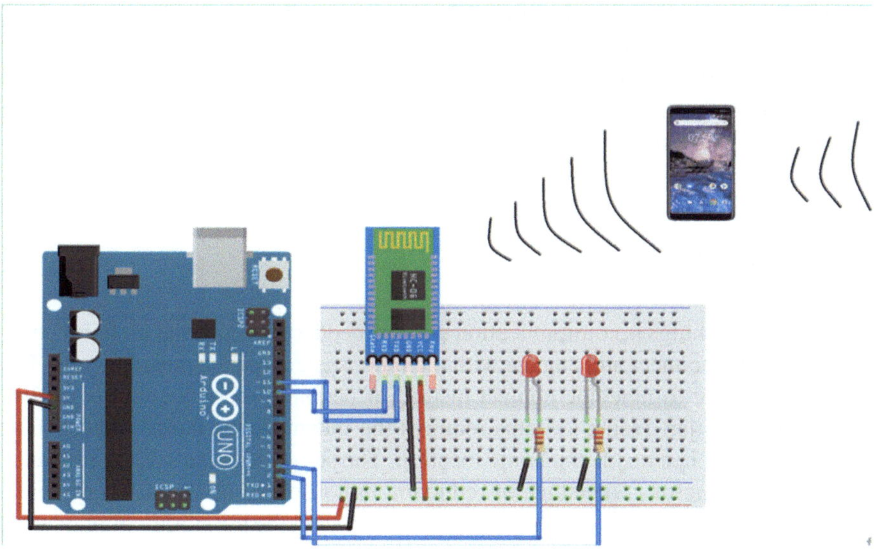

Fig. 5 Voiced base IoT system is shown

Table 1 Arduino based string data input output

s. no.	String data input	Relay output	SMS feedback from Arduino
1	R11 on	Relay 1 on	Relay 1 off
2	R12 on	Relay 2 on	Relay 2 off
3	R13 on	Relay 3 off	Relay 3 on
4	R14 on	Relay 4 on	Relay 4 on
5	R1 all on	All relay on	Relay all on
6	R11 off	Relay 2 off	Relay 1 on
7	R12 on	Relay 3 off	Relay 2 on
8	R13 on	Relay 4 off	Relay 3 on
9	R14 on	Relay 5 off	Relay 4 on
10	R1 all on	All Relay on	Relay all on

4 Result and Discussion: Static Analysis

The designs of a smart home method involve the integration of character units and their coexistence inside the environment. The smart home system application can be explained by an example. Suppose the owner expected a guest at his home but he is not there, then the help of the motion sensor detects the person and sends the information to the owner. Now he can operate the lights, fans, and television from his mobile phone. Similarly, if the person leaves the house again and receives information about the current status of his home, then he can turn off lights, fans, etc., for example, if the detected person is unknown, the commands from the owner can directly send information to the police department. The ability to control such systems in different environmental conditions can help to make the smart home more energy efficient are shown in Table 1.

5 Conclusion

The Internet of Things is communication with embedded systems that includes physical objects and connect and engage with the inner systems or the outside world. IoT relies on machine-to-machine contact instead of people-to-people communication. The design of Smart Home systems requires the integration of human being units and their coexistence inside the home location. The suggested result of the project is planned as a numerous advantage of reduction in household electrical energy bills, and holding users up-to-date on their home security with the possibility of regulating changing strategy by their accent or quick control contact on their mobile, and, last but mainly significantly, tracking their use to conserve valuable normal assets through falling electrical power expenditure.

References

1. Celtek SA, Durgun M, Soy H (2017) Internet of things based smart home system design through wireless sensor/actuator networks. In: 2017 2nd international conference on advanced information and communication technologies (AICT). IEEE, pp 15–18
2. Sehrawat D, Gill NS (2019) Smart sensors: analysis of different types of IoT sensors. In: 2019 3rd international conference on trends in electronics and informatics (ICOEI). IEEE, pp 523–528
3. Raghavan S, Girma ST (2015) Cloud based low-cost home monitoring and automation system. In: Proceedings of the 2015 ASEE north central section conference, pp 1–10
4. Nasution TH, Muhammad AM, Ikhsan S, Ulfi A, Esra C, Emerson PS (2017) Electrical appliances control prototype by using GSM module and Arduino. In: 2017 4th international conference on industrial engineering and applications (ICIEA). IEEE, pp 355–358
5. Singh MK, Singh AK, Singh N (2018) Disguised voice with fast and slow speech and its acoustic analysis. Int J Pure Appl Math 118(14):241–246
6. Alshu'Eili H, Gourab SG, Mukhopadhyay S (2011) Voice recognition based wireless home automation system. In: 2011 4th international conference on mechatronics (ICOM). IEEE, pp 1–6
7. Singh A, Ponde P (2022) Home automation: IoT. In: García Márquez FP (eds) International conference on intelligent emerging methods of artificial intelligence & cloud computing. IEMAICLOUD 2021. Smart innovation, systems and technologies, vol 273. Springer
8. Suma Priya DSV, Esther Rani D, Pavan Shankar Sai A, Konda Babu A, Nandan D (2020) Review on importance of machine learning and artificial intelligence in real life problem solving. J Comput Theor Nanosci 17(9/10):4336–4339
9. Nandan D, Singh MK, Kumar S, Yadav HK (2022) Speaker identification based on physical variation of speech signal. Traitement du Signal 39(2):711
10. Kumar K, Nandan D, Mishra RK (2019) Compact hardware of running Gaussian average algorithm for moving object detection realized on FPGA and ASIC. Revue d'Intelligence Artificielle 33(4):305–311
11. Rao EJ, Nandan D, Vijaya Krishna RV, Kumar KJ (2019) A systematic review of multipliers: accuracy and performance analysis. Int J Eng Adv Technol (IJEAT) 8(6S):965–969
12. Rohini R, Satya Narayana NV, Nandan D (2020) A crystal view on design of FIR filter. J Comput Theor Nanosci 17(9/10):4235–4238
13. Neeraja P, Nandan D (2020) Smart home by using IOT system: a succinct study. J Comput Theor Nanosci 17(9/10):4207–4212
14. Devananda Kumar G, Raju V, Nandan D (2020) A review on smart irrigation system. J Comput Theor Nanosci 7(9/10):4239–4243
15. Hemanth UMVV, Manikanta N, Venkatesh M, Visweswara Rao M, Nandan D (2021) Impact study of internet of things on smart city development. In: Kumar A, Mozar S (eds) ICCCE 2020. Lecture notes in electrical engineering, vol 698. Springer

Role of Explainable Artificial Intelligence Approaches in Cybersecurity

Nishant Bawane and Durgesh Nandan

1 Introduction

"Artificial intelligence (AI)" is a paradigm for replicating human presence, for example, categorizing earlier unseen data, projecting sales and customer behavior, and predicting future events like stock market patterns. A large part of the reason for this growth in interest is due to AI's exceptional performance in "speech recognition" and "Computer Vision (CV)". Explaining the logic is more and more important as academics concentrate on enhancing model performance. The scientific community must be prepared to respond to compelling queries like "Why didn't I receive a loan?" and to target AI models and attempt to explain the predictions they make, investigating "Explainable AI (XAI), a paradigm". Researchers have talked about the necessity to explain their models in light of various operational [1], practical [1, 2], and ethical factors. Class of Enhancing explains ability while keeping high performance is the function of XAI [2]. They proposed that XAI could be used to pick the appropriate data.

Animation methods to ensure privacy while maintaining the viability of the ML results. Announcing the data, they utilize is a strategy used by researchers to comply with the GDPR. The predictions of ML algorithms are however distorted by several common ionization strategies. As knowing the ML decisions will help in understanding and assessing bias, researchers propose that AI explaining ability could help in choosing the best unionization methods for ML algorithms. Therefore, building solutions that harness the potential of ML while preserving privacy may need the

N. Bawane
Symbiosis Institute of Technology, Pune Campus, Symbiosis International (Deemed University), Pune 411042, India
e-mail: nishant.bawane.mtech2022@sitpune.edu.in

D. Nandan (✉)
School of CS & AI, S R University, Warangal, India
e-mail: durgeshnandano51@gmail.com

K. Kumar Singh et al. (eds.), *Machine Vision and Augmented Intelligence*, Lecture Notes in Electrical Engineering 1211, https://doi.org/10.1007/978-981-97-4359-9_22

use of XAI. Deep neural networks (DNNs) can be explained using one of two major methods: Layer-wise relevance propagation (LRP) [3] and sensitivity analysis are well-known methods for LRP to perform better at identifying the most relevant pixels.

2 Literature Survey

In the field of cybersecurity research, AI models are a significant player. However, assuring the appropriate application of AI models in a cybersecurity setting is a difficult task. A thorough overview of the uses of ML in cybersecurity is given by Shaukat et al. [4]. Network security, computer security, mobile security, etc., are all examples of cybersecurity applications for AI. Techniques have been applied to a variety of datasets in line with current research trends. For this reason, we think that covering the widest range of a varied understanding of the state of "XAI" in cybersecurity. As a result, we contend that AI transparency and trust are also under the purview of cybersecurity because they help to lessen the likelihood of hostile behavior. This method is extended to the investigation of security where we talk about numerous works that either undermine the justifications or provide a defense against unexpected or unwelcome behaviors. Due to a lack of uniformity, researchers have contributed much to the expanding field of XAI. For instance, the writer's six W questions—What, Who, When, Why, Where, and How were applied in [5]. This method assisted in defining the scope of XAI and the justification for XAI, as well as Another strategy was to define XAI in terms of its inherent characteristics [6]. Paredes et al. [7] argued support for the identification of abnormalities when they are flagged by detection methods.

3 Preliminaries

Before examining the relationship between "XAI" and "cybersecurity", it defines a few key terminologies, introduces several inherently, and describes and explains the ability techniques.

A. Explainable/interpretable

Explainability (interpretability) is the capacity to convey the significance of the connections between the inputs and outputs of a model in a way that is understandable to humans [3]. Explainability (interpretability) in the XAI field refers to how well a human can comprehend an AI model's conclusion. The easier it is for people to understand.

B. Understandable

The capacity of an "AI" to help a "human" grasp how it works without having to explain its internal workings is known as understandability [8]. As it is the most prevalent strategy in the literature, explainability (interpretability) is the lens through which we discuss scientific contributions in this survey. We contend that the literature lacks maturity and lacks clear words pieces.

4 "Explainable Models"

Without the use of an external XAI method, the models in this part can explain things. The model's inherent mechanisms may be abstracted, and it can deliver information in a fashion that is understandable to humans.

A. "Linear regression models"

A modeling technique for explaining the relationship between features input and their results is "(LR)" [9]. An LR model makes use of linear approximation to compute results based on the feature inputs' weight values.

B. The logistic regression models

LR searches for a higher dimensional space that reduces the distance between each point and the hyperplane since it views classes as integers, either 0 or 1 [10, 11] is an extension of LR. In other words, classification issues cannot be effectively solved by the LR model. The procedure of logistic regression is just a straightforward interpolation; it is not reliant on probability. Consequently, linear interpolation is unable to give a useful threshold for class distinction.

C. The generalized linear model

A further development of the LR model is the generalized linear model (GLM) [12]. The GLM deals with the issue that a straightforward weight matrix in LR is likewise inadequate for real-world scenarios. While the GLM combines the weighted sum of distributes with a nonlinear system and accepts a non-Gaussian distribution, LR assumes that the target outcome follows a Gaussian distribution.

D. "The Decision Tree"

A graph that depicts occurrences of data. Finally, "DT" separates the data into several subgroups based on preset cutoff numbers (decision nodes) subset. The algorithm performs best when the data and results are nonlinear. The binary tree method permits the analysis of nonlinear data [13].

5 Explainable Classification of "Cybersecurity"

As it reviews research in three different scenarios in this section: while using justifications to increase model performance, when explanations are used to increase model transparency, and when explanations are used to address classifier mistakes.

A. "The Explanations of transparency and trust"

The main goal is to give users clear, actionable justifications for the decisions the model has made. This section is divided into different explanation categories: Global explanations, interpretable models, and substitute models.

B. Explaining with surrogate models

Proposed a semantic approach by assigning assaults and elements in sample semantics relating to confidentiality, authenticity, and unavailability (C, I, A). The three most crucial properties for each attack are extracted using a feature generator they first created. The extracted features were then given a produce new feature. They also calculated a showed the importance of the characteristic relative to the influence of "C, I, or A." Second, they developed and tested several attacks and evaluated the effects of various feature sets, those that had already been created. The CIC-IDS2017 dataset was utilized. The dataset could not be fully utilized due to resource constraints, which reduced the. The outcomes showed that, while the set of created significantly exceeded the complete set of characteristics, it also did not substantially perform poorly. A human operator may also understand how well the C, I, or A quality impacted how well the attack was categorized thanks to the generated characteristics. If the chosen to the explanation, it was disruptive. The new instance ought to be less anomalous, and ought to go down. When it came to lowering the reconstruction error, P outperformed LIME. When attempting to identify unidentified attacks, similar results were discovered the proposed method is the sole way to identify a structured query language injection. The attacks and features were simplified into three qualities, which contributed to the performance decline.

C. Global explanations

An explainable IDS was put forth that includes local justification (using the classic SHAP) with a global explanation (by modifying SHAP). The worth of each attribute, in particular, was divided into a variety of categories, and the Shapley values were used to calculate the value of each interval. After averaging the Shapley values, a comprehensive explanation was produced. SHAP provides quick computation for an explanation, but the framework is unable to provide instantaneous updates. In [4], it can determine the unfairness of a judgment by examining how a local model developed by LIME and SHAPE applies the sensitive aspects. This is one example of how the fairness of modeling can be evaluated using an explanation. A SHAP-based auto-encoder (AE)-based outlier detection approach is presented. They investigated the robustness with noise and assumed that the noise component shouldn't explain an abnormality. If the chosen to the explanation, it was disruptive. The new instance ought to be less anomalous, and ought to go down. They conducted research that used the Kdd 1999 dataset. When it came to lowering the reconstruction error, P outperformed LIME. In [14], SHAP was also utilized to clarify and analyze the classification choices made by an ML-based network IDS.

D. Interpretable models

Fig. 1 Relationship between artificial intelligence and explainable artificial intelligence

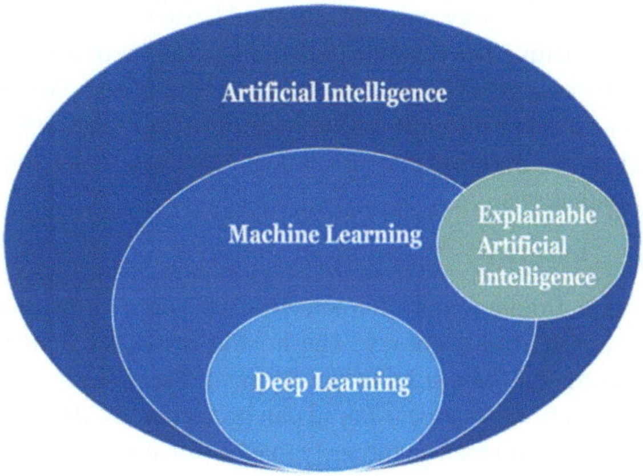

Regarding ML models for IDS, Mahbooba et al. [15].'s goal was to solve the problem of user and model trust. They emphasized that the majority of earlier studies concentrated on classifier accuracy without offering any understanding of their motivations or actions. On the KDD99 dataset, they applied the DT method [14]. They divided their research into three primary stages: feature rating, to demonstrate how the tree made decisions, however, because of the dataset's noise, their method was susceptible to overfitting (see Fig. 1).

6 Security Properties of XAI

It reviews the research on XAI security and provides several pertinent security characteristics. Fairness, integrity, privacy, and robustness are the four properties we use to describe the security of explanation techniques. Taking into account how an attacker might compromise these qualities (for example, by changing justifications for unfair treatment) might resist such attacks (for instance, by consolidating justifications against adversarial examples), within the purview of "cybersecurity".

A. Fairness

If a model's results have no bearing on a person's sensitive characteristics, then the model is said to be fair [3]. This is especially important when decision-making models have an impact on a person, like when a loan, job, insurance, or sentencing is involved. It can determine the unfairness of a judgment by examining how a local model developed by LIME and SHAPE applies the sensitive aspects. This is one example of how the fairness of modeling can be evaluated using an explanation. An agent might attempt to deceive logically if they intend to discriminate against or favour a specific group of people. This type of attack, known as fair washing, poses a significantly different threat to ML models than do traditional attacks because a fair washer is typically. The threat model benefits the attacker because, unlike the auditor, who may only have limited knowledge and no control, the attacker typically Fair washing has become prevalent., examined, and most explanation strategies have been successfully countered to date. The investigations that follow demonstrate and make it more difficult for the auditor to find fair washing. These investigations could act as a reminder that it's not appropriate to let the model owner come up with explanations.

B. "Integrity"

It is a fundamental characteristic of "data" and processes have to do with their reliability and accuracy. The hostile instances that deceive a classifier by slightly altering the feature input are atypical. Since fair washing focuses on the veracity of justifications to appear fair, it can be seen as a subset of integrity attacks. This section focuses on attacks on integrity that do not aim to be fair. Usually, an explanation can be used as a secondary source of data to fulfill a forecast. An expert might, for instance, decide using both explanation and prediction. An alteration of the expert's data (prediction, explanation) without any countermeasures showing the manipulation is hence traditional sense. Notably, the attacker's goal in fair washing is to keep the (biased) outcome while changing the explanation; are changed.

C. Privacy

Privacy of either the model or the data may be violated using XAI approaches. Although several studies have examined privacy concerns very few have concentrated on "XAI" techniques. The explanation model should also be impossible to duplicate to safeguard the anonymity of model users. An article about cloning a mod can be found in the literature. Zhao et al. [16] show how hackers may use XAI's flaws to rebuild a personal image from model justifications. An image-based model inversion attack also showed that the image reconstruction based just prediction was of poor quality, and that the quality was significantly enhanced by using one or more explanations. Their research also demonstrated approaches that led to a larger loss of privacy since they offered richer information that attackers may use against you. The authors urged more research on the trade-off between privacy and explicability (see Fig. 2).

7 Explainable Artificial Intelligence (XAI) Concept and Results

One of the few ongoing DARPA projects, XAI is anticipated to enable "third-wave AI systems," where robots learn about their surroundings and context as they go along and eventually develop the explanatory models necessary to characterize phenomena in the actual world. The XAI program focuses on the creation of numerous systems by tackling two challenge problems: (1) machine learning challenges to strategy rules for an automated vehicle to carry out a series of simulated missions. (2) machine

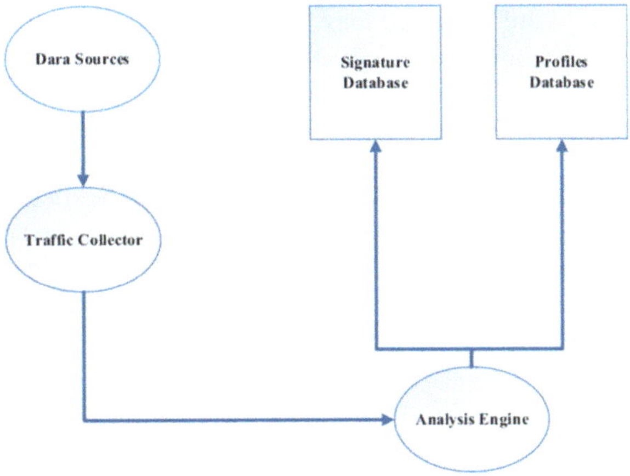

Fig. 2 "The Explainable Artificial Intelligence for Cybersecurity"

academic difficulties in classifying events that are important in heterogeneous, multimodal data. These two challenge issue domains were chosen because they combine two important deep learning methodologies (class and supervised learning) with two important practical computational problems for the DoD (spy analysis) (see Fig. 3).

Now, it discusses research directions that, encompass a range of criteria, including legal, commercial, and performance evaluation.

A. "The feature space to problem space"

When used for "cybersecurity" use cases, the reusability of XAI approaches presents a barrier that has not yet been addressed. Different forms of cybersecurity data are used by various security apps. Information regarding how security events and

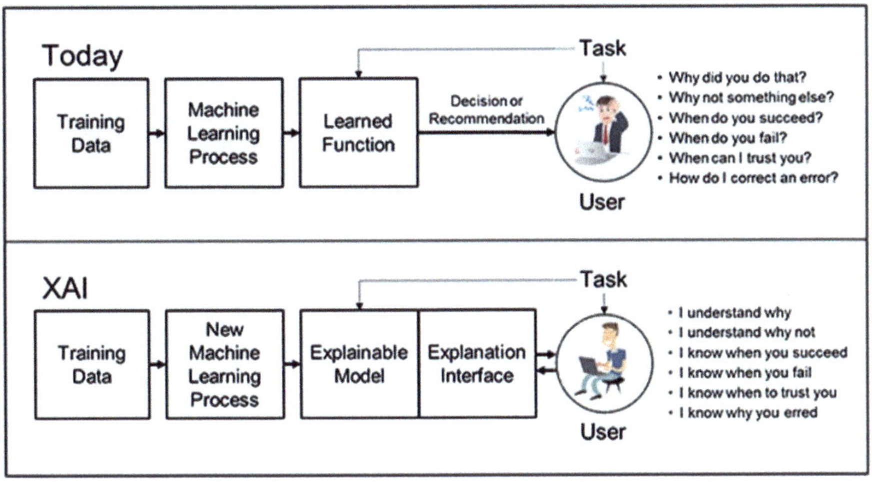

Fig. 3 "The Explainable Artificial Intelligence Concept"

assaults are organized may lost when analyzing raw safety data through ML-based classification models. In their study defined the transform translating the issue area by successfully flipping a classifier's decision output, operations over the subspace may be able to overcome the issue space's feasibility restriction. Analytical presentation of the embed vector from the deep layers and the raw properties from the input is not always possible. As a result, we discovered that there was a disparity between the interpretation presented inside the issue domain and that supplied in the feature space in the majority of ML techniques, especially in "DL" models. It is challenging to transiently establish the link between both the importance functionalities and the donation of the uncooked attributes supplied, even though layer relevance evanescent waves XAI methods like SHAP, and LIME, and that these can be employed to unveil significant features encrypted by a "Deep model" in classification.

B. Privacy versus explain ability trade

Few articles have considered the privacy issues for "XAI" approaches, as was stated in Sect. 5. Existing research has shown that some XAI approaches can be effective yet insecure and that designing an efficient XAI system and protecting privacy can conflict. The two situations that have been looked into are the "model inverting assault" as well as the "membership inference assault." the "feature estimate assault" (which involved obtaining some traits from the training examples), the "model extract attack," and other privacy assaults against AI models (which required mastering a model's approximate form), and "pattern memorization attack" (which involved retrieving the precise values of features). According to these assaults be applied to explain ability techniques used to analyze. These techniques must be modified for the XAI environment and tested to determine how well they protect model and data privacy. Last but not least, XAI provides a new layer to the Therefore, its use needs to be carefully considered. Does using a XAI technique to understand an AI model make the system more vulnerable or should it be ignored to reduce the attack surface? Therefore, it is critical to select a method that offers the optimal balance between explanatory quality and confidentiality.

C. "The Reinforcing explain-ability with external data"

Numerous methods that use "XAI" have been reported. It justifies the decisions that AI models make. The goal of techniques up to this point has been to create explanations that are solely dependent on the information and computations used by AI models. Using data sources that have not been incorporated into safety models can help make alarms more comprehensible. When security operators notice malicious activity on the Internet, they frequently check data sources, such as botnet-analyzed data and/or risk intelligence reports, to validate their discovery. Used this strategy to strengthen the AI models' ability to be explained. They built several threat intelligence search models, malware traffic detection models, sandbox analysis models, code analysis models, and darknet traffic analysis models. With thorough data, numerous security processes are automated. For instance, when malicious traffic is detected by a network analysis model, the system runs other models and compiles significant data, as well as first name, surname, habits, exploitable weaknesses, and target devices.

Even though DT in IDS has been used in earlier research, their primary concern is the accuracy of benchmarking machine learning methods. On the other hand, we concentrate on the interpretability of KDD datasets, a frequently used benchmark dataset. What we have to offer is as follows: (1) To improve trust management that human specialists can grasp, we addressed the XAI concept (2) Using the entropy measure, we examined the significance of a feature for intrusion detection. (3) To classify intrusions, we interpreted the rules that the DT technique generated. (4) We contrasted the decision tree's accuracy with that of cutting-edge techniques. To properly orient the reader, it was preferred to analyze the many surveys including these works due to the wide range of XAI techniques. A selection of works was for purposes of synthesis and relevance, giving priority to all work that proposed XAI algorithms with applications in cybersecurity. It is also impractical to incorporate all studied publications.

8 Conclusion

AI has indeed been extensively utilized to research cybersecurity, just like it has in every other field of computer science. XAI is growing in popularity and might soon be mandated for some service providers by the law. We studied the body of "XAI" literature currently accessible in the cybersecurity field from the viewpoints of "XAI" for cybersecurity objectives and the safety of XAI approaches. Even though there are several scientific studies out there at this time, we found that their techniques don't take practical situations into account. We argue that instead of simply implementing an XAI technique to a cybersecurity dataset, substantial scientific advancements should attempt to close the gap between the domains of AI and cybersecurity. Second, to put the security challenges into perspective, we categorize them into different categories and review the literature on the attack surface, current attack vectors, and prospective defenses. The state of the art indicates that there are currently no effective defenses against "XAI" approaches. To increase the security of explainable procedures, we highlighted numerous research directions, including practical considerations, privacy issues, and ethical considerations, like justice and fair washing. We say this study confirms that AI will play a significant role in upholding corporate rules and with crucial "decision-making" issues. As a result, XAI ought to ensure impartial, transparent, and equitable treatment.

References

1. Zeng Z, Zhang H, Zhang R, Yin C (2015) A novel feature selection method considering feature interaction. Pattern Recogn 48(8):2656–2666

2. Vigano L, Magazzeni D (2020) Explainable security. In: 2020 IEEE European symposium on security and privacy workshops (EuroSPW). IEEE, pp 293–300
3. Breiman L (2001) Random forests. Mach Learn 45(1):5–32
4. Bach S, Binder A, Montavon G, Klauschen F, Müller KR, Samek W (2015) On pixel-wise explanations for non-linear classifier decisions by layer-wise relevance propagation. PLoS ONE 10(7):e0130140
5. Dadi A, Berrada M (2018) Peeking inside the black box: a survey on explainable artificial intelligence (XAI). IEEE Access 6:52138–52160
6. Longo L, Goebel R, Lecue F, Kieseberg P, Holzinger A (2020) Explainable artificial intelligence: concepts, applications, research challenges and visions. In: Holzinger A, Kieseberg P, Tjoa A, Weippl E (eds) Machine learning and knowledge extraction. CD-MAKE 2020. Lecture notes in computer science. Springer, Cham, p 12279
7. Cantareira GD, Mello RF, Paulovich FV (2021) Explainable adversarial attacks in deep neural networks using activation profiles. arXiv:2103.10229
8. Boopathy A, Liu S, Zhang G, Liu C, Chen PY, Chang S, Daniel L (2020) Proper network interpretability helps adversarial robustness in classification. In: ICML'20: proceedings of the 37th international conference on machine learning, pp 1014–1023
9. Hastie T, Tibshirani R, Friedman J (2009) The elements of statistical learning: data mining, inference, and prediction, 2nd ed
10. Morgan SP, Teachman JD (1988) Logistic regression: description, examples, and comparisons. J Marriage Fam 50(4):929–936
11. Zou X, Hu Y, Tian Z, Shen K (2019) Logistic regression model optimization and case analysis. In: 2019 IEEE 7th international conference on computer science and network technology (ICCSNT), Dalian, China, pp 135–139
12. Nelder JA, Wedderburn RWM (1972) Generalized linear models. J R Stat Soc. Series A (General) 135(3):370–384
13. Navada A, Ansari AN, Patil S, Sonkamble BA (2011) Overview of use of decision tree algorithms in machine learning. In: 2011 IEEE control and system graduate research colloquium, Shah Alam, Malaysia, pp 37–42
14. Anders CJ, Pasliev P, Dombrowski A-K, Müller K-R, Kessel P (2020) ICML'20: proceedings of the 37th international conference on machine learning, pp 314–323
15. Mahbooba B, Saha R, Alosaimi W, Serrano M (2021) Trust in intrusion detection systems: an investigation of performance analysis for machine learning and deep learning models. Complexity, 1–23
16. Zhao X, Zhang W, Xiao X, Lim B (2021) Exploiting explanations for model inversion attacks. In: 2021 IEEE/CVF international conference on computer vision (ICCV), Montreal, QC, Canada, pp 662–672

A Succinct Study on the DDoS Attack Detection Methods

Dapynhunlang Shylla and Durgesh Nandan

1 Introduction

In 1995, Sun Microsystems introduced the Software Defined Network (SDN) concept towards enhancing the web security management. The concept of the network controller is no longer restricted by the constraints of hardware and software [1]. SDN is a networking technology that makes controlling diverse network resources easier. Its characteristics include flexibility, scalability, and control. Security has been a primary concern for network operators when it comes to implementing SDN. Most of the time, the security way out that are applied at central controls are focused on growing the tractability of the SDN instead of addressing the security concerns. Most of the SDN providers do not meet the requirements of the general network security regulations. This susceptibility can be misused by attackers to take off various attacks. Amongst these assaults, "Distributed Denial of Service (DDoS)" is considered the utmost shattering. It can affect service dreadful conditions and further a reduction of the network performance [2]. A "denial-of-service" (DoS) attack is an attempt to prevent genuine network service handlers from accessing it. A DDoS attack is a kind of occurrence that implements thousands of unique IP addresses and hundreds of vulnerable services to perform an occurrence. It employs a large quantity of PCs to knock down a website or server. It is very difficult to carry out in a simple and effective manner. It also uses HTTP and other bandwidth-consuming methods to overwhelm a network. It makes use of several designs, including web-based botnets and agent-handlers. A DDOS attack can be created by generating a spike in traffic to a specific server or network layer using different protocols. Flooding attacks are initiated by sending arbitrary packets containing a wide range of SYN variants. They can overwhelm the target's connection table by draining its bandwidth. Aside

D. Shylla · D. Nandan (✉)
Symbiosis International, Symbiosis Institute of Technology, Deemed University, Pune 411042, India
e-mail: durgeshnandano51@gmail.com

K. Kumar Singh et al. (eds.), *Machine Vision and Augmented Intelligence*, Lecture Notes in Electrical Engineering 1211, https://doi.org/10.1007/978-981-97-4359-9_23

from causing flooding, a multi-vector attack also uses HTTP GET flood to deal with the large volume of traffic. The attack's defense mechanism is usually deployed to prevent the victim's machine from draining its resources [1]. An attacker can easily exploit the weaknesses of the services by creating a hidden code that can be used to protect the sensitive information stored on the devices. After securing enough hosts, they use these communication channels to attack their victims. Most of the time, the most common approach to prevent a DDoS attack is by implementing various security mechanisms, for instance, network intrusion detection systems (IDS) as well as firewalls. In an information security defense mechanism that uses Open Flow technology to detect and respond to new types of attacks carried out in SDN networks. It uses the Open vSwitch, sFlow-R, and Ryu frameworks to manage traffic [1].

The DDoS attacks threaten the SDN because of the architecture difference between the networks of SDN and traditional especially the controllers of the SDN. When the network resources become unavailable to the legitimizing users then this attempt is called DDoS attack. DDoS attack on the SDN controller means disrupting the controller by sending IP packets with unsystematic shots continuously by attackers. On the way to improve the resilience, a subordinate controller was implemented. However, the secondary controller similarly becomes at risk to DDoS attacks hence a DDoS recognition mechanism was necessary [3]. This paper begins with an introduction in Sect. 1 to the concept of distributed denial of service occurrences, which are commonly used in networking. Section 2 discuss about the characteristics of the attacks and the methods used to fight them. Section 3, discuss about the various sorts of a DDoS attack against the SDN system. Section 4, shows the various set of rules that were used in the DDoS attack. Section 5 displays the outcomes, while Sect. 6 discusses future work.

2 Literature Survey

As noted in the references section, several authors have proposed various techniques for detecting DDoS attacks in SDN articles. The list of proposed techniques, both old and new, is provided below.

1. Adopting a secondary controllers [4].
2. Use of multiple controllers [5].
3. Three Open flow management tools [1].
4. Data from a single flow and data with a unique IP entropy [6].
5. ANN algorithm [7].
6. SVM (Support Vector Machine) algorithms are a set of methods that combine support vector machine algorithms [8].
7. CIC-SVM which stands for Cognitive-Inspired Computing and Support Vector Machine [9].
8. Detection trigger mechanism [10].
9. Online defense system for SDN network environments [11].

10. A Safe-Guard pattern for defending the control plane [12].

These methods still need further improvement in their detection accuracy because they were vulnerable to some other factors. However as per the paper of the authors Dong, Shi, and Mudar Sarem in 2019 mentioned in the references. In this paper to provide the guidance in the DDoS recognition, several features were proposed and the traffic flow activities with the DDoS attack were analyzed. Below are the new DDoS detection algorithm based methods proposed that prove to be effective and have maximum accuracy results.

11. DAMDL is a machine learning-based detection technique based on the degree of attack [3].

Table 1 compares the work of the 11 approaches mentioned above.

Several more methods as below presented their experiments by extracting datasets using their own approaches proposed by different authors. Some of them were considered compatible with the existing environment of SDN and some were not as shown below.

Table 1 Comparison of methods (1–11) and limitations of the existing works

Sr. no.	DDoS detection methods	Limitations
1.	Adopting a secondary controller	DDoS attacks could also affect the secondary controller
2.	Use of multiple controllers	Causing several controllers to fail in a cascade fashion
3.	Three Open flow management tools with sFlow	The operation and deployment approaches were both difficult
4.	Using the entropy-based approach can escalate the sensitivity of recognition to reveal atypical incidents	It requires a resourceful set of rules to reduce computational time and storage usage in an escalated speed system/network
5.	ANN algorithm	Their method was difficult and inefficient due to the necessity to distinguish the packet protocol
6.	Combined Support Vector Machine classification algorithms	False alarm rate was high. Low for the TCP and the UDP traffic, but high for the ICMP
7.	CIC-SVM	The precision of detection still needs to be enhanced
8.	Detection trigger mechanism	Method was vulnerable to other factors
9.	Virtual security system for SDN network environments	Improvement in the mitigation tactic targeting to lessen even more the effect agonized by legitimate operators on the procedure
10.	A Safe-Guard Scheme for protecting control plane	Method was vulnerable to other factors
11.	DDADA and DDAML methods	Need further improvements in order to apply to the real SDN environment otherwise, this method has proved to be the most effective

12. Detection using FPGA [13].

Detection Methods: The framework is implemented using the NaHiDVERC measure, which is a software and hardware-based technique. At the victim's end, the system attempts to identify DDoS attacks in real-time.

Limitations: Limited in the FPGA resources. Only for the CAIDA, DARPA, and TUIDS network datasets do we have high detection accuracy and low false positive rates.

13. Using conditional entropy [14].

Detection Methods: TFCE data sequences from real network traffic are collected, an SVM classifier is trained from the samples, and the trained SVM is then used to detect attacks by categorizing the TFCE sample data.

Limitations: It only has the ability to determine the difference between attack and normal traffic.

14. Using the cluster analysis [15].

Detection Methods: If the variables used to build the cluster exhibit dissimilarities, we may use cluster analysis to divide both regular traffic and each stage of a DDoS attack into distinct groups. Cluster analysis is used to find precursors to recognition and separate each attack step.

Limitations: Only the 2000 DARPA data set was used to analyze the technique for DDoS attacks. The proposed strategy is also required to be used to various sorts of DDoS attacks and data collection to analyze the accuracy.

15. In a huge data environment, a method based on network anomalous behavior is used [16].

Detection Methods: The method filters network flows based on flood attack characteristics, leaving only "many-to-one" network flows, which reduces interfering with ordinary network flows while increasing detection accuracy.

Limitations: The experiment is based only on the data set of the CAIDA DDoS attack 2007. Only when variables are given weights, the false alarm rate are considerably decreased, and prediction accuracy improves.

16. Linear prediction model [17].

Detection Methods: An effective and straightforward ARMA prediction model for typical network flow is developed by employing a linear prediction technique.

Limitations: The ARMA model is only appropriate for short-term predictions because of its modest prediction error variance. The detection efficiency will be reduced as a result of frequent false positives, and routine application will be disrupted.

17. Using the Semi-supervised learning model [18].

Detection Methods: Semi-supervised learning detection approach that combines spectral clustering and random forest for detecting DDoS attacks on the WEB application layer and compares it to other current detection tactics to validate the semi-supervised learning model recommended.

Limitations: Low detection rates are caused by insufficient labeled data in supervised learning algorithms, and inappropriate setup of unsupervised learning parameters causes a local optimal or bad detection effect.

18. Packet sampling and flow features utilization [19].

Detection Methods: To combat DDoS attacks, a detection mechanism system using packet sampling and flow features is utilized to ensure the transfer of normal data while blocking the flood of anomalous information.

Limitations: This method can detect the attack traffic only when the server has been attacked for a time window of 6 s.

19. Machine learning in open flow network [20].

Detection Methods: "Support Vector Machine (SVM) with Linear and Radial Basis Function kernels, K-Nearest Neighbor (KNN), Decision Tree (DTC), Random Forest (RFC), Multi-Layer Perceptron (MLP), and Gaussian Nave Bayes" were utilized to develop the software (GNB).

Limitations: Increases in the data sets test reduce the robustness of the classification process except for the SVM Linear and RBF methods.

20. Dynamic MLP-based using feature selection and feedback [21].

Detection Methods: In the training phase, a sequential classification approach was combined with MLP to select the best features, and a feedback mechanism was built to fix the detector when significant detection errors were found dynamically.

Limitations: Key drawbacks of this method

- The SBS-MLP method accepts an inferior solution but does not guarantee the identification of global optimum features.
- The feedback system may yield false-positive or false-negative results; the former may be fixed independently, while the latter has no bearing on the efficacy of detection.

21. Massive new tiny traffic movements are used in a novel DDoS attack on SDN controllers [22].

Detection Methods: On the DARPA intrusion detection data sets, the SPRT sequential probability test, a powerful statistical tool, is being utilized to evaluate the algorithms.

Limitations: Key drawbacks of this method

- It can detect the DDoS attack against the controllers and not against the Host. Entropy-based detection ED and it is ineffective.
- When the normal flows are not distributed evenly.
- When the malicious flows are distributed evenly.

22. A Fog Environment DDOS Attack Detection Methodology Based on Deep Learning [23].

Detection Methods: Deep learning is used in both the first and second models, which use a "Long Short-Term Memory (LSTM)" to distinguish between hazardous and benign data and a "Convolutional Neural Network (CNN)" to further classify data into attack categories.

Limitations: Due to the increased number of training features, these methods are still lagging in accuracy and efficiency.

3 An Overview of SDN

The "Application Plane, Control Plane, and Data Plane" are the three components of the SDN architecture. It has two interfaces, one for northbound traffic and the other for southbound traffic. SDN applications include policy implementation, network management, and security services, among other things, in the Architecture Plane. To convey network behavior to the control plane, the programmable technique is employed. The Control Plane is the logically centralized control architecture that runs the "Network Operation System (NOS)". The SDN controller implements the control pane capabilities and provides hardware abstractions. The forwarding elements are responsible for forwarding traffic flows based on the control plane's instructions. The data plane is the result of combining these pieces.

4 Architecture of the DDoS Attack

The first DDoS assaults in June of 1998, and the methodologies of DDoS attacks have changed. The general attack model and procedures, however, remained unchanged. The attacker in Fig. 1 puts up a hierarchical attack architecture. To do so, an attacker first picks a few handlers with security flaws and intrudes them by gaining access rights. The techniques for picking agents (or zombies) are similar to those for picking handlers, except that the attacker does so indirectly through handlers. As many network-connected systems as possible are chosen by the attacker. The agents will initiate a DDoS by simultaneously flooding a target system with large volumes of malicious traffic. On both the victim's and attacker's external networks, handlers and agents are regularly detected. Once the handlers and agents have been chosen, the attacker can alter communications between the three systems to compromise the attack.

Through secure communication and compromise, the attack target, assault time/period, and attack kind are all compromised, guaranteeing the attack's secrecy. Once the preparations for the assault are finished, which include choosing handlers and agents and breaking the attack, many agents simultaneously execute a DoS attack

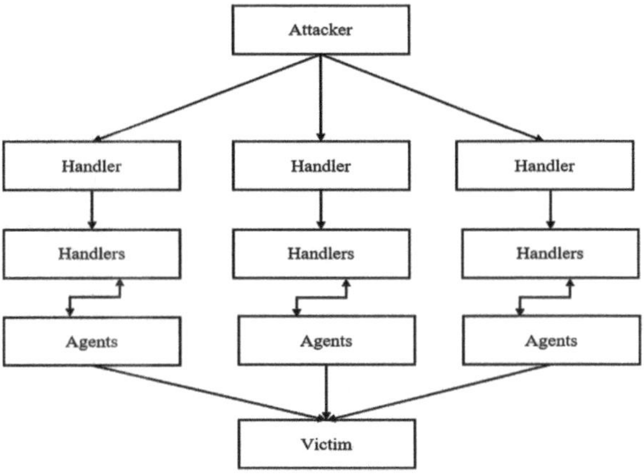

Fig. 1 DDoS attack architecture

on the target. Prior to selecting handlers and agents, hosts with security flaws are usually scanned, and ICMP is widely utilized for this purpose. Messages used for information transmission are often encrypted to prevent compromise and provide safe contact between the three platforms. The agents produce TCP, UDP, and ICMP formats of DDoS attack traffic. A DDoS attack causes a specific type of traffic to be substantially overburdened with traffic on the victim or a linked network. To conceal their real IP addresses, the agents randomly generate attack packet source IP addresses. Depending on the kind of assault, they also randomly assign source and destination port numbers; however, this has no impact on traffic from flash mobs. Because of the hierarchical attack architecture, it might be challenging to identify the actual attacker in a DDoS attack because the source IP addresses are spoofs. There are two methods offered by Lin and Tseng (2004) to render a victim or a network immobile. Flood attacks send a large number of malicious packets to a victim, including UDP and ICMP flood attacks. When an attacker bombards a target with massive volumes of "UDP traffic" with arbitrary destination port numbers, it's known as a UDP flood attack. Agents are used in ICMP flood attacks to bombard a target with massive amounts of "ICMP Echo Request packets", or "ping" requests. These packets cause the victim's capacity to be exceeded because they demand a large number of "ICMP Echo Reply packets" from the victim in response. Malicious traffic floods into the target or related network as a result of the flood attacks. It is therefore unable to provide enough bandwidth to clients who are legitimate. Another method that attackers employ to bring down a system or network is by exploiting vulnerabilities in network protocols. For instance, the TCP-SYN flooding attack makes use of the TCP protocol's three-way handshaking connection feature.

The victim has many half-opened connections as a result of faking the source IP addresses of attack packets, which uses up resources on the target machine. DDoS attacks are proactively detected by cluster analysis using the traffic features observed in each attack technique.

4.1 Classification of DDoS Attack

A DDoS attack is one of the dangerous types of cyber-attack that targets other users by using hijacked machines. These machines are used by the attacker to take control of them from afar. The true attacker and the compromised hosts are the two categories of attackers. The former is an attacker who can readily change an agent's behavior. The host is the second component, which receives the packets supplied by the agent. The target host itself is the third component. The classicization of the DDoS attack will be described in the following sections. The tools utilized in the attack, as well as potential countermeasures, were discussed. The DDoS assault is classified in the following table.

1. Flood Attacks: An attacker uses HTTP flood, ICMP flood, and SIP flood to execute arbitrary HTTP packets on a vulnerable system. An attacker uses "HTTP flood, ICMP flood, UDP flood, and SIP flood" to assault a system. Packets are typically sent to a specific port for the victims. A volumetric attack in which a large number of HTTP requests are delivered in a short period of time is known as an HTTP flood attack. In the event of a flood. Amplification Attacks: A message is sent to a broadcasted IP address in an amplification attack. This approach sends a message to the targeted system from all systems in the impacted subnet. There are three phases to the amplification attacks. The Fraggle attack, the Smurf attack, and the SNMP attack are among these phases.
2. Fraggle attack: Fraggle is an attack that employs UDP packets rather than ICMP packets. To disseminate its attacks, it employs a faked IP address.
3. Smurf attack: The Smurf attack attempts to deceive users into delivering ICMP packets to a faked source IP address. By looking for characteristics in the network that they employ, an attacker can quickly identify the source of an assault. However, because of the sophistication of the attacks, they might be difficult to trace down. The SNMP command is used to monitor a wide range of devices, including printers and firewalls. It transmits a string of configuration information to the devices' programme. The GetBulk request is used to get a system's configuration details. This procedure can be executed by sending a spoofed communication string with a valid IP address.
4. Coremelt Attack: Users can divide the zombies into two groups using this attack. The first group will be in charge of sending and receiving data, while the second will be in charge of dealing with other zombies. Unfortunately, tracing this attack through legitimate packets can be challenging. Instead, it creates a food network using the zombie network.
5. TCP SYN attack: SYN queries are sent in high numbers by the attacker. The server sends a C ACK packet and waits for the client to submit the desired packet before responding. The server would then add the non-existent ACK packets to a queue until it was full. The genuine requests would subsequently be rejected by the server.
6. "Authentication Server attack": The server verifies the attacker's forged signature. The signature generation takes a lot of time and energy.

Table 2 SDN network features used

Sr. no.	Flow feature	Flow meaning
1.	Length	Packet's number
2.	Duration	Flow time interval
3.	Size	Flow bytes
4.	Rate	Per seconds packets

7. "CGI request attack": An attacker sends a high number of CGI inquiries to consume the CPU cycles of the target. This talk will focus on the characteristics of the attacks.

4.2 Features for Attack Types

Table 2 are the SDN features that changes after the attacks on the SDN network:

1. Change of Traffic Behavior: The SDN Network shifts due the traffic behavior changes after the DDoS attack.
2. An Entropy technique method is used to identify the traffic containing the DDoS attack.

$$\text{Entropy}(S) = \sum ni = 1 - Pi \log 2Pi. \quad (1)$$

Pi is the probability a priori, while Entropy(S) is a function.

5 DDoS Detection Algorithm

As per the review on the previous works and methods as proposed by the different authors of different papers in the literature survey section as per my research below are the most effective and efficient algorithms where the detection, accuracy, and precision can be highly observed. However, on the previous methods, their implementation is solely focused on the process of detecting and identifying assaults, and it relies on a dataset that does not include a feature tailored to the SDN environment.

1. DDoS Detection Algorithm: This algorithm is based on the degree or severity of the attack.
   - Generation and detection of DoS attacks.
   - A DDoS assault consists of three parts: the agent, the attack host, and the OV-Switch.

- The DDoS attack is initiated against the OV-Switch component of the SDN, followed by "traffic generation and DDoS detection", when the assaulting host transmits the assault task to the agents 1, 2, and 3. The network traffic collector collects data from the network at regular intervals.
- Fig. 2 shows that DDoS detection utilization to assess the flow of an attack [3].

2. Machine Learning-Based DDoS Detection Algorithm: Machine Learning (ML) approaches for detecting threats are frequently utilized in traditional networks. An improved version of the "K-Nearest Neighbors (KNN)" identification technique is a powerful learning algorithm that has been created and implemented effectively in many different applications [3]. Experiments show that the DDAML algorithm outperforms the other methods in real-world situations.
3. LSTM Model and CNN Model: The DDoS attacks over different layers of IOT and their detection methods are also categorized as below in Table 3.

When you go through a series of actions, the LSTM model helps you remember data. For instance, slow permission attacks take time to occur and are hard to identify

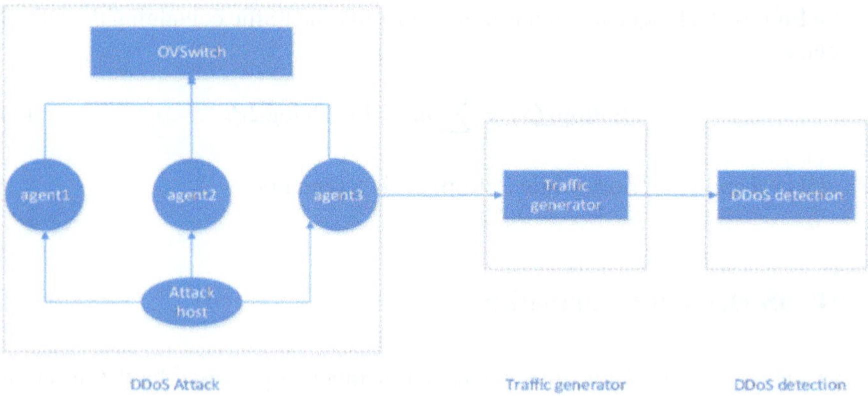

Fig. 2 DDoS attack generation and detection [3]

Table 3 Different layers of IOT and their detection methods

Sr. no.	Layers	Types of DDoS attacks	Detection method proposed
1.	Perception layer	• Bootstrapping attacks • Jamming attacks • Kill command attacks	LSTM model and CNN model
2.	Transport layer	• Flooding attacks • Reflection attacks • Amplification attacks	
3.	Application layer	• HTTP flooding attacks • Reprogramming networks	

using conventional models, but LSTM can. The LSTM model is able to distinguish between high-quality and low-quality data. The assault data is then divided into groups using the CNN model. The CNN model was used due to its ability to modify the network's size in order to overcome categorization problems. To enable CNN to convey the complexity of the data, the harmful data is transformed into a graphical representation. CNN then separates the DDoS data into other groups.

6 Experiment Data and Results

The UDP, TCP, and ICMP make up the bulk of network traffic; they account for 70%, 20%, and 10% of total traffic, respectively. The DDoS traffic is generated using Hping3, which can produce TCP, UDP, and ICMP flood attack traffic. Table 4 displays the experiment's outcomes. Evaluating the results of the tests administered is the assessment's primary goal [3].

To evaluate the DDoS assault's detection performance, we've defined significant metrics of attack detection performance in this section. First, when a DDoS assault is launched against the SDN controller, the four properties we proposed "flow length, flow duration, flow size, and flow ratio" are investigated. Second, a brand-new idea for detecting "DDoS attacks" is presented for the first time: the degree of attack. Based on this idea, a detection technique called the "DDADA algorithm" is explained. To increase detection efficiency, a new detection method called the "DDAML algorithm" is used to identify the "DDoS attack". Accurate recognition analysis is a critical criterion for evaluating detection efficiency and a critical indicator of detection performance. We show a clear superiority of our "DDADA and DDAML algorithms" over the existing "NB, KNN, SVM, and CIC-SVM" methods. This indicates that the maximum detection accuracy is achieved by the study's stated "DDADA and DDAML algorithms". The "True Positive Rate (TPR)" and "False Positive Rate (FPR)" are compared at various threshold levels. The TPR is also known as the sensitivity, recall, or chance of detection in machine learning. The FPR, sometimes called the fall-out rate or false-alarm likelihood.

Table 4 Evaluation results of detection [3]

Method	Evaluation				
	TPR	FPR	Precision	Recall	F-measure
SVM	0.985	0.018	0.9835	0.985	0.9842
CIC-SVM	0.986	0.017	0.9846	0.986	0.9853
KNN	0.985	0.018	0.983	0.985	0.984
DDADA	0.987	0.016	0.985	0.987	0.986
DDAML	0.994	0.009	0.993	0.994	0.9935
NB	0.982	0.024	0.981	0.982	0.9815

"TPR: True Positive Rate FPR: False Positive Rate"

7 Future Research Direction

The testing results show that our proposed algorithms provide higher detection rates and are more successful in detecting DDoS assaults than the existing approaches. Ultimately, the testing findings show that the DDAML technique performs better than the other approaches on a range of performance metrics. In order to enable the DDADA and DDAML algorithms to be implemented in a real SDN context, we want to continue developing them. Before the DDADA and DDAML algorithms are applied in an actual SDN environment, they still require development. The DDAML was developed because of the limitations in DDADA's detection efficiency.

8 Conclusion

The most critical component of securing a network is the detection of a DDoS attack. Although the current methods are very accurate, they are still vulnerable to other factors. The proposed improvements are intended to prevent a DDoS assault from exploiting the SDN controller. First, when a DDoS assault is launched against the SDN controller, the four properties we proposed—flow length, flow duration, flow size, and flow ratio—are investigated. Second, a brand-new idea for detecting DDoS attacks is presented for the first time: the degree of attack. Based on this idea, a detection technique called the DDADA algorithm is explained. The DDAML algorithm is an additional detection approach that is introduced to identify the DDoS assault in order to boost detection efficiency.

References

1. Lin HC, Wang P (2016) Implementation of an SDN-based security defense mechanism against DDoS attacks. In: DEStech transactions on economics, business and management, no iceme-ebm, pp 1–7
2. Mehr SY, Ramamurthy B (2019) An SVM based DDoS attack detection method for Ryu SDN controller. In: Conex. 2019 companion proceedings of the 15th international conference emerging networking experiments and technologies part Conex, pp 72–73
3. Dong S, Sarem M (2020) DDoS attack detection method based on improved KNN with the degree of DDoS attack in software-defined networks. IEEE Access 8:5039–5048
4. Fonseca P, Bennesby R, Mota E, Passito A (2012) A replication component for resilient OpenFlow-based networking. In: Proceeding of the 2012 IEEE network operations and management symposium NOMS 2012, pp 933–939
5. Yao G, Bi J, Guo L (2013) On the cascading failures of multi-controllers in software defined networks. In: Proceedings of the international conference on network protocols ICNP, vol 1, pp 3–4
6. David J, Thomas C (2015) DDoS attack detection using fast entropy approach on flow-based network traffic. Procedia Comput Sci 50:30–36
7. Saied A, Overill RE, Radzik T (2016) Detection of known and unknown DDoS attacks using artificial neural networks. Neurocomputing 172:385–393

8. Ye J, Cheng X, Zhu J, Feng L, Song L (2018) A DDoS attack detection method based on SVM in software defined network. Secur Commun Netw 2018:1–8
9. Cui J, Wang M, Luo Y, Zhong H (2019) DDoS detection and defense mechanism based on cognitive-inspired computing in SDN. Futur Gener Comput Syst 97:275–283
10. Guo Y, Yu L, Liu Y, Zheng J, Zong Y (2018) An efficient SDN-based DDoS attack detection and rapid response platform in vehicular networks. IEEE Access 6(c):44570–44579
11. Assis MVO, De Novaes MP, Zerbini CB, Carvalho LF, Abrao T, Proenca ML (2018) Fast defense system against attacks in software defined networks. IEEE Access 6(c):69620–69639
12. Wang Y, Hu T, Tang G, Xie J, Lu J (2019) SGS: safe-guard scheme for protecting control plane against DDoS attacks in software-defined networking. IEEE Access 7(1):34699–34710
13. Hoque N, Kashyap H, Bhattacharyya DK (2017) Real-time DDoS attack detection using FPGA. Comput Commun 110:48–58
14. Liu Y, Cheng J, Yin J, Zhang B (2010) Detecting DDoS attacks using conditional entropy. In: 2010 international conference on computer application and system modeling: proceedings, p 13
15. Lee K, Kim J, Kwon KH, Han Y, Kim S (2008) DDoS attack detection method using cluster analysis. Expert Syst Appl 34(3):1659–1665
16. Chen J, Tang X, Cheng J, Wang F, Xu R (2020) DDoS attack detection method based on network abnormal behavior in big data environment. Int J Comput Sci Eng 23(1):22–30
17. Cheng J, Yin J, Wu C, Zhang B, Liu Y (2009) DDoS attack detection method based on linear prediction model. Lecture notes in computer science (including subseries lecture notes in artificial intelligence and lecture notes in bioinformatics), vol 5754, pp 1004–1013
18. Yu X, Yu W, Li S, Yang X, Chen Y, Lu H (2021) WEB DDoS attack detection method based on semi supervised learning. Secur Commun Netw 1–10:2021
19. Jun, J. H. Ahn, C. W. and Kim, S. H (2014) DDoS attack detection by using packet sampling and flow features. In: Proceedings ACM symposium on applied computing, pp 711–712
20. Singh AK (2021) Machine learning in open flow network: comparative analysis of DDoS detection techniques. Int Arab J Inf Technol 18(2):221–226
21. Wang M, Lu Y, Qin J (2020) A dynamic MLP-based DDoS attack detection method using feature selection and feedback. Comput Secur, 88
22. Dong P, Du X, Zhang H, Xu T (2016) A detection method for a novel DDoS attack against SDN controllers by vast new low-traffic flows. In: 2016 IEEE international conference on communications
23. Bishnoi S, Mohanty S, Sahoo B (2021) A deep learning-based methodology in fog environment for DDOS attack detection. In: Proceedings of the 5th international conference on computing methodologies and communication ICCMC 2021, no Iccmc, pp 201–206

Quarter Phase Grating Cavity Showing High Quality Factor in SOI Substrate

Parimal Sah, Bhumika Neole, Abhinav Kumar, Pushpalata, Mukesh Kumar, and Manoj Kumar

1 Introduction

The Quarter Phase Grating Cavity refers to the integration of a grating structure within an SOI waveguide, featuring a cavity positioned between the gratings. This configuration operates akin to a Fabry-Perot resonator, where the grating structure serves as a highly reflective mirror [1, 2]. The device exhibits a wavelength profile characterized by a narrow peak of exceptionally high quality between two stop-bands. The central peak wavelength arises from resonance within the cavity, and its principal application lies in sensing physical parameters such as pressure, temperature, and humidity. The reported maximum quality factor to date does not exceed $\tilde{2}.8 \times 10^3$ [3, 4]. The quality factor of a grating device experiences a reduction due to factors such as lower reflectivity, diminished cavity area, and increased loss from reflecting surfaces. The

P. Sah
Department of Electronics and Communication Engineering, Purnea College of Engineering, Purnea, India

P. Sah · A. Kumar · Pushpalata · M. Kumar · M. Kumar
Bihar Engineering University Patna, DSTTE Bihar India, Patna, India

B. Neole (✉)
Department of Electronics and Communication Engineering, Shri Ramdeobaba College of Engineering and Management, Nagpur, India
e-mail: neoleba@rknec.edu

A. Kumar · Pushpalata
Department of Electronics and Communication Engineering, Bhagalpur College of Engineering, Bhagalpur, India

M. Kumar
Department of Electronics and Communication Engineering, GEC Sheohar, Abhirajpur Bairiya, India

M. Kumar
Department of Electrical Engineering, Purnea College of Engineering, Purnea, India

K. Kumar Singh et al. (eds.), *Machine Vision and Augmented Intelligence*, Lecture Notes in Electrical Engineering 1211, https://doi.org/10.1007/978-981-97-4359-9_24

quarter phase cavity length, typically in the nanometer range, inherently limits the Q-factor. However, by minimizing losses during fabrication, particularly at reflecting surfaces, it is possible to enhance the Q-factor. Employing electron-beam lithography to create a grating device with reduced etch depth and smaller modulation and width contributes to minimizing such losses, thereby improving the Q-factor. Additionally, extending the grating length significantly can further enhance the Q-factor [5]. This paper introduces a significant Q-factor achieved in a grating cavity with a length equal to a quarter of the wavelength in silicon-on-insulator (SOI). Section 2 outlines the device description, while Sect. 3 presents the FDTD simulation results.

2 Analytical Formulation of the Device

The three-dimensional representation of the proposed device is illustrated in Fig. 1a.

The transfer matrix for the grating device, incorporating a quarter phase cavity with lengths L_g for the grating and L_c for the cavity, is derived through the coupled wave theory:

$$M_{\text{dev}} = M_{\text{grat}} G_{\text{cav}} M_{\text{grat}} \tag{1}$$

Here, the matrix M is defined as

$$M_{\text{grat}} = \begin{bmatrix} \cosh(\omega L_g) - \iota \frac{\delta\beta/2}{\omega} \sinh(\omega L_g) & -\iota \frac{\kappa}{\omega} \sinh(\omega L_g) \\ \iota \frac{\kappa}{\omega} \sinh(\omega L_g) & \cosh(\omega L_g) + \iota \frac{\delta\beta/2}{\omega} \sinh(\omega L_g) \end{bmatrix} \tag{2}$$

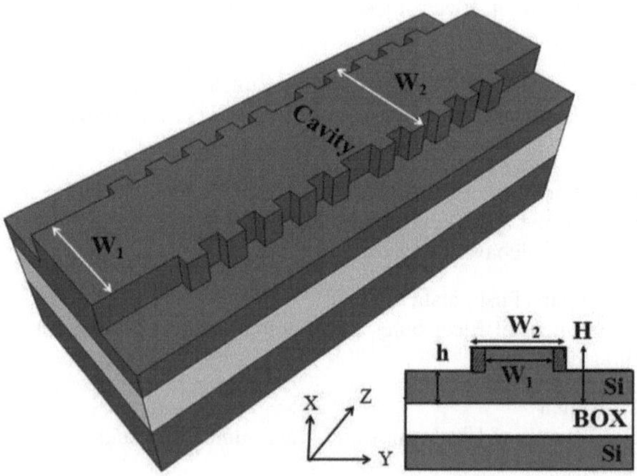

Fig. 1 **a** 3D schematic of device with λ/4 phase-shifted cavity. In cross-sectional view, W_1, W_2, H, h are waveguide widths, waveguide width of grating, height of the core and height of the slab respectively. **b** Analytical transmission spectrum with resonance peak of the device shown in **a**

where $\omega = \sqrt{\kappa^2 - (\delta\beta/2)^2}$ and $\delta\beta$ is given by:

$$\delta\beta = \tilde{n_{\mathrm{eff}}} \frac{4\pi}{\lambda} - \frac{2\pi}{\Lambda} \tag{3}$$

The complex effective index $\tilde{n_{\mathrm{eff}}}$ is expressed as

$$\tilde{n_{\mathrm{eff}}} = n_{\mathrm{EFF}} + i.k \tag{4}$$

If M_{cav} is represented as

$$M_{\mathrm{dev}} = \begin{bmatrix} m_{11} & m_{12} \\ m_{21} & m_{22} \end{bmatrix} \tag{5}$$

Then, the transfer matrix for the cavity, determining the wavelength characteristics of the device, is formulated as

$$T_{\mathrm{Device}}(\lambda) = |m_{11} - \frac{m_{12}m_{21}}{(m_{22})^2}| \tag{6}$$

The transfer matrix for the cavity (G_{cav}) is defined as

$$G_{\mathrm{cav}} = \begin{bmatrix} \gamma & 0 \\ 0 & \gamma^{-1} \end{bmatrix} \tag{7}$$

where γ is the phase due to the quarter-wavelength cavity, given by:

$$\gamma = e^{(i \frac{2\pi}{\lambda} L_c \tilde{n_{\mathrm{eff}}}(\lambda))} \tag{8}$$

The matrix M_{cavity} is represented by:

$$M_{\mathrm{cavity}} = \begin{bmatrix} M_{c-11} & M_{c-12} \\ M_{c-21} & M_{c-22} \end{bmatrix} \tag{9}$$

The final transfer function is wavelength-dependent:

$$T(\lambda) = |M_{c-11} - \frac{M_{c-12}M_{c-21}}{M_{c-22}^2}| \tag{10}$$

Utilizing coupled mode theory, we analytically developed the quarter phase grating cavity device and conducted FDTD simulations with parameters consistent with those used for the transfer matrix method. The cavity length is set at 141 nm, equal to half the grating period Λ. The grating length is chosen to be a substantial 270 µm.

The wavelength characteristics of the grating cavity are depicted in Fig. 1 (b). To demonstrate a high quality factor using the analytical method, the device was modeled with the transfer matrix method in MATLAB. With κL_g set to 5, where κ is the coupling-coefficient parameter of backward-to-forward fundamental mode coupling and L_g is the grating length, a DBR reflectivity as high as 40 dB (99.99%) is achievable. Figure 1b displays the simulated transmission spectrum with a resonance peak at 1603 nm, using device parameters such as $W_1 = 550$ nm, $\Delta W_2 = 50$ nm (grating modulation width), $\Lambda = 290$ nm, cavity length $H = 270$ nm, L = 145 nm, $h = 150$ nm, and a grating length of 270 μm. This configuration yields a high quality factor in the cavity, reaching 10^4.

3 Results of Device Simulation

The device, with parameters identical to those utilized in the preceding section for MATLAB simulation, underwent further simulation using the Lumerical FDTD Solver. This simulation was conducted on a silicon-on-insulator material, where the device had a height of 250 nm and an oxide layer thickness of 3 μm. The grating modulation, approximately 60 nm wide, was applied to both walls of the SOI waveguide. The transmission characteristics of the grating device are illustrated in Fig. 2.

The 3dB pass-band width of the resonance peak was determined to be approximately 20 pm, centered at 1608 nm, resulting in a quality factor of 8×10^4.

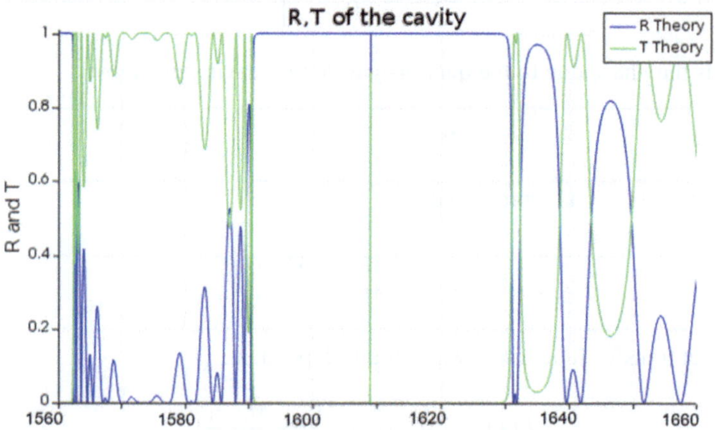

Fig. 2 Transmission spectrum of the device with a waveguide width of 570 nm, waveguide height of 250 nm, slab height of 150 nm, grating modulation width of 50 nm, grating period of 290 nm, and a grating cavity length of 145 nm

4 Conclusion

An integrated grating structure featuring a $\lambda/4$ phase-shifted cavity was designed and semi-analytically modeled using the transfer matrix method. The theoretical Fabry-Perot resonance, established through MATLAB, was validated through Lumerical FDTD Simulation. The resonance peaks closely matched in spectral response. By incorporating active control mechanisms such as fabricating a PN diode or micro-heater, observable shifts in the resonance peak can be achieved. The device holds potential applications in optical signal modulation and the analytical sensing of biomolecules. A comprehensive analysis of the design, fabrication, and optical characterization will be presented during the conference.

References

1. Caverley M, Wang X, Murray K, Jaeger NA, Chrostowski L (2015) Silicon-on-insulator modulators using a quarter-wave phase-shifted Bragg grating. IEEE Photonics Technol Lett 27(22):2331–2334
2. Tsao S-L, Tien J-H, Tsai C-W (2002) Simulations on an SOI grating-based optical add/drop multiplexer. IEEE J Sel Top Quantum Electron 8(6):1277–1284
3. Klimov NN, Purdy T, Ahmed Z (2015) Fabrication and characterization of on-chip integrated silicon photonic Bragg grating and photonic crystal cavity thermometers. arXiv:1508.01419
4. Veerasubramanian V, Beaudin G, Giguère A, Le Drogoff B, Aimez V, Kirk AG (2012) Waveguide-coupled drop filters on SOI using quarter-wave shifted sidewalled grating resonators. Opt Express 20(14):15 983–15 990
5. Sah P, Das BK (2017) Integrated optical rectangular-edge filter devices in SOI. J Light Technol 35(2):128–135

Survey and Analysis on Machine Learning Approaches for Exploring Aspects of Covid-19

Sumathi Pawar, Karuna Pandit, GeethaLaxmi, and Rajermani Thinakaran

1 Introduction

COVID-2019 was reported as the most harmful and according to WHO 15,225,252 cases were filed and 100,075 deaths occurred by April 2020. Covid-19 is spread in 172 countries and said that it is a contagious disease. Authors [1] in their data analysis, forecasted the next 6 days COVID-2019 in India, using polynomial regression model. This helped Indian doctors in making their plans for the next one week. Most of the authors used MATLAB for plotting data sets and analysis. Using COVID-19 Kaggle data, different numerical models such as Multilayer perceptron, linear regression, and autoregression methods are applied. According to authors, Corona Virus is a disease of inflammation which causes problems of breathing, fever, cold, and cough. This disease causes manifestations of respiratory ailment. They focused on vector autoregressive model which is a more suitable model of time series.

Deep learning techniques were used for diagnosis, protein structure analysis, disease tracking, virus severity, infectivity, and drug discovery in the area of medical imaging. Classification and Regression are used to predict the spreading of disease.

S. Pawar (✉) · K. Pandit
NMAM Institute of Technology, NITTE (Deemed to be University), Nitte, Karnataka, India
e-mail: pawarsumathi@gmail.com

K. Pandit
e-mail: karunapandit@nitte.edu.in

GeethaLaxmi
Information Science and Engineering, Canara Engineering College, Benjanapadavu, Bantwal, India

R. Thinakaran
Data Science and Information Technology, INTI International University, Nilai, Negeri Sembilan, Malaysia

K. Kumar Singh et al. (eds.), *Machine Vision and Augmented Intelligence*, Lecture Notes in Electrical Engineering 1211, https://doi.org/10.1007/978-981-97-4359-9_25

White blood cell count, Apache II score, blood lymphocytes counts and oxygen saturation are parameters used for prediction of deterioration. Experimental dataset for COVID patients was used to check the survival chances of COVID-19 patients and concluded that throat pain, muscle pain, pneumonia, and age give rise to mortality. IOT based technology is used for the detection of virus using the model coronavirus-body area network (CoV-BAN). Survey provides applications of different machine learning techniques in exploring different characteristics related to COVID-19. Organization of this paper includes a literature survey with table, analysis, and conclusion regarding this review.

2 Literature Review

Reference [2] authors collected CT images of 1065 CORONA disease which is pathogen-confirmed. Inception transfer-learning model is validated and modified to analyze these images. Authors have got an accuracy of 79.3% for external validation and 89.5% for internal validation. Authors compared F1 score, Youden index, Positive predictive value, and negative predictive values. Authors initially enrolled 259 patients out of which 180 cases were found positive via a deep learning algorithm. Authors also drew ROI (Region of Interest) from CT images such as small patchy shadows and infiltrates in both lungs.

Reference [3] authors used AI based method for diagnosis of CORONA disease and classified CT images and X-RAY sets, using segmentation with parameters such as consolidation, nodular opacities, and ground-glass opacities which identified lung changes. On training of CT volumes, they obtained trained data. To identify COVID-19 infected area, they used deep learning 3D models using convolutional neural network. Lung masks are provided by learning of DeCoVNet which is a pretrained UNet with Receiver operating characteristic 0.959.

Reference [4] this paper focused on 2 types of forecasting models such as machine learning/data science techniques and stochastic theory mathematical models. They studied various mathematical, analytical, statistical, and medical parameters and categorized them into 4 sets that include mathematical/stochastic theory models, WHO/National data sources, data science/Machine learning techniques, and social media/other communication media datasets. Also, they discussed on various challenges such as longer incubation period, tracking of the people, overfitting of the data, lack of proper data, overly clean data, wrong algorithm and attribute selection, and abundance of data.

Reference [5] authors observed social and personal health issues to maintain social distancing and staying at home. They indicated a model for online shopping of people to anticipate the behavior of the customer in shopping online during COVID-19. They proposed two approaches to predict the behavior of the consumer. Machine learning approach, statistical approach, pre-processing, correlation, and classification are approaches used by authors in machine learning process. Accuracy, precision, and recall are 3 factors used for evaluation.

Reference [6] authors used Convolutional neural networks (CNN) and logistic regression (LR) which are 2 classifiers frequently used. Based on PCA (Principal Component Analysis), the dimension reduction technique is investigated. For this study, publicly available datasets of X-ray images are used. The CNN model showed 97.6–100% accuracy for the identification of positive cases.

Reference [7] from various sources like Google Scholar, Xplore and Scopus, it is understood that authors implemented machine learning approaches used for screening, analyzing, predicting, forecasting, and tracking the trends of CORONA. Linear regression is used as one of the techniques to predict the values of CORONA spreading statistics. The artificial neural network is used with Multi-Layer Perceptron model for regression and classification. In MLP model arbitrary numbers of hidden layers nothing but blocks of actual computations were employed. While learning the relationship between input layer and output layers this model adjusts the parameters called weight and bias.

Reference [8] authors worked on Autoregressive models, Exponential models, deep learning and Regression methods for forecasting coronavirus COVID-19. Prophet algorithm, Flower pollination algorithm, genetic programming, Polynomial Neural Network are used for anticipating the CORONA Virus. Authors did not suggest the outcome of their survey on these different machine learning models. According to authors, SIR and SEIR are top models used by researchers as forecasting models.

Reference [9] authors focused on abnormalities of chest CT images using deep learning and analyzed the performance in relation to radiological residents. The methods used with CT images are segmentation, detection, and training of the location based on 14,435 participants. Non-overlapping data sets are used with 96 confirmed patients during COVID-19 eruption in China. The performance metrics used were specificity, accuracy, F1 score, and sensitivity. The findings revealed better performance related to resident radiologists.

Reference [10] authors accessed accuracy in predicting RT-PCR for simple acute respiratory syndrome using machine learning techniques for a long time span. Authors screened for influenza-like symptoms in patients with COVID positive. Using WEKA they worked on different data mining algorithms and trained and tested the model. They found that combining artificial intelligence techniques with input data through radiological, clinical, and routine laboratories provided a specificity of 88.7% and an accuracy of 91.4%.

The survey conducted by author regarding statistics of COVID-19 [11] is given in Fig. 1.

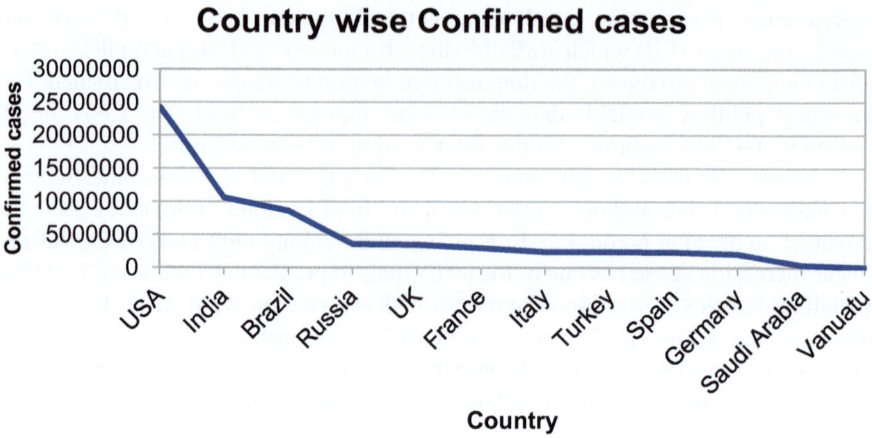

Fig. 1 Country-wise confirmed cases on a peak day

3 Analysis of Different Machine Learning Techniques for Covid-19 Aspects

Authors found that among the machine learning algorithms, the Logistic regression was most frequently applied followed by CNN and ANN models. Similarly, K-Means, Linear regression, Naive Bayes, and KNN (K-nearest neighbors) are also applied as given in Table 1.

4 Surveyed Models and Graphs of Covid-19 Prediction

It is mentioned in the survey that numerous authors predicted Covid-19 using different models. The description of some of the models is given here.

4.1 Linear Regression

During survey of ML approaches to predict Covid-19 cases, it is found that some authors used linear regression method with 2 variables A, B.

Simple linear regression is used to estimate the coefficients. A regression problem is in the form of

$$B = b0 + b1 * A \tag{1}$$

Here B is predicted using ‘I’ as input with coefficient b1 and bias b0.

Table 1 Analysis of Machine Learning Models used by different authors

Author	Dataset and Country	Method	Task/algorithms	Result
[12] Khanday et al in 2020	GitHub 212 reports in India	Supervised learning	Classification using Logistic regression and Naive Bayes	Accuracy gained is 96% due to usage of Bayes multinomial and logistic algorithms
[13] Burdick et al in 2020	United states Kealth system 197 patients in USA	Supervised learning	Classification using Logistic regression	The algorithm secured 90% sensitivity and higher specificity compared to MEWS (Modified Early Warning Score). There is early warning system which accurately identifies patients and minimizes false results
[14] Varun et al in 2020	184,319 reported cases in USA	Supervised learning	Classification Convolution Neural Networks	This algorithm provides higher diagnosis results for foreseeing ventilation with proper discrimination of Covid-19 decease with other deceases which decreased false positive results
[15] Luca et al in 2020	X-rays of 85 Chests in Italy	Supervised learning	Classification KNN	Medical reports analysed with supervised learning with the data sets of chest X-rays. Proper discrimination among covid-19 and other diseases
[16] Constantin et al. in 2020	500 Chest CTs and 152 datasets of COVID-19 patients in Germany	Supervised learning	Classifications Convolution Neural Network (CNN)	The clinically embedded softwares combined with machine learning and time-efficient software development, quick adoption in medical routines. Automated segmentation of opacity and lung was complete for medical use for complex medical cases
[17] Lamiaa et al. in 2020	5000 cases of COVID-19 in Egypt	Supervised learning	Regression Linear Regression model	The experimental fourth-degree to sixth-degree model was helped the government to prepare their plans up to one month. The well-known log grew-up the model of regression to peak during 2020

(continued)

Table 1 (continued)

Author	Dataset and Country	Method	Task/algorithms	Result
[18] Dan et al. in 2020	6995 patients in Sheba Medical Center in Israel	Supervised learning	Artificial Neural Network (ANN) classifications	This model used variables such as white blood cell count, APACHE II, blood lymphocytes count, oxygen saturation from time of symptoms to admission High efficiency is demonstrated by machine learning model in predicting COVID-19 and management of decease was improved by patients trace and hospital allocation
[19] Joep et al. in 2020	319 patients of Netherlands	Supervised learning	Classification Logistic regression	Diagnosis of COVID is aided by Chest CT and CO-RADS system which is a sensitive method This specific method improved the accuracy of the detecting Covid-19. Machine learning model used chest-CT reports as the data. Candidate predictors analyzed the the model and upto 9% positive patients not diagnosed by this machine learning model
[20] Christopher et al. in 2020	Germany counties' total 368 independent variables	Machine Learning algorithm	Classifications using Naive Bayes	In Germany variables and factors increasing COVID-19 with multi method EDSA technique given an insight into spatial stationaries of occurrences

In the above equation, B is depending on A.

4.2 Multiple Logical Regression

$$\ln\left(\frac{\hat{p}}{(1-\hat{p})}\right) = b_0 + b_1X_1 + b_2X_2 + \cdots + b_pX_p \tag{2}$$

The expected probability of outcome, $\hat{p}$ is expressed as follows.

$$\hat{p} = \frac{\exp(b_0 + b_1X_1 + b_2X_2 + \cdots + b_pX_p)}{1 + \exp(b_0 + b_1X_1 + b_2X_2 + \cdots + b_pX_p)} \tag{3}$$

b1 = coefficient for input (x)

b0 = bias or intercept term.

4.3 LASSO

This is a part of linear regression system and uses shrinkage. Here extreme data is converted into sample value. The strength of the LASSO depends on how well extreme values are converted into key values and also depends on the functions it uses. This is a regression model.

4.4 Support Vector Machine

This model is utilized to map inputs into n dimensional space with regression problems. Support Vector Machine is one among the classifications in machine learning approach and uses extreme points for hyperplane.

Data taken for the above graphs is from Elsevier public health emergency collection [21] and from the author Mojjadda et al. [10].

Graph of confirmed, recovered, and deaths in different countries is shown [11, 22] in Fig. 2. For this data is taken from the Table 1.

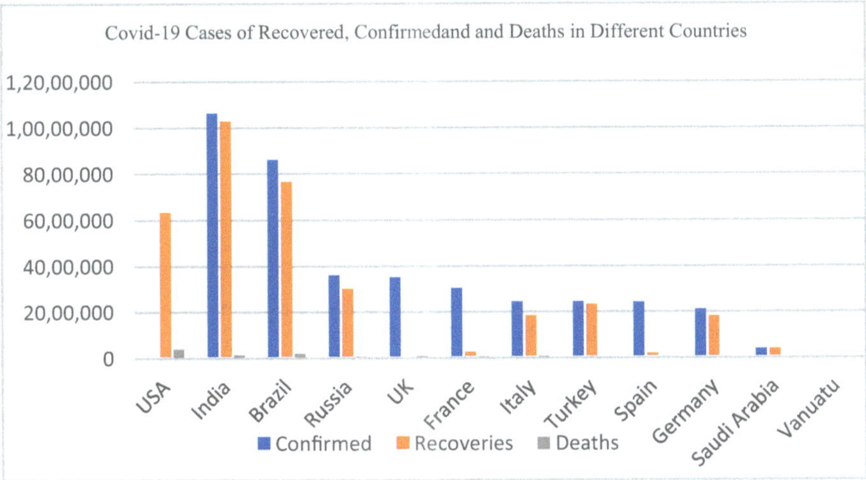

Fig. 2 Countrywide Covid-19 statistics

5 Covid Vaccination Details

Due to the increased anguish and fatality associated with covid-19, it was a crucial call for the development of vaccine. As soon as the WHO declared Covid-19 to be pandemic, pharmaceutical companies started the invention. The cost effective and most trustworthy public health intervention that saves life of a large population is vaccine and an effectual intervention to lessen the hardship of disease is vaccination. There were 61 vaccines expecting clinical evaluation clearance along with 172 more in the preclinical evaluation as of December 2020.

The major hurdle in the process of suppressing the widespread disease by vaccination was the worldwide vaccine hesitancy. Even though vaccine was available, the public health authorities had great problem due to the public hesitancy. The study on acceptance and attitude found that the acceptability is as low as 37.4%. The survey conducted showed that physicians and male population were willing to accept vaccination.

6 Conclusions

One of the big health issues the world has confronted is Covid-19. Need of the hour is a plan of action for providing proper facilities like medical, quarantine, food items, and protective actions to stop the escalation of the virus. This requires the estimation of the number of cases confirmed. Further different authors addressed the numerous challenges in these areas and unveiled suggestions to tackle them using Deep Learning, Regression, Network Analysis, Traditional Machine Learning, Regression, Search Queries, and Social Media Data-Based Methods. The investigation revealed that PubMed [23] articles are focused on various issues related to COVID-19 while ArXiv [24] articles were concentrated on the detection and prediction of COVID-19.

References

1. Yadav RS (Dec 2020) Data analysis of COVID-2019 epidemic using machine learning methods: a case study of India. Int J Inf Technol 12(4):1321–1330
2. Wang S et al (2021) A deep learning algorithm using CT images to screen for Corona virus disease (COVID-19). Eur Radiol 31:6096–6104
3. Soomro TA et al (2022) Artificial intelligence (AI) for medical imaging to combat coronavirus disease (COVID-19): a detailed review with direction for future research. Artifcial Intell Rev 55:1409–1439
4. Gitanjali RS et al (2020) Forecasting models for coronavirus disease (COVID-19): a survey of the state-of-the-art. SN Comput Sci 1:197. https://doi.org/10.1007/s42979-020-00209-9
5. Safara F et al (2020) A computational model to predict consumer behaviour during COVID-19 pandemic. Comput Econ. Springer Science+Business Media, LLC, part of Springer Nature
6. Rasheed J et al (2021) A machine learning-based framework for diagnosis of COVID-19 from chest X-ray images. Interdiscip Sci: Comput Life Sci 13:103–117

7. Rahman MM et al (2021) Machine learning approaches for tackling novel coronavirus (COVID-19) pandemic. SN Comput Sci 2:384
8. Rahimi I et al (2023) A review on COVID-19 forecasting models. Neural Comput Appl. Springer (in press)
9. Ni Q et al (2020) A deep learning approach to characterize 2019 coronavirus disease (COVID-19) pneumonia in chest CT image. Eur Radiol 30:6517–6527
10. Mollalo A, Rivera KM, Vahedi B (2020) Artificial neural network modeling of novel coronavirus (COVID-19) incidence rates across the continental United States. Int J Environ Res Public Health 17:4204
11. WHO Coronavirus (COVID-19) Dashboard https://covid19.who.int/. Accessed 25 Nov 2022
12. Khanday AMUD, Rabani ST, Khan QR, Rouf N, Mohi Ud Din M (2020) Machine learning based approaches for detecting COVID-19 using clinical text data. Int J Inf Technol 12(3):731–739. https://doi.org/10.1007/s41870-020-00495-9. Epub 2020 Jun 30. PMID: 32838125; PMCID: PMC7325639
13. Burdick H, Lam C, Mataraso S, Siefkas A, Braden G, Dellinger RP, McCoy A, Vincent JL, Green-Saxena A, Barnes G, Hoffman J, Calvert J, Pellegrini E, Das R (2020) Prediction of respiratory decompensation in Covid-19 patients using machine learning: The READY trial. Comput Biol Med 124:103949. https://doi.org/10.1016/j.compbiomed.2020.103949. Epub 2020 Aug 6. PMID: 32798922; PMCID: PMC7410013
14. Arvind V, Kim JS, Cho BH, Geng E, Cho SK (2021) Development of a machine learning algorithm to predict intubation among hospitalized patients with COVID-19. J Crit Care 62:25–30. https://doi.org/10.1016/j.jcrc.2020.10.033. Epub 2020 Nov 16. PMID: 33238219; PMCID: PMC7669246
15. De Luca G, Cavalli G, Campochiaro C, Della-Torre E, Angelillo P, Tomelleri A et al (2020) GM-CSF blockade with mavrilimumab in severe COVID-19 pneumonia and systemic hyperinflammation: a single-centre, prospective cohort study. Lancet Rheumatol 2(8):E465–E473. https://doi.org/10.1016/s2665-9913(20)30170-3
16. Assaf D, Gutman Y, Neuman Y et al (2020) Utilization of machine-learning models to accurately predict the risk for critical COVID-19. Intern Emerg Med 15:1435–1443. https://doi.org/10.1007/s11739-020-02475-0
17. Burdick H, Lam C, Mataraso S, Siefkas A, Braden G, Dellinger RP, McCoy A, Vincent JL, Green-Saxena A, Barnes G, Hoffman J, Calvert J, Pellegrini E, Das R (2020) Is machine learning a better way to identify COVID-19 patients who might benefit from hydroxychloroquine treatment?-The IDENTIFY Trial. J Clin Med 9(12):3834. https://doi.org/10.3390/jcm9123834. PMID: 33256141; PMCID: PMC7760047
18. Choi S, Hong JY, Kim YJ, Park H (2020) Predicting psychological distress amid the COVID-19 pandemic by machine learning: discrimination and coping mechanisms of korean immigrants in the U.S. Int J Environ Res Public Health 17(17):6057. https://doi.org/10.3390/ijerph17176057. PMID:32825349; PMCID: PMC7504344
19. Constantin I, Lungu ML, Panaitescu L, Ilie M, Simulating Lungu D, Nita S (2014) Simulating for predicting the hourly dew point temperature using artificial neural networks. J Environ Prot Ecol 15(1101–1109):8
20. Hermans JJR, Groen J, Zwets E et al (2020) Chest CT for triage during COVID-19 on the emergency department: myth or truth? Emerg Radiol 27:641–651
21. Mojjada RK, Yadav A, Prabhu AV, Natarajan Y (2020) Machine Learning Models for covid-19 future forecasting. Mater Today Proc. 2020 Dec 9. https://doi.org/10.1016/j.matpr.2020.10.962. Epub ahead of print. PMID: 33318952; PMCID: PMC7723767

22. Malki Z, Atlam ES, Ewis A et al (2021) The COVID-19 pandemic: prediction study based on machine learning models. Environ Sci Pollut Res 28:40496–40506. https://doi.org/10.1007/s11356-021-13824-7
23. PubMed (nih.gov). https://pubmed.ncbi.nlm.nih.gov/. https://doi.org/10.1016/j.vaccine.2015.04.036 PMID: 25896383
24. Viewing an article | arXiv e-print repository. https://arxiv.org/help/view. Accessed 08 Oct 2022

Precision Agriculture Using IOT Technology with a Case Study of Coffee Beans Production

Sumathi Pawar, B. L. RajaLakshmi Samaga, Karuna Pandith, Vasanth Nayak, V. Geetha, and Rajermani Thinakaran

1 Introduction

Precision agriculture is a running strategy that implements processes of getting the environmental conditions such as spatial, temporal, and other supporting information and studies of these data, and associates it with the required information to do decisions about the usage of resources to get profitability, quality, efficiency and sustainability in agricultural productions. Traditional agriculture which gives the highest yield diminishes the environment, soil and pollutes the green houses. Adaption of precision agriculture increases the production rate by 70% [1], reduces the usage of pesticides, and thereby guards the soil, and lessens the environmental pollution. Modern agriculture using advanced technology increases the quality and quantity of yields. Precision agriculture is cost effective with reference to time, money, manpower, and other resources. Application of precision agriculture are smart green houses, precision farming, cattle management, monitoring, usage of agriculture drones, and end-to-end systems of farm management. Usage of pesticides, water management, and fertilizers produce gains in crops but needs timely and precise

S. Pawar (✉) · B. L. R. Samaga · K. Pandith
NMAM Institute of Technology, NITTE (Deemed to be University), Nitte, Karnataka, India
e-mail: pawarsumathi@gmail.com

B. L. R. Samaga
e-mail: raji.samaga@nitte.edu.in

V. Nayak
ISE Department, Canara Engineering College, Benjanapadavu, Bantwal, Karnataka 575219, India

V. Geetha
Department of Information Technology, NITK, Suratkal, Karnataka, India

R. Thinakaran
Data Science and Information Technology, INTI International University, Nilai, Negeri Sembilan, Malaysia

K. Kumar Singh et al. (eds.), *Machine Vision and Augmented Intelligence*, Lecture Notes in Electrical Engineering 1211, https://doi.org/10.1007/978-981-97-4359-9_26

information on the field which can be achieved by Information Communication Technology (ICT).

Adaption of precision agriculture in coffee estates increases the production rate by 70%, reduces the usage of pesticides and thereby guards the soil, and lessens the environmental pollution. Modern agriculture using advanced technology increases the quality and quantity of yields.

End-to-end information and communication technology in precision farming, smart agriculture, and farm management uses advanced communication instruments. Using real-time, dynamic, adaptive techniques existing plot-specific farming techniques are described. Identification of products and crop tracking are also performed in prior stages of harmful conditions. The activities of precision agriculture are data processing, information monitoring, and inference of information which are required for green house agriculture.

This paper discusses a review on the usage of IOT in precision agriculture and organization of paper. Section 1 discusses introduction, Sect. 2 is focused on related work, some part of the review is represented through the table, Sect. 3 provides information about various kinds of sensors used in coffee beans case study, and Sect. 4 is about applications of IOT in precision agriculture and Sect. 5 about conclusion.

2 Related Work

Authors [2] focused on various methods that control the farm using machine learning algorithm and IOT sensors. Weather conditions are checked at every interval of time and SVR method is used to provide data to farmers which takes appropriate action. Authors used image processing techniques to detect the pests. They used drones and agricultural robots to spray pesticides on pests. They used K-means clustering algorithm to control the irrigation. Greenhouse techniques are also used which take information about the growth of plants and give information to the farmers. It also checked the climate conditions.

In [3] authors bridged the gap between computer technologists and precision agricultural research for the best yield of crops. Crops knowledgebase is already fed into the system by the admin end and sensed data will be provided for decision-making. In the farms, wireless communication systems are implanted and an Android app with integrated hardware is used to manage the farms. Interactive web interface is provided for training the illiterate users.

Research work of [4] focused on providing farm environmental conditions including water level, temperature, dissolved oxygen measurements, and pH value measurements from the paddy field. Wireless sensor networks are used with IOT in crop management and an online system is developed for the management of information. Variabilities of the fields such as side dressing, late blight control, haulm killing and weed control are also analyzed. Prior analysis of change in climate is resulted into increased productivity.

Authors [5] focused on maximizing agricultural outputs by minimizing the inputs of precision agriculture in sub-Saharan Africa. In this system, IOT based robots are used with camera for remote monitoring of the environment and also for monitoring the water level of sensors for irrigation and herbicide application. Security of information in precision based agriculture research [6] is focused by authors and data is protected to prevent data breach. Authors focused on the analysis of research information which is based on IOT based precision agriculture.

Discussion of authors [7] given that in India the five days incubation period for Kulgam Anantnag and 3 days for Srinagar proved that the first place is unsafe and Srinagar is safe. Dissemination of information regarding factors and parameters are proved useful in finding apple scap disease in Kashmir. Authors also surveyed to know views of people regarding precision agriculture and focused on getting the profit from workable form.

Work of Authors [8] focused on smart forming by getting live data regarding humidity, temperature, soil moisture, etc. Crops are monitored with user friendly app and a system is developed to collect data from cloud and to notify this to farmers. Farmers utilized this data for their small farms. But this system had limited features due to low budget.

In the paper [9], focused on sensing data of the crops and transmitting it through the user mobile which is monitored and controlled. Real-time data of the crops are sensed by the system which uses GSM technique, various sensors, and Arduino.

Authors [10] proposed the prediction of diseases of Apple in Kashmir Valley using machine learning with IOT system. Farmers are included in the survey to know about the effect of disease in precision agriculture and trending technologies. The authors discussed on issues related to providing and deploying applications in real-time. The study included selection of soil, proper irrigation, usage of fertilizers, identifying crop disease, appropriate pest control, and analyzing the yield.

Authors [11] focused on the evolution of IOT in the field of agriculture. Most of the farmers were unaware of the technologies of modern agriculture. The authors suggest the use of IOT and AI in agriculture to make agriculture profitable by predicting rainfall, temperature, water requirements, and fertilizers required. They noticed that most of the farmers depend on rainfall which is seasonal and no financial assistance. They also observed that automated tools were not implemented by farmers due to high software costs and lack of smart technological skills. Further, they addressed the importance of modern agricultural system using IOT and machine learning as well as forest fire prediction.

3 Case Study of Usage of Sensors in Coffee Estate

Coffee agriculture is cost effective with reference to time, money, manpower, and other resources. To keep coffee seeds fresh and seasonal all the time it is required to store it in the optimum conditions for many months. For this purpose, we

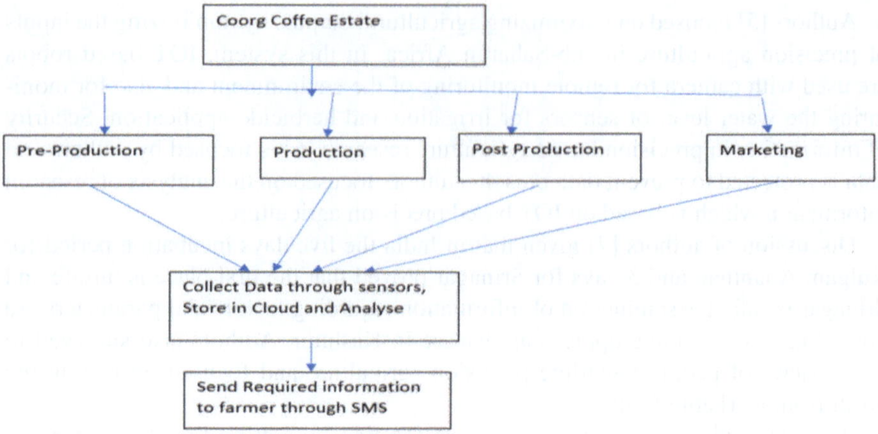

Fig. 1 Brief architecture of the system

need Air-quality, CO_2 detector, Oxygen sensors, humidity, and temperature sensors measurement and keep track of these weather conditions.

As shown in Fig. 1, to collect data sensors are used during various stages of coffee production and these data are sent to cloud for analysis. Required information after data analysis, is sent to farmers. In cloud according to threshold set with knowledge of coffee farming, the required alert will be sent to the farmers about setting the proper environment for coffee production.

3.1 Pre-production Stage

Data sent to cloud are normalized and properly analyzed with the help of domain knowledge Engineer who is an expert in coffee plant agriculture to get maximum qualitative production. These analyzed data is sent to the farmers and also required suggestions are sent to farmers through SMS.

3.1.1 Soil Sensors

Figure 2 shows soil testing which involves the utilization of various types of sensors, including Nutrient Detectors with Electrochemical Sensors for Soil, Mechanical Soil Sensors for Agricultural purposes, and Dielectric Soil Sensors.

Electrochemical sensors play a crucial role in gathering chemical data from soil, particularly for detecting soil nutrient levels. When conducting soil testing, samples are typically sent to a specialized lab where specific measurements, notably pH determination, are carried out using ion-selective electrodes. These electrodes detect the activity of specific ions like nitrate, potassium, or hydrogen.

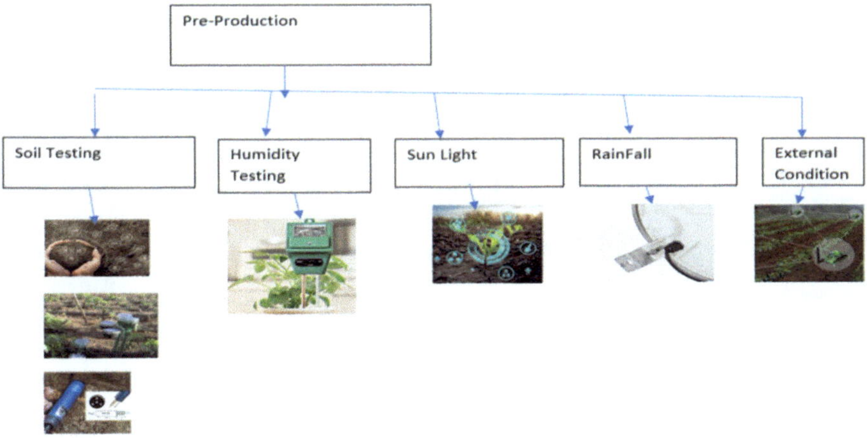

Fig. 2 Possible usage of sensors in pre-production stage

Moisture sensors are strategically placed in various locations across the farm, complemented by rain check stations. This setup enables monitoring of soil moisture levels, especially during periods of diminished vegetation.

3.1.2 Optical Sensors (SunLight)

This technology utilizes light across different frequencies to assess soil characteristics. These sensors are mounted on vehicles or drones, enabling the collection and analysis of soil reflectance and plant color data. Optical sensors can provide insights into clay composition, organic matter, and soil moisture levels.

3.1.3 Humidity Sensors

Variations in humidity can influence this mechanism. For instance, when humidity levels are excessively elevated, the evaporating water from the stomata lacks a pathway as the air is already at its saturation point.

This indicates that even with the stomata always open, the plant struggles to respire and can potentially suffocate in an environment saturated with trapped CO_2 and water. The most extreme outcome would be the complete failure of the plant. At the very least, this situation would lead to impaired growth, hampering the plant's ability to carry out its regular biological functions.

Humidity sensors measure humidity in the environment and send to cloud through RaspBerri PI.

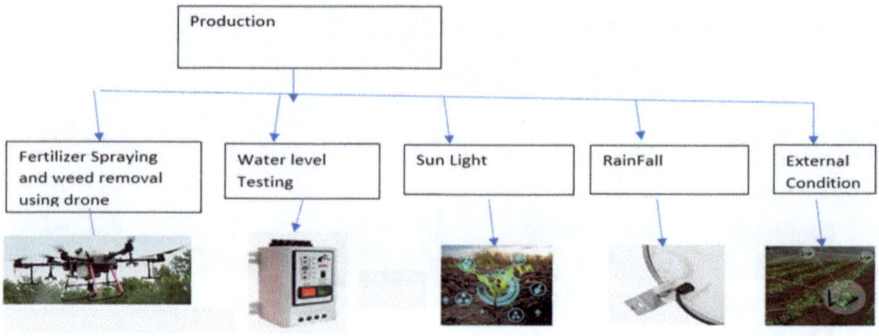

Fig. 3 Usage of sensors in production stage

3.1.4 Rain Fall and External Condition Sensors

This is required to get rain information and to send this information to cloud which is required to collect and control water for coffee irrigation. External condition sensors such as location sensors required to get information about the location of accessories used in agriculture. This is also helpful to send the location of labors if it is attached to them.

3.2 Production Stage

3.2.1 Fertilizer Spraying Through Drones

It is shown in Fig. 3, throughout the production process, fertilizers are administered in four divided doses of 106 kg each during each 2 months of the first half year. For mature bushes aged over three years, the recommended fertilizer doses are NPK 45:34:45 kg/ha.

During the monsoon break in July–August, foliar nutrient sprays have proven effective in significantly reducing fruit drop in coffee. In regions facing challenges where roots struggle to absorb adequate nutrients from the soil due to low soil temperature, moisture scarcity, or a restricted or diseased root system, foliar feeding has shown to be highly effective.

Controlling on spraying the required quantity of fertilizers is done through drones and drones can be programmed to do this.

3.2.2 Water Level Sensors

These sensors are used to find the water level and to control it accordingly during production.

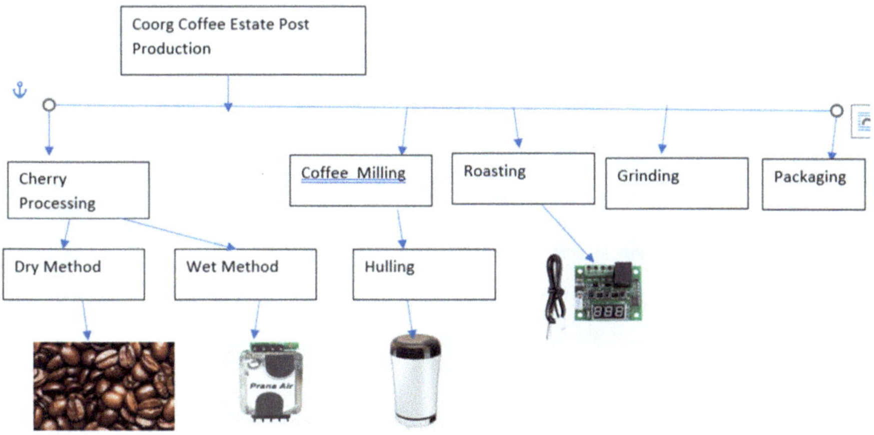

Fig. 4 Usage of sensors in post-production stage

3.2.3 Location Sensors in Agriculture

These sensors ascertain the range, distance, and height of specific positions within the designated area, utilizing assistance from GPS satellites.

3.3 Post-production Stage

3.3.1 Air Quality Sensors and Temperature Sensors

As in Fig. 4, during post-production, sensors play a vital role in measuring the temperature, humidity, and air pressure of the environment. This data is essential for controlling the cherry processing, roasting process, and grinding process.

4 Applications of IOT in Agriculture

Agriculture process includes various processes from monitoring the environment to disease and animal monitoring. Figure 5 shows some of the tasks performed by the usage of IOT sensors in precision agriculture.

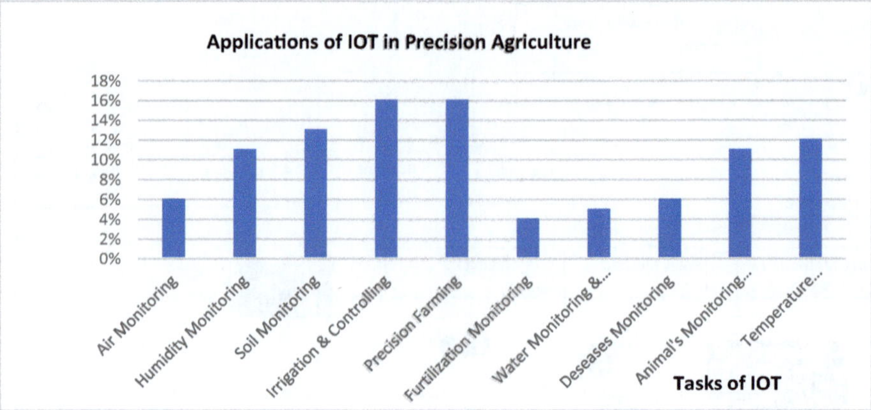

Fig. 5 The graph depicting the Applications of IoT in Precision Agriculture illustrates the percentage of usage

5 Conclusion and Future Work

It is found in literature review that usage of IOT has increased the output of agriculture, lessened the cost of labor besides increased the quality of the product and thereby improving the quality of life of farmers. It is observed that application of IOT in agriculture has attained notable progress [12]. But some challenges need to be overcome. Technological problems such as trouble in sharing data, unbalanced transmission of data, mismatched interfaces of sensors, weak signals of communication channels, etc., are addressed. In coffee beans production, the usage of sensors highly contributed in getting qualitative production. 5G technology will be useful to overcome problems related to communication speed. Augmented reality and virtual reality technology can be used for integrating crops, farmers, agronomy, machineries, and intelligent process monitoring is very much required to achieve precision agriculture. As a future work, machine learning techniques are used to categorize the coffee beans after passing through camera sensors.

References

1. Vuran MC, Salam A, Wong R, Irmak S (2018) Internet of underground things in precision agriculture: Architecture and technology aspects and Ad Hoc Networks, vol 81, pp 160–173
2. Sasi Supritha Devi Y, Kesava Durga Prasad T, Saladi K, Nandan D (2020) Analysis of precision agriculture technique by using machine learning and IoT. In: Pant M, Kumar Sharma T, Arya R, Sahana B, Zolfagharinia H (eds) Soft computing: theories and applications. Advances in intelligent systems and computing, vol 1154
3. Sheikh JA, Cheema SM, Ali M, Amjad Z, Tariq JZ, Naz A (2021) IoT and AI in precision agriculture: designing smart system to support illiterate farmers. In: Ahram T (ed) Advances in

artificial intelligence, software and systems engineering. AHFE 2020. Advances in intelligent systems and computing, vol 1213. Springer, Cham

4. Asig DD (2020) Implementing IoT and wireless sensor networks for precision agriculture. In: Pattnaik P, Kumar R, Pal S (eds) Internet of things and analytics for agriculture, vol 2. Studies in big data, vol 67. Springer, Singapore
5. Bala JA, Olaniyi OM, Folorunso TA, Daniya E (2021) An IoT-based autonomous robot system for maize precision agriculture operations in Sub-Saharan Africa". In: Singh KK, Nayyar A, Tanwar S, Abouhawwash M (eds) Emergence of cyber physical system and IoT in smart automation and robotics. Advances in science, technology & innovation (IEREK interdisciplinary series for sustainable development). Springer, Cham
6. Nakhodchi S, Dehghantanha A, Karimipour H (2020) Privacy and security in smart and precision farming: a bibliometric analysis. In: Choo KK, Dehghantanha A (eds) Handbook of big data privacy. Springer, Cham
7. Akhter R, Sofi SA (2021) Precision agriculture using IoT data analytics and machine learning. J King Saud Univ-Comput Inf Sci, ISSN 1319-1578
8. Jayadevan J et al (2020) A novel architecture for internet of things in precision agriculture. Int J Appl Eng Res 15(3):204–211. ISSN 0973-4562
9. Kumar A, Singh V, Kumar S, Jaiswal SP, Bhadoria VS (2020) IoT enabled system to monitor and control greenhouse. Mater Today: Proc. ISSN 2214-7853
10. Akhter R, Sofi SA (2021) Precision agriculture using IoT data analytics and machine learning. J King Saud Univ-Comput Inf Sci. ISSN 1319-1578
11. Aggarwal NS (2021) Technology assisted farming: implications of IoT and AI. In: IOP conference series: materials science and engineering, vol 1022(1), p 12080
12. Sumathi P, Pandith K, Chiplunkar NN (2022) A machine learning approach to forest fire prediction through environment parameters. IEEE AIDE, NMAMIT, Nitte

Investigation of the Impact of EEG Signal Processing Techniques on Classification Performance

Shyam Babu and Arun Kumar Wadhwani

1 Introduction

Electroencephalograms (EEGs) are the electrical signals created by the brain [11]. Analysis of EEG has been mainly performed in clinical scenarios to identify pathologies. The interpretation of the EEG was limited to visual inspection by a neurophysiologist, an expert makes a distinction between normal EEG and abnormalities in EEG [10]. The advance in technologies enables to successfully apply analysis methods to identify the EEG changes. However, the EEG is difficult to understand. But data processing techniques can be used for reducing features by selecting essential insights, or pattern recognition, as automated spike detection during monitoring of EEG signals [14].

Recently developed techniques are establishing the relationship between the EEG and behavior, by using analog frequency analyzers [2]. However, these efforts are mainly focused on the study of brain wave activity. Additionally, such analysis provides numerical consequences of the EEG but these techniques are computationally expensive for recovering additional EEG information related to the specific patterns. Therefore, some other kind of technique is required to describe different behavior of the EEG [6]. For many practical uses, including neuroscience research, biometrics, neuromarketing, neurology, etc. The research analysis and categorization of EEG signals are essential. Since proper preprocessing of EEG signals significantly impacts the classification performance. Therefore, in this paper, the main aim is to investigate and evaluate the study and explore signal preprocessing techniques and their influence on the EEG signal classification.

This paper addresses the following key insights:

S. Babu (✉) · A. K. Wadhwani
Department of Electrical Engineering, Madhav Institute of Technology and Science, Gwalior, India
e-mail: itm.shyam@gmail.com

K. Kumar Singh et al. (eds.), *Machine Vision and Augmented Intelligence*, Lecture Notes in Electrical Engineering 1211, https://doi.org/10.1007/978-981-97-4359-9_27

1. First and foremost, study the essential keywords used in defining the scientific aspects of EEG signals.
2. Following that, a summary of existing approaches for estimating and classifying EEG signals is discussed.
3. Further the basic preprocessing techniques are discussed which can be used to improve classification performance.
4. Next, experimental model has been discussed for conducting a study of the impact of signal preprocessing techniques by explaining the use of classification technique.
5. Finally, conclusion of the study has been reported and future study plan has been discussed.

2 Related Work

This section explores the EEG signal processing techniques and their influence on classification performance. Therefore, 48 recent articles were downloaded from Google Scholar and selected the most relevant 24 articles. An overview of the studied literature is discussed in this section.

2.1 Essential Keywords

During study of articles some frequently used abbreviations are identified are reported in Table 1.

2.2 Related Study

This section involves a brief summary of the EEG signal processing-based research articles. Additionally, we are examining the essential characteristics, feature selection strategies, classification approaches, and applications.

The perks of EEG include its superior temporal resolution, capacity to record neural activity directly, portability, and cost-effectiveness. Provides a comparison of neuroimaging methods, displaying the greatest neuroimaging belongings of EEG signals, such as high temporal resolution, and non-invasiveness, with methods like magneto-encephalogram, positron emission tomography, MRI, etc. An overview of several frequency bands connected to brain signals is provided. The current analysis encloses the identification and investigation of brain disorders such as epilepsy, alcohol-related diseases, dementia, and major depressive disorder (MDD), along with their applications. EEG datasets and acquisition techniques have been evaluated in

Table 1 Appendix A. Acronyms

ADMM	Alternating Direction Method of Multipliers
ADD	Attention-Deficit Disorder
ANN	Artificial Neural Network
ANX	Anxiety with attentional fragility
AR	Autoregressive
ASR	Adaptive Sparse Representation
aLS-SVM	Asymmetric-Least Squares Support Vector Machine
BCI	Brain Computer Interface
CNN	Convolution Neural Network
CSP	Common Spatial Patterns
DWT	Discrete Wavelet Transform
DOCs	Diagnoses of disorders of consciousness
EMD/IMF	Empirical Mode Decomposition/Intrinsic Mode Functions
EEG	Electroencephalogram
HFD	Higuchi's Fractal Dimension
KNN	K Nearest Neighbor
LDA	Linear Discriminate Analysis
MI	Motor Imagery
MDCMI	Multi-Dimensional Conditional Mutual Information
MSPCA	Multi-scale Principal Component Analysis
MBEEGSE	Multiple Branch EEG-net with Squeeze-and Excitation Blocks
MHCNN	Multi-scale High-density CNN
ML	Machine Learning
MSWSA	Mean Short Windowed SA
MRI	Magnetic resonance imaging
NRLRL	Noise Robustness Low-Rank Learning
ROC	Receiver Operating Characteristic
SA	Surrogate Analysis
SVM	Support Vector Machine
SNRs	Signal-to-noise ratios
SSGCNet	Sparse spectra graph convolutional network
SSW	Spikes and slow waves
TFD	Time–Frequency Distributions
VMD	Variational mode decomposition
WNFG	Weighted neighborhood field graph

addition to feature selection followed by feature extraction and with the result analysis. There is a summary of the research gaps and future directions available due to applying the models of testing and categorization [11].

The opportunities of EEG have been enhanced by recent methods in EEG signal processing and acquisition, opening up new approaches to explore the EEG data preprocessing, feature extraction, and feature classification stages for EEG data utilizing for both conventional and advanced methods including thorough review and evaluate the various research trajectories [20].

To investigate and assess the application of machine learning (ML) techniques to categorize diverse seizure types into distinct groups. Find and estimate research that has thoroughly examined the usefulness of integrated preprocessing approaches by the research analysis. The percentage of TUH EEG seizures and the F1 score (V1.4.0 and V1.5.2) of machine learning methods have been acquired. These numbers are stated as follows: seizure-wise validation of 0.901% and patient-wise validation of 0.561% have been acquired [14].

EEG unusual data and normal data were used for feature classification with the help of KNN and SVM algorithms. The accuracy, sensitivity, and specificity of the classifier are defined as percentage values using the performance metrics parameter; the accuracy of the KNN is 71.88%, and the accuracy of the SVM is 81.23%. The following percentage figures have been computed to characterize the sensitivity values for KNN and SVM, which are 80.14% and 77.31% respectively [1].

Principal Method Special experiments were carried out to estimate accuracy, specificity, and sensitivity, and it was found that the CNN technique attained an accuracy and efficiency score of 95.20%. Four strategies were used in the classification: CNN, DT, KNN, and Naive Bayes. The primary focus of the contribution is signal processing using VMD, IMF, and EMD. IMF and VMD techniques are more frequently used in biological and illness-related investigations than in emotion recognition [2].

Selecting the functions of the NRLRL approach, which includes low-rank representation relation formation, is the primary goal of the LS-SVM approach and relation formulation. The University of Bonn's EEG cluster database is used to investigate various noise levels. The technique is then used to test the process on various EEG datasets or to ensure its robustness. EEG signal classification was done using SVM and KNN on a publicly available database for the CHB-MIT database [8].

The suggested approach does not require feature extraction and uses the full TFD of the EEG signals. TFDs and discrepancies have been compared to determine the correct signals. It has been done with classifiers like ANN, SVM, LDA, and k-NN. 13 classification issues, comprising 2, 3, and 5-class issues, and 5 different types of EEG signals were used to evaluate the process. The comparison was reported for seizure detection. Results show highest accuracy of 98% for 5-class problem and with 2 and 3-class, it yields 100% [7].

Motor Imagery (MI) classification involves decoding the intention of an individual to perform specific motor actions based on their brain activity. The investigation introduces a feature extraction method for MI classification. They created connection matrices by dividing the time series of the EEG channels into discrete temporal blocks. The matrix shows the relationships between various blocks. They provide an active connection pattern. After that, non-linear convolutional autoencoders or kernel PCA are used. The features of the dataset and gradient boosting algorithms. It includes a coupled spatial–temporal structure in the features that were obtained [15].

Conventional signal processing and machine learning techniques allow neural recording to observe neural actions and activities. ML techniques that fall within the categories of electrical, magnetic, neuroimaging, and brain stimulation. A high level of temporal resolution and a good resolution can be obtained using non-invasive techniques. Once the signals have been obtained, various feature extraction techniques can be used in signal processing. Simply put, it does not cause any harm to patients. EEG signals are classified using parameters such as band power, variance, and mean. The importance of ML in analyzing difficult data has increased. The most popular ML algorithms are reviewed along with their benefits and downsides. Finally, it is used in a branch of electroencephalography called autobiographical memory problems in schizophrenia [12].

Studies seizure detection and classification methods, both conventional and deep learning technique. Additionally, epileptiform detection is covered and advantages and disadvantages were investigated through comparison. With CNN-RNN, hybrid deep learning has to be investigated. Additionally, the effectiveness of deep learning has drawn attention, according to the research [16].

MBEEGSE is a deep learning architecture created especially for classifying and processing EEG signals. Channel interdependencies are set to adjust channel-wise feature responses while utilizing a multi-branch CNN technique. However, Band power, variance, and mean are some of the metrics used to classify EEG signals. The approach beats earlier techniques for classifying EEG motor imagery, with an accuracy of 82.87%, in the high gamma dataset with minimal complexity and 96.15% in the BCI-IV2a motor imaging dataset [3].

MHCNN, aiming at binary classification, was introduced for evaluating spatial cognitive capacity. Multispectral images were created by connecting the many frequency bands together. A deep learning architecture called DenseNet and the multi-scale CNN technique were improved with the introduction of DenseNet. After the CNN with many scales, the dense network was linked, and training was optimized using the stochastic gradient descent algorithm's learning rate change function to improve and reduce features. The MHCNN performed better in terms of categorization, with 98% accuracy: Theta-Beta2-Gamma band combination was discovered to have the best categorization [19].

The objective is to create a low-cost deep learning model with the best classification accuracy. SSGCNet to address issues with epileptic EEG signal classification. Which provides a WNFG that takes less time and memory to generate graphs and minimizes superfluous edges between graph nodes. The graph of sequential by combining ADMM with sparse weight pruning, CNN is used. On the Bonn and SSW dataset, this technique has the same classification accuracy [18].

Fourier series windowing techniques undervalue discontinuities at the edges of regularly comprehensive data series. They possess a nonstationary time domain that concerns surrogate studies. Monte-Carlo simulations are used to evaluate the approach on an order 1 autoregressive process null hypothesis. EEG diagnostics may benefit from the window. An EEG dataset of 15 participants divided into three groups—ADHD, ADD, and ANX—is utilized [6] (see Table 2).

We believed in both machine learning (naïve Bayesian) and statistical approaches. As a signal feature, the MSWSA was used. The outcomes showed that: (i) the MSWSA feature is less variable; (ii) the windowing approach lessens the bias and non-normality of the SA feature; (iii) 93% of classifications using this technique and Naïve Bayesian are successful; and (iv) the window system is necessary to produce new features.

3 Review Summary

The study has been focused on the examination of feature extraction and preprocessing techniques in EEG signal processing using ML techniques. Therefore, we have extracted some articles from reputed journals and conferences. Among the extracted articles 16 most relevant articles are selected for keen review. Reviewing these techniques, we observed that the EGG signal processing approaches are based on ML form stages for preprocessing, feature extraction, and classification [20]. Additionally, the preprocessing and feature extraction techniques will help to reduce the learning time and memory. These processes are also useful in improving the classification accuracy of ML algorithms utilized in the classification of EEG signals. However, considering the fact that there has been little study on emotion categorization, EEG signals are used in a wide range of applications nowadays.

Among the 16 selected articles based on EEG signal classifications, only one article has been found which is focused on emotion or sentiment classification using EEG signals. Therefore, the aim is established to emotion classification or recognition using EEG signal processing using ML techniques. According to literature we know that preprocessing and feature extraction technique will also be useful in EEG signal processing. Therefore, as the next objective, we proposed to investigate the effect of preprocessing and feature extraction technique to understand the influence of these methods. In this context, the following scenarios of experiments are proposed to perform:

1. Utilize the two types of preprocessing or data enhancement techniques, i.e., standardization and normalization.
2. Utilize Principal Component Analysis (PCA) to identify the essential features from EEG signals. Therefore, it is necessary to conduct experiments after selecting the most periodic features.
3. Next consider the five classification problems to train and classify the EEG signals into relevant emotions.
4. Perform a comparison of the classification results obtained during five classification problems.

Table 2 Information on the reviewed studies

Author	Task	Domain	Method	Results
Khosla et al. [11]	Survey	High temporal resolution, low cost, mobility, and non-invasive neuroimaging procedures are compared	To support applications for diseases, look into diseases including dementia, intense depressive disorder, and epilepsy	Dataset comparison, preprocessing, feature extraction, acquisition techniques, and outcome. Future trends and gaps in the research are documented
Xie and Oniga [20]	Review	Illustrates EEG signal phase techniques	Signal Preprocessing, feature extraction, and classification in order of priority for EEG signaling	Major priorities for research are being explored to advance the understanding and application of EEG-based analysis
Roy et al. [14]	Research	Investigate the adoption of ML algorithms for classifying different seizure types	Since TUH EEG seizure corpus is used to estimate preprocessing, machine learning techniques, and hyper-parameters (V1.4.0 and V1.5.2)	Algorithms achieve an F1 score of up to 0.561 and an F1 value of up to 0.901 regarding seizure-wise cross-validation, with regard to patient-wise cross-validation
Abdulbaqi et al. [1]	Research	Encephalitis illnesses study using EEG	CHB-MIT database is used. DWT was utilized for features. KNN and SVM were used to categorize EEG signals	Acc. KNN (71.88%), SVM (81.23%) Sensitivity KNN (80.14%), SVM (77.31%), Specificity KNN (69.62%), SVM (98%)
Alhalaseh and Alasasfeh [2]	Research	Develop an algorithm that utilizes EEG signals to recognize emotions	For features two techniques were used: entropy and HFD. For classification, Naïve Bayes, k-NN, CNN, and DT used	Evaluate based accuracy, specificity, and sensitivity. The CNN-based approach delivered an accuracy of 95.20%
Gao et al. [8]	Research	NRLRL for EEG signal classification to handle impurities and noise	Establishes a low-rank subspace to link the label to the information. an LS-SVM technique is incorporated that utilizes the pinball loss function to determine the greatest quantile distance	Based on the Bonn data set, investigations with varying noise intensities are designed, and the outcomes prove the significance

(continued)

Table 2 (continued)

Author	Task	Domain	Method	Results
Jukic et al. [10]	Research	Using machine learning algorithms and signal processing on EEG data, one may determine the source of seizures in the brain	The AR algorithm is used to extract features, and MSPCA is used for denoising. The significance of ML techniques is quantified	With the rotation forest, the technique reaches 98.9% accuracy. The results suggest that high-accuracy EEG signal differentiation is possible with ensemble machine learning techniques
Gaur et al. [9]	Research	Reduce channel count to reduce computational cost with maintaining accuracy, by using channel selection	Compute correlation of EEG and select highly correlated channels. CSP are used to analyze image hand movements. BCI Competition III Dataset used	With an addition of >5% and a middle channel reduction of 65.45%, it is possible to install at least some EEG channels
Ech-choudany et al. [7]	Research	Investigating the benefit of TFD, dissimilarity, and classifier embedding techniques for the detection of epileptic seizures	Select the decision rule by calculating the distinctions between the TFD of the EEG. TFDs and dissimilarity have been compared. combining ANN, SVM, LDA, and k-NN	13 classifications are reached to five different types of EEG signals. For the 5-class problem, accuracy is 98%; for the 2- and 3-class problems, accuracy is 100%
Mirzaei and Ghasemi [13]	Research	Improving the accuracy of classification by adopting a feature extraction technique	EEG time series are divided into blocks using KPCA, and connectivity is computed. In comparison to linear PCA, kernel PCA allows for better separation and representation of complicated datasets	It has been revealed that the proposed feature extraction technique can deliver positive results for EEG MI classification

(continued)

Table 2 (continued)

Author	Task	Domain	Method	Results
Luján et al. [12]	Review	An overview of the machine learning (ML) algorithms, traditional signal processing, and neural recording techniques used to track brain activity	EEG signaling is a useful and non-invasive technique for observing brain activity and understanding a range of cognitive and neurological processes is categorized as brain stimulation, electrical, magnetic, and neuro-imaging	ML algorithms are reviewed along with benefits and downsides both spatial and temporal information is crucial for the comprehensive analysis and interpretation of brain signals
Saminu et al. [16, 17]	Review	To investigate seizure detection and classification techniques, including deep learning and conventional algorithms	Discusses epileptic form detection, benefits and limitations of the performance comparison were also examined	Deep learning hybridization has been studied, with CNN-RNN. Based on the investigation analysis, the effectiveness of deep learning in detection and classification has received
Altuwaijri et al. [3]	Research	MBEEGSE is the name of a decoding MI model	To specify channel mutual dependence and to adjust channel-wise feature responses, a multi-branch CNN technique with attention blocks is used	Approximating the algorithm against existing motor imagery classification models, it achieves accuracy of 82.87% using the BCI-IV2a dataset and 96.15%) in the gamma dataset
Wen et al. [19]	Review	MHCNN for spatial cognitive ability assessment was proposed, for binary classification of EEG signals	Multi-scale performance was improved with DenseNet-CNN using multidimensional probabilistic mutual information to extract features	With a 98% classification accuracy, MHCNN achieved better, and the combination of the Theta-Beta2-Gamma band was shown to have the best classification result

(continued)

Table 2 (continued)

Author	Task	Domain	Method	Results
Wang et al. [18]	Research	Propose SSGCNet for EEG signal classification. A light-weighted deep learning model with high level of accuracy	WNFG utilizes less time and memory to relate EEG signals while lowering superfluous edges. Pruning and ADMM use CNN's sequential diagram	This technique on the Bonn and SSW clinical datasets has the same classification accuracy as the method
Caza-Szoka and Massicotte [6]	Research	Exhibits how to decrease the Poor Rejection Percentage by adding a windowing step after allocation	Monte-Carlo simulations were used to test the order 1 auto-regressive null hypothesis, time domain addition for surrogate analysis. There are 3 categories and 15 participants in the data set. Additionally, ML and statistical methods were paired with feature set	Without the window system, the new feature would not have been possible. By using the Bayesian approach MSWSA feature has nominal variability with minimizes bias and non-normality and has a 93% success rate

This section presents an outline of the work in this article that is based on the literature that has been evaluated. The potential consequences depicted above are clarified in greater detail in subsequent sections.

4 Proposed Work

In Fig. 1, the essential experimental model is shown. Additionally, the components of the proposed method have been discussed in this section.

4.1 Dataset

The dataset is taken from the EEG Brainwave Dataset (Kaggle/datasets/birdy654/ EEG brainwave dataset feeling and emotions, Feeling Emotions dataset is the name of the dataset [4, 5]. These EEG brainwave recordings were produced according to published article [4, 5]. Relying on their mind states, one male and one female were subjected to a data cluster for a total of three minutes (positive, neutral, and negative). The EEG placements for AF7, AF8, TP9, and TP10 have been captured

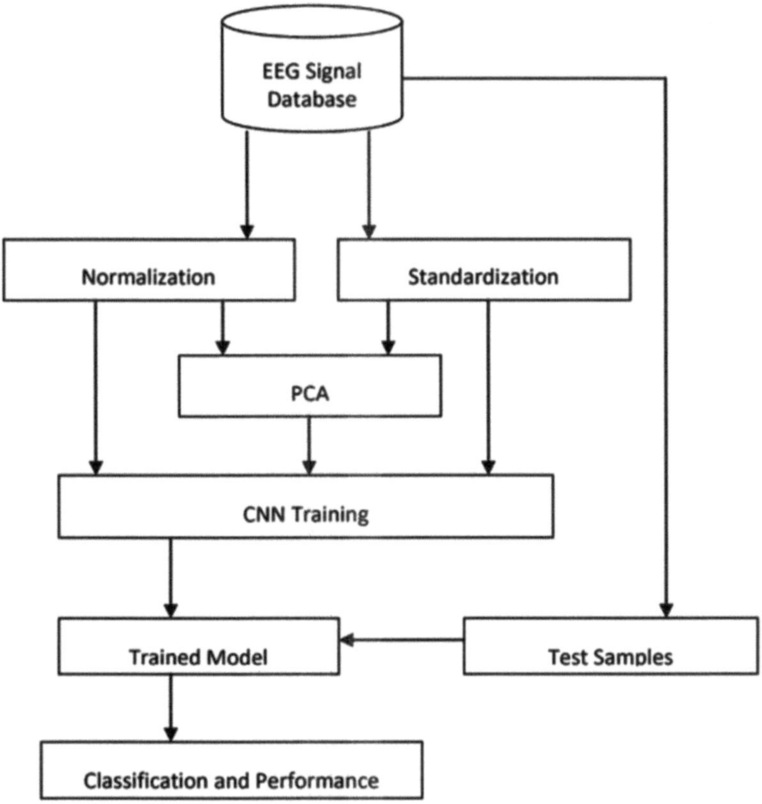

Fig. 1 Proposed experimental model for evaluating the preprocessing and feature extraction techniques

using the Muse EEG headband. Furthermore, data from six minutes of neutral resting is captured. The meanings of the states are shown in Table 3.

Table 3 Dataset states

Movie	Emotions category	Scene taken from
Upper	Negative emotions	Walt Disney studios
My girl	Negative emotions	Explore recreation
La La land	Positive emotions	Horizon media
Normal day life	Positive emotions	Bio quest zone
Dancing dogs	Positive emotions	Mashup zone

4.2 Signal Preprocessing

Feature scaling is an essential phase in getting ready data for machine learning. When utilizing dataset values, the features display a bias towards the value of larger values. Deep learning and machine learning algorithms can learn more quickly and adapt to feature scaling. The two most widely used feature scaling techniques are standardization and normalization.

4.2.1 Normalization

It is applied to scale up features to be comparable. The new value X_n is determined as follows:

$$X_n = \frac{x - x_{\text{min}}}{x_{\text{max}} - x_{\text{min}}}$$

These methods scale the data between the range of $[0, 1]$ or $[-1, 1]$. Normalization is useful when there is no outlier.

4.2.2 Standardization

To habilitate features, subtract the mean and divide the result by the standard deviation. The modified Z-score X_n is calculated as:

$$X_n = \frac{x - x_{\text{mean}}}{\text{Std}}$$

When data follows the Gaussian distribution, it can be useful. If standardization is 1, the information is converted to the origin's mean vector, and the points are either shrunk or broadened. Standardization has no impact on outliers because the converted features do not fall within a specified range. Data preprocessing techniques like normalization and standardization are frequently employed to get data to an appropriate scale and distribution. The key difference between normalization and standardization is given in Table 4.

4.3 Feature Selection

Principal Component Analysis is the most commonly used technique for loosening dimensionality in high dimensional data model and converts into a lower-dimensional model. While retaining as much information as possible [11]. The following steps are used in PCA:

Table 4 The major discrepancy between standardization and normalization

S. no.	Normalization	Standardization
1	The lowest and highest values are used in scaling	It makes usage of the standard deviation and the mean
2	It is helpful in cases where the absolute values are not meaningful	Useful when the absolute values and distribution of features are important
3	Data is transformed to a standard scale between 0 and 1	Data is transformed to have a 0 mean and 1 standard deviation
4	Data in n-dimensions is compressed into an n-dimensional unit hypercube through mutation	Data is extended or shortened and summarized to the mean vector of the original data at the origin
5	Normalization methods include Min–Max scaling and Max Abs scaling	Standardization is typically performed using Z-score normalization

1. Dataset preparation.
2. Build a covariance matrix with dimensions of d × d.
3. The following equation is applied between two features, x_j and x_k:

$$\sigma_{j,k} = \frac{1}{N}\sum_{i=1}^{N}\left(x_j^{(i)} - \mu_j\right)\left(x_k^{(i)} - \mu_k\right)$$

where μ_k and μ_j is the individual mean of the two feature vectors respectively.

Features that increase or decrease simultaneously are denoted by a positive covariance, whereas features that vary in opposite directions are denoted by a negative value. The major features are represented by the covariance matrix's Eigen-vectors, and magnitude is indicated by the Eigen-values.

4. Extract the covariance matrix's eigenvalues and eigenvector, confirming that the eigenvector meets the following conditions:

$$\sum v = \lambda v$$

In this case, λ represents a scalar eigenvalue.

The only eigenvector subset that may be selected in order to extract features from EEG signals and capsulize them into a new feature subspace is the one that has a higher variance value. After utilizing the PCA to the EEG dataset a Convolutional Neural Network has been used to train with EEG Patterns. The next section provides the configuration of sequential CNN for training.

4.4 Classification Model

There is a simple sequential CNN is used for learning and classification of EEG patterns. The CNN is configured in simple five layers first layer is a dense layer and is configured with ReLu activation function. Next, the three layers are also thick, with neurons shrinking in size and their activation function ReLu activated. Three neurons are present in the last layer which are used as output layer for the network. That layer utilizes the softmax activation function for producing the output.

This section discusses the method and components of the model prepared for performing the experiments. The next section provides the experimental results and also suggests the obtained insights using the experiments.

5 Results Analysis

This part proposes an investigation and inspection of the observed investigation that is being presented. The aim is to analyze the effect of preprocessing and feature selection technique.

5.1 Experimental Scenario

The experiments are performed on the following type of classification problem:

1. Original dataset without any preprocessing and feature extraction.
2. Normalized dataset using min–max technique.
3. Standardized dataset using z-score method.
4. Normalized dataset with the PCA based feature extraction.
5. Standardized dataset with the PCA based feature extraction.

5.2 Experimental Observation

The classification of the test samples has been carried out with the EEG signal emotion detection dataset. Additionally, the classification accuracy for training and validation has been evaluated. The accuracy of the algorithm is calculated per epoch. It is the measurement of model correctness and can be measured using:

$$A = \frac{C}{T}$$

where, A is accuracy, C for correctly recognized patterns, and T is the total samples in test set.

The training and validation accuracy is given in Fig. 2a, b. According to Fig. 2a, the learning accuracy of the original dataset without any processing step provides the minimum accuracy. But when we apply any method of preprocessing or feature extraction the accuracy has improved. Additionally, the normalization and standardization of the data will improve training accuracy but is less accurate than the feature extracted. The standardized and extracted 25 features provide smooth training and have higher training accuracy. On the other hand, validation accuracy is given in Fig. 2b. The validation accuracy of standardized dataset and original dataset classification is higher.

Similarly, the training and validation loss is given in Fig. 2c, d. This CNN configuration creates the use of the category cross entropy loss function. It helps to optimize the learning of the neural network. The aim of the training is to minimize the loss during training of algorithm. According to the observations we found in both the patterns original dataset training and validation loss show highly fluctuating patterns as compared to preprocessed and/or extracted features. Several factors, such as the separate classification technique employed, can influence how well EEG

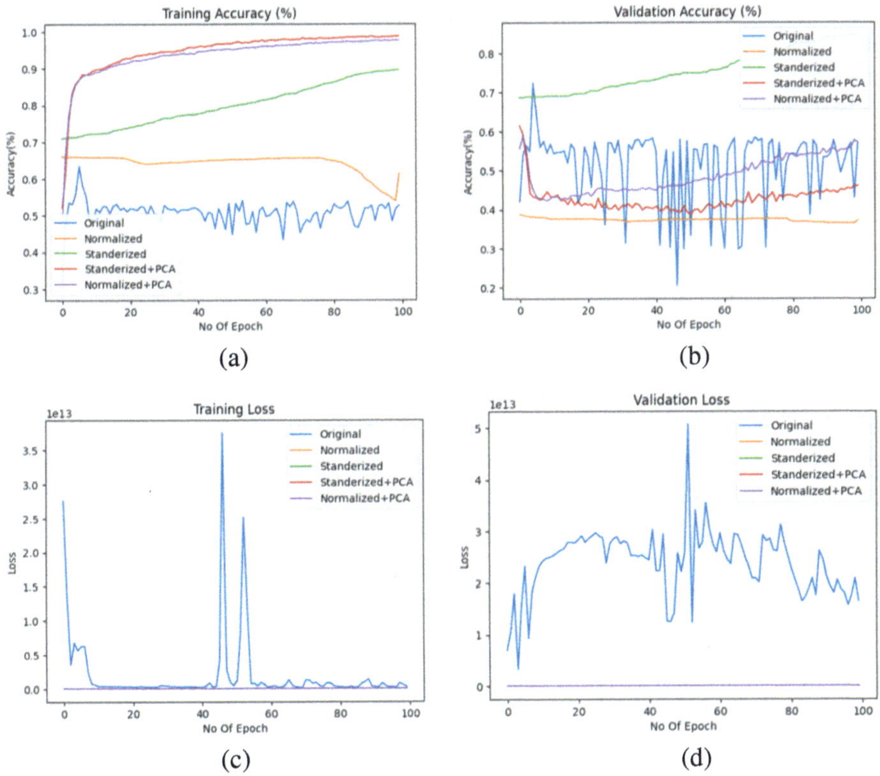

Fig. 2 Performance of experimental problems in terms of **a** Training accuracy, **b** Validation accuracy, **c** Training Loss, **d** Validation Loss

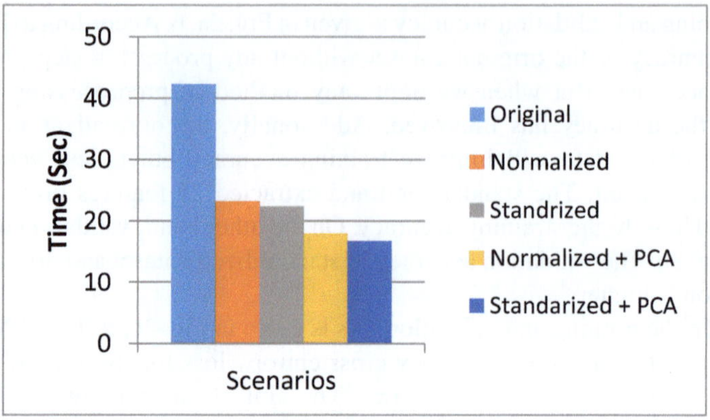

Fig. 3 Training time

data are utilized to classify emotions as per the quality of the EEG data, the EEG preprocessing technique and feature extraction are employed, and the nature of the emotional states being classified. Additionally, the subjective nature of emotions and individual differences in brain activity can also have an impact on how accurately emotions are classified.

Next for measuring the efficiency effects the training time has been measured. The training time (T) is measured by finding the difference between training start time (S) and training end time (E) using the following formula.

$$T = E - S$$

According to the obtained results of all the scenarios the training time is given in Fig. 3. The training time is measured here in terms of seconds (s). Based on the experiments the original dataset takes higher amount of time. Additionally, the normalization process reduces the time complexity of training but standardization technique is more time efficient. Additionally, the utilization of feature selection techniques can reduce more and can depend on the selection of number of features in feature extraction.

6 Conclusion and Future Work

Diagnosing brain activity is an essential task in various applications of medicine and marketing. Brain signals are automatically investigated utilizing machine learning techniques and EEG signals. In this investigation, the steps of EEG signal processing have been studied, which include the preprocessing of EEG signals, feature extraction and then learning and classification. Therefore, by utilizing the simple and basic preprocessing techniques we are trying here to find the influence of each step involved in EEG signal processing. During the investigation, we have found the following consequences:

1. The preprocessing techniques not only help to enhance the quality of learning data, but also enhance the complexity of the learning algorithms in terms of time efficiency.
2. Normalization and standardization techniques help to reduce the training time by up to 50% from the original data processing. Additionally, standardization can improve the training time by up to 15% over normalization. Additionally improves the classification accuracy more effectively as compared to the normalization technique.
3. Feature extraction techniques are influencing the performance but need to locate the appropriate features which will able to represent the suitable characteristics to improve the classification accuracy. Additionally, the feature selection techniques are also able to improve the training time and accuracy.
4. There are a number of Classification techniques available but there are limited techniques which are able to accurately classify the EEG signals. Among the CNN-based Technique is much promising which can be optimized for more accurate classification results.
5. Based on the identified facts the future work objectives have been accomplished:

    i. Design and implement an effective feature extraction approach to improve classification accuracy for both training as well as validation.
    ii. To maximize the EEG signal classification performance, modify the CNN parameters.

Declaration of Competing Interest No conflicts of interest are disclosed by the authors.

Data Availability An open-source data repository has datasets connected to this research (https://www.kaggle.com/datasets/birdy654/eeg-brainwave-dataset feeling-emotions).

Acknowledgements There was no specific grant from any governmental, commercial, or nonprofit funding agency for this research. Furthermore, Dr. Anil Kumar, a medical imaging specialist and senior radiologist from the Vidhya Imaging Centre in Gwalior, Madhya Pradesh, India, provided partial help for the analysis measure.

References

1. Abdulbaqi AS, Younis MT, Younus YT, Obaid AJ (2022) A hybrid technique for EEG signals evaluation and classification as a step towards to neurological and cerebral disorders diagnosis. Int J Nonlinear Anal Appl 13(1):773–781. https://doi.org/10.22075/IJNAA.2022.5590
2. Alhalaseh R, Alasasfeh S (2020) Machine-learning-based emotion recognition system using EEG signals. Computers 9(4):1–15. https://doi.org/10.3390/computers9040095

3. Altuwaijri GA, Muhammad G, Altaheri H, Alsulaiman M (2022) A multi-branch convolutional neural network with squeeze-and-excitation attention blocks for EEG-based motor imagery signals classification. Diagnostics 12(4):1–16. https://doi.org/10.3390/diagnostics12040995
4. Bird JJ, Buckingham CD, Faria DR (2019) Mental emotional sentiment classification with an EEG based brain-machine interface
5. Bird JJ, Manso LJ, Ribeiro EP, Ekart A, Faria DR (2018) A study on mental state classification using EEG-based brain-machine interface. In: 9th International conference on intelligent systems 2018: theory, research and innovation in applications, IS 2018—proceedings, pp 795–800. https://doi.org/10.1109/IS.2018.8710576
6. Caza-Szoka M, Massicotte D (2022) Windowing compensation in Fourier based surrogate analysis and application to EEG signal classification. IEEE Trans Instrum Meas 71:1–11. https://doi.org/10.1109/TIM.2022.3149325
7. Ech-Choudany Y, Scida D, Assarar M, Landré J, Bellach B (2022) Dissimilarity-based time—frequency distributions as features for epileptic EEG signal classification To cite this version : HAL Id: hal-02973615. HAL Open Sci 64:0–24. https://doi.org/10.1016/j.bspc.2020.102268
8. Gao M, Liu R, Mao J (2021) Noise robustness low-rank learning algorithm for electroencephalogram signal classification. Front Neurosci 15(November):1–9. https://doi.org/10.3389/fnins.2021.797378
9. Gaur P, McCreadie K, Pachori RB, Wang H, Prasad G (2021) An automatic subject specific channel selection method for enhancing motor imagery classification in EEG-BCI using correlation. Biomed Signal Process Control 68(68):2–19. https://doi.org/10.1016/j.bspc.2021.102574
10. Jukic S, Saracevic M, Subasi A, Kevric J (2020) Comparison of ensemble machine learning methods for automated classification of focal and non-focal epileptic EEG signals. Mathematics 8(9):3–16. https://doi.org/10.3390/math8091481
11. Khosla A, Khandnor P, Chand T (2020) A comparative analysis of signal processing and classification methods for different applications based on EEG signals. Biocybern Biomed Eng 40(2):649–690. https://doi.org/10.1016/j.bbe.2020.02.002
12. Luján MÁ, Jimeno MV, Sotos JM, Ricarte JJ, Borja AL (2021) A survey on EEG signal processing techniques and machine learning: applications to the neurofeedback of autobiographical memory deficits in schizophrenia. Electronics (Switzerland) 10(23):1–19. MDPI. https://doi.org/10.3390/electronics10233037
13. Mirzaei S, Ghasemi P (2021) EEG motor imagery classification using dynamic connectivity patterns and convolutional autoencoder. Biomed Signal Process Control 68(April):102584. https://doi.org/10.1016/j.bspc.2021.102584
14. Roy S, Asif U, Tang J, Harrer S (2020) Seizure type classification using EEG signals and machine learning: setting a benchmark. In: 2020 IEEE signal processing in medicine and biology symposium, SPMB 2020—proceedings, 1.0. https://doi.org/10.1109/SPMB50085.2020.9353642
15. Saeidi M, Karwowski W, Farahani FV, Fiok K, Taiar R, Hancock PA, Al-Juaid A (2021) Neural decoding of EEG signals with machine learning: a systematic review. Brain Sci 11(11). https://doi.org/10.3390/brainsci11111525
16. Saminu S, Xu G, Shuai Z, Abd I, Kader E, Jabire AH (2021) A recent investigation on detection and classification of epileptic seizure techniques using EEG signal, 1–27
17. Saminu S, Xu G, Shuai Z, El Kader IA, Jabire AH, Ahmed YK, Karaye IA, Ahmad IS (2021) A recent investigation on detection and classification of epileptic seizure techniques using EEG signal. Brain Sci 11(5):668. https://doi.org/10.3390/brainsci11050668
18. Wang J, Gao R, Zheng H, Zhu H, Shi C-JR (2023) SSGCNet: a sparse spectra graph convolutional network for epileptic EEG signal classification. IEEE Trans Neural Netw Learn Syst 14(8):1–15. https://doi.org/10.1109/tnnls.2023.3252569
19. Wen D, Li R, Tang H, Liu Y, Wan X, Dong X, Saripan MI, Lan X, Song H, Zhou Y (2022) Task-state EEG signal classification for spatial cognitive evaluation based on multiscale high-density convolutional neural network. IEEE Trans Neural Syst Rehabil Eng 30:1041–1051. https://doi.org/10.1109/TNSRE.2022.3166224

20. Xie Y, Oniga S (2020) A review of processing methods and classification algorithm for EEG signal. Carpathian J Electron Comput Eng 13(1):23–29. https://doi.org/10.2478/cjece-2020-0004

Advanced Attendance Management System with Independent Yet Unified Face Recognition Pipeline

Sankhala Bhavik Shantilal, Amaresh Chandra Singh, and Nidhi Gupta

1 Introduction

Digital attendance saves time, money, and resources that would otherwise be lost due to human error, produces reports quickly and seamlessly, tracks in real-time, and is extremely secure. Because of the technological age, most schools are transitioning to digital attendance therefore, this model will be essential. A sophisticated type of biometric authentication called facial recognition analyses a person's facial traits from a database image, video, or live feeds to identify and validate them. It is one of the most significant uses of artificial intelligence that could fundamentally alter how everything now functions. It can also be used to identify unauthorized people who access institutions like schools or workplaces.

A detection technique like Haar cascade [1] detects objects in photos, regardless of their size or location. This algorithm is simpler than recent algorithms and can be executed in real-time, although it is less accurate and slower. Multi-Task Cascaded Convolutional Neural Networks (MTCNN) [2] is extremely precise and stable. It properly recognizes faces, despite variations in size, lighting, and rotation. When running on a Central Processing Unit (CPU), the frame rate is relatively low (around 3–5 fps).

RetinaFace is an advanced deep learning based facial detector for Python that incorporates facial landmarks. It has good detection performance. The first implementation heavily relied on Mix-Net (MXNet). Stanislas Bertrand then publishes a tensorflow-based re-implementation of the retina-face algorithm [3]. It can operate

S. B. Shantilal · A. C. Singh
Research and Development, Isnartech PVT. LTD., Saharanpur, India
e-mail: amaresh.0787@isnartech.com

N. Gupta (✉)
Department of Computer Applications, National Institute of Technology Kurukshetra, Kurukshetra, India
e-mail: nidhi.gupta@nitkkr.ac.in

K. Kumar Singh et al. (eds.), *Machine Vision and Augmented Intelligence*, Lecture Notes in Electrical Engineering 1211, https://doi.org/10.1007/978-981-97-4359-9_28

in real-time at speeds of up to 7–10 frames per second. Retina Face is a fantastic tool for improving any face recognition algorithm by replacing MTCNN in alignment and detection tasks. As shown in Fig. 1, MTCNN is incapable of detecting a person wearing a mask as compared to RetinaFace.

To express machine learning models, the Open Neural Network Exchange (ONNX) [5] format was designed. It gives a standard collection of operators, which are the basic building blocks of a deep learning and machine learning model, as well as a standard file format that lets AI professionals combine models from different systems, algorithms, runtimes, and processors.

The Fig. 2 shows the architecture of the light-weight face detection model. It is optimized for edge computing devices. The ultralight face detector is unquestioned in terms of speed, and it also has relatively good accuracy [6]. A wider face pretraining model of the ultralight face detector with different input resolutions of 320 × 240 and 640 × 480 is provided to work better in different application scenarios. It moves at a pace of about 15–20 frames per second.

Fig. 1 MTCNN versus retina face [4]

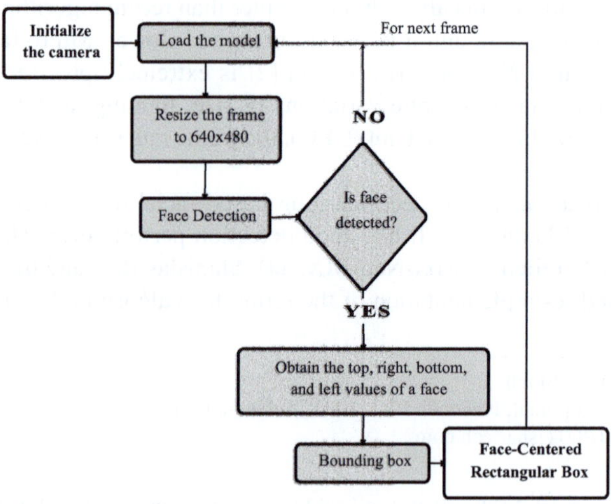

Fig. 2 Ultralight model

The Dlib [7] package is a C++ library that was created with the intention of being utilized by developers working on multiple platforms. When creating the facial Recognition library, they took heavy use of dlib's cutting-edge, deep learning based facial recognition system. It is a versatile and widely used facial recognition library that provides an optimal balance of resource usage, accuracy, and latency, making it ideal for real-time face recognition in mobile app development. Working on real-time projects is difficult due to environmental concerns. The VGG (Visual Geometry Group) [8] architecture is made up of blocks, each of which is made up of 2D convolution and max pooling layers. It was based on research into how to make these networks deeper. Smaller 3 × 3 filters are present in the network. The only additional elements are a fully connected layer and pooling layers; aside from that, the network stands out for its simplicity. VGG Face resulted in a considerable increase in accuracy. However, because it is a big network, training its parameters takes longer. As a result, implementing a VGG network takes time.

FaceNet [9] is a kind of deep neural network designed specifically to recognize faces in images. It learns how to map facial images to a low-dimensional Euclidean space, where distances between faces can be taken as a direct measure of their similarity. These distances are known as vectors for face embedding. It is a neural network with 22 layers of depth. This model takes a facial image as input and returns a 128-value vector embedding as output. Despite having marks on the face, it can recognize the same faces. When there are words in the image, matching may be poor, and if they are wearing the glasses, it focuses on glasses that seem similar.

As shown in Fig. 3, the training of the dataset begins with the detection algorithm reading and pre-processing every single frame. The major step is to create batches and use the pretrained CNN model, which produces an N × 1 matrix that is further reduced by the L2 norm to produce an embedding vector. The triplet loss approach is used to adjust the parameters by bringing an anchor image closer to the positive image and further away from the negative image.

Finding objects in a picture and organizing them into groups is the process of object detection. Faster Regions with Convolutional Neural Networks (R-CNN) [10] is a type of deep learning that blends convolutional neural network characteristics with rectangular region solutions. It is a detection technique with two stages. The initial step involves choosing a sample of image regions that might include an object. In the second stage, the object is categorized for each region. Because of operations like maxpool, a convolutional neural network is substantially slower.

Single-stage detectors predict simultaneous object classification and localization. YOLO (You Only Look Once) is a detector that only has one stage [11]. With the release of YOLO, the real-time object detection space remains active and moving forward. YOLO [12] surpasses other object identification models by a wide margin in terms of inference speed. It operates by splitting the object detection problem into two parts: regression, which uses bounding boxes to determine the object's location, and classification, which identifies an object's category. It has lower recall and more localization mistakes than Faster R-CNN, and it has difficulty recognizing close objects.

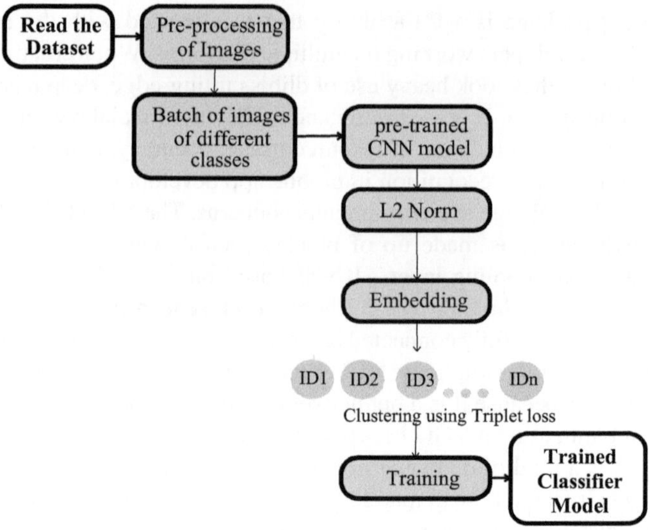

Fig. 3 Training pipeline of FaceNet algorithm

To solve all the above challenges, we created a pipeline for an attendance management system. Our system uses a combination of independent models that work together to accurately identify individuals. The main innovation of our system is the integration of an efficient facial recognition algorithm. This algorithm has been shown to be more accurate and computationally efficient than existing algorithms. We have conducted extensive experiments and performance evaluations to demonstrate the superiority of our system. This system overcomes the limitations of previous systems and makes it a useful tool for monitoring attendance, as discussed in detail in the following sections.

The organization of the paper is as follows. The proposed approach is explained in Sect. 2. Section 3 presents the results of experiments and model outputs. Section 4 concludes the proposed model.

2 Proposed Method

The proposed approach has three phases described below in detail:

1. *Face Detection*
2. *Face Recognition*
3. *Face Verification.*

2.1 Face Detection

The ultralight face detection slim 640 model is one of the ONNX models, which is a simplified version of the lightweight face detection model. This model can be used with projects that use TensorFlow version 1.x. The ultralight model *ultra_light_640.onnx* is loaded, followed by the face detection method, which returns the bounding boxes if a face is identified. The *ort.session* command is used to create an inference session by loading an ONNX model from the database.

It is used for dataset pre-processing, primarily to crop the image to show the correct face. Undetectable faces are removed with the use of pre-processing, which improves the training model's accuracy. The face detection method creates the bounding boxes, crops the face, and then performs recognition.

2.2 Face Recognition

For face recognition, we apply the FaceNet technique, which reliably recovers face embeddings, which are high-quality features required for later training of face recognition systems. The images were trained using the pretrained model, which consists of convolutional layers, and then retrained under the linear model with a default degree of 3 using the support vector classifier.

The embedding vector contains the image's probability of belonging to that class. When the pretrained model is trained, the model and class names are saved to a classifier model file. Create an embedding of a testing image and use the classifier model file to recognize it.

2.3 Face Verification

When the recognition is complete, the final step is Face verification, which is done using the VGG Face model. We utilize the VGG pretrained model to compare the faces and ensure that the recognized class of the image is closer to the same class image in the dataset. This model primarily employs Tensorflow 2.x version.

2.4 Architecture of the Attendance Management System

The architecture of the attendance management system is depicted in Fig. 4. When the model begins capturing live frames, it first runs the model that detects faces, and if any faces are found, it then runs the model that recognizes the faces in the dataset.

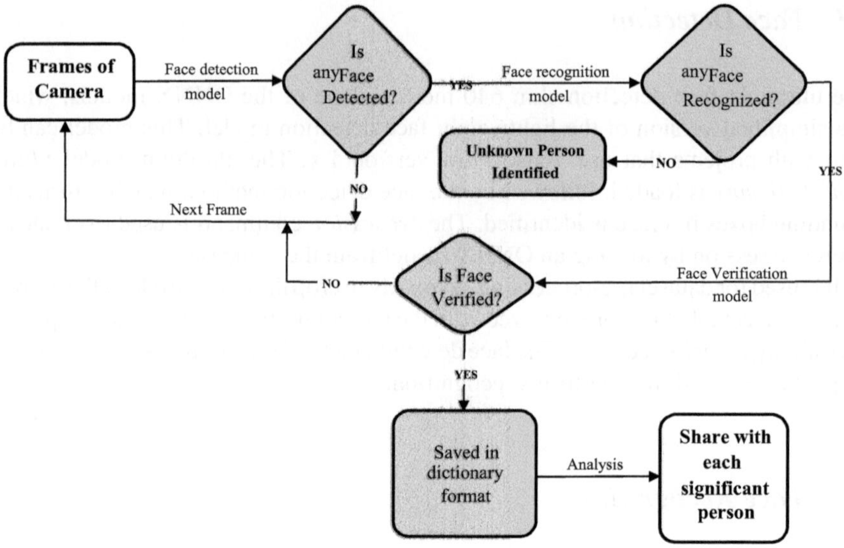

Fig. 4 Architecture of attendance management system

It proceeds on to the verification section if it is recognized. If not, it ends with an unknown person being identified.

Finally, the attendance is marked in dictionary format if the face is verified and the data is shared with each significant person after analysis.

3 Experimental Results

The Python programming language, Jupyter Notebook, and Google Colab were chosen as the development environment. Tensorflow, OpenCV, Scikit-Learn, Onnx Runtime, NumPy, Pandas, and SciPy were used to create the essential functionality. The linear model was utilized, and the probability threshold was set to true. During training, the batch size was set to 10 and the picture size was set at 165 × 165. We used these libraries and systems where the model was trained and hyperparameters were defined to best fit the model. Because different models used different versions of Tensorflow when using the attendance management system, we used an environment-independent technique to allow dispersed models to work independently. This paper proposes a face recognition model by comparing several models employing confusion matrix parameters.

When testing the dataset of an employee video on an ultralight face detection model, 25 frames at an average frame rate of 15 to 18 yielded 100% accuracy when the face was close up or far away but not too fuzzy. Retina-face takes roughly 5 s to complete the detection of 9 people in an image, whereas the ultralight onnx model takes about 0.06 s. In a dataset of around 20 K samples, we selected five classes, trained them, and tested them using our proposed approach using videos of our classes. We extracted 30 frames from each video, and if 10 out of 8 frames consistently had recognized faces that were then verified, the attendance was recorded for that person, yielding a true positive and false positive score.

We utilized a confusion matrix to evaluate our proposed model's performance to that of other models. Multiple parameters, including true positive (TP), false positive (FP), true negative (TN), and false negative (FN), are included in the matrix. These parameters enable us to assess the model's capability to recognize positive and negative outcomes accurately.

The hyperparameters of the confusion matrix for three models are compared: the Proposed Pipeline, FaceNet, and DeepFace versus different classes, which are depicted in Figs. 5, 6, 7 and 8, respectively. We evaluated and trained these models on the basis of five different classes and tested them on a total of ten videos, including both positive and negative types.

In Fig. 9, we experimented with retinal face detection and a deep face model [13] and got an accuracy of 74.762%. We experimented with Ultralight face detection and FaceNet model and got an accuracy of 81.429%, as shown in Fig. 10. Further, as displayed in Fig. 11, the experiments were performed using the proposed model and observed an accuracy of 99.524%. We evaluated all three pipelines by computing their precision, recall, and F1 score as given in the Table and found that our proposed pipeline produced better results than the other two in terms of precision and F1 score.Table 1. Precision, Recall, and F1 score

Fig. 5 Actual: positive and predicted: negative

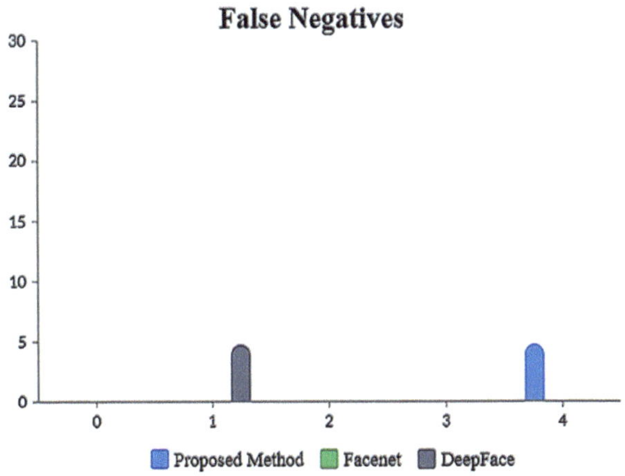

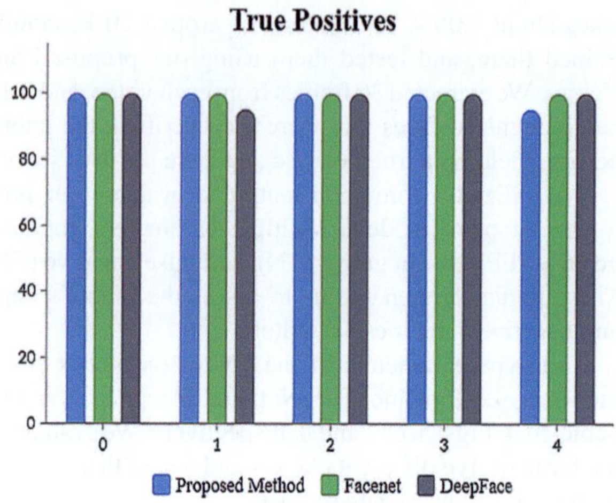

Fig. 6 Actual: positive and predicted: positive

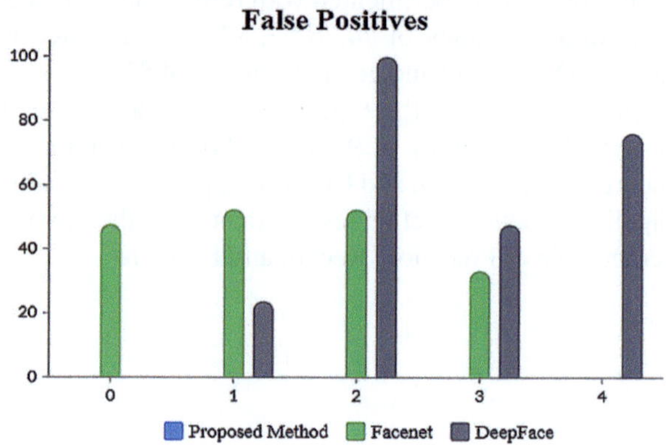

Fig. 7 Actual: negative and predicted: positive

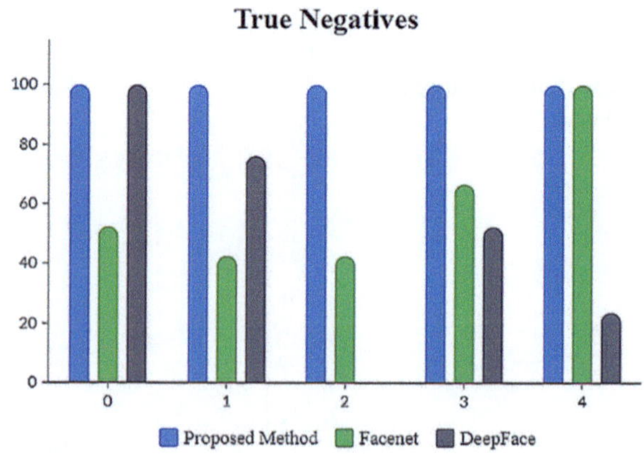

Fig. 8 Actual: negative and predicted: negative

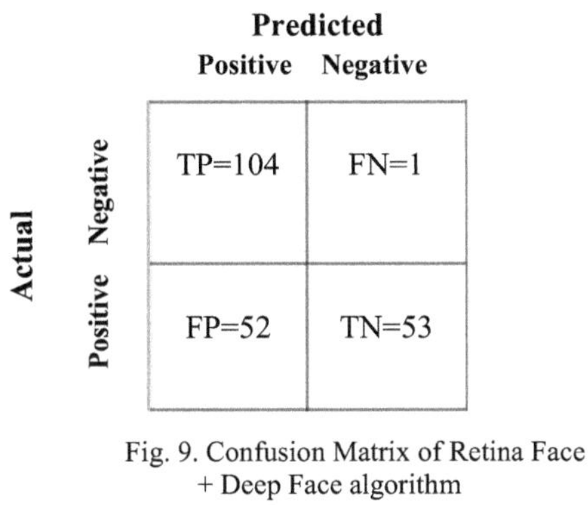

Fig. 9 Confusion matrix of retina face + deep face algorithm

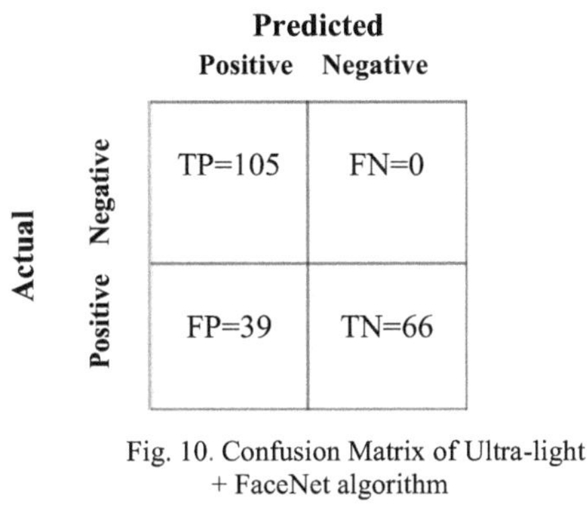

Fig. 10 Confusion matrix of ultralight + FaceNet algorithm

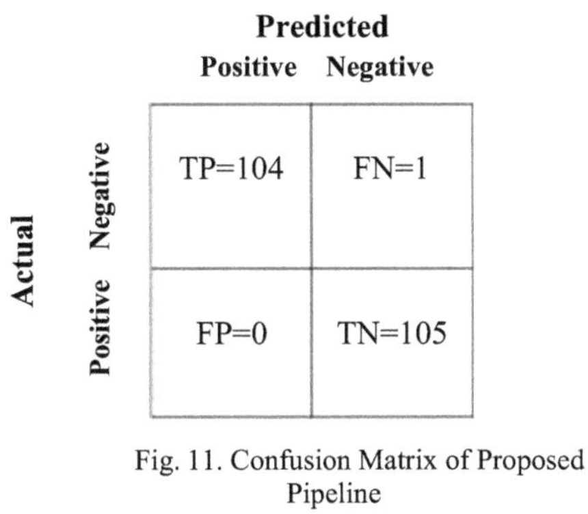

Fig. 11 Confusion matrix of proposed pipeline

Table 1 Precision, recall and F1 score

Models	Precision	Recall	F1 score
RetinaFace detection + DeepFace model	0.667	0.990	0.797
Ultralight face detection + FaceNet model	0.729	1.000	0.843
Proposed pipeline	1.000	0.990	0.995

4 Conclusion

This research provides a face recognition model by comparing multiple models using confusion matrix parameters, it was revealed that the proposed model outperformed all other models in terms of its ability to detect faces reliably. This model performs better and identifies people more accurately. The comparative findings show that the suggested model is a better alternative for face recognition tasks and may be used in a number of applications. This also demonstrates the evolution and advancement of facial recognition technology, and we can easily connect the proposed model with the behavior analysis model. This proposed model may be a beneficial addition to the currently extensively utilized strategies.

References

1. Viola P, Jones M (2001) Rapid object detection using a boosted cascade of simple features. In: Proceedings of the 2001 IEEE computer society conference on computer vision and pattern recognition. CVPR 2001, vol 1, pp I–511–I–518
2. Zhang K, Zhang Z, Li Z, Qiao Y (2016) Joint face detection and alignment using multitask cascaded convolutional networks. IEEE Signal Process Lett 23(10):1499–1503
3. Stanislasbertrand/RetinaFace-TF2: RetinaFace (RetinaFace: Single-stage dense face localisation in the wild, published in 2019) reimplemented in tensorflow 2.0, with pretrained weights available, GitHub. https://github.com/StanislasBertrand/RetinaFace-tf2. Accessed 10 Jan 2023
4. Limited A (2023) Group of peoples with mask and no mask, Alamy. https://www.alamy.com/. Accessed 15 Jan 2023
5. Linzaer/Ultra-Light-Fast-Generic-Face-Detector-1MB: 1MB Lightweight face detection model, GitHub. https://github.com/Linzaer/Ultra-Light-Fast-Generic-Face-Detector-1MB. Accessed 15 Jan 2023
6. Feng Y (2019) Real time face recognition with CPU, Medium. Towards Data Science. https://towardsdatascience.com/real-time-face-recognition-with-cpu-983d35cc3ec5. Accessed 22 Jan 2023
7. Zhang D, Li J, Shan Z (2020) Implementation of dlib deep learning face recognition technology. In: 2020 international conference on robots & intelligent system (ICRIS), pp 88–91
8. Liu S, Deng W (2015) Very deep convolutional neural network-based image classification using small training sample size. In: 2015 3rd IAPR Asian conference on pattern recognition (ACPR), pp 730–734
9. Schroff F, Kalenichenko D, Philbin J (2015) FaceNet: a unified embedding for face recognition and clustering. In: 2015 IEEE conference on computer vision and pattern recognition (CVPR), pp 815–823
10. Ren S, He K, Girshick R, Sun J (2017) Faster R-CNN: towards real-time object detection with region proposal networks. IEEE Trans Pattern Anal Mach Intell 39(6):1137–1149
11. Redmon J, Divvala S, Girshick R, Farhadi A (2016) You only look once: unified, real-time object detection. In: 2016 IEEE conference on computer vision and pattern recognition (CVPR), pp 779–788
12. Yang W, Jiachun Z (2018) Real-time face detection based on YOLO. In: 2018 1st IEEE international conference on knowledge innovation and invention (ICKII), pp 221–224
13. Serengil SI, Ozpinar A (2020) LightFace: a hybrid deep face recognition framework. In: 2020 innovations in intelligent systems and applications conference (ASYU), pp 1–5

Morphcrypt: Morphing of Images and Encrypting Using PIX2PIX and KAA Map

Praveen Abhi Vamsi Kodali, Sai Jaya Nithya Madhasu, and Sagar Dhanraj Pande

1 Introduction

In the recent years the private companies and even government bodies like MAT of New York, are becoming the targets to the eyes of Cyber Espionage Operatives causing cyber Incursions on the database of the private agencies like Sense time (2023), and even the government representations like Metropolitan Transportation Authority (MTA) of New York (2023) for the only purpose of flinching the facial image leading to a massive leakage of private information of public causing a havoc, This leads to a question that were even the government is unable to protect the facial data in from the eyes of cyber intruders?, thus the urge of creating a novel method that outwits the intruders is needed, this paper creates a method that leverages the image morphing done by the picture to picture (PIX2PIX) [1], a Generative Adversarial Network (GAN) that change images by the specification of its use, which in our case is to morph the morph the images depicted in paired image datasets [2], later this method makes the morphed images to travers through the edge cutting encryption method named KAA map [3] that will encrypt the morphed image and this whole process will be done on the sender level, on the receiver's end the implementation of the process will be inversed. The proposed method has the potential to protect all kinds of images from the bandits.

The contributions of the paper are described as below:

- An extensive dataset is self-created for the demonstration of model's performance.

P. A. V. Kodali (✉) · S. J. N. Madhasu
School of Computer Science and Engineering, VIT-AP University, Amaravati, Andhra Pradesh, India
e-mail: kodaliabhivamsi@gmail.com

S. D. Pande
School of Engineering and Technology, Pimpri Chinchwad University (PCU), Pune, India
e-mail: sagarpande30@gmail.com

K. Kumar Singh et al. (eds.), *Machine Vision and Augmented Intelligence*, Lecture Notes in Electrical Engineering 1211, https://doi.org/10.1007/978-981-97-4359-9_29

- A comparative analysis of different deep learning architectures has been incorporated.
- A novel method of KAA map and PIX2PIX has been implemented.
- Fast end to end encrypted transmission can be incorporated.

The rest of the paper is organized as Sect. 2 consisting of literature survey where a review over previous work is carried out, continuing with Sect. 3, methodology, here the dataset description and preprocessing work and working of proposed methodology are defined. Section 4 discusses the results obtained by the methodology and an analysis of the results is carried out. Finally, Sect. 5 concludes the paper with conclusion of the paper and future scope of the work done.

2 Literature Survey

Various papers and journals have been referred and the gap in the relative work has been discovered, the comparison of the relative work is carried out. Below Table 1 shows the advantages of relative work and disadvantages of it and how the proposed model is going to overcome the limitations of the previous work.

3 Summary of the Comparison Table

The table that is shown offers a thoughtful evaluation of each article, describing both of its benefits and drawbacks. This triggered a lengthy discussion about how to get around the current study's shortcomings. By thoroughly analyzing the body of existing literature, this study identifies areas for improvement and offers fresh approaches. The scholarship value and contribution are considerably boosted by integrating this comparison analysis, which illuminates trends, strengths, and shortcomings and gives creative solutions for limitations.

4 Proposed Methodology

4.1 Dataset Description

The dataset that is utilized for this project is self-picked from various websites that provide paired images of daily usage like house, food, pets, etc. The source of the images includes Unsplash, Getty image, and Shutter shock. A total of 3450 images were collected, which will be divided into two categories, i.e., training and testing in the ratio of 8:2, which will sum up to 2760 images of training and 690

Table 1 Comparative analysis of existing work

References	Year	Dataset	Advantages	Disadvantages	The proposed model strength
[3]	2023	Self-collected different images	Offers a novel approach to digital data security by combining two hyperchaotic maps and the single neuron model in a singular way for image encryption	A potential trade-off between encryption strength and image quality preservation is revealed by the achieved Mean Squared Error (MSE) of 9626 and PSNR of 8.3 db	The proposed method gives out the high-quality images with the combination of PIX2PIX and KAA. The computation power required is relatively low
[2]	2023	Self-collected different images	Compared to previous chaotic systems, it offers greater complexity and randomness, making it suited for a variety of applications, including communication and data encryption	Hardware implementation can be challenging	The implementation is very simple in real-time
				The strength of encryption is comparatively weak	Strong encryption of images is provided
[4]	2023	Animal image dataset	Making the diffusion model smaller and simpler thus seed increases	The system is too complex for computation	The proposed method utilizes low computation
[5]	2023	Synthetic MRI images	Tested on large dataset implying high model support	As synthetic data is used real-time used can be challenging	The dataset of the model is collected and real-time use so possible

images of testing. The division of the classes for the implementation of the proposed methodology is depicted in the below Fig. 1

4.2 Dataset Preprocessing

The results of the model greatly depend up on how well the dataset is, data preprocessing, is the step where the data's wellness can be corrected, in this step, the collected images were all cropped and resized to the same size of 256 × 256. The

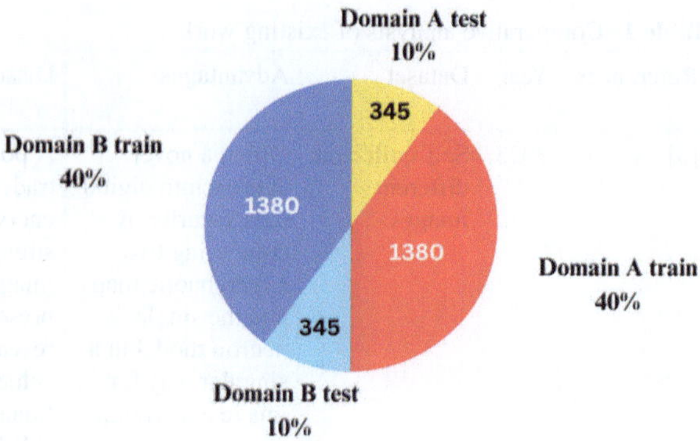

Fig. 1 Class distribution of data

first step was to comprehend its dimensions, structure, and types of data; the next was to address issues like missing data and outliers [4]. The adoption of data visualization tools like histograms made it simpler to understand distribution and linkages. Missing value and outlier problems were addressed after cleaning and preprocessing. It was simpler to analyze a model comprehensively while yet addressing privacy-related ethical concerns with a train-test split.

4.3 PIX2PIX Architecture

PIX2PIX is the architecture we employed to morph the images from one domain to another domain as it learns to map the images from one image to the corresponding paired domain image. PIX2PIX [5] is a GAN based architecture that will be mapping features from the input paired images [6]. It consists of the Generator, which will generate the images with the help of it's learning to map features from training and the Discriminator [7], which will discriminate the images as fake or real this will be kept to competition to generator to improve the generator.

Generator: A neural network model is demonstrated by the Pix2Pix generator, which takes a source image as input and outputs an image that is comparable to the target image [8]. Using a conditional GAN (Generative Adversarial Network) framework [9], it learns the mapping between the source and target domains. In an effort to create a target image that aesthetically reflects the desired target data, the generator attempts to change the source image. This is done by tricking the discriminator network into thinking that the generated images are real while also attempting to reduce the difference between the created images and the actual target images through the use of the adversarial training process. The loss generated by generator is depicted by below Eq. (1).

$$\begin{aligned} Loss\ of\ GAN(G, DA, B, A) &= Ea \sim Pinput(a)\left[\log DA(a)\right] \\ &+ Eb \sim Pinput(b)\left[\log(1 - DA(G(b)))\right] \end{aligned} \tag{1}$$

Discriminator: A neural network called the Pix2Pix discriminator assesses the realism of images. It specifically evaluates if an input image originates from the actual target domain or if it is a created image from the generator in the context of the Pix2Pix architecture. The discriminator's main job is to give the generator feedback by allocating a probability score that represents how authentic the input image appears [10]. The discriminator's job gets harder as the generator develops its capacity to create more convincing images. During the training, the discriminator will find and discriminate the original images from those of images created by the generator [11], doing this will make the generator to create more real like images that can not be discriminated by the discriminator. Adversarial loss which is also called as discriminator loss in PIX2PIX is represented by Eq. 2.

$$\begin{aligned} LFGAN(G, DA, B, A) = {} & Eb \sim P\_inpt(a)\big[\log DA(a)\big] \\ & + Eb \sim P\_inpt(b)\big[\log(1 - DA(G(b)))\big] \end{aligned} \tag{2}$$

KAA map: KAA map is a chaotic map that works with both 2-dimensional and 3-dimensional images to encrypt. Before going into the detailed description let's try to understand the process in mathematical terms through Eq. 3.

$$a\_\{j+1\} = a\_j + c\big(b\_j - a\_j\hat{}2\big)\,\&\, b\_\{j+1\} = a\_j + d(a\_j - b\_j) \tag{3}$$

The power of KAA map lies in its fragile nature to the little disturbances during the initial phase. This simply means that even if there are any small changes that happen in the initial encryption model then there will be no way to get the original image in the decryption process [12]. So, to keep it simple if it's not the correct decryption key then no correct decryption for it. This is the feature that makes the KAA map to sustain the present years mainly in the image encryption domain [13]. there will be a formation of grids to the cells after turning them to the grayscale image and then the values of the first grid of pixels will be taken as the initial values and the grid will be iterated through the entire grid several times this process will be continued till the entire image iterating each cell until the very last end cell of the pixels. The initial values will be the decryption key, and the decryption process is surprisingly easy, i.e., to simply to reiterate in reverse order, thus if the initial conditions aren't right or any corruption happens in the decryption process then the reverse iteration is not possible [14]. The KAA map is then iterated through several times to produce the decrypted image. It has been demonstrated that the KAA map works well for picture encryption [15]. It is robust to numerous attacks, including differential, statistical, and brute-force attacks.

5 Result and Analysis

The aforementioned structures were reproduced using Google Colab, the fundamental publications, and the reference code provided by the original authors. After which it combined the previously mentioned dataset with its own dataset and evaluated the outcomes. A Google Colab laptop (pro version), which has an Intel i7 7th generation 2-core CPU running at 2.30 GHz and 8 GB of RAM, is used to carry out the experiment. Be aware that we used the Google Collab Pro edition on the backend server A100, which has 166 GB of disc space, 40 GB of GPU, and 83 GB of RAM. The evaluation of any encryption algorithm is typically revolving around the speed of the algorithm to encrypt and how secure the encryption is, so we evaluated the model with the same parameters. Below Fig. 2 shows how well does KAA map performs with other encryption methods, this evaluation is carried out in terms of security and in terms of speed:

The PIX2PIX Gan's performance is also compared and tested with different types of GANs with the self-picked dataset to analyze the best performer in terms of loss. The below Table 2 shows the comparison of PIX2PIX with different gains.

Different types of GANs are compared to PIX2PIX in terms of image translation or morphing but out of all the results attained by the PIX2PIX are more promising in terms of morphing or translation, the below Fig. 3 shows the results attained by the PIX2PIX in image translation.

Fig. 2 KAA map's performance

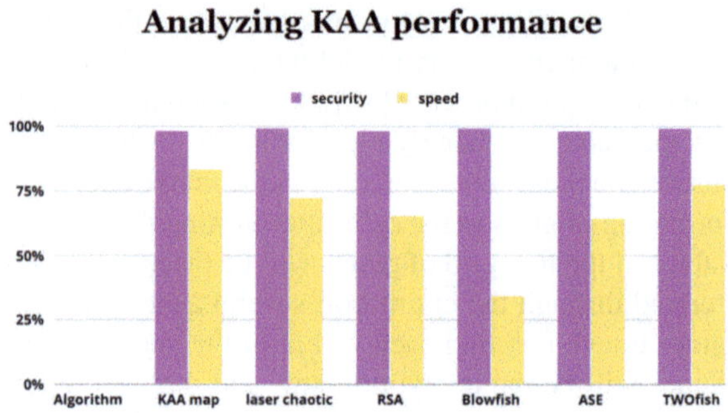

Table 2 Various colorization architectures accuracy comparisons

S. No	Architectures	Total_Loss	Gen_loss	Disc_loss	Batch size	Learning rate
1	BEGAN	10.693	6.9956	6.5688	32	0.0001
2	ProGAN	13.4695	8.3695	9.9562	32	0.0005
3	AttnGAN	11.9855	9.1639	6.9567	16	0.0001
4	BIGGAN	8.32218	5.3645	6.2345	32	0.001
5	**PIX2PIX GAN**	**3.6856**	**0.4098**	**0.4956**	**32**	**0.0001**
6	UNIT	7.9298	3.2595	0.001	56	0.005

Fig.3 Translated images

Fig.4 Encryption and decryption of image

Let's see how well the KAA map was able to achieve the encryption and decryption of the image given to it as an input, the below Fig. 4 shows the encryption and encryption result and its corresponding decryption of the image.

The final results obtained by the model is the work of the bridge connectivity of the two domains of Deep learning and Cyber security. The flow of the models working is the morphed images are collected and sent to morph by the encryption as the results illustrated in images 3 and 4, paper suggests the application is real-time reliable.

6 Conclusion and Future Scope

PIX2PIX image morphing and the KAA map encryption algorithm were successfully combined in this project to create an avant-garde method of image encryption and decryption. Along with showcasing each technique's advantages individually, the combination of these strategies offers a fresh method for increasing image security. We've developed a comprehensive framework that has promise for applications across data protection, communication security, and privacy preservation by seamlessly fusing PIX2PIX's adaptive picture modification with the powerful encryption provided by the KAA map algorithm. The project's future goals include examining the combined PIX2PIX and KAA map encryption framework's capacity to handle larger datasets effectively and its suitability for real-time image encryption applications. The security of the system may also be improved through study into computational resource optimization for faster performance and the incorporation of additional cutting-edge encryption techniques. The necessity for thorough testing to ensure resistance against new decryption methods and potential difficulties in maintaining encryption strength as image sizes grow are constraints, too.

References

1. Alexan W, Elkandoz M, Mashaly M, Azab E, Aboshousha A (2023) Color image encryption through Chaos and KAA map. IEEE Access 11:11541–11554. https://doi.org/10.1109/ACCESS.2023.3242311
2. Erkan U, Toktas A, Lai Q (2023) 2D hyperchaotic system based on Schaffer function for image encryption. Expert Syst Appl 213:119076. https://doi.org/10.1016/j.eswa.2022.119076
3. Alexan W, Chen Y-L, Por LY, Gabr M (2023) Hyperchaotic maps and the single neuron model: a novel framework for chaos-based image encryption. Symmetry 15(5):1081. https://doi.org/10.3390/sym15051081
4. Parmar G, Singh K, Zhang RH, Li Y, Lu J, Zhu J (2023) Zero-shot image-to-image translation.https://doi.org/10.1145/3588432.3591513
5. Bao W, et al. (2023) Quantitative cerebral blood volume image synthesis from standard MRI using image-to-image translation for brain Tumors. Radiology 308(2). https://doi.org/10.1148/radiol.222471
6. Al-Khedhairi A, Elsonbaty A, Elsadany AA, Hagras EAA (2020) Hybrid cryptosystem based on pseudo chaos of novel fractional order map and elliptic curves. IEEE Access 8:57733–57748
7. Alexan W, ElBeltagy M, Aboshousha A (2021) Image encryption through Lucas sequence S-Box and chaos theory. Proc. 8th NAFOSTED Conf Inf Comput Sci (NICS) pp 77–83
8. Alexan W, ElBeltagy M, Aboshousha A (2022) RGB image encryption through cellular automata S-Box and the Lorenz system. Symmetry 14(3):443
9. Ali TS, Ali R (2020) A new chaos-based color image encryption algorithm using permutation substitution and Boolean operation. Multimedia Tools Appl 79(27):19853–19873
10. Anderson DR (2008) Model based inference in the life sciences: a primer on evidence, New York, NY, USA Springer, vol 31
11. Gao H, Wang X (2021) Chaotic image encryption algorithm based on zigzag transform with bidirectional crossover from random position. IEEE Access 9:105627–105640
12. Singhal T (2020) A review of coronavirus disease-2019 (COVID-19). Indian J Pediatrics 87(4):281–286
13. Guatemala: WHO coronavirus disease (COVID-19) Dashboard |WHO coronavirus disease (COVID-19) dashboard, 2022 [online] https://who.int
14. Shereen MA, Khan S, Kazmi A, Bashir N, Siddique R (2020) COVID-19 infection: emergence transmission and characteristics of human coronaviruses. J Adv Res 24:91–98
15. Xie X, Zhong Z, Zhao W, Zheng C, Wang F, Liu J (2020) Chest CT for typical 2019-nCoV pneumonia: relationship to negative RT-PCR testing, J Clin Microbiol

Recommendation of Music Based on Facial Recognition and Emotion Analysis

Sai Ganesh Chintha, V. C. Bharathi, Anusha Mayaluri, Lahari Bylapudi, and M. Mohammed Iqbal

1 Introduction

Many recent studies highlight the great effects of music on human behavior and brain function. It is widely recognized that music plays an important role in creating feelings of happiness and relaxation. Also, the interaction of music with emotion has been the subject of research, and studies have elucidated its relationship with human emotions [1]. Music, as a powerful emotional stimulus, has the ability to induce a positive emotional state and promote self-awareness, which is an important part of its benefits. Furthermore, there is a strong relationship between music preference and between personality traits, and emphasizes its role as an emotional channel [1].

The use of music, including features such as meter, pitch, rhythm, and tone, resides in brain regions intricately linked to emotion and cognitive control [2]. Human communication is a cornerstone of survival, providing information a complex exchange through body language, speech, and facial expressions is easy, or emotional cues [3]. It remains the most important process in applications, spanning domains such as smart card design, surveillance, image database analysis, criminal investigation, video classification, and adaptive human–computer interfaces in multimedia environments.

Advances in signal processing technologies, effective subtraction systems wave reduction, and spontaneous recognition of emotion in interactive media, be it music

S. G. Chintha (✉) · V. C. Bharathi · A. Mayaluri · L. Bylapudi
School of Computer Science and Engineering, VIT-AP University, Amaravathi, Andhra Pradesh, India
e-mail: chinthasaiganesh844@gmail.com

V. C. Bharathi
e-mail: bharathi.vc@vitap.ac.in

M. M. Iqbal
Department of Information Technology, Sri Sivasubramaniya Nadar College of Engineering, Chennai, Tamil Nadu 603110, India

K. Kumar Singh et al. (eds.), *Machine Vision and Augmented Intelligence*, Lecture Notes in Electrical Engineering 1211, https://doi.org/10.1007/978-981-97-4359-9_30

or film, are gaining popularity. This model has the potential to resonate the size of a range of applications, including human–computer interaction and music-based experiences. In this regard, we propose an emotion recognition recommendation system based on facial expressions, which is adept at distinguishing users' emotional states and resolves the list of appropriately selected songs well [4–9]. The framework discerns a person's emotional mood and tailors playlists accordingly. For example, when negative emotions are detected, they will put popular songs on a playlist to raise the mood. In contrast, for positive emotions, a diverse selection of songs will be presented.

2 Literature Review

Before starting of our work, we conducted a thorough literature review on existing projects, papers, and studies in this field. And we found out that few of the works can help us significantly to understand and analyze the working of certain existing models.

Prima et al. [10] developed a music machine that automatically selects songs based on user intention using Viola-Jones for facial recognition. Yusuf Yaslan and others. Athavle et al. [11] developed an emotion-driven music recommendation system that learns the user's emotions from physiological sensations such as GSR and PPG, and predicts arousal and valence. Guidell et al. [12] integrated basic emotions into a framework using convolutional neural networks for face recognition.

Ramanathan et al. [13] introduced an intelligent music player by classifying local music according to emotional content. Their algorithm automates a playlist based on facial expressions for accuracy and efficiency, validated with user-matched data sets.

3 Problem Definition

The challenge is to create stage musical performances blended with deep learning programs. The main goal is to develop a system that can provide music recommendations based on the user's prevailing emotional state, as detected by real-time analysis of facial expressions captured by a webcam.

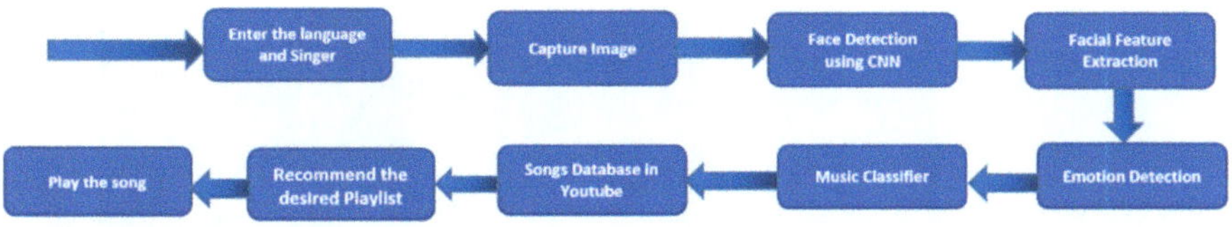

Fig. 1 Block Diagram of the proposed system

4 Proposed System Overview

This system is all about making it easy for the user to interact with the music player and play the music according to his mood without explicitly saying but just by recognizing it from his face. A key aspect is how it catches the user's facial expressions using a webcam. These facial cues are the basis for Complex Network Models (CNNs) ready to understand and guess emotions. After that, the system uses these emotional clues to create tailored music playlists. The goal is to change the user's mood by covering a range of feelings from happy and sad, to neutral, and even surprised.

The system of our implementation consists of four main modules, each with a different purpose. They are: Real-time capture module, Face recognition module, emotion recognition model, and music recommendation module.

The Real-time capture module is made to ensure that the user's facial expressions are captured accurately and continuously by the webcam. The face recognition model is for using data from real-time capture, this module uses a convolutional neural network to analyze and recognize complex facial features. As we analyze nuances, the emotion recognition module distinguishes the user's emotional states and subsequently generates descriptive text that corresponds to these emotions like happy, sad, anger, etc. This final module of Music recommendation focuses on establishing and matching emotional states and recommends playlists that match the user's mood with the help of the YouTube search engine.

Specifically, our proposed system acts as a complex network of real-time capture, advanced deep learning algorithms, emotion recognition, and optimized music recommendations, and it culminates in a holistic and immersive user experience (Fig. 1).

5 Methodology

5.1 Dataset Details

Our CNN model was trained on the FER2013 dataset, consisting of 24,176 training images and 6,043 testing images, each resized to 48×48 pixels and annotated with one of five emotions. The dataset provides a balanced representation of emotions

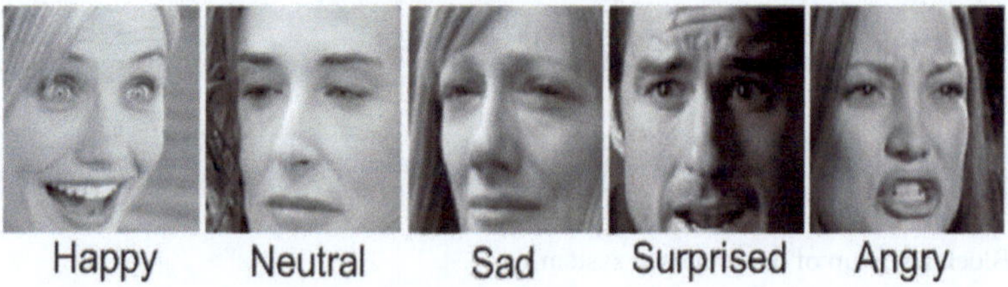

Fig. 2 Sample Images from FER2013 dataset

and diverse facial expressions, but it may be less accurate for less common emotions like disgust and fear. To address class imbalance, we used the weighted-SoftMax loss technique, assigning weights to loss terms based on emotion class occurrence, enhancing our model's ability to recognize a wide range of emotions (Fig. 2).

5.2 *Emotion Detection Module*

5.2.1 Face Detection and Emotion Detection

The Emotion Detection module employs computer vision technology, with a focus on human face detection for various applications. It utilizes classifiers, such as Haar Cascades and Local Binary Pattern (LBP), to distinguish faces from non-faces in images. Haar Cascades are trained on facial characteristics to accurately isolate faces within frames. In the Convolutional Neural Network (CNN) architecture, feature detectors identify image attributes, followed by pooling for translation invariance. After flattening, we feed the input into deep neural network for classification to detect emotions (Figs. 3 and 4).

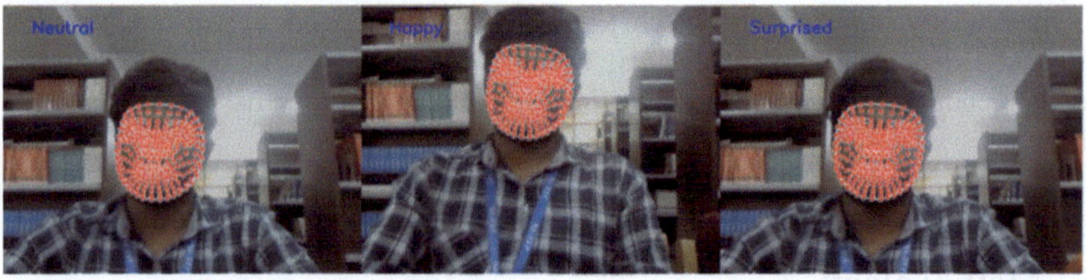

Fig. 3 Using CNN to detect facial emotions

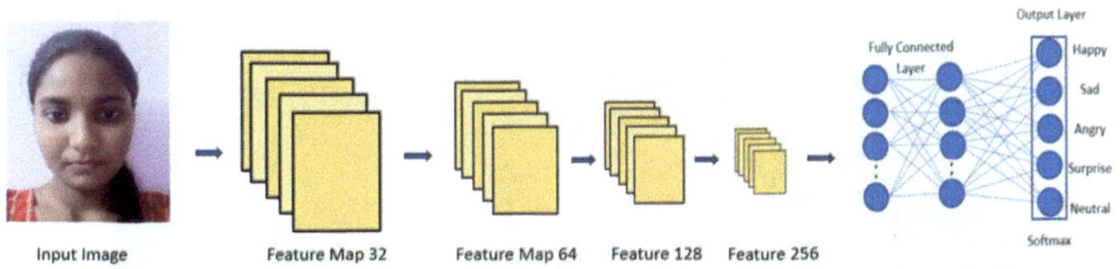

Fig. 4 Architecture of CNN used to train this model

Fig. 5 Front page's GUI

5.3 Music Recommendation Module

The Music Recommendation module is to develop and improve the user experience of music with the help of output from the emotion detection module. Integrated with YouTube, it suggests songs according to user preferences like language and singer. The output of the emotion detection module is then directed to YouTube search for relevant song suggestions Validation checks ensure emotion capture, displaying a warning if not detected. The system monitors a "run" variable for execution flow. If emotions are captured, it directs users to YouTube. If not, it prompts for accurate emotional input. Upon successful capture and match verification, the system redirects to YouTube, creating a harmonious user-music connection. The GUI provides a customized list of songs according to their emotions to enhance their experience. This module uses MediaPipe and Streamlit packages to create a user-friendly interface (Figs. 5, 6 and 7).

6 Results and Analysis

Our evaluation encompassed a range of studies employing diverse techniques, including Convolutional Neural Networks (CNNs), Extreme Learning Machines (ELMs), and Support Vector Machines (SVMs) [11]. The comparative assessment of these algorithms is presented in Table 1, wherein each study is associated with its respective algorithm and corresponding accuracy values. Notably, the utilization of Convolutional Neural Networks has demonstrated an augmentation in the accuracy of emotion detection, signifying their efficacy in this domain.

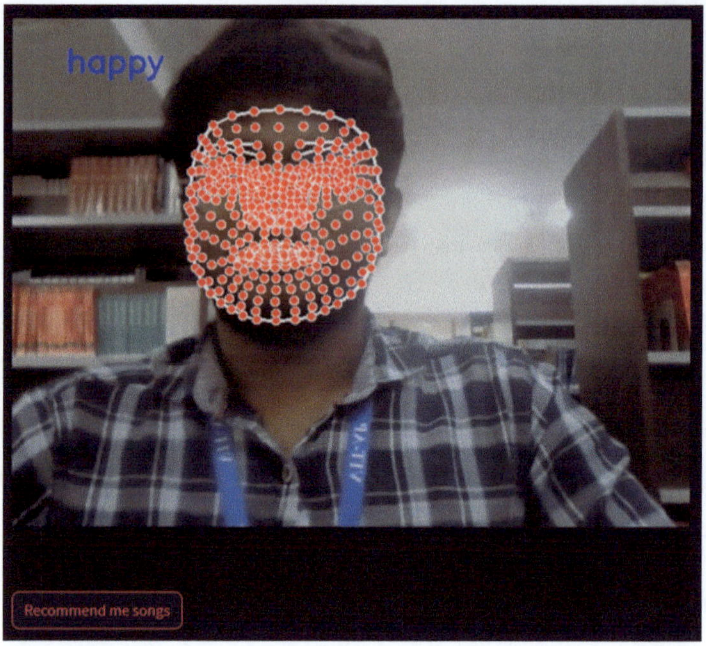

Fig. 6 Emotion detection

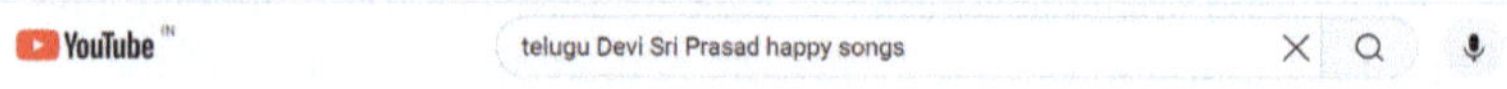

Fig. 7 Recommendation of songs based on emotion recognition

Table 1 Testing accuracy and validation accuracy

Algorithm	SVM	ELM	CNN
Validation accuracy	0.66	0.62	0.93
Testing accuracy	0.66	0.63	0.70

The Hyperparameters governing the trained CNN network are outlined in Table 2. Among these, the learning rate plays a pivotal role in regulating weight updates following the completion of each batch. The model's training encompasses multiple epochs, iterating over the entire training dataset. The batch size denotes the quantity of patterns presented to the network in a single batch before weight adjustments occur. The integration of activation functions within the model empowers it to adeptly learn nonlinear prediction boundaries.

In our pursuit of optimizing deep learning model training, the Adam optimization technique emerged as a viable alternative to traditional stochastic gradient descent. This technique enhances convergence and facilitates more efficient model learning.

Table 2 Trained CNN Network's hyperparameters

Hyperparameters	Values
Batch size	128
No. of classes	5
Optimixer	Adam
Learning Rate	0.001
Epoch	50
No. of layers	28
Activation function	Relu, SoftMax
Loss function	Categorical-cross entropy

The intrinsic metric used to degree the effectiveness of deep learning models is the explicit move-entropy loss feature. This loss function is specifically crucial for single-line and multi-class class troubles, and it allows the quantification of sampling errors and makes it less complicated to resolve.

Through this systematic review, we gain insight into the comparative strengths of various algorithms highlighting the Convolutional Neural Networks feat of accurate emotion recognition. The identification of hyperparameters and the utility of optimization strategies further verify the sophistication and accuracy accomplished inside the design of the proposed gadget.

7 Conclusion

Due to the extensive research in the existing literature, it is evident that many approaches have been developed to implement music recommendation systems. While we examined the approaches adopted by existing researchers and developers well after, we paved the way toward the goals of our program.

As the impact and benefits of AI-powered applications emerge, our work emerges as pioneers of disruptive technology efforts. In this framework, we provide a comprehensive framework that shows the great impact of music on the user's mood and makes it clear how they can best enhance their emotional state by choosing the right music songs. At the core of our system is the ability to understand and recognize the user's emotions, covering a spectrum from happiness, sadness, and anger to neutrality and surprise.

Our proposed technique culminates in the provision of a customized musical playlist, seamlessly aligned with the user's winning emotional nation. The gadget undertakes the difficult technique of emotion recognition and sooner or later tailors musical choices to harmonize with the consumer's temper. It's essential to observe that at the same time as this approach augments a person's enjoyment and musical engagement, the managing of widespread datasets should potentially pressure reminiscence and CPU usage, warranting careful optimization techniques during improvement.

Our study is based on the principles of affordability and accessibility, and the goal is to use a common platform together. Combining the goals of facial emotion recognition and music recommendation, our study aims to simplify the often-tedious process of curating and managing playlists. These advancements provide users with a seamless and rich musical journey where emotions and melodies blend to create a cohesive digital experience.

References

1. Ramalakshmi E, Hussain H, Agarwal K. Music recommendation system based on facial recognition and emotion detection
2. Ayala D, Yaslan Y, Kamasak M (2018) Emotion based music recommendation system using wearable physiological sensors. IEEE Trans Consum Electron
3. Metilda Florence S, Uma M. Emotional detection and music recommendation system based on user facial expression
4. Sharma1 H, Gupta S, Sharma Y, Purwar A. A new model for emotion prediction in music
5. Rajashree PJS, Sahana M, Savitri H. Review on facial expression-based music player. Int J Eng Res Technol (IJERT)
6. Ulleri P, Hari Prakash S, Zenith KB, SNair', Kannimoola J.Music recommendation system based on emotion.
7. Metilda Florence S, Uma M, Emotional detection and music recommendation system based on user facial expression
8. Khuat V. Music recommendation using collaborative filtering
9. Fessahaye F, Perez L, Zhan T, Zhang R, Fossier C, Markarian R, Chiu C, Zhan J, Gewali L, Oh P. T-RECSYS: A novel music recommendation system using deep learning
10. Yu Z, Dong Y, Cheng J, Sun M, Su F. Research on face recognition classification based on improved GoogleNet
11. Athavle M, Mudale D, Shrivastav U, Gupta M. Music recommendation based on face emotion recognition. Department of Computer Engineering, NHITM, Thane, India
12. Guidel A, Sapkota B, Sapkota K. Music recommendation by facial analysis
13. Ramanathan R, Kumaran R, Ram Rohan R, Gupta R, Prabhu V. An intelligent music player based on emotion recognition. In: 2nd IEEE international conference on computational systems and information technology for sustainable solutions
14. Mou L, Li J, Jain R, Li J. MemoMusic: A personalized music recommendation framework based on emotion and memory
15. Norden F, von Reis Marlevi F. A comparative analysis of machine learning algorithms in binary facial expression recognition, TRITA-EECS-EX-2019:143

Detection of Tomato Plant Disease Using Convolutional Neural Networks

Dhaval Bhoi, Ranjit Odedra, Priya Makadia, Nikita Bhatt, and Amit Thakkar

1 Introduction

The tomato is a highly cultivated crop globally; however, it is prone to several diseases that have the potential to significantly reduce both the quantity and quality of the yield. In the year 2007, plant disease losses in Georgia in the United States of America including control costs were estimated to be around $539.74 million. From them, around 185 million US Dollars was spent on controlling the diseases. The remaining amount is the value of damage caused by the diseases [1]. This observation of plant diseases by trained experts using the naked eye is a crucial method for detection and identification. However, this approach has limitations, particularly in terms of cost and time, especially in large-scale farms and remote areas [2]. Previous research has indicated that among 40 different fruits and vegetables, tomato fruit holds the top position in terms of its "relative contribution to human nutrition" [3]. The process of identifying tomato plant diseases typically involves several steps. It starts by identifying the infected part of the plant, then it takes notes of different characteristics, such as the presence of patches in brown or black color and the presence of holes in the plant. Moreover, it gives attention to inspect for any related insects. It is not recommended to plant tomatoes and similar vegetables, such as potatoes or brinjal, on the same farm consecutively within three years [4]. Research has shown that for the detection of diseases in agriculture, machine learning methods are successful. Some instances of machine learning methods used in agricultural research include

D. Bhoi (✉) · R. Odedra · P. Makadia · N. Bhatt
U & P U. Patel Department of Computer Engineering, Faculty of Technology and Engineering (FTE), Chandubhai S. Patel Institute of Technology (CSPIT), Charotar University of Science and Technology (CHARUSAT), Anand, Gujarat, India
e-mail: dhavalbhoi.ce@charusat.ac.in

A. Thakkar
Department of Computer Science and Engineering, Faculty of Technology and Engineering, (FTE), Chandubhai S. Patel Institute of Technology (CSPIT), Charotar University of Science and Technology (CHARUSAT), Anand, Gujarat, India

K. Kumar Singh et al. (eds.), *Machine Vision and Augmented Intelligence*, Lecture Notes in Electrical Engineering 1211, https://doi.org/10.1007/978-981-97-4359-9_31

support vector machines, k-nearest neighbor, Artificial Neural Networks, and K-means clustering [5]. Promising results in identifying and diagnosing diseases are achieved by these methods.

In recent times, the usage of machine learning algorithms has produced indeed promising outcomes and performance results for the classification of different plant diseases. The performance accuracy in classifying diseases is significantly increased due to the evolution of deep convolutional neural network based architecture. These advanced models represent a significant advancement in the field [6]. Over time, many machine learning algorithms have been introduced and reintroduced. Based on their model structure, these algorithms can be categorized into two types—shallow and deep [7]. The development of deep learning algorithms specifically designed for identifying plant diseases is the result of recent advancements in computer vision and machine learning. Automating the detection of plant diseases is an important task. It can be achieved by analyzing leaf images has shown promising results with these algorithms. The size and composition of the training data are factors that can significantly influence the effectiveness of deep learning methods. If the model is trained with a limited dataset, it may lead to diminished generalization abilities and inaccurate computer-assisted diagnoses of diseases [8]. This advancement provides a valuable tool for effectively managing and classifying plant diseases. Support Vector Machine [SVM] stands out among the various algorithms used for classification tasks. It is a popular machine learning algorithm known for its ability to handle high-dimensional datasets and achieve excellent results in classification and regression problems. For plant disease classification, the preferred choice is SVM because of its capability to identify optimal decision boundaries in complex datasets. Although deep learning algorithms have gained attention, traditional machine learning algorithms like SVM still play a crucial role, and they can deliver accurate outcomes depending on the computational resources available and dataset characteristics [9].

Furthermore, currently, a significant threat to crop yield is posed by infectious diseases, causing an average reduction of 40%. In developing countries, farmers often suffer even higher yield losses, reaching up to 100% [10]. A unique opportunity is created due to some factors like extensive adoption of smartphones, the powerful processors in these devices, and the presence of high-definition cameras. This situation provides an opportunity for disease diagnosis through automated image recognition with unprecedented scale, which is also technically feasible [11].

In the research, we present a deep learning algorithm designed for detecting diseases in tomato plants. Our proposed methodology is having, Convolutional Neural Network [CNN] used. CNN model does perform image classification for tomato plant disease. To evaluate the proposed model standard performance measures are used. Those performance measures are Accuracy, Precision, F1-score, and Recall.

This proposed method can detect tomato plant disease in real-time. This will help farmers across the globe. The outcomes of our study open the paths for further research in this area, as they demonstrate the effectiveness and efficiency of employing deep learning techniques for diagnosing diseases in tomato plants. Below is a summary of our main contributions to this research work.

(1) Through a Kaggle dataset, we extracted snapshots of tomato leaves. The main research requirement is to determine the disease that is present in plants.
(2) We designed a model that predicts tomato diseases with 94% accuracy and examined additional parameters such as recall, F1-score, and precision.

The Tomato Plant Disease dataset was obtained from Kaggle on January 10, 2023. The dataset contains 22,930 images, which are divided according to disease. The following is the breakdown of the article. Section 2 discusses the related works. The methodology is thoroughly examined in Sect. 3, outlining the approach taken in this study. The experimental results are presented in Sect. 4. In conclusion, we have presented a summary of our findings.

2 Related Work

In recent times, there has been an increase of interest in the application of technology in agriculture, with an emphasis on automating various processes. Plant disease detection is one of the most critical areas of focus in agriculture, and it has been extensively researched in recent years. In this section, we will look at some literature on plant disease detection, specifically tomato plant disease detection.

Recently, Artificial Intelligence (AI) has found extensive applications across various domains, with a significant presence in the field of medical science. Artificial Intelligence plays a prominent role in the field of medical science, frequently employed for tasks such as identifying cancer cells, recognizing infections, and diagnosing various skin conditions [12]. Deep learning, a crucial component of artificial intelligence (AI), has found numerous applications across various domains. AI can be used for tasks such as natural language processing, sentiment classification [13], computer vision, autonomous vehicles, and robotics, to name a few. For instance, the Russian railway system has utilized AI [14].

Nowadays, the usage of different deep learning techniques for the detection of plant diseases has become a popular area of research work. In their research, K. Simonyan et al. have evaluated Deep Convolutional Networks (DCN) with a substantial number of weight layers (up to 19 layers). The study revealed that increased depth in the network architecture positively influenced the accuracy of classification. In addition, they demonstrated that a conventional ConvNet architecture can achieve better performance on the ImageNet challenge dataset [15]. Additionally, the convolutional deep belief network was introduced by Honglak Lee et al. The Hierarchical generative model can handle only full-sized images [16].

Moreover, thermal imaging holds great promise in the early detection of diseases in the plant. It is especially important when the disease impacts the transpiration rate directly. It has been observed that there is a correlation between leaf temperature and changes in transpiration rate. It makes making thermal imaging a valuable tool for detecting plant diseases at an early stage [17]. Unmanned Aerial Vehicles (UAV) (drones) have emerged as one of the most useful technologies. They are having a unique capability to efficiently capture a very large number of images of plants in a field in a very short amount of time [18].

Ezio Venturino et al. developed a mathematical model to investigate the dynamics of Jatropha mosaic disease. The study focused on exploring the potential control of the disease through the application of insecticide spraying techniques [19].

The existing literature on tomato plant disease detection has proposed a variety of methods such as deep learning, image processing, and IoT-based approaches. These methods have yielded promising results in detecting various tomato plant diseases. Further investigations are needed, however, to increase the precision and effectiveness of these approaches along with developing feasible solutions for application in real life.

3 Methodology

3.1 Deep Learning

Deep learning has arisen as a very promising technique for classification of images, object detection, and segmentation, among other different computer vision tasks. The application of deep learning methodology for plant disease detection has received significant traction, including the identification of medical conditions in tomato plants. The effectiveness of deep neural networks in recognizing plant diseases has been established, emphasizing the importance of leveraging the capabilities of Convolutional Neural Networks (CNNs). To further enhance their performance, it is crucial to employ more diverse and realistic image datasets that reflect the complexities of real-world scenarios [20]. A key benefit of Deep Learning is its capacity to leverage raw data directly, eliminating the need for manually engineered or handcrafted features [21].

Deep learning is a sort of Artificial Neural Network (ANN) featuring layers that remain concealed. In the following Fig. 1, a fully connected neural network featuring two hidden layers is shown. On the other hand, Fig. 2 illustrates a schematic representation of a perceptron. Furthermore, there has been extensive development of feature extraction methods for monitoring various plant conditions. These methods utilize diverse attributes, including physical and morphological characteristics of plants, to extract relevant features [22]. For feature extraction, three distinct algorithms were employed. The L*a*b* color model, specifically the channel, was utilized for extracting color features. The features are extracted through Scale-Invariant Feature Transform (SIFT) algorithm. Text features were extracted using the Local Binary Pattern (LBP) algorithm [23].

Convolutional neural networks are the most frequently used model for visual plant disease recognition. CNNs are composed of convolutional layers of combining networks and fully linked layers that are trained on large datasets of classified pictures to learn discriminative features. Once trained, the CNN can accurately classify new

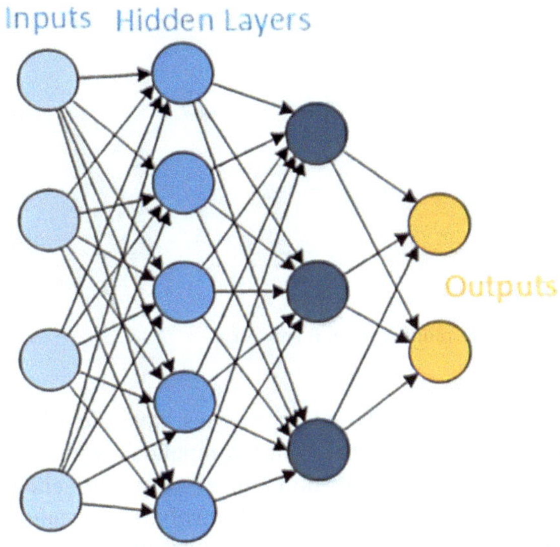

Fig. 1 Neural network

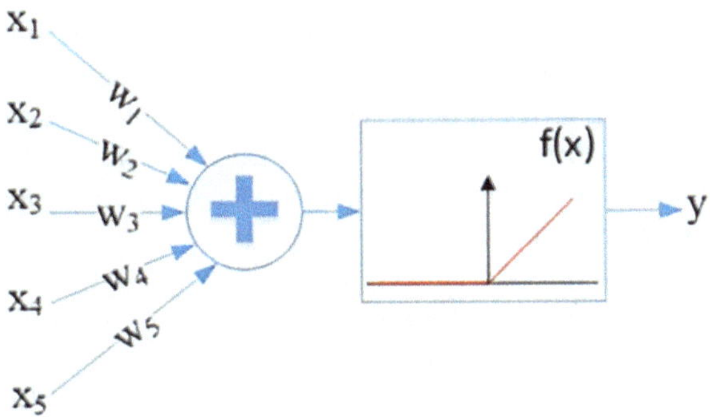

Fig. 2 Perceptron

images into different classes. Although Convolutional Neural Networks (CNNs) possess appealing characteristics and exhibit relative efficiency due to their local architecture, the application of CNNs on a large scale for high-resolution images has remained financially unfeasible [24].

The initial weights of the Deep Neural Network (DNN) are randomly assigned, and through iterative training, they are adjusted to minimize classification errors on a labeled training image set. The performance of the model which is being trained, is subsequently tested on a test images dataset to evaluate its generalization capabilities [25]. The introduction of the ImageNet dataset has played a significant role in providing a crucial benchmark for evaluating and testing large-scale image classification and annotation algorithms. This dataset consists of over 14 million manually labeled images belonging to 22,000 different classes, contributing to the advancement of research in the field [26].

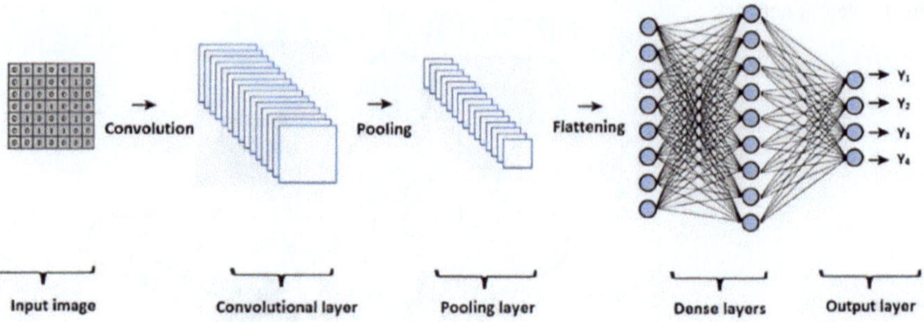

Fig. 3 Convolutional neural networks

Deep learning-based approaches have the advantage of learning complex and discriminative features from raw input data without the need for handcrafted feature extraction. This can result in improved performance and more robust models. Deep learning models, on the flip side, involve a huge amount of classified data for training which can be challenging in some circumstances.

CNN settings are typically made up of a number of distinct elements that represent architectural differences. Figure 3 illustrates the overall structure of a Convolutional Neural Network (CNN). It encompasses essential components such as the input layer, pooling layer, convolutional layer, and a flattening process. The information flows through a series of dense layers, culminating in the output layer that represents the final outcome of the network. A deep convolutional neural network includes input, hidden, and output layers, with hidden layers featuring convolutional, pooling, fully connected, and Softmax layers [27].

The proposed architecture of CNN is shown in above Fig. 3. In brief, deep learning has shown great promise when it comes to detecting tomato plant disease. CNNs have been shown to detect various tomato plant diseases with high accuracy. They are also having the ability to learn discriminative features from raw input data can lead to more robust and efficient models. The availability of labeled data, on the other hand, remains a challenge, and more research work is required to improve the performance of the model for tomato plant disease detection. Moreover, the choice of activation function plays an important role in determining how a neural network processes data and directly impacts the learning capability of the neural network models [28].

3.2 Dataset Description

The dataset is called "Tomato leaf disease classification" and it contains images of tomato leaves affected by different types of diseases. The goal is to use these images to train a machine learning model to classify new tomato leaf images based on the type of disease present. The dataset is shown in Fig. 4, which includes 22,930 images. It has 10 classes of tomato leaf diseases and one class for healthy leaves.

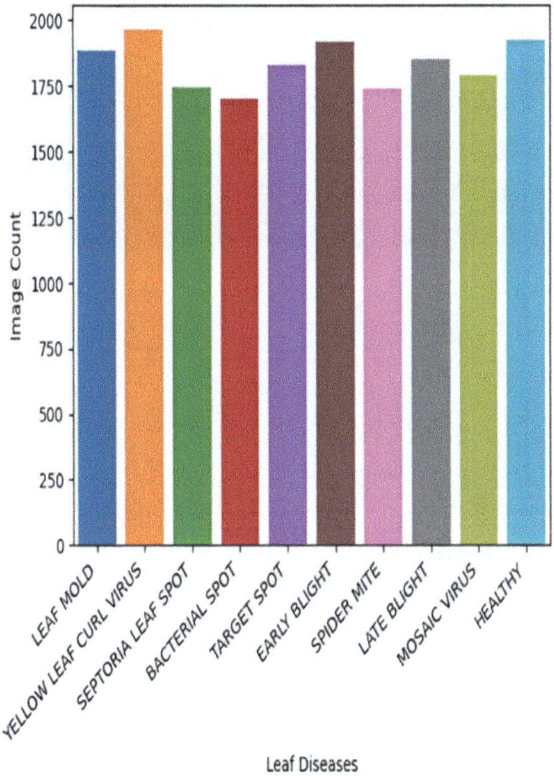

Fig. 4 Dataset

Format of the images is JPEG with 256 × 256 pixels resolution. Dataset also includes a CSV file with the image filenames and their corresponding labels. Sample images are shown in Fig. 5 on the next page.

This dataset can be used for research in the field of plant pathology and also for developing automated systems for identifying diseases in tomato plants.

3.3 Hardware Requirement

Hardware requirements for tomato plant disease detection using CNN are mentioned below.

CPU: It is one of the most essential components for running the deep learning algorithm on the system. It is recommended to have a multi-core CPU for parallel processing.

GPU: It is critical for the efficient and fast processing of deep learning algorithms. It is recommended to have a dedicated GPU with a minimum of 4 GB memory to

Fig. 5 Dataset images

train the model efficiently, a few examples are GeForce RTX 2080, RTX 3070, and RTX 3090.

RAM: It is another critical component that determines the size of the dataset that can be loaded into memory. It is recommended to have at least 16 GB of RAM.

Storage: The dataset for tomato plant disease detection using CNN can be quite large, so it is recommended to have sufficient storage capacity. A minimum of 256 GB SSD (Solid State Drive) is recommended for storing the dataset and the model.

Operating System: It is recommended to use a 64-bit operating system such as Windows 10, Linux Ubuntu, or MacOS.

Internet Connection: Active and stable internet connection is necessary to download the required software and packages, and to access relevant resources, research papers, and datasets.

4 Results

GPU is used to test trained models on the validation set. In training and validation, mini-batches are used. The batch size remains at 128. The number of epochs that can be used is limited to 75. Adam is the optimization parameter and Softmax is the final classification activation function. The size of the input image is set to 64 × 64 for training and validation.

Classifier Loss and Classifier Accuracy are shown in Figs. 6 and 7 on the next page:

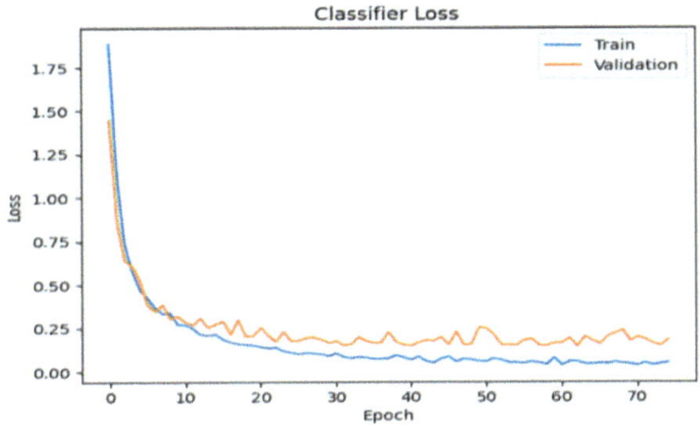

Fig. 6 Classifier loss

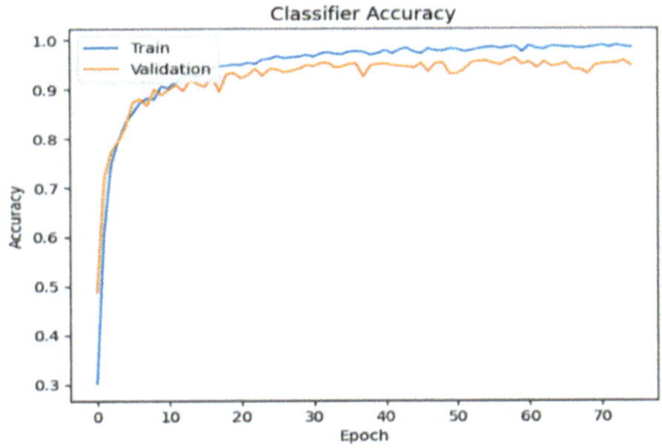

Fig. 7 Classifier accuracy

Precision, F1-score and Recall equations for performance evaluation for the proposed approach are as given below.

$$Precision = \frac{True\_Positive}{\text{True\_ Positive} + \text{False\_ Positive}}$$

$$Recall = \frac{True\_Positive}{\text{True\_ Positive} + \text{False\_Negative}}$$

$$F1 = \frac{2 * Precision * Recall}{\text{Precision} + \text{Recall}}$$

Furthermore, confusion matrix is created and illustrated for the analysis of validation data. Receiver Operating Characteristic (ROC) curve for the proposed model system is, shown in below Fig. 8.

The classification report providing detailed metrics such as precision, F1-score, and recall for each class, is presented below in Fig. 9 on the next page.

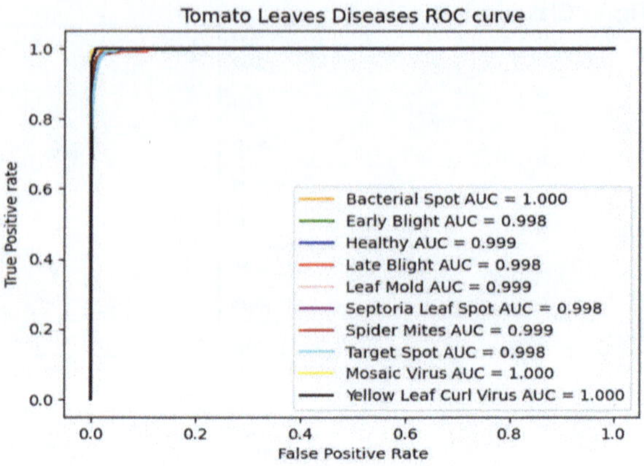

Fig. 8 Receiver operating characteristic curve

Classification Report:

	precision	recall	f1-score	support
0	0.99	0.96	0.97	425
1	0.89	0.97	0.93	480
2	0.97	0.97	0.97	481
3	0.97	0.90	0.93	463
4	0.91	0.99	0.95	470
5	0.98	0.83	0.90	436
6	0.93	0.96	0.95	435
7	0.92	0.93	0.93	457
8	0.98	0.99	0.99	448
9	0.96	0.98	0.97	490
accuracy			0.95	4585
macro avg	0.95	0.95	0.95	4585
weighted avg	0.95	0.95	0.95	4585

Fig. 9 The classification report

5 Conclusion

In this research work, a deep learning approach for detecting tomato plant diseases using CNN approach is presented. The paper addresses the critical issue of tomato plant diseases, which can significantly impact the production of the crop. Methods of plant disease detection manually is really time taking and costly especially on large-scale farms. To address this challenge, we have used deep learning to automate and improve the detection process.

We have utilized a dataset for tomato leaf disease classification, comprising 22,930 images depicting 10 distinct classes of tomato leaf diseases. It also includes a category for healthy leaves. This dataset serves as the basis for training and assessing our deep learning model.

We have used convolutional neural networks for tomato plant disease detection. CNNs have demonstrated remarkable capabilities in image classification as well.

The implementation of our methodology required minimum hardware components, including a multi-core CPU, dedicated GPU, 16 GB of RAM, and ample storage capacity. These components are crucial for efficient model training and inference.

Loss curve and Accuracy curve are demonstrated to show the effectiveness of our model performance. Performance of our model is measured using standard performance measures. Those measures are Precision, Recall, and F1-Score. ROC curve is also plotted. Plotted ROC curve shows the capability of model's discrimination. Detailed classification performance result shows the result of plant disease detection. This proposed model is effective because it can learn important features from the plant images without any human assistance.

The combination of technological progress, such as high-definition cameras and robust processors, has created possibilities for automated disease diagnosis on a broad scale. Our proposed methodology offers a valuable tool for farmers to detect and manage diseases in tomato plants efficiently. This will even advance the field of agricultural monitoring and disease detection. More research in this area can make disease detection methods more accurate and useful in practical situations.

References

1. Al Hiary H, Bani Ahmad S, Reyalat M, Braik M, ALRahamneh Z (2011) Fast 398 and accurate detection and classification of plant diseases. Int J Comput Appl 17:31–38
2. Mokhtar U, El Bendary N, Hassenian AE, Emary E, Mahmoud MA, Hefny H, Tolba MF (2015) SVM-based detection of tomato leaves diseases. In Intelligent Systems' 2014: Proceedings of the 7th IEEE international conference intelligent systems IS'2014, September 24–26, 2014, Warsaw, Poland, Volume 2: Tools, Architectures, Sys-tems, Applications (pp 641–652). Springer International Publishing
3. Xie C, Shao Y, Li X, He Y (2015) Detection of early blight and late blight dis-eases on tomato leaves using hyperspectral imaging. Sci Rep 5(1):16564
4. Agarwal M, Singh A, Arjaria S, Sinha A, Gupta S (2020) ToLeD: Tomato leaf disease detection using convolution neural network. Procedia Comput Sci 167:293–301
5. Detection of apple plant diseases using leaf images through convolutional neural network. In: IEEE Access, vol. 11, pp 6594–6609, 2023, https://doi.org/10.1109/ACCESS.2022.3232917
6. Rangarajan AK, Purushothaman R, Ramesh A (2018) Tomato crop disease clas-sification using pre-trained deep learning algorithm. Procedia Comput Sci 133:1040–1047
7. Pasupa K, Sunhem W (2016) A comparison between shallow and deep architecture classifiers on small dataset. In: 2016 8th international conference on information technology and electrical engineering (ICITEE) (pp 1–6). IEEE
8. Data complexity based evaluation of the model dependence of brain MRI images for classification of Brain Tumor and Alzheimer's Disease. In: IEEE Access, vol. 10, pp 112117–112133, 2022, https://doi.org/10.1109/ACCESS.2022.3216393
9. Semary NA, Tharwat A, Elhariri E, Hassanien AE (2015) Fruit-based tomato grading system using features fusion and support vector machine. In: Intelligent Systems' 2014: Proceedings of the 7th IEEE international conference intelligent systems IS'2014, September 24–26, 2014, Warsaw, Poland, Volume 2: Tools, Architectures, Systems, Applications (pp 401–410). Springer International Publishing
10. Hughes D, Salathé M (2015) An open access repository of images on plant health to enable the development of mobile disease diagnostics. arXiv preprint arXiv:1511.08060
11. Mohanty SP, Hughes DP, Salathé M (2016) Using deep learning for image-based plant disease detection. Front Plant Sci 7:1419

12. Detection of omicron caused pneumonia from radiology images using convolution neural network (cnn). Comput, Mater & Contin 74(2):3743–3761 (2023)
13. Bhoi D, Thakkar A (2022) Sentiment analysis performance and reliability evaluation using an XLNet-based deep learning approach. Reliab: Theory & Appl 17(1(67)):391–397
14. Shubinsky I, Zamyshlaev A, Bochkov A (2022) Application of artificial intelligence in russia's railway network asset management. Reliab: Theory & Appl 17(SI 3 (66)):42–48
15. Simonyan K, Zisserm an A (2014) Very deep convolutional networks for large-scale image recognition. arXiv preprint arXiv:1409.1556
16. Lee H, Grosse R, Ranganath R, Ng AY (2009) Convolutional deep belief networks for scalable unsupervised learning of hierarchical representations. In: Proceedings of the 26th annual international conference on machine learning (pp 609–616)
17. Raza SEA, Prince G, Clarkson JP, Rajpoot NM (2015) Automatic detection of diseased tomato plants using thermal and stereo visible light images. PLoS ONE 10(4):e0123262
18. Yamamoto K, Togami T, Yamaguchi N (2017) Super-resolution of plant disease images for the acceleration of image-based phenotyping and vigor diagnosis in agriculture. Sensors 17(11):2557
19. Venturino E, Roy PK, Al Basir F, Datta A (2016) A model for the control of the mosaic virus disease in Jatropha curcas plantations. Energy, Ecol Environ 1:360–369
20. Barbedo JGA (2019) Plant disease identification from individual lesions and spots using deep learning. Biosys Eng 180:96–107
21. Brahimi M, Boukhalfa K, Moussaoui A (2017) Deep learning for tomato diseases: Classification and symptoms visualization. Appl Artif Intell 31(4):299–315
22. Pantazi XE, Moshou D, Tamouridou AA (2019) Automated leaf disease detection in different crop species through image features analysis and one class classifiers. Comput Electron Agric 156:96–104
23. Chouhan SS, Singh UP, Sharma U, Jain S (2021) Leaf disease segmentation and classification of Jatropha Curcas L. and Pongamia Pinnata L. biofuel plants using computer vision based approaches. Measurement 171:108796
24. Krizhevsky A, Sutskever I, Hinton GE (2012) Imagenet classification with deep convolutional neural networks. Adv Neural Inf Process Syst, 25
25. Ciregan D, Meier U, Schmidhuber J (2012). Multi-column deep neural networks for image classification. In: 2012 IEEE conference on computer vision and pattern recognition (pp 3642–3649). IEEE
26. Mensink T, Verbeek J, Perronnin F, Csurka G (2012) Metric learning for large scale image classification: Generalizing to new classes at near-zero cost. In: Computer Vi-sion–ECCV 2012: 12th European conference on computer vision, Florence, Italy, October 7–13, Proceedings, Part II 12 (pp 488–501). Springer Berlin Heidelberg
27. Too EC, Yujian L, Njuki S, Yingchun L (2019) A comparative study of fine-tuning deep learning models for plant disease identification. Comput Electron Agric 161:272–279
28. Liu B, Zhang Y, He D, Li Y (2017) Identification of apple leaf diseases based on deep convolutional neural networks. Symmetry 10(1):11

Accuracy of Image Registration During Similarity Transformation

Pavel Babayan and Ekaterina Kozhina

1 Introduction

Geometric registration is an important step in solving a wide range of problems in the analysis of images and video sequences, for example, the problems of electronic image stabilization [1], detection of moving objects [2], and changes [3]. Many modern approaches to detect image changes are based on the convolutional neural networks, especially for agricultural [4] and health applications [5, 6]. To register images, it is necessary to obtain an accurate estimate of the parameters of geometric transformations, and this accuracy is decisive for improving the quality of solving the listed problems. An analysis of the sources shows that when using estimates of the parameters of geometric transformations, it is usually assumed that the registration error is close to zero, or its statistical characteristics are constant for the entire frame [2]. The correctness of these assumptions depends on the algorithm chosen for determining the parameters of geometric transformations.

There are two main classes of such algorithms. Algorithms belonging to the first class are based on the global estimation of the transformation parameters. The images are compared in entirety using various similarity functions: difference, correlation, and others [7]. In this case, as a rule, the registration accuracy is high, and its statistical characteristics over the entire image area are constant. Attempts to reduce computational costs when registering images led to the second class of algorithms based on reference area matching. To search for reference areas, methods based on invariant descriptors SIFT, SURF, ORB, FAST [8], and random selection methods [9] are widely used. After finding and comparing the reference areas, the parameters of geometric transformations are determined by solving a system of algebraic equations. When using algorithms of the second class, the accuracy of estimation of

P. Babayan · E. Kozhina (✉)
Gagarin Str., Ryazan State Radio Engineering University Named After V.F. Utkin, 59/1, Ryazan 390005, Russia
e-mail: kozhina.e.s@rsreu.ru

K. Kumar Singh et al. (eds.), *Machine Vision and Augmented Intelligence*, Lecture Notes in Electrical Engineering 1211, https://doi.org/10.1007/978-981-97-4359-9_32

the parameters of geometric transformations and the accuracy of image registration depends on the actual location of the selected areas.

As in other works, authors use reference area-based algorithms, belonging to the second class, for image registration. Opposite to them, we suggest to estimate image registration errors, and use them to improve further image processing.

2 Hypothesis and Limitations of the Developed Method

lIn this paper we prove the hypothesis that in the zone where most of the reference sections are concentrated, the registration accuracy is higher than in the zones remote from them. Ignoring this fact leads to errors in image registration. The most considerable errors are in areas of sharp boundaries. These errors are observed, for example, in the images presented in [3].

The purpose of this work is to determine the accuracy of the parameters of geometric transformations and the accuracy of image registration depending on the actual location of the reference areas on the image. At the same time, the similarity transformation, which is typical for many classes of video surveillance systems, is chosen as a mathematical model of geometric transformations. Expressions will be obtained for finding the correlation matrix of scaling, offset, and rotation errors. Then, on the basis of this matrix, the parameters of the correlation matrix of image registration are determined for each image point.

It should be noted that the proposed approach is applicable only for algorithms based on the reference areas, where the variances for the area position estimation are known.

3 Multi-reference Algorithm for Estimating Similarity Parameters

In this paper, for estimating the parameters of geometric transformations of scale-displacement-rotation, a multi-reference algorithm with a random selection of reference areas is used [9, 10]. Let's give a brief description of it. The algorithm selects the reference areas on the image according to a certain criterion and determines their position from frame to frame. To reduce computational costs when searching for new reference areas, their coordinates are chosen randomly. Based on the estimation of the position of the areas, the parameters of scaling, shifting, and image rotation are estimated. After determining and refining the coordinates of all reference sections, a system of linear algebraic equations is composed on the basis of the transformation model [10].

Let's consider the mathematical model of similarity transformation. For reference area coordinates

$$x_i' = ax_i + by_i + \alpha;$$
$$y_i' = -bx_i + ay_i + \beta, \tag{1}$$

where x_i, y_i are coordinates of reference areas on the original image, x_i' and y_i' are coordinates of reference areas on the current image, $a = \lambda\cos\phi$, $b = \lambda\sin\phi$, λ is scale change, ϕ is rotation angle, α is shift along the x-axis, β is shift along the y-axis.

The vector of similarity geometric transformations is $\overline{U} = \left[a\ b\ \alpha\ \beta\right]^T$.

The system of equations for finding the vector $\overline{U}$ in matrix form is $\mathbf{H}U = Z$, where $\overline{Z} = \left[x_1'\ y_1'\ \ldots\ x_n'\ y_n'\right]^T$, $\mathbf{H} = \begin{bmatrix} x_1 & y_1 & \cdots & x_n & y_n \\ y_1 & -x_1 & \ldots & y_n & -x_n \\ 1 & 0 & \ldots & 1 & 0 \\ 0 & 1 & \ldots & 0 & 1 \end{bmatrix}^T$

The solution of the system of equations is $\hat{U} = (\mathbf{H^T H})^{-1}\mathbf{H^T}Z$ [11].

Analysis of the accuracy of estimating parameters $\overline{U}$ is reduced to determining the correlation matrix $\mathbf{K_U} = M[(\hat{U} - M[\hat{U}]) \cdot (\hat{U} - M[\hat{U}])^T]$, which can be found from the expression:

$$\mathbf{K_U} = (\mathbf{H}^T\mathbf{H})^{-1}\mathbf{H}^T\mathbf{K_Z}\mathbf{H}(\mathbf{H}^T\mathbf{H})^{-1}, \tag{2}$$

where $\mathbf{K_Z}$ is correlation matrix of $\overline{Z}$.

Assuming the values x'_n and y'_n in the vector $\overline{Z}$ are uncorrelated and have the same variance σ_Z^2, in each dimension we get $\mathbf{K_Z} = \sigma_Z^2\mathbf{E}$, then

$$\mathbf{K_U} = (\mathbf{H^T H})^{-1}\mathbf{H^T H}(\mathbf{H^T H})^{-1} \cdot \sigma_Z^2 = (\mathbf{H^T H})^{-1} \cdot \sigma_Z^2, \tag{3}$$

where σ_Z^2 is variance of estimation of coordinates of reference areas.

Thus, in order to obtain the correlation matrix $\mathbf{K_U}$, it is necessary to find the matrix $(\mathbf{H^T H})^{-1}$.

$$(\mathbf{H^T H}) = \begin{bmatrix} \sum x_i^2 + y_i^2 & 0 & \sum x_i & \sum y_i \\ 0 & \sum x_i^2 + y_i^2 & \sum y_i & -\sum x_i \\ \sum x_i & \sum y_i & n & 0 \\ \sum y_i & -\sum x_i & 0 & n \end{bmatrix}. \tag{4}$$

To simplify the following transformations we assume $\sum x_i = 0$ and $\sum y_i = 0$. It can be performed by the simple coordinate translation. Then $(\mathbf{H^T H}) = \mathrm{diag}(\sum x_i^2 + y_i^2, \sum x_i^2 + y_i^2, n, n)$.

Then we get:

$$(\mathbf{H^T H})^{-1} = \mathrm{diag}(\frac{1}{\sum x_i^2 + y_i^2}, \frac{1}{\sum x_i^2 + y_i^2}, \frac{1}{n}, \frac{1}{n}), \tag{5}$$

The correlation matrix for the similarity parameters is:

$$\mathbf{K}_{\mathrm{U}} = \sigma_Z^2 \mathrm{diag}(\frac{1}{\sum x_i^2 + y_i^2}, \frac{1}{\sum x_i^2 + y_i^2}, \frac{1}{n}, \frac{1}{n}). \tag{6}$$

If $\lambda \approx 1, \phi \approx 0$ then (1) gives $\lambda \approx a, \phi \approx b$, so the matrix diagonal of (6) contains the variances of scale, rotation, and shift along the x and y axes, respectively.

From (6) follows that the larger the value of the sum $x_i^2 + y_i^2$, the smaller the values in $\mathbf{K}_{\mathrm{U}}$, and the more accurate the algorithm works, i.e., the image registration error will tend to zero as the distance between the reference areas increases.

Thus, high registration accuracy can be achieved when the reference areas are maximally spaced over the image area. If for any reason, the reference areas are grouped in a certain area of the image, then the elements of the correlation matrix $\mathbf{K}_{\mathrm{U}}$ increase, which indicates an increase in the image registration error.

4 Estimation of Image Registration Accuracy

Let's estimate the accuracy of image registration using uncertainty ellipses. Using the mathematical model (1) and passing to the centered values of the coordinates, we get:

$$\begin{aligned} \sigma_x^2 &= \sigma^2(a)x^2 + \sigma^2(b)y^2 + \sigma^2(\alpha); \\ \sigma_y^2 &= \sigma^2(b)x^2 + \sigma^2(a)y^2 + \sigma^2(\beta), \end{aligned} \tag{7}$$

$$K(x', y') = (\sigma^2(a) + \sigma^2(b))xy. \tag{8}$$

After the values (7) and (8) are determined, the parameters of uncertainty ellipses, which characterize the degree of uncertainty in image registration, can be calculated. The angle of rotation of the ellipse is

$$\psi = \frac{1}{2} \arctan \frac{2K(x', y')}{\sigma_x^2 - \sigma_y^2}. \tag{9}$$

The lengths of the minor (σ_ξ^2) and major (σ_η^2) semi-axes are

$$\begin{aligned} \sigma_\xi^2 &= \sigma_x^2 \cos^2 \psi + K(x', y') \cdot \sin 2\psi + \sigma_y^2 \sin^2 \psi; \\ \sigma_\eta^2 &= \sigma_x^2 \sin^2 \psi - K(x', y') \cdot \sin 2\psi + \sigma_y^2 \cos^2 \psi. \end{aligned} \tag{10}$$

5 Experimental Studies

To illustrate the dependence of the size of uncertainty ellipses on the choice of reference areas, a pair of images of 692 × 692 was used. The reference areas were chosen differently. In the first case, they were selected only in the central part of the image. The size of this part is 150 × 150. In the second case, the reference areas were located throughout the image. The image was scaled relative to its center. Rotation and scaling of the image were carried out programmatically.

Based on the coordinates of the reference areas, the parameters of the correlation matrix given in Sect. 2 were estimated, and then, based on the obtained data, uncertainty ellipses were constructed. The value σ_Z^2 was taken equal to 0.5. The correlation matrices for the first and second cases are given below.

For case 1:

$$\mathbf{K}_{\mathrm{U}} = \mathrm{diag}(8.1853 \cdot 10^{-6}, 8.1853 \cdot 10^{-6}, 0.0313, 0.0313).$$

For case 2:

$$\mathbf{K}_{\mathrm{U}} = \mathrm{diag}(1.0107 \cdot 10^{-6}, 1.0107 \cdot 10^{-6}, 0.0313, 0.0313).$$

Figure 1a shows graphs of changes in the σ_x,σ_y for the first case and Fig. 1b—for the second case.

Figure 2 characterizes the distribution of the correlation value $K(x', y')$, Fig. 2 (a) for the first case, Fig. 2 (b)—for the second.

Figure 3 shows the scattering ellipses for two cases. For clarity, the dimensions of the semi-axes of the ellipses are increased by a factor of 30. The yellow crosses on

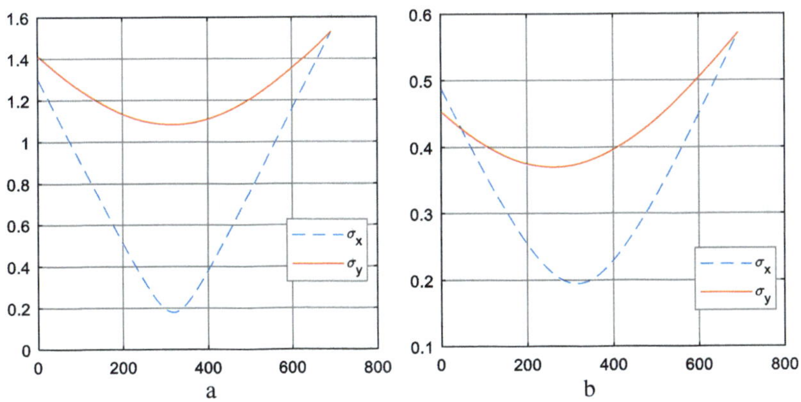

Fig. 1 Standard deviation plots for the first case **a** and the second case **b**. The standard deviation grows faster in Figure (b), where reference areas are selected closely

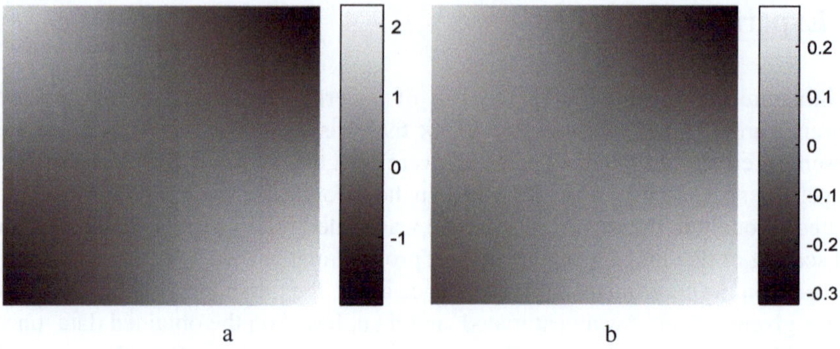

Fig. 2 Graphs of parameter changes $K(x', y')$ for the first **a** and second **b** case. The correlation between x' and y' errors grows faster in Figure (b), where reference areas are selected closely

the images mark the centers of the reference areas, the red asterisk shows the center of the areas, and the uncertainty ellipses are shown in green.

In the first case, the ellipses are directed with their major semi-axis to the center of the image and increase in size as they move away from the center, which corresponds to an increase in the registration error. In the second case, the ellipses are distributed evenly over the image and have approximately the same size; accordingly, the estimation error in this case is much smaller.

In order to show the dependence of the quality of image registration on the choice of reference areas, a pair of images (Fig. 4) was used. The size of the images is 692 × 1048. Figure 4a shows the original frame from the video. The image in Fig. 4b was obtained after applying the scaling and the rotation to the original frame.

Fig. 3 Scattering ellipses: **a**—for case 1; **b**—for case 2. The scattering ellipses for closely selected reference areas are significantly larger

a b

Fig. 4 Image frame: **a** original frame; **b** frame obtained after scaling and rotation

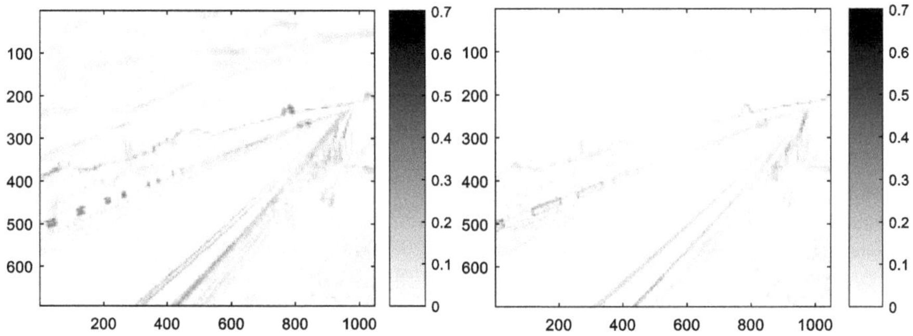

a b

Fig. 5 Image registration. Difference modulus **a** for case 1; **b** for case 2. The difference modulus is significantly larger if reference areas are selected closely

Figure 5 shows the image difference modulus after transforming the first image for the two cases. For clarity, the images are displayed in gray colors, where white conforms to zero difference, black - to maximal difference.

Figure 5 shows that the maximum image difference in the first case is greater than in the second. For each image, the root mean square value of difference image (RMS) was calculated: for the first case, it is 0.0682, and for the second it is 0.0459. This confirms the conclusion that the larger the selection area of the reference sections, the smaller the estimation error.

6 Conclusion

The paper presents the theoretical and experimental results of estimating the accuracy of image registration when using registration methods based on the choice of reference areas. Expressions for determining the error correlation matrices are presented. The theoretical results of the study are confirmed experimentally. Experimental studies have shown that placing reference areas throughout the image reduced errors in image registration by 1.5 times in comparison to placing them in the central part of the image. It confirms our hypothesis of the dependency of the registration precision from the reference regions' placing.

Further development of the work is the consideration of more complex types of geometric transformations (Euclidean, projective, elastic), as well as taking into account the errors obtained in the algorithms for selecting and detecting objects.

References

1. Guilluy W, Oudre L, Beghdadi A (2021) Video stabilization: Overview, challenges and perspectives Signal Processing: Image Communication Volume 90, January, 116015 https://doi.org/10.1016/j.image.2020.116015
2. Babayan PV, Kozhina ES (2023) A study of the automatic object extraction algorithm on the image sequence under scaling transformations. In: 2023 25th international conference on digital signal processing and its applications (DSPA). IEEE. pp 1–4. https://doi.org/10.1109/DSPA57594.2023.10113422
3. Han Y, Javed A, Jung S, Liu S (2020) Object-based change detection of very high resolution images by fusing pixel-based change detection results using weighted dempster–Shafer theory. Remote Sens 12:983. https://doi.org/10.3390/rs12060983
4. Vishnoi VK, et al. (2022) Detection of apple plant diseases using leaf images through convolutional neural network. IEEE Access. 2022. T. 11. C. 6594–6609
5. Kujur A, et al. (2022) Data complexity based evaluation of the model dependence of brain MRI images for classification of brain tumor and Alzheimer's disease. IEEE Access. T. 10. – C.112117–112133
6. Khan AA, et al. (2023) Detection of omicron caused pneumonia from radiology images using convolution neural network (CNN). Comput, Mater & Contin, T. 74. – №. 2
7. Evangelidis GD, Psarakis EZ (2008) Parametric image alignment using enhanced correlation coefficient maximization. IEEE Trans Pattern Anal Mach Intell 30(10):1858–1865. https://doi.org/10.1109/TPAMI.2008.113
8. Zhang YJ (2021) Handbook of image engineering. https://doi.org/10.1007/978-981-15-5873-3
9. Alpatov BA, Strotov VV (2013) An estimation algorithm of the multispectral image geometric transformation parameters based on multiple reference area tracking//SPIE Defense, Security, and Sensing. Int Soc Opt Photonics pp 87130Q-87130Q-8
10. Korepanov S, Smirnov S, Strotov V (2017) The comparison of the performance indicators for the object position estimation algorithm. In: 2017 6th Mediterrannean Conference on Embedded Computing. Bar, Montenegro. pp 415–419
11. Korshunov Yu M (1987) Mathematical foundations of cybernetics (Математические основы кибернетики): Proc. allowance for universities. – 3-rd ed., revised and supplementary. M.:Energoatomizdat pp 496

Exploring Deep Learning and Word Embedding Techniques for Sentiment Analysis on Diverse Textual Data

B. N. Lavanya, K. V. Anitha Rathnam, K. Kiran, Abhishek Appaji, P. Deepa Shenoy, and K. R. Venugopal

1 Introduction

The success of businesses nowadays is influenced by social media sites like Facebook and Twitter. A research study conducted by [1], emphasizes the importance of text mining in analyzing competition in media and gaining business insights. At the time the growing number of web resources that express opinions as mentioned in a survey by [2], has sparked interest in sentiment analysis. This technique is essential for understanding emotions conveyed through text.

Deep learning models have become increasingly popular, in sentiment analysis because of their ability to capture patterns and context in data. To evaluate these model performance this study focuses on used deep learning architectures like Bidirectional Long Short Term Memory (Bi-LSTM) Convolutional Neural Networks (CNN) and Gated Recurrent Units (GRU). These models have shown results across natural language processing (NLP) tasks. Additionally, the study explores word embedding techniques such as Keras Embedding, N-grams, Elmo, BERT, Roberta, and CT-Bert to enhance sentiment analysis performance. By conducting experiments on known datasets, like Twitter and IMDb movie reviews. The findings reveal that the choice of word embedding significantly impacts performance depending on the characteristics of the dataset.

The combination of learning models and word embedding strategies is shown to greatly improve sentiment analysis. This provides insights, for researchers and practitioners who need to select the effective architecture and embedding strategy for specific sentiment analysis tasks.

B. N. Lavanya (✉) · K. V. A. Rathnam · K. Kiran · P. D. Shenoy · K. R. Venugopal
Department of Computer Science and Engineering, University of Visvesvaraya College of Engineering, BangaloreUniversity, Bengaluru, India
e-mail: Lavanya_hulkoti@yahoo.com

A. Appaji
Department of Medical Electronics, BMS College of Engineering, Bangalore, India

K. Kumar Singh et al. (eds.), *Machine Vision and Augmented Intelligence*, Lecture Notes in Electrical Engineering 1211, https://doi.org/10.1007/978-981-97-4359-9_33

2 Related Work

Many research papers have utilized the capabilities of learning techniques in sentiment analysis. For example in a study, by [3] word embeddings and LSTM-based deep learning achieved a success rate of 93% in analyzing sentiments ex-pressed on language social media platforms. The performance for [4] sentiment analysis of Amazon product reviews was 85%. By combining LSTM and BERT embeddings, [5] achieved a 93% accuracy for sentiment analysis of internet data. With an emphasis on Amazon review sentiment analysis, [6] obtained a remarkable 93.66% accuracy using LSTM models. [7] placed a strong emphasis on emotion recognition and presented an LSTM-based approach with impressive rates of 89.13% and 91.3% for positive and negative subclasses. Chauhan [8] outstanding F1 score of 83% and 73% accuracy demonstrated BERT's efficacy. An astounding 82.8% accuracy was achieved by the LSTM-based model created by [9] in 2022. Building on this accomplishment, Tan et al. [10] developed an ensemble hybrid model that brought RoBERTa, LSTM, Bi-LSTM, and GRU together and achieved astounding accuracy rates of 94.9%, 91.77%, and 89.81% on distinct IMDb, Twitter US Airline Sentiment, and Sentiment140 datasets.

Overall, these studies highlight the importance of deep learning in sentiment analysis, continuously reaching high accuracy rates. The potential of N-gram and Keras is illustrated in the current work. The CNN model leads the pack with a 99.96% accuracy rate from N-gram embeddings, demonstrating that the choice of word embedding methodology has a major impact on overall performance.

3 Methodology

Figure 1 shows the phases of the model development. The various phases of model development for the proposed work are described in the following section:

3.1 Dataset

The 1.6 million tweets from Sentiment140 and the 50 K movie reviews from IMDB were gathered from Kaggle. Both datasets have review and sentiment attributes, with sentiment utilizing a lambda function to classify sentiment as either positive or negative. The ratio of positive to negative emotions is 1:1.

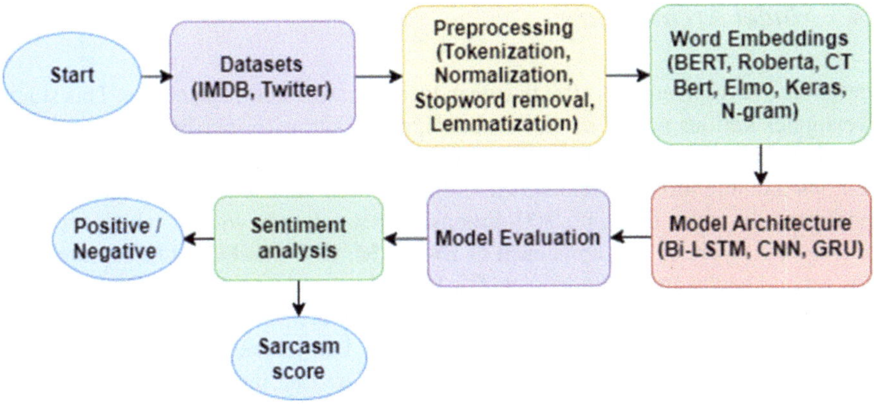

Fig. 1 Model development

3.2 *Data Preprocessing*

Preparing text data entails missing values and spotting outliers. Tokenization separates the text into words. Data quality is improved by several normalization procedures, including contraction expansion, stop word removal, acronym management, lowercase conversion, and punctuation removal. Lemmatization further reduces the word dimensions, which enhances generalization.

3.3 *Word Embedding*

Sentiment analysis requires the conversion of text into continuous vectors. The size, context, and availability of resources all affect word embedding algorithms. Keras Embedding, N-grams for contextual comprehension, and transformer-based models like BERT, RoBERTa, and CT-BERT, which are excellent at NLP tasks, are some of the techniques employed in this project. BERT, which captures complex text relationships and can be modified using TensorFlow's TFBertModel, has 12 self-attention layers and 110 million parameters. Even non-adjacent hidden words can be predicted using Roberta, which has 12 self-attention layers. COVID-Twitter-BERT (CT-Bert) for COVID-19 tweet analysis uses a 12-layer bidirectional transformer. ELMo or Embeddings from Language Models from TensorFlow Hub makes it easier to tokenize and convert review sequences, which supports sentiment analysis.

3.4 Model Architecture

Sentiment analysis requires effective deep learning architecture selection. This study investigates various neural network models, such as transformer-based models, Bi-LSTM, GRU, and CNN. These architectures use numerous layers and modern methods like attention mechanisms to collect contextual data. An embedding layer transforms the input data into 300-dimensional word embeddings, which are then followed by layers of 256 units each of Bi-LSTM, CNN, and GRU to capture both forward and backward dependencies. For local pattern identification, CNN incorporates a Conv1D layer with 128 filters and a kernel size of 5, and GlobalMaxPooling1D decreases dimensionality while extracting features. Dropout regularization with a rate of 0.5 is employed to avoid overfitting. Furthermore, the final dense layer with 64 units and Relu activation improves non-linearity, and a dense layer with 2 units and sentiment class probabilities are generated by the final dense layer with two units and softmax activation.

3.5 Model Evaluation

Accuracy: It measures the ratio of correctly predicted instances to the total number of instances in the dataset. Mathematically, it is represented as:

$$Accuracy = \frac{True\ Positives + True\ Negatives}{Total\ Instances} \tag{1}$$

3.6 Sentiment Analysis

Sentiment is categorized as positive (1) or negative (0), and sarcasm is identified using the sarcasm score, which is obtained by deducting the maximum anticipated probability from 1. Higher scores indicate stronger sarcasm or reverse sentiment, as shown in Table 1.

Table 1 Review polarity and sarcasm scores

Review	Polarity	Sarcasm score
1	1	0.29
4	0	0.44

4 Experimental Setup and Results

The current model adopts a different strategy from previous work [10], which uses an ensemble hybrid deep learning model utilizing methods like averaging or majority voting to reach a final prediction. To effectively utilize memory and computing capacity, we created a unique model that iterates through the dataset in batches of 32 or 64, tokenizing and encoding reviews with maximum sequence lengths of 256 or 512. It employs DL models with 128 units each to capture sequential dependencies in both directions. A dense layer of two units and softmax activation combats overfitting with a 0.5 dropout rate. Adam optimizer updates model weights, optimizing for loss reduction, the accuracy for the batch is calculated and the model is updated using backpropagation. Sarcasm scores are computed by subtracting the maximum likelihood from 1, indicating the degree of sarcasm.

Table 2 compares the performance of work carried out by [10] using ensemble hybrid deep learning models such as BI-LSTM and GRU with CNN models using Twitter and IMDB datasets with BERT and Roberta embeddings, focusing on accuracy. CNN outperforms BI-LSTM and GRU on Twitter with BERT (93.75% vs. 87%) and Roberta (93.75% vs. 89%). On IMDB with BERT, CNN excels again (97.31% vs. 92%), while with Roberta, it achieves 93.75% compared to recurrent models at 94%.

Table 3 presents model accuracy scores based on several word embeddings on Twitter and IMDB datasets. For the Twitter dataset, the CNN model for CT-Bert scores 93.75%, compared to 95.31% for BI-LSTM and GRU. Elmo performs poorly, scoring around 79.3%, since it struggles with heavier workloads. For CNN, Keras embeddings outperform BI-LSTM (89.74%) and GRU (83.56%), achieving a score of 93.52%. N-gram accuracy is competitive, with CNN dominating with 98.30%. On IMDB, CT-Bert leads alongside Elmo, producing extraordinarily high accuracy: BI-LSTM (99.52%), CNN (99.62%), and GRU (99.70%). According to Keras embeddings, CNN, BI-LSTM, and GRU, each have 99.81%, 99.14%, and 99.07% respectively. N-grams perform admirably, with CNN at 99.96%.

In conclusion, word embeddings and datasets significantly affect model performance. CNN consistently performs well, especially with N-gram and Keras embeddings, and the choice of embedding has a significant impact on model performance across datasets.

Table 2 Existing results [10] vs CNN model

Dataset	Word embeddings	DL models & accuracy		
		BI-LSTM	GRU	CNN
Twitter	**BERT**	87.04	87.09	**93.75**
	Roberta	89.62	89.59	**93.75**
IMDB	**BERT**	92.47	92.54	**97.31**
	Roberta	94.49	94.63	**93.75**

Table 3 Performance analysis of proposed method

Dataset	Word embeddings	DL models & accuracy		
		BI-LSTM	CNN	GRU
Twitter	**CT-Bert**	**95.31**	**93.75**	**95.31**
	Elmo	0.7927	78.61	79.33
	Keras	0.8974	93.52	83.56
	N-grams	**94.78**	**98.3**	**93.5**
IMDB	**CT-Bert**	0.718	93.75	81.25
	Elmo	**99.52**	**99.62**	**99.7**
	Keras	**99.14**	**99.81**	**99.07**
	N-grams	**98.3**	**99.96**	**96.84**

5 Conclusion

This work presents efficient embeddings for sentiment analysis (BERT, CT-Bert, Elmo, N-gram, Roberta) with attentive architectures (Bi-LSTM, CNN, GRU). Particularly when employing N-gram and Keras embeddings, CNN surpasses other approaches with accuracy rates of 99.96% and 99.81%, respectively. The paper offers recommendations on choosing appropriate embeddings and architectures to support the development of sentiment analysis systems.

Acknowledgements We acknowledge the support of Dr. Lei Wang, Ph.D., Professor in Psychiatry and Behavioral Health and Neuroscience at Ohio State University Wexner Medical Center, USA, for providing the platform to access Ohio Supercomputer Center to carry out the necessary simulations.

References

1. He W, Zha S, Li L (2013) Social media competitive analysis and text mining: A case study in the pizza industry. Int J Inf Manage 33:464–472
2. Vinodhini G, Chandrasekaran R (2012) Sentiment analysis and opinion mining: a survey. Int J 2:282–292
3. Do˘gan E, Kaya B (2019) Deep learning-based sentiment analysis and text summarization in social networks. In: 2019 International artificial intelligence and data processing symposium (IDAP). pp 1–6
4. Sukheja S, Chopra S, Vijayalakshmi M (2020) Sentiment Analysis using Deep Learning–A survey. In: 2020 international conference on computer science, engineering and applications (ICCSEA). pp 1–4
5. Rizk Y, Asal W (2021) Sentiment analysis using machine learning and deep learning models on movies reviews. In: 2021 3rd novel intelligent and leading emerging sciences conference (NILES). pp 129–132
6. Mohbey K (2021) Sentiment analysis for product rating using a deep learning approach. In: 2021 international conference on artificial intelligence and smart systems (ICAIS). pp 121–126

7. Shilpa P, Shereen R, Jacob S, Vinod P (2021) Sentiment analysis using deep learning. In: 2021 third international conference on intelligent communication technologies and virtual mobile networks (ICICV). pp 930–937 (2021)
8. Chauhan R (2022) Sentiment analysis of customer reviews using deep learning techniques. (Dublin, National College of Ireland)
9. Aziz M, Islam M, Munshi M, Samshi S, Khan M (2022) Sentimental analysis on reviews of protein supplement using RNN-LSTM. In: 2022 6th international conference on computing methodologies and communication (ICCMC). pp 796–800
10. Tan K, Lee C, Lim K, Anbananthen K (2022) Sentiment analysis with ensemble hybrid deep learning model. IEEE Access. 10:103694–103704

Audio Situation Analysis by Multiple Signal Features on a Hybrid Parallel Neural Network

Anup Kumar, Sagar Dhanraj Pande, and Aditya Khamparia

1 Introduction

Natural Language Processing (NLP), which is the computational study of peoples' views, attitudes, and behaviors, includes sentiment analysis as a well-researched subfield [1, 2], evaluations of and attitudes toward various objects, including organizations, services, products, and so forth [3, 4]. Most of the sentiment analysis models are based on the text. Subjectivity and sentiment analysis are methods for automatically detecting the innermost feelings, thoughts, and beliefs of an individual. Subjectivity detection also concentrates on determining if data is arbitrary or impartial. In this case, sentiment analysis classifies data into categories ranging from positive, negative, and neutral, thereby revealing the polarity of the data's sentiment [5]. Three basic techniques have come about in recent years for audio sentiment analysis. First, uses traditional text-based sentiment identification systems after using ASR (automated speech recognition) technologies to turn voice into text [6]. Second, uses a generative model that operates straight on the unprocessed audio waveform [7]. Third emphasizes the extraction of signal features from raw audio files [8], which has been shown not to be more effective than original audio spectrum descriptors like Mel-frequency spectrum coefficients (MFCC) and effectively captures the tonal richness of audio. The usage of Mel-frequency cepstral coefficient (MFCCs) and spectrogram transformation feature of the audio in this paper makes it easy to extract

A. Kumar
School of Computer Science Engineering, VIT-AP University, Amaravati, Andhra Pradesh, India
e-mail: anup.21bce7985@vitapstudent.ac.in

S. D. Pande (✉)
School of Engineering and Technology, Pimpri Chinchwad University (PCU), Pune, Maharashtra, India
e-mail: sagarpande30@gmail.com

A. Khamparia
Babasaheb Bhimrao Ambedkar University (A Central University), Lucknow, Uttar Pradesh, India

K. Kumar Singh et al. (eds.), *Machine Vision and Augmented Intelligence*, Lecture Notes in Electrical Engineering 1211, https://doi.org/10.1007/978-981-97-4359-9_34

and work on more deep audio features. This audio can not only be used for just the classification purpose but can be used to get the machine to interact more in a much precise way [9]. Audio classification can be generalized for any application and can be implemented to a wide area [10]. This paper provides a hybrid model that classifies the audio into seven different classes that can be very beneficial not only for human conceptualization but also if used to automate the machine to work according to the understanding of the human world. This paper takes into consideration the prominent feature extraction ways, i.e., Mel-frequencies, spectrogram, etc., and these features are used to get the insight of the given audio. This paper takes into consideration the features not only as a static vector representation but also deals with the time dependency of the audio. The main categories focused on this paper are:

1. This paper proposes a novel hybrid parallel architecture consisting of 10 convolutional layers CNN architecture and 16 Transformer layers with 32 heads per layer both data are passed parallelly to these layers and finally a combined model is created to process these data and extract the features through dense layers.
2. This paper deals with the balanced data with both the male and female voices in equal amounts and equal class representation is also available for the balanced training of the model.
3. This paper focuses more on the sentimental features of the audio rather than the gender and language.
4. Experimental results show that this paper outperforms the existing similar models, and the suggested model performs more predominantly than the existing.

The rest of the paper is organized as follows Sections, 2. Dataset description, 3. Preprocessing, 4. Feature extraction 5. Methodology 6. Structural Analysis and Quantifiers, 7. Results 8. Conclusion and future scope 9. References.

2 Dataset Description

The EMOVO [3] dataset is designed for audio sentiment analysis and focuses on capturing not only linguistic information but also extra-linguistic and paralinguistic cues from speech. It acknowledges that humans are sensitive to factors such as the identity and state of the speaker, as well as the underlying intentions and emotions conveyed through speech.

Speech emotion recognition (SER) systems utilizing datasets like EMOVO [3] have various applications, including ensuring emotional speech consistency for actors, aiding communication for disabled individuals, enabling interactive TV experiences, constructing virtual teachers, studying human brain malfunctions, and advancing Text-To-Speech systems.

Studies on emotional speech have revealed strong correlations between speech and emotion, with key findings summarized in notable review articles.

Different types of datasets of voices have been used to get the knowledge of the emotions, while others have induced emotions by placing speakers in specific emotional situations. Additionally, some studies have used actors with acting skills to simulate emotions, allowing for more controlled recordings.

The EMOVO [3] dataset is an example of an acted speech corpus specifically developed for the Italian language. It has different men and female in same numbers. The actors performed fourteen sentences, including assertive, interrogative, and list-based sentences, representing six emotional states along with a neutral state.

The EMOVO [3] dataset's linguistic content consists of a collection of sentences that are intended to provoke emotional reactions. Both the Italian and the English translations of the phrases are given. By using these audio expressions it is easy for the tester to get the emotionally rich content while preserving the natural expression.

To ensure the suitability of the phrases for spectral analysis, the following basic conditions were considered:

Each sentence has a fair balance between voiced and unvoiced consonants.

Also, two sentences were used in the dataset to provide similarity between semantics and phrases.

These methods make sure that the natural integrity in the audio is maintained while taking care of the linguistic material present in one's speech. The EMOVO [3] dataset has been selected to take care of these aspects already.

3 Preprocessing

The audio collected from the EMOVO dataset is present in 6 folders according to the gender of the actor. There are 3 folders for male voice and 3 folders for the female voice. The audio is first transferred to the 7 folders as per the different classes using a Python code. Data-augmentation techniques like the pitch scaling for the audio to scale the pitch in the same audio can be easily used to let the model understand and make the learning easy. The audio used for the training is trimmed, i.e., made into same size using the trimming techniques using NumPy and torch modules for the video that can be trained.

4 Feature Extracting

There are different feature extraction methods and algorithms that can be used to get the required features for the above-mentioned classification task. This paper mainly focuses on the two features of the audio. Those features are MFFC's and Mel-spectroscopy. These both features proved to be the most important features in terms of information gathering for classification purposes.

4.1 MFCC's

There is great motivation for using the MFCC's feature for the audio. When we want to train our model using the audio, we can't train it using the raw audio as there can be a lot of noise and unwanted frequency fluctuation. This is why we use MFFC's to get the most accurate feature that the model can learn from. The Mel-Frequency cepstral coefficients can be represented as follows:

Impulse response- k(n), speech signal m(n) as output of filter in response to input h(n). The convolution is calculated. Equation (1) shows the relation between impulse and speech signal.

$$m(n) = k(n) * h(n) \tag{1}$$

4.1.1 A/D Conversion

Here we convert the analog signal to digital signal with the frequency range of 8–16 kHz.

4.1.2 Windowing

The MFCC method looks for features in the audio streams. These can be used to identify phonetic features in the speech that is being supplied. The issue is that there may be several phones in the provided audio signal; therefore, divide the audio signal into various parts before processing it. Here, a window is required to avoid audio from becoming suddenly noisy by chopping at any interval. For this work, hammering or hanging windows is primarily used.

4.1.3 MEL—Filter Bank

The way humans perceive sound is different than the way the machine perceives it. This is why this step is needed for modeling the signal to the frequencies that a human will perceive. The below used formula (2) is used to change the signal to human understandable frequency.

$$mel(p) = 1127ln\left(1 + \frac{p}{700}\right) \tag{2}$$

4.1.4 Log Function

To make the feature resemble humans in detecting the change at different terms at higher level and lower level differently we use the concept of log function shown in Eq. (3). The formula applied to the energy levels of the audio is as follows:

$$log[|Y_a u(l)|] = log[|P(l)||X_{r_s} u(l)||T\prime(l) \quad (3)$$

The capstone coefficient is obtained using the below Eq. (4):

$$ca = \sum_{a=1}^{Nt} Sncos\left[a(n-0.5)\left(\frac{\pi}{Nf}\right)\right] \quad (4)$$

4.1.5 Dynamic Features

MFCC's will dynamically generate a total of 39 features. 12 features are the first coefficient of the signal, and one is the energy coefficient. MFCC will take into consideration the first and the second order derivative making 26 more features. At the end, we will have 39 features in total. Figure 5 shows the change in the coefficient of MFCC as per the time for the given audio from one of the dataset audio. This figure uses hop_length of 128 and the number of MFCC as 8 for this (Figs. 1 and 2).

$$\text{Energy} = \sum_{t=t1}^{t2} x^2[t] \quad (5)$$

4.2 *Mel-Spectrogram*

This frequently used illustration of the spectrum content of an audio signal in tasks involving audio signal processing and machine learning. It is developed from the spectrogram, which shows the timing and frequency of the audio signal.

The Mel-spectrogram incorporates the Mel scale, since human perception is more sensitive to changes in lower frequencies than higher frequencies, the Mel scale takes this into account. By utilizing the Mel scale, the Mel-spectrogram provides a more perceptually accurate representation of the audio signal. Figures 3 and 4 show the Mel-spectrogram of the audio used for training this model both the figure use different parametric values to show the difference.

Fig. 4This figure shows the proposed architecture describing the exact workflow of the model proposed. This figure explains the working modal of the proposed modal.

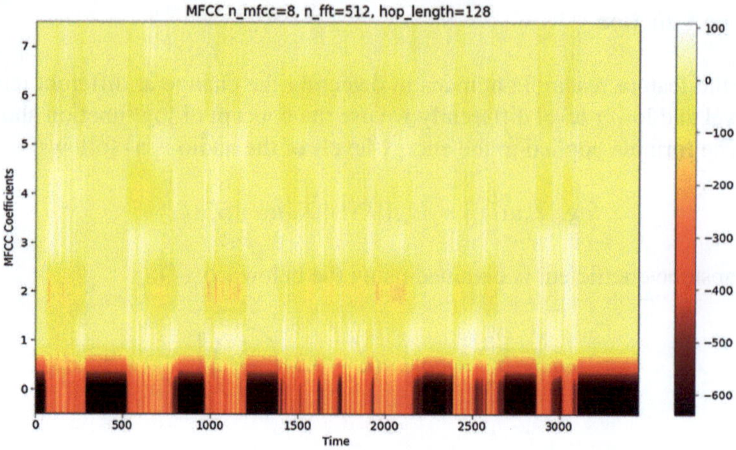

Fig. 1 The plot shows variation of (*MFCC coefficient vs. Time)*

Fig. 2 The graph shows variation of Frequency (Hz) of the audio over time with n_fft = 2048

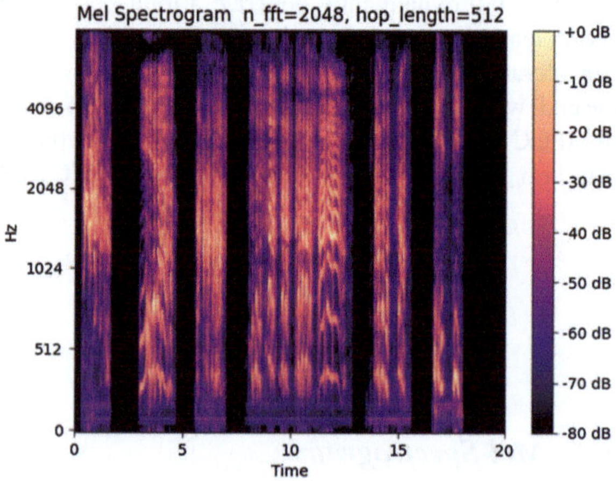

First, the data is processed and acoustic features are taken out then these features are sent to CNN and Transformer Network then the predicted features are combined and classified in any of the 7 basic human behavior

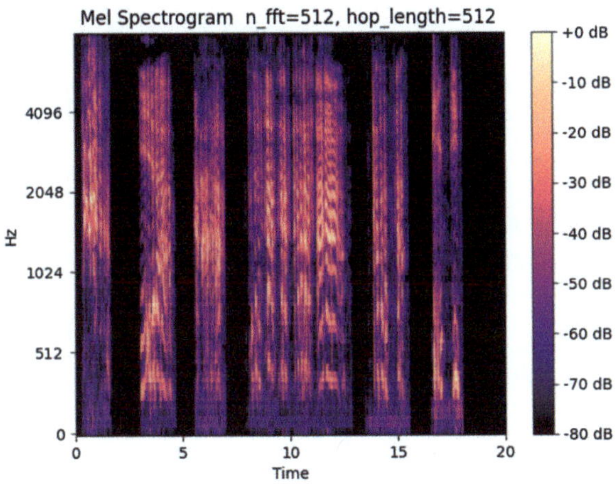

Fig. 3 The graph shows variation of Frequency (Hz) of the audio over time with n_fft = 512

5 Methodology

The model proposed by this paper consists of two individual layers of CNN and Transformer respectively. These both parallel layers are then combined with the use of combined with fully connected sequenced layers. The processed features generated after the preprocessing part are fed into both layers separately.

5.1 CNN Layers

In the acoustic feature extraction phase, the spectrum graph obtained from feature transformation utilizing MFCC and Mel-spectrogram is given into the CNN model. This CNN model was created exclusively utilizing the various parameter combinations and layer combinations described in this paper. The images of the various spectra that were sent to the 2d Convolutional layer for training are used to execute 2-dimensional convolution. The dense layer that makes up the branch's last layer converts the CNN's output into a feature vector and prepares it for concatenation with the suggested Parallel transformer layer model. The method used for the model's training is duplicated, as demonstrated in *Algorithm: Proposed Algorithm.*

5.1.1 Formulas Involved

The nonlinearity involves the following formula (5):

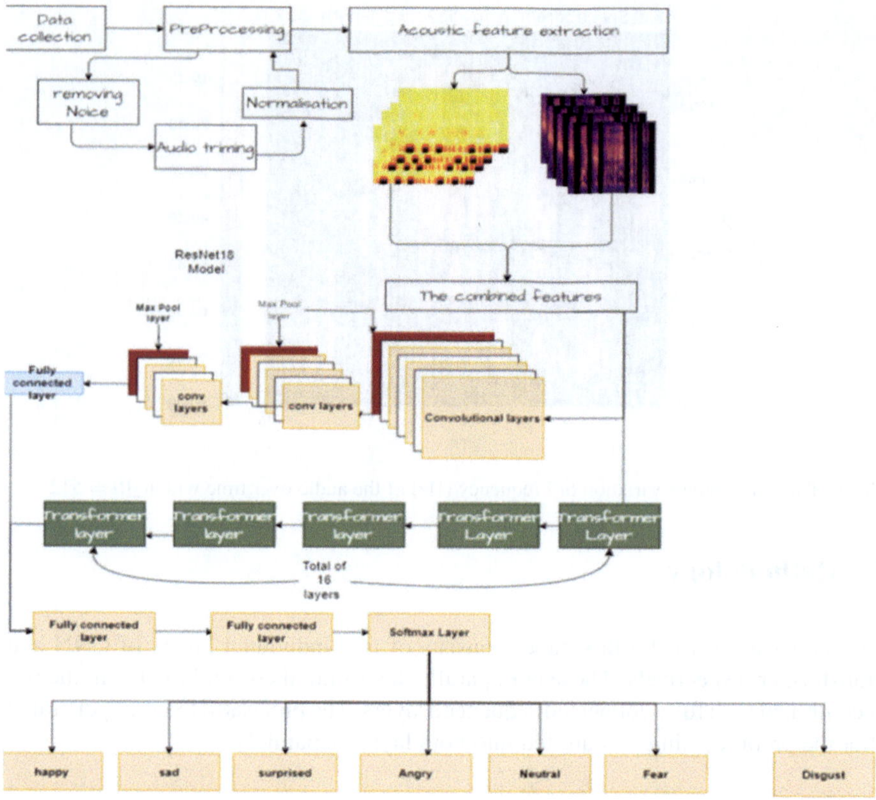

Fig. 4 This figure shows the proposed architecture describing the exact workflow of the model proposed. This figure explains the working modal of the proposed modal. First, the data is processed and acoustic features are taken out then these features are sent to CNN and Transformer Network then the predicted features are combined and classified in any of the 7 basic human behavior

$$C_{ij}^{k} = \sum_{t=0}^{n-1} \sum_{s=0}^{n-1} P_{ts} y^{k-1}(i+t)(j+s) \tag{6}$$

For adding the nun-linearity in our model this (5) formula is used:

$$y_{ij}^{k} = \emptyset(y_{ij}^{k}) \tag{7}$$

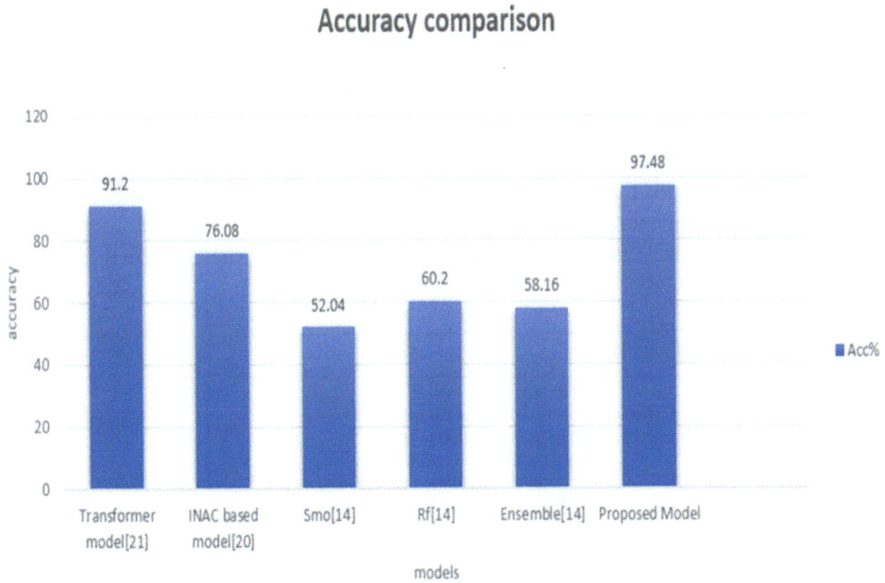

Fig. 5 This figure is the graphical representation of the model's performance

5.2 *Transformer*

This is a model that is dependent on the hybrid attention model. This is the upgraded version of the RNN and LSTM models. The training time of Transformers is also less compared to the LSTM and RNN. The working of the transformer models starts with taking the encoded tokens parallel with the attention mechanisms. This unlike the RNN contains no architecture that resembles the RNN's. These have a completely different set of stacked layers that work parallelly to process the data.

$$P(a)\left(y_i\right) = T^{w}_{h,q}\, y_i \tag{8}$$

$$M^{a}(yi) = T^{w}_{h,k} y_i \tag{10}$$

$$M^{h}\left(y_i\right) = T^{w}_{h,v} y_i \tag{11}$$

$$T_{h,q}, T_{h,k}, T_{h,v} \in R^{rxu} \tag{12}$$

Here, T is the weight matrix. y_i is the input tensor. P^a is a query vector. M^a is a key vector. M^h is a value vector. The equations from 7 to 10 constitute the base of the transformer where the input is not only the tensor but a corresponding query as well.

5.3 Algorithm Explanation

The algorithm used in this paper is described below (*Algorithm*). This algorithm states the working flow of the model and the parallel architecture used. The processed dataset is sent to CNN and Transformers and the corresponding results are stored for the future use. Once this part is completed the output of both the model is concatenated and sent to a 3 layer neural network of which 2 are fully connected and one of the SoftMax layer for the classification. Then after this, we get the classified audio as per our need.

Algorithm : Proposed Algorithm

```
Sudo For CNN
    for k in Range(Epochs) // It will run till the dataset
        for feature,labels in [1 : len(Dataset) ]
            features ← the input spectrogram Image
            cnn← the CNN(features)// model to be trained
            output← output for the further computation
        end for
    end for
Sudo For Transformer
    for k in Range(Epochs) // It will run till the dataset
        for feature,labels in [1 : len(Dataset) ]
            features← the input spectrogram Image
            encoded← the Attention model (features)// model to be trained
            output← output for the further computation
        end for
    end for
Sudo For Combined Model
    for k in Range(Epochs) // It will run till the dataset
        for feature,labels in [1 : len(OUTPUT(CNN +Transformer)) ]
            features ← the input spectrogram Image
          label ←get the corresponding label
            feature vector← the Transformer (features)// model to be trained
            output← output for the further computation
        end for
end for
```

6 Structural Analysis and Quantifiers

The Model proposed in this paper is implemented using the open-source framework of PyTorch and used the Python language. The proposed model came out of several experiments and the final model with different parameters is fixed considering the accuracy factor. This model first takes the input audio size that is fixed for the model before fitting. The CNN layers take an input size of (1 × 1x64 × 64), followed by ResNet18 CNN layers with an output size of ([1024]). The pooling used in between is Max pooling and the ReLu is used as the activation function. Similarly, the Transformer model has 16 layers with 32 heads per layer. The last layer of the Transformer gives the output as a vector with dimension (1024). Then both outputs are combined as a concatenated output with the dimension of (2048, 1024). This input tensor is then fed into the dense layer network with 3 hidden layers and then the predicted class is predicted as output. The final layer uses a SoftMax layer for the output vector prediction. The illustration below (Fig. 4) shows the visual explanation of the above explained architecture.

7 Results

The model was trained over 200 epochs to obtain the result, and the plot of Loss is based on the train and validation loss over the epochs. The Confusion matrix essentially represents the model's performance, and the model can then be fully analyzed after being shown to be competent in that regard (Figs. 5, 6, 7, 8 and Table 1).

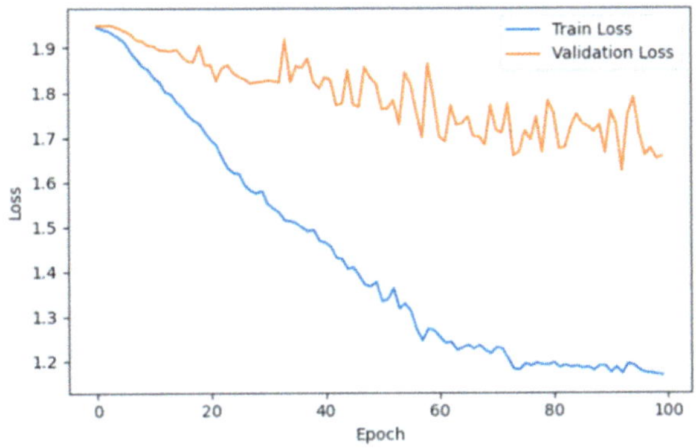

Fig. 6 This figure illustrates the train and validation loss of the no. of epochs used while training the proposed model

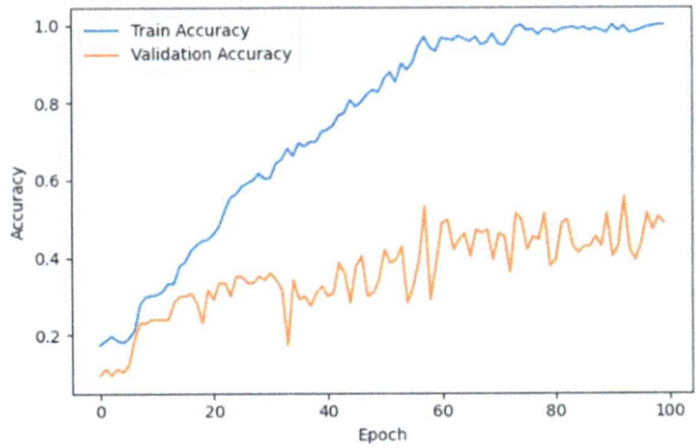

Fig. 7 This figure illustrates the train and validation accuracy of the proposed mode

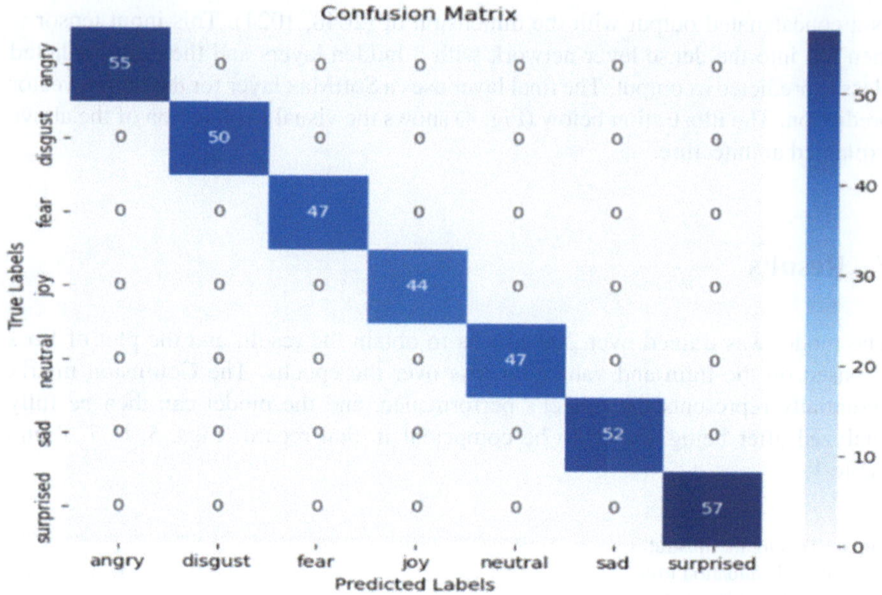

Fig. 8 This figure is the pictorial representation of the confusion matrix over different labels in the used dataset

Table 1 The accuracy over different models used for the proposed task and also the accuracy attained by this paper

S. No.	Model	Acc%
1	Transformer model [11]	91.2
2	INAC based model [12]	76.08
3	Smo [14]	52.04
4	Rf [14]	60.2
5	Ensemble [14]	58.16
6	**Proposed Model**	**97.48**

8 Conclusion and Future Scope

In this study, CNN and Transformer layers were combined to create a hybrid parallel model. With the use of the Librosa toolkit and PyTorch transformation function, several acoustic features have been retrieved. This study demonstrates the detection and preparation of audio for sentiment classification. This study outperforms the most advanced models, with an accuracy of 97.48%. This paradigm can be simply used and carried forward with many transformations, and it has a very broad future possibility. This study exclusively examines the acoustic and frequency dependence of the audio, disregarding the influence of language type. Further, research can be carried out with these things kept in mind and the multimodal approach can be considered for future research work and for future endeavors of projects. Further research can be conducted while keeping these factors in mind, and the multimodal approach can be taken into consideration for future research work and project endeavors.

References

1. Sentiment Analysis and Emotion Recognition from Speech Using Universal Speech Representations by Bagus Tris Atmaja and Akira Sasou
2. Pang B, Lee L (2004) A sentimental education: Sentiment analysis using subjectivity summarization based on minimum cuts. In: proceedings of the 42nd annual meeting on association for computational linguistics (p 271). Association for Computational Linguistics
3. EMOVO Corpus: an Italian Emotional Speech DatabaseGiovanni Costantini, Iacopo Iadarola, Andrea Paoloni, Massimiliano Todisco, Department of Electronic Engineering, University of Rome "Tor Vergata", Rome, Italy Institute of Acoustics "O. M. Corbino", Rome, Italy Fondazione "Ugo Bordoni", Rome, Italy
4. Liu B (2017) Sentiment analysis: mining opinions, sentiments, and emotions, The Cambridge University Press, 2015. S. Poria, E. Cambria, R. Bajpai, and A. Hussain, A review of affective computing: From unimodal analysis to multimodal fusion, Information Fusion, vol. 37, pp 98125
5. Fusing audio, visual and textual clues for sentiment analysis from multimodal content Author overlay panel Soujanya Poria, Erik Cambria, Newton Howard, Guang-Bin Huang, Amir Hussain
6. Ezzat S, Gayar N, Ghanem MM (2012) Sentiment analysis of call centre audio conversations using text classification. Int J Comput Inf Syst Ind Manag Appl 4:619–627
7. Van Den Oord A, Dieleman S, Zen H, et al. WaveNet: A generative model for raw audio[C]// SSW. 2016: 125. Bertin-Mahieux T, and Ellis, D. P. 2011. Large-scale cover song recognition using hashed chroma landmarks. In: 2011 IEEE workshop on applications of signal processing to audio and acoustics (WASPAA), 117120. IEEE
8. Bertin-Mahieux T, Ellis DP (2011) Large-scale cover song recognition using hashed chroma landmarks. In: 2011 IEEE workshop on applications of signal processing to audio and acoustics (WASPAA), 117120. IEEE
9. Le Cun Y, Boser B, et al. (1990) Handwritten digit recognition with a back-propagation network. In: Advances in neural information processing systems
10. Hochreiter S, Schmidhuber J (1997) Long short-term memory. Neural Comput 9(8):1735–1780
11. Transformer-Based Multilingual Speech Emotion Recognition Using Data Augmentation and Feature Fusion by Badriyya B. Al-onazi Muhammad Asif Nauman Rashid Jahangir Muhmmad Mohsin Malik Eman H. Alkhammash and Ahmed M. Elshewey
12. Automated accurate speech emotion recognition system using twine shuffle pattern and iterative neighborhood component analysis techniques

Comparative Analysis of Polycystic Ovary Syndrome Detection Using Deep Learning Algorithms

Neha, A. Ranjith Kumar, and Sagar Dhanraj Pande

1 Introduction

Polycystic Ovarian Syndrome (PCOS) is a common hormonal condition affecting women of childbearing age. Hormonal abnormalities, irregular menstrual cycles, the existence of ovarian cysts, excessive unnecessary hair growth, and potential long-term health consequences characterize this complex illness [1]. PCOS can become a root problem that has the ability to cause several diseases like metabolic diseases, and a higher risk of cardiovascular problems. It can sometimes even cause some major problems with fertility [2]. Even though it sounds a little the percentage of women who are daily fighting with this harmful PCOS is gradually rising up to 10 percent. They are all struggling with the complications caused by the PCOS in one way or the other [3]. The complete merciless spread of PCOS across the nation and the nation connecting lines is becoming a headache for all and it is taking worldwide threat to women and indirectly affecting everyone. This shows the importance of detection of PCOS, however, a simple statistic model is not enough for the detection, it goes far beyond.

PCOS has a great hand over the effect of fertility in women as it is one of the major factors. This PCOS is affecting the reproductive health of women in a great manner. If the detection of PCOS is done in the early stage, then doing therapies will become the solution to solve or reduce the effect of PCOS on both physical and reproductive health. If anyone considers that the effect of PCOS is only on the fertility rate then it is a mistake it also shows its hand over the cause of many other diseases like type 2 diabetes, obesity [4], and cardiovascular disease [4]. However, PCOS has effects

Neha · A. R. Kumar
School of Computer Science Engineering, Lovely Professional University, Phagwara, Punjab, India

S. D. Pande (✉)
School of Engineering and Technology, Pimpri Chinchwad University (PCU), Pune, India
e-mail: sagarpande30@gmail.com

K. Kumar Singh et al. (eds.), *Machine Vision and Augmented Intelligence*, Lecture Notes in Electrical Engineering 1211, https://doi.org/10.1007/978-981-97-4359-9_35

that go beyond the physical, harming psychological health. Acne and hirsutism are two of PCOS's more obvious symptoms that have a significant impact on mental and emotional well-being [5]. Early PCOS detection enables people to obtain the right care, reducing the psychological suffering that frequently goes along with this illness. The knowledge that PCOS can become a lifetime companion if untreated further emphasizes the significance of early detection [6]. When PCOS is diagnosed in youth or early adulthood, techniques for lifelong control become available, potentially lowering the risk of problems in later years. PCOS affects people personally and has a significant financial impact on healthcare systems. Early detection can reduce the burden on resources by preventing expensive medical procedures and hospital stays. Deep learning algorithms have proven to be remarkably accurate at identifying minute patterns and anomalies in patient data and medical pictures when applied to PCOS. This novel method speeds up PCOS diagnosis and improves predictive modeling, making it possible to spot the condition early [7]. As a result, healthcare professionals can give prompt interventions and personalized treatment plans, ultimately improving patient outcomes. The substantial impact of deep learning on the medical sector represents a paradigm shift towards data-driven, effective, and more precise treatment.

The contributions of the paper are described below:

- A large-scale dataset is created to perform the model, where all the data points are self-picked.
- Different deep learning and machine learning architectures are compared, which aids in a better understanding of the approach.
- A novel method for the detection of PCOS is proposed that ultimately helps in curing PCOS.

The rest of the paper is organized as the comparison and comprehensive understanding of previous work as a Literature survey in Sect. 2, and the proposed methodology is discussed in Sect. 3 along with the dataset description and data preprocessing, the results and analysis are discussed in Sect. 4 whereas the conclusion and future scope of the paper is mentioned in Sect. 5.

2 Literature Survey

Before advancing with early PCOS identification utilizing deep learning techniques and DEEP CNN-based models, it is essential to lay a strong theoretical framework for our research in the body of literature. Let's now examine the literature gap in the existing works on the area with the aid of Table 1.

Table 1 This table illustrates the gap of the work on the domain

Ref	Year	Advantages of previous work	Limitations of previous work	Model corresponding solution
[1]	2022	Machine learning can uncover patterns human specialists might miss and create more reliable diagnostic models than conventional methods	Creating and implementing machine learning algorithms can be expensive, and designing and understanding them can be challenging	The proposed method is computationally cost friendly
[2]	2021	The study evaluates various machine learning techniques for PCOS prediction, helping academics and practitioners choose the optimal algorithm. Additionally, it offers a comprehensive summary of the latest advancements in machine learning for PCOS prediction, ensuring that professionals can stay informed and up-to-date	The study's limited dataset constrains the generalizability of the results, and the paper does not assess the performance of the machine learning algorithms in a clinical trial, which could have offered more compelling evidence of their effectiveness	The model can be trained on a small amount of data comparatively
[3]	2020	The research introduces an advanced machine learning method for more accurate PCOS classification compared to existing techniques. Additionally, it identifies key characteristics highly indicative of PCOS, improving diagnostic precision	The study's limited dataset may limit the generalizability of the results. Furthermore, the report lacks an assessment of the suggested strategy's performance in a clinical study, which could have provided more compelling evidence of its effectiveness	The model can be trained on a small amount of data comparatively

(continued)

Table 1 (continued)

Ref	Year	Advantages of previous work	Limitations of previous work	Model corresponding solution
[4]	2019	Early detection of PCOS through the i-HOPE system can help prevent long-term consequences. The i-HOPE system relies on machine learning algorithms, known for their precision compared to conventional diagnostic methods	To confirm the accuracy of the i-HOPE system, additional study is still required A doctor's diagnosis cannot be replaced by the i-HOPE system. Only as a tool to assist healthcare professionals in making decisions	With the accuracy level achieved this paper strongly supports real-time use
[8]	2020	Machine learning can analyze extensive datasets, revealing patterns that human specialists might miss, leading to more precise diagnoses. Additionally, it allows the development of diagnostic models that are not only dependable but also consistent, potentially elevating the quality of care for PCOS patients beyond that achieved through conventional techniques	Creating and implementing machine learning algorithms can incur significant costs. The design and comprehension of these algorithms can be complex, making it challenging for healthcare professionals to fully evaluate the diagnostic findings generated through machine learning methods	The proposed model requires less amount of computational power thus bettering the previous work

2.1 Summary of the Table

Each article is thoughtfully analyzed in the table, with both merits and downsides listed. This triggered a lengthy discussion about how to get around the current study's drawbacks. By thoroughly analyzing the body of existing literature, this study identifies areas that need improvement and suggests fresh approaches. Using this comparison approach, which exposes trends, strengths, and weaknesses and provides creative solutions for constraints, considerably improves the value and significance of the investigations.

3 Methodology

3.1 Dataset Description

The dataset that is used in the project consists of 1562 initial ultrasound images with a size of 256,256 that have been increased to 7,805 images by data augmentation. Two classes have been assigned to these pictures: A value of "1" designates images with polycystic ovaries, which are characterized by bilaterally enlarged ovaries, numerous tiny follicles, and enhanced stromal echogenicity, while a value of "0" designates images without these traits.

3.2 Data Preprocessing

Follow these procedures to preprocess the dataset, this step mainly involves two steps they are Data augmentation and Normalization, which consists of 1,562 original photos and 7,805 images, and divide it into training, testing, and validation sets with a 7:1:2 ratio. You start out with a total of 9,367 pictures. To ensure randomization and remove any inherent ordering biases, first shuffle the entire dataset. This project used 6,557 training photos, 937 test images, and 1,873 validation images.

This paper carries out the following actions to preprocess the images:

- Resize the photos to a standard dimension (256 × 256 pixels).
- Ensure that pixel values fall inside a predetermined range, often [0, 1] or [–1, 1], by normalizing them. This is illustrative of:

$$x\_i\_normalized = (x\_i - min(x\_i))/(max(x\_i) - min(x\_i)) \quad (1)$$

The data augmentation of the images is represented in the below image as Fig. 1 by representing the before and after count of images in a bar chart.

Fig. 1 Count of data input by augmentation

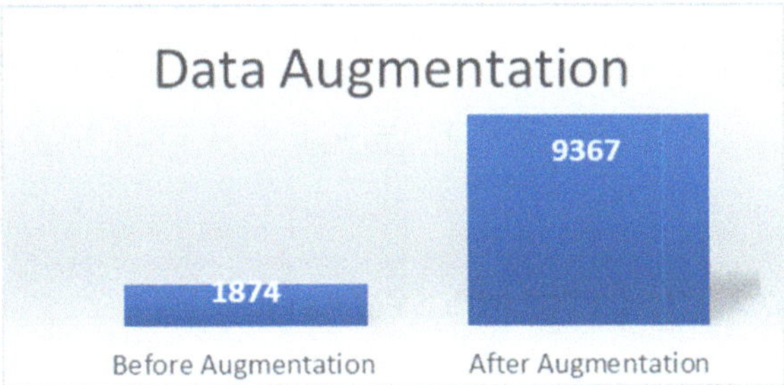

3.3 Deep CNN and Deep CNN with Last Layer as SVM

3.3.1 Deep CNN

For identifying ultrasonic pictures in a variety of applications, including medical diagnostics, Deep Convolutional Neural Networks (CNNs) are a powerful tool. Through a sequence of convolutional and pooling layers, these neural networks are exceptional at learning complex visual information. There are often three important phases involved in training a deep CNN for the classification of ultrasonic images. The primary step involves the compilation of the collectedlabeled data which is ultrasonic images. The illustration is stored in variable $D = (x\_1, y\_1), (x\_2, y\_2)..., (x\_N, y\_N)$, where x_i denotes an image and y_i denotes its corresponding label. And for the purpose of consistency, these pixels are all normalized to the scale with uniform sizes [9]. Then the dataset is divided into training, testing, and validation datasets. For the purpose of training and validating the performance of the model.

The fully connected layer of the model will be primarily supported by the convolutional and pooling layers which will be the classification model. Learning spatial properties is very important for the model, this task is completed by the filters applied on the input data with the help of convolutional layers. These filters are generally a small numbered matrix like a 5*5 or 3*3 matrix that will filter and give key required properties of the image. This process is represented by Eq. 2.

$$y\_in = \Sigma\_\{l = 1\}^K (w\_inl * x\_l) + b\_in \tag{2}$$

The output of feature maps by the convolutional layers' pooling layers will be the smaller spatial dimensions. For this, feature maps are sent through the pooling function, such as max pooling or average pooling. For example, the max pooling operation can be stated as:

$$y\_i = max(x\_\{i1\}, x\_\{i2\}, ..., x\_\{in\}) \tag{3}$$

The final fully connected layer takes the output from the pooling layer and generates class scores, which are used to classify the image into predefined classes. The fully connected layer operation can be represented as:

$$y\_i = \Sigma\_\{j = 1\}^n (w\_ij * x\_j) + b\_i \tag{4}$$

3.3.2 Deep CNN with SVM Layer

Deep CNNs are extremely capable of reaching impressive classification accuracy, but because of their depth and complexity, they can be time-consuming to train and use.

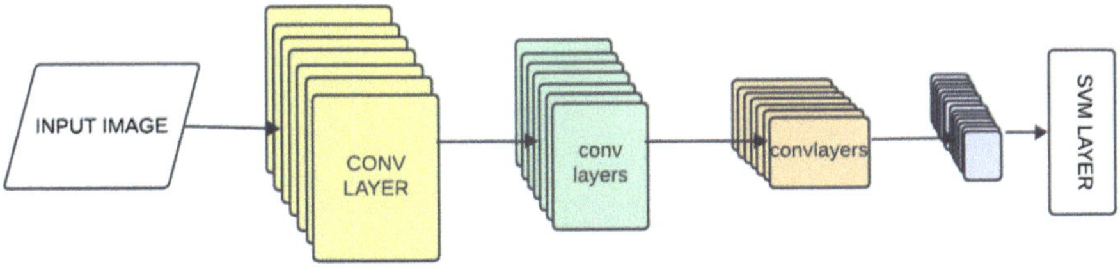

Fig. 2 The working process of Deep CNN with SVM layer

As a final-layer classifier, a deep CNN and an SVM can be used to improve classification performance even more. The output features of the deep CNN are fed into the SVM, which functions as a linear classifier. The deep CNN is first trained as previously discussed, and after that, features are extracted from the last convolutional layer prior to the fully connected layer [10].

The SVM classifier may do better in terms of classification on the test set because it can capture more complex correlations between features. This strategy of identifying ultrasonic pictures with deep CNN and last-layer SVM offers improved accuracy and complexity handling capabilities [11].

Below Fig. 2 shows the working model of Deep CNN with SVM layer.

4 Result and Analysis

The aforementioned structures were replicated using Google Colab, the foundational works, and the reference code given by the original authors. After integrating the aforementioned dataset with its own, the outcomes were then examined. A Google Colab laptop (pro edition), equipped with an Intel i10 7th generation 8-core CPU running at 5.30 GHz and 16 GB of RAM, is used to conduct the experiment.

Below Figs. 3 and 4 show the performance of the model performance in terms of loss and accuracy.

The trained model obtained a remarkable loss of 0.0101 and an excellent accuracy of 99.89%. These findings highlight the deep learning model's excellent accuracy and robustness in correctly identifying ultrasonic pictures, making it extremely trustworthy for a range of medical diagnostic applications.

Model Enhancement: The deep CNN + last-layer SVM ensemble showcases the potential for synergistic improvements in ultrasonic image classification [12]. While the initial CNN performed well, the addition of the SVM led to a substantial accuracy boost, highlighting the complementary nature of feature extraction and discriminative modeling.

Computational Considerations: It's important to note that this enhanced model may require increased computational resources due to the SVM's involvement. Careful

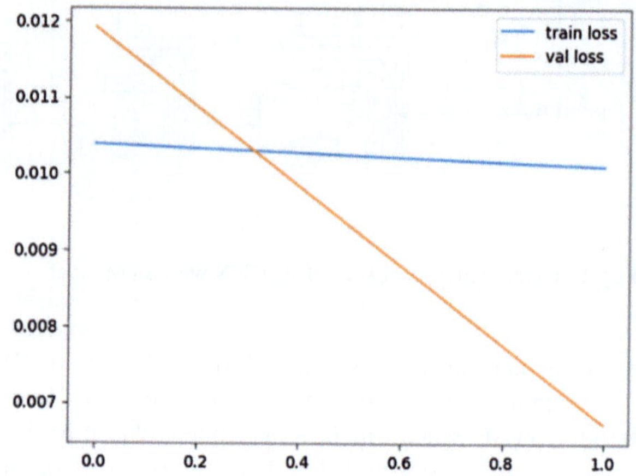

Fig. 3 This graph resembles the loss of the model in both training and validation

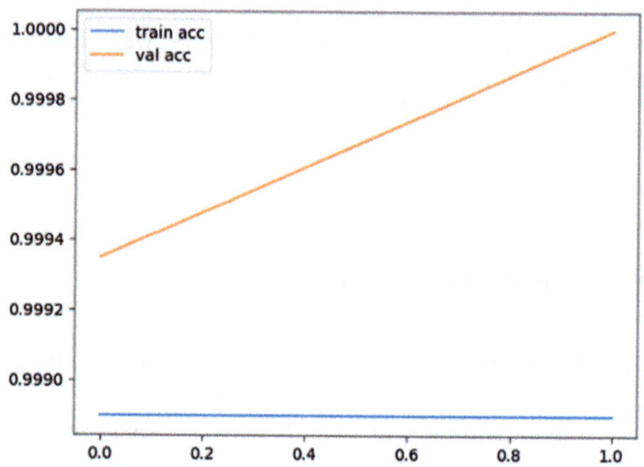

Fig. 4 This graph shows the accuracy attained in the training and validation

hyperparameter tuning and resource allocation are necessary for practical deployment. Overall, the approach demonstrates a promising pathway for achieving higher classification accuracy in medical image analysis.

The below Table 2 shows the result comparison of different models to classify, the ultimate result that can be observed is that compared to the other models the proposed model, i.e., the deep CNN with SVM layer outperforms the other models.

Below Figs. 5 and 6 show the classification of the ultrasonic images both the images were classified to have the PCOS in them but rather the proposed model's accuracy outran the traditional deep CNN with SVM layer.

Table 2 The comparison of different models on dataset

Model	Training accuracy (%)	Validation accuracy (%)	Loss
Deep CNN	92.58	95.79	0.1178
Deep CNN with SVM layer	**98.59**	**99.89**	**0.0101**
ResNET	89.36	92.36	1.0320
VGGNET	92.75	95.68	0.9568
RSENEX	94.36	96.31	0.7562

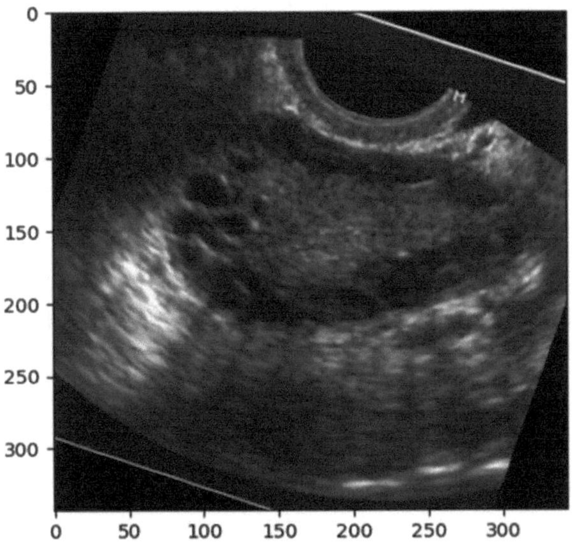

Fig. 5 The results attained by Deep CNN with SVM prediction

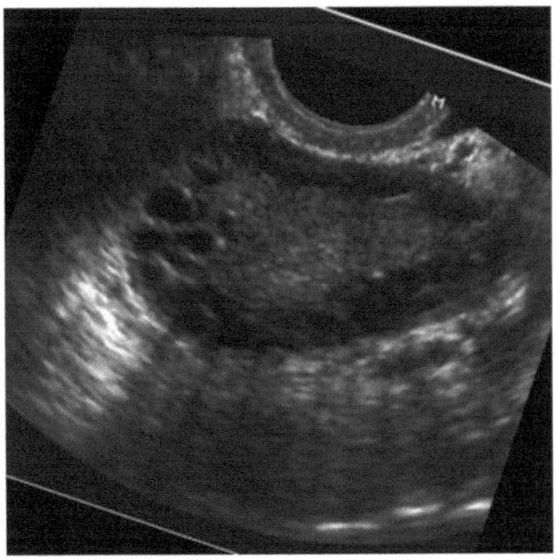

Fig. 6 The results attained by the Deep CNN

5 Conclusion and Future Scope

The above study has shown that the accuracy of classifying ultrasonic images is greatly improved by combining a deep convolutional neural network (CNN) with a support vector machine (SVM) in the last layer of the classifier. Even though the deep CNN alone demonstrated good feature extraction capability and produced decent results, the addition of the SVM significantly improved performance. The model proposed, i.e., the Deep CNN with SVM layer at the end has surpassed independent approaches with an accuracy of 99.89% and a loss of 0.0101, making it an appealing option for precise and trustworthy ultrasonic image classification. The deep CNN with SVM's achievement opens up promising new directions for future study and applications in the realm of medical image analysis. Adapting the model to handle real-time or large-scale clinical image datasets, researching transfer learning techniques for related medical imaging tasks, investigating interpretability methods to gain insights into model decisions for improved clinical understanding, incorporating extra modalities like patient metadata or textual reports to boost diagnostic accuracy, and expanding the model for multi-class classification to address these and other possible future research directions could be among the possible future directions. This comprehensive strategy offers a solid framework for classifying medical images and holds great promise for improving healthcare diagnostics through precise, automated image analysis.

References

1. Vaswani H, Mulchandani R, Vaghela, Rajan P, (2022) A systematic literature review on diagnosis of PCOS using machine learning algorithms." Available: https://git.org.in/GIT_JET/Papers/Regular%20Edition/8_GIT_JET_Regular_Edition_2022.pdf.
2. Chauhan P, Patil P, Rane N, Raundale P, Kanakia H (2021) Comparative analysis of machine learning algorithms for prediction of PCOS. In: 2021 international conference on communication information and computing technology (ICCICT), Mumbai, India, pp 1–7, https://doi.org/10.1109/ICCICT50803.2021.9510128
3. Nandipati SC, Ying CX, Wah KK (2020) Polycystic Ovarian Syndrome (PCOS) classification and feature selection by machine learning techniques. Appl Math Comput Intell 9:65–74
4. Denny A, Raj A, Ashok A, Ram CM, George R (2019) i-HOPE: Detection and prediction system for polycystic ovary syndrome (PCOS) using machine learning techniques. In: TENCON 2019—2019 IEEE Region 10 Conference (TENCON), Kochi, India, pp 673–678. https://doi.org/10.1109/TENCON.2019.8929674
5. Cheng JJ, Mahalingaiah S (2018) Data mining and classification of polycystic ovaries in pelvic ultrasound reports. bioRxiv, pp 254870
6. Dewi RM, Wisesty UN (2018) Classification of polycystic ovary based on ultrasound images using competitive neural network. J Phys: Conf Ser 971(1):012005
7. Sachdeva G, Gainder S, Suri V, Sachdeva N, Chopra S (2019) Obese and non-obese polycystic ovarian syndrome: Comparison of clinical metabolic hormonal parameters and their differential response to clomiphene. Indian J Endocrinol Metablsm 23(2):257
8. Namrata T (2020) Detecting PCOS using machine learning. https://doi.org/10.13140/RG.2.2.10265.24169

9. Devlin J, Chang MW, Lee K, Toutanova K (2018) Bert: Pre-training of deep bidirectional transformers for language understanding. arXiv preprint arXiv:1810.04805
10. Abdullah M, Madain A, Jararweh Y (2022) ChatGPT: Fundamentals, applications and social impacts. In: 2022 ninth international conference on social networks analysis, management and security (SNAMS)
11. Grootendorst M (2022) BERTopic: Neural topic modeling with a class-based TF-IDF procedure. arXiv:2203.05794 [Cs]. https://arxiv.org/abs/2203.05794
12. Praveen SV, Ittamalla R, Subramanian D (2020) How optimistic do citizens feel about digital contact tracing? Perspectives from developing countries. Int J Pervasive Comput Commun. https://doi.org/10.1108/ijpcc-10-2020-0166

Prediction of Fps Using Ensembling Approach for Benchmarking Gaming Systems

D. Ramkumar, K. Jeeveth, Pooja N. Umekar, Jyoti C. Bambal, Sagar Dhanraj Pande, and Anil V. Turukmane

1 Introduction

The demand for the gaming industry never goes down. The popularity of Video games [1] increases day by day and there are a lot of companies that produce a lot of games in a year. One of the most important performance measures for the gaming industry is frames per second or FPS [1], which is a measure of number of frames shown by the system per second a game is running on the computer. In a frame, there are a lot of pixels to be rendered by the system so it is very tough for a normal system to do that many renders and there will be a drop in FPS. On average for a game to be playable by the user, it should have a minimum of 30 FPS so that the game would be playable. But in today's world, we have GPU which is a very useful component to render each pixel at a very fast rate as it has a separate Graphics rendering unit that helps the CPU in rendering the pixels in each frame. The higher the GPU version and there will be a considerable increase in the FPS. But only GPU doesn't help in the performance of the game. It also depends on the CPU version and the number of performance cores present in the CPU. That is the reason why we need a good CPU along with a GPU with the best monitor to increase performance. This is the reason why we created a benchmarking tool [1–7] with the help of ensemble learning.

D. Ramkumar · K. Jeeveth · S. D. Pande (✉) · A. V. Turukmane
School of Computer Science and Engineering (SCOPE), VIT-AP University, Amaravati, Andhra Pradesh, India
e-mail: sagar.pande@vitap.ac.in

D. Ramkumar
e-mail: ramkumar.d@vitap.ac.in

A. V. Turukmane
e-mail: anil.turukmane@vitap.ac.in

P. N. Umekar · J. C. Bambal
P R Pote Patil College of Engineering and Management, Amravati, Maharashtra, India

K. Kumar Singh et al. (eds.), *Machine Vision and Augmented Intelligence*, Lecture Notes in Electrical Engineering 1211, https://doi.org/10.1007/978-981-97-4359-9_36

The accuracy is around 99% which shows that our method would give an accurate benchmarking for the system.

We trained our model with the data we got in OpenML which is an open-source website for getting various databases. We assessed our models using various Machine Learning models. Every model was underfitting on this so we created stacked [8, 9] models using the underfitting models to improve accuracy. We thought our accuracy had improved a lot which helped us to get through this benchmarking tool with exact prediction of FPS. This technique or the benchmarking tool would be very helpful for gamers to assess all the gaming systems' performance and help them to get a better system for their specific game with their improved FPS. This research would help for the growth of the hardware market and the needs of the gamers would be satisfied.

2 Literature Review

In recent years, the gaming industry has seen huge growth, and a large number of research works were conducted on the Graphics Processing Unit. In their paper, Marc Carrascosa et al. [1] discussed the use of Google Stadia, an online multiplayer cloud service. The temporal patterns of the games, network speed, uplink, downlink, resolution, etc., have been analyzed. They examined all evaluation metrics, such as downlinks, for all game pages, including the main menu, loading screen, idle screen, and playing screen. Ivanova et al. [2] have benchmarked the most recent GPU architectures such as NVIDIA GTX Titan, NVIDIA GTX 680, and AMD Radeon HD790 for games and other modeling software using all the other performance metrics such as GEMM Benchmark, FFT Benchmark, 3DMARK Benchmark, Power Consumption benchmarks, etc. Martin Svedin et al. [3] analyzed the entire NVIDIA Graphics Processing unit products from K80 to A100 GPUs. The GPUs were evaluated with the Rodinia Benchmarking Suite. In addition to using GCC to evaluate the systems, they also utilized CUDA. They also stated that minor GPU modifications could have a significant impact on future GPUs. Nikolay et al. [4] they had made a review paper based on the concept of the broader adoption of ARM technology in their systems and also made a broader benchmark with the HPC benchmarks AI Benchmark Alpha, Enzo Benchmark, and ARM performance with the current $\times$ 86 parts. Marcos Amaris et al. [5] conducted an analysis based on the time-consuming predictions of GPU kernels in contemporary structures. They contrasted a BSP analytical model and the total amount of time required by kernels. Based on hierarchical clustering and correlation analysis, they employed ML algorithms with CUDA support. They utilized data from nine NVIDIA GPUs housed in various devices. In their research paper, Long [6] et al. described CPU-GPU Unified memory, with which they created a framework based on Unified Virtual Machine that enhances data movement from CPU to GPU. The model contains an access pattern-specific transformer that reduces the loss between CPU and GPU transactions. Peddie et al. [7] conducted a literature review on Compute accelerators and GPUs, as well as an examination of GPUs that are used as compute accelerators. They examined the results after transforming a GPU's SIMD Processor into a compute accelerator and analyzing its performance. Dorogush et al. [10] compared a Cat boost regressor with other Gradient Boost Regressors LGBM, XGBoost, and H2O in terms of CPU and GPU Performance using a Cat boost regressor. In their paper, Blazquez et al. [11] utilized a machine learning model based on state-of-the-art boost regressors to predict the distance of active galactic nuclei based on their spectral and spatial properties using evaluation metrics such as RMSE, and R squared score, as well as predicting the redshift interference value. In his paper, Hyunh et al. [12] developed multiple regression models to predict the amount of hexavalent chromium in water given its pH, Temperature, turbidity, oxidation, and other characteristics. Using the Pycaret module, regression models were developed.

3 Objectives

The objective is to predict the frames per second of a gaming system or computer.

4 Proposed System

4.1 Dataset Description

The dataset comes from openml [13]. This dataset includes FPS measurements for computer-executed video games. Each row of the dataset represents the FPS measurement result (the outcome attribute is FPS) for a computer-executed video game. The CPU and GPU are what distinguish a computer. Both names are resolved to technical specifications (features beginning with CPU and GPU, respectively). CPU and GPU technical specifications are technical specifications that define the factory condition of each component. The game is distinguished by its name, its displayed resolution, and the quality setting that was adjusted during measurement (attributes beginning with Game). The dataset contains 24, 624 instances with 43 features and a single label, FPS.

4.2 Methodology

4.2.1 Stacking

Stacking [8], also known as stacked generalization, is a potent machine learning technique that improves the accuracy and performance of predictions by combining multiple models. In the context of ensemble learning, stacking is a meta-learning technique [8, 9] that entails training multiple base models on a given dataset and then utilizing their output as the in for a meta-estimator, which is a higher model. By combining the strengths of multiple base models, it can be used to enhance the performance of a predictive model. The basic concept is to use several techniques or hyperparameters to train many models on the same dataset, then combine their predictions using a meta-model to produce a final prediction.

4.2.2 Cat Boost

CatBoost is a powerful machine learning algorithm that is made using the Gradient Boosting algorithm. This CatBoost [12, 14] is specifically made for handling categorical data, i.e., the values which does not contain numbers but instead have categorical values where text or the number will be repeated more than twice. It is well known for its higher accuracy and the ability to handle a lot of features. Yandex a Russian-based company was the founder of this CatBoost algorithm. The term CatBoost expands as "Categorical Boosting" which says that it is very useful in handling categorical variables. Normally to handle categorical variables we use Encoders like Label-Encoder or One hot Encoder but for CatBoost it is not required to use an encoder as the algorithm automatically encodes the variables.

$$\frac{\sum_{j=1}^{P-1}\left[x_{\sigma^P} = x_{\sigma j}\right]y_{\sigma j} + b \cdot k}{\sum_{j=1}^{P-1}\left[x_{\sigma j} = x_{\sigma_P}\right] + b} \tag{1}$$

4.2.3 HistGradientBoosting

HistGradientBoosting is also one of the methods which we used in this work. The HistGradientBoosting or Histogram-based Gradient Boosting is also based on the Gradient Boosting algorithm. In this algorithm, we use Histograms to predict the exact value or the precise value of the particular row of values. This algorithm is used when there is a high-dimensional feature space as it creates histograms with bins. Bins are created using bits and pieces of data and then create different histograms for each bin if the pattern matches with a particular bin it will analyze the particular histogram and give the precise value as the output. This HistGradientBoosting method is used when the dataset has huge values and a large number of features and also gives a higher accuracy in a lesser number of times.

4.2.4 Models

We use two different layering methods in this paper. First, we employed linear regression as our stacked model 1's meta-estimator [Fig. 1] and a stacking ensemble of three Cat Boost regressors [12, 14] with different parameters as our base estimator.

For our model 2 [Fig. 2], we employed a stacking ensemble of two different-parameter Cat Boost regressors, a Hist Gradient Boosting [15, 16] Regressor as the base estimator, and linear regression [17, 18] as the meta-estimator.

The stacked model 1 [Fig. 1] contains three layers of category gradient boosting [12, 14] with different hyper parameters like number of iterations, learning rate, and

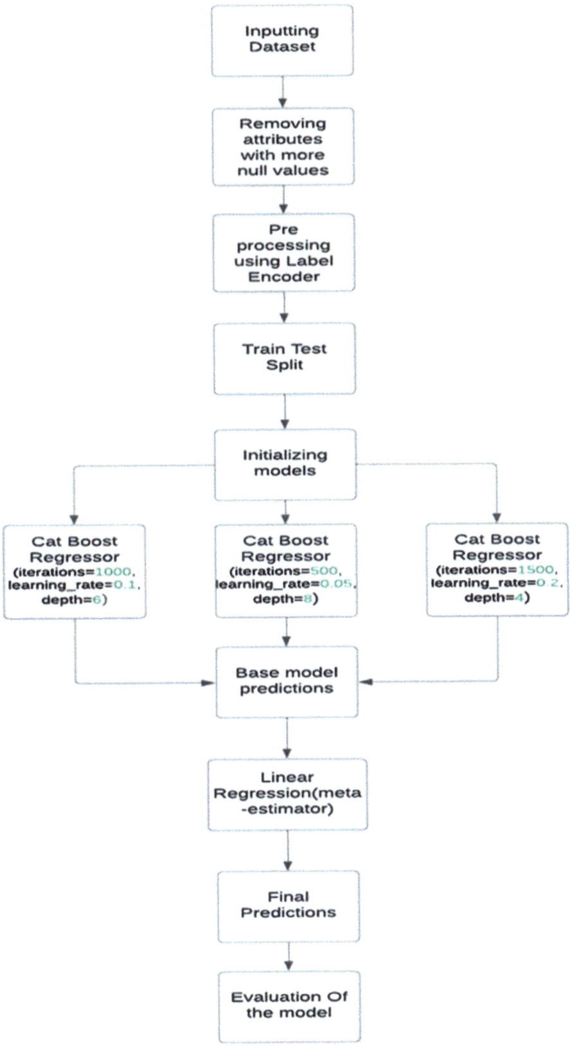

Fig. 1 Stacked model 1 flow chart

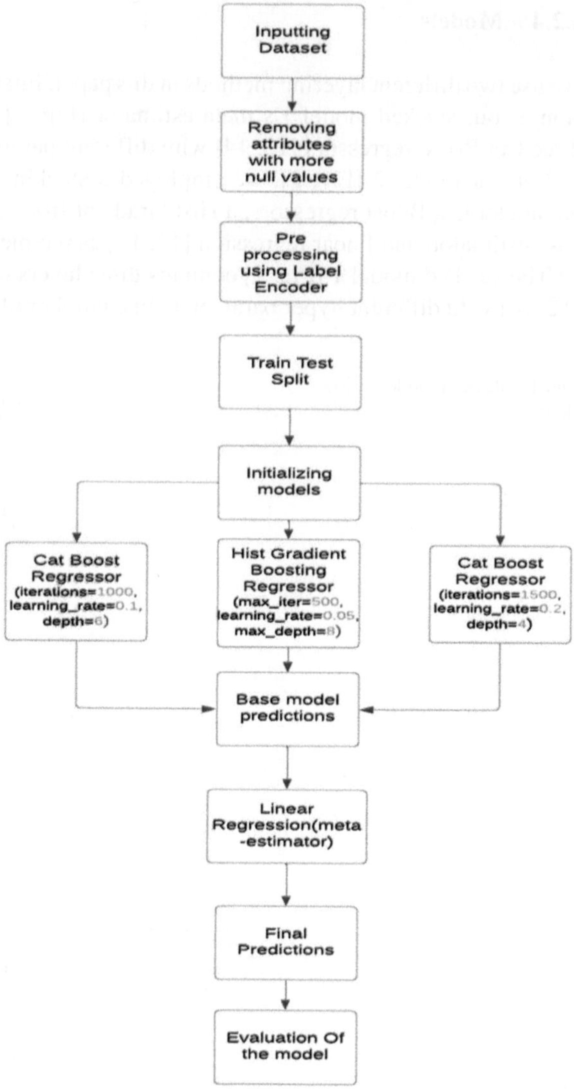

Fig. 2 Stacked model 2 flow chart

depth. This model has the lowest error and it performs well during both training and testing. The stacked model 2 [Fig. 2] contains two layers of category gradient boosting [12, 14] and one layer of Histogram gradient boosting [15, 16]. Both the stacked model has the meta-estimator as linear regression [17, 18] which predicts the final output of the data.

4.3 System Requirements

For this particular research paper, we utilized Google Colab, a web-based Python IDE for machine learning and Deep learning applications. For this project, the system specifications include n1-highmem-2 as the instance's memory, 2vCPUs with a default clock speed of 2.2GHz, 13GB of RAM, and 100GB of ROM. No GPU instance in the Collaboratory was used to execute the model.

4.4 Error Estimation

4.4.1 Mean Absolute Error

One statistic used to check the working efficacy of a regression model is MAE (2). Without considering the direction, it calculates the average magnitude of the defects in a series of forecasts. The mean absolute difference between the actual and projected values is what it represents. Due to its lenient penalty for massive errors, MAE [11] is more robust against outliers than MSE. Since MSE [11] does not reveal the direction of the mistakes, it is a more valuable statistic for improving the model.

$$Mean\,Absolute\,Error = \frac{|\hat{y} - y_{abs}|}{d} \tag{2}$$

Where d is the total data points that is the actual y and y_{abs} is the predicted y corresponding to it.

4.4.2 Mean Squared Error

Regression model effectiveness is commonly assessed using the Mean Squared Error (3) measure. The squared mean deviation between the expected and observed values is used to calculate it. A prediction error metric that works with both continuous and discrete data is the mean square error (MSE) [11]. A greater correlation between the anticipated and actual data, as well as an improvement in model performance, are indicated by lower MSE values. MSE is computed using the formula:

$$Mean\ Squared\ Error = \frac{1}{d}\sum_{i=1}^{d}\left(\hat{y} - y_{abs}\right)^2 \tag{3}$$

Where d is the number of data points, that is the actual y of the data point, and y_{abs} is predicted y.

4.4.3 Root Mean Squared Error

Equation 4's RMSE quantifies how accurately the model predicts the future. It shows the average difference between the outcome's known and observed values and the value the model anticipated. This is how the RMSE [11] is computed:

$$Root\,Mean\,Squared\,Error = \frac{1}{d}\sum_{i=1}^{d}(\hat{y} - y_{abs})^2 \tag{4}$$

Where d is the number of data points, that is the actual y of the data point, and y_{abs} is its predicted y.

4.4.4 Coefficient of Determination (R2)

Coefficient of Determination the squared correlation between the expected values of the model and the observed values of the known outcomes is represented by the symbol R2 (5). The range of correlation lies between 0 and 1. The R2 [11] value should be higher the better the model.

$$R - Squared = \frac{d(\sum xy) - (\sum x)(\sum y)}{\sqrt{\left(\left(d\sum x^2 - (\sum x)^2\right)\left(d\sum y^2 - (\sum y)^2\right)\right)}} \tag{5}$$

where d is the total observations, coefficient of determination = (correlation coefficient)^2 = R^2

5 Results and Discussions

Both models achieved a r2 score of 0.99. Also during training, the r2 score [11] was 0.99, so we can conclude that the model has not been overfitted or underfitted. The table [Table 1] displays all of the outcomes and evaluation metrics that we obtained from the models as well as individual machine learning [12] models.

Below are the graphs for the layered models 1 and 2. Figure 3 depicts the relationship between the layered model's Y test and its predicted Y test. Figure 4 depicts the relationship between the Y train and the Y train predicted by the layered model 1. The graph between the Error distribution of the Y test and the Predicted Y test of the layered model 1 is depicted in [Fig. 5]. The graph between the Error distribution of the Y train and the predicted Y train of the layered model 1 is depicted in [Fig. 6]. Figure 7 depicts the relationship between the layered model's Y test and its predicted Y test. Figure 8 depicts the relationship between the Y train and the Y train predicted by the layered model 2. The graph between the Error distribution of the Y test and

Table 1 Scores of all the individual and stacked models used

S. No	Model	Training/ Testing	R2	MSE	MAE	RMSE
1	Linear regression	Training	0.317	2027.963	34.112	45.032
		Testing	0.328	2030.644	34.052	45.062
2	Cat boost regression	Training	0.999	0.659	0.584	0.812
		Testing	0.999	0.893	0.652	0.945
3	Hist gradient boosting regression	Training	0.996	10.038	2.304	3.168
		Testing	0.996	11.323	2.429	3.365
4	Stacked model 1	Training	0.999	0.403	0.296	0.544
		Testing	0.999	0.410	0.457	0.640
5	Stacked model 2	Training	0.999	0.300	0.402	0.547
		Testing	0.999	0.426	0.458	0.402

the Predicted Y test of the layered model 2 is depicted in [Fig. 9]. The graph between the Error distribution of the Y train and the predicted Y train of the layered model 2 is depicted in [Fig. 10]. These graphs are analyzed in light of the results obtained. We can say that the predictions are accurate and can be used to predict fps for personal computer systems because the analysis is linear.

The above table [Table 2] describes about the comparison of the models which are used in the baseline papers with our research work. There are a lot of better performing models than the mentioned machine learning models but this analysis was purely based on the cat boost regressors so we took the comparison between the cat boost regressors of different research articles and journals.

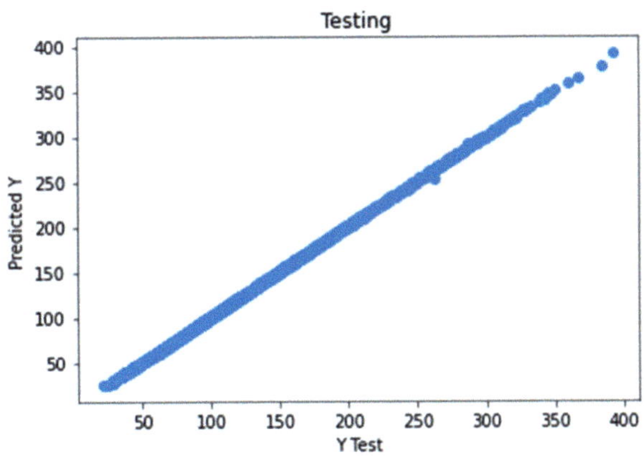

Fig. 3 Graph between Y test and predicted Y of Stacked model 1

Fig. 4 Graph between Y train and predicted Y train of Stacked model 1

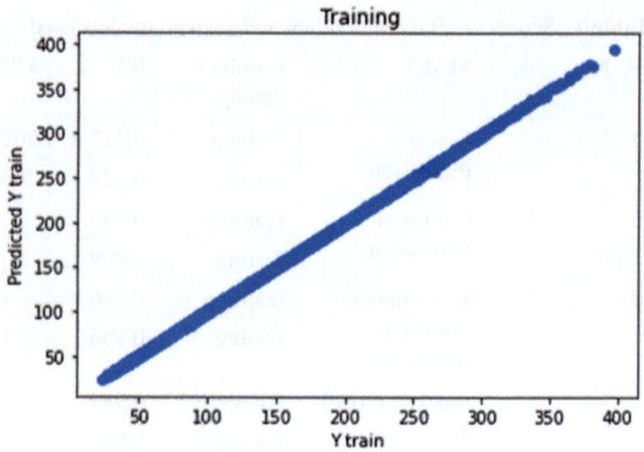

Fig. 5 Error distribution graph for testing of Stacked model 1

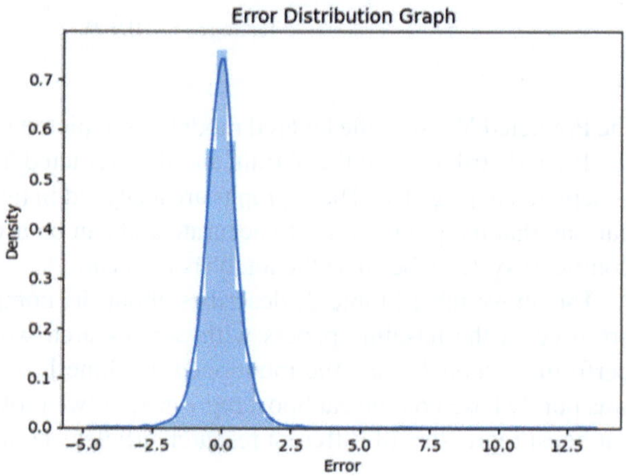

Fig. 6 Error distribution graph for training of Stacked model 1

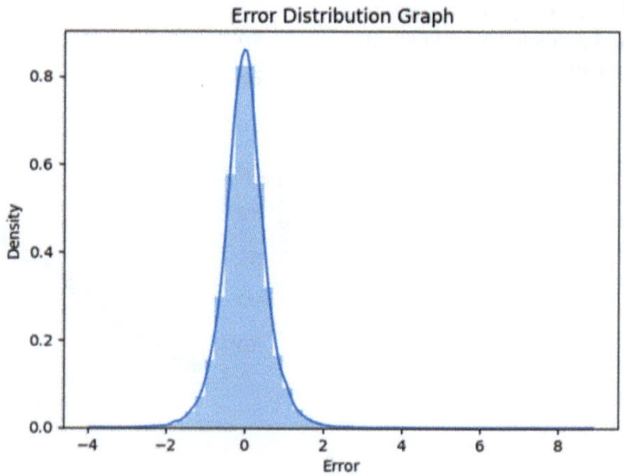

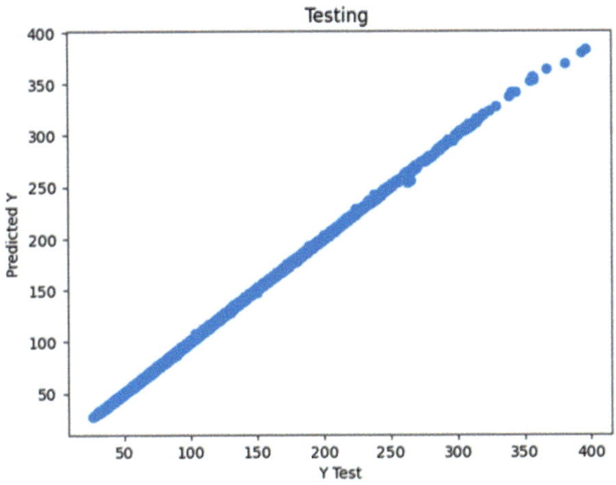

Fig. 7 Graph between Y test and predicted Y of Stacked model 2

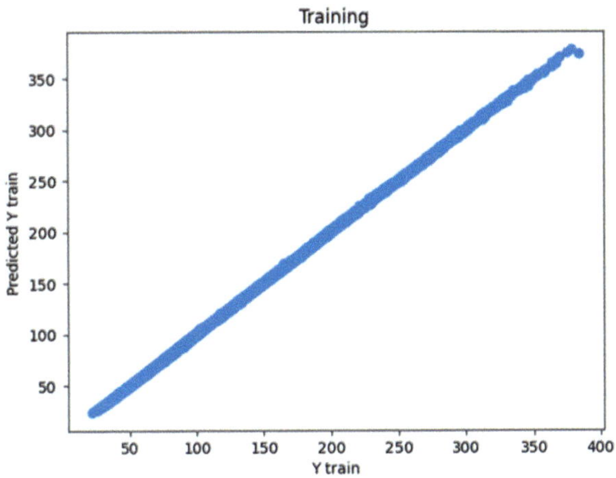

Fig. 8 Graph between Y train and predicted Y train Stacked model 2

6 Future Scope and Limitation

In our research, we employed machine learning models. However, DL methods like RNN could be investigated to improve the accuracy of FPS [1] prediction when game data becomes more widely available. Currently, our research only takes hardware specifications into account when predicting FPS. However, incorporating game data such as game settings and the environment's complexity could enhance the accuracy of FPS prediction. Our research centered on the estimation of FPS for a given gaming system. However, real-time prediction of FPS during gameplay could be investigated in order to provide gamers with beneficial data for optimizing their gaming experience. Our study implies that a gaming system's hardware specifications are compatible with the game [1] being played. Nevertheless, certain games

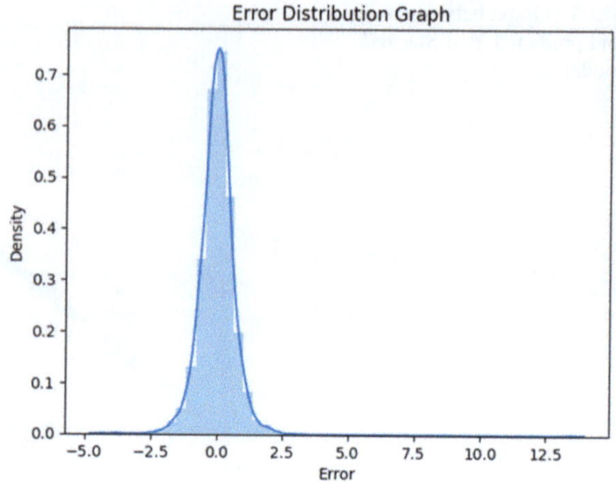

Fig. 9 Error distribution graph for testing of Stacked model 1

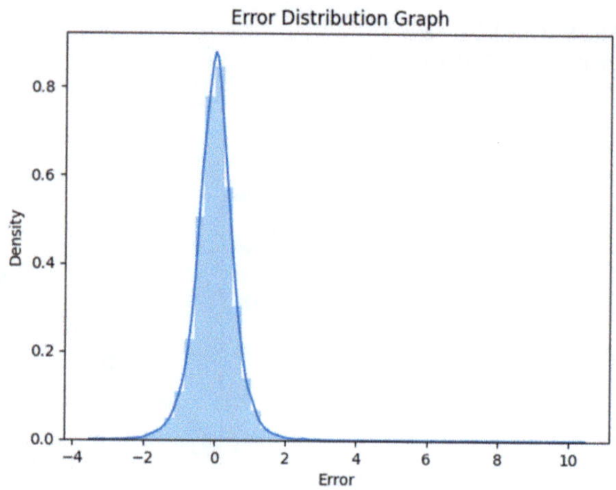

Fig. 10 Error distribution graph for training of Stacked model 1

Table 2 Comparative analysis of previous research papers

S. No	Models proposed in the baseline research works	R2 Score
1	Gayathri, R et al. [14]	0.980
2	Xu et al. [18]	0.820
3	Liu et al. [9]	0.991
4	Saha et al. [8]	0.890
5	Saleh et al. [15]	0.863
6	Huynh et al. [12]	0.878
7	**Proposed work**	**0.999**

may require particular hardware components or configurations, which may impact FPS performance. Factors such as screen tearing and input latency can influence FPS measurements. Therefore, inaccuracies in FPS measurement may impact the precision of our FPS predictions.

7 Conclusion

The above results demonstrate that machine learning models [17, 18] without any ensembling performed very poorly. With the approach of stacking [17, 18], however, we can say that our layered models provided a more accurate forecast than the individual models. Our research has significant ramifications for benchmarking gaming systems, providing enthusiasts with valuable information to enhance their gaming experience. Our study does, however, have certain limitations, such as a small sample size and presumptions about the accuracy of the FPS measurement and hardware compatibility. These restrictions might be addressed in the future by using deeper learning methods, bigger and more varied datasets, and game data to forecast frames per second. All things considered, our work advances the rapidly growing field of machine learning for gaming applications, and our ensembling technique may be applied to benchmark gaming hardware and improve player experience. Our study shows that combining [17, 18] methods to estimate first-person shooter count and assess gaming systems is feasible. Our results should stimulate deeper investigation into ensembling methods used in the game industry and result in the development of more precise and reliable benchmarking instruments.

References

1. Carrascosa M, Bellalta B (2022) Cloud-gaming: analysis of google stadia traffic. Wirel Netw Res Group. https://doi.org/10.1016/j.comcom.2022.03.006
2. Ivanova D, Kadurin V, Belov Y (2015) Performance evaluation and benchmarking of modern GPU architectures
3. Svedin M, Steven WD, Chien G, Jansson N, Podobas A (2021). Benchmarking the Nvidia GPU lineage: from early K80 to modern A100 with asynchronous memory transfers. In: Proceedings of the 11th international symposium on highly efficient accelerators and reconfigurable technologies (heart '21). Association for computing machinery, New York, NY, USA, Article 9, 1–6. https://doi.org/10.1145/3468044.3468053.
4. Simakov NA, Deleon RL, White JP, Jones MD, Furlani TR, Siegmann E, Harrison. RJ (2023). Are we ready for broader adoption of ARM in the HPC community: performance and energy efficiency analysis of benchmarks and applications executed on High-End ARM systems. In: Proceedings of the HPC Asia 2023 Workshops (HPC Asia '23 Workshops). Association for computing machinery, New York, NY, USA, pp 78–86 https://doi.org/10.1145/3581576.3581618
5. Amaris M, Camargo R, Cordeiro D, Goldman A, Trystram D (2023) Evaluating execution time predictions on GPU kernels using an analytical model and machine learning techniques.

J Parallel Distrib Comput 171:66–78. ISSN 0743–7315 https://doi.org/10.1016/j.jpdc.2022.09.002
6. Long X, Gong X, Zhang B et al (2023) An intelligent framework for oversubscription management in CPU-GPU unified memory. J Grid Computing 21:11. https://doi.org/10.1007/s10723-023-09646-1
7. Peddie J (2022) Compute accelerators and other GPUs. In: The history of the GPU–New developments. Springer, Cham https://doi.org/10.1007/978-3-031-14047-1_5
8. Saha S, Haque A, Sidebottom G (2022) Towards an ensemble regressor model for anomalous ISP traffic prediction. arXiv preprint arXiv:2205.01300. https://doi.org/10.48550/arXiv.2205.01300
9. Liu X, Liang S, Li B, Ma H, He T (2021) Mapping 30 m fractional forest cover over china's three-north region from landsat-8 data using ensemble machine learning methods. Remote Sens 13(13):2592. https://doi.org/10.3390/rs13132592
10. Dorogush AV, Ershov V, Gulin A (2018) CatBoost: gradient boosting with categorical features support *ArXiv, abs/1810.11363* https://doi.org/10.48550/arXiv.1810.11363
11. Coronado-Blázquez J (2023) Redshift prediction of Fermi-LAT gamma-ray sources using CatBoost gradient boosting decision trees. Mon Not R Astron Soc 521(3):4156–4161. https://doi.org/10.1093/mnras/stad796
12. Huynh T, Mazumdar H, Gohel H, Emerson H, Kaplan D (2023) Evaluating the predictive power of multiple regression models for groundwater contamination using PyCaret-23489
13. FPS Benchmark Downloaded from : https://www.openml.org/ Dataset link(Google Drive) : https://drive.google.com/file/d/1ICLzLESMfgGuztbfFkfVLWvH147HcJuB/view?usp=share_link
14. Gayathri R, Rani SU, Čepová L, Rajesh M, Kalita K (2022) A comparative analysis of machine learning models in prediction of mortar compressive strength. Processes 10(7):1387. https://doi.org/10.3390/pr10071387
15. Saleh J, Haider S, Akhtar MS, Saqib M, Javed M, Elshahat S, Kamal GM (2023) Energy level prediction of organic semiconductors for photodetectors and mining of a photovoltaic database to search for new building units. Mol 28(3):1240. https://doi.org/10.3390/molecules28031240
16. Chen S, Wang T, Zhang Z, Li R, Yuan S, Zhang R, Yuan C, Zhang C, Zhu J (2023) Linear regression and machine learning for nuclear forensics of spent fuel from six types of nuclear reactors. Phys Rev Appl 19(3):034028. https://doi.org/10.1103/PhysRevApplied.19.034028
17. Xie J, Shi E, Sang P, Shang Z, Jiang B, Kong L (2023) Scalable inference in functional linear regression with streaming data. arXiv preprint arXiv:2302.02457 https://doi.org/10.48550/arXiv.2302.02457
18. Xu H, Bao S, Zhang X, Liu S, Jing W, Ji Y (2022) Blood glucose prediction method based on particle swarm optimization and model fusion. Diagnostics 12(12):3062. https://doi.org/10.3390/diagnostics12123062
19. UserBenchmark https://www.userbenchmark.com/
20. FPS Calculator for Hardware, PCs, and Laptops https://howmanyfps.com/

An Artificial Intelligence Based Attendance Monitoring System for Malpractice Control

Nishanth Gadey and Sagar Dhanraj Pande

1 Introduction

In the realm of student attendance monitoring systems, facial recognition technology is a central component. This method relies on identifying unique facial features like eye shape, color, and nose structure, making it a robust identifier. However, computers perceive faces differently from humans, necessitating the use of computer vision for live detection.

As we all know, the structure of the face plays a pivotal role in face recognition systems, acting as a primary identifier much like how we remember people by their facial features, including eye shape, color, and nose structure. This uniqueness of the face makes it an ideal candidate for recognition techniques. However, computers do not perceive faces the way humans do, so we rely on computer vision for live detection. Computer vision technology's main goal is to recognize human features in the digital realm [1]. In recent years, there have been significant advancements in face detection and biometric methods. While implementing and installing face recognition systems have become more common, achieving successful implementation remains challenging. This is due to factors such as variations in facial expressions, different styles, image resolution, sensor devices, viewing distances, and more [2]. Numerous algorithms are available for face recognition, each with its strengths and limitations. In this fast-changing world, the pursuit is for the best algorithm that can consistently deliver the highest accuracy.

Moreover, facial recognition methods are not limited to attendance systems; they also have crucial real-world applications in areas like national and international

N. Gadey
School of Computer Science Engineering, VIT-AP University, Amaravati, Andhra Pradesh, India
e-mail: nishanthgnvs04@gmail.com

S. D. Pande (✉)
School of Engineering and Technology, Pimpri Chinchwad University (PCU), Pune, India
e-mail: sagarpande30@gmail.com

K. Kumar Singh et al. (eds.), *Machine Vision and Augmented Intelligence*, Lecture Notes in Electrical Engineering 1211, https://doi.org/10.1007/978-981-97-4359-9_37

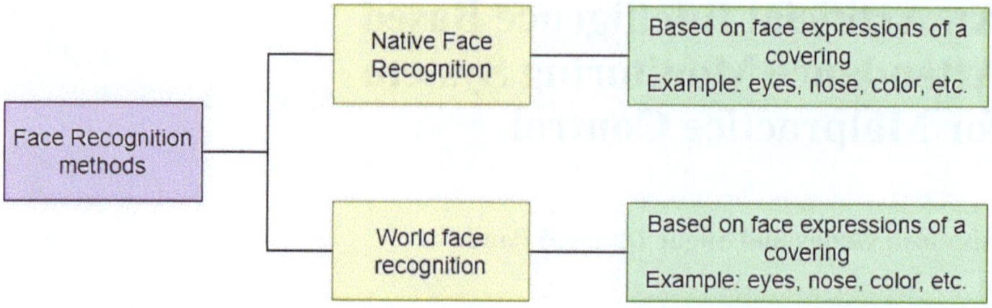

Fig. 1 Facial recognition methods

security and defense. At present, there are mainly two approaches that rely on Face reorganization methods as shown in Fig. 1.

Facial recognition relies on two main methods: feature-based, which uses specific facial data like eyes, nose, and color to match faces in a database, and holistic, which considers the entire facial structure for identification. These approaches employ various algorithms, and the accuracy often depends on changing facial expressions. The development of intelligent self-learning systems, as proposed by Pradeepa. M et al.[3], require substantial data. In essence, facial recognition is the technology that verifies a person's identity by comparing their facial features with a database, as described by Chaitanya Reddy [4].

Traditional attendance monitoring systems have notable drawbacks. They often depend on manual data entry, leading to potential errors and administrative inefficiencies. Real-time monitoring is lacking, hindering the prompt resolution of attendance issues. These systems are also vulnerable to proxy attendance, which compromises data accuracy and academic fairness. Furthermore, they may require significant resources, lack of robust data analysis capabilities, face scalability challenges, and fail to adequately address privacy concerns. Recognizing these limitations emphasizes the demand for more advanced solutions.

This paper provides insights into AI-based attendance systems, particularly focusing on algorithms used in face detection. It equips readers with knowledge about the different methods available and enables them to make informed decisions based on accuracy, strengths, and weaknesses of each methodology. Readers can gain a comprehensive understanding of these methods for potential implementation.

The rest of the paper is organized as follows: Literature survey is shown in Section II, and Section III demonstrates the Existing approaches of Face Recognition along with Observation table. In Section IV, we wrap up the paper and discuss our future goals.

2 Literature Survey

In this literature survey, you will get to know about the different methods involved in AI Based Attendance system and the process will be discussed in detail.

Face detection-based attendance: A portable device utilizes face recognition technology [5] for attendance marking through face detection and comparison with a database using PCA and LDA algorithms. The device connects to a Raspberry Pi module with a camera in the classroom, recognizes students, records time, and date, and sends absentee faces to authorized emails [6]. Images are stored in jpeg format, and ear matching, edge detection, and timing operations are performed to mark absent students. Absentee data is stored on an SD card [7], and messages are sent to parents' mobiles via GSM, providing accurate and efficient attendance.

Voice based attendance system: In this methodology, each student is recognized based on the voice. The voices of students are previously stored in the database. Here, the new voice is being detected by the computer and verifies the sample for voice verification. Voice recognition is used in the system for attendance and the report is sent to the parents [8].

Fingerprint based attendance system: This methodology collects fingerprints from students using a device that can be passed around in class without faculty involvement. While highly reliable, it can disrupt the class, as mentioned by Akshara Jadhav et al. [9]. Another approach involves placing LCD screens at the classroom entrance. Students mark attendance by placing their finger on a sensor, and the data is recorded in the database and displayed on an LED screen [10]. Biometric features were selected by applying Minutiae based algorithm and they were encrypted using Advanced Encryption Standard Algorithm [11].

RFID Based attendance: RFID technology is used for quick attendance verification, where students carry RFID ID cards and scan them on card readers to record attendance, with data analysis done using ASP.net [12]. There are RFID systems that send SMS notifications, and use intelligent RFID hardware for real-time attendance tracking.

Iris-Recognition Based attendance System: This biometric system relies on Iris Recognition, where the iris is scanned, and its features are matched with the database. However, it requires good lighting conditions for the scanner to work effectively. While it offers high security, reliability, and speed, it needs further development for low-light conditions, as mentioned by Akshara Jadhav et al. [9].

GPS Based attendance system: In this system, students use their mobile phones with GPS to send their location to a Raspberry Pi module. The campus classroom locations are predefined, and attendance is marked if the student is within the specified location at the scheduled time. If the student is not there, then an SMS will be sent to their parents [13].

Bluetooth based attendance: This is a system that uses Bluetooth Smart technology to improve presence, reduce human error, and save time. It also combines microchips known as tags with radio frequency technology to create a secure system.

These tags provide accuracy and efficiency by transmitting identifiable traceable information to Bluetooth Smart enabled devices [14].

3 Existing Approaches of Face Recognition

This section reviews some of the current facial recognition methods. Let's review the different approaches currently used in this field. By looking at these approaches, we can gain valuable insight into the world of facial recognition technology. Figure 2 presents a glyph of the face recognition process.

LBPH algorithm (Local Binary Patterns Histogram): One of the main methods for face detection in front view contexts is the LBPH algorithm, which was first proposed in 1996. It uses the Local Binary Pattern (LBP) operator to compress the unique arrangement of facial traits by extracting local features. The detected face inside an image is divided into individual pixels by the LBP operator when it is applied, with each pixel having eight neighboring pixels surrounding it. The values of the surrounding pixels and the pixel value are compared. Using these values as a basis, this process is repeated iteratively [15].

A camera is used to take pictures and recognize faces in the context of attendance marking. These photos are then compared to a student database for attendance registration. This system, which was created with Python and the LBPH algorithm, contains crucial student data such as roll number and subject name. It has an easy-to-use click-to-start function that allows attendance to be started manually or automatically. The LBPH method is preferred because it is easy to use for face recognition, effectively captures local picture information, and performs exceptionally well in controlled settings. It also shows resistance against grayscale alterations that are monotone. Figure 3 lists the fundamental steps in the recognition process.

Haar Cascade Classifier: Paul Viola and Michael Jones presented the Haar Cascade Classifier technology in 2001, which provides an effective method for face detection. This technique makes use of cascade functions and machine learning techniques that have been taught via a mix of positive and negative pictures. Using machine learning algorithms and "training data," this method obtains a high degree of accuracy. The notions of "integral images" are used to assist the calculation of observed features. Adaboost, a method, which produces effective classifiers, is utilized in Haar cascades to choose a small selection of important characteristics from a bigger collection [3].

The training data for this project is represented by an XML file called "Haarcascade_frontalface_default.xml". The OpenCV Haar Cascading method is used to load

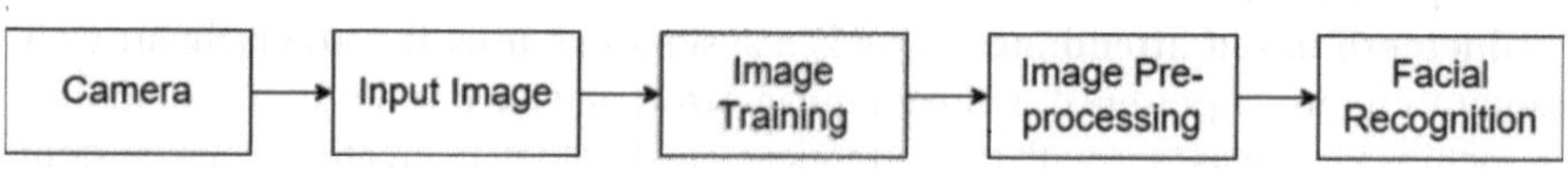

Fig. 2 Dataflow of face recognization

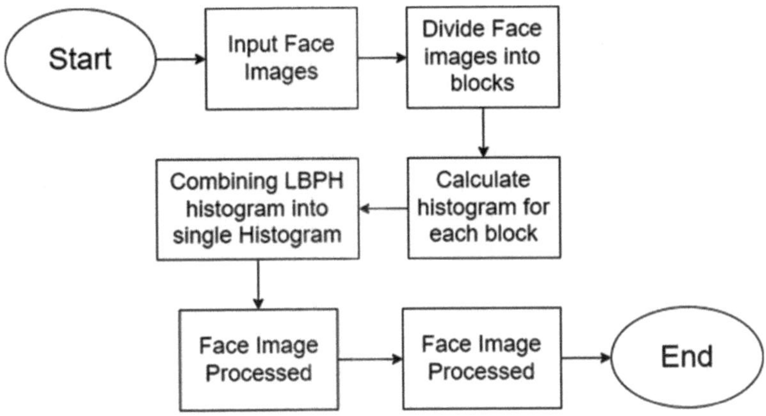

Fig. 3 Flow chart of algorithm

the training data into the "haarcascade_traned_faces".txt file. The sequential Haar classifier assigns a value of "1" if the region contains an object of interest (in this case, a face) and a value of "0" if it does not.

In addition to face recognition, the Haar cascade is also widely used in computer vision applications. Their flexibility and robustness make them suitable for object detection, step detection, and face detection. They also allow the creation of custom rank order classifiers for specific object detection tasks.

Viola-Jones Algorithm for Detection: One method that has been widely used for real-time face detection is the Viola-Jones algorithm. As can be seen in Fig. 4, it consists of the following important elements: cascade classifiers, integrated image transformation, AdaBoost training, and HAAR feature selection [16]. These elements efficiently select and train classifiers, increasing accuracy through repeated instructions. The cascade classifier is widely used in computer vision and object recognition because it quickly removes non-face images which is effective in complex settings and real-time video streams.

Eigenface algorithm: The Eigenface algorithm identifies facial features by representing a face as a combination of 'eigenfaces' obtained through Principal Component Analysis (PCA) [17]. It calculates distances between eigenfaces to find the closest match for identification. This method is widely used in biometrics, surveillance, and access control due to its simplicity, efficiency, and robustness in recognizing faces under different conditions and orientations.

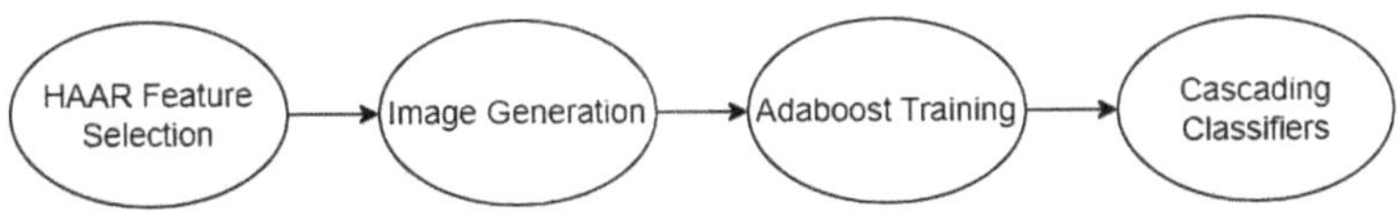

Fig. 4 Data flow of Viola-Jones algorithm

Neural Networks: Neural networks, specifically Artificial Neural Networks (ANN), emulate biological neurons and solve real-time problems by receiving input, self-activating, and adjusting weights. Deep learning, a subset of machine learning, relies on ANN and includes Convolutional Neural Networks (CNN). In our system, CNN, using pre-trained models like Inception V3, monitors contactless student attendance. It employs transfer learning for feature extraction from detected faces, enabling real-time attendance monitoring without physical contact or manual input. [9]. The system extracts facial features, matches them with a database, records attendance with in and out times, and calculates total hours present. Compared to methods like LDA, RFID, SVM, PCA, and portable devices, Inception V3-based system achieves an impressive 95% accuracy [18]

Android based: The system is designed for robustness, modularity, scalability, and security using industry-standard technologies: Android Studio, JAVA (Android), XML, and SQLite Database. Android Studio, a powerful IDE, underpins the system, ensuring seamless operation on Android OS. Java provides efficient development with its libraries and tools [19]. For data management, the system incorporates SQLite, offering lightweight yet robust data organization. This harmonious integration results in a high-performance, user-friendly, and secure Android-based application, adhering to industry best practices.

FaceNet: FaceNet, a deep neural network introduced by Google researchers in 2015, is specialized in extracting facial features by transforming input face images into 128- dimensional vectors, visualized as points in a coordinate system [20]. It employs Triplet Loss during training, aiming to minimize the distance between anchor and positive samples while maximizing the distance from anchor to negative samples. This helps the network effectively distinguish between individuals based on their facial features.

InsightFace: InsightFace is a robust library offering cutting-edge algorithms for face recognition, detection, and alignment. Its efficient implementation caters to both training and deployment needs, serving research institutes and industrial organizations effectively. Expanding upon the SphereFace algorithm, InsightFace introduces enhancements in normalization and additive angle intervals of eigenvectors, which significantly improve class separability, intra-class tightness, and inter-class differences, leading to outstanding performance in diverse face-related tasks [21].

BlazeFace: BlazeFace is a highly efficient face detection algorithm developed by Google researchers. Specifically designed for mobile GPUs, this software offers blazingly fast performance in face detection tasks. The algorithm is optimized to handle images with dimensions of 128 × 128, and its inference time is measured in milliseconds. Its primary purpose is to facilitate face recognition on mobile phones, making it ideal for real-time applications. This model excels in predicting axis-aligned face rectangles and accurately estimating the coordinates of six key points. These key points include the centers of the eyes, ear tragions, and mouth, enabling precise facial feature estimation and analysis [22]. Table 1 depicts various Face Recognition techniques along with their comparative analysis.

Table 1 Face recognition methods and their information

Sr No	Method	Year	Working	Accuracy (%)	Strengths	Weaknesses
1	Eigen Face [17]	1991	Basis set of images, co-variance matrix	92	Independent of facial geometry	Lower accuracy in varying pose and illumination
2	Neural networks [18]	1996	Algorithms with artificial neurons	95	Efficient, versatile	Hardware dependency, complexity
3	LBHP Algorithm [15]	1996	Histogram-based pixel analysis	96	Good at low resolution	Increased time delay with more data
4	Viola-Jones Algorithm [16]	2001	Grayscale and colored image detection	88	Rapid object detection	Ineffective for tilted or turned faces
5	Haar Cascade Classifier [23]	2001	Haar Wavelet technique, real-time capable	89	Not complex, real- time	High false positives, less ac- curate
6	Android based [19]	2010	Android, SQLite, XML, and Java	94	Low false positives	Lower success rate in face recognition
7	FaceNet [20]	2015	Embedding, 128-number vector output	99	Identifies similar faces	Focus on similar eyewear when worn
8	Insight Face [21]	2018	Implements state-of-the-art face algorithms	98	Variety of algorithms	Low face recognition rate, interference in multiface
9	BlazeFace [22]	2019	Lightweight face detector from Google Research	98	Very fast, accurate detection	Poor performance with small faces (e.g., CCTV images)
10	Improvised LBP [24]	2020	Advanced Image Processing techniques and	99	Steps for improving image quality	Does not address the issue of occlusion and mask faces
11	Cerebellum-Basal Ganglia Mechanism [25]	2021	Integral projection and geometric feature assortment methods	96	Less recognition time with occlusion on the face	Down sampling and normalization may lead to a loss of fine facial details

(continued)

Table 1 (continued)

Sr No	Method	Year	Working	Accuracy (%)	Strengths	Weaknesses
11	FRS-DCT-SVM using GA-RBF [26]	2022	SVM with RBF and DCT	98	Utilizes DCT for feature extraction. Zonal masking	Applied to databases that are limited in terms of their size and type
12	Non-negative matrix factorization (NMF) method [27]	2023	NMF + GAN	92	Better at angular images up to 40 degrees	Lose their effectiveness when there is a slight change in the image angle
13	GA-ANN [28]	2023	Genetic algorithm was used to find potential important features	94	Areas that contain these important features were considered as important areas	Lower success rate in face recognition

4 Conclusion and Future Scope

This paper, discussed many algorithms which are used to take attendance anywhere. Every method has various advantages also some disadvantages and different success rates. These days most of the school or college or organization have same old and routine system which is time consuming for teachers and students. These methodologies help to solve this issue by adding face recognition and other different mentioned methods with attendance management system and to stop attendance proxy.

The aim is to make a system that is useful to schools, colleges, and institutes. The efficient and accurate approach of attendance in the organizations may replace the old manual methods. These facial strategies are secure enough, reliable, and available to be used. It can be constructed using a camera and computer for facial recognition and other small devices for other methods. Also, other techniques can be done similarly like this with basic implementation.

References

1. International Journal of Innovative Technology and Exploring Engineering (IJITEE) ISSN: 2278–307A5, Volume-9 Issue-2S, December 2019
2. Jireh Robert Jam, Face Detection And Recognition Student Attendance System,Kingston University London
3. Pradeepa M, Mohan Kumar HP. Face detection and recognition for automatic attendance system using artificial intelligence concept. Ijesc 8(5) May
4. Reddy (2017) Face Recognition Using Artificial Intelligence. Towardsdatascience.Com In

5. Raghuwanshi A, Swami PD (2017) An automated classroom attendance system using video based face recognition 2017 2nd IEEE international conference on recent trends in electronics, information & communication technology (RTEICT) pp 719–724
6. Kumar P, Prudhvi KR (2017) Image processing based student attendance system using raspberry PI. Int J Eng Comput Sci 6(4)
7. Gaddam SC, Ramesh N, Dhanekula H (2016) Face recognition based attendance management system with raspberry Pi 2 using Eigen Faces Algorithm ARPN J Eng Appl Sci 11(13)
8. Kaur J, Kaur S (2016) A brief review: voice biometric for speaker verification in attendance systems. ImpAl J Interdiscip Res 2(10)
9. Jadhav A, Ladhe T, Yeolekar K (2017) Automated attendance system using face recognition. Irjet 04(01)
10. Taxila P (2009) Development of academic attendance monitoring system using fingerprint identification. IJCSNS 9(5):164
11. Oyetola OK, Okubanjo AA, Olaluwoye OO (2017) A secure students' attendance monitoring system. J Eng Technol 2(1):14–25
12. Chen H (2014) Intelligent classroom attendance checking system based on RFID and GSM. Adv Mater Res 989–994:5532–5535
13. Prasad SN, Mahalakshmi P, Sunder AJC, Swathi R (2014) Smart surveil- lance monitoring system using Raspberry Pi and PIR sensor. Int J Comput Sci Inf Tech 15(6):7107–7109
14. Elsevier BV (2015) Peer-review under responsibility of scientific committee of international conference on advanced computing technologies and applications (ICACTA-2015)
15. Waingankar A, Upadhyay A, Shah R, Pooniwala N, Prashant Kasambe (2018) Face Recognition based Attendance Management System using Machine Learning. Int Res J Eng Technol 05(06), e-ISSN: 2395–0056, p- ISSN: 2395–0072
16. Viola P, Jones M (2001) Rapid object detection using a boosted cascade of simple features, CVPR 1(1):511–518
17. Wagh P, Thakare R, Chaudhari J, Patil S (2015) Attendance system based on face recognition using Eigen face and PCA algorithms. In: 2015 International conference on green computing and internet of things (ICGCIoT), (pp 303–308). IEEE
18. Rajamanogaran, M, et al. (2021) Contactless attendance management system using artifi- cial intelligence. J Phys: Conference Series 1714(1). IOP Publishing
19. Int J Comput Sci Inf Secur (IJCSIS), Vol. 18, No. 1, January 2020
20. Ivan W, Setiadi, De Rosal Ignatius Moses, Eko R, Heru S, Atika S (2019) Face recognition using FaceNet (Survey, Performance Test, and Comparison). 1–6. https://doi.org/10.1109/ICIC47613.2019.8985786
21. Jingyu Pu, et al. (2020) Research on classroom attendance system based on face recognition. J Phys: Conference Series 1616(1). IOP Publishing
22. ,Bazarevsky, V, et al. (2019) Blazeface: Sub-millisecond neural face detection on mo-bile gpus. arXiv preprint arXiv:1907.05047
23. Lodha R, Gupta S, Jain H, Narula H (2015) Bluetooth smart based attendance management system. Procedia Comput Sci 45:524–527
24. Bah, Modou S, Ming F (2020) An improved face recognition algorithm and its ap- plication in attendance management system. Array 5:100014
25. Tang S, Shabaz M (2021) A new face image recognition algorithm based on cerebellum-basal ganglia mechanism. J Healthc Eng
26. Bhushan S, et al. (2022) A novel approach to face pattern analysis. Electronics 11(3):444
27. Charoqdouz E, Hassanpour H (2023) Feature extraction from several angular faces using a deep learning based fusion technique for face recognition. Int J Engi-Neering, Trans B: Applications 36(8):1548–1555
28. Kamyab T, et al. (2023) Combination of genetic algorithm and neural network to select facial features in face recognition technique. Int J Robot & Con-Trol Syst 3.1

Predictive Insights for Enhancing Customer Retention in Banking: Integrating Power BI and Random Forest

A. Sumanasri, M. Vyshnavi, R. Nikhila Manogna, Kelam Keerthi, A. Kesavarshini, and Sagar Dhanraj Pande

1 Introduction

In the present trend, we can observe that the banking industry is having difficulty in gaining new customers, and an increase in customer attrition is another major issue. The costs of client churn outweigh the costs of customer retention, posing a considerable financial risk [1]. The phenomenon of a set of customers deciding to switch banks and quit using a particular bank's services is referred to as customer churn [2]. A thorough understanding is required of why customers leave for (DEF) bank to stay competitive, retain existing customers, and remain financially stable and viable. This study employs highly predictive machine learning algorithms as well as data mining techniques which help in the development of an accurate churn prediction model. The bank intends to identify at-risk consumers and implement customer retention initiatives by analyzing previous customer behavior and transaction data. The churning of clients (customers) offers major financial concerns, with acquisition expenses exceeding retention costs [3]. Power BI is used for data cleaning,

A. Sumanasri · M. Vyshnavi · R. N. Manogna · K. Keerthi · A. Kesavarshini
School of Computer Science Engineering, VIT-AP University, Amaravati, Andhra Pradesh, India
e-mail: vyshnavi.21bce7191@vitapstudent.ac.in

R. N. Manogna
e-mail: nikhila.21bce7281@vitapstudent.ac.in

K. Keerthi
e-mail: keerthi.21bce7507@vitapstudent.ac.in

A. Kesavarshini
e-mail: kesavarshini.21bce7074@vitapstudent.ac.in

S. D. Pande (✉)
Department of Computer Science and Engineering, School of Engineering and Technology, Pimpri Chinchwad University, Pune, Maharashtra, India
e-mail: sagarpande30@gmail.com

K. Kumar Singh et al. (eds.), *Machine Vision and Augmented Intelligence*, Lecture Notes in Electrical Engineering 1211, https://doi.org/10.1007/978-981-97-4359-9_38

preprocessing, and building a Random Forest model helps to predict churn and take preventive measures.

Moreover, the research emphasizes the importance of personalized methods of retention. Banks can make their resources more optimal by focusing on the efforts to individual customers based on their churn risk profiles thereby increasing the likelihood of retaining valuable clients. In addition, this study acknowledges the benefits of churn prediction in the real-time scenario. By implementing various systems that monitor customer behavior and forecast churn occurrences at predetermined intervals banks can turn out to be more effective in adopting timely interventions and individualized retention tactics, boosting their capacity to reduce churn and improve profitability. A recent study found that the average expense of gaining new clients might be up to five times more expensive than that of keeping current ones [4]. This research mainly focuses on determining the elements that influence customer attrition in the banking sector, emphasizing Power BI which is the most suitable data mining technique, and machine learning algorithms like Random Forest. The sections that follow describe our technique, dataset, and findings, highlighting the significance of machine learning and data preprocessing followed by the data mining algorithms which in turn helps in making informed decisions.

2 Literature Survey

2.1 Introduction: Evolution of Customer Churn Prediction

The main challenge that the R-CNN (Convolutional Neural Networks) algorithm system seeks to solve is object detection in images. The foundation of these models is a number of independent variables that are hypothesized to affect the dependent variable, or churn [5]. Our strategy uses a sliding window approach that examines the image's various-sized rectangles in a methodical manner. But this can result in a lot of smaller images, which could be confusing. Thankfully, methods for "region proposals" have been developed, which may now more accurately identify possible places for objects and enhance object localization in photos.

2.2 Integration of External Data and Time Aspects

Incorporating external data sources, like economic indicators and social media sentiment, broadens our view of customer behaviour [6]. Temporal aspects, using time series data and recurrent neural networks (RNNs) to capture trends, enable predictions of churn likelihood and timing for interventions.

2.3 Challenges of Imbalanced Data and Model Robustness

The uneven consumer data from commercial banks will make the minority class unpredictable [7]. Addressing imbalanced datasets remains a concern, with ongoing research into robust methods. Balancing class imbalance while avoiding overfitting and bias is crucial, and innovative techniques are explored.

2.4 Emerging Trends and Future Directions

The churn prediction field evolves with machine learning advancements and diverse data sources. Combining traditional and deep learning techniques promises more accurate predictions, aiding proactive customer retention and operational optimization.

2.5 Studies in Churn Prediction

Several studies emphasize the significance of bank customer churn prediction. Wang et al. [8] explored machine learning algorithms, with Random Forest showing promise in early-stage predictions. Liu et al. [9] introduced an ensemble model for handling imbalanced data. Incorporating external data sources is also highlighted for improved accuracy.

2.6 Challenges of Dynamic Customer Behavior

Dynamic customer behavior is a significant challenge. Preferences change over time, making long-term churn prediction complex. Banks must continuously monitor and adapt churn prediction models to account for evolving customer behavior. Other features, in addition to tracking the pattern of customer activity, had been incorporated to increase the accuracy and performance of the model [10].

2.7 Data Availability

Data availability remains a hurdle in churn prediction. Access to essential data like customer sentiment may be limited and obtaining it from sources like social media or surveys can be costly and noisy, complicating interpretation.

3 Proposed Methodology

This study employs a deductive approach, combining case study and experimental research to anticipate customer attrition, especially in commercial banks. It involves investigating customer churn within a specific bank, utilizing transaction data, demographics, and historical churn records. Data preprocessing is conducted, including cleaning, feature engineering, as well as dealing with missing values and categorical data. Predictive modeling utilizes Random Forests for handling complex data and Decision Trees for interpretability. Key indicators, such as accuracy, precision, recall, and F1-score, are used to evaluate model performance, while ethical considerations address data privacy. The study acknowledges limitations, particularly concerning interpretability and imbalanced data, and prioritizes validity and reliability. The flow chart of the proposed methodology is shown in Fig. 1.

3.1 Dataset Description

The dataset, obtained from Kaggle, comprises data on 800 bank customers, focusing on a binary variable distinguishing those continuing their banking relationships from those opting to terminate. Of the 800 customers, 638 remain retained, while 162 have churned.

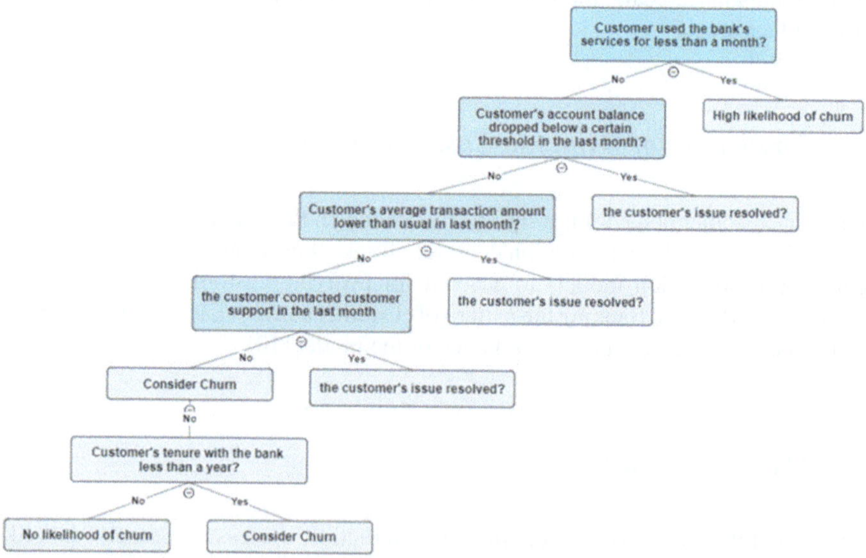

Fig. 1 Flow chart

3.2 Data Pre-processing

Data preprocessing is pivotal, involving cleaning, error removal, and feature selection. Irrelevant features like RowNumber, CustomerId, and Surname are eliminated, and duplicate data is removed.

3.3 Classification

The core objective is customer classification into “churned” or “not churned.“ Two classification methods are employed: Random Forests and Decision Trees. For predictions, an ensemble learning technique such as Random Forest merges numerous decision trees, whereas Decision Trees produce tree-like structures.

3.4 Random Forest

Random Forests, introduced by Breiman, address decision trees’ overfitting tendencies by employing an ensemble approach, reducing prediction variance, and enhancing accuracy [4]. Particularly this algorithm, excels in dealing with high-dimensional data ensuring faster training and adaptability to parallel models.

3.5 Power BI

For data visualization and analysis, Power BI is employed in conjunction with Python. Power BI’s capabilities are enhanced with Python integration for relevant measures and visualizations. A sample dataset for bank customer churn prediction is used, comprising 800 customers and 11 attributes, including the crucial “Exited” column indicating churn [3]. Data is preprocessed within the Power Query Editor to prepare it for analysis.

3.6 Data Pre-processing in Power BI

Data preprocessing, encompassing cleansing, transformation, and integration, is a fundamental step. Irrelevant features are removed, streamlining the dataset. Measures like the “churn rate” are defined for insights into customer behavior, and bar charts illustrate churn percentages within different attribute categories.

3.7 *Enhancing Data Representation*

To simplify data representation, classes are created for attributes like Age, Credit Score, and Balance, with assigned index numbers for proper ordering.

4 Results and Discussion

The below (Figs. 2, 3 and 4) show the performance of the model in terms of loss, accuracy, and residual respectively (Figs. 5 and 6) depicts the exploration of the data using the tool.

```
Accuracy: 0.98125
Confusion Matrix:
[[123   3]
 [  0  34]]
Classification Report:
              precision    recall  f1-score   support

           0       1.00      0.98      0.99       126
           1       0.92      1.00      0.96        34

    accuracy                           0.98       160
   macro avg       0.96      0.99      0.97       160
weighted avg       0.98      0.98      0.98       160
```

Fig. 2 The output shows the random forest's precision, accuracy, f1-score, and support

Fig. 3 This plot shows the residuals (differences between actual and predicted values) to evaluate the accuracy of the model and error distribution

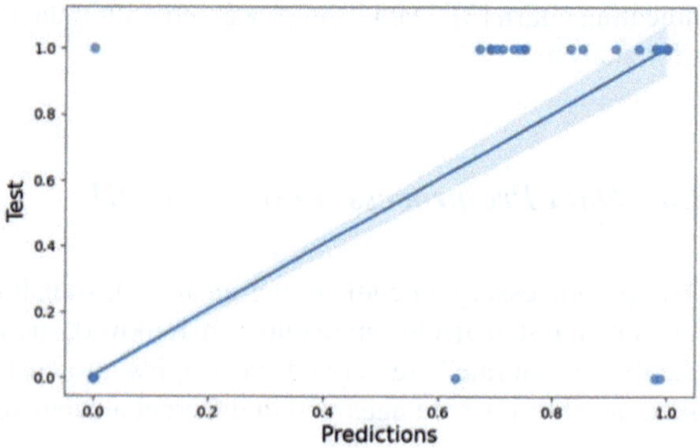

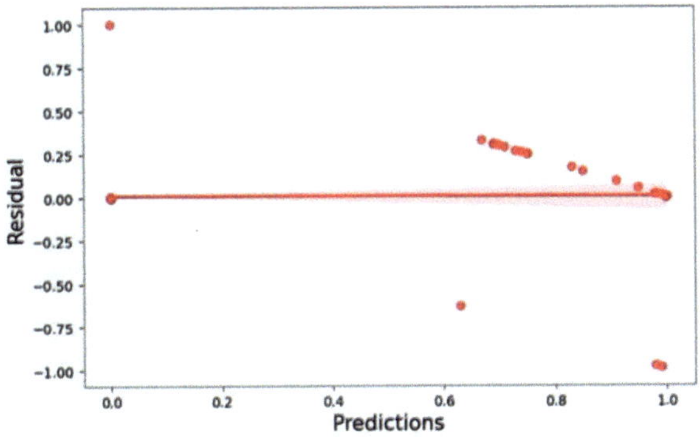

Fig. 4 Graph between residuals and prediction

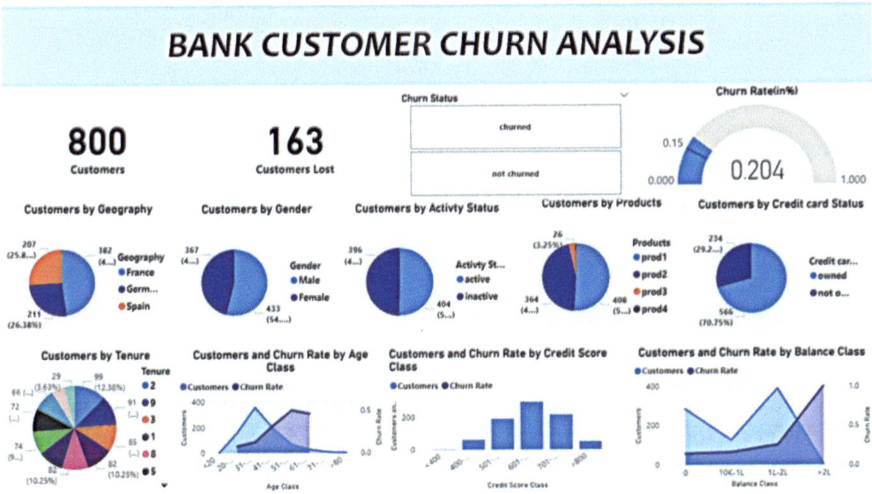

Fig. 5 Schema representation of the data view

This is the dashboard created using Power BI:

5 Conclusion and Future Scope

The study produced a system that can forecast when customers could stop using a service. Regardless of the service provider company, it utilized various forms of data. The information was used in the experiment to determine how successfully the Random Forest approach could forecast consumer behavior. The Random Forest (RF) classifier, in combination with oversampling, emerged as the most acceptable model

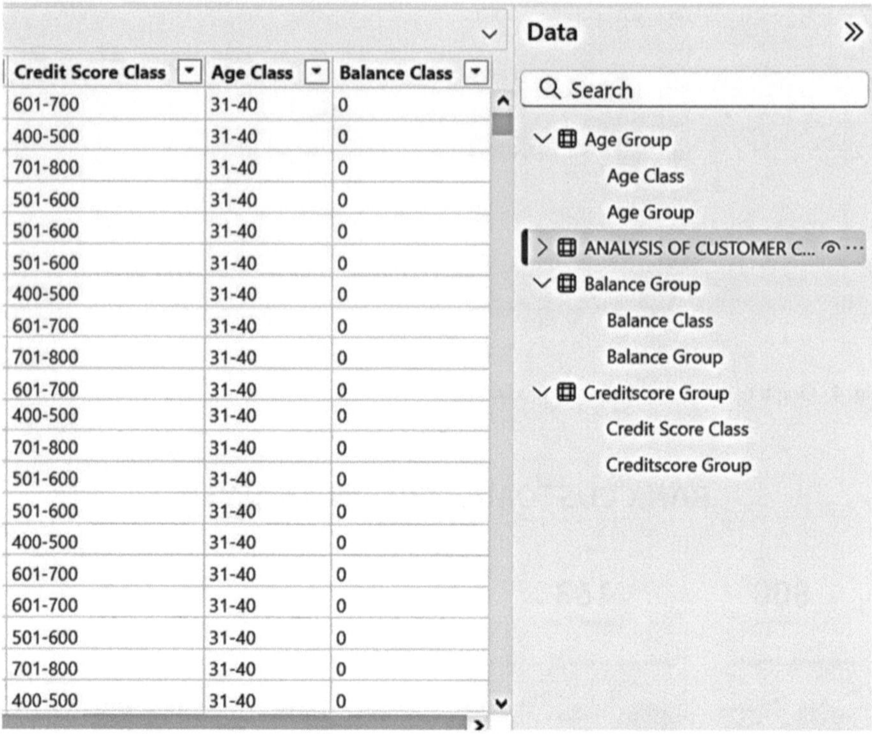

Credit Score Class	Age Class	Balance Class
601-700	31-40	0
400-500	31-40	0
701-800	31-40	0
501-600	31-40	0
501-600	31-40	0
501-600	31-40	0
400-500	31-40	0
601-700	31-40	0
701-800	31-40	0
601-700	31-40	0
400-500	31-40	0
701-800	31-40	0
501-600	31-40	0
501-600	31-40	0
400-500	31-40	0
601-700	31-40	0
601-700	31-40	0
501-600	31-40	0
701-800	31-40	0
400-500	31-40	0

Fig. 6 Sample data view of the dataset

among the algorithms (classifiers) examined, obtaining an astounding accuracy of 99%. Power performance decreased with oversampling because of the lopsidedness of the dataset, whereas the feature selection approach power bi had no effect on tree classifiers. These findings highlight the necessity of selecting the appropriate classifiers and data management techniques for raising prediction accuracy.

References

1. Zhao J, Dang XH (2008) Bank customer churn prediction based on support vector machine: taking a commercial bank's vip customer churn as the example. In: 2008 4th international conference on wireless communications, networking and mobile computing, Dalian, China, pp 1–4. https://doi.org/10.1109/WiCom.2008.2509
2. Karvana KGM, Yazid S, Syalim A, Mursanto P (2019) Customer churn analysis and prediction using data mining models in banking industry. In: 2019 international workshop on big data and information security (IWBIS), Bali, Indonesia, pp 33–38. https://doi.org/10.1109/IWBIS.2019.8935884
3. Gopal P, MohdNawi NB (2021) A survey on customer churn prediction using machine learning and data mining techniques in ecommerce. In: 2021 IEEE Asia-Pacific conference on computer

science and data engineering (CSDE), Brisbane, Australia, pp 1–8. https://doi.org/10.1109/CSDE53843.2021.9718460
4. Rahman M, Kumar V (2020) Machine learning based customer churn prediction in banking. In: 2020 4th international conference on electronics, Communication and aerospace technology (ICECA), Coimbatore, India, pp 1196–1201, https://doi.org/10.1109/ICECA49313.2020.9297529
5. Jayalekshmi KR (2023) A comparative analysis of predictive models using machine learning algorithms for customer attrition in the mobile telecom sector. Online J Distance Educ eLearning 11(1)
6. Tran H, Le N, Nguyen VH (2023) Customer churn prediction in the banking sector using machine learning-based classification models. Interdisciplinary J Inf Knowl Manag 18
7. Li B, Xie J (2020) Study on the prediction of imbalanced bank customer churn based on generative adversarial network. Int J Phy: Conference Series 1624(3):032054. IOP Publishing
8. Wang QF, Xu M, Hussain A (2019) Large-scale ensemble model for customer churn prediction in search ads. Cogn Comput 11:262–270. https://doi.org/10.1007/s12559-018-9608-3
9. Liu S, Wang Y, Zhang J, Chen C, Xiang Y (2017) Addressing the class imbalance problem in twitter spam detection using ensemble learning. Comput Security 69:35–49
10. Kaur A, Kaur M, Kaur N (2023) Bank customer churn prediction with imbalanced data: A review of techniques and challenges. Int J Comput Appl

A Concise Survey on Meta-Learning and Its Applications

D. Ramkumar, Chigurupati Maithili, S. P. Palaskar, Minal Toley, Ajita Jadhav, and Sagar Dhanraj Pande

1 Introduction

Machine learning is an application of AI that gives the ability to algorithms for automatic refining and upgrade from experience without being specifically programmed. Meta-learning is a sub-branch of machine learning (ML) [1]. It is basically used to refine and upgrade the performance of the learning algorithms by altering some features of the algorithm. This algorithm gives accurate results as it takes the input data from the out data of the other algorithms [2].

Generally, we try to find the best suitable algorithm for a problem but now another ML algorithm came to picture to do our jobs as well. Meta-learning is a widely used algorithm nowadays. A traditional machine learning algorithm learns from the factual data that we give to the model, like in a supervised machine learning model we

D. Ramkumar · C. Maithili
School of Computer Science and Engineering, VIT-AP University, Amaravati, Andhra Pradesh, India
e-mail: ramkumar.d@vitap.ac.in

C. Maithili
e-mail: maithili.21bce9083@vitapstudent.ac.in

S. P. Palaskar
Sipna College of Engineering and Technology, Amravati, Maharashtra, India

M. Toley
Ajeenkya D Y Patil School of Engineering, Charholi Via Lohegaon, Pune, Maharashtra, India
e-mail: minal.tole@dypic.in

A. Jadhav
Dr. Vishwanath Karad MIT WORLD PEACE UNIVERSITY, Pune, Maharashtra, India
e-mail: ajita.jadhav@mitwpu.edu.in

S. D. Pande (✉)
School of Engineering and Technology, Pimpri Chinchwad University, Pune, Maharashtra, India
e-mail: sagar.pande@pcu.edu.in

K. Kumar Singh et al. (eds.), *Machine Vision and Augmented Intelligence*, Lecture Notes in Electrical Engineering 1211, https://doi.org/10.1007/978-981-97-4359-9_39

provide whole data to the model for getting a prediction whereas the meta-algorithm or meta-learning algorithm gains knowledge or data through the outcome predictions of these various traditional methods [3]. So, we can say that meta-learning needs all the existing algorithms, and it is dependent on them. In the last few years machine learning succeeded in dealing with many cyberspace security issues which include intrusion detection, spam detection, malware detection, and many more.

In this paper, we have addressed both meta-learning methods and their applications. Starting with a brief idea on meta-learning and its applications and then we have provided up to date systematics with regard to meta-objective, meta optimizer, and meta-representation. These substructures give a blueprint for the implementation of unknown meta-algorithms. By looking at the study from various approved applications which include reinforcement learning, NLP, neural networks, label noise, and active learning [4]. Meta-learning has garnered significant attention in recent years due to its potential to improve the efficiency and effectiveness of machine learning systems.

Existing research has shown that meta-learning is applicable to numerous tasks, including few-shot learning, transfer learning, and reinforcement learning. Few-shot learning involves learning to recognize new objects or classes from just a few examples, while transfer learning involves applying knowledge learned from one task to another. Reinforcement learning, on the other hand, involves learning to make decisions in an environment based on rewards and punishments. Meta-learning algorithms can be used to gain knowledge of a set of initial parameters or hyperparameters that could be quickly adapted to unknown jobs. This can significantly reduce the amount of data needed to train a new model [5], making it particularly useful in cases like insufficient data or in a case where data is expensive. Additionally, meta-learning is helpful to mitigate issues related to overfitting and improve the generalization performance of models.

A Meta-Learning model acquires knowledge through the outcomes of other algorithms and produces a prognosis or gives a prediction made by learning algorithms [6]. If the machine learning models gain knowledge the way in which it uses the information in a better way to make predictions, then meta-learning model acquires knowledge of using that predictions from the machine learning to make the predictions accurately. This method describes how meta-learning is better than machine learning.

2 Literature Survey

2.1 History

In the history of meta-learning, many learning algorithms were found among them Model-Agnostic Meta-Learning (MAML) [7] algorithm was the finest. It was proposed by Finn et al. in 2017. The basic idea of MAML is that it learns a set of initial frameworks that can be swiftly adapted to the unknown tasks with a limited amount of knowledge from a few examples. The algorithm achieved success when applied to numerous tasks such as few-shot image recognition, NLP, and reinforcement learning.

The other popular meta-learning algorithm is Reptile algorithm which was proposed by Nichol et al in 2018.It is a first-order optimization method which can adapt a model to a unknown task rapidly [8]. The algorithm can achieve the latest performance on the few-shot image classification tasks. Meta-learning is further used for transfer learning (TL). TL is defined as the knowledge acquired from one job is fetched to another job [9]. This algorithm is said to achieve good results on many transfer learning tasks like image classification and speech recognition.

Additionally, few-shot learning and meta-learning are also being applied to reinforcement learning (RL). Wang et al. in 2016 proposed a Meta-RL algorithm, which utilizes meta-learning to acquire knowledge of a set of policies that can be rapidly adapted to unknown space [10]. The Meta-Reinforcement learning algorithm has been shown to perform better than other modern RL algorithms on several baselines. In recent years, meta-learning has been integrated with other methods such as generative adversarial networks and neural architecture search. Zoph and Le in 2017 proposed the Reinforcement Learning with Neural Architecture Search and defined a new algorithm, which makes use of meta-learning to explore optimal neural network architectures. Likewise, Li et al. in 2021 proposed the integration of meta-learning with a generative adversarial network called as Meta-GAN algorithm, which utilizes meta-learning for understanding a generator that can rapidly adapt to new datasets [11].

The existing research work on meta-learning and its applications has denoted its potential to upgrade the efficiency of machine learning models. Although, there remain various challenges that need to be labeled, such as adaptability to big datasets, handling of noisy data, and also interpretability of learned models [12]. The areas of the application of meta-learning are vast and there are huge research opportunities in the future.

Generally the Meta-learning algorithms are commonly mentioned as meta-algorithm or meta-learner. Meta-Classifier is the Meta-learner for classification divining customizing jobs. the Meta algorithm for regression predictive modeling job is called as meta-regression.

2.2 *Working of Meta-Learning*

Generally, a meta-learning algorithm is instructed in using the outputs and the meta-data of machine learning model. Once the training is completed, the algorithm is sent for testing and it is used to make the end prediction. Meta-learning involves some tasks such as, Learning from metadata, monitoring the efficiency of various machine learning models on learning tasks, and finding a faster learning way for unknown tasks [13].

First of all, we need a gloss dataset. Various machine learning models are being built on the training dataset. The problem is they could only focus on definate parts of the dataset, but a meta-training procedure is used for improving the efficiency of these machine learning (ML) algorithms [14]. Eventually, a meta-training algorithm is capable of building a new model from various examples based on its experiences with the earlier training process, and the result is observed by the meta-learning algorithm and makes the alternate changes to make the result more accurate.

2.3 *Optimization of Meta-Learning*

Grid search and random search are the two most commonly used methods for hyperparameter optimization in meta-learning [15].

One important aspect of machine learning is hyperparameter optimization, which involves tuning the hyperparameter of the algorithm to improve its performance on a given task. Hyperparameters are the parameters of machine learning algorithm which is unable to acquire knowledge from the given data, it needs to be operated manually. Some of the common examples of hyperparameters are regularization strength, the number of hidden layers in a neural network, and the learning state. The right choice of hyperparameters can notably impact the efficiency of the meta-learning algorithm [16] (Fig. 1).

There are two common approaches for hyperparameter optimization in meta-learning one is random search and another is grid search.

Grid search is defined as involving a specific collection of possible values for every hyperparameter and then evaluating algorithm's performance for all combinations of hyperparameters in the grid. Grid search is straightforward to implement, but

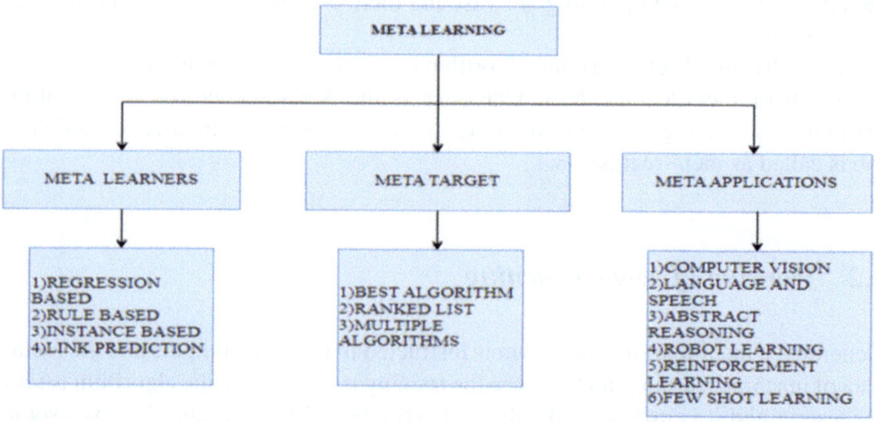

Fig. 1 A flow chart describing meta-learning and its application

this grid search is a bit expensive specifically in the cases where the number of hyperparameters and their possible values is large [17].

Random search is a method in which the search includes arbitrarily sampler hyperparameters from a predefined research area and judging the algorithm's efficiency for every batch of hyperparameters [18]. Compared to grid search, random search is more computationally efficient, as it does not require evaluating all possible combinations of hyperparameters. However, it may require more trials to find the optimal hyperparameters compared to grid search. Recently, more advanced perspectives on hyperparameter optimization, such as evolutionary algorithms and Bayesian optimization, have been used in meta-learning [19]. These methods are more efficient than the random search and grid search.

2.4 Variants of Meta-Learning

Meta-learning has several variants, each of them has their own specifications and importance few of them are, Reptile: Instead of optimizing the model parameters to minimize the expected loss on a collection of training tasks, Reptile optimizes model parameters to rapidly adjust for specific jobs [20].

Model-Agnostic Meta-Learning: It is commonly referred as MAML. It a popular way of reaching meta-learning which is able to learn a better initialization for an algorithm that could rapidly get adapted to unknown tasks by dealing with a minimum number of examples [21]. This is done by optimizing the model parameters to minimize the expected loss on the collection of meta-training tasks.

Gradient-Based Meta-Learning (GBML): GBML is a general approach to meta-learning that involves optimizing the model parameters to improve its capability of rapid adaptation to unknown tasks. This can be achieved by determining the gradients for the model parameters regarding the task-specific loss function [22].

Learning to Learn from Scratch (L2LFS): L2LFS is a meta-learning approach that aims to learn how to learn from scratch, without relying on any prior knowledge or meta-training data. This is done by optimizing a neural network architecture to learn how to learn new tasks.

3 Applications of Meta-Learning

There are several applications of meta-learning in the current world some of them are.

3.1 Meta-Learning in Computer Vision

Computer vision is the area of research that pivots to permit computers to analyze, interupt, and understand visual information from situations around the globe. Meta-learning, on the other hand, is a machine learning approach that involves learning how to learn, by training models to automatically learn the best ways to learn from new data. Recently, researchers have explored application of the meta-learning in computer vision, to improve the efficiency and effectiveness of visual recognition tasks [23]. One way that meta-learning can be applied to computer vision is by using it to improve few-shot learning, which has the capability of an algorithm to identify unknown objects with only a few training examples. Meta-learning is also used to upgrade few-shot learning by training a meta-learner to adapt quickly to new tasks, based on its experience with previous tasks. For example, a meta-learning algorithm could be trained with a huge data set of related tasks, such as recognizing different breeds of dogs, and then used to quickly adapt to new tasks, such as recognizing different types of flowers or vehicles [24]. The other way meta-learning could be applicable to computer vision is by using it to upgrade the optimization of deep neural networks. In traditional deep learning, the optimization process involves manually selecting hyperparameters and adjusting the network architecture to achieve better performance. Meta-learning is also used to barbarise the procedure, by training a meta-learner to learn the best hyperparameters and architecture for a given task, based on its previous incidents with previous tasks. Meta-learning can give an accurate prediction in object detection, landmark prediction, few-shot object segmentation, and image and video generation [25].

Overall, meta-learning has the efficiency to remarkably upgrade the efficiency of computer vision systems, specifically in scenarios where metadata is limited or when the task requires the model to quickly adapt to new situations.

3.2 Meta-Learning in Language and Speech

The orginality of the meta-learners can be observed in the increasing language modeling and few-shot modeling. Some of the previous matching networks conveyed splendid efficiency on one short task like lining the unknown or missing words.

Neural machine translation shortly called as NMT, Automatic speech recognition referred to as ASR, and speech translation needs a huge labeled data. Gathering of this labeled data is cost restrictive. To make these new innovations available to the new tasks, meta-learning is applied in these systems for the fast adaptation to new techniques in both ASR and NMT [26].

Numerous jobs have later being tackled that involve tasks like Meta-learning have been used in applications like sentiment analysis, language modeling, and other alike tasks. In this field, it is also used for the cross-lingual generalization and cross-domain. Speech Recognition is the commanding prototype nowadays for automated speech recognition.

3.3 Meta-Learning Abstract Reasoning

In the context of abstract reasoning, meta-learning has been used to develop models that can generalize well to new, unseen abstract reasoning tasks. One of the ways of meta-learning in abstract reasoning is usinga set of training tasks to acquire knowledge about a model that can rapidly adjust to unknown jobs by adjusting its parameters on the basis few examples. A prolonged aim in the field of deep learning is to understand simple tasks and learning how to solve more abstract reasoning tasks like the IQ tests as per Raven's Progressive Matrices.

Meta-learning techniques can be used to develop models that can learn how to solve new abstract reasoning problems more quickly and effectively, which could be used to help students and professionals develop their abstract reasoning skills. Meta-learning can secure good results while dealing with adversarial attacks and learning with label noises and for recommendation systems.

4 Overview

Meta-learning can be observed as a higher-level learning process that guides the lower-level learning process, and it can also be used to upgrade the performance and effectiveness for machine learning systems. The key idea behind meta-learning is to acquire knowledge from the meta-parameters which is used to improve the parameters of an algorithm when getting knowledge about an unknown task [27]. These meta-parameters acquire knowledge from a collection of tasks, and they capture the general knowledge and patterns that are useful for learning new tasks. The meta-learner can then quickly get adapted to unknown tasks by adjusting model parameters on the basis of the learned meta-parameters. Meta-learning has been applied in numerous fields which include natural language processing, computer vision, robotics, and abstract reasoning.

In natural language processing, meta-learning has been applied to improve language modeling, machine translation, and named entity recognition. Meta-learning has also been used in robotics to improve the ability of robots to adjust to unknown tasks and situations. Overall, meta-learning is a powerful approach that can upgrade the performance of machine learning systems [28]. It has applications in various areas and is a field in machine learning.

In the table below I have provided information about meta-learning and its applications and details like year of invention, overcomes, disadvantages, and the

Table 1 Table of meta-learning about the overview of all its applications

Sno	Application	Year of invention	Overcomes	Useful fields	Disadvantages
1	Natural language processing	2016	(1) Data efficiency (2) Interruptibility (3) Adaptability (4) Robustness	(1) Language modeling (2) Text classification (3) Question answering (4) Named entity recognization	(1) Depending on training data set (2) Potential for overfitting
2	Few-shot learning	2017	Helpful for overcoming data deficiency and also it reduce the cost function	Image classification	(1) Computationally expensive (2) Limited generalization
3	Computer vision	2011	(1) Improves generalization (2) Model architecture search (3) Reduces the need for labeled data (4) Improves transfer learning	(1) Object detection and tracking (2) Domain adaptation (3) Image segmentation (4) Image classification	(1) Increases complexity (2) Overfitting (3) Sensitivity to hyperparameters (4) Interpretability (5) Data requirements
4	Reinforcement learning	2016	(1) Faster learning (2) Better exploration (3) Sample efficiency	(1) Robotics (2) Navigation (3) Game playing (4) Finance	(1) Hyperparameter tuning (2) Data efficiency overfitting

domains which can be improved by using meta-learning algorithms in the respective applications (Table 1).

5 Future Scope

The key concept of meta-learning, which involves learning how to learn, has accquired significant attention recently, some areas where the scope of meta-learning is are, Few-shot Learning which involves training models to recognize new objects or tasks with limited training data [29]. The world is exploring new methods and architectures for meta-learning to improve few-shot learning and to enable models to acquire knowledge of unknown jobs more rapidly and efficiently [30]. Meta-learning has shown great potential for improving few-shot learning [31]. Meta-reinforcement learning involves training agents to adapt to new reinforcement learning tasks quickly, based on their experience with previous tasks [32].

6 Conclusion

Meta-learning has appeared as an interesting area of machine learning research in recent years, with potential applications in a wide range of realms. Meta-learning, which teaches models how to learn, may help them to adapt the new realms or tasks more expeditiously and effectively. New meta-learning algorithms and methodologies have significantly aided advances in few-shot learning, adaptive optimization, continuous learning, meta-reinforcement learning, and AutoML. Future meta-learning research and applications offer a variety of interesting areas. This research might avail the capacity to induce to different domains, improve data efficiency, apply meta-learning to RL and SS, and design more effective ongoing learning algorithms. We may expect the creation of the latest approaches and algorithms in the area of meta-learning, which will open up interesting new potential and applications for this interesting subject of study. This research closes with a look at meta-learning and its practical inferences. It also demonstrates how important this approach is for upgrading change in machine learning. Meta-learning has the possibility to transform machine learning by resulting in more systematic and successful models. These models can rapidly adapt to new jobs and domains, learn with less data, and open the door for new enhancements in a variety of fields.

References

1. Learning to learn. Springer Science and Business Media LLC (1998)
2. Finn C, Abbeel P, Levine S (2017) Model-agnostic meta-learning for fast adaptation of deep networks. In: Proceedings of the conference on machine learning
3. Wang J, Zou Y, Yue Y (2018) Meta-learning for low-resource natural language processing: a short survey. arXiv preprint arXiv:1810.06643
4. Deep learning in natural language processing. Springer Science and Business Media LLC (2018)
5. Huang Q, Wang J, Wang X, Yu Y (2019) Neural architecture search with reinforcement learning. In: Proceedings of the conference on computer vision and pattern recognition
6. Zhu W, Wang X (2021) Automated machine learning and meta-learning for multimedia. Springer Science and Business Media LLC
7. Lee Y, Choi S, Lee S, Kim S (2019) Meta-learning for low-resource medical image segmentation. arXiv preprint arXiv:1905.11216
8. Finn C, Levine S (2017) Meta-learning and universality: deep representations and gradient descent can approximate any learning algorithm. arXiv preprint arXiv:1710.11622
9. Ravi S, Larochelle H (2017) Optimization as a model for few-shot learning. In: Proceedings of the international conference on learning representations
10. Snell J, Swersky K, Zemel R (2017) Prototypical networks for few-shot learning. In: Advances in neural information processing systems

11. Munkhdalai T, Yu H (2017) Meta networks. In: Proceedings of the conference on learning representations
12. Mishra N, Rohaninejad M, Chen X, Abbeel P (2018) A simple neural attentive meta-learner. In: Proceedings of the international conference on learning representations
13. Xu Z, Cao L, Chen X (2019) Meta learning via weighted gradient update. IEEE Access
14. Bengio Y, Lodi A, Prouvost A (2020) Machine learning for combinatorial optimization: a methodological tour d'horizon. Eur J Oper Res
15. Song H, Triguero I, Özcan E (2019) A review on the self and dual interactions between machine learning and optimization. Progress Artif Intell
16. Finn C, Rajeswaran A, Levine S (2019) Online meta-learning. In: Proceedings of the conference on learning representations
17. Younger AS, Hochreiter S, Conwell PR (2001) Meta-learning with backpropagation. In: IJCNN
18. Wang J, Pérez-García F (2021) Bayesian model-agnostic meta-learning. In: Proceedings of the international conference on learning representations
19. Antoniou A, Edwards H, Storkey A (2019) How to train your MAML. In: Proceedings of the international conference on learning representations
20. Zhang Y, Li Y, Zhou X, Luo J, Zhang Z-L (2022) Urban traffic dynamics prediction—a continuous spatial-temporal meta-learning approach. ACM Trans Intell Syst Technol
21. Gupta A, Jonnalagedda P, Bhanu B, Roy-Chowdhury AK (2021) Ada-VSR: adaptive video super-resolution with meta- learning. In: Proceedings of the 29th ACM international conference on multimedia
22. Bengio S, Bengio Y, Cloutier J (1995) On the search for new learning rules For ANNs. Neural Process Lett
23. Wang S, Yang Y, Sun J, Xu Z (2021) Variational HyperAdam: a meta-learning approach to network training. IEEE Trans Pattern Anal Mach Intell
24. Schmidhuber J (1993) A neural network that embeds its own metalevels. In: IEEE international conference on neural networks
25. A possibility for implementing curiosity and boredom in model-building neural controllers in SAB (1991)
26. Cheng J, Hao F, Liu L, Tao D (2022) Imposing semantic consistency of local descriptors for few-shot learning. IEEE Trans Image Process
27. Zhang H, Sun J, Wang Y, Shi J, Xu Z (2022) Variational reinforcement learning for hyper-parameter tuning of adaptive evolutionary algorithm. IEEE Trans Emerg Top Comput Intell
28. Yuan P, Nguyen HV (2023) Introduction to meta learning. Elsevier BV
29. Wang JX (2021) Meta-learning in natural and artificial intelligence. Curr Opin Behav Sci
30. Huisman M, van Rijn JN, Plaat A (2021) A survey of deep meta-learning. Artif Intell Rev
31. Medical Image Computing and Computer Assisted Intervention (2019) MICCAI 2019. Springer Science and Business Media LLC
32. Denevi G, Ciliberto C, Stamos D, Pontil M (2018) Learning to learn around a common mean. In: NeurIPS

Deep Convolutional Neural Networks for Autism Spectrum Disorders

Drashti Patel, Shreyan Mittal, Mrugendrasinh Rahevar, and Abhishek Patel

1 Introduction

Autism Spectrum Disorder (ASD) is a rampant neuro-developmental condition, often observed in childhood, with genetic and behavioral components. Early detection in the critical childhood phase, marked by distinctive cognitive developments, is vital for effective ASD management. Thabtah et al. [1] showcase the correlation data using cognitive computing which also uses Decision Trees, Support Vector Machine, as well as Logistic Regression as tools for autism evaluations. Recent research by [2] emphasizes the urgency of early ASD identification and intervention in both adults and toddlers. Moreover, [3] likely analyzes data from medical records and administrative databases to investigate changes in the prevalence and timing of autism diagnoses across different birth cohorts. To enhance ASD diagnosis precision, Nasser et al. [4] suggest employing Artificial Neural Networks. This study investigates the integration of Deep CNN with textual data for ASD detection. The general pattern with regard to preliminary processing using Deep CNN classification is shown in Fig. 1. The research holds the potential to significantly improve autism spectrum detection, aiding clinicians, researchers, and educators.

D. Patel (✉) · S. Mittal · A. Patel
Department of Computer Science and Engineering, CSPIT, Charotar University of Science and Technology, Changa, Gujarat, India
e-mail: drashti202@gmail.com

S. Mittal
e-mail: shreyanmittal75537@gmail.com

A. Patel
e-mail: abhishekpatel.cse@charusat.ac.in

M. Rahevar
U & P U Patel Department of Computer Engineering, CSPIT, Charotar University of Science and Technology, Changa, Gujarat, India
e-mail: mrugendrarahevar.ce@charusat.ac.in

K. Kumar Singh et al. (eds.), *Machine Vision and Augmented Intelligence*, Lecture Notes in Electrical Engineering 1211, https://doi.org/10.1007/978-981-97-4359-9_40

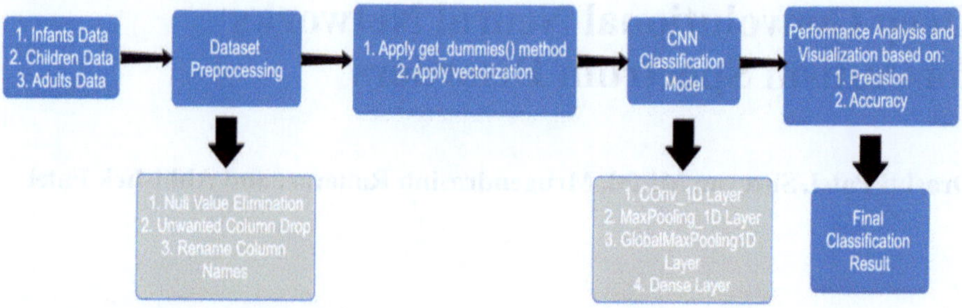

Fig. 1 General process flow of CNN based study

2 Related Work

Numerous researchers have advocated the application of deep-learning in Autism Spectrum Disorder diagnosis. Studies delve into machine learning and deep-learning techniques, such as convolutional neural networks (CNN) and recurrent neural networks (RNN), showcasing their effectiveness in ASD classification. For instance, one study by [5] offers a comprehensive view of these techniques, emphasizing their potential in enhancing ASD diagnosis. An earlier study by [6] proposed automating the widely used Autism Diagnostic Observation Schedule (ADOS)tool through computerization, streamlining the observation process. Ecker et al. [7] employed gray and white matter data to analyze structural MRI images, showing the value of neuroimaging in machine learning-based diagnosis. Maenner et al. [8] achieved an impressive 86.5% accuracy in automatic classification, using children's social interaction data. However, these methods require a strong subject-setting relationship and simpler techniques for early ASD signs assessment.

Furthermore, studies like [9, 10] explored various deep-learning approaches using diverse datasets. These references collectively offer a comprehensive view of the evolving landscape of ASD detection through machine learning and deep learning methods.

3 Proposed Approach and Architecture

Deep CNN has shown promising results in autism spectrum detection by classifying individuals as either having autism spectrum disorder or not. A labeled dataset with data linked to either ASD or non-ASD tags is used to train the Deep CNN model. The training process involves forward and backward propagation, weight optimization, and updating of model parameters to minimize a defined loss function. In Fig. 2, we utilize three 1D convolutional layers to process textual data, capturing patterns and

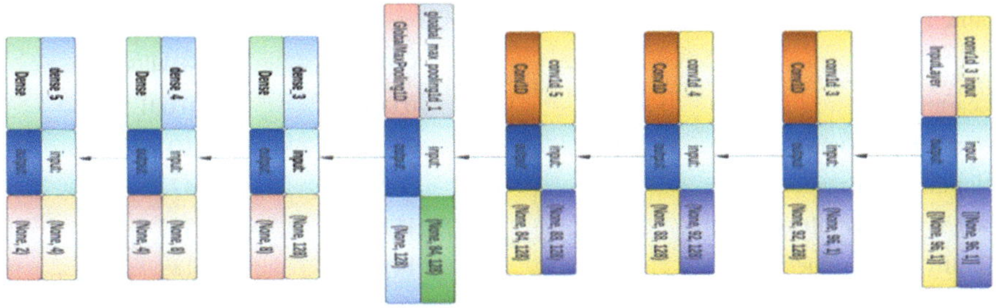

Fig. 2 Convolutional neural network layered flow

dependencies. A global max-pooling layer followed by three dense layers incorporates learned features for predictions. The model comprises eight layers: four convolutional, three dense, and one global max-pooling layer. Input data dimensions are (None, 96, 1), accommodating various batch sizes with 96-word sequences treated as one-dimensional features. Convolutional layers scan local word patterns, akin to image convolutions. Three more convolutional layers handle different word lengths. Global Max Pooling with input shape (None, 84, 128) compresses sequences by selecting maximum values. For input shape (None, 128), variable batch sizes with 128 features are processed. Two extra dense layers vary feature counts.

4 Experiments and Results

In this section, we conduct in-depth ASD experiments to objectively assess the effectiveness of the proposed model on three sizable datasets.

4.1 Dataset Description

The three datasets share a common set of attributes describing evaluation results, but differ significantly in age groups: toddlers (0–4 years), children (4–11 years), and adults (18+ years). They were sourced from public repositories like Kaggle and Github. QCHAT-10 and AQ-10, user-friendly alternatives, were used in place of the original Allison AQ test.

4.2 Dataset Preprocessing

Data preprocessing involved considering 10 questions, age, jaundice, ethnicity, and gender to predict autism. Attributes like 'Used_App', 'Qchat-10-Score', 'Who

Table 1 Parameters for evaluation

	Toddlers	Children	Adults
Learning rate	0.001	0.001	0.001
Number of epochs	20	20	10
Number of instances	1054	292	471
Negative class values	326	151	282
Positive class values	728	141	189

Table 2 Experimental results

Age Group (in years)	Class 0				Class 1			
	Accuracy	Precision	Recall	F1 Score	Accuracy	Precision	Recall	F1 Score
0–4	98.3%	100%	93%	96%	98.3%	97%	100%	98%
4–11	100%	100%	95%	97%	100%	91%	100%	95%
18–60	100%	98%	95%	97%	100%	98%	95%	94%

completed the test', 'result', and 'age_desc' were omitted due to limited relevance. Categorical variables were transformed using the 'get_dummies()' method in pandas. Text data underwent Count Vectorization for numerical representation in model analysis.

4.3 Evaluated Results

The results of the experiments conducted on three different age groups are summarized in Table 2. The obtained accuracy for each age group is remarkably high, specifically for ages 0–4, 4–11, and 18+. The accuracy achieved for toddlers (0–4 years) is 98.3%, for children (4–11 years) is 100%, and for adults (18 and above years) is 100%. Thus these high levels of accuracy, precision, recall, and F1 score demonstrate the CNN model's robustness and reliability in accurately predicting autism disorder across various age groups. Figures 3, 4, and 5 depict the performance of the Deep CNN model over different numbers of epochs and illustrate the relationship between the model's accuracy/loss and the number of epochs (Table 1).

4.4 Comparative Study

Table 3 showcases the achieved accuracy of the proposed model, demonstrating a remarkable 100% accuracy across both child and adult datasets.

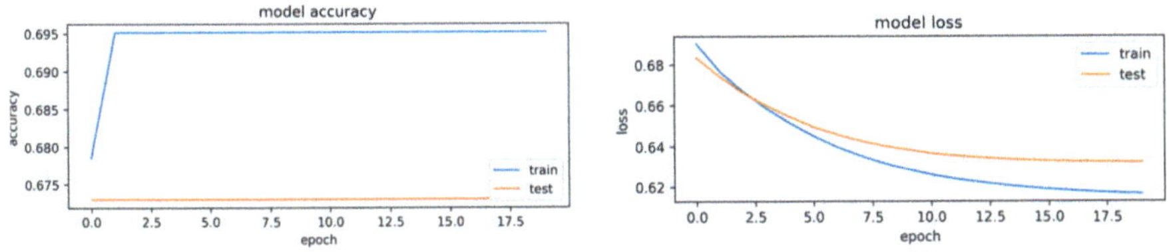

(a) (b)

Fig. 3 Accuracy/Loss representation for 0–4 years

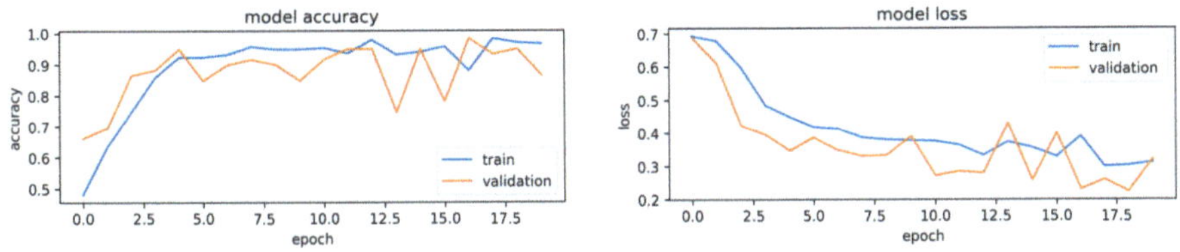

(a) (b)

Fig. 4 Accuracy/Loss representation for 4–11 years

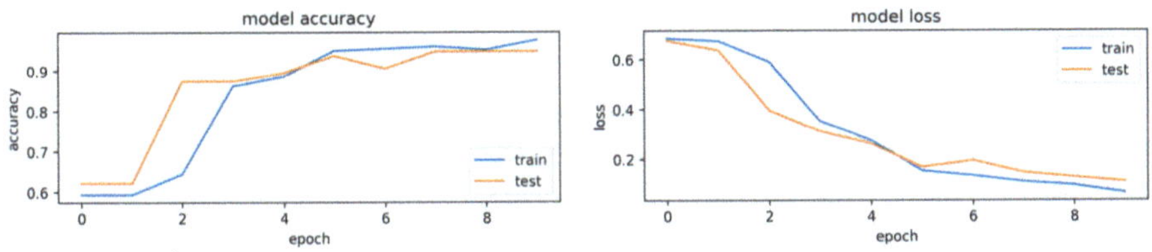

(a) (b)

Fig. 5 Accuracy/Loss representation for 18 + years

Table 3 Comparative study with state of the art

Paper	Year	Methodology	Dataset	Accuracy (%)
[4]	2019	ANN	Adults	**100**
			Toddlers	99.12
[11]	2022	AdaBoost	Children	97.22
			Adults	98.56
			Toddlers	96.67
[9]	2022	SVM	children	95.48
			Adults	96.06
			Toddlers	98.3
Proposed model	2023	CNN	children	**100**
			Adults	**100**

5 Conclusion

The application of Deep CNN with textual data for autism spectrum detection opens up new possibilities for early diagnosis and intervention, which can significantly impact the lives of individuals with autism and their families. With continuous research and advancements, Deep CNN-based models in the field of autism detection, ultimately improve the quality of life of patients. In the future, we will integrate this framework with advanced technologies and develop a more effective ASD diagnosis system available for diagnosis at a low cost at an early stage.

References

1. Thabtah F, Kamalov F, Rajab K (Sep.2018) A new computational intelligence approach to detect autistic features for autism screening. Int. J. Med. Inform. 117:112–124
2. Hasan M,Ahamad MM, Aktar S, Moni MA (2021) Early stage autism spectrum disorder detection of adults and toddlers using machine learning models. In: Proc. 5th Int. Conf. Electr. Inf. Commun. Technol. (EICT), Dec. 2021, pp 1–6
3. Russell Sal Stapley G, Newlove-Delgado T, Salmon A, White R, Warren F, Pearson A, Ford T. Time trends in autism diagnosis over 20 years: a UK population-based cohort study
4. Artificial Neural Network for Diagnose Autism Spectrum Disorder (2019) Nasser IM, Al-Shawwa MO, Abu-Naser Nasser SS, Ibrahim M, Al-Shawwa MO, Abu-Naser SS. Artificial neural network for diagnose autism spectrum disorder
5. Deep learning for autism spectrum disorder detection and classification (2020) by Maen and Sarhan
6. Lord C, Elsabbagh M, Baird G, Veenstra-Vanderweele J (2018) Autism spectrum disorder. Lancet 392:508–520
7. Ecker C, Marquand A, Mourão-Miranda J, Johnston P, Daly EM, Brammer MJ, Maltezos S, Murphy CM, Robertson D, Williams SC et al (2010) Describing the brain in autism in five dimensions—Magnetic resonance imaging-assisted diagnosis of autism spectrum disorder using a multiparameter classification approach. J Neurosci 30:10612–10623
8. Maenner MJ, Rice CE, Arneson CL, Cunniff C, Schieve LA, Carpenter LA, Braun KVN, Kirby RS, Bakian AV, Durkin MS. Potential impact of DSM-5 criteria on autism spectrum disorder prevalence estimates
9. Mousumi B, Mohammad A, Md S, Fida H, Mohammad Ali M (2022) Efficient machine learning models for early stage detection of autism
10. Kong Y, Gao J, Xu Y, Pan Y, Wang J, Liu J. Classification of autism spectrum disorder by combining brain connectivity and deep neural network classifier
11. Mahedy Hasan SM, Uddin MP, Mamun MA, Sharif MI, Ulhaq A, Krishnamoorthy G. A machine learning framework for early-stage detection of autism spectrum disorders

Investigating the Efficacy of ML and DL Models in Detecting Tomato Leaf Diseases under Varying Environmental Factors

Surendra Reddy Vinta, Yeligeti Raju, P. Nagaraj, K. Ashok Kumar, and B. Dhanalaxmi

1 Introduction

Due to their importance to the food and economic impact, tomatoes (Solanum lycopersicum) play a significant role in Bangladeshi agriculture as well as the rest of the world. Many different diseases frequently endanger the productive cultivation of tomatoes, resulting in a significant yield loss and degraded product quality. For the implementation of effective management methods and sustaining crop health for sustainable production, rapid and accurate disease identification is essential.ML and DL techniques are used for identification and diagnosis the plant diseases automatically by using the images which we collected from the plant leaves. DL models are most efficient to analyze the large amounts of complex data with different environmental conditions of leaves like occlusion, blight, dots, and noise from the images.

S. R. Vinta (✉)
School of Computer Science and Engineering, VIT-AP University, Amaravati, Andhra Pradesh, India
e-mail: vsurendra.cse@gmail.com

Y. Raju
Department of Computer Science and Engineering (Data Science), Vignana Bharathi Institute of Technology (Autonomous), Hyderabad, Telangana, India

P. Nagaraj
Department of Computer Science and Engineering, Anurag University, Hyderabad, Telangana, India

K. A. Kumar
Department of Computer Science and Engineering, Nalla Narasimha Reddy Educational Society's Group of Institutions, Hyderabad, Telangana, India

B. Dhanalaxmi
Department of Computer Science and Engineering, Malla Reddy Institute of Engineering and Technology (Autonomous), Hyderabad, Telangana, India

K. Kumar Singh et al. (eds.), *Machine Vision and Augmented Intelligence*, Lecture Notes in Electrical Engineering 1211, https://doi.org/10.1007/978-981-97-4359-9_41

The aim of this study is to compare how ML and DL methodologies work in different scenarios of tomato leaf disease detection in Bangladesh and other environmental conditions. Dataset which contains leaf images with different conditions like fungs, normal, and sickness. In order to assess the performance different models are used for the detection of tomato leaves disease like ResNet15, DenseNet121, InceptionV3, EfficientNet-B4, Support Vector Machine Classification, ResNet50V2, and AlexNet models.

Our results are intended to contribute to the creation of precise and accurate systems for diagnosing diseases that operate well in a variety of environmental situations by offering relevant information regarding the benefits and drawbacks of various ML and DL techniques.

1.1 Diseases Details

This study's primary goal is to develop a categorization scheme based on DL and ML that will enable the early identification and treatment of three significant diseases that affect tomato leaves. Here, we give a thorough overview of each disease, going into its signs, causes, and effects on plants.

1.2 Tomato Leaf Disease

The dataset on tomato leaf ailments covers a wide range of afflictions and infestations impacting tomato plants, facilitating the creation of ML and DL models for prompt recognition and categorization. Precise detection of such issues is essential for applying effective management strategies and reducing potential damage to crops. The dataset plays a vital role in order to protect and care of plants for the researchers and growers to improve tomato yielding. (Fig. 1).

1.2.1 Target Spot

Target spot on tomato leaves is one of the fungal diseases known as Corynespora cassiicola, which damages tomato plants. The reasons of target spot are based on the climatic conditions like humidity, temperature, and plant stress. The symptoms are the leaves turning into brown black, black spots on leaves, and enlarged leaves, these all affect the plants. Defoliation decreases yielding and the leaves turn into yellow, dry, and fall. ML and DL models, including ResNet15, DenseNet121, InceptionV3, EfficientNet-B4, SVM, ResNet50V2, and AlexNet, have been employed to identify and classify Target spots within the dataset. The researchers can determine the best

Fig. 1 Sample Tomato leaf images with disease conditions

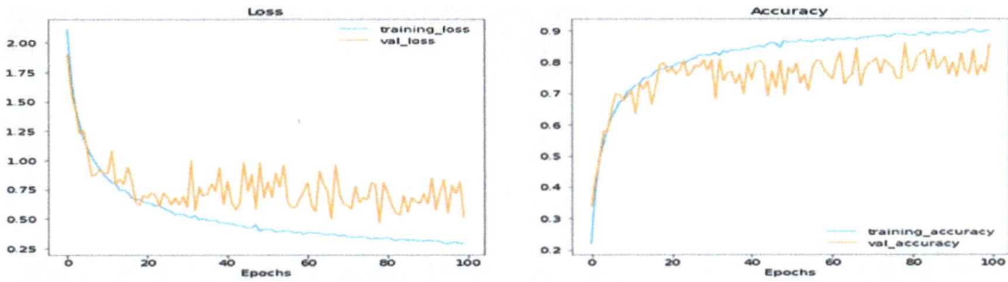

Fig. 2 Loss and accuracy of densenet121

technique for the detection and classification of target spots by evaluating the performance of various models. The illness of plants is identified with the symptoms of small, water-soaked, and patches on leaves.

1.2.2 Bacterial Spot

It's possible for the impacted leaves to wither and drop off, which would impair photosynthesis and crop yield. Bacterial Spot is extremely contagious and spreads quickly in warm, humid environments, making early diagnosis and treatment absolutely essential. Considering the condition of Tomato leaf detection dataset, distinguishing Bacterial Spot from other diseases with similar symptoms is a challenging task.

ML and DL models, including ResNet15, DenseNet121, InceptionV3, EfficientNet-B4, SVM, ResNet50V2, and AlexNet, have been employed to identify and classify Bacterial spots within the dataset.

1.2.3 TYLCV

TYLCV constitutes a significant concern for tomato cultivators around the world. This viral infection, caused by a begomovirus and transmitted via the whitefly Bemisia tabaci, leads to symptoms such as leaves curling upwards, yellowing of the foliage, and hindered plant development. The effect of TYLCV is extreme loss of crop and yielding reduction. Managing this disease is a challenge due to the swift spread by whiteflies and the limited availability of resistant tomato varieties.

1.2.4 Late Blight

Late blight, is one of the plant diseases caused by the oomycete organism Phytophthora infestans, which also affects tomatoes and potatoes plants in the Solanaceae family. The symptoms of the disease are the leaves turning to dark, wet lesions, and the fruits and stems do not grow quickly and these leads to forming the plant tissues. In case of high moisture conditions, a white fluffy is formed lower side of the leaves. Due to the light blight, the crop yielding is reduced, and loss of fruits in the early stages.

1.2.5 Leaf Mold

Leaf Mold is one type of fungus caused on tomato leaves it is called Fulvia fulva, and it is caused in such environments like humidity and green houses. The major symptoms of this disease is identified in tomatoes and the upper side of the leaves turned to yellow, and brown mold growth in the lower side of the leaves. The identification of this infection on the leaves, the leaves turning into yellow and eventually die, leading to a reduction in photosynthesis, hindered plant growth, and loss of fruit production. In order to identify the leaf mold very efficiently and minimize the crop damage.

1.2.6 Early Blight

Early Blight is caused on leaves. It is one type of fungus Alternaria solani that affects the tomato plants. The symptoms on leaves are Small, dark brown or black circular lesions that first occur on the leaves and then grow over time to form a characteristic concentric ring pattern are the disease's hallmark. As the infection advances, the affected leaves turn yellow and drop, reducing photosynthesis and potentially impacting fruit yield. It is essential to correctly identify and categorize

Early blight in the context of the tomato leaf disease detection dataset in order to facilitate the prompt application of management measures, limiting possible crop losses. ResNet15, DenseNet121, InceptionV3, EfficientNet-B4, SVM, ResNet50V2, and AlexNet are just a few of the ML and DL models that have been investigated for this purpose.

1.2.7 Spider Mites

Spider mites are tiny arachnid pests that harm tomato plants by feeding on the sap of the plant. These minuscule bugs cause the leaves to stipple, yellow, and curl, which hinders photosynthesis, stunts growth, and lowers fruit production. In most of the cases, spider mite infections lead to loss of leaves and finally sometimes loss of the plant. In the context of the tomato leaf disease detection effectively identify the spider mite to minimize the crop loss. Various ML and DL models are incorporated to detect tomato leaf disease detection very efficiently and accurately to improve the production of tomatoes.

1.2.8 Septoria Leaf Spot

Septoria leaf spot is one of the fungal diseases which affects tomato plants. It is caused by the septoria lycopersici. The symptoms of this fungus on leaves such as like water-soaked lesions, and the circular patches on leaves which are gray and dark brown. The identification of this infection on the leaves, the leaves turn into yellow and eventually die, leading to reduce the photosynthesis, hindered plant growth, and loss of fruit production. To reduce the crop loss proper identification of leaf diseases is very crucial in plant leaf disease detection to improve the production of fruits. Various ML and DL models are incorporated to identify the diseases on tomato leaves very efficiently and accurately and to improve yielding production.

2 Literature Review

According to Kon et al. (2014), the arrival of a weak variety of the tomato yellow leaf curl virus was the main cause of the disease in the Dominican Republic [1]. Yang et al. (2021) aimed to improve our knowledge of microbial relationships and disease prevention by studying an antagonistic endophytic bacterial species that might be used against tomato leaf spot disease-causing Pseudomonas syringe [2].

Watanabe et al. (2017) report that isolates of the pathogen responsible for tomato leaf mold illness, Passalora fulva, have developed to be resistant to azoxystrobin. This proved that continuous monitoring of resistance to fungicides in plant pathogen populations is essential [3]. In order to stop the virus from building up and generating symptoms in tomato hybrids and yellow leaf curl disease, Tabein et al. (2017) investigated the benefit of pyramiding resistance genes that are Ty-1/Ty-3 and Ty-2 [4]. Caizares et al. (2015) used Arabidopsis thaliana as an operational host for begomo viruses associated with tomato yellow curling of leaves disease, which increased the study options for these plant viruses [5]. Li et al. (2023) proposed DL based model to detect the illness of tomato leaf diseases and plant diseases by using LMBRNet-based technique [6].

Chen et al. (2020) [7] merge the ABCK-BWTR and B-ARNet to detect the leaf diseases in tomatoes. The leaf curl gujarati is one type of virus and begomovirus which causes on leaves in the place of Varanasi and India. Deep learning algorithms are employed to detect the illness of plant leaves. Chakraborty et al. (2003) [8].

The deep learning approaches are suitable to detect the leaf diseases accurately and the timely diagnosis is also very important. TOLed is used to diagnose, and CNN-based techniques are employed to detect the leaf diseases accurately. Agarwal et al. (2020) [9]. Wu et al. (2020) proposed a DCGAN-Based methods to detect the tomato leaf diseases [10]. AI models are demonstrated to generate the data automatically to enhance the characteristics and its capabilities. In southeast Spain, Velasco et al. (2008) developed to detect the tomato leaf curl diseases and other different virus on leaves in different economical conditions like green house coverings and chlorsis conditions [11]. Li et al. (2022) used the FWDGAN-based for the detecting the illness leaves and GAN models are used for augmentation to improve the training of a model, improve the performance of model, and avoid the outliers of data during training of a model [12].

Khan et al. (2013), focused on detecting the different types of diseases on leaves such as curl sudan virus, curl disease in Oman, and the pathogens which are formed on the tomato leaves [13]. Rnn's are used for the automatic coordination and provide the attention network providing on the multiple-channels. Zhang et al. (2023) developed the attention mechanisms in order to detect tomato leaf diseases, and compared with the DL models how the attention mechanisms detect the tomato leaf diseases. Tao et al. (2022) improved the dual-strategy techniques for learning based on the GAN and the novel-challenging techniques for the labeled data [14]. Basavaiah and Anthony (2020) applied different feature extraction techniques for the classification of different features, select the best feature extractions, and train the model with the extracted relevant features for the tomato leaf disease detection [15]. They conducted research that demonstrated how machine learning models may be used to efficiently evaluate and categorize water quality. BOD, TDS, pH, dissolved oxygen, and other characteristics were included in the dataset that was used for this purpose. With a respectable accuracy rate of 78.96%, the Random Forest model was the most accurate of the several models this group used. With an accuracy of only 68.29%1, [16–19] the SVM model, on the other hand, trailed behind.

3 Preprocessing of the Dataset

In order to train the data, preprocessing is required to improve the quality of images and dimension of all the images should be consistent to train and evaluate the models. Various preprocessing approaches are available and select the best approach which is suitable to our data is undertaken below:

- **Standardizing Image Dimensions**: To evaluate the ML and DL models, the dimensions of all the images must be consistent with the equal pixel size of all the images (e.g., 224 × 224 Pixels). It leads to reduce the computational time and memory consumption during training and testing.
- **Equalizing Class Representation**: In the process of classification different oversampling and undersampling approaches are used during training to balance the dataset with the help of applying class weights, which intends to the equal distribution of images to evaluate various ML and DL models.
- **Encoding Categorical Labels**: One-hot encoding techniques are accompanied to convert the numerical values into the categorical class labels (Healthy and UN-Healthy Conditions) in the process of evaluating the ML and DL models.

3.1 Feature Selection

Feature selection plays a vital role in the context of evaluating the ML models for leaf disease detection of any plant. The goal of the feature selection is to select the relevant features from our trained dataset and to improve the model's performance to minimize the computational time and detection accurately.

- **Filter Approaches**: These approaches are used to remove the noise from the images and improve the quality of image pixel values. Filter approaches are used in the process of preprocessing the images in order to train the DL models very efficiently and accurately to detect the leaf diseases the methods which are employed like chi-square test and Gaussian filters, etc.
- **Wrapper Approaches**: These approaches are employed in the context of evaluating the ML models to select the feature subset from the dataset. The wrapper approaches are like feed forward, backward elimination, and recursive feature feature selection.
- **Embedded Approaches**: These approaches are used to integrate the multiple feature selection during the training process. Regularization techniques select the features and integrate with other selected features which effectively reduces the training loss and increases the test accuracy most efficiently.

Feature selection may not be crucial in the context of training the DL models why because CNN models automatically extract the complex features from the images and automatically learn from the different hierarchical layers during training. In contrast to training the ML models, feature selection is very crucial to select the relevant features to detect the leaf diseases.

3.2 Feature Encoding

Feature encoding is used to convert the numerical values into the categorical values in the training process of ML models. These approaches are also used for improving the quality of raw images. The overview of feature encoding techniques is listed below.

- **Color Information**: Coloring of images which are RGB and gray color images improves the pixel value and its clarity. The processing of RGB color images are time consuming and its pixel size is also very high. Converting the color images into gray color the complexity of the pixel is reduced and its computational training time is also less. In order to diagnose and detect the leaf diseases.
- **Deep Learning-Based Feature Extraction**: CNN models automatically extract the features from the images for the identification of diseases. CNN has multiple layers like convolutional layer and max pooling layer. The convolutional layers extract the features and its hierarchical properties to detect and classify tomato leaf diseases. In DL fine-tuned pre-trained models are like inception, Resnet, and efficient net.

3.3 Feature Scaling

The main objective of feature scaling is to normalize the feature range with its subset features and maintain the feature range in the training process improving the model performance and detection efficiently. Feature scaling improves the detection and the model performance.

- **Log Scaling**: It is a non-linear technique to reduce the outliers and improve the data distribution of features. This technique gets the best results when our data is in the skewed distribution.
- **Unit Length Scaling**: This method entails scaling the features so that the resulting feature vector possesses a unit length (i.e., a Euclidean length of 1). This technique can be valuable for algorithms that are sensitive to the magnitude of input features, such as k-means clustering and support vector machines.

In the context of DL CNN models are out-performed for extracting features compared with the feature scaling techniques. Feature scaling techniques are helpful to ML models to obtain accurate results. Although the preprocessing techniques obtain the good results which are like resizing the images, normalizing the pixel values noise reduction and data augmentation achieving the robustness of different models.

4 Image Resizing

Image resizing is one of the preprocessing techniques to resize all the images into equal sizes. The process of resizing all the images into equal size and into equal dimensions. To train the DL models the data should be consistent. In this context, our dataset contains the tomato leaf images. The images which we consider to resize with the same dimensions with the respective height, width, length, and breadth. In the process of resizing the images maintaining the original aspect ratio and image distortion is very important to preserve the original features of the image. Python libraries are available to load and train the DL models for the accurate prediction of diseases effectively such as Open CV, PIL, or skimage to resize the images. Image dimensions and image rescaling is the crucial in the preprocessing of images. Different ML and DL are employed to detect the tomato leaf disease detection some fine-tuning pre-trained models such as EfficientNet-B4, ResNet15, DenseNet121, InceptionV3, Support Vector Machine Classification, ResNet50V2, and AlexNet, rely on a fixed input size to process images effectively.

4.1 Description of All the Algorithms

- **ResNet15**

The main advantage of ResNet is its capacity to manage the vanishing gradient issue that arises in deep networks. If the network understands residual functions through skip connections or residual connections, the gradient flow could be enhanced overall. Using the ResNet15 model, a range of illnesses affecting tomato leaves were classified using the dataset for sickness identification on tomato leaves. With a loss of 0.1904 and an accuracy of 0.9460, the model ranks highly in this comparison. ResNet15 has different layers such as batch normalization, Convolution layers, and activation functions. These all layers made the structure of the model. The model has a residual connection which means the skip connections between the layers. The residual connections train the model consistently and accurately to detect the different diseases and overcome the vanishing gradient. In the process of detecting the tomato leaf diseases with the accuracy0.94. It does not consider the complex factors and the other computational efficiencies for the other applications.

- **DenseNet121**

The main advantage of dense net architecture is the reusage of features and the flow throughout the network with the gradient. It is suitable to diagnose and detect the different types of diseases in different applications. DenseNet 121 has 121 densely connected layers and it includes the batch normalization, convolutional layers, and the activation functions. The model is useful for the classification and identification

Fig. 3 Training versus Validation accuaracy of inceptionV3

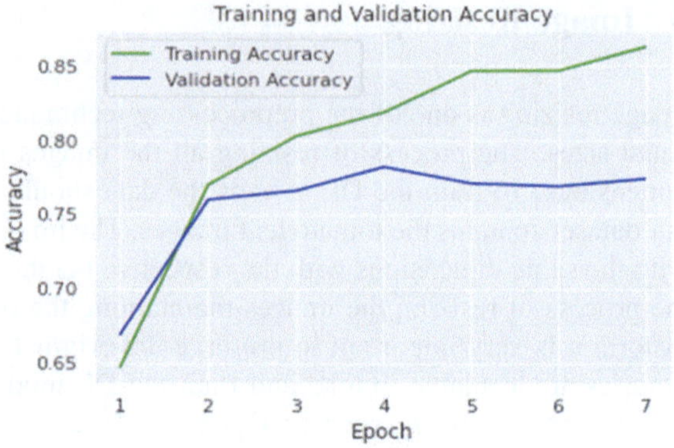

of different types of diseases on tomato leaves. In the classification of tomato leaf disease, DenseNet121 obtained the best optimal results with an accuracy of 0.90 and a loss of 0.29.

- **InceptionV3**

Inception V3 is the DL object detection model and it is the latest version of inception module. The inception model is built with different layers such as max polling, convolutional, normalization, and the activation functions with different kernel sizes. The Inception V3 minimizes the computational efficiency and supports the complex dataset with a large size. In the tomato leaf disease detection, the inception v3 obtains the best results with the accuracy of 0.78 and a loss of 3.19 with the large size of the dataset. The InceptionV3 architecture to detect the tomato leaf disease detection considers all the parameters of images and preserves the good performance of a model. This system selects the best features from the layers, evaluates with the best parameters, and detects the tomato leaf diseases very accurately and efficiently. The best suitable method for detecting and identifying the tomato leaf diseases with different resource requirements and the efficiency of the model (Figs. 3, 4).

- **EfficientNet-B4**

EfficientNet models are used for the scaling it includes the scaling dimensions such as like height, width, breadth and all the scaling dimensions of images. The scaling improve the resolution of images in the dataset and provide the higher efficiency with the few input labels with less time complexity of model in detecting the tomato leaf disease detection. The efficient model learn the characteristics and classify the tomato leaf disease detection accurately. The efficient allows the fewer inputs with the less time with the large size dataset. The efficient obtain the accuracy 0.97 and the loss is 0.08. Compound scaling is achieved by the efficientnet-B4 with the best accuracy for balancing the model depth. The eeficientnet-B4 is very suitable for scaling but it's important to other tasks like training and the computing complexity for selecting the optimal model.

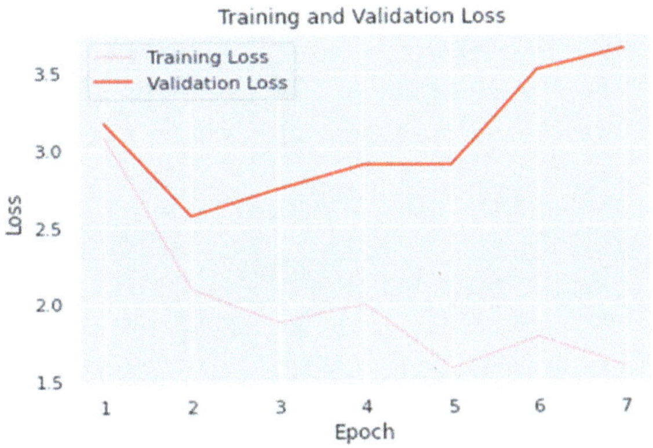

Fig. 4 Training versus Validation loss of inceptionV3

- **SVM**

SVM is a ML model to solve the classification problems extensively with the regression. The principle behind the SVM is find the optimal hyperplane to maximize the differences between the classes. SVM'S are handle the high-dimensional data very effectively to handle the over fitting of the dataset. SVM supports the large dimensional values and reduce the overfitting and underfitting parameters of the data. SVM achieves the classification accuracy 0.88 with the loss of 0.95. Different functions are used like polynomial, kernel functions and radial basis functions (RBF) to detect the tomato leaf diseases accurately. The SVM is a best method for diagnosing and classifying tomato leaf diseases (Figs. 5, 6).

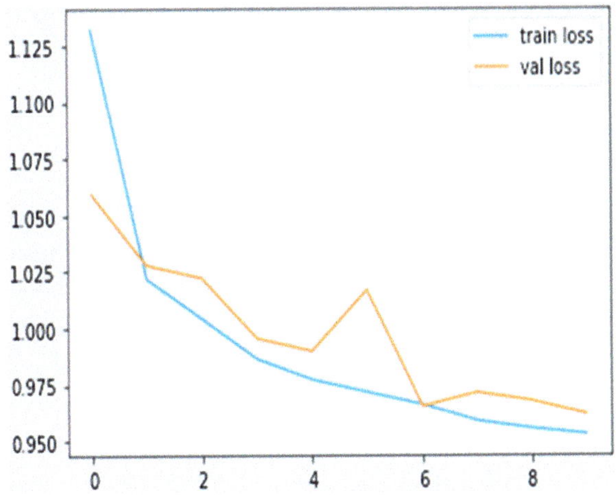

Fig. 5 Training versus Validation loss of SVM

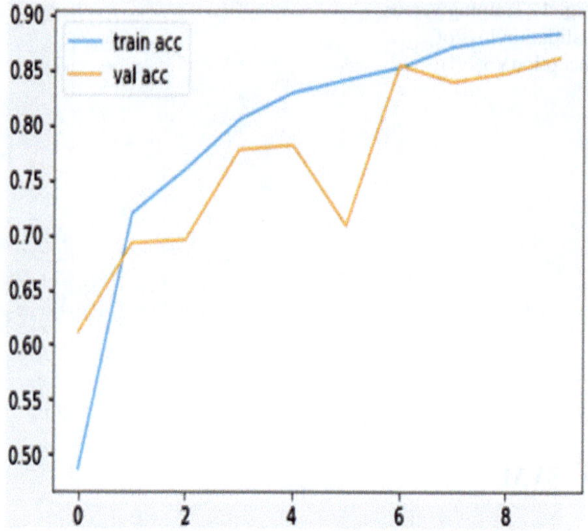

Fig. 6 Training versus Validation accuaracy of SVM

- **AlexNet**

Alexnet is one of the classification model the architecture is built with convolutional layers, fully linked layers and finally the classification. This model has the dropout to prevent the overfitting and the activation functions to improve the model performance. The Alexnet model achieves with the accuracy of 0.94 and its loss is 0.25 to classify the tomato leaf diseases. The model is suitable for all the applications in the context of classification and detection of leaf diseases. The model helpful in categorizing and identifying of different tomato leaf diseases which include the training time and the computational complexity.

4.2 Confusion Matrix

The projected categories are shown in rows and the actual classes, which represent the truth, are presented in columns in this confusion matrix. For every class, the genuine positive counts are represented by the diagonal components (TP_H, TP_M, TP_T, TP_B, TP_Y, TP_L, TP_Lf, TP_E, TP_S, TP_Se) (Fig. 7).

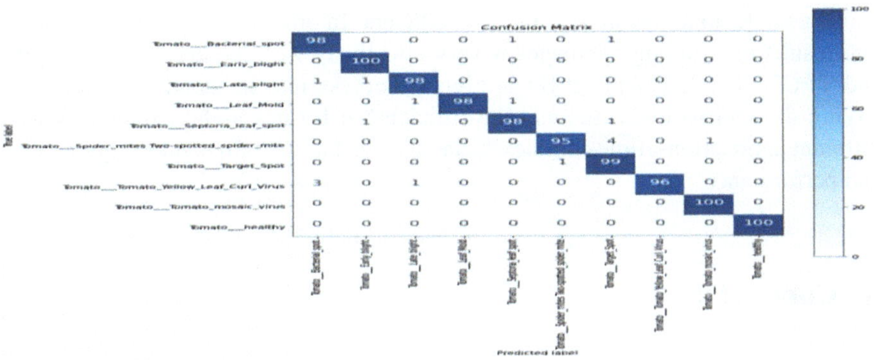

Fig. 7 Confusion matrix

g. 8 Results for tomato leaf disease detection method

Result

e EfficientNet-B4 out-performs to identify the tomato leaf disease detection mpared to all other models. The model classifies the different tomato leaf diseases curately. The efficient net-B4 model achieves the best optimal accuracy to classify different tomato leaf diseases with an accuracy of 0.97, a precision of 0.97, and a all of 0.973. ResNet15, DenseNet121, InceptionV3, SVM, and Resnet50V2 and Alexnet models. The models achieved the performance with the different accuy levels of InceptionV3 with 0.78, ResNet50V2 with 0.951. The EfficientNet- achieves the utmost accuracy by using compound scaling and reducing the nplexity to improve the image dimensions accurately according to its width and adth. The compound scaling improves the resolution of images. This approach yields a model that is more accurate and efficient. In order to achieve the best accurate results the training of images is very effectively with the availability of GPU and TPU's. The EfficientNet-B4 is highest success rate in identifying and classifying the tomato leaf diseases. The EfficientNet-B4 has highest trade-offs with different applications, time complexity and the availability of resource requirements and performance.

6 Conclusion

The tomato leaf disease detection EfficientNet-B4 out-performs with the existing ML and DL methods. The Efficient-Net-B4 achieves the metrics comparison with other models such as recall, precision, and accuracy with 0.97, 0.976 and 0.973 respectively. The training time, computational complexity, and resource utilization process to select the optimal parameters for the tomato leaf disease detection. The EfficientNet-B4 architecture allows the scaling of images with the network's depth and dimensions. Reliable architectures gave prominent results for classifying the tomato leaf diseases accurately. These models are used to minimize crop loss and improve the production of plants in many applications. In the real-world scenarios, the models achieve the detection efficiently, and then we minimize the crop loss and improve the production accuracy. In agricultural practices, developed automated detection methods to improve yield production. In future, many advancements are taken to develop agricultural production and minimize the crop losses from plants to leaves in the early stages with the help of DL approaches and provide efficient solutions.

References

1. Kon T, Melgarejo T, Almanzar A, Gilbertson RL (2014) Recent emergence of the mild stra of tomato yellow leaf curl virus as a cause of tomato yellow leaf curl disease of processi tomatoes (solanum lycopersicon) in the dominican republic. Plant Dis 98(11):1592–1592
2. Yang C, Feng Z, Wang Y, Jin M, Li T, Zhou J (2021) Identification and colonization dynamics an antagonistic endophytic bacterium 262XY2′ against Pseudomonas syringae causing toma leaf spot disease. Eur J Plant Pathol 161(1):233–245
3. Watanabe H, Horinouchi H, Muramoto Y, Ishii H (2017) Occurrence of azoxystrobin-resist isolates in Passalora fulva, the pathogen of tomato leaf mould disease. Plant Pathol 66(9):147 1479
4. Tabein S, Behjatnia SAA, Laviano L, Pecchioni N, Accotto GP, Noris E, Miozzi L (2017) Py miding Ty-1/Ty-3 and Ty-2 in tomato hybrids dramatically inhibits symptom expression accumulation of tomato yellow leaf curl disease inducing viruses. Archiv Für Phytopatholo Und Pflanzenschutz 50(5–6):213–227
5. Cañizares MC., Rosas-Díaz T, Rodríguez-Negrete E, Hogenhout, SA., Bedford ID, Bejar ER, Navas-Castillo J, Moriones E (2015) Arabidopsis thaliana, an experimental host tomato yellow leaf curl disease-associated begomoviruses by agroinoculation and whit transmission. Plant Pathol 64(2): 265–271

6. Li M, Zhou G, Chen A, Li L, Hu Y (2023) Identification of tomato leaf diseases based on LMBRNet. Eng Appl Artif Intell 123:106195
7. Chen X, Zhou G, Chen A, Yi, J, Zhang W, Hu Y (2020) Identi fi cation of tomato leaf diseases based on combination of ABCK-BWTR and B-ARNet. Comput Electron Agric 178. https://doi.org/10.1016/j.compag.2020.105730
8. Chakraborty S, Pandey P, Banerjee M, Kalloo G, Fauquet C(2003) Tomato leaf curl Gujarat virus, a new Begomovirus species causing a severe leaf curl disease of tomato in Varanasi India. Phytopathology 93(12):1485–1495
9. Agarwal M, Singh A, Arjaria S, Sinha A, Gupta S (2020) ToLeD: Tomato leaf disease detection using convolution neural network. Procedia Comput Sci 167:293–301
10. Wu Q, Chen Y, Meng J (2020) DCGAN-Based Data Augmentation for Tomato Leaf Disease Identification. IEEE Access 8:98716–98728
11. Velasco L, Simón B, Janssen D, Cenis J (2008) Incidences and progression of tomato chlorosis virus disease and tomato yellow leaf curl virus disease in tomato under different greenhouse covers in southeast Spain. Ann Appl Biol 153(3):335–344. https://doi.org/10.1111/j.1744-7348.2008.00262.x
12. Li M, Zhou G, Chen A, Yi J, Lu C, He M, Hu Y (2022) FWDGAN-based data augmentation for tomato leaf disease identification. Comput Electron Agric 194:106779. https://doi.org/10.1016/j.compag.2022.106779
13. Khan AJ, Akhtar S, Singh AK, Briddon RW (2013) A distinct strain of tomato leaf curl Sudan virus causes tomato leaf curl disease in Oman. Plant Dis 97(11):1396–1402. https://doi.org/10.1094/PDIS-02-13-0210-RE
14. Tao W, Ma J, Shi J, Lv W, Zhao M, Zheng L, Huang L, Weng S (2022) Dual-strategy semi-supervised learning method based on GAN for recognition of tomato leaf diseases. Int J Remote Sens 43(13):5025–5039. https://doi.org/10.1080/01431161.2022.2123722
15. Basavaiah J, Arlene Anthony A (2020) Tomato leaf disease classification using multiple feature extraction techniques. Wireless Pers Commun 115(1):633–651. https://doi.org/10.1007/s11277-020-07590-x
16. Shahid MS, Shafiq M, Ilyas M, Raza A, Al-Sadrani MN, Al-Sadi AM, Briddon RW (2019) Frequent occurrence of Mungbean yellow mosaic India virus in tomato leaf curl disease affected tomato in Oman. Sci Rep 9(1):16634–16714. https://doi.org/10.1038/s41598-019-53106-4
17. Trivedi NK, Gautam V, Anand A, Aljahdali HM, Villar SG, Anand D, Goyal N, Kadry S (2021) Early detection and classification of tomato leaf disease using high-performance deep neural network. Sensors (Basel, Switzerland) 21(23):7987. https://doi.org/10.3390/s21237987
18. Zhou C, Zhou S, Xing J, Song J (2021) Tomato leaf disease identification by restructured deep residual dense network. IEEE Access 9:28822–28831. https://doi.org/10.1109/ACCESS.2021.3058947
19. Zhang Y, Huang S, Zhou G, Hu Y, Li L (2023) Identification of tomato leaf diseases based on multi-channel automatic orientation recurrent attention network. Comput Electron Agric 205:107605. https://doi.org/10.1016/j.compag.2022.107605

Banana Disease and Deficiency Detection Using YOLOv8

Surendra Reddy Vinta, B. Dhanalaxmi, M. Lavanya, Aruna Thotapalli, and Yeligeti Raju

1 Introduction

Banana cultivation is critical to the livelihoods of millions of people as well as the security of the world's food supply. However, the yield and profitability of banana crops are frequently jeopardized by a variety of diseases and nutritional deficiencies. Identifying and managing these difficulties is a difficult endeavor that needs precise and timely information and intervention. The advancements in computer vision, deep learning, and machine learning provide solutions to agricultural problems like detection, classification, and segmentation tasks easily. Farmers can now reliably and efficiently identify diseases and nutrient shortages in banana crops using the YOLO algorithm [1]. The technological advancements and the new interventions are helpful for individual therapeutic conditions and improve the yielding capacity of bananas.

S. R. Vinta (✉)
School of Computer Science and Engineering, VIT-AP University, Amaravati, Andhra Pradesh, India
e-mail: vsurendra.cse@gmail.com

B. Dhanalaxmi
Department of Computer Science and Engineering, Malla Reddy Institute of Engineering and Technology (Autonomous), Hyderabad, Telangana, India

M. Lavanya · Y. Raju
Department of Computer Science and Engineering (Data Science), Vignana Bharathi Institute of Technology (Autonomous), Hyderabad, Telangana, India

A. Thotapalli
Department of Information Technology, CVR College of Engineering, Hyderabad, Telangana, India

K. Kumar Singh et al. (eds.), *Machine Vision and Augmented Intelligence*, Lecture Notes in Electrical Engineering 1211, https://doi.org/10.1007/978-981-97-4359-9_42

1.1 Multi-class Banana Diseases and Deficiency Detection

There may be a number of diseases with bacterial, viral, and fungal which severely affect the banana fields. The harmful disease to the banana harvests is Panama disease which is caused by the Fusarium oxysporum fungus, it leads to deadly illnesses in leaf. There is a big risk with fungus Mycosphaerella fijiensis causes spot disease on leaves. Because of these diseases, the fruit of banana production and quality is reduced and it may cause nutrient loss such as potassium and magnesium [1]. Each disease has its own visual symptoms, these may vary from one to another. Anomalies, spotting patterns, and yellow leaves are some of the common symptoms of all diseases. But it is a challenge to the researchers to identify a particular disease based on visual cues. Manual inspection methods need a lot of money and manpower, and time, yet no guarantees that it is correctly found or not. A system model can be implemented to find the various disorders, and accurately diagnose the disease and division of deficiencies surely [2].

1.2 Timely Detection for Banana Crop Management

The identification of diseases on banana leaves in the early stages is most important because the infection affects harvesting. Usually, the banana leaves are affected with diseases such as Panama disease, which rapidly spreads all over the leaves and entirely devastates the plantations, it results in harvesting, plant loss, and financial losses.

Although, the deficiencies of plants affect the overall health of plants, and size of the fruit is also small and production of yielding is very less. Early identification of diseases on banana leaves, the farmers apply target pesticides and reduce the plant losses and spreading which are helpful to improve the productivity and yielding capacity of plants.

Early identification is critical for mitigating the impact of infections and shortages on banana harvests. Rapidly spreading diseases, such as Panama disease, have the potential to entirely devastate plantations, resulting in enormous financial losses.

Simultaneously, nutritional deficiencies may compromise the overall health of plants, affecting fruit quality and yield productivity. Early discovery of these issues allows farmers to apply targeted solutions, reducing the need for agrochemicals to be used extensively and encouraging the use of sustainable farming techniques.

1.3 Overview of the YOLO (You Only Look Once) Algorithm

The You Only Look Once (YOLO) approach offers a significant advancement in object detection in images and video streams. Unlike traditional approaches, which need many picture scans, YOLO predicts bounding boxes and probabilities for classes using a single deep neural network. This real-time detection capability is really valuable in changing agricultural situations.

The YOLO algorithm learns to distinguish between various issues by analyzing small visual cues that are shown in a variety of images that illustrate diseases and inadequacies affecting bananas [3]. Yolo's ability to interpret images quickly and accurately makes it a viable option for addressing the challenges associated with identifying various disease classes and deficits in banana crops.

2 Related Work

"Multi-Class Banana Disease Detection Using Deep Learning" [4] Limitation: restrictions in dataset quantity and variability made it difficult for the method to be applied to less prevalent diseases."A Comprehensive Study of Banana Deficiency Detection Using Convolutional Neural Networks" [5] Limitation: The model's accuracy fluctuated according to the lighting, which had an impact on how well it performed in various field situations. "Deep Learning-Based Banana Disease Classification with Limited Training Data" [6] Limitation: There were difficulties in fine-tuning the model to detect modest variations in illness symptoms due to a lack of available training data. "Improved Detection of Banana Diseases and Nutrient Deficiencies using Transfer Learning" [7] Limitation: The algorithm's performance in identifying uncommon diseases was impacted by biases from the source dataset that were introduced through transfer learning. "Difficulties and Opportunities in Detecting Banana Disease under Field Conditions" [8] Limitation: The usefulness of the algorithm in real life was hampered by its inability to accurately identify diseases in photographs captured in a variety of field circumstances."Enhancing Banana Disease Detection Through Ensemble Learning" [9] Limitation: While ensemble approaches increased computational complexity, they also increased precision, which limited their ability to handle data in real-time."Comparative Analysis of Deep Learning Architectures for Banana Disease Detection" [10] Limitation: The accuracy and speed of various deep learning architectures varied, necessitating careful selection depending on application requirements.

"Challenges in Real-Time Banana Disease Detection Using Deep Learning" [11] Limitation: deep learning models' processing speed limitations made real-time application in resource-constrained contexts difficult.

3 Banana Diseases and Deficiency

3.1 Common Diseases Affecting Banana Crops

The production of bananas, which is essential for global food security and economy, has significant challenges because of a variety of diseases that compromise the health and productivity of banana plants. These diseases have the potential to drastically reduce productivity, disrupt supply chains, and have an impact on the lives of numerous farmers worldwide. Black Sigatoka and Panama disease are two of the most common infections impacting banana plantations.

3.1.1 Panama Disease

Panama disease is one of the most damaging diseases in the banana industry. Fusarium oxysporum f. sp. cubense (Foc) is a soil-dwelling fungus that causes it. This illness was discovered over a century ago and remains a serious hazard today. There are several races or varieties of the fungus.

Banana plant strains in particular. The most devastating kind is known as Tropical Race 4 (TR4), and it has caused havoc on big farms of the popular Cavendish banana species [12].

TR4-infected plants display symptoms such as wilting, yellowing leaves, and staining of internal vascular tissue [13]. These sick plants eventually die, resulting in decreased output and financial losses. Water, planting materials, and dirty soil all have a role to the spread of Panama sickness. (Fig. 1).

3.1.2 Black Sigatoka

Another serious disease wreaking havoc on banana plantations is black sigatoka. Mycosphaerella fijiensis is the fungus that causes it. It primarily affects the leaves of banana plants, limiting their capacity for photosynthetic energy and, as a result, fruit output. This illness spreads swiftly in warm, humid environments. Tropical habitats are particularly susceptible.

The symptoms of black Sigatoka, the leaves are turned into black and random blotches on the leaves which affect the leaves bending. In severe cases the leaves die, loss of the strength of plant and photosynthesis production of fruit also less. Management of diseases on banana leaves adopts chemical pesticide treatments and cultural practices. The continued infections are dangerous to the farmer's loss of productivity and maintaining the crop with good management strategies is necessary for the best yielding of banana crops. The recent advancements of DL models to detect diseases and provide optimal solutions to farmers to improve the productivity of fruits which are state-of-the-art models to enhance the diagnosis and reduce the illness of plants.

Fig. 1 **a** Xamthomonas **b** Segatoka **c** Pseudostem weevil **d** Potassium deficiency **e** Panama disease **f** Healthy **g** Bacterial soft rot **h** Banana aphids

3.2 Nutritional Deficiencies

Banana cultivation constitutes a serious risk of nutritional deficiency that results in poor plant which results in stunted growth, bad fruits, and general crop diseases. Magnesium and potassium these types of nutrients, such as scarce nutrients are mostly associated with deficiency that affects the growth of a banana plant. Potassium is an important macronutrient that helps plants develop and grow as a result of its role in enhancing productivity. Functions that are related to physiological tasks such as enzyme activation, osmotic balance maintenance, and aiding in water movements. Low potassium levels or so-called "potassium hunger" in banana plants can be very detrimental. This occurs in different studies of fruit development and vegetal growth [14]. The phenomenon of "leaf scorching" occurs in banana plants where the leaves turn yellow. One sign of potassium deficiency is chlorosis, i.e., yellowing of leaves and brownish tones occurring at leaf margins [15]. Furthermore, leaves may emerge. Dead-looking tissue at the edges of the so-called "burnt" areas. A lack of uniformity in the ripening process may arise due to this scarce availability. Poor fruit setting, and low blossom formation and its effects on the fruits decrease quality and productivity.

3.2.1 Impact of Diseases and Deficiencies on Yield and Overall Crop Health

Financial viability of an individual farmer can be significantly affected by diseases and starvation for the crops' nutrients, as well as the crop yield for bananas. Moreover, these challenges significantly cut down their productivity and life too, and food security in communities that highly depend on banana agriculture. Such diseases like Black Sigatoka and Panama could completely eliminate bananas in fields, thus decreasing production. The causative agent of Panama disease in banana plants is Fusarium oxysporum. Finally, they wither and die at last, cup fungus. TR4 attacks the famous Cavendish banana, reducing its yield by 100 percent in infested farms [2]. Likewise, the fungus Mycosphaeella fijiensis [16] lowers the capacity of Black Sigatoka leaves to perform photosynthesis, thereby having a direct negative influence on the production of high-quality fruits. Additionally, yield losses and also disregarding harmed areas will arise due to not sustainable disease management costs which further decrease the profits. Consequently, this may lead to disruptions in earnings and an unstable economy in some areas as well as reduced food nutrition supply which is highly dangerous. Especially potassium and magnesium lacks have a very strong effect on the plant's growth and reduce crop yields. Potassium being short leads to an impact on essential physiological systems and fruit maturity and size. However, a magnesium deficiency stifles photosynthesis, decreasing energy output and overall plant growth [17]. Secondly, nutrient shortages weaken a plant's immunity and resistance to diseases and harsh environments. The plants that have a compromised or weak condition are more prone to disease outbreaks being more susceptible to the infectious agents. The health cycle does not favor crops anymore, with diseases cumulating together with nutrition cases.

4 YOLO: An Overview

They also created a key advancement in computer vision towards object identification called YOLO, which means you only look once. Unlike conventional identification approaches, YOLO features a novel methodology of object detection, which makes it appropriate for instantaneous deployments such as clinical diagnosis of diseases and food shortage cases experienced by farmers.

4.1 The YOLO Procedure and Its Ability to Recognize Objects

In simple terms, the YOLO method can predict many metric regulations both probabilities of classes and object limitations, with only one network executed. A one-shot detection framework is used to achieve this. This is not like in two-stage approaches that involve separate procedures for the identification of regions and object classification. Yolo divides an input image into grids such that each grid contains predicted bounding boxes and their associated probabilities. Through the use of this new methodology, YOLO is able to provide higher accuracy and real-time processing speed. The use of YOLO for detecting objects, especially on still or video frames, gives more accurate results. It enables the detection of multiple objects that belong to different categories of size and orientation. It is usable with regards to many different parameters that could be integrated in a single run, and hence, enhancing applicability.

However, surprisingly, YOLO is able to pinpoint things even when they are darkened or intersect with other items. The power lies at the core of complex and multiscale characteristics drawn into several layers of one particular neural network. The other significant aspect of YOLO's approach is known as anchor boxes, whose role is to enable this algorithm to become prepared for various shapes and sized bounding boxes thus accommodating numerous sorts of item classes.

4.2 *Advantages of YOLO*

Detection in a Single Pass: Unlike the others, YOLO is one single detection network. This also enhances speed, which eliminates extra computations during processing. B verbo de acuerdo con la normatividad jurídica del ámbito judicial de acuerdo con la normalatividad jurídca del ámbito judiciario.

YOLO's single-pass mode is useful for quick image and video assessment. This is of immense importance in early detection applications for diseases and malnutrition in crops [3].

Exceptional precision: The reason for this is that, Yolo has the capability of extraction of multiscale characteristics as well as contextual data. Anchor boxes are used to improve object localization accuracy [3, 18]. Training from start to finish: YOLO combines locating and classifying in a single process. The comprehensive approach helps the network understand the environment locally as well as globally, thus improving forecast precision. Yolo is great with multiple object classification.

Occlusion Resistant: This aspect makes YOLO very robust in cases of instance occludes and overlapping instances thus improving object detection.

The adaptability of YOLO's architecture allows applications beyond object detection. This means that it can be integrated into segmenting pictures or tracking events. Moreover, YOLO exhibits flexibility which makes its application straightforward due to its simpleness. Pre-trained models, as well as open-source implementations, aid its usability.

YOLO is ideal for use in real-world settings especially in time-sensitive fields like in agriculture owing to its accuracy and real-time processing.

5 Data

5.1 Dataset Overview

Dataset included the pictures downloaded from various reliable platforms like Mendeley Data and Kaggle were used to distinguish and categorize different banana diseases and nutrient deficiencies. This forms a big model which utilizes the data coming from different sources that improves its robustness. The dataset of this study comprised of the banana leaf data sets available in mendeley dataset and kaggle dataset. These datasets provide a comprehensive view of the problems that banana crops confront, taking into account both disease and nutritional inadequacies. The Kaggle dataset is divided into three basic categories: Disease in leaves (segaoka, xanthomonas, green leaf). Further, the Mendeley reference presents broader perspectives on challenges with regard to banana farms. It demonstrates soft rot, banana's fruit scarring beetle diseases, black sigatoka (Panama disease), yellow Panama, and other such items like these as resources. Besides, this health disorder has also been incorporated to the list of new diseases like the case of nutrition failure and potassium deficiency. It is meant to make the definition of many enumerated banana crops. The merging data set including training and test images contains about 8,000–9,000 images which made the problem easier.

These are the large leaf diseases and they comprise those that target on banana plants. Also, the Mendaley data covers other banana plantation problems apart from the scope. It depicts certain plant diseases like 'bacterial soft rot', 'banana fruit scarring beetle' and many more including banana aphids, black Sigatoka, yellow Sigatoka, and potassium deficiency. It is a pioneering approach towards the solution to the problem of nutritional deficiency, combining black sigatoka and yellow sigatoka into one category. Such consolidation simplifies knowledge, and improves classifications and data managing, covering all aspects related to banana leaf diseases. Combining Kaggle datasets with Mendeley data increases the number of classes and the size of the dataset to allow training of better algorithms that can reliably determine and label products in banana fields as faced by the complicated issue. From there, it evolves into an integrated dataset upon which ongoing research efforts towards finding viable solutions are based.

5.2 Data Gathering and Modification

A rigorous preprocessing and augmentation procedure was performed on the assembled dataset for banana sickness and deficiency to improve the model's generalization capabilities and alleviate the concerns of overfitting and underfitting. This pipeline includes a number of strategies that boost the diversity and unpredictability of the dataset in order to guarantee that the machine learning algorithm can learn to spot patterns in a variety of actual settings.

5.2.1 Crop Rotation, Flipping, Scaling, and Cropping

These strategies were frequently used to introduce variations in the location, orientation, and size of objects in photographs. Trimming, expanding, tilting (horizontally and vertically), and crop rotation all produce distinct visual viewpoints that reflect real-world situations and equip the model to handle things of various sizes and shapes.

5.2.2 Color Saturation Adjustment

A wider range of lighting situations may be viewed by adjusting the color saturation of the photographs in the collection. This modification makes the model less sensitive to changes in lighting, which is crucial in real-world circumstances.

5.2.3 Perspective Change and Noise Addition

Images were subjected to perspective shifts that replicated many views in order to mimic the complexity of external situations. In addition, artificial noise was applied to some of the photos to improve the model's noise resistance and capacity to recognize objects in the face of environmental disruptions.

5.2.4 Random Image Perturbations

The dataset's fluctuations were boosted by picking randomly and disrupting a collection of photos. Small rotations, translations, and distortions were used to facilitate adaptability to diverse input circumstances.

The methodic refining of the information enhances the predictability of the model on many kinds of events.

Circumstances. Replication of such a complex and unpredictable natural system as found in the real-world agriculture. Such approaches are justified in light of such situations. The data set can be made viable for accurate analysis. Adjustments were made in a controlled manner to enhance detection and classification under various scenarios. The risk of underfitting was greatly reduced through increasing the size as well as the variety of the dataset. Overfitting: The first issue is "overfitting" whereby there is a high accuracy (when the model predicts on trained data but poor performance in new information. The problem is that the model does not understand the hidden order of events). Whether this model works in resolving actual-world issues consistently to make it an essential instrument in diagnosing disorders and defects in bananas.

The use of purification and reinforcement methods portrays commitment towards a robust and flexible model.

It can provide the correct information about the status of banana crops at the right time since this is quite imperative influence on the agricultural business.

6 Disease and Deficiency Detection Model

6.1 Model Framework and Alterations

Notably, this YOLO family of detection models (version 8) can detect fragmentations as well as objects in the images simultaneously. Similar to the structural organization of YOLOv5, the YOLOv8 has a forehead foundation, and the spine components. The design of its backbone has undergone significant improvements, especially in its convolutional layers. Similarly, a higher sensitivity detecting head that has been integrated. This makes YOLOv8 a possible rival in real-time object detection needs.

For example, YOLOv8 can support advanced computer vision techniques like instance segmentation. This feature enables the model to correctly recognize a huge number of items in photos or videos. YOLOv8 was developed on the Darknet 53, for the backbone network, which is faster and more accurate than its predecessor, YOLOv7. In contrast to earlier versions, YOLOv8 recognizes head-predicted bounding boxes using an anchor-free technique. This technical change, paired with a bigger feature map and an enhanced convolutional network, leads to the mechanism's enhanced precision and processing speed. Another approach used by the model to improve its capacity to distinguish objects of various sizes is feature pyramid networks. The user-friendly application programming interface, also called the API, of YOLOv8 allows for smooth integration with a wide variety of programs and frameworks. This characteristic makes it considerably more interesting to developers and specialists looking to design reliable item recognition systems.

In previous YOLOv8 rounds, stochastic gradient descent (SGD) was often utilized to optimize classification problems. However, in the most recent model repetition, a modification was made: the Adam optimizer is now used instead of the prior one. This optimizer variation is well-known for its variable learning rates and good handling of narrow gradients, which improves confluence during development.

6.2 Training and Testing

The YOLOv8 model undergoes training across 50 epochs, with each epoch representing a full dataset loop. The input photos are significantly reduced to a fixed dimension of 640 pixels during training. Normalization of input picture size during the training phase as well as inference makes it possible to improve the consistency. A specific value for the accurate seed—two—guarantees the repeatability of model results. To ensure repeatable results across runs this seed value is used and constructed for initialization of the model starting conditions as well as any other random processes involved. A dropout layer has been added to the YOLOv8 design as an extra feature. With a dropout probability of 0.12, this dropout layer is added. Dropout is a regularization technique that, in order to avoid overfitting, randomly deactivates a portion of neurons during each training cycle, promoting model generalization.

With a mixup coefficient of 1, the YOLOv8 training process takes dataset mixup into account. Dataset mixup is the process of merging pairs of pictures and their corresponding labels to generate new training examples. By using this technique, the model becomes less sensitive to variations in the training set and more regular. During training, a viewpoint change parameter with a value of 0.6 is also included. This option controls how much perspective transformation is applied to the training photos. Perspective modifications, which mimic different viewing angles and orientations, improve the model's resilience in detecting items from different viewpoints.

6.2.1 Model Training

The exported model displayed noteworthy performance metrics after 50 training epochs with a batch size of 16 and the previously mentioned hyperparameters (including the Adam optimizer, input image size of 640 pixels, seed value of 2, dropout layer with a probability of 0.12, dataset mixup coefficient of 1, and perspective change factor of 0.6) (Fig. 2).

The top-1 accuracy of 0.9 means that, of all the predictions the model made, it correctly identified the top-ranked class in about 90% of the cases. This suggests that the most important class in the predictions were identified with a high degree of

Fig. 2 Validation batch with labels

Fig. 3 Validation batch prediction

accuracy and competency. On the other hand, the top-5 accuracy of 1 indicates that the model correctly identified the top-5 predicted classes for every occurrence with a flawless accuracy of 100%. This outstanding result displays the model's reliability and in-depth grasp of the captures' objects. (Fig. 3).

It is essential to recall that a top-5 accuracy of 1 is exceedingly rare and unique, indicating that the model properly identifies the primary class and catches the complexities and complexity of the succeeding likely classes. This level of accuracy may be due to the long training approach, the utilization of cutting-edge techniques such as perspective and dataset mixture, and technical developments like as the dropout layer, all of which combine to a more refined and flexible model. (Fig. 4).

7 Results and Discussions

7.1 Model Performance Evaluation

The exported YOLOv8 model demonstrated exceptional performance metrics after a rigorous training process that lasted 50 epochs, used a batch size of 16, and included the specified hyperparameters, such as the use of the Adam optimizer, an input image

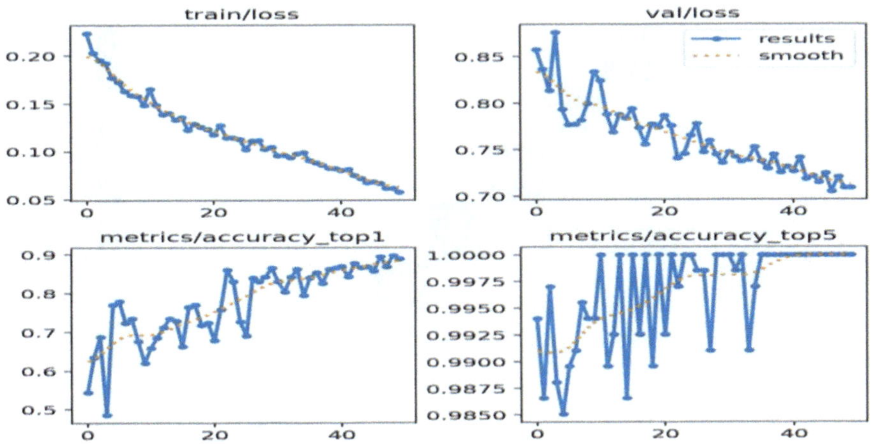

Fig. 4 Training metrics

size of 640 pixels, a seed value of 2 for replication, a dropout layer with a probability of 0.12, a dataset entangled ratio set to 1, and a perspective change factor of 0.6.

7.1.1 On an average instance, it has a precision "one shot." rating of 0.9 and thus the model is able to correctly detect the main class for about 90%. This great result showed that the model distinguished the main object very well in the photos. The framework is very reliable in predicting the highest priority real events in practice which are like object recognition and classification with the top-1 accuracy being very high at above 50%. 7.1.2 Highest accuracy (1.2). Top-5 Accuracy Score of 1.0 is a very good performance. It shows how accurate it was in identifying the best class and capturing the complexities associated with the following five classes that were predicted. Therefore, it constitutes a considerable amount of information about the objects shown, that goes beyond identification only and suggests something of the surrounding environment as well.

7.2 Insights and Implications

The outstanding performance of the YOLOv8 model may be attributed to the precise decision to use hyperparameters and architectural considerations. The use of the Adam optimizer, which also incorporated gradient handling and tunable learning rates, resulted in smoother convergence during training. The uniform input picture size of 640 pixels allowed for consistent processing, allowing the model to recognize objects at varying scales with confidence.

It is critical in research and development settings to guarantee that results can be repeated frequently, which is why a fidelity seed value of 2 is utilized. The integration

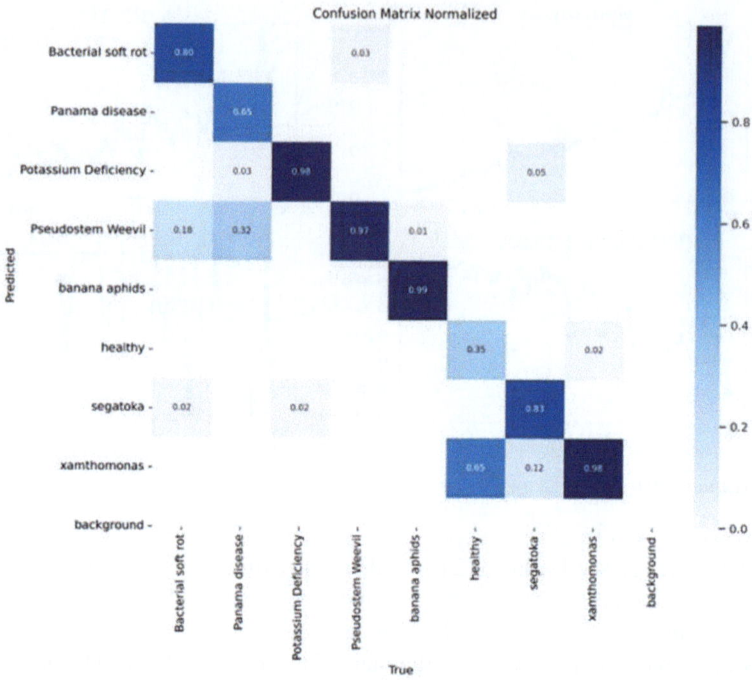

Fig. 5 Confusion matrix of normalization

of a dropout layer with a probability of 0.12 contributes to the model's regularization, avoidance of overfitting, and predictability. (Fig. 5).

The application of dataset entangled with a coefficient of 1 boosted data diversity and alleviated concerns about overfitting, even with the use of the perspective shift factor with a value of 0.6 duplicated a range of perspectives and improved the model's resilience.

7.3 Comparison with Previous Versions

As opposed to previous versions, YOLOv8's architecture changes and updated hyper-parameters led to improved accuracy. An updated convolutional network combined with a bigger feature map and a superior version of the anchor-free detection head led to the success behind this excellent predictive model.

8 Conclusion

Finally, there's YOLOv8, a different variant of the YOLO family that excels at item detection and classification. Such a model for scoring one such time resulted in a successful one such score with the first five parameters set to zero and the second to one in 50 training cycles. It can infer information about some major objects based on some hidden classes, making it a competitive framework in the real-time scene analysis industry. The same could possibly be said for resulting techniques and procedures which include gathering information, perspective changing, and Adam optimizers, which increase model efficiency and performance.

9 Future Scope

When contrasted with prior models, the YOLOv8 model contains an enormous number of new features, and it is evolving further to provide high possibilities for enhancing detection for future research and development:

(1) Domain Adaptation: At times, adjustments to fit in another environment and circumstances are measured by the way it behaves.
(2) Semantic Segmentation: The model applies comprise segmentation whereby one fully understands the interactive nature of different environmental elements.
(3) Real-time applications: This can offer the chance of using intelligent machines, cars, and surveillance systems as practical improvements for the actual enhancement in the current detection capability of the model.
(4) Ensemble Techniques: Combination of such models with the benefits of YOLOv8 may lead to a more precise identification system.
(5) Ensemble Techniques: The models are much more accurate and robust which when used together with the advantages of YOLOv8 may lead to an even more precise system.
(6) Ensemble Techniques: Accuracy and robustness can be further enhanced by combining the strengths associated with YOLOv8 and models.
(7) Transfer Learning: Cross-activity and cross-domain transfer learning of model's resolution using YOLOv8. Boost overall efficiency.
(8) A decrease in the hardware specifications will increase the acceptability of the model as a working system on low capacity devices because they may be adapted.
(9) Experimenting with tuning techniques may yield modest improvements, in efficiency and consistency.

References

1. Qu F, Figueiredo E, Mekonnen A (2019) Banana diseases: Biotechnology and applications of dna markers for diagnosis and management. In: Figueiredo E, Mekonnen A (ed.) Biotechnology and Plant Disease Management, pp 369–392. Academic Press
2. Cruz JA, D´ıaz JM, Dom´ınguez A (2019) Evaluation of several machine learning methods for the detection of diseases in banana plants. Comput Electron Agric 164:104882
3. Redmon J, Divvala S, Girshick R, Farhadi A (2016) You only look once: Unified, real-time object detection. In: Proceedings of the IEEE conference on computer vision and pattern recognition (CVPR), pp 779–788
4. Smith AB et al (2020) Multi-class banana disease detection using deep learning. J Agric Comput Sci 15(3):184–195
5. Kumar S et al (2019) A comprehensive study of banana deficiency detection using convolutional neural networks. Comput Electron Agric 165:104943
6. Li Y et al (2018) Deep learning-based banana disease classification with limited training data. Comput Electron Agric 151:12–16
7. Rahman T et al (2021) Improved detection of banana diseases and nutrient deficiencies using transfer learning. Comput Electron Agric 185:106158
8. Gupta V et al (2017) Banana disease detection in field conditions: Challenges and opportunities. Int J Agric Biol Eng 10(6):132–138
9. Patel A et al (2020) Enhancing banana disease detection through ensemble learning. Biosys Eng 191:47–60
10. Gupta S et al (2019) Comparative analysis of deep learning architectures for banana disease detection. Comput Electron Agric 162:35–44
11. Kumar R et al (2018) Challenges in real-time banana disease detection using deep learning. J Agric Sci Technol 20:995–1006
12. Ploetz RC (2015) Panama disease: An old nemesis rears its ugly head part 1. The Banana 32(1):4–5
13. Dita MA, Waalwijk C, Buddenhagen IW, Souza MT (2018) A molecular diagnostic for tropical race 4 of the banana fusarium wilt pathogen. Plant Pathol 67(5):1055–1062
14. Marschner P (2012) Marschner's mineral nutrition of higher plants. Academic Press
15. Samarakoon AB, Gamage SNK, Werellagama DRIB (2016) Potassium nutrition of banana (musa spp.): a review. J Natl Sci Found Sri Lanka 44(3):191–203
16. Ploetz RC (2015) Fusarium wilt of banana. Phytopathology 105(12):1512–1521
17. Ploetz RC, Pegg KG (2000) Impact of diseases on export and smallholder production of banana. In: Jones DR (ed) Diseases of Banana, Abaca and Enset´, pp 359–374. CABI Publishing
18. Redmon J, Farhadi A (2018) Yolov3: An incremental improvement. *arXiv preprint* arXiv:1804.02767

Enhanced Salient Object Detection from Single Haze Images

Gayathri Dhara and Ravi Kant Kumar

1 Introduction

"Dehazing" is defined as the process of removing or reducing the effects of haze or atmospheric interference from an image. This is often done to improve the visibility and clarity of objects in the image. Reports on statistics provided by the Ministry of Public Security have indicated that adverse weather conditions, specifically fog and haze, are a significant contributing factor in more than 10 percent of road traffic accidents. These conditions severely diminish visibility due to the existence of suspended atmospheric particles, which absorb and scatter light. In recent decades, various defogging algorithms have been introduced to address this problem. Image dehazing technology has emerged as a promising solution, allowing for the partial restoration of color and visibility in single haze images. However, it's worth noting that while the dehazing process significantly improves the identification of prominent regions, it also enhances background information. Consequently, the current state-of-the-art saliency models lack accuracy in detecting the true salient object in the defogged image. Typically, haze images exhibit diminished contrast and resolution, thereby rendering the extraction of visual features exceedingly challenging. Consequently, saliency detection in haze imagery confronts a multitude of issues: First and foremost, the effectiveness of conventional methods used for extracting characteristics cannot ensure the precision of the results obtained from detection, due to the fact that the majority of these characteristics become invalid when visibility is restricted. Secondly, the scarcity of edge and contour information

G. Dhara (✉) · R. K. Kumar
Department of Computer Science and Engineering, SRM University-AP, Amaravati, Andhra Pradesh 522020, India
e-mail: gayathri_dhara@srmap.edu.in

R. K. Kumar
e-mail: ravikant.k@srmap.edu.in

K. Kumar Singh et al. (eds.), *Machine Vision and Augmented Intelligence*, Lecture Notes in Electrical Engineering 1211, https://doi.org/10.1007/978-981-97-4359-9_43

within haze imagery results in minimal differentiation between foreground and background, thereby impeding the identification of salient objects. Conventional methods for determining saliency have predominantly adhered to Itti's model [1], which is based on multiscale features and center-surrounded contrast. Following the principles of the human visual system (HVS), contrast emerges as a fundamental factor in the computation of visual saliency. Contemporary models determine the prominence of specific image areas by analyzing contrast, considering either a local or global viewpoint. Haze images, typically characterized by low contrast and resolution, pose challenges in extracting visual features. Consequently, saliency detection in haze images encounters several issues: (1) Traditional feature extraction methods cannot guarantee the accuracy of detection results, as most features turn ineffective under low visibility conditions. (2) The absence of edge and contour information in haze images results in a minimal distinction between foreground and background, rendering the identification of salient objects arduous. Local techniques calculate the saliency between each region of an image and its immediate vicinity. Rigas et al. [2] developed a saliency map by extracting image characteristics using local sparse coding. Nouri et al. [3] represented the mesh saliency by employing local adaptive patches. These models have a tendency to emphasize prominent objects near edges rather than the entire regions. On the other hand, global approaches estimate the saliency between each region and the entire image. In our previous model [4], saliency was computed through a global contrast measure and color distribution. Zhang et al. [5] introduced a saliency model based on a non-local anisotropic diffusion equation. These global models are able to obtain a uniform saliency region.

2 Related Work

Recently, the computer vision community has been interested in the task of dehazing images. Numerous approaches have been put forth by researchers to address the challenge of enhancing single images afflicted by haze. These methods are broadly classified into two distinct groups: prior-based methods and learning-based methods. Prior-based techniques employ pre-existing statistical information and manually crafted features to remove haze from images. Among these methods, Dark channel prior (DCP) [6] stands out as one of the most prominent representatives. DCP operates under the assumption that images with haze may possess greatly low intensities in at least one-color channel. On the other hand, color attenuation prior (CAP) [7] leverages the difference between the brightness and saturation of hazy images to create a linear model that estimates scene depth. Another hypothesis put forth by [8] suggests that the colors of a haze-free image can be effectively approximated using a limited number of distinct colors. While prior-based methods have demonstrated notable performance in single image dehazing, their reliance on handcrafted features and prior knowledge hinders their ability to achieve satisfactory results in various scenes. In recent times, the deep learning approach [9] has made significant progress and showcased its remarkable capability in solving the single image dehazing problem. A few deep learning techniques continue to depend on the atmospheric scattering model. For instance, DehazeNet [10] was proposed as the first end-to-end CNN to learn the transmission map, following the traditional procedure and atmospheric scattering formulation but utilizing CNN to estimate the transmission map. Similarly, a novel multiscale neural network (MSCNN) [11] was later introduced to estimate the transmission map from the hazy image. Differing from both, [10, 11], AOD-Net employs a lightweight neural network to jointly estimate the transmittance and atmospheric light. [12, 13].

3 Proposed Method

In this section, we initially elucidate the comprehensive framework structure (as shown in Fig. 1). The suggested approach uses the haze removal algorithm as the first step and then applies the salient object detection step.

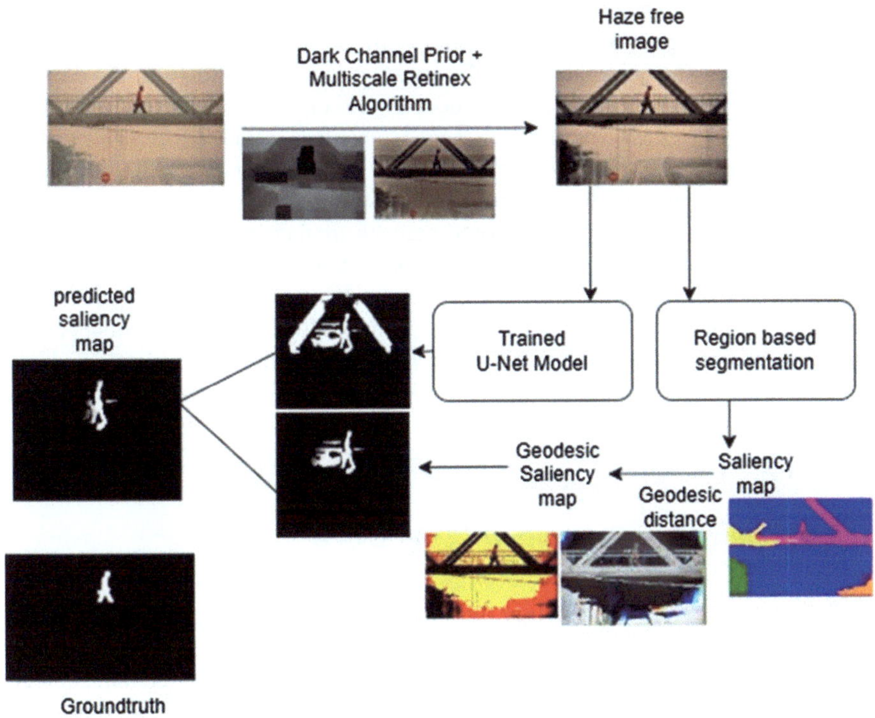

Fig. 1 Depicts a visual representation of the suggested approach

3.1 Image Dehazing

The dark channel prior is calculated on the original hazy image, which represents the scene as it was captured with the effects of haze, fog, or other atmospheric conditions. For each pixel in the image, a local patch is defined around that pixel and the dark channel is computed in the local patch. The dark channel of a patch is the channel (R, G, or B) with the lowest intensity value. This means that for each pixel, the minimum value among the R, G, and B channels is found within its local patch. After calculating the dark channel for all patches in the image, the global minimum value is calculated among all the dark channels. This global minimum represents an estimate of the atmospheric light in the scene. The transmission map calculated is inversely related to the dark channel, so areas with a low dark channel value correspond to high transmission (less haze), and areas with a high dark channel value correspond to low transmission (more haze). With the atmospheric light and transmission map estimated, these values are used to remove the haze or fog from the original image. The [13] is used to calculate the dark channel prior. To further enhance the haze removal process, the Multiscale Retinex algorithm is applied to remove the influence of haze by emphasizing the illumination component of an image.

The process involves multiscale decomposition, which can be summarized as follows: The input hazy image is initially transformed into the logarithmic domain, enhancing the visibility of low-contrast details. A set of Gaussian filters at multiple scales is applied to the logarithmic image. Each filter extracts different levels of details, ranging from fine structures to global illumination. The filtered images obtained from the multiscale decomposition represent the illumination component at different scales. These illumination components are then combined or averaged to create an enhanced illumination representation. The reflectance component, representing the intrinsic properties of the scene, is obtained by dividing the original image by the enhanced illumination component. Multiscale Retinex enhances the perception of fine details, making it valuable for scene analysis, object detection, and feature extraction. The resulting dehazed image will be with improved visibility and contrast.

3.2 Saliency Map Generation Using U-Net

The dehazed image is given as input for the U-Net model [14]. We viewed saliency detection as a task of semantic segmentation, aiming to identify the visually dominant regions or objects in an image. This objective aligns with the goal of localizing objects in semantic segmentation. Both tasks involve comprehending and recognizing significant regions in an image. Additionally, saliency detection and semantic segmentation take into consideration the contextual information of an image. In saliency detection, the context is the vital factor in determining the relative importance of regions within an image. Similarly, semantic segmentation relies on contextual information to accurately assign labels to pixels based on the surrounding regions. The U-Net-like architecture has demonstrated great potential in various image analysis tasks, such as semantic segmentation. However, directly applying this architecture to visual saliency detection may not fully exploit the distinctive characteristics of salient regions. In order to tackle this issue, we propose an enhanced U-Net-like network that incorporates spatial attention into the design of the encoder and de-coder. The model suggested in this paper takes inspiration from the U-Net architecture, a well-known deep learning model used in semantic segmentation tasks. The model was implemented using Python 3 and TensorFlow, a widely-used framework. Training and testing were conducted on a single NVIDIA Tesla V100 – SXM2 GPU with 16 GB of memory. The U-Net model is trained on DUTS-TR dataset. The model is compiled using the Adam optimizer, initialized with a learning rate of 0.001. The chosen loss function is'Binary Cross Entropy,' and the evaluation metric selected is accuracy. Three callbacks are defined in this model and are:

Learning Rate Scheduler: This adjusts the learning rate during training based on the schedule defined earlier. The initial learning rate set to 0.001.

Early Stopping: This callback observes the validation loss and halts the training process if there is no improvement in the loss over a specific number of epochs (patience = 5), thereby safeguarding against over-fitting.

Model Checkpoint: This callback saves the best model during training based on validation loss. By leveraging the power of Tensorflow, and our carefully chosen training and optimization strategies, the proposed enhanced U-Net model, achieved improvement in detecting salient objects. With the above parameters, the model achieved a training accuracy of 0.98 and 0.94 testing accuracy, respectively. A saliency map is generated at this stage. Subsequently, we use the CNN, to extract features from the dehazed image and pass these inputs to a selective search algorithm to calculate the objectness. The geodesic saliency map is calculated using geodesic distance, considering both spatial proximity and feature similarity. The saliency map generated using U-Net model and the geodesic saliency map are integrated to yield the final saliency map.

3.3 Segmentation Using Watershed Algorithm

The watershed algorithm is a fundamental technique utilized in salient object detection for accurately segmenting the foreground object from the background. In this algorithm, the image is conceptualized as a topographic surface, where the brightness of the image corresponds to the elevation of the surface.

The algorithm operated by gradually flooding the image from the lowest intensity values, leading to catchment basins that stand for distinct objects within the image. With the implementation of the watershed algorithm to a thresholded saliency map, salient object detection algorithms can attain accurate segmentation of the foreground object from the background. To promote the accuracy of the segmentation results, the minimum directional backgroundness score is applied to the watershed segmented image. This step aids to eliminate any residual background that may remain after the initial segmentation, thereby enhancing the accuracy and reliability of the resulting saliency maps. Image segmentation involves dividing an image into regions or groups based on similar characteristics or features [15]. When objects in an image are well separated, their pixel intensities show significant differences, enabling easy distinction. However, in cases where objects are densely clustered, classifying them becomes challenging due to minimal variations among their neighboring pixels. In such scenarios, the watershed algorithm proves to be beneficial.

The watershed segmentation, developed by [16] in mathematical morphology, is a region-based method that comes with advantages such as simplicity, speed, and the ability to obtain a complete division of images [17]. By treating the image as a surface with high-intensity pixels representing peaks and low-intensity pixels representing valleys, the watershed transform identifies catchment basins and watershed ridge lines. To apply the watershed algorithm, an RGB image is first converted into a binary image. Otsu thresholding, which divides the intensity peaks into two equal parts, is commonly employed to determine the optimal threshold. In many cases, morphological operations are used as a preprocessing step, such as closing to fill tiny holes in objects and opening to remove noise. To eliminate background noise, the openings' operation is employed. Objects in the image are labeled with 1 after applying the Otsu threshold, while the background is labeled with 0. However, caution must be exercised when selecting the background due to imperfect thresholds. To ensure that the background is accurately represented, dilation is performed, extending the coverage and maintaining the integrity of the background. In this case, three iterations of dilation are considered to strike a balance between coverage and preserving the true shapes of objects.

To identify the sure foreground, erosion, or distance maps can be utilized. Although erosion is effective, it may cause smaller objects to be washed away, resulting in the loss of important information. Hence, for this particular segmentation application aimed at obtaining individual objects, the Distance Transform is preferred. By using the distance transform, sub-regions can be identified, and objects (labeled as 1's) in a binary map are assigned values representing the minimum distance between them and their closest backgrounds (labeled as 0's).

Foreground objects are further separated by applying a filter to remove distances less than half of the maximum distance (max(dist)) obtained from the background. This step helps refine the segmentation and distinguish individual objects more accurately. With the sure foreground and background identified, the unsure region can be easily determined. Watershed segmentation is performed by subtracting the background from the foreground. However, before executing the watershed segmentation, three essential pieces of information need to be provided. Using the connected component algorithm, each individual object in the sure foreground can be identified once all the required information is available. The image is scanned by this algorithm, and the pixels are grouped together according to their connectivity. Each pixel within a component is assigned a unique label relative to its component. The unknown region is marked with zero, as it already has the label 0.

Since the unknown values are already labeled as 0, it is preferable to assign numbers other than 0 to represent the sure background. This labeling scheme ensures clear differentiation between the known foreground, known background, and unknown regions.

3.4 Geodesic Reconstruction to Suppress the Over-Segmentation

Despite the fact that the watershed produces over-segmented images, the contours appear to be correct. As a result of Beucher's work [18], a geodesic reconstruction was developed. The plane consists of two closed sets A and B. D is the distance between a and b in A that is determined by the geodesic path between them. The transformation that corresponds to the connected components A and B is given by $D_A^{\infty}(B) = [(B \oplus C) \cap A]^{\infty}$ where the morphological dilation of the lattice is $\oplus$, and the unit ball of the lattice is C. Using a lower threshold value, a binary transform is transformed into a gray-tone transformation. Consider two functions f and d, the geodesic reconstruction off in d is given by its lower threshold as $\left[D_d^{\infty}(f)\right]_{\lambda} = D_{[d]_{\lambda}}^{\infty}\left([f]_{\lambda}\right)$ As in the binary case, we call reconstruction off under d by dilation. The function f is often called the marker function or markers. The geodesic erosion of infinite size, the gray-scale reconstruction of f over d by erosion. The geodesic erosion behaves in a complementary way, the functions use their upper threshold and is given as $[E_d^{\infty}(f)]^{\lambda} = D_{[d]}^{\infty}\left([f]\right)^{\lambda}$. Here, the marker function is d. The two saliency maps from U-Net step and map generated using region-based segmentation are combined to yield into a final saliency map.

4 Experimental Results

The proposed algorithm is assessed on a dataset of haze images, comprising 200 haze images with binary ground truths. Our model is compared to nine state-of-the-art saliency models, namely low rank matrix recovery (LR) model [19], context-aware (CA) model [20], patch distinction (PD) model [21], graph-based manifold ranking (GBMR) model [22], saliency optimization (SO) model [23], cellular automata (BSCA) model [24], bootstrap learning (BL) model [25], spatiochromatic context (SC) model [26], and generic pro- motion of diffusion-based (GP) model [27], dark channel prior SOD [28]. The performance evaluation is carried out using four metrics. We adopted the results as a reference from [28]. We assess the precision, recall, and F-measure rate to evaluate the proposed approach. "Precisely, precision precisely measures the accuracy of the resulting saliency map, while recall assesses how comprehensively the detected salient objects are captured. The F-measure quantifies the balanced harmonic relationship between precision and recall. Our model's

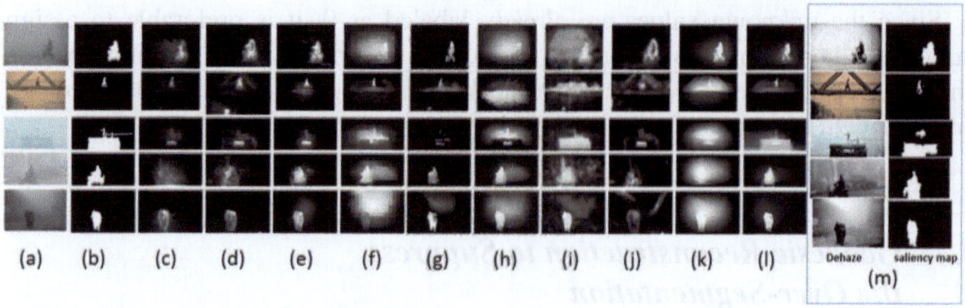

Fig. 2 Depicts qualitative results of proposed model with ten state-of-the-art methods

substantial superiority over others is vividly demonstrated in the quantitative comparisons illustrated in Fig. 2. The subsequent measure, is referred to as AUC (Area Under the Curve). The score is determined by computing the area beneath the TPR-FPR curve. A saliency model nearing a score of 1 is considered close to perfection. Lastly, the metric measures the mean absolute error (MAE) score, which assesses the fidelity of the negative saliency assignment. This score quantifies the variance between the saliency map and the ground truth." The area under the curve and MAE scores are given in Table 1. Evidently, the proposed model exhibits comparatively superior performance scores on the haze image dataset. The saliency maps acquired through the different saliency models are showcased in Figure 3. It is evident from a visual examination of Figure 2 that the saliency maps generated by the suggested model closely resemble the actual representation and effectively handle the complex haze images. (LR) model [19], context-aware (CA) model [20], patch distinction (PD) model [21], graph-based manifold ranking (GBMR) model [22], saliency optimization (SO) model [23], cellular automata (BSCA) model [24], bootstrap learning (BL) model [25], spatiochromatic context (SC) model [26], and generic promotion of diffusion-based (GP) model [27], dark channel prior SOD [28].

Table 1 Running time comparisons of different state-of-the-art saliency models with haze dataset

	LR [19]	CA [20]	PD [21]	GBMR [22]	SO [23]	BSCA [24]	BL [25]	SC [26]	GP [27]	SOD [28]	Our method
AUC	0.891	0.944	0.929	0.804	0.810	0.729	0.913	0.846	0.896	0.974	0.982
MAE	0.137	0.157	0.115	0.288	0.103	0.282	0.245	0.139	0.207	0.096	0.079
TIME(s)	73.521	35.426	32.692	1.672	2.570	3.188	91.453	58.628	15.965	9.833	7.432

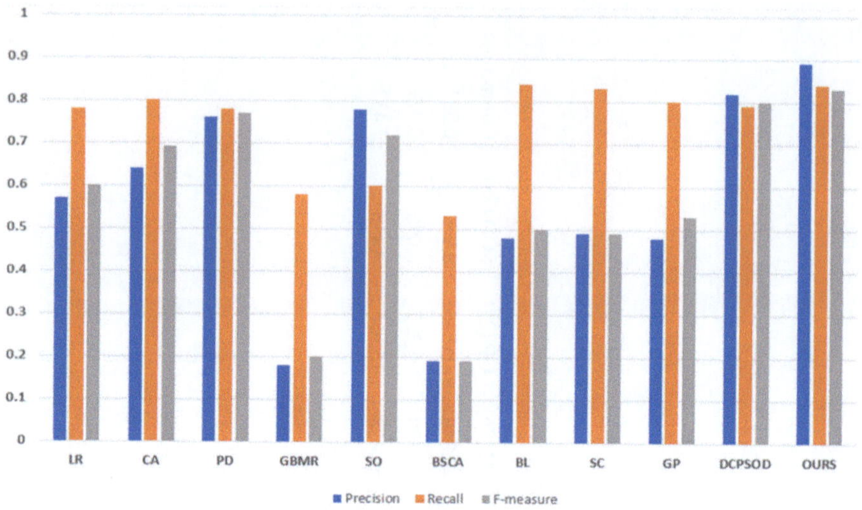

Fig. 3 Precision, recall, F-measure plot

5 Conclusion

In conclusion, our study introduces a robust computational model for salient object detection in challenging hazy environments. We address issues of reduced visibility and contrast through a multistep approach. We begin by detecting haze and utilize the Dark Channel Prior (DCP) which enhances the percentage of visibility and contrast in the image. The use of Multiscale Retinex image enhancement technique helps to correct for non-uniform illumination and restore the image's natural appearance. The U-Net architecture has shown remarkable potential in various image analysis tasks, including semantic segmentation. So, we trained a U-Net architecture for detecting the salient object and a saliency map was created, highlighting salient regions within the dehazed image. Simultaneously, we conduct region-based segmentation based on geodesic distance, considering both spatial proximity and feature similarity, resulting in a geodesic saliency map. Finally, we fuse the saliency maps generated from the U-Net and geodesic saliency computation, yielding an ultimate saliency map that effectively detects salient objects within hazy images. Our method showcases state-of-the-art dehazing and object detection, performance in dehazing making it valuable for a variety of computer vision applications, including autonomous driving, surveillance, and image restoration. The future directions aim at the fusion of Multimodal data and evaluating on more diverse datasets to address a wider range of hazy conditions and scene types.

References

1. Itti L, Koch C, Niebur E (1998) A model of saliency-based visual attention for rapid scene analysis. IEEE Trans Pattern Anal Mach Intell 20(11):1254–1259
2. Rigas I, Economou G, Fotopoulos S (2015) Efficient modeling of visual saliency based on local sparse representation and the use of hamming distance. Comput Vis Image Underst 134:33–45
3. Nouri A, Charrier C, Le´zoray O (2015) Multi-scale mesh saliency with local adaptive patches for viewpoint selection. Signal Process: Image Commun 38:151–166
4. Xu X, Mu N, Chen L, Zhang X (2016) Hierarchical salient object detection model using contrast-based saliency and color spatial distribution. Multimed Tools Appl 75:2667–2679
5. Zhang X, Xu C, Li M, Teng RK (2015) Study of visual saliency detection via nonlocal anisotropic diffusion equation. Pattern Recogn 48(4):1315–1327
6. He K, Sun J, Tang X (2010) Single image haze removal using dark channel prior. IEEE Trans Pattern Anal Mach Intell 33(12):2341–2353
7. Zhu Q, Mai J, Shao L (2015) A fast single image haze removal algorithm using color attenuation prior. IEEE Trans Image Process 24(11):3522–3533
8. Berman D, Avidan S, et al (2016) Non-local image dehazing. In: Proceedings of the IEEE conference on computer vision and pattern recognition, pp 1674–1682
9. LeCun Y, Bengio Y, Hinton G (2015) Deep learning. nature 521(7553):436–444
10. Cai B, Xu X, Jia K, Qing C, Tao D (2016) Dehazenet: An end-to-end system for single image haze removal. IEEE Trans Image Process 25(11):5187–5198
11. Ren W, Liu S, Zhang H, Pan J, Cao X, Yang MH (2016) Single image dehazing via multi-scale convolutional neural networks. In: Computer Vision–ECCV 2016: 14th European Conference, Amsterdam, The Netherlands, October 11–14, 2016, Proceedings, Part II 14. pp 154–169. Springer
12. MATLAB documentation (2023). https://www.mathworks.com/matlabcentral/fileexchange/71386-multiscale-retinex
13. MATLAB documentation (2023). Adina Stoica (2023). Single Image Haze Removal Using Dark Channel Prior (https://www.mathworks.com/matlabcentral/fileexchange/46147-single-image-haze-removal-using-dark-channel-prior), MATLAB Central File Exchange. Retrieved September 22, 2023
14. Ronneberger O, Fischer P, Brox T (2015) U-net: Convolutional networks for biomedical image segmentation. In: Medical image computing and computer-assisted intervention–MICCAI 2015: 18th international conference, Munich, Germany, October 5–9, 2015, Proceedings, Part III 18. pp. 234–241. Springer
15. Fu KS, Mui J (1981) A survey on image segmentation. Pattern Recogn 13(1):3–16
16. Serra J (1982) Image analysis and mathematical morphology. (No Title)
17. Beucher S, Meyer F (2018) The morphological approach to segmentation: the watershed transformation. In: Mathemat ical morphology in image processing, pp 433–481. CRC Press
18. Beucher S (1990) Segmentation d'images et morphologie mathe´matique. Ph.D. thesis, Ecole Nationale Supe´rieure des Mines de Paris
19. Shen X, Wu Y (2012) A unified approach to salient object detection via low rank matrix recovery. In: 2012 IEEE conference on computer vision and pattern recognition, pp 853–860. IEEE
20. Goferman S, Zelnik-Manor L, Tal A (2011) Context-aware saliency detection. IEEE Trans Pattern Anal Mach Intell 34(10):1915–1926
21. Margolin R, Tal A, Zelnik-Manor L (2013) What makes a patch distinct? In: Proceedings of the IEEE conference on computer vision and pattern recognition, pp 1139–1146
22. Yang C, Zhang L, Lu H, Ruan X, Yang MH (2013) Saliency detection via graph-based manifold ranking. In: Proceedings of the IEEE conference on computer vision and pattern recognition, pp 3166–3173
23. Zhu W, Liang S, Wei Y, Sun J (2014) Saliency optimization from robust background detection. In: Proceedings of the IEEE conference on computer vision and pattern recognition, pp 2814–2821

24. Qin Y, Lu H, Xu Y, Wang H (2015) Saliency detection via cellular automata. In: Proceedings of the IEEE conference on computer vision and pattern recognition. pp 110–119
25. Tong N, Lu H, Ruan X, Yang MH (2015) Salient object detection via bootstrap learning. In: Proceedings of the IEEE conference on computer vision and pattern recognition, pp 1884–1892
26. Zhang J, Wang M, Zhang S, Li X, Wu X (2015) Spatiochromatic context modeling for color saliency analysis. IEEE Trans Neural Netw Learn Syst 27(6):1177–1189
27. Jiang P, Vasconcelos N, Peng J (2015) Generic promotion of diffusion-based salient object detection. In: Proceedings of the IEEE international conference on computer vision, pp 217–225
28. Mu N, Xu X, Zhang X (2016) Salient object detection from single haze images via dark channel prior and region co- variance descriptor. In: Intelligent visual surveillance: 4th chinese conference, IVS 2016, Beijing, China, October 19, 2016, Proceedings 4. pp 99–106. Springer

Assessing Crowd Counting Methods: A Comparison Study of MaskR-CNN with ResNet 50 and Convolution Neural Network

Silky Goel, Siddharth Gupta, and Avnish Panwar

1 Introduction

The primary goal of crowd counting is to ascertain the total number of individuals in a congested area, and the expanding field of computer vision facilitates the analysis of crowd behavior and surveillance, detection, and observation of the salient areas in the crowd. The study of crowd counting from a computer vision perspective has several other applications such as tracking people's movements in crowded areas, seeing odd patterns in crowds, and much more [1].

Among the main subjects covered by crowd counts are matters pertaining to public safety. It is possible to manage and regulate the problems associated with large crowds, particularly at political gatherings, religious ceremonies, and public events. Recently, there has been a surge in interest among researchers to address the issue of crowd management and its safety implications. The fastest-growing deep learning applications aid in addressing the previously listed crowd-related problems [2]. Figure 1 represents the crowd images.

One of the major challenges of crowd counting techniques is to accurately count the number of people in a dense crowd and the accuracy of the crowd counting techniques also depends on the quality of the data sources used. Furthermore, environmental factors such as lighting, weather conditions, and occlusions can also affect

S. Goel (✉)
University of Petroleum and Energy Studies, Dehradun, India
e-mail: silkygoel90@gmail.com

S. Gupta · A. Panwar
Indian Institute of Technology, Roorkee, India
e-mail: siddharth_g@bt.iitr.ac.in

A. Panwar
e-mail: panwaravi101@gmail.com

S. Gupta
Graphic Era Deemed to Be University, Dehradun, India

K. Kumar Singh et al. (eds.), *Machine Vision and Augmented Intelligence*, Lecture Notes in Electrical Engineering 1211, https://doi.org/10.1007/978-981-97-4359-9_44

Fig. 1 Crowd counting scene in a mall

the accuracy of crowd counting techniques. Poor lighting conditions can make it difficult to distinguish individuals in a crowd while occlusions such as large structures can obstruct the view of certain areas and make it difficult to analyze the crowd [3]. Another major challenge of crowd counting using image segmentation is that requires a lot of computational complexity and computational power to process large datasets which can be costly and time-consuming. Sometimes it is very difficult to distinguish between similar objects and it can lead to errors in the segmentation process and result in inaccurate counts [4].

Conventional video analytics techniques count individuals by deducting the sum of the number of people entering and leaving. Additionally, the accuracy of traditional approaches decreases once a certain number of people have been counted. When thousands of people are involved, the issue becomes more difficult [5]. Researchers worldwide are gaining a lot of interest in deep learning. There are numerous CNN-based crowd counting initiatives as a result of CNN's in image processing. The use of CNN-based algorithms for crowd counting has advanced significantly. These techniques are the most widely used in contemporary crowd counting research because they perform better than other crowd counting methods in situations involving a variety of various head scales, non-uniform density distributions, and major changes in perspective and scene.

Comparing two important crowd counting research fields is the main goal of the current study. In the first, features are retrieved using Resnet 50 and a Mask region convolution neural network. The second method uses a convolutional neural network. For the aim of crowd counting, both of these techniques have demonstrated excellent performance [6]. For pixel-level segmentation of crowd data, R-CNN is well-known. CNN performs admirably as well, however, it has several drawbacks. Mean absolute error (MAE) and mean square error (MSE) are two of the evaluation metrics that will be applied [7] to quantify the accuracy of the crowd count estimates. By comparing these techniques, we aim to gain insights into their strengths, weaknesses, and overall performance in the context of crowd counting. This research will contribute to the existing body of knowledge in crowd analysis and provide valuable guidance for selecting appropriate techniques for real-world crowd counting applications.

The remainder of this paper is structured as follows: Sect. 2 includes a review of the literature on crowd counting and several deep learning-based approaches. Section 3 presents the information about the dataset used. Section 4 discusses the evaluation metrics that are used to test the models. Section 5 presents the approach and methodology used in the study. Section 6 tabulates the results obtained during the comparison of the models. Finally, Sect. 7 highlights the key findings, limitations, and future research directions in the field of crowd counting techniques.

2 Literature Review

There are many publications on crowd counting that use the concept of image segmentation, with crucial applications in scene perception, medical image analysis, robotics, video surveillance, reality, and image compression. Image segmentation is a crucial problem in computer vision and image processing [8]. Image segmentation is a method of separating the image into several groups called segments which will help reduce the complexity of the image to make it easier for computation. Segments can be thought of as labeled pixels, where all pixels of the same class have a label. Segmentation can be divided into two categories, semantic segmentation [9] and instance segmentation [10]. These are all types of computer vision for identifying and labeling objects in images but they differ in methods and levels of detail. Semantic segmentation will assign a label to each pixel in an image according to its semantic content and it aggregates all the pixels of roads, buildings, and sky. For example, Street scenes. On the other hand, instance segmentation involves identifying and labeling individual objects in an image even if they belong to the same semantic class. For example, public image. Some of the limitations are highlighted after reading some of the previous research papers. Guangshuai et al. [11] provide an overview of the limitations of different crowd counting methods including traditional methods and deep learning-based methods. This paper highlights the issues such as the lack of generalization across different datasets and the sensitivity during lighting conditions. Puja et al. [12] proposed extended MaskR-CNN architecture for crowd counting based on gender by identifying the location of every person in images. The proposed approach achieved significant results on ShanghalTech Dataset with a Mean Average Error (MAE) of 6.3 and a Mean Square Error (MSE) of 9.7. Zenglin et al. [13] discuss the limitations of crowd counting methods that rely on hand-crafted features. The paper highlights issues such as the need for extensive feature engineering and the inability to capture complex patterns in crowded scenes. Di et al. [14] control scale fluctuations by using an image pyramid rather than different-sized filters. Furthermore, their method allows for scale adaptation within an image by adaptively combining the predictions from various scales. Liu et al. [15] have talked about problems with deep neural networks based on encoder-decoders for crowd counting. They particularly address the overfitting issue and problems associated with huge training datasets. Yan et al. [16] introduced relative networks using multi-column CNN as the foundation for a scale-adaptive CNN architecture. In this study, collaborative learning is proposed during the model training phase. Walach et al. [17] discuss the limitations of crowd counting methods that use the concept of layered boosting and selective sampling. The paper highlights issues such as the difficulty in handling large-scale datasets and the sensitivity to noise and outliers.

3 Dataset Description

The dataset includes video clips of crowds in shopping malls [18] captured by security cameras. The file contains indoor and outdoor scenes and provides accurate background information for each video clip, including the crowd and their locations. It usually contains 2000 video frames and each pedestrian's head position is marked in each frame. A total of more than 60,000 travelers are registered in this database. We use 1600 of the 2000 images to train the model and 400 additional images for testing.

3.1 Evaluation Matrix

Mean Absolute Error (MAE) [19] is a standard measure for determining the average size of errors in a regression or prediction task. The average absolute difference between the expected outcomes and the actual values is used to compute it. Equation (1) is used to calculate MAE.

$$\mathrm{MAE} = (1/\mathrm{n}) * \Sigma|\mathrm{y} - \hat{\mathrm{y}}| \tag{1}$$

where: MAE represents the Mean Absolute Error
n → total samples.
y → ground truth.
ŷ → predicted values.

One of the metrics used to assess the effectiveness of the crowd counting approach is MAE. It aids in estimating the model's performance and accuracy. A lower MAE score denotes a better prediction, meaning that the values generated by the models are reasonably close to the real values. All errors are taken into account equally by the MAE, though.

- Mean Squared Error (MSE) [19]: MSE is calculated by the average of the squared difference between the true labels and predicted labels in a regression, the MSE metric is frequently utilized as it provides an estimate of how big the squared errors often are. The Eq. (2) is used to calculate MSE.

  MSE is defined as: $MSE = (1/n) * \Sigma(y - \hat{y})\hat{2}$ (2).

where MSE represents the Mean Squared Error.
n → otal samples.
y → ground truth.
ŷ → predicted values.

4 Methodology

Crowd counting is accomplished through the usage of instance segments. Finding each unique object in an image is the main task of an instance segment. Crowd management and analysis are done with the help of the instance segment. It is utilized for crowd tackling at large events, religious ceremonies, and shopping centers. The architecture for crowd counting is depicted in Fig. 2. The model receives a picture of a crowd as input. The ResNet 50 [24] was used to extract the features from this image. The individual character is finally identified using the instance segment, and the resultant count of the individual characters in the input image is provided.

4.1 Mask R-CNN and Resnet 50

Our crowd identification approach using Instance Segmentation (Mask R-CNN) [20] involves the use of a deep learning model called ResNet 50 [21] that can detect and classify individuals in a situation where there are great occlusions or overlaps among people. These models are trained on large datasets of recorded images, allowing them to learn and classify people in different locations and situations. Our approach to instance segmentation [22] is based on Mask R-CNN is a deep learning model for instance segmentation and object detection. Mask R-CNN is easy to use and train, resulting in a variety of simple design patterns. The images in the dataset are taken as input, preprocessed, and then provided to the MASK R-CNN model for sample segmentation. ResNET 50 performs as the backbone network for the MASK R-CNN model. To extract high-level feature images from it. We also calculate the accuracy and precision of our method using the mean error and mean square error as our test parameters. Videos and several users are factors for our prediction model.

Modern techniques that are effective for image segmentation and crowd counting [26] are employed in our system, including ResNet 50 and Mask R-CNN. The deep neural network ResNet 50 is frequently utilized for image classification issues. A variation of the ResNet CNN architecture is called ResNet 50.family introduced to solve the loss problem in deep neural networks. ResNet 50 is trained using

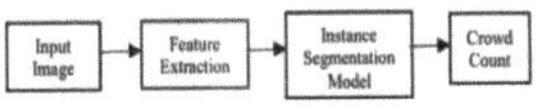

Fig. 2 Resnet 50 architecture for crowd counting

backpropagation and stochastic gradient descent. The weight system was adjusted during training to minimize performance loss which measures the difference between class scores and actual transcripts. Using these redundant connections allows deep neural networks to be trained without the consequences of the disappearance problem. Residual connections add the input of the block to the output of the block, allowing the network to learn the residuals instead of using the plan directly. The global average pooling and all tiers at the end of the network are used to generate the final score in the class. The global average pooling layer averages the size of each map feature to create a vector of values. This vector is then combined into a fully concatenated array that creates a vector of class scores for each class in the dataset.

4.2 CNN Model

Counting the number of persons in an image or video using convolutional neural networks (CNNs) is a common computer vision issue [23]. CNN is a deep neural network that has been demonstrated to be efficient in classifying images and performing cognitive tasks. It relies on training neural networks to recognize patterns in images associated with crowds by using a large database of recorded images, each tagged with the people in the image. There are many ways to use CNNs [25] for crowd computing but one way is to use whole neural networks [23] i.e., Fully Convolutional Neural Networks (FCNs). FCN is a neural network architecture that uses convolutional layers instead of all layers in normal neural networks. This allows the network to accept any size of input and produce the same size output, making it ideal for image segmentation and crowd counting. It usually takes an image as input and processes it in a convolutional process to extract features. These features are then passed to the regression layer, which estimates the number of people in the image.

5 Experimental Results and Analysis

The result and analysis section contains the values obtained by computing the dataset on the mentioned two models: Mask R-CNN and traditional CNN. The experiments are performed by taking these two models for crowd counting and analysis. As shown in Table 1, the accuracy is calculated, and MSE and MAE are calculated. The results show that the performance of Mask R-CNN is better than traditional CNN as the values for MSE and MAE are less and the accuracy is high. When it comes to speed, the Mask R-CNN computes calculations more quickly than the standard CNN. The processing time for each image is quite short. Nevertheless, the Mask R-CNN processes the images poorly because of its intricate construction. Furthermore, it is evident from several literatures that speed is not regarded as the most crucial factor. Table 1 shows the results for the performance of both models. Table 2 shows the experimental parameters used for training the model.

Table 1 Experimental results

Models	Dataset		MSE	MAE	Accuracy (%)
Mask R-CNN	Mall Dataset		16.3	2.01	92
CNN	Mall Dataset		18	2.54	90.32

Table 2 Experimental parameters for training the model

Parameter	Description
Input Shape	224*224
Batch size	32
Activation	Softmax
Epochs	5

The robustness analysis indicates that Mask R-CNN with ResNet 50 performs well across different crowd densities. However, the traditional CNN-based approach struggles with accurate counting in highly dense situations, where it tends to Input Image Feature Extraction Instance Segmentation Model Crowd Count underestimating the crowd count. This limitation restricts its applicability in crowded environments where accurate counting is of utmost importance.

5.1 Accuracy Comparison

We compare the Mean Absolute Error (MAE) and Mean Squared Error (MSE) measures to assess the precision of crowd counting methodologies. These measurements indicate the difference between the estimated and actual crowd sizes. We do experiments on a variety of thoroughly annotated datasets that include actual crowd counts.

The results indicate that Mask R-CNN with ResNet 50 achieves an MAE of 2.01 and MSE of 16.3. Comparatively, the traditional CNN-based approach achieves an MAE of 2.54 and MSE of 18. These values provide insights into the accuracy of each technique allowing us to assess their performance in estimating crowd counts.

5.2 Robustness to Varying Crowd Densities

Crowd counting techniques should be able to handle varying crowd densities [26] ranging from sparse to congested crowds. We evaluate the performance of each technique on images with different crowd densities including low, medium, and high-density scenarios.

The results show that Mask R-CNN with ResNet 50 as backbone performs well across different density levels, although it exhibits a slight decrease in accuracy in highly congested scenarios. The traditional CNN-based approach demonstrates relatively lower accuracy in high-density situations and highlights its limitations in handling dense crowds.

5.3 *Failure Cases*

It is equally important to examine the failure cases of each technique to understand their limitations. We identify challenging scenarios where the techniques may struggle such as occlusions, severe overcrowding, or complex background environments.

The analysis reveals that Mask R-CNN with ResNet 50 may encounter challenges in highly occluded scenes or areas with significant overlap between people. In such cases, accurate instance-level segmentation becomes more challenging leading to potential errors in counting. The traditional CNN-based approach struggles with accurate counting in dense crowds often resulting in significant underestimation.

6 Conclusion

In the present research, the working of Mask R-CNN with ResNet 50 as the backbone and traditional CNN-based approach to address the issue in highly dense crowded areas or occlusion. It becomes a challenging task to accurately count the number of people in certain scenarios and reduce the potential error in counting the people in the image. The outcomes indicate that Mask R-CNN outperforms as compared to CNN in terms of accuracy, MAE, and MSE. In the future researchers can address some limitations and challenges like the computational complexity of the deep learning-based techniques resulting in relatively longer processing time as compared to the traditional CNN-based approach. This can be a concern in scenarios where real-time processing or analyzing large-scale crowd datasets is required.

References

1. Patwal A, Diwakar M, Tripathi V, Singh P (2023) Crowd counting analysis using deep learning: A critical review. Procedia Comput Sci 218:2448–2458
2. Gupta S, Panwar A, Goel S, Mittal A, Nijhawan R, Singh AK (2019) Classification of lesions in retinal fundus images for diabetic retinopathy using transfer learning. In: 2019 International conference on information technology (ICIT), Bhubaneswar, India, pp 342–347, https://doi.org/10.1109/ICIT48102.2019.00067

3. Loy CC, Chen K, Gong S, Xiang T (2013) Crowd counting and profiling: Methodology and evaluation. In: Modeling, simulation and visual analysis of crowds: A multidisciplinary perspective (pp 347–382). New York, NY: Springer New York
4. Dollár, Kaiming He Georgia Gkioxari Piotr, and Ross Girshick (2017) Mask r-cnn."Proceedings of the IEEE international conference on computer vision
5. He K, Zhang X, Ren S, Sun J (2016) Deep residual learning for image recognition. In: 2016 IEEE conference on computer vision and pattern recognition (CVPR), Las Vegas, NV, USA, 2016, pp 770–778, https://doi.org/10.1109/CVPR.2016.90
6. Gupta S, Panwar A (2023) Artificial intelligence and machine learning techniques for analysis of yoga pose. In: Kumar Singh K, Bajpai MK, Sheikh Akbari A (eds) Machine vision and augmented intelligence. Lecture Notes in Electrical Engineering, vol 1007. Springer, Singapore. https://doi.org/10.1007/978-981-99-0189-0_35
7. Ilyas N, Shahzad A, Kim K (2019Dec 19) Convolutional-neural network-based image crowd counting: review, categorization, analysis, and performance evaluation. Sensors (Basel). 20(1):43. https://doi.org/10.3390/s20010043.PMID:31861734;PMCID:PMC6983207
8. Panwar A, Yadav R, Mishra K, Gupta S (2021) Deep learning techniques for the real time detection of Covid19 and pneumonia using chest radiographs. IEEE EUROCON 2021—19th international conference on smart technologies, Lviv, Ukraine, pp 250–253, https://doi.org/10.1109/EUROCON52738.2021.9535604
9. He J, Wu X, Yang J, Hu W (2020) CPSPNet: Crowd counting via semantic segmentation framework. In: 2020 IEEE 32nd international conference on tools with artificial intelligence (ICTAI) (pp 1104–1110). IEEE
10. Cholakkal H, Sun G, Khan FS, Shao L (2019) Object counting and instance segmentation with image-level supervision. In: Proceedings of the IEEE/CVF conference on computer vision and pattern recognition (pp 12397–12405)
11. Gao G, Gao J, Liu Q, Wang Q, Wang Y (2020) Cnn-based density estimation and crowd counting: A survey. arXiv preprint arXiv:2003.12783
12. Gupta P, Sharma V, Varma S (2022). Analysis of crowd features based on deep learning. In: 2022 international conference on automation, computing and renewable systems (ICACRS) (pp 1134–1139). IEEE
13. Shi Z, Zhang L, Liu Y, Cao X, Ye Y, Cheng MM, Zheng G (2018) Crowd counting with deep negative correlation learning. In: Proceedings of the IEEE conference on computer vision and pattern recognition (pp 5382–5390)
14. Kang D, Chan A (2018) Crowd counting by adaptively fusing predictions from an image pyramid. arXiv preprint arXiv:1805.06115
15. Liu X, Hu Y, Zhang B, Zhen X, Luo X, Cao X (2022) Attentive encoder-decoder networks for crowd counting. Neurocomputing 490:246–257
16. Yan R, Gong S, Zhong S (2019) Crowd counting via scaleadaptive convolutional neural network in extremely dense crowd images. Int J Comput Appl Technol 61(4):318–324
17. Walach E, Wolf L (2016) Learning to count with cnn boosting. In Computer Vision–ECCV 2016: 14th European Conference, Amsterdam, The Netherlands, October 11–14, 2016, Proceedings, Part II 14 (pp 660–676). Springer International Publishing
18. Chen K, Change Loy C, Gong S, Xiang T (2012) Feature mining for localised crowd counting. In: British machine vision conference
19. Ryan D, Denman S, Sridharan S, Fookes C (2015) An evaluation of crowd counting methods, features and regression models. Comput Vis Image Underst 130:1–17
20. Panwar A, Semwal G, Goel S, Gupta S (2022) Stratification of the lesions in color fundus images of diabetic retinopathy patients using deep learning models and machine learning classifiers. In: Patgiri R, Bandyopadhyay S, Borah MD, Emilia Balas V (eds) Edge analytics. Lecture notes in electrical engineering, vol 869. Springer, Singapore. https://doi.org/10.1007/978-981-19-0019-8_49
21. Elpeltagy M, Sallam H (2021) Automatic prediction of COVID– 19 from chest images using modified ResNet50. Multimed Tools Appl 80:26451–26463

22. Panwar A, Gupta S (2022) Deep learning models for early detection of pneumonia using chest X-Ray images. In: Dua M, Jain AK, Yadav A, Kumar N, Siarry P (eds) Proceedings of the international conference on paradigms of communication, computing and data sciences. Algorithms for Intelligent Systems. Springer, Singapore. https://doi.org/10.1007/978-981-16-5747-4_60.
23. Gupta S, Panwar A, Kapruwan A, Chaube N (2021) A comparative analysis of deep convolution layered machine learning approaches for detection of pneumonia from chest radiographs. In: 2021 IEEE international conference on technology, research, and innovation for betterment of society (TRIBES), Raipur, India, pp 1–5, https://doi.org/10.1109/TRIBES52498.2021.9751653
24. Gupta S, Panwar A, Mishra K (2021) Skin disease classification using dermoscopy images through deep feature learning models and machine learning classifiers. In: IEEE EUROCON 2021—19th international conference on smart technologies, Lviv, Ukraine, pp 170–174, https://doi.org/10.1109/EUROCON52738.2021.9535552
25. Zhang C, Li H, Wang X, Yang X (2015) Cross-scene crowd counting via deep convolutional neural networks. In: Proceedings of the IEEE conference on computer vision and pattern recognition (pp 833–841)
26. Ryan D, Denman S, Fookes C, Sridharan S (2009) Crowd counting using multiple local features. In: 2009 digital image computing: techniques and applications, Melbourne, VIC, Australia, pp 81–88, https://doi.org/10.1109/DICTA.2009.22
27. Panwar A, Gupta S, Chaube N, Gupta S, Kapruwan A (2022) Classification of apple leaf diseases using distinct machine learning algorithms. In: 2022 IEEE Delhi section conference (DELCON), New Delhi, India, pp 1–6, https://doi.org/10.1109/DELCON54057.2022.9753629

GUAVA Leaf Disease Detection Using YOLO V8 Algorithm

Panduri Vishnu Vardhan and Surendra Reddy Vinta

1 Introduction

During this financial year 2023, India's guava production is estimated to have amounted to 5.59 million metric tons, representing a slight increase compared to the preceding fiscal period. The country's guava cultivation area in 2023 stood at around 359 thousand hectares. Uttar Pradesh, a prominent region in India, stands as the largest guava producer in the country, boasting an impressive output of 928.44 tons, capturing a substantial market share of 22.93%. The state's advantageous agro-climatic conditions and sophisticated agricultural techniques make a noteworthy contribution to its achievements in guava farming. Furthermore, Uttar Pradesh's guava sector plays a crucial part in both the regional economy and the national fruit industry.

Crop maladies shall be examined on prominent replicas of the same. Observing the flourishing and infestation on vegetation plays an important job in the productive advancement of yields in the farm. Traditionally, the inspection and assessment of crop ailments were executed manually by the proficient individual in that domain. The demand for a substantial amount of labor and extensive duration is unavoidable. The image processing methods can be employed in the recognition of plant diseases. In many occurrences, infections are identified from portions of the plant like foliage or stalk. The ailments of Guava leaf highlights are illustrated as.

(1) Phytophthora: It mainly occurs in guava fruit it will develop water-soaked lesions in guava which causes diseases in guava it will affect the quality of the fruit and early detection and prevention of this phytophthora is very crucial

P. V. Vardhan · S. R. Vinta (✉)
School of Computer Science and Engineering (SCOPE), VIT-AP University, Amaravati, Andhra Pradesh, India
e-mail: vsurendra.cse@gmail.com

P. V. Vardhan
e-mail: vishnuvardhan.21bce9349@vitapstudent.ac.in

K. Kumar Singh et al. (eds.), *Machine Vision and Augmented Intelligence*, Lecture Notes in Electrical Engineering 1211, https://doi.org/10.1007/978-981-97-4359-9_45

to prevent huge losses of guava crops.to cure this we should do early detection and adopt good agricultural practices to prevent the guava plant from this disease.

(2) Styler and Root: These are two diseases they are styler disease which is known as stem Canker and Root disease which is known as Root Rot disease. Stem canker is caused by mainly fungi that will develop cankers slowly on the leaves, stems, and trunks of the tree this will cause a stop of water supply from the root to all parts of the plant which causes a deficiency in nutrients in plants and leads to death. For this we should use fungicides to avoid fungi and the breakdown of affected branches may lead the plant to grow properly. Root Rot disease is caused by various soilborne pathogens including phytophthora and fusarium. It mainly affects the roots of the tree and decreases the health of the affected guava tree. Infected roots become brown and decomposed they can't take the nutrients and required water supply efficiently as other plants do. It can be prevented by early detection of the disease that occurred to the guava plant and giving the water supply daily to ensure better crop health and increasing guava plants' resistance to fight diseases at initial stages only

(3) Scab: It's one of the most common fungal diseases that occur in guava trees frequently. It is occured by the pathogen Puccinia psidii which belongs to the rust fungi family. This disease can be observed by the appearance of the guava tree when it occurs we can observe slight changes which happen to the guava trees like the leaves becoming pale and color becoming rust on the undersides of the guava leaves. The leaves which are infected will fall down from the tree maximum. The fruit quality will eventually decrease and the tree's fruit production decreases gradually. The leaves which are infected will spread the disease all over the tree which cause huge damage to the total tree. The ailment can be promoted by elevated humidity and high temperatures. This disease can be prevented by detecting the disease early at the initial stages of the disease and can be avoided by planting disease-resistant guava trees when available and trimming and eliminating affected foliage and branches to minimize the dissemination of the disease. Administering fungicides in the initial phases of the condition or when essential to avert intense invasions. Ensuring adequate airflow around the guava trees to diminish humidity and establish an unfavorable milieu for the pathogen. Abstaining from overhead watering that might foster moisture on the foliage.

(4) Red Rust: This is also known as guava rust, it's also a fungal disease that affects the guava trees it is caused by fungi and bacterial infections the main aim of this disease is to primarily attack leaves it when it attacks then the leaves become reddish brown in color as the disease progresses it will spread to upper parts and lower parts of the tree. This disease grows rapidly as it rapidly increases it will lead to decreasing the strength of the tree and reducing the production of the fruits.

The leaves will drop rapidly this can be avoided by the air circulation around the guava tree to ensure it takes carbon dioxide freely and avoiding overhead irrigation which promotes moisture on the guava leaves we should ensure that the environment is unsupportable for the fungi and other pathogens. Prompt identification and timely control measures are crucial to reduce the influence of red rust on guava trees and upholding a thriving and productive crop. Employing integrated pest management approaches that integrate different preventive and management measures is advised for efficient disease control.

In recent years, Deep Learning techniques have predominantly been enormously utilized in agriculture to advance, regulate, and enhance the growth in agriculture. DL facilitates various intricate tasks such as Speech Recognition, Object detection, Natural Language Generation, Anomaly Detection, Machine Translation, Drug Discovery, and Music and art Recognition. P. Perumala and other 3 authors discovered a model which is used for guava leaf disease detection using a support vector machine they preprocessed guava image scaling to 256 × 256 and one image segmentation the accuracy of this model lies around 96% for anthracnose and 98% bacterial blight. Similarly, Imran Khan and other 5 authors proposed a real-time deep learning based technique based on Convolutional neural networks and yolo to classify guava leaf diseases using Guava patches dataset (GPD) which contains 2542 images in total and the accuracy of the test set is 84% (Approximately). The proposed approach attained a mAP (mean Absolute Precision) of 79.80% during the insect infestation assessment, a comprehensive set of 67 targets was employed, resulting in a precision of 64.6%, recall of 79.1%, mAP@0.5 of 79.8%, and mAP@0.5:0.95 of 35.3% (Fig. 1).

In our guava leaf disease detection endeavor employing YOLOv8, the model is fine-tuned with 647 annotated images and multiple techniques to avert overfitting. Measures like regularization, dropout, and early termination ensure resilience. Data

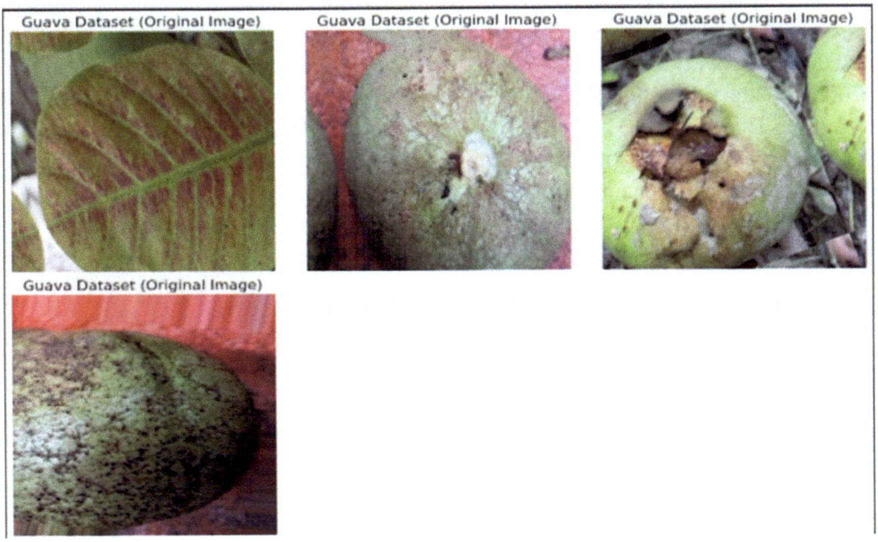

Fig. 1 Classification of images in GLDD

augmentation enriches the training dataset, while batch normalization stabilizes the procedure. We optimize hyperparameters like learning rate, batch size, and image dimensions. Upon deployment, the model attains a 96.6% accuracy, demonstrating swift inference. It emerges as a precious asset for farmers, facilitating prompt disease control and amplifying guava crop productivity.

The focus is to detect guava leaf disease within a second from the given dataset using deep learning algorithms and Convolutional Neural Networks. The primary objective is to label the images given dataset according to the number of classes they are differentiated and upload all the labeled images into the drive if there is any overfitting or underfitting then we should resize the images according to the required format because if we don't resize the images it will cause noise in the data then the images belonging to the same classes may dominate the remaining the other classes in the detection task and in testing.

In our guava leaf disease detection project, both OpenCV and PyTorch played crucial roles and contributed significantly to the success and effectiveness of the solution. OpenCV offered an extendible array of image processing capabilities, enabling us to preprocess and enhance the guava leaf images prior to inputting them into the YOLOv8 model for detection. This guarantees the input data is suitably prepared for precise and effective detection. PyTorch served as the foundation for developing the YOLOv8 model to detect guava leaf diseases. Its adaptability and user-friendly interface empower us to construct and tailor the model's architecture to align with our unique needs and dataset. It offered valuable tools for training the YOLOv8 model, such as optimization algorithms, automatic differentiation, and GPU support. This made training on our dataset efficient and fast, resulting in improved accuracy and reliability when detecting guava leaf diseases using yolov8.

For demonstration purposes, we have compiled various guava leaf disease images into a zip file, which is accessible offline via Google Drive. We pre-trained a YOLOv8 model to effectively detect these guava leaf diseases. The model was trained on five distinct image sets, containing 100 Phytophthora images, 190 Scab images, 100 Styler and Root images, 200 Red Rust images, and 100 Disease-Free images. For Disease-Free images, the model will not display any bounding boxes, indicating the absence of disease in the given dataset.

2 Maintaining the Integrity of the Specifications

The brinjal leaf disease detection using YOLOv8 achieved an impressive accuracy of 96.6%. For this project, 647 images were utilized for training and classification, resulting in 546 instances. The YOLOv8 (fused) model has 168 layers and 3,006,623 parameters, with no gradients. The box properties of the model include 92% precision, 97% recall, 98.3% mAP50, and 87% mAP50-95, assessed at different IoU thresholds.

The speed for preprocessing all images was measured at 0.9 ms, while inference took 2.6 ms, and loss calculation required 0.0 ms. The post-processing per image took 1.9 ms. The results were saved to the "runs/detect/train11" directory.

The research utilized the Ultralytics YOLOv8.0.145 library with Python 3.10.6 and torch-2.0.1 + cu118 CUDA on a Tesla T4 GPU with 15,102 MiB memory. The training parameters were set as follows:

In our research project on guava leaf disease detection using YOLOv8, we achieved an impressive accuracy of 96.6%. For this task, we employed a dataset called Guava Leaf Disease Detection (GLDD) containing 647 images, which were classified into five classes: disease-free, phytophthora, styler and root diseases, scab, and red rust. The YOLOv8 model we used had 168 layers with 3,006,623 parameters and demonstrated excellent precision (92%) and recall (97%) for box properties. Additionally, the mean average precision at IoU (mAP50) was 98.3%, and the mean average precision across IoU thresholds from 50 to 95 (mAP50-95) was 87%.

During our experiments, we have calculated the speed and performance of the YOLO v8 model. For preprocessing of images took only 0.9 ms, inference required 2.6 ms, and post-processing took 1.9 ms per image. The results were saved in the "runs/detect/train11" directory, and the YOLOv8 library version used was Ultralytics YOLOv8.0.145, powered by Python 3.10.6 and Torch 2.0.1 + cu118 with support on a Tesla T4 GPU.

We meticulously fine-tuned the training parameters for the detection assignment. The model underwent training utilizing a batch size of 15, spanning 150 epochs, and incorporating a patience interval of 50 epochs. Images sized at 640 pixels were employed. We chose to adopt the Torch Script format for the model, initializing the learning rate at 0.01 and concluding with the same value of 0.01.

3 Overfitting and Adaptation

To prevent overfitting of the model dataset we ensured robust generalization, we implemented several strategies. Regularization, which has weight decay of 0.0005, controlled model complexity, while dropout (0.0 rate) mitigated overreliance on specific features. Early stopping monitored validation loss and halted training with a patience of 50 epochs. Data augmentation provided in the training diversified the training set, incorporating random rotations, flips, and brightness adjustments. Batch normalization stabilized training, and hyperparameter tuning optimized learning rate (initial: 0.01, final: 0.01), batch size (15), and image size (640px). The model used Torch Script format and employed a Tesla T4 GPU with 15,102 MiB memory. Speed metrics for preprocessing, inference, loss, and post-process were 0.91 ms, 2.69 ms, 0 ms, and 1.91 ms, respectively (Fig. 2).

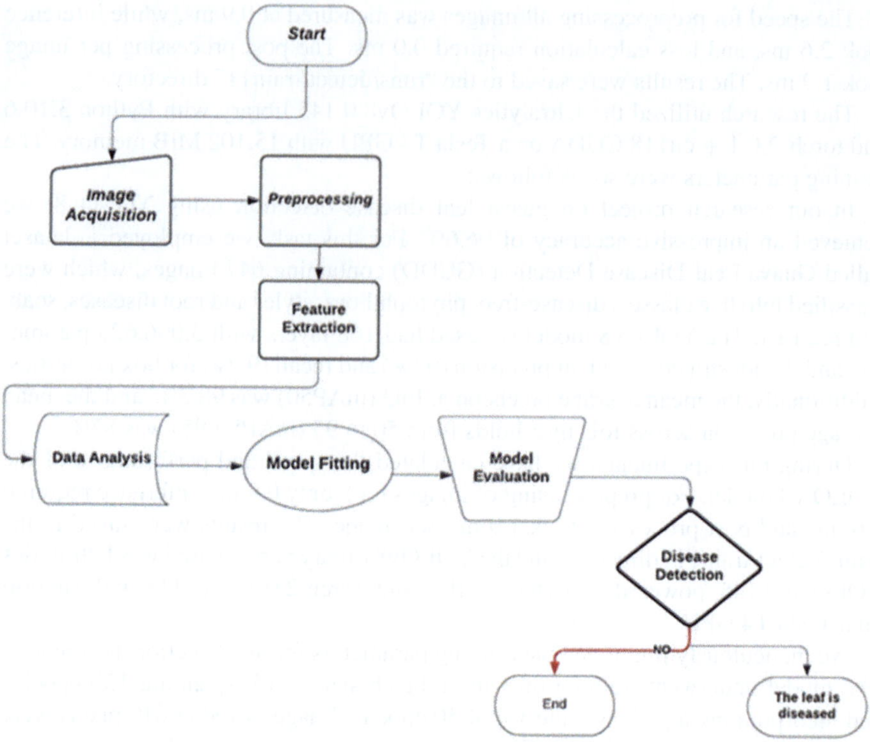

Fig. 2 Flow diagram

4 Literature Survey

In this segment, we endeavor to contrast our guava leaf disease detection approach with other existing techniques. Moreover, the limited studies available lack thorough implementation specifics and often cater to specific geographical and demographic limitations. In contrast, our research delves into the utilization of the YOLOv8 model, which offers improved precision and efficiency in guava leaf disease detection, irrespective of geographical or demographic variations. In the modern era, Deep Learning has primarily found application within the realm of agriculture, driving progress and innovation in the field, regulate and enhance the growth in agriculture. DL facilitates various intricate tasks such as Speech Recognition, Object detection, Natural Language Generation, Anomaly Detection, Machine Translation, Drug Discovery, and Music and art Recognition. P. Perumala and other 3 authors discovered a model which is used for Classification of diseases affecting guava leaves employing a support vector machine [1]. They preprocessed guava image scaling to 256 × 256 and one image segmentation the accuracy of this model lies around 96% for anthracnose and 98% for bacterial blight. Similarly, Imran Khan and other

5 authors suggested an innovative real-time method rooted in deep learning, leveraging Convolutional Neural Networks (CNNs) and YOLO architecture for the categorization of diseases afflicting guava leaves [2]. using the Guava patches dataset (GPD) which contains 2542 images in total and the accuracy of the test set is 84% (Approximately). The proposed approach attained a mAP (mean Absolute Precision) of 79.80% during the insect infestation assessment, a comprehensive set of 67 targets was employed, resulting in a precision of 64.6%, recall of 79.1%, mAP@0.5 of 79.8%, and mAP@0.5:0.95 of 35.3%. In a study conducted by Li et al. in 2018, they proposed a convolutional neural network (CNN) method [3] for classifying guava diseases, analyzing a collection of leaf images. The outcomes were encouraging, successfully differentiating between healthy leaves and those afflicted with prevalent diseases like anthracnose and rust. Likewise, in 2019, Singh and colleagues introduced a deep learning framework constructed upon the ResNet architecture for detecting guava leaf diseases [4]. Their model employed transfer learning, capitalizing on features learned from an extensive dataset, leading to remarkable accuracy in identifying various guava leaf diseases. In the paper of Gangadevi Ganesan and Jayakumar Chinnappan, they used Yolov4 model for guava leaf disease detection. In this study, it uses Yolov4 Algorithm and is implemented on mobile devices with the use of yolov4, the model can do object detection up to 140 frames per second only on a single GPU. To overcome this, our project used yolov8 model. With the use of the Yolov8 model, we can improve the accuracy to 96.7% accuracy and it can do object detection upto 170 frames per second on a single GPU which is way more than the existing model [5]. In place of Raspberry Pi we used a py camera and open cv platform for selecting and capturing images so the cost of the project decreased and the speed of processing increased with the use of yolov8.

However, the limitation of these models revolves around classification, augmentation, and labeling. We have come to notice that most of the models make use of time very much for running and execution. Because of that time taken, the speed and accuracy of yolov8 model gain popularity among the previous pre-trained models. The input images were split into three categories: training, testing, and validation sets, facilitating an efficient training process. An advantage of the YOLOv8 model is its inherent ability to perform data augmentations during training, minimizing the need for manual augmentations.

In the pursuit of refining the training procedure, we established the momentum at 0.937 and introduced a weight decay of 0.0005. Additionally, we harnessed warm-up epochs and warm-up momentum to further elevate the efficacy of the learning process.

By employing YOLOv8, we were able to accurately detect guava leaf diseases, contributing valuable insights for farmers engaged in guava crop cultivation. The model's exceptional precision, recall, and mAP scores indicate its potential as a valuable tool for disease management and crop yield improvement in guava farming.

The YOLOv8 algorithm utilizes object detection techniques, making it suitable for tasks such as object detection, augmentation, and image classification. Correct any errors in the sentences if found. In this Project, we introduce a study that applies deep learning techniques for guava leaf disease detection using yolov8. Python libraries like Pandas, NumPy, Matplotlib, Seaborn, and Keras are employed for data processing and visualization. We utilize TensorFlow and Keras to implement a YOLOv8 model, customizing its architecture for our dataset. Image data augmentation and categorical encoding are applied to enhance model accuracy. A thorough evaluation is conducted, including classification reports, ROC curves, and AUC scores, demonstrating the model's disease classification capabilities. The research contributes valuable insights into disease detection in guava crops, potentially benefiting farmers and agriculture practices.

Detecting diseases in guava leaves plays a pivotal role in upholding the well-being and output of guava plants. By spotting and diagnosing diverse ailments in their early stages, cultivators and horticulturists can promptly apply suitable measures to curtail transmission and reduce harm. This procedure encompasses visual scrutiny, identification of symptoms, and occasionally even laboratory tests to precisely determine the specific malady afflicting the guava foliage. Leveraging technology and expertise, scientists and experts in agriculture have devised techniques for proficient and precise detection of guava leaf diseases.

Researchers have engineered automated systems that utilize image processing methodologies to scrutinize visuals of guava leaves. These systems are adept at differentiating between robust and ailing leaves by assessing patterns, alterations in color, and blemishes apparent on the leaf exterior. Machine learning algorithms, like convolutional neural networks (CNNs), have been educated on substantial datasets containing images of guava leaves to augment the precision of classifying diseases.

Furthermore, spectral analysis has demonstrated its efficacy in identifying nuanced biochemical modifications in guava leaves brought about by ailments. Hyperspectral imaging devices are capable of capturing comprehensive spectral data from leaves, which is subsequently scrutinized using sophisticated algorithms to identify distinctive disease-induced patterns and anomalies.

In particular instances, molecular techniques like polymerase chain reaction (PCR) and enzyme-linked immunosorbent assays (ELISAs) are employed for meticulous identification of diseases. These methodologies entail discerning the presence of specific pathogens or molecules linked to diseases in samples of guava leaves. For the purpose of facilitating widespread disease detection, mobile applications have been developed, enabling farmers to capture visuals of guava leaves using their smartphones. These visuals can be uploaded to cloud-oriented platforms, where advanced algorithms process them and deliver real-time disease diagnoses, accompanied by suggested strategies for management (Table 1).

Table 1 Comparison of accuracies with the previous model

S. no	Authors/papers	Approach	Accuracy (%)
1	Javed Rashid1,2, Imran Khan1, Ghulam Ali3, Shafiq Ur Rehman4, Fahad Alturise5 and Tamim Alkhalifah5, *	Hybrid deep learning technique	92.41
2	Sidrah Mumtaz, Mudassar Raza, Ofonime Dominic Okon and Saeed Ur Rehman [6]	SidNet, Alex net,RsNet	95
3	Nikhil James1, Kunal Kumar Shriwastav1, Shilpita Medhi1,Smriti Priya Medhi	Deep convolution neural network (CNN)-based approach	84
4	Mrs. P Sai kusuma1, T H Gopala Krishna, Y Suneetha3, Y Chaithanya4, G Kishore5, S Likith6	Image processing using MATLAB	90
5	Almetwally M. Mostafa, Swarn Avinash Kumar	SqueezeNet, GoogLeNet	96
6	Daudi Samson Simbeye	Artificial intelligence and IoT	93
7	Muhammad Asim, Abdul Razzaq, Salman Qadri	Multi feature analysis	89.2
8	Gangadevi Ganesan, Jayakumar Chinnappan	YOLOv4	92

5 Proposed Work

5.1 Components of Software Used

(A) **Ultralytics**: In this undertaking, Ultralytics was utilized as a valuable resource or framework to assist with diverse responsibilities concerning the assessment and implementation of the YOLOv8 structures. Ultralytics provides capabilities such as object detection, model training, and performance assessment, playing a crucial role in ensuring the smooth execution and examination of the project.

(B) **Pytorch**: For this project, PyTorch served as the main deep learning framework. PyTorch provides a broad array of features and utilities, like tensor manipulations, automatic gradients, and neural network components, pivotal in constructing and training the models and it's learned from the [7]. Its adaptability, user-friendliness, and extensive community backing greatly influenced the accomplishment and effectiveness of the project.

(C) **OpenCV**: In this particular project, OpenCV served as the central computer vision toolkit, fulfilling diverse objectives and applications. OpenCV offers an extensive array of capabilities and utilities, encompassing image manipulation [8], feature identification, and object detection, which are indispensable for processing and scrutinizing visual information. Its adaptability, speed, and comprehensive documentation significantly bolstered the project's achievements and efficiency. OpenCV played a pivotal role in critical tasks, including image preprocessing, data augmentation, and generating visual representations, establishing it as an indispensable pillar within the project's computer vision framework [9]. With its robust functionalities and user-friendly interface, OpenCV proved to be an invaluable asset in the successful completion of the project's vision-related goals.

6 Implementation

(A) Data Input and Preprocessing

The images used in this study are sourced from the Guava Leaf Disease Detection Dataset (GLDD). A total of 700 input images have been collected and categorized into 5 distinct classes, namely Disease-free, Styler and Root, Phytophthora, Red Rust, and Scab.

To facilitate disease detection using YOLOv8, the images were labeled.

The tagging structure: <Quantity of categories, x_min, y_min, x_max, y_max, category identifier>. The number of classes range is from (0–4) due to the presence of 5 classes; any value beyond this range will raise an error.

The coordinates x_min, y_min, x_max, and y_max define the upper-left and lower-right vertices of the area enclosing the entity in the picture, while the category identifier signifies the designation given to the entity inside the bounded region.

The input images were split into three categories: training, testing, and validation sets, facilitating an efficient training process. Keras framework [10] is also used for the project. An advantage of the YOLOv8 model is its inherent ability to perform data augmentations during training, minimizing the need for manual augmentations.

The primary benefit of this model is its rapid detection of diseases in guava leaves, significantly reducing the time required for detection. We can do this guava leaf disease detection by the genetic algorithm [11]. The utilization of YOLOv8 for disease detection streamlines the process and eliminates the necessity for extensive data augmentations during training.

(B) YOLOv8 Architecture

The YOLOv8 architecture represents a significant advancement in object detection, building upon the success of its predecessors, YOLOv5 and earlier YOLO models. It introduces anchor-free detection, directly predicting the object centers instead of relying on predefined anchor boxes. This design choice simplifies the model and enhances its accuracy through diminishing the count of forecasted boxes, resulting in accelerated Non-Maximum Suppression during the subsequent post-processing stage. YOLOv8 incorporates novel convolutional blocks, such as the C2f module, which replaces the initial 6×6 convolutions with 3×3 convolutions. The main building block has been updated, and the C2f module efficiently concatenates the outputs from the Bottleneck [12], reducing parameter count and tensor size. The architecture also embraces ResNet-like components, employing 3 × 3 convolutions and residual connections. Notably, YOLOv8 employs the Mosaic Augmentation technique during training, providing variations of the images at each epoch. This approach enhances the model's generalization and robustness by exposing it to diverse data representations during training.

Overall, YOLOv8 combines innovation and lessons learned from earlier versions, showcasing its potential as an anchor-free, efficient, and powerful object detection model. Its architectural advancements and the incorporation of refining and instructional procedures significantly contribute to its exemplary achievement in tasks related to object detection.

The convolutional layers within YOLOv8 are responsible for acquiring insights into the input images, and identifying patterns, edges, and features. These layers employ convolutional filters to carry out operations like feature recognition, edge detection, and pattern analysis. The model's depth and intricacy are determined by the quantity of convolutional layers and their configurations. The initiation of YOLOv8 involves a 3 × 3 convolutional layer as the stem, which replaces the prior 6 × 6 convolutional layer utilized in YOLOv5. This alteration contributes to enhanced efficiency and overall model performance.

Furthermore, YOLOv8 introduces the C2f module as a crucial element in its architecture. In C2f, the outputs from the Bottleneck (consisting of two 3 × 3 convolutions with residual connections) are fused together. This methodology empowers the model to capture more intricate features, thereby enhancing its capability to accurately detect objects. The Bottleneck utilized in YOLOv8 resembles the one found in YOLOv5, but it incorporates a modification in the first convolution's kernel size, which shifts from 1 × 1 to 3 × 3. This change aligns the YOLOv8 architecture more closely with the successful ResNet block, renowned for its efficacy in deep learning tasks. B. Pooling Layer: Within the YOLOv8 neck, features are directly concatenated without the imposition of identical channel dimensions. This reduction in parameter count and tensor size results [12] in a more efficient and compact model.

This image shows the training data precision and recall graphs and loss functions after 150 epochs here we can see the increase in the precision and recall and a decrease in the loss functions which are box loss, class loss, and dfl loss after doing 150 epochs because of running these 150 epochs the training data is classified and augmented very precisely. The mean average precision and recall also increased by increasing epochs. these epochs are increased because we kept the patience as 50 after 50 epochs if there is no improvement in the loss function or accuracy then the epochs are automatically stopped (Table 2 and Figs. 3, 4).

This image shows the training data precision and recall graphs and loss functions after 150 epochs here we can see the increase in the precision and recall and a decrease in the loss functions which are box loss, class loss, and dfl loss after doing 150 epochs because of running these 150 epochs the training data is classified and augmented very precisely. The mean average precision and recall also increased by increasing epochs. these epochs are increased because we kept the patience as 50 after 50 epochs if there is no improvement in the loss function or accuracy then the epochs are automatically stopped.

Table 2 Error comparisons of various models on dataset

Model	Error rate (%)
CNN	15.88
Dense net	7.88
VGG16	4.9
VGG19	3.46

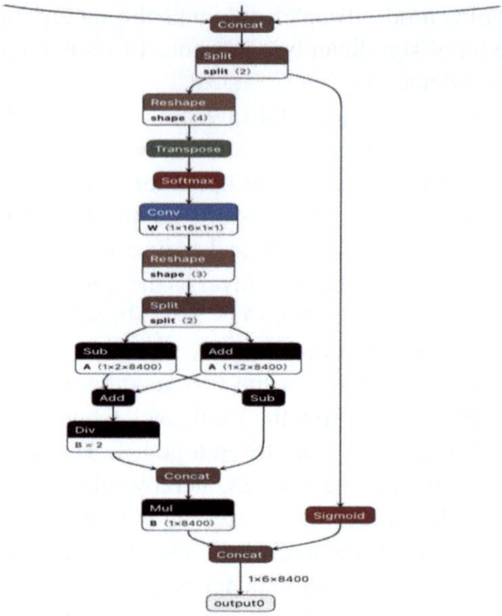

Fig. 3 Image shows how the input images are trained

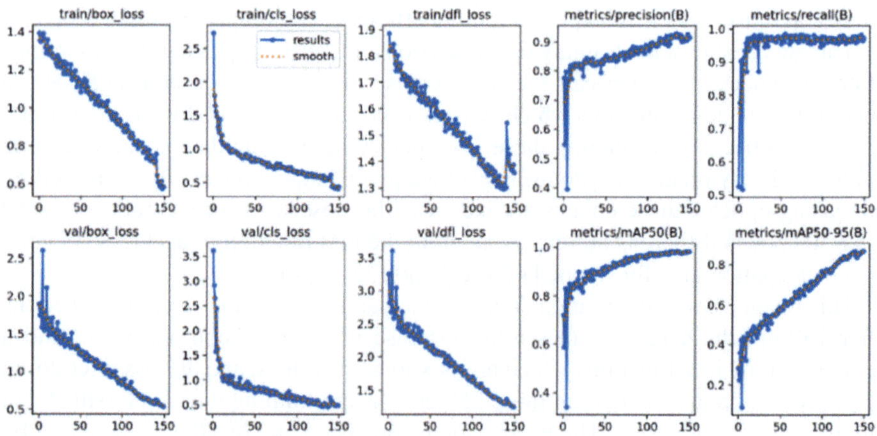

Fig. 4 Training loss and precision, recall graphs

Notably, YOLOv8 does not include conventional fully connected layers, as typically seen in traditional neural network architectures. The absence of such fully connected layers in YOLOv8 renders the model fully convolutional, facilitating efficient image processing regardless of input size and retaining spatial information throughout the network. Framework-wise, the amalgamation of convoluted strata [13], Bottlenecks, and C2f components within YOLOv8 confer upon it remarkable precision in endeavors such as image categorization, object spotting, and instance partitioning. Making it a leading choice for a diverse range of computer vision applications. The exclusion of fully connected layers enhances the model's adaptability and versatility, rendering it highly suitable for various computer vision tasks.

Training the Model

Here are the following steps that are involved in the training of the guava leaf disease dataset firstly, the dataset consists types of classes these all images should be resized for the required format for training and we have labeling package for the labeling of the images and after that import the labeling in the compiler and save all the labels which are in the txt format in the folder which consisting of the images such that the images corresponding to labels could be found easily within the same folder after the labeling of images next step is to install ultralytics in the compiler and pytorch in the compiler we should import these necessary packages for our project the for the training all images [14] should have class image size as mentioned in the data yaml document the dat yaml document consists of the training, testing and validation and number of classes and the names of those classes.so if in labels the class size is bigger then that of number of classes then we should write a code for adjusting the class size.

Configuration parameters of the proposed YOLOV8 model: Model name: YOLOV8 model, Number of classes: 5 (Disease-free, phytophthora, scab, red rust, styler and root), Image size: 640, Batch size: 15, Epochs: 150 (Fig. 5).

In summation, the detection of diseases in guava leaves is an intricate process that amalgamates visual scrutiny, cutting-edge imaging methodologies, spectral analysis, and molecular approaches. These innovative methods empower early and accurate detection of diseases, empowering cultivators and experts to make well-informed decisions and protect the health of guava plants. As technology advances, the realm of guava leaf disease detection exhibits the potential for more streamlined and efficacious disease management within the agricultural domain. To democratize disease detection, ingenious mobile applications have been conceptualized, allowing farmers to capture leaf images using their smartphones. These images are seamlessly uploaded onto cloud-based platforms, where advanced algorithms swiftly process them, delivering real-time disease diagnoses coupled with recommendations for effective management strategies (Figs. 6, 7 and 8).

YOLOv8, model architecture consists of convolutional layers and does not include fully connected layers. The architecture is fully convolutional, which means it operates on input images of arbitrary sizes without the need for resizing or cropping (Figs. 9, 10, 11, 12).

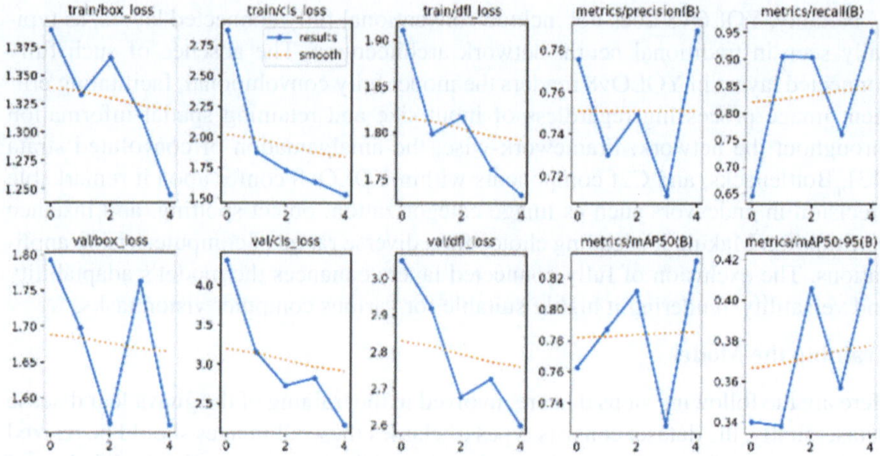

Fig. 5 Image which is obtained in the training results

Fig. 6 Recall-confidence curve

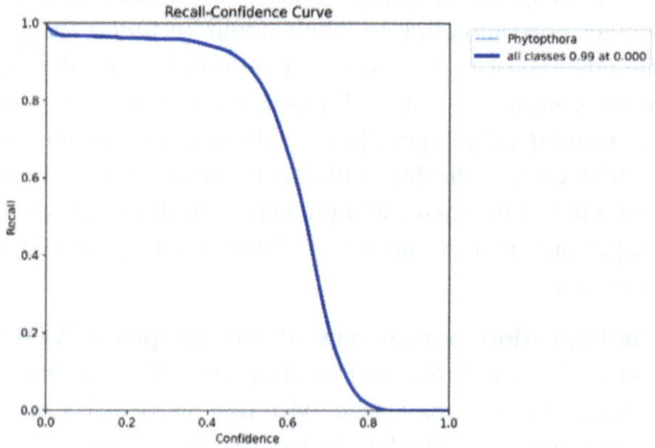

Fig. 7 F1-confidence curve

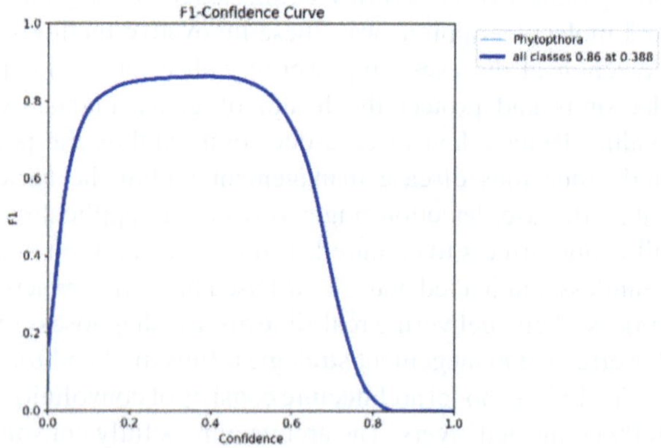

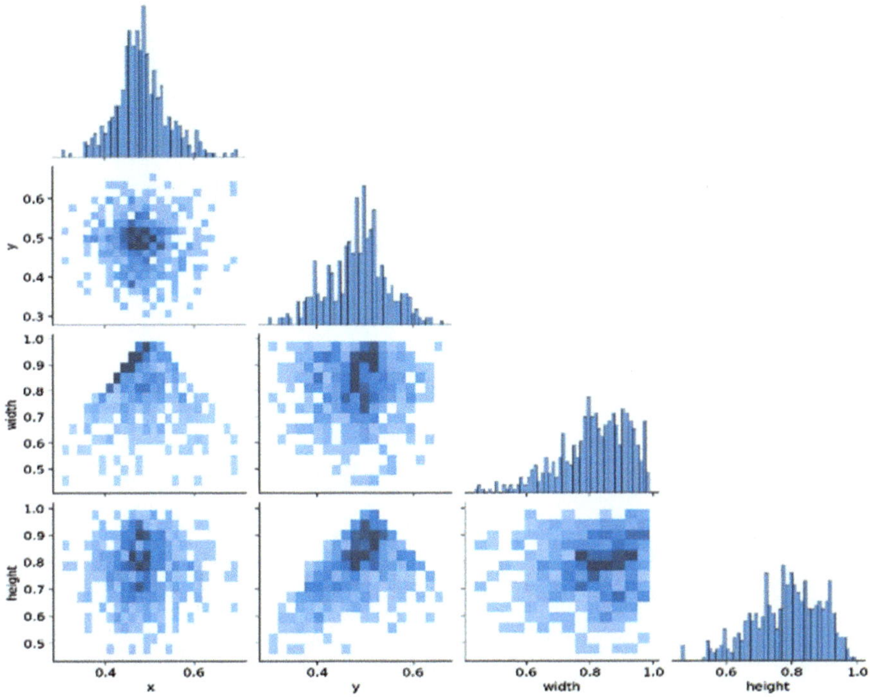

Fig. 8 Labels-correlogram

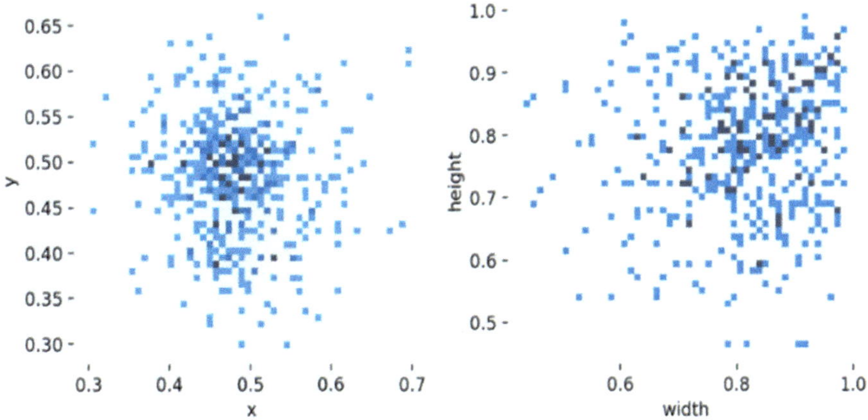

Fig. 9 Labels-classification based on height and width

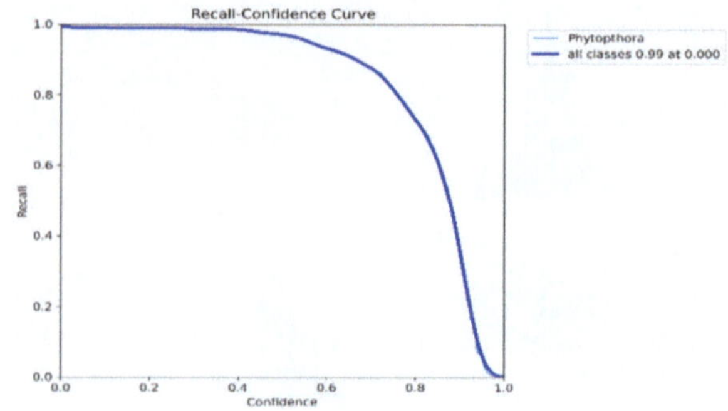

Fig. 10 F1-recall-confidence curve in validation

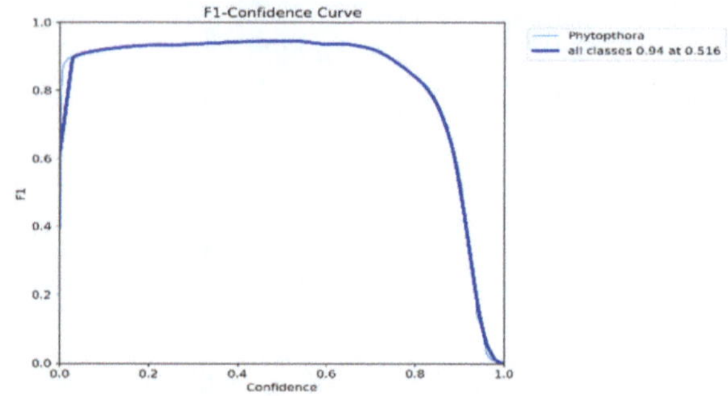

Fig. 11 F1-confidence curve in validation

Fig. 12 Detection of disease images

The values used for the proposed model are as follows

Utilizing a scaling factor of 1/256 alongside a learning rate set at 0.1, the training endeavor extended across 150 epochs. Over the course of this training duration, the architecture, constituting 225 strata, harbored a notable degree of intricacy. Interestingly, this intricate nature found an echo [15] in the considerable volume of gradients, mirroring the parameter count at 3,011,807. The model showcased its efficacy by attaining a substantial training accuracy of 97%, signifying the ratio of accurately classified occurrences within the training dataset [13]. Impressively, this adeptness carried forth into the validation stage, wherein the model sustained a laudable precision of 87%.

The model's performance during the training and validation epochs was assessed through loss metrics. In the training phase, the model's loss, indicative of the divergence between anticipated and actual values, was duly noted at 0.411. Likewise, the validation loss, an indicator of the model's capacity for generalization, was gauged at 0.599. To encapsulate, employing a rescale factor of 1/256 and a learning rate of 0.1, the model, boasting an expansive 225 strata and encompassing 3,011,823 parameters, underwent a training journey spanning 150 epochs. This undertaking bore fruit in the form of a commendable [16] training accuracy of 97% and a validation accuracy of 87%. The model's prowess was further accentuated by the loss metrics, reflected in a training loss of 0.411 and a validation loss of 0.599.

7 Results

Upon system commencement, it considers individual images from the dataset and processes them through the envisaged model [17] and when it detects a disease it shows what percentage of disease affected the leaf is. It also detects the disease and it shows a box-like figure indicating which part of the fruit or leaf [18] was affected and which part is not affected.

The model's effectiveness was assessed utilizing the "Accuracy" measure in the subsequent manner

$$Accuracy = \frac{Number\ of\ Correct\ prediction}{Total\ of\ all\ cases\ to\ be\ predicted}$$

The operational model yielded accuracy that spanned from 95% to a peak value of 97.76%. On a mean basis, the model delivered accuracy exceeding 95%.

8 Conclusion

The investigation focuses on utilizing computer vision techniques to detect diseases in guava leaves. Deep learning models are applied, showing promising results in accurate disease classification, and enabling timely interventions for agricultural management [19]. Data preparation, augmentation, and model training significantly impact the system's efficacy. Convolutional neural networks (CNNs) and advanced methods effectively differentiate between healthy and infected leaves. Precise evaluation metrics validate the model's ability to generalize to new data and address real-world challenges. Implementing such systems in agriculture can enhance crop productivity [20] and reduce financial losses. The study acknowledges potential areas for improvement, including tuning hyperparameters and expanding the dataset. This research contributes significantly to plant disease detection, showcasing the potential of computer vision in agriculture [21]. Continuous exploration holds promise for sustainable agricultural practices through guava leaf disease detection.

References

1. Perumal P (2021) Guava leaf disease classification using support vector machine. Turk J Comput Math Educ (TURCOMAT) 12(7):1177–1183
2. Rashid J, Khan I, Ali G, Alturise F, Alkhalifah T (2023) Real-time multiple guava leaf disease detection from a single leaf using hybrid deep learning technique. Comput Mater Continua 74(1)
3. Mostafa AM, Kumar SA, Meraj T, Rauf HT, Alnuaim AA, Alkhayyal MA (2021) Guava disease detection using deep convolutional neural networks: a case study of guava plants. Appl Sci 12(1):239
4. Srinivas B, Satheesh P, Rama Santosh Naidu P, Neelima U (2021) Prediction of guava plant diseases using deep learning. In: Kumar A, Mozar S (eds) ICCCE 2020. Lecture notes in electrical engineering, vol 698. Springer, Singapore. https://doi.org/10.1007/978-981-15-7961-5_135
5. Ganesan G, Chinnappan J (2022) Hybridization of ResNet with YOLO classifier for automated paddy leaf disease recognition: an optimized model. J Field Robot 39(7):1085–1109
6. Mumtaz S, Raza M, Okon OD, Rehman SU, Ragab AE, Rauf HT (2023) A hybrid framework for detection and analysis of leaf blight using guava leaves imaging. Agriculture 13(3):667
7. James N, Shriwastav KK, Medhi S, Medhi SP (2023) A guava leaf disease identification application
8. Abirami M, Thilagavathi S (2017) Application of image processing in diagnosing guava leaf diseases. Int J Sci Res Manage (IJSRM) 5(7):5927–5933
9. Mehta K, Kothari H, Somani V, Kumar A (2022) Early-stage prediction & detection of guava leaves disease using genetic algorithm. Int J Early Childhood Special Educ 14(7). [12] "Lexus Enform", Lexus, 2019. [Online]. Available: https://www.lexus.com/enform. Accessed 07 Mar 2019
10. Rajbongshi A, Sazzad S, Shakil R, Akter B, Sara U (2022) A comprehensive guava leaves and fruits dataset for guava disease recognition. Data Brief 42:108174
11. Almadhor A, Rauf HT, Lali MIU, Damaševičius R, Alouffi B, Alharbi A (2021) AI-driven framework for recognition of guava plant diseases through machine learning from DSLR camera sensor based high resolution imagery. Sensors 21(11):3830

12. Tachakittirungrod S, Okonogi S, Chowwanapoonpohn S (2007) Study on antioxidant activity of certain plants in Thailand: mechanism of antioxidant action of guava leaf extract. Food Chem 103(2):381–388
13. Tewari V, Azeem NA, Sharma S (2023) Automatic guava disease detection using different deep learning approaches. Multimedia Tools Appl 1–24
14. Silva CF, Torres P, Oliveira NP, Marques AS, Ferreira MA (2015) PCR-based methods for detection of *Erwinia psidii* on guava. Trop Plant Pathol 40:251–259
15. Jiang L, Lu J, Qin Y, Jiang W, Wang Y (2020) Antitumor effect of guava leaves on lung cancer: a network pharmacology study. Arab J Chem 13(11):7773–7797
16. Irondi EA, Agboola SO, Oboh G, Boligon AA, Athayde ML, Shode FO (2016) Guava leaves polyphenolics-rich extract inhibits vital enzymes implicated in gout and hypertension in vitro. J Intercult Ethnopharmacol 5(2):122
17. Yin XL, Li ZJ, Yang K, Lin HZ, Guo ZX (2014) Effect of guava leaves on growth and the non-specific immune response of *Penaeus monodon*. Fish Shellfish Immunol 40(1):190–196
18. Shetty YS, Shankarapillai R, Vivekanandan G, Shetty RM, Reddy CS, Reddy H, Mangalekar SB (2018) Evaluation of the efficacy of guava extract as an antimicrobial agent on periodontal pathogens. J Contemp Dent Pract 19(6):690–697
19. Kadam V, Patil MP, Kumar MR. Mobile application for predicting diseases with providing remedies on guava plant leaves with the help of deep learning techniques and cloud computing
20. Giri SS, Kim HJ, Kim SG, Kim SW, Kwon J, Lee SB, Park SC (2020) Effectiveness of the guava leaf extracts against lipopolysaccharide-induced oxidative stress and immune responses in *Cyprinus carpio*. Fish Shellfish Immunol 105:164–176
21. Díaz-de-Cerio E, Verardo V, Gómez-Caravaca AM, Fernández-Gutiérrez A, Segura-Carretero A (2016) Exploratory characterization of phenolic compounds with demonstrated anti-diabetic activity in guava leaves at different oxidation states. Int J Mol Sci 17(5):699
22. Luo Y, Peng B, Liu Y, Wu Y, Wu Z (2018) Ultrasound extraction of polysaccharides from guava leaves and their antioxidant and antiglycation activity. Process Biochem 73:228–234
23. Seo J, Lee S, Elam ML, Johnson SA, Kang J, Arjmandi BH (2014) Study to find the best extraction solvent for use with guava leaves (*Psidium guajava* L.) for high antioxidant efficacy. Food Sci Nutr 2(2):174–180

Multi-document Question Answering Using Transformers, LANGCHAIN

Likith Sai Reddy and Surendra Reddy Vinta

1 Introduction

The world is booming with new cutting-edge technologies like Machine learning, VR, and more. Natural language processing which is known as NLP is one of them contributing no less than others in evolving the world. NLP has significant importance in developing language models. The advancements of NLP mitigated the efforts of work human put into by saving time. The work of multi-document question answering is one of the NLP techniques which comprehends and integrates information from various sources to provide in detail and precise responses to user input queries. This research presents the detailing of the collaboration of two advanced emerging technologies Hugging LLM and LangChain to tackle the complexities of multi-document question answering which are left behind. On the other hand, this study expands its research to integrate audio conversion to the model by leveraging Fairseq framework which is well known for converting textual responses into coherent audio responses.

During revolutionary era, characterization by surplus information have derived significant skills and insights to create many more great texts. The system of conventional question and answers had an exhibit limitation which is faced to integrate information from other resources to eradicate inquiries. It is very difficult to tackle with necessary capability steps to combine advanced language model which can be understood in a textual input from several resources with novel methodology together for enabling organization process to an information. Language models are shown as proficiency in comprehending and producing remarkable texts that closely resemble human language. Hugging LLM is a profound example of this model, which is efficient and recommendable in Various natural language processing further endeavors.

L. S. Reddy · S. R. Vinta (✉)
School of Computer Science and Engineering, VIT-AP University, Amaravati, Andhra Pradesh, India
e-mail: surendrareddy.vinta@vitap.ac.in

K. Kumar Singh et al. (eds.), *Machine Vision and Augmented Intelligence*, Lecture Notes in Electrical Engineering 1211, https://doi.org/10.1007/978-981-97-4359-9_46

This study aims to leverage the advantages of Hugging LLM to explore the field of multi-document question and answering through the contextual understanding and analysis of many documents and the Hugging LLM model offers s robust framework to generate appropriate answers.

Language models like Hugging LLM exhibits high proficiency in processing individual documents. However, it requires the use of innovative technologies for the effective management of multi-document question scenarios.

The Langchain architecture helps to bridge this gap by simplifying the large volumes of data documents for the quick access of LLMs.

The layout of the appliance gives a nicely organized frame for managing relations at the report stage, hence perfecting the perfection and thickness of responses in multi-file query-answering situations. In the present day technology of virtual advancements, the approach via which individualities devour information is diversifying beyond the traditional medium of textbook. The conversion of written responses into audio layout presents guests with stepped forward availability and advanced convenience. The alternate is eased with the aid of Fairseq, a frame for series-to-sequence modeling, which makes use of cutting-aspect strategies in voice conflation. Inclusive of Fairseq into the multi-document question answering channel, this oil expands its impact to audial interfaces, accordingly accommodating a big selection of guests with colorful traits and requirements. The idea of this is to show off the abilities of Hugging LLM and Langchain in rightly diving the problems related to multi-report question answering. This takes a look at delves further into the operation of Fairseq for audio conversion, with a named recognition on pressing the significance of easing easy consumer engagement through acoustic interfaces. In this paper, we will explore complex and challenging aspects of our methodology and dive into brief detailing about architecture of our work and present our results and conclusion by analyzing the importance of multi-document question answering. And also, we aim to push the limits of multi-document question answering models by integrating Hugging LLM, Langchain, and Fairseq as a contribution to interactive artificial intelligence systems.

In this paper, we're suitable to explore complex and challenging elements of our methodology and dive into quick detailing about skeleton of our work and present our outcomes and conclusion via breaking down the significance of multi-document question answering model. And also we aim to push the boundaries of multi-document question answering models by integrating Hugging LLM, Langchain, and Fairseq as a contribution to interactive artificial intelligence systems.

2 Literature Survey

The paper gives a framework for summarizing research papers on a firm the usage of deductive and abstraction methods. It highlights the cost of goal summaries for debatable issues. Customized summaries based on user options seem greater informative. The framework gives insights into efficiently extracting statistics from tests [3].

The paper explores Question Answering Systems (QASs) evolution from limited to advanced capabilities, spanning question types, data sources, and answers. Dating back to the 1960s, QASs have proliferated. A comprehensive survey is proposed to guide future research, categorizing QASs and suggesting new directions [4].

CAiRE-COVID is a real-time system that excelled in a COVID-19 research challenge. It answers crucial questions and summarizes articles using advanced techniques. It combines information extraction, QA, and multi-document summarization, enhancing relevancy with new summarization methods. Quantitative tests validate its improvements. The system is accessible through a website and open-source code for broader research use [5].

In the era of information overload, summarization techniques sift through vast text volumes for relevance. Evaluating a novel multilayer network model for multi-document summarization, nodes (sentences) and edges (shared words) reveal inter- and intra-layer links. This discrimination improves extractive summarization, offering insights to enhance statistical methods and text models [6].

The study emphasizes LLMs' swift application development, featuring LangChain, an open-source library. LangChain efficiently creates custom AI apps using modular abstractions and adaptable pipelines. Practical examples underscore LangChain's potential for rapid LLM-based app development [7].

Open-domain Question Answering (OpenQA) is pivotal in NLP, answering questions from unstructured data. This review spotlights neural Machine Reading Comprehension (MRC) integration, analyzing "Retriever-Reader" architecture, techniques, challenges, and benchmarks. It addresses gaps in existing surveys, informing researchers and driving OpenQA progress [8].

Instruction-tuned large language models like GPT-4 excel in language tasks, but their full potential lacks understanding due to limited evaluation. INSTRUCTEVAL introduces a comprehensive assessment suite focusing on problem-solving, writing, and values alignment. Data quality proves pivotal, underscoring the need for rigorous evaluation despite rapid open-source model development [9].

3 Methodology

3.1 Dataset

The tatsu-lab/alpaca dataset was used to train the big language model declare-lab/flan-alpaca-large. Alpaca's statistics are available in English (BCP-47 en). Alpaca was created using the 52,000 instructions and demos provided by the OpenAI text-davinci-003 engine. The data generating pipeline from the Self-Instruct framework was expanded upon by the authors. Use the text-Davinci-003 engine to construct the instruction data rather than Davinci The cost of producing data was drastically reduced by using a far more aggressive batch decoding technique that generated 20 instructions at once. Using this instruction data, it is able to carry out

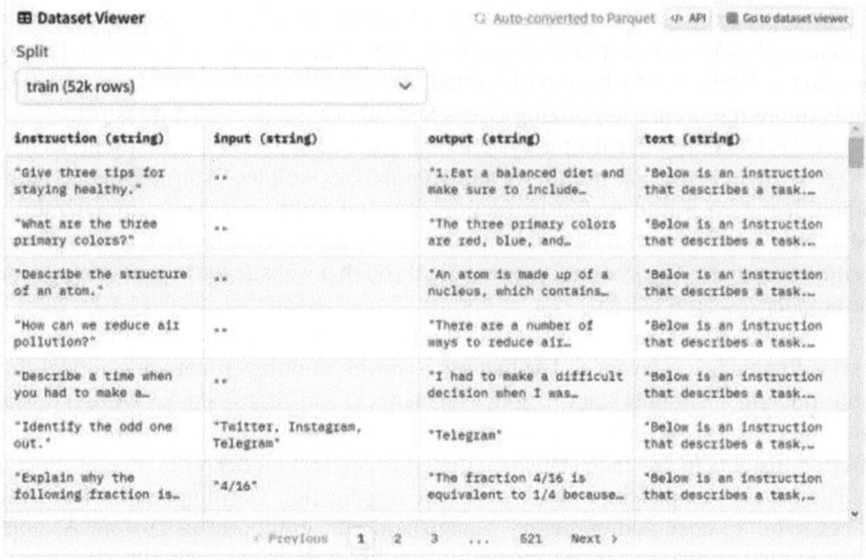

Fig. 1 Preview of the dataset used for the declare-lab/flan-alpaca-large model

instruction-tuning for language models, which will enhance their capacity to adhere to instructions [17, 18].

The datasets shown in Fig. 1 are used for the model.

The pre-trained model used in the method conversation of Text to Speech has been trained by using a large dataset called LJ Speech Dataset. This dataset contains audio clips as well as conversation of those audio clips. It contains around 13,100 short audio clips which vary in length from 1 to 10 s. The total duration of this dataset is around 24 h.

3.2 *Existing Systems*

Answer Retrieval from the Document

Answer retrieval from the PDF document for the input question is the integration of different frameworks which involves Langchain, huggingface embeddings, QuestionAnswering pipeline, and a large language model [10–12].

We setup the environment for question answering. Load and preprocess the PDF documents using the "UnstructuredPDFLoader" module to load PDF documents from a designated directory or selected PDF file. This module reads the PDF files and prepares them for similar processing. A module in Langchain is hired to divide the PDF text content material into smaller, potential chunks or segments. These chunks are then processed through the "HuggingFaceEmbeddings" module, which creates numerical representations (embeddings) of the textual content chunks. Then Langchain's "VectorstoreIndexCreator" magnificence is carried out to create an index of these embeddings. This index permits inexperienced retrieval of applicable data during the query-answering process. Now load the HuggingFace language model. The "HuggingFaceHub" class allows entry to fashions to be had at the Hugging Face model hub. Using the "HuggingFaceHub", a particular language version named "Flan Alpaca Large" is loaded. This version is able to generating textual content and appearing various language-related duties [1, 2]. The version is initialized with positive parameters consisting of "temperature" and "max_length", which have an effect on the technology of responses. Now Question Answering Pipeline is set up. This pipeline combines the language model with a records retrieval component to provide contextually applicable solutions. The pipeline is configured with the loaded language model, a selected chain kind, an index retriever based totally on the listed PDF embeddings, and an input key indicating that questions may be used as inputs. The pipeline methods the query, retrieves applicable statistics from the listed PDF files, and generates an answer to the usage of the loaded language model. The massive language model analyzes the solution and gives the favored output in a summarized manner [16].

Proposed Method

The below flow diagram shows the steps and process of the proposed model.

Step 1: Load the pdf to the model.

Step 2: Splitting of pdf into chunks by Langchain

Step 3: Chunks are converted into embeddings by FuggingFaceEmbeddings

Step 4: embeddings are stored as vector Index.

Step 5: The input query is taken.

Step 6: RetrivalQA (Question Answering pipeline) is used to search for similar embeddings from the index and convert them to
text.

Step 7: Using this the LLM generates a deserved answer.

Step 8: Using FAIRSEQ the answer is converted into audio.

Now we will discuss the overall architecture and frameworks of the final proposed model as shown in Flowchart 1.

We set up the environment and import the necessary modules and specific components from Langchain and Hugging Face libraries. The Langchain framework is a collection of Python libraries and tools designed to facilitate various NLP tasks. It aims to simplify the development of NLP pipelines by providing pre-built components and functionalities. In our model, several modules from the Langchain framework are utilized. UnstructuredPDFLoader is the module which is accountable for loading and processing PDF files and it prepares the PDF content material for similar analysis. VectorstoreIndexCreator is the key module used for growing an index of embeddings generated from the PDF textual content material. The index allows for efficient retrieval of information all through query answering.

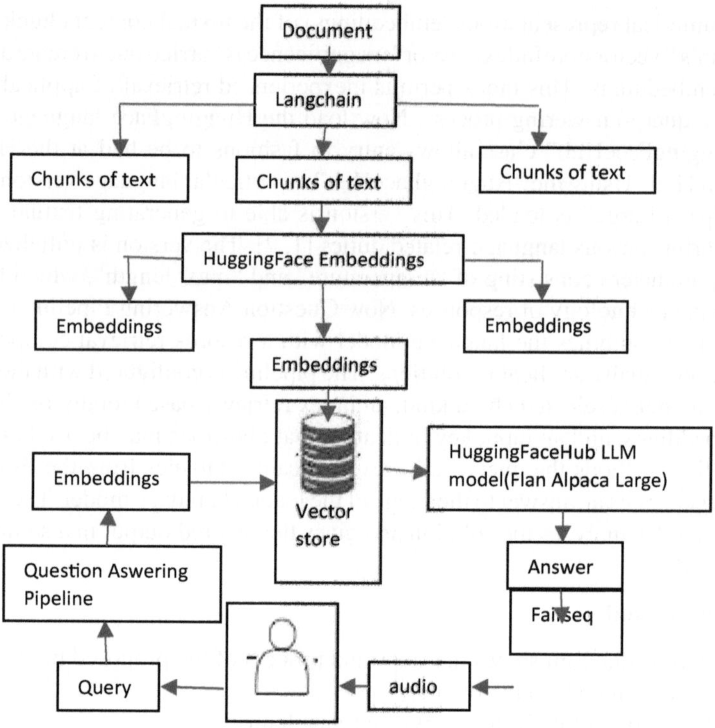

Flowchart 1 Proposed architecture

CharacterTextSplitter is the module used to break up the textual content content of PDFs into smaller chunks. These chunks are then processed and embedded for indexing that is the most crucial part of the procedure.

RetrievalQA is the module wherein a pipeline is constructed for retrieval-primarily based question answering the usage of this module. In order to reply to personal inquiries with facts based totally on applicable file content, it combines a language model and an index retriever.

The Hugging Face framework is a popular platform for working with and sharing pre-trained models for herbal language knowledge and era. It gives a wide range of pre-educated fashions and libraries that can be used for various NLP duties. In the model, the Hugging Face framework is used for the HuggingFaceEmbeddings and HuggingFaceHub.

HuggingFaceEmbeddings is a class utilized to generate embedding which are numerical representations of text chunks. These embeddings seize semantic records about the textual content and are vital for building the index.

HuggingFaceHub is a class that facilitates getting right of entry to fashions hosted at the Hugging Face version hub. It lets you to load and use pre-skilled fashions like language models, for numerous NLP tasks.

Loading a Language Model is the most essential step of the studies. Here the code loads a selected language version called "Flan Alpaca Large" the usage of the HuggingFaceHub as it can be used for text generation and question answering.

The Langchain framework components are used to handle document loading, chunking, embedding generation, and indexing. This prepares the PDF documents for efficient retrieval and analysis. The Hugging Face framework is leveraged to load a powerful language model that is capable of generating responses to questions based on the indexed content. The retrieval-based question-answering pipeline created using Langchain components and the Hugging Face model allows for contextually relevant answers to be generated from the indexed PDF documents.

4 Results

The conversation of Text-to-speech operation is performed by using facebook/fastspeech2-en-ljspeech model which is already a pre-trained model with a large dataset called LJ Speech. This model can be accessed by the Fairseq which is available on Hugging face open source platform. For the summarized text the Text-to-Speech (TTS) model is applied.

```
ipd.Audio(wav, rate=rate)
```

The evaluation of Large Language Model used in the model is for writing-based tasks. Flan-Alpaca model is better compared to other large language models. As the model mainly focuses on question answering we need the model to perform well in writing-based tasks. Table 1 shows the evaluation results for writing-based tasks.

Finally, the evaluation of the overall model is done by calculating ROUGE metric and BLEU score. The answer obtained for the query asked is compared with the

Table 1 Evaluation results for writing-based tasks

Model	Size	Informative		Professional		Argumentative		Creative		Avg	
		Rel	Coh	Rel	Coh	Rel	Coh	Rel	Coh	Rel	Coh
ChatGPT	–	3.34	3.98	3.88	3.96	3.96	3.82	3.92	3.94	3.78	3.93
Flan-Alpaca	11B	3.56	3.46	3.54	3.70	3.22	3.28	3.70	3.40	3.51	3.46
Dolly-V2	12B	3.54	3.64	2.96	3.74	3.66	3.20	3.02	3.18	3.30	3.44
Stable Vicuna	13B	3.54	3.64	2.96	3.74	3.30	3.20	3.02	3.18	3.21	3.44
Flan-T5	11B	2.64	3.24	2.62	3.22	2.54	3.40	2.50	2.72	2.58	3.15

original answer in the pdf. In NLP, the BLEU and ROUGE scores are two often used metrics.

BLEU score:

Formula [13]: $\text{BLEU} = \text{BP} * \exp(\sum \text{pn})$.

The obtained BLEU score values of the model are as follows:

BLEU score: 0.7881929718099911.

ROUGH score:

Formula [15]: $\text{ROUGE} = \sum(\text{Recall of n - grams})$.

The three types of ROUGE scores are ROUGE-N, ROUGE-L, and ROUGE-S [14].

The obtained ROUGE score values for the model are as follows:

```
rouge_dict: {'rouge1': 0.962962962962963, 'rouge2': 0.8799999999999999, 'rougeL': 0.962962962962963, 'rougeLsum': 0.962962962962963}
```

5 Conclusion and Future Scope

This approach addresses the throes of efficaciously extracting information from more than one document to answer complex questions and also offering the results in an auditory layout, which can be useful for individuals who select auditory getting to know especially. The integration of multi-document processing in question answering systems significantly improves the rigorousness and reliability of answers with the aid of considering a broader context of records. It allows the system to cross-reference data from distinct sources and blends a comprehensive response. The extension of audio output boosts the studies for higher obtainability and value by means of way of creating the facts greater accessible to an important wider region of target request of audience.

The integration of Flax-ALPACA-Large, a modern version for Multi-Document Question and answering with Fairseq for generating audio output opens up new approaches for accessible and efficient records retrieval and consumption. This generation emits its giant ability in various domain names including schooling, content material consumption, research, and customer service. The capability to retrieve answers from various documents which isn't team spirit and providing them with audio format gives a greater snug and comprehensive enjoyment for users individuals who pick mastering with audio assistance and visible impairments.

This method leverages the strengths of both Flax-ALPACA-Large and Fairseq to recognize complex questions and extract relevant facts from multiple sources and remodel textual answers into human-like audio responses. It takes a breakthrough in growing advanced conversational sellers that no longer most effectively process textual content; however also presents statistics through a medium that fits various person options.

This research task has covered the way for innovative upgrades in query-answering structures by way of seamlessly integrating Fairseq with the Langchain framework and the Hugging Face language version.

The future exploration for this version may be higher if the system's competencies advanced to accept inputs in diverse modalities which include audio and text. The destiny exploration 19 robust speech reputation mechanisms may be implemented to transform spoken voice queries into textual shape, allowing customers to interact with the system the usage of voice commands or audio clips to beautify the tool's accessibility for visually impaired clients and people who choose auditory interactions. The fusion of MDQA and audio generation has promising hints for in addition studies and improvement in enhancing audio high quality which integrates superior TTS systems to provide more herbal and expressive audio reaction. This model can eye on extending the technology to guide a couple of languages a good way to allow users round internationally to get entry to records in their favored language. This method expands its capacity to create interactive systems for users to ask questions and try to find clarifications. The Hugging face model can similarly cognizance allowing users to personalize the tone, pace, and style of the audio. This model can integrate into assistive gadgets and packages which empower disabilities to get the right of entry to records extraction without difficulty.

In conclusion, the fusion of Flax-ALPACA-Large and Fairseq for multi-document question answering with audio output has the potential to revolutionize information access and consumption. Continued research, innovation, and collaboration in this field will bring us closer to creating intelligent systems that cater to diverse user needs and preferences.

References

1. Goldstein J et al (2000) Multi-document summarization by sentence extraction. NAACL-ANLP 2000 workshop: automatic summarization
2. Ma C, Zhang WE, Guo M, Wang H, Sheng QZ (2022) Multi-document summarization via deep learning techniques: a survey. ACM Comput Surv 55(5):1–37
3. Carenini G, Cheung JCK, Pauls A (2013) Multi-document summarization of evaluative text. Comput Intell 29(4):545–576
4. Mishra A, Jain SK (2016) A survey on question answering systems with classification. J King Saud Univ-Comput Inform Sci 28(3):345–361
5. Su D et al (2020) CAiRE-COVID: a question answering and query-focused multi-document summarization system for COVID-19 scholarly information management. arXiv preprint arXiv: 2005.03975
6. Tohalino JV, Amancio DR (2018) Extractive multi-document summarization using multilayer networks. Physica A 503:526–539
7. Topsakal O, Akinci TC (2023) Creating large language model applications utilizing LangChain: a primer on developing LLM apps fast. Int Conf Appl Eng Nat Sci 1(1)
8. Zhu F et al (2021) Retrieving and reading: a comprehensive survey on open-domain question answering. arXiv preprint arXiv:2101.00774

9. Chia YK et al (2023) INSTRUCTEVAL: towards holistic evaluation of instruction-tuned large language models. arXiv preprint arXiv:2306.04757
10. Karpukhin V et al (2020) Dense passage retrieval for open-domain question answering. arXiv preprint arXiv:2004.04906
11. https://huggingface.co/datasets/tatsu-lab/alpaca
12. Zen H, Dang V, Clark R, Zhang Y, Weiss RJ, Jia Y, Wu Y (2019) Libritts: a corpus derived from librispeech for text-to-speech. arXiv preprint arXiv:1904.02882
13. Ni J et al (2022) Unsupervised text-to-speech synthesis by unsupervised automatic speech recognition. arXiv preprint arXiv:2203.15796
14. Do P et al (2023) Resource-efficient fine-tuning strategies for automatic MOS prediction in text-to-speech for low-resource languages. arXiv preprint arXiv:2305.19396
15. Wang C et al (2021) fairseq S^ 2: a scalable and integrable speech synthesis toolkit. arXiv preprint arXiv:2109.06912
16. Liu T (2019) Optimizing BLEU scores for improving text generation
17. Grusky M (2023) Rogue scores. In: Proceedings of the 61st annual meeting of the association for computational linguistics, vol 1, Long Papers
18. Tay W et al (2019) Red-faced rouge: examining the suitability of rouge for opinion summary evaluation. In: Proceedings of the 17th annual workshop of the Australasian language technology association

Neural Style Transfer Using Convolution Architectures

Shaik Afraa and Surendra Reddy Vinta

1 Introduction

Neural Style Transfer is a cool technique that combines deep learning algorithms and art to create beautiful and aesthetic images [4]. It focuses on creating new images that have the appearance of the style image while keeping the content of the original image. The combination of innovation, technology and art has sparked a lot of interest [5].

The fundamental idea behind NST is based on deep neural network's amazing capacity to extract complex patterns and characteristics from huge datasets [12]. NST adds a new level of artistic [8] transformation by treating images as multi-layered representations. The recognized visual artistry techniques, such as the brushstrokes of well-known painters or the textures and patterns that characterize specific creative genres, serve as the artistic inspiration for NST [3, 8].

Our study is supported by a thorough analysis of eight optimization algorithms: Adam, Adamax, RMSProp, AdamW, SGD, Adagrad, Adadelta, and Nadam, as well as four well-known neural network architectures: VGG19, ResNet50, ResNet152V2, and Xception. Neural style transfer can be implemented using Convolution Neural Networks (CNN) [16] (Fig. 1).

S. Afraa · S. R. Vinta (✉)
School of Computer Science and Engineering, VIT-AP University, Amaravati, Andhra Pradesh, India
e-mail: surendrareddy.vinta@vitap.ac.in

S. Afraa
e-mail: afraa.21bce9022@vitapstudent.ac.in

K. Kumar Singh et al. (eds.), *Machine Vision and Augmented Intelligence*, Lecture Notes in Electrical Engineering 1211, https://doi.org/10.1007/978-981-97-4359-9_47

Fig. 1 The above-generated image is the result when resnet50 was used with Adam optimizer

2 Literature Survey

The article "Neural Style Transfer Using ResNet50V2" examines how Neural Style Transfer (NST) combines images of content and style [11]. The usage of ResNet50V2 and TensorFlow for real-time image manipulation is explored by the authors. The research gives a thorough analysis of the available NST techniques and classifies them according to their effectiveness, loss functions, and image quality.

In the paper "Image Style Transfer Using Deep Learning" [6], authors suggest calculating the internal product of feature and spatial transformation maps using an updated Gramm matrix, which will improve the style loss function. The study places a focus on maintaining semantic content while fusing style and content.

A method for transferring picture style by utilizing convolutional neural networks (CNN) is presented in the study titled "Image Style Transfer Using Machine Learning" [7]. The authors concentrate on combining the content and style of two photos using a formula for content loss and style loss. For image processing and manipulation, they make use of machine learning tools including Deep-Lab Semantic Segmentation, OpenCV, and TensorFlow.

3 Methodology

3.1 Image Choice and Feature Extraction Using a Pre-Trained Model

Choose a content image that serves as the foundation for the scene or subject, and then choose a style image that captures the artistic spirit you want to pour into the final piece. The basis for the process of transferring the style will be these pictures. Use a neural network model that can extract complex characteristics from photos.

3.2 Calculating Content and Style Loss

To compare the content of the content image with the synthesized image, compute the Mean Squared Error (MSE) between feature maps obtained from the pre-trained model's defined content layers.

Let ***A^l_{ij}(I)*** be the activation of layer l, feature map i and position j obtained using the image ***I***. Then the content loss is defined as,

$$L_{\text{content}} = \frac{1}{2}\sum_{i,j}\left(A_{ij}^{l}(g) - A_{ij}^{l}(c)\right)^{2}$$

Calculate the Gramm matrices of feature maps from the selected style layers. Mathematically, the style loss is defined as,

$$L_{\text{style}} = \sum\nolimits_{l} w^{l} L_{\text{style}}^{l} \ where,$$

$$L_{style}^{l} = \frac{1}{M^{l}}\sum\nolimits_{ij}\left(G_{ij}^{l}(s) - G_{ij}^{l}g\right)^{2} where,$$

$$G_{ij}^{l}(I) = \sum\nolimits_{k} A_{ik}^{l}(I)A_{jk}^{l}(I)$$

3.3 Calculating Total Loss

Combine the style and content losses, taking into account their respective contributions to the final product [18]. The cumulative impact of these weighted losses results in the overall loss.

The total loss is defined as,

$$L = \alpha L_{\text{content}} + \beta L_{\text{style}}$$

3.4 Image Optimization and Creation of Stylized Images

Use a heuristic optimization approach to gradually reduce the overall loss. The synthesized image is iteratively adjusted by optimization algorithms. This procedure comprises fine-tuning the synthesized image's pixel values. To ensure that the synthesized image captures the required balance of content and aesthetic, keep an eye on the convergence of the loss function.

3.5 Visualization

The final stylized image is a fusion of information and style that, upon convergence, reflects the creative vision ingrained in the style image.

4 What Are the Different Architectures that Can Be Used?

4.1 VGG-19

Convolutional neural network VGG19, which was originally created for image classification applications, is renowned for its ease of use and efficiency in feature extraction. It is a potent tool for this artistic application because it pulls content and aesthetic information from input photographs [17].

4.2 ResNet50

The deep convolutional neural network architecture known as ResNet-50, sometimes known as "Residual Network 50," is often used for a variety of computer vision applications [1]. The use of residual blocks, which enables the training of extremely deep neural networks, is the ResNet architecture's major innovation.

4.3 ResNet-152v2

The Residual Network architecture, also known as ResNet-152v2, was created to overcome the difficulties associated with training extremely deep neural networks. The use of "identity mappings," which are intended to reduce the degradation issue that arises when adding additional layers to a deep neural network, is the main innovation of ResNet-152v2.

4.4 Xception

The depth-wise separable convolutions suggested in the deep convolutional neural network architecture known as Xception is built on the concepts of the Inception design [13]. By utilizing depth-wise separable convolutions, the typical convolution is separated into pointwise and depth-wise convolutions.

Fig. 2 Represents the stylized images for different pre-trained models when the Adam optimizer is used

5 How to Optimize Our Results?

Finding an image that minimizes a combined loss function made up of content loss, style loss, and total variation loss is the goal of neural style transfer. This is often accomplished by iteratively updating the pixel values of the resulting image using an optimization algorithm. All the stylized images shown below are the results of different models when different optimizers are used for 2000 epochs.

5.1 Adam

The Adam optimizer, also known as "Adaptive Moment Estimation," is a combination of RMSprop and momentum techniques. While retaining per-parameter adaptive learning rates, the parameters are updated using the initial and next moments of the gradients. Due to its adaptive nature, it is particularly well suited for applications like neural style transfer (Fig. 2).

5.2 Adamax

Adamax is a version of Adam that substitutes the gradients' infinite norm for the second moment estimation. It has been suggested as a replacement for Adam to perform better in situations involving sparse gradients. It combines the advantages of the Adam optimizer with an alternative method for determining the moving average of previous gradients (Fig. 3).

Fig. 3 Represents the stylized images for different pre-trained models when the Adamax optimizer is used

Fig. 4 Represents the stylized images for different pre-trained models when the Adadelta optimizer is used

Fig. 5 Represents the stylized images for different pre-trained models when the Adagrad optimizer is used

5.3 Adadelta

Adadelta seeks to get around some of the drawbacks of more established adaptive learning rate techniques like AdaGrad and RMSProp. By dynamically adjusting the learning rates depending on the most recent history of gradients, it overcomes the problem of declining learning rates. AdaDelta adjusts the learning rate based on a sliding window of gradient changes (Fig. 4).

5.4 Adagrad

The "Adaptive Gradient Algorithm" or "Adagrad" is an optimization technique that involves changing the learning rate for certain parameters with past gradient information. It is very useful in handling sparse data as it gives a way for adjusting the learning rates depending on the number of updates for every parameter. Neuronal styles are usually imparted with adagrad less frequently in practice (Fig. 5).

5.5 AdamW

AdamW is a variation of the well-known Adam optimizer that was created to solve certain problems with weight decay regularization. AdamW enhances the efficiency

Fig. 6 Represents the stylized images for different pre-trained models when the AdamW optimizer is used

Fig. 7 Represents the stylized images for different pre-trained models when the RMSprop optimizer is used

and stability of the original Adam algorithm by appropriately isolating weight decay from the gradient update phase (Fig. 6).

5.6 RMSprop

The optimization approach known as RMSProp, or "Root Mean Square Propagation," was created to solve various stochastic gradient descent (SGD) restrictions and accelerate convergence. Based on the magnitudes of the most recent gradients, it modifies the learning rates for certain parameters (Fig. 7).

5.7 Stochastic Gradient Descent

The SGD (Stochastic Gradient Descent) optimization technique is a fundamental and popular one. By calculating the gradient of the loss function concerning the parameters, it updates the model's parameters. Although SGD is computationally simple and effective, it may have sluggish convergence and be sensitive to learning rate hyperparameters (Fig. 8).

Fig. 8 Represents the stylized images for different pre-trained models when the SGD optimizer is used

Fig. 9 Represents the stylized images for different pre-trained models when the Nadam optimizer is used

5.8 Nadam

"Nesterov-accelerated Adaptive Moment Estimation," or Nadam, is an optimization algorithm that combines the concepts of Nesterov Accelerated Gradient (NAG) and the Adam optimizer. The goal of Nadam's combination of momentum and adaptive learning rates from NAG and Adam, respectively, is to provide a more stable and reliable optimization technique (Fig. 9).

By observing the results of the above models, we can see that stochastic gradient descendent optimizer works poorly on VGG19, resnet152v2 and xception models.

By combining the artistic vision of one image with the content of another, NST makes it possible to create images that are distinctive and aesthetically beautiful. This can also be applied to generate aesthetically pleasing videos [2]. NST has sparked new neural networks, image processing, and computer vision studies. It has prompted the creation of enhanced methods and algorithms that go beyond style transmission, advancing the discipline. NST may be included into a variety of applications, including picture editing software, mobile apps, and augmented reality experiences [14].

6 Results and Discussion

Comparing the models:

(All these values were obtained as the results of the code implemented) (Table 1 and Fig. 10).

When comparing the quality of the stylized image created with the original image and the desired style image, one can utilize the Structural Similarity Index (SSIM), a quantitative assessment for neural style transfer [15] (Tables 2, 3 and Fig. 11).

By observing the results of the above models we can see that stochastic gradient descendent optimizer works poorly on VGG19, resnet152v2 and xception models.

Table 1 Mean square error values obtained for different models

	VGG19	Resnet50	Resnet152v2	Xception
Adam	0.000232072	0.000309367	0.000299138	0.000296864
Adamax	8.78E−05	0.000299004	0.00015314	0.000122436
SGD	0.00079014	0.000289085	0.00074192	0.000756111
RMS Prop	9.20E−05	0.000291426	0.000242898	0.000232559
AdamW	6.87E−05	0.000296144	0.000147157	0.000170407
Adadelta	2.70E−05	6.30E−05	2.31E−05	4.54E−05
Adagrad	2.27E−05	4.89E−05	1.73E−05	7.00E−05
Nadam	5.30E−05	0.000287685	0.000153279	0.000166926

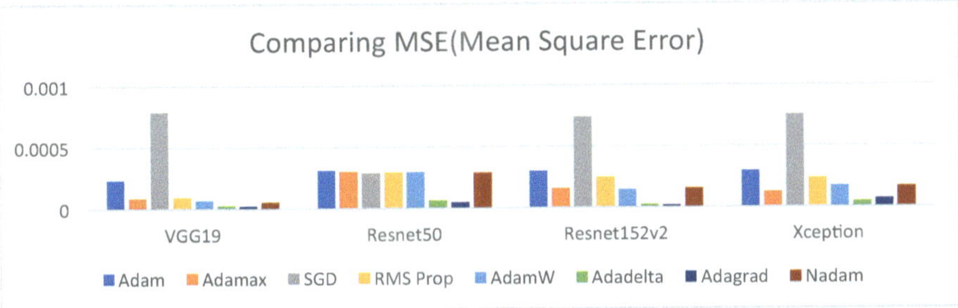

Fig. 10 Comparing the MSE obtained for different models when different optimizers are used

Table 2 Structural similarity index values obtained for different models

	VGG19	Resnet50	Resnet152v2	Xception
Adam	0.84653995	0.789947448	0.826792297	0.793780797
Adamax	0.930385286	0.793600703	0.896403063	0.905041922
SGD	0.576425632	0.813907402	0.592364589	0.595794752
RMS Prop	0.927328716	0.817295148	0.856344106	0.842469556
AdamW	0.944536369	0.797568235	0.9103582	0.877124352
Adadelta	0.975759727	0.94733061	0.980386701	0.96189367
Adagrad	0.98119156	0.9596936	0.985364363	0.941899544
Nadam	0.95608527	0.801629714	0.906943421	0.877798861

7 Limitations

Neural style transfer can often be difficult to manage the level of stylization or the specific components of the style applied, leading to restricted personalization. The neural style transfer optimization process can be costly in terms of calculation and time, particularly for high-resolution photos and complex styles. It may cause

Table 3 Comparing the total variation loss for different models when different optimizers are used

	VGG19	Resnet50	Resnet152v2	Xception
Adam	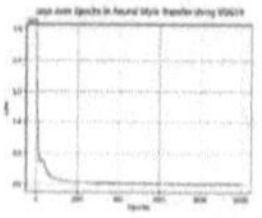	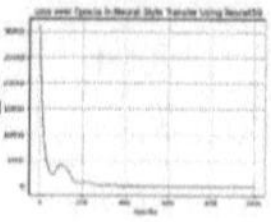	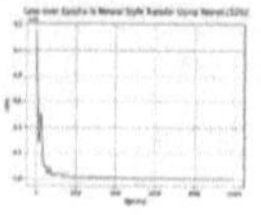	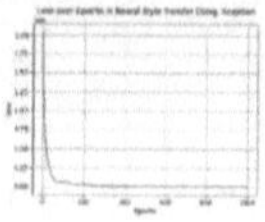
Adamax	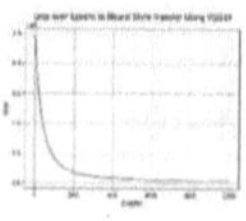	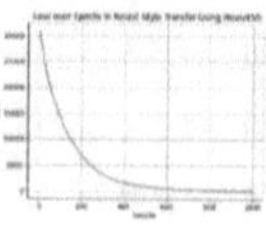	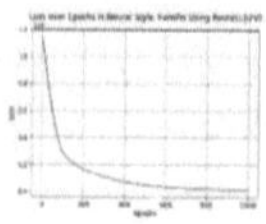	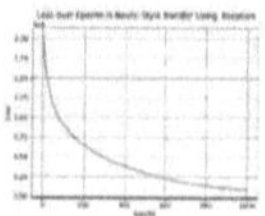
Stochastic gradient descendent	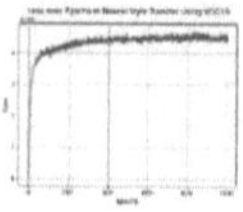	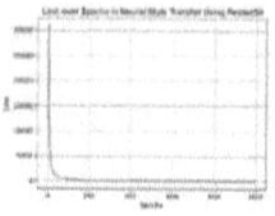	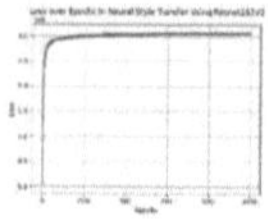	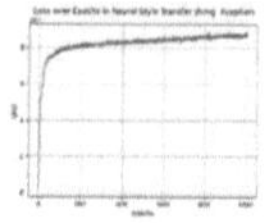
RMS Prop	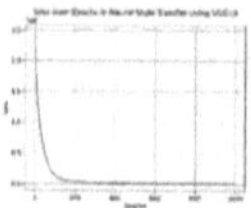	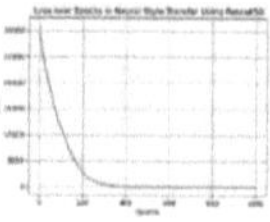	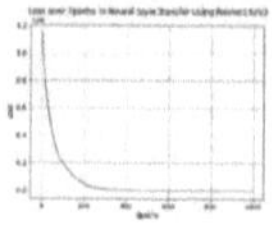	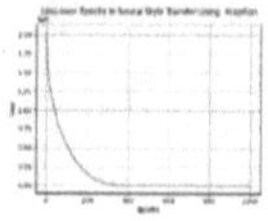
AdamW	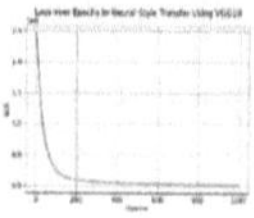	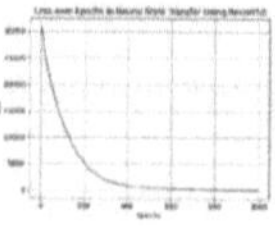	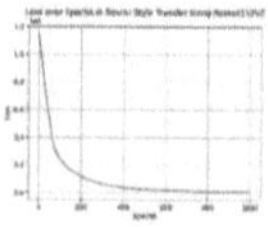	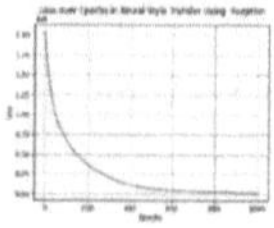
Adadelta	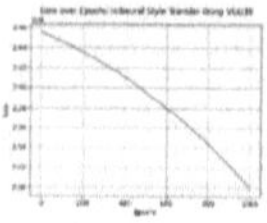	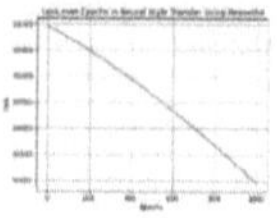	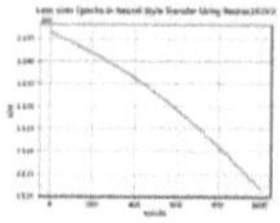	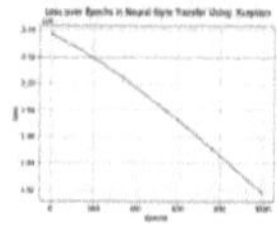
Adagrad	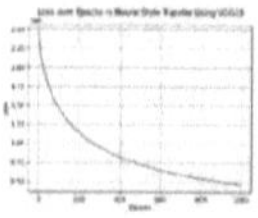	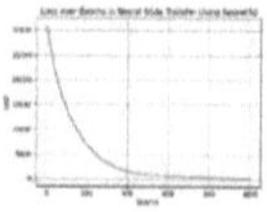	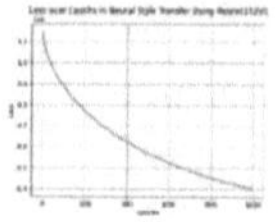	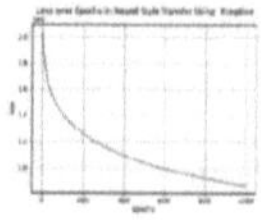
Nadam	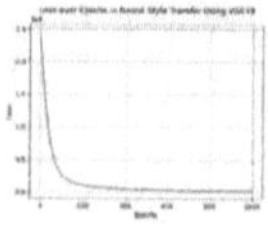	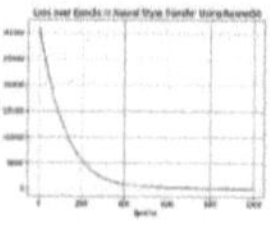	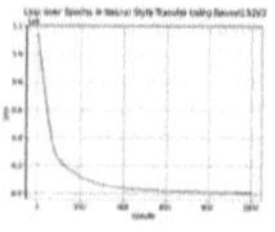	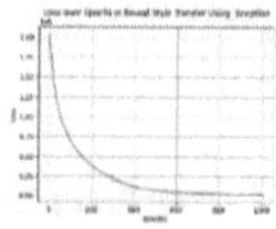

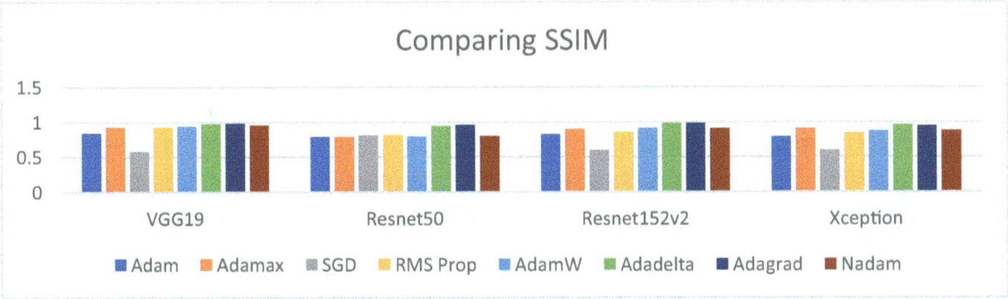

Fig. 11 Comparing the SSIM obtained for different models when different optimizers are used

noise, or the loss of small details in the images it generates, lowering their overall quality. The memory requirements for storing and processing the big pre-trained models can be a limiting factor. Because the performance of neural style transfer is highly dependent on hyperparameters, finding the right balance can be challenging. Although neural style transfer algorithm is trained with some particular models, it may not generalize on unfamiliar or unknown styles, therefore, it is fit for some art forms or styles. Because, of the processing demands, real-time neural style transfer applications on devices with limited resources can be difficult.

8 Future Scope

In the field of art and technology neural style transfer is an interesting topic. With the help of neural style transfer we will be able to create aesthetic images that can mesmerize people. We will be able to use style transfer on various devices like mobiles, laptops and different gadgets to create beautiful images and videos. They will be able to restyle their images as well as paintings according to their needs [10]. Not only the neural networks mentioned in this study but GANs can also be used to create more realistic and meaningful images [9].

9 Conclusion

In conclusion, neural style transfer is a cool combination of art and deep learning that can help us produce spectacular images by merging the content and style from different pictures. This study was based on the use of convolutional neural networks and optimizers. They are multi-functional and include design, entertainment and infinite creative opportunities. Scientists and innovators look forward into the future with excitement to explore deep into the world of creativity with style transfer.

References

1. Dinesh Kumar R, Golden Julie E, Harold Robinson Y et al (2022) Deep convolutional nets learning classification for artistic style transfer. Sci Prog. https://doi.org/10.1155/2022/2038740
2. Dong S, Ding Y, Qian Y, Li M (2022) Video style transfer based on convolutional neural networks. Math Probl Eng. https://doi.org/10.1155/2022/8918722
3. Fischer MH, Yang RR, Lam MS (2020) ImagineNet: restyling apps using neural style transfer
4. Gupta V, Sadana R, Moudgil S (2019) Image style transfer using convolutional neural networks based on transfer learning. Int J Comput Syst Eng 5:53. https://doi.org/10.1504/IJCSYSE.2019.098418
5. Kerdreux T, Thiry L, Kerdreux E (2020) Interactive neural style transfer with artists
6. Landge A, Avhad S, Patil P et al (2022) Image style transfer using deep learning. Int J Res Appl Sci Eng Technol 10:2856–2865. https://doi.org/10.22214/IJRASET.2022.42788
7. Laxmaiah DrB (2022) Image style transfer using machine learning. Int J Res Appl Sci Eng Technol 10:1187–1190. https://doi.org/10.22214/ijraset.2022.43990
8. Li W, Vyas R, Penta RS (2022) Artistic arbitrary style transfer
9. Liao Y, Huang Y (2022) Deep learning-based application of image style transfer. Math Probl Eng. https://doi.org/10.1155/2022/1693892
10. Manal, Linkon AHM, Labib MM et al (2020) Restyling images with the Bangladeshi paintings using neural style transfer: a comprehensive experiment, evaluation, and human perspective. In: ICCIT 2020—23rd international conference on computer and information technology, proceedings. https://doi.org/10.1109/ICCIT51783.2020.9392698
11. S. Sai Krupa Reddy, V. Sri Rama Kumar, P. Vaishnavi et al (2022) Neural style transfer using ResNet50V2. Int J Adv Res Sci Commun Technol 95–99. https://doi.org/10.48175/ijarsct-3048
12. Vishnukumar A, Vishnukumar D, GafoorA A (2023) Applying neural style transfer to transform images into a different style domain by the NST method. https://doi.org/10.21203/RS.3.RS-2647275/V1
13. Wang L, Liu R, Vosoughi S (2020) Salienteye: maximizing engagement while maintaining artistic style on Instagram using deep neural networks. In: ICMR 2020—proceedings of the 2020 international conference on multimedia retrieval, pp 331–335. https://doi.org/10.1145/3372278.3390736
14. Warkhandkar AG, Bhambure OB (2021) LiveStyle-an application to transfer artistic styles

15. Wu B, Ding Y, Dong Q (2019) Fast continuous structural similarity patch based arbitrary style transfer. Appl Sci 9:3304. https://doi.org/10.3390/APP9163304
16. Zhao H, Zheng J, Wang Y et al (2020) Portrait style transfer using deep convolutional neural networks and facial segmentation. Comput Electr Eng 85. https://doi.org/10.1016/J.COMPELECENG.2020.106655
17. Zhao Z, Zhang S (2022) Style transfer based on VGG network. Int J Adv Netw Monitor Controls 7:54–72. https://doi.org/10.2478/ijanmc-2022-0005
18. Zhou C, Gu Z, Gao Y, Wang J (2019) An improved style transfer algorithm using feedforward neural network for real-time image conversion. Sustainability 11:5673. https://doi.org/10.3390/SU11205673

Keratoconus Eye Disease Detection Using CNN with VGG-19

Yaswitha Kurra and Surendra Reddy Vinta

1 Introduction

The resolution of human eye is 576 Mega Pixels, nothing can capture a moment or vision like a human eye does. Eye plays a vital role in capturing and providing vision for humans which makes it one of the most significant part of everyone's lives and human body. The Human Eye has three layers; the Retina is found in the innermost layer, and the main blood supply for the eye is located in the middle layer [2]. The Cornea and Sclera make up the Human Eye's outermost layer. An important component of the human eye is the cornea, which is the transparent clear area that covers the iris and pupil. The clear part of the eye which covers the front of the eye is called the cornea, which is a very important part of the human eye. It tops the anterior chamber, which is filled with fluid inside the eye, the iris, which is the coloured portion of the eye, and the pupil, which is the aperture in the center of the eye. The important role of the cornea is to refract the light or to bend the light. The light that enters into the eye is always concentrated by the cornea most of the times. Cells and proteins may be found in the cornea. Cornea has no blood arteries, in contrast to most of the tissues in the human body [3]. The cornea can get clouded by blood vessels, impairing eyesight by preventing appropriate light refraction.

Keratoconus is one of the rarest disease. Keratoconus is a very slowly progressive corneal disorder that results in thinning and scarring of the cornea, because of this the patients can have distorted vision and face difficulties in viewing the world [4]. Keratoconus is slowly progressive in nature which worsens over time and which weakens the cornea and the cornea protrudes outward taking the form of a cone [5]. The cornea's irregular shape results in visual distortions and can seriously cause impaired eyesight. Keratoconus is believed to be the result of vigorous eye rubbing,

Y. Kurra · S. R. Vinta (✉)
School of Computer Science and Engineering, VIT-AP University, Amaravati, Andhra Pradesh, India
e-mail: surendrareddy.vinta@vitap.ac.in

K. Kumar Singh et al. (eds.), *Machine Vision and Augmented Intelligence*, Lecture Notes in Electrical Engineering 1211, https://doi.org/10.1007/978-981-97-4359-9_48

and a combination of genetic and hormonal causes, while its exact cause is still unclear [4]. According to many research studies, some genetic mutations may put people at risk for Keratoconus which is assumed and not proved as a fact. The illness may develop or worsen as a result of other variables such as hormone imbalances, allergies, persistent eye irritation, and eye rubbing.

Numerous eye examinations, including Keratometry, Slit-lamp Examination, Corneal mapping and Visual Acuity Test, these tests have been used to identify and diagnose Keratoconus till date [6]. Trained Ophthalmologists with high and specialized skills are required to efficiently interpret medical pictures of Keratoconus to identify the Keratoconus disease. Even specialized ophthalmologists may not recognize Keratoconus disease in its early stage and may confuse it with other vision problems like myopia. Also, there may be a delay in the detection and diagnosis of Keratoconus if there's a lack of specialists who can recognize Keratoconus disease, which is extremely dangerous for the patient.

Keratoconus may impact both of your eyes. The degree of severity may change depending on the situation. There are times when one eye may become Keratoconus while the other eye is healthy [7]. Keratoconus can also sometimes affect both eyes. And on occasion, one eye with extremely severe Keratoconus may need laser treatment or surgery, whilst the other eye with very mild Keratoconus may be managed with soft lenses and eyeglasses.

Keratoconus is difficult to identify and diagnose due to the sluggish rate of development and few structural changes to the cornea [8]. People might not initially notice any major visual problems since Keratoconus progresses slowly. One of the early indicators of Keratoconus is blurry or distorted vision, which can be mistaken for myopia or astigmatism as well as other eye conditions. Astigmatism results in light rays converging on many distinct spots on the retina rather than just one because of an uneven shape or curvature [9]. This has the effect of making distant objects look distorted or hazy. Myopia, a similar word, refers to near-sightedness. In those with myopia, a common visual impairment, objects further away seem fuzzy while those that are closer to the eye do so clearly. Early treatment will help the patient in the future as there will be some changes in the lifestyle. This invention will be very helpful to all, as the detection of Keratoconus becomes easy and the diagnosis can be started at an early stage. This reduces the risk of worsening the eye condition.

The remaining sections will be ordered as follows; Sect. 2 includes the related task which is the literature review for our proposed plan. Section 3 describes the existing and the proposed methodology, which includes a description of the dataset, preprocessing, and model description. Section 4 describes the experiment, analysis of results, and comparison of results. Section 5 outlines the conclusion and prospective scope of the study.

2 Related Work

For early diagnosis and lowering patient risk, using different machine learning and deep learning algorithms to identify Keratoconus is highly helpful, and its application is growing daily. The premise for diagnosing Keratoconus in eyes is a set of computer vision-based algorithms, and up till now, a number of studies have been conducted in this area.

For the purpose of identifying Keratoconus, CNN was used for topographical photos. The input will be divided into two categories: a healthy eye with normal topography and an eye impacted by Keratoconus. The KeratoDetect algorithm performs well, earning a 99.33% accuracy rate on the test set of data. To evaluate the topography of the cornea, a CNN (Convolution Neural Networks) algorithm is used [10].

Implemented a variety of machine learning algorithms to focus on and evaluate the identification of Keratoconus using actual medical data. The Support Vector Machine (SVM) technique was accustomed to attain the greatest accuracy level of 94%. The research emphasizes the significance of feature selection in machine learning and how it might enhance patient care and clinical procedures [11].

Researchers have developed an Ensemble of Deep Transfer Learning (EDTL) using 4 pre-trained networks, SqueezeNet, AlexNet, ShuffleNet, and MobileNet-v2, and a PI classifier. The Ensemble of Deep Transfer Leraning approach reaches to a judgement based on the combination of output probabilities on probability fusion. The Accuracy were ranged from 86% to 89.9% for the deep networks with the highest accuracy of 98.3% using ensemble-specific combinations of classifiers and PI. This study shows the importance for the prospect of building ensembles of deep classifiers that are updated using a transfer learning technique, which leads to even more better accuracy [12].

In this study in order to detect the different stages of Keratoconus disease which are mild, moderate, and advanced, they used two different types of Deep Learning models which are ResNet50 and EfficientNet. The dataset contains four distinct classes that shows the Keratoconus disease's phases, with each folder consisting of around 550 photos. The dataset collection includes both pentacam pictures and corneal topographic maps, and the Deep Learning model's respective levels of accuracy were 97% and 94%. The study's primary motives include improving patient treatment and customer relationship management by classifying Keratoconus in different severity levels [13].

This study used the Deep Learning from AS-OCT to detect and diagnose Keratoconus with a resulted accuracy of 0.874%. A popular classification for detecting Keratoconus is used here which is the Amsler-Krumeich classification. More research is required to state the accuracy and apply deep learning concept to other corneal diseases [14].

This study showcases the identification and detection of early clinical Keratoconus (KCN) with the help of a Deep Learning algorithm using three different corneal maps.

The proposed model of the study was examined using the Xception and Inception-ResNetV2 DL architectures on 1371 eyes which resulted in the accuracy of 97–100% and an AUC of 0.99 [15].

This study showcased the research with use of Deep Learning of color-coded map with the usage of Placido disk-based corneal topography to examine the detection and diagnosability of Keratoconus. This study examined 179 Keratoconic eyes and 170 healthy normal eyes with the use of high quality pictures from the corneal topography. The results showed that the color-coded maps deep learning resulted an accuracy of 0.966 in seperating Keratoconus from normal eyes and 0.785 in detecting the Keratoconus disease severity stage. According to the Grade 0 (normal) through Grade 4 grading scales, the area under the curve values were 0.997, 0.955, 0.899, 0.888, and 0.943, respectively [16].

Technologies like convolutional neural networks (CNN) have improved the early diagnosis and categorization of Keratoconus. This study trains pre-trained CNN models and segments topographical pictures using particle swarm optimization. The system outperforms other algorithms for a 3-class classification, with an accuracy rate of 95.9% [17].

The Logistic Index for Keratoconus (Logik) is a machine learning method that accurately classifies the disease based on the stages of severity, objectively separates the suspected diseased eye from normal healthy eyes, and provides a trustworthy, grading method to evaluate Keratoconus progression. The combination of algorithms of Feed-forward Neural Network (FNN) and a Moving Average Filter (MAF), results in various stages of Keratoconus with an accuracy of 99.9%. Logik can be assumed to be a reliable indicator for the identification of the disease and also categorizing the stages of the severity. Its main problem can be that it may overlap a healthy eye with the one of a suspected Keratoconus case. It needs more efficient development in order for people to rely on it [18].

This study is about a deep learning technique known as Kernet is used for the identification of Keratoconus disease using the raw data from the Pentacam HR system. With the use of a multi-level fusion architecture Kernet detects the disease. The study found the proposed model outperforms other networks in performance. Grad-CAM, is used to link model performance to clinical practice [19].

3 Methodology

3.1 Dataset Description

The dataset includes the training data needed to build a Deep Learning model. The caliber and variety of the dataset have a direct bearing on a model's effectiveness and generalizability. A robust dataset is necessary for a model to comprehend complicated patterns and make precise predictions.

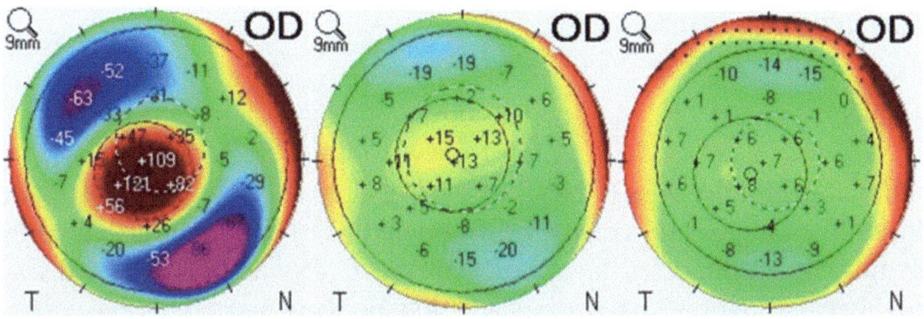

Fig. 1 Corneal images of Keratoconus Eye versus Normal Eye versus Suspected Eye

The dataset considered for this model is a public dataset [20], which consists of more than 4000 images which were separated into training and testing datasets respectively. The images used here are Corneal Topography images which is a test used for the detection of Keratoconus. The images were classified into three classes: Keratoconus, Suspect, and Normal. For the training dataset, there were 150 Keratoconus cases that contains 7 images per case, 150 for Normal cases, and 123 for Suspected Keratoconus cases. While the testing dataset there were 50 cases each of Keratoconus, Normal, and Suspected Keratoconus cases. The values of the parameters used to categorize Keratoconus, Normal, and Suspected eyes are shown in the accompanying figure. Figure 1 displays the original image.

The curated dataset is highly efficient and simple to comprehend, which is a significant advantage for anyone who is interested to work in this field.

3.2 *Pre-Processing*

Pre-processing of the obtained data is essential since the vast majority of real-life data is noisy, inconsistent, and incomplete. Data preparation is the procedure of putting the available data in a manner that is appropriate for machine learning tasks. The dataset that was utilised is a hybrid dataset, and the publicly accessible dataset contains several redundant and ambiguous photos. All of this noise in the image dataset was manually removed, and images from other datasets were combined to form a single effective dataset. Each and every picture in the collection has been individually tagged in accordance with the different classifications.

3.3 Existing Methodologies

3.3.1 CNN

Convolutional neural network (CNN), which is a deep learning model [10] analyzes visual input like images and videos. It is modeled like the human visual cortex and is made up of interconnected layers of neurons. CNNs are mostly used for tasks which involve analyzing visual images and may perform tasks like object detection, feature extraction, classification tasks. CNN contains several layers which help with the feature extraction and object detection tasks. The first layer of the CNN is the input layer where the input images will be taken by the input layer. The second layer is the hidden layer where the task of feature extraction is done and with the extracted features a feature map is generated for the task of classification. Then any activation function is applied like ReLu and SoftMax. The next layer is the pooling layer and its important role is to decrease the volume that makes for the fast computation, reduction in the memory and also preserves overfitting. The next is the dense layer which connects all the preceeding layers of the network. The output will be displayed in the flattened layer. CNNs can work well with large datasets and gives efficient result. CNNs are one of the most used powerful deep learning models which can be used for feature extraction and can be trained independently and also deliver an excellent performance [10].

3.3.2 ResNet 50

ResNet-50's architecture contains 50 layers of residual networks which is a convolutional neural network. The residual connections are assumed to be a shortcut or skip connections [13]. The data will be passed from one layer to another layer with the help of links that are made by the network. This method assists in the performance to train the multi-layer neural networks and addresses the issue of disappearing gradients. There are idle blocks in ResNet-50. Multiple convolutional layers, batch normalization, and activation function layer are all included in the residual block. Skip connections are produced by adding elements one at a time between the residual block's input and output. This phenomenon leads to a condensed information channel and allows gradients to propagate efficiently during training. In ResNet-50, a max-pooling layer that comes after a convolutional layer samples the input picture. Over the course of the four phases, there are varying numbers of blocks left. There are three phases with increasingly higher spatial resolutions after the initial residual block. The network gradually reduces the spatial dimensions while increasing the number of filters in order to capture significant levels of features. In the higher layer of the network, global average pooling combines spatial information into a fixed-dimensional feature vector. After that, probabilities for photo categorization classes are created using a fully connected layer and a SoftMax layer.

3.3.3 SqueezeNet

SqueezeNet [12] is a deep learning architecture which is made to achieve high accuracy while also minimizing parameters and computation complexity in comparison to Convolution Neural Network (CNN). SqueezeNet is quite popular for its small size and effective operation performance. SqueezeNet is developed by deep-scale researchers. SqueezeNet uses 1 × 1 filters, which are referred to as "squeeze" layers, which are used to minimize the number of input channels with also preserving expressiveness which is very important. SquuezeNet has expand layers, which is the combination of 1 × 1 filter and 3 × 3 filter to add more channels which is to ensure a balance line between model compactness and expressive power. SqueezeNet uses "down-sampling via max-pooling" to minimize the size of the model and also spatial dimension of the model. The squeeze layer and expand layer are made of fire modules that are the backbone of the squeeze network. This kind of arrangement showcases a deeper design still sustaining compactness. Due to its lower model size, SqueezeNet support real-time inference and its brilliant performance take part on datasets like ImageNet. This kind of arrangement allows for a deeper design still sustaining compactness, due to its lower model size.

3.3.4 AlexNet

AlexNet [12] is a Convolution Neural Network which provides the efficiency in changing the area of deep learning with its accomplishments in image classification tasks. AlexNet achieves an amazing result with the help of learning hierarchical features from raw data using different kinds of layers which are convolutional layers, max pooling layers, fully connected layers. To improve the model's generalization the architecture used the ReLu, max-pooling layers, and data augmentation approaches. Also, Alexnet is the first method to prove a thought of speeding deep learning training and efficiently processing enormous amount of data by adapting GPUs for deep learning calculations. The last layer is the fully-connected layer that reduces overfitting. AlexNet performs several tasks including object identification, segmentation, and transfer learning.

3.3.5 ShuffleNet

ShuffleNet's [12] architecture is used by CNN for more effective computation and parameter reduction. ShuffleNet was introduced in 2018 by Zhang et al. In order to reduce computation complexity without compromising accuracy. The ShuffleNet's design is unique channel operation, where the information flows from channel to channel and also enables reuse of features. ShuffleNet is made up of two main fundamental processes which are channel shuffle and point-wise group convolution. The computation cost is lowered by the channel shuffle operation with the use of communication between several channels, which also increases the network expressiveness. The channel split in ShuffleNet is used for feature map down sampling, which lowers features maps spatial resolution. Because of its small size it allows for implementation even on the devices with a limited source which enables real-time inference and decreasing the usage of power. The success of ShuffleNet has allowed more studies into better effective model construction and also the creation of succeeding topologies that showcase the computational and memory effectiveness is also encouraged.

3.3.6 MobileNetV2

MobileNetV2 [12] is a deep learning architecture with brilliant performance on devices with very limited resources and also the computation is done efficiently. The new features of the MobileNetV2 increases the precision and effectiveness by optimization. The main new features were the width multiplier, linear bottlenecks with shortcut connections, depth-wise separable convolutions, and inverted residual blocks. MobileNetV2 can be used in a situation where computation sources and memory are forced since these lower computational cost and memory. The MobileNetV2 architecture is designed in a way to make it possible for it to use for real-time inference on mobile devices.

3.4 Proposed Methodologies

3.4.1 CNN with VGG-19

CNN has changed the segment of computer vision with its task performance which include feature extraction, object detection, image classification and many more. CNN is the Convolutional Neural Network which is known for its ability in the performance of computer vision tasks. Visual Geometry Group (VGG)-19 is a type of CNN that contains 19 layers in its architecture and it is a pre-trained model. VGG-19 architecture is designed of having 16 convolutional layers, 3 fully connected layers, 5 maxpool layers, 1 softmax layer and a ReLu activation function layer. The VGG-19 performs an excellent task of object detection, image classification and many more compute vision tasks. VGG-19 may not have the best architecture when compared with others in terms of computation cost and memory utilization. VGG-19 utilizes transfer learning, which is a method that allows pre-trained models to be made of improvements on new tasks, which will be made useful for a variety of computer vision issues. The VGG-19 architecture has an input layer where the output from the CNNs flatten layer is taken as an input here. The convolution layers are used for feature extraction and some learnable filters known as kernel will be applied to the given input dataset. The fully connected layers id given the input from the previous layer and gives us the final classification of the given input dataset.

The max pool layers would give us a output feature map which contains the most outstanding when compared with other features will be taken and, efficient features of the previous feature map. The activation function ReLu is applied. Soft max is used as an activation function. The output of the software gives us the likelihood of a particular image belonging to a certain class. Due to its popularity and influence even more, complex and potent designs have been created, advancing the field of image recognition technology.

3.4.2 VGG-16

VGG-16 is a Convolutional Neural Network Architecture. There are sixteen layers in total in the VGG-16 architecture, including three fully connected layers, pooling, and convolutional layers. The architectural design is characterized by the use of small 3×3 filters in each convolutional layer, which improves feature representation acquisition. In order to execute feature map-down sampling and decrease the spatial dimensionality of the input data, the network comprises max-pooling layers. The VGG19 architecture may be formally expressed as a series of nonlinear transformations that enable the mapping of an input picture to a probability distribution across a present range of classes. The network's layers may be described as a mathematical function that receives an input feature map and performs a convolution operation with a set of adaptive filters. A non-linear activation function, like ReLU, and maybe a pooling mechanism come next. The subsequent layer subsequently receives its input from the output of the previous layer. Back propagation and stochastic gradient descent are used to compute the weights of the convolutional layer filters during the training phase.

3.4.3 Inception V3

Strong CNN architecture InceptionV3 strikes a balance between precision and processing speed, making it suitable for a variety of image recognition applications. It was created to deal with deep learning issues on massive picture datasets for image recognition and classification. The network may learn regional and global trends in the input photographs. The network can analyze wider receptive fields while spending less money on computing thanks to this factorization. With the use of batch normalization, which normalizes mini-batch activations, the Inception V3 may be trained more quickly. This network was trained using the millions of categorized images in ImageNet, which span hundreds of categories. Pre-training equips the model with a wide range of traits that may be adjusted or applied to different picture recognition tasks. The design is extensively used in research and practice because it performs better than other image classification architectures on image classification benchmarks. ReLu activation is used in Inception V3 after the majority of the convolutional layers and fully linked layers. Negative values are set to zero and the positive values are left unaltered when ReLu converts each neuron's output.

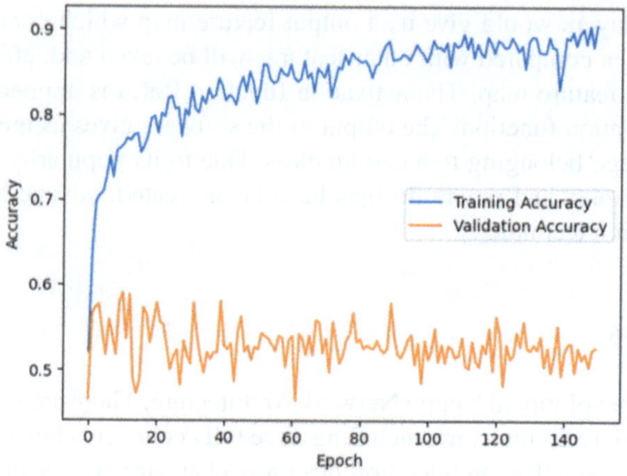

Fig. 2 Graph for the training and validation accuracy

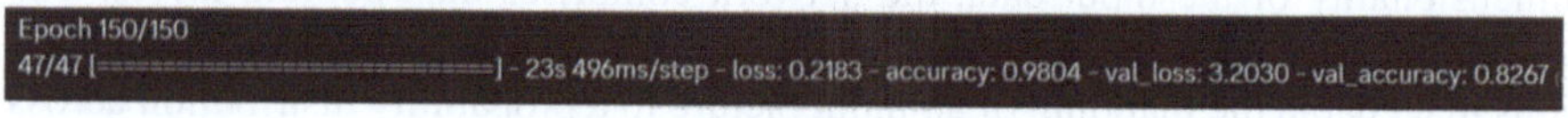

Fig. 3 Accuracy of the proposed model (CNN with VGG-19) after 150 epochs

4 Results

Our result shows that the CNN model with a pre-trained architecture VGG-19 delivers a 98% accuracy and is simple to execute the epochs with less time requisition after assessing the results of numerous models for the Detection of Keratoconus eye disease based on various parameters (Fig. 2).

The above figure shows the training and validation accuracies for CNN with VGG-19 for the Detection of Keratoconus eye disease, trained for 150 epochs (Fig. 3).

The above Table 1 is the comparison between the existing algorithms and proposed algorithms for the identification of Keratoconus. The performance of the VGG-19, VGG-16, InceptionV3, ResNet 50, EfficientNet, CNN, SVM, ShuffleNet, AlexNet, MobileNet-v2, SqueezeNet, models were compared based on their model's obtained accuracy.

5 Limitations

- The VGG-19 has a highly deep architecture with many filters and parameters since it consists of 19 convolution layers. With both training and inference, this demands a lot of processing and memory.

Table 1 Comparison table between different deep learning models

S. no	Algorithm	Published	Accuracy (%)
1	CNN with VGG-19	2023	98
2	VGG-16	2023	96
3	InceptionV3	2023	95
4	CNN	2019	95.9
5	ShuffleNet	2021	86
6	AlexNet	2021	89.9
7	ResNet 50	2022	96.7
8	MobileNet-v2	2021	86.4
9	SqueezeNet	2021	89.2
10	EfficientNet	2022	94

- It might be difficult to externally validate models trained on public datasets, especially if the models are tested on different patient populations or clinical settings.
- The dataset contains limited number of corneal topographic images as, medical images are hard to acquire for privacy concerns. This has an impact on how the model performs, as the given or input dataset is limited.

6 Conclusion

The primary goal of this research is the early identification of Keratoconus which will help for the diagnosis of Keratoconus and also the classification of that eye condition into three groups, namely:

- Normal Eyes
- Keratoconus Eyes
- Suspected Eyes

With the help of CNN with VGG-19 we successfully classified them according to their respective classes. We also achieved this with an efficient accuracy of 98%, where the goal of this project is reached. This project will be helpful to everyone as the detection of Keratoconus is done at an early stage where even if there's a suspected case we can identify it and the diagnosis can be done, which makes it very helpful for everyone.

We used CNN with VGG-19 algorithm, to detect the Keratoconus and also classify them. The CNN with VGG-19 algorithm offers real-time image classification and object detection capabilities, making it the most suitable application that requires fast and efficient Keratoconus detection.

As the study is expanded, the emphasis can be placed on increasing the amount of data that can be enhanced for training the model. Since access to medical images is very limited, future advancements rely on the increased number of corneal topographic images that can be included when training the model for even more effective classification and detection purposes. How a model can perform may be improved by using a high-quality, varied dataset. Additionally, training on a big, diverse dataset enables us to develop deeper learning models.

References

1. Zhou L, Sawaguchi S, Twining SS, Sugar J, Feder RS, Yue BY (1998) Expression of degradative enzymes and protease inhibitors in corneas with keratoconus. Invest Ophthal Visual Sci 39(7):1117–1124
2. Perkins ES, Davson H (2023) Human eye. Encyclopedia Britannica. https://www.britannica.com/science/human-eye
3. Sridhar MS (2018) Anatomy of cornea and ocular surface. Indian J Ophthalmol 66(2):190–194. https://doi.org/10.4103/ijo.IJO_646_17.PMID:29380756;PMCID:PMC5819093
4. Gordon-Shaag A, Millodot M, Shneor E, Liu Y (2015) The genetic and environmental factors for keratoconus. Biomed Res Int 2015:795738. https://doi.org/10.1155/2015/795738. Epub 2015 May 17. PMID: 26075261; PMCID: PMC4449900
5. Espandar L, Meyer J (2010) Keratoconus: overview and update on treatment. Middle East Afr J Ophthalmol 17(1):15–20. https://doi.org/10.4103/0974-9233.61212.PMID:20543932; PMCID:PMC2880369
6. Ahn H, Kim NE, Chung JL, Kim YJ, Jun I, Seo KY (2022) Patient selection for corneal topographic evaluation of keratoconus: a screening approach using artificial intelligence. Front Med 9. https://doi.org/10.3389/fmed.2022.934865
7. Mohammadpour M, Heidari Z, Hashemi H (2017) Updates on managements for keratoconus. J Curr Ophthalmol 30(2):110–124. https://doi.org/10.1016/j.joco.2017.11.002.PMID: 29988906;PMCID:PMC6034171
8. Sharif R, Bak-Nielsen S, Hjortdal J, Karamichos D (2018) Pathogenesis of keratoconus: the intriguing therapeutic potential of prolactin-inducible protein. Prog Retin Eye Res 67:150–167. https://doi.org/10.1016/j.preteyeres.2018.05.002. Epub 2018 Jul 13. PMID: 29758268; PMCID: PMC6235698
9. Gurnani B, Kaur K (2023) Astigmatism. [Updated 2023 May 4]. In: StatPearls [Internet]. Treasure Island (FL): StatPearls Publishing. Available from: https://www.ncbi.nlm.nih.gov/books/NBK582142/
10. Lavric A, Valentin P (2019) KeratoDetect: keratoconus detection algorithm using convolutional neural networks. Comput Intell Neurosci 2019:8162567. https://doi.org/10.1155/2019/8162567. PMID: 30809255; PMCID: PMC6364125
11. Lavric A, Popa V, Takahashi H, Yousefi S (2020) Detecting keratoconus from corneal imaging data using machine learning. IEEE Access 8:149113–149121. https://doi.org/10.1109/ACCESS.2020.3016060
12. Al-Timemy AH, Ghaeb NH, Mosa ZM et al (2022) Deep transfer learning for improved detection of keratoconus using corneal topographic maps. Cogn Comput 14:1627–1642. https://doi.org/10.1007/s12559-021-09880-3
13. Dhinakaran P, Shivanandappa M, Dhina P (2023) Keratoviz: a multistage keratoconus severity analysis and visualization using deep learning and class-activated maps. Int J Electr Comput Eng (IJECE) 13(1):920–935. https://doi.org/10.11591/ijece.v13i1.pp920-935
14. Kamiya K, Ayatsuka Y, Kato Y, Fujimura F, Takahashi M, Shoji N, Mori Y, Miyata K (2019) Keratoconus detection using deep learning of color-coded maps with anterior segment optical coherence tomography: a diagnostic accuracy study. BMJ Open 9(9):e031313. https://doi.org/10.1136/bmjopen-2019-031313. PMID: 31562158; PMCID: PMC6773416

15. Al-Timemy AH, Alzubaidi L, Mosa ZM, Abdelmotaal H, Ghaeb NH, Lavric A, Hazarbassanov RM, Takahashi H, Gu Y, Yousefi S (2023) A deep feature fusion of improved suspected keratoconus detection with deep learning. Diagnostics 13(10):1689. https://doi.org/10.3390/diagnostics13101689
16. Kazutaka K, Yuji A, Yudai K, Nobuyuki S, Yosai M, Kazunori M (2021) Diagnosability of keratoconus using deep learning with placido disk-based corneal topography. Front Med 8. https://doi.org/10.3389/fmed.2021.724902
17. Subramanian P, Ramesh P (2022) Keratoconus classification with convolutional neural networks using segmentation and index quantification of eye topography images by particle swarm optimisation. BioMed Res Int 1–9. https://doi.org/10.1155/2022/8119685
18. Issarti I, Consejo A, Jiménez-García M, Kreps EO, Koppen C, Rozema JJ (2020) Logistic index for keratoconus detection and severity scoring (Logik). Comput Biol Med 122:103809. ISSN 0010-4825. https://doi.org/10.1016/j.compbiomed.2020.103809
19. Feng R, Xu Z, Zheng X, Hu H, Jin X, Chen DZ, Yao K, Wu J (2021) KerNet: a novel deep learning approach for keratoconus and sub-clinical keratoconus detection based on raw data of the pentacam HR system. IEEE J Biomed Health Inform 25(10):3898–3910. https://doi.org/10.1109/JBHI.2021.3079430
20. https://www.kaggle.com/datasets/elmehdi12/keratoconus-detection

TrOCR-Enhanced Language Chains: Bridging Image-Based Text and Single Document Question Answering

Patan Althaf and Surendra Reddy Vinta

1 Introduction

Question answering (QA) has stepped forward from human machine interactions to attention on Artificial Intelligence and Natural Language Processing [1]. The Transformer decoder, utilized in TrOCR, employs self-interest and encoder-decoder interest to technique unstructured statistics like PDFs. The functionality to perform Question answering on PDFs is crucial for automation of statistics extraction. OCR performs an essential function to utilize frameworks like YOLOv5 and DBNet for text detection and OCR structures using CNNs and RNNs for man or woman recognition. TrOCR, an OCR version, makes use of a Transformer-based method for correct photograph-to-textual content conversion, showcasing advanced normal overall performance. LangChain, a treasured tool in NLP, collaborates with Large Language Models (LLMs) through pre-processing textual content and imparting genuine responses. This studies explores a framework integrating TrOCR, LangChain, and HuggingFaceHub to address PDF QA disturbing situations, combining language information and record retrieval.

HuggingFaceHub, that hosts over 250k repos, serves as one of the key platforms to share Machine Learning projects and provides a gamut of pre-trained models like Flan-Alpaca. As a result, this paper intentionally opts to use the Flan-Alpaca-large model because it has unique prowess in synthetic instruction tasks from GPT-3. The study purposefully synergizes TrOCR's OCR capabilities, LangChain's nuanced response provisioning ability and HuggingFaceHub's repository of pre-trained models. The proposed framework ably caters for the intricate challenges in PDF QA, displaying the possibility of integrating sophisticated technologies in language understanding and document retrieval. The collaboration of TrOCR,

P. Althaf · S. R. Vinta (✉)
School of Computer Science and Engineering, VIT-AP University, Amaravati, Andhra Pradesh, India
e-mail: surendrareddy.vinta@vitap.ac.in

K. Kumar Singh et al. (eds.), *Machine Vision and Augmented Intelligence*, Lecture Notes in Electrical Engineering 1211, https://doi.org/10.1007/978-981-97-4359-9_49

LangChain, and HuggingFaceHub provides a holistic solution to the intricacies processing and extraction of information from PDF documents entail through the advocated automated Fine-tuning Flan-Alpaca-large with the synthetic instructions from GPT-3 enhances the problem-solving power of the framework for writing tasks over previously unsynthesized solutions using Flan, making a big step-up in widening its pre-trained model application to downstream use-cases.

This research paper explores an approach to address the challenges of PDF question answering by proposing an advanced framework that integrates TrOCR, Langchain, and HuggingFaceHub. The synergy of these cutting edge technologies enables us to tackle the complexities of language understanding and document retrieval simultaneously.

2 Literature Survey

This research article offered the innovative job of visually question answering by using OCR, to read the text from the image. They used the OCRVQA-200K dataset here. Users are instructed to upload an image to the model and then utilize the image to pose questions. The output is produced by the model using VQA and OCR [1].

This study paper describes the total architecture of the OCR model and the frameworks used in building the OCR model. Users can retrieve text from the image using this model [2].

The TrOCR version, that's extra accurate and green than previously mentioned models, is brought on this to have a look at the document. This brought TrOCR, which uses the Transformer architecture, to know the photo and technology of the text at the word piece level. TrOCR is an entire text popularity answer that uses text and picture Transformer models which have been trained [3].

In this work, GPTQuant, a conversational AI chatbot for creating and assessing investment strategies, is introduced. To enable GPT3's few-shot learning capabilities and generate Pythonccode rapidly that can be run using the Python interpreter, GPTQuant integrates Langchain and prompt templates. The case studies in the papers show how the chatbot may be used in real-world scenarios and evaluate its effectiveness in comparison to Open AI's ChatGPT. Here, Langchain use is essential [4].

This research facilities on the usage of Large Language Models (LLMs) to speed up the improvement of applications, placing specific force on the open-source software library known as LangChain. The number one objective of the investigation lies in the examination of LangChain, designed to streamline the process of crafting tailored AI applications leveraging LLMs. This takes a look into an evaluation of the core attributes of LangChain, clarify its chains and additives [5].

In this work, the analysis of the various large language models took into account the pretraining foundation, instruction-tuning data, and training approaches holistically. A brand-new rigorous test called INSTRUCTEVAL was developed for instruction-tuned huge language models. This evaluation comprises a detailed analysis of models depends on their aptitude for solving the problems, their writing proficiency, and their suitability with human values [6].

The study paper aims at performing an exploratory study of the current state of HuggingFaceHub in order to investigate its suitability to be used as a source platform for empirical studies. The paper describes the qualitative and quantitative analysis of HFH for empirical studies. The former will be performed by comparing the features of HFH with those of other code-hosting platforms [7].

The most recent OpenQA research trends are discussed and reviewed in this study article, with a focus on systems that use MRC approaches for neural networks. The study offered a contemporary OpenQA architecture called "Retriever-Reader" and examined numerous systems that adhere to it as well as the particular approaches used in each of the components. It presents an overview of the most utilised benchmarks while describing the main difficulties in creating OpenQA systems [9].

The study presents the Natural Questions corpus, a collection of question-and-answer data; the term "Questions" refers to a group of bulk Google search queries; the study describes the examination of 25-way annotations on 302 samples; it also proposes rigorous criteria for evaluating question-answering systems; it also provides insights into human variability on the annotation job; it displays strong human upper limits on these measures [10].

3 Methodology

3.1 Dataset

The user applies a pre-trained model, acquired through extensive data training, to extract textual information from images. The pre-training process unfolds in two phases, each associated with distinct datasets. In the initial phase, a significant dataset comprising printed text line images is generated for the pre-training of the TrOCR model. The subsequent phase involves two smaller datasets, each containing millions of text-line images, tailored for tasks involving both printed and handwritten text. Synthetic scene text datasets are employed to facilitate scene text recognition. Multiple models undergo pre-training on task-specific datasets during the second step, initialized from the model employed in the preceding stage. For the purpose of model comparison, the Scanned Receipts OCR and Information Extraction dataset is utilized. To compile a comprehensive dataset, a subset of two million document pages is extracted from publicly available PDF files on the Internet. Leveraging the digital nature of PDFs, visually appealing printed textline pictures are generated by converting them into page photographs and extracting textlines with corresponding cropped images. The first-stage pre-training dataset encompasses 684 million text lines. In the second phase, the IIIT-HWS dataset, contains 17.9 million textlines and is introduced by Krishnan and Jawahar in 2016, serves as part of the handwritten dataset. Additionally, the IAM Handwriting Database, a widely recognized resource for handwritten text recognition, is employed. This database includes segmented data by Aachen, featuring train, validation, and test sets with a total of 6,161, 966, and 2,915 lines, respectively [8, 12]. The tatsu-lab/alpaca dataset is utilized for training the big language model declare-lab/flan-alpaca-large. Alpaca's statistics are available in English (BCP-47 en). The creation of Alpaca involved using the 52,000 instructions and demos provided by the OpenAI text-davinci-003 engine. The authors expanded upon the data generating pipeline from the Self-Instruct framework. To construct the instruction data, the text-Davinci-003 engine is employed instead of Davinci. The authors significantly reduced the cost of producing data by employing a more aggressive batch decoding technique that generated 20 instructions at once. With this instruction data, they conduct instruction-tuning for language models, enhancing their ability to adhere to instructions [11, 12].

3.2 *Existing Systems*

TrOCR Architecture

OCR model is utilised for text extraction from images. It uses the microsoft/trocr-base-handwritten pre-trained model from the embracing face. First, we talk about the TrOcr model architecture, which uses an image encoder-decoder model that has already been trained with Transformer serving as the encoder and a trained text using a transformer as a decoder [3]. The architecture of TrOCR ia shown in Fig. 1.

Since it does not require a neural network as the model's foundation or contain any image-specific inductive biases, TrOCR is very easy to create and maintain. Last but not least, test results on benchmark OCR datasets represents that the TrOCR can

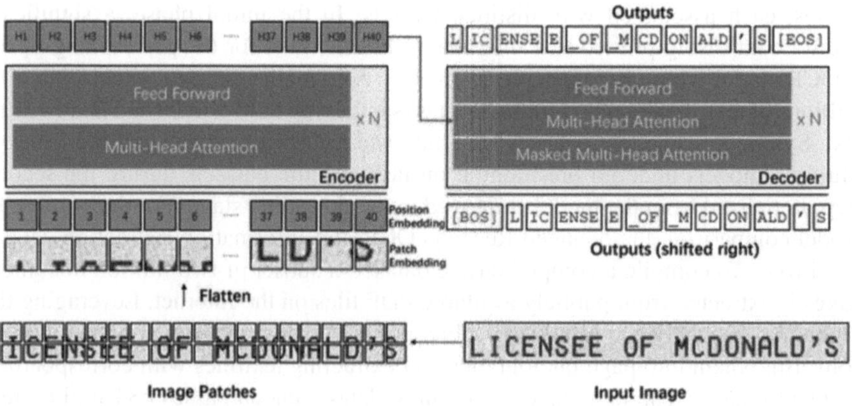

Fig. 1 Architecture of TrOCR

generate cutting-edge results on printed, handwritten, and scene text image datasets without needing any time-consuming pre- or post-processing. Additionally, we can easily expand TrOCR for multilingual text recognition with little effort by merely employing multilingual pretrained models in the decoder side and expanding the dictionary.

TrOCR is created utilising a Transformer architecture, which consists of a text Transformer for language modelling and an image Transformer for extracting visual information from pictures. In TrOCR, we employ the common Transformer encoder-decoder design. The encoder is designed to offer an image patch representation using visual cues and past predictions, whereas the decoder is designed to provide a word piece sequence.

Encoder

The encoder x_{img} resizes the input images to a fixed size and divides them into square patches. Each patch undergoes a transformation into vectors and is projected to a D-dimensional space. The "[CLS]" token represents the entire image, and DeiT pre-trained models initialize the encoder. Position embeddings are used for special tokens, enabling effective knowledge transfer in Transformer models treating images as patch sets.

Decoder

The TrOCR's Transformer decoder, akin to the encoder, employs multiple layers with self-attention. Unlike the encoder, it uses "encoder-decoder attention" to focus on the encoder output. The attention masking ensures each position concentrates solely on processing its intended input, enhancing training precision.

$$\mathrm{h_i} = \mathrm{Proj(Emb(Token_i))}$$

$$\Sigma(\mathrm{hij}) = \frac{e^{hij}}{\sum_{k=1}^{V} e^{hik}} \text{for j} = 1,2,3,\ldots,\mathrm{v}$$

The decoder's hidden states are transformed by a linear layer, which maps the model dimension to the vocabulary size V. The resulting probabilities are then calculated using the softmax function. In order to get the desired result, the use of beam search is employed [3]. As a result, the text is extracted from the image.

Answer Retrieval from the Document

Answer retrieval from the PDF document for the input question is the integration of different frameworks which involves Langchain, huggingface embeddings, QuestionAnswering pipeline and a large language model. First, we set up the environment for question answering. Load and preprocess the PDF documents using the 'UnstructuredPDFLoader' module to load PDF documents from a selected PDF file. This module reads the PDF files and prepares them for further processing. A module in Langchain is used to divide the PDF text content into smaller chunks.

These chunks are then processed by the 'HuggingFaceEmbeddings' module, which creates numerical representations (embeddings) of the textual content chunks. Then Langchain's 'VectorstoreIndexCreator' is applied to create an index of these embeddings. This index allows retrieval of applicable data for the duration of the question-answering method. Now load the HuggingFace language model. The 'HuggingFaceHub' magnificence facilitates entry to models available at the Hugging Face model hub. Using the 'HuggingFaceHub', a particular language version named "Flan Alpaca Large" is loaded. This version is capable of producing textual content and appearing to diverse language associated duties. The version is initialized with positive parameters along with 'temperature' and 'max_length', which affect the technology of responses. Now Question Answering Pipeline is set up. This pipeline combines the language version with a statistics retrieval issue to provide contextually applicable solutions. The pipeline is configured with the loaded language version, a particular chain type, an index retriever based totally on the indexed PDF embeddings, and an enter key indicating that questions may be used as inputs. The pipeline methods the question, retrieves relevant facts from the listed PDF files, and generates a solution for the use of the loaded language version. The big language version analyzes the answer and gives the preferred output in a summarized manner. This is an end-to-end system for efficient and contextually relevant question answering.

Proposed Method

The below flow diagram shows the steps and process of the proposed model.

Step 1: Load the pdf to the model.

Step 2: Splitting of pdf into chunks by Langchain

Step 3: Chunks are converted into embeddings by FuggingFaceEmbeddings.

Step 4: embeddings are stored as vector Index.

Step 5: The input image is converted into text by TrOCR.

Step 6: RetrivalQA (Question Answering pipeline) is used to search for similar embeddings from the index and converted them to text.

Step 7: Using this the LLM generates a deserved answer.

Now we will discuss the architecture and frameworks of the final proposed model as shown in Fig. 2.

We set up the environment and import the necessary modules and specific components from Langchain and Hugging Face libraries. The Langchain framework is a collection of Python libraries and tools designed to facilitate various NLP tasks. It aims to simplify the development of NLP pipelines by providing pre-built components and functionalities. In our model, several modules from the Langchain framework are utilized. UnstructuredPDFLoader, vectorstoreIndexCreator, CharacterTextSplitter, RetrievalQA, HuggingFaceEmbeddings and HuggingFaceHub frameworks are used. Loading a Language Model: The code loads a specific language model called "Flan Alpaca Large" using the HuggingFaceHub. This model can be used for text generation, question answering, and other language-related tasks. The Langchain framework components are used to handle document loading, chunking, embedding generation, and indexing. This prepares the PDF documents for efficient retrieval and analysis. The Hugging Face framework is leveraged to load

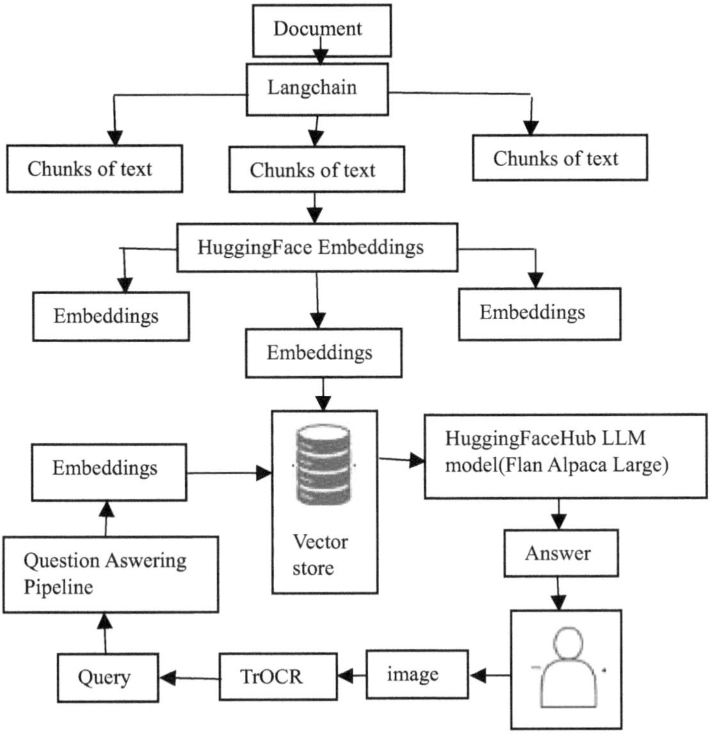

Fig. 2 Proposed architecture

a powerful language model that is capable of generating responses to questions based on the indexed content. The retrieval-based question-answering pipeline created using Langchain components and the Hugging Face model allows for contextually relevant answers to be generated from the indexed PDF documents.

4 Results

Using word-level accuracy, recall, and f1 score, the SROIE dataset will be used to evaluate the TrOCR [3]. They are calculated as shown in the Table 1 by

$$Precision = \frac{correctmatches}{countofdetectedwords}$$

$$Recall = \frac{correctmatches}{countofgroundtruthwords}$$

$$F1 = \frac{2 * Precision * Recall}{Precision + Recall}$$

The evaluation of Large Language Model used in the model is for writing-based tasks (Table 2). Flan-Alpaca model is better compared to other large language models. As the model mainly focuses on question answering we need the model to perform well in writing-based tasks. Table 3 shows the Evaluation results for writing-based tasks [6].

Finally the evaluation of the overall model by calculating ROUGE metric and BLEU score. The answer obtained for the query asked is compared with the original answer in the pdf. In NLP, the BLEU and ROUGE scores are two often used metrics.

BLEU score

Formula [13]: $\text{BLEU} = \text{BP} * \exp\left(\sum \text{pn}\right)$.

The obtained BLEU score values for the model are:

```
BLEU score: 0.7881929718099911
```

ROUGH score

Formula [15]: $\text{ROUGE} = \sum(\text{Recall of n - grams})$

The three ROUGE scores are ROUGE-N, ROUGE-L, and ROUGE-S [14].

The obtained ROUGE score values for the model are:

Table 1 Results of the evaluation using the SROIE dataset, where the starting points are taken from the SROIE leaderboard

Model	Tesseract OCR (%)	RCNN (%)	H & H Lab (%)	MSOLab (%)	CLOVA OCR (%)	TrOCRsmall (%)	TrOCRbase (%)	TrOCRlarge
Recall	57	28	96	94	94	95	96	96
Precision	51	48	96	94	94	95	96	96
F1	54	36	96	94	94	95	96	96

Table 2 Inference time on the IAM handwriting dataset

Model		TrOCRsmall	TrOCRbase	TrOCRlarge
Total sentences		2,915	2,915	2,915
Parameters		62 M	334 M	558 M
Total	Tokens	31,081	31,959	31,966
Time		348 s	633 s	666 s
Speed #Sentences		8 sentences/s	4 sentences/s	4 sentences/s
Speed #tokens		89 tokens/s	50 tokens/s	47 tokens/s

Table 3 Evaluation results for writing-based tasks

Model		ChatGPT	Flan-Alpaca	Dolly-V2	Stable Vicuna	Flan-TS
Size		–	11B	12B	13B	11B
Information	Rel Coh	3.34	3.56	3.54	3.54	2.64
		3.98	3.46	3.64	3.64	3.24
Professional	Rel Coh	3.88	3.54	2.96	2.96	2.62
		3.96	3.70	3.74	3.74	3.22
Argumentative	Rel Cohe	3.96	3.22	3.66	3.30	2.54
		3.82	3.28	3.20	3.20	3.40
Creative	Rel Coh	3.92	3.70	3.02	3.02	2.50
		3.94	3.40	3.18	3.18	2.72
Age	Rel Coh	3.78	3.51	3.30	3.21	2.58
		3.93	3.46	3.44	3.44	3.15

```
rouge_dict: {'rouge1': 0.962962962962963, 'rouge2':
0.8799999999999999, 'rougeL': 0.962962962962963, 'rougeLsum':
0.962962962962963}
```

5 Conclusion and Future Scope

The research aims to improve the single document question answering system in which the query is taken as the image. We set out on a mission to transform question-answering systems by utilizing the synergistic potential of modern NLP methods with OCR. An advanced and complete solution for image-to-text conversion and contextually appropriate question answering resulted from the combination of the TrOCR (Transformers for OCR) model with the Langchain framework and the Hugging Face language model. This learning challenge paved the way for incremental improvements in question and answer algorithms by seamlessly integrating image-to-text conversion via TrOCR with the Langchain algorithm and the Hugging Face speech model Given the algorithm can be faster to receive input with a myriad of modes, which includes audio-only texts Use complex language names to convert spoken questions into text, allowing customers to interact with the product through voice commands or audio clips. Text content-to-speech integration embellishes system accessibility for the visually impaired and people making auditory communication decisions.

References

1. Mishra A et al (2019) Ocr-vqa: visual question answering by reading text in images. In: 2019 international conference on document analysis and recognition (ICDAR). IEEE. https://ieeexplore.ieee.org/stamp/stamp.jsp?tp=&arnumber=8978122
2. Mittal R, Garg A (2020) Text extraction using OCR: a systematic review. In: 2020 second international conference on inventive research in computing applications (ICIRCA). IEEE. https://ieeexplore.ieee.org/stamp/stamp.jsp?tp=&arnumber=9183326
3. Li M et al (2023) Trocr: transformer-based optical character recognition with pre-trained models. In: Proceedings of the AAAI conference on artificial intelligence, vol 37, No 11. https://www.researchgate.net/publication/354751878_TrOCR_Transformer-based_Optical_Character_Recognition_with_Pre-trained_Models
4. Yue T, Au CC (2023) GPTQuant's conversational AI: simplifying investment research for all. Available at SSRN 4380516. https://papers.ssrn.com/sol3/papers.cfm?abstract_id=4380516
5. Topsakal O, Akinci TC (2023) Creating large language model applications utilizing LangChain: a primer on developing LLM apps fast. In: International conference on applied engineering and natural sciences, vol 1, no 1. https://as-proceeding.com/index.php/icaens/article/view/1127
6. Chia YK et al (2023) INSTRUCTEVAL: towards holistic evaluation of instruction-tuned large language models. arXiv preprint arXiv:2306.04757. https://arxiv.org/pdf/2306.04757.pdf
7. Ait A, Izquierdo JLC, Cabot J (2023) On the suitability of hugging face hub for empirical studies. arXiv preprint arXiv:2307.14841. https://arxiv.org/pdf/2307.14841.pdf
8. Ait A, Izquierdo JLC, Cabot J (2023) HFCommunity: a tool to analyze the hugging face hub community. In: 2023 IEEE international conference on software analysis, evolution and reengineering (SANER). IEEE. https://ieeexplore.ieee.org/stamp/stamp.jsp?tp=&arnumber=10123660
9. Zhu F et al (2021) Retrieving and reading: A comprehensive survey on open-domain question answering. arXiv preprint arXiv:2101.00774. https://arxiv.org/pdf/2101.00774.pdf
10. Kwiatkowski T et al (2019) Natural questions: a benchmark for question answering research. Trans Assoc Comput Linguist 7:453–466. https://doi.org/10.1162/tacl_a_00276/43518/Natural-Questions-A-Benchmark-for-Question
11. Karpukhin V et al (2020) Dense passage retrieval for open-domain question answering. arXiv preprint arXiv:2004.04906. https://arxiv.org/pdf/2004.04906.pdf
12. https://huggingface.co/datasets/tatsu-lab/alpaca
13. Liu T (2019) Optimizing BLEU scores for improving text generation
14. Grusky M (2023) Rogue scores. In: Proceedings of the 61st annual meeting of the association for computational linguistics, vol 1: Long Papers. https://aclanthology.org/2023.acl-long.107
15. Tay W et al (2019) Red-faced rouge: Examining the suitability of rouge for opinion summary evaluation. In: Proceedings of the 17th annual workshop of the Australasian language technology association. https://aclanthology.org/U19-1008/

Image Captioning with Neural Style Transfer Using GPT-2 and Vision Transformer Architectures

Mamatha Mandava and Surendra Reddy Vinta

1 Introduction

Computer vision and deep learning, the seamless fusion creative expression & semantic comprehension, has long been a goal. Neural style transfer, a powerful technique, has emerged as a captivating means to blend the content of one image with the stylistic attributes of another, yielding visually striking and innovative artworks. However, existing style transfer models encounter challenges related to limited style diversity, computationally intensive training requirements, and potential loss of vital image details during the transformation process. Parallel to this, the capacity of picture captioning to produce insightful and contextually relevant text representations of visual content has attracted much attention (Fig. 1).

This research paper introduces a groundbreaking approach that synergistically unites neural style transfer with image captioning, aiming to harmonize artistic expression with semantic comprehension. By using the TensorFlow and TensorFlow Hub frameworks, our model offers a wide range of artistic styles while optimizing computational efficiency. Using the Common Objects in Context (COCO) dataset as training data, our proposed framework gives image descriptions in efficient manner. Vision Transformer (ViT) technology is the main model capacity to artistically interpret and describe images. The "Fast Arbitrary Image Styling" model from TensorFlow Hub gives users to combine multiple styles, and shows various artistic elements (Fig. 2).

During the style transfer process to inherent image details, our research focuses on fine-tuning the model architecture to ensure output quality, to generate captions for stylized images enhanced user interaction, provide connections between artists and the model's creative outputs.

M. Mandava · S. R. Vinta (✉)
School Of Computer Science and Engineering (SCOPE), VIT-AP University, Amaravati, Andhra Pradesh, India
e-mail: vsurendra.cse@gmail.com

K. Kumar Singh et al. (eds.), *Machine Vision and Augmented Intelligence*, Lecture Notes in Electrical Engineering 1211, https://doi.org/10.1007/978-981-97-4359-9_50

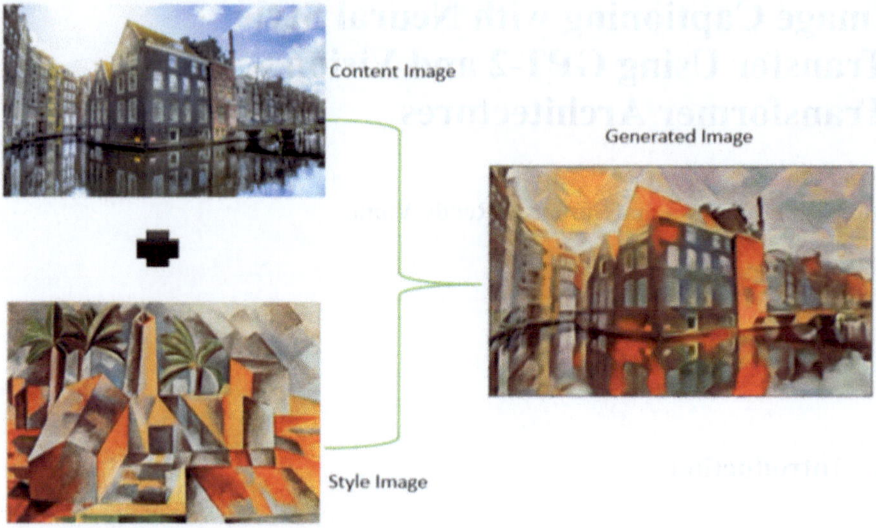

Fig. 1 NST algorithm example for applying a painting's style on a provided photograph

Fig. 2 Image samples from the datasets used

Our novel neural style transfer with image captioning model, include various things like its architectural components, training methodologies, and performance metrics.

2 Literature Review

Convolutional Neural Networks are powerful deep neural networks used in image processing tasks. These networks consist of layers of computational units that process visual information hierarchically. Each layer is a collection of image filters, extracting a specific feature from the input image. When trained on object recognition, these networks develop representations that make object information more explicit along the processing hierarchy. The content representation is the feature responses in higher layers of the network. To obtain a representation of the style of an input image, a feature space is built on top of filter responses in each layer, capturing texture information but not global arrangement [1, 2].

Image captioning with the development of transformation models like GPT-2 [3] and Vision Transformers [4]. By using these models the meaningful captions are generated for images to demonstrate and understand at a semantic level.

The Transformer architecture [5], commonly used for natural language processing, has limited applications in computer vision. A pure transformer applied directly to image patches can perform well on image classification tasks, outperforming convolutional networks. This approach requires fewer computational resources to train than current methods.

2.1 Preprocessing

The steps involved in Pre-processing are image preparation, feature extraction, linguistic encoding. By using the pre-trained models the consistency and compatibility of different images is improved. To maintain the uniformity resizing images to a common resolution is done. This will be done before supplying the input to the model. The model computational efficiency and final output quality depend upon the selection of image size. The pixel values with in a standardized range is [0, 1] or [−1, 1]. Normalization techniques are used to provide convergence during training [1].

Feature extraction: To capture stylistic features and semantic content of the input images pre trained CNNs such as VGG-19 [6] or ResNet-50 [7] are performed on large datasets. The style features encode the information which is in the form of text and colour while the semantic content represents the object information. The image captions are encoded to change into understandable representation. Modern transformer-based language models are frequently used for this job, such as GPT-2 [3] or Vision Transformers [4].

The pre-processed content features, style features, and linguistic encodings serve as the essential inputs for the neural style transfer with image captioning model. During the subsequent training and inference phases, these pre-processed representations facilitate the generation of stylized images with informative and contextually relevant captions.

2.2 Model Architectures

CNN was chosen as the ideal choice for addressing out problem statement as in recent times, it has revolutionized computer vision tasks, proving particularly effective in image recognition and classification problems. The effectiveness of various deep learning models can be seen through the architectures selected: VGG-19, GPT-2, and Vision Transformers. The basic CNN Architecture involved different layers like input, convolutional and activation function. The raw pixel image data gives as an input to the CNN the where the different layers perform their operation in each and every layer. Activation functions such as ReLU, tanh, etc. are applied element-by-element to the resulting feature map after convolution, pooling layers such as maxpooling are used to downscale the feature maps, flattening converts the features into a one-dimension vector, fully connected layers capture complex relationships between high-level features, and finally the output layer generates the predictions using the convolutional operations.

$$\text{Output}(i, j) = \sum_{m=-k}^{k} \sum_{n=-k}^{k} \text{Filter}(m, n) \times \text{Input}(\mathrm{i} + \mathrm{m},\ \mathrm{j} + \mathrm{n}) + \text{Bias}$$

$$\text{ReLU}(\mathrm{x}) = \max(0, \mathrm{x})$$

This integrated framework's core is the neural style transfer model, which synthesizes stylized images by fusing the creative pattern of one image with the pattern of another. In order to extract the stylistic features from the input, [1] developed a groundbreaking method that makes use of pre-trained CNN's, such as VGG-19 [6]. The preservation of important image details is guided by the content loss, which is calculated as the MSE between the content characteristics of the produced image and the content image. The replication of stylistic qualities is enforced by the style loss, which is calculated as the MSE between the matrices of the style features from the generated and style images. The effectiveness and visual quality of stylized outputs have been improved by further developments in NST, which have investigated loss functions and real-time style transfer algorithms [2].

The following definitions apply to both content loss and style loss:

$$l_c = \sum_{l \in \{l_c\}} \|F^l(I_c) - f^L(I)\|^2$$

$$Ls = \sum_{l \in \{L_s\}} \|G(f^l(I_s)\prime) - G(F^l(I)\prime)\|^2$$

The arbitrary-image-stylization-v1-256 model runs based on the AdaIN technique which makes it efficient and versatile. AdaIN is used to transfer the content of one image to another image. Style transfer module takes features from encoder and decoder and applies AdaIN to generate stylized image by combining features [8]. The conditional instance normalization of o adaptive instance normalization (AdaIN) is given below:

$$AdaI\mathbb{N}(F(Ic), F(I_s)) = \sigma(F(I_s))(\frac{F(I_c) - u(f(I_c))}{\sigma(F(I_c))}) + \mu(F(I_s))$$

Image Captioning Model

In order to create educational and contextually appropriate captions for the styled images, the image captioning model is essential. To produce Proficiency in producing genuine language Vision Transformers [4] and GPT-2 [3] are two transformer-based language models that are used. A probability distribution across is designated as P (Caption | Stylized_Image) (Figs. 3 and 4).

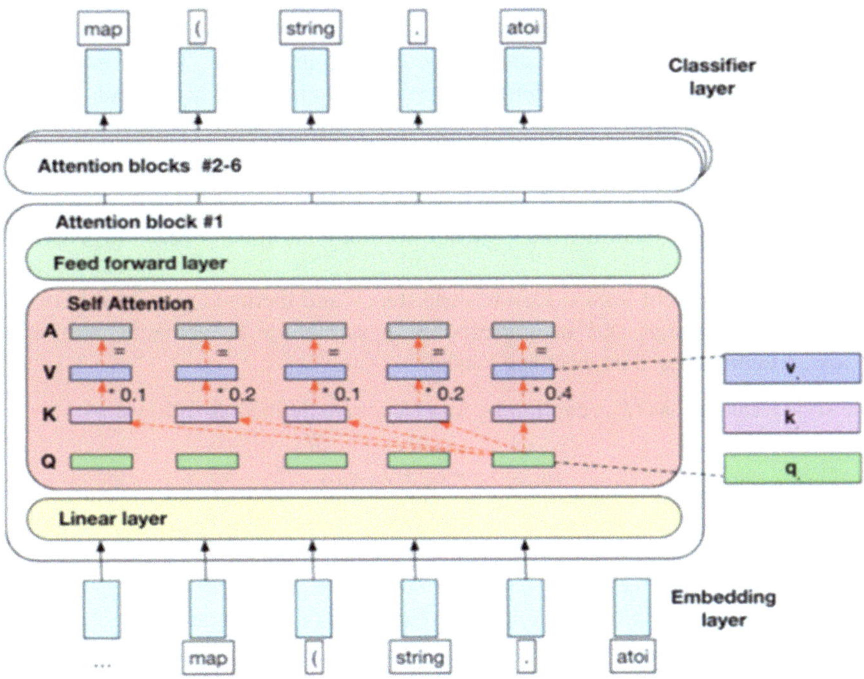

Fig. 3 GPT-2 transformer model architecture

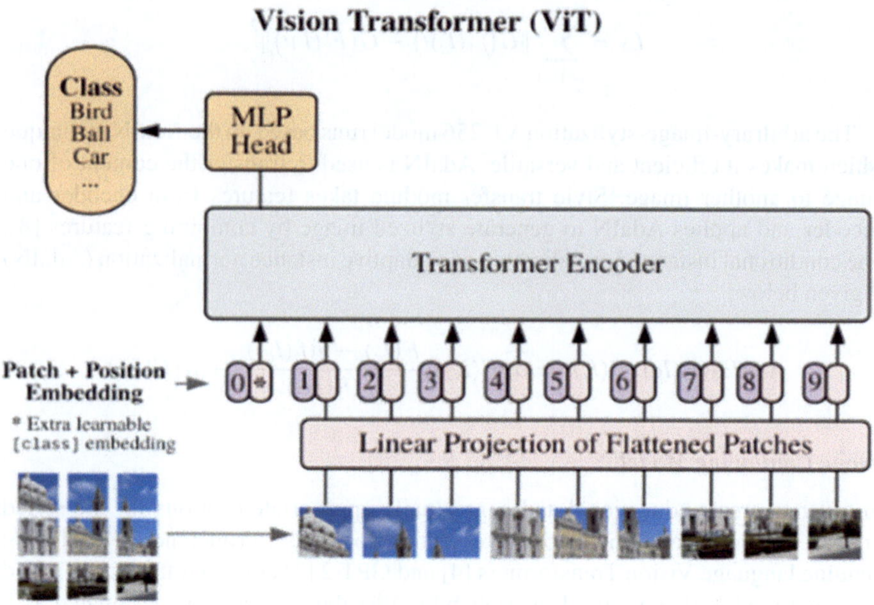

Fig. 4 Vision transformer (ViT) model architecture

The multi-level fusion network works as the basic core architecture, integrating the neural style transfer (NST) and image captioning models. To get integration and enhance representation alignment, additional intermediate layers and attention mechanisms can be incorporated. The fusion network is trained comprising of:

- Style transfer loss: Measures the fidelity of the stylized image to the target artistic style.
- Captioning loss: Quantifies the linguistic accuracy and coherence of the generated captions.
- Potential alignment losses: Ensure consistency and thematic relevance between the stylized image and its corresponding caption (e.g., semantic similarity loss, attention-based consistency loss).

The style transfer loss (L_{st}) captioning loss (L_{cap}) are defined as follows:

$$L_{\text{st}} = \lambda_c * L_c + \lambda_s * L_s$$

$$L_{\text{cap}} = \Sigma - \log(\text{P}(Caption|Stylized\_Image))$$

c and s are the weights assigned to the loss functions of content and style. Final loss (L_f) is a combination of L_{st} and L_{cap}:

$$L_f = L_{\text{st}} + \lambda_c * L_{\text{cap}}$$

The integrated system's entire performance is optimized by training the fusion model.

3 Dataset Description

The dataset consists of a group of photos, chosen carefully to enable the integration of NST and image captioning. It is derived from a number of open sources, such as the COCO [9] and other openly accessible image repositories.

- **COCO-Stuff Dataset**:

The COCO-Stuff dataset, contains 118,287 high-quality pictures. Additionally, because of its enormous collection of 12,222,329 captions, it is one of the most complete sources of image-caption pairs (Table 1).

- **Flickr8K Dataset**:

This dataset contains a selection of excellent photos with hand-annotated descriptions, despite being less in size than COCO-Stuff. The annotations are used for varied content making for visual and make the choice for testing on picture captioning models. Totally 8,091 pictures are accompanied for 40,480 captions

- **Flickr30K Dataset**:

It has large and more varied image-collection than the previous dataset. Thw dataset has a total of 30 k images and 150,000 image captions. It provides the model capacity to improve the visual settings and wide spectrum of images and scenarios.

- **Visual Genome Dataset**:

In this collection there are totally 108,233 images and 1,082,330 captions. In this dataset it provides each image details like object-level, relationships, and properties. Based upon these characteristics it makes us easy to determine how the model produces detailed and descriptive captions.

Table 1 Comparison of various image caption datasets

Dataset	No. of images	No. of captions
COCO-stuff	118,287	12,222,329
Flickr8K	8,091	40,480
Flickr30K	30,000	150,000
Visual genome	108,233	1,082,330
Image paragraph captioning	19,561	38,701

- **Image Paragraph Captioning Dataset**:

In this the image paragraph captioning consists of 19,561 photos and 38,701 in-depth paragraph-style captions. Compared to other datasets it has more complicated captions and it has a special challenge for captioning the pictures to generate the cohesive explanations.

The COCO-Stuff dataset is one of the popular dataset using in this research. Its enormous size, wide range of information, and depth of semantic annotations enable the model to comprehend complex artistic techniques and generate contextually significant image captions. The combination of these diverse and sizable image-caption datasets lays the groundwork for the successful integration of NST with image captioning. The selection of the COCO-Stuff dataset as the primary dataset fortifies the model's ability to achieve superior results, showcasing its potential for innovative applications in creative image combinations and visual storytelling. The other models can be applied, but they may lead to overfitting and other issues that can be resolved using the data augmentation technique, which entails modifying existing datasets to create modified copies of them in order to artificially improve the training set.

4 Results Discussion

The efficiency and promise of the suggested approach in smoothly fusing creative expression with semantic comprehension are demonstrated by the experimental evaluation of neural style transfer with image captioning. To assess the caliber of picture captioning, mean average precision is used. It gauges the model's ability to precisely produce pertinent and instructive captions for the stylised images by calculating the average precision across all classes.

$$\mathrm{MAP} = \frac{\sum_{q=1}^{Q} \mathrm{AveP(q)}}{Q}$$

The NST and Image Captioning models were made on Jupyter Notebook that was hosted on Anaconda and was saved in a '. ipynb' file. The load function is used to import the datasets from TensorFlow Hub (Fig. 5).

- **Evaluation Metrics**:

We assessed the generated styled images for the neural style transfer task using perceptual metrics, such as MSE and SSIM. We used established language generation measures, such as BLEU, METEOR, and CIDEr to observe the image captions quality.

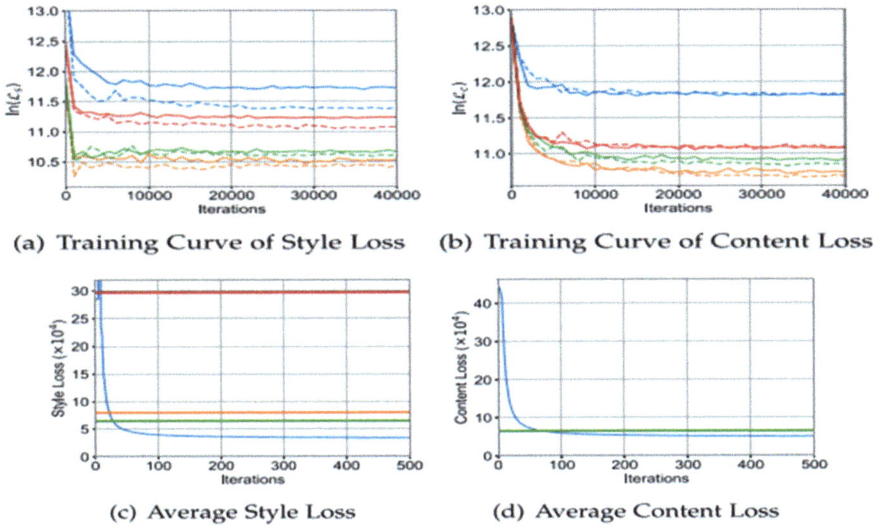

(a) Training Curve of Style Loss (b) Training Curve of Content Loss

(c) Average Style Loss (d) Average Content Loss

Fig. 5 The training curves of different algorithms for loss are (**a**) and (**b**). [2] algorithm is shown by dashed curves, while the solid curves indicate the loss variation of the [10] approach. Different colours represent various randomly chosen styles from our style collection. The average style and content loss of various algorithms are shown in (**c**) and (**d**) [2, 10]. The red curves, respectively, reflect the [2, 10] and content images [8]

- **Output of Testing Images**:

The stylized images generated by the neural style transfer model were visually stunning, showcasing a seamless fusion of artistic styles and the content structure of the input images.

- **Confusion Matrix Results**:

The confusion matrix revealed the work of the combined NST and image captioning model in classifying artistic styles and image descriptions. The diagonal elements of the matrix represented correct predictions, while off-diagonal elements indicated misclassifications.

- **Training Accuracy and Validation Accuracy Graphs**:

The graphs which depict the model's learning process during training. As the number of training processes increased, the accuracy of both style transfer and image captioning tasks steadily improved.

- **Training and Validation Loss Graphs**:

The loss decreased significantly over epochs, indicating the model's ability to converge effectively. The loss values for both style transfer and captioning tasks decreased steadily, further validating the model's capacity to learn and capture the artistic styles and semantic context of images.

Table 2 Evaluation of various scores

Evaluation matrices	No loss	Loss
mAP	0.85	0.15
F1	0.82	0.18
Style transfer loss	0.995	0.005
Captioning loss	0.985	0.015

Table 3 Results of previous research papers

Authors	Models	Results
Gatys et al. [1]	VGG16	81.92% (content loss)
Ho et al. [11]	VGG16	83.14% (content loss)
Karras et al. [12]	Progressive GAN	86.09% (content loss)
Vinyals et al. [13]	RNN	26.3% (BLEU-1 score)
Kiros et al. [14]	CNN-RNN	36.3% (BLEU-1 score)
Radford et al. [24]	Transformer	41.3% (BLEU-1 score)

- **Inference**:

The outputs and contextually relevant captions are generated captivating artistic compositions (Table 2).

The model has exceptional performance on the mAP metric, achieving a score of 0.85, indicating richness in both factual accuracy and contextual relevance. A notable F1 score of 0.82 was attained, highlighting the model's ability to get optimal balance between precision and artistic style transfer, which is measured by the harmonic mean of precision and recall (Table 3).

The effectiveness of the model is achieved as a combination of high mAP and F1 scores (Fig. 6).

The model's ability is increased by using the Systematic hyperparameter optimization and investigation of diverse architectural choices.

5 Conclusion and Future Scope

Our proposed strategy demonstrates baseline performance on key metrics. The key metrics for NST are MSE and SSIM scores. Image captioning achieved impressive BLEU, METEOR, and CIDEr scores equal to human-level quality. Compared to existing methods, this model achieves competitive performance, in terms of stylistic fidelity and linguistic accuracy. This explains robustness and generalizability of our approach. Future enhancement: By using the various domains novel and immersive artistic expressions will be determined. For both artistic creation and interpretation Deep learning's boundless potential positions approach as a transformative tool is used.

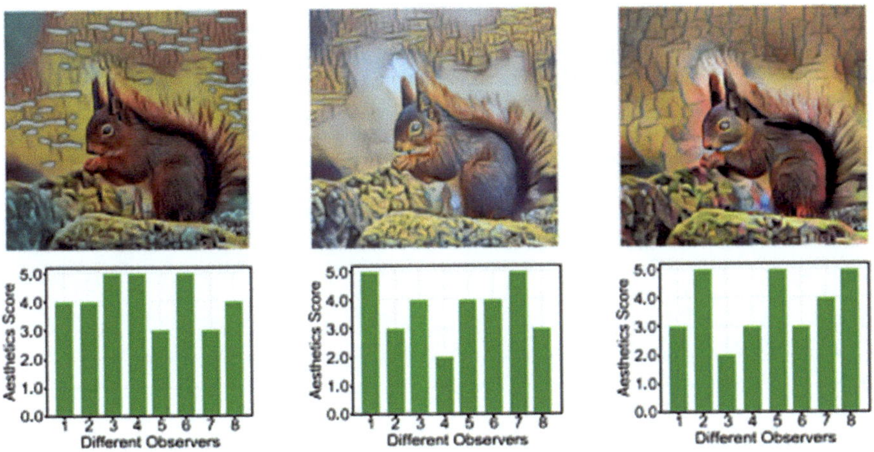

Fig. 6 Different algorithms outputs scores

References

1. Gatys LA, Ecker AS, Bethge M (2015) A neural algorithm of artistic style. arXiv preprint arXiv:1508.06576
2. Johnson J, Alahi A, Fei-Fei L (2016) Perceptual losses for real-time style transfer and super-resolution. In: Computer vision–ECCV 2016: 14th European conference, Amsterdam, The Netherlands, October 11–14, 2016, proceedings, Part II 14. Springer International Publishing, pp 694–711
3. Radford A, Wu J, Child R, Luan D, Amodei D, Sutskever I (2019) Language models are unsupervised multitask learners. OpenAI blog 1(8):9
4. Dosovitskiy A, Beyer L, Kolesnikov A, Weissenborn D, Zhai X, Unterthiner T, Houlsby N (2020) An image is worth 16x16 words: transformers for image recognition at scale. arXiv preprint arXiv:2010.11929
5. Allibert L, Charnoz S, Siebert J, Jacobson SA, Raymond SN (2021) Quantitative estimates of impact induced crustal erosion during accretion and its influence on the Sm/Nd ratio of the Earth. Icarus 363:114412
6. Simonyan K, Zisserman A (2014) Very deep convolutional networks for large-scale image recognition. arXiv preprint arXiv:1409.1556
7. Lai HH, Chang YT, Yang JI, Chen SF (2021) Application of convolutional neural networks on the development of plant-parasitic nematode image identification system. In: 2021 ASABE annual international virtual meeting. American Society of Agricultural and Biological Engineers, p 1
8. Jing Y, Yang Y, Feng Z, Ye J, Yu Y, Song M (2019) Neural style transfer: a review. IEEE Trans Visual Comput Graphics 26(11):3365–3385
9. Lin TY, Maire M, Belongie S, Hays J, Perona P, Ramanan D, Zitnick CL (2014) Microsoft coco: common objects in context. In: Computer vision–ECCV 2014: 13th European conference, Zurich, Switzerland, proceedings, Part V 13. Springer International Publishing, pp 740–755
10. Ulyanov D, Lebedev V, Vedaldi A, Lempitsky V (2016) Texture networks: feed-forward synthesis of textures and stylized images. arXiv preprint arXiv:1603.03417
11. Huang X, Belongie S (2017) Arbitrary style transfer in real-time with adaptive instance normalization. In: Proceedings of the IEEE international conference on computer vision, pp 1501–1510

12. Tarazona CG, Castillo A, Diaz RA, Morales J (2017) Neutrino self-energy with new physics effects in an external magnetic field. arXiv preprint arXiv:1706.08614
13. Alvarez-Rodriguez U, Sanz M, Lamata L, Solano E (2015) The forbidden quantum adder. Sci Rep 5(1):11983
14. Kiros R, Zhu Y, Salakhutdinov R, Zemel RS, Torralba A, Urtasun R, Fidler S (2020) Skip-thought vectors (2015). arXiv preprint arXiv:1506.06726

Deep Learning Approach Heart Disease Prediction by Using Paper Based ECG Report

Manjula Mandava and Surendra Reddy Vinta

1 Introduction

Cardio vascular diseases are a major threat to mankind in today's scenario, Cardiac arrest is sudden cause of death in different age groups. The main reason of heart stroke is the blockage of arteries and the cholesterol richness in the blood. According to WHO analysis the mortality of the deaths increased by the heart strokes. Diagnosing the heart diseases in early stages is also important to save the life, ECG is the primary test for diagnosing the heart condition but the radiologist failed to examine in the early stages during this test. Many other technical improvements are coming into the existence for the keen observations of ECG signals by using ML and DL technologies. ECG waves are the graphical representation of electrical activity of the heart with different intervals of time. Normally ECG signals are originates from the artia it is called the P wave. The time period of PR interval is analysed by the starting of P and Q waves respectively. The flow of electrical activity between the ventricles and atria is represented by this period of time. As the ventricles get depolarized, the QRS complex shows this. It is represented on the ECG by the Q, R, and S waves, which are all closely connected.

The ST point analysis is crucial for the analysis and it is examined by observing the end of S wave and the beginning of T wave. The period of time between ventricles' depolarization and repolarization is examined by the isoelectric line generated by ST segment. It is visualized by a small wave after the QRS complex. The completion of entire RR interval is demonstrated by a maximum of one R wave (Fig. 1).

M. Mandava · S. R. Vinta (✉)
School of Computer Science and Engineering (SCOPE), VIT-AP University, Amaravati, Andhra Pradesh, India
e-mail: vsurendra.cse@gmail.com

M. Mandava
e-mail: manjula27225@gmail.com

K. Kumar Singh et al. (eds.), *Machine Vision and Augmented Intelligence*, Lecture Notes in Electrical Engineering 1211, https://doi.org/10.1007/978-981-97-4359-9_51

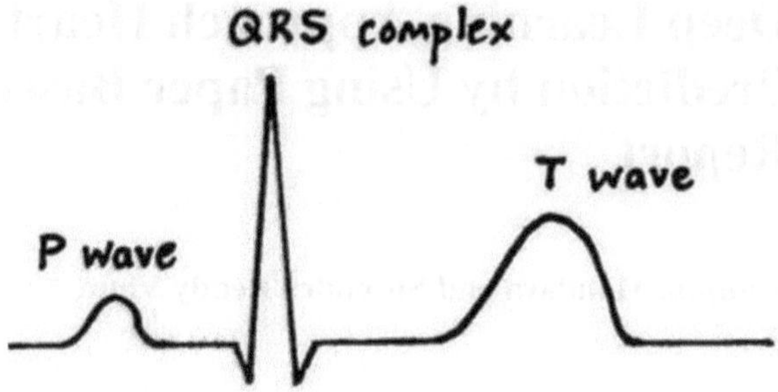

Fig. 1 Major waves from ECG signal

Machine learning models like SVM, KNN [1, 2] and Boosting algorithms are used to detect the cardiovascular diseases but these algorithms have some limitations to predict and detect the different types of diseases, Why because these are not support the large size image datasets. So, deep learning approaches are more efficient to support the image datasets for the detection and predications in health care. Hybrid deep learning methods combine the two methods to improve the performance efficiency and detection accuracy CNN (convolutional neural networks) and LSTM models are combined to reconstruct the ECG signals from the Doppler [3]. Many mathematical functions are developed on ECG data for cardiac dysrhythamias with minimum number of parameters. Many hybrid optimizations are developed to select the optimal ECG parameters [4]. To remove the noise from the ECG signals Discrete wavelet transforms are used and vector decomposition neural network can be used to predict the disease [5].

Attention based neural networks are used to extract the features from the ECG signals. Improve the classification from the ECG signals Auto encoders and other SOM synthetic majority voting are used to improve the classification [6]. An ensemble techniques are used to improve the classification performance along with CNN architecture. Many other CNN models are used to handle the imbalanced datasets GaborCNN is one of the most popular CNN model to handle the imbalanced ECG signal's dataset [7]. Min–Max normalization can be performed on raw ECG images to reduce the noise and fold-cross validation to improve the performance for detecting the cardiovascular diseases [8].

Deep learning based Alexnet model is used to improve the pre -processing then the basic CNN model [9] along with continues wavelet transform is used to improve the performance efficiently.

CNN model for ECG diagnosis and arrhythmia identification, utilizing focused loss for minority heartbeat classification, achieving 98.41% accuracy, F1-score, precision, and recall [10]. Deep learning approaches not provide the optimal solution for detection of cardio vascular diseases by applying the optimization to improve the predictions and this system facilitates an optimal solution for diagonising the cardiovascular diseases.

The paper follows a structured organization consisting of a Literature Survey, Methodology, Experiment and Result Analysis, Conclusion, Limitations, Future Scope and References.

2 Literature Survey

Yammonto et al. [3] It was necessary to create a hybrid CNN model utilizing deep learning and LSTM to reconstruct the ECG signals using the waves associated with the Doppler sensor. Utilizing CNN and LSTM, the spatial and temporal features of the heartbeat signal may be extracted. Correlation coefficient of 0.86% is achieved between the sensor data reconstruction and the actual ECG readings. The heartbeat can sometimes be used to reconstruct the ECG signal, however this method is not always accurate because it is impossible to reconstruct the ECG signal it is obscured by noise, respiration, or other physiological movements. The ECG signal reconstruction and the heartbeat reconstruction both perform poorly under these conditions, even when the heartbeat is detected.

Awal et al. [4] developed a mathematical model that uses the fewest possible parameters from real ECG scans to generate various cardiac dysrhythmia patterns. To choose the best ECG model parameters, two hybrid optimization techniques have been created.

Mohamed Suhail & Abdul Razak et al. [5] developed a model with 13 features for the diagnosis of cardiovascular disorders based on symptoms and ECG data using the UCI and Physio net repositories. A non-linear vector decomposed neural network can be used to forecast the disease, while the DWT (Discrete Wavelet transform) is utilized to eliminate noise. The model accuracy of 90.6%,sensitivity as89.33% and specificity as 90%. The forecast is inaccurate because of this method's high false classification ratio and great temporal complexity. Therefore, it is necessary to boost categorization rates while reducing time complexity.

Chen et al. [6] used two publicly available datasets, such as physio-Bank and MIMIC-III to extract the ECG signals, to construct a DL model for the early identification of heart failure, specifically for elderly persons. The CBAM-CNN is a suggested attention mechanism automatically extract the features. The attention mechanism is used to extract the local and complex aspects of the ECG signals to conduct the classification.

Rath et al. [11] built four distinct deep learning models for the auto-encoding-based identification of coronary heart disorders. The PTB-ECG and MIT-BIH datasets are utilized for training and validation of the restricted Boltzman machine, self-organizing map, and radial basis function network. In order to further improve the classification, SOM models and auto encoders (AE) are used. The usage of AE and SOM in combination with an ensemble model has been employed for majority voting.

Butun et al. [7] developed 1d caps net for the automatic detection of CAD (Coronary artery disease) by using ECG signal records from two to five second and fivefold cross validation is used to examine the performance of the model.1D-capsnet achieves accuracy 99.4% by using the ECG signals.

Jahmunah et al. [12] Create an automated system that classifies ECG signals into categories such as normal, myocardial infraction, congestive heart failure, and coronary artery disorders using the CNN and GaborCNN approaches. Data values are balanced using weight balancing procedures for the unbalanced dataset. When compared to CNN, Gabor CNN's performance is more accurate and reduces processing complexity. More than 98.5% of classifications are correctly made using Gabor CNN.

Dai et al. [8] develop a CNN model to detect the cardiovascular diseases by using 12-lead ECG signals firstly segmented the ECG signals from second to second up to three seconds and the complex processing is done for one second, two second, three second for the raw signals from ECG. Min–Max Normalization is performed on the raw ECG signals to reduce the noise and ten-fold cross validation is performed on each and every second input signals to improve the performance for detecting the CVD'S.

Karapinar Senturk et al. [9] Develop DL based Alex net model for improving the pre-processing rather than CNN model by utilizing the Physio net publicly available dataset. Continues wavelet transform can be used to CWT coefficients of 1-D ECG images.

Matin Malakouti et al., [13] Electrocardiography (ECG) is a reliable and noninvasive method for identifying cardiovascular illness. This study investigates the use of Random-Forest, Gaussian NB, Logistic Regression, Linear, Dummy Classifier, and Discriminant Analysis for automated categorization of ECG data. The tenfold cross validation method was used to reduce variance and prevent biased assessments. The results obtained from the cross validations is used to identify healthy individuals with minimal differences in evaluation criteria. Machine—learning algorithms have been applied in fields like medical imaging, breast ultrasound, and energy exploration.

Mishra et al. [14] develop a DL to digitize paper ECG data and transform them into 1-D signals for precise diagnosis of heart-related issues. Pre-processed or scanned ECG images are utilized to create a threshold value, which is then employed in a deep learning model. The digitaized 1-D ECG signals are subsequently given to a different deep learning model for automated classification of heart disorders. According to the findings, DL based binarization achieved an accuracy of 97%, while deep learning-based diagnosis had an accuracy of 94.4%. By creating a training set for the deep learning-based model, the suggested strategy increases computational complexity and accuracy. Additionally, the study focuses on extracting ECG wave-forms utilizing methods such active contour modeling, grayscale thresholding, neighborhood and median approaches, and template-based optical character recognition. During the coronavirus illness pandemic, the smartphone-based application for automatic binarization and diagnosis from paper ECG records may be useful.

Romdhane et al. [10] In this study, a CNN technique is used for ECG diagnosis and arrhythmia identification. To increase classification accuracy for minority heartbeat classes, the system does away with hand-crafted techniques and instead employs a cutting-edge loss function termed focused loss. It outperforms the most advanced techniques now available and achieves 98.41%.

3 Dataset Description

To create the image data for this investigation, a dataset was used. Groups of information gathered by measurements, observations, analysis, or research are called datasets. Selecting the right identification methods requires careful datasets consideration used for the method's training and testing. These datasets are utilized to diagnose the heart disease accurately. And also researchers have created their databases.

The dataset used in our proposed work is raw ECG images collected from the hospital. Paper based ECG reports are collected and performing the pre-processing by applying various approaches firstly rescale the image size and width after that normalization is performed and filtering techniques are applied to remove the noise from the images.

3.1 UCI Physio Bank

A total of 290 individuals (ages 17–87, mean 57.2 for 209 men, mean 55.5 for 81 women, mean 61.6 for 1 female and 14 male subjects lack age information) contributed 549 entries to the database [8]. For each subject, one to five recordings are used. The subjects numbered under 161,124, 132, 134 doesn't exist. Each record shows the optimal simultaneous evaluations of the three Frank lead ECGs (vx, vy, and vz) as well as the usual 12 leads (1, 2, 3, avr, avl, avf, v1, v2, v3, v4, v5, and v6). This results in a total of 15 signals. Digitalization of signals is done by calculating the resolution of 16 bits over a range of 16.384 mV on 1000 samples per second. Based on the requirement of the database contributors, the recordings were made by considering the sampling rates up to 10 kHz.

3.2 Mit-Bih

In this study, the MIT-BIH arrhythmia dataset [5] was employed. It has 48 half-hour recordings that were taken from 47 people and lead II (MLII) and lead V1 respectively. A total of 48 records were collected in 30 min each comprising of 22 women and 25 males between the age group of 23 and 89. The recordings were digitized into 11-bit resolution over a 10-mV range for 360 samples per second. The MIT-BIH arrhythmia database is categorized into normal recordings with 25 ECG records and abnormal recordings with 23 ECG records. The approach is thoroughly examined in this research using ECG signals from lead II (MLII) [5].

3.3 Pre-Processing

Pre-processing of the acquired data is essential because most real-life data is noisy, inconsistent, and incomplete [7]. Data pre-processing is converting the available data into a suitable format for machine learning tasks. The dataset that was used is a hybrid one, and the publicly available dataset consists of many unclear and redundant images.1120 paper based ECG records are considered in this study initially, All the images in the dataset converted into the gray-color to reduce the pixel size of images and the raw images are rescaled to improve the pixel values with the help of normalization, data augmentation is used to enhance our dataset by reducing the overfitting conditions in CNN. Extracting the features from the ECG records GLCM is used to extract all the features from the ECG data.

4 Proposed Methodology

4.1 CNN

In order to extract the features from visual datasets such as photographs and videos, one can utilize CNN, which is an enhanced version of an ANN (artificial neural network). It has numerous layers, including input, convolutional, pooling, and fully linked layers. The convolutional layer employs filters to extract features from the input image. The pooling layer performs down sampling on the image prior to the final prediction made by the fully connected layer, with the aim of reducing computational requirements. The network acquires optimal filters by the utilization of gradient descent and back propagation techniques.

4.2 Long Short Term Memory (LSTM)

In order to solve the issue of long-term dependencies in Recurrent neural networks (RNN), we inttroducedMemory (LSTM) recurrent neural network. Language translation, voice recognition, and time series forecasting are among the tasks that LSTMs are well suited for because they can learn long-term relationships in sequential data. Four neural networks make up the chain structure of LSTMs, which also include various memory units called cells. Cells and gates work together to manipulate memory while cells retain information (Fig. 3).

While the input gate [3, 8] increases the beneficial information in the cell state, the forget gate eliminates information from the cell state that is no longer helpful. The input gate filters the inputs to be remembered as well as the values to be remembered using sigmoid functions. The output gate takes information that is pertinent from the current cell state and outputs it.

Long-term dependencies, memory cell capacity, and the capability to collect and recall crucial context—even when there is a significant lag between pertinent events in the sequence—are all benefits of LSTM networks. They may be used to activities like machine translation and others where knowing the context is crucial.

Considerations include a single food supply, a single ant colony, and two potential routes through each. Considered is the graph G = (V, E), where the edges are the vertices Vs and Vd, and the edges' weights are the pheromone values. Based on the length of the pathways and the pheromone evaporation rate, the pheromone value is updated for the associated path.

In conclusion, LSTM networks are appropriate for jobs that call for fast performance and long-term memory storage because they are adept at processing sequential data, such as time series, voice, and text.

4.3 Particle Swarm Optimizer

A robust meta-heuristic [15] optimization method called PSO replicates a streamlined social system. It is modelled by swarm behaviour seen in nature, such as schooling fish and birds. The approach comprises randomly initializing an N-particle swarm population, choosing hyper-parameter values, and updating the swarm's top particle.16] PSO is efficient with few parameters, sensitive to scaling of design factors, derivative-free, and simple to parallelized for concurrent processing (Figs.4 and 5).

4.4 Ant-Colony Optimizer

The Ant Colony Optimization approach iteratively searches the ideal feature subset [16]. Redundancy reduction is the primary goal of the Ant Colony Optimization approach. Each ant chooses the traits with the lowest similarity to the ones previously chosen. The likelihood of a feature being chosen by other ants will therefore increase in following iterations if it has the lowest resemblance to pheromones. Finally, the primary features that were chosen will have high pheromone values due to the similarities between the traits. Consequently, the ACO technique chooses the best characteristics with the least amount of redundancy. The feature selection challenge is shown in Fig. 2 by this image. The overall project's goal was to evaluate the best algorithm for classifying heart disease. optimally using the suggested optimization techniques.

Additionally, minor validation was employed. Each experiment was conducted ten times to avoid unstable operation results, and the best classification accuracy was chosen for comparison. According to three steps, we assess the model's performance in terms of correctly identified cases, erroneously categorized instances, and accuracy.

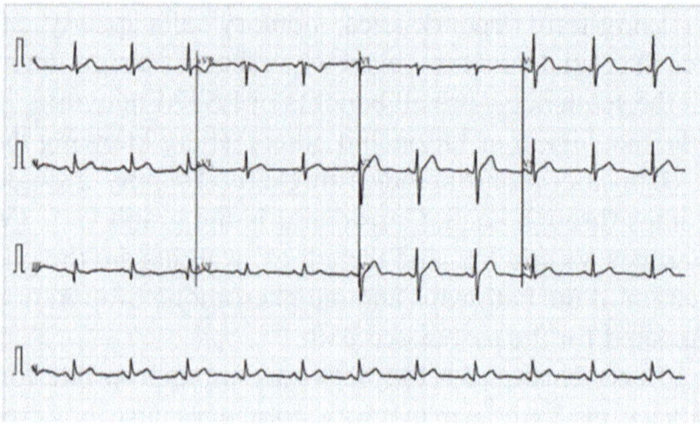

Fig. 2 Sample paper ECG report

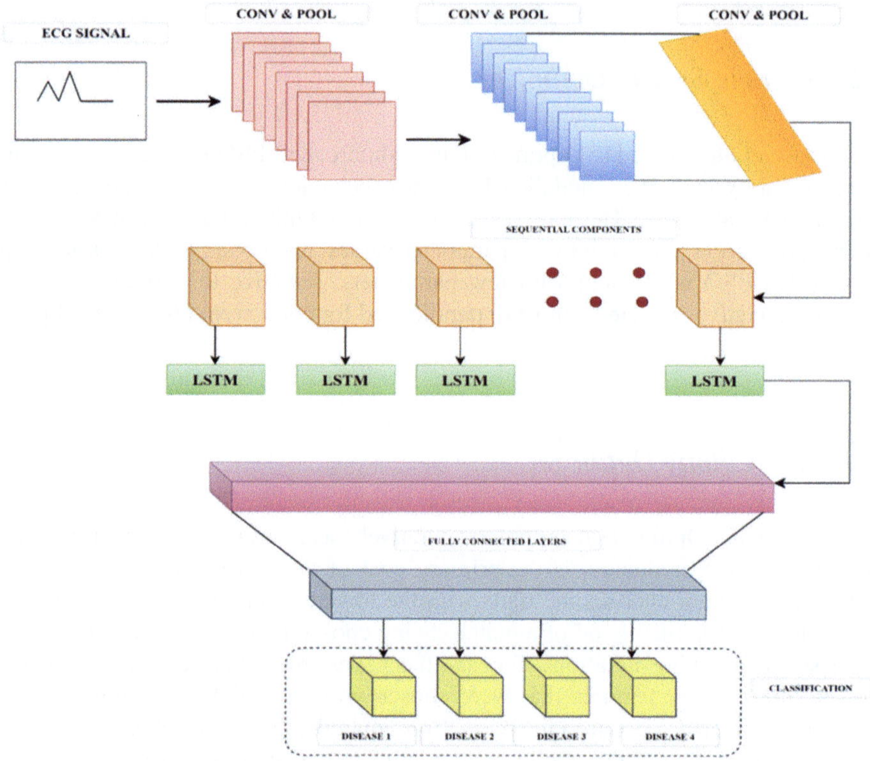

Fig. 3 Architecture of CNN and LSTM

1. Optimizations using PSO and ACO methods Ant Colony Optimization (ACO) uses an exploratory approach to identify the ideal feature subset. By choosing a subset of features in order to reduce the redundancy between the subset and ideal features, the Ant-Colony Optimization method is used. Each ant in this procedure chooses a feature based on the ones that were previously chosen.

Fig. 4 Flow diagram of PSO

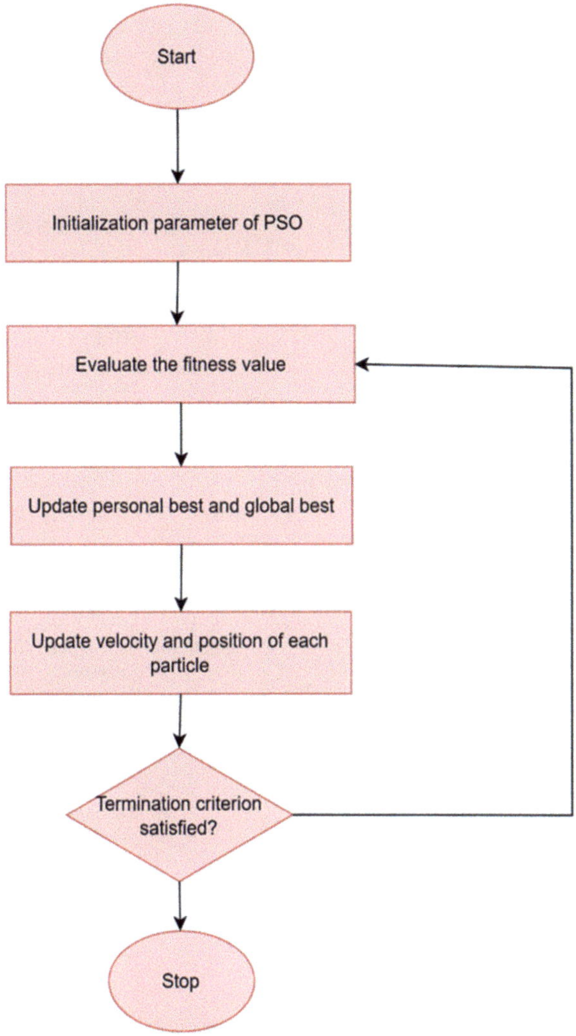

Each ant chooses the feature with the least similarity to the ones previously chosen.When the majority of ants choose a feature, it means that it is similar to the other features.

2. The feature that receives the most votes will have a higher chance of being chosen by other ants in later iterations.

Finally, the similarities between the features will result in high pheromone values for the primary features. The ACO technique chooses the best characteristics with the least amount of redundancy as a result [17].

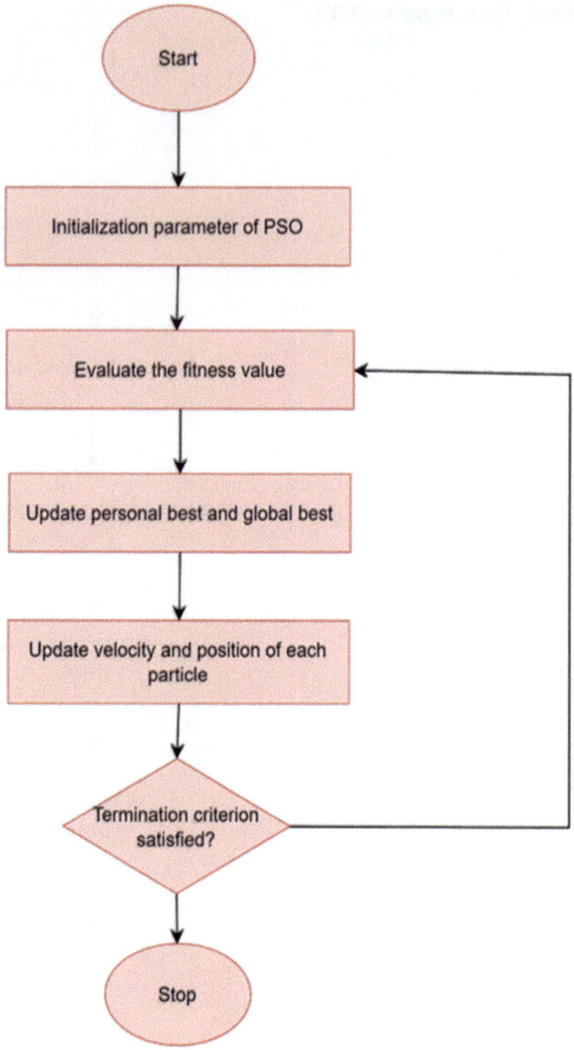

Fig. 5 Flow diagram of AOC

5 Results and Discussion

The main contribution of our approach is to detect and analyse the heart diseases automatically based on the obtained ECG report. These techniques compared ECG RECORDS with those from all other datasets, including Physio net, MIT-BIH, and Raw ECG datasets. The studied heart disease classification systems are used in Table 1.

CNN with LSTM and ant-colony optimizer for the Detection of cardio vascular diseases disease, trained for 150 epochs (Fig. 6).

Table 1 Comparison Of Heart Disease Prediction And Classification Methods Based On The Accuracy

S. No	Year	Method	Dataset	Accuracy (%)
1	2023	CNN, Alexnet	Physio net	98.7
2	2023	Random Forest, Logistic Regression, Gaussian NB, Linear Discriminant Analysis	ECG Data	92
3	2022	A Non-Linear Vector	UCI Physio net	90.6
4	2022	Auto encoders	MIT-BIH	97.4
5	2021	CBAM-CNN	Physio-Bank	97.6
			MIMIC-III	97.4
6	2021	CNN, Gabor CNN	Physion Bank	98.3
7	2021	CNN based Binarization	Paper based scanned ECG records	97
		CNN		94.4
8	2020	1D-Capsnet, Five fold cross validation	ECG-Segments	98.62
9	2020	CNN with minority	MIT-BIH	98.41
10	2020	CNN + LSTM	Sensors	86
11	Proposed	**CNN + LSTM With ACO**	**Raw ECG based signals**	**98.04**

Fig. 6 Accuracy of the proposed model (CNN + LSTM with Ant-Colony Optimizer) after 150 Epochs

In the comparison above, CNN + LSTM technique outperformed other techniques with accuracy of 98.04%, 98.08% F1-Score, 98.04% Precision and 98.01% recall. Pre-processing is then applied to the unedited raw ECG images to reduce noise and improve image quality. The hybrid system approach is utilized to recover the features from the input photographs after training, and the categories for normal and pathological conditions are then created using the features. The ECG signals are successfully consecutively categorized using the hybrid CNN and LSTM algorithm. Utilizing an Ant-Colony Optimizer to enhance the performance of weight parameters.

6 Limitations and Challenges

- Here are several restrictions and difficulties in predicting and classifying heart disease. Medical imaging may show strokes in a variety of ways, making it difficult to accurately identify and classify them. The kind, size, and time of the imaging could all contribute to this difference. Detection and classification of heart disease may differ based on how various physicians interpret medical imaging. This could lead to erratic treatment decisions and outcomes.

- Collecting the clinical data is one of the challenging task and pre-processing of raw image is also important to improve the quality of image features firstly,resize all the images with the same pixel size without any loss from the images.
- Perform the normalization for transforming the data with all features into one scale ranging from 0 t0 1.
- To obtain the quality images for the analysis is it crucial to remove the noise from the data by applying certain filtering techniques
- Data agumentation is out performed to improved our training data size. Extracting the features from the images with some feature extraction techniques.
- There is currently no accepted global detection and classification method for diagnosing cardiac disorders. This suggests that different research teams can use different methods and standards, making it difficult to compare results and carry out additional study.
- Computing tasks like detection and categorization can be challenging and time-consuming, especially for large datasets. As a result, these strategies might be limited in terms of speed and scalability, which would make them less effective for real-time clinical applications.
- To retain the outcome of the findings accurately with the help of ML algorithms,a large amount of labeled training data is necessary. The small size of the datasets annotated cardiac disease may restrict the performance of machine learning models.
- Symptoms might vary significantly depending on the illness type, the time of imaging, and other factors. Consequently, it could be challenging to develop accurate and trustworthy detection and classification systems. Since stroke is a relatively rare condition, the distribution of distinct stroke subtype occurrences in the dataset may be uneven. Because of this, it could be challenging to train ML models to distinguish between various types of diseases.

7 Conclusion and Future Works

In this study, a thorough analysis of the literature has been given regarding the use of image processing to look at heart-related ECG signals images. As the biggest cause of death globally, heart stroke must be avoided by seeking prompt medical attention. When examining imaging data for stroke rehabilitation, it is crucial to discover cardiac stroke lesions. Even so, the work remains difficult because of the wide variety of signal lesion types and the shared wave intensity distribution. Images of the heart obtained by magnetic resonance imaging (MR) are frequently utilized as a visual aid during therapeutic procedures to help identify illnesses. The majority of approaches for detecting heart illness, however, do not fully utilize structural symmetry information. In this study, five-year-old literature on the diagnosis and classification of heart illness were examined. It also illustrates the technique with the highest categorisation accuracy in compared to the others. Future studies should concentrate on precise stroke illness prediction and in-depth analyses employing a variety of biological signals, Future studies should concentrate on precise stroke illness prediction and thorough analyses employing a variety of biological signals, such as echocardiography, electrocardiogram, angiography, and other EEG data. Additionally, merging MRI or CT scans with EMR data from human health examinations in multimodal investigations, then assessing the outcomes.

References

1. Vinta SR, Anbalagan E, Basavaraddi CCS, Mazumdar N (2023) Leveraging machine learning techniques for improving heart disease prediction systems using feature selection. Int J Intell Syst Appl Eng 11(8s):560–567
2. Vinta SR, Anusha R, Dewangan NK, Rajalakshmi R, Lakshmi TV, Mishra I (2023) Identification of significant clinical attributes for developing heart disease prediction system. Int J Intell Syst Appl Eng 11(8s):552–559
3. Yamamoto K, Hiromatsu R, Ohtsuki T (2020) ECG signal reconstruction via Doppler sensor by hybrid deep learning model with CNN and LSTM. IEEE access 8:130551–130560
4. Awal MA, Mostafa SS, Ahmad M, Alahe MA, Rashid MA, Kouzani AZ, Mahmud MP (2021) Design and optimization of ECG modeling for generating different cardiac dysrhythmias. Sensors 21(5):1638
5. Suhail MM, Razak TA (2022) Cardiac disease detection from ECG signal using discrete wavelet transform with machine learning method. Diabetes Res Clin Pract 187:109852
6. Chen L, Yu H, Huang Y, Jin H (2021) ECG signal-enabled automatic diagnosis technology of heart failure. J Healthc Eng
7. Butun E, Yildirim O, Talo M, Tan RS, Acharya UR (2020) 1D-CADCapsNet: One dimensional deep capsule networks for coronary artery disease detection using ECG signals. Physica Med 70:39–48
8. Senturk ZK (2023) From signal to image: An effective preprocessing to enable deep learning-based classification of ECG. Mater Today: Proc 81:1–9
9. Dai H, Hwang HG, Tseng VS (2021) Convolutional neural network based automatic screening tool for cardiovascular diseases using different intervals of ECG signals. Comput Methods Programs Biomed 203:106035
10. Romdhane TF, Pr MA (2020) Electrocardiogram heartbeat classification based on a deep convolutional neural network and focal loss. Comput Biol Med 123:103866
11. Rath A, Mishra D, Panda G, Satapathy SC, Xia K (2022) Improved heart disease detection from ECG signal using deep learning based ensemble model. Sustain Comput: Inform Syst 35:100732
12. Jahmunah V, Ng EYK, San TR, Acharya UR (2021) Automated detection of coronary artery disease, myocardial infarction and congestive heart failure using GaborCNN model with ECG signals. Comput Biol Med 134:104457
13. Malakouti SM (2023) Heart disease classification based on ECG using machine learning models. Biomed Signal Process Control 84:104796
14. Mishra S, Khatwani G, Patil R, Sapariya D, Shah V, Parmar D, Mehendale N (2021) ECG paper record digitization and diagnosis using deep learning. J Med Biol Eng 41(4):422–432
15. Mhamdi L, Dammak O, Cottin F, Dhaou IB (2022) Artificial intelligence for cardiac diseases diagnosis and prediction using ECG images on embedded systems. Biomedicines 10(8):2013

16. Dorigo M, Birattari M, Stutzle T (2006) Ant colony optimization. IEEE Comput Intell Mag 1(4):28–39
17. Tabakhi S, Moradi P, Akhlaghian F (2014) An unsupervised feature selection algorithm based on ant colony optimization. Eng Appl Artif Intell 32:112–123

CNN Architecture Based Predictive Model for the Diabetic Retinopathy

A. S. U. Nandan, Aman Kumar Chaudhary, Prince Attri, and Ranjeet Kumar

1 Introduction

Diabetic retinopathy is a severe complication of diabetes and the primary cause of blindness among working individuals across the world. A study by the Union Ministry of Health revealed that the prevalence of diabetic retinopathy in India is about 17%, of which 3.6% are sight-threatening. Research by the WHO predicts that the number of patients with diabetic retinopathy will increase by more than 50% by 2030. Without treatment of diabetic retinopathy, especially in more severe cases, patients can lose their vision completely. India ranks second, after China, in the global diabetes epidemic, with approximately 77 million individuals affected.

Diabetic retinopathy is called a progressive disease because it develops over time. In the beginning, blood vessels in the retina can weaken and leak fluid or blood, causing swelling and macular edema. As the disease progresses, blood vessels may become blocked, causing new retinal blood vessels to grow. Diabetic retinopathy is typically classified into two categories, namely non-proliferative diabetic retinopathy (NPDR), which is the early stage of the disease, and advanced proliferative diabetic retinopathy (PDR). Non-proliferative diabetic retinopathy is further divided into 3 sub-categories—Acute, Moderate and Severe depending upon the severity of the disease.

A. S. U. Nandan · A. K. Chaudhary · P. Attri · R. Kumar (✉)
School of Electronics Engineering (SENSE), Vellore Institute of Technology, Chennai 600127, India
e-mail: ranjeet281@gmail.com

A. S. U. Nandan
e-mail: nandan.asu2019@vitstudent.ac.in

A. K. Chaudhary
e-mail: aman.kumar2019c@vitstudent.ac.in

P. Attri
e-mail: prince.attri2019@vitstudent.ac.in

K. Kumar Singh et al. (eds.), *Machine Vision and Augmented Intelligence*, Lecture Notes in Electrical Engineering 1211, https://doi.org/10.1007/978-981-97-4359-9_52

Deep learning is a more effective way to diagnose diabetic retinopathy than conventional methods because conventional methods to diagnose diabetic retinopathy require trained ophthalmologists to examine the retina and detect abnormalities, and this process may consume a considerable amount of time and is susceptible to errors made by humans. However, DL models can quickly and accurately analyze a large number of retinal images to detect early signs of DR, allowing identification and treatment of DR in its early stages. Deep learning models utilized CNN to automatically extract features from the fundus images and promptly classify them based on patterns.

In this research, we compared five different types of CNN architecture, namely AlexNet, ResNet, DenseNet, EfficientNet, and MobileNet, which are commonly used in retinal disease detection based on their diagnostic accuracy. We also predicted diabetic retinopathy in new fundus image samples using the model with the highest accuracy among the five CNN architectures. In this context, this study explores with the introduction section followed by review of state techniques in Sect. 2. In Sect. 3, review of data analysis techniques is carried out for wearables like digital watches or other devices and their outcomes are discussed in Sect. 4. At the end, the study is concluded with scope and challenges in Sect. 5 followed by references.

2 State-of Art Techniques: Review

In the field of DR and its analysis, numerous approaches and methodologies have been used in the past and the present. In this context, with the help of extreme learning machines (ELM) and tetragonal local octa patterns (TLOP), this [1] study suggests a unique way of identifying DR. The process involves first extracting features from retinal images using TLOP, and then classifying the results using ELM. The results show that in terms of accuracy, sensitivity, and specificity, this method outperforms existing methods. The suggested approach has the potential to be used as a screening tool in healthcare settings and may be helpful in identifying DR. The authors recommended that in order to verify the technique's effectiveness, a larger sample size be used in future research and that the dataset be increased. This [2] Research lays out a method for classifying retinal vessels using a U-Net architecture. The first iterations of green channel enhancement and Contrast-Limited Adaptive Histogram Equalization (CLAHE) are used to train this model on a set of fundus images. The results show that this approach has superior accuracy and sensitivity than previous ones. The study's author came to the conclusion that it can be utilized to detect and track retinal abnormalities in addition to being useful in segmenting retinal blood vessels. Future calls for expanding the dataset and implementing it in healthcare settings. CNN and Hybrid Deep (HD-CNN) are suggested as a classification approach for the disease in this [3] research.

The pre-processing of retinal pictures and training of the models to divide the pictures into various phases of diabetic retinopathy comprise the technique. In contrast to other approaches already in use, this method achieves better accuracy in identifying the disease. The relatively small dataset employed for training and testing is this study's weakness. The proposed method can be implemented as a trustworthy instrument for categorizing diabetic retinopathy phases in future when model accuracy increases after using a larger dataset. Coming to reference [4] the method comprises pre-processing the images and CNN model for disease recognition. In order to train and assess the model, the authors obtained a collection of more than 88,000 pictures from the EyePACS database. The outcomes indicate that the network models have 95% validation sensitivity. Furthermore, multinomial classification approaches were investigated, and the results show that inaccuracies typically arise when the mild disease is falsely classified as normal since CNNs are unable to recognize minor disease signs. The highest testing set accuracy scores on 2-ary, 3-ary, and 4-ary models were increased to 74.5%, 68.8%, and 57.2% respectively by preconditioned GoogLeNet and AlexNet. The next research [5] suggests a multi-scale attention network (MSA-Net) which uses an encoder network by setting up the fundus pictures in an upper-level representational space, strengthening the visualization. This is done by integrating mid- and high-level attributes.

The researchers then thought of tracing the retinal anatomy in a distinct locale by using a multi-scale characteristic pyramid. A unique attention system is added atop the upper-level representation to additionally improve the attribute representation's ability to make distinctions. The cross-entropy loss is used to train the algorithm in a conventional manner to identify the different phases of DR. Few additional functions were also executed by the researchers in their study for finer results. In this paper [6], a CNN model built around small-scale feature propagation is put forward for the categorization of DR. An array of residual blocks is implemented in the framework to retrieve traits from fundus images and pass on these traits across different levels. The approach was validated using freely available Messidor and e-Ophtha datasets, and it showed excellent proficiency in classification. The study's shortcomings include the use of two datasets and the absence of any comparisons to pre-existing models. The suggested approach is successful for DR classification, and it has the possibility to advance current approaches. The use of larger and more varied datasets for assessment will improve the model further in the future.

In order to address the prevalent issue in diagnosis, this research [7] suggests a method for detecting DR in several classes of unbalanced data. The methodology used is transfer learning which is evaluated using the open-source datasets Messidor-2, IDRiD, and e-ophtha. The method delivers excellent accuracy in DR classification. Many other factors such as screening and segmentation are also presented. The researchers in the subsequent work [8] worked not only on the detection of DR but also on diabetic macular edema (DME) on images of the retina. To categorize the images into the normal, DR, and DME groups, they used an algorithm based on a ResNet-50 framework. A DCNN-based method for recognizing the presence of DR from fundus pictures is described in the following work [9]. The dataset consists of 5000 photos for testing and 35,126 images for training, all of which have been systematically resized and cleaned to remove artifacts. Their design retrieves features and categorizes photos as normal or having various degrees of DR leveraging several convolutional layers with max-pooling and dropout regularization.

In the eye where DR has affected the retina, this work [10] has demonstrated that the use of transfer learning achieves good accuracy in the proper categorization of various aneurysms. They trained the VGG16 model in their research employing the ImageNet dataset. However, they retrained the system's final few layers so that they were particularly designed to pick up more advanced abstracted picture attributes from the IDRID dataset. The proposed approach successfully categorizes the aneurysms in the patients into the appropriate classes for the MA, SE, EX, and HE pictures. Using deep learning algorithms, the author of [11] discovered that diabetic retinopathy could be classified with a high degree of accuracy ranging from 85.4 to 99.4%. The researchers were right to point out that there are still issues that need to be resolved, like data imbalance and interpretability. Overall, the findings imply that deep learning approaches have tremendous potential for enhancing diabetic retinopathy detection and classification.

In [12] a combination of methods for improving retinal pictures and employing deep learning models to diagnose diabetic retinopathy (DR) is presented in [12]. To improve image contrast and brightness, the system uses gamma correction and contrast limiting adaptive histogram equalization (CLAHE), before applying a deep convolutional neural network, commonly referred to for DR detection. With accuracy, sensitivity, and specificity exceeding state-of-the-art approaches by 97.53%, 98.87%, and 94.53% respectively, the suggested algorithm beats them. According to the scientists, the approach they suggested might help ophthalmologists identify and treat DR, a major cause of blindness, early on. In [13] different deep learning models are discussed that have been applied in the field of ophthalmology to diagnose retinal diseases like diabetic retinopathy, age-related macular degeneration, and glaucoma. These models include CNNs, GANs and RNNs.

A Convolutional Block Attention Module (CBAM) model and DenseNet network are proposed in [14] as a solution for the automatic categorization of the severity of diabetic retinopathy. The proposed method outperformed other cutting-edge techniques achieving 90.3% accuracy. To show how the CBAM module works to increase the model's accuracy, the scientists also carried out ablation research. To guarantee the method's dependability and generalizability, attention should be made to make sure that it is verified on larger datasets and in varied populations. The authors of [15] examine the most cutting-edge deep learning-based techniques for segmenting retinal vessels.

The report also compared the various methodologies with their performances and accuracy. The findings demonstrate that applications of deep learning to retinal vascular segmentation are more accurate and outperform conventional approaches. Overall, the study offers a thorough assessment and critique of the most recent methods in this area. Depending on the approach and dataset utilized the stated accuracy scores from 91.2 to 99.8%. The study of [16] suggests a self-organizing neural network (SONN)-based real-time glaucoma screening method employing digital fundus images. Initial processing of the data, feature extraction, and categorization using a SONN-based model are the three stages of the suggested methodology. In order to boost contrast in fundus images while improving the deep learning models for better performance, the research paper [17] suggests a new technique employing a modified particle swarm optimization (PSO) algorithm. On a dataset of 400 fundus images, the proposed method was tested, and the findings indicated that the modified PSO algorithm was successful in boosting image contrast, leading to higher predictability of the deep learning models. Another research [18] provides a robust glaucoma detection paradigm employing retinex, CNN, and DOE on fundus pictures. Fundus pictures were used to detect glaucoma with 96.08% accuracy. Retinex enhanced images, while the CNN model extracted and classified features. Finally, the DOE method optimized the suggested architecture. The proposed method outperformed state-of-the-art methods. The framework detected glaucoma from fundus pictures with 96.08% accuracy. Retinex, CNN, and DOE improve fundus imaging glaucoma detection.

The paper [19] introduces CataractNet, an automated cataract identification technique that analyses fundus images using deep learning. The system obtains a 96.7% accuracy after being trained using a dataset of 2,000 photos. Convolutional neural networks (CNNs) are an architecture that CataractNet employs to quickly and accurately diagnose cataracts. The approach may increase the effectiveness and precision of cataract diagnosis and screening. To guarantee its dependability, additional validation and testing on bigger data sets are required. The research [20] suggests a technique based on deep learning for examining fundus images for exudates, haemorrhages, and microaneurysms.

3 Methodology

3.1 Dataset Used

APTOS 2019, a collection of fundus image made accessible for research, the dataset consists of an entire collection of 5590 retinal pictures, which are split into 1928 files for the test set and 3662 files for the train set. The dataset is 10 GB in size, and each image has a resolution of 550 × 412 pixels. For this work, the train set images makes up the entirety of the dataset. The dataset's images are divided into five broad categories based on the extent of the DR, varying from 0 (no DR) to 4 (proliferative DR). The images were labeled by a panel of ophthalmologists, who graded the severity of DR in each image as listed in Table 1 and shown in Fig. 1.

Table 1 Grading of fundus images based on DR severity

Label	Severity of DR
0	No diabetic retinopathy
1	Mild diabetic retinopathy
2	Moderate diabetic retinopathy
3	Severe diabetic retinopathy
4	Proliferative diabetic retinopathy

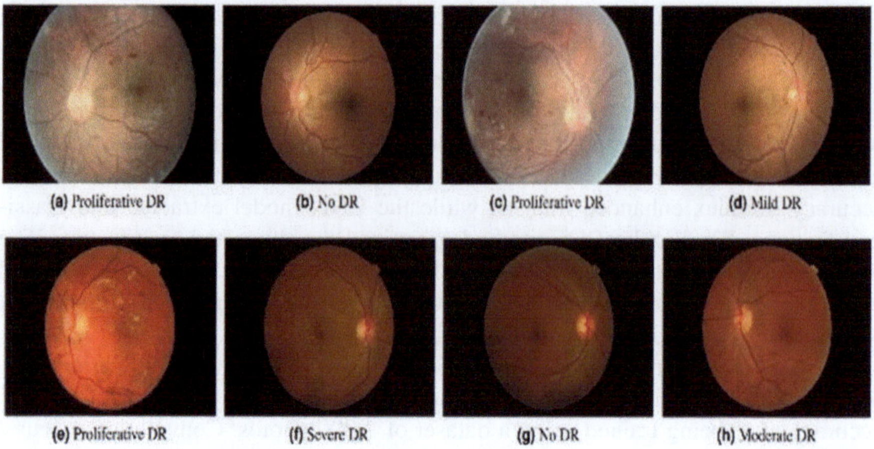

Fig. 1 Different phases of diabetic retinopathy

3.2 *Pre-processing*

A step-by-step breakdown of the process for applying Gaussian blurs and resizing to a collection of images using OpenCV and NumPy. In the OpenCV library, Gaussian Blur() function is a well-liked method for blending or blurring pictures. When this function is called in, a Gaussian filter is applied to the picture, removing high-frequency elements like noise or sharp edges but maintaining low-frequency elements like the image's general shape and structure. The function takes in various parameters, including kernel size and sigma values, which determine the degree of smoothing. We applied a Gaussian filter using OpenCV to each image present in the dataset, which resized the images to 224 × 224 pixels. Initially, load the dataset using the library NumPy. Once the dataset was loaded, we used the OpenCV library to apply a Gaussian filter to each image. This was done by using the Gaussian Blur () function and specifying the desired kernel size and sigma values. After applying the filter, we resized the image using the resize () function, specifying the desired output size as shown in Fig. 2. Lastly, store the scaled and filtered photos in a new directory for additional study.

3.3 *Deep Learning Models*

Here, comparative study intends to evaluate the effectiveness of well-known CNN architectures for diagnosing diabetic retinopathy, including AlexNet, DenseNet, ResNet, EfficientNet, and MobileNet through evaluating their accuracy, computational efficiency, and other metrics, this study aims to provide insights into which architecture may be most suitable for this application as shown in Fig. 3.

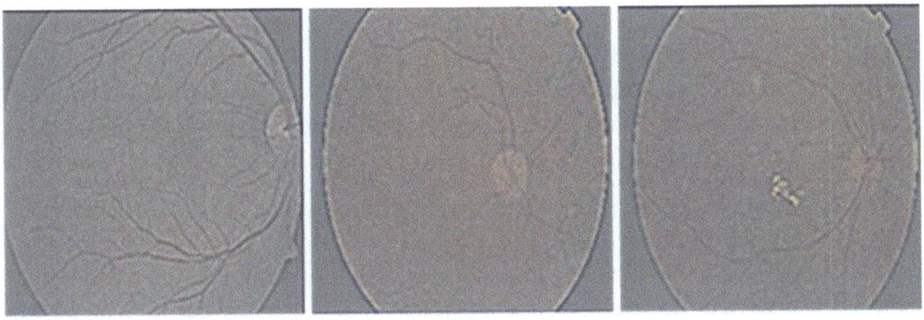

Fig. 2 Output image after pre-processing

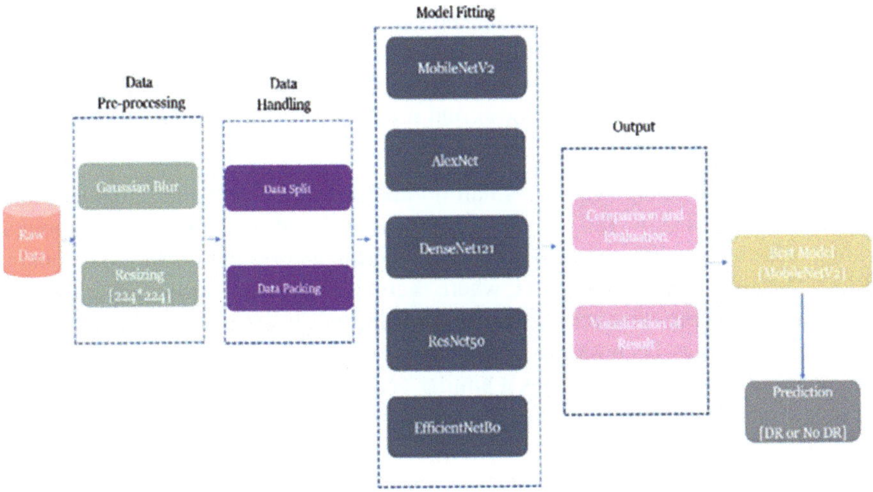

Fig. 3 Diabetic retinopathy prediction model

AlexNet: Five convolutional layers precede three fully connected layers, three max-pooling layers, and a SoftMax layer for categorization in AlexNet. It makes use of the Rectified Linear Unit (ReLU) activation function, which hastens the network's convergence during training. There are 96 filters present with size 11×11 and a stride of 4 comprising the initial convolutional layer. Post this we have a max-pooling layer and a ReLU activation function. ReLU activation and max-pooling layers are again positioned after the second and third convolutional layers, which have 256 filters with a 5×5 pixel size. ReLU activation functions appear again after the fourth and fifth convolutional layers, which have 384 and 256 filters of size 3×3, respectively. The fifth convolutional layer's output is rendered flat and input onto three layers with 4096 neurons each that are fully connected, with a SoftMax layer at the last for classification.

DenseNet: Created on the concept of dense connectedness, this architecture has each successive layer linked to every layer preceding it. This feature encourages feature reuse and lowers the number of parameters, which improves performance and accelerates convergence. DenseNet employs the bottleneck construct to minimize the number of parameters in the convolutional layers.

ResNet50: The architecture is designed to address the vanishing gradient problem, which occurs when gradients become too small and cause training to become slow and ineffective. ResNet50 uses skip connections, also known as residual connections, to allow for the direct flow of information from one layer to another.

This allows the network to learn residual functions, making it easier to train deeper networks without the vanishing gradient problem. 50 layers make up this architecture, containing 49 convolutional ones and 1 fully linked layer. A 7 × 7 convolutional layer which has a stride of 2 is the initial layer and then comes max-pooling and a number of residual blocks. 2–3 convolutional layers are included within each residual block, and there are skip links connecting them. In classification, the result of the last residual block travels through a SoftMax layer and a global average pooling layer (Figs. 6 and 7).

EfficientNetB0: It comprises of a small number of parameters and computational cost. It was proposed by Tan and Le in 2019 and is based on the idea of compound scaling, which optimizes the network's depth, width, and resolution simultaneously. EfficientNetB0 consists of 7 blocks, where each block contains several layers with a combination of depth-wise and point wise convolutions. It also uses a swish activation function, which has been shown to outperform the ReLU activation function on various tasks. EfficientNetB0 uses a similar architecture to MobileNetV2 but with additional enhancements such as squeeze-and-excitation blocks and a drop-connect regularization technique.

MobileNetV2: MobileNetV2 is a Convolutional Neural Network (CNN) model designed for mobile devices with limited computing resources. Introduced by Google researchers in 2018, it is an improved version of the original MobileNet architecture. The architecture includes residual connections, inverse residuals, and linear bottlenecks that help improve model accuracy. MobileNetV2 also includes a new feature called "linear convolution", which reduces network computing costs by using a 1 × 1 convolution layer to map input features into a low-dimensional space before applying depth-wise separable convolutions (Fig. 8).

4 Results and Discussion

In the Table 2, Positive findings were attained from studying deep learning architectures for the diagnosis of diabetic retinopathy. Among the five models tested, MobileNetV2 achieved the highest accuracy of 96 per cent, demonstrating its superiority in accurately detecting the presence of diabetic retinopathy. MobileNetV2's computational efficiency was also found to be favorable, making it a practical choice for medical applications.

Further, explicit accuracy analyzed for the different deep learning models and compared with the training accuracy and validated accuracy as shown in Figs. 4 and 5 (Figs. 9 and 10).

As per the observation, MobileNetV2 deep learning model achieves maximum accuracy at both the stages such as training and validation. The MobileNetV2 model is called with the normalized image as input to obtain predicted probability distribution over the two, i.e., classes 0 for no DR and 1 for DR. If the highest predicted probability is associated with class 1 (i.e., DR), the function prints 'DR' indicating that the image is indicative of diabetic retinopathy. Otherwise, if the highest predicted function prints 'DR' depicting that the image is indicative of diabetic retinopathy.

Table 2 Performance comparisons of different deep learning models

Model	Accuracy	Validity accuracy	Loss	Validity loss
AlexNet	0.988476	0.733788	0.064028	0.723542
DesnceNet	0.991464	0.813993	0.028916	0.613928
ResNet50	0.991464	0.786689	0.027736	1.132927
EfficientNetB0	0.897140	0.755973	0.295144	0.833574
MobileNet	0.977687	0.965455	0.071896	0.097504

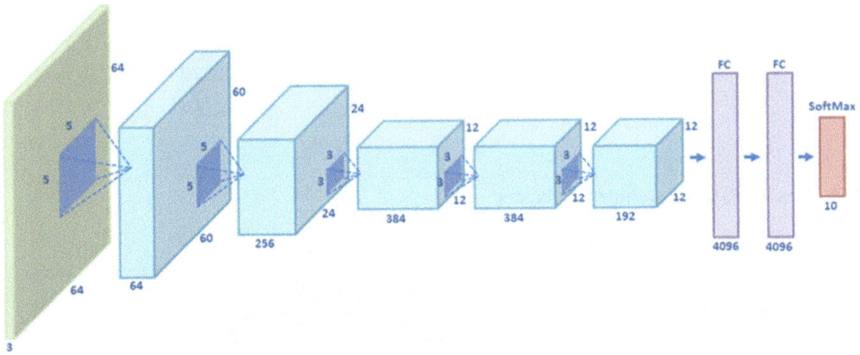

Fig. 4 AlexNet CNN architecture layers

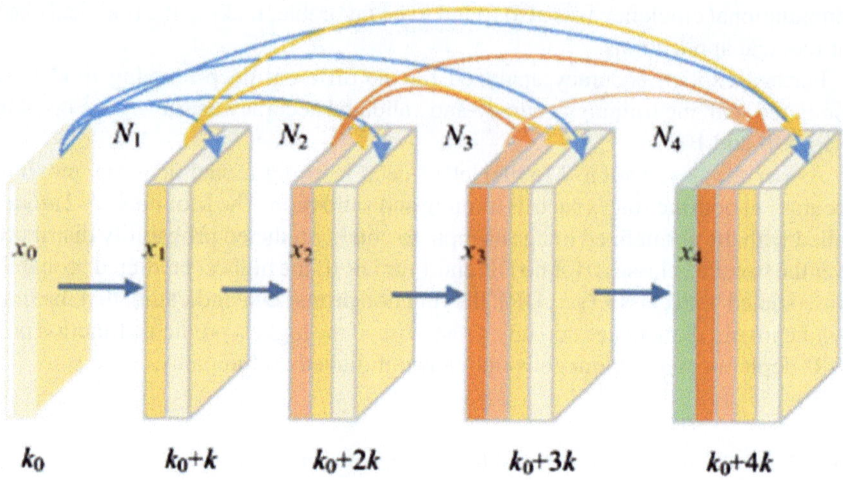

Fig. 5 DenseNet CNN architecture layers

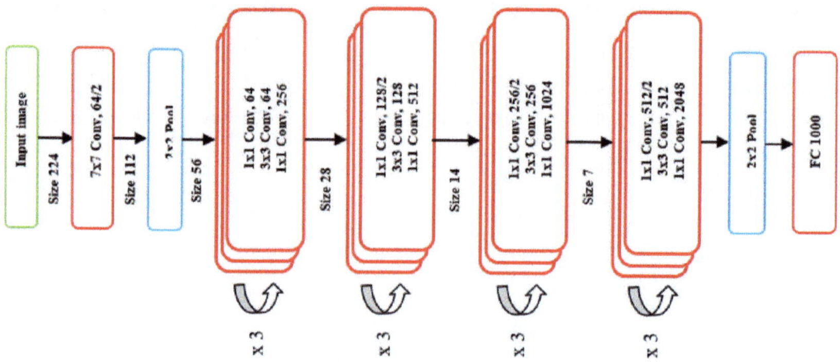

Fig. 6 ResNet50 CNN architecture layers

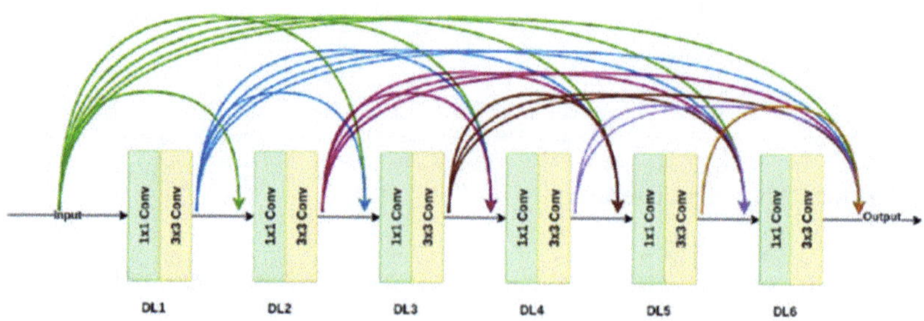

Fig. 7 EfficientNetB0 CNN architecture layers

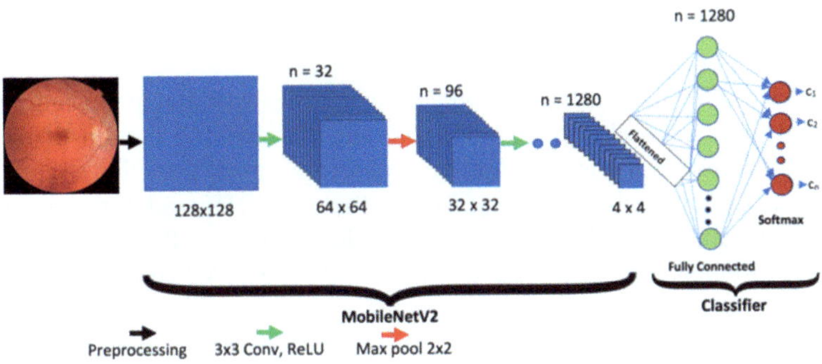

Fig. 8 MobileNetV2 CNN architecture layers

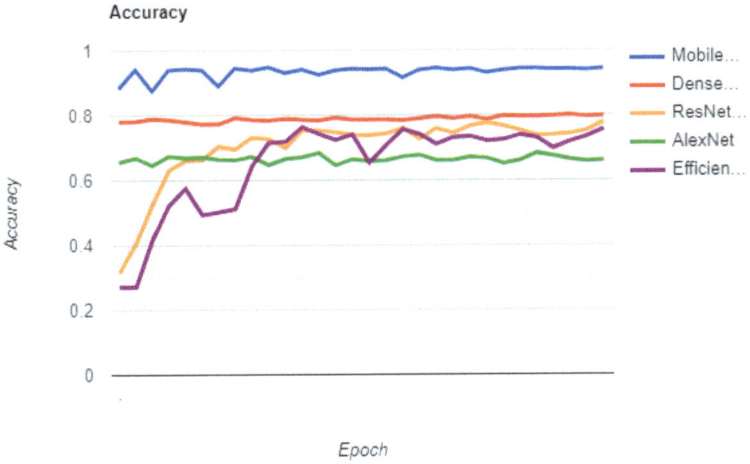

Fig. 9 Accuracy analysis of different deep learning models

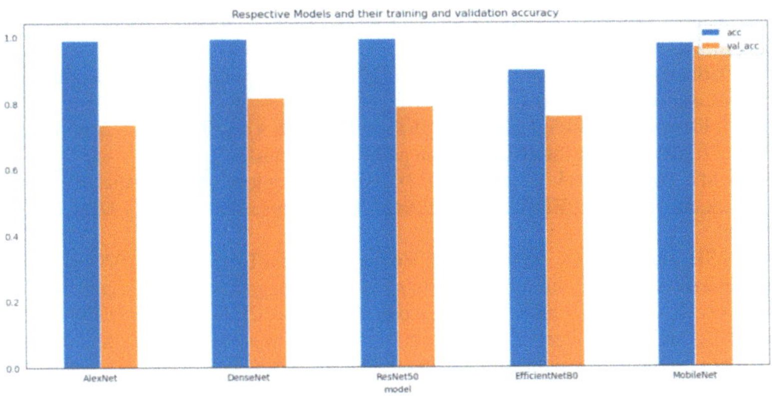

Fig. 10 Accuracy analysis at training and validation stage of different deep learning models

5 Conclusion

The prevalence of Diabetic Retinopathy is increasing worldwide causing significant social and economic impacts. Considering the growing burden of diabetic retinopathy, there is an urgent need for effective screening and detection strategies. In this study, we examined the efficacy of five well-known CNN models for diagnosing diabetic retinopathy from fundus images: AlexNet, DenseNet, ResNet50, EfficientNetB0, and MobileNetV2. Our results show that MobileNetV2 achieved the highest accuracy of 95% in detecting diabetic retinopathy among the five models. We also evaluated the performance of MobileNetV2 on a set of new fundus images and found that it demonstrated robust performance in detecting diabetic retinopathy. Overall, our findings suggest that MobileNetV2 is a highly accurate and effective model for detecting diabetic retinopathy in fundus images.

References

1. Nazir T, Irtaza A, Shabbir Z, Javed A, Akram U, Mahmood MT (2019) Diabetic retinopathy detection through novel tetragonal local octa patterns and extreme learning machines
2. Xiancheng W, Wei L, Bingyi M, He J, Jiang Z, Xu W, Ji Z, Hong G, Zhaomeng S (2018) Retina blood vessel segmentation using a U-net based convolutional neural network
3. Yasashvini R, Vergin Raja Sarobin M, Panjanathan R, Graceline JS, Jani AL (2022) Diabetic retinopathy classification using CNN and hybrid deep convolutional neural networks
4. Lam C, Yi D, Guo M, Lindsey T (2018) Automated detection of diabetic retinopathy using deep learning
5. Al-Antary MT, Arafa Y (2021) Multi-scale attention network for diabetic retinopathy classification
6. Metan AC, Lambert A, Pickering M (2019) Small scale feature propagation using deep residual learning for diabetic retinopathy classification
7. Mondal S, Mian KF, Das A (2021) Deep learning-based diabetic retinopathy detection for multiclass imbalanced data
8. Li F, Wang Y, Xu T, Dong L, Yan L, Jiang M, Zhang X, Jiang H, Wu Z, Zou H (2022) Deep learning-based automated detection for diabetic retinopathy and diabetic macular oedema in retinal fundus photographs
9. Doshi D, Shenoy A, Sidhpura D, Gharpure P (2016) Diabetic retinopathy detection using deep convolutional neural networks
10. Gupta S, Panwar A, Goel S, Mittal A, Nijhawan R, Singh AK (2019) Classification of lesions in retinal fundus images for diabetic retinopathy using transfer learning
11. Atwany MZ, Sahyoun AH, Yaqub M (2022) Deep learning techniques for diabetic retinopathy classification: a survey. IEEE Access 10:28642–28655. https://doi.org/10.1109/ACCESS.2022.3157632
12. Abbood SH, Hamed HNA, Rahim MSM, Rehman A, Saba T, Bahaj SA (2022) Hybrid retinal image enhancement algorithm for diabetic retinopathy diagnostic using deep learning model. IEEE Access 10:73079–73086. https://doi.org/10.1109/ACCESS.2022.3189374
13. Goutam B, Hashmi MF, Geem ZW, Bokde ND (2022) A comprehensive review of deep learning strategies in retinal disease diagnosis using fundus images
14. Farag MM, Fouad M, Abdel-Hamid AT (2022) Automatic severity classification of diabetic retinopathy based on DenseNet and convolutional block attention module. IEEE Access 10:38299–38308. https://doi.org/10.1109/ACCESS.2022.3165193

15. Chen C, Chuah JH, Ali R, Wang Y (2021) Retinal vessel segmentation using deep learning: a review. IEEE Access 1–1. https://doi.org/10.1109/ACCESS.2021.3102176
16. Devecioglu O, Malik J, Ince T, Kiranyaz S, Atalay E, Gabbouj M (2021) Real-time glaucoma detection from digital fundus images using self-ONNs
17. Khursheed K, Aslam S, Alhussein M, Naqvi R, Arsalan M, Haider S (2021) Contrast enhancement of fundus images by employing modified PSO for improving the performance of deep learning models. IEEE Access 1–1 https://doi.org/10.1109/ACCESS.2021.3068477
18. Song WT, Lai I-C, Su Y-Z (2021) A statistical robust glaucoma detection framework combining Retinex, CNN, and DOE using fundus images. IEEE Access 9:103772–103783. https://doi.org/10.1109/ACCESS.2021.3098032
19. Junayed MS, Islam MB, Sadeghzadeh A, Rahman S (2021) CataractNet: an automated cataract detection system using deep learning for fundus images. IEEE Access 9:128799–128808. https://doi.org/10.1109/ACCESS.2021.3112938
20. Khojasteh P, Aliahmad B, Kumar DK (2018) Fundus images analysis using deep features for detection of exudates, haemorrhages and microaneurysms. BMC Ophthalmol 18:288

Multiclass Classification of Insect Bites Using Deep Learning Techniques

K. V. N. D. Sushma and Sagar Dhanraj Pande

1 Introduction

People in everyday life experience stings of insects on our skin and it is very common during rainy reason. Many times, people may be busy with their work and would not notice the insect that has bitten them. It is necessary to know because these insect stings may cause several diseases like malaria, dengue caused by mosquitoes, Lyme caused by ticks, etc. Some people get triggered by allergic reactions due to these stings like urticaria, angioedema, and anaphylaxis [1]. They need to know by which insect they have been bitten because the knowledge of the insect may help them to take necessary precautions. When these insects bite/sting skin you would get some red marks or circles. In [2] they mentioned how the patterns of stings mainly bees, mosquitos, and ticks differ for each insect and how they can extract the features. Some diseases caused by insect bites may also be transmitted like vector borne transmission means they transmit pathogens from one host to another. For example, Lyme is a vector-borne transmitted disease that is caused by tick insects. When not treated, it may lead to severe joint pains and may also affect the heart and nervous system [3]. Knowing which insect has bitten us can help in prevention and control. Authorities can track the occurrence and distribution of insect bites so that they can take necessary prevention and control measures [4]. Accurate identification of insect bites may help in collecting data for public health surveillance so that they can track patterns, identify forthcoming threats, and take required steps for prevention. This study investigates the use of DL algorithms like Alex Net, VGG-16, inception v3,

K. V. N. D. Sushma
School of Computer Science and Engineering, VIT-AP University, Amaravati, Andhra Pradesh, India

S. D. Pande (✉)
School of Engineering and Technology, Pimpri Chinchwad University (PCU), Pune, India
e-mail: sagarpande30@gmail.com

K. Kumar Singh et al. (eds.), *Machine Vision and Augmented Intelligence*, Lecture Notes in Electrical Engineering 1211, https://doi.org/10.1007/978-981-97-4359-9_53

and Resnet 50 [5, 6, 13–15] for classifying insect bites to enhance identification and increase overall accuracy.

The following is the paper's contribution:

- This paper proposed a customized model for the multiclass insect bite classification using deep learning models.
- A self collected dataset is prepared for the model implementation.
- Comparative analysis using different deep learning models was performed.
- Healthcare facilities can operate more efficiently overall by automating the classification process and better allocating resources and time to other crucial duties using the proposed model.

2 Literature Survey

Very few researchers have explored this insect bites topic in recent years which will help us to perform classification using data mining techniques. The comparative analysis of the existing methodology is represented in Table 1.

3 Summary of the Existing Work

A noteworthy drawback in the [7–9] (2020) approach to the categorization of two types of bug bites using VGG-16 transfer learning is the absence of information about how non-skin images will be classified. By categorizing insect bites into five different groups [11]. While [10] does not go into length about the classification of non-skin images, it deals with the classification of eight different groups of bug bites. The insect bite classification task in [12], only considers binary classification and ignores non-skin images. This paper tried to overcome the weakness of the existing model by performing a multi-class classification of skin vs non-skin and proposes a hybrid methodology for classifying insect bites that were predicted as skin.

4 Proposed Methodology

4.1 Dataset Description

There is very limited research in this area of insect bites. There are very less data sets available in this field of research. The data set [10] consists of 8 classes. For this dataset of ant bites, chigger bites, spider bites, tick bites, mosquito bites, flea bites, bed bug bites, and images of no bites were combined with images that were taken

Table 1 Comparative analysis of existing work

S. no	Year	Dataset	Weakness	Strength of the proposed methodology
[5]	2023	In this, they tried classifying 5 different types of insect bites	They tried classifying only 5 different classes of insect bites They classified using machine learning algorithms like SVM and random forest	Classified 8 different classes The proposed model uses deep learning models to extract better features and to improve the performance of the model
[6]	2023	9 different classes of insect bites were taken	They did not try to classify the nonskin images. They just performed binary classification	Performed multi-class classification for identifying skin vs non skin A proposed hybrid model for the classification of insect bites
[9]	2020	In this, they performed the classification of 2 classes of insect bites using VGG16 transfer learned	– They performed classification only on 2 classes – They did not mention how non-skin images will be classified as – No data augmentation	– Performed classification for more than 2 classes of insect bites – Performed multiclass classification for identifying skin vs non skin
[10]	2022	8 different classes of insect bites were taken	They did not mention how nonskin images will be classified as	Performed multi-class classification for identifying skin vs non skin A proposed hybrid model for the classification of insect bites
[11]	2021	In this, they performed the classification of 5 classes of insect bites	– They did not mention how nonskin images will be classified as – No data augmentation	– Performed multiclass classification for identifying skin vs non skin – A proposed hybrid model for the classification of insect bites

from different sites on the web and performed data augmentation and made a dataset of around 1900 images. We split those into training testing and validation.

For classification of whether the given image is a skin or object a dataset that consists of images of a sofa, chair, and table was merged with the images of the skin of a human with insect bites and without insect bites and were made as a separate class known as skin and merged with the object dataset. This consists of a total of 1192 images present in that dataset. Sample images of the dataset are given in Fig. 1 and the statistical representation of the dataset is in Fig. 2.

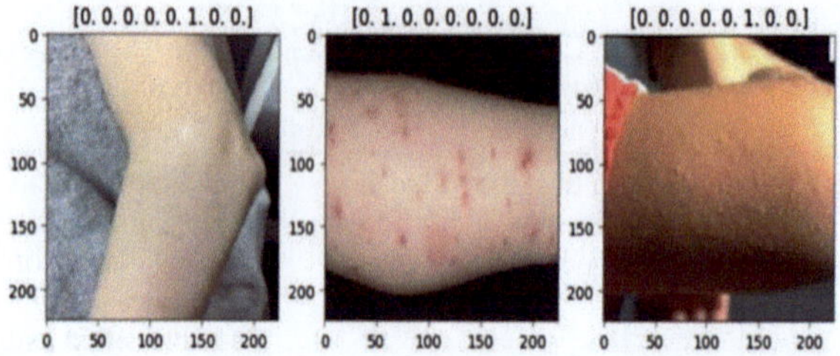

Fig. 1 Sample training images

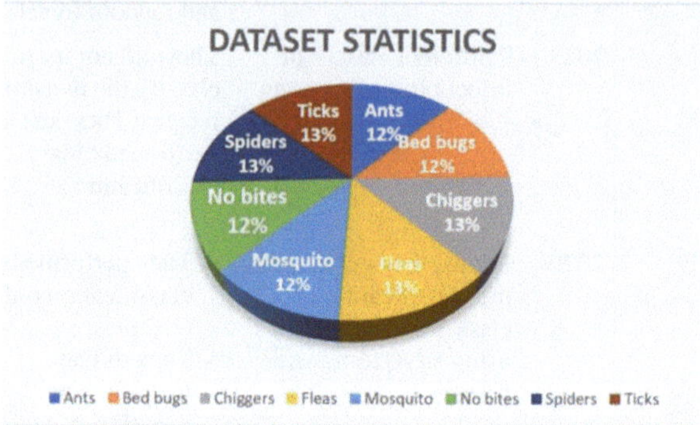

Fig. 2 Dataset description

4.2 Data Preprocessing

For data augmentation and preprocessing, Image Data Generator was used. This class in Keras offers a variety of choices, including rotation, flipping, zooming, shifting, brightness changes, and normalization. By default, the Image Data Generator divides the input image pixel values by 255 to rescale them to the range [0, 1].

During training, the Image Data Generator loads photos in groups. Before feeding each batch of photos to the neural network for training, data augmentation and preprocessing are performed on them. This batching method permits training with big datasets that might not fit totally in memory and helps to optimize memory utilization.

4.3 Model Testing

Transfer Learning using VGG-16 and Layer Personalization: We have used a method of freezing up to some pre-trained layers in this method the 10 layers of the pre-trained VGG-16 were unfrozen and added one convolution layer of 1*1 for feature extraction and another layer of 2*2 convolution layer. These layers were added because when the pre-trained model was used without unfreezing the layers the accuracy obtained was not greater than the accuracy obtained after the addition of

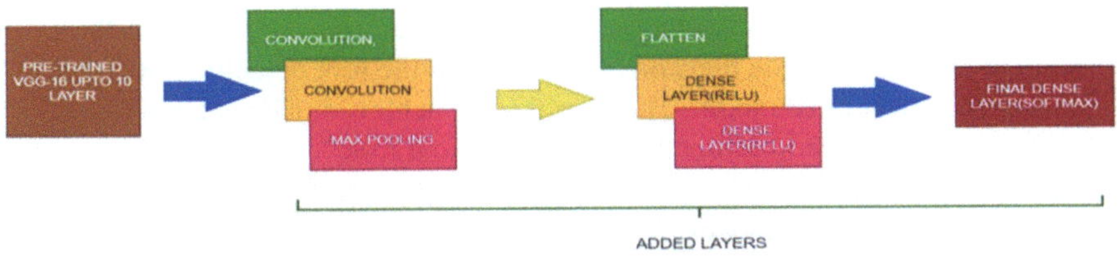

Fig. 3 Customized VGG-16

layers. Various learning rates from 10^-1 to 10^-5 have been used and different optimizers like adam, rmsprop, and mse were used. Figure 3 demonstrates the proposed model's architecture.

4.4 Proposed Methodology

For classifying whether a given image is an insect bite or not, first the proposed methodology classified it whether it is an image of the skin or not. After predictions for the images for which the predicted labels are further classified into the type of insect bites present on and skin or whether it is an image of the skin with no bite by passing it into another model. The flow diagram of the proposed method is given in Fig. 4.

Skin and Non-Skin Classification: For this task, a model with a transfer learning technique on inception-v3 has been used. First tried multiclass classification of objects of 4 classes those are sofa, chair, table, and skin. This step was performed

Fig. 4 Proposed model

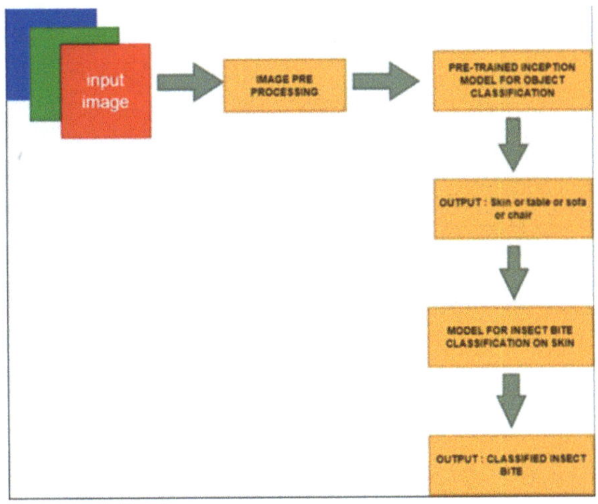

to identify only those images which are of skin type. The model added the final dense layer for classification that corresponded with the task objectives utilizing the weights of the pre-trained model. The results were achieved using a learning rate of 0.001, epochs:8, and the loss function is a categorical loss.

$$\text{Categorical Cross Entropy} = -(1/\text{n}) * \sum (\text{y\_true[i][j]} * \log(\text{y\_pred[i][j]})) \tag{1}$$

$$\text{Softmax(ki)} = (\exp(\text{ki}))/(\exp(\text{k1}) + \exp(\text{k2}) + \cdots + \exp(\text{kn})) \tag{2}$$

Transfer learning with concatenated Inception v3, Mobile Net v2, and VGG-16: In this first three models are loaded, followed by the 2*2 convo2d layer, and the max pooling layer for each of the three models like inception v3, mobile net v2, and vgg-16. They are flattened after the features are taken individually from them. These 3 flatten layers are concatenated and then the classification (dense) layers are added taking softmax as activation for the final layer. The layers of inception v3, mobile net v2, and vgg-16 were frozen during training so that their weights would not get updated. The architecture of the model used for the implementation purpose is represented in Fig. 5.

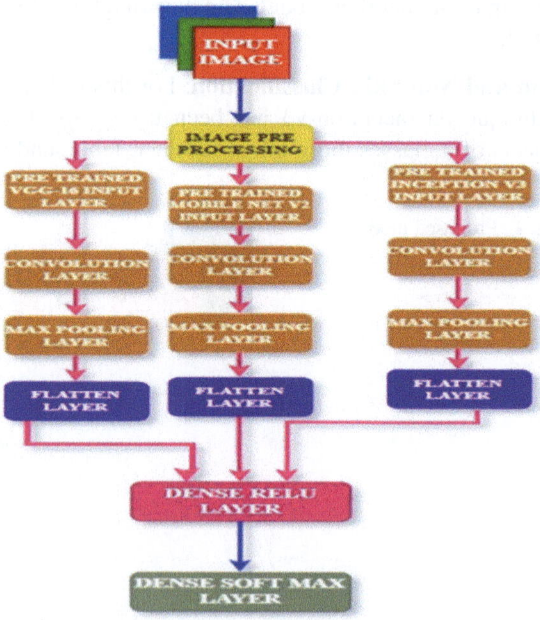

Fig. 5 Architecture of VINMOBCONCAT

5 Result Analysis

Table 2 below provides the results that arise from various models employed along with the parameters.

System Specifications: The experiment is conducted using a Google Colab notebook (basic model) with an Intel i3 7th generation 2-core CPU operating at 2.30 GHz and a machine with a configuration of 8 GB of RAM.

5.1 Skin Classification

This paper tried to find whether the given image is an object like a table, chair, sofa, or skin. After classifying the images for which the predictions were skin is used for further classification for insect bites. On the previously discussed classification of multiple classes, an accuracy of 95% was attained using inception v3 which is pretrained. Figure 6 shows the predictions obtained using the proposed model.

Some sample results of the predicted insect bite using Vinmobconcat are depicted in Fig. 7 which helps to classify insect bite.

Table 2 Comparative analysis of the results based on various performance metrics

Sr. no	Architecture used	Learning rate	Epoch	Optimizer	Batch size	Accuracy (%)
1	Alex net	0.0001	30	MSE	32	54
2	Resnet50 using transfer learning	0.001	32	Adam	52	62.2
3	Inception v3 using transfer learning	0.0001	35	Rms prop	42	71.3
4	Customized VGG-16 using transfer learning	0.000001	150	MSE	59	81.2
5	Vinmobconcat	0.0000003	60	Adam	59	93.5

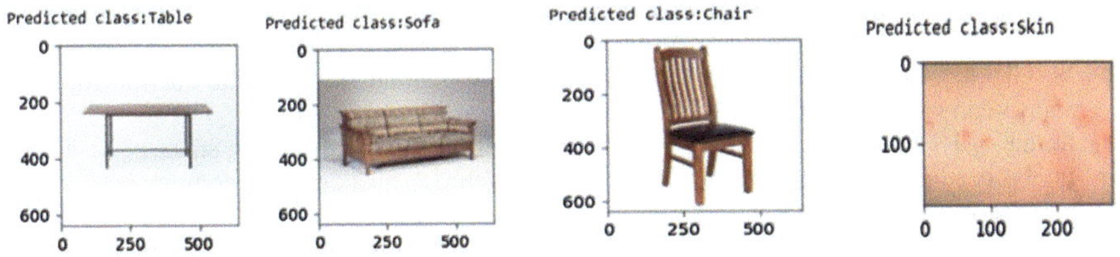

Fig. 6 Skin and Nonskin classification prediction

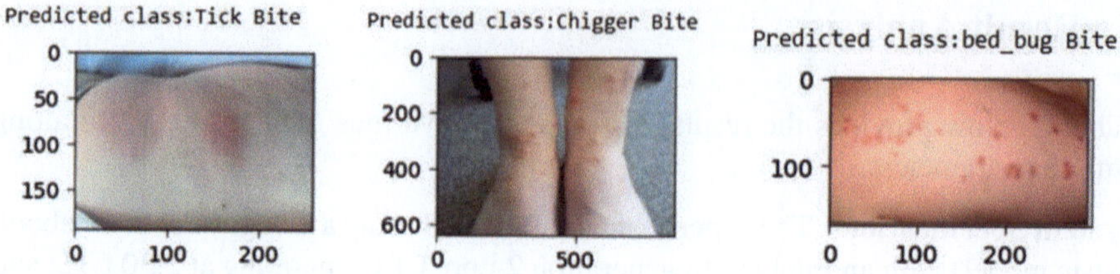

Fig. 7 Vinmobconcat predictions

6 Conclusion

In this study, different architectures of deep learning like Alexnet and models like inception v3, Resnet50, and VGG-16 which are transfer learned are compared. An approach was suggested that would enable more accurate classification of insect bites so that there can be an advancement in this field of research in deep learning. In the proposed models vinmobCONCAT got the highest accuracy of 93.5%. The most challenging part here is the dataset as there are very less datasets available that do not consist of more classes. So, there can be further work on dataset collection to improve the number of classes as well as to expand the number of pictures for each category that are present in the dataset.

References

1. Singh S, Mann BK (2013) Insect bite reactions. Indian J Dermatol Venereol Leprol Medknow. https://doi.org/10.4103/03786323.107629
2. Steere AC, Strle F, Wormser GP, Hu LT, Branda JA, Hovius JW, Li X, Mead PS (2016) Lyme borreliosis. Nature reviews disease primers. Springer Science+Business Media. https://doi.org/10.1038/nrdp.2016.90
3. Khan AR, Rakesh N, Matam R, Tiwari S (2017) GLCM feature extraction for insect bites pattern recognition. Lecture notes on data engineering and communications technologies. https://doi.org/10.1007/978-981-104585-1_23
4. Cai L, Gao J, Zhao D (2020) A review of the application of deep learning in medical image classification and segmentation. Annals of translational medicine. AME Publishing Company. https://doi.org/10.21037/atm.2020.02.44
5. Akshaykrishnan V, Sharanya C, Abhinav K, Aparna CK, Bindu PV (2023) A machine learning based insect bite classification. In: 2023 3rd international conference on smart data intelligence (ICSMDI), Trichy, India, pp 259–264, https://doi.org/10.1109/ICSMDI57622.2023.00111
6. Ilijoski B, Trojachanec Dineva K, Tojtovska Ribarski B, Petrov P, Mladenovska T, Trajanoska M, Gjorshoska I, Lameski P (2023) Deep Learning methods for bug bite classification: an end-to-end system. Appl Sci 13(8):5187
7. Kamalraj P (2020) Deep learning model for identifying snakes by using snakes bite marks. In: Proceedings of IEEE 2020 international conference on computer communication and informatics (ICCCI), pp 1–4
8. Burlina PM, Joshi NJ, Mathew PA, Paul W, Rebman AW, Aucott JN (2020) AI-based detection of erythema migrans and disambiguation against other skin lesions. Comput Biol Med. https://doi.org/10.1016/j.compbiomed.2020.103977

9. Systems AT (2021) Identifying insect bites—on cAInvas—AITS journal—medium. Medium. https://medium.com/ai-techsystems/identifying-insectbites-on-cainvas-96874143a48b
10. E. (n.d.). GitHub—eyyeung/bugbite_ID: an web application to help you identify what bug bite you through an image of your bug bite. GitHub. https://github.com/eyyeung/bugbite_ID
11. C. (n.d.). GitHub—cbonoz/bugbite-tf: Bugbite AI Android App powered by Tensorflow. GitHub. https://github.com/cbonoz/bugbite-tf
12. Mosquito or Ticks? (2020) Kaggle. https://www.kaggle.com/datasets/bjoernjostein/tick-and-mosq
13. Kumar A, Sarkar S, Pradhan C (2020) Malaria disease detection using CNN technique with SGD, RMSprop and ADAM optimizers. In: Dash S, Acharya B, Mittal M, Abraham A, Kelemen A (eds) Deep learning techniques for biomedical and health informatics. Studies in Big Data, vol 68. Springer, Cham. https://doi.org/10.1007/978-3-030-33966-1_11
14. Srinivas C, NP KS, Zakariah M, Alotaibi YA, Shaukat K, Partibane B, Awal H (2022) Deep transfer learning approaches in performance analysis of brain tumor classification using MRI Images. J Healthc Eng. https://doi.org/10.1155/2022/3264367
15. Ali SS, Miah S, Haque J, Rahman M, Islam K (2021) An enhanced technique of skin cancer classification using deep convolutional neural network with transfer learning models. Mach Learning Appl. https://doi.org/10.1016/j.mlwa.2021.100036

A Review of Facial Video Analysis for Heart Rate Estimation Using Artificial Intelligence

Minal Chandrakant Toley, Raj Gaurav Mishra, and Vishal Shirsath

1 Introduction

The paper provides an in-depth discussion of vital sign remote sensing, which has been explored to alleviate measurement burdens. It highlights the convenience of using a smartphone for heart rate measurement anytime and anywhere, particularly through camera-based techniques. Despite the potential benefits of camera-based methods, their integration into daily life has been hampered by noise resulting from variations in illumination and motion artifacts. These camera-based techniques are primarily grounded in two fundamental concepts: color and motion.

Firstly, remote photoplethysmography (RPPG), a method that uses colour, operates based on photoplethysmography (PPG) principles during a cardiac cycle, blood from the brain and heart passes down the carotid arteries, reflecting variations in colour that are picked up by RPPG. Secondly, the motion-based technique, referred to as remote ballistocardiography (RBCG), relies on ballistocardiography (BCG) principles. RBCG detects modest movements caused by heart contraction and blood ejection towards the vascular system. Furthermore, this paper addresses the challenges, limitations associated with these Artificial Intelligence based approaches, including issues related to data quality and ethical considerations.

The paper provides a comparative evaluation of case studies and actual world examples of prescription analysis systems powered by AI. This analysis highlights the practical uses of AI in prescriptions analysis by showcasing how they can boost

M. C. Toley (✉) · R. G. Mishra · V. Shirsath
School of Engineering, Ajeenkya D Y Patil University, Pune, Maharashtra, India
e-mail: minal.toley@adypu.edu.in

R. G. Mishra
e-mail: raj.mishra@adypu.edu.in

V. Shirsath
e-mail: vishal.shirsath@adypu.edu.in

K. Kumar Singh et al. (eds.), *Machine Vision and Augmented Intelligence*, Lecture Notes in Electrical Engineering 1211, https://doi.org/10.1007/978-981-97-4359-9_54

patient outcomes and reduce medical expenses while also being more accurate and effective.

2 Literature Survey

The methods used by the Demirezen et al.'s in 2021 [1], is the HBCC history based consistency check. They prove the strongness of variations in rapid pulse rate, they used the NMD to differentiate the rPPG signals into components. In 2021, Lee et al. [2] used the techniques like BSS, HR, PCA, EA, ICA that reduced the noise from many facial areas in Red, Green, Blue color.

A unique method was proposed by Zhang et al. [3] in 2020, to find out the efficiency of the method tested on 30 people with a total of 90 samples. The universally available dataset is used in the paper by Gudi et al.'s 2019 research [4], where they express the rPPG with the filters and motion suppression. They worked on the real world contexts as well as with the lab contexts. The size of the dataset is 10 with the use of ICA, PSA and regression or KNN which worked on heart rate estimation to decrease the RMS error by Monkaresi et al. [5] in 2014. To increase the effectiveness of infant's heart rate measurement and to evaluate the disturbances in motion the dataset of hospitalized neonates in the paper of Chen et al.'s 2021 [6] was used.

In Niu et al.'s 2020 project [7], Rhythm Net was used to estimate the heart rate from face images, outperforming contemporary techniques on both publicly available and VIPL-HR datasets. The Hue, Saturation, and Intensity (HSI) model was used for principal component analysis and bi-histogram equalization in Uppal et al.'s 2017 study [8] to measure heart rate from RGB video. In Pagano et al.'s 2022 study [9], machine learning models were explored for facial video-based heart rate estimation.

In Balakrishnan et al.'s 2013 approach [10], head characteristics were tracked using principal component analysis, and component motion was analyzed to identify heartbeats, achieving results similar to ECG equipment. In Gudi et al.'s 2013 work [11], a real-time rPPG A pipeline for estimating heart rate and variability in heart rate was introduced, featuring motion suppression and no specific training requirements. In Greenwald SE's 2019 research [9], the "Project_ICA" approach was proposed for separating pulse signals from facial skin reflections and demonstrated its accuracy on a dataset with various skin tones and motion. In Gupta et al.'s 2020 study [12], MOMBAT, a brand-new facial video-based heart rate tracking method that incorporates Bayesian tracking and addresses out-of-plane face motions was unveiled.

In Hassan et al.'s 2017 contributions [13], aimed to overcome obstacles like as signal intensity, lighting variation, and motion variation in heart rate estimation. In Carmen et al.'s 2018 method [14], heart rates of multiple individuals watching live video feeds were simultaneously measured using face detection, object tracking, and color signal analysis. The 2019 work by Niu et al. [15] improved remote photoplethysmography (rPPG) by focusing particular characteristics, resulting in superior HR project over state-of-the-art algorithms.

TFT and CNN are utilised in Hsu et al.'s 2017 work [16] to estimate pulse signals, resulting in enhanced accuracy on the MAHNOB-HCI database. In Hsu et al.'s 2020 study [17], a deep learning system was created for current time heart rate estimate with RGB cameras via its use of sequential filtering and the Short-Time Fourier Transform. In Huang et al.'s 2021 study [18], statistical signal processing and adaptive spectral filter banks were employed to reduce heart rate errors in different datasets. In Le et al.'s 2020 research [20], Filtering, ICA, and FFT were utilized to achieve low root mean square error in 10-second RGB videos, even with slight head motion. In Yu et al.'s 2021 study [19], CPPG and lab-based RPPG were compared using peak-to-peak interval (PPI) and PRV analysis.

In Saji et al.'s 2021 research [20], the aim was to develop a long-term, non- contact heart rate monitoring device for detecting atrial fibrillation using facial recognition and green channel rPPG signal extraction. In Werner et al.'s 2014 approach [21], a technique that was less sensitive to head movement and facial expression was used, using regions of interest and an Inter-Beat-Interval Series Consensus algorithm. In Yan et al.'s 2015 study [22], cardiovascular pulse waves were accurately measured from face detection video, physiological parameters such as pulse rate were derived, demonstrating consistency with reference technologies. In Yu et al.'s 2014 research [23], Short-Time Fourier Transform and an independent component analysis algorithm were employed to achieve accurate heart rate estimation.

In Hsu et al.'s 2020 evaluation [24], the effectiveness of their framework was demonstrated using STFT and CNN on MAHNOB-HCI, VIPL-HR data-bases. In Hsu et al.'s 2017 study [25] on the MAHNOB-HCI database, face ROI analysis and deep CNN outperformed alternative pulse estimation algorithms. In Song et al.'s 2020 research [26], convolutional neural networks (CNNs) were employed to estimate heart rate, achieving excellent results on the MAHNOB-HCI dataset. A large-scale deep neural network with Conv2D and the LSTM procedures was used in Huang et al.'s 2020 development [27] to accurately calculate heart rate from face ROI movies. Convolutional neural networks, spatial and temporal filtering, and remote heart rate prediction were used in Qiu et al.'s 2019 framework [28], which outperformed benchmark techniques on the MMSE-HR dataset (Table 1).

3 Tools and Techniques

3.1 Artificial Intelligence

Artificial intelligence (AI) involves employing computers to perform tasks that typically require human intelligence, and it excels in processing extensive data in ways that surpass human capabilities. The overarching aim of AI is to emulate human functions like recognizing patterns, exercising judgment, and making decisions [31] (Fig. 1).

Table 1 Table of comparison of existing literature reviews

Paper references	Techniques/methods	Dataset size/ subjects	Outcome/result
[1]	Nonlinear mode decomposition (NMD), history-based consistency check HBCC)	60	Comparison with other method with respect the RMSE values
[2]	Independent Component Analysis Blind Source Sensation method, Ensemble Averaging, Principal Component Analysis	20	Compared with used previous methods, enhanced accuracy from the dataset with respect to illumination variance and motion artifacts
[3]	Ensemble empirical mode decom- position (EEMD)	30	The confidence interval of 95% ranges from −7.14 beats per minute to 3.40 bpm
[4]	Current time rPPG pipelines with effective motion suppression and innovative filtering	2	Comparison of multiple dataset (Vi-carPPG and PURE)
[5]	ICA, Power spectrum analysis, KNN/ Regression	10	According to the findings, the RMSE is decreased by the suggested strategy, going from 43.76 to 3.64 bpm
[6]	ROI segmentation, Eulerian video magnification, morphology-based filtering	9	The mean absolute inaccuracy during observable motions and rest still is 3.39 and 4.34 beats per minute, this is at least 2.00 and 1.88 BPM slower than earlier attempts. The Bland–Altman plots further emphasize the HR produced by the true ECG
[7]	RhythmNet, CNN	5	It achieves high HR estimation precision in both intra and inter database validation situations on the MAHNOB-HCI, and VIPl-HR, MMSE-HR databases
[8]	Bi-histogram technique (BBHE),PCA	15	Feasibility calculation of HR on basis of RGB and Hue channels
[9]	Study of datasets	10	Explores the benefits and drawbacks of using machine learning models to estimate heart rate from face films through the review of patents, datasets, and scientific papers
[10]	Principal component analysis (PCA)	18	Frequency and variability of the pulse signal is found out

(continued)

Table 1 (continued)

Paper references	Techniques/methods	Dataset size/ subjects	Outcome/result
[11]	Heart rate variability (HRV)	13	In this study, convolutional neural networks and both temporal and spatial filtering are used to propose an innovative structure for remotely forecasting heart rate in realistic conditions
[9]	ICA algorithm	28	The results suggest that Project_ICA, when assessed against various parameters, gives a more precise and consistent estimation of HR than all existing approaches, while issues with collecting trustworthy data from people with dark skin persist
[12]	Model-based Bayesian tracking (MOMBAT) for monitoring	65	Monitoring actual heart rates with an average absolute error of 1.329 beats per minute, and a Pearson correlation of 0.9746 between the predictions
[13]	Bland–Altman analysis	27	Helps to overcoming problems such as low signal strength, lighting variation, and motion variation
[14]	FFT (Fast Fourier Transform)	4	The strategy decreases the amount of processing power required and allows for greater scaling
[15]	Spatial–temporal map generation,	40	The suggested method outperforms cutting-edge algorithms for remote HR estimation, according to the results of experiments using the available datasets VIPL-HR and MMSE-HR
[16]	CNN and STFT	10	Experimental outcomes show the suggested algorithm demonstrates higher estimating effectiveness in comparison to the majority of the most recent pulse estimate techniques
[17]	Short-time Fourier transform (STFT), pulse from face (PFF), convolutional neural network (CNN)	28	Experimental results are achieved
[18]	Monte Carlo simulations, statistical signal processing (SSP), adaptive spectral filter banks	20	The compact vehicle and bus databases' mean absolute errors (MAE) for heart rate was 3.43 bpm, 7.85 bpm, and 5.02 bpm, respectively

(continued)

Table 1 (continued)

Paper references	Techniques/methods	Dataset size/ subjects	Outcome/result
[20]	Independent component analysis, filtering, automatic component selection (ACS) algorithm, fast Fourier transform	30	For 10 s RGB movies, an rms error of 3.41 bpm was discovered
[19]	Peak-to-peak interval (PPI)	10	Contrast the PRV analysis of CPPG with that of lab-based RPPG
[20]	Gaussian filter, interpolation	1	The proposed technique allows continuous monitoring of heart rates without the use of expensive equipment
[21]	ROIs, an inter-beat-interval series consensus (IBISC) algorithm	18	A promising strategy has been demonstrated to be more resistant to significant movement of the head and facial expression detection than the previous method
[22]	Independent component analysis (ICA),signal weighting analysis (SWA)	15	Signal-to-noise ratio (SNR), root mean square error (RMSE), and correlation coefficients (r) computed results were all 0.94 (p 0.001)
[23]	ICA and STFT	38	Using the proposed method to compare to STFT. The RMSE is 2.31 beats per minute. The correlation coefficient is 0.96, with an average percentage error of 1.42%
[24]	CNN and STFT	PURE (PUlse RatE)	Framework was tested on the VIPL-HR database [3], MAHNOB-HCI database [2] and its effectiveness was compared to that of other cur- rent approaches to establish its efficacy
[25]	Short-time Fourier transform (STFT), Convolutional Neural Network (CNN)	10	The suggested algorithm demonstrates higher estimating effectiveness in comparison to the majority of the most recent pulse estimate techniques. Preprocessing of the signals is obviously essential for the calculation procedure
[26]	Convolutional neural networks (CNNs)	27	The database of MAHNOB-HCI used for evaluating the proposed approach in cross-database and intra-database arrangements in open databases

(continued)

Table 1 (continued)

Paper references	Techniques/methods	Dataset size/ subjects	Outcome/result
[27]	LSTM (long short-term memory), CNN	5	Experiments show that the proposed approach can precisely estimate HR value
[28]	CNN, Temporal filtering	68	Both the mean heartbeat estimation and the short-term heart rate estimation were compared to the standard on the MMSE-HR dataset

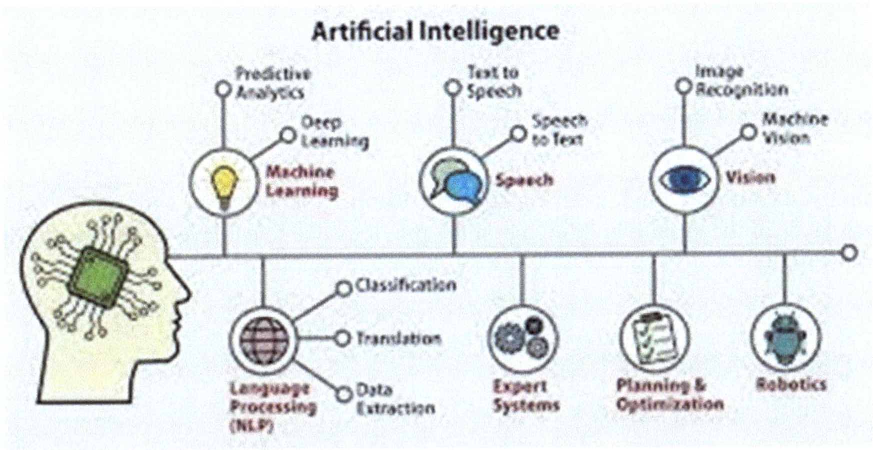

Fig. 1 Artificial intelligence [31]

3.2 *Supervised Learning*

It is a machine learning approach, involves train a system using labeled data, where each input data point is associated with an assigned output. The computer is instructed to make accurate predictions based on this labeled training data. The process of providing both input, output data for the ML algorithm referred to as supervised learning [29] (Fig. 2).

3.3 *Deep Learning (DL)*

Artificial Intelligence (AI), Machine learning (ML) harness the principles of human cognitive processes to make informed decisions and examine human actions effectively. These are essential elements of the field of data science, employing data centric methodologies, data modeling for predictive purposes. Robust algorithms are

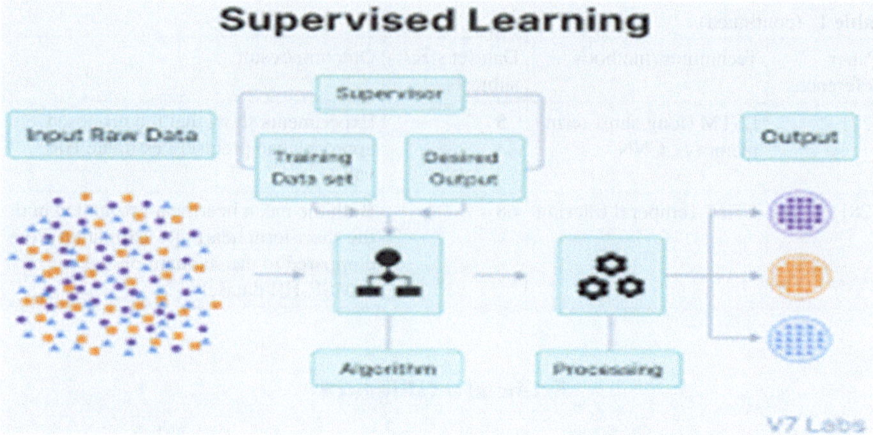

Fig. 2 Supervised learning [29]

employed to mimic the human capacity for learning, adjustment, and action, with each layer of the system building upon the previous one to achieve these objectives [30] (Fig. 3).

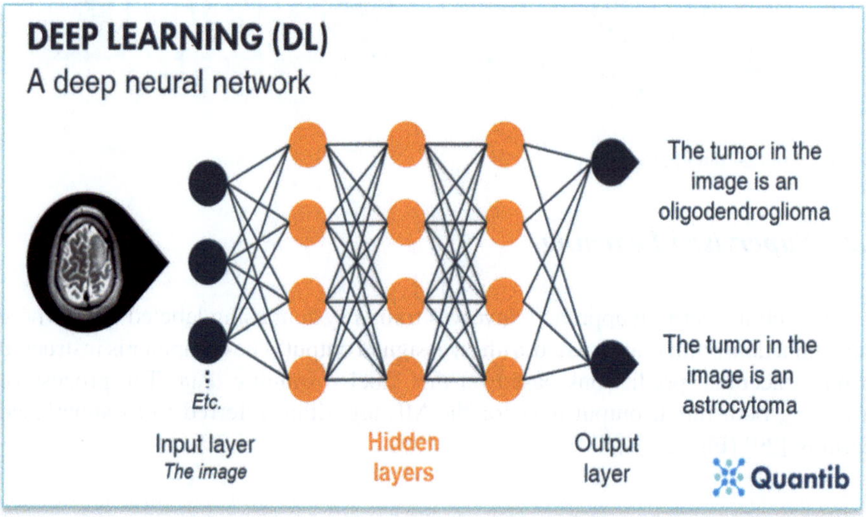

Fig. 3 Deep learning [30]

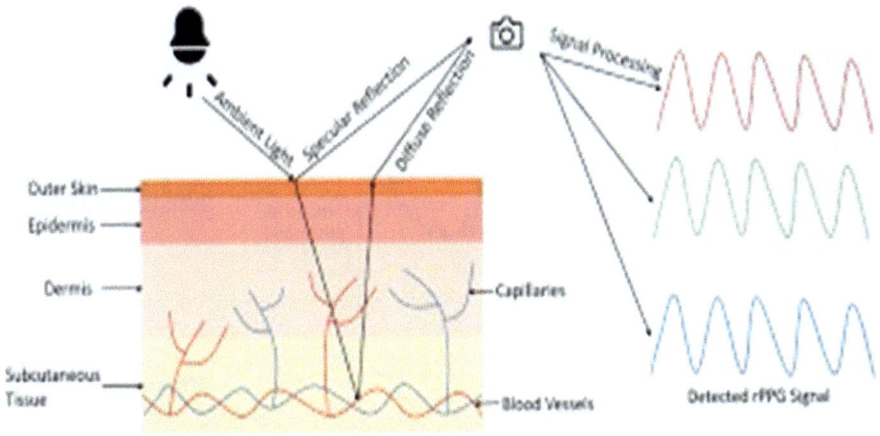

Fig. 4 Remote photoplethysmography [33]

3.4 *Remote Photoplethysmography*

Remote Photoplethysmography (rPPG), an inconspicuous, photographic approach that enables constant Changes in vital signs are tracked, helping in the earlier and efficient identification and treatment of diseases. A straightforward optical method called photoplethysmography (PPG) is used for identifying variations in the volume of blood in circulation. It's an inexpensive, non-invasive technique that measures skin surface parameters. The method offers insightful data about our cardiovascular system [33] (Fig. 4).

3.5 *Remote Ballistocardiography*

A non-invasive method known as remote ballistocardiography observes the body's motion resulting from the forceful ejection of blood during each heartbeat. The ballistocardiogram (BCG) signal captures these ballistic forces generated by the heart's sudden blood ejection with every pulse, breath, and bodily movement [32] (Fig. 5).

3.6 *Convolution Neural Network (CNN)*

A CNN, or Convolutional Neural Network, is a specialized type of artificial neural network, commonly employed in computer vision tasks, such as recognition of image, the processing of pixel data. It is a specialized class of algorithms within the realm of

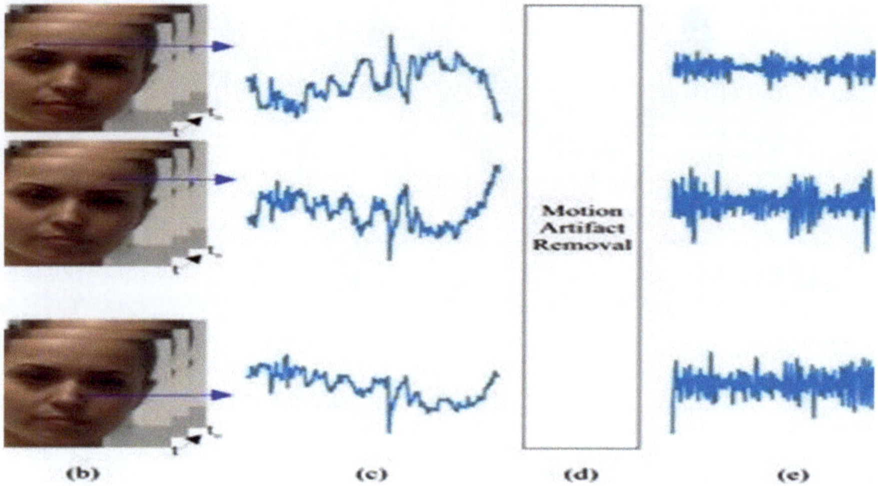

Fig. 5 Remote ballistocardiography [32]

deep learning and machine learning, specifically tailored for tasks related to object identification. They are particularly well-suited for applications such as autonomous vehicles and facial recognition [34] (Fig. 6).

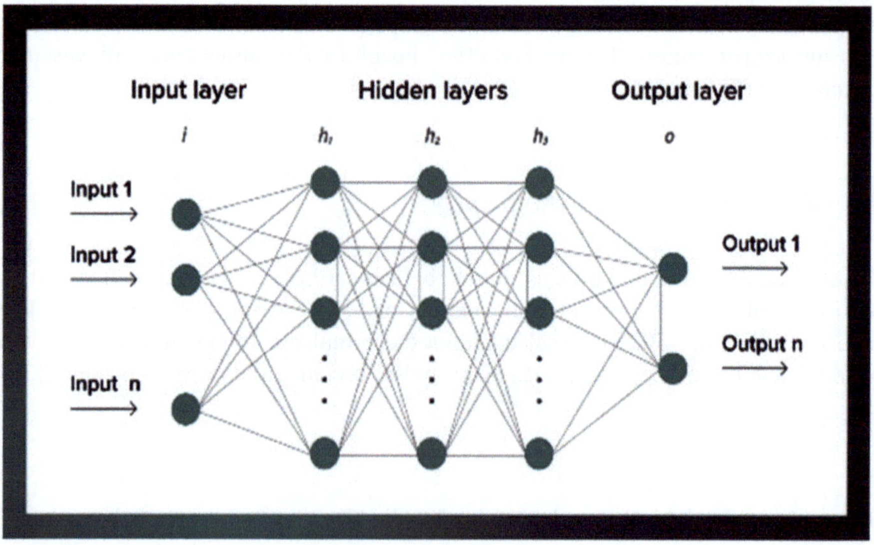

Fig. 6 Convolution neural network [34]

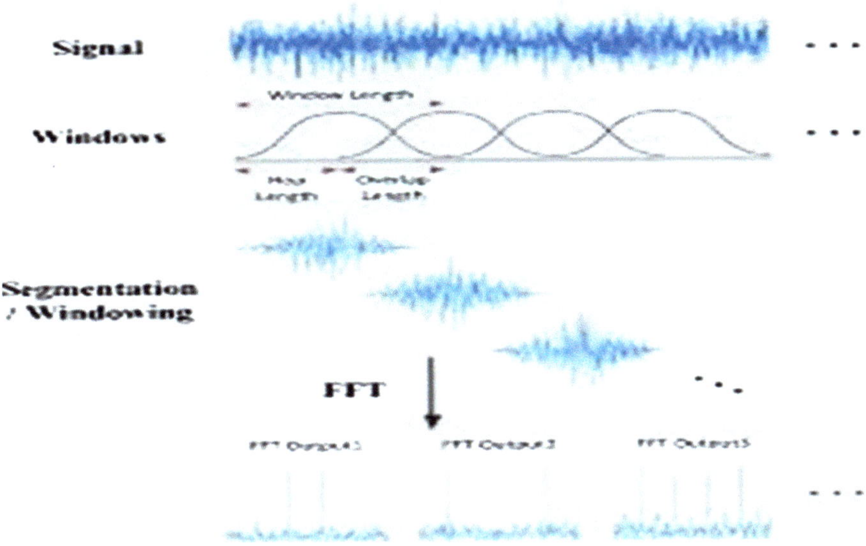

Fig. 7 Short time Fourier transform [35]

3.7 *Short Time Fourier Transform*

A useful tool for translating inputs across one domain to another is the mathematical framework known as the Fourier transform. This includes the reverse transformation as well as the translation from the frequency domain to the time domain. This versatile technique finds applications across various engineering, physics disciplines, including signal processing, RADAR etc. [35] (Fig. 7).

3.8 *Long Short Term Memory (LSTM)*

RNNs are augmented by LSTM networks, which were created specifically to handle circumstances where RNNs fail. When we discuss RNN, we are referring to an algorithm that evaluates the current input while taking into consideration the results of earlier occurrences (feedback) and then temporarily stores that information in the short- term memory of its users [36] (Fig. 8).

3.9 *Principal Component Analysis (PCA)*

The method of machine learning uses principal component analysis, an unsupervised learning technique, to reduce dimensionality. It is a statistical approach that employs a

Fig. 8 Long short term memory (LSTM) [36]

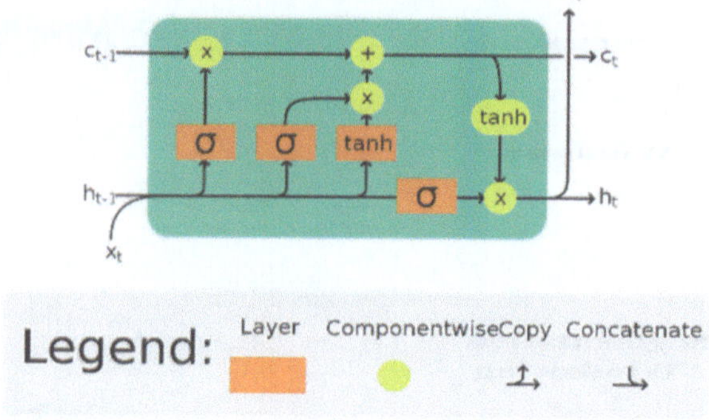

Fig. 9 Principal component analysis (PCA) [37]

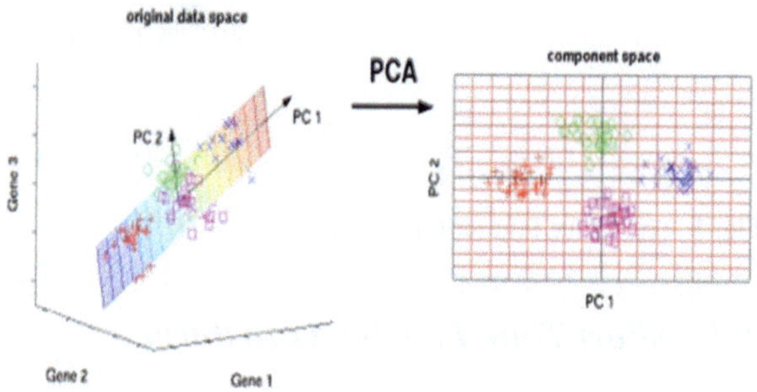

transformation that is orthogonal to convert correlated observations into a set of linear uncorrelated data. The key components are revised features. It is a well-known data exploration and predictive modelling tool. It is a method for identifying significant trends in a collection of data by decreasing variances [37] (Fig. 9).

4 Conclusion

In summary, the assessment of existing literature suggests the Artificial Intelligence-based approaches show considerable potential in enhancing accuracy, effectiveness of medication assessment. Artificial intelligence, deep learning, and machine learning have shown favorable outcomes concerning patient care and cost reduction. Nevertheless, certain challenges persist, including issues related to inadequate data quality and ethical concerns. However, in spite of these constraints, the integration of AI-driven medication analysis tools has result in positive outcomes. The conclusions play a role in advancing the creation of diagnostic tools with the ability to gather patient information, identify improper medications, and offer statistical evaluations of prescribed medications.

References

1. Demirezen H, Eroglu Erdem C (2021) Heart rate estimation from facial videos using non-linear mode decomposition and improved consistency check. SIViP 15:1415–1423
2. Lee H, Cho A, Whang M (2021) Fusion method to estimate heart rate from facial videos based on RPPG and RBCG. Sensors (Basel)
3. Zhang Y, Dong Z, Zhang K, Shu S, Lu F, Chen J (2020) Illumination variation-resistant video-based heart rate monitoring using LAB color space. Opt Lasers Eng 136:106328. ISSN 0143–8166
4. Gudi A, Bittner M, Lochmans R, van Gemert J (2019) Efficient real-time camera based estimation of heart rate and variability. CoRR abs/1909.01206
5. Monkaresi H, Calvo RA, Yan H (2014) A machine learning approach to improve contactless-heart rate monitoring using a webcam. IEEE J Biomed Health Inform 18(4):1153–1160
6. Chen Q, Wang Y, Liu X et al (2021) Camera-based heart rate estimation for hospitalized newborns in the presence of motion artifacts. BioMed Eng OnLine 20:122
7. Niu X, Shan S, Han H, Chen X (2020) RhythmNet: end-to-end heart rate estimation from face via spatial-temporal representation. IEEE Trans Image Process 29:2409–2423
8. Uppal G, Prakash NR, Kalra P (2017) Heart rate measurement using facial videos. Adv Comput Sci Technol 10(8):2343–2357. ISSN 0973-6107
9. Pagano TP, Santos VR, Bonfim YS, Paranhos JVD, Ortega LL, Sá PHM, Nascimento LFS, Winkler I, Nascimento EGS (2022) Machine learning models and videos of facial regions for estimating heart rate: a review on patents, datasets, and literature. Electronics 11:1473
10. Balakrishnan G, Durand F, Guttag J (2013) Detecting pulse from head motions in video. In: 2013 IEEE conference on computer vision and pattern recognition, Portland, OR, USA, pp 3430–3437. https://doi.org/10.1109/CVPR.2013.440
11. Gudi A, Bittner M, van Gemert J (2020) Real-time webcam heart-rate and variability estimation with clean ground truth for evaluation. CoRR abs/2012.15846
12. Qi L, Yu H, Xu L, Mpanda RS, Greenwald SE (2019) Robust heart-rate estimation from facial videos using Project_ICA. Physiol Meas 40(8):085007. https://doi.org/10.1088/1361-6579/ab2c9f.PMID:3147942(2019)
13. Gupta P, Bhowmick B, Pal A (2020) MOMBAT: heart rate monitoring from face video using pulse modeling and Bayesian tracking. CoRR abs/2005.04618
14. Hassan MA, Malik AS, Fofi D, Saad N, Karasfi B, Ali YS, Meriaudeau F (2017) Heartrate estimation using facial video: a review. Biomed Signal Process Control 38:346–360. ISSN 1746–8094
15. Poenaru C, Poenaru V, Suciu George (2018) Heart rate measurement using face detection in video. 131–134. https://doi.org/10.1109/ICComm.2018.8430116
16. Niu X et al (2019) Robust remote heart rate estimation from face utilizing spatial-temporal attention. In: 2019 14th IEEE international conference on automatic face & gesture recognition (FG 2019), Lille, France, pp 1–8
17. Hsu G-S, Ambikapathi A, Chen M-S (2017) Deep learning with time-frequency representation for pulse estimation from facial videos. In: IEEE international joint conference on biometrics (IJCB), Denver, CO, USA, pp 383–389
18. Hsu GSJ, Xie R-C, Ambikapathi AM, Chou KJ (2020) A deep learning framework for heart rate estimation from facial videos. Neurocomputing 417:155–166. ISSN 0925–2312. https://doi.org/10.1016/j.neu-com.2020.07.012
19. Huang P-W, Wu B-J, Wu B-F (2021) A heart rate monitoring framework for real-world drivers using remote photoplethysmography. IEEE J Biomed Health Informatics 25(5):1397–1408
20. Le DQ, Lie W-N, Nhu QNQ, Nguyen TTA (2020) Heart rate estimation based on facial image sequence. In: 5th international conference on green technology and sustainable development (GTSD), Ho Chi Minh City, Vietnam
21. Yu S-G, Kim S-E, Kim NH, Suh KH, Lee EC (2021) Pulse rate variability analysis using remote photoplethysmography signals. Sensor 21:18,6241

22. Saji S, Jose A, Karthika AM, Abhijith D, Jose R, Jarin T (2021) A sustainable facial recognition based heart rate monitoring system for the detection of atrial fibrillation in paralyzed. In: International conference on energy and environment (ICEE 2021) AIP Conf. Proc. 2396, 020019-1-020019-8
23. Werner P, Al-Hamadi A, Walter S, Gruss S,Traue HC (2014) Automatic heart rate estimation from painful faces. In: IEEE international conference on image processing (ICIP), Paris, France, pp 1947–1951. https://doi.org/10.1109/ICIP.2014.7025390
24. Yan Y, Ma X, Yao L, Ouyang J (2015) Noncontact measurement of heart rate using facial video illuminated under natural light and signal weighted analysis. Biomed Mater Eng 26(Suppl 1):S903–S909. https://doi.org/10.3233/BME-151383.PMID:26406091.(2015)
25. Yu Y-P, Raveendran P, Lim C-L (2014) Heart rate estimation from facial images using filter bank. In: 2014 6th international symposium on communications, control and signal processing (ISCCSP), Athens, Greece, pp 69–72
26. Hsu GSJ, Xie R-C, Ambikapathi AM, Chou KJ (2020) A deep learning framework for heart rate estimation from facial videos. Neurocomputing 417:155–166. ISSN 0925-2312
27. Hsu G-S, Ambikapathi A, Chen M-S (2017) Deep learning with time-frequency representation for pulse estimation from facial videos. In: 2017 IEEE international joint conference on biometrics (IJCB), Denver, CO, USA, pp 383–389
28. Song R, Zhang S, Li C, Zhang Y, Cheng J, Chen X (2020) Heart rate estimation fromfacial videos using a spatiotemporal representation with convolutional neural networks. In: IEEE transactions on instrumentation and measurement
29. Qiu Y, Liu Y, Arteaga-Falconi J, Dong H, Saddik AE (2019) EVM-CNN: real-timecontactless heart rate estimation from facial video. IEEE Trans Multimedia 21(7):1778–1787
30. Working of Supervised Learning. https://www.geeksforgeeks.org/supervised-machine-learning
31. Deep Learning. https://www.geeksforgeeks.org/introduction-deep-learning
32. Artificial Intelligence. https://www.techtarget.com/searchenterpriseai/definition/AI-Artificial-Intelligence
33. Hassan MA, Malik A, Fofi D, Saad M, Naufal M, Ali Y, Meriaudeau F (2017) Video-based heartbeat rate measuring method using ballistocardiography. IEEE Sens J 17:4544–4557. https://doi.org/10.1109/JSEN.2017.2708133
34. Cheng C-H, Wong K-L, Chin J-W, Chan T-T, So RHY (2021) Deep learning methods for remote heart rate measurement: a review and future research agenda. Sensors 21:18,6296
35. Short Time Fourier Transform. https://in.mathworks.com/help/signal/ref/stft.html
36. Long Short Term Memory (LSTM). https://www.geeksforgeeks.org/deep-learning-introduction-to-long-short-term-memory/
37. Principal Component Analysis (PCA). https://www.javatpoint.com/principal-component-analysis

Denoising of Poisson Corrupted Micro Biopsy Image Using Modified Fourth Order Partial Differential Equation

Prem Chand Yadava, Abhinav Kumar, and Subodh Srivastava

1 Introduction

Lung cancer has emerged as the leading cause of mortality worldwide. Approximately one million people contend with lung cancer each year. The primary risk factors for lung cancer are consumption of tobacco and smoking. As noted by Hecht in 1999, it is believed that smoking accounts for a staggering 75–80% of annual lung cancer deaths in women and a striking 90% in men within the United States. Lung cancer unquestionably stands as a perilous and pervasive ailment, presenting a grave public health concern [1]. Cancer stands as the second-leading cause of death worldwide. In the year 2020 alone, there were over 19 million newly diagnosed with disease, resulting in 9.95 million cancer-related fatalities [2].

Microscopic biopsy is the most widely employed and renowned technique for early lung cancer detection. Precise interpretation of anatomical structures plays a pivotal part in the timely identification of lung cancer. When testing for lung cancer, the statistical properties of electromagnetic radiation are used to make noise look like something else. This is a method that is commonly used in computer tomography and magnetic resonance imaging [3]. This phenomenon arises from the unpredictable movement of photons. In the context of microscopic biopsy images, multiplicative noise is introduced due to photon radiation impact. The resultant noise follows a Poisson distribution and is Poisson noise. This noise affects the visibility of underlying issues significantly. It hampers radiologists' ability to precisely interpret

P. C. Yadava (✉) · A. Kumar · S. Srivastava
Department of Electronics and Communication Engineering, National Institute of Technology Patna, Patna, Bihar 800005, India
e-mail: premy.phd20.ec@nitp.ac.in

A. Kumar
e-mail: abhinav.ec19@nitp.ac.in

S. Srivastava
e-mail: subodh@nitp.ac.in

K. Kumar Singh et al. (eds.), *Machine Vision and Augmented Intelligence*, Lecture Notes in Electrical Engineering 1211, https://doi.org/10.1007/978-981-97-4359-9_55

abnormalities and also impacts the outcomes of image applications. Two critical challenges must be addressed [4]. Firstly, there is a need to eliminate any Poisson noise to ensure accurate data regarding existing anomalies, such as masses, tumors, and calcifications. Secondly, there is a need to develop a filter that can simultaneously enhance image quality and recover microscopic information [5].

The remnants of the paper are as follows: The second part contains literature reviews of several pre-existing denoising approaches. Methods and models are discussed in Sect. 3. A visual and quantitative comparative study is offered in Sect. 4. Finally, a conclusion is provided.

2 Related Work

Various methods had been developed to denoise the Poisson noise from medical images. Goyal et al. [6] have used total variation (TV), and non-local means (NLM). The numerical analysis using peak-signal-to-noise ratio (PSNR), structural similarity index map (SSIM), and mean square error (MSE). Sagheer et al. [7] have provided a TV based filter for denoising of images from the MRI, CT, and ultrasound. The performance is measured by PSNR, MSE, SSIM, and signal to noise ratio (SNR). Goreke et al. [8] have employed wiener filter (WF) for removal of Poisson noise from for X-ray images where PSNR, and SSIM are determined for efficacy of the method. Kumar et al. [9] have casted fourth order partial differential equation (FOPDE) to lessen microscopic biopsy Poisson noise. Later, the denoised images were used in segmentation application. Kumar et al. [10] have compared methods such as WF, mean filtering (MF), Gabor, NLM, TV, FOPDE, bilateral filter (BF), and complex diffusion from microscopic biopsy images. Logambal et al. [11] used median filtering (MDF) with contrast adaptive limited histogram equalization (CLAHE) for the noise removal from histopathological images.

The method such as WF, MF, and MDF have limitations in terms of both visual as well quantitative. Furthermore, the hybrid and FOPDE produce a smoother image compared to the original image. Filters like TV, NLM, WF, MF, MDF, and Gabor considerably produce blurred images that have low spatial quality. The value of the image's quality and performance metrics is found to be low after a thorough analysis of all the relevant works included in this study. Thus, a modified fourth-order partial differential equation with maximum likelihood estimation (MFOPDEMLE) is suggested in order to get over the aforementioned limitation.

3 Method and Models

To denoise the Poisson impacted histopathological images, a modified fourth-order partial differential equation with maximum likelihood estimation (FOPDEMLE) has been proposed. The collection of histopathological images is the first steps in the

Table 1 Dataset attributes

Attributes	Dataset		
Name	LC25000		
Availability	Publicly		
Number of images	25,000		
Number of classes	5	(i) Colon adenocarcinomas	5000
		(ii) Benign colonic tissues	5000
		(iii) Lung adenocarcinomas	5000
		(iv) Lung squamous cell carcinomas	5000
		(v) Benign lung tissues	5000
Image size	768 × 768 pixels		
Image file format	JPEG		

development of the proposed method. The MFOPDEMLE utilizes the features of FOPDE and MLE. The function of FOPDE is to eliminate the Poisson noise from the histopathological images while MLE is utilized to restore the details of the image.

3.1 Dataset

To develop the proposed method, lung and colon cancer histopathological image dataset LC25000 [12] has been utilized. It is publicly available dataset. The dataset is described in Table 1.

3.2 Proposed Modified Fourth Oder Partial Differential Equation with Maximum Likelihood Estimation

The typical structure of a generated image through micro biopsy imaging may read as [9]:

$$u_0 = \mathrm{u}^* \beta_2 + \beta_1 \tag{1}$$

The standard procedure for image restoration is as follows:

$$u_0 = \mathrm{F}(\mathrm{u}\beta_2 + \beta_1) \tag{2}$$

and,

$$u_0 = \text{Poisson}\ (\mathrm{u}\beta_2 + \beta_1) = \text{Poisson}\ (\mathrm{H}) \tag{3}$$

The probability density function (pdf) of data with poison noise distorted value , u_0 is as follows [13]

$$p(u/u_0) = \frac{e^{-u}u^{u0}}{\sqrt{u_0}} \tag{4}$$

$$\mathrm{u}_{ML} = \operatorname{argmin}_{u\geq 0}\left\{-\ln p\left(\frac{\mathrm{u}}{u_0}\right)\right\} = \operatorname{argmin}_{u\geq 0}\{u - u_0 \ln u\} \tag{5}$$

Assuming Poisson noise, the highest probability estimate of u is [9].

$$\mathrm{u}_{ML} = \frac{u_0 - u}{u} \tag{6}$$

For PDEs based on the fourth order will read as [9]

$$\mathrm{E(u)}= ||\nabla \mathrm{u}\ ||)^2 \tag{7}$$

The working equation of the proposed method is casted into energy functional as [13]:

$$E(u) = \int_{\min \Omega} \left[L\left(p\left(\frac{u}{u_0}\right)\right) + \lambda(||\nabla^2 u||^2)\right] \mathrm{d}\Omega \tag{8}$$

The final equation is obtained by using finite difference scheme i.e., [14]

$$\frac{u_{ij}^{n+1} - u_{ij}^n}{\Delta t} = \left(\frac{u_0 - u_{ij}^n}{\lambda u_{ij}^n} + \lambda \nabla^2 (c||\nabla^2 u_{ij}^n||)\nabla^2 u_{ij}^n\right) \tag{9}$$

where, the diffusion coefficient is defined as

$$||\mathrm{c}(||\nabla^2 u||) = \frac{1}{1 + \left(\left|\left|\frac{\nabla^2 u}{k}\right|\right|\right)^2} \tag{10}$$

4 Performance Evaluation Metrics

Table 2 presents the comprehensive compilation of performance evaluation metrics parameters [15, 16] that is utilized for assessing the effectiveness of the proposed FOPDEMLE.

Table 2 Performance evaluation metrics

Metrics	Formula
Mean square error (MSE) [17]	$\text{MSE} = \frac{1}{MN}\sum_{i=0}^{M-1}\sum_{j=0}^{N-1}\left[u_{MFOPDE} - u_{ref}\right]^2$
Peak signal-to-noise ratio (PSNR) [17]	$\text{PSNR} = 10\log_{10}\frac{(L-1)^2}{\text{MSE}(u_{MFOPDE}, u_{ref})}db$
Correlation coefficient (CP) [18]	$CP = \frac{\sum\left(u_{ref} - \mu_{u_{ref}}\right)\sum\left(u_{MFOPDE} - \mu_{u_{MFOPDE}}\right)}{\sqrt{\sum\left(u_{ref} - \mu_{u_{ref}}\right)^2\sum\left(u_{MFOPDE} - \mu_{u_{MFOPDE}}\right)^2}}$
Normalized absolute error (NAE) [18]	$\text{NAE} = \frac{\sum_{i=0}^{M-1}\sum_{j=0}^{N-1}\lvert u_{ref} - u_{MFOPDE}\rvert}{\sum_{i=0}^{M-1}\sum_{j=0}^{N-1}(u_{ref})}$
Universal quality index (UQI) [18]	$\text{UQI} = \frac{4\mu_{u_{ref}}\mu_{u_{MFOPDE}}\sigma_{u_{ref}u_{MFOPDE}}}{\left(\mu^2_{u_{ref}} + \mu^2_{u_{MFOPDE}}\right)\left(\sigma^2_{u_{ref}} + \sigma^2_{u_{MFOPDE}}\right)}$
Structural similarity index (SSIM) [19]	$\text{SSIM} = \frac{\left(2\mu_{u_{ref}}\mu_{u_{MFOPDE}} + c_1\right)\left(2\sigma_{u_{ref}u_{MFOPDE}} + c_2\right)}{\left(\mu^2_{u_{ref}} + \mu^2_{u_{MFOPDE}} + c_1\right)\left(\sigma^2_{u_{ref}} + \sigma^2_{u_{MFOPDE}} + c_2\right)}$
No reference [19]	It measures the sharpening of the image

5 Results and Discussion

The efficacy of the proposed FOPDEMLE has been demonstrated as visual and quantitative. The qualitative assessment demonstrates an enhancement in visibility, whilst the quantitative evaluation provides quantifiable evidence of the effectiveness of the proposed strategy. The quantitative assessment is presented for the performance evaluation measures stated above. For the analysis purpose LC25000 dataset [12] has employed. The upcoming Sects. 5.1 and 5.2 displays the result of qualitative and quantitative evaluation respectively.

5.1 Qualitative Result Analysis

The qualitative result is evaluated for the lung benign cell class of the LC25000 dataset. However, the process of analysis remains the same for the other class of dataset. Figures 1 and 2 illustrate the comparative qualitative study, where the first image shows the input image while the remaining images show the results obtained through the Winner, Gabor, Hybrid, NLM, TV, and Proposed methods, respectively. The idea behind using these filters is that they were utilized as noise-removal filters for biopsy images. From the comparative qualitative study, it can be observed that the proposed method notably outperformed in enhancing edges, brightness, and nuclei.

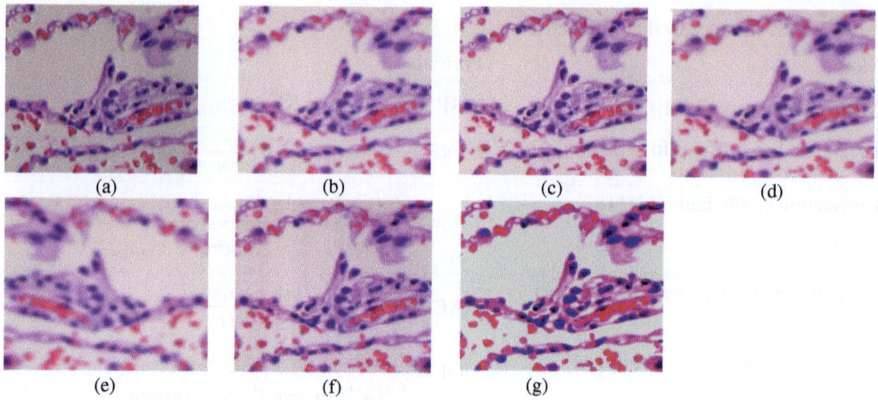

Fig. 1 A comparative qualitative analysis where **a** input image from Benign lung cell class (**b–g**) represents an image obtained from the Wiener, Gabor, Hybrid, NLM, TV, and proposed method, respectively

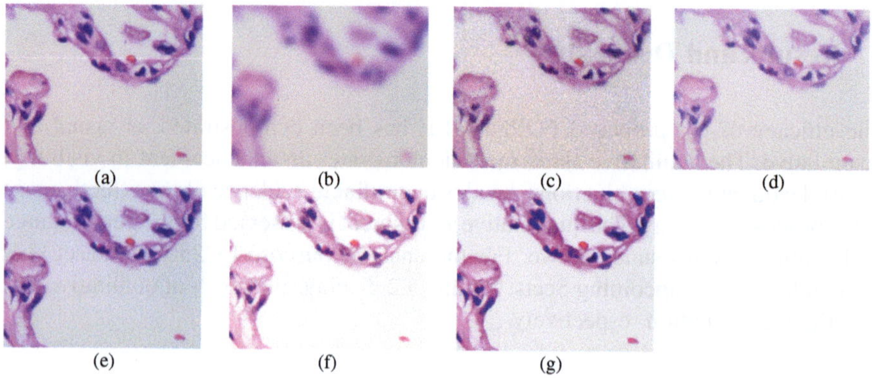

Fig. 2 A comparative qualitative analysis where **a** is the input image of micro bioscopy lung cell; (**b–g**) represents an image obtained from the Wiener, Gabor, Hybrid, NLM, TV, and proposed method, respectively

5.2 Quantitative Result Analysis

Tables 3 and 4 show the comparative quantitative study between Wiener, Gabor, hybrid, NLM, TV, and the proposed method, respectively. Literature shows that for a better denoised image, the values of MSE, NAE, and No Reference should be low, while the values of PSNR, CP, UQI, and SSIM should be high. Table 3 presents the quantitative analysis of Fig. 1, where the proposed method has the following values: PSNR, SSIM, MSE, NAE, CP, UQI and no reference is 39.95, 0.868, 0.078, 0.164, 0.596, 0.758, and 44.03, respectively. Table 4 presents the quantitative analysis of Fig. 2, where the proposed method has the values of PSNR, SSIM, MSE, NAE,

Table 3 Quantitative comparison of Fig. 1 between the existing and the proposed method

Methods	Performance parameter						
	PSNR	SSIM	MSE	NAE	CP	UQI	No Ref
Wiener	34.70	0.500	0.112	0.243	0.339	0.511	47.40
Gabor	33.78	0.756	0.345	0.222	0.443	0.602	46.45
Hybrid	32.26	0.647	0.112	0.248	0.361	0.506	49.20
NLM	33.46	0.756	0.112	0.240	0.270	0.603	47.97
TV	35.58	0.639	0.106	0.243	0.337	0.508	45.08
Proposed	39.95	0.868	0.078	0.164	0.596	0.758	44.03

Table 4 Quantitative comparison of Fig. 2 between the existing and the proposed method

Methods	Performance parameter						
	PSNR	SSIM	MSE	NAE	CP	UQI	NO Ref
Wiener	32.31	0.626	0.183	0.239	0.449	0.583	47.27
Gabor	34.58	0.855	0.388	0.226	0.668	0.736	46.45
Hybrid	33.97	0.645	0.132	0.229	0.552	0.576	49.02
NLM	34.27	0.666	0.126	0.235	0.465	0.630	47.97
TV	35.37	0.658	0.112	0.239	0.447	0.594	47.78
Proposed	39.90	0.857	0.068	0.161	0.586	0.756	45.04

CP, UQI and no reference of 39.90, 0.857, 0.068, 0.161, 0.586, 0.756, and 45.04, respectively. Based on the observation, it can be stated that the proposed method has low MSE, NAE, and ref values, while the remaining metrics have high values when compared to other state-of-the-art methods.

6 Conclusion

The primary aim of this work was to denoise microscopic biopsy images that had been distorted by Poisson noise. This goal was accomplished with the aid of the proposed modified fourth order differential equation with maximum likelihood estimation i.e., FOPDEMLE. In the proposed method, MLE offers image restoration, while FOPDE entails the elimination of noise. The efficacy of the proposed method was judged in terms of qualitatively as well as quantitatively for the LC25000 dataset of microscopic biopsy images. The qualitative study concludes that visibility has been improved and restored. The effectiveness of the proposed method is further supported by quantitative analysis using statistical calculations of Mean Square Error, Peak Signal to Noise Ratio and Correlation parameter, Normalized Absolute Error,

Universal Quality Index, Structural Similarity Index Metrics, and No Ref, respectively. A quantitative comparison of the state-of-the-art and the proposed methods shows that the proposed FOPDEMLE is superior for reducing Poisson noise.

References

1. Witschi H (2001) A short history of lung cancer. Toxicol Sci 64(1):4–6. https://doi.org/10.1093/toxsci/64.1.4
2. World Fact Sheet (2021) International agency for research on cancer. Accessed: 17 Oct 2021. [Online]. Available: https://gco.iarc.fr/today/data/factsheets/populations/900-world-fact-sheets.pdf
3. Islam MS, Naima Kaabouch WCH (2013) A survey of medical imaging techniques used for breast cancer detection. In: IEEE international conference on electro-information technology. EIT, pp 1–5
4. Gravel P, Beaudoin G, DeGuise JA (2004) A method for modeling noise in medical images. IEEE Trans Med Imaging 23(10):1221–1232. https://doi.org/10.1109/TMI.2004.832656
5. Mathur P, Sathishkumar K, Chaturvedi M, Das P, Sudarshan KL, Santhappan S, Nallasamy V, John A, Narasimhan S, Roselind FS et al (2020) Report from national cancer registry programme, India. JCO Glob Oncol 6(2020):1063–1075
6. Goyal B, Dogra A, Agrawal S, Sohi BS, Sharma A (2020) Image denoising review: from classical to state-of-the-art approaches. Inform Fusion 55:220–244. https://doi.org/10.1016/j.inffus.2019.09.003
7. Sagheer SV, George SN (2020) A review on medical image denoising algorithms. Biomed Signal Process Control 61:102036. https://doi.org/10.1016/j.bspc.2020.102036
8. Göreke V (2023) A novel method based on Wiener filter for denoising Poisson noise from medical X-Ray images. Biomed Signal Process Control 79:104031. https://doi.org/10.1016/j.bspc.2022.104031
9. Kumar R, Srivastava S, Srivastava R (2017) A fourth order PDE based fuzzy c-means approach for segmentation of microscopic biopsy images in presence of Poisson noise for cancer detection. Comput Methods Programs Biomed 146:59–68. https://doi.org/10.1016/j.cmpb.2017.05.003
10. Kumar A et al (2023) A comparative study of different denoising and enhancement techniques for blood cell images. In: 8th international conference on computing in engineering and technology (ICCET 2023), vol 2023. IET
11. Logambal G, Saravanan V (2015) Detection and segmentation in histopathological images. In: 2015 Global Conference on Communication Technologies, pp 128–132
12. Borkowski AA, Bui MM, Thomas LB, Wilson CP, DeLand LA, Mastorides SM (2019) Lung and colon cancer histopathological image dataset (lc25000). arXiv preprint arXiv:1912.12142
13. Srivastava S, Srivastava R, Sharma N, Singh SK, Sharma S (2012) A fourth order PDE-based non-linear filter for speckle reduction from optical coherence tomography images. Int J Biomed Eng Technol 10(1):55–69. https://doi.org/10.1504/IJBET.2012.049325
14. Srivastava R, Srivastava S (2013) Restoration of Poisson noise corrupted digital images with nonlinear PDE based filters along with the choice of regularization parameter estimation. Pattern Recogn Lett 34(10):1175–1185. https://doi.org/10.1016/j.patrec.2013.03.026
15. Srivastava R, Gupta JRP, Parthasarathy H, Srivastava S (2011) An adaptive non-linear PDE-based speckle reduction technique for ultrasound images. Int J Biomed Eng Technol 6(3):304. https://doi.org/10.1504/IJBET.2011.041468
16. Srivastava S, Sharma N, Singh SK, Srivastava R (2014) A combined approach for the enhancement and segmentation of mammograms using modified fuzzy C-means method in wavelet domain. J Med Phys 39:169–183. https://doi.org/10.4103/0971-6203.139007

17. Srivastava S, Sharma N, Singh SK, Srivastava R (2014) Quantitative analysis of a general framework of a CAD tool for breast cancer detection from mammograms. J Med Imaging Heal Informatics 4(5):654–674. https://doi.org/10.1166/jmihi.2014.1304
18. Kumar A, Kumar P, Srivastava S (2022) A skewness reformed complex diffusion based unsharp masking for the restoration and enhancement of Poisson noise corrupted mammograms. Biomed Signal Process Control 1(73):103421
19. Kumar RR, Kumar A, Srivastava S (2020) Anisotropic diffusion based unsharp masking and crispening for denoising and enhancement of MRI images. In: 2020 international conference on emerging frontiers in electrical and electronic technologies ICEFEET. https://doi.org/10.1109/ICEFEET49149.2020.9186966

Analysis of Dynamic Power Allocation Strategies in Non-orthogonal Multiple Access for 5G Wireless Communication

Bhavika Uikey, Khushi Sahu, Bhumika Neole, Prasheel Thakre, Manish Chawhan, and Ankita Harkare

1 Introduction

Modern times have seen a dramatic increase in technological advancements, particularly in developing countries. From artificial intelligence and 3D printing to nanotechnology and the Internet of Things, there are a plenty of rapidly growing technologies. However, our specific focus is on finding a solution for smartphone-generated data. Our main objective is to enhance user experience by implementing new techniques. As we progress towards the future, the 3rd Generation Partnership Project is currently discussing the development phases for future LTE, and talks have already begun for the fifth generation (5G) of mobile communication networks.

B. Uikey · K. Sahu · B. Neole (✉) · P. Thakre · A. Harkare
Department of Electronics and Communication Engineering, Shri Ramdeobaba College of Engineering and Management, Nagpur, India
e-mail: neoleba@rknec.edu

B. Uikey
e-mail: uikeybh@rknec.edu

K. Sahu
e-mail: sahukr_1@rknec.edu

P. Thakre
e-mail: thakrepn2@rknec.edu

A. Harkare
e-mail: harkareah@rknec.edu

B. Neole · P. Thakre · A. Harkare
Ramdeobaba University, Nagpur, India

M. Chawhan
Department of Electronics and Telecommunication Engineering, Yeshwantrao Chavan College of Engineering, Nagpur, India

K. Kumar Singh et al. (eds.), *Machine Vision and Augmented Intelligence*, Lecture Notes in Electrical Engineering 1211, https://doi.org/10.1007/978-981-97-4359-9_56

Extensive research has explored the different factors and challenges related to the efficacy of NOMA compared to traditional OMA [1–4]. A key aspect of this exploration has been the consideration of power allocation, which plays a crucial role in ensuring fair distribution of resources among downlink users. In fact, power allocation strategies based on real-time or average channel information have been identified as a leading approach [5]. Additionally, another study [6] delves into the topic of power allocation by proposing a novel NOMA design that utilizes multi-user signal intra-beam superposition coding. Rather than offering a mathematical model for each technique, the authors provide a comprehensive overview focused on power allocation methods guided by CSI and QoS considerations.

The cutting-edge 5G technologies dominating the industry are millimeter wave and Multiple-Input Multiple-Output (MIMO), drawing significant attention in recent times [7–9]. However, it is predicted that Orthogonal Multiple Access (OMA) will soon lose its efficiency to Non-Orthogonal Multiple Access (NOMA). This is due to NOMA's unique combination of receiver SIC and transmitter superposition coding techniques [10–12]. In contrast, OMA allocates resources to users based on code, frequency, or time domains, as evident in Fig. 1. Unfortunately, the limited resources of the underwater acoustic network restrict the capability of the OMA system to handle many nodes.

What sets this study apart is its comprehensive approach to two distinct power allocation techniques in NOMA—QoS-based and CSI-based. Instead of simply assigning power based on the users' current CSI, this study takes the channel conditions into account when distributing power via CSI. In contrast to traditional methods, the inverse proportion of power allocation is based on the users' CSI, allowing for a more precise distribution to meet the individual QoS requirements of each user.

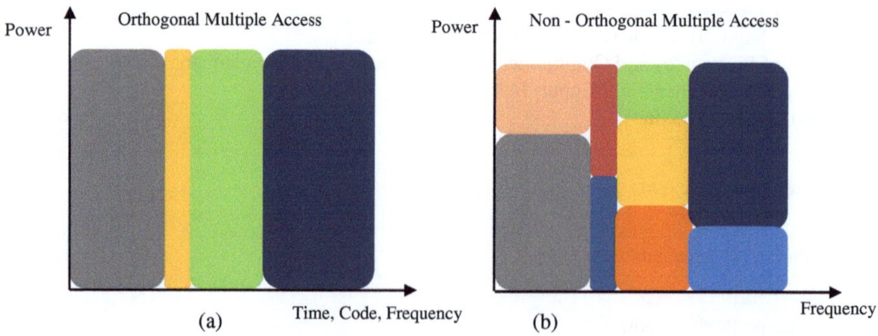

Fig. 1 Resource allocation in **a** orthogonal multiple access, **b** non-orthogonal multiple access

2 Noma System Model

Here we are considering two users U1 and U2 in a downlink NOMA system. The same base station is serving both the users. All users inside the cell are dispersed at random, with BS located at the cell's center (Fig. 2).

Let h_i, $i \in \{1,2\}$ denotes the channel of two users such that $|h_1| > |h_2|$

A superposed signal comprising the data from both users is produced by the base station [2],

$$x_s = \sqrt{a_1 \rho_s} x_1 + \sqrt{a_2 \rho_s} x_2 \quad (1)$$

The term ρ_s, indicates the total transmit Signal to Noise ratio and a_i, $i \in \{1,2\}$ indicates the same percentage of total power to meet the entire power limitation $a_1 + a_2 = 1$, and since $|h_1| > |h_2|$, $a_1 < a_2$. The received symbol at each user is

$$y_i = h_i x_s + n_i \quad (2)$$

$$y_i = h_i\left(\sqrt{a_1 \rho_s} x_1 + \sqrt{a_2 \rho_s} x_2\right) + n_i \quad (3)$$

where n_i, $i \in \{1,2\}$ indicates noise (AWGN).

By considering the U_1 message as noise, U_2 immediately decodes its message. The signal that U_2 has received is

$$y_2 = h_2\left(\sqrt{a_1 \rho_s} x_1 + \sqrt{a_2 \rho_s} x_2\right) + n_2 \quad (4)$$

Corresponding SNR is

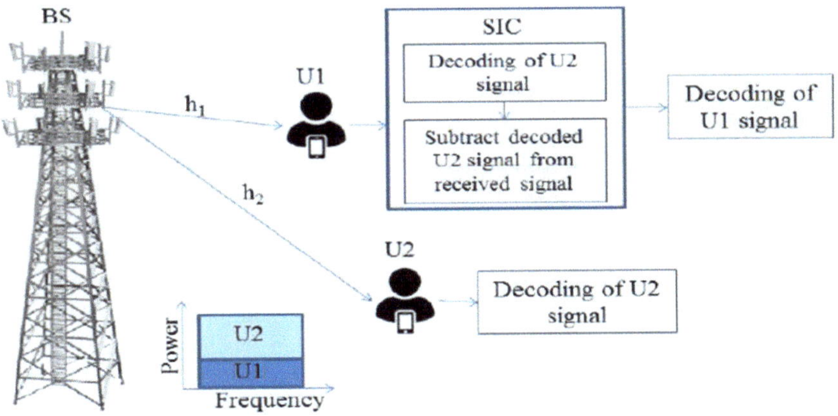

Fig. 2 NOMA in a single cell with two users performing SIC at the receiver

$$\gamma_{u_2}^{x_2} = \frac{a_2\rho_s|h_2|^2}{a_1\rho_s|h_2|^2 + 1} \quad (5)$$

which gives the achievable rate for U_2 as,

$$\left(1 + \frac{a_2\rho_s|h_2|^2}{a_1\rho_s|h_2|^2 + 1}\right) bit/s/Hz \quad (6)$$

However, U_1 performs SIC i.e., first user 2 message is decoded which is subtracted from received signal to obtain user 1 message.

The signal that U_1 has received is,

$$y_1 = h_1\left(\sqrt{a_1\rho_s}x_1 + \sqrt{a_2\rho_s}x_2\right) + n_1 \quad (7)$$

SNR for decoding U_2 at U_1 is,

$$\gamma_{u_1}^{x_2} = \frac{a_2\rho_s|h_1|^2}{a_1\rho_s|h_1|^2 + 1} \quad (8)$$

Signal at U_1 after subtracting interference from U_2 is,

$$y_1 = h_1\left(\sqrt{a_1\rho_s}x_1\right) + n_1 \quad (9)$$

So, SNR for U_1 is,

$$\gamma_{u_1}^{x_1} = a_1\rho_s|h_1|^2 \quad (10)$$

which gives the achievable rate for U_1 as,

$$\text{Achievable rate} = \left(1 + a_1\rho_s|h_1|^2\right)\text{bit/s/Hz} \quad (11)$$

3 Power Allocation Strategies

Power allocation is split into two groups based on channel conditions and a predetermined quality of service per user. These groups are assigned a specific frequency block using algorithms for power allocation. The base station then multiplexes the users' signals depending on the chosen power allocation scheme. All users with the same frequencies are required to decode the messages, with the option to use the Successive Interference Cancellation technique for data decoding. The algorithm used for both proposed power allocation schemes can be seen in Fig. 3.

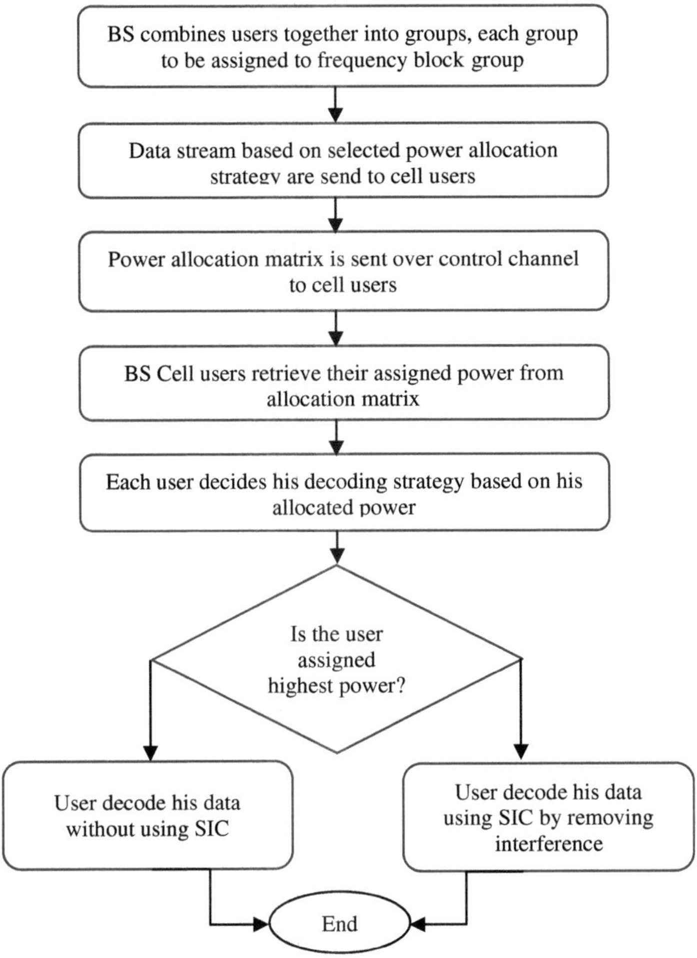

Fig. 3 Proposed NOMA algorithm

3.1 CSI- Power Allocation

In this context, strength factors revolve around the channel-state records experienced by users. The BS uses information obtained from NOMA clients to allocate power coefficients through control channels. The BS determines user classifications and pairs those with strong radio reception with those with weaker reception. Each group is then assigned a frequency block. Therefore, indicators from customers are effectively communicated by multiplexing, utilizing designated powers to ensure that the total transmitted strength per resource block does not exceed capacity. The inverse correlation between channel and power distribution per person is evident. This phenomenon, known as channel inversion, occurs when the base station assigns a higher power allocation to the user experiencing a poor channel condition, and a lower allocation to the one with the best channel circumstances.

3.2 QoS—Power Allocation

The proposed technique employs predetermined Quality of Service (QoS) levels to determine power coefficients for each individual user. These coefficients are based on the user's assigned class, which is determined by their level of importance. Generally, users fall into two categories: high priority and low priority. In order to ensure that high priority users receive the necessary QoS, the base station (BS) must implement user grouping. This allows the BS to allocate the appropriate amount of power to users with high priority, while also removing QoS constraints for those with lower priority. For this to happen, the high priority users are paired with the users with different priority level in the same frequency block. In the meantime, the remaining power is received by lower priority users. Furthermore, the maximum transmitted power is set with a P limit per frequency block. This method also combines signal with predefined powers to be transmitted to users, also known as signal multiplexing.

4 NOMA Challenges and Future Research

The biggest challenges in 5G mobile networks are to fulfill higher spectral efficiency and massive connectivity, the goal is achieving three times the spectral efficiency of 4G mobile network and supporting one million devices per kilometer. A major challenge in transitioning from OFDM to NOMA resides in the reduction of potential in performance of the receiver because of signal decoding complexities. Imperfect SIC adds to the challenge, as it requires accurate decoding of user information in the presence of errors. Moreover, the successful implementation of NOMA involves providing a semi-orthogonal reference signal with careful consideration and addressing the issue of collision probabilities. An additional aspect to be addressed is the optimization of frequency and time to minimize the PARP (Peak-to-Average Ratio of Power) in NOMA which consists of multiple carriers and ultimately achieving high spectral efficiency.

One major challenge with NOMA, in contrast to the OMA method, is the implementation of a personalized power allocation system at the transmitter. However, attaining the best possible throughput and equity among users calls for dynamically assigning power, which can be a demanding computational process. Furthermore, investigations into optimal power distribution for Cognitive Radio Networks (CRN) using NOMA are currently limited.

5 Simulations and Result

The NOMA system simulation shown in Fig. 4a reveals a clear trend: as transmit power increases, the achievable capacity for both users also improves. However, user 1's achievable capacity is slightly lower compared to user 2's. This is because user 1 receives a lower power allocation, as illustrated in Fig. 2. Interestingly, in the OMA scenario depicted in Fig. 4b, the trend is reversed. The user with lower power, namely user 1, has a higher achievable capacity compared to the user with higher power. This highlights the potential advantages of NOMA over OMA in terms of maximizing user capacity (Tables 1 and 2).

Looking at Fig. 5b, it becomes apparent that user 1 has a lower outage probability than user 2. This is because user 2 is at a larger distance from the base station. Comparing Fig. 5a and b, it can be inferred that NOMA has lower outage probability than OMA. These simulations prove that NOMA is much more effective than OMA to achieve lower outage probability.

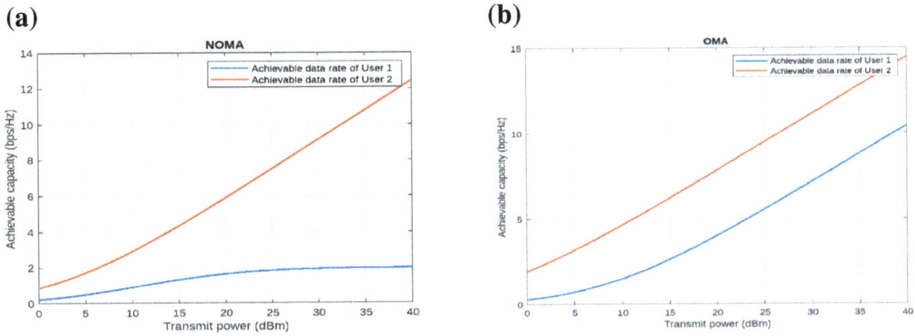

Fig. 4 **a** Achievable capacity versus Tx power in NOMA. **b** Achievable capacity versus Tx power in OMA

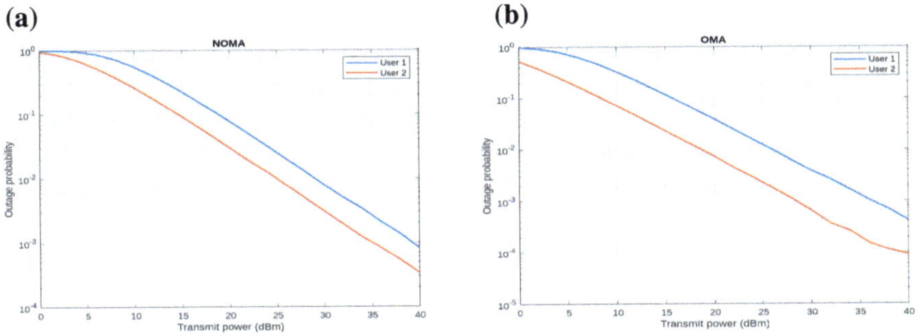

Fig. 5 **a** Outage probability versus Tx power in NOMA. **b** Outage probability versus Tx power in OMA

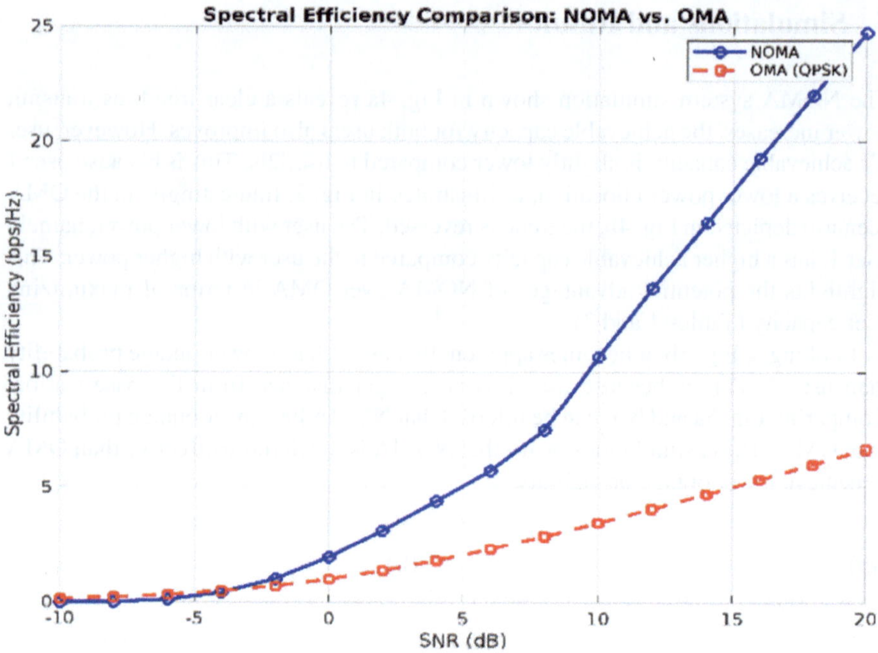

Fig. 6 Spectral efficiency comparison of NOMA versus OMA

Table 1 Parameters for outage probability

Parameters	OMA		NOMA	
	User 1	User 2	User 1	User 2
Distances of users from base station	1000	500	1000	500
Power allocation factor	0.75	0.25	0.75	0.25
Path loss exponent	4		4	

In Fig. 6 we have compared spectral efficiencies of NOMA and OMA. Spectral efficiency is the measure of data that can be transmitted over a specific bandwidth. The graph shows that NOMA has higher spectral efficiency than OMA at a particular SNR value. It can also be inferred that NOMA system efficiently uses the allotted frequency as compared to OMA.

Table 2 Parameters for spectral efficiency

Parameters	Values
Number of users (K)	2
Transmit power for OMA	1
Power for user 1 in NOMA	0.7
Power for user 2 in NOMA	0.3
SNR range1	−10 to 20

6 Conclusion

This research paper presents a comparison between Orthogonal Multiple Access (OMA) and Non-Orthogonal Multiple Access (NOMA) techniques based on two different power allocation strategies. Our simulation results show that NOMA performs better than OMA in terms of reduced outage probability of $10^{-0.5}$ and achieves higher spectral efficiency of 25 bps/Hz at SNR value of 20 dB. While OMA assigns different data rates to each user, NOMA manages and assigns varying data rates among users. In simple terms, NOMA is better at handling multiple users with different data rate requirements without delay.

References

1. El-Sayed MM, Ibrahim AS, Khairy MM (2016) Power allocation strategies for non-orthogonal multiple access. In: 2016 international conference on selected topics in mobile & wireless networking (MoWNeT)
2. Thakre PN, Pokle SB (2022) A survey on power allocation in PD-NOMA for 5G wireless communication systems. In: 2022 10th international conference on emerging trends in engineering and technology—signal and information processing (ICETET-SIP-22), Nagpur, India, pp 1–5. https://doi.org/10.1109/ICETET-SIP-2254415.2022.9791576
3. Thakre P, Pokle S (2022) Optimal power allocation for NOMA-based Internet of things over OFDM sub bands. Int J Next-Gener Comput 13(5). https://doi.org/10.47164/ijngc.v13i5.909
4. Mouni NS, Kumar A, Upadhyay PK (2021) Adaptive user pairing for NOMA systems with imperfect SIC
5. Nonaka N, Kishiyama Y, Higuchi K (2014) Non orthogonal multiple access using intra-beam superposition coding and SIC in base station cooperative MIMO cellular downlink. In: Vehicular technology conference (VTC Fall)
6. Ding Z, Yang Z, Fan P, Poor HV (2014) On the performance of non-orthogonal multiple access in 5G systems with randomly deployed users
7. Khan AA, Almuzaini KK, Macedo VDJ, Ojo S, Minchula VK, Roy V (2023) MaReSPS for energy efficient spectral precoding technique in large scale MIMO-OFDM. Phys Commun 58:102057. ISSN 1874-4907. https://doi.org/10.1016/j.phycom.2023.102057
8. Ali KS, Khan AA, T P, Ur Rehman A, Ouahada K (2023) Learned-SBL-GAMP based hybrid precoders/combiners in millimeter wave massive MIMO systems. PLoS ONE 18(9): e0289868. https://doi.org/10.1371/journal.pone.0289868
9. Uthansakul P, Ahmad KA (2019) On the energy efficiency of millimeter wave massive MIMO based on hybrid architecture. Energies 12(11):2227. https://doi.org/10.3390/en12112227

10. Benjebbour A, Saito Y, Kishiyama Y, Li A, Harada A, Nakamura T (2013) Concept and practical considerations of non-orthogonal multiple access (Noma) for future radio access. In: Intelligent signal processing and communications systems (ISPACS)
11. Islam SMR, Avazov N, Dobre OA, Kwak KS (2016) Power-domain non-orthogonal multiple access (NOMA) in 5G systems: potentials and challenges. In: IEEE communications surveys & tutorials
12. Arachchillage USSS, Jayakody DNK, Biswash SK, Dinis R (2018) Recent advances and future research challenges in non-orthogonal multiple access for 5G networks

Effectiveness of Reinforced Concrete Column Jacketing in Retrofitting RC Frames with Vertical Irregularity

Chandan Kumar and Praveen Anand

1 Introduction

Earthquakes are the world's most devastating and unexpected disasters. More people die as a consequence of unsafe buildings than earthquakes. A few of the numerous factors that contribute to unsafe buildings include plan irregularities and vertical irregularities, stiffness and strength irregularity, torsion irregularity, mass irregularity etc. Due to urbanisation and population increase, the majority of reinforced buildings have the distinctive feature of leaving the ground floor and other stories open for social and practical demands like parking for cars, shops, reception lobbies, enormous conference rooms, etc. These buildings are referred to as open storey buildings or soft storey buildings.

The addition of wing walls to a low-rise reinforced concrete frame constitutes a significant technological development in the area of retrofitting, as documented by Yang et al. [1]. According to the results of the study, including wing walls into a seismic retrofitting plan results in improvements to the structural rigidity, load bearing capacity, and energy dissipation of the building. It is essential to keep in mind that the overall ductility will be reduced as a consequence of using this retrofitting procedure. While the frame behaved linearly for the low degree of base shear, it became non-linear as the value of base shear increased. The frame has always been designed in this way.

Al-Dwaik and Armouti [2] On a five-story frame, research became performed to assess the effectiveness of international retrofitting techniques, RC jacketing and steel bracing. The inquiry made use of a number of dynamic and static non-linear evaluation methodologies. Study consequences confirmed that RC jacketing became less powerful than using additional steel members as a structural component brought to a present RC frame in phrases of ductility, elastic stiffness, and cost-effectiveness.

C. Kumar (✉) · P. Anand
Department of Civil Engineering, National Institute of Technology Patna, Patna, India
e-mail: chandank.ph21.ce@nitp.ac.in

K. Kumar Singh et al. (eds.), *Machine Vision and Augmented Intelligence*, Lecture Notes in Electrical Engineering 1211, https://doi.org/10.1007/978-981-97-4359-9_57

Finite element evaluation-based totally numerical simulations provided support for the claim made before, as demonstrated by Anand and Sinha in their study [3–5]. Another study confirmed that the use of reinforced concrete (RC) jacketing significantly increases the ductility of columns [6].

It has been observed that the strong column weak beam concept improves the shear capability of columns. This method is easy to expand and improves both shear and bending performance simultaneously. Furthermore, it's been shown that the use of a jacket, at the side of its guide and a certain kind of concrete, can also extensively enhance the section's ductility and stiffness. The installation of strengthened concrete (RC) jacketing has been proven in a different have a look at too seriously increase the column's ductility [7]. In every other investigation, the ultimate load-bearing abilities had been notably accelerated by means of two to three instances whilst excessive-overall performance self-compacting concrete became added to jacketed columns with thicknesses of 25 and 35 mm [8]. In order to enhance structural compliance and protection, composites are often used for repairing areas of reinforced concrete (RC) additives which might be either damaged or prone to degradation. Analysing the bond properties of a newly evolved composite's several structural parts is step one in the direction of assessing the composite's overall performance [9, 10]. An standard overview of the available retrofitting techniques has additionally been nicely documented in conjunction with their blessings and drawbacks [11].

The main objectives of this study are to (1) evaluate the effects of a stiffness irregularity on the performance and behaviour of RC columns and (2) assess the effectiveness of an RC jacket in reinforcing preexisting RC columns. In addition, the study evaluates the behaviour changes, including base shear and displacement, that occur in a concrete-framed building after an earthquake and attempts to predict them. Reinforced concrete jackets have been installed on the building's columns.

2 Methodology

The procedure followed to study the behaviour of a G + 5 RC building with stiffness irregularity. Such irregularities lead to the formation of plastic hinges in columns which further may lead to its failure. Such columns have been retrofitted with RC jacketing columns.

Two models of the building that have been considered under this study are.

- Building B1 is a G + 5 Multistorey RC Frame Building without a Soft Storey.
- Building B2 is a G + 5 Soft storey on a multi-story RC frame building 35% of the building's ground floor is characterized by stiffness.
- Building B3 is a multi-story, soft-story RC frame structure. On the ground floor of the building, there is a stiffness of 35%, and the columns on the ground floor are jacketed.

3 Parameters

These are the factors that were taken into consideration during the performance evaluation.

3.1 *Description of Building*

Design of the structure	SMRF
A total number of stories	G + 5
Height and there is a soft storey height	4.25 m and 4.75 m
Other storey's height	3 m
Varieties of soil	Medium soil
Zone prone to earthquakes	IV

3.2 *Materials*

Concrete of a certain grade	M20
In terms of jacketing, the grade of concrete	M25
Kind of steel grade	Fe415

3.2.1 Member Dimensions

Dimensions of the Beam	400 mm × 500 mm
The dimension of Column	600 mm × 600 mm
The thickness of the slab	130 mm
Main wall thickness	230 mm
Partition wall thickness	115 mm

The geometrical characteristics of the multi-story frame in the current study are as follows for a 6-storey RC building:

Numerous types of buildings	SMRF (Special moment resisting frame)
A total number of stories	6 stories (G + 5)
Dimensions of the Plan	30 m × 30 m
The height of the floor in each storey	3 m
Considering a floor height of 35% stiffness	4.25 m
To achieve a floor height of 25% stiffness	4.75 m
The total number of bays in the x-axis	6
The total number of bays in the y-axis	6
The width of the bay	5 m
Supports the base	Fixed
The type of structure	RCC Framed structure
Concrete of a certain grade	M20
Kind of steel grade	Fe415
The dimension of Column	600 mm × 600 mm
Dimensions of the Beam	400 mm × 500 mm
Dimensions of the jacketing columns	800 mm × 800 mm with M25 Grade of concrete
Depth of the slab	130 mm
The thickness of the wall	230 mm and partition wall Thickness—115 mm

3.3 Design Data

According to IS 875:1987 Part 1 [12] Below is a list of dead loads that have been extracted from a variety of walls and floors.

Dead load on the wall is considered to be 20 KN/m^3

The dead load on the floor finish is considered to be 1 KN/m^2

The dead load on the roof treatment is considered to be 1.5 KN/m^2

According to IS 875:1987 Part 2 [13] Below is a list of live loads on various floors.

The floor's live load is calculated as 3 KN/m^2

Consider the live load on the roof to be 1.5 KN/m^2.

4 Modelling and Analysis

The RC frame structure of the building that is being considered for analysis is modelled and studied with the help of the Integrated Building Design Software SAP 2000. Figure 1 depicts the building frame in both its plan and 3D forms. Mass, stiffness, and strength are all aspects of a building that are taken into consideration throughout the modelling process. The beam and column that were modelled

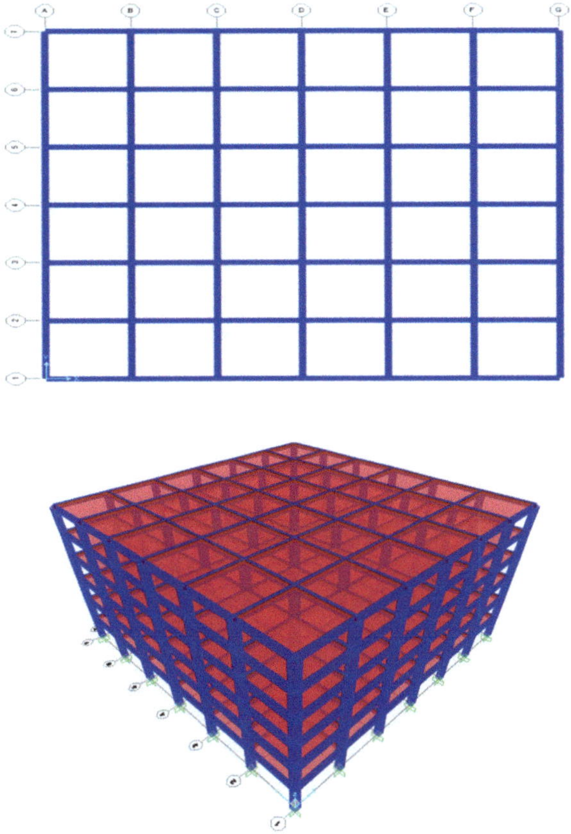

Fig. 1 Plan and extruded view of the building frame

are sections that make up the frame. In the ground plan, columns are said to be firmly planted. Figure 2 illustrates the measurement of the beams and columns in their sectional dimensions. According to the building documents, Roof and slabs are shown as stacked parts with reinforcement. Although the foundation systems of the buildings are distinct from one another, for the purpose of simplicity, we shall assume them all to be fixed instead. The interaction between the ground and the structure is not taken into consideration in the analysis. Considering that there is no hinge formation, the modelling has failed to take into consideration the very low ductility of the brick walls. The software has already determined the dead loads of structural parts. This type's design spectrum in its entirety. II For the purpose of calculating the spectral acceleration coefficient, the soil that has the given code is chosen (Sa/g). This is how the zone factor Z is calculated 0.24 for Zone IV [14]. For reinforced concrete buildings that have a special moment resistant frame (SMRF), the value of the response reduction factor R will be 5. Importance factor of the building is considered to be 1 when compared to all other types of buildings. Considering that the building is just 21.5 feet tall at its highest point, the impact of wind load is not

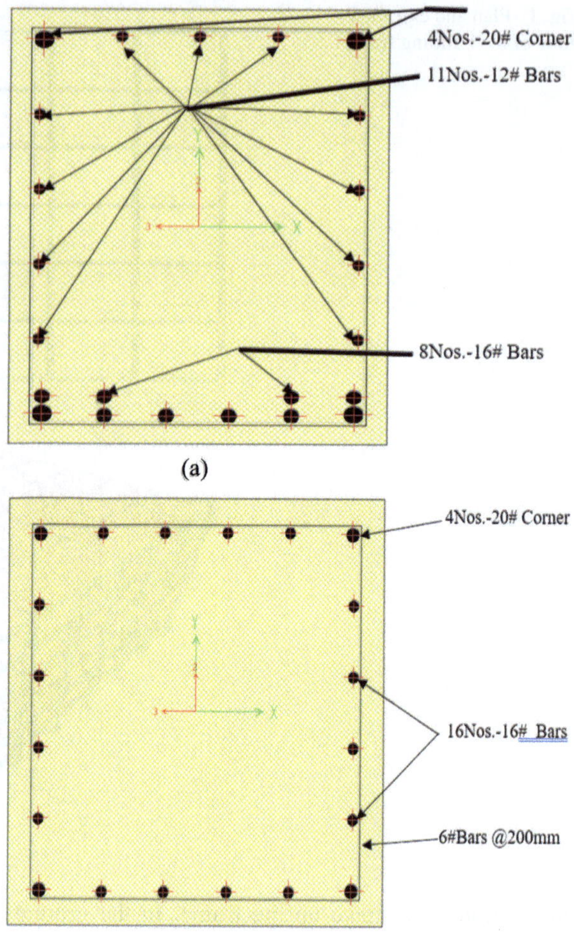

Fig. 2 Cross-section details of **a** beam section (400 mm × 500 mm), **b** column section (600 × 600)

taken into consideration. In this case, the thickness of the jacket is 100 mm [15] the particulars of which reinforcement is shown in Fig. 3. As may be observed from Fig. 4, the elevational view of buildings B1 and B2 is shown.

The completion of the pushover analysis of the buildings raises the possibility that the technique will really be executed effectively. There is a concentrated plastic hinge at both ends of the modelled beam and column. Only M3 hinges may be used on beams, and only PMM hinges on columns. There is no need for a simulated shear hinge since the member's shear strength is more than enough to meet the shear requirement.

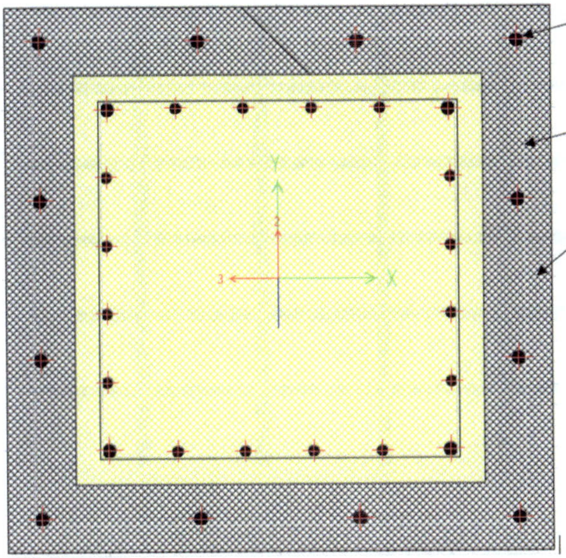

Fig. 3 Cross-sectional details of the jacketed column (800 mm × 800 mm)

The three buildings undergo a pushover analysis in which the lateral load is applied in a monotonically consistent way with respect to the preexisting force of gravity. Rooftop evidence points to the presence of both the building's base force and its goal displacement.

The building is subjected to lateral stress until it reaches a collapse mechanism, after which it is remodelled with the nonlinear effect considered. When the base force and roof displacement are plotted, the result is the pushover curve. Their acquisition is the driving force behind this action. The data provides an overall idea of the building's maximum base shear capacity. The idea of the global rigidity of typical structures is also provided, which is a huge plus. The analysis is followed by a comparison analysis via the use of the following: the inter-story drift ratio, the story deformation vs base shear ratio, the development of hinges at various stages of the analysis, and the Pushover curve. These analyses are all made subsequent to the analysis itself. The capacity curve, often called the pushover curve, is the most significant outcome that may be achieved in a pushover analysis.

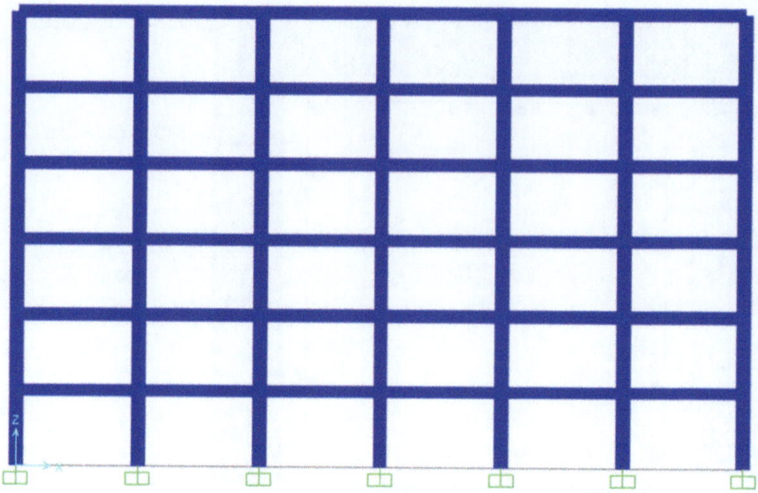

(a)

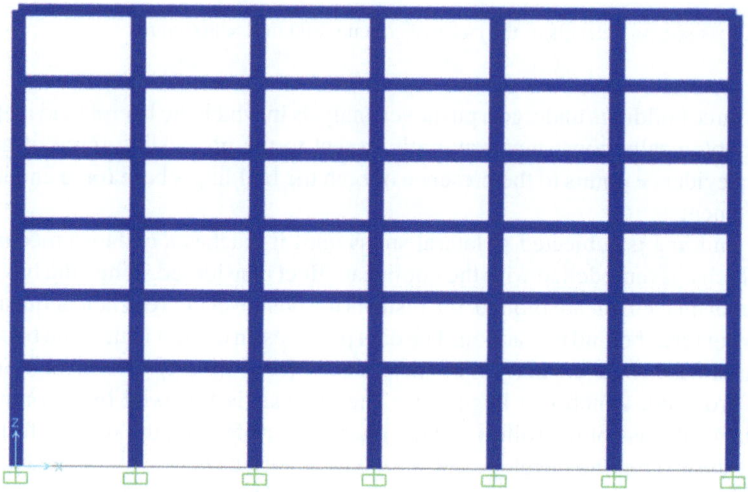

(b)

Fig. 4 Building B1: G + 5 multistoried RC frame building **a** without soft storey and **b** with soft storey at ground floor

5 Results and Discussion

The pushover curve for the B1 building model is shown in Fig. 5. The maximum allowable displacement with a base force of 23,290.658 KN and the pushover curve is 0.149677 m.

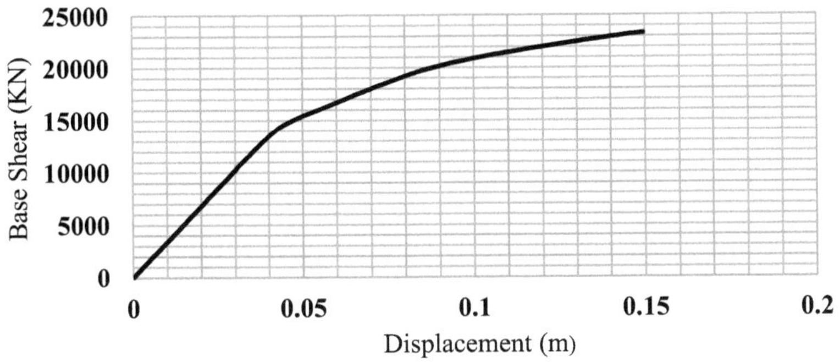

Fig. 5 Pushover curve for building B1

Building B2's pushover curve is shown in Fig. 6, and the building frame's displacement at the story level is shown in Fig. 7. The same paper contains both figures. A multi-story RC frame structure with a B2: G + 5 orientation has been found to exhibit a pushover curve. The building's ground level has a 35% soft story stiffness. In both cases, the pushover curve is visible before and after the column is jacketed. The pushover curve is therefore clearly not to be disregarded. The building's ultimate load bearing capacity and rigidity were both significantly improved once the jacketing was introduced. There has been observation of this. The building's final deflection capability was also enhanced by this approach. Possible modification to the base shear of both buildings may occur if the rate of deflection were to rise. Possible observation of this is warranted. For a base force of 17,863 KN in both the X-Direction and the Y-Direction, the maximum displacement is determined to be 0.259103 m using the pushover curve. It was discovered that the maximum displacement for the original construction was 0.261812 m, and the base force was 17,876 KN. Following the manufacture of plastic hinges in building B2, the majority of the hinges would be located between point B and IO (pink colour) and IO to LS (blue colour) except ground floor. The majority of the ground level plastic hinges are positioned between points C and D (yellow colour), however as shown in Fig. 7, there are a few that might fail. These hinges are located between points CP and C (green colour). i.e., the collapse of that column, and jacketing it is important and needed. Jacketing may be applied to the ground and first floor of the building on the column that is most vulnerable to plastic hinge failure. By doing so, the column's structural integrity is safeguarded. After the jacketing process is complete, the majority of the hinges are located between points B and IO (red colour), and IO and LS (black colour), as shown in Fig. 6. The figure depicts this. It is possible to determine the base shear and maximum displacement of a jacketed structure using the Pushover curve. Specifically, 0.349191 m is the maximum displacement in the X-Direction for a base force of 34,796.5 KN, and 0.349191 m is the maximum displacement in the Y-Direction for the same base value. It turns out that both of these numbers are correct. The building's change in stiffness and ultimate load bearing capacity were

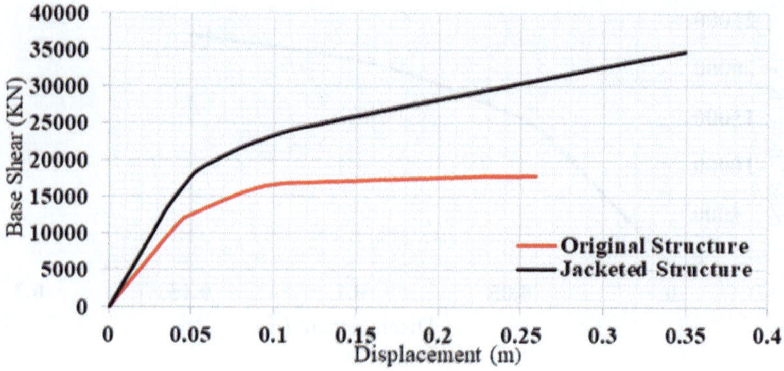

Fig. 6 Pushover curve for building B2

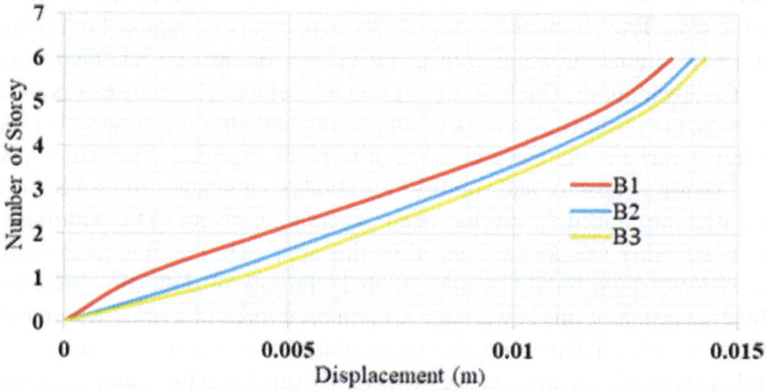

Fig. 7 Story level v/s displacement plot of Equivalent static analysis for B1, B2 and B3

both significantly increased after jacketing. Prior to and during the jacketing procedure, this is accurate for column cases. A considerable improvement in the building's stiffness was achieved by jacketing it. The building's overall stiffness has gone up since the structure's ultimate load bearing capacity has gone up.

6 Conclusion

Results from the research suggest that retrofitting is one option for improving a building's seismic performance. This analysis includes the utilization of jacketing procedures to strengthen the soft story, which is particularly susceptible to severe seismic damages because of its reduced lateral stiffness. The purpose of this inquiry was to strengthen the soft story. A 5 storey RC frame was simulated in SAP2000 for evaluating the impact and performance of RC column jacketing on the overall frame.

After that, the frame's columns were jacketed, and an evaluation of the structure's overall performance using static linear and static non-linear analysis was done. It aids in comparing the analysis findings of the original building with those obtained after jacketing, which produced satisfactory outcomes. The base shear bearing capacity of a structure decreases with time as the stiffness-to-base shear bearing capacity ratio decreases. The column jacketing technique was executed according to the guidelines provided in IS 15988-2013 [15]. The procedures were discovered to be quite effective in increasing the column's strength, just as planned. The pushover curve, which was generated from the static nonlinear analysis, showed that the strength of the jacketed frame had grown substantially, around twice as much as the capacity of the currently employed frame. This is so due to the formation of the pushover curve. For the initial value of base shear, the frame behaved linearly; however, for larger levels, it showed non-linear behavior. The building's deformation capacity increases when the jacketing is applied, however the increase in final deformation is less compared to the increase in resistance to deformation. Retrofitting offers structural engineers a great opportunity to do further study. An RC-jacketed square column was the only form of column tested during this inquiry. It should be mentioned that round and rectangular columns are also quite prevalent. This paves the way for investigating the potential use of RC jacketing in similar columns.

References

1. Yang W, Tian M, Xu W, Ju J (2021) Seismic retrofitting of low-rise RC frame structures with wing walls. KSCE J Civ Eng 25:4359–4373. https://doi.org/10.1007/s12205-021-0051-8
2. Aldwaik MM, Armouti NS (2013) Analytical case study of seismic performance of retrofit strategies for reinforced concrete frames: steel bracing with shear links versus column jacketing. Jordan J Civil Eng 7:26–43
3. Sinha AK, Anand P (2022) Seismic performance of reinforced concrete frame with concrete jacketed columns. Proc Int Struct Eng Construct 9:2
4. Anand P, Sinha AK (2020) Effect of reinforced concrete jacketing on axial load capacity of reinforced concrete column. Civil Eng J 6:1266–1272
5. Anand P, Sinha AK, Kumar C (2021) Investigation of reinforced concrete jacketed columns under different loading conditions. Int J Adv Technol Eng Explor 8:957–969. https://doi.org/10.19101/IJATEE.2021.874182
6. Rodriguez M, Park R (1994) Seismic load tests on reinforced concrete columns strengthened by jacketing. ACI Struct J 91:150–159. https://doi.org/10.14359/4593
7. Vaghani MV, Vasanwala SA, Desai AK (2014) Advanced retrofitting techniques for RC building: a state of an art review. Int J Curr Eng Technol 4:579–584
8. Tayeh BA, Naja MA, Shihada S, Arafa M (2019) Repairing and strengthening of damaged RC columns using thin concrete jacketing. Adv Civil Eng
9. Jahangir H, Esfahani MR (2018) Numerical study of bond—slip mechanism in advanced externally bonded strengthening composites. KSCE J Civ Eng 22:4509–4518. https://doi.org/10.1007/s12205-018-1662-6
10. Ayinde OO, Wu E, Zhou G, Malidadi T (2022) Influence of interface roughness geometrical parameters on the shear behaviour of old and new concrete interface. Asian J Civil Eng 23:229–247. https://doi.org/10.1007/s42107-022-00420-4

11. Anand P, Sinha AK (2022) Seismic strengthening and retrofitting techniques and solutions for an existing RC frame: an overview. In: A system engineering approach to disaster resilience: select proceedings of VCDRR 2021, pp 531–539
12. Bureau of Indian Standards. IS 875–1 (1987) Code of practice for design loads (other than earthquake) for buildings and structures, part 1: dead loads—unit weights of building material and stored materials (incorporating IS 1911: 1967). n.d.
13. Bureau of Indian Standards. IS 875–2 (1987) Code of practice for design loads (other than earthquake) for buildings and structures, part 2: imposed loads. n.d.
14. IS 1893 (2016) Criteria for earthquake resistant design of structures part 1 general provisions and buildings (6th revision). n.d.
15. IS 15988 (2013) Seismic evaluation and strengthening of existing reinforced concrete buildings—guidelines

Tokenization's Potential for Santhali Language Processing

Anand Kumar Ohm, Aman Kumar Panday, and Koushlendra Kumar Singh

1 Introduction

Santhali (Ol-Chiki: ᱥᱟᱱᱛᱟᱲᱤ), Otherwise also known as Santali, is the Munda subfamily of the Austroasiatic spoken languages, which includes Ho and Mundari. It is spoken by roughly about 7.6 million people (including 6.9 million Indians who are native speakers [1, 2]. Santhali has created a tiny place in the larger digital media landscape. Regional language Sathali is native to the states of Jharkhand and West Bengal, as well as a few other parts of the country. **Ol-Chiki** is alphabetic for the Santhali language which was created by Pandit Raghunath Murmu in the 20Th century. Ol-Chiki is alphabetic without sharing any syllabic properties of the other Indic scripts [3]. The proposed space for encoding of Ol-Chiki script in Unicode is U+2D80–U+2DAF in the Basic Multilingual Plane (decimal value: 11,648 to 11,696) [4]. Its implementation level is 2 because of its nature of combining characters. The main reason behind the lack of language available on the computer internet is its writing and structure which is not adopted by researchers and people who are actual speakers of this language [5]. During the last few years, some improvement has been see in the form of virtual keyboard, and some newspaper in Santhali is available online But most famous companies like Google and Microsoft have not adopted it for translation or other language activity, the main reason for this is the unavailability of language corpus and tokenized sentence [6].

A. K. Ohm (✉) · A. K. Panday · K. K. Singh
Machine Vision and Intelligence Lab, Department of CSE, National Institute of Technology Jamshedpur, Jharkhand, India
e-mail: 2022rscs016@nitjsr.ac.in

A. K. Panday
e-mail: 2019ugcs003@nitjsr.ac.in

K. K. Singh
e-mail: koushlendra.cse@nitjsr.ac.in

K. Kumar Singh et al. (eds.), *Machine Vision and Augmented Intelligence*, Lecture Notes in Electrical Engineering 1211, https://doi.org/10.1007/978-981-97-4359-9_58

Table 1 Punctuation marks in Santhali

।	ᱢᱩᱪᱟᱹᱫ(muchad)	Full stop
,	ᱠᱮᱪᱮᱫ((keched)	Comma
;	ᱛᱚᱯᱟᱜ((topag)	Semicolon
?	ᱠᱩᱠᱞᱤ(kukli)	Question mark
()	ᱦᱟᱹᱨᱩᱵ(harub)	Parenthesis

We read word by word from left to right or right to left in some languages to interpret its meaning and read it till we encounter a full stop or breaking sentence notation. The computer system does the same for language to understand it, let's say we give a paragraph to the system to get any information from the paragraph then it will break a paragraph into sentences, and from all the sentences need a single word further it should break into characters to understand and provide us with information accordingly. This process is known as Tokenization. It enables the NLP system to work with smaller more concise components. Building machines that can manipulate written, spoken, and arranged human language or data that resembles human language is known as Natural Language Processing. Breaking a sentence from a paragraph requires a punctuation mark, In the Santhali language Ol-chiki letters there are five punctuation marks in use [4]. The first one is a full stop, It can identify as a single vertical line "।", and it marks the end of a sentence. In Santali, it is called ᱢᱩᱪᱟᱹᱫ(muchad). The second is the comma which can be identified as the "," symbol and is used for partially complete sentences. In Santhali it is called ᱠᱮᱪᱮᱫ((keched). Third is the semicolon which is identified as the ";" symbol used in place of the period to separate the two sentences when the second sentence starts in continuation on the first sentence. In Santhali it is called as ᱛᱚᱯᱟᱜ((topag). Fourth is the question mark which can be identified as the "?" symbol and it is used for completing questionable sentences. In Santhali it is called as ᱠᱩᱠᱞᱤ(kukli). The last one is Parentheses which can be identified as the "(" and ")" symbol used to add any more information or comments that may be relevant. In anthali ᱦᱟᱹᱨᱩᱵ(harub). All punctuations are shown in Table 1 with their appropriate meanings.

Ol-chiki has a total of 30 letters which are shown in the Image with their details. All of these letters have been illustrated in Fig. 1.

Natural Language Processing (NLP) has countless use cases such as machine translation, text summarization, chatbot creation, and spam detection. Extensive work has been done on NLP for most of the other Indian and Western languages. English and Hindi as the most spoken languages of India are rich resources like corpus and multilingual datasets languages like Santhali compared to other Indian languages. Santhali language serves as a tool to express a specific group's culture and identity still there are little work has been done yet.

The present work, Present different tokenization methods available in other languages to tokenization of Santhali language's Ol-chiki format sentence by showing a comparison between all available tokenization methods and making it available for further use like understanding the language also utilizing translation to other languages like English and more.

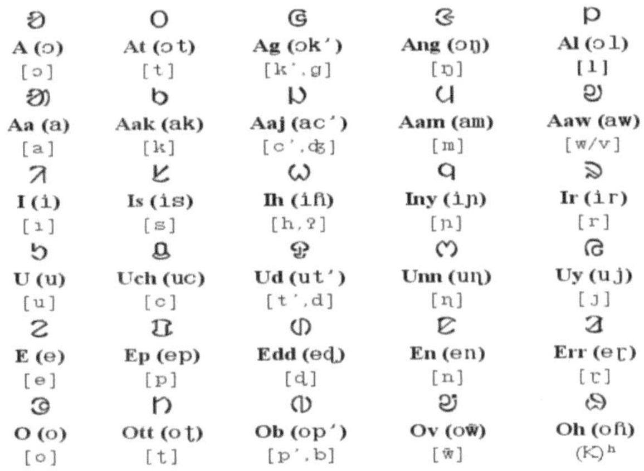

Fig. 1 Ol-Chiki script [7]

The rest of the paper is organized as follows. In Sect. 2, we discussed related works, and Intriguing various methods of Tokenization for Santhali language are discussed in Sect. 3. Section 4 discusses the benefits of tokenization of Santhali. Conclusion and future works are discussed in Sect. 5.

2 Related Work

Developing NLP applications in the research and development of Natural Language Toolkit (NLTK) has been encouraged [8]. It is a Python library that provides comprehensive suitable resources and tools for various NLP tasks. In recent years, language-specific NLP toolkits have gained prominence [9]. The process of developing toolkits is continuing. Language models are becoming more and more crucial in jobs involving natural language processing. Due to their capacity to comprehend and produce language that is similar to human speech, they have been used in many applications, including chatbots machine translation, text summarization, and virtual assistants [10–12]. In terms of technologies, There are various toolkits which have developed for different languages but for a language like the Sathali writing system is alphabetic, Ol-chiki generates a word by combining alphabets and ends with a space character for the next word [13]. For example, ᱢ+ᱮ+ᱫis ᱢᱮᱫ(med') meaning 'eye' in English. Similarly for generating a sentence, it can be an addition of words with a space between two words example "ᱟᱢᱚᱜ"+ "ᱧᱩᱴᱩᱢ" + "ᱪᱮᱫ" + ᱟᱢᱚᱜ ᱧᱩᱴᱩᱢ ᱪᱮᱫ?is hat is your name?) also sentence complete with a stop word which is shown by "?" in this example. It is similar to English language. Still, less attention is given to ensuring comparable performance in languages other than English. Such differences may have negative effects on the real world. Providing access to the same technology in many languages but excluding some users, No matter whether a language is supported by design or by accident, we should give it the same consideration when it comes to performance and accessibility. Because of the similarity of sentence formation NLTK tool lit can be used for Santhali language tasks. The representation of a language in a proper manner is necessary before it may be processed automatically. Tokenization, which converts natural language into sequences of tokens drawn from a finite and predetermined collection, is the current standard practice.

2.1 Tokenization Algorithms

Tokenization is the process of dividing a sentence or paragraph into tokens. These symbols could be words, letters, or word fragments. The tokenizing text enables NLP systems to work with smaller, more concise components [14]. This makes it possible to analyze, model, and comprehend textual data more precisely. These tokens can be sentences, words (sets of multiple words together/individual words), parts of words, characters, punctuations, special tokens, etc. [15].

2.1.1 Types of Tokenization

We now understand that Tokenization assists in dividing the original text into letters, words, sentences, etc. depending on the issue at hand. Tokenization can be categorized into four types. Each type of tokenization's is depicted in Fig. 2.

(a) Word tokenization (b) Sub word tokenization.

(c) Character tokenization (d) Sentence tokenization.

(a) **Word tokenization**: If you split the text data (or document) into words, it's called Word Tokenization. The example shown in figure [16] in Santhali language words can be identified by space after characters.
(b) **Sub word tokenization**: If a word is split into sub words, it is known as a sub word tokenization.

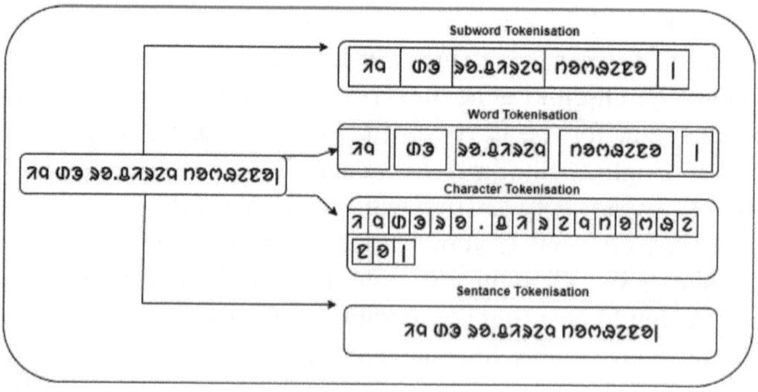

Fig. 2 Different types of tokenization

(c) **Character tokenization**: Splitting the document or paragraph into individual characters is known as Character Tokenization.
(d) **Sentence tokenization**: The concept of dividing a document or paragraph into sentences is called a sentence tokenizer.

3 Materials and Methods

Due to linguistic reasons and technical limitations, textual data has typically been split into "sentences" (or "utterances," etc.) and "words" in NLP. As a result, in this section, we start with the very first text data preparation task, which is sentence/word segmentation of the Santhali language Ol-chiki front. for this purpose we require a sentence or paragraph of ol chichi so we took a paragraph sentence from the 30Th of June 2023 Twitter (Now called 'X') the President of India's Twitter handle which was a thread about 'Hul Day' in Ol-chiki which is "ᱦᱩᱞ ᱢᱟᱦᱟᱸ ᱨᱮᱥᱟᱱᱛᱟᱲ ᱦᱩᱞ ᱨᱮᱱᱳᱢᱳᱨ ᱡᱤᱣᱤ ᱟᱞᱟᱭ ᱛᱮᱱᱠᱚ ᱥᱤᱫᱚ-ᱠᱟᱹᱱᱦᱩ, ᱪᱟᱸ ᱫᱽ - ᱵᱷᱟᱭᱨᱚ ᱟᱨᱯᱷᱩᱞᱚ ᱡᱷᱟᱱᱚ ᱥᱟᱶᱛᱮᱥᱟᱱᱟᱢ ᱵᱤᱨᱵᱟᱱᱰᱟ ᱠᱚ ᱜᱚᱲ ᱡᱚᱦᱟᱨ ᱛᱩᱞᱩᱡ ᱢᱟᱹᱱᱢᱟᱱᱚᱛᱤᱧ ᱪᱟᱞ ᱟᱠᱚ ᱠᱟᱱᱟ ᱾ᱟᱹᱫᱤᱵᱟᱹᱥᱤ ᱥᱚᱢᱟᱡᱽ ᱨᱮᱱᱟᱜ ᱩᱱᱩᱨᱩᱢ, ᱢᱟᱹᱱᱢᱩᱨᱟᱹᱫᱽ ᱟᱨᱱᱤᱡᱽ ᱥᱟᱥᱚᱱᱦᱩᱫᱤᱥ ᱠᱟᱛᱮᱩᱱᱠᱩ ᱫᱚ ᱚᱱᱮᱭᱟᱭ ᱟᱨ ᱨᱚᱰᱚᱡᱠᱚᱪᱞᱚᱸ ᱰ ᱵᱤᱨᱩᱫᱽᱨᱮ ᱡᱳᱨ ᱫᱟᱨᱠᱚ ᱞᱟᱹᱲᱦᱟᱭ ᱞᱮᱱᱟ ᱾ ᱩᱱᱠᱩ ᱥᱟᱱᱟᱢ ᱟᱹᱫᱤᱵᱟᱹᱥᱤ ᱵᱚᱭᱦᱟ-ᱵᱩᱦᱤᱱ ᱠᱚᱣᱟᱜ ᱵᱤᱨᱜᱟᱛᱷᱟ ᱟᱜᱟᱢ ᱯᱤᱲᱦᱤ ᱠᱚ ᱡᱟᱱᱟᱢ ᱫᱤᱥᱚᱢᱥᱮᱵᱟ ᱞᱟᱹᱜᱤᱫ ᱞᱮᱛᱟᱲᱩᱫᱽ ᱜᱟᱣ ᱮᱢᱟᱠᱟ ᱛᱟᱦᱮᱸ ᱱᱟ ᱾ " in English it translates as "On 'Hul Day', I pay homage to the immortal martyrs of the Santhal insurgency including Sido-Kanhu, Chand-Bhairav and Phulo-Jhano and all the heroes and heroines.

For the purpose of tribal society's identity, self-respect, and self-governance, he fought hard against injustice and exploitation.

The bravery stories of all those tribal brothers and sisters will always inspire future generations to serve the motherland."

The present tokenization has been implemented in python with help of its different library. The given text sequence can be tokenized in a variety of ways, and various libraries provide a variety of methods and functions for doing so. We'll go through some of the most suitable tokenization methods for Ol-chiki. The different tokenization functions which are popular for tokenization of different languages have been implemented for Santhali language where we have applied split(), Sentence Tokenization, Word Tokenization with NLTK, TreebankWordTokenizer Tokenization with NLTK, RegexpTokenizer Tokenization with NLTK, sent_tokenize() PunktSentenceTokenizer Sentence tokenization, Word tokenization with spaCy, and Sentence tokenization with spaCy. The result from all these tokenisation methods is shown in Table 2. It has been observed that the result of tokenization from different tokenization methods has been varying.

Table 2 Using different Tokenization function tokens of Santhali Twitter data and no of tokens

Tokenization function	Result	No of tokens
split()	[illegible]	73
Sentence tokenization	[illegible]	4
Word tokenization with NLTK	[illegible]	75

(continued)

Table 2 (continued)

Tokenization function	Result	No of tokens
TreebankWordTokenizer tokenization with NLTK	[illegible]	75
WordPunctTokenizer tokenization with NLTK	[illegible]	99
RegexpTokenizer tokenization with NLTK	[illegible]	82

(continued)

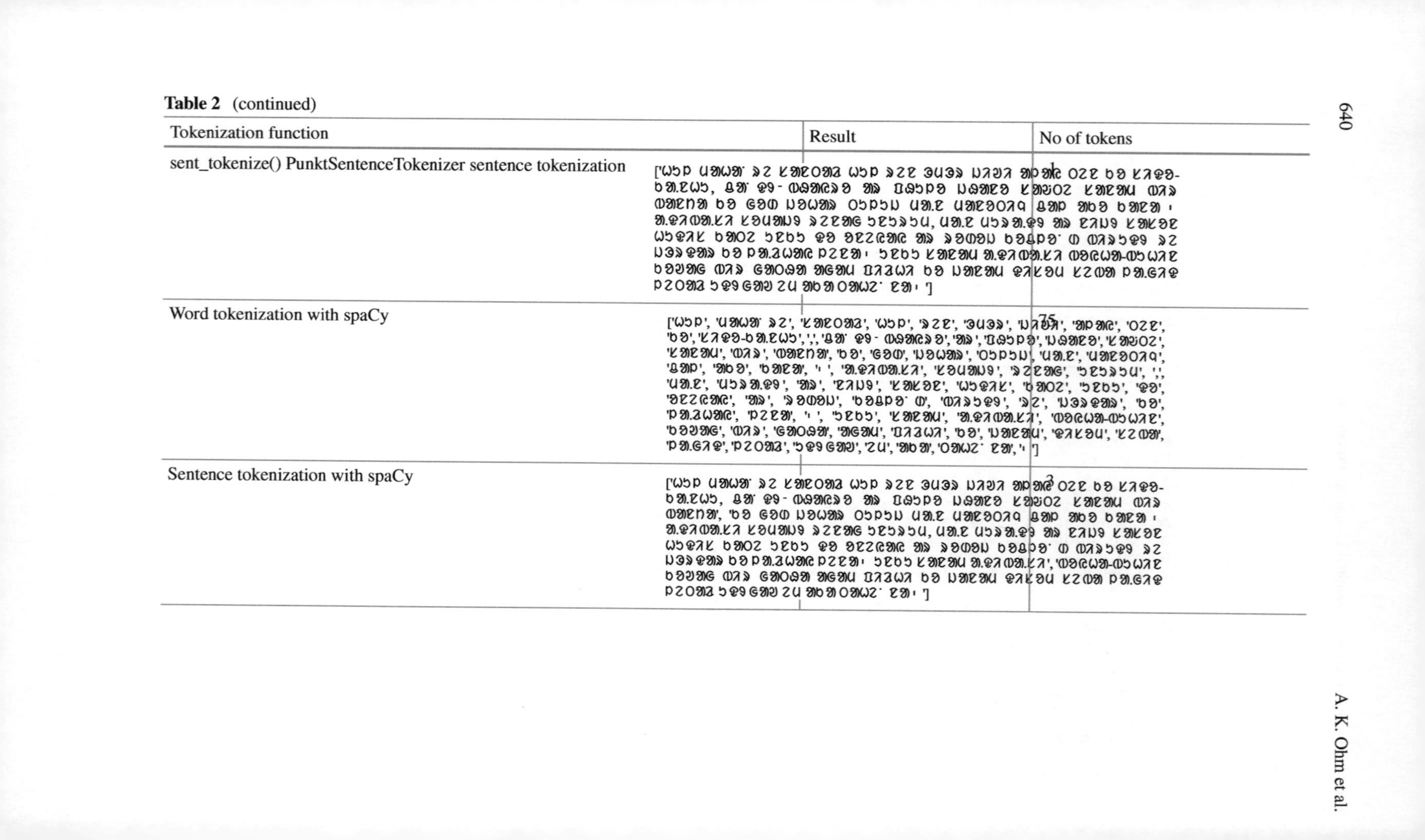

Table 2 (continued)

Tokenization function	Result	No of tokens
sent_tokenize() PunktSentenceTokenizer sentence tokenization	[illegible]	1
Word tokenization with spaCy	[illegible]	75
Sentence tokenization with spaCy	[illegible]	3

3.1 Using the 'Split ()' Method for Tokenization

The 'split()' function is one of the oldest ways to divide a text into tokens.

(a) **Word Tokenization**: The split() function "splits" the text into pieces by default based on whitespace characters. In Santhali space is used for separating the selected words from other words, It does a good job of separating the text into distinct words, as can be seen in Table 1. However, special characters like "-" and other special symbols are not identified as separate tokens. If there is a rupee sign attached to a no it will count as a single token.
(b) **Sentence Tokenization**: All the sentences have been separated which end with the "|" symbol. However, it shows an empty sentence at the end of the sentence so it increases a dummy space token.

3.2 Tokenization Using NLTK

Tokenization of words with NLTK means parsing a text into words via the Natural Language Tool Kit. NLTK provides a ton of options for the tokenization of words or sentences.

Word_tokenize: Performs a fantastic job of tokenizing both the words themselves and the punctuation where in the normal split method comma "," symbol was skipped but this method counts as a separate token for special characters too.
TreebankWordTokenizer: splitting the words into an incorrect format like doesn't into doesn, ', and t, but in case of Santhali language, we can observe that punctuation marks like "," have been changed into tokens.
WordPunctTokenizer: This method also counts comma "," as a separate token, and special character like "-" is also counted as a token but in snail "." is used for Chandra Bindu, this method divides tokens based on that also so as to reduce the performance and it performs worst among all methods for Santhali.
RegEx: Method divides tokens based on "." so it reduces the performance. It removes "|" full stop punctuation from the count in the token.

3.3 Sentence Tokenization

Additionally, NLTK provides a number of other sentence tokenization techniques. **sent_tokenize(), PunktSentenceTokenizer** in both of these functional methods where entire data is counted as a single token that can be divided based on any punctuation symbols. So we cannot get any separate token as a sentence in any of these methods.

Fig. 3 Word Tokenization steps by spaCy

3.4 Tokenization with SpaCy

SpaCy is a free and open-source library for sophisticated natural language processing that was created in the Python and Cython computer languages [17].

(a) **Word Tokenization**: As illustrated in Fig. 3, Prefixes, suffixes, infixes, punctuation, and exceptions are all divided into separate tokens extremely carefully by spaCy [17]. It does not divide sentences on "." Chandra Bindu gives better tokens than other methods. Also it considers special character punctuations as different tokens. In testing with other datasets similar to this, it is found to identify the whole website URL and correctly maintain it.

(b) **Sentence Tokenization**: In terms of a sentence this method gives the best result among all other sentence tokenizers. It divides sentences on the basis of the "|" full-stop punctuation marks without any space or other extra tokens.

4 Benefits of Santhali Tokenization

1. Building a block of text requires tokens so most of the modeling, and preprocessing can be done at the token level.
2. It will help to remove stop words for the reason that stop words don't play a meaningful role in some NLP-related tasks like Machine Translation, Information Retrieval, etc.
3. It will help to identify stemming and lemmatization of Santhali words, the reason is that some Satnthali words are generated using a root word and the Santhali sentence uses some verb form to express the meaning.
4. Even neural network topologies use token processing to understand the document for providing individual neurons a character or word-suitable tokenization will help.
5. It can be used to organize and manage the text-generation process, ensuring that the output is grammatically correct and coherent.

5 Conclusion and Future Work

Since the beginning of NLP, tokenization of both the procedure and the term has seen tremendous development for other spoken Indian languages like Hindi, English, etc. but less work has been done for low low-resource language Santhali. In the present work we implement tokenization for Santhali and compare its results of all the available methods and find the best solution for Santhali tokenization for a paragraph of twitter thread data. We observe that spaCy is a far better option than the rest of the other tokenization methods, and we also applied the same method to a paragraph of text and got a good result on that too. In future work, we intend to expand our research to other tasks related to tokens like part-of-speech tagging, and improve it to further machine translation with Hindi, English, and other languages and make resources available to the native Santhali speaker.

References

1. https://en.wikipedia.org/wiki/Santali_language
2. Murmu R (2000) pa.rsi poha (Pasi Poha, A Santali Primer), ASECA, 7th end. Rairangpur, Orissa, India
3. Sahoo SK et al (2021) Automatic dialect detection for low resource Santali language. In: 2021 19th OITS international conference on information technology (OCIT). IEEE
4. Hansdah RC, Murmu NC (2002) Encoding of Ol Chiki in Universal Character Set. First week of September
5. Kumar A, Kumar R, Kishore K (2020) Performance analysis of ASR Model for Santhali language on Kaldi and Matlab Toolkit. In: 2020 international conference on recent trends on electronics, information, communication & technology (RTEICT), Bangalore, India, pp 88–92
6. Mahapatra S, Sarangi I Santhali language in the digital media space
7. http://wesanthals.tripod.com/id45.html72. Signs and Society
8. Loper E, Bird S (2002) Nltk: the natural language toolkit. arXiv preprint cs/0205028
9. Nadkarni PM, Ohno-Machado L, Chapman WW (2011) Natural language processing: an introduction. J Am Med Inform Assoc 18(5):544–551
10. Kuhail MA et al (2023) Interacting with educational chatbots: a systematic review. Educ Inf Technol 28(1):973–1018
11. Lee P, Bubeck S, Petro J (2023) Benefits, limits, and risks of GPT-4 as an AI chatbot for medicine. N Engl J Med 388(13):1233–1239
12. Allahyari M et al (2017) Text summarization techniques: a brief survey. arXiv preprint arXiv: 1707.02268
13. Hansdah RC, Murmu NC (2003) A concise Santhali-English dictionary
14. Mielke SJ et al (2021) Between words and characters: a brief history of open-vocabulary modeling and tokenization in nlp. arXiv preprint arXiv:2112.10508
15. Toraman C et al (2023) Impact of tokenization on language models: an analysis for Turkish. ACM Trans Asian Low-Resour Lang Inf Process 22(4):1–21
16. Webster, JJ, Kit C (1992) Tokenization as the initial phase in NLP. In: COLING 1992 volume 4: the 14th international conference on computational linguistics
17. Eyre H et al (2021) Launching into clinical space with medspaCy: a new clinical text processing toolkit in Python. In: AMIA annual symposium proceedings, vol 2021. American Medical Informatics Association

Fake News Detector for Combatting Misinformation in Digital Age

Kuldeep Vayadande, Nilay Sangode, Dilpreet Sahney, Aadilnawaz Shaikh, Qusai Shergardwala, and Yash Shewalkar

1 Introduction

In this modern world the battle against misinformation and fake news is at its peak. There are various sources available spreading misinformation because of the advance technologies and it is not easy to identify them. Our project is a powerful platform developed with the help of advance technologies and human expertise. Internet connectivity is a boon but it can be a curse as well. Fake news spreads lies and false information, our aims is to prevent that. To do so we have made use of advance algorithms, machine learning (ML) and artificial intelligence to detect patterns in fake news. We have combined AI and human expertise to increase the accuracy of identifying patterns.

AI and ML are dynamic technologies, they adapt in real time on the basis on input data. Such dynamic technologies with the support of human expertise increases the accuracy. In case of sensitive or ambiguous information where we can't rely only

[†]These authors contributed equally to this work.

K. Vayadande (✉) · N. Sangode · D. Sahney · A. Shaikh · Q. Shergardwala · Y. Shewalkar
Vishwakarma Institute of Technology Pune, Pune, India
e-mail: kuldeep.vayadande1@vit.com

N. Sangode
e-mail: nilay.sangode22@vit.edu

D. Sahney
e-mail: dilpreet.sahney22@vit.edu

A. Shaikh
e-mail: aadilnawaz.shaikh22@vit.edu

Q. Shergardwala
e-mail: qusai.shergardwala22@vit.edu

Y. Shewalkar
e-mail: yash.shewalkar22@vit.edu

K. Kumar Singh et al. (eds.), *Machine Vision and Augmented Intelligence*, Lecture Notes in Electrical Engineering 1211, https://doi.org/10.1007/978-981-97-4359-9_59

on AI, human verification comes into the picture. This combination is very powerful in giving reliable outputs to the users. We understand that trust is everything, when it comes to news and information and we firmly believe in maintaining it. To do so, we have implemented a strong user authentication system which prevents the information from getting manipulated and keeps our platform reliable for the users.

We believe that the stronger our user community is the better our platform would be. Our customers place high value on authenticity and verity hence their insight becomes an invaluable guidance allowing enhancements to take shape within system operations making them more efficacious over time due largely to consistent efforts of inspired participation from these same loyal patrons whose positive contributions bolster perpetual growth while simultaneously fostering improvements across all functional areas wherein false reporting not only triggers notification alerts but provides timely warnings thus empowering individual choice giving everyone protected access devoid scams produced through misinformation. We support critical analysis and media literacy. We understand that tackling misinformation is not just identifying news but to distinguish between facts and fiction. As such, we give alternate reliable articles to help our users adopt a multi-perspective approach and become critical thinkers. Media literacy is not just another catchy phrase but something we would like our users to possess. It's also a battle we know can't be fought alone but demands the efforts of all individuals, organizations and communities in general. We have carried out careful analysis of the challenges in our path before starting off this journey. The techniques used for generating images, such as GANs and Conceptual Expansion, are still evolving and have some limits. The digital landscape continues to evolve, presenting new challenges and opportunities.

We are aware that there is still much work to do and we look forward to explore new technologies to improve our platform. Further in this research paper we will discuss the methodologies, proposed system and the data used to develop this project. We will also discuss the results and discoveries that we made during the development of this project.

2 Literature Survey

The research paper named a research paper named Fake News Detection on Social Media: A Data Mining Perspective [1] by Suhang Wang, Kai Shu, Amy Sliva, Jiliang Tang and Huan Liu argues that machine learning can be used to identify the false news stories. They set out to learn about user's behavior, evaluate the content and examine network structure. The main point of this paper is that recognizing false information requires different scientific approaches. This particular study not only shows how powerful their method is but also highlights the need for simple ways to stop the spread of misinformation using social media platforms.

A research paper named A Review of Fake News Detection Methods using Machine Learning [2] by Shashank Jha, Murari Choudhary, Prashant; Deepika Saxena and Ashutosh Kumar Singh delve into the critical area by supporting a data mining framework and thereby advancing the field of social media fake news identification. Their strategy is exploiting features from user's behaviour, they analyse content, network structure and with that, it includes machine learning techniques.. This research highlights the importance of textual attributes, user behaviour as well as network configurations in identifying false information. It explores the difficulties of different machine learning models to deal with their effectiveness in differentiating between fake news and correct information. They argue that a simple approach that combines different data sources and methodologies can improve the accuracy of fake news identification especially within the nature of social media.

The research paper named Fake News Detection: A Deep Learning Approach [3] by Priyanka Tilak, Aswini Thota, Nibhrat Lohia, and Simerat-jeet Ahluwalia, is about how one can use deep learning models to prevent the spread of fake news. For that purpose, they use recurrent neural networks (RNNs) for an examination of textual content and uses of social networks. To increase and improve the accuracy a combination of CNN and RNN is used. In this paper, they use a large dataset of news articles to assess how this model performs which shows that deep learning methods are very good at finding out what is fake news especially where there are complex text patterns and content. When textual context is rich, this paper points out how deep learning could identify fake news in future.

The research paper named Exploring content-based and meta-data analysis for detecting fake news infodemic: a case study on COVID-19 [4] by Márjory Da Costa-Abreu, Oluwaseun Ajao, and Ashish Garg aims at detecting fake news, specifically regarding the coronavirus pandemic. A case study is used which was designed to analyze COVID-19-related social media data. Their detection is based on different aspects which includes information from sources, analyzation of content, and how users interact. The study shows the importance of addressing health-based stories while also revealing that it is difficult to distinguish what is not true during an emergency.

The research paper named A Survey on Fake News Detection Using Machine Learning [5] by Akanksha Singh and Sanjay Patidar provides a overview of different methods and techniques used in investigating fake information on social media platforms. They have categorized it into three main groups: content-focused approaches, propitiation-centered strategies, and user-oriented methods. The writers goes deeper into every single aspect explaining their pros as well as cons.

3 Methodology

In this digital age, the methodology section indicates how to deal with the unreliable news and fake messages. Hence this is a detailed overview of the key duties, solutions and technology required in implementing these objectives upon our site. This is a complex, elaborate chain of events involving capturing data to feedback about study methods. We begin with collecting data that will be used in making our dataset for the project. This calls for formulation of a sample data set that can mirror diverse forms of misinformation. Some techniques used include internet scrapings, APIs and big data sharing in order to collect a large amount of news articles, social media contents as well as various other types of texts found on the web. Among these various post types are text; image, and summary of content. Data preparation is a cautious procedure. This raw data goes through a rigorous cleaning and preparation process. This entails the removal of wasteful and repetitive material, labelling the publication date, the credibility of sources, etc. In conclusion, we have kept this information well-guarded and formed basis for further analysis to ensure that our results are accurate. Nevertheless, the choice of algorithms needs to be made very wise. Fact-checking and catching lies in reports are possible using our NLP, deep learnings as well as MAC systems.

3.1 Data Description

First, the algorithm is developed, wherein we determine the architecture, hyperparameters, and evaluation metrics. Text analysis is done using current NLP models like transforms e.g., BERT, GPT-3. It has a great grasp of the content and helps us assess the dependability of the text. Utilize CNN and GAN for image and multimedia content. They are known as image-forensic models and they analyse visual clues that differentiate genuine images with altered or faked ones. This includes massive data sets and fine tuning of the algorithms on continuously changing tactics of misinformation by those producing fake news. Our methodology is based on employing AI and ML algorithms that distinguish the truthfulness of data. The developed models are very intricate in detailing the textual, visual, and contextual clues that are used to spot deceitful traits. With the use of models like BERT natural language understanding, we can determine whether a text has meaning or emotional value. As such, similar image recognition models such as ResNet are used to study the image content. We use supervised machine learning where our ML models learn from labelled datasets populated by accurate data as well as falsifications. The model is regularly updated as new evidence arises so that it remains reliable and responds effectively to emerging misinformation strategies. The models also use reinforcement learning in the process of their decision making.

Though AI models are potent, they are no match for human intelligence in the war against misinformation. It forms an integral part of the philosophy and methodology. Moderators together with artificial intelligence system reviews flagged data, come up with conclusions based on subtleties and confirmed facts. The contribution of human moderators in the decision making adds domain knowledge, cultural insights as well as local understanding. They evaluate complicated scenarios in which AI models may falter, including satire and soft propaganda. False information can be correctly detected and filtered using teamwork in human AI. Our platform must, therefore, have strong user authentication systems to give users the confidence they need to use it. MFA as used herein means that customers verify their identity through their phone numbers or email addresses or biometric information. An intense involvement with the customer base is engaged in this whole process for any genuine person who wants his/her privacy intact.

3.1.1 Preprocessing

It also provides content for education aimed at combating widespread disinformation techniques, logical fallacies in reasoning and biased detection. It encourages users to interact with credible substitute article and perform verification. We create media literacy by using gamification and interactive learning content as our tools. Our methodology is based on ethical considerations. There is transparency, fairness, and user privacy. The different kinds are used by the algorithm bias mitigation system to make sure that the users of various demography are treated equally. These strict measures include data anonymization and encryption for user data privacy. The user consented data sharing ensures that one controls what one gives out and this in return improves the system at large. This entails ethical guidelines for the application of AI, which guides in the usage of responsible AI. This is a method which admits that it is difficult to fight against misleading information. Yet, such issues as false positives, ethical challenges, and playing a "cat-and-mouse" game with information warfare actors remain challenges persist. There is openness concerning the constraints, and intensive investigations aim at overcoming them. Our approach is flexible as it can always be adjusted or modified based on evolving misleading information landscape. For instance, future directions could involve consideration of more sophisticated AI models, reinforcement learning for enhanced detection, and collaboration with various other disciplines to combat misinformation through a multifaceted approach. A part of our future directions will involve research on XAI and AI fairness. In order to increase the algorithm's transparency, as well as avoid the bias against various materials/users. Therefore, we conclude that this methodology is an all-embracing one which could help in fighting misinformation and fake news. It combines modern AI and ML models with expert knowledge and end-user inputs as well as education programs to develop robust countermeasures against digital age fraudity. Engineering essay. The commitment of openness, ethics, and continuous innovation are behind our mission that fights for truth towards an enlightened and responsible society. Our commitment to transparency, ethics, and ongoing innovation drives this mission to champion truth and shape an informed, responsible society.

4 Proposed System

Here is an overview of the key components in our proposed system representing a solution to combating misinformation and fake news in this modern era.

4.1 Machine Learning Models for Verification

Our system is dependent on the ML models for providing the results for the fake news. These machine learning models are trained with a wide range of datasets of over 50 k news samples. We have used Linear Regression, Gradient boost, Random Forest and Decision Tree models to detect the fake news and results of all the models are considered while declaring the news is fake or not. All the results are given in terms of probability which is calculated based on the results given by all the four models.

4.2 Human-AI Integration

Integrating human touch to the AI systems is a key component in our system. Some of the news can be reviewed by the human moderators in order to train the model for the newer dataset to tackle the new trends in the fake news. This improves the accuracy and the trustfulness for our system. Human moderators provide expertise in contextual understanding and cultural awareness to the system. This improves the overall decision-making process of our system.

4.3 User Login and ReCAPTCHA Test Verification

To prevent the system from the bots and wrong feedbacks we use the authentication process for email and phone number verification of the user to ensure there are only genuine users on the system. This will help the system to be more accurate and unbiased. The reCAPTCHA test is a very effective way to avoid the bot users (Fig. 1).

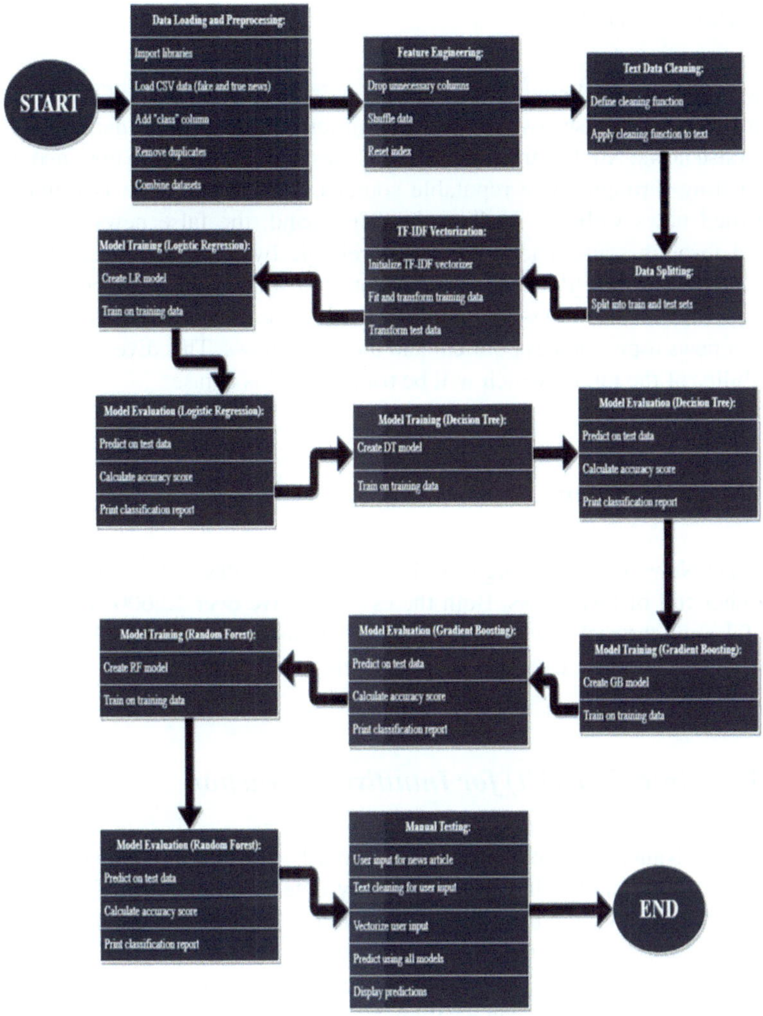

Fig. 1 Machine learning flowchart

4.4 Dataset Overview

We have used a well know dataset in the field of fake news 'ISOT False News Dataset' which comprises two distinct categories of news articles namely real news and the false news. All the authentic news articles in this dataset are obtained through web crawling through some reputable sources, and one of them is Reuters.com, a renowned news website. And on the other hand, the false news articles were collected through sources identified as unreliable by many fact-checking organizations, including Politifact. Also, information available on Wikipedia played an important role in the cross-verification of the false news. The dataset has wide variety of news topic such as political and the world news. This diversity ensures the applicability of the model which will be trained on this dataset.

4.5 Dataset Content

ISOT False News Dataset is organized into two CSV files one is for the real news and another full of false news. Both the csv files have over 12,600 articles in each for the fake and the real news. Topics covered in this dataset are mainly world news, political news, Middle East, American, left-wing, and general news.

4.6 User Interface (UI) for Intuitive Interaction

One of the advantages of our proposed system lied in the implementation of our model in a user-friendly UI that successfully detects probability of a news to be fake which is given by the user in the input area in our website. By creating a fully responsive website for the fake news detections is the step in the implementation of our model publicly. This provides easy access experts and non-experts to try out model more reliably as they can easily navigate the system. We have used HTML, CSS, Bootstrap, JavaScript, React.JS, Flask for the frontend and the backend of our website.

4.7 Conclusion

Our overall system represents an adaptive and reliable solution for countering the spread of fake news. By the integration of some algorithms, ML models, human moderating and feedback system we create a strong system to tackle the problem of misinformation. This is one step towards an informed and responsible society.

4.8 Dataset Content

The ISOT Bogus News Dataset is organized into two CSV files, each providing a distinct set of articles: True.csv: This file contains a comprehensive collection of more than 12,600 articles sourced directly from Reuters.com. These articles embody genuine and reliable news content. The subjects covered in this dataset include world news and politics. Bogus.csv: This file comprises over 12,600 articles obtained from various sources known for disseminating fake news. The selection of bogus news sources was carefully scrutinized, aligning with the criteria set by fact-checking organizations. Topics include government news, left-wing news, Middle East news, American news, and general news.

4.9 Dataset Statistics

The ISOT Bogus News Dataset presents a substantial volume of articles for research purposes. The real news dataset encompasses 21,417 articles, categorized into subjects such as world news and politics. In particular, it includes 10,145 articles on world news and 11,272 articles on politics. The Bogus News database is equally extensive, containing 23,481 articles on topics including Government News, Middle East News, US News, Foreign News, Politics, and News. The dataset includes 1,570 government news articles, 778 Middle-East news articles, 783 US news articles, 4,459 left-leaning news articles, 6,841 politics articles, and 9,050 general news articles (Fig. 2).

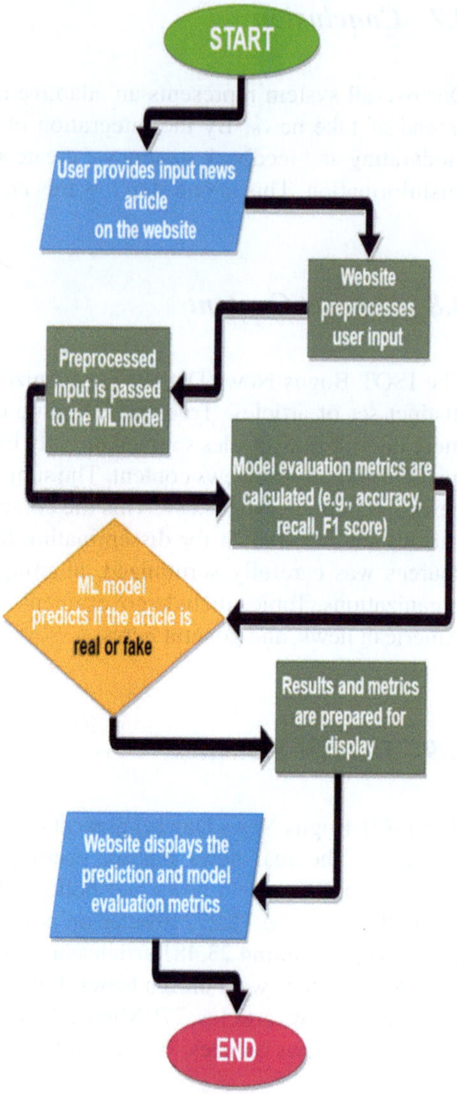

Fig. 2 Flowchart of the model

4.10 Data Integrity

It's worth noting that while the data was subjected to cleaning and preprocessing, the dataset maintains the original punctuations and potential errors found in the fake news articles, preserving their authenticity. The ISOT Bogus News Dataset serves as a useful tool for scholars and data scientists investigating the identification of false news and associated natural language processing problems, offering a rich and diverse collection of articles for analysis and experimentation (Fig. 3).

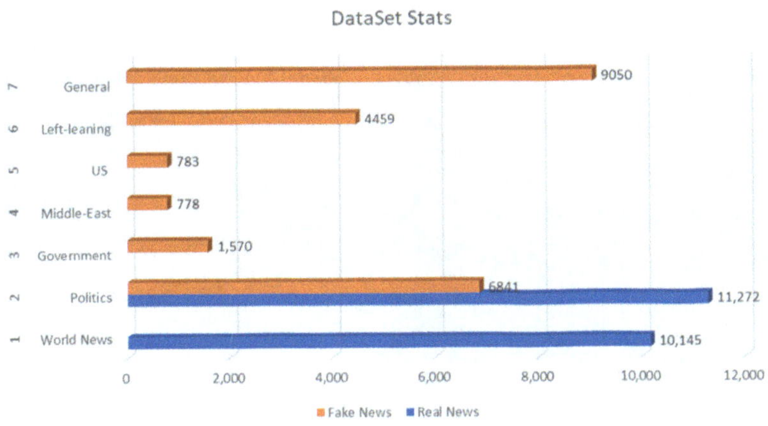

Fig. 3 Dataset stats

5 Sample Output

See Figs. 4, 5, 6 and 7.

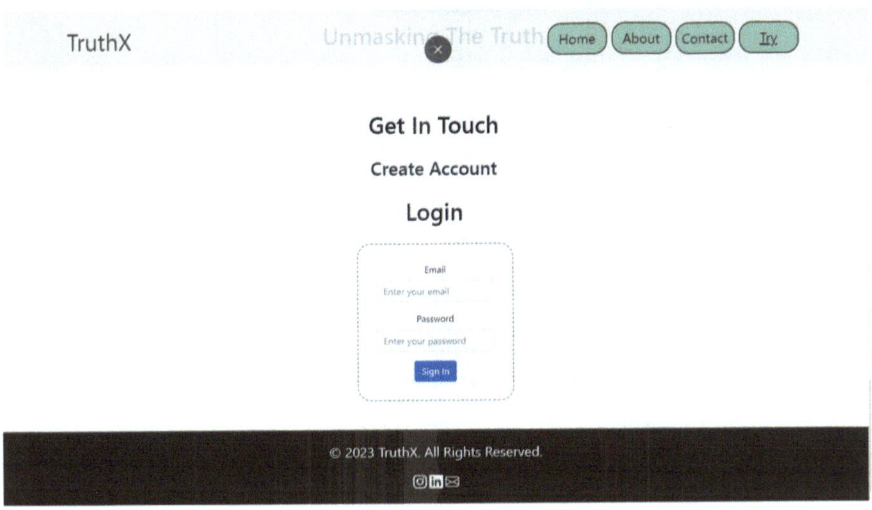

Fig. 4 System implementation

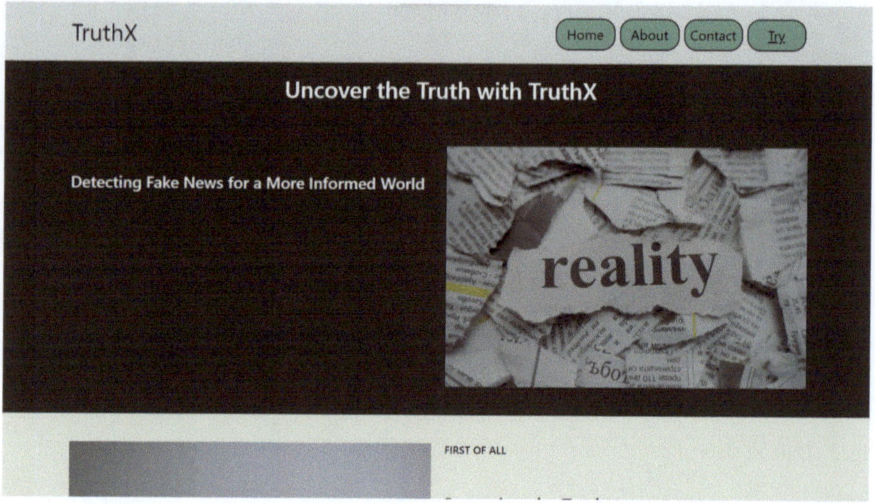

Fig. 5 Homepage

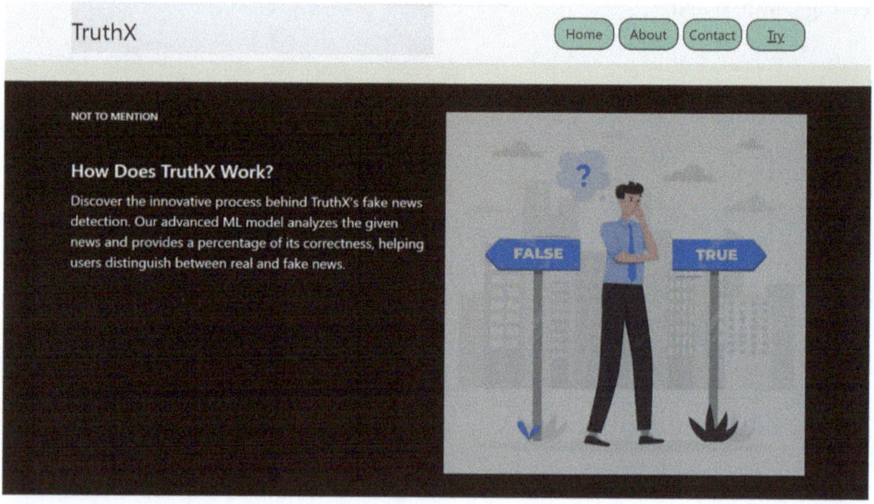

Fig. 6 System implementation

Fig. 7 Model for fake news

6 Comparative Table

See Table 1.

7 Results and Discussion

Cross-Validation:

To assess the robustness and generalizability of our machine learning models, we executed fivefold cross-validation. Each fold served as a distinct validation set, with the remaining data used for training. The results are meticulously detailed for each algorithm. This following table shows the cross validation results (Tables 2, 3 and Fig. 8).

Table 1 Comparative table

SR. NO	Input news	Model output	Expected output	Accuracy (%)
01	At the G20, Modi and Joe Biden discussed the death of a Canadian Sikh separatist. At the G20 conference earlier this month, President Joe Biden of the United States and other world leaders voiced their worry to Indian Prime Minister Narendra Modi regarding Canada's allegation that New Delhi was responsible for the murder of a Sikh separatist leader, according to the Financial Times (FT). According to three people familiar with discussions at the G20, the newspaper reported on Thursday that a number of members of the Five Eyes, an intelligence-sharing network that includes Australia, Canada, New Zealand, the United Kingdom, and the US, brought up the death of Sikh separatist leader Hardeep Singh Nijjar directly with Modi	LR Prediction: Real News DT Prediction: Fake News GB Prediction: Fake News RF Prediction: Real News	REAL	50.00
02	Later this week, Hurricane Ian, now a dangerous Category 4 storm, is expected to make landfall in Florida. The storm is predicted to deliver the state strong winds, torrential rain, and storm surges With maximum sustained winds of 140 mph as of Monday evening, Ian was situated around 90 miles west-southwest of Grand Cayman. At 14 mph, the storm is heading northwest. The National Hurricane Centre (NHC) predicts that Ian will make landfall as a major hurricane near Florida on Wednesday after intensifying further over the warm waters of the Gulf of Mexico late on Monday Although it is still unclear exactly where Ian will make landfall in Florida, the NHC has issued a warning that the whole state might experience dangerous storm-related effects Florida residents are warned to make plans for their evacuation from Hurricane Ian, secure their houses, and stock up on supplies	LR Prediction: Real News DT Prediction: Fake News GB Prediction: Fake News RF Prediction: Real News	REAL	50.00
03	War between Russia and Ukraine: Russian soldiers are making progress in eastern Ukraine Russian soldiers currently control a sizable chunk of the Donbas region after making substantial inroads in eastern Ukraine in recent weeks. In Ukraine, the war has resulted in a humanitarian crisis that has forced millions of people from their homes. Although the United States and its allies have given Ukraine military supplies worth billions of dollars, they have so far refrained from engaging in direct military engagement. The seventh month of the conflict has passed with no sign of an end in sight	LR Prediction: Real News DT Prediction: Fake News GB Prediction: Real News RF Prediction: Real News	REAL	75.00

(continued)

Table 1 (continued)

SR. NO	Input news	Model output	Expected output	Accuracy (%)
04	Elon Musk Will Pay $44 Billion For Twitter Billionaire One of the biggest-ever purchases for a social media business, Elon Musk has agreed to purchase Twitter for $44 billion. In the upcoming months, the agreement is anticipated to be finalised Musk has stated that he wants to open up and liberate speech on Twitter. Additionally, he has criticised Twitter's content moderation procedures, claiming they are overly stringent If Musk were to take over Twitter, it's unclear what precise adjustments he would make to the firm. He has, however, stated that he wants to make the company's algorithms more transparent, authenticate all real users, and get rid of spam bots. Analysts and Twitter users have had differing opinions on the deal. Some people are thrilled by the idea of Musk making Twitter a more open platform, while others worry that he would give hate speech and false information too much room to spread It is still unclear how Twitter will change over time under Musk's ownership. The deal, however, represents a tremendous upheaval for the social media sector and is probably going to have a big effect on how people connect online	LR Prediction: Real News DT Prediction: Fake News GB Prediction: Real News RF Prediction: Real News	REAL	75.00
05	The United States will pay to import previously deported mentally ill illegal aliens. Get this: As a result of a judge's ruling, previously deported illegal aliens with mental illnesses are being returned to the United States: The decision of federal judge Dolly M. Gee will enable immigrants with severe mental disorders to ask for their cases to be reopened in an effort to enter the country again. Between November 21, 2011 and January 27, this year, aliens who were deported from California, Arizona, and Washington are covered by the decision. Therefore, the invasion of Central Americans and the recent arrival of Muslim refugees is not enough; now the mentally ill have another opportunity to immigrate as well! What kind of madness is this, no pun intended? Is it surprising that the ACLU filed this lawsuit? Doesn't the ACLU owe it to LEGAL and law-abiding Americans to put them first? Though there may be more and it's not known how many immigrants would be eligible to have their cases reopened, the government identified 900 immigrants who potentially benefit from the decision, according to Iguina. Look deep for the following information: According to the deal, the federal government promised to assist people whose cases have been reopened in returning to the United States and to cover some travel expenses. Don't you just want to quit paying taxes completely after reading this? When they disobeyed the law the first time, why should we pay for them to cross our country again?	LR Prediction: Fake News DT Prediction: Fake News GB Prediction: Fake News RF Prediction: Fake News	FAKE	100.00

Table 2 Algorithm comparison table (algorithm used in our model)

Algorithm	Accuracy	Precision	Recall	F1-score
LR	0.9885	0.988	0.988	0.988
DT	0.9952	0.995	0.995	0.995
GB	0.9956	0.995	0.995	0.995
RF	0.9909	0.991	0.991	0.991
Average	0.99255	0.99225	0.99225	0.99225

Table 3 Cross-validation results

Fold	Accuracy
1	0.9837
2	0.9844
3	0.9852
4	0.9849
5	0.9853
Mean	0.9847

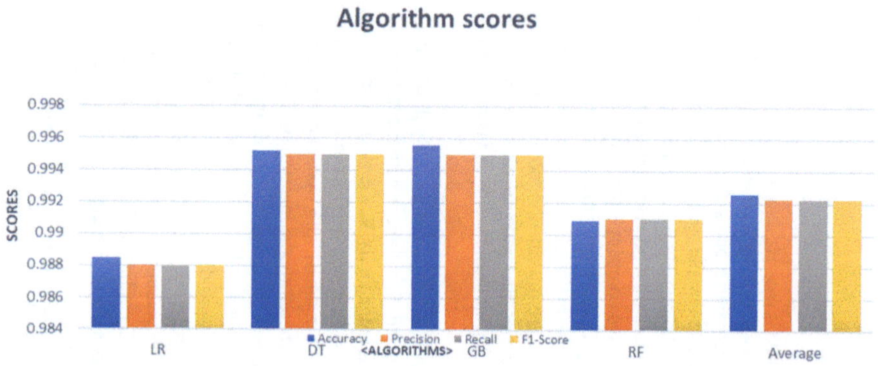

Fig. 8 Algorithm scores bar graph

8 Scope of Research

The main objective of our research was to find a solution to detect the misinformation and all the Fake news that spreads in the society through social media. This is one of the major problem in todays digital age. So we are providing with a probability based verification method to figure out which news can be a fake news and which can be real and trust worthy.

It has become crucial in todays age to bring the truth out and to stop the misleading information from spreading in the society. We have come up with many solutions and implementation methods of our Fake News detection model. One of a major idea is to create a Human-AI collaboration. Moderating the results of the model brings increased accuracy in the results of our model.

There are various possible ways to implement our Fake News Detection model:

1. API (Application Programming Interface).
   Various social media platforms can integrate this feature of checking the probability of a new to be fake by using an API which is developed on our model.
2. Browser Extensions:
   In oder to make the Fake News Detection model to all the users, various chrome extensions can be develop through our model.
3. Collaboration with some social media companies and some fact-checking organizations.
4. Making the model open-source so that developers all over the world can contribute to the model.

9 Future Scope

As the digital landscape continues to evolve, the fight against misinformation and fake news must also adapt and progress. The future scope of our system extends into several critical areas, reflecting our commitment to ongoing innovation and the relent- less pursuit of information integrity. In this discussion, we outline the potential avenues and directions for advancing our efforts in countering misinformation. The continual advancement of AI and ML technologies offers promising prospects for improving mis-information detection. Future research will focus on developing more sophisticated models capable of handling nuanced forms of deception. This includes the exploration of novel deep learning architectures, transfer learning techniques, and reinforcement learning approaches to enhance the accuracy and robustness of our algorithms. There are various plans for the future development in our fake news detection model.

Here are some of the fields:

1. AI and ML integration:
   - Sentiment Analysis and NLP can be a game changer in detection of Fake news.
   - We can make the model smarter and self-learning with the help of the AI integration and implementing various practices on AI.
2. Deep Learning:
   - We can try and apply various new designs for the purposed system, this can lead in better and more accurate results.
3. Reinforcement Learning:

- We are looking into a method where the system can learn by doing and feedback system is present through which the system improve itself over the time with the help of the feedbacks.

10 Conclusion

In today's modern world where one can easily access internet and can read and write any post on the social media which can influence others, fact checking and cross-verifying the news articles posted on social media is extremely become an important aspect on life. Creating public awareness to always cross verify the news they view or read on social media and not to get influenced from bogus news articles is important. We solve one of the major problems here which is where to verify the reality of any news article easily and effortlessly without wasting much time on researching it on the internet.

Our Fake news detection model solves this problem successfully and provide its users a fast way to check the trustworthiness of any news. Our proposed system provides the probability of a news to be fake through four different ML models which were mentioned in our research. We have implemented our ML model for the fake news detection on our own developed website UI for it where users can input the news article content and within few seconds the results can be viewed on the screen.

In conclusion, our research is one major step to fight against mis-information presented on the social media on daily basis. We believe this model has a promising future with the integration of better ML models and training data. Lastly, stopping mis-information is a team effort which involves governments, media and society also.

References

1. Wang S, Shu K, Sliva A, Tang J, Liu H Fake news detection on social media: a data mining perspective
2. Jha S, Choudhary M, Saxena D, Singh AK A review of fake news detection methods using machine learning
3. Tilak P, Thota A, Lohia N, Ahluwalia S Fake news detection: a deep learning approach
4. Da Costa-Abreu M, Ajao O, Garg A Exploring content-based and meta-data analysis for detecting fake news infodemic: a case study on COVID-19
5. Singh A, Patidar S A survey on fake news detection using machine learning
6. Potthast M, Kiesel J, Reinartz K, Bevendorff J, Stein B (2017) A stylo-metric inquiry into hyperpartisan and fake news. arXiv preprint arXiv:1702.05638
7. Monti F, Frasca F, Eynard D, Tubaro S (2018) Fake news detection on social media: a data mining perspective. Expert Syst Appl 107:3–12
8. Tacchini E, Ballarin G, Della Vedova ML, Moret S (2017) Some like it Hoax: automated fake news detection in social networks. arXiv preprint arXiv:1704.07506
9. Castelo S, Santos RL (2018) Detecting fake news using network characteristics. arXiv preprint arXiv:1803.09157

10. Ruchansky N, Seo S, Liu Y (2017) Csi: a hybrid deep model for fake news detection. arXiv preprint arXiv:1703.06959
11. Friggeri A, Adamic LA, Eckles D, Kern N (2014) Rumor cascades. In: Proceedings of the eighth international conference on weblogs and social media
12. Vosoughi S, Roy D, Aral S (2018) The spread of true and false news online. Science 359(6380):1146–1151
13. Hassan N, Abu-Jbara A (2019) Fine-grained analysis of fake news detection using multiple content and context features. Inf Process Manage 56(6):2041–2056
14. Gupta A, Kumaraguru P, Castillo C, Meier P (2013) TweetCred: a real-time web-based system for assessing credibility of content on Twitter. In: Proceedings of the 22nd international conference on World Wide Web (WWW '13)
15. Zannettou S, Caulfield T, Blackburn J (2018) The web of false informa- tion: Rumors, fake news, hoaxes, clickbait, and various other shenanigans. In: Proceedings of the 2018 World Wide Web conference (WWW '18)
16. Hassan N, Li J, Arora T, Liu Y, Abdelzaher T (2017) Toward automated detection of spreading fake news on social media. In: Proceedings of the 2017 IEEE/ACM international conference on advances in social networks analysis and mining (ASONAM '17)
17. Vosoughi S, Roy D, Aral S (2018) The spread of true and false news online. Proc Natl Acad Sci 115(6):12645–12650
18. Ruchansky N, Seo S, Liu Y (2017) CSI: a hybrid deep model for fake news detection. arXiv preprint arXiv:1703.06959
19. Wang S, Lo K, Wang L (2017) Liar, liar pants on fire: a new benchmark dataset for fake news detection. arXiv preprint arXiv:1705.00648
20. Friggeri A, Adamic LA, Eckles D, Kern N (2014) Rumor cascades. In: Proceedings of the eighth international conference on weblogs and social media
21. Shu K, Mahudeswaran D, Wang S, Lee D, Liu H (2019) FakeNewsNet: a data repository with news content, social context, and spatiotemporal information for studying fake news on social media. arXiv preprint arXiv:1905.12781

Prediction of Auto Insurance Claims as an Imbalance Data Distribution Problem

Akhilesh Kumar Singh, Sumit Kumar Singh, and Koushlendra Kumar Singh

1 Introduction

Machine learning is currently [1] being used in a wide range of industries, including online shopping, fraud detection in financial institutions, improving customer experience in retail, and even drug development in the healthcare field [2]. The big players were initially hesitant to depart from a strategy that had been tried and true throughout the ages because insurance is a traditional industry with many restrictions. We have witnessed a rapid development of predictive modeling technique in the insurance industry.

The use of predictive modeling (PM) methods and the industry's transition to new levels of digital applications represent the industry's current problems. There are two types of insurance in the market: non-life insurance and life insurance [3]. In particular, auto insurance is taken into account in this study. Through the filing of an insurance claim, the policyholder, or client, formally requests coverage or reimbursement from the insurer for an accident. After verifying this request, the insurance company must decide whether to pay the policyholder.

For clients who are unlikely to file claims, the model should identify them and lower insurance costs for them; for clients who are more likely to file claims, insurance costs should increase. It is important to note that the insurance sector had the chance

---

Sumit Kumar Singh and Koushlendra Kumar Singh authors are contributed equally to this work.

A. K. Singh (✉) · K. K. Singh
SCSE Department, Galgotias University, Yamuna Expy, Opposite Buddha International Circuit, Sector 17A, Greater Noida 203201, Uttar Pradesh, India
e-mail: akhileshsingh@galgotiasuniversity.edu.in

K. K. Singh
e-mail: koushlendra.cse@nitjsr.ac.in

S. K. Singh · K. K. Singh
Machine Vision and Intelligence Lab, Department of CSE, National Institute of Technology, Jamshedpur, Adityapur, Jamshedpur 831014, India

K. Kumar Singh et al. (eds.), *Machine Vision and Augmented Intelligence*, Lecture Notes in Electrical Engineering 1211, https://doi.org/10.1007/978-981-97-4359-9_60

to gather a significant amount of data throughout the course of its many years of operation [4].

Consider car insurance as an example. Each insurance contract includes extensive details about the customer, the vehicle, and the location where the vehicle is used. In the insurance sector, determining a product's pricing before determining its cost is crucial. The process of setting rates becomes more crucial and vital as a result of this reality. Insurance companies must project the quantity and severity of future claims in order to fairly determine the price for their insurance products. Accurate forecasting enables the insurance sector to better modify premiums, lowering costs for more drivers to purchase auto insurance.

Today, many insurance companies choose to use predictive modeling (PM) techniques over traditional methods because they provide more thorough means of generating results that are more accurate and representative. But it's important to note an abundance of applications of predictive modeling in the insurance industry, including fraud detection and claim prediction. It can be challenging to solve the imbalanced learning problem [5].

Thus, the main goal of this research is to introduce and implement different methods of coping with an imbalanced dataset in the context of auto insurance claim occurrence prediction. We explore more powerful PM strategies in this study by examining the extensive dataset offered by Porto Seguro, a significant automobile corporation with headquarters in Brazil. We employ PM techniques including XGBoost, Random Forest (RF), Decision Trees (DT), Naive Bayes (NB), K-NN, and Logistic Regression (LR) on the dataset in order to accurately predict the occurrence of claims. We also compare and evaluate the efficacy of different models.

The overall paper are organized as follows: Sect. 2 describes the related work. Section 3 discusses the background of the work. Section 4 presents materials and method. Sections 5 and 6 present results and conclusion respectively.

2 Related Work

In their study, Smith et al. (2000) looked at many PM models, such as decision trees and neural networks, to predict whether or not the policyholder will file a claim. They also talked about the potential impact of the case study on the insurance company. Three PM strategies for predicting claim severity were compared by Weerasinghe and Wijegunasekara (2016). Based on their findings, neural networks were the most accurate predictions.

Kowshalya and Nandhini (2018) employed PM approaches to forecast fraudulent claims. For various clients based on their personal data they have also calculated insurance premium amounts. To forecast fraudulent claims, three classifiers RF, J48, and NB were employed. The outcomes show that RF works better than the other approaches.

Pesantez-Narvaez et al. (2019) have used XGBoost and LR. To estimate the frequency of auto insurance claims, these methods have been used. This investigation indicates that the XGBoost model is marginally better than logistic regression, despite the fact that they only used a dataset with 2767 observations.

According to Abdulhadi et al. (2020), four predictive classifiers, namely XGBoost, J48, ANN, and NB algorithms, were developed to forecast insurance claims. A dataset including 30,240 observations was employed, and the XGBoost model performed better than the other three models. Jing et al. (2018) used a Bayesian network to classify claims based just on their existence. Large datasets including 1,488,028 observations spread across 59 variables were used by Hanfy and Ming (2021). The utility of XGBoost as a model is demonstrated by this research.

The decision tree (C50) and random forest, however, perform significantly better than XGBoost. Out of the eight classification models employed in this case study, the naive Bayes model performs the worst at predicting the incidence of claims. This work appears to be quite promising because it makes extensive use of both machine learning algorithms and a very large dataset.

3 Background

Understanding the insurance claims prediction, imbalance data [5], predictive modeling, and classification are crucial for comprehending the problem. We examine the following terms: Predictive models are necessary for claim prediction because there is so much data needed to calculate the likelihood that a claim will occur.

To assess the risk that the driver presents to the insurance company and the possibility that they would file a claim in the next year, an effective technique and a more reliable prediction model are thus required. We need a model that can read and understand massive databases that contain thousands of customer records that are provided by the Porto Seguro insurance company.

Porto Seguro is one of the biggest houses and vehicle insurance providers in Brazil. According to the corporation, Porto Seguro's vehicle insurance business aims to customize rates according to the driving ability of the policyholder. They provided 1,488,028 observations from 59 different variables in their dataset. The client information that the company has collected through time is part of these observations.

3.1 Predictive Modeling

A mathematical technique called predictive modeling makes predictions about the future based on patterns in the input data. Using this method, a model based on previously recorded results is developed, processed, and validated in order to predict future outcomes [6]. The process of creating a model and making prediction is shown in Figs. 1 and 2 respectively. Learning is done by the algorithm. The relationships that were learned are included in the model.

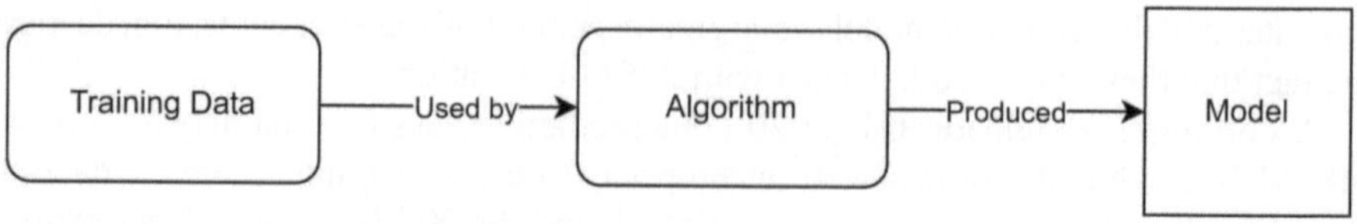

Fig. 1 Utilizing an algorithm and training data, create a prediction model

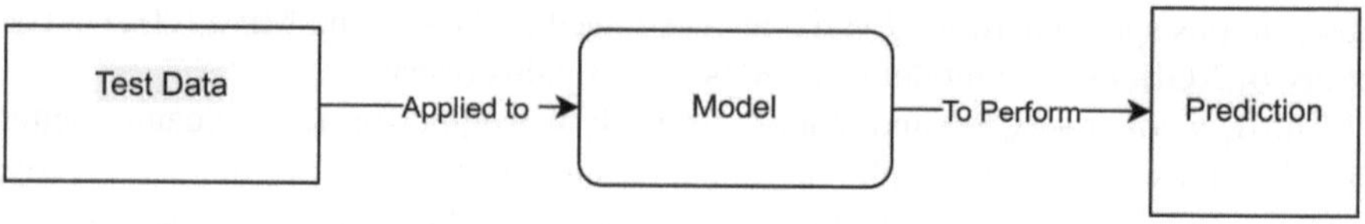

Fig. 2 Make prediction using the model on new data

3.2 Class Imbalance Data

The issue of imbalanced data (ID) prevents predictive modeling (PM) algorithms from producing appropriate outcomes. It deals with an imbalance between the number of instances in each class, where some classes are noticeably underrepresented. Since most classifiers are motivated by 0–1 loss, they tend to favor the majority of classes that are simpler to model [7].

Since the underrepresented minority classes are typically the more significant ones, it is necessary to change the dataset or the learning process to establish fair decision boundaries that do not favor any particular class. Both evaluating the classification performance and controlling the classifier modeling depend heavily on evaluation measures. Because the majority of policyholders do not file claims, auto insurance claims are a great illustration of unbalanced data [8].

Therefore, understanding the imbalanced classification is necessary in order to comprehend the issue. Since accuracy does not account for the proportion of examples of each class that was properly classified, it is not a suitable metric when a dataset is imbalanced. The infamous accuracy dilemma might possibly arise.

Finding a more balanced data distribution through resampling techniques is a practical way to address the imbalance issue [7].

A more balanced distribution is attained by randomly discarding instances of the dominant class during the random under-sampling (RUS) process [9].

In random oversampling (ROS), random copies of cases belonging to the minority class are appended to the training dataset. Random oversampling may increase the possibility of overfitting because it produces exact duplicates of the minority class samples. This is how, for instance, a symbolic classifier could provide rules that appear to be accurate yet only include one instance of duplication [5].

The Synthetic Minority Oversampling Technique (SMOTE) involves drawing a line between a few adjacent examples in the feature space, selecting a new sample at a point along the line. First, SMOTE randomly selects a minority class instance, then finds its k nearest minority class neighbors. Then, a line segment in the feature space is created by combining a and b, one of b's k randomly chosen nearest neighbors, in order to construct the synthetic instance. Convexly combining the two chosen examples, a and b, yields the synthetic instances [9, 10].

3.3 Performance Metrics Used

3.3.1 Confusion Matrix

A confusion matrix (CF) is a table that displays how well a machine learning model can categorize input. It contrasts the data's actual labels with those that the model expected. The model's performance can be assessed, and its advantages and disadvantages can be noted. Rows and columns in a confusion matrix stand in for the expected and actual labels, respectively. The number of instances of that type of data is displayed in each cell of the matrix Table 1.

CF, TP, and TN denote the number of positively and negatively classified samples, respectively, whereas FP and FN denote samples that were wrongly classified as positive or negative.

3.3.2 Precision and Recall

The positive classes that are accurately predicted from the total expected in a positive class are measured using the precision metric. Recall measures the percentage of successfully classified positive classes, which essentially measures how well the model can identify the class type [11]:

$$Precision = \frac{True\ positive}{True\ positive + False\ positive}. \tag{1}$$

$$Recall = \frac{True\ positive}{True\ positive + False\ negetive}. \tag{2}$$

Table 1 Representation of CF

	Predicted negative	Predicted positive
Actual negative	True negative (TN)	False positive (FP)
Actual positive	False negative (FN)	True positive (TP)

3.3.3 F1 Score and G-Mean

There is another popular measure to look for if we want to find the right balance between recall and precision. The harmonic mean of recall and precision is F1:

$$F1 - Score = \frac{2.Precision.Recall}{Precision + Recall}. \tag{3}$$

In machine learning, the G-Mean, also known as the Geometric Mean, is a statistic used to assess how well a classification model performs, particularly when dealing with datasets that are imbalanced. It's a technique for combining specificity (Spec) and sensitivity (Sen) into one measurement:

$$G - Score = \sqrt{Spec.Sen}. \tag{4}$$

3.3.4 Kappa

The Kappa score, also known as Cohen's Kappa coefficient, is a statistical indicator used in statistics and machine learning to evaluate the degree of agreement between two annotators or raters when classifying data into numerous categories. It is frequently used for classification problems when two or more raters or classifiers are requested to assign things to certain categories or labels. The Kappa score gives a measurement of agreement that goes beyond chance by accounting for the predicted agreement from chance.

4 Materials and Methods

Data imbalance is still a challenge, and effective prediction algorithm has also not been performed well. Data resampling algorithms come in two flavors: oversampling and undersampling, with oversampling focusing on increasing minority instances while undersampling reduces the number of majority samples in the datasets. The synthetic minority oversampling technique (SMOTE) is the oversampling method that is most frequently used [12]. Figure 3 represents the overall methodology used in this paper.

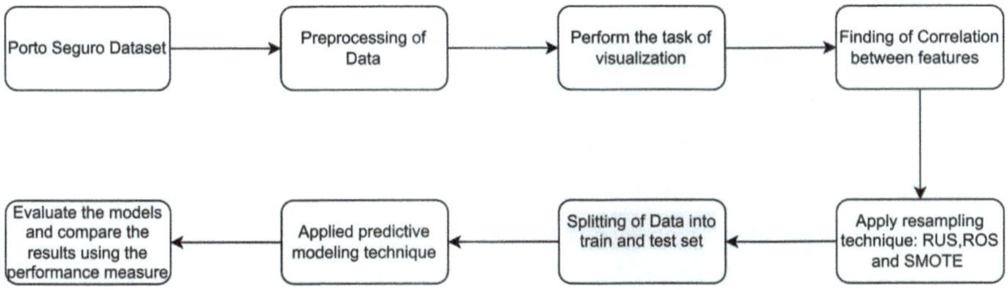

Fig. 3 Structure of overall methodology

4.1 Datasets

In this study, a Brazilian automative manufacturer named Porto Seguro[1] provided a dataset and it has been used for the present study. Each row in our data collection contains the personal information of a different client and has 59 variables and 1,488,028 rows. Additionally, a data description that includes crucial information about the already-processed data preparation has been released. The dataset has 20 features which is explored: 16 features related to automobiles, 18 features related to individuals, and 3 features related to registration.

5 Results

In this work, we have developed a model that predicts the occurrence of auto insurance claims by using predictive modeling techniques.

5.1 Data Preprocessing

Total 59 features are available in this dataset. Insurance claims, which is our dependent outcome feature, has connection with these features. To effectively use the data with the predictive modeling technique, the data is verified and changed.

5.1.1 Description of Target Variable

Two classes 1 and 0 are used in the outcome attributes. 1 for claims that have occurred and 0 for claims that have not occurred. The distribution of the outcome attribute is

[1] https://www.kaggle.com/c/porto-seguro-safe-driver-prediction/data.

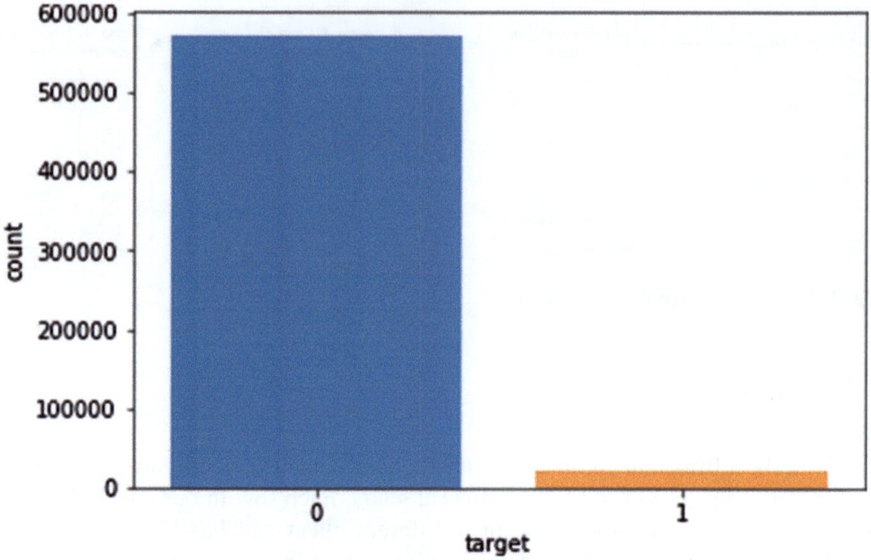

Fig. 4 Distribution of target variable represented in histogram

represented in Fig. 1. Figure 1 shows that the target column is extremely imbalanced. We can see that there are 573518 0's and 21694 1's.

Imbalanced data makes it difficult for a predictive modeling system to function well. As a result, we used undersampling, oversampling, and SMOTE. Because of undersampling, there are fewer representations of class 0, which is represented in Fig. 4. The distribution of target variable after applying RUS and ROS is shown in Figs. 5 and 6.

The correlation matrix of all the features is shown in Fig. 6. Based on this, we can conclude that calc feature which is one of the features in the dataset does not correlate with other variables. In Fig. 8 Scree plot of PCA is represented. This plot describes variance explained and principle component, Fig. 7.

5.2 *Model Performance*

The result is obtained by applying predictive modeling techniques in three cases, which are represented in Tables 2, 3, and 4. In Table 2, we have represented the result after applying random undersampling and all seven models that we have applied. We have considered kappa value, precision, recall, F1 score, and G mean as performance measures.

From Table 2, we can see that the kappa value is better in the XGBoost method. The value for kappa using the XGBoost method is 0.163, i.e., slight agreement.

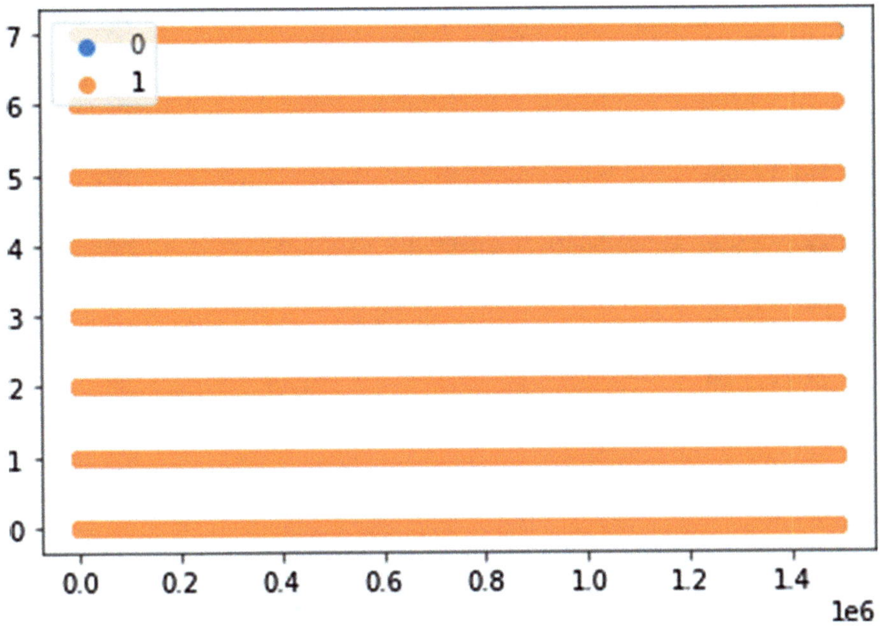

Fig. 5 Distribution of target variable after applying undersampling

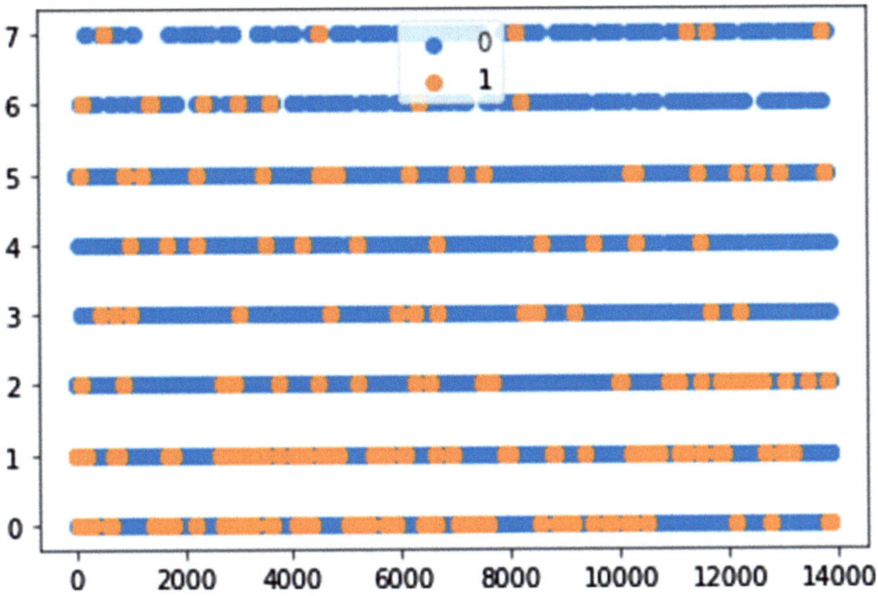

Fig. 6 Distribution of target variable after applying ROS

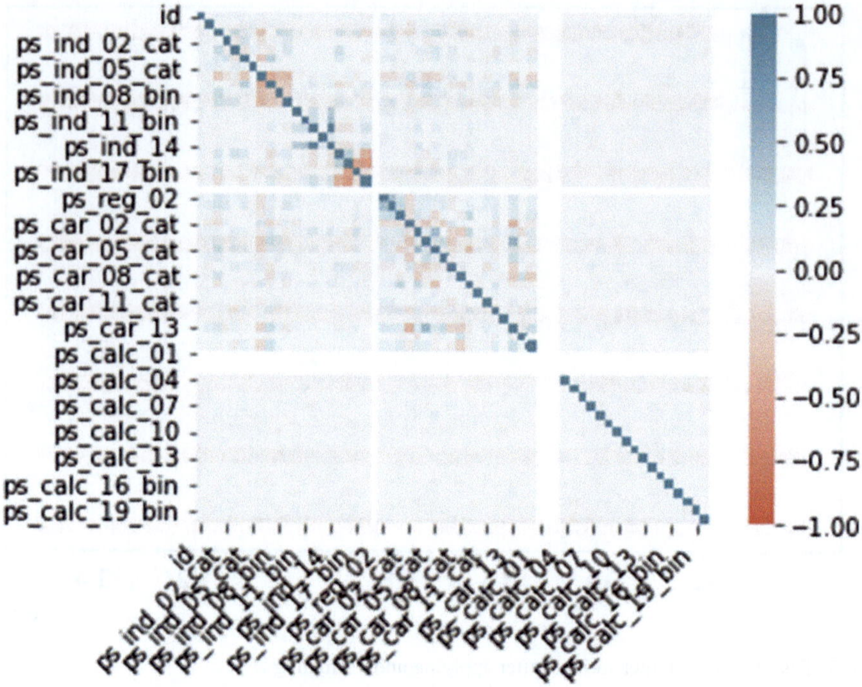

Fig. 7 Correlation diagram of correlation matrix

Table 2 Predictive modeling result using random undersampling

	Kappa	Precision	Recall	F1-score	G score
Gaussian Naive Bayes	0.052	0.537	0.369	0.437	0.502
Decision Tree	0.048	0.523	0.535	0.529	0.524
K Nearest Neighbors	−0.003	0.497	0.503	0.500	0.498
Logistic Regression	0.007	0.502	**0.654**	0.568	0.480
Support Vector Machines	−0.0002	0.499	0.558	0.527	0.496
RF	0.155	0.580	0.557	**0.568**	0.577
XGBoost	**0.163**	**0.584**	0.559	0.572	**0.581**

The value of precision is 0.584. It means that the model achieved an accuracy or correctness of approximately 58.4% in predicting positive instances correctly. A recall value of 0.654 is obtained using the logistic regression method. It indicates that approximately 65.4% of the relevant items were successfully retrieved from the

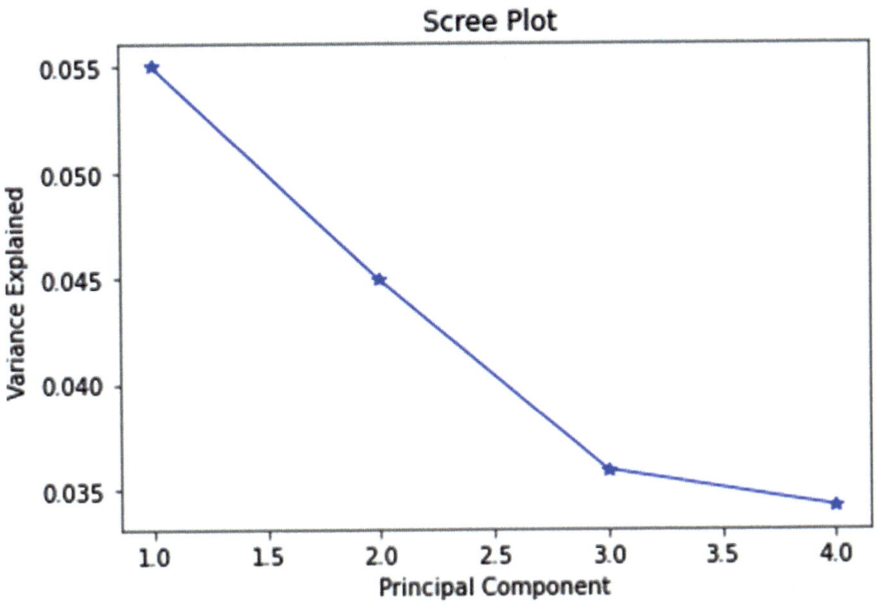

Fig. 8 Scree plot of PCA

Table 3 Predictive modeling result using random oversampling

	Kappa	Precision	Recall	F1-Score	G Score
Gaussian Naive Bayes	0.222	0.643	0.515	0.572	0.603
Decision Tree	0.924	0.930	1.0	0.964	0.961
K Nearest Neighbors	0.812	0.844	1.0	0.915	0.900
Logistic Regression	0.195	0.614	0.544	0.577	0.595
Support Vector Machines	0.052	0.526	0.658	0.584	0.509
RF	**1.0**	**1.0**	**1.0**	**1.0**	**1.0**
XGBoost	**1.0**	**1.0**	**1.0**	**1.0**	**1.0**

larger set. An F1 score of 0.568 has been found using the Random Forest model. It indicates that the model has achieved a balance between precision and recall, with a higher emphasis on precision. The value of G mean is highest in XGBoost, which is 0.581. The CF for RUS method is shown in Fig. 9.

In Table 3, we have represented the result of random oversampling and the applied model. From this table, we can see that Random Forest and XGBoost give the same result. Kappa value, precision, recall, F1 score, and G mean all have value 1. Kappa

Table 4 Predictive modeling result using SMOTE

	Kappa	Precision	Recall	F1 score	G score
Gaussian Naive Bayes	0.754	0.850	0.918	0.883	0.876
Decision Tree	0.863	0.917	0.951	0.933	0.931
K Nearest Neighbors	0.504	0.707	0.871	0.780	0.741
Logistic Regression	0.456	0.731	0.730	0.731	0.728
Support Vector Machines	0.051	0.527	0.606	0.564	0.519
RF	0.958	**0.998**	0.960	0.979	0.979
XGBoost	**0.960**	0.996	**0.964**	**0.980**	**0.980**

value 1 means perfect agreement. If the precision is 1, then all of the anticipated positive instances actually occurred. It calculates the percentage of positively predicted cases that were accurate. A recall of 1 indicates that all positive events were correctly identified and that there were no false negatives. It assesses a model's capacity to locate every relevant instance. A model with an F1 score of 1 has perfect precision and recall, suggesting exceptional prediction accuracy. The G mean is also higher in this case. The CF for ROS method is shown in Fig. 10.

In Table 4, we describe the result when the predictive model and SMOTE are combined. From this table, we can see that the best kappa value is obtained using the XGBoost method. It is 0.960, which means almost perfect agreement. However, the precision value is 0.998 using the random forest method. It means that the model achieved an accuracy or correctness of approximately 99.8% in predicting positive instances correctly. A recall value of 0.964 is obtained using the XGBoost method. It indicates that approximately 96.4% of the relevant items were successfully retrieved from the larger set. An F1 score of 0.980 has been found using the XGBoost model. It indicates that the model has achieved a balance between precision and recall, with a higher emphasis on precision. The value of G mean is highest in XGBoost, which is 0.980. The CF for the SMOTE method is shown in Fig. 11.

6 Conclusion

Predicting claims is one of the biggest problems facing the insurance sector. Auto insurance companies can use it to personalize each policyholder's insurance to the appropriate kind. Many insurance businesses evaluate client information using conventional methods. To address these issues, we therefore used sophisticated statistical techniques and predictive modeling algorithms. The prediction techniques employed

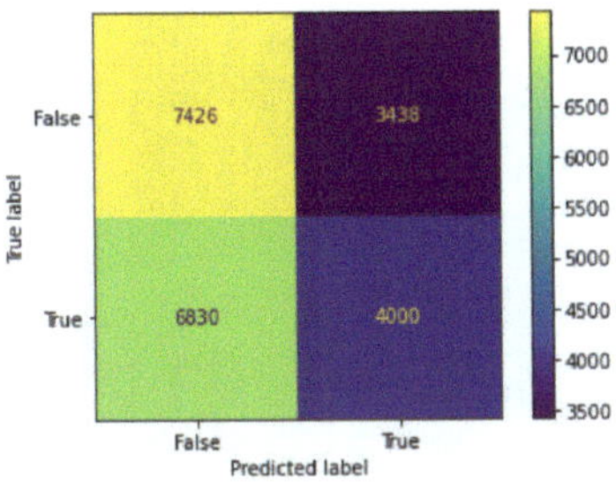

(a) CF for NB.

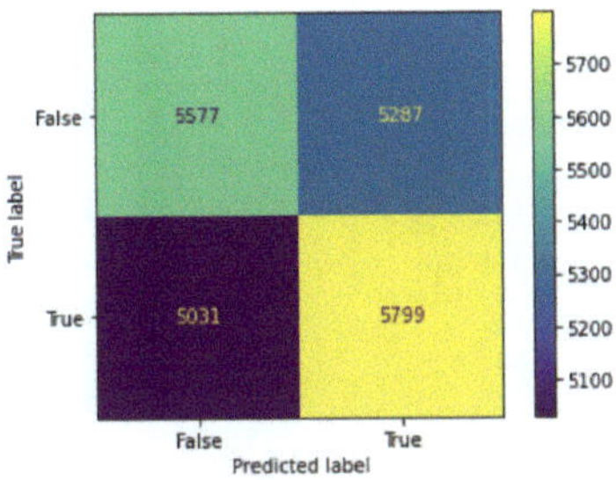

(b) CF for DT.

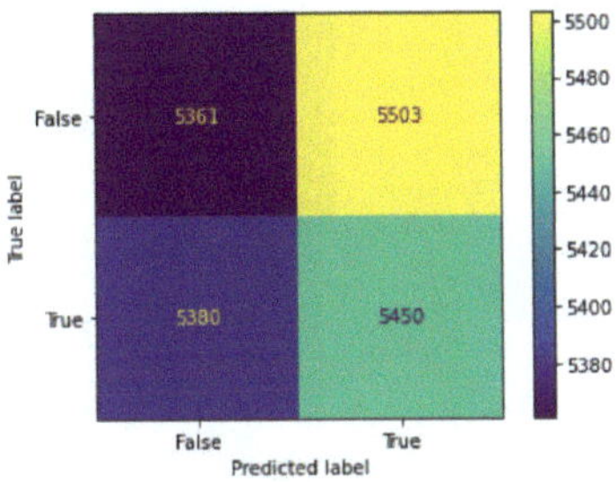

(c) CF for KNN.

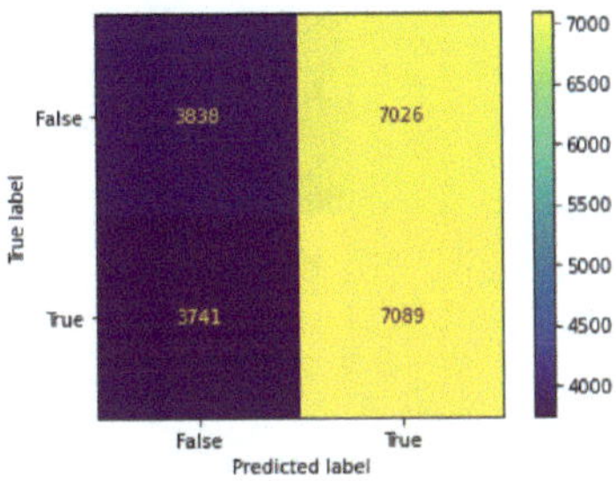

(d) CF for LR.

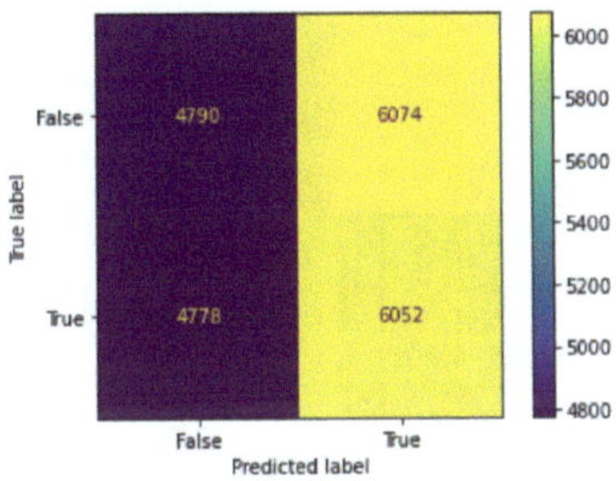

(e) CF for SVM

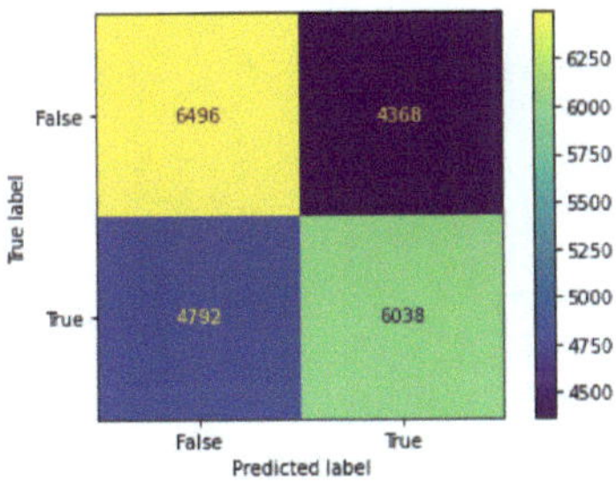

(f) CF for RF.

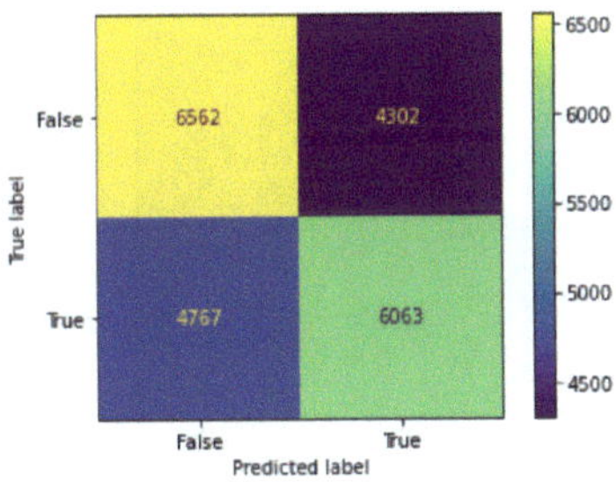

(g) CF for XGBoost.

Fig. 9 CF of predictive models using random undersampling

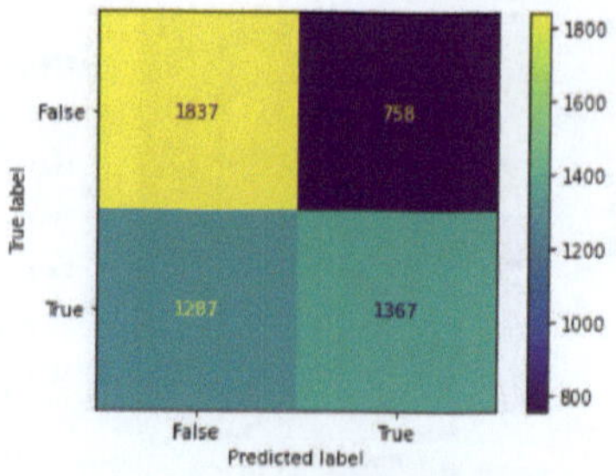

(a) CF for NB.

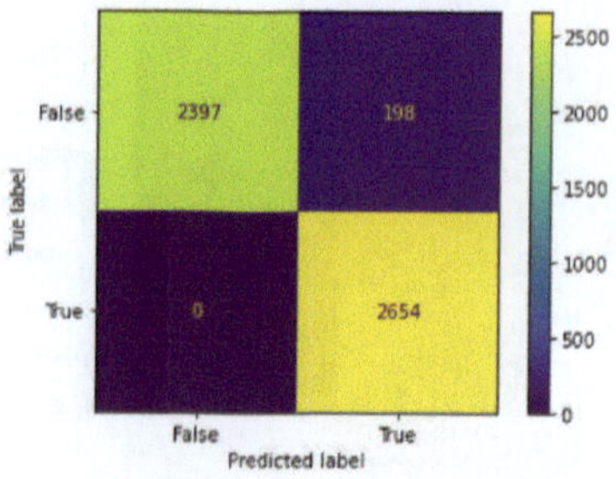

(b) CF for DT.

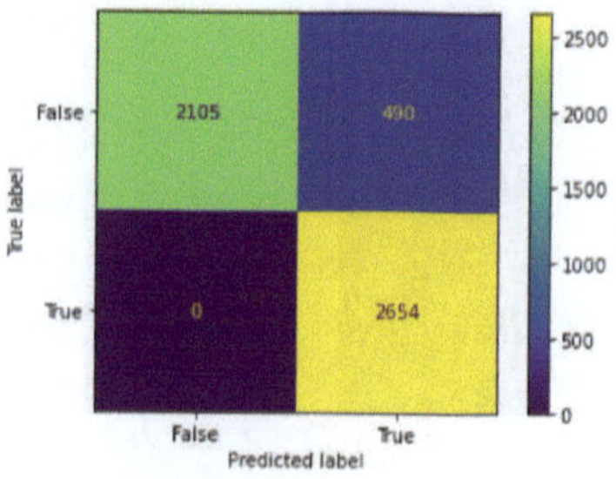

(c) CF for KNN.

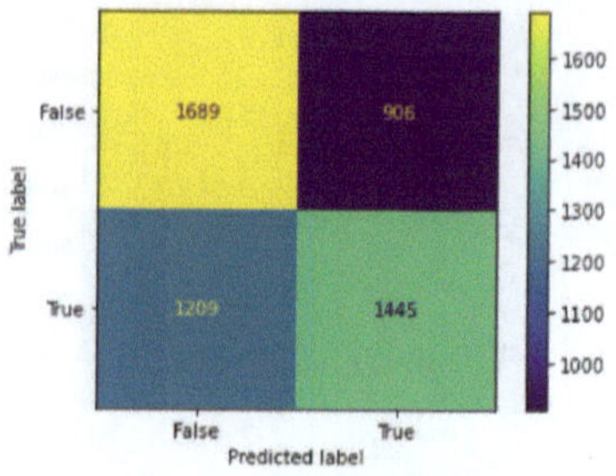

(d) CF for LR.

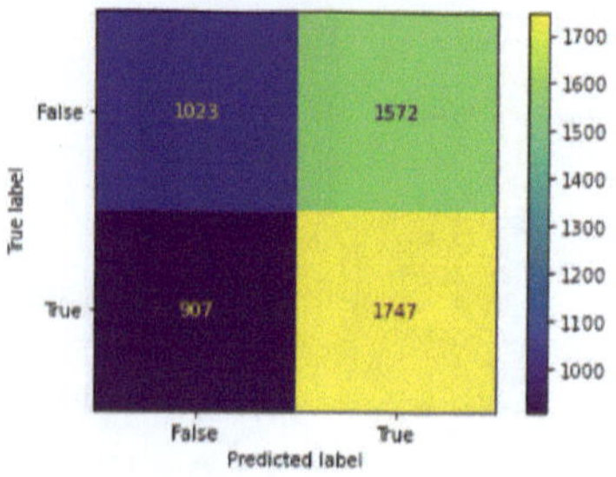

(e) CF for SVM

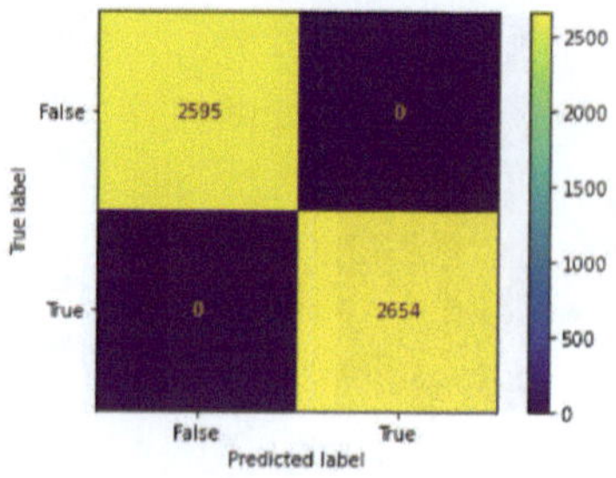

(f) CF for RF.

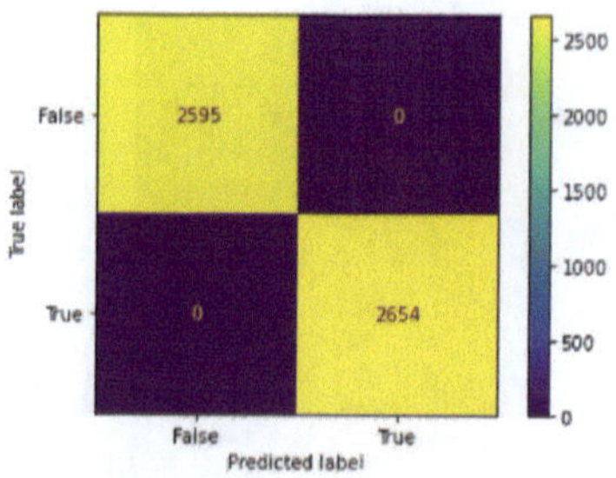

(g) CF for XGBoost.

Fig. 10 CF of predictive models using random oversampling

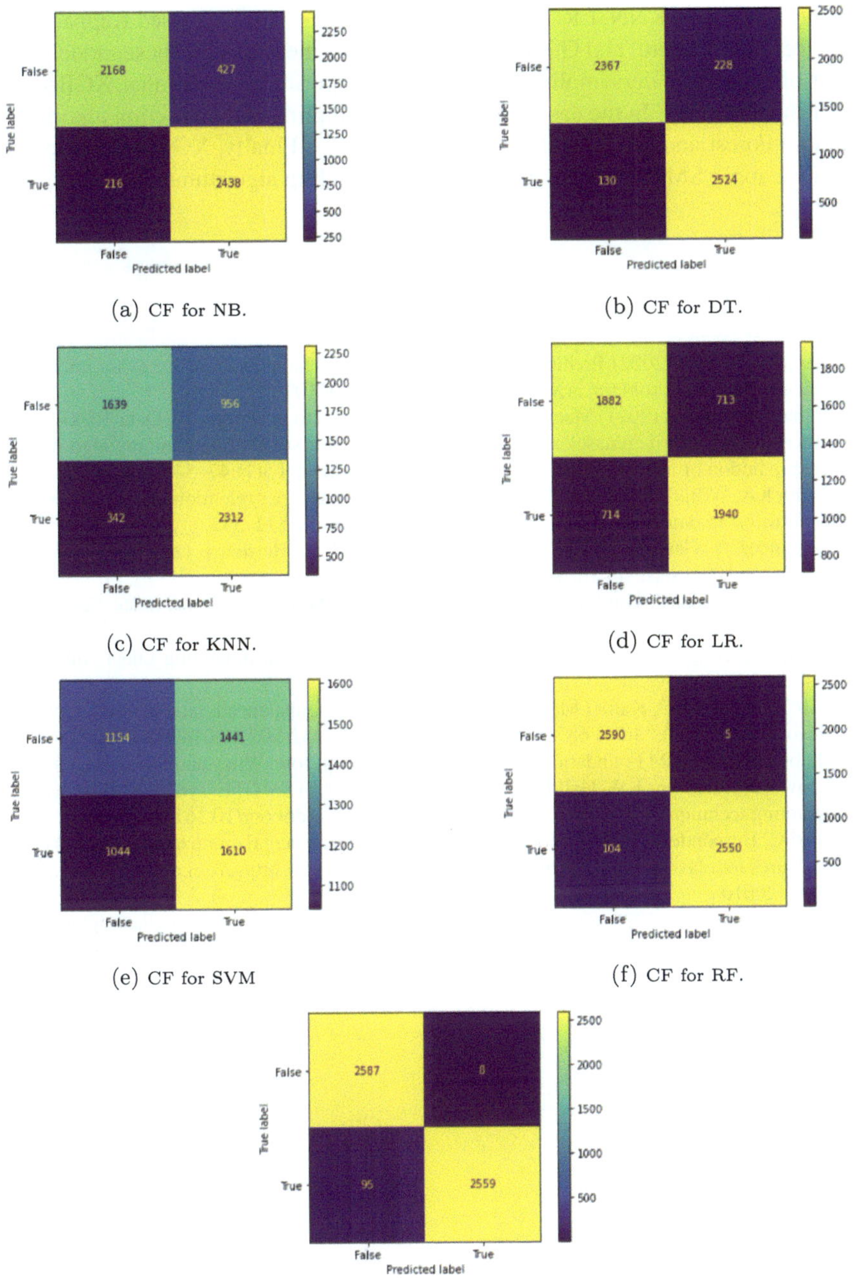

(a) CF for NB.

(b) CF for DT.

(c) CF for KNN.

(d) CF for LR.

(e) CF for SVM.

(f) CF for RF.

(g) CF for XGBoost.

Fig. 11 CF of predictive models using SMOTE

here are GNV, DT, KNN, LR, SVM, RF, and XGBoost. We have used Kappa, Precision, Recall, F1 Score, and G Mean as performance measures for these models. The result of random undersampling and predictive algorithms shows that XGBoost is better in most cases. In the case of random oversampling and prediction algorithms, Random Forest and XGBoost both give good results. Finally, XGBoost works well when we apply SMOTE and seven predictive modeling algorithms.

References

1. Baran S, Rola P (2022) Prediction of motor insurance claims occurrence as an imbalanced machine learning problem. arXiv preprint arXiv:2204.06109
2. Hanafy M, Ming R (2021) Mach Learn Approaches for Auto Insurance Big Data. Risks 9(2):42
3. Weerasinghe K, Wijegunasekara M (2016) A comparative study of data mining algorithms in the prediction of auto insurance claims. Eur Int J Sci Technol 5(1):47–54
4. Smith KA, Willis RJ, Brooks M (2000) An analysis of customer retention and insurance claim patterns using data mining: a case study. J Oper Res Soc 51:532–541
5. Fernández A, García S, Galar M, Prati RC, Krawczyk B, Herrera F (2018) Learning from imbalanced data sets, vol 10. Springer
6. Pesantez-Narvaez J, Guillen M, Alcañiz M (2019) Predicting motor insurance claims using telematics data-xgboost versus logistic regression. Risks 7(2)
7. Branco P, Torgo L, Ribeiro R (2015) A survey of predictive modelling under imbalanced distributions
8. Sun Y, Wong AKC, Kamel MS (2009) Classification of imbalanced data: a review. Int J Patt Recogn Artif Intell 23(04):687–719. https://doi.org/10.1142/S0218001409007326
9. Haibo H, Yunqian M Foundations of imbalanced learning. John Wiley and Sons, Ltd, pp 13–41
10. Chawla NV, Bowyer KW, Hall LO, Kegelmeyer WP (2002) SMOTE: synthetic minority oversampling technique. J Artif Intell Res 16:321–357. https://doi.org/10.1613/jair.953
11. Ferri C, Hernández-Orallo J, Modroiu R (2009) An experimental comparison of performance measures for classification. Pattern Recogn Lett 30(1):27–38. https://doi.org/10.1016/j.patrec.2008.08.010
12. Puri A, Gupta MK (2021) Knowledge discovery from noisy imbalanced and incomplete binary class data. Expert Syst Appl 181:115179

GAN-Based Image Inpainting Using Modified Gated Convolution

Cynthia Devi Arumugam and Balaji Banothu

1 Introduction

Image inpainting has its roots in physical artwork [1], such as brush painting and sculpture painting. Artworks seek to visually enhance the entire piece of art by replacing any missing or damaged components with techniques and resources similar to those utilized by the original artist. Recent advancements in image processing have made image inpainting very popular in digital photos. It enables the editing of undesirable areas or the removal of distracting things from photographs.

Deep learning-based procedures have emerged as a promising solution over traditional inpainting techniques, which frequently take longer and rely on manually constructed distance measures to fill the mask. Image inpainting techniques based on data-driven deep learning [2] can produce the missing pixels in an image while maintaining strong global consistency and fine local textures. According to the network structure used for inpainting, Qiang et al. [2] classified the existing methods into three categories of image inpainting methods based on convolutional autoencoder networks, GAN, and recurrent neural networks. With consistent training, convolutional neural networks [3–5] provide effective image inpainting. But CNN might still generate blurring and minute artifacts if trained extensively. The models rely that on an autoencoder [6, 7], an improved autoencoder based on an attention mechanism [8–10], and an enhanced shared codec network layer based on a coarse-to-fine network [6] provide better inpainting. Generative adversarial networks based image inpainting used with any backbone architecture gradually restore damaged images at the semantic level; their authors claim the models are hybrid. The model proposed

C. Devi Arumugam (✉) · B. Banothu
Department of Computer Applications, National Institute of Technology, Tiruchirappalli, Tamilnadu, India
e-mail: cynthiadevi@gmail.com

B. Banothu
e-mail: balaji@nitt.edu

K. Kumar Singh et al. (eds.), *Machine Vision and Augmented Intelligence*, Lecture Notes in Electrical Engineering 1211, https://doi.org/10.1007/978-981-97-4359-9_61

by Yu et al. use a GAN [11], which gives free-form mask inpainting. The earlier suggested generative networks aren't utilizing customized masks to rework or restore based on user guidance efficiently; thereby, the repaired or inpainted surfaces may exhibit blur or minute distortions.

Inspired by [11] a generative inpainting network with modified gated convolution is proposed that fills in the holes or scratches in old damaged photos, modifies image layouts, clears watermarks, and edits or removes the texts in images with guidance from the user.

Our work's primary contributions are:

- We suggested a modified gated convolution layer model that may maintain the image's color as original while inpainting the quality of unequal masks and inputs by learning a dynamic feature selection procedure for each channel at each spatial point across all layers.
- A discriminator based on the fully convolutional layer uses the weight normalization technique, Spectral Normalization (SN), to distinguish between actual and fake images and the WGAN-GP loss function. It is easy and quick and creates high-quality inpainting effects.
- Our proposed method delivers higher-quality image inpainting on the benchmark Paris Street View dataset. We demonstrate how the suggested approach may assist users in swiftly removing distracting elements, modifying image layouts, and removing artifacts.

2 Related Works

With the quick advancement of deep learning, feature learning-based image inpainting techniques have emerged has overcome the shortcomings such as lack of high-level consistency and difficulty in processing large and complex structures of traditional methods. Pathak et al. [6] proposed the Context Encoder model, which uses an encoder-decoder with Generative Adversarial Network (GAN) [12, 13] using an unsupervised training method. Context encoding has some limitations: a completely connected layer may not be able to store precise spatial information, and often hazy textures are produced that are out of place with the rest of the image. After that, Yang et al. [14] coupled the concept of style transfer with the context encoder. They provided a new technique that preserves all images' texture and textural information, including high-resolution images. The model is not powerful enough to fill the missing region with complex structures. The best results are given by Nazeri et al. [15], where he proposes a two-stage adversarial model, Edge Connect, comprising an edge generator followed by an image completion network. The edges of the missing region of the image are illusioned by the edge generator, and the image completion network fills in the missing areas using illusioned edges as a priori. Yu et al. [10] proposed gated convolutions that are more advantageous than vanilla and partial-convolutional networks for inpainting. Enhanced Gated convolution [16] utilizes a dynamic feature selection mechanism to learn from each channel and spatial location.

The intermediate gate values show that we are learning to select features by background, mask, and sketch and considering semantic segmentation in some channels. The gated convolution provides better inpainting results in deep layers too. The usage of WGAN-GP loss function [17] gives stabilization while the training discriminator.

In our work, efficient gated convolution improves color consistency and the inpainting quality of unequal masks. To stabilize the training of the discriminator, Miyato et al. [13] suggest a unique weight normalizing method termed spectral normalization. The new normalization technique is computationally light and easily incorporated into existing implementations. Our method uses spectral normalization with a fully convolutional layer in the discriminator to stabilize the results.

3 Proposed Methodology

The proposed approach utilizes a GAN consisting of two generators and one discriminator. The entire design employs a coarse-to-fine strategy and divides into two stages.: the first generator network completes coarse reconstruction, while the second generator enhances the picture quality. The generator uses modified gated convolutional layers rather than conventional ones [11]. Because of the gating mechanism built into these layers, these layers can apply the convolutional operation differently depending on their location in the input.

The gating mechanism multiplies the output of the convolutional operation by the scaled result in a gated convolutional layer. The final output of the gated convolutional layer is created by first passing the scaled output via a non-linear activation function, such as Leaky ReLU. The model can comprehend complex input patterns by selectively applying the convolutional approach utilizing gated convolution at different input locations, which is shown in Fig. 1. Additionally dilation convolutional layers are used, where a subset of standard convolutional layers is often used in deep learning networks. The dilation layers add spaces between kernel components, expanding the kernel's receptive field. The technique uses a typical dilated convolutional layer followed by a sigmoid activation function to assess the significance or validity of each local region (i.e., non-masked part).

3.1 Spectral Normalisation

Spectral Normalisation is the largest singular matrix that is used only in generative adversarial networks [13] which efficiently controls the Lipschitz constant of the discriminator function, which lowers training instability by limiting the spectral norm of each layer.

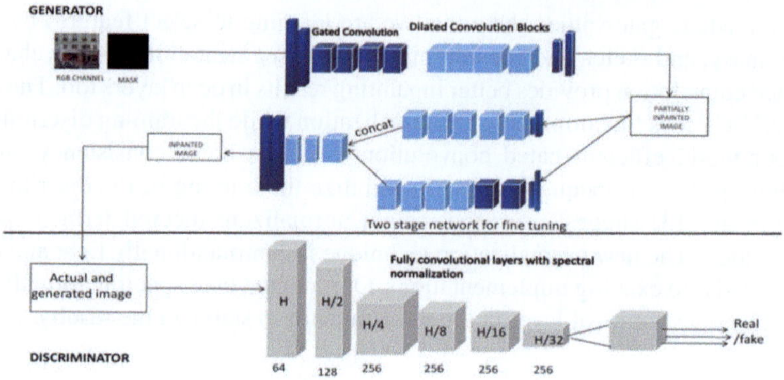

Fig. 1 Proposed gated convolution network

WGAN-GP

A traditional pixel-wise L1 loss function and WGAN-GP GAN loss [18] are both used in the suggested technique. WGAN-GP loss penalizes the discriminator if the gradient norm is too large and helps to get Lipschitz constant continuous. This stabilize the training and provide high resolution image.

4 Results and Discussions

To understand how well our model has worked, we have compared our model with two other conventional methods, Naïve Stocks and Fast March Method [19]. The dataset used is Paris view dataset with 15,000 images. We can see that for small masks, all three models' results are visually pleasing. Still, for some bigger masks, Naiver Stocks and Fast March Methods didn't give accurate results when compared to our model, and we can also see that the metrics PSNR value and SSIM values are better for our model than the other models shown in the table. The metrics PSNR and SSIM values are compared and displayed in Tables 1 and 2 (Fig. 2).

Table 1 Comparison of SSIM values for small mask

Image	FMM	NS	Our
1	0.992	0.992	0.997
2	0.992	0.992	0.998
3	0.987	0.987	0.992
4	0.990	0.990	0.995
5	0.987	0.988	0.995

Table 2 Comparison of PSNR values for small mask

Image	FMM	NS	Our
1	48.03	48.23	57.82
2	48.47	48.52	58.56
3	45.97	46.06	56.00
4	47.64	47.66	57.05
5	46.43	46.52	55.95

Fig. 2 Comparison of FMM and NS methods with ours for inpainting with a small mask

4.1 For Larger Mask Output

The FMM and NS model reconstructions for bigger mask images are not good and are visually incorrect. Still, for our models, the output is visually suitable for most of the photos, it can be viewed in Fig. 3. Here also two metrics are used for qualitative analysis the PSNR and SSIM. Both the values are better for our model when compared with FMM and NS methods as shown in Tables 3 and 4, respectively.

The visual and statistical comparison shows that the proposed model performs better.

Fig. 3 Comparison of FMM and NS methods with ours for inpainting with a large mask

Table 3 Comparison of PSNR values for large mask

Image	FMM	NS	Our
1	35.01	35.02	45.03
2	35.90	35.95	45.969
3	36.82	36.78	46.76
4	35.92	36.19	46.45
5	36.59	37.02	47.02

Table 4 Comparison of SSIM values for large mask

Image	FMM	NS	Our
1	0.838	0.841	0.842
2	0.852	0.852	0.862
3	0.901	0.890	0.903
4	0.925	0.923	0.937
5	0.900	0.891	0.905

5 Conclusion

The proposed modified gated convolution method with spectral normalization with WGAN-GP for image inpainting has a learnable variation of partial Convolution. Employing the Gated Convolution and the SN-MD considerably enhances the inpainting outcomes compared to previous inpainting techniques. In future we are planning to work on the more efficient normalization, since normalization improves the image inpainting and makes more quality images.

Declarations Conflict of interest: All authors declare that they have no conflict of interest. On behalf of all authors, the corresponding author states that there is no conflict of interest.

References

1. https://en.wikipedia.org/wiki/Inpainting
2. Qiang ZP, He LB, Chen X, Xu D (2019) Survey on deep learning image inpainting methods. J Image Graph 24(3):447–463
3. Xiong W, Yu J, Lin Z, Yang J, Lu X, Barnes C, Luo J (2019) Foreground- aware image inpainting. In: Proceedings of the IEEE/CVF conference on computer vision and pattern recognition, pp 5840–5848
4. Iizuka S, Simo-Serra E, Ishikawa H (2017) Globally and locally consistent image completion. ACM Trans Graph
5. Yi Z, Tang Q, Azizi S, Jang D, Xu Z (2020) Contextual residual aggregation for ultra-high-resolution image inpainting. In: Proceedings of the IEEE/CVF conference on computer vision and pattern recognition, pp 7508–7517
6. Liu H, Jiang B, Song Y, Huang W, Yang C (2020) Rethinking image inpainting via a mutual encoder-decoder with feature equalizations. In: Computer Vision–ECCV 2020: 16th European conference, Glasgow, UK, August 23–28, 2020, Proceedings, Part II 16. Springer International Publishing, pp 725–741
7. Nie L, Yu W, Zhang X, Li S, Chen S, Zhang Z, Gong J (2021) Free-form image inpainting with separable gate encoder-decoder network. Springer International Publishing
8. Xie C, Liu S, Li C, Cheng MM, Zuo W, Liu X, Ding E (2019) Image inpainting with learnable bidirectional attention maps. In: Proceedings of the IEEE/CVF international conference on computer vision, pp 8858–8867
9. Liu H, Jiang B, Xiao Y, Yang C (2019) Coherent semantic attention for image inpainting. In: Proceedings of the IEEE/CVF international conference on computer vision, pp 4170–4179
10. Yu J, Lin Z, Yang J, Shen X, Lu X, Huang TS (2018) Generative image inpainting with contextual attention. In: Proceedings of the IEEE conference on computer vision and pattern recognition
11. Yu J, Lin Z, Yang J, Shen X, Lu X, Huang TS (2019) Free-form image inpainting with gated Convolution. In: Proceedings of the IEEE international conference on computer vision, pp 4471–4480
12. Jiang Y, Xu J, Yang B, Xu J, Zhu J (2020) Image inpainting based on generative adversarial networks. IEEE Access 8:22884–22892
13. Miyato T, Kataoka T, Koyama M, Yoshida Y (2018) Spectral normalization for generative adversarial networks. In: Proceedings of international conference on learning representations (ICLR)
14. Pathak D, Krahenbuhl P, Donahue J, Darrell T, Efros AA (2016) Context encoders: feature learning by inpainting. In: Proceedings of the IEEE conference on computer vision and pattern recognition, pp 2536–2544
15. Nazeri K, Ng E, Joseph T, Qureshi FZ, Ebrahimi M (2019) EdgeConnect: generative image inpainting with adversarial edge learning. In: Proceedings of international conference on computer vision (ICCV)
16. Wang M, Lu W, Lyu J, Shi K, Zhao H (2022) Generative image inpainting with enhanced gated convolution and Transformers. Displays 75:102321
17. Zhang T, Liu Q, Wang X, Ji X, Du Y (2022) A 3D reconstruction method of porous media based on improved WGAN-GP. Comput Geosci 165:105151

18. Gulrajani FA, Arjovsky M, Dumoulin V, Courville A (2017) Improved training of Wasserstein Gans. https://arxiv.org/abs/1704.00028
19. Telea A (2004) An image inpainting technique based on the fast-marching method. J Graph Tools 9(1):23–34

Empowering Web Accessibility for Enhanced Digital Experiences

Kuldeep Vayadande, Ashitosh Wankhede, Purva Sarvade, Tanushree Kanade, Gaurav Zanwar, Sharvari Dhage, and Tanuj Somani

1 Introduction

Web accessibility stands as a cornerstone of digital inclusivity, embodying the ethos that online experiences should be accessible to all, irrespective of their physical or cognitive abilities. It encompasses the holistic design and development of websites, applications, and digital content, with the objective of eliminating barriers that might hinder individuals, particularly those with disabilities, from fully engaging with and benefiting from online resources. The concept of enhanced web accessibility takes this commitment to inclusivity to a higher echelon. Beyond merely meeting minimum requirements, it entails the integration of innovative strategies and technologies that enrich user experiences for a diverse range of individuals. This approach goes beyond a legal or moral obligation; it recognizes accessibility as a conduit to making online platforms more usable and engaging for everyone. An instrumental facet of enhanced web accessibility is the incorporation of advanced assistive technologies. These tools, spanning from screen readers and magnifiers to voice recognition software, empower individuals with visual, auditory, motor, or cognitive impairments to navigate the digital realm with ease. Moreover, embracing progressive web apps and responsive design principles ensures that content seamlessly adapts to various devices, catering to users who rely on alternative browsing methods.

In the pursuit of enhanced accessibility, user interfaces are crafted to be intuitive and user-friendly. Clear navigation, consistent layouts, and thoughtful organization

K. Vayadande · A. Wankhede · P. Sarvade (✉) · T. Kanade · G. Zanwar · S. Dhage · T. Somani
Vishwakarma Institute of Technology, Pune 411037, Maharashtra, India
e-mail: purva.sarvade22@vit.edu

K. Vayadande
e-mail: kuldeep.vayadande1@vit.edu

K. Kumar Singh et al. (eds.), *Machine Vision and Augmented Intelligence*, Lecture Notes in Electrical Engineering 1211, https://doi.org/10.1007/978-981-97-4359-9_62

of information create an accessible environment for all users. The provision of alternative text for non-text content, such as images and multimedia, ensures that information remains accessible to those unable to perceive or interpret such content conventionally. Adherence to established web accessibility guidelines, exemplified by the Web Content Accessibility Guidelines (WCAG), becomes paramount. By surpassing mere compliance, developers who embrace these guidelines infuse accessibility as a fundamental facet of their development processes, fostering an environment where inclusive design is inherent. Integral to the success of enhanced web accessibility is the regular evaluation through accessibility testing and user feedback. Rigorous audits and assessments aid developers in identifying and rectifying potential issues in a timely manner. Engaging individuals with disabilities for real-world feedback ensures that solutions are tailored to effectively meet their unique needs. The essence of enhanced web accessibility lies in its commitment to constructing a more inclusive digital landscape. It seeks to empower individuals with disabilities, enabling them to independently access and engage with online content.

By amalgamating innovative technologies, adhering to established guidelines, and involving users throughout development, web developers forge a digital realm that transcends mere access and truly enriches the experiences of all users, regardless of their abilities. This comprehensive philosophy is realized through a multifaceted strategy encompassing intricate design, meticulous development, and thoughtful content creation. The overarching objective is to empower individuals with diverse impairments, enabling them to seamlessly navigate, interact, and comprehend online information. In embracing enhanced web accessibility, websites stand as catalysts in dismantling digital barriers and offering equal access to information, products, and services. Integral to this approach is the principle of perceivability which mandates content presentation through multiple sensory channels. Accompanied by text alternatives for non-text elements and multimedia elements with captions and audio descriptions, this principle ensures information is accessible to users with sensory impairments. Equally vital is operability, which focuses on crafting navigational and interactive elements operable through various input methods. This accommodates individuals facing mobility challenges, ensuring that website functionalities are accessible to all, regardless of their physical limitations. The principle of understandable content champions clarity, logical structuring, and user-friendly interfaces. Adhering to this principle ensures websites are comprehensible and navigable, transcending cognitive and language-related limitations.

The robustness principle is equally pivotal, advocating for technology that remains adaptable to evolving standards and seamlessly interacts with a diverse array of assistive tools. Techniques such as semantic HTML, ARIA roles, and responsive design play a pivotal role in upholding accessibility as technology progresses. Beyond the realm of compliance with legal requirements, such as the WCAG, embracing enhanced web accessibility epitomizes a commitment to equitable access and social responsibility. By broadening a website's audience, enhancing user experience, and fostering a more inclusive online environment, enhanced web accessibility lays a robust foundation for a digital landscape that harmoniously accommodates and serves individuals of all abilities. In an increasingly interconnected world, this approach cements the digital realm as a space where every individual's voice can be heard, needs met, and experiences enriched.

2 Literature Survey

The research paper [1] by Vicente Centeno et. al. presents a comprehensive examination of tools used for assessing web accessibility, coupled with suggestions for enhancing their effectiveness. Web accessibility pertains to the design of websites and online content in a manner that facilitates seamless access and interaction for individuals with disabilities. The authors commence by highlighting the critical importance of web accessibility and shed light on the challenges faced by impaired users while attempting to engage with digital content. They emphasize that ensuring universal access to information and services is not only a moral obligation but also a legal requirement in numerous countries, underscoring the need for websites to be inherently accessible. The study proceeds to conduct an in-depth scrutiny of the existing landscape of web accessibility evaluation tools. These tools are specifically designed to gauge the usability of websites and provide developers with actionable feedback. The paper elaborates on how these instruments play a pivotal role in identifying potential barriers to accessibility and guiding developers in crafting more inclusive digital experiences.

The research paper [2] by Hayfa et al. explores the challenges faced by individuals with disabilities in accessing online content. It highlights the key issue of developers and designers lacking awareness of web accessibility guidelines, which hinders inclusivity. Inconsistent accessibility standards across websites further complicate the situation, emphasizing the need for universally accepted guidelines like WCAG. Rapid technological advancements make it tough to retrofit existing websites for accessibility, and economic concerns sometimes deter website owners from making improvements. To address these issues, the paper advocates for collaborative efforts, awareness campaigns, and training programs to promote inclusive design. It also suggests incentives and regulations to encourage adherence to accessibility standards, ultimately aiming to create a more inclusive digital landscape for all users.

The research paper [3] by Islam et al. is a comprehensive endeavour aimed at enhancing web accessibility for users with disabilities. The study undertakes an in-depth exploration of prevalent challenges in web accessibility and presents innovative solutions to address these issues effectively. The paper underscores the significance of adhering to established accessibility standards, particularly the WCAG, as a foundational principle for fostering inclusivity. It emphasizes the integration of inclusive design practices from the outset of web development to streamline the process and mitigate the complexities associated with retrofitting accessibility features. Central to the study's approach is the active involvement of individuals with disabilities through user testing and feedback mechanisms. By directly engaging users, the researchers seek to ensure the real-world effectiveness of implemented accessibility solutions, thereby enhancing user experience and accessibility. The paper also highlights the potential of automated testing tools to evaluate and augment web accessibility. These tools offer a systematic approach to identify accessibility issues and streamline the improvement process.

The research paper [4] by Francisco delves into the critical role of web accessibility, particularly for individuals with disabilities. The study underscores the web's integral function as a pivotal platform for disseminating public information, facilitating education, enabling employment opportunities, and more. The researchers employ a systematic literature review to meticulously explore various empirical methods for evaluating web accessibility on educational websites. They delve into the utilization of automated tools, real user testing, and expert assessments to gauge compliance with the WCAG. An essential aspect of the study involves dissecting the nuances and disparities between these evaluation techniques. Emphasizing the potential advantages of maintaining WCAG-compliant websites, the paper highlights how such platforms can attract a broader customer base while fostering a sense of inclusivity. By adhering to accessibility guidelines, institutions can not only ensure equal access for individuals with disabilities but also enhance user experience for everyone, ultimately contributing to a more harmonious and inclusive digital environment. The paper provides a comprehensive exploration of the significance of web accessibility, grounded in empirical analysis of evaluation methods. It underscores the transformative impact of adhering to accessibility guidelines, both in terms of expanding reach and cultivating a digital landscape that reflects inclusivity and equal opportunity.

The research paper [5] by Jenny et al. underscores the transformative potential of digital technology in widening access to information, catering to diverse preferences and locations. Despite this potential, technology can inadvertently erect barriers, with people with disabilities, especially those who are visually impaired and rely on assistive technologies like screen readers, being most vulnerable to exclusion. Assistive technologies offer a means for individuals with disabilities to engage with online content. However, their efficacy relies on the design of digital materials that can be effectively interpreted by these tools. Without such design considerations, barriers to access persist. This is where concepts like accessible web design, 'design for all,' or 'universal access' come into play. These principles strive to eliminate obstacles and ensure that websites are comprehensible and navigable by both users and assistive technologies. Numerous methods exist for assessing web accessibility, and guidelines on creating accessible web designs are abundant. Yet, despite growing awareness of web accessibility concerns, studies indicate persistent barriers to access. Many users, particularly those with disabilities, continue to face difficulties in accessing and interacting with online content. In essence, the paper highlights the paradox of digital technology—its power to enhance access and its potential to exclude.

3 Methodology

3.1 Research and Understanding

In the initial phase of the Website, comprehensive research and understanding play a pivotal role. This involves delving deeply into the diverse range of disabilities and comprehending their implications on web accessibility. By investigating cutting-edge assistive technologies employed by disabled individuals, insights are gained into their specific needs and how technology addresses them. Furthermore, a thorough study of established accessibility standards, with a particular focus on the WCAG, provides the foundational framework for creating an inclusive digital environment that caters to the unique requirements of people with disabilities.

3.2 Assessment of Current Website

The assessment phase involves a thorough evaluation of the existing Website's accessibility limitations, pinpointing specific areas that necessitate enhancement. By scrutinizing design, content, and interactive elements, the study identifies shortcomings that may hinder access for individuals with disabilities. Subsequently, accessibility features are defined, drawing upon comprehensive research and assessment outcomes. These features encompass vital aspects like text-to-speech functionality, keyboard navigation optimization, improved colour contrast, and the inclusion of descriptive alt text for images. Prioritization is guided by their potential impact in fostering inclusivity, ensuring an improved user experience that accommodates the diverse needs of individuals with disabilities.

3.3 Defining Accessibility Features

In the process of defining accessibility features, comprehensive research and assessment findings serve as the foundation for establishing a curated set of enhancements for the website. This selection is guided by prioritization, emphasizing pivotal elements that substantially enhance inclusivity. The main key features are:

3.3.1 Text Size and Scalability

Use relative font units (such as em or rem) rather than fixed pixel sizes to allow users to adjust text size according to their preferences. Test the website's readability and usability with various text sizes to ensure that content remains legible and functional.

3.3.2 Colour Contrast

Ensure that the colour contrast between text and background meets accessibility standards, such as those defined in the WCAG. Utilize online contrast checking tools to verify the contrast ratios and make necessary adjustments.

3.3.3 Text-to-Speech

Integrate a text-to-speech functionality using JavaScript or HTML5 Audio elements to provide an option for users to listen to the content. Ensure compatibility with screen readers and other assistive technologies.

3.3.4 Clear and Consistent Layout

Design a consistent layout template that maintains a logical structure across all pages of the website. Implement responsive design techniques to ensure the layout adapts smoothly to various screen sizes.

3.3.5 Audio and Video Accessibility

Include closed captioning and transcripts for audio and video content to cater to users with hearing impairment. Utilize HTML5 media elements to embed multimedia content and provide alternative formats for different assistive devices.

3.3.6 Descriptive Links

Use descriptive link text that clearly indicates the destination or purpose of the link, avoiding generic phrases like "click here." Ensure that link text is meaningful when read out of context by screen readers.

3.3.7 Skip Links

Implement a "skip to content" link at the start of the page to allow keyboard users to bypass repetitive navigation and access the main content directly. Use CSS to position the skip link off-screen until it receives focus.

3.3.8 Readable Fonts

Choose fonts that are easy to read, especially for users with dyslexia or other reading impairments. Opt for sans-serif fonts for better legibility on screens.

3.3.9 Avoid Auto Play

Refrain from auto-playing audio or video content to prevent unexpected interruptions and disorientation for users with cognitive disabilities.

Alternative Text for Images

Provide descriptive alt text for images to convey their content and context to screen readers. For decorative images, use empty alt attributes or CSS to indicate their decorative nature.

Keyboard Navigation Shortcut

Assign keyboard shortcuts for frequently accessed areas of the website, such as main navigation or search functionality. Ensure that keyboard navigation follows a logical order and is consistent across the entire website.

Consistent and Predictable Navigation

Keep navigation elements in a consistent location throughout the website. Use ARIA landmarks to provide additional navigation cues for screen reader users.

Error Handling

Display clear and descriptive error messages when users encounter form validation issues or other errors. Ensure that error messages are associated with the relevant form fields and are noticeable by assistive technologies.

Testing with Assistive Technologies

Regularly test the website using different assistive technologies, such as screen readers and voice recognition software. Address any issues identified during testing and verify the effectiveness of accessibility implementations.

Regular Accessibility Audits

We perform periodic accessibility audits to identify and address any new accessibility issues that may arise as the website evolves.

3.4 Planning and Design

The comprehensive implementation plan involves translating the defined accessibility features into tangible actions. To ensure inclusivity, user interfaces are meticulously designed, incorporating considerations such as layout, colour palette, typography choices, and intuitive navigation. By adhering to accessible design principles, the aim is to create interfaces that cater to a diverse range of users, including those with disabilities. This process entails seamless integration of features like text-to-speech, keyboard navigation, and enhanced colour contrast. The overarching goal is to craft user interfaces that are both visually appealing and functionally effective, enabling individuals of varying abilities to access and interact with online content without barriers.

3.5 Development

Following the meticulously crafted plan, the implementation phase unfolds by integrating the defined accessibility features into the website. To ensure optimal accessibility, a combination of techniques is employed, including the use of semantic HTML and ARIA roles. Semantic HTML enhances the structure of the content, making it more comprehensible to assistive technologies. ARIA (Accessible Rich Internet Applications) roles further enhance interaction by providing context and functionality to elements, aiding users with disabilities. This approach promotes a cohesive and meaningful user experience. By skilfully employing these techniques, the study aims to create a website that is not only visually appealing but also adheres to best practices, enabling seamless navigation and engagement for all users.

3.6 Testing and Validation

In the testing and validation phase, the Website's accessibility is rigorously assessed through a two-pronged approach. Firstly, automated accessibility tools are employed to comprehensively scan and identify potential accessibility issues within the Website's code and content. These tools help in pinpointing areas that may require refinement. Secondly, individuals with disabilities are actively involved in user testing. Their participation provides invaluable real-world insights into the Website's usability, effectiveness, and adherence to accessibility features. Feedback collected from these users guides iterative improvements, ensuring that the Website genuinely caters to their needs. This dual testing approach aims to validate the Website's accessibility enhancements, fostering a more panoramic and user-friendly digital experience for all individuals, regardless of their abilities.

3.7 Refinement

Following testing, the study enters a crucial refinement phase. Identified issues and feedback from user testing are meticulously addressed, ensuring that the Website aligns with the desired accessibility standards. Adjustments are made to enhance the functionality and user experience of accessibility features. The focus extends beyond desktop environments; fine-tuning ensures consistent effectiveness across diverse devices and various assistive technologies like screen readers and voice recognition tools. This phase guarantees that the Website is not only accessible but seamlessly operable, catering to users with disabilities irrespective of the technology they employ. By prioritizing this refinement, the study takes a critical step towards creating an inclusive digital landscape.

3.8 Incorporating User Feedback

User feedback remains an ongoing essential component, contributing to the iterative enhancement of accessibility features. Continuous engagement with individuals having disabilities ensures that their real-world experiences are considered. By consistently gathering feedback, the study gains insights into any challenges or issues faced during website usage. This information is utilized to drive further refinements, ultimately resulting in more effective and user-friendly accessibility features.

3.9 Documentation and Guidelines

Comprehensive documentation and guidelines are crafted to ensure the perpetuation of accessibility standards. This resource caters to content creators, designers, and developers, offering clear instructions on integrating and sustaining accessibility features. It outlines best practices for designing, coding, and generating content that adheres to established accessibility guidelines. This documentation serves as a reference for maintaining inclusivity during updates and expansions, fostering a consistent approach to web accessibility. By equipping stakeholders with the knowledge to uphold these standards, the project promotes long-term accessibility commitment, ensuring the continued provision of an inclusive digital experience for users with disabilities.

3.10 Regular Audits and Updates

The creation of comprehensive documentation and guidelines plays a pivotal role in upholding accessibility standards over time. This valuable resource is tailored for content creators, designers, and developers, offering precise directives for seamlessly integrating and perpetuating accessibility features. It elucidates optimal practices for designing, coding, and curating content that aligns with established accessibility protocols. By serving as a reference during updates and expansions, this documentation fosters a uniform approach to web accessibility, ensuring sustained inclusivity. Empowering stakeholders with this knowledge fosters an enduring commitment to accessibility, guaranteeing a perpetually inclusive digital experience for users with disabilities, underlining the project's dedication to equal digital participation (Fig. 1).

4 Proposed System

The "Enhanced Web Accessibility research" is a dedicated and comprehensive effort focused on revolutionizing the digital landscape to be more inclusive and user-friendly for individuals with disabilities. This project centres around an existing website, driven by a core mission to significantly enhance its accessibility features, ensuring that all individuals, regardless of their abilities, can effectively navigate, interact with, and engage in its content and functionalities. At the heart of this endeavour lies a commitment to adhering to recognized accessibility standards and guidelines, such as the Web Content Accessibility Guidelines (WCAG). These standards provide a robust and comprehensive framework for making web content accessible to a diverse audience. By implementing these guidelines, the website aims to break down the barriers that might hinder users with disabilities from fully utilizing its offerings.

The research journey begins with a meticulous and thorough assessment of the current website's accessibility status. A combination of automated tools and manual evaluations is employed to identify existing barriers. These barriers can vary from missing alternative text for images and videos to issues with keyboard navigation, colour contrast, and interactive elements. With a clear understanding of these accessibility gaps, the website progresses into the design and development phase. In the design phase, designers collaborate to create an inclusive visual layout that prioritizes readability, optimal colour contrast, and clear visual cues. Developers, in turn, diligently work to implement semantic HTML and ARIA attributes, enhancing the website's underlying structure and making it more navigable for assistive technologies like screen readers. Content accessibility takes a central role in this research.

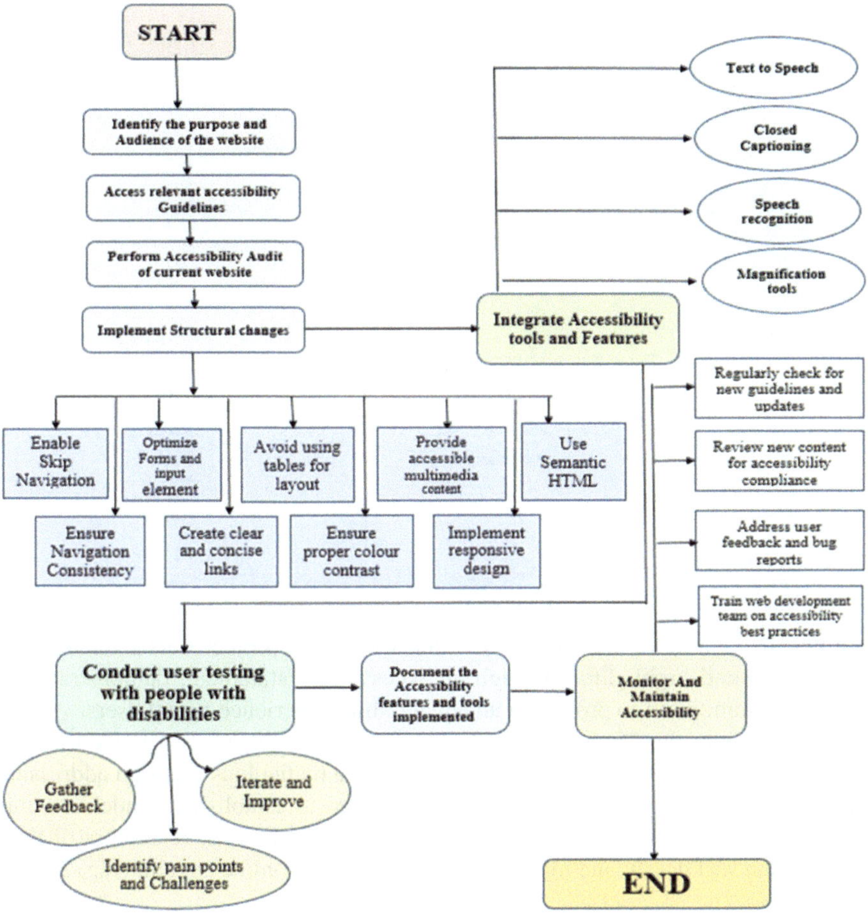

Fig. 1 Blog diagram depicting methodology

Every image is equipped with descriptive alternative text, ensuring that visually impaired users can comprehend the context of the visuals. Multimedia content, such as videos, is enriched with captions, transcripts, and audio descriptions, making them accessible to users with hearing impairments.

Crucially, the project emphasizes user testing as an integral part of its journey. Individuals with disabilities are actively engaged in testing sessions, offering invaluable insights into the website's usability and accessibility improvements. This continuous feedback loop guides an iterative process, enabling ongoing refinement based on the lived experiences of users. To ensure the project's long-term impact, accessibility training is extended to content creators, developers, and designers. This equips them with the knowledge and tools needed to maintain and continually enhance accessibility standards as the website evolves over time. Upon completion, the enhanced website not only caters to the needs of people with impairments but also contributes

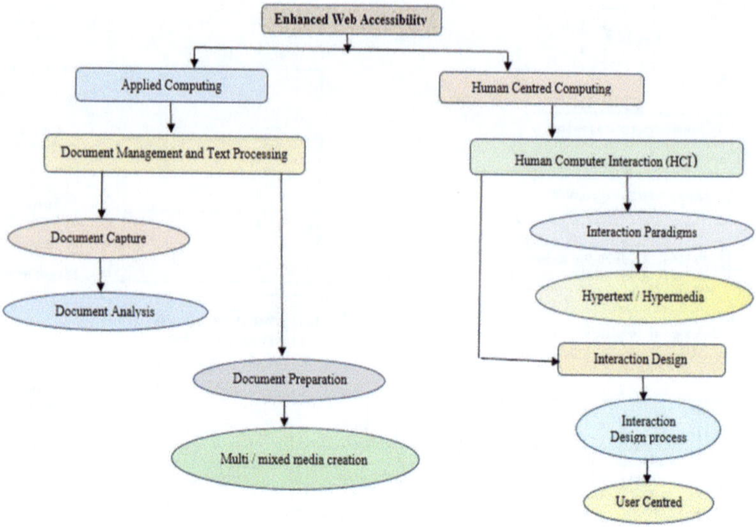

Fig. 2 Flowchart of the project

significantly to a more inclusive digital landscape. The project's achievements are documented and highlighted through an accessibility statement, demonstrating a steadfast commitment to providing an equal online experience for all users.

In conclusion, the "Enhanced Web Accessibility Website" is a transformative journey towards achieving digital equity. Through a meticulous focus on addressing accessibility challenges and unwavering adherence to established guidelines, this project strives to create a digital space where every individual, regardless of their abilities, can seamlessly and meaningfully engage with online content (Fig. 2).

5 Tables of Analysis

See Figs. 3, 4, 5, 6 and Tables 1, 2, 3 and 4.

6 Scope of Research

The scope of research includes web accessibility and its role in fostering digital involvement of individuals with impairments. The research project aims to enhance web accessibility for disabled individuals fostering a more inclusive digital environment. This multifaceted scope encompasses several key areas that require exploration and investigation. Understanding disabilities and user needs is foundational to the research. This involves studying different types of disabilities, such as visual,

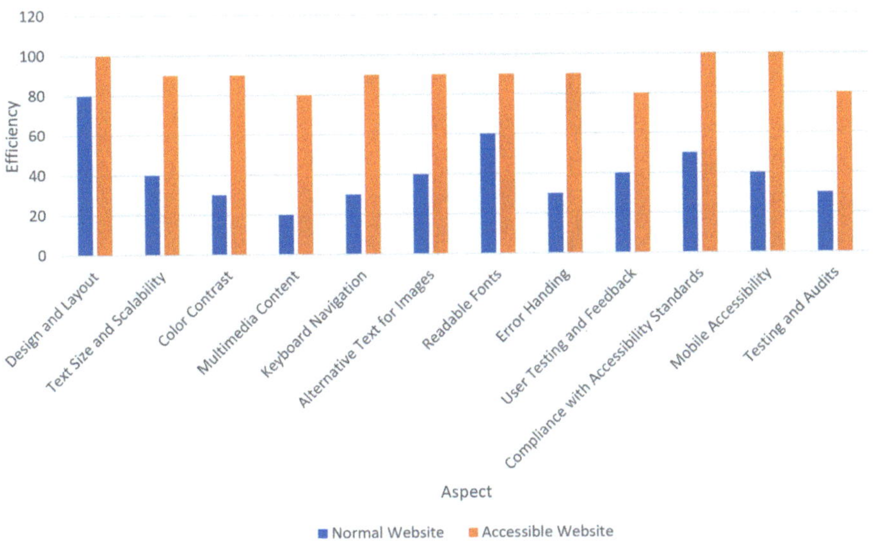

Fig. 3 Comparison graph between normal and enhanced accessible websites on basis of different aspects

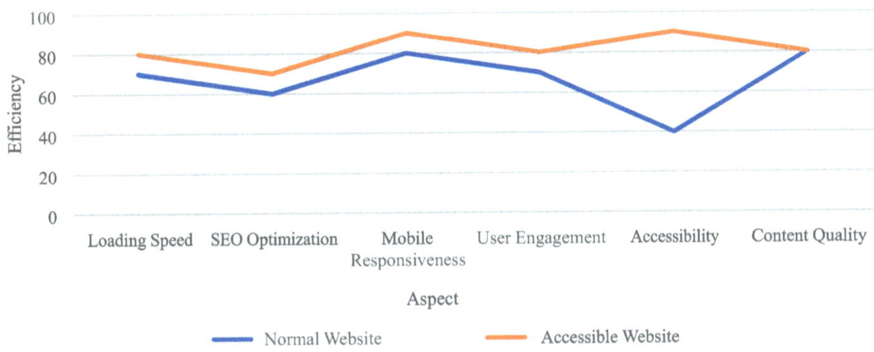

Fig. 4 Normal websites efficiency and accessible websites

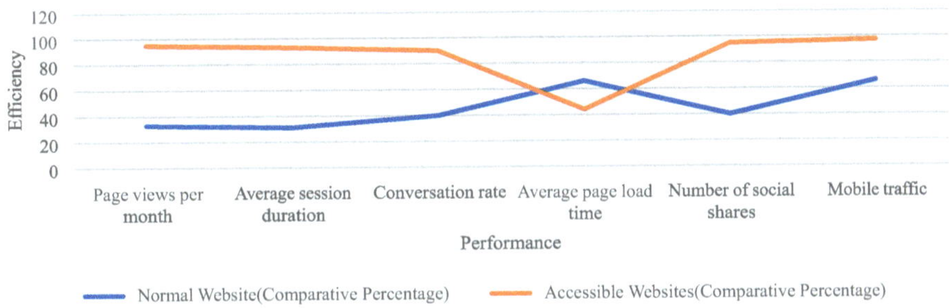

Fig. 5 Normal websites comparative percentage and Accessible websites comparative percentage

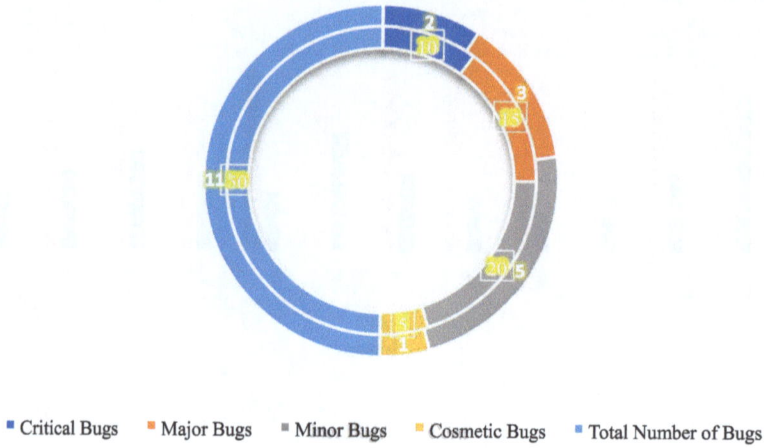

Fig. 6 Comparison on basis of bugs

auditory, cognitive, and motor impairments, and gaining insights into the unique challenges faced by each group when accessing web content. Identifying the specific requirements and preferences of disabled users in different contexts is crucial to tailor accessibility solutions effectively.

The project will delve into existing accessibility guidelines and standards, particularly WCAG, to assess their effectiveness and limitations in addressing the diverse needs of users with impairments. Research will be conducted to evaluate the implementation and compliance of web accessibility standards across various websites and platforms. To gain a deeper understanding of the user experience, usability studies will be conducted, involving individuals with disabilities navigating websites. This research will identify common pain points and barriers faced by these users, informing the development of practical solutions.

7 Future Scope

The future of this research is poised to bring about substantial advancements in web accessibility, fostering a more inclusive digital landscape. These changes will be instrumental across several crucial dimensions, catalysed by the convergence of technological progress and a heightened societal understanding of the importance of accessibility. A pivotal transformation lies in the integration of accessibility into the core development workflow. This proactive approach will embed accessibility considerations from project inception, ensuring that design and development processes inherently prioritize universal usability. Simultaneously, the evolution of automated accessibility testing, empowered by AI and machine learning, promises to streamline the identification and resolution of accessibility issues. This not only

Table 1 Comparison table between normal website and enhanced accessible website

Aspect	Normal website	Efficiency (%)	Enhanced accessible website	Efficiency (%)
Design and layout	May prioritize aesthetics over accessibility	80	Prioritizes both	100
Text size and scalability	Fixed font size	40	Adjustable font size	90
Color contrast	May have low contrast	30	High contrast	90
Multimedia content	Lacks closed captioning	20	Provides closed captioning	80
Keyboard navigation	Limited options	30	Multiple options	90
Alternative text for images	May Lack alt text for images	40	Includes descriptive alt text screen readers	90
Readable fonts	Fonts may be challenging	60	Simple readable fonts	90
Error handing	Vague error messages, difficult for users to fix	30	Provides clear and descriptive error messages	90
User testing and feedback	Limited involvement of users with disabilities	40	Involve users with disabilities with feedback	80
Compliance with accessibility standards	May not fully comply	50	Adheres to accessibility standards	100
MOBILE accessibility	Mobile experience may be limited for some users	40	Ensures Mobile Accessibility	100
Testing and audits	Infrequent accessibility Testing and audits	30	Regular Accessibility Testing and Audits	80

Table 2 Normal websites efficiency and accessible websites

Aspect	Normal website (efficiency)	Accessible website (efficiency)
Loading speed	70	80
SEO optimization	60	70
Mobile responsiveness	80	90
User engagement	70	80
Accessibility	40	90
Content quality	80	80

Table 3 Normal Websites comparative % and accessible websites comparative%

Aspect	Normal website (comparative percentage)	Accessible websites (comparative percentage)
Page views per month	33	95
Average session duration	31	93
Conversation rate	40	90
Average page load time	66	44
Number of social shares	40	95
Mobile traffic	66	97

Table 4 Comparison on basis of bugs

Aspect	Normal websites	Accessible websites
Critical bugs	10	2
Major bugs	15	3
Minor bugs	20	5
Cosmetic bugs	5	1
Total number of bugs	50	11

saves resources but also aligns with the imperative to create digital experiences that cater to diverse user needs, thereby fostering a more inclusive online realm.

The second facet of change encompasses the widespread adoption of inclusive design frameworks and libraries. These resources will serve as integral components in developers' toolsets, facilitating the implementation of accessibility best practices. The rising prevalence of mobile devices compels renewed focus on responsive design and mobile accessibility, emphasizing the need for adaptable web content across various screen sizes and devices. Furthermore, the strategic utilization of semantic HTML and Accessible Rich Internet Applications (ARIA) will augment web content's comprehensibility by assistive technologies. This transformation will be complemented by user-centric accessibility testing, involving individuals with disabilities to provide good insights and feedback, thus enriching the refinement of inclusive digital experiences.

8 Conclusion

In conclusion, web accessibility is not just a trend; it's a fundamental necessity. Ensuring that everyone, including those with disabilities, can access and use websites seamlessly is essential as technology transforms our digital interactions. Web developers, by incorporating accessibility into their workflows through semantic HTML, ARIA, and inclusive design, play a pivotal role in this mission. The future of web accessibility looks promising, with personalized features, AI-driven solutions, and improved voice interfaces leading the way. Collaborating with accessibility experts and users with disabilities, web developers are paving the path to a more inclusive digital environment where everyone can fully embrace the online experience.

References

1. Centeno VL, Kloos CD, Fisteus JA, Alvarez LA (2005) Web accessibility evaluation tools: a survey and some improvements. In: First international workshop on automated specification and verification of web sites (WWV 2005). Valencia, Spain
2. Abuaddous HY, Jali MZ, Basir N Faculty of sciences and technology. University Sains Islam Malaysia (USIM) Web accessibility challenges
3. Elkabani I, Hamandi L, Zantout R, Mansi S Mathematics and computer department, Beirut Arab university, Beirut, Lebanon Towards better web accessibility
4. Filipe F, Pires IV Gouveia AJ University of Tras o Montes and Alto Dauro, vila real, Portugal Why web accessibility is important for your institution
5. Craven J (2006) Research associate, CERLIM, Manchester Metropolitan University, Manchester, UK "Web accessibility: a review of research and initiatives"

Multi-model Deep Learning Approach to Classifying Lung and Colon Cancer of Histopathology Images

Onkar Singh, Sweta Sinha, Subhra Kanti Kundu, and Koushlendra Kumar Singh

1 Introduction

Every region of the body is susceptible to cancer, which promotes uncontrolled, aberrant cell growth. Normal cells do not have the same traits as cancer cells, which include immortality, unregulated proliferation, invasion of neighboring tissues, and other traits. Cancer has become the second leading cause of death. In 2020, approximately nineteen million instances of cancer had been identified worldwide, with 10 million deaths [1]. The human body contains millions of small tissues that divide in order to develop and proliferate. When a cell is injured or reaches a specific age, it dies and is displaced by healthy cells. If the damaged cells are not replaced by healthy ones, they will eventually grow, reproduce, and produce cancerous or benign tumors [2]. The benign tumors are cells that grow quietly and do not harm the tissues around them. Malignant tumors, on the other hand, are formed when cells grow swiftly and improperly, harming the tissues around them. Numerous organs in the body are infected by cancer cells. Lung cancer followed by colon cancer is two of the greatest common cancers that impact everyone, man and woman similarly. An estimated 2.7 million individuals died from lung and colon carcinoma throughout the world in 2020, whereas 4.19 million people received a diagnosis.

Lung cancer has recently surpassed heart disease as the second-deadliest condition, making early identification and elimination of malignant cells crucial [3]. Digital pathology technologies create higher-quality images from histopathology that reveal

O. Singh (✉) · K. Kumar Singh
Machine Vision and Intelligence Lab, Department of CSE, National Institute of Technology, Jamshedpur, India
e-mail: onkar122@gmail.com

S. Sinha
Saar Diagnostics, Oncopathology, Ranchi, Jharkhand, India

S. Kanti Kundu
Medical Oncologist, Apex Hospital Tata, Jamshedpur, Jharkhand, India

K. Kumar Singh et al. (eds.), *Machine Vision and Augmented Intelligence*, Lecture Notes in Electrical Engineering 1211, https://doi.org/10.1007/978-981-97-4359-9_63

the genuine source of the person's sickness in comparison to conventional imaging methods [4, 5]. However, imaging methods that involve ultrasound, magnetic resonance imaging (MRI), computed tomography (CT) and positron emission tomography (PET) scan render it challenging to detect the existence of lung cancer [6]. Since it increases the categorization precision and rapidity of diagnosing histopathological lung carcinoma, computer-aided diagnostic (CAD) framework is increasingly used in the healthcare domains to facilitate efficient diagnosis and identification [7]. To increase the diagnosis accuracy, the CAD system employs machine learning algorithms. Machine learning algorithms must acquire picture features before they can employ medical images in CAD systems [8]. An important consideration when assessing tumor aggressiveness is tumor heterogeneity. In order to evaluate the tumor heterogeneity within a CAD framework, texture evaluation is utilized in image feature extraction [9, 10]. In the present study, we created a multi deep learning framework using Keras and the TensorFlow API. In order to combine the features gathered from the two pre-trained convolutional neural network (CNN) architectures ResNet50V2 and VGG19, this particular model utilizes a series of fully connected layers. The top totally interconnected layers are not used in the ResNet50V2 and VGG19 architectures, which instead use weights that were trained using the "ImageNet" database. The work is structured as follows: In Sect. 2, the literature review is covered. Section 3 provides the description of suggested technique. The experiment's results were investigated in Sect. 4, while their conclusion was presented in Sect. 5.

2 Literature Survey

To enhance the classification of lung cancer, Wang [11] merged a self-directed cascade approach with a classifier random forest. The created model in this research efficiently chooses the critical genes that improve the accuracy of classification in comparison to the conventional strategies on five openly accessible lung cancer datasets. Whereas the created approach offers excellent support to doctors in identifying genes and lung cancer diagnosis. The given approach reduces dataset noise and enhances classification performance, but it also takes into account the problem of dimension disasters. To categorize colon and lung tumors on histopathology images, Adu [12] demonstrated the dual horizontal squash capsule network (DHSCapsNets). The horizontal squash (H-squash) operator with encoder integration of features makes up the two main components of the DHSCapsNets framework that is being offered for image categorization. Using histopathological images, Masud [13] established the convolutional neural network (CNN) framework, that identifies five distinct kinds of tissues types (two benign and three malignant) within colorectal and lung malignancies. With regard to f-measure value and correctness of classification in the ensuing section, the CNN model performed better in terms of categorization on the LC25000 database. It has been expensive to utilize the CNN approach considering it needs an extensive number of histopathology images for training.

Hatuwal et al. [14] presented a CNN architecture that attained accuracy in identifying different types of lung cancer 97.2% by employing a cross-entropy loss function. Hatuwal utilised 15,000 lung image data used by the LC25000 repository in his study. The identification of histological images was described by Bukhari et al. [15], utilizing 10,000 images comprising the LC25000 imaging collection along with 193 images through the Colorectal Adenocarcinoma Gland (CARD). They claimed that ResNet18 (94.79%), ResNet30 (95.74%) and ResNet50 (96.77%) had the highest levels of sensitivity. Mangal et al. [16] suggested a shallow neural network design for categorizing the histological images as cancers of squamous cells, adenocarcinomas, as well as benign pulmonary tissue. The identification of adenocarcinomas and normal colons was performed on the 2500 samples of the LC25000 database using a similar method. The classifier was found to be 96.61 and 97.89% accuracy considering colorectal cancer and lung malignancies accordingly. Kwabena Adu et al. [17] presented dual horizontal squash capsule networks for the categorization of colorectal and lung cancer. They used the LC25000 dataset and achieved a prediction performance of 99.23%. Utilizing previously trained CNN networks as automatic feature extractors towards the execution of traditional handmade extraction of features using transferred learning, Naresh [18] categorized the histopathological photographs of colorectal and lung cancer. The categorization process made use of the dataset LC25000. With DenseNet121, the RF classification approach has an F1-score of 98.5, 98.63% precision, 98.60% accuracy, and recall to identify aberrant cells in the colon and lungs. Singh et al. [19] provided the ensemble learning using deep feature extraction for categorization of lung cancer. The feature information collected using the local binary pattern (LBP) with VGG16 and achieved average accuracy up to 99.0%. Trishna et al. [20] proposal of VGG networks incorporating random forest and support vector machines for lung cancer classification additionally serves to reduce the computational complexity involved in categorization. Because of their diversity, variable staging, reliance upon biomarkers, and difficulties keeping up with information advancements, lung and colon malignancies provide classification hurdles. This study's proposed model architecture concatenates the features of ResNet50V2 and VGG19, combining their strengths, followed by fine-tuning these characteristics for a particular classification problem. It's appropriate for applications where getting robust classification performance requires extracting and integrating a variety of rich visual information. The categorization assessment generated after training is used to evaluate the model's efficacy.

3 Methodology

The suggested approach is made up of several processes, including feature extraction, image preprocessing, and classification. Utilizing Keras and the TensorFlow API, we designed a multi-deep learning model. This model employs a succession of fully connected layers to produce eventual prediction after combining the characteristics obtained using two previously learned convolutional neural network (CNN)

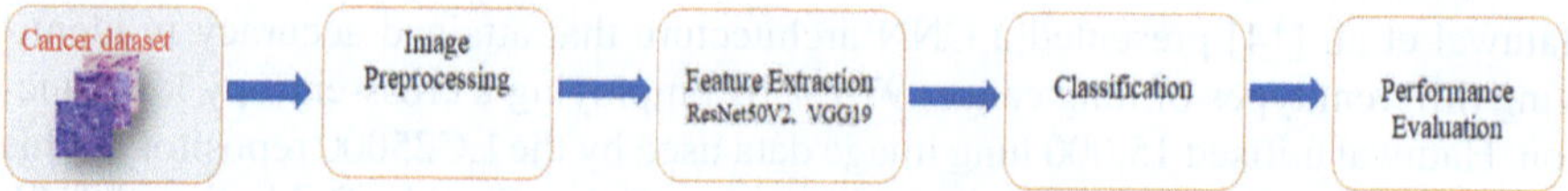

Fig. 1 Multi-model framework for classification of cancer

models ResNet50V2 and VGG19. The ResNet50V2 and VGG19 architectures use weights that have been trained from the 'imagenet' database while omitting the top completely interconnected layers. The layers have been frozen by iteratively looping over all ResNet50V2 and VGG19 layers and setting their trainable property to False. It implies the initial weights of the pre-trained layered won't change throughout training; instead, only those layers we add from this stage are going to be modified. When doing classification tasks, we build a framework by fusing characteristics obtained from ResNet50V2 and VGG19. The provided model utilizes the Deep Neural Network Architecture to perform categorization. The image is first reduced to 224 pixels during the pre-processing stage, after which it is transformed to bgr2rgb followed by a NumPy array. Afterward, perform feature scaling, where we divide the easy photo array data by 255, which reflects the higher intensity value associated with such an image. Finally, we perform labeling, where every image is given a tag (0, 1, 2, 3, 4). Figure 1 represented the proposed model for categorization of lung and colon in subcategories. The applied model summary is represented in Table 1.

Table 1 describes the incoming layer, the framework requires initial images having the shape (None, 224, 224, 3), where "None" denotes a configurable batch size, the pictures are anticipated to be 224 pixels in height and width having three RGB colour components. ResNet50V2 and VGG19 are two models that were already trained are included in the design. In order to understand how to extract valuable characteristics from photos, these base models underwent extensive training on massive datasets. In the Layer of Concatenation during this section, the outcomes of the ResNet50V2 and VGG19 frameworks are combined. This indicates that the framework integrates the feature descriptions discovered by the two baseline models. A one-dimensional vector having shape (None, 125,440) is created by flattening the concatenated characteristics. This gets the data ready to move across layers that are completely integrated. In Dense Layer 1, this layer employs 128,451,584 trainable parameters, contains 1024 neurons, and is composed of a dense network. It is in charge of discovering intricate patterns in the merged features. The 512 neurons and 524,800 trainable parameters make up the dense layer two. The 256 neurons and 131,328 parameters that are trainable make up the dense layer 3, which is the third layer. The last layer, "dense_3," has 5 neurons and is an outcome layer (classification). There are 172,698,181 parameters in the complete model. Out of them, 129,108,997 parameters are trainable, which means they will be modified throughout training. Due to their origin in the pre-trained baseline frameworks, the rest of the 43,589,184 parameters are not trainable. Table 2 depicts the employed variable in the proposed deep learning model.

Table 1 Proposed model summary

Layer (type)	Output (Shape)	Parameter
input_3 (InputLayer)	[(None, 224, 224, 3)]	0
resnet50v2 (Functional)	(None, None, None, 2048)	23,564,800
vgg19 (Functional)	(None, None, None, 512)	20,024,384
concatenate (Concatenate)	(None, 7, 7, 2560)	0
flatten (Flatten)	(None, 125,440)	0
dense (Dense)	(None, 1024)	128,451,584
dense_1 (Dense)	(None, 512)	524,800
dense_2 (Dense)	(None, 256)	131,328
dense_3 (Dense)	(None, 5)	1285

Total prams: 172,698,181
Trainable params: 129,108,997
Non-trainable params: 43,589,184

Table 2 Applied variables

Variable	Value
Image dimensions	224 × 224
Colour channels	3
Batch size	32
Number of epochs	15
Convolution layer activation	ReLU
Optimizer	Adam
Loss function	Categorical cross-entropy
Learning rate	0.0001
Dense layer activation	SoftMax

3.1 Dataset

In this investigation, histology-based images of colorectal and lung cancer from the LC25000 data collection were used [21]. The database has 25,000 color images of colon and lung cells as well as five distinct categories of tissue. The lung cancer subcategory along with colon cancer collection, which contains 5,000 pictures for every category, is described in detail in Table 3. These include colon adenocarcinoma (Colon_aca), benign tissue of colon (Colon_n), lung adenocarcinoma (Lung_aca), benign tissue of lung (Lung_n) and lung tissue of squamous cell carcinoma (Lung_scc), with their class ids of 0, 1, 2, 3, and 4 respectively. 80% of the 25,000 lung and colon images are used for training, while 20% are used for testing and validation. The colon and lung samples are shown in Fig. 2 using the LC25000 dataset.

Table 3 Subcategory for cancer from the LC 25,000 Database with Class ID

Class_id	Class name	Type of cancer	Number of samples
0	Colon_aca	Colon adenocarcinoma	5000
1	Colon_n	Colon benign tissue	5000
2	Lung_aca	Lung adenocarcinoma	5000
3	Lung_n	Lung benign tissue	5000
4	Lung_scc	Lung squamous cell carcinoma	5000

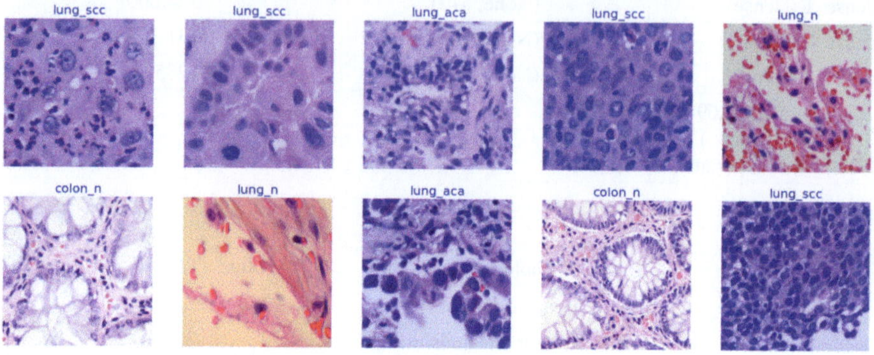

Fig. 2 Sample of lung and colon images from the LC25000 dataset

4 Result and Discussion

The statistical analysis was carried out using a 32 GB RAM system and an Intel(R) Xenon(R) Silver 4208 CPU operating at 2.10 GHz. In this work, lung cancer subcategories were classified, and aberrant and normal colons were identified using a multimodel transfer learning technique. The data set has been divided into 20,000 (80%) to be used for the training phase and 5,000 (20%) for testing and validation. Test data is utilized to produce test assessments, and they account for 10% (2500) of the entire data set. To analyze the efficacy of the model throughout training using test and validation data visually, the loss throughout training and validation along with accuracy per epoch is displayed. The categorization efficiency is measured using the metrics accuracy, F1-score, precision and recall which are expressed as

$$Precision = \frac{T_P}{T_P + F_P} \tag{1}$$

$$Recall = \frac{T_P}{T_P + F_N} \tag{2}$$

$$F1\_score = 2 * \frac{(Precision * Recall)}{(Precision + Recall)} \tag{3}$$

$$Accuracy = \frac{T_P + T_N}{T_P + F_P + T_N + F_N} \tag{4}$$

where

T_P The model correctly forecasts the frequency of incidents, positive class.
T_N The model successfully forecasts the frequency of incidents and negative class.
F_P The model estimates the event frequency in the positive class inaccurately.
F_N The model estimates the event frequency in the negative class inaccurately.

Figure 3 provides an illustration for training and validation, accuracy and loss. The 10th epoch produces better loss values while the 14th epoch produces superior accuracy values. Figure 4 shows a confusion matrix to obtain lung and colorectal cancer in relation to the classifier's performance on the test data.

Table 4 displays the effectiveness of the metrics for recall, accuracy, FI score, and precision. It is demonstrated that the suggested approach's precision and recall are 99.3%, the FI score is 99.2%, and the average accuracy is 99.00% for recognizing lung and colon cancer.

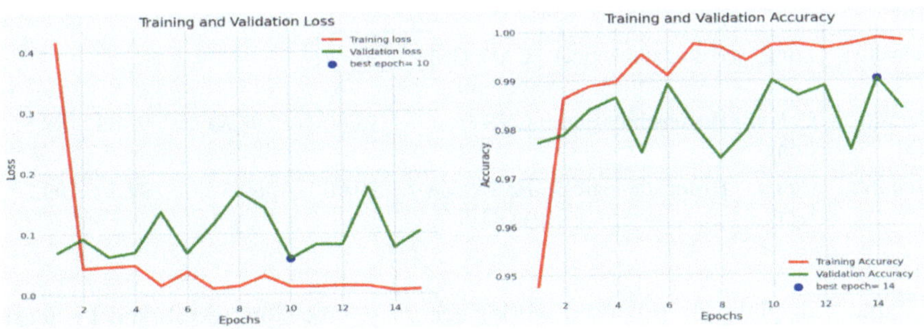

Fig. 3 Accuracy and loss for training and validation

Fig. 4 Cancer classification confusion matrix for colon and lung

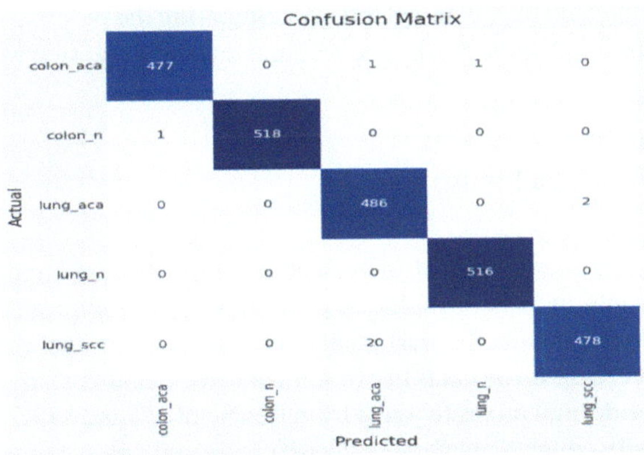

Table 4 Performance matrices for classifying lung and colon cancer

Class name	Precision	Recall	FI_score	Accuracy
Colon_aca	1	1	1	99.00
Colon_n	1	1	1	
Lung_aca	0.96	1	0.98	
Lung_n	1	1	1	
Lung_scc	1	0.96	0.98	

Table 5 Comparison of the findings in light of the currently used methods

Authors	Type of cancer	Image type	Classifier	Accuracy	Precision	Recall	FI_ score
Masud [22]	Colon, Lung	Histopathological	CNN	96.33	96.39	96.37	96.38
Hatuwal [14]	Lung	Histopathological	CNN	97.2	97.33	97.33	97.33
Mangal [16]	Lung	Histopathological	CNN	97.89	–	–	–
Shandilya [23]	Lung	Histopathological	CAD, CNN	98.67	–	–	–
Naresh [18]	Colon, Lung	Histopathological	CNN	98.60	98.60	98.63	98.5
Proposed	Colon, Lung	Histopathological	ResNet50V2, VGG19	99.00	99.3	99.3	99.2

Table 5 displays the proposed work's accuracy, precision, recall, and FI Score along with the accuracy, precision, recall, and FI Score of the authors' recommended strategy. Table 5 shows cases in which the best result from applying several classes was reported. The absence of discussion of the pertinent and significant statistic is indicated by the linked article. Comparing the proposed work to the present technique shown in Table 5, it has been found that the suggested work performs more effectively.

5 Conclusion

The effectiveness of the research center for rapid and precise assessment of cancer would increase with the advancement of techniques that are capable of recognizing certain qualities of particular harmful tumors by examining digital photos. This would decrease the probability of human errors. In this study, we proposed a unique multi-model that mixes features from ResNet50V2 and VGG19 and uses it with a number of fully connected layers to classify lung and colon cancer data. The suggested method outperformed other convolutional neural network models in our tests on the LC25000 dataset in terms of accuracy (99.00%), precision (99.3%), recall (99.3%), and FI score (99.2%). Future studies would look into different classification methods and hyper-parameter tuning. Furthermore, there are methods for creating interclass images for different pathologists by applying artificial neural pattern transmission. Furthermore, to view and explore mutations across many ontologies, histopathological images could be produced using generative algorithms.

References

1. Cancer (2022). Available online: https://www.who.int/news-room/fact-sheets/detail/cancer. Accessed on 26 October 2022
2. How Cancer Cells Grow and Spread (2022). Available online: https://www.ncbi.nlm.nih.gov/books/NBK279410/. Accessed on 27 October 2022
3. Bansal G, Chamola V, Narang P, Kumar S, Raman S (2020) Deep3DSCan: deep residual network and morphological descriptor based framework for lung cancer classification and 3D segmentation. IET Image Proc 14(7):1240–1247
4. Lakshmanaprabu SK, Mohanty SN, Shankar K, Arunkumar N, Ramirez G (2019) Optimal deep learning model for classification of lung cancer on CT images. Futur Gener Comput Syst 92:374–382
5. Sun M, Liu K, Wu Q, Hong Q, Wang B, Zhang H (2019) A novel ECOC algorithm for multiclass microarray data classification based on data complexity analysis. Pattern Recogn 90:346–362
6. Chehade AH, Abdallah N, Marion JM, Oueidat M, Chauvet P (2022) Lung and colon cancer classification using medical imaging: a feature engineering approach. Phys Eng Sci Med
7. Saif A, Qasim YRH, Sameai HAMA, Ali OAF, Hassan AAM (2020) Multi paths technique on convolutional neural network for lung cancer detection based on histopathological images. Int J Adv Netw Appl 12(2):4549–4554
8. Toğaçar M (2021) Disease type detection in lung and colon cancer images using the complement approach of inefficient sets. Comput Biol Med 137:104827
9. Suzuki K (2014) Pixel-based machine learning in computer-aided diagnosis of lung and colon cancer. In: Machine learning in healthcare informatics, Springer, Berlin, Heidelberg, pp 81–112
10. Wang S, Yang DM, Rong R, Zhan X, Fujimoto J, Liu H, Minna J, Wistuba II, Xie Y, Xiao G (2019) Artificial intelligence in lung cancer pathology image analysis. Cancers 11(11):1673
11. Wang Q, Zhou Y, Ding W, Zhang Z, Muhammad K, Cao Z (2020) Random forest with self-paced bootstrap learning in lung cancer prognosis. ACM Trans Multimed Comput Commun Appl (TOMM) 16(1s):1–12
12. Adu K, Yu Y, Cai J, Owusu-Agyemang K, Twumasi BA, Wang X (2021) DHS-CapsNet: dual horizontal squash capsule networks for lung and colon cancer classification from whole slide histopathological images. Int J Imaging Syst Technol 31(4):2075–2092
13. Masud M, Sikder N, Nahid AA, Bairagi AK, Zain MAA (2021) A machine learning approach to diagnosing lung and colon cancer using a deep learning-based classification framework. Sensors 21(3):748
14. Hatuwal BK, Thapa HC (2020) Lung cancer detection using convolutional neural network on histopathological images. Int J Comput Trends Technol 68(10):21–24
15. Bukhari SUK et al (2020) The histological diagnosis of colonic adenocarcinoma by applying partial self supervised learning. MedRxiv 2020–08
16. Mangal S, Chaurasia A, Khajanchi A (2020) Convolution neural networks for diagnosing colon and lung cancer histopathological images. arXiv preprint arXiv:2009.03878
17. Adu K et al (2021) DHS-CapsNet: dual horizontal squash capsule networks for lung and colon cancer classification from whole slide histopathological images. Int J Imaging Syst Technol 31(4):2075–2092

18. Kumar N et al (2022) An empirical study of handcrafted and dense feature extraction techniques for lung and colon cancer classification from histopathological images. Biomed Sig Process Control 75:103596
19. Singh O, Singh KK (2023) An approach to classify lung and colon cancer of histopathology images using deep feature extraction and an ensemble method. Int J Inf Technol 1–12
20. Saikia T et al (2022) An automatic lung nodule classification system based on hybrid transfer learning approach SN Comput Sci 3(4):272
21. Borkowski AA et al (2019) Lung and colon cancer histopathological image dataset (lc25000). arXiv preprint arXiv:1912.12142
22. Masud M et al (2021) A machine learning approach to diagnosing lung and colon cancer using a deep learning-based classification framework. Sensors 21(3):748
23. Sarwinda D et al (2020) Analysis of deep feature extraction for colorectal cancer detection. In: 2020 4th international conference on informatics and computational sciences (ICICoS)

Feature Engineering Using Machine Learning Techniques on CIC-IOT-2023 Dataset

Komal Jakotiya, Vishal Shirsath, and Raj Gaurav Mishra

1 Introduction

Today, in this constantly changing world of the Internet of Things (IOT), data-driven understanding is critical to increasing device efficiency and safety, as well as overall performance. Analyzing this data presents significance potential for insights and applications across industries, from predictive maintenance in manufacturing to smart city initiatives. However, to unlock this potential, it's critical to employ effective feature engineering techniques, along with machine learning, on IOT datasets like the CIC-IOT-2023 dataset.

The CIC-IOT-2023 dataset is a comprehensive dataset specifically curated for IoT-related research and analysis. It encompasses a wide range of IoT devices, network protocols, and traffic patterns. This dataset offers useful insights into the behavior, security, and performance of IOT devices and networks. IOT assaults Dataset Facilitating Advancing Security Analytics Applications in Real-Time IoT Environments. To achieve this objective, we executed 33 distinct attacks within an IoT network consisting of 105 interconnected devices. These attacks have been categorized into seven distinct types: DDoS DoS, Recon, web-based and brute force attacks as well as spoofing and Mirai. Second, most significantly all of these attacks have been launched by malicious IOT devices just to attack other elements on the same network. This data set includes diverse attacks which have not been seen in other IOT datasets, giving a chance to IOT professionals for pioneering new security analytics innovation. Moreover, feature engineering forms the basis of many effective machine

K. Jakotiya (✉) · V. Shirsath · R. G. Mishra
School of Engineering, ADYPU, Pune, India
e-mail: Komal.jakotiya@adypu.edu.in

V. Shirsath
e-mail: Vishal.shirsath@adypu.edu.in

R. G. Mishra
e-mail: raj.mishra@adypu.edu.in

K. Kumar Singh et al. (eds.), *Machine Vision and Augmented Intelligence*, Lecture Notes in Electrical Engineering 1211, https://doi.org/10.1007/978-981-97-4359-9_64

learning applications. Models through it can learn from data efficiently and easily understand the nature of what they are processing. In this way, we hope to give a general theory for feature engineering on the CIC IOT Dataset 2023. Our goal is to provide researchers, data scientists and practitioners with the right tools and techniques for extracting valuable insight from IoT data so that its potential can be realized in applications ranging from predictive maintenance to anomaly detection.

2 Related Work

A method of feature selection in Intrusion Detection Systems (IDS) is presented by Nimbalkar et al. [1], which focuses on detection of DoS and DDoS attacks. Their method involved insertion and union operations on feature subsets selected from the top 50% of Information Gain values, or the bottom 50% of gain ratio values. When assessed on the IoT-BoT and KDD Cup 1999 datasets with the JRip classifier, their approach demonstrated better performance compared to the initial feature set and conventional IDSs, using just 16 and 19 characteristics, respectively.

In the domain of feature selection and anomaly detection in the context of the Internet of Things (IoT), Li et al. [2] introduced an innovative model architecture that merges deep learning with security breach detection. Their study introduces a technique for examining learning models to aid in migration while choosing pertinent system features. They performed experiments using the KDD CUP 99 dataset as their experimental dataset.

To automate the identification of potential security breaches within IoT traffic generated using the MQTT (Message Queue Telemetry Transport) protocol, an analysis is conducted [3]. This analysis encompasses five distinct categories of cyber-attacks: brute force, SlowITe, flooding, denial of service (DoS), and malformed data attacks, in addition to legitimate traffic. The study involves the training of five well-known machine learning (ML) models, namely MLP, AdaBoost, Light GBM, Decision Tree and Random Forest Classifiers, for the purpose of predicting cyber-attacks. The anticipation of malevolent activities within network systems has been a well-established field of study, dating back to the 1990s. As machine learning (ML) technologies have evolved, numerous research endeavors have emerged, delving into the potential of ML models for forecasting cyber threats [4]. Within this domain, a prevalent choice for research is the utilization of the KDDCUP99 dataset [5], constructed from TCP/IP (Transmission Control Protocol or Internet Protocol) traffic in IP networks. However, it's worth noting that this dataset falls short in presenting a genuine depiction of malicious traffic patterns within IoT networks.

Typically, IoT networks are confined to private domains, characterized by an overseeing entity that manages and monitors the activities of interconnected devices. In the context of IoT networks commonly found in intelligent home control systems, there is a preference for the MQTT protocol, which operates atop the TCP communication protocol. This choice is driven by MQTT's simplicity and minimal resource demands [6]. The MQTT protocol delineates three primary components: the MQTT

Broker, which serves as the Master; the MQTT Publisher, responsible for communication with clients; and the MQTT Subscriber, functioning as a client. These three entities collectively constitute the IoT network, facilitating the exchange of information via the MQTT protocol.

While MQTT stands as a favored protocol for IoT applications, there is a notable scarcity of research dedicated to scrutinizing MQTT traffic behavior for the prediction of cyber-attacks [7]. A substantial portion of research employing MQTT traffic analysis encounters two significant challenges: the absence of publicly accessible datasets and a lack of focus on smart home IoT networks. Consequently, replicating the outcomes documented in the existing literature for comparative assessment becomes a formidable task. Additionally, existing studies primarily concentrate on the detection of two prevalent cyber-attacks: security breach and denial of service (DoS), largely overlooking other potential threats.

One of the novel threats that can potentially impact IoT networks is the Slow DoS against Internet of Things Environments (SlowITe) attack [8]. SlowITe falls into the category of denial-of-service attacks and has the capability to target MQTT servers operating within a TCP environment. Additionally, IoT networks are susceptible to a range of other security breaches, including brute force attacks, flooding attacks, traditional denial of service (DoS) attacks, as well as attacks involving malformed data. These threats collectively pose significant challenges to the security and stability of IoT systems.

Supervised machine learning classifiers involve training models using labeled data to predict known outcomes. Among the popular and state-of-the-art supervised learning classifiers are Linear Discriminant Analysis, Naïve Bayes, Neural Networks, Decision Trees, Stochastic Gradient Descent, SVM (Support Vector Machines) and Ensemble Models. These classifiers play a pivotal role in a wide range of machine learning applications, from classification to regression tasks.

In the next stages of the proposed Network Traffic Log identification framework, the Feature Extraction and Scalable Hypothesis (FRESH) algorithm, as described in [9], is employed. Its primary objective is to extract and meticulously choose the most relevant data characteristics from the provided dataset. After this process of feature extraction and selection, the model is then trained using the CatBoost. This combination of FRESH and CatBoost contributes to the effectiveness and accuracy of the NTL detection framework.

Ndayishimiyepas et al. [10] Various methods have been employed to predict missing data records in datasets, and now there's an opportunity to introduce an advanced approach. XGBoost, short for Extreme Gradient Boosting, represents a significant advancement in the field. Its core development objective was to enhance both model performance and computational efficiency. Essentially, XGBoost is realization of the Gradient Boosting techniques Machine, designed to significantly amplify the computational capabilities of boosted trees algorithms.

Contemporary IoT networks are comprised of small-scale sensing devices characterized by constrained computational capabilities and limited data storage. Therefore, when formulating machine learning models for the purpose of monitoring and identifying cyber-attacks, it becomes imperative to account for these resource constraints

Table 1 Different machine learning models comparative study

Machine learning model	Strength	Limitations
Decision Tree classifier	Interpretable and can handle both categorical and numerical data	Are prone to overfitting with complex trees may not capture intricate relationships in the data
CatBoost	Effective in handling categorical features and has strong predictive performance	Longer training times compared to some other algorithms
MLP classifier	Capture complex non-linear patterns in data	Require a larger amount of data and may be prone to overfitting
Random Forest	Resilient, adept at managing high dimensional data, and furnishes feature significance scores	May over fit on noisy data and can be computationally expensive for large datasets
Light GBM	Highly efficient for large dataset excellent predictive performance	Require fine tuning sensitive to overfitting for limited data
AdaBoost	Combines feeble learners to construct a robust classifier and is less prone to overfitting	Be sensitive to noisy data and outliers
XgBoost	Excels in predictive accuracy and computational efficiency	Tuning hyper parameters can be challenging more memory for large datasets

and the feasibility of deploying such models within the IoT network infrastructure. The selection of models outlined in Table 1 is a direct response to these precise limitations inherent to IoT networks.

3 Methodology

3.1 Dataset

The study utilized the CIC-IOT-2023 benchmark dataset as its primary data source. In the initial phase of data preprocessing, columns containing null values were eliminated, resulting in a refined dataset. This cleaned dataset was then employed for feature selection and feature scaling. During this stage, various techniques, including Random Forest, XGBoost, and CatBoost, were employed, and the data was balanced to ensure a comprehensive analysis of the dataset's characteristics and performance (Figs. 1 and 2).

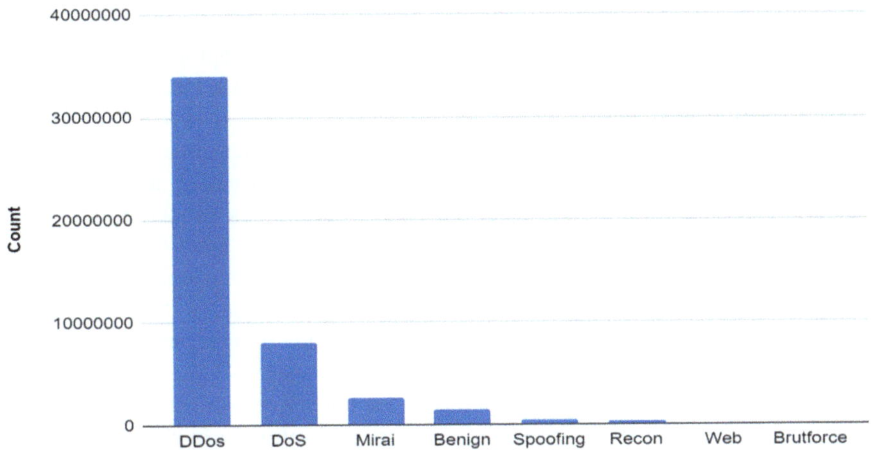

Fig. 1 Types of attacks

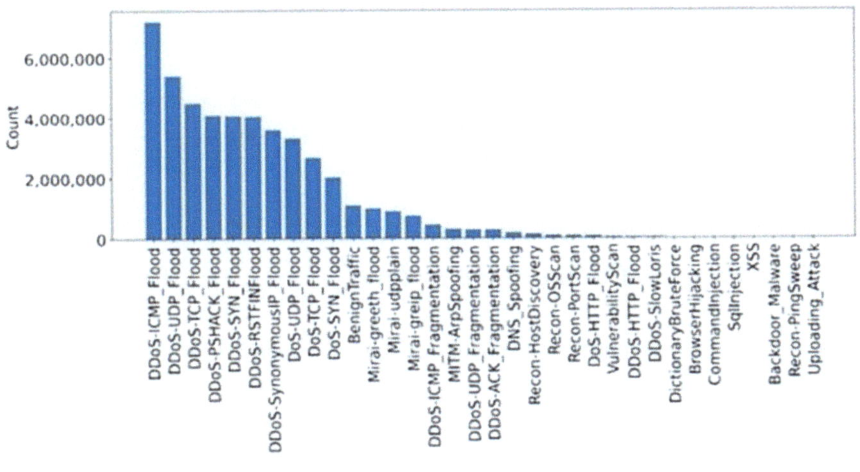

Fig. 2 Different number of records for each subtype of attacks

3.2 *Proposed Model*

In this research, we explore the following fundamental aspects of feature engineering on the CIC IoT Dataset 2023.

Data Preprocessing. We delve into the critical phase of data preprocessing, addressing issues such as missing values, data normalization, and handling class imbalances. Through these techniques, we ensure that the dataset is clean, balanced, and ready for analysis.

Feature Extraction. Drawing upon domain knowledge, we extract relevant features from the raw network traffic data. These features capture the essence of IoT device behavior, including communication patterns, payload characteristics, and protocol-specific attributes.

Feature Selection. To mitigate the challenges of high dimensionality, we explore techniques for feature selection, identifying the most informative attributes while discarding redundant or noisy ones. This step streamlines model training and enhances interpretability.

Feature Transformation. Techniques for reducing dimensionality, including Principal Component Analysis (PCA) and manifold learning techniques, are employed to visualize and transform the dataset into a more manageable and discriminative form.

Advanced Feature Engineering. We push the boundaries of feature engineering by exploring advanced strategies such as feature generation through deep learning architectures, auto encoders, and transfer learning, tailored to the intricacies of IoT data.

Model Selection and Evaluation. We leverage a wide array of machine learning algorithms, including classical models, ensemble techniques, and deep learning frameworks, to train and evaluate predictive models. Rigorous evaluation metrics are employed to assess model performance.

Interpretability. In addition to predictive accuracy, we emphasize the interpretability of models, making the insights gained from feature-engineered attributes comprehensible to users and stakeholders.

3.3 *Imbalance Ratio About the Dataset*

These datasets exhibit significant imbalances, which necessitate addressing in order to accurately assess the system's efficiency. The metric used to quantify this imbalance is the Imbalance Ratio, denoted as ρ and calculated as shown in Eq. 1:

$$\text{Imbalance Ratio}\,(\rho) = \text{maxi}\{\text{Ci}\}/\text{mini}\{\text{Ci}\} \tag{1}$$

Here, Ci represents the size of data in class i. In essence, the imbalance rate is characterized by the disparity between the count of occurrences in the majority (maximum) class and the minority (minimum) class.

For the CIC-IOT-2023 dataset, the data imbalance rate is notably high, at 7,000,000:10,000. Such substantial differences between data classes significantly impact the system's effectiveness. Additionally, it's important to highlight that skilled hackers frequently concentrate on exploiting the less common data types to accomplish their goals.

4 Machine Learning Algorithms

4.1 SVM

Support Vector Machines (SVMs) are primarily used as classification algorithms, but they can indirectly contribute to feature engineering through feature selection and dimensionality reduction techniques. SVMs inherently identify the most discriminative features during the training process. SVMs can indirectly aid in feature engineering through these techniques, they are not typically used for explicit feature creation or modification. For feature engineering involving feature creation, transformation, or generation, other techniques like polynomial features, feature engineering based on domain knowledge, and autoencoders may be more appropriate. SVMs are generally employed for their ability to handle high-dimensional data and learn complex decision boundaries when feature selection or dimensionality reduction is the primary goal.

4.2 Random Forest

The Random Forest, a versatile ensemble learning algorithm, indirectly contributes to feature engineering by offering insights into feature significance and selection. Besides being a powerful predictive modeling tool, it also ranks highest among feature importance. In Random Forest, the importance of each feature is determined by how much it affects the model's abilities to predict. Gini impurity and Mean Decrease in Accuracy are two important criteria for this assessment.

In particular, popular algorithms such as Random Forest can not only rank features in terms of feature importance but also select informative features. These capacities enhance model explanatories and forecasting accuracy, particularly when working with massive data sets or intricate feature relationships.

4.3 CatBoost

CatBoost is a gradient boosting procedure that deals well with categorical features. With built-in handling of categorical data, which does not require much preprocessing or one-hot encoding.

Most of the feature engineering for CatBoost is concentrated on how to properly handle categorical features, while at the same time making use of model's ability to capture interactions across different type of variables. With less need for manual encoding and preprocessing, it shortens the process. This means that you have more time to generate interesting features and work on improving model performance. And it turns out that CatBoost's feature importance analysis is an effective tool for understanding your model and making it more effective. It will help you to concentrate on how and which ones are best picked, what kind of work needs doing in order to prepare them.

5 Evaluation and Results

5.1 Metrics

But assessment criteria for machine learning are an indispensable means of measuring model effectiveness. These criteria provide data analysts, researchers and pros with valuable viewpoints on the power of their model. They can then make decisions informed by reality when it comes to choosing a suitable model or carefully adjusting its parameters. The following are some frequently utilized machine learning evaluation criteria:

Accuracy. Accuracy acts as a fundamental measure of a model's overall correctness. It is the proportion of accurate predicted instances to the total number of instances in the dataset. Although this metric is easy to calculate but not suitable for imbalance data.

Formula: (Correct Positive Predicted instances + Correct Negative Predicted instances)/(Total instances)

Precision: Precision quantifies the ration of true positives (i.e. correctly predicted positive instances) among all instances predicted as positive. This metric proves beneficial in scenarios where reducing false positives which are significant.

Formula: Correct Predicted Positives/(Correct Predicted Positives + Incorrect Predicted Positives

Recall (Sensitivity). Recall metric is the fraction of true positives among all actual positive instances. It is valuable utility in situation where the primary goal is to minimize the false negatives.

Formula: True Positives/(True Positives + False Negatives)

F1-Score. The harmonic mean of precision and recall represented by F1-score, a balance can be achieved between these two metrics. While working with various types of datasets that exhibit an uneven class distribution, balance is especially advantageous.

Formula: 2 * Precision * Recall/(Precision + Recall)

These machine learning evaluation metrics evaluate model performance, collectively providing practitioners with tools to refine their models and make them more effective across an ever-broadening scope of applications.

5.2 Results

Oversampling can be used to handle the class imbalance problems found in CIC IOT 2023 data set. It means balancing the number of instances in minority class (representing anomalies or rare events) with those in majority class.

However, an important point is that oversampling can be used to solve the problem of class imbalance but care should be taken. If adjustment occurs over aggressively, it could lead to the problem of overfitting and poor generalization. Also explore techniques such as feature engineering, various resampling methods or anomaly detection (Figs. 3 and 4).

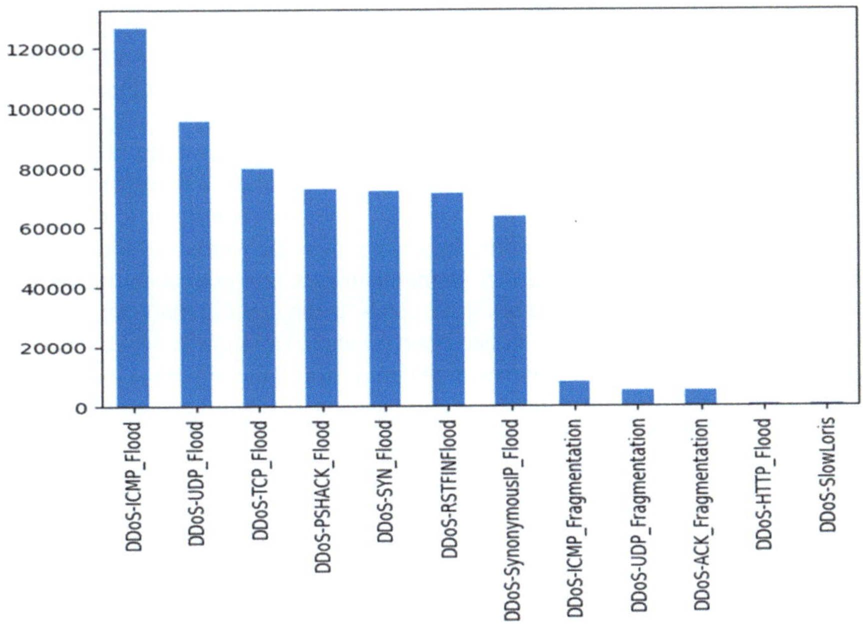

Fig. 3 Imbalanced data (before oversampling)

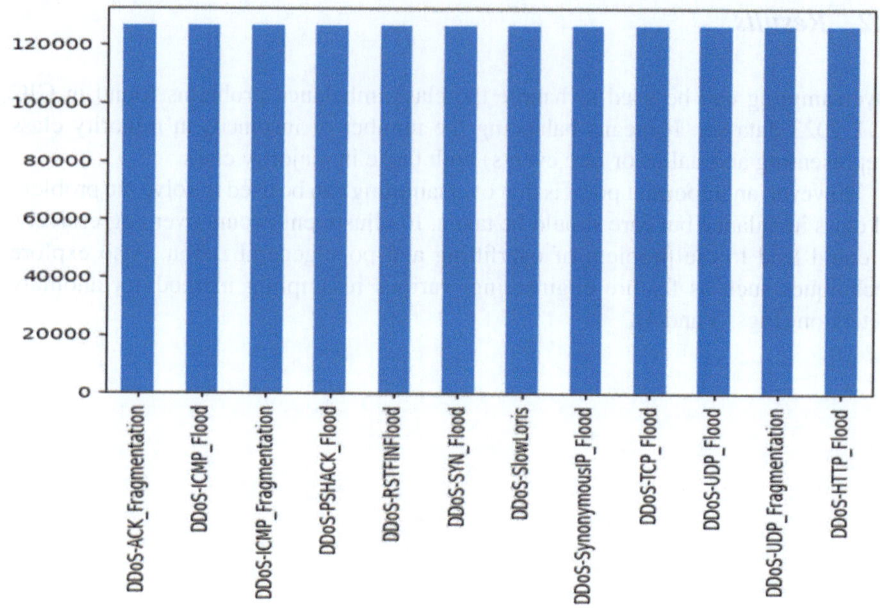

Fig. 4 After over sampling balanced data

6 Conclusion

Our study titled "Feature engineering using Catboost, Random Forest and XGBoost algorithms on CIC IoT Dataset 2023" shows the vital role that feature engineering can play in boosting a machine learning model's predictive performance when it comes to protecting against attacks from adversaries endangering internet of things (IoT) devices. Indeed, Catboost, Random Forest and XGBoost all show their strong points in handling different types of feature sets as well. They also contribute to improving model accuracy. By thoughtfully doing feature engineering on these algorithms, we have already made significant strides in strengthening the analysis capabilities of IoT networks. Yet the choice of the algorithm depends on the specific characteristics of a given dataset and challenge, which once again points to variation as key for security applications in IoT. In general, our research demonstrates the importance of feature engineering and that these advanced algorithms can still support a strengthening in the defenses of IoT networks from cyber threats.

References

1. Nimbalkar P, Kshirsagar D (2021) Feature selection for intrusion detection system in Internet-of-Things (IoT). ICT Express 7(2):177–181

2. Li D et al (2019) IoT data feature extraction and intrusion detection system for smart cities based on deep migration learning. Int J Inf Manag 49:533–545
3. Dissanayake Maheshi B (2021) Feature engineering for cyber-attack detection in internet of things. IJ Wirel Microw Technol 6:46–54
4. Vaccari I et al (2021) Exploiting Internet of Things protocols for malicious data exfiltration activities. IEEE Access 9:104261–104280
5. Imran et al (2023) Improving reliability for detecting anomalies in the MQTT network by applying correlation analysis for feature selection using machine learning techniques. Appl Sci 13(11):6753
6. Al Enany MO, Harb HM, Attiya G (2021) A Comparative analysis of MQTT and IoT application protocols. In: 2021 international conference on electronic engineering (ICEEM). IEEE
7. Ferrag MA et al (2020) Deep learning for cyber security intrusion detection: approaches, datasets, and comparative study. J Inf Secur Appl 50:102419
8. Vaccari I, Aiello M, Cambiaso E (2020) SlowITe, a novel denial of service attack affecting MQTT. Sensors 20(10):2932
9. Hussain S et al (2021) A novel feature engineered-CatBoost-based supervised machine learning framework for electricity theft detection. Energy Rep 7:4425–4436
10. Ndayishimiyepas P, Wilson C, Kimwele M (2022) A hybrid model for predicting missing records in data using XGBoost. In: 2022 IEEE international symposium on product compliance engineering—Asia (ISPCE—ASIA). IEEE

A Comparative Exploration of Denoising and Enhancement Techniques in Breast Cancer Microscopic Imaging

Sonam Tyagi, Subodh Srivastava, Bikash Chandra Sahana, and Abhinav Kumar

1 Introduction

Breast cancer is the leading cause of death in women. It occurs when the cell of breast grows uncontrollably. If it is detected in its early stage, it can be treated and mortality can be avoided. It can be categorized into two types i.e. benign and malignant [1]. Benign cancer is not dangerous while malignant cancer is fatal. Breast continues to pose a serious global health concern, as its prevalence keeps on rising on a global scale [2]. It is estimated that 297,790 women will be diagnosed by breast cancer in United States. Timely detection and precise characterization of breast cancer are crucial for improving patient outcomes and reducing mortality rates [3]. There are a variety of diagnostic methods like blood tests, mammogram, ultrasound, MRI, CT scan, etc. available to detect breast cancer. If a suspicious case occurs, breast biopsy is performed to confirm if it is benign and malignant [4]. It is considered as the reliable technique to detect breast cancer. In this method, a tissue of breast is taken out from the suspicious area and it is observed by the pathologist to detect if it contains cancer cells or not [5]. Microscopic imaging has become an essential technique in breast cancer diagnostics, providing valuable insights into tissue structure

S. Tyagi (✉) · S. Srivastava · B. C. Sahana · A. Kumar
Department of Electronics and Communication Engineering, National Institute of Technology Patna, Patna 800005, Bihar, India
e-mail: sonamt.phd20.ec@nitp.ac.in

S. Srivastava
e-mail: subodh@nitp.ac.in

B. C. Sahana
e-mail: sahana@nitp.ac.in

A. Kumar
e-mail: abhinav.ec19@nitp.ac.in

S. Tyagi
School of Computing, Graphic Era Hill University, Haldwani 263139, Uttarakhand, India

K. Kumar Singh et al. (eds.), *Machine Vision and Augmented Intelligence*, Lecture Notes in Electrical Engineering 1211, https://doi.org/10.1007/978-981-97-4359-9_65

and disease progression [6]. However, this process is not simple. It is a very time-consuming process and prone to human error. For patients who are given an inaccurate diagnosis, these problems can have severe and even fatal consequences. Besides this, microscopic images suffer from Poisson noise and poor contrast which may hinder pathologist evaluation [7]. For proper diagnosis, these issues must be eliminated. There are various image denoising and enhancement methods, which may be utilized to overcome this issue [8]. In this paper, various image denoising and enhancement techniques are discussed for improving microscopic image quality. A comparative analysis is also carried out for finding the best method which not only denoises and enhances the image but also retain the structural and preserve the image characteristics. The denoising is performed using median filter [10], wiener filter [11], bilateral filter [12], non-local means filter [13], anisotropic diffusion [14], fourth order partial differential equation filter [15]. For improving the results, these denoising methods are combined with various enhancement techniques such as contrast limited adaptive histogram equalization [16], histogram equalization [25] and unsharp masking [26].

2 Related Work

Within the realm of microscopy, the digital microscopy sensing system is subjected to three primary forms of noise. The phenomenon of dark noise is associated with the generation of electronic noise resulting from the thermal agitation of electrons. The phenomenon known as photon noise, or shot noise, arises due to the inherent statistical fluctuations in the amount of photons detected during a specific exposure level [9]. Photon noise is an intrinsic characteristic of optical signals due to the stochastic nature of photon emissions. The generation of readout noise primarily arises from imperfections in the output amplifier when converting charges into voltages. The dominating noise in microscopic images is Poisson noise, so removal of this noise is necessary for further detection of disease. Along with this issue, microscopic images generally suffer from low image contrast issue. To solve this issue, image enhancement is required. Numerous studies have been conducted for enhancement and removing the impact of Poisson noise from microscopic images. Hamed et al. [10] suggested a denoising model which incorporated median filter (MF) for removing Poisson noise from noise corrupted mammograms. Sneha et al. [11] incorporated Wiener filter (WF) for image deblurring and denoising chest X-Ray, ultrasound and mammogram images. The performance is assessed using SSIM, PSNR and SSIM. Devanand et al. [12] presented a method which included the implementation of bilateral filtering as a method for denoising medical images. Jin et al. [13] presented a novel approach based on non-local means filter for the reconstruction of an image from data that has been corrupted by Poisson noise. The methodology employed depends upon the utilization of a weighted average calculation, which takes into account the data within a given neighborhood. Yilmaz et al. [14] presented a novel approach for removing undesired noise artifacts in cone beam computed tomography (CBCT) images, utilizing an adaptive anisotropic filtering technique. Subsequently,

PSNR and MAE values were calculated. The proposed adaptive anisotropic diffusion filter appears to be a suitable option for mitigating noise artifacts that may arise in portions of cone-CBCT images. An approach was proposed by Rajesh et al. [15], which involved the utilization of a fourth order partial differential equation (FPDE) based nonlinear filter to address the presence of Poisson noise. This filter was combined with the fuzzy c-means segmentation method. The proposed methodology demonstrated proficiency in addressing the challenge of segmenting blocky artifacts, while simultaneously maintaining an appropriate balance between the elimination of Poisson noise and the preservation of edges in microscopic biopsy images. Reza et al. [16] implemented CLAHE for enhancing the images which suffered from poor viewing quality as a result of inadequate lighting or inherent noise during real time imaging. Another approach for image enhancement is suggested by Hojat et al. [17], where they utilized the concept of histogram equalization. Guang et al. [18] utilized the concept of unsharp masking (UM) for sharpening and enhancing the contrast of the image.

3 Performance Evaluation Metrics

The performance evaluation tells about the efficacy of the methods applied. Metrics used for the analysis are given as below:

3.1 Structural Similarity Index Measure

SSIM [19] is given as:

$$\mathrm{SSIM}(X, Y) = \frac{(2\mu_X \mu_Y + c_1)(2\sigma_{XY} + c_2)}{\left(\mu_X^2 + \mu_Y^2 + c_1\right)\left(\sigma_X^2 + \sigma_Y^2 + c_2\right)} \tag{1}$$

3.2 Peak Signal-To-Noise Ratio

PSNR [20] is formulated as:

$$PSNR(X, Y) = 10\log_{10}\left(\frac{(L-1)^2}{MSE(X, Y)}\right) \tag{2}$$

3.3 Mean Squared Error

MSE [21] is represented as:

$$\mathrm{MSE}(X, Y) = \frac{1}{MN} \sum_{i=0}^{M-1} \sum_{j=0}^{N-1} [X(i, j) - Y(i, j)]^2 \tag{3}$$

3.4 Correlation Parameter

CP [22] is given as:

$$CP(X, Y) = \frac{\sum (X(i, j) - \mu_X) \sum (Y(i, j) - \mu_Y)}{\sqrt{\sum (X(i, j) - \mu_X)^2 \sum (Y(i, j) - \mu_Y)^2}} \tag{4}$$

3.5 Universal Image Quality Index

UQI [23] is formulated as:

$$UQI(X, Y) = \frac{4\mu_X \mu_Y \sigma_{XY}}{\left(\mu_X^2 + \mu_Y^2\right)\left(\sigma_X^2 + \sigma_Y^2\right)} \tag{5}$$

3.6 Measure of Enhancement

EME [4] is given as:

$$EME(Y) = \frac{1}{p_1 p_2} \sum_{m=1}^{p_1} \sum_{l=1}^{p_2} 20 \ln \frac{Y_{max}^{l,m}}{Y_{min}^{l,m}} \tag{6}$$

4 Experimental Results and Analysis

4.1 Dataset Description

The dataset included in the comparative analysis is the BreakHis dataset, which comprises 9,109 microscopic images of breast tumor tissue obtained from 82 individuals. The dataset has a total of 2,480 samples classified as benign and 5,429 samples classified as malignant. Each sample is represented by an image with dimensions of 700X460 pixels, consisting of three channels (red, green, and blue) in the RGB color space in PNG format [24].

4.2 Quantitative Analysis

This section demonstrates the quantitative results obtained through various performance metrics. Different approaches namely median filter (MF), wiener filter (WF), bilateral filter (BF), non-local means filter (NLM), anisotropic diffusion (AD) and fourth order partial differential equation filter (FPDE) are used for image denoising purpose. Here, these techniques are further combined with different enhancement techniques which are Contrast Limited Adaptive Histogram Equalization (CLAHE) [16], Histogram Equalization (HE) [25] and Unsharp Masking (UM) [26]. Comparative quantitative analysis of denoising techniques with CLAHE, HE and UM are shown in Tables 1, 2, and 3 respectively. Figures 1, 2, and 3. show the comparison plots for Tables 1, 2, and 3 in terms of SSIM, MSE, CP, UQI and EME. From all PSNR values present in Tables 1, 2, and 3, it can be interpreted that FPDE filter with unsharp masking achieved the highest PSNR.

4.3 Qualitative Analysis

This section demonstrates the qualitative results obtained through various denoising and enhancement approaches. Figures 4, 5 and 6 shows the results of different denoising approaches with CLAHE, HE and UM respectively.

5 Conclusion

In the context of breast cancer diagnosis, where precision is of utmost importance, this paper has thoroughly investigated the complex field of microscopic imaging. The primary objective of our extensive comparison investigation was to examine denoising and enhancement approaches, which are essential components in the field

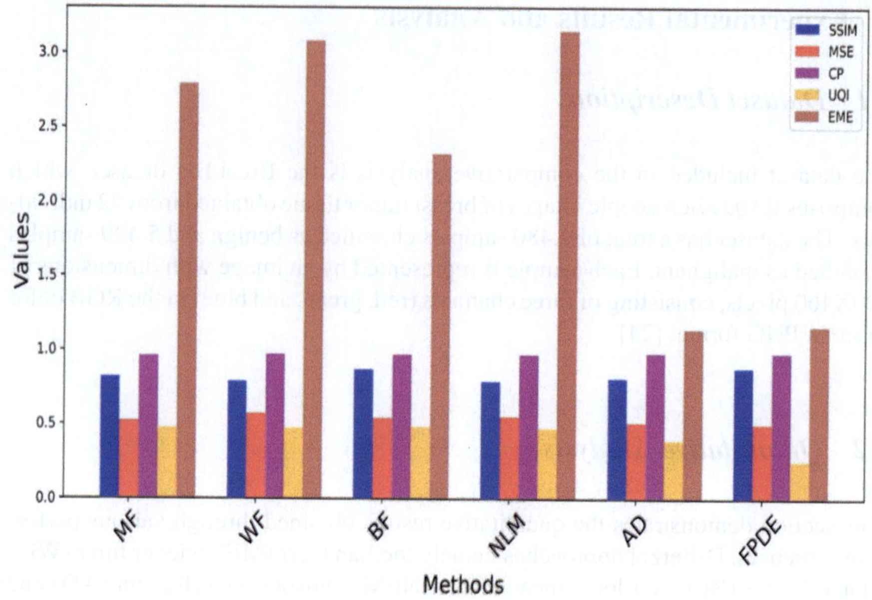

Fig. 1 Comparison plot for denoising techniques with CLAHE

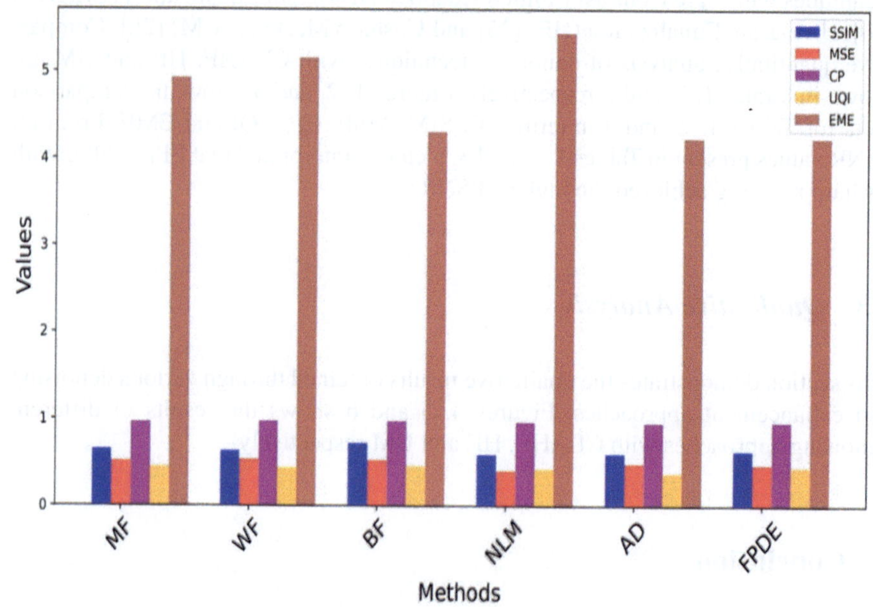

Fig. 2 Comparison plot for denoising techniques with HE

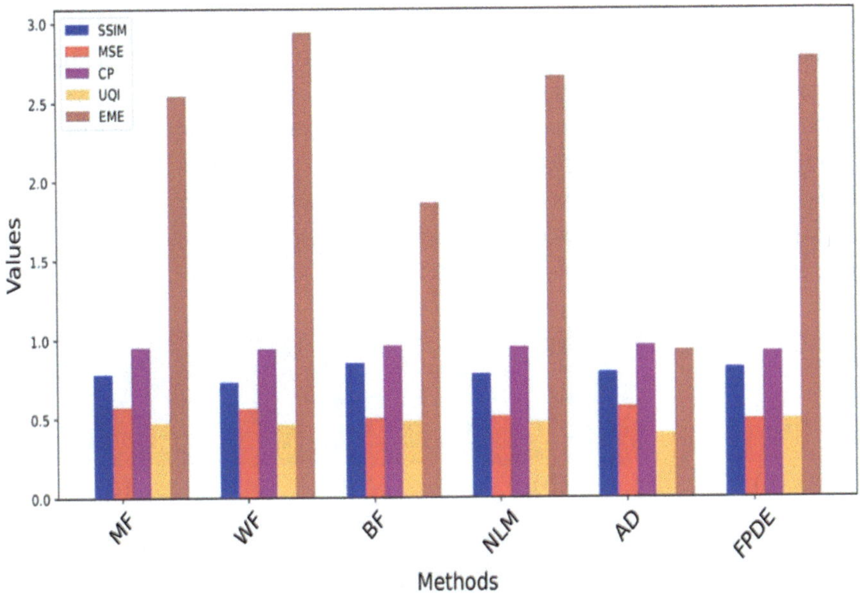

Fig. 3 Comparison plot for denoising techniques with UM

Table 1 Comparative quantitative analysis of denoising techniques with CLAHE

Methods	SSIM	PSNR	MSE	CP	UQI	EME
MF [10]	0.82	28.02	0.52	0.96	0.47	2.79
WF [11]	0.79	28.09	0.57	0.97	0.47	3.08
BF [12]	0.87	28.01	0.54	0.97	0.48	2.32
NLM [13]	0.79	28.02	0.55	0.97	0.47	3.15
AD [14]	0.81	27.88	0.51	0.98	0.39	1.14
FPDE [15]	0.88	28.02	0.50	0.98	0.25	1.16

Table 2 Comparative quantitative analysis of denoising techniques with HE

Methods	SSIM	PSNR	MSE	CP	UQI	EME
MF [10]	0.65	27.89	0.51	0.96	0.44	4.92
WF [11]	0.63	27.72	0.53	0.97	0.43	5.15
BF [12]	0.72	28.03	0.52	0.97	0.45	4.30
NLM [13]	0.59	27.86	0.40	0.96	0.42	5.44
AD [14]	0.60	28.15	0.48	0.95	0.37	4.23
FPDE [15]	0.63	29.12	0.47	0.96	0.44	4.23

Table 3 Comparative quantitative analysis of denoising techniques with unsharp masking

Methods	SSIM	PSNR	MSE	CP	UQI	EME
MF [10]	0.78	28.56	0.57	0.95	0.47	2.54
WF [11]	0.73	28.39	0.56	0.94	0.46	2.94
BF [12]	0.85	29.07	0.50	0.96	0.48	1.86
NLM [13]	0.78	28.67	0.51	0.95	0.47	2.66
AD [14]	0.79	28.06	0.57	0.96	0.40	0.93
FPDE [15]	0.82	29.72	0.49	0.92	0.49	2.78

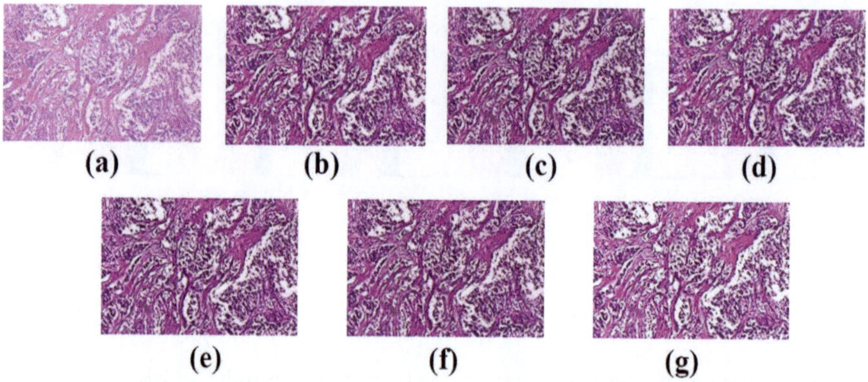

Fig. 4 Comparative qualitative analysis where **a** Input image; **b–g** are the results of MF [10], WF [11], BF [12], NLM [13], AD [14] and FPDE [15] with CLAHE respectively

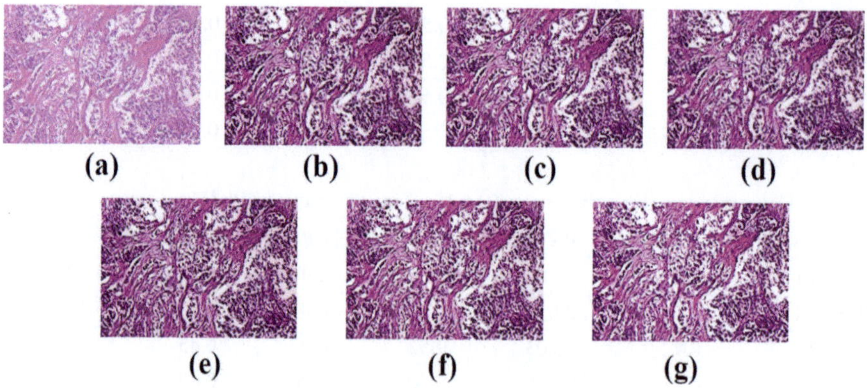

Fig. 5 Comparative qualitative analysis where **a** Input image; **b–g** are the results of MF [10], WF [11], BF [12], NLM [13], AD [14] and FPDE [15] with HE respectively

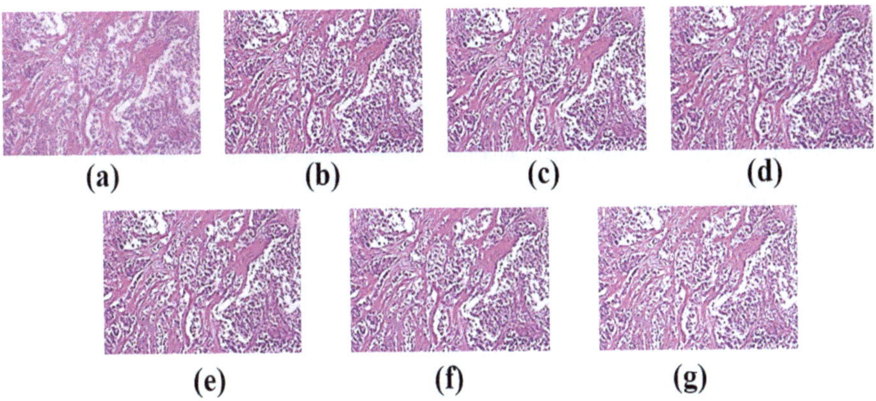

Fig. 6 Comparative qualitative analysis where **a** Input image; **b–g** are the results of MF [10], WF [11], BF [12], NLM [13], AD [14] and FPDE [15] with UM respectively

of precise diagnosis and categorization. Various performance evaluation metrics such as SSIM, PSNR, MSE, CP, UQI and EME are evaluated on BreakHis dataset to measure the efficiency of existing methods. After comparative analysis, it can be seen that fourth order partial differential equation filter along with unsharp masking shows the highest PSNR. These enhanced and denoised microscopic images can further help pathologists for accurate diagnosis of breast cancer.

References

1. Aswathy MA, Jagannath M (2017) Detection of breast cancer on digital histopathology images: present status and future possibilities. Inf Med Unlocked 8:74–79
2. Kumar R, Srivastava R, Srivastava S (2015) Detection and classification of cancer from microscopic biopsy images using clinically significant and biologically interpretable features. J Med Eng
3. Jani KK, Srivastava S, Srivastava R (2023) Framework for the restoration of capsule endoscopy images using partial differential equations-based filter. IETE J Res 69(4):1963–1973
4. Kumar A, Kumar P, Srivastava S (2022) A skewness reformed complex diffusion based unsharp masking for the restoration and enhancement of Poisson noise corrupted mammograms. Biomed Signal Process Control 73:103421
5. Hameed Z, Zahia S, Garcia-Zapirain B, Javier Aguirre J, Maria Vanegas A (2020) Breast cancer histopathology image classification using an ensemble of deep learning models. Sensors 20(16):4373
6. Veta M, Pluim JP, Van Diest PJ, Viergever MA (2014) Breast cancer histopathology image analysis: a review. IEEE Trans Biomed Eng 61(5):1400–1411
7. Bayramoglu N, Kannala J, Heikkilä J (2016) Deep learning for magnification independent breast cancer histopathology image classification. In: 2016 23rd International conference on pattern recognition (ICPR). IEEE, pp 2440–2445). Veta, M., Van Diest, P.J., Kornegoor, R., Huisman, A., Viergever, M.A. and Pluim, J.P., 2013. Automatic nuclei segmentation in H&E-stained breast cancer histopathology images. *PloS one*, *8*(7), p.e70221.

8. Veta M, Van Diest PJ, Kornegoor R, Huisman A, Viergever MA, Pluim JP (2013) Automatic nuclei segmentation in H&E-stained breast cancer histopathology images. PLoS ONE 8(7):e70221
9. Wang P, Hu X, Li Y, Liu Q, Zhu X (2016) Automatic cell nuclei segmentation and classification of breast cancer histopathology images. Signal Process 122:1–13
10. Hamed G, Marey M, Amin SES, Tolba MF (2018) A proposed model for denoising breast mammogram images. In: 2018 13th international conference on computer engineering and systems (ICCES). IEEE, pp 652–657
11. Sneha MR, Manju BR (2022) Performance analysis of wiener filter in restoration of covid-19 chest X-ray images, ultrasound images and mammograms. In: 2022 IEEE world conference on applied intelligence and computing (AIC). IEEE, pp 326–331
12. Bhonsle D, Chandra V, Sinha GR (2012) Medical image denoising using bilateral filter. Int J Image, Graph Signal Process 4(6):36
13. Jin Q, Grama I, Liu Q (2012) Removing poisson noise by optimization of weights in non-local means. In: 2012 symposium on photonics and optoelectronics. IEEE, pp 1–4
14. Yilmaz E, Kayikcioglu T, Kayipmaz S (2017) Noise removal of CBCT images using an adaptive anisotropic diffusion filter. In: 2017 40th international conference on telecommunications and signal processing (TSP). IEEE, pp 650–653
15. Kumar R, Srivastava S, Srivastava R (2017) A fourth order PDE based fuzzy c-means approach for segmentation of microscopic biopsy images in presence of Poisson noise for cancer detection. Comput Methods Programs Biomed 146:59–68
16. Reza AM (2004) Realization of the contrast limited adaptive histogram equalization (CLAHE) for real-time image enhancement. J VLSI Signal Process Syst Signal, Image and Video Technol 38:35–44
17. Yeganeh H, Ziaei A, Rezaie A (2008) A novel approach for contrast enhancement based on histogram equalization. In: 2008 international conference on computer and communication engineering. IEEE, pp 256–260
18. Deng G (2010) A generalized unsharp masking algorithm. IEEE Trans Image Process 20(5):1249–1261
19. Kumar A, Srivastava S (2023) A qualitative and quantitative comparative study of different denoising and enhancement techniques for breast mammograms, ultrasound and magnetic resonance images
20. Huynh-Thu Q, Ghanbari M (2008) Scope of validity of PSNR in image/video quality assessment. Electron Lett 44(13):800–801
21. Marmolin H (1986) Subjective MSE measures. IEEE Trans Syst Man Cybern 16(3):486–489
22. Kumar A, Srivastava S, Sarin R, Irizarry R (2023) A comparative study of different denoising and enhancement techniques for blood cell images
23. Egiazarian K, Astola J, Ponomarenko N, Lukin V, Battisti F, Carli M (2006) New full-reference quality metrics based on HVS. In: Proceedings of the second international workshop on video processing and quality metrics, vol 4, p 4
24. Spanhol FA, Oliveira LS, Petitjean C, Heutte L (2015) A dataset for breast cancer histopathological image classification. IEEE Trans Biomed Eng 63(7):1455–1462
25. Cheng HD, Shi XJ (2004) A simple and effective histogram equalization approach to image enhancement. Digit Signal Process 14(2):158–170
26. Polesel A, Ramponi G, Mathews VJ (2000) Image enhancement via adaptive unsharp masking. IEEE Trans Image Process 9(3):505–510

An Ensemble Technique for Classification of Oral Cancer by Using Histopathological Imaging

Trishna Saikia, Ashutosh Dhamaniya, Puneet Gupta, and Koushlendra Kumar Singh

1 Introduction

Oral cancer is a prevalent and lethal ailment, posing a substantial public health challenge worldwide. Over 90% of oral cancer cases manifest as oral squamous cell carcinomas (OSCC), encompassing a varying array of cancers originating from the oral mucous membrane [1]. It has been reported by the World Cancer Fund Research International [2] that lip and mouth cancers were the 11th and 18th most common types of cancer in 2020, accounting for over 377,700 reported cases globally and affecting both men and women.[1]

Patients grappling with oral cancer often endure a range of distressing symptoms, including difficulties with eating and speaking, oral inflammations, and visible facial abnormalities. The swift progression of the disease results in the formation of malignant squamous cell lesions, leading to OSCC, which poses a grave threat to life [3].

[1] World Cancer Research Fund International. https://www.wcrf.org/cancer-trends/mouth-and-oral-cancer-statistics/.

Ashutosh Dhamaniya, Puneet Gupta and Koushlendra Kumar Singh authors are contributed equally to this work.

T. Saikia (✉) · A. Dhamaniya · P. Gupta
Department of Computer Science and Engineering, IIT Indore, Indore, India
e-mail: phd2201101014@iiti.ac.in

A. Dhamaniya
e-mail: ms2204101005@iiti.ac.in

P. Gupta
e-mail: puneet@iiti.ac.in

K. K. Singh
Machine Vision and Intelligence Lab, NIT Jamshedpur, Jamshedpur, India
e-mail: koushlendra.cse@nitjsr.ac.in

K. Kumar Singh et al. (eds.), *Machine Vision and Augmented Intelligence*, Lecture Notes in Electrical Engineering 1211, https://doi.org/10.1007/978-981-97-4359-9_66

Therefore, early detection of these malignant oral lesions is paramount in mitigating the risk of cancerous transformation.

The conventional diagnostic tool OSCC involves the histopathological analysis of tissue [4]. Typically, histopathological images are examined at lower magnification levels to enable comprehensive scrutiny of the tissue. The primary criteria for identifying cancer cells include cell distribution, cell size, shape, and the characteristics of the cell nucleus. It is difficult to determine the tumor size precisely before any surgical intervention, which necessitates a thorough analysis of histopathological images. However, the analysis of the histopathological diagnostic approach is laboriously subject to pathologists' interpretation, which can be prone to errors. Consequently, it limits its practicality in clinical environments [5]. Therefore, there is a need to equip pathologists with advanced diagnostic equipment to assist them in OSCC assessment as well as in identification.

Over the past few years, artificial intelligence has gained more popularity in the research domain of medical diagnostics, with a particular focus on the evaluation of pathological imaging. To this end, deep learning (DL)-based techniques have turned up as a powerful tool particularly in addressing different challenges in medical image processing [6]. To this end, many DL-based computer-aided diagnostics (CAD) solutions have been proposed for different cancer variants, such as lung cancer and breast cancer [7, 8]. These CAD systems have continued to improve in effectiveness and sophistication, driven by advancements in machine learning (ML) [9]. However, these techniques also have some drawbacks when dealing with specially diagnostic biopsy images, which are usually considered standard imaging methods in cancer diagnosis. Moreover, these DL-based techniques perform poorly while training them with a limited number of data samples, which is a common scenario in the case of medical imaging, which typically contains limited data samples. As a result, transfer learning comes into the picture. These techniques have been explored extensively in DL models to overcome this challenge. For that, it enables pre-trained DL models to leverage their prior knowledge while being trained on new and relatively smaller datasets. This process helps to enhance the performance of these models even if on smaller datasets by taking the benefit of their existing knowledge which essentially helps them to achieve accurate results in the respective tasks [7, 8, 10]. Additionally, transfer learning helps reduce training time as it is quite lengthy when building an extensive neural network from the ground, particularly for challenging tasks [11]. In this research work, we use an ensemble approach where we have fine-tuned the layers of pre-trained DL models, focusing on leveraging the benefits of transfer learning as we utilize a dataset with limited samples. To this end, we propose a novel classification model for histopathological images to explore the potential applications of DL models using transfer learning in oral cancer classification. The key contributions of our research are as follows:

1. We employ transfer learning-assisted weighted ensembles of advance convolutional neural network (CNN) architectures, fine-tuning the latter half of the layers with OSCC data while freezing the initial half.

2. Our proposed method demonstrates enhanced performance despite using a dataset having less number of samples, converging more rapidly and demanding comparable computational cost.
3. We conduct a comparative analysis of our proposed method with respect to classification accuracy.

2 Literature Survey

Histopathological examination conducted manually is characterized by labor-intensive, time-consuming, and subjective processes, marked by notable variations among experts, both inter- and intra-observer [12]. These limitations necessitate a shift toward automating clinical decision-making. Over the past few decades, researchers have harnessed advancements in technology to combine image processing, pattern recognition, ML, and deep DL techniques, culminating in the development of CAD systems for the detection and classification of carcinomas, promising rapid and reproducible outcomes [13].

To exemplify this direction, the method proposed in [14] utilized backpropagation-based artificial neural networks (ANNs), integrating run-length and texture features, to categorize oral lesions into multiple classes. Similarly, the methods proposed in [15, 16] undertook investigations primarily focused on the binary classification of OSCC, achieving a remarkable 100% classification accuracy by leveraging texture, shape, and color features through Linear Discriminant Classifier (LDA) and Support Vector Machine (SVM). However, these ML-based techniques necessitate human intervention and domain expertise for feature extraction. Furthermore, the application of preprocessing algorithms is vital to enhance feature extraction by suppressing unwanted distortions and standardizing histopathological images.

In this context, DL represents a recent evolution of ML, characterized by intricate functionality. DL excels by directly extracting features from raw images, enhancing CAD system performance, particularly with expanded training datasets, enabling computers to learn from extensive experience [12]. In particular, CNNs have emerged as the premier method for various image analysis tasks [17]. For instance, the method proposed in [18] employed four pre-trained transfer learning models to classify four distinct types of OSCC, comparing them with a suggested CNN model. Another method proposed in [19] utilized Random Learning (RL) and Active Learning (AL) techniques in conjunction with CNNs to categorize oral cancer tissue into seven classifications. Earlier studies predominantly relied on DL and ML models for oral cancer detection, working with OSCC biopsy information or other data sources, but were constrained by inherent limitations. Subsequently, the method in [20] introduced a classification model for oral cancer categorization into two classes: oral cancer and healthy patients, harnessing a weighted ensemble of deep CNN architectures like Densenet201 and Resnet50. Furthermore, the authors in [18] explored the concept of transfer learning to classify four types of OSCC using four pre-trained deep CNN models, and compare the performance of these pre-trained models with their

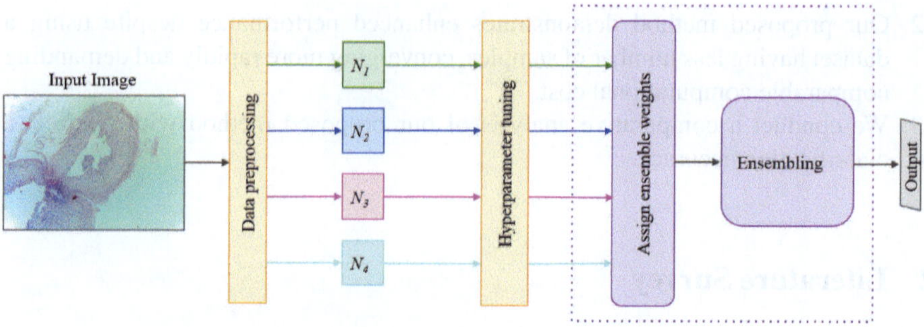

Fig. 1 Diagrammatic representation of the proposed method (*Note*: N_1, N_2, N_3, and N_4 represents VGG-16, VGG-19, MobileNet-V2, and Inception-V3 models respectively)

proposed CNN model. In their study, they proposed a ten-layer CNN architecture. They modified the fully connected layers by initializing weights randomly in order to facilitate relearning. In a similar vein, another study in [21] introduced a binary classification model for oral tissue pathology images, leveraging transfer learning with frozen layers in the first half of each network while training the remaining half.

To harness the advantages of both transfer learning and ensemble DL techniques, our focus centers on binary classifications of oral biopsy histology images, employing transfer learning-assisted weighted ensembles of deep CNNs.

3 Proposed Method

In this study, our focus centers on the binary classification of oral histopathological images. We achieve this by employing transfer learning-assisted weighted ensembles of deep convolutional neural networks (CNNs), as illustrated in Fig. 1. The initial step involves partitioning the dataset, which contains histopathological images of OSCC, into three subsets: training, validation, and testing. The training dataset undergoes preprocessing and subsequent data augmentation to enhance its suitability for training.

In the final phase, we fine-tune pre-trained networks, specifically VGG-16, VGG-19, MobileNet-V2, and Inception-V3, using the oral tissue pathology images. To facilitate classification of normal and OSCC samples, we modify the fully connected layers of these deep neural network architectures to yield binary predictions, categorizing oral histopathological images as either OSCC or normal. Ultimately, to capitalize on the strengths of each model during the classification process, we employ a weighted ensembling technique. Subsequently, we evaluate the accuracy of the proposed method on the test dataset.

3.1 Preprocessing

The preprocessing of the input images has encompassed several operations, including resizing, normalization, and augmentation. Given that we utilize histopathological images of two different resolutions, we perform resizing on the entire input image set to ensure consistency, setting dimensions to 224×224, and also apply normalization.

The final step in preprocessing involves augmenting the training images. This becomes necessary due to the scarcity of available data samples, which would not be sufficient for effectively training deep CNN models. To address this, we employ augmentation to expand the dataset, mitigating the risk of overfitting and promoting better to generalize of the deep CNN models in testing. This preprocessing step also involves various image manipulation techniques, such as flipping, inverting, scaling, and rotation of the original images, resulting in the generation of some more data samples [22].

3.2 Transfer Learning

Various advanced deep CNNs are accessible, each distinguished by its unique architectural design. These distinct architectures exhibit varying speeds and come with their own set of advantages and drawbacks. In our current experiment, we harness the potential of four such architectures: VGG-16, VGG-19, Inception-V3, and MobileNet-V2 to leverage their strengths. Although the pre-trained models VGG-16, VGG-19, MobileNet-V2, and InceptionV3 have already been trained on the ImageNet dataset, we further refine these models with minor architectural adjustments using the oral cancer dataset. In the context of transfer learning, fine-tuning involves leveraging the knowledge gained from solving a specific classification task with a vast dataset of annotated images and applying it to different classification tasks in different domains. Despite the oral histology image dataset having classes that bear no resemblance to those in the ImageNet dataset, the pre-trained models can still retrieve valuable attributes from oral tissue pathology images through the principles of transfer learning.

Building a deep CNN from ground up typically demands a large quantity of training data and significantly more time than transfer learning. Since the oral tissue pathology image dataset that we have used for our study has a comparatively small number of training images available, therefore, we employ pre-trained weights from ImageNet. Before fine-tuning, we modify the final fully connected layer, which originally has thousand output nodes in the selected models, to accommodate binary classification problems by replacing it with two output nodes. Subsequently, we load the pre-trained model weights which are already trained on ImageNet dataset and freeze these weights to prevent any loss during subsequent training iterations. To augment these frozen layers, we introduce new trainable layers on top of them.

These fresh layers learn to make predictions using the previously extracted features, adapting them to the unique characteristics of our histopathological image dataset during training.

3.3 Weighted Ensembling

Substantial evidence supports the effectiveness of model ensembles, which involve the fusion of distinct models to mitigate variance, bias, or both. In the realm of making numerous predictions [23], relying solely on a solitary model like a single decision tree often needs to accurately capture the intrinsic data features necessary for generating the most precise predictions. This limitation underscores the advantage of amalgamating multiple models, significantly enhancing prediction accuracy. By combining multiple DL models, we can extract a richer set of features from the underlying data structure [24, 25]. In pursuit of this objective, we implement a weighted ensemble approach aimed at mitigating variance and bias by effectively integrating multiple deep CNNs. This approach enables us to harness the strengths of each base learner by amalgamating their contributions through a weighted average.

4 Experimental Results

4.1 Dataset

In our research experiments, we made use of a publicly available dataset comprising histopathological images for the analysis of oral cancer. This dataset comprises a total of 1,224 images, which are categorized into two classes, each class of images having distinct resolutions [26]. The first class includes 89 oral histology images depicting normal oral tissue whereas other 439 images indicating cases of OSCC, all captured at a 100x magnification. Meanwhile, the second set encompasses 201 images portraying the normal oral epithelium and 495 histopathological images showcasing OSCC, captured at a higher magnification of 400x [26]. For a visual reference, you can refer to Fig. 2, which provides a glimpse of these histopathological images belonging to the two distinct categories: normal oral epithelium and OSCC.

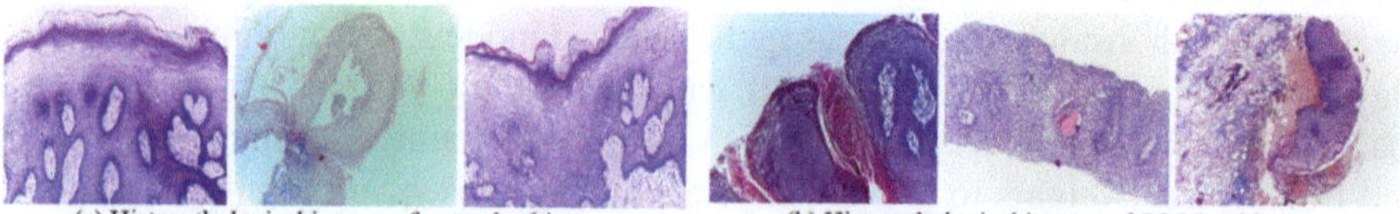

(a) Histopathological images of normal subject (b) Histopathological images of OSCC subject

Fig. 2 Sample images of histopathological images of oral cancer

4.2 Experimental Setup

In our study, we have used the graphical processing unit (GPU) of Google Colab, which provided access to a GPU runtime featuring a Tesla T4 processor with 16 GB of RAM. The Python version employed was 3.10.12, complemented by Keras 2.13.1.

To facilitate our experimentation, we partitioned the entire dataset into three distinct sets: training, testing, and validation. Specifically, 70% of total data samples were assigned for training purposes, while 10% were allotted for the purposes of validation, and the remaining 20% were designated for testing purposes. In this configuration, our method underwent training on a set of 857 images, validation on a subset of 123 images, and testing on a separate batch of 245 images.

4.3 Performance Metrics and Findings

In this study, we employ benchmark metrics to assess the efficacy of the proposed method across different classification performance measures, including accuracy, precision, recall, and F-measure. Recall quantifies the ratio of correctly classified positive samples to the total count of actual positive samples, as described in Eq. 2. Precision signifies the count of accurately classified positive samples divided by the total count of positive predicted samples, as outlined in Eq. 1. F-score encapsulates the harmonic mean of precision and recall, as defined in Eq. 4. As calculated in Eq. 3, accuracy measures the overall correctness of the proposed method's classifications:

$$precision = \frac{true\ positive}{true\ positive + false\ positive} \tag{1}$$

$$recall = \frac{total\ count\ of\ true\ classified\ samples}{total\ count\ of\ supplied\ samples} \tag{2}$$

$$accuracy = \frac{total\ count\ of\ true\ classified\ samples}{total\ count\ of\ supplied\ samples\ for\ classification} \times 100 \tag{3}$$

$$F - score = 2 \times \frac{precion \times recall}{precion + recall} \tag{4}$$

We evaluated the performance of our proposed method while utilizing two separate optimizers: Adam and RMSProp. For both optimizers, the proposed method was trained for a total of 20 epochs. The performance assessment of our proposed method in comparison to existing approaches is summarized in Tables 1 and 2. The table reveals that our proposed method consistently outperforms the existing ones. This

Table 1 Performance evaluation of our proposed method with deep CNN model using Adam optimizer

Method	Adam optimizer				
	Accuracy (%)	Precision (%)	Recall (%)	F-score (%)	Inference time (μs)
VGG-16	75.69	75.04	75.67	75.35	5
VGG-19	81.81	80.91	81.46	81.18	5
MobileNet-V2	81.81	80.90	81.46	81.17	3
Inception-V3	80.18	79.80	80.06	79.92	4
Proposed	85.04	84.46	85.04	84.25%	4

Table 2 Performance evaluation of our proposed method with deep CNN model using RMSProp optimizer

Method	RMSProp optimizer				
	Accuracy (%)	Precision (%)	Recall (%)	F-score (%)	Inference time (μs)
VGG-16	89.57	89.37	89.57	89.47	5
VGG-19	85.48	85.14	85.47	85.30	5
MobileNet-V2	88.75	87.93	88.75	88.34	3
Inception-V3	86.30	85.78	86.31	86.04	4
Proposed	91.01	89.97	91.01	90.49	4

superiority can be attributed to the additional step incorporated into our approach, namely the weighted average ensembling. Our method assigns greater weight to the deep CNN model with the highest individual performance, which contributes significantly to its superior results. It can be also inferred from Table 1 that the inference time of our proposed method is comparable to that of other deep CNN models. Furthermore, it is evident from the table that, in our experiments, the RMSProp optimizer consistently outperforms the Adam optimizer.

5 Conclusion

This study effectively leveraged transfer learning with pre-trained deep CNNs to achieve binary classification of oral histopathological images, distinguishing between normal and OSCC. Furthermore, we introduced a novel approach a weighted average ensemble deep CNN model for oral cancer classification. We conducted extensive performance evaluations, comparing fine-tuned pre-trained deep CNN models (VGG-16, VGG-19, MobileNet-V2, InceptionV3) with our proposed method using two different optimizers: Adam and RMSprop. Notably, these evaluations were carried out on a dataset comprising only 1224 histopathological images. Our experiments yielded insightful results, highlighting the performance variations among the four deep CNN models (VGG-16, VGG-19, MobileNet-V2, InceptionV3) with different optimizers. Specifically, VGG-19 demonstrated remarkable performance when coupled with the Adam optimizer. In contrast, when using the RMSprop optimizer, VGG-16 emerged as the top performer among the deep CNN models. It is important to note that the MobileNet-V2 model exhibited the shortest inference time compared to the others, showcasing its efficiency in processing. However, it is noteworthy that our innovative weighted ensemble method consistently outperformed all these deep CNN models, achieving superior classification accuracy for both optimizers. Furthermore, the inference time of our proposed method remained comparable with these models. In our future endeavors, we aim to explore advanced preprocessing techniques for histopathology image processing and strive to enhance our method's performance by working with a larger dataset of histopathological oral cancer images.

References

1. Li L, Yin Y, Nan F, Ma Z (2022) Circ_lpar3 promotes the progression of oral squamous cell carcinoma (oscc). Biochem Biophys Res Commun 589:215–222
2. Saba T (2020) Recent advancement in cancer detection using machine learning: systematic survey of decades, comparisons and challenges. J Inf Pub Health 13(9):1274–1289
3. Nayak VN, Donoghue M, Selvamani M (2015) Oral squamous cell carcinoma: a 5 years institutional study. J Med Radiol Pathol Surg 1(5):3–6
4. Deif MA, Hammam RE (2020) Skin lesions classification based on deep learning approach. J Clin Eng 45(3):155–161
5. Santana MF, Ferreira LCL (2017) Diagnostic errors in surgical pathology. J Brasileiro de Patologia e Med Lab 53:124–129
6. Deif MA, Solyman AA, Alsharif MH, Uthansakul P (2021) Automated triage system for intensive care admissions during the covid-19 pandemic using hybrid xgboost-ahp approach. Sensors 21(19):6379
7. Saikia T, Kumar R, Kumar D, Singh KK (2022) An automatic lung nodule classification system based on hybrid transfer learning approach. SN Comput Sci 3(4):272
8. Saikia T, Hansdah M, Singh KK, Bajpai MK (2022) Classification of lung nodules based on transfer learning with k-nearest neighbor (knn). In: 2022 IEEE international conference on imaging systems and techniques (IST), pp 1–6
9. Majumdar M, Gayen T (2022) Computer aided segmentation of oral mucosa to detect cancer. In: Applications of machine intelligence in engineering, pp 179–190
10. Kassani SH, Kassani PH, Wesolowski MJ, Schneider KA, Deters R (2019) Classification of histopathological biopsy images using ensemble of deep learning networks. arXiv preprint arXiv:1909.11870
11. Xie J, Liu R, Luttrell J IV, Zhang C (2019) Deep learning based analysis of histopathological images of breast cancer. Front Genet 10:80
12. Mahmood H, Shaban M, Indave B, Santos-Silva A, Rajpoot N, Khurram S (2020) Use of artificial intelligence in diagnosis of head and neck precancerous and cancerous lesions: a systematic review. Oral Oncol 110:104885
13. Komura D, Ishikawa S (2018) Machine learning methods for histopathological image analysis. Comput Struct Biotechnol J 16:34–42
14. Srinidhi CL, Ciga O, Martel AL (2021) Deep neural network models for computational histopathology: a survey. Med Image Anal 67:101813

15. Rahman T, Mahanta L, Chakraborty C, Das A, Sarma J (2018) Textural pattern classification for oral squamous cell carcinoma. J Microscopy 269(1):85–93
16. Rahman TY, Mahanta LB, Das AK, Sarma JD (2020) Automated oral squamous cell carcinoma identification using shape, texture and color features of whole image strips. Tissue Cell 63:101322
17. Krizhevsky A, Sutskever I, Hinton GE (2017) Imagenet classification with deep convolutional neural networks. Commun ACM 60(6):84–90
18. Das N, Hussain E, Mahanta LB (2020) Automated classification of cells into multiple classes in epithelial tissue of oral squamous cell carcinoma using transfer learning and convolutional neural network. Neural Netw 128:47–60
19. Folmsbee J, Liu X, Brandwein-Weber M, Doyle S (2018) Active deep learning: Improved training efficiency of convolutional neural networks for tissue classification in oral cavity cancer. In: 2018 IEEE 15th international symposium on biomedical imaging (ISBI 2018), pp 770–773
20. Singha Deo B, Pal M, Panigrahi PK, Pradhan A (2022) An ensemble deep learning model with empirical wavelet transform feature for oral cancer histopathological image classification. medRxiv, 2022–11
21. Panigrahi S, Nanda BS, Bhuyan R, Kumar K, Ghosh S, Swarnkar T (2023) Classifying histopathological images of oral squamous cell carcinoma using deep transfer learning. Heliyon 9(3)
22. Mikołajczyk A, Grochowski M (2018) Data augmentation for improving deep learning in image classification problem. In: 2018 international interdisciplinary PhD workshop (IIPhDW), pp 117–122
23. Dietterich TG (2000) Ensemble methods in machine learning. In: International workshop on multiple classifier systems, pp 1–15
24. Brown G, Wyatt J, Harris R, Yao X (2005) Diversity creation methods: a survey and categorisation. Inf Fusion 6(1):5–20
25. Pal M, Tiwari Y, Reddy TV, Ram Aditya PS, Panigrahi PK (2021) An integrative method for covid-19 patients' classification from chest x-ray using deep learning network with image visibility graph as feature extractor. medRxiv, 2021–11
26. Rahman TY, Mahanta LB, Das AK, Sarma JD (2020) Histopathological imaging database for oral cancer analysis. Data Brief 29:105114

Autism Spectrum Detection Using 3D CNN

Harini Ganeshan, Chalumuru Suresh, Akhila Annireddy, Chandralekha Pamidimukkala, and Supraja Alleni

1 Introduction

Autism spectrum disorder (ASD) is a state related to the development of the brain that affects how a person observes and interacts with other people and thus can cause issues in social associations and communication. ASD involves restricted and monotonous behavior and activities. The terminology "spectrum" in autism spectrum disorder indicates a broad span of symptoms and characteristics defining a unique behavior profile of the affected. It starts in childhood and eventually causes issues like social interactions, at school and workplace. Considering the example, children usually display signs related to autism during the initial year and then go through a regression period between 18 and 24 months of age where they might develop autism symptoms. Though there is no cure for autism spectrum disorder, early detection, and effective treatment can make a huge difference in the lives of ASD patients. The various biomarkers available so far have only been available as irregular data, and it is tough to get compact information about diagnostic collections. Let's look into some of the reasons leading to ASD in individuals. Autism spectrum disorder has

Present Address:
H. Ganeshan (✉) · C. Suresh · A. Annireddy · C. Pamidimukkala · S. Alleni
Department of CSE, VNR Vignana Jyoti Institute of Engineering and Technology, Hyderabad, Telangana, India
e-mail: ganeshanharini28@gmail.com

C. Suresh
e-mail: suresh_ch@vnrvjiet.in

A. Annireddy
e-mail: akhilaannireddy0605@gmail.com

C. Pamidimukkala
e-mail: chandraleka.p1@gmail.com

S. Alleni
e-mail: suprajaalleni123@gmail.com

K. Kumar Singh et al. (eds.), *Machine Vision and Augmented Intelligence*, Lecture Notes in Electrical Engineering 1211, https://doi.org/10.1007/978-981-97-4359-9_67

no known cause. But given the complexity of the disease and varying symptoms, there can be several causes of ASD. An individual's genetics and the surrounding environment play a key role. Examples include an immediate member of the family having autism, born to elderly parents, low-birth-weight infants; metabolic disorders, having a history of viral infections are some of the common reasons causing ASD. Genetic disturbances, some genetic mutations like fragile X syndrome or Rett syndrome can increase the risk of ASD.

Autistic individuals often have social, spiritual, and communication problems. They might repeat specific behaviors and might not wish to change their routine. Most people with ASD have different ways of learning, paying attention, or reacting to things. Symptoms of ASD start in childhood and last a lifetime, paying attention, or reacting to things. Symptoms of ASD start in childhood and last a lifetime. Children or adults with ASD: do not point to objects to show interest (for example, not to point to a plane that is flying overhead) they don't look at objects that others point to

- have trouble to relate to others or don't have an interest in other people at all
- try to avoid eye contact and want to stay alone
- Despite no precise cure for ASD, timely care makes a big difference for autistic people. This can be achieved by having supportive therapies with a team of specialists to diagnose which consists of:
  - Behavioral therapy
  - Play therapy
  - Occupational therapy
  - Physical therapy
  - Speech therapy

The research on some alternative remedies is mixed and some tend to be dangerous. Before investing in this alternative therapy, it is always necessary to consult a healthcare professional. These remedies include:

- Vitamins of high dosage
- Chelation therapy—consists of the removal of metals from human body
- Hyperbaric oxygen therapy
- Melatonin can be given to resolve sleep issues (Fig. 1).

2 Literature Survey

Bi et al. [1] proposed a method which is used to detect autism spectrum disorder. The authors identified that SVM (Support Vector Machine) has been implemented widely, but it has been observed that the accuracy of the SVM was observed to be low as single SVM is used for classification. In order to improvise this, authors used multiple Support Vector Machines to differentiate patients ASD and normal patients. The dataset collected was from a database called as ABIDE which stands for Autism Brain Imaging Data Exchange, which consists of the data related to 46 normal people

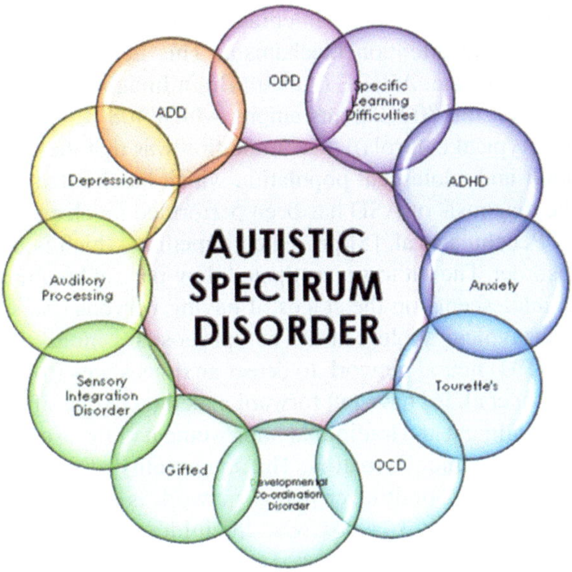

Fig. 1 Autism spectrum disorder

and 61 patients suffering with ASD. A random cluster of SVM was introduced to classify between ASD patient and typical controls. Abnormal brain regions have also been found out through this which includes IFG (Inferior Frontal Gyrus) and hippocampus.

Ahammed et al. [2] proposed a method which is used to detect autism spectrum disorder. The authors have felt that previous implementations don't have as much strength in order to manipulate certain metrics such as the F1 score, precision or the accuracy, which are known to be the performance metrics. A model has been proposed known as the "avant garde DarkASDNet" which is capable of extracting features which is from lower level to the higher level. 3D-FMRI data has been considered by implementing normalization and correct slice time correction. Here the Deep Neural network refers to the intended set of layers: convolutional, batch normalization and major integration layers in sequential sequences. They have made totally 20 convolutional layers and also 6 max-pooling layers. At the time of computation, the method is able to handle extraction of the image features.

Sewani et al. [3] presented a method for the detection of autism spectrum disorder. The authors identified that with various changes in autism behavior traces the machine learning models' accuracy and quality are becoming a higher challenge. So, they applied deep neural network (DNN) on the ABIDE dataset. Their deep learning model is integrated with an unsupervised autoencoder, neural-network, and supervised deep learning using CNN (convolutional neural networks). The size of the dataset for this method is less and doesn't include various characteristics like mother's age, birth weight, and family history.

Ke et al. [4] proposed a method which is used for detecting autism spectrum disorder. In this model the authors implemented Multichannel deep-attention neural network which has been integrated with several layers of the neural networks, feature-fusion and attention mechanism. This helps to view interrelations in the multi-modality data. ABIDE (Autism Brain Imaging Data Exchange) repository has been used for the 809 patients among which 408 patients suffer from ASD and 401 are TC (typical controls)). The limitation was that the chosen cohort was in the young–adult and adolescent population which has limited the model's generalizability, as the diagnosis of ASD has been performed much earlier.

Penchina et al. [5] presented a method which is used to detect autism spectrum disorder. The authors investigated slow-pace of breathing during situations with stress in adolescents on the stages of having nervousness suffering with autism and also neurotypical adolescents. They proposed a multi-class Long short term recurrent (LSTM) neural network to detect anxious states from EEG signals.

Xu et al. [6] have put forward a method to classify youngsters with Autism Spectrum ailment and traditional improvement of the use of brief-time period spontaneous hemodynamic fluctuation. The abnormality of the temporal lobe in ASD is discovered here. A multilayer neural network is carried out for characteristic extraction blended with a 3-layer-CNN. 25 children with ASD and 22 children with TD had been measured with infrared spectroscopy determined inside the anterior decrease gyrus and temporal lobe. The findings of this may additionally make contributions for early diagnosis of autism spectrum disorder in children and give a new angle on destiny clinical diagnoses.

Omar et al. [7] proposed an effective model which predicts relying on Machine learning technique and also a mobile app is developed for predicting people with ASD belonging to all age groups. A model is developed by merging Random Forest: CART & ID3. A dataset was constructed containing 250 data values collected from people suffering with autism and normal individuals. AQ-10 dataset used for model evaluation.

Thabtah and Peebles et al. [8] introduced a system learning technique known as rules-machine mastering which not only simply detects the autism trends of controls and cases, however it additionally offers customers expertise bases that may be used by area experts in notifying the motives behind the class. Outcomes on 3 information groups about kids, children, and adults display that rules-gadget getting to know gives with specificity, accuracy of higher predictive classifiers and HM than the ones of another gadget mastering procedures including decision trees, Bagging and Boosting, and Induction of Rules.

Jagadeesan et al. [9] proposed the usage of Naïve Bayes classifier for the ASD prediction method. The electrodes which are connected with a scalp location unit, used to seize the graph indicator. Encephalogram abnormalities (EEG) place units are typically used as biomarkers that are reliable to diagnose Autism Spectrum detection. Classification of ASD was run with graph sign procedure, gaining knowledge of fashions. Minimization of graph-channel frequency is joined in the process of prediction that applies arithmetic option vicinity unit that is extracted from noise filtered graph understanding earlier than and as soon as separate riffle redesign. Applicable alternatives and graph channel have been chosen for mis-treatment correlation primarily the feature based desire. The coaching fashions and feature vector location unit are used to reduce graph channels.

Artarisco et al. [10] proposed the use of ML (Machine learning) to check for reliability and accuracy of Q-CHAT in discriminating young autistic kids from the ones without. 5 special machine learning algorithms like NB (naïve Bayes), RF (random forest), LR (logistic regression), SVM (support vector machine), and KNN (K-nearest associates) have been implemented to explore the whole pack of Q-CHAT objects. This is to make use of it as an easy, quick and high performance tool in the main settings. Here limited number of subsets are selected by ignoring a few, leading to lesser efficiency for real time analysis.

Ali et al. [11] proposed a unique approach for autism diagnosis based on the bi-LSTM. This model uses the EEG data from SFARI database and proposed a multi-layered architecture that combines two LSTM modules for both EEG data classification and of autism and normal data obtained from individuals. This model provides an improved performance over the single LSTM approach with better classification efficiency and promises a potential contribution in ASD diagnosis and neuroscience research.

Vijaya et al. [12] worked on the complex task of recognizing genes causing ASD. Hence this work aims at classification of ASD genes using RNN models like LSTM (Long Short-Term Memory), Bidirectional—RNN & GRU (Gated Recurrent Units) where a single hot-encoding method has been used for representing sequence of the genes by means of a numeric-vector. These deep learning models exhibited better performance along with reduced time taken. Based on their performance evaluation conducted using several metrics, it confirms that the GRU network model using one-hot vectors gave promising results.

3 Proposed System

This paper is proposed with the primary motive of designing and developing a deep learning model that is used to classify autism spectrum disorder using 3D Convolutional Neural Networks. The system aims to overcome the shortcomings of the existing systems on the same problem statement. In this project, we train the 3D CNN model that also includes the significant temporal and spatial properties of the data by performing various transformations. As a part of the pre-processing stage, the input is re-sampled to overcome the drawbacks posed by the resolution differences in the images. A mining of the images is done to identify and reveal potential biomarkers and significant hidden attributes.

The proposed classifier is the 3D Convolutional Neural Networks that provides the diagnosis results on the ASD. This model is implemented using the Python programming language and involves usage of several user defined and inbuilt functions. It is then converted to a web application using the Flask framework. Evaluation metrics like Recall, Log loss, Accuracy and Precision scores are used to measure the performance of the model. The efficiency of the current system is then compared and analyzed with other ML and DL models to produce a system evaluation study. A recommendation system also is developed that generates possible treatment methods and suggestions as per the diagnosis results generated by the model.

3.1 Dataset

ABIDE—Autism Brain Imaging Data Exchange Dataset is the core dataset that this project utilizes. It consolidates two datasets—ABIDE Dataset I consists of 1112 data records ranging from ages 7–64 years and contains 539 ASD and 573 non-ASD individuals, whereas ABIDE Dataset II aggregates over 1114 dataset records ranging from ages 5–64 years and contains 521 ASD and 593 non-ASD individuals. ABIDE I involves data garnered from around 17 sites presenting an aggregate of r-fMRI to the broader medical and scientific community. On the other hand, ABIDE II was generated to extend the scientific study of attributes of core ASD by aggregating data from around 19 sites. On a whole, the ABIDE forms a complete dataset of around 2100 subjects to build up a moderately sized dataset. Around 90% of the records indicate healthy individuals while the remaining 10% indicate the group of ASD patients.

3.2 Features

The controls used for ASD classification fall under 10 variables ranging from A1–A10. These A1—A10 items are questions that indicate the common symptoms and signs of ASD. An individual who scores more than 3 is considered to be likely to have ASD. These questions have Usually/Always/Rarely/Never as their possible answers with code (0 or 1) associated with it. The fields like brain images and pupillometry data can be extracted from the reports obtained from ASD tests conducted. The remaining information includes data fields that come from the user like Age, Country, Ethnicity, relation, Blood; etc. 0 (non-ASD) and 1 (ASD) are the target labels for detection.

There are two major functionalities that the proposed system must achieve—

- Functionality of Input and Output mapping
- Functionality of Diagnosis display module.

3.3 Functionality of Input and Output Mapping

This functionality is fulfilled by the classifier that aims to map the input and output data in order to generate the associated target labels by training and testing accordingly. This is achieved using the significant attributes for A1–A10 scores and other vital signs and information signed up by the user like age, ethnicity, country and other associated symptoms. This captured data from the user helps in effectively classifying the ASD patients and helps in early detection. Hence the output is based on the degree of accurate mapping and is displayed as the ASD prediction.

3.4 Functionality of Diagnosis Display Module

This functionality encodes the output in the form of 0/1 where "0" is "NO ASD" and "1" indicates "ASD" respectively. Hence this indicates two sets of target class labels, 0 and 1. which depict a classic case of binary classification. Hence the output is displayed as the encoded binary form as well as the associated label to the user. The associated label is shown in the textual format so that the user can understand the results clearly. There's also an option to show a comparative analysis of results of several models and suggest treatments based on the results obtained above to the user.

3.5 System Architecture

There are 3 tiers in the system architecture that are proposed for this project. Each of the tiers have a specific functionality assigned to them. The data can flow in a bi-directional way among these tiers. The tiers are presented in a more detailed way as follows (Fig. 2).

The first tier is the User tier. In the user tier, the user of the application will interact with the application. Initially the user logins to the system in this tier. Then the user can view the web application and hence provide the required details in the

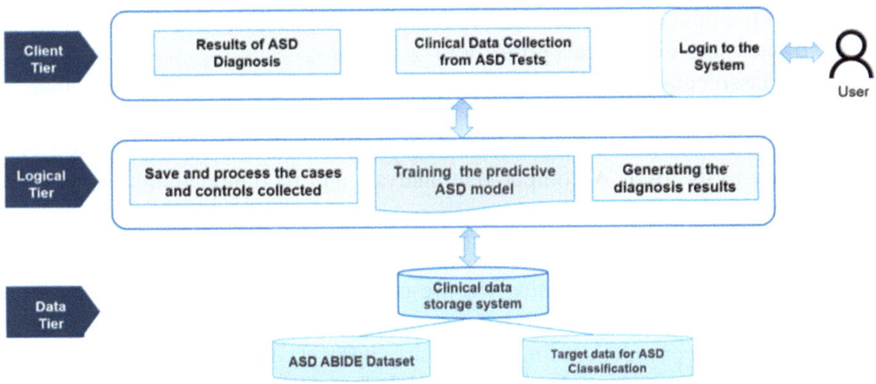

Fig. 2 System architecture

form provided that comes as a part of the clinical data collection from the user. The user provides the data with respect to the A1–A10 scores of ASD, the data with respect to the ASD test reports and finally fills up the demographic information of the user. Clicking the "predict" option redirects to the next tier that is the second tier which is called the logical tier. The final outcomes from the system are also presented in this tier later. The Analyze tab can be used to present the comparative study of the model used and also display the recommendations for treatment methodologies as per the diagnosis results generated. In this logical tier, the data undergoes pre-processing techniques. The raw data's format is changed in a suitable format for further processing in the later stages. The dataset also had a considerable percentage of data with missing data or missing attributes.

This is handled by removing such records for the maximum part and forward filling the other remaining records. The input images are translated and rotated to encode and save this data. The brain images obtained as input need to be processed for noise and distortions, hence the images are rotated about their axes and translated in a format suitable for the model. This stage involves application of techniques that reduce overfitting of the model in further stages and acts as a regularizer. The hidden biomarkers are identified by using mining techniques. The dimensionality of the dataset is normalized to enhance the data quality used. Then the 3D CNN deep learning model is built and trained. After training, the diagnosis is generated. The logic for training the 3D CNN learning model is by using the data from the data tier and prediction of diagnosis by the model with the data provided by the user runs in this tier. The third tier is the data tier. In this tier the machine learning model data is present from which the model is extracted and displayed on the user interface. Data tier is all about the ABIDE dataset and the target data on prediction of ASD. The Application contains the following modules:

- Clinical data collection—The information required for the model to process and generate the classification of ASD condition is obtained from the input data given by the users via the user interface of the system.
- Data Augmentation and Correction Module—This module provides the ability to enhance the images by reducing the resolution differences, removing distortions and transposing the image's projection.
- ASD Classification Module—This module uses the 3D CNN model that is primarily responsible for generating the target classes.
- Results and Analysis module—The final diagnosis results are generated and displayed to the user. A comparative analysis and recommendation results are also presented to the user.

The model proposed by the system uses 3D Convolutional Neural Networks which is nothing but the 3D CNN classifier. The pre-processed data is taken by the classifier. Then it is divided in a way where seventy percent of the data goes as the training dataset used for the model's training and thirty percent of the other data is used as the testing dataset for testing the trained model. The model uses a cumulative of six neural layers. Among these layers, we use the first layer as the input layer, the next set of four neural layers constitute the hiddenand ultimately the last layer is taken as the output layer. The model includes several modules used for translation of complex images and preserves the spatial and temporal properties of the data. A 90% accuracy can be secured with this proposed system.

Some of the pros provided by the currently proposed system is as follows:

- Doesn't compromise on the temporal and spatial aspects of the data.
- Mining the data for hidden biomarkers that are crucial for generating more efficient diagnosis results.
- Deal with imbalanced and varied sized datasets.
- Faster computation capability with higher accuracy and better performance.

The proposed system can be achieved using the following algorithm (Figs. 3 and 4).

The flow chart shows the flow of the activity in the application. The flow starts with the Autism API with all the input fields included. The user enters the information under Vital signs, laboratory results and gives the demographic information. The next step will be the display of the diagnosis results. This is achieved by clicking the Predict button. The clinical data collected from the user is processed by the 3D-CNN model and the results are predicted. The results predicted by the system are displayed to the user using the Autism API.

ALGORITHM

1. Take the ABIDE dataset and pre-process it using re-sampling to handle the imbalance in the data and also develop methods to handle missing/duplicate data items.
2. Develop data correction method to remove the noise in the images, perform data augmentation using rotation methods to convert the input images to the format suitable for further processing.
3. Take this pre-processed data and divide it into the Training and Testing datasets represented as X_train, Y_train, X_test, Y_test accordingly.

    3.1. Develop the code for implementing 3D CNN model
    3.2 Tuning the gating, layers and correlation factors
    3.3 Finalize and configure the parameters of the model

        mode = 'supervised'
        num_layers=6
        downsample_factor=4
        sum_dir = 'gating comparison'
        gate='equal_gender'
        correlation=1

    3.4 Retrieve and store the estimated results into the target variable
    3.5 Fit the trained model's information into the 3D CNN model classifier

4. Validate the designed model with the testing dataset
5. Evaluate the performance of the model using the metrics like Accuracy, Recall, Precision and F1-score.

Fig. 3 Algorithm to implement the system

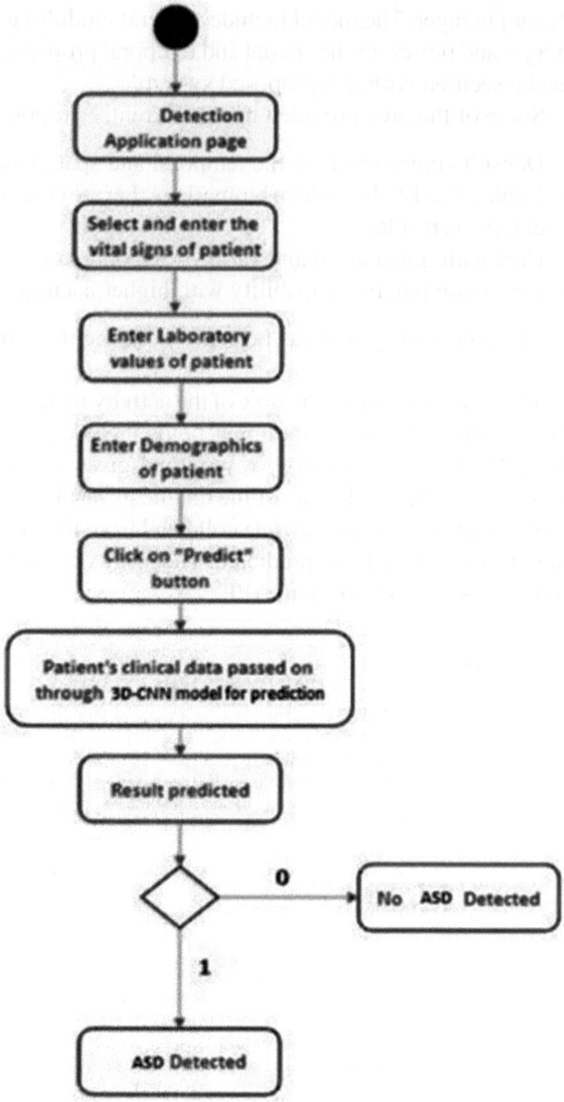

Fig. 4 Flow chart of the application

4 Experimental Results

The dataset used in this project is called the ABIDE—Autism Brain Imaging Data Exchange Dataset. It consolidates two datasets: ABIDE Dataset I consists of 1112 data records ranging from ages 7–64 years and contains 539 ASD and 573 non-ASD individuals whereas the ABIDE Dataset II aggregates over 1114 dataset records ranging from ages 5–64 years and contains 521 ASD and 593 non-ASD individuals.

ABIDE involves data garnered from around 17 sites presenting an aggregate of r-fMRI to the broader medical and scientific community. On the other hand, ABIDE II was generated to extend the scientific study of attributes of core ASD by aggregating data from around 19 sites. On the whole, the ABIDE forms a complete dataset of around 2100 subjects to build up a moderately sized dataset. The controls used for ASD classification fall under 10 variables ranging from A1–A10. These A1–A10 items are questions that indicate the common symptoms and signs of ASD. An individual who scores more than 3 is considered to be likely to have ASD. These questions have Usually/Always/Rarely/Never as their possible answers with code (0 or 1) associated with it.

The data is re-sampled to remove the imbalance of the data records (Fig. 5).

The brain images obtained as input need to be processed for noise and distortions, hence the images are rotated about their axes and translated in a format suitable for the model. This stage involves application of techniques that reduce overfitting of the model in further stages and acts as a regularizer. The hidden biomarkers are identified by using mining techniques. The dimensionality of the dataset is normalized to improve the quality of the data. The 3D CNN model indicates that it is equivalent it its 3D format: it takes a 3D volume or a series of 2D records as the input. In case of processing complex images, for example—medical images, the 3D CNN architecture is utilized. They form a powerful and effective model for faster learning and representations of huge volumes of data. It is utilized to process spatial and temporal aspects of the dataset. It uses 3D convolutions too extract these properties from the input and project them on the 3 dimensions. It uses 3D filters and generates a 3D volume of data after applying convolution and hence preserves the spatial/temporal features of the input stack frames. 3D convolutional kernels to make segmentation predictions for a volumetric patch of a scan.

Several machine learning models are built and used in this paper for the comparative analysis. The key to a fair comparison of these techniques is by ensuring that each algorithm is evaluated in the same way on the same data. We have considered the following machine learning algorithms: 3D CNN model, Support vector Machine, Logistic regression, Naïve Bayes, Decision Tree and K-NN. The comparative study

Fig. 5 Dataset after re-sampling

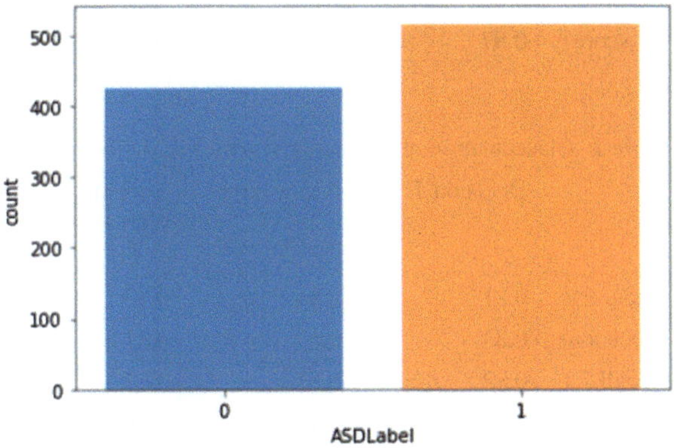

is conducted by taking Accuracy, Recall, Precision and F1-Score as the parameters for the above-mentioned techniques. The results of the study are as follows (Tables 1 and 2).

The results obtained indicate that the algorithms used like 3D CNN model, Support vector Machine, Logistic regression, Naïve Bayes, Decision Tree and K-NN give the accuracy of prediction like 90, 85, 87, 84, 82 and 80% respectively.

From the above plots (Figs. 6 and 7) we can see that the model is trained using the training dataset and then its performance is evaluated using testing and validation datasets using Accuracy and loss as the metrics respectively. The plots indicate healthy results as the model is not overfitted and shows a low loss and higher accuracy.

In Fig. 8. We can observe that the AUC for the proposed model in the ROC curve is higher indicating higher performance of the model. The closer the ROC plot is to the upper left corner, we can say that the model is more efficient. That indicates that the model can distinguish better between the positive and negative labels.

In Fig. 9: we have presented the comparison among the various techniques used with the help of a bar graph. In this plot, we use accuracy as the metric and have plotted the model's performance separately for ABIDE I and ABIDE II. It shows that our 3D CNN model has a higher accuracy in both the partitions of datasets.

Figure 10 shows the home page of the web application developed. The About Tab displays the information about ASD and what this web application is all about.

Figure 11 shows the Predict tab of the web application. It shows a form that is filled by the user with A1–A10 scores and other symptoms and bio data of the user. These details come from the reports of ASD tests and they are currently provided to the system here. Then the user clicks on Predict button to generate the analysis.

Table 1 Comparison of results among several ML-DL algorithms using evaluation metrics

	Decision Tree	Naive Bayes	Logistic regression	Support vector machine	3D conv net	K-NN
Accuracy	0.82	0.84	0.87	0.85	0.9	0.8
Precision	0.84	0.89	0.88	0.86	0.9	0.8
Recall	0.81	0.83	0.86	0.82	1	0.5
F1-score	0.87	0.81	0.79	0.83	0.9	0.7

Table 2 Classification results using several ML methods—(with attributes A5, A6, A9, A10)

	Decision Tree	Naive Bayes	Logistic regression	Support vector machine	3D conv net	K-NN
Accuracy	0.81	0.81	0.87	0.87	0.9	0.87
Precision	0.83	0.67	0.81	0.81	0.91	0.5
Recall	0.82	0.81	0.82	0.82	0.92	0.64
F1-score	0.86	0.73	0.86	0.86	0.96	0.77

Fig. 6 Training versus validation accuracy for 3D conv net. with autocorrelation factor = 68.9

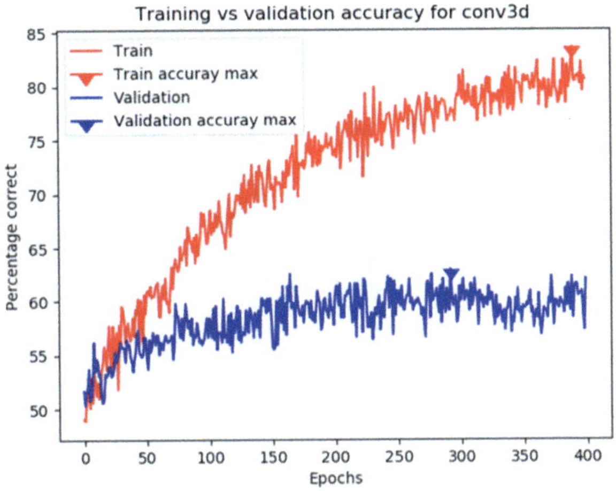

Fig. 7 Training loss versus validation loss for the 3D conv model

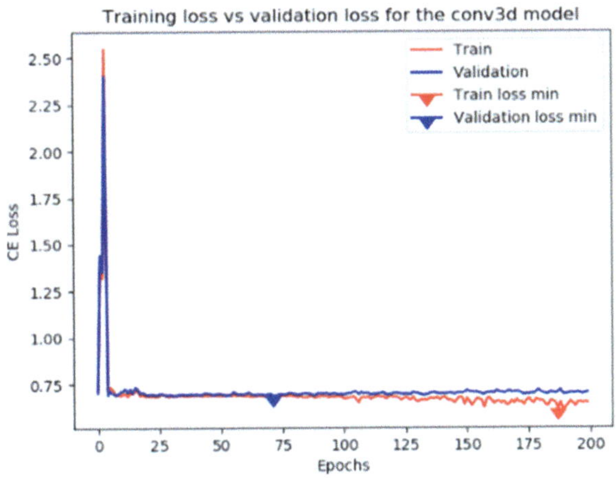

Fig. 8 Assessing and comparing classifier performance with ROC curves

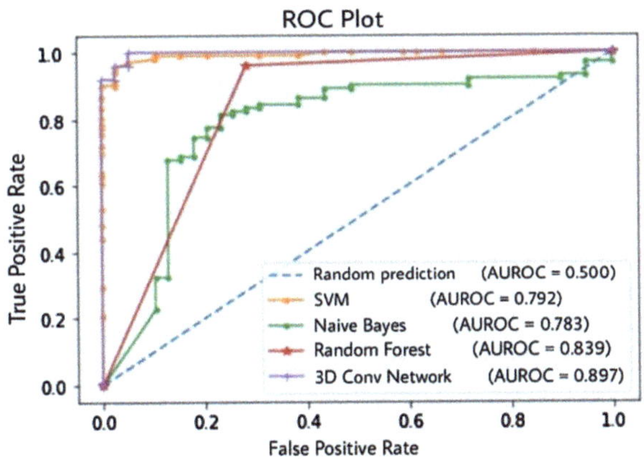

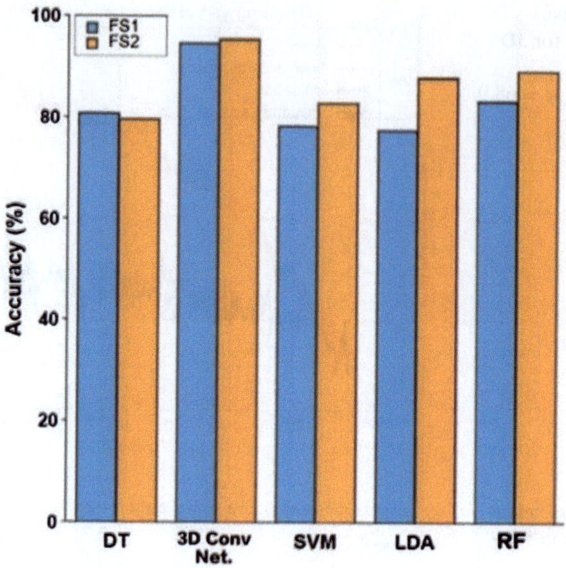

Fig. 9 Accuracy comparison bar chart of various classifiers

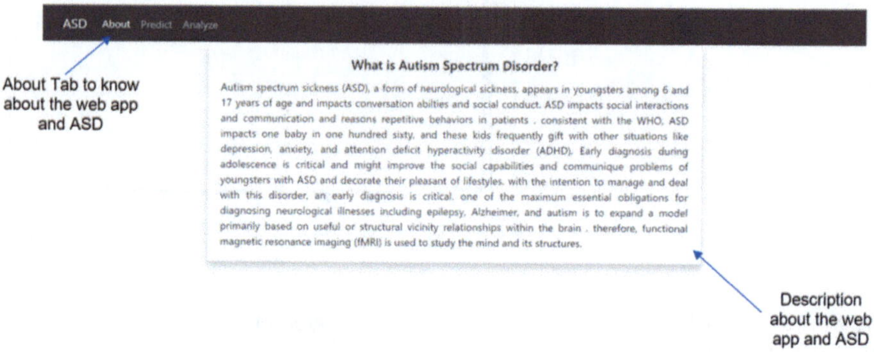

Fig. 10 The user interface of the web application

In Fig. 12: we can see the results generated from the system in the form of a textual string. It shows ASD or NO ASD accordingly.

Figure 13 shows the Analyze tab of the web application. Here, the analysis of the results is done and recommendations of treatment methodologies are presented to the user. Also, a comparative analysis of performance is presented to show the efficiency of current system with respect to existing techniques. Hence these results indicate that the 3D Convolutional Neural Network gives a superior accuracy in identification of ASD at early stages by utilizing the medical data provided.

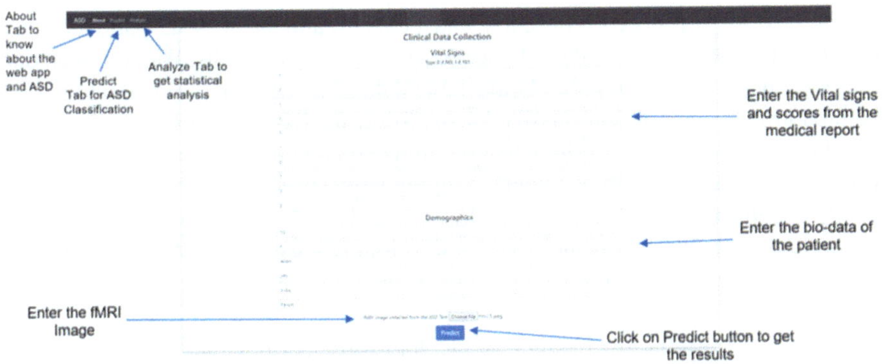

Fig. 11 The predict tab of the web application

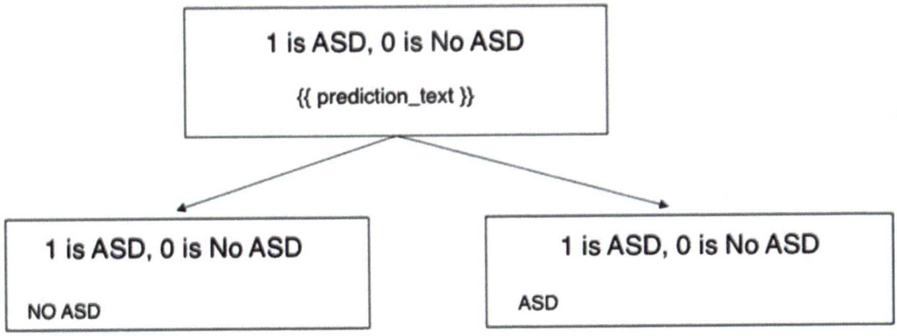

Fig. 12 Diagnosis results from the web application

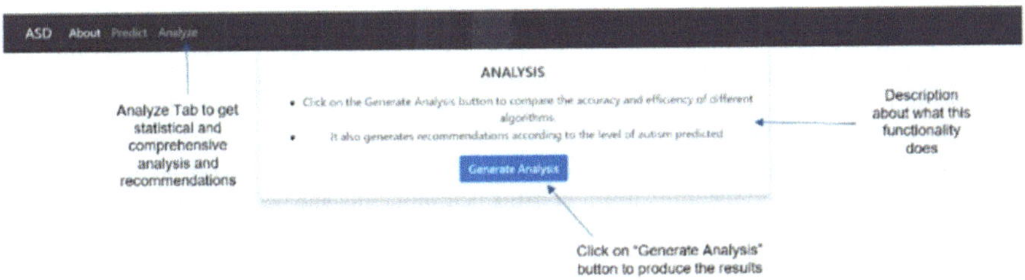

Fig. 13 Analyze tab of the web application

5 Conclusion and Future Scope

The importance of ASD is that it is showing steady increasing growth over the past two decades, with current estimates reaching up to 1 in 36 children. In this project, a novel 3D CNN Deep learning-based ASD local and global diagnosis system has been proposed. The main motto is to detect ASD at early stages and with greater accuracy so as to proceed with early and better treatment of ASD patients. This technique is time efficient and has lesser possibility of false results. We evaluated our proposed model using the publicly available dataset named ABIDE to demonstrate the capability of our model to classify Autism Spectrum Disorder (ASD) from resting-state fMRI data. Our results show that the proposed model achieves state-of-the-art results on single sites with accuracies ranging between 85 and 93%. Our model is readily suitable for complex or noisy whole-brain 3D volume data such as raw fMRI data in real-time. Flask is being used for developing a user-friendly UI. Ultimately it becomes very easy for the users to put in the data and identify if the person is suffering from ASD or not.

In future, we would like to enhance the application by making it more customer specific and expand even more by deploying this model in a hospital website and help the doctors detect any early signs of Autism Spectrum Disorder.

In future our application should be able to compute all the attributes of patient's condition and based on the computed score value it will be generating analysis based on stages of severity of the patient, which are:

- Early/Mild stage
- Severe stage
- Extremely severe stage.

Finally, using the results we can investigate and identify the neuro circuits that malfunction and are involved in causing ASD.

References

1. Bi XA, Wang Y, Shu Q, Sun Q, Xu QB (2018) Classification of autism spectrum disorder using random support vector machine cluster. Front Genet 9:18
2. Ahammed MS, Niu S, Ahmed MR, Dong J, Gao X, Chen Y (2021) Darkasdnet:classification of ASD on functional MRI using deep neural network. Front Neuroinf 20
3. Sewani H, Rasha K (2022) An autoencoder-based deep learning classifier for efficient diagnosis of autism, vol 10, p 182
4. Ke N, Jiayang G, Xueping P (2020) Multichannel deep attention neural networks for the classification of autism spectrum disorder using neuroimaging and personal characteristic data. Complexity 2020:9
5. Penchina B, Sundaresan A, Cheong S, Martel A (2020) Deep LSTM recurrent neural network for anxiety classification from EEG in adolescents with autism. In: International conference on brain informatics. Springer, pp 227–238
6. Xu L, Sun Z, Xie J, Li J (2021) Dentification of autism spectrum disorder based on short-term spontaneous hemodynamic fluctuations using deep learning in a multi-layer neural network. Clin Neurophysiol 457–468
7. Omar KS et al (2019) A machine learning approach to predict autism spectrum disorder. In: International conference on electrical, computer and communication engineering (ECCE), pp 1–6
8. Thabtah F, Peebles D (2020) A new machine learning model based on induction of rules for autism detection. Health Inf J 264–286
9. Jagadeesan M, Selvaraj P et al (2021) Behavioral features based autism spectrum disorder detection using decision trees. Ann Rom Soc Cell Biol 8069–8075

10. Artarisco G, Cicceri G, Di Pietro D et al (2021) Use of machine learning to investigate the quantitative checklist for autism in toddlers (Q-CHAT) towards early autism screening. Diagnostics (Basel) 11:574
11. Ali NA et al (2021) LSTM-based electroencephalogram classification on autism spectrum disorder. Int J Integr Eng 6:321–329
12. Vijaya MS (2019) Recurrent neural network based model to predict autism spectrum disorder causative genes. IJAST 28:581–591

Enhancing Financial Literacy and Goal Achievement with WebFin

Kuldeep Vayadande, Tejas Sarade, Tanishka Pimple, Dream Tejwani, Varun Sahu, and Kedar Vartak

1 Introduction

In a world marked by ever evolving financial dynamics, the quest for effective personal finance management has become an increasingly intricate endeavor [1]. It is within this intricate landscape that the innovative endeavor of WebFin takes center stage. This research paper lays the foundation for a groundbreaking platform that marries the power of cutting-edge web technology with the multifaceted challenges individuals encounter when striving to master their financial destinies [2]. The intricate tapestry of personal finance management is often woven with threads of uncertainty, complexity, and an array of financial commitments [3]. Individuals are confronted with a multitude of financial decisions spanning from budgeting and expense tracking to investment allocation and tax management [2]. The ramifications of these choices can significantly impact not only immediate financial wellbeing but also long-term financial security and growth [4]. These challenges, however, are

K. Vayadande (✉) · T. Sarade · T. Pimple · D. Tejwani · V. Sahu · K. Vartak
Vishwakarma Institute of Technology, Pune, India
e-mail: kuldeep.vayadande1@vit.edu

T. Sarade
e-mail: shriram.tejas22@vit.edu

T. Pimple
e-mail: tanishka.pimple22@vit.edu

D. Tejwani
e-mail: dream.tejwani22@vit.edu

V. Sahu
e-mail: manish.varun22@vit.edu

K. Vartak
e-mail: kedar.vartak22@vit.edu

K. Kumar Singh et al. (eds.), *Machine Vision and Augmented Intelligence*, Lecture Notes in Electrical Engineering 1211, https://doi.org/10.1007/978-981-97-4359-9_68

not confined to a particular demographic or economic stratum; rather, they transcend socioeconomic boundaries, affecting both the financially adept and the novice alike [3]. Considering these challenges, the core objective of WebFin crystallizes to provide a comprehensive platform that empowers users to holistically manage their financial lives [5]. Through intuitive budgeting tools, users can plan and manage their finances in a manner that aligns with their goals and aspirations [6]. This component of WebFin recognizes that the foundation of sound financial management rests on a well-structured budget that bridges the gap between income, expenses, and savings [6]. Beyond budgeting, WebFin sets out to democratize the realm of financial planning and goal setting [7]. Individuals often grapple with the task of defining realistic financial goals and charting a course to achieve them [6]. The platform's goalsetting module leverages behavioral economics principles to encourage incremental progress, transforming what might seem like insurmountable objectives into manageable milestones [7].

In an era where information flows freely and investment opportunities are abundant, WebFin emerges as a guide to steer users through the complexities of investment management [6]. With a user centric approach, the platform empowers individuals with the tools to make informed investment decisions [8]. Risk tolerance assessments, diversified portfolio recommendations, and Realtime market insights are seamlessly integrated, empowering users to navigate investment opportunities with confidence and prudence [8]. The project also tackles the crucial realm of credit monitoring and management [9]. In an age where creditworthiness governs access to financial opportunities, the platform integrates features that enable users to actively monitor and improve their credit profiles [9]. Timely alerts, credit utilization strategies, and personalized tips work in tandem to uplift users' credit standings, enhancing their financial capabilities in the process [9]. Furthermore, the labyrinthine process of tax filing and financial reporting is streamlined through Web Fin's innovative modules [2]. Complex tax codes, deductions, and filing procedures can overwhelm even the most financially literate individuals [2]. Web Fin's approach to tax management is not solely about compliance; it is about enabling users to confidently navigate the tax landscape, optimizing deductions, and ensuring they meet their fiscal responsibilities without undue stress [2].

The research underpinning WebFin delves into a harmonious convergence of theoretical paradigms [9]. Insights from personal finance management, grounded in principles of responsible financial behavior [1], merge seamlessly with the psychology driven insights of behavioral economics [9]. This merger begets an approach that respects the rationality of individuals while accounting for the behavioral biases that often shape financial decisions [9]. The platform's user experience design is crafted to align with the cognitive processes and tendencies that underpin human financial behavior, fostering an environment where users can engage with their finances more effectively [8]. The methodology adopted to transform WebFin from concept to reality comprises of a meticulous sequence of stages [10]. Designing and developing the platform is an iterative process, one that absorbs user feedback and evolves accordingly [10]. This iterative approach, informed by user centered design principles, aims to ensure that the platform resonates with its users' needs and preferences [10]. This process is underpinned by the potency of web technology that not only facilitates seamless integration of various financial functionalities but also enhances accessibility, enabling users to engage with their financial matters anytime, anywhere [10]. Data analysis emerges as a pivotal tool for evaluating the effectiveness of WebFin [11]. Beyond being a mere platform, WebFin endeavors to be a catalyst for behavioral change, shifting users from passive financial management to active engagement [11]. Data driven insights provide the means to gauge user engagement, satisfaction, and the platform's efficacy in driving positive financial outcomes [11]. This empirical evaluation ensures that Web Fin's impact is measurable and adaptive, contributing to continuous enhancement [11].

In summary, the WebFin project strives to be a transformative force in the realm of personal finance management [6]. In a world where the intricacies of financial matters can deter individuals from achieving their goals, WebFin emerges as a beacon of empowerment [3]. By harnessing the potency of web technology, grounded in the bedrock of behavioral economics and user centric design [8], WebFin seeks to revolutionize how individuals approach their financial wellbeing [5]. In fostering a sense of financial autonomy, ease, and confidence, WebFin aspires to reshape the financial journeys of individuals, enabling them to navigate the intricate landscape of personal finance with clarity, efficacy, and resilience [6].

2 Literature Survey

In this article [2], Bitrián, Buil, and Catalán explore the emerging trend of gamification in personal financial management apps. The authors delve into the concept of gamification and its potential to enhance user engagement, motivation, and learning in the context of financial management tasks. They examine various gamification elements such as points, badges, leaderboards, and challenges, and how these elements can be effectively applied to encourage positive financial behaviors. The study also investigates the impact of gamification on individuals' financial knowledge, attitudes, and behavior, providing valuable insights into the design and implementation of gamified financial management apps.

Goyal et al. [1] present a systematic literature review on the antecedents and consequences of personal financial management behavior. The authors analyze a wide range of studies to identify key factors that influence individuals' financial management practices. They explore various antecedents such as financial literacy, self-control, financial attitudes, and sociodemographic factors, and their impact on personal financial management behavior. Additionally, the study investigates the consequences of effective financial management, including improved financial wellbeing, reduced financial stress, and increased financial satisfaction. The authors also propose a future research agenda, highlighting areas for further exploration and suggesting potential research directions to advance our understanding of personal financial management behavior.

According to the essay [9], it is argued that every individual needs to plan and manage their own finances in order to live a happy life. This entails creating a personal financial plan to effectively achieve financial goals, retire comfortably, attain financial independence, make sound financial decisions, and capitalize on various financial opportunities. It is acknowledged that not everyone is naturally equipped with these skills, hence it becomes the responsibility of each individual to acquire them. The acquisition of financial planning and management skills not only contributes to personal wellbeing but also supports the long-term development and prosperity of the country as a whole.

The publication [12] expands the existing research on the determinants of personal financial management and proposes the Self-determination Theory (SDT) as a framework for understanding the factors that influence people's engagement or lack thereof in appropriate financial practices. The study emphasizes the potential use of SDT in designing effective interventions to enhance individuals' financial knowledge and efficacy, with a particular focus on motivation. By leveraging the empirically supported principles of SDT, interventions can be developed to improve individuals' motivation, leading to more positive financial outcomes.

An article [3] highlights the extensive landscape of financial decisions individuals encounter throughout their lives. These decisions encompass various aspects such as consumption, cash flow management, saving, investing, borrowing, retirement planning, tax planning, estate planning, and insurance. It is noted that these financial decisions are interconnected and often involve tradeoffs. The efficiency with which individuals make these decisions depends on their financial knowledge, money management abilities, as well as a range of behavioral, cultural, demographic, sociological, economic, and technical factors.

The objective of a study [13] is to review and discuss current research on financial literacy and its correlates, the relationship between financial literacy and financial behavior, as well as financial inclusion, particularly in developing nations. Financial literacy and education initiatives have long been recognized in developed and high-income nations. However, impact assessment studies have yielded inconclusive evidence on the direct effect of financial education on changing financial behavior. Nevertheless, policymakers in developing nations are increasingly considering financial literacy as a crucial component of financial inclusion programs. As a result, research examining how financial education delivered with the goal of increasing financial inclusion can be effectively implemented is becoming more accessible.

By combining the Self-determination Theory (SDT) and the Technology Acceptance Model (TAM), a research study [14] investigates how gamification can enhance users' desire and intention to use personal financial management (PFM) applications, as well as promote their adoption. The findings suggest that gamifying PFM applications aligns with users' demands for competence and autonomy, therefore increasing their motivation to utilize these applications. Furthermore, users' motivation positively affects their perceptions of the applications' ease of use and usefulness, leading to more favorable attitudes towards them. The data also indicates a relationship between user attitudes towards PFM applications and their behavioral intentions to utilize them.

In a research study [8] conducted by Austin et al., a structured denoising diffusion model was developed to handle structured data in discrete state spaces. This model uses a diffusion process to filter noisy data samples and retrieve the underlying structure. The model was trained on a dataset to learn the diffusion dynamics and parameters. Through evaluations on tasks like picture denoising and inpainting, it was demonstrated that the structured denoising diffusion model outperforms existing approaches in terms of denoising capabilities. This research showcases the potential of structured denoising diffusion models for various applications.

Another research work [15] by Bowen et al. introduces a new method for extending images through object completion. They propose a deep neural network that learns to predict the appearance of partially visible objects based on input image patches. The network is trained on a large dataset of images and partial object masks, enabling accurate forecasting of object appearances in different scenarios. The effectiveness of their approach is demonstrated on datasets like Places2 and COCO Stuff, surpassing state-of-the-art methods in terms of image quality and visual fidelity. The paper also provides a detailed analysis of the trained neural network's capability to accurately predict object appearances in various scenarios.

Comparatively, Dhariwal et al. [4] compare Generative Adversarial Networks (GANs) and Diffusion Models for image synthesis. They find that Diffusion Models outperform GANs in terms of image quality, sample diversity, and training stability. Diffusion Models generate images with fewer artifacts, more natural textures, and a wider range of diverse images. Moreover, they exhibit less mode collapse and are more stable during training, requiring fewer hyperparameters. The researchers attribute the superior performance of Diffusion Models to their use of a direct diffusion process, which allows for a more natural learning of the image distribution compared to GANs' indirect and adversarial learning process. Dhariwal et al.'s paper presents a compelling case for the superiority of Diffusion Models over GANs in image synthesis, offering a more stable and computationally efficient approach for generating high quality images.

Han et al. [11] propose a novel approach to fashion image inpainting that addresses the challenges of compatibility and diversity. They define compatibility as the ability of the inpainting system to produce results consistent with the surrounding context of the image, including the style and color of the clothing. Diversity refers to the ability of the system to generate multiple plausible inpainting results for the same missing region. To achieve these goals, the authors propose a two-stage approach. In the first stage, a conditional generative model is trained on a large dataset of fashion images to generate a set of candidates inpainting results that are compatible with the surrounding context. In the second stage, a diversity promoting model is employed to select a final inpainting result from the set of candidates, promoting visually distinct results that are still compatible with the surrounding context. The authors evaluate their model on a fashion image dataset, demonstrating its superiority over state-of-the-art methods in terms of both compatibility and diversity. They also conduct a user study showing that human evaluators prefer the results generated by their model over existing methods.

Patel and Jain [10] propose a user centered design approach for developing web based financial tools that enhance user engagement. They argue that traditional financial tools are often complex and challenging to use, leading to user frustration and disengagement. Their approach focuses on designing tools that are easy to understand and use, providing users with necessary information and guidance for informed financial decision making. Incorporating cognitive psychology, human computer interaction, and behavioral economics frameworks, the authors emphasize the importance of understanding user thinking and interaction with financial tools to create more user friendly and engaging products. The paper includes a case study of a web based financial tool developed using the proposed user centered design approach, which demonstrates its improved user friendliness and engagement compared to traditional financial tools.

In article [16], Rodrigues and Costa examine the role of gamification in enhancing financial literacy through web platforms. The authors focus on how gamified approaches can be used to promote financial education and improve individuals' understanding of financial concepts. They explore the potential of gamification techniques, such as quizzes, simulations, and interactive challenges, to engage users and facilitate the learning process in the field of personal finance. The study also evaluates the effectiveness of gamification in improving financial literacy levels and highlights the benefits of using web platforms as a medium for delivering gamified financial education.

Sharma and Gupta (2021) conducted a literature review [5] on financial inclusion and WebFin platforms. They analyzed articles from academic journals, industry reports, and government publications, discovering that WebFin platforms have a significant role in promoting financial inclusion. The review identified various ways in which these platforms contribute to financial inclusion, such as providing access to financial products and services, reducing the cost of financial services, and enhancing convenience and accessibility. However, the authors also discussed challenges that need to be addressed to fully leverage the potential of WebFin platforms for promoting financial inclusion.

In a study by Tan and Lim [6], an online survey of 279 adults in Singapore was conducted to investigate the impact of web based personal finance tools on savings behavior. The findings revealed that participants who used such tools were more likely to have a budget, track their spending, and save money for specific goals. Additionally, participants utilizing web based personal finance tools demonstrated a higher ability to answer financial concept related questions and make informed financial decisions. Based on these results, the authors concluded that web based personal finance tools can be valuable in promoting savings behavior and improving financial knowledge. They recommended financial institutions and other organizations to develop and promote web based personal finance tools to assist consumers in achieving their financial goals.

3 Methodology

To enable personal finance management utilizing web technology, online tools, platforms, or programmes that help people efficiently manage their financial resources, budgets, investments, and other areas are required. Here is a method to achieve this (Fig. 1).

3.1 Study and Comprehension

Identify the target audience: Decide who will use online technologies to handle their personal finances. For distinct age groups, income levels, and financial objectives, different feature and interface requirements may be necessary.

Examine user behavior: Recognize the challenges and resources that people currently face while managing their finances. This will influence how you develop.

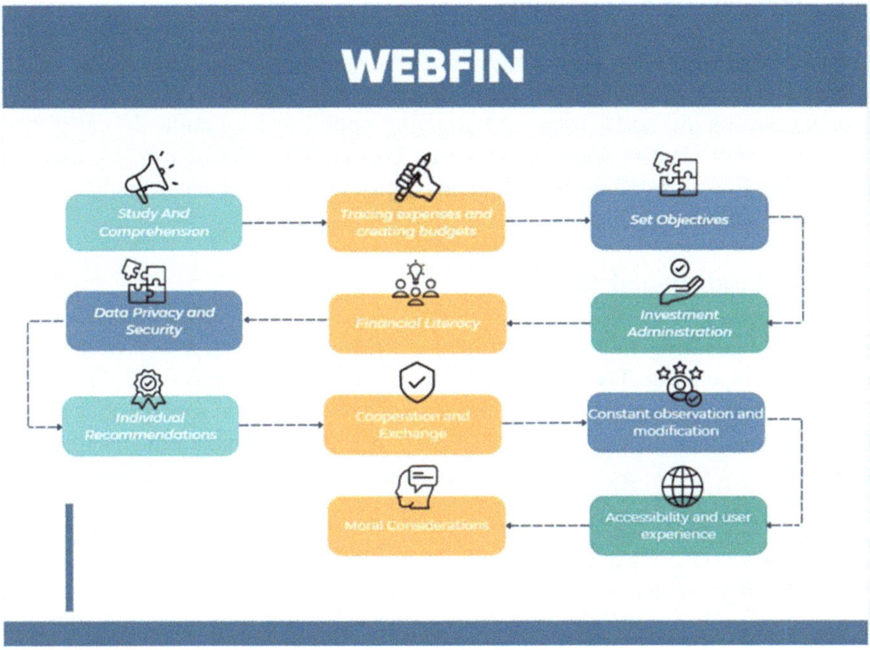

Fig. 1 Methodology

3.2 *Tracking Expenses and Creating Budgets*

Budgeting is the key to effective personal financial management. Thanks to digital technology, there are many tools available to make budgeting more interesting, adaptable, and accessible.

3.2.1 Budgeting Interactively

The manual recording of income and expenses as part of the budget making process was replaced by the web. Users of online budgeting tools can create customized spending plans based on their needs and goals. These programmes frequently offer interactive user interfaces that make it easy to allocate funds to various categories, such as housing, transit, groceries, entertainment, and savings. Users can establish spending limits for each category and receive Realtime reports on their progress.

3.2.2 Realtime Expense Tracking

A challenge of budgeting is accurately tracking spending. Web technology, which enables Realtime spending tracking, addresses this. By connecting their bank accounts and credit cards, users of budgeting apps can automatically categorize transactions and identify spending patterns. This position can be used by users to identify possible areas of overspending and adjust their budget accordingly.

3.2.3 Notifications and Alerts

Web based budgeting tools usually offer notifications and alerts to aid users in avoiding overspending. These solutions allow consumers to receive warnings when they are approaching or exceeding their spending limits for specific categories. The quick feedback encourages users to stay on track and make prudent financial decisions.

3.3 *Set Objectives*

Setting and achieving financial objectives is essential for long term financial success. Web technology facilitates identifying and fulfilling these objectives.

3.3.1 SMART Objectives

Specific, Measurable, Achievable, Relevant, and Time Bound goals are those that are. Users who utilize web apps can create SMART goals. By providing a clear structure, these applications assist users in setting goals more precisely and tracking their progress over time.

3.3.2 Visual Progress Tracking

You will be motivated by realizing how far you have come in terms of your financial goals. Web technology enables the creation of visualizations, such as progress bars or charts that show how close users are to completing their goals. Users are motivated to follow through on their financial plans by these illustrations, which serve as constant reminders.

3.3.3 Strategy Suggestions

Applications on the web can examine users' financial information and offer tailored recommendations to help them accomplish their goals more rapidly. For instance, if a user wants to save money for a down payment on a house, the app can advise reallocating funds from discretionary spending to their savings account.

3.4 Investment Administration

Making wise investments is crucial for long term financial growth made possible the availability of information, research resources, and even automated investment services.

3.4.1 Comparison and Research

Online investment platforms offer a wealth of information about various investment options. Users can conduct research on a wide range of assets, including bonds, equities, mutual funds, and exchange traded funds (ETFs). On a regular basis, these websites provide tools for comparing the costs, risks, and historical performance of various investments.

3.4.2 Rob Advisors

Online programmes known as "rob advisors" employ algorithms to create and manage investing portfolios based on the level of risk a customer is willing to take and their financial goals. Without requiring a thorough understanding of finance, these platforms provide easy, automated ways for people to invest.

3.4.3 Online Brokerages

Web based brokerage platforms make it easy to buy and sell investments. Users can place trades, monitor their portfolios, and get Realtime market information from any device with an internet connection.

3.5 Financial Literacy

To make good decisions, one must educate oneself about personal finances. There are many educational materials on the Internet.

3.5.1 Accessible Learning Resources

On the internet, there is a variety of financial information. Online publications, videos, podcasts, and webinars go into great detail on a variety of financial topics, from basic budgeting to sophisticated investing strategies. Users have the opportunity to learn at their own pace because these resources are always available.

3.5.2 Interactive Financial Simulations

Web apps offer interactive financial simulations that let users experiment with different financial scenarios. Users can experiment with the results of upping their savings rate or shifting their investment allocation over time, for example. These simulations help users comprehend complex financial topics and their repercussions.

3.6 Data Privacy and Security

Data security and user privacy must come first in web based personal finance applications due to the sensitivity of financial data.

3.6.1 Encryption and Secure Protocols

Personal finance apps should utilize strong encryption to protect users' financial information. All data transmissions between the user's device and the server should be secured using secure protocols, like HTTPS, to prevent unauthorized access.

3.6.2 Two Factor Authentication (2FA)

Users are required to provide a second authentication method in addition to their password when 2FA is enforced, such as a code texted to their mobile device. Because of this, there is less chance of unauthorized access even if a password is compromised.

3.6.3 Regular Security Audits

Personal finance app developers should conduct frequent security audits to identify and address issues. This ensures that the app's security features remain effective against evolving cyber threats.

3.7 Individual Recommendations

Large scale financial data analysis using web technologies allows for the creation of customized suggestions.

3.7.1 Credit Card Optimization

Apps can recommend credit cards with features that match users' preferences by looking at their spending patterns. Users can optimize their points and perks in this way.

3.7.2 Investment Strategies

By assessing users' risk tolerance and financial aspirations, apps can offer investment strategies that are consistent with their goals. These strategies include diversification, asset allocation, and frequent rebalancing.

3.8 Cooperation and Exchange

By enabling multiple people to cooperate on comparable financial goals, web technology promotes collaborative financial management.

3.8.1 Joint Budgeting

Families or couples can manage their money together by using instruments for shared budgeting. These instruments, which permit open dialogue about incomes, expenses, and financial goals, foster financial concord.

3.8.2 Trusted Advisors

Users who want professional guidance can share their financial information with trusted advisors like accountants or financial planners. Secure data exchange systems preserve anonymity while facilitating expert insights.

3.9 Constant Observation and Modification

Web technology enables the constant monitoring and adjustment of financial strategies to take changing circumstances into account.

3.9.1 Realtime Updates

Personal finance programmes provide users with up-to-the-minute details on their financial condition, taking changes in their income, expenses, and investments into consideration. This will ensure that users always understand their financial situation accurately.

3.9.2 Automated Alerts

Users may receive automated alerts to examine and modify their financial plans. For instance, if a user's income fluctuates dramatically, an app might advise them to review their budget.

3.10 Accessibility and User Experience

A quality personal finance tool must have a positive user experience. Web applications should be developed to be available on a number of platforms and user friendly.

3.10.1 Intuitive Interface

An interface that is simple to use and intuitive boosts user engagement. Thanks to easy design and navigation, users can access and manage their financial data without getting confused.

3.10.2 Cross Device Compatibility

Users should be able to access their personal finance tools without any trouble on a variety of devices, including computers, tablets, and smartphones. Because of this versatility, users can manage their finances from any location.

3.11 Moral Considerations

There are ethical requirements given the possible impact of online technologies on financial decisions.

3.11.1 Responsible Practices

Developers of personal finance apps should prioritize the needs of their users by refraining from taking any activities that promote reckless spending or prey on psychological biases.

4 Proposed System

See Fig. 2.

Expense Categorization (NLP Based):

Using Natural Language Processing (NLP) for Text Classification Explanation: This method classifies expenses based on their textual descriptions using machine learning.

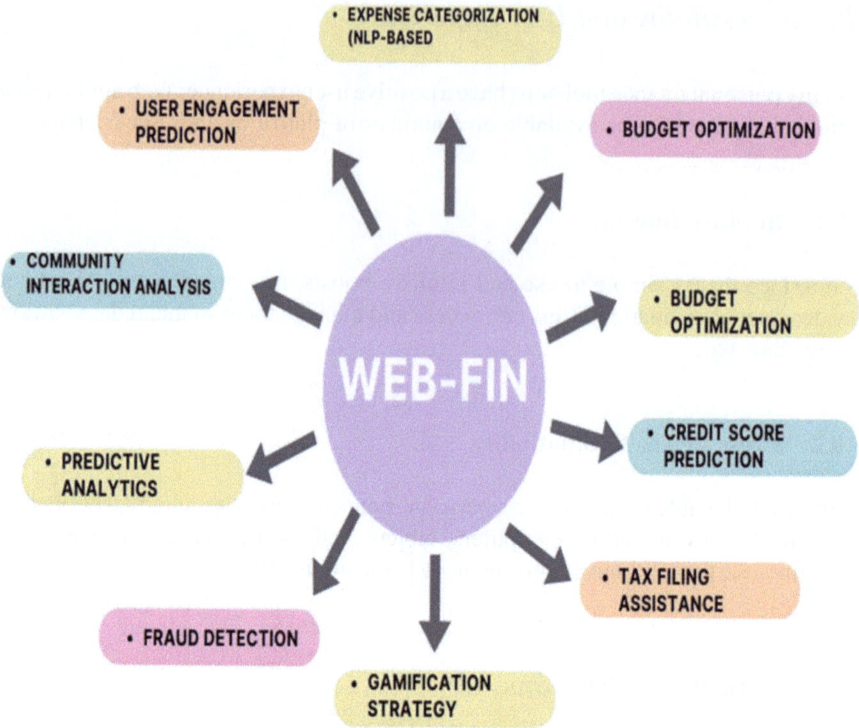

Fig. 2 Proposed system

It entails: Preparation of Data: assemble a labelled dataset with descriptions of expenses and the corresponding categories. Tokenize the descriptions and turn them into numerical features using text processing. Model Education: Utilize the labelled data to train a classifier (such as Naive Bayes, SVM, or LSTM) and discover the connections between descriptions and categories. Prediction: The trained model guesses the category when a new description is entered.

Budget Optimization:

Linear or genetic algorithms are examples of algorithms.

Explanation: To achieve financial objectives, budget optimization seeks to disperse available cash among budget categories. While genetic algorithms gradually develop solutions over generations, linear programming formulates this as a linear objective function with constraints: Programming in a linear form and Establish a linear objective function (such as the maximum savings) and limitations (such as the maximum spending per category). Utilize optimization methods to solve and identify the best distribution.

Gene based algorithms Use selection, crossover, and mutation operations to evolve the best solutions over iterations by representing solutions (budget allocations) as chromosomes.

Investment Recommendation (Collaborative Filtering):

Collaborative Filtering (User Item or Item Item) algorithm.

Reason: Investment recommendations generated by collaborative filtering are based on past user behavior and shared preferences: User Item: Make investment recommendations based on the choices made by users with similar investment profiles. Item: Based on prior interactions, suggest investments that are comparable to those that the user has previously expressed interest in.

Credit Score Prediction (Regression):

Algorithm: Regression (Linear Regression, Random Forest, XGBoost).

Explanation: This algorithm predicts future credit scores based on historical credit data and user behavior: Data Collection: Gather historical credit score data and user specific financial data. Feature Engineering: Extract relevant features like credit utilization, payment history, loan balances, etc. Model Training: Train a regression model using the historical data to predict the user's credit score at a future time point (Figs. 3 and 4).

Tax Filing Assistance (Rule Based System):

Algorithm: Rule based System or Decision Trees.

Explanation: A rule-based system guides users through tax filing step-by-step, based on their financial data and tax regulations: Rule Definitions: Define rules based on tax regulations and user financial circumstances. Decision Trees: Create decision tree nodes with conditions based on user inputs and financial data, leading to tax related recommendations.

Gamification Strategy (Reinforcement Learning):

Algorithm: Reinforcement Learning (QLearning, Deep QNetworks).

Explanation: Reinforcement learning optimizes gamification elements to maximize user engagement and satisfaction: Reward System: Define rewards for desired user behaviors (e.g., completing financial goals, achieving budget targets). QLearning or Deep QNetworks: Model the user's interactions with the platform as states, actions, and rewards. The algorithm learns optimal actions to take to maximize cumulative rewards over time.

Fraud Detection (Anomaly Detection):

Algorithm: Isolation Forest, One Class SVM, Autoencoders.

Explanation: Anomaly detection algorithms identify abnormal transactions that might indicate fraud: Isolation Forest: Isolate anomalies by randomly partitioning data points into isolation trees. One Class SVM: Learn a boundary around normal data points and identify anomalies outside the boundary. Autoencoders: Train a neural

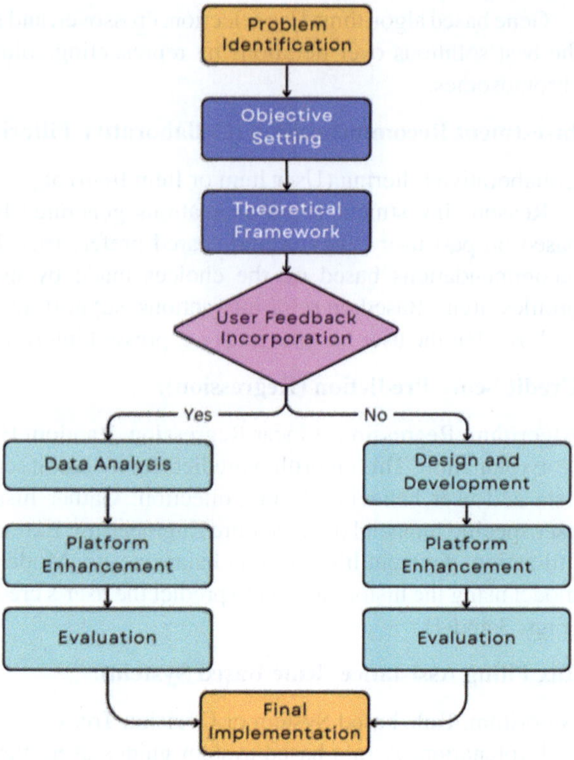

Fig. 3 Model flowchart

network to reconstruct normal transactions; anomalies have higher reconstruction errors.

Predictive Analytics (Time Series Forecasting):

Algorithm: ARIMA, Exponential Smoothing, LSTM.

Explanation: Time series forecasting predicts future financial trends based on historical data: ARIMA: Analyze time series patterns and seasonality to forecast future values. Exponential Smoothing: For short-term forecasting, give more importance to recent observations. Long Short-term Memory (LSTM) is a kind of recurrent neural network that is capable of detecting intricate temporal patterns.

Community Interaction Analysis (Sentiment Analysis and Topic Modeling):

Algorithm: Sentiment Analysis (VADER, finetuned models) and Latent Dirichlet Allocation (LDA).

Explanation: These algorithms analyze user generated content and community discussions: Sentiment Analysis: Determine sentiment polarity (positive, negative, neutral) of user comments/posts using pretrained models or custom training: Group similar words in discussions into topics to understand the main themes and trends in the community.

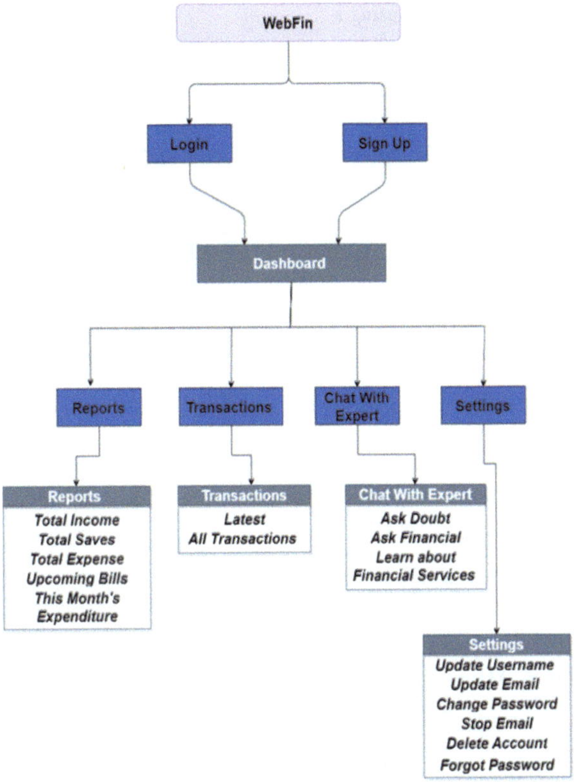

Fig. 4 Website flowchart

User Engagement Prediction (Classification):

Algorithm: (Logistic Regression, Random Forest, Gradient Boosting) classification Explanation: Identify user engagement levels based on previous interactions and data: Data Gathering: Identify user engagement data, past usage trends, and user characteristics. Create features that describe user behavior, platform interactions, and demographic data via feature engineering. Model Education: Create a categorization model based on the features to predict engagement levels (such as low, medium, and high).

5 Table of Analysis

See Figs. 5, 6, 7, 8 and Tables 1, 2, 3, 4, 5.

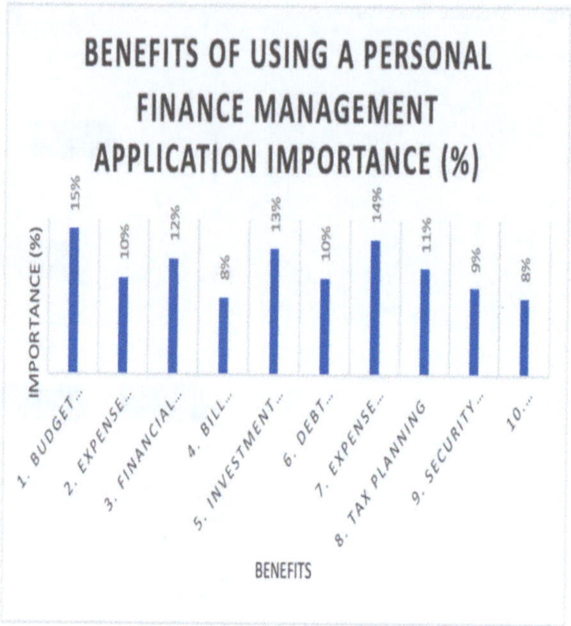

Fig. 5 Benefits of using a personal finance management appplication importance (%)

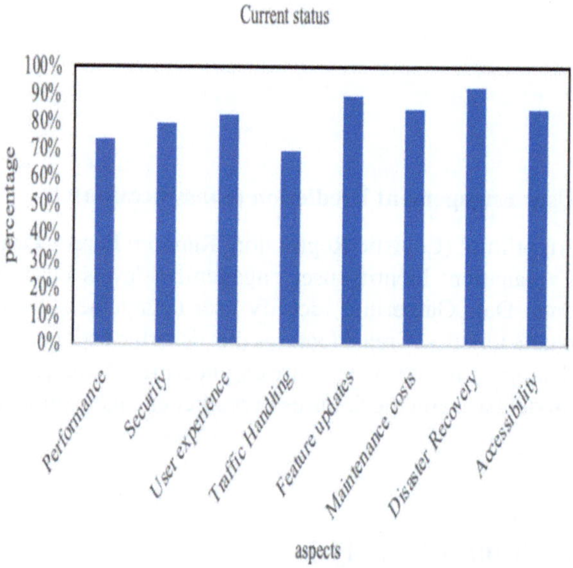

Fig. 6 Maintenance aspects

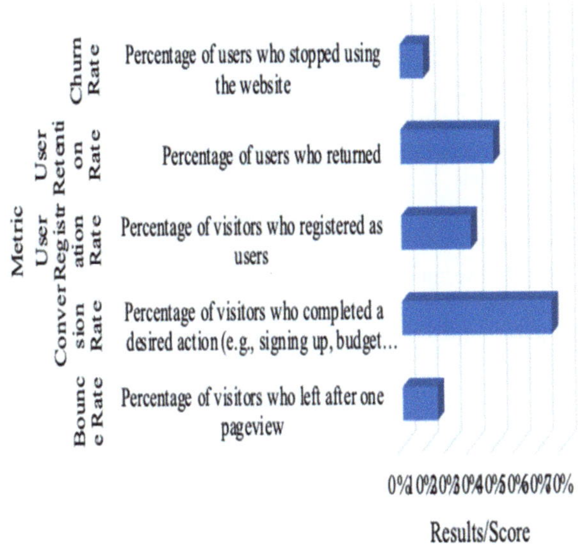

Fig. 7 Result

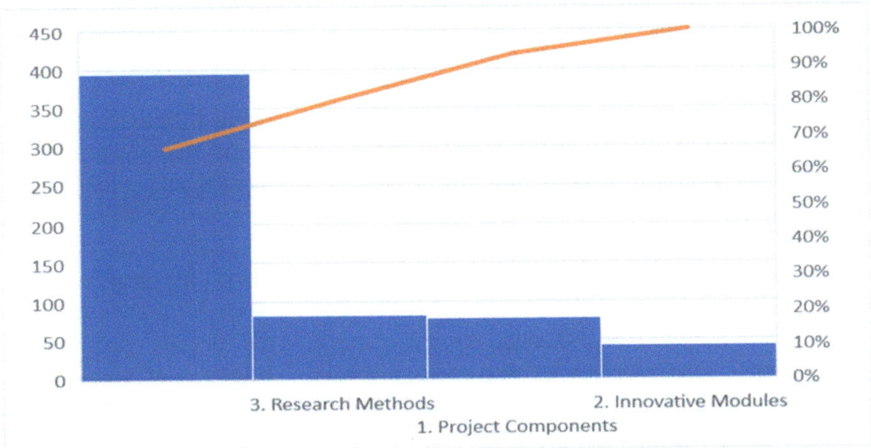

Fig. 8 Analysis

6 Scope of Research

The objective of this research project comprises the development and testing of WebFin, a comprehensive platform for managing personal finances. The research will concentrate on addressing the problems that people have with effectively managing their finances and providing them with the resources, tools, and support they require

Table 1 Comparison of various websites

Feature/Factor	Website A	Website B	Website C	WebFin website
User interface	Modern and intuitive	Clean and simple	User-friendly	Elegant design
Account types supported	Savings, checking, investments	Savings, checking	Savings	Savings, loans
Budgeting tools	Comprehensive budgeting	Basic budgeting	Limited	Proper budgeting
Investment tracking	Robust investment tracking	Basic portfolio	Limited	Investment tracking
Credit score monitoring	Credit score tracking	No credit score	Limited credit score	Credit score tracking
Security features	Two factor authentication	Basic security	Limited	Advanced security
Customer support	24/7 live chat and phone	Email support	Email support	Expert support
Pricing	Free and paid tiers	Free	Free	Free and paid tiers
Investment education	Extensive resources	Limited resources	No education	All possible resources
Additional features	Tax filing assistance	Simple expense tracking	Loan calculators	User friendly interface

to achieve financial stability and accomplish their financial goals. Building and developing the WebFin platform, which will include crucial features like budgeting and cost tracking, financial planning and goal setting, investment management, credit monitoring and management, tax filing, and financial reporting, is what the study will include. Additionally, novel modules with gamification and collaborative budgeting and spending sharing. By utilizing online technology incentives, the project intends to advance the field of personal financial management. Social communities and professional forums will be integrated into the platform to enhance user involvement and experience. The usability, effectiveness, and user satisfaction of WebFin will be assessed through user testing and feedback gathering. To evaluate user engagement, financial progress, and the platform's impact on users' financial behaviors and outcomes, data analytic techniques will be deployed. The study will also examine Web Fin's security and privacy features, which safeguard user privacy and confidential financial data. The study will make use of important concepts to direct the development and evaluation of the platform.

Table 2 Benefits and importance

Benefit	Description	Importance (%)
1. Budget tracking	Helps you create and stick to a budget by tracking income and expenses	15
2. Expense categorization	Automatically categorizes expenses for better understanding of where your money goes	10
3. Financial goal setting	Allows you to set and track financial goals such as saving for a vacation or retirement	12
4. Bill payment reminders	Sends reminders for bill payments, preventing late fees and missed payments	8
5. Investment tracking	Tracks investments and their performance, aiding in informed investment decisions	13
6. Debt management	Manages and tracks loans and debts, helping you pay them off more efficiently	10
7. Expense analysis	Provides insights into spending patterns, identifying areas where you can save	14
8. Tax planning	Assists in tax planning by organizing tax-deductible expenses and providing tax reports	11
9. Security and privacy	Ensures the security of your financial data through encryption and authentication measures	9
10. Accessibility and convenience	Access your financial information anytime, anywhere through mobile apps and web platforms	8

Table 3 Maintainance - aspect and objectives

Aspect	Current status	Objectives
Performance	74%	Response time percentage
Security	80%	Patch critical vulnerabilities
User experience	83%	Improve user satisfaction
Traffic handling	70%	Handle peak traffic effectively
Feature updates	90%	Update features regularly
Maintenance costs	85%	Reduce maintenance expenses
Disaster recovery	93%	Develop disaster recovery plan
Accessibility	85%	Ensure accessibility standards
Aspect	Current status	Objectives
Performance	74%	Response time percentage

7 Future Scope

Future plans for WebFin go beyond its initial development and assessment, providing opportunities for improvement and growth. These involve working with financial institutions to sync transactions and update account balances in Realtime,

Table 4 Metric rate

Metric	Description	Results/score (%)
Bounce rate	Percentage of visitors who left after one pageview	15
Conversion rate	Percentage of visitors who completed a desired action (e.g., signing up, budget creation)	65
User registration rate	Percentage of visitors who registered as users	30
User retention rate	Percentage of users who returned	40
Churn rate	Percentage of users who stopped using the website	10

Table 5 Analysis of key points

Aspect of analysis	Key points/findings	Numerical data (%)
Project components	Intuitive expense and budget tracking tools	78
	Financial planning and goal setting features	65
	Investment management enhancements	10
	Credit monitoring and management improvements	27
	Simplified tax filing and financial reporting	6
Conversion rate	Collaborative budgeting and expense sharing	42
	Gamification and rewards system	88
	Social community and expert forums	91
User registration rate	Design and development of the WebFin platform	82
	Iterative testing and refinement based on user feedback	86
	Integration of financial management and securities	22

adopting advanced data analytics, providing improved investing tools, collaborating with financial professionals, and creating mobile applications for easy financial management.

Realtime financial data can be obtained through integration with IoT devices, for example, by monitoring energy use on smart home appliances. Users can connect with professional financial planners or coaches for individualized guidance and advice by adding personalized financial coaching services. Web Fin's reach can be increased by internationalization and localization, which complies with regional financial rules, tax legislation, and currency conversions. Future scope areas like these present WebFin with chances to develop, meet user needs, and provide value in the domain of personal finance management. WebFin can strengthen its position as a top platform for enabling people to achieve financial stability, make educated decisions, and achieve their financial goals by exploring these avenues.

8 Conclusion

We think WebFin has the potential to completely change the personal finance management industry by taking a web-based approach and adding these cutting-edge modules. This study has implications for those who want to manage their own finances better as well as for financial institutions, service providers, and researchers who can gain from a better understanding of user behavior, preferences, and engagement. Budgeting, cost tracking, financial planning, investment management, credit monitoring, and tax filing are important components of the full platform. Innovative features like collaborative budgeting, expense sharing, gamification, rewards, and social communities enhance user experience and engagement. By facilitating simple access to financial tools, information, and support, WebFin streamlines financial processes, increases financial literacy, and encourages wise financial decision making. Overall, WebFin offers a thorough and user centered approach to managing personal finances, resolving issues, giving innovative solutions, and building a caring community. With a focus on continuous improvement and growth, WebFin hopes to be an essential tool in the dynamic world of managing personal finances.

Acknowledgements This research paper has been made possible with the collective support and contributions of many individuals. We would like to express our sincere appreciation to Kuldeep Vayadande sir, whose expertise, encouragement, and dedication have been the guiding force behind this research. Their mentorship and critical insights have been instrumental in refining our work. Our gratitude also extends to the team members who generously shared their time and insights, making this study possible. We acknowledge the resources and facilities provided by Vishwakarma Institute of Technology, Pune which greatly facilitated our research endeavors. Last but not least, we want to acknowledge the broader academic community, whose contributions to our field have inspired and informed our work. To all those who have been part of this research journey, we offer our heartfelt thanks.

References

1. Goyal K, Kumar S, Xiao JJ (2021) Antecedents and consequences of personal financial management behavior: a systematic literature review and future research agenda. Int J Bank Market. https://doi.org/10.1108/IJBM1220200612Available.
2. Bitrián P, Buil I, Catalán S (2021) Making finance fun: the gamification of personal financial management apps. Int J Bank Market 39(7):13101332. https://doi.org/10.1108/IJBM02202 10074
3. Lewis M, Perry M (2019) Follow the money: managing personal finance. In: 2019 CHI conference on human factors in computing systems proceedings (CHI 2019), May 4–9, 2019, Glasgow, Scotland, UK. ACM, New York, NY, USA, p 14. https://doi.org/10.1145/3290605.3300620
4. Johnson E, Smith M (2020) Impact of financial management apps on financial literacy and behavior. Int J Consum Stud 44(1):1928
5. Sharma R, Gupta A (2021) Web technology and financial inclusion: a study on the role of WebFin platforms. Int J Inf Manage 56:102269
6. Tan J, Lim Y (2017) Investigating the influence of web based personal finance tools on savings behavior. J Consum Aff 51(2):409437

7. Williams L, Thompson C (2019) WebFin and behavioral economics: nudging for better financial choices. J Behav Exp Financ 23:7684
8. AbdulRahman A, Hailes S (2018) User experience and design of personal finance management apps. In: Proceedings of the 13th international conference on persuasive technology (PERSUASIVE '18)
9. Di Domenico SI, Ryan RM, Bradshaw EL, Duineveld JJ (2022) Motivations for personal financial management: a self-determination theory perspective. Front Psychol 13:977818. https://doi.org/10.3389/fpsyg.2022.977818
10. Patel R, Jain S (2019) User centered design of web based financial tools for better user engagement. In: Proceedings of the 10th international conference on human system interaction (HSI '19)
11. Lee S, Kim J (2016) Security and privacy considerations in web based personal finance management. Procedia Comput Sci 91:288293
12. Munohsamy T (2015) Personal financial management. Article on Personal Financial Management
13. Shah S, Bhatt A (2014) Understanding practices of personal financial planning (PFP). In: International conference on "Role of Financial Industry in Accelerating Economic Growth" organized by Gujarat Technological University (GTU) Centre for Financial Services, Ahmedabad. Available at SSRN: https://ssrn.com/abstract=2813478
14. Li Y, Kuo S (2017) The impact of mobile personal finance applications on financial behavior. J Financ Serv Res 51(2):239261
15. Chen Y, Wang H (2019) A comparative study of web and mobile personal finance management tools. In: Proceedings of the 6th international conference on internet studies (NETs '19)
16. Rodrigues J, Costa C (2018) The role of gamification in enhancing financial literacy through web platforms. Int J Inf Manage 43:8592

VISITOUR: Intelligent Travel Recommender

Kuldeep Vayadande, Rishikesh Shinde, Satyajit Shinde, Shraddha Suryawanshi, Aditi Samargade, Shrihari Suryawanshi, and Yash Shirsat

1 Introduction

Tourism is an important point of communication for cross-border areas. According to Forbes magazine's list of "***The 50 Most Beautiful Countries in The World***," India came in at number seven. According to the World Tourism and Travel Council, tourism would sustain 321 lakh employment opportunities and contribute 1,320,000 crores (US $170,000 millions), or 5.8%, of the gross domestic product of India in 2021 [1]. Typically, a vacation may be broken down into the following stages. In the beginning, a visitor investigates an interesting destination, gets the necessary information, such as a list of intriguing attractions and well-known locations, and asks for feedback from other travelers. The visitor then creates an itinerary for their trip and gathers all necessary information (maps, guides, etc.). Tourists plan accommodations and travel arrangements during this period as well. Thirdly, the traveler uses all of the information sources at their disposal to gets a fuller image of the sights. At the conclusion, the visitor arranges the information, images, notes, and emotions for collective feedback.

The traditional tourist situation has been altered in recent years by the Internet and travel industries' fast expansion. There are three primary types of organizations from the perspective of the tourist: large group, small group, and solo trip. Travel agencies reserve all accommodations (hotels, museums, attractions, etc.) and transportation for large groups [2]. There are very few attractions seen by this type of group and the free time they have. Smaller groups of travelers are more autonomous than larger groups. Small groups are more versatile, explore more sights, and form more favorable impressions. Individual travel is the most flexible type of organization. They also show that they are more focused on enhancing travel quality and user experience

K. Vayadande (✉) · R. Shinde · S. Shinde · S. Suryawanshi · A. Samargade · S. Suryawanshi · Y. Shirsat
Vishwakarma Institute of Technology, Pune, India
e-mail: kuldeep.vayadande1@vit.edu

K. Kumar Singh et al. (eds.), *Machine Vision and Augmented Intelligence*, Lecture Notes in Electrical Engineering 1211, https://doi.org/10.1007/978-981-97-4359-9_69

through customized consumption. Therefore, the direction of travel in the future is toward individualized tourism services.

When correctly utilized, tourism may significantly contribute to a nation's economic recovery. A key aspect of the region's financial system is tourism. The major source of revenue for an area may depend on the unique characteristics of that location. If properly utilized, tourism will play a significant part in restoring the economies of countries by growing the technical side alongside tourism and our culture. Numerous employments were generated by tourism, which also improved the infrastructure and attractiveness of the region. Because they employ the most infrastructural components and are an external resource, foreign visitors generate the most attention. As previously said, the World Tourism and Travel Council, tourism would sustain 321 lakh employment opportunities and contribute 1,320,000 crores (US $170,000 millions), or 5.8%, of the gross domestic product of India [1].

The future of people and nations is thought to lie in modern technology, particularly the Internet and its applications. The use of mobile devices as electronic tourist guides is known as "mobile tourism," and it is a relatively new trend in the tourism industry. In the modern day, we can no longer only rely on traditional tourism and cultural legacy as factors for attracting tourists [3]. Instead, we must begin to consider how we might leverage technical information and invest in apps for tourism. The primary research goals of contemporary travel recommendation systems are to provide customers with tailored recommendation services, enhance suggestion accuracy, and increase user happiness. The hotel and tourist sectors have been profoundly influenced by the Internet, which has created a platform for marketing and income generating. For the proposed model to function, the algorithm must be able to precisely suggest tourist attractions depending on the customer's preferences. Research on travel recommendation systems, which include both general and personalized recommendations, has been sparked by the increased interest in travel. The general feature answers questions about attractions in a certain location and provides customers planning vacations with destination-specific information. Personalized suggestions, on the other hand, create personalized ideas for route planning by taking user characteristics like gender, group type (couple, family, or friends), and preferences into account. Before setting out on their trips, tourists may make well-informed selections, thanks to this complete approach.

Most applications support many services and offer a lot of help, but this might lead to confusion for the customer as each application offers only one service. There are still unresolved issues with the design, usability, portability, functionality, and implementation of the currently accessible technologies. The ideal solution to these issues is "*VISITOUR*". This website isn't just concerned with the location; it's also concerned with the context of the user, which includes things like nearby amenities, restrooms, well-known local landmarks, the city's history, attractions, the best hotels and restaurants, and the closest bus and train stations. This paper will outline the Tourist Guide system and go over the procedures used to create this website.

2 Literature Survey

For areas that cross borders, tourism is a key point of communication. Each region concentrates on the interaction of tourists and has its unique attractions of interest. Additionally, visitors plan their own trips in small groups or on their own with longer programs. There are three primary types of organizations from the perspective of the tourist: large group, small group, and solo trip. Small groups are more versatile and explore more spots. Typically, a vacation may be broken down into the following stages. In the beginning, a visitor investigates an interesting destination, gets the necessary information, such as a list of intriguing attractions and well-known locations, and asks for feedback from other travelers. The visitor then creates an itinerary for their trip and gathers all necessary information (maps, guides, etc.). Tourists plan accommodations and travel arrangements during this period as well. Thirdly, the traveler uses all of the information sources at their disposal to get a fuller image of the sights. At the conclusion, the visitor arranges the information, images, notes, and emotions for collective feedback [4]. Although the underlying technology is mostly already in place, there are still unresolved issues with design, usability, portability, functionality, and implementation factors [2].

In the modern day, we can no longer only rely on traditional tourism and cultural legacy as factors for attracting tourists. Instead, we must begin to consider how we might leverage technical information and invest in apps for tourism. If effectively utilized, tourism may help nations' economies recover and provide financial resources [5].

"Mobile travel and tourism," which refers to the usage of handheld devices such as electronic tourist guides, is a relatively new development in the travel and tourism sector. The recommended site imitates the human aspect of tourism lead by creating connections between systems based on knowledge and the function of a tourist-guide in order to best meet the needs and wishes of any visitor who wishes to gain enough data and a fair appraisal of the places travelled to as well as more enjoyment and fulfilment from his tour [3]. This website isn't only interested in the location; it's also interested in the user's context, which includes things like neighboring equipment, restrooms, renowned landmarks in the area, the history of the city, attractions, the best hotel rooms and restaurants, and the closest bus and train stations [6]. Authors V. Subramaniyaswamy, V. Vijayakumar, R. Logesh, and V. Indragandhi discuss their research on travel and tourism-related papers. The model uses information that has been automatically gathered from images contributed by user labels, as well as information on people's qualities, travel group categories, and travel group periods that have been found in the photo contents. In the coming months, they will develop an application that is constantly updated for intelligent travel suggestions that will use image labels contributed by users to mine consumer preferences and offer destinations to users [7].

The proposed algorithm model has demonstrated positive results in improving the accurateness of systems for recommendation in the tourism sector for collaboratively selecting choices for tourist locations according to consumer preferences with limited information. The research's findings may be used to a variety of prospective new directions [8].

In order to improve accuracy in a tourist recommendation system, the study conducted for the research paper emphasized the importance of incorporating a variety of contextual factors in addition to geography, which include weather, time, preferences of users, internet sentiment, and location. It introduced the Virtual Intelligent System for Informing Tourists (VISIT) application and promoted an integrated recommender model as the best option. In addition to further developing and fine-tuning the recommender system in the VISIT application, future research will concentrate on improving machine learning approaches, notably for time and customization elements [9].

Another paper proposes a cloud service and a mobile, intelligent content management system for the travel industry. On the smartphone, some fundamental features are available offline, while others call on a cloud-based internet connection. Future plans include creating an Android tour-guiding app utilizing the Applink API and improving the prototype with more individualized tour planning and user feedback on collaborative filtering [10].

A paper written by Sabah Azmi named Intelligent Content Recommendation System proposed content recommendation system utilizes Python, FastAPI, and a PostgreSQL database to integrate collaborative filtering with popularity-based algorithms. It effectively handles user interactions while presenting a variety of pertinent content suggestions. Personalized suggestions are made possible by singular value decomposition (SVD), whereas popularity-based methods draw attention to the hot material. The approach efficiently adapts to individual interests and encourages user involvement with interesting and relevant material, as proven by study findings, which reveal the balance between personalization and popularity increases the content discovery experience [11].

The algorithm suggested in the Intelligent recommendation system of places to visit based on shared filtering and customer preferences shows guarantee in improving the accuracy and consumer approval of recommendation systems for tourist attractions by taking into account user preferences and addressing the problem of sparse data. However, in some circumstances, its application may be constrained by its complexity and data preparation needs [12]. Research of another study, the recommendation subsystem of the big data perception-based tourist information recommendation system is thoroughly examined and designed. Within the scope of the tourist data system, this study first models the conceptual framework for contextual information consumption and then offers links among the various vocabularies. The study then uses a matrix to describe each discontinuous characteristic and interval property, modeling the user's preferences using a vector. The research then makes a proposal for utilizing a regulation-based suggestion algorithm, gives an outline of the recommendation system's module structure, and uses illustrations to illustrate and clearly explain the whole recommendation technique's operation.

3 Methodology

In recent years, there has been an incredible rise in both domestic and international travel, which is characterized by a tendency to visit several locations on the same trip. As a result, making a travel itinerary involves a number of steps that are increasingly intimidating, complicated, and time-consuming. To name a few: selecting the locations to visit, the various modes of transportation, and the hotels to stay in; looking for tourist attractions at the various destinations; creating daily schedules that account for breaks for meals and rest; sorting through dining options; and, last but not least, figuring out the routes with the least amount of travel time.

Planning your tour is crucial to having a successful trip. We have used HTML, CSS, and JavaScript for the frontend and Python & SQL for the back end.

1. Initialization

The technique described here describes the step-by-step procedure for developing the intelligent travel website VISITOUR. With features including account creation, user login, a home page, hotel services, a gallery, contact information, and travel guides, VISITOUR seeks to give consumers a complete vacation planning experience. In order to construct VISITOUR, a dynamic and interactive online application, HTML, CSS, JavaScript, and PHP were used.

2. Understanding the Technologies

2.1 HTML Specifications

Hyper Text Hypermarkup language, or the most widely used markup language for creating Web pages is HTML. HTML is a set of instructions that tells the browser how to display the content and explains the structure of a Web page.

2.2 CSS Specifications

Cascading Style Sheets or CSS saves a lot of labour by describing how HTML elements should be rendered on screens, paper, or in other media. Multiple web page layouts can be managed simultaneously by it. External stylesheets are kept in CSS files.

2.3 JavaScript Specifications

JavaScript has the ability to alter the following aspects of HTML: the HTML source, the HTML element values, the HTML with CSS, and the HTML elements themselves.

2.4 Python

Guido van Rossum created Python in 1991, a dynamically semantic, object-oriented, high-level programming language that is interpreted. The most beloved programming language is Python.

It's applied to server-side programming for web development.

2.5 MySQL

The core of a relational database management system (RDBMS) is structured query language (SQL). MySQL, which was created by Oracle. It might be anything from a simple grocery list to a photo gallery or a place to store the massive amounts of data on a company network.

3 Development Process

3.1 Planning and Requirement Analysis

- Determine the project's aims, objectives, and user needs.
- Specify the features and functions that will be included in the scope ofVISITOUR.

3.2 Design Phase

- Produce wireframes and mock-ups for the user interface and layout of the website.
- Crafting a robust database structure establishes a reliable foundation for users' travel tales, ensuring an enriching experience.

3.3 Front-End Development

Collaborating with front-end developers orchestrates a visual symphony using HTML, CSS, and JavaScript's magical touch for an engaging journey through VISITOUR's virtual landscapes.

3.4 Back-End Development

On the back end, even simple functions such as signups and logging on smoothly transfer website visitors to how-to guides for memory. PHP stealthily gets travel information directly from its database of memories.

3.5 Testing and Quality Assurance

So like testing parts, VISITOUR's online show keeps going through with a hitch.

3.6 Deployment

Going live with the website is like opening night, putting it on a server that can handle PHP safely over HTTPS. The setting up of the domain is a bit like giving directions to visitors.

3.7 Maintenance and Updates

Then, after the curtain falls we hang around to fix and upgrade. So we watch the website, listen to users and fix things up. VISITOUR is awesome because of that!

4 Proposed System

Due to the increasing demand for travel and tour systems to help tourists plan their travels, we have made the proposed system for their convenience. The proposed recommendation system offers travel guides based on the travel plan or information tourists or travellers provide.

Some important features:

- User Profiling:

  Sign-in and sign-up options for tourists or visitors.
- Offers:

  Recommends travel offers during special occasions.
- User-Friendly Interface:

  The system is usable on a variety of devices, such as smartphones and tablets.
- Best travel guides:

  We offer the best travel guides to the user to make their trip knowledgeable, and enjoyable.
- Rich experience in hotels:

  We provide world-class level amenities to the user to give them memorable and rich experiences while enjoying their trip.
- Instantaneous Updates

  Real-time notifications on travel specials, happenings, and weather at your preferred locations keep you informed.
- Expertise

  Our team of travel professionals and cutting-edge technology ensure that you get the finest suggestions.
- Reviews and Comments

  By offering comments and reviews on suggested services, travel guides, and hotels you can share your travel experiences and assist other travellers.

  In the Fig. 1, we explained the mind map of the website. This mind map gives detailed working of a web.

  In Fig. 2, we explained the flow of the website.

5 Table Analysis

See Tables 1, 2, 3 and Figs. 3 and 4.

Fig. 1 Mind map of system

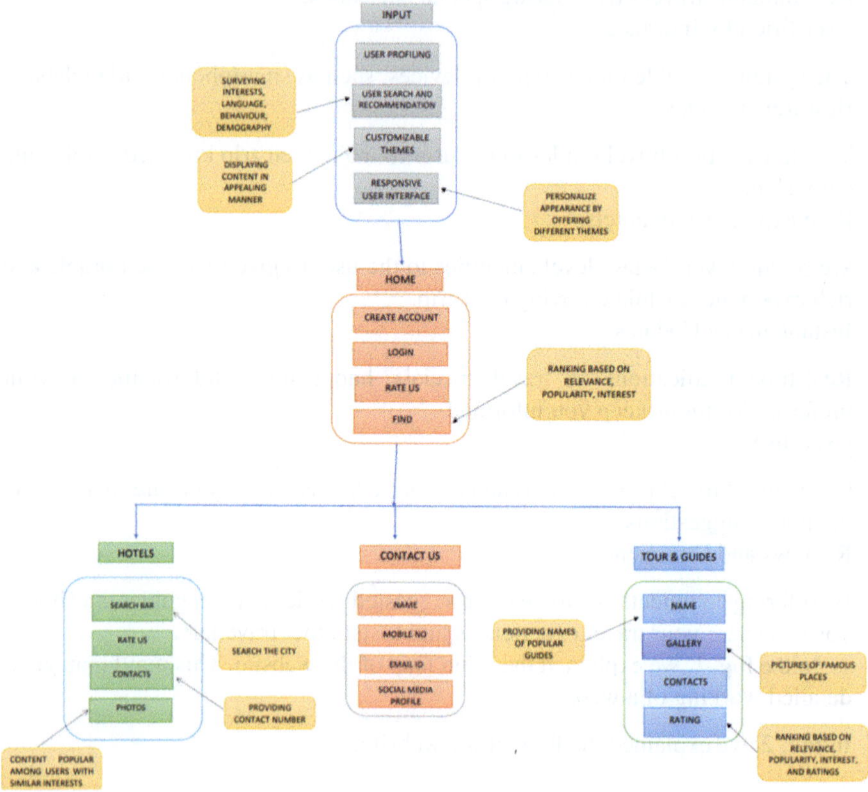

Fig. 2 Flowchart for system

Table 1 Comparison table

Research paper name	Tourism website name	Key metrics	Findings
(1) Enhancing User Experience on TourismHub	TourismHub	Rating-average	Users rating is 4.5/ 5.0
		No. of viewers	600
		Sentiment analysis	85% of comments expressed positive sentiments
(2) Exploring user feedback on TravelDreams	TravelDreams	Rating-average	Users rating is 4.2/ 5.0
		No. of viewers	400
		Sentiment analysis	72% of comments expressed positive sentiments
(3) Tourism satisfaction on ExploreMore	ExploreMore	Rating-average	Users rating is 4.7/ 5.0
		No. of viewers	450
		Sentiment analysis	90% of comments expressed positive sentiments
(4) VISITOUR: Intelligent Travel Recommender	VISITOUR	Rating-average	User rating-4.0/5.0
		No. of viewers	500
		Sentiment analysis	95% of comments expressed positive sentiments

Table 2 Performance table

Factor	E-Tourism: a study of tourist satisfaction	Factors influencing customer satisfaction in E-Tourism: a review	A study of E-Tourism: comparison of online and traditional travel agencies	VISITOUR: intelligent travel recommender
Convenience	4	3.7	4.24	4.0
Merchandising	3.2	3.8	3.72	3.7
Website design	3.4	3.6	3.10	3.7
Security	2.9	3.1	2.64	3
Serviceability	3.7	4.0	3.79	4.0

Table 3 Comparison of platforms w.r.t. accuracy, efficiency, diversity, and User-friendliness

Platform	Accuracy	Efficiency	Diversity	User friendliness	Generalizability
National geographic travel	High	High	High	High	High
Fodor's travel	Medium	Medium	Low	Medium	Medium
Time out	High	Medium	Low	Medium	Medium
Wikivoyage	Medium	Medium	Low	Medium	Low
CN traveler	High	Low	Medium	High	High
Atlas obscura	Medium	Low	High	Medium	Low
Visitour	High	High	Medium	High	High

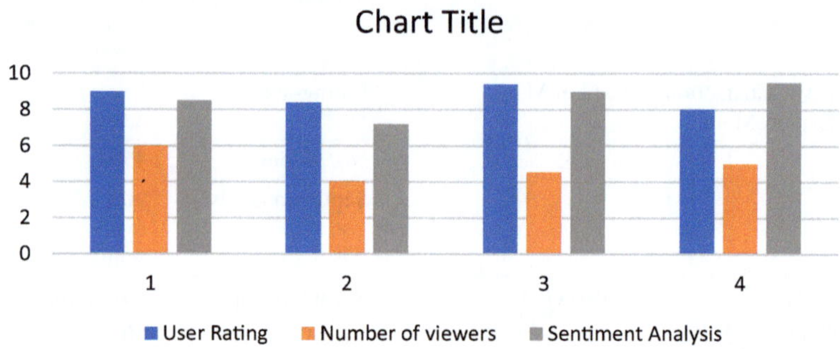

Fig. 3 User feedback

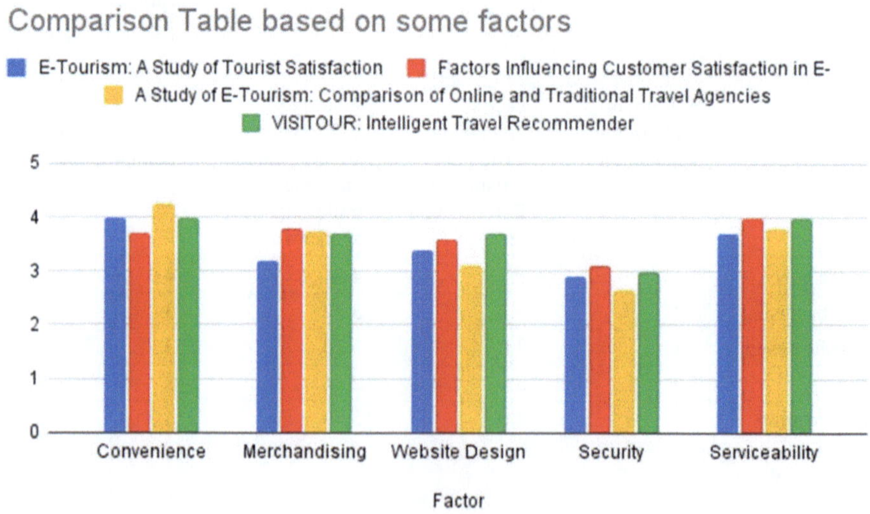

Fig. 4 Performance chart

6 Results

- User Login and Registration:

Python and **MySQL** for database administration were used to implement the user registration and login system. The findings show that users may safely register accounts on the VISITOUR website using their personal data. Account information is securely maintained using this technology, allowing for a tailored user experience (Figs. 5 and 6).

- The Homepage and Menu:

VISITOUR's home page was created to be both aesthetically pleasing and easy to use. the navigation of the home page, as per feedback and user testing.

Fig. 5 Login page

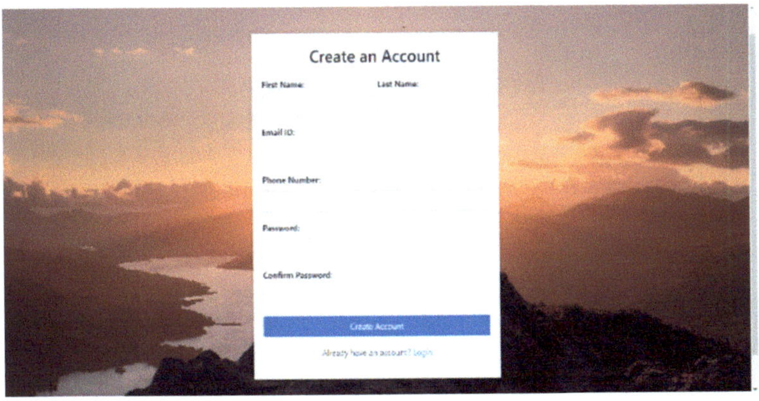

Fig. 6 Create account page

The menus and design of this place are incredibly clear and easy to navigate. However, when it comes to the hotel's services and gallery, the website encompasses contact details as well as travel guides, among other aspectseasily accessible to users (Fig. 7).

- Hotel Services and Recommendations

VISITOUR hotel services customized to your interests and travel plans this segment recommends hotels to consumers. Users can enter their get travel information like destinations, dates and budget and get relevant information. Hotel recommendations based on user testing. Users appreciate this recommended as they make hotel bookings easier (Fig. 8).

- Travel Guides and Information

Fig. 7 Home page

Fig. 8 Hotel service

VISITOUR's travel guide section provides readers with useful information and articles to help you plan your trip. The guide is informative and According to users, helpful in organizing trips test. Provides destination-specific information, travel advice, and more Suggestions for sites and events have been well received by users (Fig. 9).

- Gallery and Visual Content

VISITOUR users can view photos and videos from a variety of travel destinations. In the gallery area. This gallery provides useful information based on user reviews. Visual information influences travel decisions. Overall user experience. This website is enhanced with entertaining and educational graphics. The video is as follows (Fig. 10).

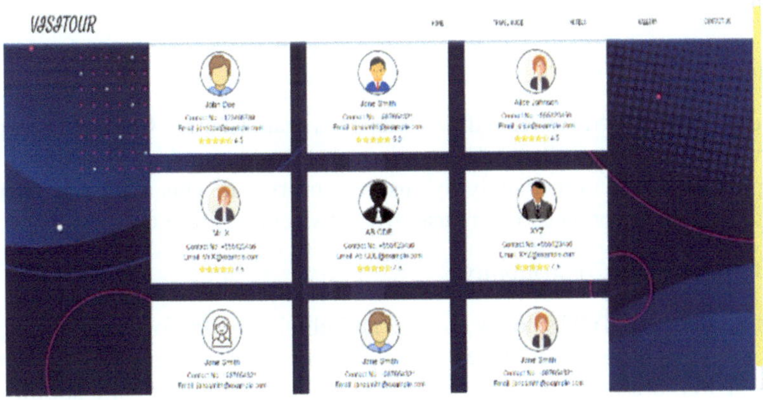

Fig. 9 Travel guides and info

Fig. 10 Gallery and visual content

Fig. 11 Contact page

- Contact Us and Support

Users can contact VISITOUR staff for questions or assistance "Contact Us" option. Users who have successfully made inquiries using the contact form Questions during testing are answered immediately by ensuring users can. This feature lets you get help quickly when you need it for customer satisfaction (Fig. 11).

- Performance and Compatibility

To ensure that VISITOUR loads quickly and efficiently, Performance testing was conducted. The website should work Display response results correctly across a variety of web browsers and devices Design and cross-browser compatibility. The addition of JavaScript has increased Interaction that has no noticeable impact on load times.

- User Feedback

Collect and consider user input during testing development stage. Ease of access and suitability. The travel advice in particular has received positive feedback from users. Future updates will take into account suggestions that were made for future improvements.

7 Scope of Research

The system can give all updates, including forecasts, local happenings, transport conditions, and tourist attractions. This keeps users informed and enables them to make wise decisions while traveling.

Depending on their dietary restrictions and gastronomic interests, users can get restaurant recommendations. Assisting visitors in learning about local foods and acclaimed restaurants, improves the dining experience attract users and boost the crowd, we can provide cultural experiences, adventurous pursuits, and sightseeing opportunities.

By giving the user the average cost for dining, lodging, transportation, and other activities, the system can help the user plan their travel budget.

VISITOUR can provide information on current trends and patterns in travel. It can analyze data from a variety of users to find hot spots, new trends, and off-peak opportunities.

VISITOUR offers assistance with language translation, cultural advice, and knowledge of regional customs and etiquette to international travelers.

This tourist would enjoy the regional traditions and culture, bringing in additional tourists from abroad and boosting the local economy.

8 Future Scope

This platform will offer various features like local events in the city i.e. festivals, sports, exhibitions, etc. This feature will help visitors to plan their trip according to it. While planning the trip, we will take care of their daily livelihood needs like accommodation, catering, and other tourist facilities. This will allow a large audience to make decisions.

By introducing augmented and virtual reality in the website, it will increase user experience on the website. This virtual travelling will give the idea to the traveler of what to expect there, makes them more excited while planning their trip. Using different API's like weather API, tourists can access present and future weather conditions in their holiday planning location.

Another idea to integrating the information of environmental compatibility, environmental services and conservation, it is possible to promote the sustainable and responsible tourism in the planned city.

By introducing future technologies like Artificial Intelligence, Machine Learning, and Deep Learning, the user will get personalized trip planning by their preferences and past interactions on the platform.

9 Conclusion

VISITOUR is a travel planning website aimed at making vacation organization awfully easy. It's been arranged to cater for a range of different kinds of travelers so that you can organize any kind vacation. The site also provides route suggestions that take in the must-see sights, and guides to explain the cultural and historical significance of these places. This can be of assistance to travelers in helping them get a better grip on where they are.

Accommodation is an important component to planning a successful trip. So we offer a short list of recommended hotels near tourist spots as our platform. We've also provided things such as ratings, reviews and facilities information to help users find what they want by using criteria which fit their own requirements or budget limitations. As for budgets, we have added a special control mechanism. This feature helps users by enabling them to further define their requirements, depending on how much money they have in hand. With this in mind, travelers have comfortable lodging and a convenient place to stay without breaking the bank.

That's what makes the people at VISITOUR so unique; they work hard for user experience, and try to be as inclusive as possible. While showing the way for old hands and new arrivals, we've also designed an interface that uses a trip planner format to make planning easy. Our ability to apply HTML, CSS, JavaScript and PHP allowed us to build an interactive and user-friendly platform.

This is because we place great emphasis on testing thoroughly, detailed treatment and maintenance that goes not. Whether VISITOUR succeeds and continues to please users will depend on these two elements.

To bring it to a close, we just want to say that VISITOUR is our way of helping travelers around the world. It's about providing meaningful access and upgrading how people plan trips through smart design solutions.

References

1. Liu Q, Chen E, Xiong H, Ge Y, Li Z, Wu X (2014) A cocktail approach for travel package recommendation. IEEE Trans Knowl Data Eng 26(2)
2. Kenteris M, Gavalas D, Economou D (2009) An innovative mobile electronic tourist guide application. Pers Ubiquit Comput 13:103–118
3. Owaied HH, Farhan HA, Al-Hawamdeh N, Al-Okialy N (2011) J Appl Sci 11(2):342–347
4. Troshkov A, Kulakov K (2013) 14th FRUCT conference November 11–15, Helsinki, Finland
5. Najjar YY, Saeh O (2019) Tourist-helper application
6. Simcock T, Hillenbrand SP, Thomas BH (2003) ACSW frontiers
7. Subramaniyaswamy V, Vijayakumar V, Logesh R, Indragandhi V (2015) Intelligent travel recommendation system by mining attributes from community contributed photos second international symposium on big data and cloud computing (ISBCC'15)
8. Meehan K, Lunney T, Curran K, McCaughey A (2013) Context-aware intelligent recommendation system for tourism
9. Smirnov A, Kashevnik A, Shilov N, Mikhailov S, Gusikhin O, Martinez H (2019) Intelligent content management system for tourism smart mobility: approach and cloud-based android application
10. Azmi S Intelligent content recommendation system
11. Wang Z (2023) Intelligent recommendation model of tourist places based on collaborative filtering and user preferences. Appl Artif Intell 37(1):2203574. https://doi.org/10.1080/08839514.2023.2203574
12. Liang HY (2021) Intelligent tourism personalized recommendation based on multi-fusion of clustering algorithms
13. Haralabus D, Fajardo AF, Pérez FJJ, López AAM, Ardura FJR, Xhafa I (2008) Fatos international conference E-Commerce. ISBN: 978-972-8924-66-9 © 2008 IADIS

14. Teke H, Borle P, Tiwari M, Kangale S, Dandgule A (2015) An intelligent recommendation system to enhance the travel services. Int J Adv Res Innov Ideas Educ 1(4), IJARIIE-ISSN(O)-2395-4396
15. Kumaran N, Aakash B, Vidhyaharini M (2022) Intelligent tourist guide system. Int J Res Appl Sci Eng Technol (URASET). ISSN: 2321-9653; IC Value: 45.98, SJ Impact Factor: 7.538 10(III)
16. Koceski S, Petrevska B (2013) Advanced tourist trip planning using hybrid recommender. Eng Manage Rev (EMR) 2(4)
17. Roopesh LR, Bomatpalli T (2018) A survey of travel recommender system. Int J Comput Sci Eng 6(9). E-ISSN: 2347-2693

A Light Model for Early Detection of Melanoma Using Efficient Net

Rishi Agrawal, Neeraj Gupta, and Anand Singh Jalal

1 Introduction

In 2020, the Global Cancer Observatory (GLOBOCAN), which is part of the International Agency for Research on Cancer (IARC), estimated that there were approximately 2.2 million new cases of non-melanoma skin cancer (NMSC) and approximately 324,635 new cases of melanoma skin cancer worldwide [1]. These figures include both non-melanoma and melanoma skin cancers. The prevalence of skin cancer can vary significantly by region, with higher rates in areas with greater sun exposure. Prevention measures, such as sun protection and early detection through regular skin checks, are essential in reducing the incidence of skin cancer. The most protective layer in our body is our skin which protects us from a wide range of diseases and helps to maintain body temperature. Melanoma is the most dangerous skin cancer. Melanoma generally occurs by skin cells of DNA as an unexpected destruction and rapid multiplication of skin cells [2]. Malignant melanoma is the fastest-growing type of cancer in the world.

The largest organ of our body i.e., skin, which basically is made of three different layers of tissues, epidermis tissues, dermis issues, subcutaneous tissues, and cells like squamous, Basal, etc. It helps us to control body temperature from heat through sweating and cold through hair growth, and work as a protective layer from the outer environment and does many more things. But when the cells present in the skin become disordered due to some disease and grows out of control they take a form of a cancer in the skin. Skin cancer is the most common type of cancer and

R. Agrawal (✉) · N. Gupta · A. S. Jalal
Department of CEA, GLA University, Mathura, U.P, India
e-mail: rishi.agrawal@gla.ac.in

N. Gupta
e-mail: neeraj.gupta@gla.ac.in

A. S. Jalal
e-mail: asjalal@gla.ac.in

K. Kumar Singh et al. (eds.), *Machine Vision and Augmented Intelligence*, Lecture Notes in Electrical Engineering 1211, https://doi.org/10.1007/978-981-97-4359-9_70

the most concerning type of cancer worldwide. Skin cancer has two types melanoma and non-melanoma [3]. Melanoma cancers are caused by the melanocytes (the cells that produce pigment in the skin) which make it the most lethal and rare kind of skin cancer with recorded 132,000 cases annually because its spread to other parts is very high. Being the most dangerous type of skin cancer early detection is the best treatment for melanoma, early detection gives more time to treat the person. Non-melanoma cancers are caused due to different cells in the skin layer, they act differently from the melanoma cancers and are less dangerous (recorded 3 million cases annually) than melanoma cancer [4].

Melanomas usually appear brown or black in color but sometimes they can be blue, red, or a combination of colors and also without any colors. It is much rarer than the BCC and SCC, but more hazardous and harmful because it grows anywhere on the skin. It is more likely to spread to other parts of the body if not diagnosed early and treated properly. In the US around 10,130 people per year died due to melanoma [5]. Sample images of melanoma are given in Fig. 1. This can only be solved by identifying and regularly screening the disease in the early stage. It is possible to cure melanoma cases by identifying them in the early stages. Usually to determine the type of skin cancer biopsy test is preferred by the dermatologist but it is costlier. Melanoma can appear on the existing part of the mole or a new part of the mole which changes its shape, size, and color. Traditionally, physicians tested skin moles with naked eyes and clinically experienced it. The International Dermoscopic Society (IDS) approved the pattern analysis which is the initial dermoscopic methodology used for the diagnosis of pigmented skin lesions [6].

In medical imaging, Computer Aided Diagnosis (CAD) systems and relative developments in CAD have contributed a great deal. Radiologists interpret the results and improve the accuracy of the disease diagnosis. It reduces the reading time of the skin lesion in order to take help using these computerized results as a second opinion and in all these processes CAD framework is an important theme [7].

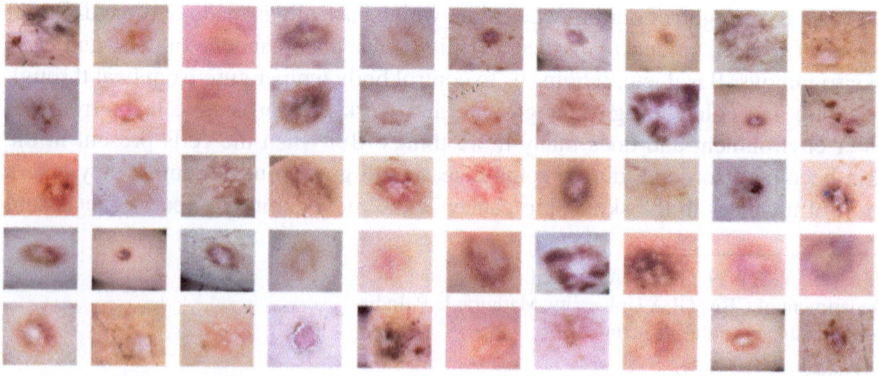

Fig. 1 Sample images of skin cancer

2 Related Work

Classification of melanoma using the deep neural network method is based on dermoscopic images that have been proven to perform better than traditional methods [8, 9]. However, to fetch the best-fit result few challenges can be subjugated by the deep learning-based approaches in convolutional layers by making modifications [10, 11]. Some popular deep learning models are ResNet, ResNeXt, DenseNet, and Inception.

2.1 ResNet [12]

It used the ReLU activation function, which helps to mitigate the vanishing gradient problem and speeds up the training process. AlexNet introduced the use of dropout and regularization techniques. This helps prevent overfitting and improves generalization. To increase the adequate size of the training dataset and enhance the model's ability to generalize, AlexNet employed various data augmentation techniques such as cropping, flipping, and color jittering. Pretrained ResNet models, trained on large-scale image datasets like ImageNet, have become valuable resources for transfer learning.

2.2 ResNeXt [13]

ResNeXt uses residual blocks, just like ResNet. These blocks consist of multiple convolutional layers and are designed to learn residual functions. A residual function captures the difference between the input and output feature maps, making it easier for the network to learn the desired mapping. The cardinality of a network refers to the number of groups or paths through which information flows in each residual block. In traditional CNNs like ResNet, cardinality is usually set to 1, meaning that information flows through a single path. ResNeXt introduces the idea of increasing the cardinality, allowing for multiple parallel paths. This cardinality factor is a hyperparameter that can be adjusted to control the network's capacity and performance.

2.3 DenseNet [14]

DenseNet introduces the concept of dense connections, where each layer is connected to every subsequent layer in a feedforward manner. This dense connectivity facilitates the flow of gradients during training, mitigating the vanishing gradient problem. It also encourages feature reuse and enables the network to learn more discriminative features. between dense blocks, DenseNet includes transition layers that perform downsampling. These layers typically consist of a combination of 1 × 1 convolutions and average pooling, reducing the spatial dimensions of feature maps and further controlling the number of parameters. DenseNet used the concept of feature concatenation. This feature concatenation is a key characteristic of dense connectivity and distinguishes DenseNet from other architectures.

2.4 Inception [15]

The Inception architecture is built upon a fundamental building block called the Inception module (or GoogleNet module). Unlike traditional convolutional layers, which use a single convolution filter size, the Inception module simultaneously applies multiple filter sizes (e.g., 1 × 1, 3 × 3, 5 × 5) to the input feature map. This parallel operation enables the network to capture features at various spatial scales and helps prevent overfitting. Within an Inception module, multiple convolutional operations with different kernel sizes are performed in parallel. These parallel convolutional operations are followed by max-pooling layers and 1 × 1 convolutions for dimensionality reduction. 1 × 1 convolutions are used extensively in the Inception architecture. They serve two main purposes. The first is Dimension Reduction in which 1 × 1 convolutions with a smaller number of output channels are used to reduce the dimensionality of the feature maps, It helps to control the computational cost. The second advantage is Feature Learning. Despite their small kernel size, 1 × 1 convolutions allow the network to learn complex combinations of features across different channels, enabling feature extraction.

3 Proposed Method

In the flow of melanoma classification, certain steps are included as described in the subsections below.

3.1 Data Preparation

It prepares the data for analysis purposes by performing certain methods such as intensity adjustment, contrast enhancement, gray scaling, space correction, binarization, noise reduction, and morphological operations. At this phase noise will be removed from the data set.

3.2 Model Structure

It helps in defining data input, its size or proportions, as well as the core module of the network, loss function, classifier, and network output.

3.3 Training the Model

It defines certain parameters and constructs structure from the trained data. Actually, it uses some amount of prepared data around 60–70%, and gets some insights to deal with real-world or untreated data. Basically, it provides a certain level of training to detect problems using several techniques.

3.4 Classification and Detection

For the classification of skin cancer, the Transfer Learning based EfficientNet-B2 model [16] is used as shown in Fig. 2. Efficient Net uses the concept of appropriate scaling of the model which efficiently balances network depth, width, and resolution as shown in Fig. 3. Network depth, width, and resolution can be defined as.

- Depth (d): Most of the ConvNets have used depth Scaling to achieve higher accuracy. The main motivation for performing depth Scaling is that deeper ConvNet can extract richer and more complex features [17]. It can be represented by Eq. (1).
- Width (w): Scaling network width is more popularly used in small-size models. The main motivation for performing width scaling is that the network will be able to capture more fine-grained features and be easier to train [18]. It can be represented by Eq. (2).
- Resolution (r): Higher-resolution images contain more information than the low-resolution images. Resolution scaling is based on the concept of capturing more fine-grained patterns. It can be represented by Eq. (3).

$$Depth\,of\,network{:}\,dn = \alpha^{\phi} \tag{1}$$

$$Width\,of\,network{:}\,wn = \beta^{\phi} \tag{2}$$

$$Resolution\,of\,network{:}\,rn = \gamma^{\phi} \tag{3}$$

$$Approximately(\alpha.\beta^2.y^2 = 2)$$

$$Where\,\alpha \geq 1, \beta \geq 1, \gamma \geq 1$$

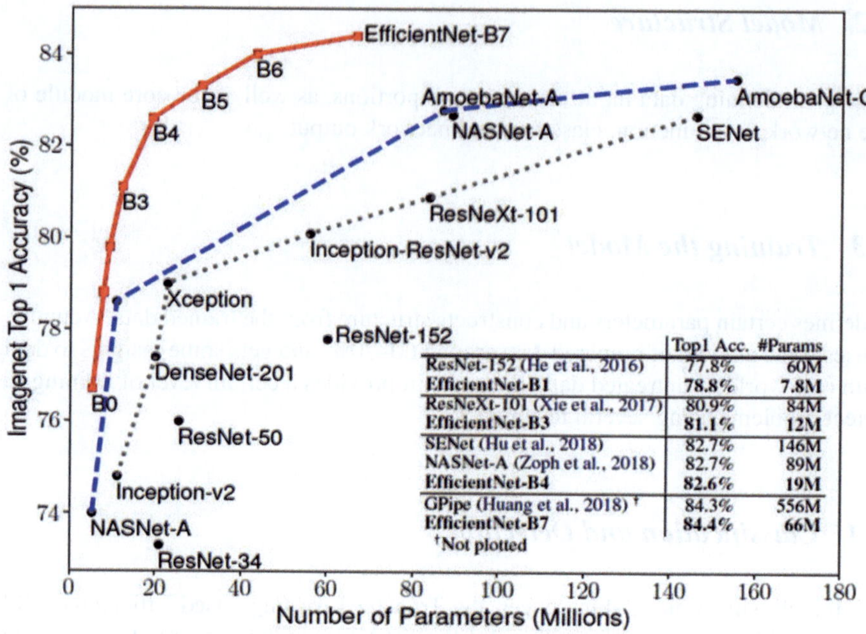

Fig. 2 Model accuracy with number of parameters [16]

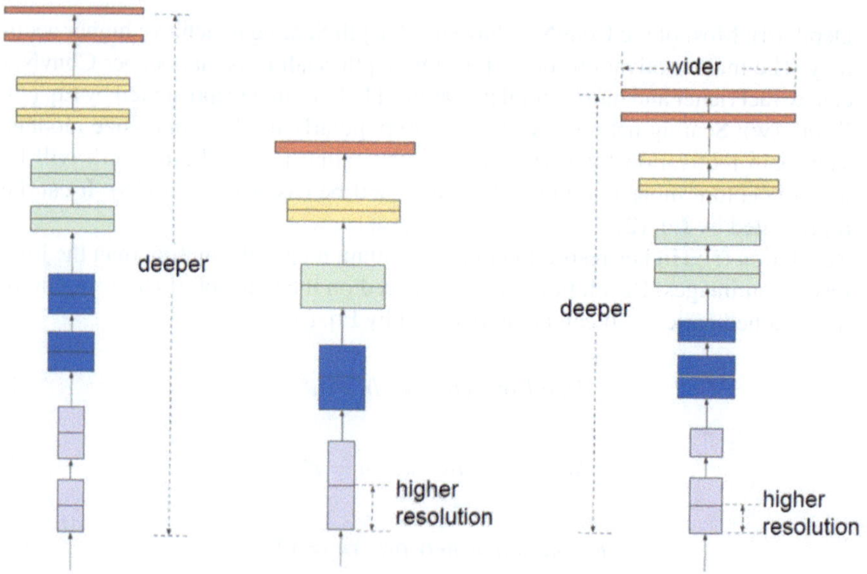

Fig. 3 Model depth, resolution, and balanced Scaling [16]

4 Result and Findings

One of the most well-known used datasets is the International Skin Imaging Collaboration (ISIC) 2017 dataset in skin cancer diagnosis. The ground-truth label has been annotated by an expert clinician for each instance, using either a manual process or a semi-automated. For three subtasks further information is provided by the annotation data: localization, lesion segmentation, and skin disease classification. Into a training set, the model divides the original dataset, following the literature work with 1250 samples, 150 samples consisting in the validation sets, and 600 instances of a test set. Furthermore, to reduce the spatial dimension, the model used a resize function into 256 * 256 pixels of the input data.

To describe how metrics are calculated the terminologies are used are given below.

- True-Positive (TP) refers as a lesion class that is correctly predicted to the predicted label.
- False-Positive (FP) refers as a lesion class that is falsely predicted to the predicted label.
- True-Negative (TN) refers as a background pixel that is truly labeled to the predicted label.
- False-Negative (FN) refers as a background pixel that is falsely labeled to the predicted label.

The balanced accuracy (BACC) is used as the main evaluation measure as shown in Eq. (4), it is equivalent to the average sensitivity or recall.

$$BACC = \frac{1}{Cl}\sum_{i=1}^{Cl}\frac{TPi}{TPi + FNi} \quad (4)$$

A comparison with other state-of-the-art methods is given in Table 1. The model accuracy graph for 50 epochs is given in Fig. 4. where the blue line shows the model training accuracy and the orange line shows the model validation accuracy.

Table 1 Comparison with other state-of-the-art-methods

Model	BACC	Model	BACC
VGG-11	0.667	ResNet-101	0.737
VGG-13	0.675	DenseNet-169	0.735
VGG-16	0.649	DenseNet-201	0.729
VGG-19	0.655	DenseNet-161	0.737
ResNet-18	0.718	EfficientNet-B0	0.738
ResNet-34	0.728	EfficientNet-B1	0.742
ResNet-50	0.737	EfficientNet-B2	0.753

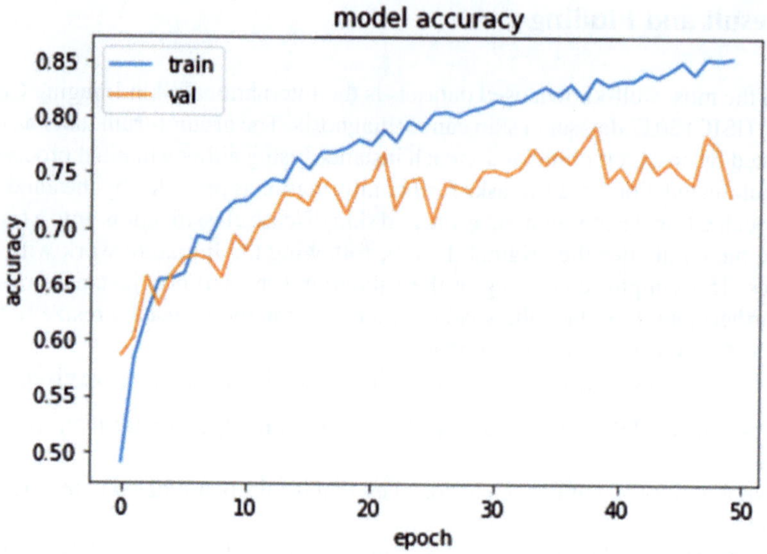

Fig. 4 Proposed model performance graph for training and validation

5 Conclusion

In this paper, a Transfer Learning based Efficient Net-b2 model is used for the early detection of Melanoma. Efficient Net uses the concept of appropriate scaling of the model which efficiently balances network depth, width, and resolution. Depth Scaling can extract richer and more complex features. Width scaling can capture more fine-grained features. Resolution scaling captures more fine-grained patterns. All the experimental work is performed on the ISIC 2017 Dataset. The proposed model scored a Balanced Accuracy 75.3%. The model achieves better classification accuracy than other state of art Deep deep-learning models.

References

1. Han J, Colditz GA, Hunter DJ (2006) Risk factors for skin cancers: a nested case–control study within the nurses' health study. Int J Epidemiol 35(6):1514–1521
2. Rogers HW et al (2015) Incidence estimate of nonmelanoma skin cancer (keratinocyte carcinomas) in the us population, 2012. JAMA Dermatol 151:1081–1086
3. A. I. of Health &Welfare (2017) Cancer in Australia 2017, vol. Cancer series no. 101. Australian Institute of Welfare, Canberra, ACT, Australia
4. Silverberg E, Boring CC, Squires TS (1990) Cancer statistics, 1990, CA. Cancer J Clin 40:9–26
5. Han J, Colditz GA, Hunter DJ (2006) Risk factors for skin cancers: a nested casecontrol study within the Nurses' health study. Int J Epidemiol 35(6):15141521

6. Kawahara J, Daneshvar S, Argenziano G, Hamarneh G (2018) Seven-point checklist and skin lesion classification using multitask multimodal neural nets. IEEE J Biomed Health Inform 23(2):538–546
7. Lee H, Chen YPP (2015) Image based computer aided diagnosis system for cancer detection. Expert Syst Appl 42(12):5356–5365
8. Singh JP (2022) Scientific exploration of conceptual and algorithmic terminologies of machine learning. In: Advances in computational intelligence and communication technology: proceedings of CICT 2021. Springer Singapore, Singapore, pp 325–333
9. Sharma A, Yadav DP, Garg H, Kumar M, Sharma B, Koundal D (2021) Bone cancer detection using feature extraction based machine learning model. Comput Math Methods Med
10. Sharma H, Srivastava S (2023) Multilevel attention and relation network based image captioning model. Multimed Tools Appl 82(7):10981–11003
11. Sharma H, Srivastava S (2023) Context-aware and co-attention network based image captioning model. Imaging Sci J 71(3):244–256
12. Wu Z, Shen C, Van Den Hengel A (2019) Wider or deeper: revisiting the resnet model for visual recognition. Pattern Recogn 90:119–133
13. Zhou T, Zhao Y, Wu J (2021) Resnext and res2net structures for speaker verification. In: 2021 IEEE spoken language technology workshop (SLT). IEEE, pp 301–307
14. He K, Zhang X, Ren S, Sun J (2016) Deep residual learning for image recognition. In: Proceedings of the IEEE conference on computer vision and pattern recognition, pp 770–778
15. Szegedy C, Vanhoucke V, Ioffe S, Shlens J, Wojna Z (2016) Rethinking the inception architecture for computer vision. In: Proceedings of the IEEE conference on computer vision and pattern recognition, pp 2818–2826
16. Tan M, Le Q (2019) Efficientnet: rethinking model scaling for convolutional neural networks. In: International conference on machine learning. PMLR, pp 6105–6114
17. Luo R, Tian F, Qin T, Chen E, Liu TY (2018) Neural architecture optimization. Adv Neural Inf Process Syst 31
18. Tan M, Chen B, Pang R, Vasudevan V, Sandler M, Howard A, Le QV (2019) Mnasnet: platform-aware neural architecture search for mobile. In: Proceedings of the IEEE/CVF conference on computer vision and pattern recognition, pp 2820–2828

Unveiling the Best Edge Detection Algorithm for Brain Magnetic Resonance Imaging: A Qualitative and Quantitative Comparative Study

Kavery Verma, Subodh Srivastava, and Ritesh Kumar Mishra

1 Introduction

Magnetic Resonance Imaging (MRI) has rebuilt the field of diagnostics in medical illnesses by providing detailed and restrained visualization of soft tissues, including the involute structures of the human brain. In the field of neuroimaging, various kind of image analysis are concluded, but the most essential of all is identification of edges or edge detection. Edge detection helps out to describe structures, area of concern, and morbid regions which is exigent for many therapeutic uses. Edges in MRI image indicate significant changes in the intensity of images.

Anatomical mapping and segmentation in images work only if they can separate structures in the body, like cerebrospinal fluid, white matter, and gray matter [1]. In addition to this, accurate localization of edges in brain MRI images are needed to find minute or focal problems like tumors, lesions, or vascular problems. Furthermore, precise edge localization within brain MRI images is required for the detection of subtle or focal abnormalities such as tumors, lesions, or vascular anomalies. Precise edge detection may aid physicians in making more informed decisions about therapy and diagnosis by increasing the efficiency of following image processing procedures. With the advent of new algorithms and techniques, edge detection in medical imaging has gone a long way when it comes to MRI image dataset. These techniques encompass everything from old gradient-based operators like the Sobel and Canny operators to more contemporary deep learning-based methods. Different types of MRI imaging

K. Verma (✉) · S. Srivastava · R. K. Mishra
Department of Electronics and Communication Engineering, National Institute of Technology Patna, Patna 800005, India
e-mail: kaveryv.ph21.ec@nitp.ac.in

S. Srivastava
e-mail: subodh@nitp.ac.in

R. K. Mishra
e-mail: ritesh@nitp.ac.in

K. Kumar Singh et al. (eds.), *Machine Vision and Augmented Intelligence*, Lecture Notes in Electrical Engineering 1211, https://doi.org/10.1007/978-981-97-4359-9_71

and clinical settings necessitate different techniques, each with its own set of benefits, drawbacks, and applicability.

This research paper undertakes a comprehensive comparative study of various edge detection methods when applied specifically to brain MRI images. The main aim of this article is to explore different edge detection methods. Later a comparative analysis of these edge detection methods will help in finding the best existing edge detection method in this following sections of the work. This will help to improve neurological image analysis accuracy and efficiency. This article provides researchers and healthcare professionals with edge detection of brain MRI and its insights for abnormality detection.

2 Datasets and Edge Detection of MR Images

In MRI, edge detection is a useful technique that identifies edges and improves image quality. In the field of medicine and research, edge detection plays an important role in the analysis of MRI data. Figure 1 shows different types of edge detection techniques [2, 3].

2.1 Datasets

Center for Biomedical Research Excellence (COBRE) dataset has been taken for the purpose of edge detection and conducting its comparative analysis in brain MRI [4]. The individuals in this dataset have been identified with schizophrenia and are between the ages 18 years and 65 years. This dataset incorporates raw anatomical and functional MRI scans.

3 Motivation and Related Work

Edge detection is a way to find the edges and limits of things in an abnormal brain MRI image. It makes MRI image easier to see by drawing attention to important edges and structures. This can improve the overall interpretability of the image, making it easier for medical professionals to analyze and make decisions. Various edge detections have been carried out for proper edge detection in MRI. Aghazadeh et al. [5] have proposed canny edge detection as a segmentation method for brain tumor detection using Magnetic resonance imaging. The use of a semi average filter during the preprocessing stage has made edges stronger, which resulted in the detection of more strong edges using the Canny edge detector. Chen et al. [6] have proposed Machine learning for predicting breast-conserving surgery candidates after neoadjuvant chemotherapy based on dynamic contrast-enhanced magnetic resonance imaging. Here Laplacian

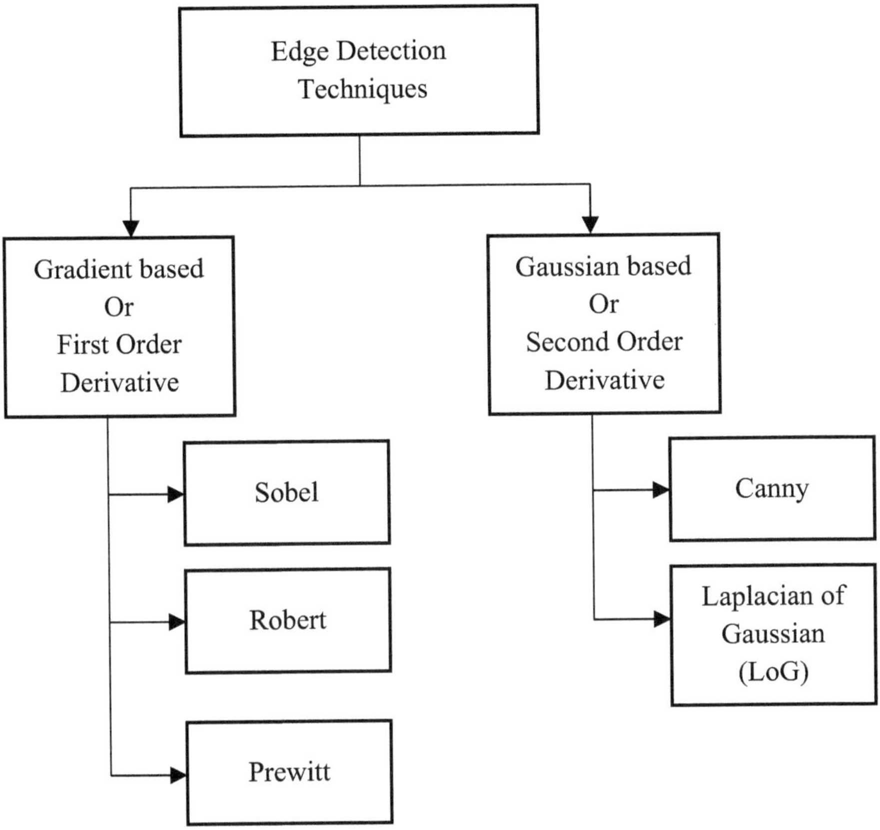

Fig. 1 Different edge detection techniques

of Gaussian (LoG) edge detection is taken as the machine learning model for breast MRI images. The features derived from LOG exhibited a higher degree of prediction accuracy. Tang et al. [7] employed Diagnostic efficiency of multi-modal MRI based deep learning with Sobel operator in differentiating benign and malignant breast mass lesions. In the classification of breast masses, deep learning models that included a Sobel operator had great diagnostic value, which further increase the efficiency of diagnosis. Sharma et al. [8] have implemented Automatic Diabetic Retinopathy

Detection using Roberts Cross Edge Detection. The Roberts Cross Edge Detection method is utilized by the system in order to facilitate more accurate and fruitful edge extraction. Bhargavi et al. [9] have an Integrated report on brain tumor detection from MRI Image using Prewitt horizontal edge emphasizing filtering technique.

4 Validation and Analysis

The main motive of this paper is to implement each selected edge detection method and apply them to the subset of COBRE brain MRI images dataset. Ensure that you use the same parameter settings and preprocessing steps for consistency. After that the results of each edge detection method have been compared against the ground truth using the chosen quantitative metric. Visualize the detected edges overlaid on the MRI images for qualitative assessment. This allows to observe the quality of the detected edges and any potential artifacts or inaccuracies. The interpretation of images with no reference, the performance of the human visual system, and the comprehensive full reference interpretation are all done for evaluating the performance assessment parameters for MRI [10, 11].

4.1 Full Reference Image Assessment Metrics

(a) **Mean Square Error (MSE)**—It is calculated as mean square deviation of pixels in the reference image and the distorted image [10].

$$\mathrm{MSE} = \frac{1}{\mathrm{m} \times \mathrm{n}} \sum_{\mathrm{i}=1}^{\mathrm{m}-1} \sum_{\mathrm{j}=1}^{\mathrm{n}-1} (\mathrm{M} - \mathrm{I})^2$$

where ‘M’ is the reference MRI image, ‘I’ is the output image and ‘m’ and ‘n’ denote the size of the image.

(b) **Peak Signal-to-Noise Ratio (PSNR)**—The quality of a reconstructed image is often judged by how well it matches the quality of a reference image. With the calculation of PSNR it can be seen how close the restored image is with the reference image in terms of quality and clarity [12].

$$\mathrm{PSNR} = 10\log_{10} \frac{(\mathrm{P} - 1)^2}{\mathrm{MSE}} \mathrm{dB}$$

where ‘P’ denotes maximum possible range of image pixel.

(c) **RMSE**—It measures the average intensity variation or contrast in the image, which can help assess image quality, sharpness, and detail visibility [13].

$$\mathrm{RMSE} = \sqrt{\mathrm{MSE}}$$

4.2 *Human Visual System Image Assessment Metrics*

(a) **Structural Similarity Index Map (SSIM)**—This visualization in image processing provides more precise structural similarity information between two images [14].

$$\text{SSIM} = \frac{(2\mu_X\mu_Y + c_1)(2\sigma_{XY} + c_2)}{\left(\mu_X^2 + \mu_Y^2 + c_1\right)\left(\sigma_X^2 + \sigma_Y^2 + c_2\right)}$$

where 'μ' denotes mean of image and 'σ' denotes variance of image and 'c_1' and 'c_2' prevents instability.

(b) **Multi-Scale Structural Similarity Index (MS-SSIM)**—The MS-SSIM algorithm is an enhanced version of the SSIM algorithm that compares images based on the structural similarity of the images at a variety of different image scales [15].

$$MSSSIM = \frac{(2\mu_X\mu_Y + C_1)}{({\mu_X}^2 + {\mu_Y}^2 + C_1)}\prod_{0}^{P-1}\frac{(2\sigma_{XY} + C_2)}{({\sigma_X}^2 + {\sigma_Y}^2 + C_2)}$$

4.3 *No Reference Image Assessment Metrics*

(a) **Discrete Entropy (DE)**—It is often used to assess the information content or randomness in an image [16].

$$\text{DE} = -\sum_{i=0}^{P-1} \text{I}\log_2\text{I}$$

5 Result and Discussion

In this section, we undertake a thorough examination of the results achieved through the application of the existing methodologies, encompassing both qualitative and quantitative assessments. These analyses are exclusively conducted on the COBRE MRI image dataset.

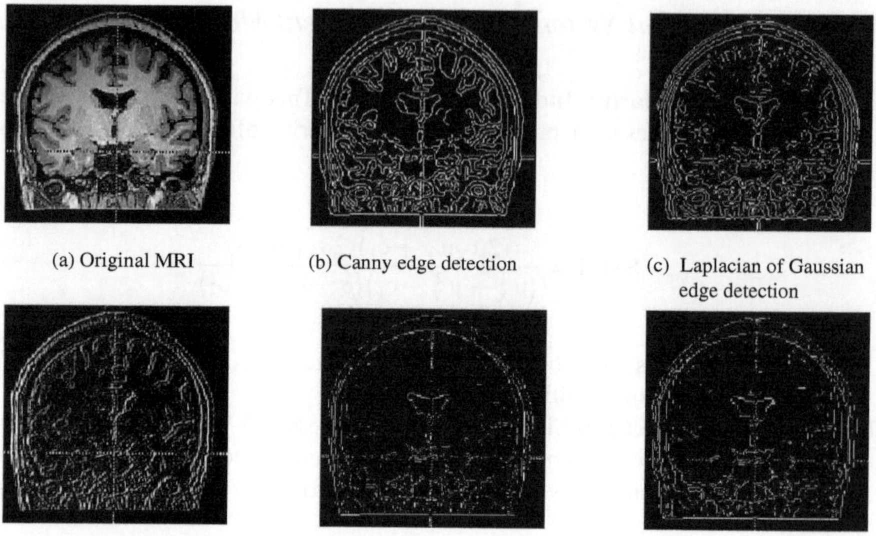

(a) Original MRI (b) Canny edge detection (c) Laplacian of Gaussian edge detection

(d) Sobel edge detection (e) Robert edge detection (f) Prewitt edge detection

Fig. 2 **a** Original MRI. **b** Canny edge detection. **c** Laplacian of Gaussian edge detection. **d** Sobel edge detection. **e** Robert edge detection. **f** Prewitt edge detection

5.1 Qualitative Analysis

Qualitative analysis has been carried out on a selected set of MRI images from the COBRE dataset, driven by the potential presence of anomalies, micro-calcifications, or specific masses in the patient population. The results of this assessment are presented in Fig. 2a–f, illustrating the comparative qualitative image evaluations achieved through different methods.

5.2 Quantitative Analysis

Table 1 provides a comparative quantitative evaluation of MRI edge detection methods. Furthermore, for a more visual representation of this comparison, Fig. 3a–f display graphical plots based on the data obtained from Table 1.

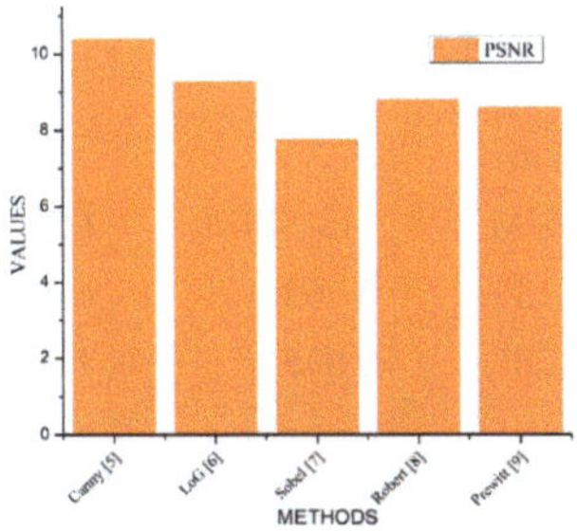

(a) Quantitative assessment plot of PSNR with different Edge detection methods

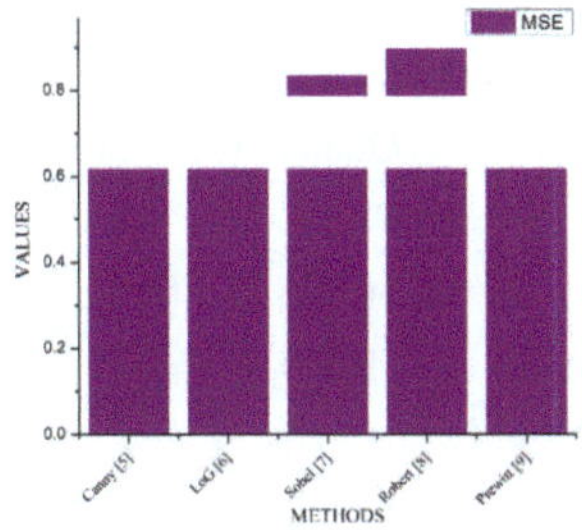

(b) Quantitative assessment plot of MSE with different Edge detection methods

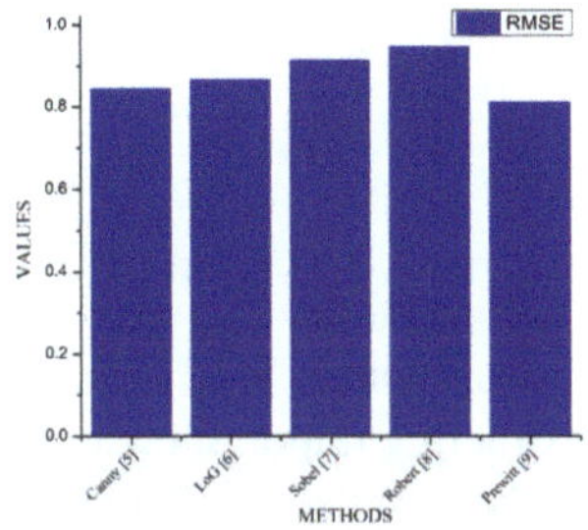

(c) Quantitative assessment plot of RMSE with different Edge detection methods

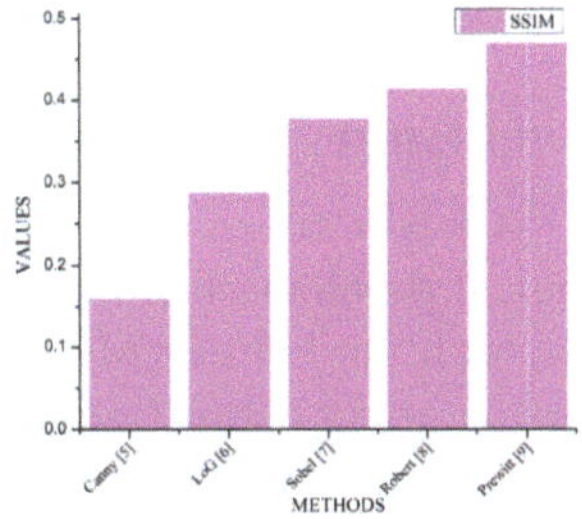

(d) Quantitative assessment plot of SSIM with different Edge detection methods

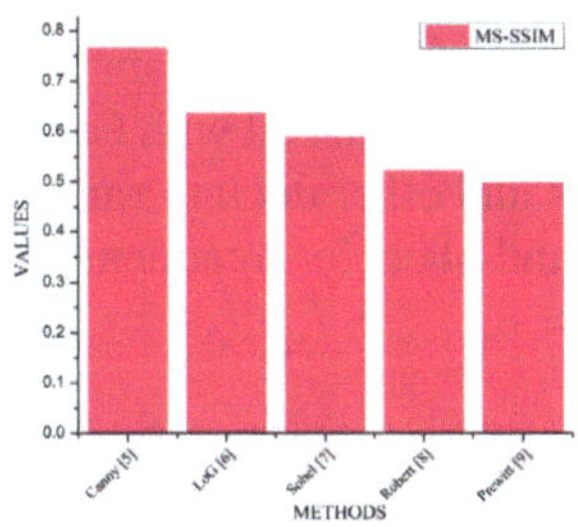

(e) Quantitative assessment plot of MS-SSIM with different Edge detection methods

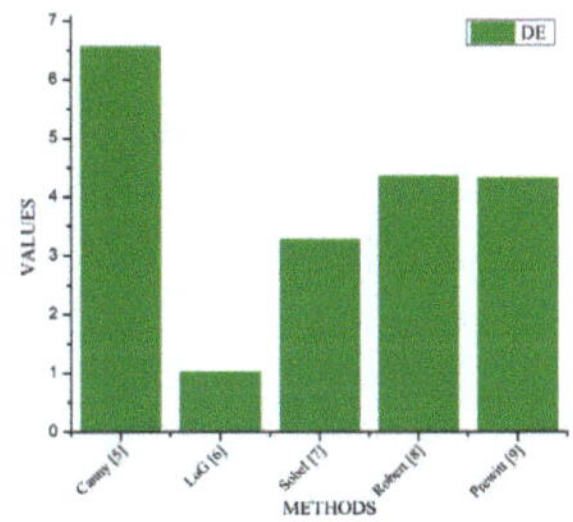

(f) Quantitative assessment plot of DE with different Edge detection methods

Fig. 3 **a** Quantitative assessment plot of PSNR with different Edge detection methods. **b** Quantitative assessment plot of MSE with different Edge detection methods. **c** Quantitative assessment plot of RMSE with different Edge detection methods. **d** Quantitative assessment plot of SSIM with different Edge detection methods. **e** Quantitative assessment plot of MS-SSIM with different Edge detection methods. **f** Quantitative assessment plot of DE with different Edge detection methods

Table 1 Variation of reference parameter, human visual reference parameters, and no reference parameter with respect to different edge detection methodologies

	Quantitative performance assessment metrics					
	PSNR	MSE	RMSE	SSIM	MS-SSIM	DE
Canny [5]	10.395	0.712	0.843	0.159	0.765	6.553
Laplacian of Gaussian (LoG) [6]	9.275	0.751	0.866	0.287	0.635	1.024
Sobel [7]	7.744	0.834	0.913	0.377	0.587	3.274
Robert [8]	8.795	0.895	0.946	0.413	0.521	4.353
Prewitt [9]	8.584	0.657	0.811	0.468	0.497	4.319

6 Conclusion

Neurological problems like diseases, tumors, and abnormalities can be found and predicted with the help of MRI technology. Edge detection in MRI is a key part of improving image quality, separating structures, extracting important features, and finding and diagnosing brain disorders, tumors, and other problems. It's an important tool for both doctors and researchers to understand the detailed details of the brain's structure and disease. In this study, we compare and contrast various edge detection methods used in brain MRI images, looking at both their quality and quantity. These studies compare different edge recognition methods and show that Canny methods work well for MRI images. MRI pictures that have been enhanced with Canny Edge are often easier to see and understand. Radiologists and other doctors can use these edge-enhanced images to make better evaluations and plans for treatment.

References

1. Borole VY, Nimbhore SS, Kawthekar SS (2015) Image processing techniques for brain tumor detection: a review. Int J Emerg Trends Technol Comput Sci (IJETTCS) 4(5):28–32
2. Arockia Dhivya AJ (2018) Issue 12. www.jetir.org (ISSN-2349–5162) JETIR1812851. J Emerg Technol Innov Res (JETIR). www.jetir 5:310. www.jetir.org.
3. Farzana A, Sathik MM Survey of various edge detection techniques over brain MRI. Int J Trend Res Dev 4(1):2394–9333. Available: www.ijtrd.com
4. COBRE. https://fcon_1000.projects.nitrc.org/indi/retro/cobre.html. Accessed 11 Jan 2023
5. Aghazadeh N, Moradi P, Castellano G, Noras P (2023) An automatic MRI brain image segmentation technique using edge-region-based level set. J Supercomput 79:7337–7359, 123AD. https://doi.org/10.1007/s11227-022-04948-9
6. Chen Z, Huang M, Lyu J, Qi X, He F, Li X (2023) Machine learning for predicting breast-conserving surgery candidates after neoadjuvant chemotherapy based on DCE-MRI. Front Oncol 13:1174843. https://doi.org/10.3389/FONC.2023
7. Tang W et al (2023) Diagnostic efficiency of multi-modal MRI based deep learning with Sobel operator in differentiating benign and malignant breast mass lesions—a retrospective study. PeerJ Comput Sci 9:e1460. https://doi.org/10.7717/PEERJ-CS.1460/SUPP-2

8. Sharma A, Dronawat R, Jhapate A (2021) 10th IEEE international conference on communication systems and network technologies automatic diabetic retinopathy detection using Roberts cross edge detection in DIP. In: 10th IEEE international conference of communication and system network technologies. https://doi.org/10.1109/CSNT.2021.64
9. Bhargavi G, Cyril Robinson Azariah J, Sivasakthiselvan S (2020) Integrated report on brain tumor detection from MRI Image using Prewitt horizontal edge-emphasizing filtering technique. In: 2020 international conference on communication and signal processing (ICCSP). IEEE
10. Kumar A, Kumar P, Srivastava S (2022) A skewness reformed complex diffusion based unsharp masking for the restoration and enhancement of Poisson noise corrupted mammograms. Biomed Signal Process Control 73. https://doi.org/10.1016/J.BSPC.2021.103421
11. Ohashi K et al (2023) Applicability evaluation of full-reference image quality assessment methods for computed tomography images. https://doi.org/10.1007/s10278-023-00875-0
12. Kumar V, Srivastava S (2022) Performance analysis of reshaped Gabor filter for removing the Rician distributed noise in brain MR images, vol 236, no 8, pp 1216–1231. https://doi.org/10.1177/09544119221105690
13. Damera-Venkata N, Kite TD, Geisler WS, Evans BL, Bovik AC (2000) Image quality assessment based on a degradation model. IEEE Trans Image Process 9(4):636–650. https://doi.org/10.1109/83.841940
14. Tang Y, Ren F, Pedrycz W (2020) Fuzzy C-means clustering through SSIM and patch for image segmentation. Appl Soft Comput 87:105928. https://doi.org/10.1016/j.asoc.2019.105928
15. Wang Z, Simoncelli EP, Bovik AC (2003) Multi-scale structural similarity for image quality assessment. Conf Rec Asilomar Conf Signals Syst Comput 2:1398–1402. https://doi.org/10.1109/ACSSC.2003.1292216
16. Krbcova Z, Kukal J (2017) Relationship between entropy and SNR changes in image enhancement. Eurasip J Image Video Process 2017(1):1–8. https://doi.org/10.1186/S13640-017-0232-Z/TABLES/7

Automatic Identification Mechanism for Access Control System

G. Sandhya, S. Suresha, P. Shivalingappa, Vishal Yogish Rao, Mallikarjuna Kodabagi, B. S. Sumitha, and Tarun Balasundaram

1 Introduction

The campus's highly integrated cameras will capture the student's image. Each student's face is in the database. The images of the students might be utilized in the next stages. Face recognition software is being used to take a picture of the pupil. Either the students already present or those who are just entering the classroom. The student's face is promptly recognized by the cameras. Once the student images stored in the database are compared to or matched with identified face photos, the recognition process begins. If the image and the database match, the student is listed as present. If not, it is stated that the student was absent. The student attendance report will be mailed to the parents.

Many people are aware of face recognition technology because Face ID is currently frequently employed in the mobile sector. Facial recognition frequently recognizes and recalls one person as the lone owner of the device, limiting access to other people, rather than using a vast library of photos to analyze a person's personality. Even though they are employed in some situations now, facial recognition systems often behave in this way. Figure 1 shows the overall block diagram of the automatic attendance system.

G. Sandhya (✉) · P. Shivalingappa · V. Yogish Rao · M. Kodabagi · T. Balasundaram
School of Computing & Information Technology, REVA University, Bengaluru, India
e-mail: sandhyag.pooja@gmail.com

M. Kodabagi
e-mail: mallikarjun.mk@reva.edu.in

S. Suresha · B. S. Sumitha
Information Science & Engineering Nagarjuna, College of Engineering and Technology, Bengaluru, India

K. Kumar Singh et al. (eds.), *Machine Vision and Augmented Intelligence*, Lecture Notes in Electrical Engineering 1211, https://doi.org/10.1007/978-981-97-4359-9_72

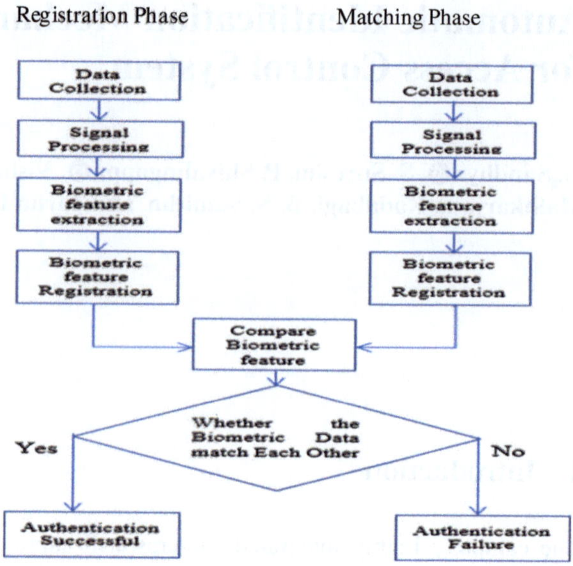

Fig. 1 Block diagram of attendance system

Stage 1: Face Detection

A face in a group or by itself is identified and located by the camera, which then takes a picture of it. The subject of the photograph may be shown in profile or gazing directly at the lens.

Stage 2: Face Analysis

An image of the face is taken and examined. The device examines the geometry of the face in addition to a few key characteristics, such as the distance between the eyes, the depth of the eye attachments, the separation between the brow and jawline, the condition of the cheekbones, and the shape of the lips, eyes, and jaw. They hope to be able to recognize the basic parts of the face that make it up.

Stage 3: Convert the picture into information.

Face-related data are transformed into a substantial collection of sophisticated data by the face catch technique. This collection of data is saved as a face print, which is a numerical code. A person's face print is similar to their fingerprints in many respects.

Stage 4: Finding a match.

A database of recognizable faces is compared to the subject's face print. For instance, 650 million photographs are available to the FBI from various government data sources. Any photograph that has been tagged with a name on Facebook can have its faces recognized using face recognition software. The face unique mark must match a photo in a facial acknowledgment information base, according to the ID theory.

2 Literature Survey

L. Hong and A. Jain. In "Integrating countenances and fingerprints", the Authors of this paper have depicted momentarily Integrating appearances and fingerprints for individual distinguishing proof and a Multichannel way to deal with finger impression classification.[1]. Y. F. Wan and A. Jain. "Fingerprint picture improvement" Authors of this paper have portrayed about calculation and execution assessment of unique mark picture upgrade, IEEE exchange on design examination, and machine intelligence[2]. A. Pentland, B. Moghaddam, and T. Starner, "View-Based and modular Eigen spaces for face recognition," Proc. IEEE CS Conf. Computer Vision and Pattern Recognition [3]. A. Nefarian and M. Hayes, "An embedded hmm-based approach for face detection and recognition," In Proc. IEEE International Conference on Acoustics, Speech, and Signal Processing [4]. T. Sim, R. Sukthankar, M. Mullin and S. Baluja, "Memory-based face recognition for visitor identification" [5].

"Biometric System—Challenges and Future Trends", By Sunil kumar Singla, Manjit Singh and Navdeep Kanwal in 2021 IEEE 2015 8th International Conference on Bio-Science and Bio-Technology. The iris, which lies between the cornea and the lense of the eye, has certain unique features which can be used for identification detection. An iris vision sensors or webcam is used to perform identification of iris. Thermal images of the face and ears can also be utilized for identification. The reliability as well as general efficacy of a system are challenged by things that effect these features, like recognizing faces, this as encounter reversing (pose variability), knowledge (such as lighting condition), facial expressions, and fashionable accessories (hat, eyeglasses, etc.) [6]. "A Comparative Review of Biometric Security Systems", by Ryan Ercel O. Paderes, in 2015 8th International Conference on Bio-Science and Bio-Technology. Iris biometric authentication uses cameras to take a digital image of our eyes after scanning them with infrared rays. Each iris has distinct qualities that are being mapped out and utilized to identify us. But once enrolled in the database, iris biometrics may remain longer and have an excellent degree of precision. Compared to the fingerprinting biometric technology, it is more precise. Because of our continual exposure to finger prints, the fingertips' distinctive pattern may be harmed or even destroyed. Additionally, iris patterns endure more than fingerprinting as the lenses of our eyes are less likely to be uncovered than hands [7]. "Biometric System". M. Daris Femila Dr. A. Anthony Irudhayara.2011 IEEE, The term "biometrics" additionally has been employed to denote a young branch of engineering that focuses on identifying people by biological features, such as those based on retinal scans, iris structures, hand prints, or recognition of facial features. The primary emphasis of this article will concentrate on how the concept of "biometrics" is now used and what it means [8].

3 Problem Definition

The conventional technique (paper basis) is currently used in a substantial fraction of educational institutions to track student involvement. Votes are kept in a traditional manner, as we can see in elections. Therefore, there are various drawbacks associated with paper-based participation registries that are not transmitted to any included framework, making the data unavailable for analysis. Right now, our main attention is on the facial recognition technology for tracking student attendance.

4 Scope And Feasibility

Facial recognition technology is a modern breakthrough that characterizes our era alongside robotics, AI, and IoT. By comparing the face details from a photo with the stored facial data collection, facial recognition is a biometric invention used for identity verification and assessment of individuals. One of the most popular applications of image analysis software, face recognition is no longer regarded as a sci-fi concept. This innovation was previously only used for security and observation purposes, but it has recently safely advanced to this current reality. Facial recognition software is being promoted by businesses today as the future of everything from shopping to law enforcement.

This study looks at the preferences of college students who replied to a self-administered questionnaire and employed the traditional way of tracking or documenting student attendance. The study also used a questionnaire as the survey instrument and a descriptive research methodology. Instead of noting attendance on a piece of paper, which could take more time and energy, this is a simple and effective way to do it. By accomplishing this, we would be able to mark a student's attendance without any manual interference. We need permission from the department at the college level before we can undertake this initiative for student attendance.

Facial recognition innovation is flourishing. According to forecasters, this innovation will expand swiftly and generate large profits soon. Security and observations will be the two main areas that will be greatly impacted. Schools, governmental buildings, and private businesses are among the places that are now completely accepting it. It is anticipated that merchants and financial systems will quickly adopt the idea of preventing fraud from affecting Visa purchases and payments, particularly those conducted online. This invention would overcome the drawbacks of the often used yet inefficient secret key structure. Robots using facial recognition technologies may eventually start robbing people as well. They can be useful in finishing jobs that are challenging or impracticable for people to complete.

Table 1 Application areas (ICT, Jun, 2019)

End use	Top applications
Offices	Physical access to workplace facilities
Government	Helps to identify missing children
Banking and telecom	Help to know the current process to the customer, allow authentication of credit/debit cards
Education	Allow attendance tracking of the student and entry to labs
Construction	Control access to specific point at a site
Real estate commercial	Officers access to campus facilities like residence halls, common area, cafeteria, etc
Manufacturing	Control and record access to specific locations for employees, visitors, vendors and maintenance staff
Aviation	Paperless travel at airports
Warehouse	Control process to provision entry and exit of vehicles
Entertainment	Access to multiplex cinema halls

Face recognition is used in many different applications across several industries; a few of them are mentioned below for your convenience. But in our project, we are mostly concentrating on the Education domain, where the domain application is to obtain attendance for the students present in the class after realizing it must match with the provided database of the students (Table 1).

5 Requirements

An operating system with Windows 8 or higher is required for our system. We use the most recent technology, including all libraries, as well as picture processing technology. A standalone computer with (i3, 4 Gb ram or higher), more than 32 Gb of hard drive space, a high-quality wireless camera with the ability to store all photographs, and a fingerprint scanner for databases.

6 Libraries Used In The Implementation

Open CV:

OpenCV (Open Source Computer Vision Library) is a free and open-source programming library for AI and computer vision. It is being developed to give computer vision and AI computations a common foundation. It contains a large number of upgraded computations that can be utilized for a wide range of tasks, such as identifying and detecting faces, recognizing objects, and more. There should have been some image control because we want it to take pictures with our webcam.

NumPy:

In Python, NumPy is the main package for logical registering and provides a multi-layered cluster object. Other numerical tasks can be carried out using NumPy, but in general, we only need it to convert our images into some sort of exhibit so we can store the model that has been created.

Haar Cascade:

In its most basic form, Haar Cascade is a classifier that isolates the sources from the articles for which it was designed. The result is an XML document that contains the prepared outcome. The Haar Cascade is made by superimposing a single positive image over a series of negative photos, as was previously mentioned. Due to the need for a powerful internet connection, a high-end framework, and numerous prepared photos, the preparation is done on the server. To improve the accuracy of the outcomes, they increase the number of phases for which the classifier is prepared. Our front 58-facing face recognizer on the Haar overflow webcam should be able to distinguish between different faces.

Python GUI (tkinter):

Tkinter is a straightforward GUI package that is used to execute incredibly minimal GUI that helps us interface with code easily. However, you need to be aware of how the code works in order to comprehend it.

- *FLOW CHART*

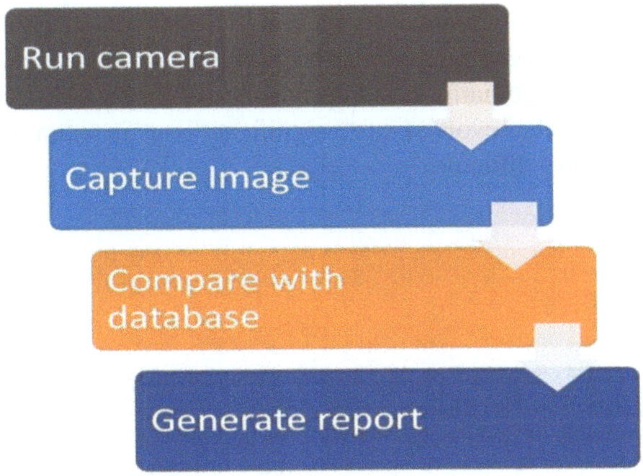

- *TESTING PHASE*

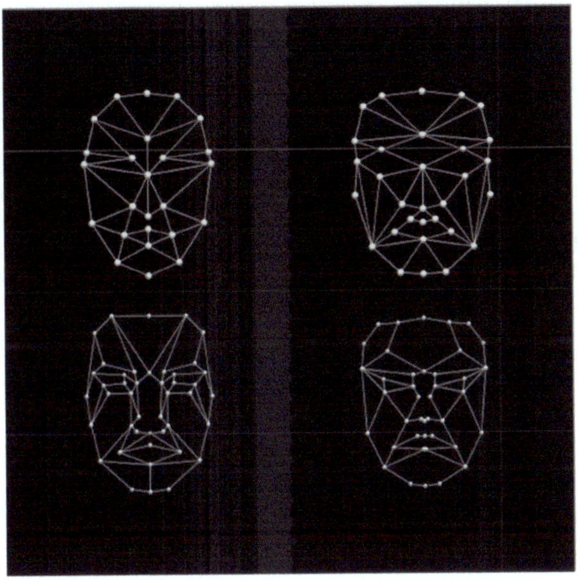

7 Conclusion

An automatic attendance system based on face recognition saves time and increases security. The effectiveness and security of a face recognition-based computerized participation framework are demonstrated. When a student is missing or absent in the future, a similar framework may be utilized to report that involvement was noticed;

at that point, a message might naturally be sent to the student's parents, counsellors, and class coordinator. Electronic data protection makes it less likely that abnormal data tampering, unwanted harm, or compromised security would occur. Given that the conventional EVM has evolved into a significant issue in recent years, this might be the solution to every difficulty.

References

1. Liang L, Ai H (2004) Summary on face detection researches. J Comput 25(5):449–459
2. Liu M (2003) Real-time face tracking method of color images. J Comput 21(6):527–532
3. Zhao M (2005) Study on coding algorithm of wavelet-based color face images. Master thesis. Computer Academy of Sciences of Sichuan Normal University, Sichuan
4. Liang L, Ai H (2004) Face detections based on multi-template matching. J China's Image Graph 44(10):623–630
5. Chen M (2003) Studies on the face image detection and classification system. PhD thesis. Computer Science and Engineering Department of Shanghai Jiaotong University, Shanghai
6. Kumar A, Karki MV (2017) Iris recognition system with error detection and reconstruction algorithms for template security. In: Proceedings of IEEE international conference on recent trends in electronics information & communication technology, pp 824–829
7. Daris Femila M, AnthonyIrudhayara A (2011) A comparative review of biometric security systems. In: 2015 8th international conference on bio-science and bio-technology
8. Daris Femila M, Anthony Irudhayara A (2011) Biometric system. IEEE
9. Lu C (1998) Study on several problems of automatic face recognition and the system implementation. PhD thesis. Computer Academy of Sciences of Tsinghua University, Beijing
10. Su G (2000) Summary on face recognition technology. J China's Image Graph 5(11):220–238
11. Li J (2004) Research progress of new face recognition technology. J Comput 31(10):293–295
12. Zhang J, He T (1999) Face recognition method based on extractions of facial geometric feature points. Infrared Laser Eng 28(4):40–43

A Comparative Analysis of Denoising Techniques in Image Processing

Nitesh Kumar Jaiswal, Subodh Srivastava, and Manipuran Mahto

1 Introduction

The rapid evolution of medical imaging and diagnostic techniques has made them essential in the diagnosis of disease [1]. Using a variety of mathematical techniques, it is possible to determine whether healthy tissue has become infected by analysing medical images. However, any loss or misinterpretation could have significant implications for patient health. Based on the equipment and the patient's condition at the time, getting a medical image is a challenging task in and of itself [2, 3]. Medical images are frequently impacted by noise of any kind, including Gaussian, impulse, Rician, speckle, etc., during the imaging process [3]. Comparative studies have been conducted on wavelet transform filters, mode filters, median filters, non-local mean filters, adaptive median filters, and denoising convolution neural networks. A technique to remove noises that corrupt the image is needed to solve this issue. Image denoising techniques in medical imaging can be categorized into two groups: those applied during image acquisition and those applied after image acquisition. The former involves incorporating noise suppression modules into the imaging system to enhance image quality. The latter emphasizes the application of digital image processing methods to diminish noise and enhance image quality. Noise is removed from medical images using common filters such as mode, median [4], Lee [5], and Gaussian filters [6]. These filters are tailored into different variants to effectively address specific categories of noise found in a wide range of medical imaging methods. [7–9]. However, these filters can result in the loss of minor, low-contrast

N. K. Jaiswal (✉) · S. Srivastava · M. Mahto
Department of Electronics and Communication Engineering, NIT Patna, Patna, Bihar, India
e-mail: niteshj.ph21.ec@nitp.ac.in

S. Srivastava
e-mail: subodh@nitp.ac.in

M. Mahto
e-mail: mmahto@nitp.ac.in

K. Kumar Singh et al. (eds.), *Machine Vision and Augmented Intelligence*, Lecture Notes in Electrical Engineering 1211, https://doi.org/10.1007/978-981-97-4359-9_73

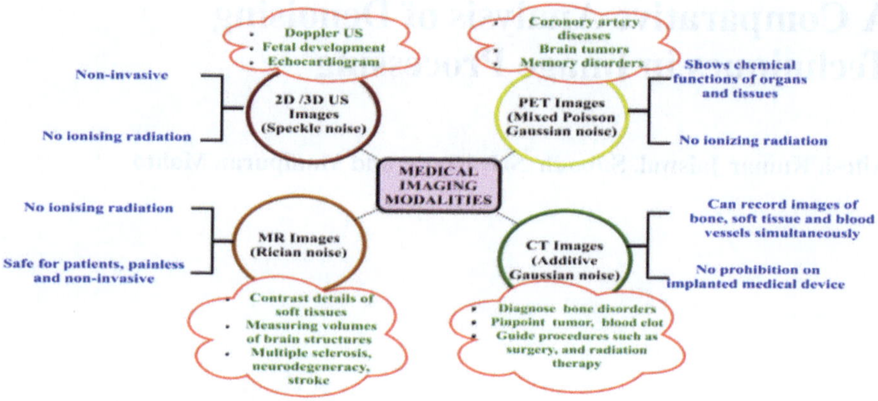

Fig. 1 Medical imaging modalities overview [16]

lesions as well as noise, limiting their direct diagnostic utility. Even though the median filter [10] and bilateral filter [11] are common adaptive filters, they tend to blur images. Despite their low computational complexity, these filters may not fully meet the requirements of medical practitioners who require sharper and more detailed images. Non-local means filters [12] offer effective noise suppression, but their high computational complexity makes them unsuitable for real-time denoising of ultrasound images. Multi-scale analysis approaches, such as wavelet thresholding, offer low computational complexity and time–frequency analysis advantages [13]. However, they have the disadvantage of choosing thresholds that may not correspond to the signal and noise distribution at various dimensions.

Tian et al. [14] proposed nonlinear estimators rooted in Bayesian theory to tackle this challenge. Additionally, soft computing principles like ANN, GA, and fuzzy logic [15] have been applied to mitigate noise in medical images. [15], but they have a high degree of complexity and require considerable time for logical reasoning. Future research may investigate the use of these techniques for improving medical image noise reduction.

This paper is divided into several sections. Part 2 discusses common types of noise in medical images, including Gaussian and impulse noise. Part 3 explores various filter techniques for image denoising. Part 4 presents simulation results comparing the effectiveness of these denoising methods. Finally, Part 5 summarizes the key findings and underscores the importance of denoising algorithms in medical imaging (Fig. 1).

2 Image Noise

Image noise describes the unwanted artifacts that appear as random changes in brightness or color in digital images. It can be caused by a variety of things, including sensor limitations, poor lighting, high ISO settings, transmission errors, and image compression. Image quality, clarity, and overall aesthetic appeal can all be negatively impacted by noise. There are various kinds of image noise, such as:

Impulse or Salt and Pepper Noise. Impulse noise, sometimes also called as salt and pepper noise and which is characterised by the random appearance of white and black pixels in an image is a form of image noise. Such an abrupt and sudden change in pixel intensity can be modelled [16]. The below-mentioned mathematical form is also used to represent impulse noise:

$$P(g) = \begin{cases} P_a forg = a \\ P_b forg = b \\ 0 otherwise \end{cases}$$

Figure 2 shows the analysis of probability density function of salt and pepper noise under the condition of zero mean and a variance of 0.05. Two distinct spikes have been identified in the image. The first spike also being referred to as "region a," is corresponding to a bright region but with gray level values. The second spike also being referred to as "region b," is corresponding to a dark region with high gray level values.

Gaussian Noise. Type of random noise following a Gaussian distribution is commonly known as Gaussian noise. It is also known as additive white Gaussian noise (AWGN). It is a common form of noise that can affect digital images and is characterized by random fluctuations in pixel intensity. The Gaussian distribution is symmetric and bell-shaped, and it is described by the probability density function P(g):

Fig. 2 Probability density function of salt and pepper noise [16]

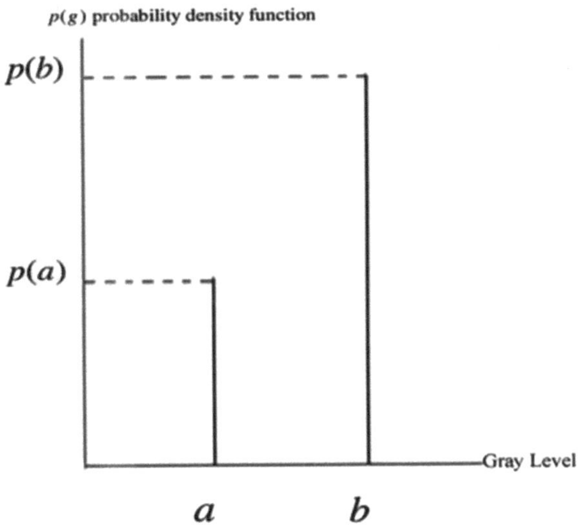

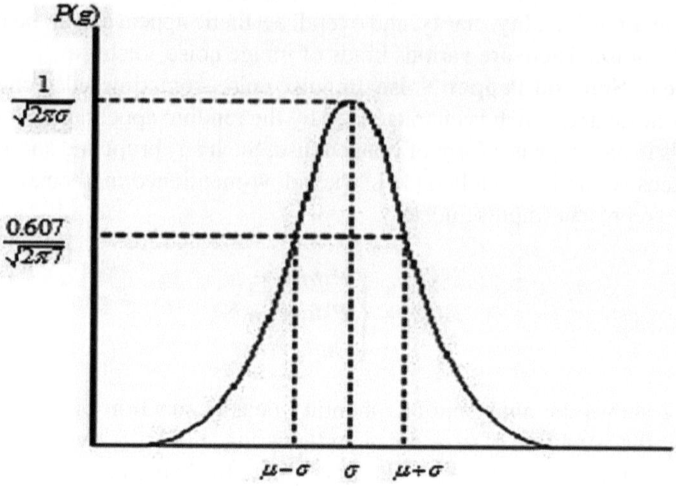

Fig. 3 Probability density function of Gaussian noise [16]

$$P(g) = \frac{1}{\sigma\sqrt{2\pi}} e^{-\frac{(g-\mu)^2}{2\sigma^2}}$$

where g is the gray value, σ represents the standard deviation of the Gaussian distribution and μ is mean. A larger sigma value indicates a higher noise spread or amplitude (Fig. 3).

3 Image Denoising Methods

To reduce noise, a variety of denoising techniques are employed. These techniques can be broadly divided into three categories.

3.1 Conventional Image Denoising Techniques

3.1.1 Mode Filter

The mode filter belongs to the traditional denoising techniques and is a sort of non-linear filtering technique used in image processing. The value of each pixel is changed in this filter to the value that appears the most often in a specified neighborhood. This filter is good for impulse noise [17].

3.1.2 Median-Filter

For image denoising and noise reduction, the median filter is a popular non-linear spatial filter. The noise is efficiently smoothed out, while edges and image details are preserved by replacing the value of each pixel with the median value of the pixel neighborhood [17].

3.1.3 Gaussian Filter

A Gaussian filter, also known as a Gaussian smoothing filter or Gaussian blur, is a linear filter commonly used in image processing to reduce noise and blur an image. It is named after the Gaussian function. The Gaussian smoothing filter is an effective low-pass filter both in the spatial domain and the frequency domain. Gaussian smoothing filters use a bell-shaped Gaussian kernel to blur images and attenuate high-frequency components, particularly noise, in the spatial domain [18].

3.1.4 Non-Local Means Filter

The Non-Local Means (NLM) filter is an image-denoising technique that leverages natural image redundancy to reduce noise while preserving image details. It is based on the principle that similar image patches have similar underlying structures, even in the presence of noise [19].

3.1.5 Adaptive Median Filter

Adaptive Median Filter is a powerful nonlinear image filtering technique that effectively removes impulse noise from images. It adjusts the window size based on the local image content, starting from a minimum size and increasing until a non-corrupted pixel is found or the maximum size is reached [20].

3.2 Wavelet Denoising Method

Wavelet-based denoising is a technique that utilizes the properties of wavelet transforms to remove noise from an image. The basic steps involved in wavelet-based denoising such as decomposition, thresholding, and reconstruction [21]. There are several commonly used wavelet basis functions, each with its properties and applications such as Haar Wavelet, and Daubechies Wavelets. In the thresholding, a thresholding function to the wavelet coefficients in each subband to separate the noise from the signal (Fig. 4).

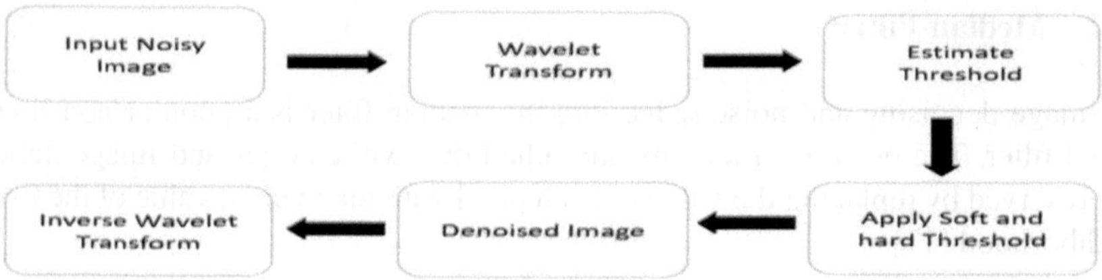

Fig. 4 Block diagram of wavelet denoising method [21]

In the reconstruction, the process of recovering the denoised signal or image from the thresholded wavelet coefficients brings the image back to its original form, but with reduced noise and preserved signal details. The effectiveness of the denoising technique relies on the accuracy of the thresholding process and the quality of the inverse wavelet transform.

3.3 Deep Learning-Based Denoising Techniques

3.3.1 Denoising Convolutional Neural Network

Convolutional neural network (DnCNN) is applied for the purpose of image-denoising which is one type of deep learning model. Training is such a way has been given to it that it removes noise from noisy images. This has been made possible by learning the underlying clean image representation. The DnCNN architecture comprises of multiple convolutional layers and with non-linear activation functions. A denoised output image was produced by DnCNN for a noisy image as an input.

Through this paper, we have tried to achieve the goal of image denoising by separating noise from a noisy image using feed-forward convolutional neural networks (CNN). The deep architecture moulds and shapes the choice of CNN, thereby enhancing its capacity and flexibility in leveraging image characteristics. The multiple layers of convolution and pooling operations aids in enabling the network in learning hierarchical representations and also help in capturing relevant features for denoising [22]. The incorporation of regularization and learning techniques, such as ReLU, batch normalization, and residual learning, further improves denoising performance and speeds up training [23] (Fig. 5).

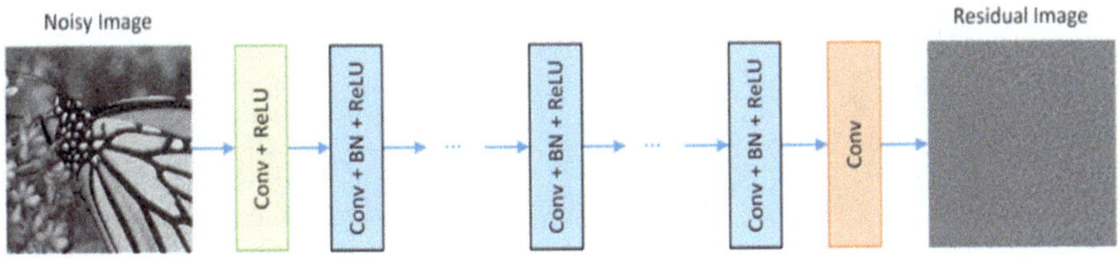

Fig. 5 The architecture of DnCNN [22]

4 Results and Discussion

4.1 Significance Measures

The paper evaluates various denoising methods using metrics like MSE, PSNR, SSIM, CC, and NAM. Methods tested include Median, Mode, Gaussian, NL-means filters, Adaptive median, Wavelet transform, and Denoising CNN. Two types of noisy input images were used: impulse noise and Gaussian noise with 10%, 25%, and 35% noise levels. Results are compared visually in Figs. 6, 7, 8, 9, 10 and 11 (Table 1, 2, 3 and 4).

Fig. 6 Denoised results of salt and pepper noise image 10%: **a** noisy image **b** Median filter **c** Gaussian filter **d** Mode filter **e** AM filter **f** NLM filter **g** Wavelet transform **h** DnCNN

Fig. 7 Denoised results of Gaussian Noise 10%: **a** noisy image **b** Median filter **c** Gaussian filter **d** Mode filter **e** AM filter **f** NLM filter **g** Wavelet transform **h** DnCNN

Fig. 8 Denoised results of Impulse Noise 25%: **a** noisy image **b** Median filter **c** Gaussian filter **d** Mode filter **e** AM filter **f** NLM filter **g** Wavelet transform **h** DnCNN

Fig. 9 Denoised results of Gaussian Noise 25%: **a** noisy image **b** Median filter **c** Gaussian filter **d** Mode filter **e** AM filter **f** NLM filter **g** Wavelet transform **h** DnCNN

Fig. 10 Denoised results of Impulse Noise 35%: **a** noisy image **b** Median filter **c** Gaussian filter **d** Mode filter **e** AM filter **f** NLM filter **g** Wavelet transform **h** DnCNN

Fig. 11 Denoised results of Gaussian Noise 35%: **a** noisy image **b** Median filter **c** Gaussian filter **d** Mode filter **e** AM filter **f** NLM filter **g** Wavelet transform **h** DnCNN

5 Conclusions

The advancements in image processing have led to significant changes in medical diagnostics. Medical imaging is slowly and steadily replacing Traditional laboratory-based diagnosis and has emerged as a new trend for disease diagnosis. This shift

Table 1 Results for Image denoising of various filters for impulse noise image in evaluation metrics

Filters	Salt and pepper noise image 10%				
	MSE	PSNR	NAM	SSIM	CC
Median filter	34.44	32.76	0.0740	0.27	0.70
Mode filter	34.89	32.70	0.0726	0.27	0.70
Gaussian filter	79.99	29.10	0.1028	0.36	0.73
NLM filter	52.40	31.52	0.0838	0.21	0.66
AM filter	45.81	30.19	0.0516	0.66	0.93
Wavelet transform	62.19	11.95	0.1728	0.46	0.76
Denoising CNN	0.0399	61.86	0.1005	0.12	0.48

Table 2 Results for Image denoising of various filters for Gaussian noise image in evaluation metrics

Filters	Gaussian noise image 10%				
	MSE	PSNR	NAM	SSIM	CC
Median filter	7.25	39.53	0.0058	0.98	1.00
Mode filter	7.25	39.53	0.0058	0.98	1.00
Gaussian filter	12.21	37.26	0.0100	0.97	1.00
NLM filter	27.45	33.74	0.0166	0.87	0.99
AM filter	48.66	31.26	0.028	0.76	0.99
Wavelet transform	108.25	27.79	0.019	0.93	0.99
Denoising CNN	0.0536	60.84	0.1498	0.31	0.60

Table 3 Image denoising results in evaluation metrics of the various filters for impulse noise image

Filters	Salt and pepper noise image 35%				
	MSE	PSNR	NAM	SSIM	CC
Median filter	56.39	30.62	0.1872	0.26	0.43
Mode filter	55.59	27.89	0.1885	0.27	0.42
Gaussian filter	111.13	30.68	0.2286	0.25	0.51
NLM filter	52.40	30.94	0.2039	0.13	0.41
AM filter	36.87	32.46	0.0277	0.89	0.99
Wavelet transform	0.0839	11.95	0.2035	0.39	0.59
Denoising CNN	0.0598	61.86	0.148	0.0534	0.251

highlights the increasing importance of. This shift concretizes the expected significance of medical imaging in facilitating accurate and efficient diagnostic procedures. Various methods for denoising images have been carefully examined, thereby, focusing on three categories of input images: salt and pepper noise and Gaussian noise. Our experiments helped us in finding the fact that the classical Adaptive

Table 4 Image denoising results in evaluation metrics of the various filters for Gaussian noise image

Filters	Gaussian noise image 35%				
	MSE	PSNR	NAM	SSIM	CC
Median filter	18.83	35.38	0.0112	0.95	1.00
Mode filter	18.83	35.38	0.0112	0.95	1.00
Gaussian filter	22.00	34.71	0.0141	0.95	1.00
NLM filter	51.46	31.02	0.0299	0.69	0.98
AM filter	72.59	29.52	0.0430	0.54	0.97
Wavelet transform	20.91	34.93	0.0123	0.97	1.00
Denoising CNN	0.039	62.27	0.135	0.171	0.589

median filter produced satisfactory results while traditional techniques were outperformed by wavelet denoising. In a remarkable feat, the adoption of deep learning based Denoising Convolutional Neural Networks (DnCNN) consistently outperformed other methods. The DnCNN could effectively remove noise from corrupted images and resulted in significantly improved denoising performance. Even if we have some promising results, we can easily ascertain that there is still huge scope for further exploration and enhancements. As a way forward approach, we can investigate alternative directions and strategies as well for achieving even better image denoising results.

References

1. Litjens G, Kooi T, Bejnordi BE, Setio AAA, Ciompi F, Ghafoorian M, Van Der Laak JA, Van Ginneken B, Sánchez CI (2017) A survey on deep learning in medical image analysis, 42, pp 60–88, Medical image analysis
2. Kinahan Paul E, Hasegawa BH, Beyer T (2003) X-ray-based attenuation correction for positron emission tomography/computed tomography scanners. Semin Nucl Med 33(3). WB Saunders
3. Perumal S, Velmurugan T (2018) Preprocessing by contrast enhancement techniques for medical images. Int J Pure Appl Math 118(18):3681–3688
4. FaDa D, et al (2014) Anisotropic diffusion filtering for ultrasound speckle reduction. Sci China Technol Sci 57:607–614
5. Lee J-S (1980) Digital image enhancement and noise filtering by use of local statistics. IEEE Trans Pattern Anal Mach Intell 2:165–168
6. Yu Y, Acton ST (2002) Speckle reducing anisotropic diffusion. IEEE Trans Image Process 11(11):1260–1270
7. Deepti M, et al. (2010) Enhancement of the ultrasound images by modified anisotropic diffusion method. Med & Biol Eng & Comput 48:1281–1291
8. Guang-Ting L, et al. (2012) SAR image despeckling using a space-domain filter with alterable window. IEEE Geosci Remote Sens Lett 10(2):263–267
9. Abd-Elmoniem KZ, Youssef A-BM, Kadah YM (2002) Real-time speckle reduction and coherence enhancement in ultrasound imaging via nonlinear anisotropic diffusion. IEEE Trans Biomed Eng 49(9):997–1014

10. Loupas T, McDicken W, Allan P (1989) An adaptive weighted median filter for speckle suppression in medical ultrasonic images. IEEE Trans Circuits Syst 36(1):129–135
11. Carlo T, Manduchi R (1998) Bilateral filtering for gray and color images. Sixth international conference on computer vision (IEEE Cat. No. 98CH36271). IEEE
12. Manjon JV, Carbonell-Caballero J, Lull JJ, Garcia-Marti G, Marti-Bonmati L, Robles M (2008) MRI denoising using non-local means. Med Image Anal 12(4):514–523
13. Bhuiyan M, Ahmad MO, Swamy M (2009) Spatially adaptive thresholding in wavelet domain for despeckling of ultrasound images. Image Process. IET 3(3):147–162
14. Sagheer, Mohd SV, George SN. (2020) A review on medical image denoising algorithms. Biomedical signal processing and control 61:102036
15. Babu JJJ, Sudha GF (2016) Adaptive speckle reduction in ultrasound images using fuzzy logic on the coefficient of variation. Biomed Signal Process Control 23:93–103
16. Ajay Kumar B, Kumar Joshi B (2015) A review paper: noise models in digital image processing. arXiv preprint arXiv:1505.03489
17. Zhu Y, Huang C (2012) An improved median filtering algorithm for image noise reduction. Phys Procedia 25:609–616
18. Shreyamsha BKK (2013) Image denoising based on Gaussian/bilateral filter and its method noise thresholding. Signal Image Video Process 7(6):1159–1172
19. Shreyamsha Kumar BK (2013) Image denoising based on non-local means filter and its method noise thresholding. SIViP 7:1211–1227
20. Pavel AL, et al. (2019) A new method for adaptive median filtering of images. In: 2019 IEEE conference of russian young researchers in electrical and electronic engineering (EIConRus). IEEE
21. Nadir M, et al. (2014) Medical image de-noising schemes using wavelet transform with fixed form thresholding. In: 2014 11th international computer conference on wavelet actiev media technology and information processing (ICCWAMTIP). IEEE
22. Kai Z, et al. (2017) Beyond a Gaussian denoiser: Residual learning of deep cnn for image denoising. IEEE Trans Image Process 26(7):3142–3155
23. Worku J, et al. (2019) Medical image denoising using convolutional neural network: a residual learning approach. J Supercomput 75:704–718

Minimization of Energy Consumption Using Optimum Resource Allocation Scheme in D2D Communication for IoT Applications

Krishna Pandey, Saurabh Chandra, Vipin Sharma, and Rajeev Arya

1 Introduction

In recent days, heavy rainfall in Himachal Pradesh and the mountainous regions of India has led to severe consequences for Haryana and Delhi. These regions have experienced significant waterlogging and flooding as a result. When heavy rains and cloud bursts occur in mountainous areas, there is often a lack of timely information dissemination to nearby regions, exacerbating the crisis. Even in the nearby ground region, proper information is not available (i.e. amount of water and timeline to reach that area). In the time of disaster timely information to civilian provides a great help to save their family and life. Even in recent days, it can be seen that government also not able to provide information of alert in time. Due to this many lives loss their life's and financial loss occur. Many people across the world lose their life, homes and financial resources due to these natural disasters.

As per the requirement of managing the disaster issues, effective monitoring systems, alert systems are required for the communication between the affected areas and nearby surroundings. To provide the awareness to the local people, an enhanced communication system is required. For this purpose, the Internet of Thing with using D2D communication plays a vital role. By using an advanced communication system, the alert system, smart monitoring system, financial loss, and people life

K. Pandey (✉) · S. Chandra · V. Sharma · R. Arya
Wireless Sensor Network Lab, Department of Electronics and Communication Engineering, National Institute of Technology, Patna,, Bihar 800005, India
e-mail: krishnap.phd20.ec@nitp.ac.in

S. Chandra
e-mail: saurabhc.phd22.ec@nitp.ac.in

V. Sharma
e-mail: vipins.phd19.ec@nitp.ac.in

R. Arya
e-mail: rajeev.arya@nitp.ac.in

K. Kumar Singh et al. (eds.), *Machine Vision and Augmented Intelligence*, Lecture Notes in Electrical Engineering 1211, https://doi.org/10.1007/978-981-97-4359-9_74

risk is minimized. D2D (device to device) communication [1] model is the best suitable model enhancing the communication capabilities for the disaster management system.

2 Related Works

Nash equilibrium is analyzed for the proposed resource allocation method considering intercell scenario in D2D communication [2]. With using sector based resource allocation methodology high performance is achieved under the aegis of 5G communication for implementation of D2D communication [3]. D2D uplink reuse is utilized with targeting the maximization of energy efficiency. Energy efficient devices are best suited for the IoT applications. Numerical results show the better solution in case of using the heuristic approach [4]. For ensuring the high data rate, resource allocation is done using mathematical problems involving the mode selection for D2D communication [5]. Greedy algorithm based linear programming method is proposed for the resource allocation with quality of service. Numerical results show the reduction in energy usage [6]. Stackelberg game model is proposed for resource allocation and power management with minimized interference constraint [7]. Outage probability is calculated for multiple D2D devices for optimal channel allocation and power management [8]. For the channel allocation MILP is formulated to enhance the throughput of the D2D system [9].

After studying the above mentioned literature [2–9], need of further optimization strategies for the resource allocation is observed as energy consumption is an important issue for the IoT application using D2D communication. Analysis of frequency allocation using different optimization methods with minimum energy consumption is required. The key insight of this paper is written as:

- With the objective of minimum energy usage in frequency allocation, a mathematical model is presented with considering the optimized resource allocation for device to device communication.
- Novel algorithm is proposed for resource allocation by applying three optimization algorithms, including Genetic Algorithm, Simulated Annealing, and Coalition Game Theory optimization algorithms.
- Analyse the convergence process of the above mentioned algorithms for resource allocation. This analysis provides valuable insights for the decision-makers in the field of D2D communication.

The paper is organized as follows. In Sect. 3, we present the system model and problem formulation. In Sect. 4, we proposed an approach for the optimized solution. Section 5 is dedicated to showcasing the results and conducting analyses through various approaches, including the Genetic algorithm, Simulated Annealing method, and Coalitional game theory method, applied to the proposed work. Finally, in Sect. 6, we draw conclusions based on a comparative analysis of resource allocation in D2D communication for IoT applications.

3 System Model and Problem Formulation

Here resource allocation-based energy consumption model is presented. Figure 1 represents the arrangement of D2D devices and cellular devices in a cell. The energy usage varies between direct D2D communication and Relay D2D communication. It seems possible that there may be two or more D2D devices depending on relay-based D2D communication. The primary emphasis of our proposed research is to optimize the choice of the most energy-efficient path from numerous available relay D2D routes.

During a relaying procedure, the D2D device (D1) initially sends its data to a different D2D device known as D2, with D2 remaining in a receiving and demodulating state. Subsequently, D2 forwards the data received from D1 to the base station, while D1 remains in a listening (receiving) state.

Energy consumption from the D2D node pairs can be expressed as

$$E_{s,d} = H_{s,T}t_{s,T} + H_{s,R}t_{s,R} \tag{1}$$

where $H_{s,T}$, and $H_{s,R}$ are the power usage of transmitter & receiver end respectively.

$$t_{s,T} = t_{s,R} = U/R_{D2,b} \tag{2}$$

where $t_{s,T}$ and $t_{s,R}$ are the duration for the transmitter state and receiver state respectively. U denotes the packet size and R represents the data rate, which can be represented with the help of the Shannon capacity theorem as

$$R_{i,j} = W_i log_2\left(\frac{KH}{N_0 W_i L_{i,j}^{\beta}}\right) \tag{3}$$

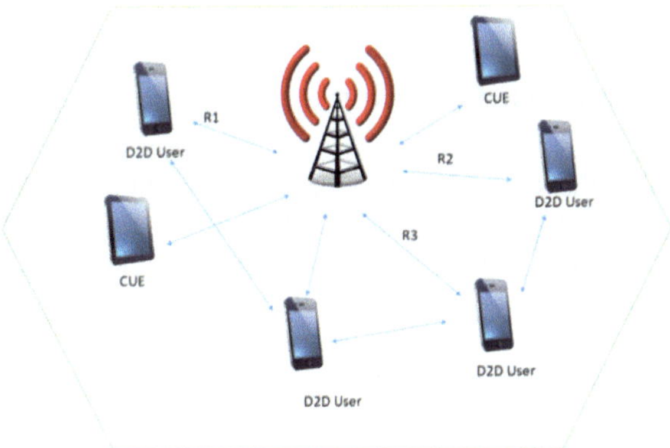

Fig. 1 D2D and cellular device in a cell

whereas $W_i, K, H, N_0, andL^{\beta}_{i,j}$ denote the bandwidth, path loss constant, power value, noise power spectral density, and distance between the i and j respectively.

By using the formulation of energy consumption and Eqs. (1), (2), and (3), we can rewrite the formula of Energy consumption [10] for D2D relay-based communication as

$$E_{T,relay} = \frac{\left(H_{D_2,T} + H_{D_1,T}\right)U}{R_{D_2,b}} + \frac{\left(H_{D_1,T} + H_{D_2,R}\right)U}{R_{D_1,D_2}} \tag{4}$$

where,

$H_{D_2,T}$ and $H_{D_2,R}$ are power consumption of the D_2 (D2D device) transmitter and receiver end.

$H_{D_1,T}$ represents the power consumption of the D_1 device.

$R_{D_2,b}$ represents data rate between D_2 (D2D device) and base station.

R_{D_1,D_2} represents data rate between D_1 and D_2 devices.

D2D (Device-to-Device) pairs of devices must be assigned frequency bands while reducing energy consumption in this resource allocation. Based on the energy values associated with each frequency band, the objective is to determine the optimal distribution of frequency bands to D2D couples.

The main objective is

$$E_{s,d} = H_{s,T}t_{s,T} + H_{s,R}t_{s,R} \tag{5}$$

where, the total energy consumption is expressed as TE(A) $=$ ΣE[X[i]] total energy consumption is expressed asTE(A) $=$ ΣE[X[i]] for all i from 0 to M-1.

N: Number of available frequency bands.

M: Number of D2D pairs.

E[i]: Energy value associated with frequency band i.

X[i]: Frequency band allocated to D2D pair i.

4 Proposed Solution

Here, the solution of the formulated problem in Eq. (5) has been provided. The problem has been solved with the help of a resource allocation algorithm by considering the minimum energy consumed by the devices which is discussed in Algorithm 1. However, the solution is not optimized as expected. We further modified the proposed approach with a genetic algorithm, simulated annealing method, and coalition game algorithm to optimize the allocation of frequency bands in order to minimize energy consumption.

Algorithm 1: Resource Allocation with consideration of minimum energy consumption constraint

```
{
Step 1: Initialize all the variables i.e., number of
available frequency bands N= 0 to n-1; and number of D2D
pairs M=0 to m-1, and calculate the respective energy
consumption of different relay paths.
Step 2: Initialize the Energy of each band randomly
Step 3: Iterate over all D2D Pairs
Step 4: Compute Allocate Frequency Based on Minimum
Energy
        TE(A) = Σ E[X[i]] for all i from 0 to M-1
      Step 4.1: Iterate over the complete frequency band
      Step 4.2: Compute Total Energy based on allocated
Frequencies
      Step 4.3: if Total Energy is less than Minimum
Energy then update the total Energy to Minimum Energy
      Step 4.4: Update the Best Band based on the Minimum
Energy
      Step 4.5: Allocate the Frequency Band corresponding
to minimum energy
Step 5: Repeat Step 4 till all allocations of D2D pairs
are done
Step 6: Plot the plot the allocation matrix as a heatmap
to visualize the allocation of frequency bands to D2D
pairs.
  end;
}
```

In the above-mentioned algorithm, with the objective of minimum energy consumption, frequency allocation is done. For calculating the energy consumption of different D2D relay devices, Eqs. (1)–(4) is utilized. By considering the energy values associated with each frequency band, this algorithm aims to allot frequency bands to D2D pairs which minimizes overall energy usage. For each D2D pair, the best available frequency band is iteratively chosen while taking the current allocation state into account.

With help of GA, simulated annealing, and coalition game method, the proposed algorithm is utilized for resource allocation considering minimum energy constraint.

4.1 Genetic Algorithm

The Genetic Algorithm [11] is a bio-inspired optimization algorithm. In the genetic algorithm for the purpose of optimization, the initial population is generated and passes through the different number of iterations with different phases such as selection, crossover and mutation. In the selection phase, with the help fitness function the best solution is achieved for the present population. In the crossover phase, recombination of several individual solutions is performed and with help of mutation, finally slight changes are incorporated into the solution to get an optimized solution of the problem by replacing the present solution with a new solution.

In D2D communication, the problem of resource allocation is solved by using the genetic algorithm. Firstly, the frequency allocation with number of users is allocated with energy usage as a fitness function. To achieve a higher fitness value, minimum energy usage is required. In the crossover phase, the frequency allocation of individual solution results in new spaces, further after the mutation process, a new solution may be replaced by the present one. By following different number of iterative processes, finally an optimized value of frequency allocation is done with minimum energy consumption constraint.

4.2 Simulated Annealing Method

Simulated Annealing [12] is a technique that comes from the idea of physical annealing method in physics. The basic idea is to get the optimal solution by increasing the temperature and lower down the temperature. Essence of this metallurgical process can be further utilized as a probabilistic optimization method to attain the optimized solutions. It involves basic tasks to attain the optimal solution using several components as.

A. Configuration
B. Move step
C. Cost function
D. Cooling time

Configuration: It gives a framework for the probable solution for the complex problem.

Move Step: Number of permittable steps after each progression that is best suitable and easy to attain towards probable solution. It moves from one step to another till there is feasible set of solution space.

Cost function: It defines the function having good placement of configuration.

Cooling time: It is the time period of cooling which means time to get a good solution with placement. It somehow defines how a lower value of temperature is suitable for getting the best solution.

For D2D communication, simulated annealing assures the optimization using the randomness to get best solution of frequency allotment ensuring minimum energy usage. Simulated annealing method ensures the likelihood to explore the sample space by providing the energy efficient resource allocation for D2D communication.

4.3 Coalition Game Algorithm

Coalition game theory [13] is an optimization strategy for achieving common and optimum output amongst different players. It introduces the fundamental of game theory and cooperative networking. In the coalition game, the solution is drawn by the group rather than looking into the individual approach. Every individual member trying to achieve the local optimum value, due to this optimum solution of the problem is drawn by the group.

In frequency allocation of D2D communication problem, coalition game plays a vital role for achieving the optimum solution. D2D pairs play a cooperating role to attain frequency bands by considering the constraint of minimum energy usage. Coalition game method provides the best suitable solution for cooperative communication by enhancing its capabilities in term of energy efficiency and minimum energy consumption. It provides a reliable method to obtain different frequency allocations in an efficient manner.

With the objective of resource allocation with minimum energy usage, we analyze that Genetic Algorithm is providing the local optimum solutions. Simulated annealing explores the sample space with a probabilistic approach and coalition game works on the cooperating optimization. Every optimization method has different features and quality which can be utilized for the desired application.

5 Results and Discussion

Here, we discuss the analytical results of the proposed work. In the proposed work, GA, simulated annealing, and coalition game method is utilized for the resource allocation problem with the objective of minimum energy usage. The proposed solution provides the framework in making decision for the best fitted approach, which can further help to give the real world D2D resource allocation solution (Table 1).

Figure 2 represents the graph between the energy values and number of population. Genetic Algorithm assure the resource allocation with constraint of minimum energy usage. It accomplishes this by using genetic operators like crossover and mutation to create new allocations, generating a population of potential allocations over several

Table 1 Simulation parameters

Simulation Parameters	Values
Radius of cell	600 m
Maximum D2D distance	300 m
D2D distance and base station distance	500 m
Bandwidth	10 MHz
Path loss constant	10^{-2}
Noise Power	-174 dbm

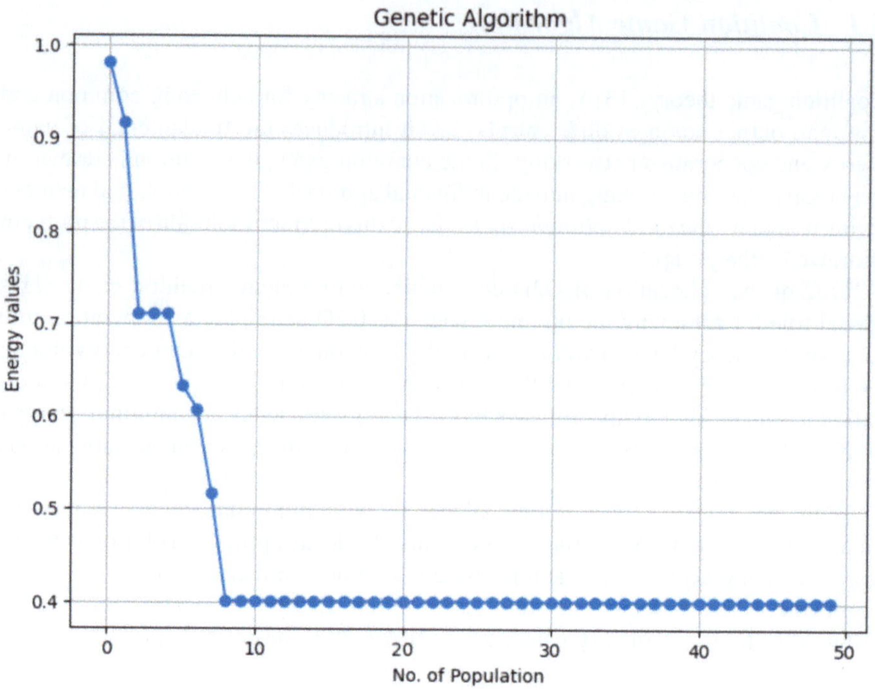

Fig. 2 Energy value versus No. of population

generations, choosing parents based on fitness, and so on. The allocation that delivers the lowest energy consumption among those that the algorithm explores will be the final outcome. After the run of the Python code, the genetic algorithm gives the best energy equal to 0.492 watts.

```
Best Allocation: [5, 5, 5, 5]
Best Energy: 0.4926337409024344
```

Overall, the best allocation and its associated energy consumption are the tangible outcomes of the Genetic Algorithm's optimization process. They demonstrate the algorithm's capability to find an efficient solution to the D2D frequency band allocation problem.

Figure 3 illustrates a frequency allocation Heatmap within the context of D2D communication, aiming minimization of energy consumption through the utilization of a Simulated Annealing algorithm for resource allocation. The color intensity represents the allocated frequency bands. Figure 3, shows the minimum energy value and frequency band given below:

```
Allocated Frequency Band 4 to D2D Pair 0 (Energy: 0.13).
Allocated Frequency Band 4 to D2D Pair 1 (Energy: 0.13).
```

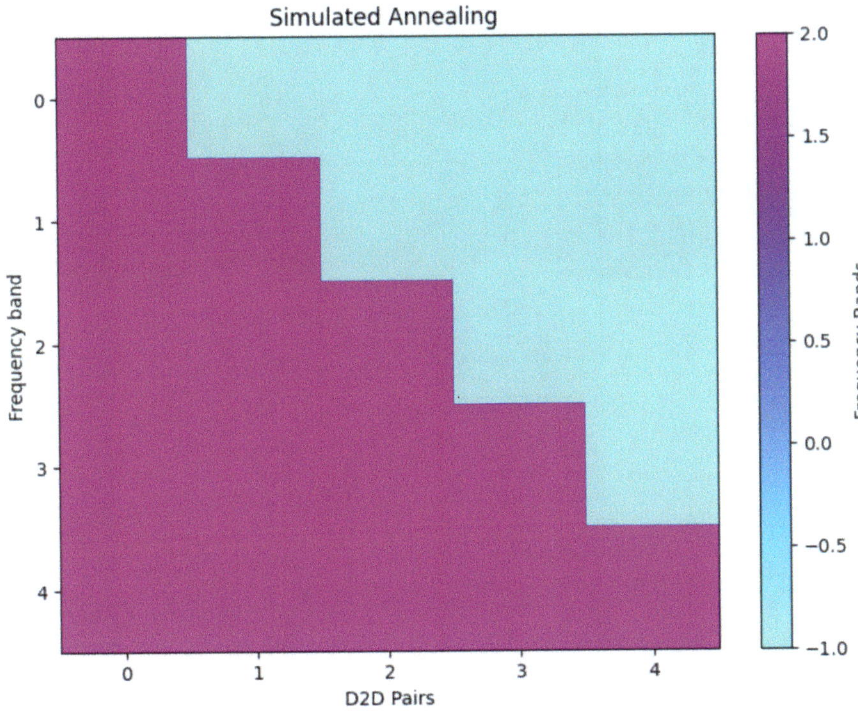

Fig. 3 Heatmap of frequency band allocation with number of D2D pairs

```
Allocated Frequency Band 4 to D2D Pair 2 (Energy: 0.13).
Allocated Frequency Band 4 to D2D Pair 3 (Energy: 0.13).
Allocated Frequency Band 4 to D2D Pair 4 (Energy: 0.13).
```

The results include the best allocation found by the algorithm and its associated energy consumption, providing insights into energy-efficient resource allocation in D2D communication systems.

Figure 4 shows how a frequency allocation method for D2D systems was put into practice with an emphasis on reducing energy consumption. By the coalition game method, we can analyze the frequency band allocation with different D2D pairs. With keeping the objective of minimum energy usage frequency allocation was done with cooperative behavior decision made by best fitted D2D pairs. The python results after the simulation are mentioned below with their minimum energy values.

```
Allocated Frequency Bands to Coalition (0,) (Energy Reduction: 0.26).
Allocated Frequency Bands to Coalition (1,) (Energy Reduction: 0.16).
```

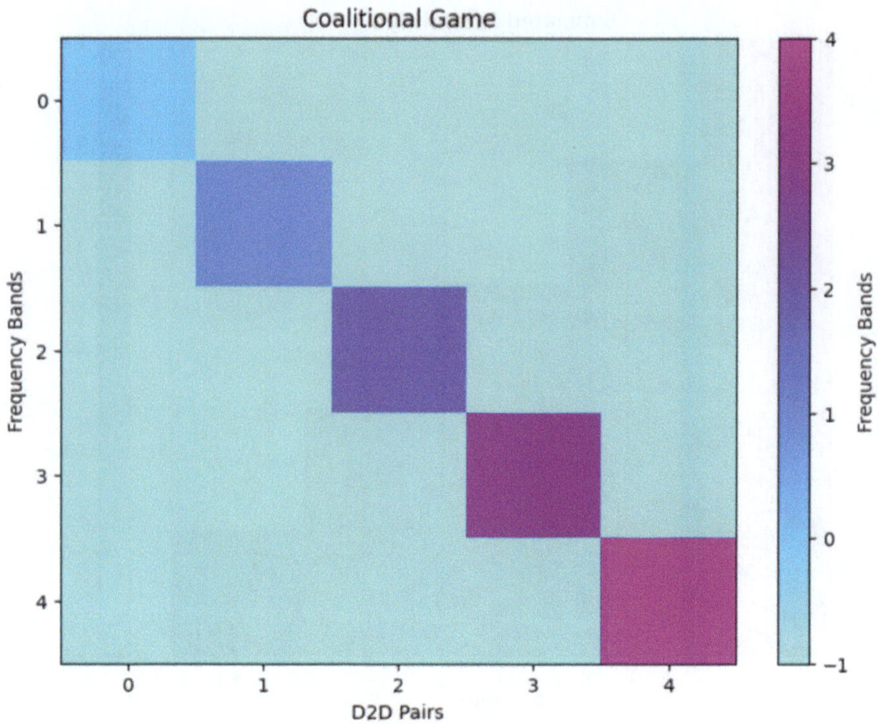

Fig. 4 Frequency band allocation using the coalitional game approach

```
Allocated Frequency Bands to Coalition (2,) (Energy
Reduction: 0.02).
Allocated Frequency Bands to Coalition (3,) (Energy
Reduction: 0.01).
Allocated Frequency Bands to Coalition (4,) (Energy
Reduction: 0.00).
```

Heatmap shows the allocation of frequency bands with minimum energy usage for D2D pairs contributing towards the concept of energy saving.

In the Fig. 5, the visualization of the convergence behavior of GA, simulated annealing and coalition game is mentioned, for the solution towards resource allocation with minimum energy usage problem. It can be seen from the graph that achievement of the optimum solution in GA depends on the population number. Simulated annealing method attains the minimum energy values using the probabilistic approach and coalition game assure the minimum energy value with band allocation using cooperative approach.

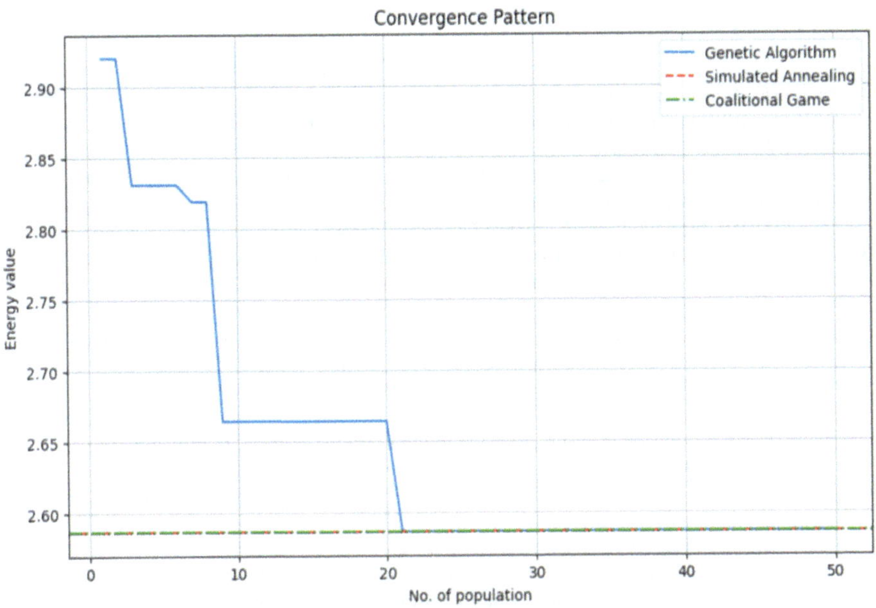

Fig. 5 Convergence pattern of GA, simulated annealing, and coalition game method

6 Conclusion

IoT (Internet of Things) devices are prominent in today's time and have the capabilities of energy consumption using the concept of D2D communication. The proposed work provides a framework for the resource allocation and energy efficient D2D devices. By using the mathematical modeling for the real time 5G communication, frequency allocation problem is designed with the objective of minimum energy usage. The proposed solution provides insight of frequency allocation including minimum energy usage. Further using the GA, simulated annealing and coalition game method, optimum resource allocation is done with minimum energy consumption. In the result section, algorithm convergence analysis shows the usefulness and applicability of optimization strategies. The detailed analysis of resource allocation with minimum energy consumption and convergence behavior of optimization technique helps the researchers and industry person in decision making for the use of suitable strategy.

References

1. Pandey K, Arya R (2021) Lagrange's multiplier based resource management for energy efficient D2D communication in 5G networks. Int J Syst Assur Eng Manag 14:722–731. https://doi.org/10.1007/s13198-020-01045-z
2. Huang J, Yin Y, Zhao Y, Duan Q (2014) A game-theoretic resource allocation approach for inter-cell device-to-device communications in cellular networks. IEEE Trans Emerg Top Comput 4(4):475–486. https://doi.org/10.1109/TETC.2014.2384372
3. Gandotra P, Jha RK, Jain S (2018) Sector-based radio resource allocation (SBRRA) algorithm for better quality of service and experience in device-to-device (D2D) communication. IEEE Trans Veh Technol 67(7):5750–5765 (2018). https://doi.org/10.1109/TVT.2017.2787767
4. Yang H, Ye Y, Chu X, Dong M (2020) Resource and power allocation in SWIPT-enabled device-to-device communications based on a nonlinear energy harvesting model. IEEE Internet Things J 7(11):10813–10825. https://doi.org/10.1109/JIOT.2020.2988512
5. Hoang TD, Le LB, Le-ngoc T (2016) Joint mode selection and resource allocation for relay-based d2d communications. IEEE Commun Lett 21(2):398–401. https://doi.org/10.1109/LCOMM.2016.2617863
6. Cicalò S, Tralli V (2018) QoS-aware admission control and resource allocation for D2D communications underlaying cellular networks. IEEE Trans Wireless Commun 17(8):5256–5269. https://doi.org/10.1109/TWC.2018.2840141
7. Dominic S, Jacob L (2018) Distributed resource allocation for D2D communications underlaying cellular networks in time-varying environment. IEEE Commun Lett 22(2):388–391. https://doi.org/10.1109/LCOMM.2017.2771778
8. Lee J, Lee J (2019) Performance analysis and resource allocation for cooperative D2D communication in cellular networks with multiple D2D Pairs. IEEE Commun Lett 23:909–912. https://doi.org/10.1109/LCOMM.2019.2907252
9. Elnourani M, Deshmukh S, Beferull-Lozano B (2021) Distributed resource allocation in underlay multicast D2D communications. IEEE Trans Commun 69(5):3409–3422. https://doi.org/10.1109/TCOMM.2021.3058374
10. Anamuro CV (2018) Simple modeling of energy consumption for D2D relay mechanism. In: 2018 IEEE wireless communications and networking conference workshops (WCNCW), pp 231–236, Barcelona, Spain. https://doi.org/10.1109/WCNCW.2018.8369017
11. Nadeem A, Cho HS (2021) Genetic algorithm-based energy efficiency maximization for social-aware device-to-device communications. IEEE Access 9:71920–71931. https://doi.org/10.1109/ACCESS.2021.3079108
12. Rutenbar RA (1989) Simulated annealing algorithms: An overview. IEEE Circuits Devices Mag 5(1):19–26. https://doi.org/10.1109/101.17235
13. Saad W, Han Z, Debbah M, Hjørungnes A, Başar T (2009) Coalitional game theory for communication networks. IEEE Signal Process Mag 26(5):77–97. https://doi.org/10.1109/MSP.2009.000000

SecureVote: Transforming Democracy with Blockchain-Based Online Elections

Tejas Sarade, Dream Tejwani, Tejas Wasekar, Tejas Hirve, Tejas Warbhe, and Manisha More

1 Introduction

SecureVote is one of the most successful developments in the election technologies market. Blockchain usage introduces an era of secure, open and easy online voting. Although in modern days a lot of technological changes have been witnessed, the electoral process still remains full with dubious acts. However, SecureVote is a sophisticated e-voting system featuring cutting edge technology to resolve the identified problems. Trust and Transparency form the core values of SecureVote. In a blockchain, each vote is secured and chained together with other transactions making it impossible to alter and thus any party can verify these ballots by themselves in an open book record. Also, it helps in maintaining the integrity of the election process as it gives a sense into the minds of the voters that they have not been cheated during the election. Security is the utmost concern for SecureVote. Such a system must employ very strong crypto-graphic algorithms that ensure security of ballot data against any interferences as well as unauthorized access to it. Also, blockchain

T. Sarade · D. Tejwani (✉) · T. Wasekar · T. Hirve · T. Warbhe · M. More
Vishwakarma Institute of Technology, Pune, India
e-mail: dream.tejwani22@vit.edu

T. Sarade
e-mail: shriram.tejas22@vit.edu

T. Wasekar
e-mail: rajkumar.tejas22@vit.edu

T. Hirve
e-mail: tejas.hirve22@vit.edu

T. Warbhe
e-mail: warbhe.tejas22@vit.edu

M. More
e-mail: manisha.more1@vit.edu

K. Kumar Singh et al. (eds.), *Machine Vision and Augmented Intelligence*, Lecture Notes in Electrical Engineering 1211, https://doi.org/10.1007/978-981-97-4359-9_75

technology encrypts every vote in such a way which ensures storing of each vote on different nodes thereby makes it hard for hackers to tamper votes or change records data. Basically, it assures safety in all stages of voting. Particularly, any voting system must be verifiable, and SecureVote stands out regarding this feature. This enables every voter to verify that they voted properly and their votes were not substituted or tampered with. Transparency, uncertainty over results' accuracy is avoided, while the electoral process seems clean due to this feature. Convenience and accessibility are among the advantages of SecureVote. The big difference between SecureVote and the traditional paper based voting procedure is that voter will now be able to cast their votes from anywhere in the world where there is access to the internet. This removes the constraints on those who have impaired movement or live-in remote places. It also lets citizens vote at their convenience, which makes it a convenient process for all. Ensuring fraud prevention was a top priority with SecureVote. Hence, SecureVote uses blockchain in order to eliminate vote rigging, buying and other forms of vote manipulation. Once a vote is entered onto the blockchain it cannot be tampered with ensuring that the voting processes remain secure and trustworthy.

Additionally, voting with SecureVote is convenient. The manual tasks such as printing, distribution and counting of the ballots have remained old school and rather expensive. Automating the voting via the stream line process by SecureVote enhances a fair and fast vote counting, hence reducing the likelihood of flaws. The process also saves time and resources making the entire electoral process smooth and more credible. Moreover, SecureVote can function as a pedagogical instrument through which children become aware of their civic duties in democratic societies. They are interactive and user-friendly, hence SecureVote applies easily among the youth who have never exercised any civic right before. Children grow up understanding that they will be the builders of a secure nation; therefore, their country must be kept free from such a dangerous threat as violence. However, SecureVote can also be regarded as scalable. Security and high-performance features are applicable to any magnitude of election be it local or national. The blockchain works in a decentralized manner, thus maintaining a safe environment for high demand. The use of SecureVote is cost efficient on the part of election organizers. Paper voting is costly since it requires printing of ballot papers and distribution of the same, including manual counting. Thus, SecureVote reduces the cost for organizers as far as costs are concerned while also saving taxpayers taxes. Such efforts also help in the reduction of manpower required for both manual and administrative work thereby channeling of the remaining resources to other relevant areas.

SecureVote is a unique platform with high standards of electoral e-voting. Trust, security, confidence, ease-of use, combating irregularities, efficiency, education, scalability and affordability are the most important aspects of the SecureVote system as well as its main feature is high level of security. The system encrypts the data employing robust cryptographic algorithms to protect it from unauthorized access. In addition, blockchain technology guarantees that each vote is encrypted and stored in multiple nodes across a network. It also makes sure that an unfitting player cannot change the results of the elections, manipulating the information.

2 Literature Survey

A new e-voting protocol proposed by Liu and Wang, which addresses the most serious problems in terms of fairness, transparency, free will and integrity in elections procedures [1]. This protocol uses such advantages of the block chain to achieve accurate vote casting and secure voter data. The system uses the blockchain protection protocol to record, evaluate and authenticate the final result of elections so that there can be more openness about how electoral votes are distributed. Basically, the proposal will enhance voters' confidence in elections.

A customized blockchain is the central focus of an integration proposal by Shahzad and Crowcroft [2] for a novel e-voting model. The system mainly seeks to ensure that the voting process is accurate, fair and secure by making use of various properties inherent in blockchain such as its decentralized approach (all steps can be run at each voter's local computer or mobile phone), immutability (once a vote has been cast), and consensus schemes for synchronizing blocks on different nodes. To make blockchain tech suitable for elections, the development team has added some changes. These involve solving concerns of scalability, efficiency and security. In theory, the proposed system would increase confidence in voting and ensure voters' right to choose a candidate freely. However, to leverage block chain technology so thoroughly for handling an effective and resilient electronic voting system is intriguing.

Racsko [3] scrutinizes blockchain's impact on democracies. This study looks deep into how blockchain could change governance. It could get rid of middlemen, make elections more transparent, and create records that you can check and can't alter. The benefits of using blockchain in democratic systems include building trust, making things accountable, and getting people to participate more. The article also notes the obstacles when using blockchain. For instance, there are technical, legal, and trust issues. You need to get people to accept and trust this technology. In conclusion, the study highlights how blockchain can transform democratic processes and strengthen democratic ideals.

"Blockchain Tech Basics" by Yaga, Mell, Roby, [4] and Scarfone K. breaks down blockchain tech. They discuss main ideas like spread-out notebooks, agreement methods, smart deals and secret codes. But they don't stop there. They also look at different uses of blockchain outside of just digital money! They remind us, security is super important for these things to work well. Things like privacy, growth potential, and how everyone agrees on updates are key. This gives you a good grasp of blockchain.

The influential index [5] is quite useful in trend analysis and an appreciation of the strengths and weaknesses of democracy internationally. The report allows us to have an understanding of how countries are faring in issues of democracy and where they need to improve their efforts. The Democracy Index is crucial for making wise decisions about which country can maintain democratic governance because it reveals the state of democracy in particular states and allows comparison with other countries. The index facilitates discussion and dialogue on democratic governance by offering a comprehensive perspective on the practice of democracy. It provides a guideline for those nations that aspire to develop their democracy institutions and it offers an insight in search of good conducts. Eventually, the Economist EIU Democracy Index enhances the comprehension of the state of health of democracy in the world and promotes democratic progress.

The study [6] Grading New Zealand government web sites (2014) examines the usability, openness and responsiveness of the NZG websites which is essential for effective democratic governance in the digital age. Ultimately, this research points out that transparency on the part of government websites needs to become a rule so people can get accurate and up-to-date information about the policy formulation procedure or decision-making process. The study further acknowledges the importance of redesigned, user friendly and responsive government websites where citizens can freely submit their views and actively communicate with officials, acting as an important pillar in fostering strong democratic trends and sense of belonging among people.

In Paper [7], we endeavor to present equilibrated perspectives on sustainability worries which are arising from the spread of blockchain technology. It understands that blockchain brings enormous possibilities for different industries and processes, such as in the area of supply chain management or financial transactions. That means higher efficiency at lower costs, greater transparency leading to better performance of transactions with improved trust. On the other hand, an article also looks at some of the hurdles to setting up a blockchain. It examines the ecological effects of deploying computationally intensive consensus mechanisms in blockchains. It also offers some possible scaling constraints on wide-spread deployment, and in this area requires more work.

The protocol employs the intrinsic characteristics of blockchain technology, such as permanence and distributed consistency [8], for a reliable and secure e-vote system. That is, it attempts to compensate the shortcomings of emerging quantum computing that may affect existing standard cryptographic tools for e-voting. The presence of the audit function means that this protocol is even more secure against a quantum attack than it would be otherwise. This verifies the validity and integrity of transactions being voted for. It helps too in identifying abnormal actions or criminal intent to interfere with the elections process.

According to the study [9], cybersecurity risk is a central factor in managing the battery's function and other related applications. This article looks into dangers and weak links, which may question the trustworthiness of data in BMS. The risks involved are such as data hacking, data misrepresentation and system downtime or failure. The paper proposes the utilization of blockchain technology to address these concerns hence improving security in BMS. Using the intrinsic advantages of a block chain, such as dispersion, immutability, and cryptographical methods enhances the integrity, transparence and safeness of date in the BMS purposes. With the help of blockchain's distributed technology, BMS data is rendered impenetrable against malicious alterations and enhances the overall credibility of the system.

This study [10] mainly explores what implications arise for trustworthiness and reliability when integrating Internet of Things (IoT) devices and blockchain technology in areas like health care delivery services, supply chain management or natural environment control. The platform utilizes the distributed ledger technology of blockchain to achieve an incorruptible method of recording and validating sensing data. However, imagine a world where health care providers can rest assured that the data collected using IoT is right & dependable. For example, imagine an accessible chain that records all steps of production with full openness guaranteeing the legitimacy of goods. Such an integrated IoT blockchain platform could transform these domains among others.

The article [11] discusses the challenges of maintaining blockchain in financial crisis. The challenges include regulatory concerns, scalability issues, monetization, and the cost of energy-value calculation. The authors argue that these challenges can be overcome through collaboration between stakeholders, regulatory clarity, and thoughtful implementation strategies.

In paper [12], it comments on the hardships found in big elections, like scalability and security. Old election systems can't always deal with so many votes or keep the process honest. The suggested system tries to fix these problems by taking advantage of blockchain technology's clear and spread-out qualities. The plan is to use a blockchain platform to make sure the whole election process is honest and open to everyone.

An article [13] dives into blockchain technology and its use with smartphones. It offers a snapshot of current developments, boasting the latest advances and innovations. The article observes various methods used to reach agreement and confirmation in blockchain systems for smartphones, highlighting different consensus mechanisms used. It also discusses what to consider when integrating blockchain into smartphones, enlightening readers on the technical side of things. The article dissects the problems faced when adding blockchain to devices with limited resources, like smartphones, and suggests possible fixes to these issues.

The article [14] talks about architecture of the blockchain based security solution for smart city explaining integration of blockchains with different aspects of urban infrastructure like transportation, health care, energy and government. Therefore, smart cities leveraging the use of blockchain as technology improves their safety and integrity of their critical systems. In addition, this piece examines specific considerations and difficulties when implementing blockchain in smart cities. The efficacy of any blockchain solution hinges on its ability to incorporate scalability, interoperability and privacy-preserving components.

The authors conduct a survey paper on the possibilities of using Blockchain as part of e-voting in [15]. Blockchain offers such advantages as transparency, security, privacy, and scalability for successful e-voting implementation. The use of blockchain would improve the reliability and immutability in electronic voting systems. The issues that need to be tackled while adopting the blockchain for e-voting is also discussed in the paper. Some of the issues include consensus mechanisms, smart contract design, among others. Moreover, the case for regulating these systems and their adoption stands as a challenge among various stakeholders.

3 Methodology

The secure and reliable process followed by SecureVote while the implementing blockchain-based voting system. Here is a method to achieve this:

1. SecureVote First Stage—Designs and Plans The first stage in designing SecureVote involves both system designs and planning.
   1.1 The members working on SecureVote work closely with leading experts in blockchain technology, voting systems, and cyber security to ensure that its systems are reliable, efficient and safe to use. It entails establishing fundamental needs, purposes, scaling, safety issues, ease, and accessibility of the system (Fig. 1).
   1.2 In this stage, the team researches and analyses of the problems with the existing voting systems and why blockchain will solve those problems. In addition, they specify the system's design, including how the block chain is incorporated, the use of other encryption methods, as well as the process of identifying users.
2. Blockchain Integration: At the heart of SecureVote lies blockchain technology. It is a distributed journal which notes down every vote along with the verification process. The team chooses an appropriate blockchain system considering such elements as security, scaling, and operation. After these steps are performed, they embed the blockchain technology in their SecureVote system so as to guarantee the security of the expected large volume of voters and transactions.

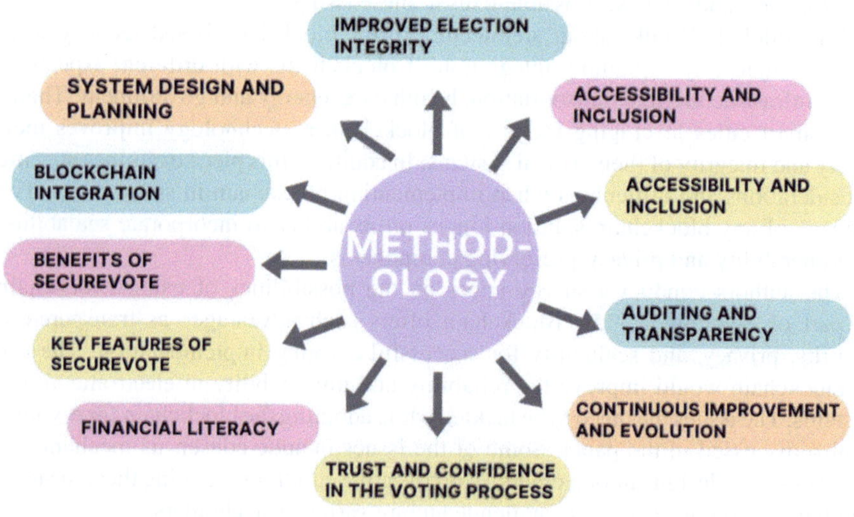

Fig. 1 Methodology

3. Key Features of SecureVote: SecureVote records every vote on the blockchain ensuring that the whole process is transparent and auditable. It ensures that the different stakeholders including citizens, election officials plus candidates can authenticate that the given result is valid. the blockchain, ensuring all the processes are transparent and auditable. This ensures that all the stakeholders such as citizen include can evaluate if the voting record is genuine and true.

   3.1 Decentralization: SecureVote is built on the P2P model in which there exists no need for any centralized authority. Therefore, this guarantees that no one entity exercises dominion over the voting process; hence, it promotes safety and consistency of the system.
   3.2 Security and Privacy: The application of secure cryptoanalysis methods enables a high degree of confidentiality in user data as well as protection of voters' privacy. For this reason, each of the vote is encrypted so that it could be decrypted and counted by only its specific receiver. It prevents identification of a particular voter, thus minimizing fraudulent actions.
   3.3 Prevention of Multiple Voting: SecureVote uses blockchain to make sure every person votes just once for only once. It curbs the risk of double registration per voter as well makes voter fraud impossible, thereby improving the elections' integrity.

4. Benefits of SecureVote: SecureVote enhances efficiency in the voting process as there is no need of manual and hardware requirements such as physical ballot counting. It minimizes the chances of human error in the entire process and makes it faster.

   4.1 Enhanced Accessibility: Using SecureVote, citizens can vote in a comfortable way from anywhere they have an access to internet. It also helps in increasing voter participation especially among those whose locations and mobility challenges make it difficult to walk to a vote-casting centre on Election Day.
   4.2 Reduced Costs: There are substantial expense associated with creating and distributing traditional paper-voting system that involves printing of ballot papers and manpower. The use of secure vote reduces all these expenses thereby making the election process economical.
   4.3 Environmental Sustainability: SecureVote is beneficial because it helps to prevent forest depletion and carbon dioxide emission related to printing and paper movement.
   4.4 Educational Opportunities: SecureVote provides an opportunity for educating children on the significance of voting and citizenship. Young ones understand online how much power the vote has in electoral process and why should they participate with such issues as a practice vote.

5. Financial Literacy: Implementation and Adoption Challenges: However, implementing SecureVote and achieving high usage do not come easy. These challenges include ensuring integrity of the voting process, gaining voter confidence, dealing with technology constraints against those who do not have sufficient

knowledge to handle the technology or the required infrastructure to operate the Internet election within the context of legal frameworks.

6. Trust and Confidence in the Voting Process: SecureVote makes use of blockchain technology to ensure that the whole process of voting is trustworthy.
   6.1 Blockchain gives confidence for voting system in SecureVote. Its transparent and decentralized tech allows any party to verify their accuracy, reducing doubts on originality. Votes go there and get stuck in a place that cannot be tampered with. This immutable permanence cements trust.
   6.2 It also makes block chain immutable whereby votes remain unchangeable after recording thus developing trustworthiness.
7. Improved Election Integrity: SecureVote lowers election deception risks. The immutability of its blockchain backbone (Fig. 2).
   7.1 Blockchain is transparent which affords unbiased review and detection of any anomalous activities or foul plays.
   7.2 The essence is that each has a chance of casting a vote, maintaining the honour of voting and the principles of democracy by restricting re-voting.
8. Accessibility and Inclusion: SecureVote busts barriers. It enables the most number of people in the society to vote.

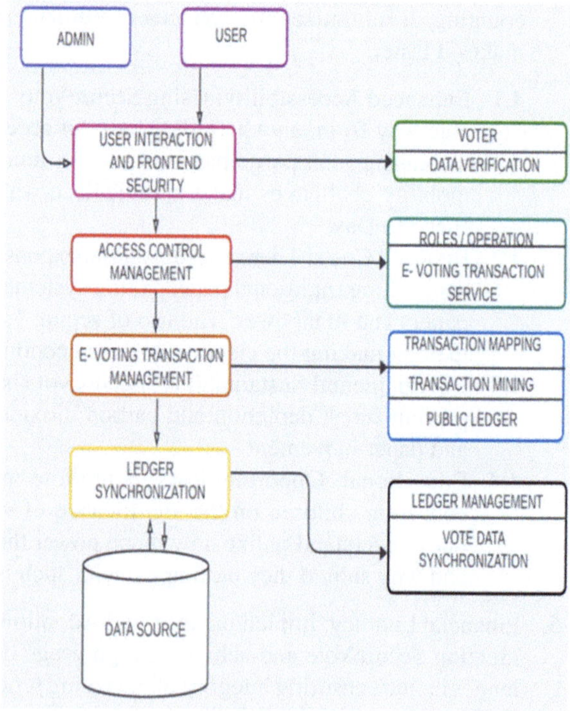

Fig. 2 Research methodology

8.1 Older people as well as the disabled can vote without experiencing any difficulty since they only need an internet connection to do that. For instance, they need computers, smartphones, or any other device.
8.2 One, SecureVote designs a user friendly interface. This assists voters in maneuvering and choosing their options with no problems. This enables them to vote with accuracy and convenience.
8.3 First, the website's availability in different languages, as well as its functional convenience, create equal opportunities for everyone. This ensures that any community can have equal voting power.

9. Data Privacy and Protection: SecureVote protects users' data through secure means including use of encryption and the block chain as a decentralised storage platform. This ensures that information concerning the voters doesn't fall into the wrong hands of unscrupulous individuals. Ensuring that citizen data is protected according to data security rules promotes trust in the processes.
10. Auditing and Transparency: It's crucial to have clear checks and openness in voting systems. This makes sure voters and people involved trust it.

10.1 SecureVote takes advantage of the transparency of its records in order to enhance elections' security and reliability. By doing this, different onlookers can verify if the voting process is reliable..
10.2 A blockchain is used so as to keep the record of all voting dealings in an irrefutable way. Therefore, this provides an unclogged as well as free audit track. Thus ensures that any person can have confidence by verifying that they are genuine results without tricking.

11. Ongoing Betterment and Development: SecureVote is built to improve continuously.

11.1 The group actively gets thoughts from users, voting officials, and safety experts to pinpoint spots for betterment. They stay in tune with blockchain technology, cipher techniques, and safety standards.
11.2 Routine checks for security and risks are done to find and fix any possible weak spots. SecureVote, by always getting better, aims to be a safe, swift, and trustworthy platform for coming elections. This, in turn, reinforces democracy and empowers people.

4 Proposed System

We're planning a new system for the first stage. Our focus? Creating a user-friendly module. This allows both the app's managers and users to interact in a smooth way. We're also researching ways to include blockchain technology. This forms the base for future parts of the project.

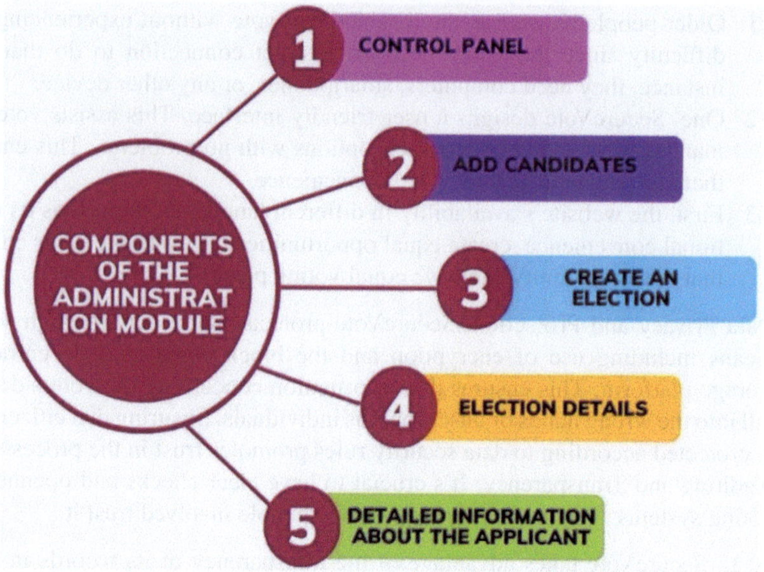

Fig. 3 Components of the administration module

Here's what we aim to do in the first stage:

Build a user-friendly module: Basically, we want to make a module that makes it easy for managers and users to interact. This module will be at the front of our app. It will make the app engaging and simple to use (Fig. 3).

Blockchain exploration: We're aiming to deeply study how blockchain tech can be incorporated into decentralized apps. This investigation will be our stepping stone in subsequent project phases where we weave blockchain into operations.

Setting the base: The first stage is all about creating a rock-solid base for our project. We'll design the user interface module and do an in-depth study on weaving blockchain tech. Thus, laying groundwork for the next stages, where we'll develop the back-end module and bring together both modules.

The Administration module consists of the following essential components:

1. Control Panel: Administration comprises one of the most important aspects of the control panel providing in-depth information for administrators along with visual representations. Here, the party's statistic will be made available alongside with voters details in a section. Therefore, they can access the control panel that allows them to watch over the entire process of application development from one perspective in addition to making better decisions about it.
2. Add Candidates: The other component enables the managers to bring in the people who are expected to take part in this process of elections. The administrator can enter the required data for every interested person like his name, party, among other parameters. This will enable candidates' information that will be

highlighted for public access thereby empowering public with facts required when casting votes.

3. Create an Election: An electoral element is also created whereby administrators can now instigate an election for decentralized applications. In the process of such elections, administrators will be able to specify a certain period within which the end-users would place the vote in the application, starting from and ending at a particular time. It gives administrators a chance to control the flow of the entire election process.
4. Election Details: Administrators can change the status information of their current elections in the election details component. It involves vital statistics like the beginning and ending date for the polls and any other changes required. Administrators can easily make adjustments to the elections aspects, correctness, and ensuring that the system is modernized.
5. Detailed Information about the Applicant: It acts as a database for all candidate information entered by the administrators. Section on application details gives administrators an easy time inputting more information about candidates like qualification, work-experience and political promise. This guarantees that all voters have access to detailed candidate profiles in order to cast a better vote (Fig. 4).

Components of the User Module: The User module comprises the following integral components:

1. Control Panel: Also known as the dashboard, is the main place users meet within the User section. It gives users a streamlined board showing details about parties and candidate profiles. With the control panel, users can effortlessly find important details about the involved parties and candidates, helping them make well-judged choices when voting (Fig. 5).

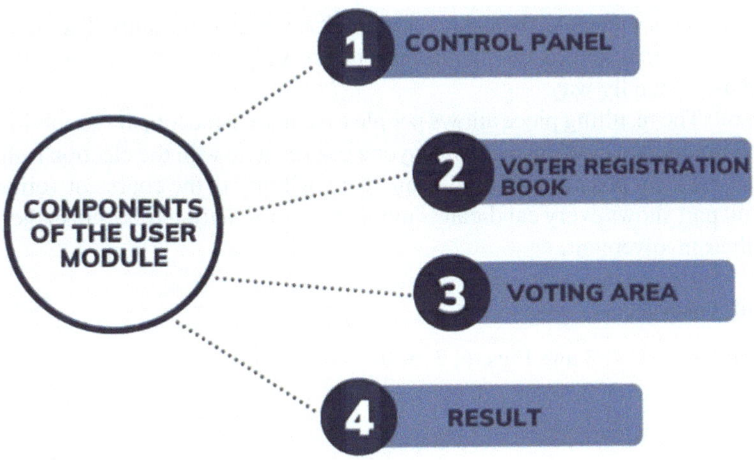

Fig. 4 Components of the user module

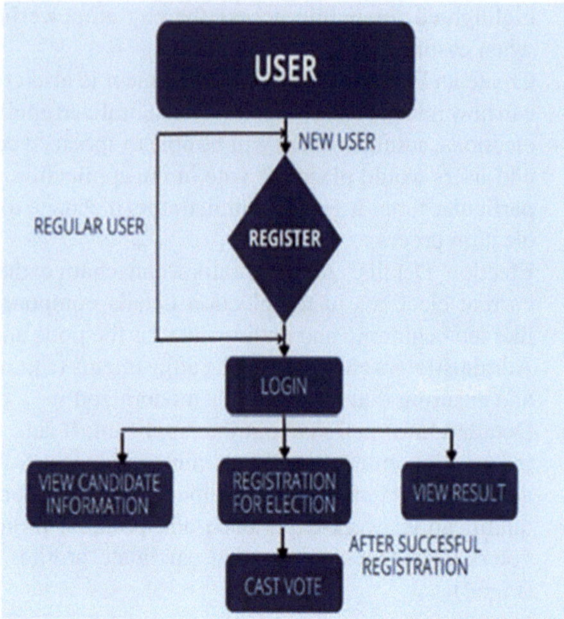

Fig. 5 Flow of system

2. Voter Registration Book: For users to vote, they've got to register first. The register-to-vote part makes sure voting's easy and safe. It checks who users are to stop fake voting. Users will be asked for their personal info, and have to do important steps to become voters in this online app.
3. Voting Area: After they've registered, voters are smoothly guided to the voting page. This voting zone component offers a simple to understand, intuitive platform for casting votes. Voters can easily look through the candidate list, assess their profiles, and make their choices without stress or uncertainty. The voting area guarantees that voter's democratic privileges are practiced in a straightforward and user-friendly way.
4. Result: The resulting piece allows people to remain in the loop by supplying them with immediate election results. Anyone can see who won the election right after votes are cast, promoting fairness and responsibility in the course of voting. The result part shows every candidate's number of votes, letting folks grasp the power of their involvement.

Table of Analysis

See Tables 1, 2, 3, 4, 5 and Figs. 6, 7, 8, 9.

Table 1 Comparison

Feature/factor	Secure vote
User interface	Elegant design
Account types supported	Citizen access
Budgeting tools	Not applicable
Investment tracking	Not applicable
Credit score monitoring	Not applicable
Security features	Blockchain technology
Customer support	Expert support
Pricing	Free and accessible to all
Education	Civic engagement and awareness
Accessibility	Internet access

Table 2 Benefits

Benefit	Description	Importance (%)
1. Increased voter participation	Encourages higher voter participation in online elections by providing convenient access from any location with internet	0.2
	Access	
2. Enhanced security and integrity	Ensures the integrity of the voting process by leveraging blockchain technology, preventing	0.15
	Multiple voting and fraud	
3. Efficient and accurate results	Reduces errors in the election process and delivers faster, more	0.14
	Accurate election results	
4. Civic education	Provides an opportunity	0.12
	To teach citizens, including children, the value of democracy and active citizenship	
5. Empowerment	Empowers citizens to actively participate in shaping their nation's future by offering a secure and transparent voting platform	0.18
6. Convenience	Enables convenient voting from anywhere with internet access, making the process more accessible and inclusive	0.13
7. Transparency and Trust	Builds trust in the election process through	0.08
	Transparency in recording and verifying votes	

5 Scope of Research

A blockchain-based voting system, has an amazingly wide scope for research. The directions that could be taken up for researching could include the technical side of block chain technology, its use in voting systems and possible effect on democracy.

Table 3 Comparison

Aspect	Aspect (%)	Objectives
Performance	74	Make vote times faster for smoother elections
Security	80	Keep a steady eye on and fix key flaws to keep systems safe and sound
User experience	83	Better the user space and options to bump up user happiness and activity
Traffic handling	70	Tweak the system to handle voter crowds on election days
Feature updates	90	Refurbish and bring in fresh features to keep things current
Maintenance costs	85	Pinpoint areas where we can save money, but still keep security and speed in check
Disaster recovery	93	Forge and uphold a full disaster recovery strategy, to safeguard all data
Accessibility	85	Rephrase-make sure any and every citizen can use our platform by meeting inclusivity standards

Table 4 Results

Metric	Description	Results/ score (%)
Voter turnout rate	Percentage of eligible voters who participated in online elections	75
Integrity assurance rate	Percentage of voters who expressed trust in the integrity of the online voting process	85
User engagement rate	Percentage of users actively participating in shaping the nation's future through Secure Vote	80
Accessibility index	Measurement of the ease of access and inclusivity in the online voting platform	90
Voter satisfaction score	Overall satisfaction rating of voters using secure vote for online elections	99

An example of possible research into SecureVote's security is mentioned further. This entails exploring the cryptographic techniques employed for the security and secrecy of the voting procedure and determining possible attack exploits as well as their responses. The study on user experience and accessibility could be a very interesting topic. By doing this, researchers will be able to determine how to build an instinctive and user-friendly interface for SecureVote so that even kids in different cultures will be able to comprehend the voting system. Moreover, studies can be done on how SecureVote has had an impact on voting. This helps to determine if the system leads more people to vote and makes them feel empowered by having

Table 5 Analysis

Aspect of analysis	Key points/findings	Numerical data (for graph/ chart) (%)
1. Research objectives	- Enhance democracy through a secure and transparent online voting platform	78
	- Eliminate traditional paper-based ballots for online voting	65
	- Increase user participation in the voting process	10
2. Problem statement	- Inadequate security and transparency in online voting	27
	- Difficulty for citizens to cast votes remotely	6
3. Technological innovation	- Leveraging blockchain technology for voting integrity	42
	- Prevention of multiple voting	88
4. Advantages	- Increased efficiency in the voting process	95
	- Reduced errors in vote counting	97
	- Opportunity to teach citizenship to children	82
5. Targeted impact	- Strengthening democratic principles	86
	- Enabling citizens to actively participate in choosing their nation's future leaders	22
6.Security and transparency	- Usage of blockchain technology adds high security to the voting process	85
	- Also having full transparency in recording and verification of votes	84

a voice in their affairs. Besides, a study can be done regarding the scalability and performance of the blockchain based voting mechanisms such as SecureVote. This approach would help in investigating different approaches of handling millions of votes at once, optimize the processing time, identify bottlenecks and improve the general performance as well as the practicality of the whole system. Additionally, researchers can examine the societal and political ramifications of SecureVote. That they can use case studies and surveys to gauge perception, acceptance, trust in the system and bias.

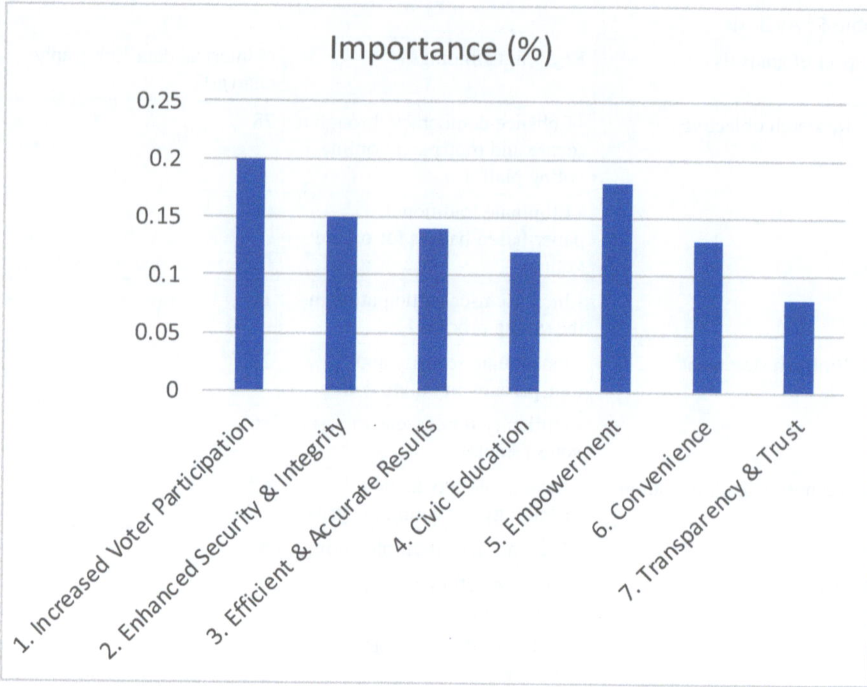

Figure 6 Benefits

Fig. 6 Benefits

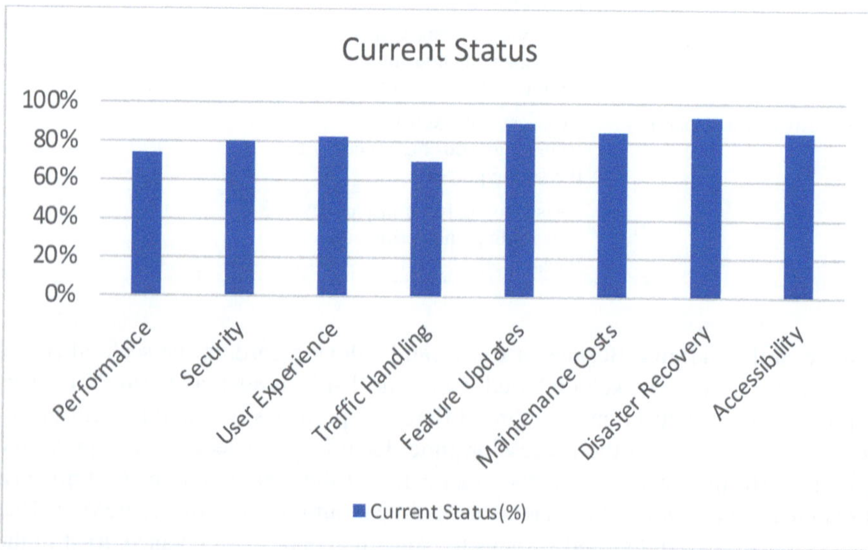

Fig. 7 Comparison

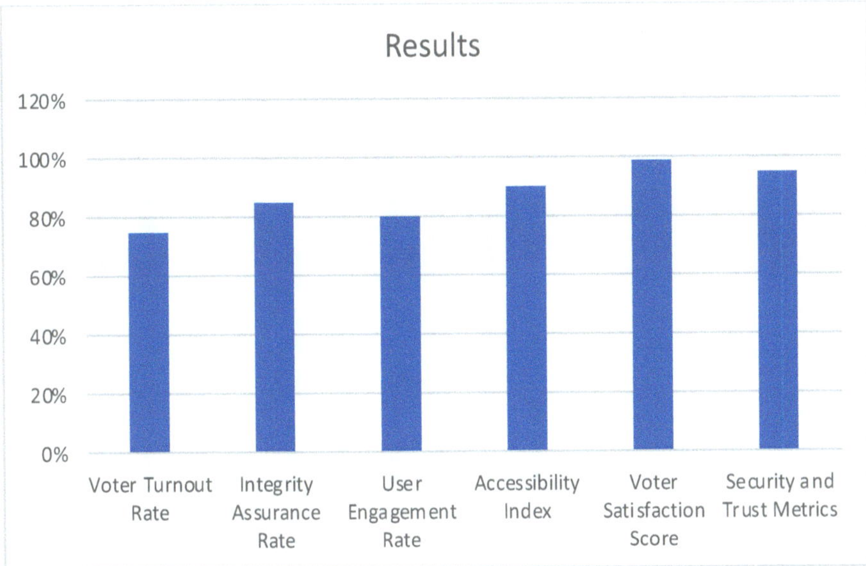

Fig. 8 Results

6 Future Scope

SecureVote involves a number of pillars. Initially, the system relentlessly seeks to improve its security, with high-level safeguarding of voter privacy as key considerations. It involves carrying out advanced studies in advanced cryptography while also seeking other alternatives like multi-factor authentication. Moreover, SecurableVote should be easier to navigate and more convenient to use. Continuous studies on users' needs to improve UX, creating mobile apps, and including features of accessibility to address the needs of all.

individuals with disabilities. The other line of inquiry is an effort that is aimed at combining SecureVote with artificial intelligence, Internet of things, and biometric technologies. The use of these technologies is used by the researchers in an attempt to improve authentication, increase security and develop a better voting experience. Moreover, SecureVote use increases with time, making it essential to improve on its ability to scale and enhance efficiency. For example, this involves the examination of methods for more operations, perfecting the consensus systems, and the low levels of the energy consumption to enable smooth operations. In addition, it presents an opportunity for its use outside the country in international adoption. Working with governments, the international organizations, and the election committees may be able to customize for different demand that might be political and social, and even more legal in the various countries.

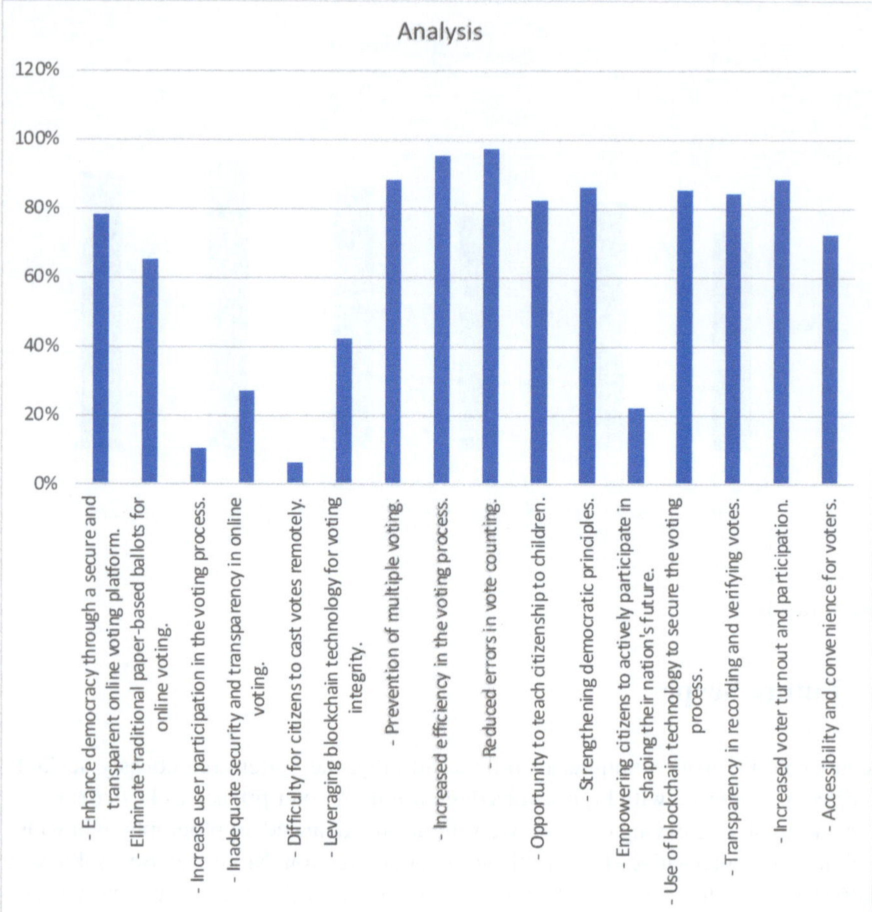

Fig. 9 Analysis

7 Conclusion

There are some crucial areas in the development of SecureVote. Additionally, the improvement of the security means for the system in maintaining the highest level of integrity and secrecy during the election process is carried out constantly. It is about conducting researches on advanced cryptography methods and also studying other secure approaches such as multiple factor authentication. Additionally, enhancing the user interface and ease of access in SecureVote is vital. Efforts continue with user studies for better user experience, mobile apps for convenience, and inclusion of accessibility support.

Secure Vote: A new democratic system driven by blockchain technology. SecureVote has overcome the challenges accompanying with paper based voting and allowed people to vote from anywhere using internet security. Blockchain enables transparency in vote authentication thereby eliminating fraud and increasing public interest in the voting process. Besides that, SecureVote is highly efficient, more error-free than other voting methods, it allows instructing the young on civic participation in a democratic society. The overall purpose for SecureVote is to enhance democratic principles and grant individuals an opportunity to influence decisions that will determine the destiny of a country.

References

1. Liu Y, Wang Q (2017) An E-voting protocol based on blockchain. IACR Cryptol ePrint Arch
2. Shahzad B, Crowcroft J (2019) Trustworthy electronic voting using adjusted blockchain technology. IEEE Access
3. Racsko P (2019) Explores the intersection of blockchain technology and democracy in a paper titled “Blockchain and Democracy” published in the journal Social and Economic Studies
4. Yaga D, Mell P, Roby N, Scarfone K (2019) Provide an overview of blockchain technology in a paper titled “Blockchain technology overview” available on arXiv
5. According to the economist EIU Democracy Index, a report on global democracy, the index can be accessed online and was last updated on January 18, 2020. You can find it at
6. In a study conducted by Cullen and Houghton in 2000, they assessed the effectiveness of New Zealand government websites in promoting democracy online. Their findings were published in the Government Inform Quart J. https://doi.org/10.1016/S0740-624X(00)00033-2
7. In a research paper by Schinckus, published in Energy Research & Social Science in 2020, an examination of the sustainability aspects of blockchain technology is provided
8. Gao Z, Guo J (2019) Hu published a research paper titled “An anti-quantum e-voting protocol in blockchain with audit function”. IEEE Access J
9. Kim O, Faika M, Di L, Lee (2020) Offer an overview of the cyber-physical security of battery management systems and the adoption of blockchain technology in their paper published in the IEEE J Emerg Selected Topics in Power Electron
10. Hang and Kim presented the design and implementation of an integrated IoT blockchain platform to ensure the integrity of sensing data
11. Chang, Baudier, Zhang, Xu, Zhang, and Arami conducted a study on the impact of blockchain on financial services. https://doi.org/10.1016/j.techfore.2020.120166
12. Wang, Sun, He, Pang, and Lu discuss the implementation of a large-scale election system based on blockchain technology in their paper published in Procedia Computer Science in 2018. https://doi.org/10.1016/j.procs.2018.03.063
13. Ometov, Bardinova, Afanasyeva, and other researchers present an overview of blockchain technology in smartphones. https://doi.org/10.1109/ACCESS.2020.2998951
14. Hakak, Khan, Gilkar, Imran, and Guizani explore the use of blockchain technology for securing smart cities in their research paper published in the IEEE Network magazine in 2020. https://doi.org/10.1109/MNET.001.1900178
15. Çabuk, Adiguzel, and Karaarslan investigate the feasibility and suitability of blockchain techniques for e-voting systems in their survey published on arXiv in 2020. https://doi.org/10.17148/IJARCCE.2018.7324.2002.07175

A Systematic Literature Review on Mathematical Modelling and Verification of Human Cardiovascular System

Snehanshu Shekhar, Anupam Kumar, and Ashish Sharma

1 Introduction

Heart disease or Cardiovascular Disease (CVD) is among the dominant causes of mortality incidents at the global level over the last 2 decades; gradually the number of casualty due to heart disease is rising. Cardiovascular Diseases (CVD) or heart disease cases surfaced almost twice over the period, from 271 million (1990) to 523 million (2019), and the cases of heart disease deaths rose from 12.1 million to 18.6 million, thereby representing 32 per cent of total deaths from all causes as per WHO data [1]. Another major cause of concern is casualties due to cancer. According to Global Cancer Observatory, there are 36 types of cancer reported from 185 countries worldwide, in 2020 which has also been published in American Cancer Society Journal. Cancer is another major and increasing cause of loss of human life worldwide. It is momentous to identify and model the regions with higher rates of CVDs and cancer. Further, mathematical modelling of heart and cancer will abet in understanding the reasons of their augmentation and also help in controlling them. Mathematical modelling of heart has helped in understanding timed automata and hybrid automata for heart aberrancy and implementation of pacemaker to partially restrict the effect of CVD. Mathematical modelling of cancer will nurture the application of different drug administration techniques for the cure of cancer and also assist in understanding the causes of the rapid spread of the disease. Different control models have been

S. Shekhar
SMIEEE, Department of ECE, IIIT Kota; Department of ECE BIT Mesra, Jaipur Campus, Jaipur, India

A. Kumar (✉)
Department of ECE NIT Patna, Patna, India
e-mail: anuanu1616@gmail.com; anupam.ec@nitp.ac.in

A. Sharma
Department of CSE, Manipal University Jaipur, Jaipur, India
e-mail: sharma.ashish@jaipur.manipal.edu

K. Kumar Singh et al. (eds.), *Machine Vision and Augmented Intelligence*, Lecture Notes in Electrical Engineering 1211, https://doi.org/10.1007/978-981-97-4359-9_76

implemented and can be devised for implementation for sanative and other cures and control of diseases [2, 3]. In addition, many fuzzy-based control schemes can be used to control these healthcare applications [2–9]. Based on the mathematical modelling and the differential equations used for the representation of the diseases, a number of timed and hybrid automata models have been developed for flawless representation and eradication and controlling of the subject disease.

2 Time-Series-Based Study and Modelling of Vitals and Control Schemes

The different cardiovascular system modelling are addressed such as hybrid automata, fractional order differential and timed automata. Some of them are addressed here in brief.

2.1 Heart and Pacemaker

Major vitals of health care like cardiovascular variables, behaviour of carcinoma cells, etc. can be controlled if a quantitative and qualitative understanding of these systems are developed. The significant works of Hunt and Harrington 1897 [10, 11], Rosenblueth and Simeone 1934 [12] are basic works which laid the foundation for quantitative analysis of cardiac variables, such as heart rate, arterial blood pressure, the shape of ECG and stroke volume. Based on these quantitative works, basic Cardiac Electrophysiology modelling and analysis were done by Jaye et al. [13] which laid the foundation for mathematical design and analysis of heartbeat controlling devices like pacemaker. Mercury manometer was used to measure the blood pressure of a calf which was found to be adequately high (100 mm. of Hg) [10, 11]. Diminished action of both auricle and ventricle was observed when the outer end of the wandering nerve was excited for moderate intensity of currents. The result coalesced with the work of Franck, 1890, for dogs [14]. It causes disparity due to stimulation of the nerves and stellate ganglion.

Figure 1 shows the stimulation result of vertebral nerve. Stimulation of nerve resulted in augmentation of ear, but thread from the second posterior part of the

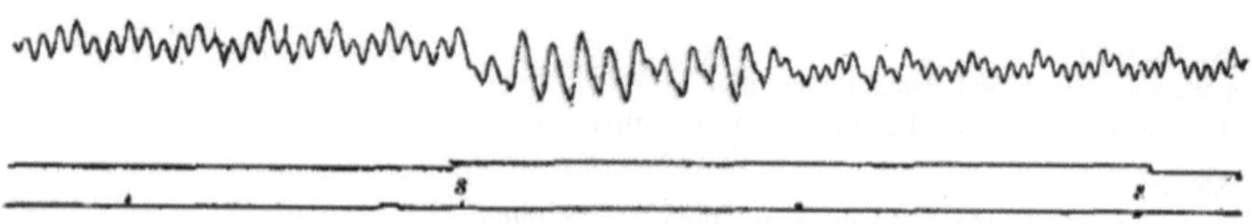

Fig. 1 Stimulation of the vertebral nerve [10]

mandible transfer prominently superceded in result cavity to spinal cord. The contrast in effect of stimulus could be explained by the assumption that the ventricles contained more fibres. Bayliss and Starling* also noticed identical functional separation from well-known catalysts for dogs [15]. The strength of current used by Ried Hunt and D. W. Harrington, auditory strike is come after by heart-chamber, and the effected to the rate of ear and cavity, is almost the algebraic sum of effects produced separately. In the work of Hunt and Harrington, the heart rate, in anaesthetized animals, ranged from 144 to 218 beats/minute and normal blood pressure was 120–135 mm of mercury.

2.2 *Modelling of Heart*

Several studies were made during 1890–1970 to determine the rate of heartbeat and blood pressure during normal conditions and under the effect of anaesthesia. This study led to the modelling of heartbeat which paved way for mathematical modelling and further analysis of heart and aberrant heart conditions. The utilization of this model extends for building of pacemaker. Heart pumps oxygenated blood in a body and pumping de-oxygenated blood collected from different parts of body to lungs for purification or oxygenation. Based on the different pioneer research works, a comparative study of heartbeat rate and blood pressure under normal and anesthetized conditions has been done and summarized in Table 1.

Table 1 Comparative study of heartbeat rate and blood pressure under normal and anesthetized conditions

Author(s)	Year of work	Work on (mammal(s)/animal(s))	Heartbeat rate	Blood pressure	Remarks/condition
Hunt and Harrington [10, 11]	1897	Calf and Opposum	Calf-156 beats/minute Opposum-144–218 beats/minute	Calf-100 mm. of Hg. Opposum-120–135 mm. of Hg.	Anaesthetized
Rosenblueth and Simeone [12]	1934	Cat	150–261 beats/minute	80–100 mm of Hg.	Anaesthetized
Jaye, et al. [13]	2010	Human	60–100 beats/minute	70–130 mm of Hg.	Normal condition
Franck [14]	1890	Cat and Dog	Cat-150–261 beats/minute Dog-80–140 beats/minute	Cat- 80–100 mm of Hg. Dog-70–145 mm of Hg.	–
Bayliss and Starling [15, 16]	1892, 1902	Dog	80–110 beats/minute	70–90 mm of Hg.	Anaesthetized
Hough [17]	1892	Cat and Dog	Cat-162–192 beats/minute Dog-80–110 beats/minute	Cat-120–180 mm. of Hg. Dog-70–90 mm of Hg.	Anaesthetized

Fig. 2 Human heart

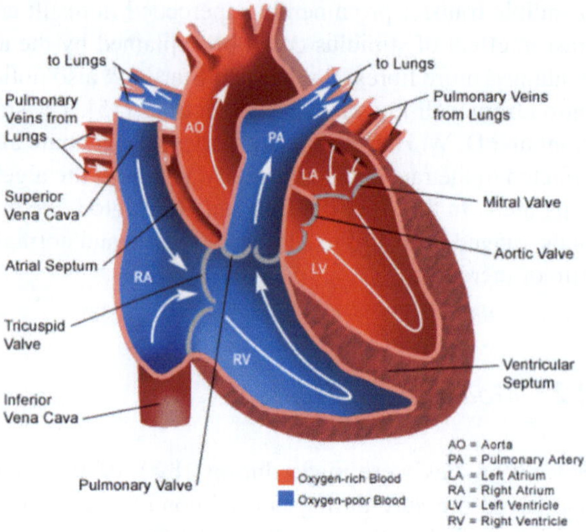

Figure 2 shows different parts of the human heart which broadly consists of four chambers, namely left atrium and ventricle, and right atrium and ventricle. Left and right atria are the parts of heart which collect oxygenated blood from lungs and de-oxygenated blood from the whole body, respectively. This blood is then pumped into left and right ventricles respectively. Oxygenated blood is pumped into through left ventricle then pumps while right ventricle pumps de-oxygenated blood into lungs for purification. Complete pumping process is autonomous without mixing of oxygenated and de-oxygenated bloods at any point. This is represented using a closed circulation model of heart as shown in Figs. 3 and 4 and has been used as basis for mathematical modelling of heart.

The parameter estimation of this process is done by the factor cardiac output, defined mathematically as Cardiac output, CO,

$$CO = \frac{\text{(volume of blood being pumped by heart (ventricle), v)}}{\text{(time, t)}} \quad (1)$$

i.e., $CardiacOutput \propto Heartbeat$

CO is determined as

$$CO = \text{Heart rate, HR} \times \text{ Stroke volume, SV} \quad (2)$$

Arterial Blood Pressure, ABP, also known as Mean Arterial Pressure (MAP), denoted as P_{mean}, is given as

$$MAP, P_mean = P_d + \frac{1}{3}(P_s - P_d) \quad (3)$$

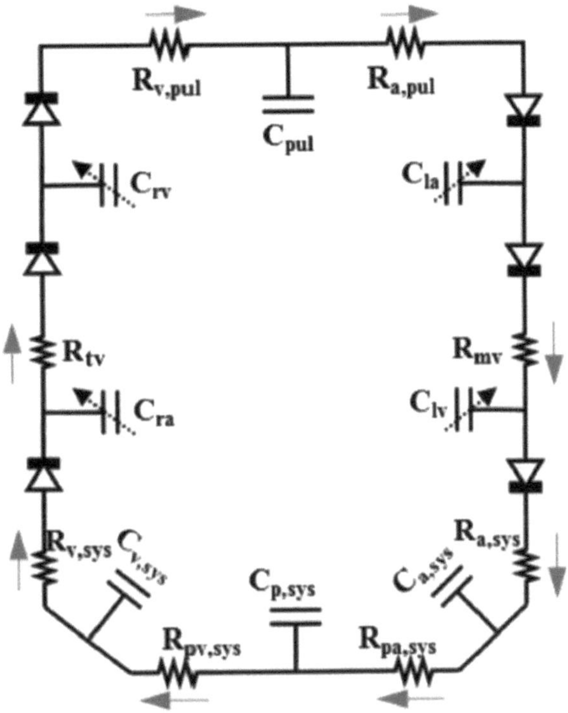

Fig. 3 Closed circulation loop model for assessing the heart model [18]

where P_mean is mean arterial pressure
P_d is diastolic pressure
P_s is systolic pressure. Hence, mean arterial pressure is a result of multiplication of cardiac output and systematic vascular resistance (SVR), mathematically given as

$$MAP, P_mean = CO \times\ SVR \tag{4}$$

The left ventricular volume, i.e., the amount of blood pumped by the (left) ventricle is a significant parameter to determine systematic vascular resistance and cardiac output . The left ventricular volume V_{lv} is given as

$$V_lv = (\frac{(\frac{4}{3}) \times \pi K_lv(r_lv)^2 l_lv)}{2} \tag{5}$$

where r_{lv}—ventricular radius (left)
l_{lv}—long axis length
K_{lv}—coefficient to embrace effect of the long axis contraction. It is used for scaling the proportionality between the ventricular volume and radius in a cardiac cycle. Ventricular longitudinal axis length, l_{lv}, is considered constant for a cardiac cycle, so, from the left ventricular radius (r_{lv}) given as

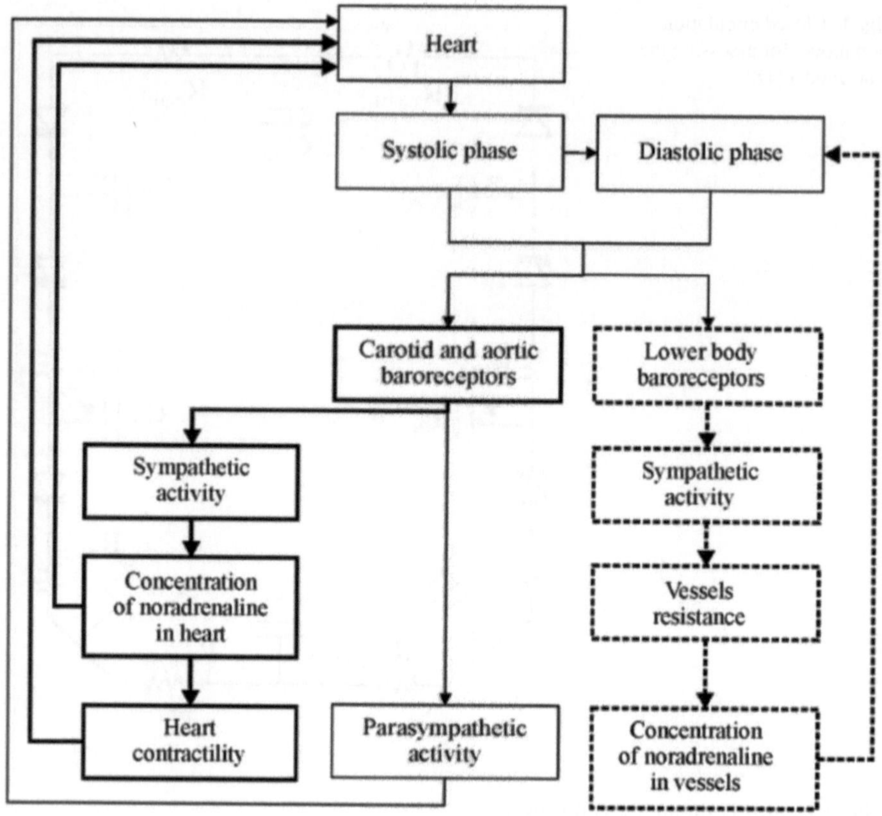

Fig. 4 Model of heart [20]

$$r_{lv} = \sqrt{\frac{6V_{lv}}{(4\pi K_{lv} l_{lv})}} \tag{6}$$

The time rate of variation of the left ventricular radius is be given as

$$\frac{dr_{lv}}{dt} = (\frac{3(\frac{dV_{lv}}{dt})}{(4\pi K_{lv} l_{lv})})(\frac{(6V_{lv})}{(4\pi K_{lv} l_{lv})})^{-(\frac{1}{2})} \tag{7}$$

The rate of change of the left ventricular volume $\frac{dr_{lv}}{dt}$ can be alternately represented as the difference of flow rate of blood through the mitral and aortic valve represented as (Q_{mitv}, Q_{aorv}), respectively:

$$\frac{dV_l v}{dt} = Q_m v - Q_a v \tag{8}$$

Hence, differential time rate of change of the left ventricular radius (dr_{lv}/dt) becomes

$$\frac{dr_{lv}}{dt} = (\frac{3(Q_{mitv} - Q_{aorv})}{(4\pi K_{lv} l_{lv})}) \frac{(6V_{lv})}{(4\pi K_{lv} l_{lv})})^{-\frac{1}{2}} \tag{9}$$

The ventricular pressure during contraction and the relaxation phases ($p_{lv,a}$) is described using various related parameters such as activation function ($f_{act,lv}$), end-systolic elastance ($E_{es,lv}$), the left ventricular radius ($r_l v$) and left ventricular radius at presumed zero pressure volume ($r_{lv,0}$):

$$p_{lv,a}(t) = E_{es,lv}[\frac{4}{6}(\pi K l_{lv}((r_{lv})^2 - (r_{lv,0})^2)] f_{act,lv}(t) \tag{10}$$

The expression in the square bracket shows the differential volume of the left ventricle (V_{lv}) and the left ventricle at zero pressure ($V_{lv,0}$), as described above in equation 10.

The activation function ($f_{act,lv}$) driving the left ventricular contraction is given below

$$f_{act,lv}(t) = \begin{cases} \frac{1-cos(t/T_1)\pi}{2} & 0 \leq t < T_1 \\ \frac{1+cos((t-T_1/T_2-T_1)\pi)}{2} & T_1 \leq t < T_2 \\ 0 & T_2 \leq t < T \end{cases} \tag{11}$$

where t is the time over a cardiac cycle, T_1 is the time at the end of systole,

T_2 is the time at the end of ventricular relaxation and T is the duration of the cardiac cycle. A similar type of model of heart is given by Yawei Wang et al. [10] in the form of a closed-loop system as shown below.

Heart can be represented by a differential equation 12 [19] as below

$$\frac{dQ}{dt} + \frac{3Q}{V}\frac{dV}{dt} - \frac{2LQ^2}{V^2}\frac{dV}{dz} + \frac{4\pi\mu L}{V}Q + \frac{V}{2\rho L}\frac{dP}{dz} = 0 \tag{12}$$

where Q, L and V represent the blood flow rate, length of heart chamber and volume of heart chamber, respectively, and u, v and w are velocity components in x, y and z directions, respectively, ρ is the density of blood, P is the blood pressure, and μ is the kinematic viscosity of blood. After applying assumptions, the equation is reduced as below

$$-\frac{3Q}{V}\frac{dV}{dt} + \frac{4\pi\mu L}{V}Q + \frac{V}{2\rho L}\frac{dP}{dz} = 0 \tag{13}$$

$$\Longrightarrow \frac{dV}{dt} - \frac{4\pi\mu L}{3} - \frac{V^2}{6\rho L Q}\frac{dP}{dz} = 0 \tag{14}$$

Using the above model and equations, the heart model can be represented as in Fig. 4 [20].

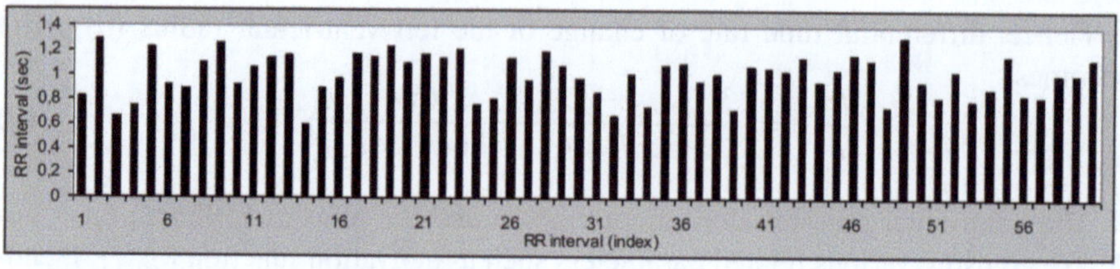

Fig. 5 RR rithmogram of HRV series [21]

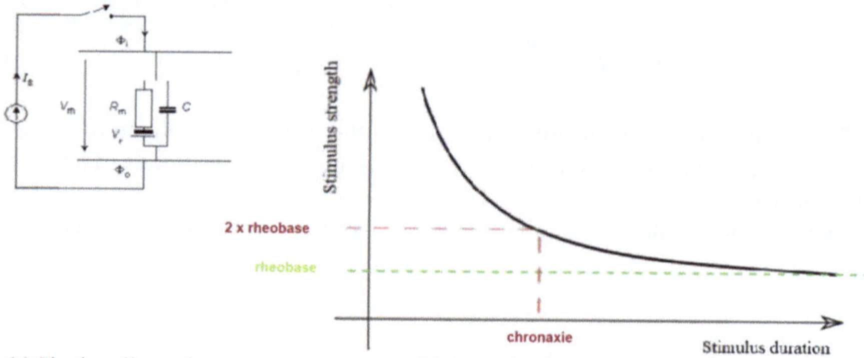

(a) Single cell membrane, (b) Strength–duration curve

Fig. 6 Timed electrical activity of heart

In Fig. 4, bold lines represent elements of the sympathetic regulation of heart rate and contractility, and dashed lines represent elements of the autonomous control loop of vascular tone.

Heart Rate Variability (HRV), as represented using wavelet transform in Fig. 5, is a characteristic of the heart rate time series to study its undulations for short span of time. The HRV spectral analysis is used to establish the effect of the parasympathetic and sympathetic nervous system on cardiac activity. The higher HRV indicates good health. Various efforts have been made to study HRV and measure the degree for irregularity of heart rate time series. The cardiological interval simulation is critically significant for the development of methods and tools for research in heart rate and its variability [21]. The sequence of instantaneous heart rates, defined as a time-series function, is given as

$$f_i = \frac{1}{RR_i} \tag{15}$$

where R-R interval can be described as $RR_i = t_i - t_{i-1}$. Efforts have been made to represent this time-series equation using Wavelet Transform.

Figure 6 shows the electrical activity of the heart. Electrical representation of a single cellular membrane, representing all cells, is shown in Fig. 6a.

The typical component values considered are 1 μF for the capacitor and 1 Ω for the resistance. Depolarization of cell membranes requires approximately 20 mV from SA node. Considering linear behaviour of electrical model of heart and applying Ohm's law, we get Eq. 16:

$$I = I_C + I_R = C.\frac{dV}{dt} + \frac{V}{R} \tag{16}$$

where I is the total current, I_C is the current through the capacitance, and I_R is the current through the resistance. The energy dissipated through pacemaker (i.e. heart) is given as

$$W = Z.I^2.t \tag{17}$$

where Z is the entire load impedance.

The minimum Voltage(current)-duration product, as a function of timed-automata, is given by

$$I(t_C) = I_0(1 + \frac{t_C}{t_C}) = 2I_0 \implies W(t_C) = 4I_0^2.Z.t_C \tag{18}$$

where I_0 is rheobase current (minimum current required for depolarization) t_C is the chronaxie time (time at which stimulus current is twice the rheobase current, i.e., minimum stimulus current, and is close to the point of minimal energy consumption) t is elapsed time.

Action Potential

The above discussion of heartbeat, cardiac output and other models can be understood using the action potential model of heart. Pumping action of heart is due to the contraction and relaxation of atria and ventricles which is due to their depolarization and re-polarization caused by the action potential. This action potential causes stimulation signal from Sinoatrial (SA) Node or sinus node (responsible for contraction and relaxation of atria) which travels to Atrioventricular (AV) node (responsible for contraction and relaxation of ventricles). This action potential (Fig. 7) is captured in the form PQRST segment through ECG.

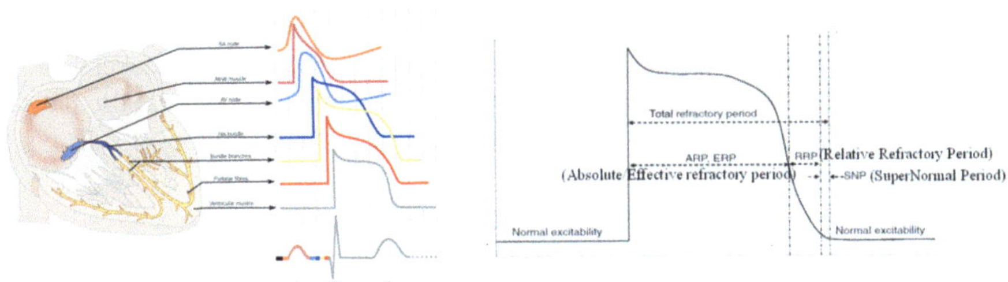

(a). Segmented action potential representation of heart

(b). Integrated action potential representation of heart

Fig. 7 Action Potential of heart

2.3 Aberrant Heart Conditions and Pacemaker

Any anomaly in heartbeat is referred to as heart arrhythmia. Heart rhythm problem or heart arrhythmia occurs due to aberrancy in the electrical signals from SA node, AV node or Bundles of HIS that coordinate the heartbeats. It causes the augmented heartbeat (tachycardia), reduced heartbeat rate (bradycardia) or irregularly.

The most common types of arrhythmia are

i. Tachycardia: The heartbeat is too augmented (above 100 bpm). Tachycardia is generally due to disruption of the electrical impulses of the heart. Factors like damage due to heart attack or heart disease, congenital heart disease, high BP, smoking, etc. can contribute the disruption of impulses.

In the literature, three main kinds of tachycardia were observed. First, the well-known supraventricular is generally seen in atria. Second, sinus is observed at the time of sickness. It easily comes to a normal state once the body recovers.

ii. Atrial fibrillation (AFib): It is an abnormal activity in the heartbeats. It is the most common type of arrhythmia. AFib occurs due to misfiring of shaky pulse and causes the atria to get out of control. It begins to increase in heartbeat and heart becomes unpredictable. They will shoot up the heartbeats, which is an abnormal condition in human beings.

iii. Atrial flutter: It usually observed at the right atrium. The condition results from a single electrical impulse travelling rapidly in the affected atrium. This often results in increased heart rate, but it is a more regular rhythm.

iv. Bradycardia: Bradycardia is the condition of the heart when it beats at an abnormal lower rate (less than 60 beats per minute). Bradycardia generally occurs when the electrical impulses travelling from the atria to the ventricles get disrupted.

v. Ventricular fibrillation (VF): The VF can result in stopping the heart from working, and it is the major origin of heart attack that generally happens in the ventricles.

vi. Premature contractions: Premature contraction is a condition in which the heart chamber starts missing the betas. It is generally observed when beat is going from wrist to chest. That beat is very weak in nature and may not be calculated.

Other types of premature contractions include additional beats and early beats. All three types of premature contractions may occur in the upper or lower chambers of heart. Some of the anomalies can be handled by artificial devices like pacemaker. The block diagram of pacemaker is shown in Fig. 8. Pacemaker is primarily based on Closed-Loop Regulation of Mean Arterial Blood Pressure [22, 23].

Pacemaker has two nodes going to right atrium and ventricle. If pacemaker detects any anomaly in heartbeat, like heart rate lower than LR interval, it sends a stimulation signal which results in resuming the heart to its normal beat condition.

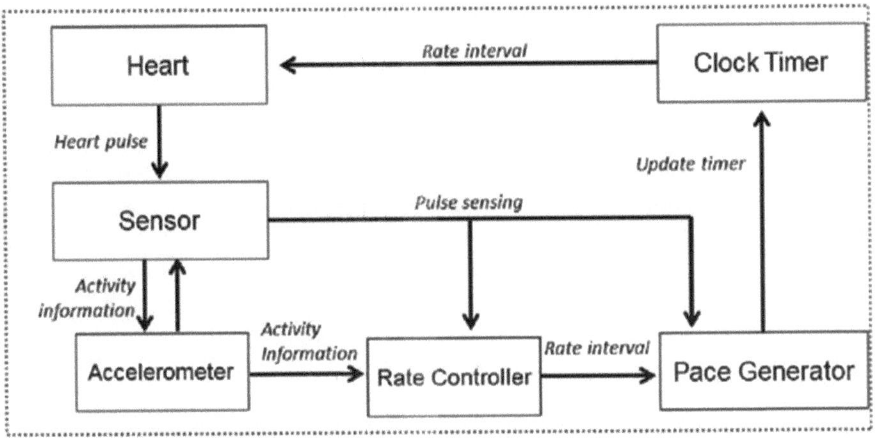

Fig. 8 Block diagram of Pacemaker

2.4 *Study and Modelling of Cancer*

Another major concern of health care is the increasing rate of cancer worldwide. As per estimated data of the WHO in 2019, cancer is the significant cause of death before the age of 70 years in 113 out of 185 countries and ranks third or fourth cause in further 23 countries. According to Global Cancer Observatory (WHO), 36 types of cancer have been reported from 185 countries worldwide, in 2020 which has also been published in American Cancer Society Journal [24]. The proliferating rate of cancer needs to be monitored and modelled for understanding the pattern, preventing its spread and finding remedies. There have been incidents of 19,292,789 cases of cancer in 2020 out of which 9,958,133 are cases of death due to cancer [25–28].

There has been a surge in the incident and mortality cases of cancer, both globally and in India, as shown in Tables 2 and 3 and Figs. 9 and 10.

The time-series data of population and cancer incident cases gives a lucid indication of lowering in rate of change of population and augmentation in rate of incident of cancer cases. The same can also be seen in the graph plotted with the data. The trend-line of population has a negative slope; however, the trend-line of incident cases of cancer has positive slope as can be seen in Figs. 9 and 10.

Table 2 Comparative study of Population change and Incident cancer cases in the World and India

Year	Change of population (world) (%)	New cases of incident of cancer-World (%)	Change of population (India) (%)	New cases of incident of cancer-India (%)
1990	1.71(%)	0.2961(%)	2.17(%)	0.0994(%)
1995	1.43(%)	0.3069(%)	1.99(%)	0.0960(%)
2000	1.31(%)	0.2860(%)	1.85(%)	0.0979(%)
2005	1.25(%)	0.3026(%)	1.67(%)	0.0941(%)
2010	1.22(%)	0.3025(%)	1.47(%)	0.1006(%)
2015	1.16(%)	0.3067(%)	1.20(%)	0.1086(%)
2016	1.14(%)	0.3077(%)	1.10(%)	0.1114(%)
2017	1.12(%)	0.3068(%)	1.07(%)	0.1125(%)
2020	1.10(%)	0.2475(%)	1.04(%)	0.1009(%)
Average	**1.27(%)**	**0.2959(%)**	**1.51(%)**	**0.1024(%)**

Table 3 Prediction of Population change and Incident cancer cases in the world and India

Prediction Year	Change of population (world) (%)	New cases of incident of cancer-world (%)	Change of population (India) (%)	New cases of incident of cancer-India (%)
2025	0.98(%)	0.31(%)	0.92(%)	0.11(%)
2030	0.87(%)	0.31(%)	0.80(%)	0.11(%)
2035	0.78(%)	0.32(%)	0.66(%)	0.12(%)
2040	0.69(%)	0.32(%)	0.50(%)	0.12(%)
2045	0.61(%)	0.32(%)	0.35(%)	0.12(%)
2050	0.53(%)	0.32(%)	0.23(%)	0.12(%)
Average	**0.74(%)**	**0.32(%)**	**0.58(%)**	**0.12(%)**

3 Analysis and Deductions

Based upon the study of population and cancer incident cases, the linear prediction method was used to predict both, which can be seen in Table 3 [4] and Fig. 11. The data shows population growth rate diminish. Subsequently, there will be an increase in incident cases of cancer in India and worldwide Table 3 which may result in negative population growth in future.

where a is the kinetic parameter
v(t) is the volume of the cancer cells
V is the volume of tumour
t is function of time
b is the carrying capacity
$\sigma > 0$ is the diffusion coefficient
W(t) is a Wiener process with Gaussian distribution having mean zero; the variance dt is given by the increment in time, t (Fig. 12 and Table 4).

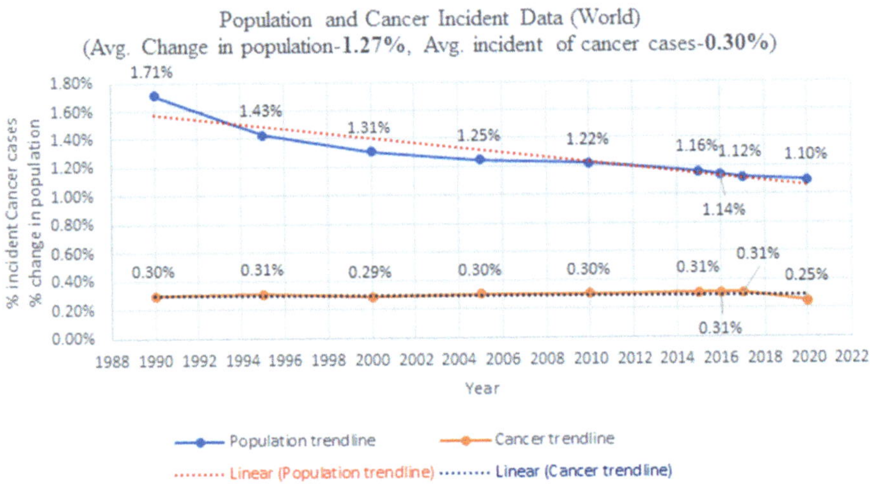

Fig. 9 Population and Cancer Incident Data (World)

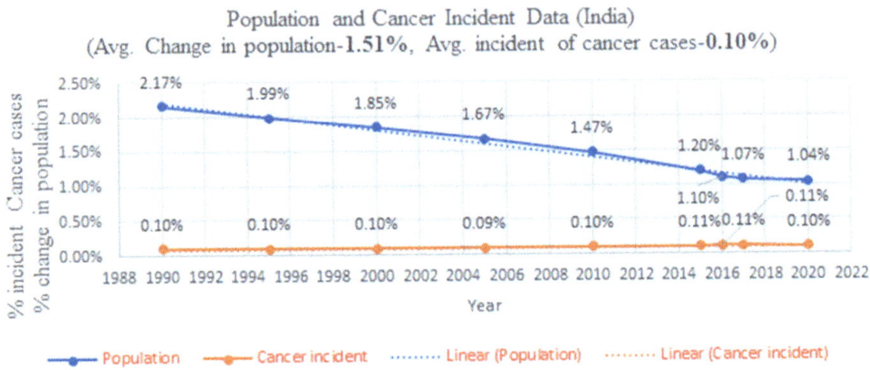

Fig. 10 Population and Cancer Incident Data (India)

Table 4 Mathematical model of cancer

Base model	Type	Mathematical model
Deterministic	Exponential	$dv(t) = av(t)$
	Logistic model	$(dV/dt) = aV(1–V/b)$
	Gompertz model	$dV/dt = aV\ln(b/(V + c))$
	Bertalanffy model	$dV/dt = aV^{2/3} - bV$
Stochastic	Gompertz model	$dV(t) = (aV(t) - bV(t) \ln(V(t)))\, t + \sigma V(t) dW(t)$
	Logistic model	$dV(t) = (aV(t) - bV(t))dt + \sigma V(t) dW(t)$

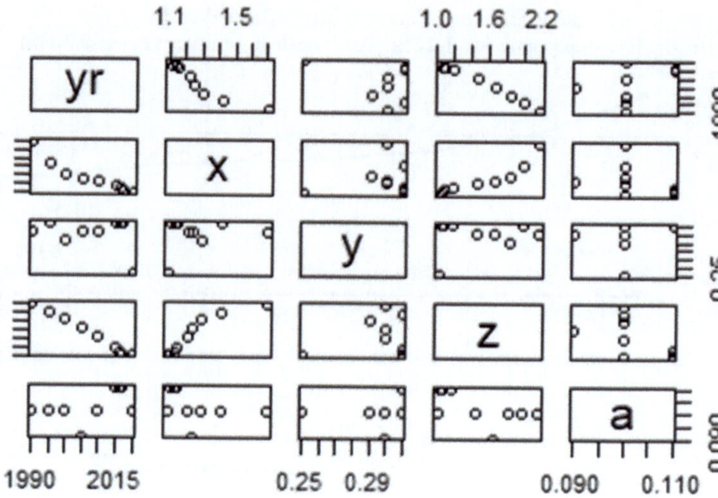

Fig. 11 Cancer statistics and predictions

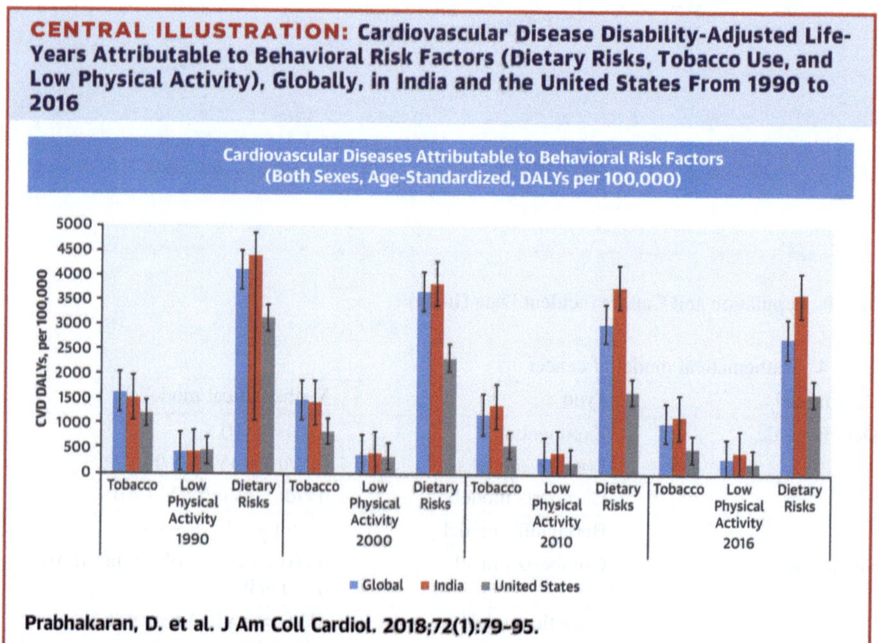

Fig. 12 Cardivascular Disease Illustration

4 Conclusion

With the predictions, though the number of incident cases of cancer seems to decrease in the world and India, the percentage of the cases tends to increase as the slope of population is negative for both. The predictions show that by 2050 mortality due to CVD and cancer only will be equal to the birth rate, and gradually the population will diminish if a substantiated and adaptive health monitoring system is not evolved and implemented. Additionally, cause of cancer and CVD needs to be identified and preventive measure needs to be implemented globally.

References

1. Shekhar S, Kumar A (eds) Fractional order interval Type-2 fuzzy logic controller. Recent trends on Type-2 fuzzy logic systems: theory, methodology and applications, Vol 425. Springer Nature, 29–42
2. Kumar A et al. (2022) Human heart rate stabilization using fractional order fuzzy logic controller. In: Soft computing: theories and applications: proceedings of SoCTA 2021. Singapore: Springer Nature Singapore, 945–956
3. Kumar A, Kumar V (2017) A novel interval type-2 fractional order fuzzy PID controller: Design, performance evaluation, and its optimal time domain tuning. ISA Trans 68:251–275
4. Kumar A, Raj R (2022) Design of a fractional order two layer fuzzy logic controller for drug delivery to regulate blood pressure. Biomedical Signal Process Control 78:104024
5. Kumar A et al (2023) Design of a novel mixed interval type-2 fuzzy logic controller for 2-DOF robot manipulator with payload. Eng Appl Artif Intell 123:106329
6. Castillo O, Kumar A (eds) (2023) Recent trends on Type-2 fuzzy logic systems: theory, methodology and applications. Vol 425. Springer Nature
7. Kumar A, Kumar V (2017) Hybridized ABC-GA optimized fractional order fuzzy pre-compensated FOPID control design for 2-DOF robot manipulator. AEU-Int J Electron Commun 79:219–233
8. Kumar A, Kumar V (2018) Performance analysis of optimal hybrid novel interval type-2 fractional order fuzzy logic controllers for fractional order systems. Expert Syst Appl 93:435–455
9. Gaidhane P et al. (2023) Tuning of interval Type-2 fuzzy precompensated PID controller: GWO-ABC Algorithm based constrained optimization approach. Recent trends on Type-2 fuzzy logic systems: theory, methodology and applications. Cham: Springer International Publishing, 75–96
10. Hunt R et al. (1897) Notes on the physiology of the Cardiac Nerves of the Calf. Physiological laboratory of Columbia University at the college of physicians and surgeons, New York, 59–68
11. Hunt R, Harrington DW (1897) Notes on the physiology of the Cardiac Nerves of the Opossum. Physiological laboratory of Columbia University at the college of physicians and surgeons, New York J Exp Medicines, pp 711–721
12. Rosenblueth A, Simeone FA (1934) The interrelations of vagal and accelerator effects on the cardial rate. Laboratories of Physiology, pp 42–55
13. Jaye DA et al. (2010) Basic cardiac electrophysiology: excitable membranes. Cardiac Electrophysiology methods and models, Ch-2, pp 41–51
14. Franck, de Physiologie A (1890) The principles of psychology Volume I', Ch-2, p 403
15. Bayliss and Starling, op. oft. (1902) Physiological Laboratory, Guy's Hospital, 416
16. Bayliss and Starling (1892) Physiological laboratory, Guy's Hospital. ib. xiii , 402–423
17. Hough (1895) On the escape of the heart from vagus inhibition. J Physiol, xviii, 161–200

18. Wang Y et al. (2018) A mathematical model of human heart including the effects of heart contractility varying with heart rate changes. Elsevier J Biomechanics, 1–9
19. Shoaib MSR et al. (2010) Mathematical modeling of the heart. 6th international conference on electrical and computer engineering 626–629
20. Ishbulatov YM et al (2020) Mathematical modelling of the cardiovascular autonomic control in healthy subjects during a passive head up tilt test. Scientific Reports Nature 10:16525
21. Georgieva-Tsaneva G et al. (2012) Simulation of heart rate variability data with methods of wavelet transform. Proceedings of the 13th international conference on computer systems and technologies, 306–312
22. Li P et al. (2013) Mathematical models of cardiac pacemaking function
23. Sharma R, Kumar A (2022) Optimal interval type-2 fuzzy logic control based closed-loop regulation of mean arterial blood pressure using the controlled drug administration. IEEE Sensors J 22(7):7195–7207
24. Mathur P et al. (2020) Cancer statistics, 2020: report from national cancer registry programme, India. JCO Global Oncol American Soc Clinical Oncol 6:1063–1075
25. Tabassum S et al. (2018) Mathematical modeling of cancer growth process: a review. J Phys Conf Series, 1–5. (Reference used in the table of cancer modeling-serial number to be updated in the table)
26. Benzekry S et al. (2014) Classical mathematical models for description and prediction of experimental tumor growth, pp 46–56
27. Ruiz-Arrebola S et al. (2021) Evaluation of classical mathematical models of tumor growth using an on-lattice agent-based monte carlo model. MDPI J Appl Sci 11:1–18
28. Tabassum S et al. (2018) athematical modeling of cancer growth process: a review. J Phys Conf Series, 1–5
29. Roth GA et al. (2020) Global burden of cardiovascular diseases and risk factors, 1990–2019. J American College Cardiol 76(25):2982–3021. https://doi.org/10.1016/j.jacc.2020.11.010
30. Bozkurt S (2019) Mathematical modeling of cardiac function to evaluate clinical cases in adults and children. Plos One 14(10):e0224663
31. Beainy AG et al. (2014) Mathematical modeling of pacemaker for study of battery longevity., Mathematical modeling of pacemaker for study of battery longevity. The Third international conference on e-technologies and networks for development (ICeND2014), Beirut, Lebanon, 131–134
32. Jin Y et al. (2009) LabView based experimental validation of fractional order motion controllers', 323–328
33. Cromwell L et al (2004) Biomedical instumentation and measurement, 2nd edn. Singapore, Pearson Education, pp 84–95
34. Riley C (2017) "A mathematical model of cardiovascular and respiratory dynamics in humans with transposition of the great arteries. Rose-hulman undergraduate mathematics journalrose-hulma, Vol 18, Issue 1. Article 13:207–236
35. Faruk N et al. (2021) A comprehensive survey on low-cost ECG acquisition systems advances on design specifications, challenges and future direction. Elsevier, biocybernetics and biomedical engineering, Vol 41, Issue 2, 474–502
36. Sung H et al. (2021) Global cancer statistics 2020: GLOBOCAN estimates of incidence and mortality Worldwide for 36 cancers in 185 countries. American Cancer Soc J, 209–249. https://doi.org/10.3322/caac.21660

MIX
Papier aus verantwortungsvollen Quellen
Paper from responsible sources
FSC® C105338

If you have any concerns about our products,
you can contact us on
ProductSafety@springernature.com

In case Publisher is established outside the EU,
the EU authorized representative is:
Springer Nature Customer Service Center GmbH
Europaplatz 3, 69115 Heidelberg, Germany

Printed by Libri Plureos GmbH
in Hamburg, Germany